Music
Reference
and
Research
Materials

MUSIC REFERENCE AND RESEARCH MATERIALS

An Annotated Bibliography

FIFTH EDITION

VINCENT H. DUCKLES
IDA REED

Michael A. Keller, *Advisory Editor*

Indexed by **Linda Solow Blotner**

SCHIRMER BOOKS
An Imprint of Simon & Schuster Macmillan
New York

Prentice Hall International
London   Mexico City   New Delhi   Singapore   Sydney   Toronto

Schirmer Books
An Imprint of Simon & Schuster Macmillan
1633 Broadway
New York, NY 10019

Library of Congress Catalog Card Number: 97-11148

Printed in the United States of America

printing number
2 3 4 5 6 7 8 9 10

Library of Congress Cataloging in Publication Data
Duckles, Vincent H. (Vincent Harris), 1913-
Music reference and research materials: an annotated bibliography.—5th ed. / Vincent H. Duckles, Ida Reed; Michael A. Keller, advisory editor; indexed by Linda Solow Blotner.
p. cm.

ISBN 0-02-870821-0

1. Music—Bibliography. 2. Music—History and criticism—Bibliography. 3. Music—Bibliography—Bibliography. I. Reed, Ida. II. Keller, Michael A. III. Title.
ML113.D83 1997
016.78—dc21

97-11148
CIP
MN

This paper meets the requirements of ANSI/NISO Z39.48-1992 (Permanence of Paper).

CONTENTS

INTRODUCTION TO THE FIFTH EDITION

It has been 10 years since the Fourth Edition of *Music Reference and Research Materials* was published. In that time, the research library world has changed considerably. Access to information about online holdings of not only local libraries but also an international range of other collections has become commonplace. The easy access to this information has vastly increased both the amount and the currency of reference material immediately available to the music library user, whether beginning student or established scholar. Accordingly, the rationale behind the compilation of this work has changed from that of a bibliography gathering useful works for the music researcher to a bibliography selectively compiling titles from a wide array of available choices. Each decision to include a source in the present edition has been influenced both by the traditions established in the four earlier editions (and one revision) of *Music Reference and Research Materials* and by the current working editor's desire to present a balance of classic historic titles, dependable standard works, and important newly written tools, with the mix perhaps thrown occasionally askew by a small number of the unusual and arcane. It must be emphasized that no single section of the text is meant to be other than selective. In fact, no single section is able to be other than selective. The past decade's increase in the number of music reference titles published has meant that most of the chapters of this volume could be expanded to fill a volume of their own, a challenge for other compilers to undertake.

The format of the entries in this edition is based on the *Chicago Manual of Style,* 14th ed., with the entries arranged by author or editor; the secondary influence on the format is the title page rather than current or past library cataloging practice. The numbering of the individual entries in this edition reflects the chapter and the entry's position in it, instead of the through-numbered entries of the past. The works are cited by their most recent nonreprint edition; reprint editions are listed in the work's publication history, unless they present an additional distinguishing feature. The pagination given in the bibliographic citation includes the work's Roman-numbered pages if there are over 20 (xx) cited, informing the reader that considerable prefatory material exists. About 15% of the entries included in the Fourth Edition, Revised, have been omitted, generally because they have been superseded by more recent works; there are also listed over 175 new editions of previously cited titles, and over 1,100 newly included titles. In about 25 entries titles previously cited as separate entries are combined, for the convenience of the user. The length of the publishing history of each entry and the number of reviews cited have been increased, the former to show a work's growth and the latter to provide examples of the reception given to it by the musical community at large. The abbreviations used to provide needed space are given a table, in which, it should be noted, the abbreviations for the states are given in the format preferred by the *Chicago Manual of Style* rather than by the U.S. Postal Service. With one exception, the cutoff date of publication for inclusion is December 1995, although works announced as anticipated for publication in 1996 are often indicated in the publishing history, and in some instances reviews have been cited from material published up to the time of this work's publication.

Space considerations have curtailed both the duplicate entries of past editions and the generous cross-references previously supplied in the body of the text. There is more subdivision of topics than in past editions, and users will note that many sections are headed by a landmark work in the subject area, separated by a printer's mark (➤) from the main part of the section. (Thus, Coover's *Music Lexicography* begins the dictionaries and encyclopedias chapter, *Baker's Biographical Dictionary* that chapter's section on international biography, and so on.) As the passage of time has demanded, there are a number of new subject sections, and other established sections have been relabeled. An effort has been made to segregate reference indexes in their home sections because of their special utility for the user.

At the request of many users, the four indexes of the last edition have become one, redesigned and compiled under the supervision of Linda Solow Blotner, a prize-winning indexer and Head of the Music Library, Hartt Conservatory of Music.

CONTRIBUTORS

The time has passed when a title such as this could be the work of one person. Without the help of the people listed here, I would be working on this edition for many years to come. The following 10 colleagues compiled and in many cases originated important sections of this book. Their individual expertise can only make this work more valuable. In the order of their work's appearance in the text, I would like to acknowledge the work of and publicly thank Ruthann Boyles McTyre, Fine Arts Librarian, Baylor University, who devised and expanded the list of Source Readings (Chapter 2); Dr. Lauriejean Reinhart, National Humanities Center, who completely reorganized and rewrote the overview of Guides to Musicology (Chapter 3); Professor Cynthia Cyrus, Blair School of Music, Vanderbilt University, who took in hand the fledgling section on Performance Practice (Chapter 3) and built it into a unified whole; Philip Vandermeer, Head of Reference and Circulation, Music Library, University of Maryland, who organized and wrote two new sections of ethnomusicology, that for print sources in Chapter 4 and the ethnodiscography section in Chapter 10; Sarah McCleskey, Collection Manager, Music Library, University of North Carolina at Chapel Hill, who used her reference experience with various song indexes to compile and write a new and useful section of collections of song texts and translations (Chapter 5); Leslie Bennett, Head, Music Services Department, Knight Library, University of Oregon, who contributed inspired work on popular, musical theater, and jazz discographies, including an extended section on recordings of individual popular performers (Chapter 10); Carol Tatian, Music Librarian, Brown University, who made sense of the geographic guides to music resources and events (Chapter 11); Brad Short, Music Librarian, Gaylord Music Library, Washington University, who gathered resources for the rapidly changing electronic resources scene, and who helped with the hard decisions about what to omit (Chapter 12); Steve Mantz, Music Librarian, Davidson College, who organized a pithy and varied section on Music Business and Law (Chapter 13); and Jill Shires, Music Cataloger, Music Library, University of North Carolina at Chapel Hill, who updated the section on music cataloging, while leaving enough of the old to allow for a historical perspective (Chapter 13). These colleagues generously gave of their professional knowledge, time, and energy to make this volume an infinitely richer one. We all owe them appreciation and thanks.

In addition, Professor James Pruett, lately Chief of the Music Division, Library of Congress, and Professor Lilian Pruett, North Carolina Central University, my dear friends, were kind enough to wield a blue pencil in the early chapters and to give advice and assistance and to listen to this editor's ramblings whenever approached; Jim's editorial skill and Lilian's fluency in a multitude of mid-European languages were both especially appreciated. I was also fortunate to have my generous and knowledgeable UNC-CH library colleagues Nadia Zilper, Slavic Bibliographer, Hsi-Chu Bolick, East-Asian Cataloger, and Joseph Collins, Germanic Languages and Fine Arts Cataloger, act as consultants in their specialties, as did my longtime friend Professor Maryellen Bieder, Romance Languages Department, Indiana University.

In the formative stages of this work and beyond, I received help and valuable advice from Dr. David Hunter, Music Librarian, University of Texas, Austin, and Book Review Editor of Notes; and Dr. Daniel Zager, Librarian, Conservatory Librarian, Oberlin College, and Editor, Notes. The three of us have spent time and thought with this work from the early days of the Fourth Edition's publication, and the wisdom of these colleagues assisted immeasurably with what changes are found between these covers. In addition, Edwin A. Quist, Head Librarian of the Arthur Friedheim Library, Peabody Conservatory of Music, and Professor Richard Green, Northwestern University, gave thoughtful responses to earlier versions in the period before publication. Margaretta Yarborough, Assistant Head of the Cataloging Department, Davis Library, UNC-CH, and a professional proofreader with the University of North Carolina Press and Oxford University Press, read much of the manuscript numerous times, always to improve it; she saved this editor from much future embarrassment and left a debt that I can never repay.

In addition, I have been fortunate enough to have received help and advice from conductor Gillian Anderson (late of the Music Division, Library of Congress); Ann P. Basart, the founder and publisher of Fallen Leaf Press; my colleagues in the Mary Biddle Duke Siemans Music Library, Duke University, John Druesedow, Tim Cherubini, and Pat Canovai, for many kindnesses and cooperative acts; Sarah Dorsey, Music Librarian, University of North Carolina at Greensboro, Diane Steinhaus Pettit, Public Service Librarian, and Sarah McCleskey, Collection Manager, Music Library, UNC-CH; Paula Hinton and Tommy Nixon, Reference Department, Davis Library, UNC-CH; Scott Barker, Director of Computing and Telecommunications, and Gillian Debreczeny, Librarian, School of Information and Library Science, UNC-CH; Elizabeth Chenault, Reference Librarian, Rare Books Collection, UNC-CH; Philip Rees, Art Librarian, UNC-CH; Professor James B. Coover, Baird Music Library, SUNY, Buffalo; Michael Gray, Voice of America; Dr. Kevin Kelly, University of Georgia; Kathryn Logan, Head of the Music and Art Department, the Carnegie Library of Pittsburgh; Professor William R. Meredith, Director of the Ira Brilliant Beethoven Center, San Jose State University; Joan Redding, BBC Music Library; Dr. Norris L. Stephens, Music Librarian, University of Pittsburgh; Suzanne Thorin, late of the Library of Congress and currently Dean of Libraries, Indiana University; my latest class in Music Librarianship at UNC-CH's School of Information and Library Science, including Barbara Aschenbrenner, Elizabeth Dain, Paul Dinsmoor, Tara Guthrie, Jane D. Harris, Arleen Myers, and Earla Pope; Alice Bordsen; Kim Christopher; Deborah Coclanis; Betsy and Westy Dain; Barbara Friedell Davidson; Jeanne Hart Dickey; Bonnie Jo Dopp, University of Maryland; Christine Dvonch; the Rev. Tambria Lee; Loretta Lopipare; Eileen McGrath; Van and Peggy Quinn; Joanne Vimont Shore; Professor Ruth Weidner, West Chester State University; Professor Ann Thomas Wilkins, Duquesne University; and Page Zyromski. I especially appreciate the special help given by my music library mentor, Irene Millen, who founded the valuable Music Division at the Carnegie Library of Pittsburgh; and by Professors William S. Newman, Henry Woodward, and Howard Smithers.

Two special groups of people deserve acknowledgment. At the University of North Carolina at Chapel Hill libraries, thanks go to Dr. Joe Hewitt, Associate Provost for University Libraries, for generously and wholeheartedly supporting my request for leave to work on this project; to Dr. Marcella Grendler, Associate University Librarian for the Special Collections and Planning, for substantial help and encouragement at the start of this adventure; and to Diane Wheeler Strauss, Associate University Librarian for Public Service and on her own a most successful veteran of this type of activity, for valuable and encouraging consultative sessions throughout my four years of compiling, writing, and rewriting. There is no question that without the assistance of Dr. Vivian Clark; Dr. W. Woodrow Burns; Dr. Edwin Cox, late of Duke University; Stella Waugh, of Duke University; Dr. Deidre Teaford of Wake Forest University; and, most lately, Drs. Joseph Wiley, Eileen Powell, Mark Graham, and Julian Rosenman of the University of North Carolina at Chapel Hill, this project would not have been completed. The support and assistance they provided were extraordinary, and my knowing that they were all at hand for additional help as needed made all the difference to my peace of mind.

And finally, to Michael Keller, who trusted me to work on the project that meant so much to him. The faith he placed in me to update the work on which he spent so much time, thought, and energy was gratefully received. There are few more generous colleagues. Richard Carlin and Jill Lectka of Schirmer Books gave continued encouragement during the early days of this project. And Anna Savini McAliley understood how much this project meant and did what she could to see that it was finished.

This editor has come to understand clearly the challenges of compiling a work of this type and the many possibilities for error, great and small. It is hoped that its users will forgive the missteps they find and will bring them to the attention of the undersigned, where they will be gratefully received.

Ida Reed
University of North Carolina at Chapel Hill
Chapel Hill, North Carolina
1996

INTRODUCTION TO THE FIRST EDITION

A bibliography can be regarded as the relatively inert by-product of scholarly activity, or it can be treated as an active ingredient in the learning process. The latter perspective has been adopted in this guide to Music Reference and Research Materials. While no one but a professional bibliographer may be expected to come for his leisure reading to a list of books, most of us can respond with interest to an organized survey of the literature of a particular field. A bibliography, in fact, offers one of the best means of gaining an over-all impression of a subject area. It throws the essential patterns of a discipline into relief, casting light on what has been accomplished and drawing attention to the shadows where work still needs to be done. This guide has been designed to illuminate the bibliographical resources for musical scholarship. It is, above all, intended to serve a teaching purpose. Implicit in its organization is the concept that bibliography is an approach to knowledge, a way in which the student can progress toward mastery in his chosen field of specialization within the larger dimensions of the field of music. The guide was developed, through a series of editions beginning in 1949, as a text for a graduate seminar entitled "An Introduction to Musical Scholarship" given in the Music Department of the University of California at Berkeley. If its pattern has been determined to some extent by the way in which music bibliography is taught in a specific institution, its structure is still flexible enough to permit other teachers to use it in their own way.

The work is actually intended to fulfill the requirements of two groups: graduate students who need to become acquainted with the resources of musical research, and music reference librarians whose job it is to help others find the information they want. While the needs of the two have much in common, there are points at which their interests diverge. Much more is listed here than will be required for reference services in any but a large music research library, and there is material included which the scholar would rarely need to consult unless he moved outside of the traditional framework of historical musicology.

The present volume is much larger than any of its predecessors, yet it remains a selective list. One limitation in coverage, strictly enforced, is the selection of titles that pertain directly or exclusively to music. This criterion eliminates a great deal of valuable reference material, particularly important in areas that lie on the borderline between musicology and other disciplines: liturgics, the theater arts, literature, the dance, etc. No musicologist can afford to neglect such general reference tools as the *Encyclopedia of Religion and Ethics,* or Cabrol's *Dictionnaire d'archéologie chrétienne et de liturgie,* or, in another area, the *Census of Medieval and Renaissance Manuscripts in the U.S. and Canada,* by Seymour de Ricci, or Paul O. Kristeller's valuable survey of the catalogs of *Latin Manuscript Books before 1600.* The fact that these tools are indispensable only serves to demonstrate that musicology is far from being a self-sufficient and self-contained discipline. But an attempt to list all of the peripheral resources would inflate the present work and destroy its focus. There are excellent bibliographies of general reference works currently available. Perhaps the best service to be offered to the young musicologist here is to direct him to Constance M. Winchell's *Guide to Reference Books* (7th ed., 1951, and later supplements) or to Theodore Besterman's *World Bibliography of Bibliographies* (3rd ed., 1955–56). If all else fails, he should be urged to rely on that universal repository of fact and resource, the reference librarian, who sits behind a desk in every large library, prepared to guide the inquiring student through the complex paths of information retrieval. But there is a distinct advantage to be gained in approaching the general reference tools from the musician's point of view. Recently Keith E. Mixter has furnished such an approach in his manual on *General Bibliography for Music Research* (1962), published as Number 4 in the *Detroit Studies in Music Bibliography.* It is a pleasure to be able to point to that work as a useful complement to this one.

A few further statements should be added to make clear what ground this guide is, and is not, intended to cover. It does not represent the well-rounded library of musical literature; it contains no entries for biography, no local histories, no monographs or studies devoted to most of the subject areas into which the field of music can be subdivided. It is certainly not a basic list of titles which every music library should acquire; but it does provide a list from which the essential materials for a music reference collection can be selected. It can best be described as a bibliography of music bibliographies, its emphasis being on those works which themselves serve as points of departure for further investigations: lists, inventories, alphabetized compilations of facts about music. The one section which falls most conspicuously outside of this pattern of bibliographic emphasis is the section on *Histories and Chronologies.* This is the only category in which books are listed for what they contain intrinsically rather than for their function as guides to further information.

In its preliminary forms this book has been put to use in a number of courses in music bibliography throughout the country, and as a result has benefited from the suggestions of several generous-minded critics. I am particularly indebted to Professor Albert T. Luper of the State University of Iowa, and to Professor Otto Albrecht of the University of Pennsylvania for their help in this respect. The form of the annotations owes much to Richard Angell of the Library of Congress, who placed his notes at my disposal. My colleagues in the Music Library of the University of California at Berkeley, Harriet Nicewonger and Minnie Elmer, have made their influence felt on nearly every page in matters that have to do with the selection of titles, the framing of the annotations, and the reading of proof.

One feature which has been introduced for the first time in the current edition is the citation of book reviews. These are offered as practical aids to the evaluation of the items. No effort has been made to achieve complete coverage: reviews are cited only for the more recent items, and are confined largely to those published in the English-language journals.

The entries are numbered throughout this book, and for the most part, each title is entered once. There are some instances of duplicate entries, however, when the content of the item calls for its listing in more than one category. Eitner's *Quellen-Lexikon* is a case in point. This title is entered once as a dictionary of biography, and again as a bibliography of early music.

Abbreviations are used sparingly. What they save in space in a work of this kind is rarely commensurate to the inconvenience caused to the user. They are confined to the standard symbols for the dictionaries and journals most frequently cited in reviews: *Grove for Grove's Dictionary of Music and Musicians,* 5th edition; *MGG for Die Musik in Geschichte und Gegenwart; Acta M for Acta Musicologica; JAMS for Journal of the American Musicological Society; MQ for the Musical Quarterly;* and *Notes for Music Library Association Notes,* 2nd series.

A bibliographer's work is never done. Even as this edition goes to press, I am troubled by the submerged voices of would-be entries which may have been overlooked, and entries which may have been misplaced or misrepresented. Other music bibliographers proceed, unconcerned, with their work, the results of which will eventually call for supplements, or even substantial revisions in our present pattern of organization. But if one were too attentive to such considerations a work of this kind would never reach the point of publication. Now that it has made its appearance, I hope that it will attract collaboration, in the form of corrections, additions, or suggestions for improvement, from all who have occasion to use it.

Vincent Duckles
1964

SYMBOLS AND ABBREVIATIONS

*	New title added.
AACR2	*Anglo-American Cataloging Rules,* 2nd ed.
Ala.	Alabama
AM	*American Music*
AMISJ	*Journal of the American Musical Instrument Society*
AMISN	*Newsletter of the American Musical Instrument Society*
AMS	*American Musicological Society*
AMT	*American Music Teacher*
ARBA	*American Reference Books Annual*
ARG	*American Record Guide*
Ariz.	Arizona
Ark.	Arkansas
ARSCJ	*Association for Recorded Sound Collections Journal*
B.C.	British Columbia
BPM	*Black Perspective in Music*
Calif.	California
CD	compact disc
CM	*Current Musicology*
CMC	Canadian Music Centre
Colo.	Colorado
cols.	columns
Conn.	Connecticut
CNV	*Cum Notis Variorum*
CRME	*Bulletin of the Council for Research in Music Education*
CUNY	City University of New York
D.C.	District of Columbia
Del.	Delaware
DEUMM	*Dizionario enciclopedica universale della musica e dei musicisti*
ed.	edition
eds.	editions
EKJ	*Early Keyboard Journal*
EM	*Early Music*
EP	extended-play recording
Fla.	Florida
Fontes	*Fontes Artes Musicae*
Ga.	Georgia
IAML	International Association of Music Libraries
ICS	International Clarinet Society
IFMCY	*International Folk Music Council Yearbook*

Ill.	Illinois
Ind.	Indiana
IPA	International Phonetic Alphabet
IRASM	*International Review of the Aesthetics and Sociology of Music*
ISAMN	*Institute for Studies in American Music Newsletter*
ISBN	International Standard Book Number
ISSN	International Standard Serial Number
ITGJ	*International Trumpet Guild Journal*
JAMS	*Journal of the American Musicological Society*
JEMFQ	*John Edwards Memorial Foundation Quarterly*
JLSA	*Journal of the Lute Society of America*
JM	*Journal of Musicology*
JMR	*Journal of Musicological Research*
JMT	*The Journal of Music Theory*
JRME	*Journal of Research in Music Education*
Kans.	Kansas
KWIC	key word in context
Ky.	Kentucky
l.	leaf
La.	Louisiana
LAMR	*Latin American Music Review*
LC	Library of Congress
LJ	*Library Journal*
ll.	leaves
LP	long-playing record, usually, 12 inch, 33 1/3 rpm
LQ	*Library Quarterly*
M&L	*Music and Letters*
MA	*Musical America*
MARC	Machine-readable cataloging
Mass.	Massachusetts
Md.	Maryland
MEJ	*Music Educators Journal*
MGG	*Die Musik in Geschichte und Gegenwart*
Minn.	Minnesota
MLA	Music Library Association
MOMA	Museum of Modern Art
Mo.	Missouri
Mont.	Montana
MQ	*Musical Quarterly*
MR	*Music Review*
MT	*Musical Times*
NATS	*National Association of Teachers of Singing Journal*
N.C.	North Carolina
NCM	*Nineteenth-Century Music*
Neb.	Nebraska

N.J.	New Jersey
N.M.	New Mexico
no.	number
nos.	numbers
Notes	*Music Library Association Notes*
N.Y.	New York
N.Z.	New Zealand
OCLC	Online Library Information Center
OJ	*Opera Journal*
Okla.	Oklahoma
ON	*Opera News*
Ont.	Ontario
OQ	*Opera Quarterly*
Ore.	Oregon
p.	page
Pa.	Pennsylvania
PMS	*Popular Music and Society*
PNM	*Perspectives of New Music*
pp.	pages
pseud.	pseudonym
R.I.	Rhode Island
RIAA	Recording Industry Association of America
RIdIM	*Répertoire International d'Iconographie Musicale*
RILM	*Répertoire International de Littérature Musicale*
RIPM	*Répertoire International de la Presse Musicale*
RISM	*Répertoire International des Sources Musicales*
RMA	Royal Musical Association
rpm	revolutions per minute
RQ	*Reference Quarterly*
SMT	*Society for Music Theory*
SSB	*Sonneck Society Bulletin*
SSN	*Sonneck Society Newsletter*
SUNY	State University of New York
Tex.	Texas
TLS	*Times Literary Supplement*
trans.	translated
Va.	Virginia
VdGSAJ	*Journal of the Viola da Gamba Society of America*
vol(s).	volume(s)
Vt.	Vermont
Wash.	Washington
Wisc.	Wisconsin
W. Va.	West Virginia

1

DICTIONARIES AND ENCYCLOPEDIAS

Dictionaries and encyclopedias are reference works in which the subjects covered are generally listed alphabetically. Theoretically, encyclopedias provide more detailed coverage than dictionaries, although the two terms are often used interchangeably. Many 1-vol. reference works are labeled encyclopedias; on the other hand, *The New Grove Dictionary of Music and Musicians* (**1.48**) is an impressive 20 volumes. James B. Coover has compiled the most comprehensive bibliography of music dictionaries and encyclopedias, *Music Lexicography* (**1.1**), which, with his subsequent writings on the subject, codifies the history of these fundamental music reference tools. More concise coverage is given by Harold Samuel in "Dictionaries and Encyclopedias" in *The New Harvard Dictionary of Music* (**1.320**), and Vincent Duckles offers his philosophical overview in "Music Lexicography," *College Music Symposium* 11 (1971): 115–22.

The present list includes the most important music dictionaries and encyclopedias in current use, in modern languages, cited under their latest edition. It also offers a selection of titles available as modern reprints, of continuing value for historical study, from the work of Johannes Tinctoris in 1495 to the present, showing through the centuries the ever-changing view of various elements of music and its study. The works are arranged by type of coverage: general works that include both terms and biographies; international biographical sources; nationally oriented dictionaries; separately published indexes to biographical sources; dictionaries of musical terms; dictionaries and encyclopedias of popular music, of musical instruments and their makers, of music for opera, theater, and film, of sacred music, of musical quotations (prose and melodic), of compositional devices, and of lists and handbooks. Some of these areas are newly subdivided to unite like titles.

GENERAL WORKS

1.1 Coover, James. *Music Lexicography: Including a Study of Lacunae in Music Lexicography and a Bibliography of Music Dictionaries.* 3rd ed., revised and enlarged. xxxix + 175 pp. Carlisle, Pa.: Carlisle Books, 1971.

First published as *A Bibliography of Music Dictionaries* (Denver, Colo.: Denver Public Library, 1952, 81 pp.; Bibliographical Center for Research. Rocky Mountain Region, Denver. Special bibliographies, 1). The 2nd ed. was *Music Lexicography: Including a Study of Lacunae in Music Lexicography and a Bibliography of Music Dictionaries* (Denver, Colo.: Bibliographical Center for Research, Rocky Mountain Region, Denver Public Library, 1958, xxx + 126 pp.).

A comprehensive overview of music dictionaries. The bibliography and its appendix have 1,801 entries arranged alphabetically by author, editor, or title; each entry cites all known editions of the work. These citations are preceded by a general discussion of the history of music lexicography and existing lacunae between 1500 and 1700. There are indexes to personal names, to topics and type, and, by date of publication, to dictionaries before 1900, as well as lists of "Some 17th-Century Works with 'Appended' Music Dictionaries," "Some 18th-Century Musical Works with 'Appended' Music Dictionaries," and "General Dictionaries to 1700 Which May

Contain Musical Items." Nyal Williams and Peggy Daub provide additions and corrections in "Coover's *Music Lexicography:* Two Supplements" in *Notes* 30 (1974): 492–500.

Glen Haydon reviews the 1st ed. in *Notes* 10 (1953): 281–82, Irene Millen reviews the 2nd ed. in *Notes* 16 (1959): 383–84 (giving some errata not corrected in the 3rd ed.), and Nyal Williams reviews the 3rd in *Notes* 30 (1974): 517–18.

The New Grove Dictionary of Music and Musicians (**1.48**) contains Coover's "Dictionaries and Encyclopedias of Music," an extended essay on the early history of dictionaries, divided into several chronological spans, each with a chronologically arranged bibliography of dictionaries. There is a separate section on encyclopedias, with a bibliography, organized by country, followed by a selective section on dictionaries of terms. International biographical and then national or regional biographical dictionaries are listed and discussed; dictionaries devoted to specific topics are selectively listed, arranged alphabetically by topic. There are a chronology, "Landmarks in Musical Lexicography," and a bibliography. Coover's article is the distillation of a lifetime of bibliographic work on the genre. As an extended postscript, Coover published "Lacunae in Music Dictionaries" in *CNV* 115–16 (1987) and, in the five subsequent issues, "A Non-Evaluative Checklist of Music Dictionaries and Encyclopedias," a classified bibliography. Together, these complement and update *Music Lexicography* and the article and bibliography in *The New Grove*.

1.2 Åstrand, Hans. *Sohlmans musiklexikon.* 2nd ed., revised and updated. 5 vols. Stockholm: Sohlmans Förlag, 1975–79.

First ed., edited by Gosta Morin and Carl Allan Moberg, 1948–52, 4 vols.

The major modern Swedish encyclopedia with an excellent overview of music's contemporary scene. This is an extensive work with contributions by leading Scandinavian musicologists, planned by a Scandinavian editorial board, providing brief entries on a wide variety of musical topics, including many biographies. The 2nd ed. is greatly revised; each vol. has a list of earlier articles deleted from the new ed., a feature that obliquely gives an account of the evolving Swedish musical world. The 5th vol. includes a classified index to topical articles. The longer articles are signed, with bibliographies. There are many musical examples and unusual illustrations, photographs, and charts, with a fair percentage in color. The variety of topics covered is wide-ranging: Popular music (including jazz), ethnic dance forms, musical technologies, and geographic topics are discussed.

The 2nd ed. is reviewed by Sven Hansell in *Fontes* 24 (1977): 194–96 and, briefly, by Stephen M. Fry in *Notes* 33 (1976): 307.

1.3 Albert Torrellas, Alberto. *Diccionario enciclopédico de la música.* 4 vols. Barcelona: Central Catalana de Publicaciones, 1947–52.

Supersedes *Diccionario de la música ilustrado,* 1927–29, 2 vols.

A Spanish encyclopedia whose major contributors include composers and musicologists from Spain, Portugal, and Latin America. The 1st vol., *Terminología, tecnología, morfología, instrumentos,* contains technical terms in many languages, including Greek and some Asian languages (transliterated), without bibliography or documentation. Vols. 2 and 3, *Biografías, bibliografía, monografías, historia, argumentos de operas,* have biographies of composers, performers, and musicologists, with emphasis on Spanish and Latin American musicians, including works lists for major composers and a classified works list for minor ones. There are historical articles under the individual countries, with extended articles for Spanish provinces, covering such areas as folk music, history, composers, and institutions but omitting bibliographical references. The 4th vol., *Apéndice,* has corrections and extensive additions to the first 3 vols. in all subject areas.

1.4 Allorto, Riccardo. *Nuovo dizionario Ricordi della musica e dei musicisti.* 730 pp. Milan: G. Ricordi, 1976.

Compiled using parts of the *Dizionario Ricordi della musica e dei musicisti,* 1959, edited by Claudio Sartori (1,155 pp.).

A quick-reference work with a wide overview. The entries are short and the bibliographies brief. The vol. is beautifully printed, with 16 color plates illustrating the history of musical notation. There are many musical examples and multilingual (French, German, and English) tables of terms; nontabular definitions include the Latin, Greek, Spanish, and Russian equivalents.

The *Dizionario* is reviewed by Jack A. Westrup in *M&L* 41 (1960): 80–81 and by James B. Coover in *Notes* 17 (1960): 564–66.

1.5 Ammer, Christine. *The HarperCollins Dictionary of Music.* 3rd ed. 512 pp. New York: HarperPerennial, 1995.

Revised 2nd ed. in paperback issued as the *HarperCollins Dictionary of Music* by HarperCollins, 1991; 2nd ed. issued as *The Harper Dictionary of Music* (Harper & Row, 1987, 493 pp.). First ed., *Harper's Dictionary of Music* (New York: Harper & Row, 1972, 414 pp.). English ed., Robert Hale, London, 1972.

A versatile dictionary for the general music lover. Musical terms, forms, instruments, and composers are covered, with detailed explanations and examples of both art music and popular music in over 3,500 entries, accompanied by line drawings and musical examples. It includes phonetic pronunciations and numerous selective lists (such as ballets, baroque composers, dynamic marks, operettas, oratorios, song cycles, symphonic poems, and symphonies).

The 1st ed. is reviewed by Nyal Williams in *Notes* 29 (1973): 449–50. The 2nd ed. is reviewed by Detlef Gojowy in *Neue Zeitschrift* 149 (January 1988): 61 and by Carol June Bradley in *ARBA* 19 (1988): no. 1275.

1.6 Arnold, Denis. *The New Oxford Companion to Music.* 2 vols. 2,017 pp. Oxford; New York: Oxford University Press, 1983.

Reprinted, with corrections, in 1984, 1988, 1990, and 1994. First published in 1938 as *The Oxford Companion to Music,* edited by Percy A. Scholes and issued under his direction in 8 additional eds. through 1955. 10th ed., edited by John Owen Ward, 1970 (1,189 pp.). In 1940 Scholes's *A List of Books about Music in the English Language, Prepared as an Appendix to the Oxford Companion to Music* was published by Oxford University Press (64 pp.). The French ed. of the *New Oxford Companion,* trans. by Marie-Stella Parias, was published as *Dictionnaire encyclopédique de la musique* (Paris: Robert Laffont, 1988, 2 vols., 2,158 pp.).

A classic and comprehensive work designed for the general reader, reborn in a new, 2-vol. format, the product of 90 contributors, including its first and its latest editors. Intended to be complete in themselves, the few articles with bibliographies cite recent English-language titles; *The New Grove* (**1.48**) is cited as the source for "more facts." The pronunciation guide of foreign or difficult terms and names, as well as the compilations of "Misattributed Compositions" and "Nicknamed Compositions" included in most of the earlier editions, have been abandoned. The inclusion of jazz, some additional popular music, and non-Western music shows the new editor's broader world view. Nevertheless, the inclusion of some of Scholes's classic articles reveals a dated approach.

Other much-edited descendants of Scholes's original work include *The Oxford Dictionary of Music* (**1.27**) and the *Concise Oxford Dictionary of Music.*

The 1st ed. is reviewed by C. B. Oldman in *M&L* 20 (1939): 72–74, the 8th ed. by Charles Warren Fox in *Notes* 8 (1950): 177–78, and the 9th ed. by Vincent Duckles in *Notes* 13 (1955): 70–72. Reviews of *The New Oxford Companion* include those by Clifford Bartlett in *Brio* 20 (1983): 61–62, Brian Newbould in *MT* 125 (1984): 570–71, Karen Pendle in *OQ* 2 (1984): 170–72, James Porter in *Ethnomusicology* 31 (1987): 128–31, Denis Stevens in *EM* 13 (1985): 85–89, Michael Tilmouth in *M&L* 65 (1984): 303–6, and by Ross Wood in *ARBA* 15 (1984): no. 889.

1.7 Basso, Alberto. *Dizionario enciclopedico universale della musica e dei musicisti.* 13 vols. Turin: Unione Tipografico-Editrice Torinese, 1983–90.

Contents: Prima parte, *La lessico,* Vols. 1–4 (1983–84); Seconda parte, *Le biografie,* Vols. 1–8 (1985–88); *Appendice* (1990, 770 pp.).

Successor to *La musica* (Turin: Unione Tipografico-Editrice Torinese, 1966–71, 2 vols. in 6).

The leading Italian encyclopedia of music, nicknamed *DEUMM* by its publisher. The coverage is international, with 37,000 entries (12,000 more than *The New Grove*) and selective bibliographies. The dictionary of terms has extensive signed articles, with many illustrations, charts, and tables, as well as generous cross-references. The biographical section features signed articles on composers, performers, and other musical figures. The composer articles have works lists, although the standard thematic catalog numbers are often omitted. *The New Grove* (**1.48**) is often mentioned as an additional reference source. The *Appendice* contains additional citations, expanding and deepening the areas of coverage; errata are not included.

Reviewed by David Fallows in *EM* 12 (1984): 93–95; by Hans Lenneberg in *Notes* 42 (1986): 538–40, 45 (1988): 72–74, and 46 (1989): 83–84; and by Frederick W. Sternfeld in *M&L* 72 (1991): 407–8.

1.8 Blom, Eric. *The New Everyman Dictionary of Music.* 6th ed. Edited by David Cummings. 876 pp. London: J.M. Dent; Toronto: Fitzhenry & Whiteside, 1988; New York: Weidenfeld and Nicolson, 1989. (Everyman's reference library)

Paperback ed., New York: Grove Weidenfeld, 1991. First ed. published in London by J.M. Dent & Sons, 1947, as *Everyman's Dictionary of Music;* American ed. (Philadelphia, Pa.: David M. McKay, 1948, 706 pp.); 2nd ed., 1954 (687 pp.); 3rd ed., 1958; 4th ed., 1962, revised by Sir Jack Westrup; revised ed., 1965; further revised ed., 1968. Fifth ed., 1974 (793 pp.), revised by Jack Westrup, John Caldwell, Edward Olleson, and R. T. Beck; Spanish ed. published in Buenos Aires by Editorial Claridad in 1985 (1,035 pp.).

A popular quick-reference book of terms and biographies (composers, performers, and writers on music). Rich in information and generous with musical examples, the *Dictionary* has kept its relatively compact size in part through the extensive use of abbreviations. The summary lists of composers' works include the date of composition for each work.

The 1st ed. is reviewed by W. McNaught in *MT* 88 (1947): 223–24; the 2nd ed. by Vincent Duckles in *Notes* 13 (1955): 70–72; and the 6th ed. by Noël Goodwin in *Opera* 39 (1988): 1059–60, by William J. Waters in *LJ* 114 (1989): 68, and by Arthur Jacobs in *M&L* 70 (1989): 236–37.

1.9 Blume, Friedrich. *Die Musik in Geschichte und Gegenwart: Allgemeine Enzyklopädie der Musik.* 17 vols. Kassel, Germany; Basel: Bärenreiter-Verlag, 1949–86.

The first 14 vols., originally issued in fascicles, make up the main body of the work; Vols. 15 and 16, the *Ergänzungs-Bände,* published 1973–79, correct and supplement the earlier volumes; Vol. 15 also provides individual entries for those originally covered in very large family articles; errata are also given in Vols. 3, 7, and 10. The *Register Band,* Vol. 17 (1986), edited by Elisabeth and Harald Heckmann, is an extensive and valuable index, making many otherwise obscured matters accessible and succinctly using graphic symbols to point out a variety of special features.

A comprehensive music reference work of the highest scholarly merit, written in German, but international in scope and coverage, commonly called *MGG.* There are 9,414 articles, some of monographic length, embodying contemporary research by 1,300 specialist contributors from more than 40 countries. Over half the entries are for composers; the information on those deemed more significant includes detailed works lists (noting publisher and date of premiere) and bibliographies, with both features notoriously difficult to read because of their abbreviations and formatting. There are many relevant illustrations. Each of the pre-*Ergänzungs-Bände* contains indexes to the individual volume, arranged by title and by author, as well as a list of illustrations.

Four of Blume's major survey articles were trans. by M. D. Herter Norton and published by W.W. Norton in two vols.: *Renaissance and Baroque Music: A Comprehensive Survey* (1967, 180 pp.) and *Classic and Romantic Music: A Comprehensive Survey* (1970, 213 pp.). The former is reviewed by Vernon Gotwals in *Notes* 24 (1968): 488–89.

Along its way to completion, various sections of *MGG* were reviewed by Willi Apel in *JAMS* 3 (1950): 142–45, 4 (1951): 160–63 and 261–62, 5 (1952): 56–57 and 138–39, 6 (1953): 68–69, and 8 (1955): 43–45; by Charles Warren Fox in *Notes* 7 (1950): 466–67, 10 (1953): 451–52, and 12 (1954): 92–93; and by Paul Henry Lang in *MQ* 36 (1950): 141–43 and 38 (1952): 477–79.

The publication of *Grove Dictionary*'s 5th ed. in 1954 prompted some critical comparisons between *Grove* and *MGG;* see Richard S. Hill in *Notes* 12 (1954): 85–92 and A. Hyatt King, "*Grove V* and *MGG,*" in the *Monthly Musical Record* 85 (1955): 115–19, 152–57, and 183–85. For a fascinating discussion of the genesis, organization, and production of *MGG,* see Friedrich Blume's "*Die Musik in Geschichte und Gegenwart:* A Postlude" in *Notes* 24 (1967): 217–44. Blume also wrote a preface to *MGG*'s *Supplement* in *Notes* 26 (1969): 5–8. Paul Henry Lang's "*Die Musik in Geschichte und Gegenwart:* Epilogue," in *Notes* 36 (1979): 271–81, is a panegyric to Blume and the others who worked on *MGG,* as well as a comment on the state of musicology. See also Jack Westrup, "Kritische Anmerkungen zu *Die Musik in Geschichte und Gegenwart,*" volumes 9–14," trans. by Ludwig Finscher in *Die Musikforschung* 22 (1969): 217–25.

The facsimiles in *MGG* of pre-1600 polyphonic music are indexed by Terence Ford in *Notes* 39 (1983): 283–315; Dominique-René de Lerma and Michael Phillips compiled "Entries of Ethnomusicological Interest in *MGG:* A Preliminary Listing" in *Ethnomusicology* 13 (1969): 129–38, including biographies and an index of contributors.

A new ed. of *MGG,* elegantly redesigned in format, edited by Ludwig Finscher, began to be issued in 1994 (Kassel, Germany: Bärenreiter; Stuttgart: Metzler) and is scheduled to arrive at the rate of 2 volumes a year for 10 years; the new format segregates musical subjects (*Sachteil,* 8 vols., and *Register,* to be published 1994–98) and biography (*Personenteil,* 12 vols., to be published 1998–2004), in the style of the 12th ed. of Riemann (**1.45**), as edited by Gurlitt. The editor describes the *Sachteil* as an encyclopedia rather than a lexicon, thus omitting all brief entries of musical terminology, as is found in *The New Grove* (**1.48**) or *DEUMM* (**1.7**).

The 1st vol. of the new ed. is reviewed by David Fallows in *EM* 23 (1995): 151–52 and, more thoroughly, by Mark Germer in "The New *Musik in Geschichte und Gegenwart:* First Impressions" in *Notes* 52 (1995): 39–44.

1.10* Candé, Roland de. *Nouveau dictionnaire de la musique.* 670 pp. Paris: Seuil, 1983.

First ed., *Dictionnaire de musique,* published in Paris by Éditions du Seuil, 1961 (283 pp.). The 1st ed. was also published in a Spanish trans., *Diccionari de la música,* in Barcelona by Edicions 62 in 1967 (223 pp.) and in an Italian trans., *Dizionario di musica,* in Milan by Tascabili Bompiani in 1968 (285 pp.).

A beautifully printed, liberally illustrated French dictionary of music for the concertgoer, with brief composer biographies and musical definitions. The illustrations include photographs, musical examples, charts, manuscript facsimiles (some in color), title-page reproductions, and family trees. There are a discography (pp. 610–52) that gives label names but no manufacturer numbers, a charted chronology (pp. 654–57), a classified bibliography, and a subject index.

1.11 Cooper, Martin. *The Concise Encyclopedia of Music and Musicians.* 4th ed., revised. 480 pp. London: Hutchinson, 1978.

The 1st ed. was published in London by Hutchinson and in New York by Hawthorn Books, 1958 (516 pp.); the 2nd ed., revised, was published in 1971 (481 pp.). The 3rd ed., revised, was published in London by Hutchinson in 1975 (481 pp.).

A work designed for the average music lover. There are 17 contributors in addition to the editor. The biographical entries are brief, with longer discussions of major terms and forms, but no bibliographies. The volume is well illustrated, with 16 color plates and more than 100 in monochrome.

The 1st ed. is reviewed by Hans F. Redlich in *MR* 20 (1959): 340–41 and by Robin Hull in *MT* 99 (1958): 487–88.

1.12 Dahlhaus, Carl, and **Hans Heinrich Eggebrecht.** *Brockhaus Riemann Musiklexikon in vier Bänden und einem Ergänzungsband.* 5 vols. Mainz: Schott; Munich: Piper, 1995. (Serie Musik Piper-Schott)

The *Ergänzungsband* was first published in 1989 and updated in 1995. An earlier ed. was the *Brockhaus–Riemann-Musiklexikon* (Wiesbaden: Brockhaus; Mainz: B. Schott's Söhne, 1978–79, 2 vols.).

A general music dictionary based on the format laid out in the 1882 Riemann's *Musik-Lexikon* (**1.45**). Areas covered include musical terms and biographical entries (for composers, musicologists, and performers, historical and current, classical and popular). Phonetic pronunciation, musical examples, and selective bibliographies are included as appropriate. Abbreviations and sigla are extensively used. The entries are brought up to date by the *Supplement* (120 pp.), which adds information for previous entries as well as new topics.

The 1979 ed. is reviewed by Wolfgang Burde in *Neue Zeitschrift* 140 (1979): 74–75 and by Hubert Unverricht in *Musik und Bildung* 11 (1979): 127–28; its 1st vol. is also reviewed by Stephen M. Fry in *Notes* 36 (1980): 901–2. The 1989 ed. is reviewed by Herbert Höntsch in *Tibia* 15 (1990): 143 and by Susan T. Sommer in *Notes* 47 (1990): 408.

1.13 Eaglefield Hull, Arthur. *A Dictionary of Modern Music and Musicians.* 543 pp. London: J.M. Dent, 1924. (Bernard J. Naylor collection)

Reprinted by Da Capo Press and by Scholarly Press, New York, in 1971, as well as in 1973 by AMS Press, New York. A German ed., *Das neue Musiklexikon, nach dem Dictionary of Modern Music and Musicians,* was edited, with many additions and corrections, by Alfred Einstein and published by M. Hesse in Berlin, 1926 (729 pp.). In turn, much of the content of *Das neue Musiklexikon* was incorporated in the 11th ed. of Riemann's *Musik-Lexikon* (**1.45**).

A predominantly biographical dictionary that includes terms related to then-contemporary music. It has excellent international coverage of music from 1880 to 1920 and was written with numerous foreign collaborators. There are entries for publishers, musicologists, organizations, and new instruments, among others. Corrections and additions are included in the 1938 ed. of Slonimsky's *Music since 1900* (**2.84**).

1.14* Eggebrecht, Hans Heinrich. *Meyers Taschenlexikon Musik in 3 Bänden.* Edited in cooperation with the Redaktion Musik des Bibliographischen Instituts under the direction of Gerhard Kmiatkowski. 3 vols. Mannheim, Germany: Bibliographisches Institut, 1984.

A concise ed., *Meyers kleines Lexikon,* was published by the Institut in 1986, 491 pp.

A generously illustrated, multivolume German dictionary, international and far-ranging in scope, covering 8,000 persons (composers, performers, and instrument makers), musical instruments, and terms, with selective bibliographical references.

1.15 Framery, Nicolas Étienne, the **Abbé Jean Étienne Feytou,** and **Pierre Louis Ginguené.** *Encyclopédie méthodique, ou par ordre de matières: par une société de gens de lettres, de savants et d'artistes . . . La Musique.* 2 vols. Paris: Chez Panckoncke, 1791–1818.

Publisher varies. Tome II, Paris: Chez Mme veuve Agasse; in this vol. the name of Jérôme Joseph de Momigny replaces that of the Abbé Feytou. Vol. 1 has a musical appendix (74 pp.); Vol. 2 (114 pp.).

Reprinted by Da Capo Press, New York, 1971.

A large general work of which the two volumes cited are concerned with music. These volumes are of considerable historical importance because they incorporate all of Rousseau's *Dictionnaire de musique,* 1768 (**1.324**) and articles from the Diderot–d'Alembert *Encyclopédie* (1751–72), along with more recent commentary. The articles are signed.

1.16 Goléa, Antoine, and **Michel Vignal.** *Larousse de la musique.* 2 vols. Paris: Librairie Larousse, 1982.

A 1-vol. abridgment was published in 1985. The 1st ed. (1957, 2 vols.) was edited by Norbert

Dufourcq with Félix Raugel and Armand Machabey. An Italian version of the 1st ed. was issued as *Dizionario musicale Larousse,* edited by Delfino Nava (Milan: Edizioni Paoline, 1961, 3 vols.).

An encyclopedic dictionary with more than 8,000 entries, principally on Western music from its origins to the present. The emphasis is generally French, with brief but authoritative articles: biographies (composers, performers, musicologists, editors, instrument makers, critics, and writers), works (operas, ballets, and historical manuscripts, with about 2,000 entries under the titles of individual compositions), and subjects (terms, places, schools, forms, and genres), and some articles on non-Western music. Special features include lists of published thematic catalogs and lists of works performed at certain festivals. There is a bibliography, arranged by subject, at the end of the 2nd vol., as well as a name and title index.

The 1st ed. is reviewed by Paul Henry Lang in *MQ* 45 (1959): 120–23 and by James B. Coover in *Notes* 16 (1959): 381–83.

1.17* Goodman, Alfred A. *Musik von A–Z, vom gregorianischen Choral zu Jazz und Beat: Komponisten, Werke, Interpreten, Orchester, Opernhäuser, Kammermusikvereinigungen, Bands, Geschichte, Theorie und Instrumente.* 640 pp. Munich: Südwest Verlag, 1971.

One man's attempt to meet the needs of a wide range of music-lovers. It is liberally illustrated (multiple examples per page), international in scope, with musical excerpts and a wide range of coverage. A large percentage of the entries are biographical, with only the most major composers given works lists; there are no bibliographies.

1.18 Griffiths, Paul. *The Thames and Hudson Encyclopaedia of Twentieth-Century Music.* 207 pp. London; New York: Thames & Hudson, 1986.

A concise British approach to contemporary Western art music. A subject entry at the beginning of this "encyclopedia" (an overly grandiose label) organizes entries by nationality, and a chronology at the end lists first performances year-by-year. The 500+ brief composer entries include selected works lists and bibliographies; the terminology entries are clear and succinct.

Reviewed by Ann P. Basart in *CNV* 113 (1987): 5, by George Louis Mayer in *ARBA* 18 (1987): no. 1231, by Peter Owens in *M&L* 68 (1987): 298–99, and by Marion S. Gushee in *Notes* 45 (1989): 756–57.

1.19* Hadley, Benjamin. *Britannica Book of Music.* 881 pp. New York: Doubleday/Britannica Books, 1980.

Musical offspring of a venerable parent. Newly commissioned entries are combined with excerpts from the *Encyclopedia Britannica* to produce a reference work intended for the nonspecialist reader. The biographical entries include both composers and performers; however, composers active in popular music and musical theater can be located only in articles on those subjects. Also included are entries for musical terms and historical eras. There are some basic bibliographies, occasional brief discographies (without performance or label information), illustrations, diagrams, and musical examples. A few of the longer articles are signed.

An earlier, similar title from the 11th ed. of the same parent source was Donald F. Tovey's *Musical Articles from the Encyclopedia Britannica,* published by Oxford University Press in 1944 (256 pp.), which was reprinted as *The Forms of Music* in 1956 by Meridian Press, New York. Its 28 articles, of varying length, are on the larger aspects of music (harmony, madrigals, sonata, and sonata forms).

Britannica Book of Music is reviewed by Margaret Downie in *AMISN* 10 (1981): 6 no. 1 and by George R. Hill in *ARBA* 13 (1982): no. 1037.

1.20 Herzfeld, Friedrich. *Das neue Ullstein Lexikon der Musik.* 9th ed. 819 pp. Frankfurt am Main: Verlag Ullstein, 1993.

The 1st ed. was published as *Lexikon der Musik,* Berlin, 1957 (551 pp.), and the 3rd ed. (1965, 631 pp.) was *Ullstein Musiklexikon.* The 7th, *Ullstein Lexikon der Musik* (1974, 631 pp.), and 8th, *Das neue Ullstein Lexikon der Musik* (1989, 819 pp.) follow. Also published as *DBG-Musiklexikon* by the Deutsche Buch-Gemeinschaft, Berlin, 1965.

A popular, ready-reference source. This frequently revised but seldom expanded 1-vol. music dictionary is profusely illustrated with small-scale portraits, musical examples, and brief, quickly outdated discographies.

1.21 Honegger, Marc. *Dictionnaire de musique.* 4 vols. Paris: Bordas, 1970–76.

Contents: Part I, *Les hommes et leurs oeuvres* (2 vols.); Part II, *Science de la musique: Techniques, formes, instruments* (2 vols.).

Part I was reprinted in 1974 and revised in 1979; a new ed. of Part I, also 2 vols., was published in 1986, reprinted in 1993. There is a revised German ed. originally published as *Das grosse Lexikon der Musik in acht Bänden,* edited by Marc Honegger and Günther Massenkeil (Freiburg; Basel: Herder, 1978–83); 2 final vols., a German trans. of Gerald Abraham's *The Concise Oxford History of Music* (**2.3**), were added in 1983, with the set published as *Das grosse Lexikon der Musik.* Spanish ed. of the 1st part, *Diccionario de la música: Los hombres y sus obras* (Madrid: Espasa-Escalpe, 1987–93, 2nd ed.), 2 vols.

One of the most substantial modern French music encyclopedias. With particularly excellent coverage of French topics, although with brief entries, this handsome, well-illustrated work was produced with the collaboration of 186 authorities and is international in scope, with musical examples and bibliographical references.

The 1986 ed. of Part I is reviewed by Roger Nichols in *M&L* 71 (1990): 524–26.

1.22 Jacobs, Arthur. *The Penguin Dictionary of Music.* 5th ed. 447 pp. London; New York: Penguin Books, 1991. (Penguin reference books)

First published as the paperback *A New Dictionary of Music,* 1958, followed by a hardcover ed. with a new introduction and corrections, published in London and Chicago, Ill., 1961. The 2nd ed., Penguin, in Baltimore, Md., 1967 (424 pp.); the 3rd ed., 1973 (425 pp.). The 4th ed., Harmondsworth, England, *The New Penguin Dictionary of Music,* 1977 (457 pp.). The 6th ed. anticipated, 1996.

A pocket dictionary "for the inquiring music lover," with brief identifications of people, terms, specific composition titles, and other musical topics.

The 1961 ed. is reviewed by Harold E. Samuel in *Notes* 20 (1963): 657–58.

1.23 Jurík, Marián. *Malá encyklopédia hudby.* 642 pp. + 32 pp. of plates. Bratislava: Obzor, t. Pravda, 1969.

An illustrated Slovak bio-bibliography and dictionary of music. There are no bibliographical references with the articles, although there is a bibliography at the end of the volume (pp. 629–42).

1.24* Kao, T'ien-k'ang. *Yin yüeh chih shih tz'u tien.* 840 pp. Kan-su jen min ch'u pan she: Kan-su sheng hsin hua shu tien fa hsing, 1981.

A Chinese dictionary of music, containing general music terms for and information on folk songs, drama, music theory, and musical instruments, defining terms and containing information on composers. There are both subject and character stroke indexes. The text is printed in simplified characters.

1.25 Keldysh, Iuriĭ Vsevolodovich. *Entsiklopedicheskii muzykal´nyi slovar´.* Edited by B. S. Shteinpress and I. M. Iampol´skii. 326 pp. Moscow: Gos. Nuach. Izd.-vo "Bol´shaia sovetskaia entsiklopediia," 1959.

A standard Soviet encyclopedia of music, containing partially revised articles from the general *Bol´shaia sovetskaia entsiklopediia.*

1.26 Keldysh, Iuriĭ Vsevolodovich. *Muzykal´naia entsiklopediia.* 6 vols. Moscow: "Sov. Entsiklopediia—Sov. Kompozitor," 1973–82.

The official music encyclopedia of the Soviet Union, containing extensive, signed articles, many with bibliographies and works lists. Though international in scope, coverage is provided in greater depth for figures in socialist countries and includes musical figures cited in no other reference work, enabling the reader to acquire information and opinion otherwise unavailable. I. M. Iampol'ski's article "Muzykal'noi bibliografiia" uses a typical approach, surveying music bibliographical works without chronological or geopolitical boundaries, but with substantial coverage of works done in socialist countries, particularly the Soviet Union.

1.27 Kennedy, Michael, and **Joyce Bourne.** *The Oxford Dictionary of Music.* 2nd ed. 985 pp. Oxford; New York: Oxford University Press, 1994.

First published in 1985 (810 pp.), a revised, enlarged ed. of the *Concise Oxford Dictionary of Music* (3rd ed., 1980, 724 pp.). The latter's Preface describes it as "the first complete and radical overhaul since Dr. Scholes' original compilation," in turn based on the original by Percy A. Scholes, first published in 1952 (xxx + 655 pp.). The 2nd ed., 1964, was reissued as a paperback by Oxford in 1968 (636 pp.); 3rd ed. was reprinted in paperback, with corrections, in 1988. In 1991, a Chinese trans. of the 3rd ed., *Niu-chin chien ming yin yueh tzu tien,* was published in Pei-ching.

A quick-reference source for music. This ed., adding 1500+ new entries, includes entries for musical terms and instruments, many short bibliographies for composers, vocal and instrumental performers, and conductors, as well as hundreds of entries on individual compositions. Of the 11,000 entries, about 4,000 are biographical; many new entries have been added to those remaining from previous editions.

The first ed. is reviewed by Michael Tilmouth in *M&L* 67 (1986): 305–6. The 2nd ed. is reviewed by Nicky Hind in *Brio* 32 (1995): 46–47.

1.28 Kovačević, Krešimir. *Muzička enciklopedija.* 2nd ed. 3 vols. Zagreb: Jugoslavenski leksikografski zavod, 1971–79.

The 1st ed., edited by Josip Andreis, was published in 2 vols., 1958–63.

The work of the former Yugoslavia's leading musicologists. There are condensed biographical entries and extended subject entries, with well-organized bibliographies and works lists; the biographies, though international in coverage, exclude living performers and emphasize Slavic composers. Excellent in content and appearance, it is liberally illustrated.

The 1st ed. is reviewed by Josef Brozek in *Notes* 21 (1963): 128–29.

1.29 Lavignac, Albert. *Encyclopédie de la musique et dictionnaire du conservatoire.* 2 parts in 11 vols. Paris: C. Delagrave, 1913–31.

Contents: Part I, *Histoire de la musique;* Part II, *Technique, esthétique, pédagogie.*

Originally published in fascicles.

A work designed in the tradition of the French encyclopedists as a universal repository of musical knowledge. It is international in scope, although most of the contributors are French. Many of the studies are full-scale monographs and for years ranked among the more important surveys of their fields. History is treated by country. Among the chief contributors are Maurice Emmanuel, Amédée Gastoué, Oscar Chilesotti, Romain Rolland, Henry Expert, and Rafael Mitjana.

Part II deals with music theory, instruction, and aesthetics in all aspects, including acoustics, notation, instrument making, choreography, and institutions. There are many illustrations, both pictorial and musical. Major articles include those by Charles Koechlin, Paul Rougnon, and Vincent D'Indy.

The *Encyclopédie* lacks an index, but the detailed tables of contents at the end of each part can be most useful as a guide to its contents. A partial index compiled by Robert Bruce appears in *Notes* ser. 1 (May 1936): 1–40.

The 4th vol. is reviewed by R. O. Morris in *M&L* 2 (1921): 85–86 and the 5th vol. is reviewed by A. H. Strangways and Robert Lachmann in *M&L* 4 (1923): 290–92.

1.30* Lebrecht, Norman. *The Companion to Twentieth-Century Music: An Enlightening and Entertaining Guide to the Music of Our Century—from Puccini and Mahler to the Composers and Performers of Today.* 418 pp. New York: Simon & Schuster, 1992.

A dictionary of terms, festivals, musical compositions, and musicians (composers, performers, and conductors) from both the popular and the art music worlds. The entries for the latter are the reverse of the usual: A statement placing the subject and his or her musical philosophy in time is followed by an abbreviated biographical statement. There is a chart showing the new music performed, arranged by year, with parallel columns listing events in the rest of the arts and in the rest of the world.

1.31 Lindlar, Heinrich. *Rororo Musikhandbuch.* 2 vols. Reinbek bei Hamburg: Rowohlt, 1973.

Contents: Vol. 1, *Musiklehre und Musikleben;* Vol. 2, *Lexikon der Komponisten, Lexikon der Interpreten, Gesamtregister.*

Originally issued as *Meyers Handbuch über die Musik,* 1961.

A miscellaneous array of facts about music and musical life, from a European perspective. There are lists of libraries, societies, research institutes, and performers, with a wide scope but shallow coverage.

1.32 Lissa, Zofia, and **Elżbięta Dziebowska.** *Encyklopedia muzyczna PWM.* 4 vols. to date. Cracow: Polskie Wydawn. Muzyczne, 1979– .

A modern, illustrated Polish encyclopedia of music, providing bio-bibliographical information and entries on terms and topics.

1.33 Meguro, Sansaku. *Hyōjun ongaku jiten / Standard Music Dictionary.* 2 vols. Tokyo: Ongaku no Tomosha, 1966–73.

A multivolume Japanese dictionary of music.

1.34 Michel, François. *Encyclopédie de la musique.* Edited in collaboration with François Lesure, Vladimir Fédorov, and an editorial committee composed of Nadia Boulanger et al. 3 vols. Paris: Fasquelle, 1958–61.

The Spanish adaptation, *Enciclopedia Salvat de la música* (Barcelona: Salvat Editores, S.A., 1967, 4 vols.), was revised and adapted by Manuel Valls Gorina.

A mixture of extended subject essays and short biographical articles, especially valuable for its coverage of modern music, generally called "Fasquelle." In the 1st vol., before the dictionary proper, is a 200-page introduction, labeled by Coover (**1.1**) as "sometimes-interesting, momentarily useful"; the "Informations générales" gives a guide to French publishers, festivals, concerts, music associations, copyright laws, institutions, and music education current in the 1950s. A "Livre d'or" (pp. 35–76) contains portraits and facsimile pages from the manuscripts of leading contemporary composers, and there is a chronological table of music history (pp. 202–38). Despite this opening section and the French nationality of most contributors, the *Encyclopédie* covers Europe and the Americas. Ideas and principles are emphasized more than individuals and musical works. Although the biographical articles are short, the range of biographical coverage is unusually extensive; there are bibliographical references, although most are to *MGG* (**1.9**). Works lists are included for major composers. There are many signed articles and excellent illustrative material, both musical and pictorial.

The 1st vol. of the French ed. is reviewed by James B. Coover in *Notes* 16 (1959): 381–83; Vols. 2 and 3 are reviewed by James B. Coover, with a biographically oriented errata list by Nicolas Slonimsky in *Notes* 18 (1961): 421–23. The Spanish ed. is reviewed by Daniel Devoto in *Revue de musicologie* 57 (1971): 87–88.

1.35 Moore, John W. *Complete Encyclopaedia of Music, Elementary, Technical, Historical, Biographical, Vocal, and Instrumental.* 1,004 pp. Boston, Mass.: J.P. Jewett and Co.; New York: Sheldon, Lamport and Blakeman, 1854.

Appendix to Encyclopedia of Music, Containing Events and Information Occurring Since the Main Work was Issued, was published in Boston by Oliver Ditson in 1875 (45 pp.) as part of their American culture series. The *Complete Encyclopaedia* was first printed by Ditson in 1852, and was reprinted by them in 1880. Reprinted in 1973 by the AMS Press, New York.

The first comprehensive American musical dictionary. The *Complete Encyclopaedia* contains more than 5,000 terms, 4,000 biographical citations, and 200 general articles, many drawn from such European sources as Gerber (**1.78**), Choron and Fayolle (**1.68**), Burney (**2.7**), Hawkins (**2.19**), Schilling (**1.51**), and Fétis (**1.75**), with substantial additions from *Dwight's Musical Journal* and the *New York Musical Times.* The *Complete Encyclopaedia* is especially rich in notices of 18th- and 19th-century musicians, but somewhat weak in early Americana.

1.36 Moore, John W. *A Dictionary of Musical Information, Containing Also a Vocabulary of Musical Terms, and a List of Modern Musical Works Published in the United States from 1640 to 1875.* 211 pp. Boston, Mass.: Oliver Ditson, 1876.

The 1st ed. was reprinted by Burt Franklin in New York, 1971, and by the AMS Press, New York, 1977.

Using the author's *Complete Encyclopaedia* (**1.35**) as a foundation, the "musical information" is chiefly biographical entries, and those quite brief; the "vocabulary of musical terms" is a pronunciation dictionary; and the "list of modern musical works" is alphabetical by title, including many anthologies.

1.37* Morehead, Philip D., and **Anne MacNeil.** *The New American Dictionary of Music: From Dvorak to Dylan, Machaut to Motown.* 608 pp. New York: Dutton, 1991.

British ed. published as *Bloomsbury Dictionary of Music* in London by Bloomsbury Publishing, 1992. Paperback ed. published by Meridian in New York as the *New International Dictionary of Music,* 1992.

Designed as the "first stop for quick information on a wide variety of musical topics." However, some topics seem to have been left behind: Ironically, in a work labeling itself as American, there is no entry for Oscar Sonneck. Included are entries for terms of both art and popular music, biographies of art and popular composers and performers (current and historical, solo and ensemble), music publishers, instrument manufacturers, titles of musical compositions (including major national anthems) and broadcast programs, and musical movements and styles. Few composition titles are given in the biographical entries. Some musical examples and line drawings are included.

1.38 Moser, Hans J. *Musik Lexikon.* 4th ed. 2 vols. Hamburg: H. Sikorski, 1955.

Nachtrag, 1958 (71 pp.); *Ergänzungsband, A–Z,* 1963 (287 pp.).

First published 1932–35; 2nd ed., 1943; 3rd ed., 1951.

Brief authoritative articles, with special emphasis on bibliographies and lists of early music in new editions. The contents were originally intended for German readers, but the later editions have become increasingly international in scope. The 4th ed., the first to appear in 2 vols., was extensively revised, with many new articles and bibliographical additions.

1.39 *Ongaku daijiten: Encyclopaedia musica.* 6 vols. Tokyo: Heibonsha, 1981–83.

The 1st ed., *Ongaku jiten,* edited by Yasazuro Shimonaka, was issued in 12 vols., 1954–57.

A major Japanese encyclopedia of music. The 6th vol. serves as an index to the set.

1.40 Pena, Joaquín, and **Higinio Anglés.** *Diccionario de la música Labor.* 2 vols. Barcelona: Labor, 1954.

Begun in 1940 as an adaptation of Riemann (**1.45**) and developed as a new dictionary of music for professional musicians and the general user in Spanish-speaking countries. The contributors are Spanish and Spanish-American. The foreign biographies are drawn from such standard authorities as Riemann, Grove (**1.48**), and Baker (**1.62**). The coverage includes bio-bibliography, musical technique, and music history. There is an extensive list of music periodicals, classified by country, with a short bibliography on musical journalism.

1.41* Pérez Gutierrez, Mariano. *Diccionario de la música y los músicos.* 3 vols. Madrid: Ediciones ISTMO, 1985. (Colección fundamentos, 87–89)

A Spanish dictionary of brief entries on music and musicians (composers and performers, historical and contemporary), intended for the music amateur.

1.42 Pratt, Waldo S. *The New Encyclopedia of Music and Musicians.* New and revised ed. 969 pp. New York: Macmillan, 1929.

First published in 1924.

Originally planned as an abridgment of the 2nd ed. of *Grove* (**1.48**) and instead developed as an independent work. The coverage is primarily of the 18th to 20th centuries, with emphasis on living musicians and the American musical scene. The definitions of musical terms are excellent. The body of the work is arranged in three main categories: terms, biographies, and institutions and organizations. There are appendixes of bibliographies, persons before 1700, and operas and oratorios since 1900, as well as various additional death dates.

1.43 Prieberg, Fred K. *Lexikon der neuen Musik.* 495 pp. Freiburg; Munich: K. Alber, 1958.

Primarily a biographical dictionary, but with some articles on aspects of and trends in contemporary music (such as film music, radio operas, polytonality, 12-tone music, and musique concrète). The approach is factual rather than critical, covering the education, activities, and principal works of 20th-century composers.

1.44 Randel, Don Michael. *Harvard Concise Dictionary of Music.* 577 pp. Cambridge, Mass.: Harvard University Press, 1978.

Successor to the Willi Apel and Ralph T. Daniel *Harvard Brief Dictionary of Music,* 1960 (341 pp.), which was an offshoot of the *Harvard Dictionary of Music* (**1.269**). A paperback ed. was published by Washington Square Press in New York, 1961, and a Spanish ed., *Diccionario Harvard de música,* was published by Editorial Diana, Mexico City, 1984 (559 pp.). Followed by Randel's complete retooling, *The New Harvard Dictionary of Music,* 1986 (**1.320**).

A reference tool for students enrolled in a college-level music appreciation course. This descendant of a distinguished line has 6,000 entries, including short articles on musical topics, musical compositions, and 2,000 composers, as well as definitions of musical terms.

Reviewed by Stanley Sadie in *MT* 120 (1979): 220–21 and by Linda I. Solow in *Notes* 36 (1979): 93–94.

1.45 Riemann, Hugo. *Riemann Musik-Lexikon.* 12th ed. Edited by Wilibald Gurlitt. 5 vols. Mainz: B. Schott's Söhne; New York: Schott Music Corporation, 1959–75.

The first 2 vols. are a biographical dictionary, issued 1959–61; the 3rd is a subject dictionary, edited by Hans Heinrich Eggebrecht and published in 1967. Two supplementary vols. of biographical entries, addenda, and errata, *Ergänzungsbände,* were edited by Carl Dahlhaus, 1972–75. The 12th ed. is the latest in a series based on Riemann's work, which was first published in 1882, and is the first in which terms and biographies are listed separately. The 9th–11th eds. were supervised by Alfred Einstein, who added much to the scope and authority of the work. *Brockhaus Riemann Musiklexikon* (**1.12**) is the current heir to the Riemann mantle.

An international dictionary of music, covering all times and places and incorporating the achievements of German musical scholarship. It is superior to Moser (**1.38**) in typography and organization, and to Baker (**1.62**) in bibliographical coverage. Lists of works are included in the bodies of the articles; modern editions of early works and bibliographical references are given in separate paragraphs. The 3rd vol., the *Sachteil,* is similar to the *New Harvard Dictionary of Music* (**1.320**), defining terms, describing musical instruments, and covering other musical subjects; one important article is a small-scale version of Heyer (**5.511**), listing composers' collected works and monuments of music, complete with a composer index. The *Ergänzungsbände* incorporate new information, corrections, and additions to the articles and bibliographies in the first 3 vols., as well as offering new articles. The 5th vol. includes a supplementary necrology covering persons in the dictionary who died before 1975.

Riemann's work has been widely translated, and most of the translations incorporate new material of national interest. The principal translations are as follows:

Dictionnaire de musique. Trans. after the 4th ed. by Georges Humbert. Paris: Perrin, 1895–1902. 2nd ed., Paris: Perrin, 1913. 3rd ed., entirely reset and augmented, under the direction of André Schaeffner, with the collaboration of Marc Pincherle, Yvonne Rokseth, and André Tessier. Paris: Payot, 1931 (1,485 pp.).

Dictionary of Music. New ed., with many additions by the author. Trans. by J. S. Shedlock. London: Augener, 1893. Also published in 1897 as the *Encyclopedic Dictionary of Music,* with later eds. in 1902 and 1908. The 1908 ed. was reprinted by Da Capo, New York, in 1970.

Muzykal´nyi slovar´. Moscow: P. Iurgenson, 1901–4. A Russian trans. from the 5th German ed.

Nordisk Musik-lexikon, trans. by H. V. Schytte. Copenhagen: W. Hansen, 1888–1902, 2 vols., with a *Supplement,* 1906.

The 12th ed.'s *Personenteil* is reviewed by Vincent Duckles in *Notes* 16 (1959): 240–42 and 18 (1961): 572–74, by Paul Henry Lang in *MQ* 45 (1959): 563–66, by Hans Heinrich Eggebrecht in *Die Musikforschung* 12 (1959): 221–23, and by Charles van den Borren in *Revue belge de musicologie* 14 (1960): 137–38. The 12th ed.'s *Sachteil,* Vol. 3, is reviewed by Jack Alan Westrup in *M&L* 49 (1968): 256–57, by François Lesure in *Revue de musicologie* 54 (1968): 115–16, by Vincent Duckles in *Notes* 27 (1970): 256–58, and in a review article, "Hugo Riemann und der 'neue Riemann,'" by Walter Wiora in *Die Musikforschung* 22 (1969): 348–55. The *Ergänzungsbände* are briefly reviewed by Stephen M. Fry in *Notes* 32 (1976): 782.

1.46 Robijns, Jozef, and **Miep Zijlstra.** *Algemene muziek encyclopedie.* 10 vols. Haarlem, The Netherlands: De Haan, 1979–84.

Earlier ed. issued as *Algemene muziekencyclopedie, onder leiding van August Corbet en Wouter Paap.* J. Robjins: Redactiesecretaris (Antwerp: Zuid-Nederlandse Uitg., 1957–72, 7 vols.).

The most comprehensive Dutch music encyclopedia. The latest edition increases the coverage of all aspects of music, including ethnomusicology, popular music, and jazz, and is especially valuable for its wide biographical range; its brief biographies include performers, musicologists, composers, and dancers. Major articles are signed by contributors from England, Israel, the U.S., the USSR, and other countries. Subject bibliographies, discographies, and brief works lists are included for composers.

1.47 Roche, Jerome, and **Elizabeth Roche.** *A Dictionary of Early Music: From the Troubadours to Monteverdi.* 208 pp. New York: Oxford University Press, 1981.

A selective dictionary of the medieval through the early baroque periods. About 700 of the 1,000 entries are for composers of interest to the modern performer and listener, another 100 concern musical instruments, and the final 200 deal with a miscellaneous assortment of technical terms, musical forms, major manuscript and printed sources, the principal renaissance music publishers, and the more important theorists and writers on music. Modern scholarly editions are often cited as bibliographies for the individual entries.

Reviewed by François Lesure in *Fontes* 29 (1982): 149, by John Caldwell in *EM* 10 (1982): 76+, and by Allie Wise Goudy in *ARBA* 14 (1983): no. 932.

1.48 Sadie, Stanley. *The New Grove Dictionary of Music and Musicians.* 20 vols. London: Macmillan; Washington, D.C.: Grove's Dictionaries of Music, 1980.

First published 1879–90, 4 vols.; 2nd ed., 1904–10, edited by J. A. Fuller-Maitland; 3rd ed., 1927–28, edited by H. C. Colles; 4th ed., 1940, edited by H. C. Colles. A supplementary volume to the 3rd ed. appeared in 1940, covering 1928–40, adding new information on the earlier entries. The *American Supplement,* edited by Waldo S. Pratt, containing material on the Americas, was published in 1920 and again in 1928. The 5th ed., edited by Eric Blom, was published in 1954 by Macmillan, 9 vols.; a supplementary vol., edited by Eric Blom with Denis Stevens as associate editor, was published in 1963 (493 pp.). The 5th ed. was reissued in paperback by St. Martin's Press, New York, 1970. The 1980 6th ed. was reissued in paperback, 1995.

The standard and the largest comprehensive music encyclopedia in English and the work to which all others are currently compared. In contrast to similar works of this type, all 20 vols. were issued at the same time. Only 3% of *The New Grove* comes from previous editions. Its entries are on music history, theory and practice, musical terminology, the music of various locations ranging from continents to units as small as a city, and an outstanding selection of biographies. More than half of the biographical entries are on composers; the others cover the range of people connected with the art and business of music, both historical and current: performers, conductors, historians and scholars, writers on music, librettists, printers, instrument makers and dealers, patrons, dancers, and the like. The longer biographical entries for composers include generally well-organized lists of works, with multiple catalog numbers if appropriate (and, occasionally, indexes to individual sections of the lists), and extensive bibliographies, given in chronological order and occasionally classified; the shorter biographical entries summarize works lists and bibliographical material. The format of the individual bibliographical citations is in the European mode, identifying the author by first initial and last name only, giving the date and place of publication and omitting the publisher's name; citations for articles generally list only the initial page number. Musical examples and relevant illustrations are included. All but the shortest entries are signed; an appendix in the last volume lists the almost 2,500 contributors, an international gathering, and gives the last known professional address of those still living.

The editorial committee is best described as Anglo-American, with prominent national advisers. This edition clearly favors the interests of music scholars rather than those of informed amateurs and performers. It succeeds *MGG* (**1.9**) as the major music reference work supporting and informing musical scholarship. *The New Grove* lacks a general index; its vast body of information is less accessible than it could be. There is a helpful index to ethnomusicological terms, a reflection of the extensive coverage of non-Western and folk music. Other reference tools attempt to deal with parts of the indexing problem. Robert Cowden, in his *Concert and Opera Singers* (**1.250**), indexes singers in *The New Grove.* Ann P. Basart in *CNV* 117–34 (1987–89) compiled an "Index to the Manuscripts in the *New Grove* Articles on 'Sources.'" Ann Viles put together an index of viol players cited in *VdGSAJ* 27 (1990): 55–75.

The publication of *The New Grove* brought a flood of commentary, most of it highly favorable. Stanley Sadie, the general editor, provided a preview of the complexities of organizing such a project in the article *"The New Grove"* in *Notes* 32 (1975): 259–68. The text of *The New Grove* was set by computer and, since its publication, parts have reappeared, revised and updated, in a varied series of volumes. The whole work has been reprinted with a few alterations.

MQ devotes an entire issue, 68 (1982): 153–286, to assessments of certain broad topics in *The New Grove.* Ethnomusicologists divide *The New Grove* coverage geographically in *Ethnomusicology* 29 (1985): 138–76 and 314–51. Similar treatment is given *The New Grove* in *Notes* 38 (1981): 45–59, by Susan T. Sommer, William Morris, Virgil Thomson, Michael Tilson Thomas, and the reference staff of the Music Division of the New York Public Library. Joshua Rifkin reviews *The New Grove* in *JAMS* 35 (1982): 182–99, as does Desmond Shawe-Taylor in the *New Yorker* (November 23 1981): 218–25. A controversial (and lengthy) review is that by Charles Rosen in the *New York Review of Books* (May 28 1981). Donald W. Krummel's review appears in *Choice* (February 1981): 762–66 and George R. Hill reviews it in *ARBA* 12 (1981): no. 1016. Andrew Jones, Robin Orr, and Michael Greenhalgh review portions of *The New Grove* in *MT* (March 1981) and reviews by Christopher Hogwood and Derrick Puffett appear in the April 1981 issue.

The 5th ed. of *Grove* is reviewed by Richard S. Hill in *Notes* 12 (1954): 85–92.

Articles from *The New Grove* and books originating with such articles are cited as nos. **1.1, 1.220, 1.469, 1.488, 3.3, 3.15, 3.64, 4.66, 5.504, 5.523, 5.530, 5.542, 5.583, 9.1,** and **13.11.**

1.49* Sadie, Stanley, and **Alison Latham.** *The Norton/Grove Concise Encyclopedia of Music.* 850 pp. New York: W.W. Norton, 1988.

The British ed. was published in London by Macmillan Press Ltd. as *The Grove Concise Dictionary of Music.*

A well-designed 1-vol. reference work of 10,000 entries for music-lovers and students, with a slight British bias. This is not a condensation or updating of *The New Grove* (**1.48**), but is compiled with the same scope and "along broadly the same principles as informed *The New Grove.*" There are entries for musical terms, 1,000 titles of musical works, instruments, 5,600 biographies (composers, conductors, and theorists), institutions, over 1,000 musical compositions, and national musics. A wide variety of music is covered, international in scope. The entries have no bibliographies and the works lists included are severely condensed.

Reviewed by William S. Brockman in *ARBA* 21 (1990): no. 1230 and by Geraldine Ostrove in *Notes* 47 (1991): 796–97. The British ed. is reviewed, with errata, addenda, and misprints listed, by Michael Kennedy in *M&L* 70 (1989): 517–18.

1.50 Sartori, Claudio. *Enciclopedia della musica.* 6 vols. Milan: Rizzoli, 1972–74.

First ed. published by Ricordi in 4 vols., 1963–65.

A major modern Italian encyclopedia of music, well printed and handsomely illustrated. There are contributions by 232 international specialists; the longer articles are signed, and there is good bibliographical coverage.

1.51 Schilling, Gustav. *Enzyklopädie der gesammten musikalischen Wissenschaften, oder, Universal-Lexikon der Tonkunst.* 2nd ed. 6 vols. Stuttgart: F.H. Köhler, 1840.

Supplement-Band was issued in 1842. There was a reprint ed. by Georg Olms Verlag, 1974. The 1st ed. was published 1835–38.

One of the leading 19th-century repositories of musical knowledge. This is a comprehensive work with an emphasis on the subject aspects of the topic, but also with numerous biographies displaced or reduced in later reference works. A 1-vol. condensation, *Universal-Lexikon der Tonkunst,* was published in 1849; many of its entries are more comprehensive than in the original edition.

1.52 Seeger, Horst. *Musiklexikon in zwei Bänden.* 2 vols. Leipzig: Deutscher Verlag für Musik VEB, 1966.

The biographical entries were updated and reissued in 1981 as Seeger's *Musiklexikon: Personen A–Z* (**1.109**), 860 pp.

A representation of the Marxist approach to music lexicography, with articles by 44 then–East German contributors. The biographical entries have summary lists of composers' works; there are illustrations, but no bibliographies, even for articles on major topics.

1.53 Śledziński, Stefan. *Mała encyklopedia muzyki.* 3rd ed. 1,278 pp. Warsaw: Panstwowe Wydawn. Naukowe, 1981.

First issued in 1924; later eds. published in 1960, 1968, and 1970.

A popular Polish dictionary, international in coverage, with definitions of terms, fairly extensive signed articles on topics, and brief biographies covering composers, performers, and critics. There are short bibliographies for major subjects and extensive indexing: A biographical index organizes all references to individuals throughout the volume, and a title index gives the musical form and the composer of the work in question, as well as the page location for musical compositions.

1.54* Smolka, Jaroslav. *Malá encyklopedie hudby.* 737 pp. + 48 plates. Prague: Supraphon, 1983.

Supervised by a joint committee of Czech and Slovak scholars, a dictionary liberally illustrated with portraits, facsimiles of musical scores and signatures, musical examples, and line drawings of musical instruments. International in scope, the coverage includes biographies of composers as well as terms of sacred and secular music, both art and popular. The volume ends with chronologically arranged illustrative plates and a classified bibliography.

1.55 Szabolcsi, Bence, and **Aladár Tóth.** *Zenei lexikon.* 4 vols. Budapest: Zeneműkiadó, 1965.

A related work, edited by Gábor Darvas, was *Zenei Minilexikon* (Budapest: Zeneműkiadó, 1974, 298 pp.).

A high-quality, general music encyclopedia, a revision and expansion of a work first issued 1930–31. Its major articles are signed by outstanding musicologists, Hungarian and foreign. There are long articles on national music, musical forms, and music for various instruments. The biographical articles discuss major works and list others by category. There are short bibliographies.

Reviewed by J. Gerely in *Revue de musicologie* 53 (1967): 185–87.

1.56 Thompson, Oscar. *The International Cyclopedia of Music and Musicians.* 11th ed. Edited by Bruce Bohle. 2,609 pp. New York: Dodd, Mead, and Company, 1985.

First published in 1938; its Board of Associates included Marion Bauer, Gilbert Chase, Nicolas Slonimsky, Walter H. Rubsaman, and Goddard Lieberson. The 4th–8th eds. were edited by Nicolas Slonimsky, the 9th ed. was edited by Robin Sabin, and the 10th ed. was edited by Bruce Bohle. The 11th ed. has an appendix of additional articles and new information to add to articles appearing in the 10th ed.; it is thus a reprint of the 10th ed., with a section of addenda and corrigenda.

A good American 1-vol. general dictionary of music. It has a strong list of contributors, with extensive signed articles for major persons and subjects and a large number of title entries for music compositions. Of particular value are the detailed lists, given in tabular form, of works by major composers. Through the 8th ed., the work carried an appendix of opera plots and an extensive bibliography of music literature.

The 4th ed. is reviewed by Charles Warren Fox in *Notes* 4 (1947): 169–71. The 5th ed. is reviewed by Charles Warren Fox in *Notes* 7 (1950): 291–92. The 9th ed. is reviewed by Irene Millen in *Notes* 22 (1965): 733–35. The 10th ed. is briefly reviewed by Stephen M. Fry in *Notes* 32 (1975): 557 and the 11th ed. by William J. Dane in *ARBA* 17 (1986): no. 1289.

1.57 Törnblom, Folke H. *Bonniers Musiklexikon.* 528 pp. Stockholm: Bonniers Förlag, 1983.

First published in 1975, edited by Åke Engström and Folke H. Törnblom, based on entries in the *Bonniers Lexikon* of 1961–67 (446 pp.) and the *Tonkonsten* of 1955–57 (2 vols.). The Danish ed., *Gads Musikleksikon,* edited by Soren Sorensen, John Christiansen, and Finn Slumstrup, was published by G.E.C. Gad in Copenhagen, 1976 (502 pp.), based on the *Bonniers Musiklexikon* of 1975.

A liberally illustrated (by photographs and line drawings) music dictionary in Swedish, including over 7,000 entries, covering such categories as biography (composers, performers, scholars, ensembles), terms (including popular and jazz), musical works, and musical instruments. Also present are detailed tables and diagrams depicting such subjects as mutes for stringed instruments, solmization, a typical orchestra seating chart, musical ornaments, and organ construction. The endpapers carry a chronological chart of music history (700 B.C. to 1970), with parallel columns devoted to art, literature, philosophy, and political history.

1.58 Vinton, John. *Dictionary of Contemporary Music.* 834 pp. New York: E.P. Dutton, 1974.

The British ed., *Dictionary of Twentieth-Century Music,* was published in London by Thames and Hudson, 1974.

A focus on concert music of the Western tradition from the late 19th century, with an emphasis on the 20th century. Many of the composer entries are based on questionnaires completed by the composers, and the extended subject entries were written by distinguished scholars; there are entries for both new terms and established terms with new meanings. The editor's preface suggests that one way to use this book is to regard it as a slice of history reported largely by some of its makers. The articles include lists of principal compositions and short bibliographies. There is much more content than in the similarly aimed Griffiths (**1.18**). Some of the editor's musings and conclusions appear in his *Essays after a Dictionary: Music and Culture at the Close of Western Civilization* (Lewisburg, Pa.: Bucknell University Press, 1977), 170 pp.

Reviewed by Peter S. Odegard in *JAMS* 29 (1976): 153–56.

1.59 Walther, Johann G. *Musikalisches Lexicon oder musikalische Bibliothek.* 659 pp. + 22 folding plates. Leipzig: Wolffgang Deer, 1732.

A facsimile reprint, edited by Richard Schaal, was published by Bärenreiter (1953 and 1986) (Documenta musicologica, I/3).

A landmark in the history of music reference and the first music dictionary in German. This *Lexicon* established the pattern for modern dictionaries that combine terms and biographies, such as Riemann (**1.45**) and Moser (**1.38**). It is also a primary source of information about late baroque musical knowledge and practice, expanding Brossard's work (**1.280**).

1.60 Westrup, Jack, and **Frank L. Harrison.** *The New College Encyclopedia of Music.* Revised by Conrad Wilson. 608 pp. New York: W.W. Norton, 1976.

Published first in England as *Collins Music Encyclopedia,* 1959, and in the U.S. as the *New College Encyclopedia of Music,* 1960, 739 pp. The present ed. was reprinted in Britain as *Collins Encyclopedia of Music.* The 1976 ed. was reprinted in the U.S. in 1981 and in Britain in 1984.

An encyclopedia less scholarly than informative. Its focus is on standard composers, terms, and titles, with brief attention given to early and modern topics. There are works summaries for most important composers. There are occasional bibliographical references in the articles and some illustrations, with musical quotations.

The 1960 ed. is reviewed by James B. Coover in *Notes* 17 (1960): 564–66.

1.61 Willemze, Theo. *Spectrum Muzieklexicon.* 4 vols. Utrecht: Het Spectrum, 1975.

A compendium of very brief entries, with composers, authors, and titles of pieces of music, as well as definitions of terms. There are many cross-references from the major European languages to Dutch, with extensive coverage of a broad span of Low Country musical culture. In 1981, the biographical entries were slightly updated and published separately in two volumes as *Componistenlexicon.*

INTERNATIONAL BIOGRAPHY

In this section are dictionaries and encyclopedias, international in coverage, in which the emphasis is exclusively or mainly on people engaged in music-related activities, such as composers, performers, scholars, critics, and impresarios. The line that separates biographical dictionaries from volumes of collected biography is rather arbitrary. The distinction is essentially between works that contain numerous brief entries, alphabetically arranged, and works that are collections of essays on a fairly limited group of musicians. This latter category is not included in the following list.

1.62 Baker, Theodore. *Baker's Biographical Dictionary of Musicians.* Revised by Nicolas Slonimsky. 8th ed. xxxv + 2,115 pp. New York: Schirmer Books, 1991.

A 3-vol. French ed., *Dictionnaire biographique des musiciens,* adapted and augmented by Alain Paris, was published in Paris by R. Laffont in 1995 (lx + 4,728 pp.).

First published in 1900, with subsequent eds. appearing in 1905, 1919, 1940, 1958, 1978, and

1984. The 1958 ed. was reprinted in 1965, with a 143-page *Supplement.* There were also a 1971 *Supplement* (262 pp.), *The Concise Baker's Biographical Dictionary of Musicians* (1988, 1,407 pp.), *The Concise Edition of Baker's Biographical Dictionary of Musicians* (1994, 1,155 pp.), and *The Portable Baker's Biographical Dictionary of Musicians,* edited by Richard Kostelanetz (1995, 291 pp.).

The most authoritative and extensive biographical dictionary in English, a standard work from its 1st ed. Its main emphasis is on musicians and musical figures in the world of art music. Through the 3rd ed., early figures were treated briefly, with references to *Grove* (**1.48**) and Eitner (**5.544**). For the 4th ed., these biographies were rewritten as independent articles (by Gustave Reese, Gilbert Chase, and Robert Geiger). The 5th ed. was greatly revised and enlarged and checked carefully for accuracy. The 6th ed. was extensively revised from the 5th ed. and the 7th from the 6th.

The editor's introduction (in the 6th, 7th, and 8th eds.) is a landmark essay on the techniques necessary for biographical research. Slonimsky's thumbnail opinion of his subjects can often be found in his introductory description, preceding the subject's nationality: Musicologists and their like (Bukofzer, Dahlhaus, Einstein, Grout, Grove, Lang, and Schrade) are "eminent"; sopranos (Callas, Sills, and Sutherland) are "celebrated"; George Gershwin was "immensely gifted," whereas Ira was "talented"; Clara Schumann was "famous," whereas Robert was "great"; Lili Boulanger was "talented," whereas Nadia was "illustrious"; Elvis Presley was "fantastically popular," whereas Dolly Parton is "successful"; and Russian composer Sergei Slonimsky was "greatly talented," whereas his uncle Nicolas was "legendary." His evaluations reflect his notable sense of humor.

Robert Cowden's *Instrumental Virtuosi: A Bibliography of Biographical Materials* (**1.251**) lists the instrumentalists found in *Baker's,* and his *Concert and Opera Conductors: A Bibliography of Biographical Materials* (**1.249**) does the same for conductors.

The 4th ed. with *Supplement* is reviewed by Charles Warren Fox in *Notes* 7 (1950): 291–92. The 5th ed. is reviewed by Brooks Shepard, Jr., in *Notes* 16 (1959): 239–40 and by Philip L. Miller in *MQ* 45 (1959): 255–58. The 1971 *Supplement* is reviewed by Gloria Rose in *Notes* 29 (1972): 253–54. The 6th ed. is reviewed by Stanley Sadie in *Notes* 36 (1979): 81–83. The 7th ed. is reviewed by François Lesure in *Fontes* 33 (1986): 218 and by Ross Wood in *ARBA* 17 (1986): no. 1232. The 1988 *Concise Edition* is reviewed by Marion S. Gushee in *Notes* 45 (1989): 755–56. The 8th ed. is reviewed and placed in historical context by Susan T. Sommer in *Notes* 49 (1992): 67–70.

⬿

1.63 Altmann, Wilhelm, and **Paul Frank.** *Kurzgefasstes Tonkünstler-Lexikon für Musiker und Freunde der Musik.* 15th ed. Vols. 1–2, books 1 and 2. Wilhelmshaven, Germany: Heinrichshofen's Verlag, 1971–78.

Vol. 1 is a reprint of the 14th ed. published in Regensburg by G. Bosse, 1936, while correcting and augmenting the 14th by adding over 16,000 new entries. The 2nd vol. was edited by Burhard Bulling, Florian Noetzel, and Helmut Rösner. The 1st ed. was published in 1860 as Paul Frank's *Kleines Tonkünstler-Lexikon;* the title varies slightly in subsequent eds. Paul Frank was the pseudonym of Carl Wilhelm Merseburger.

One of the most popular prewar German dictionaries of musical biography, useful for quick reference and for identifying the pseudonyms of composers. The *Tonkünstler-Lexikon* has extremely wide coverage, but with minimal data. There are over 18,000 entries, including composers, librettists, performers, and musicologists, with many minor figures; the 2nd vol. is more international and popularly oriented than the 1st vol. Much-abbreviated entries for individuals and groups (such as the Beatles and the Amadeus Quartet) give birthplace and date, educational history, and career details. There are no works lists or bibliographical references. There is a multilingual table of abbreviations.

The 1st vol. of the 15th ed. is reviewed by Nyal Williams in *Notes* 29 (1973): 448.

1.64 Bertini, Giuseppe. *Dizionario storico-critico degli scrittori di musica e de'piu celebri artisti di tutte le nazioni si antiche che moderne.* 4 vols. in 2. Palermo, Italy: Dalla Tipografia reale di Guerrà, 1814–15.

An early Italian dictionary of musical biography. Bertini leaned heavily on Choron and Fayolle (**1.68**) for information while adding much new material, especially on Italian composers. His "Discorso preliminare" is a perceptive discussion of the role of bibliography in enhancing musical knowledge.

1.65 Bingley, William. *Musical Biography: Memoirs of the Lives and Writings of the Most Eminent Musical Composers and Writers Who Have Flourished in the Different Countries of Europe during the Last Three Centuries.* 2nd ed. 2 vols. London: H. Colburn, 1834.

Reprinted in New York by Da Capo Press, 1971 (Da Capo music reprint series). The 1st ed. was issued in 1814.

Brief, anecdotal accounts grouped chronologically and by national schools.

1.66 Brown, James Duff. *Biographical Dictionary of Musicians, with a Bibliography of English Writings on Music.* 637 pp. Paisley; London: A. Gardner, 1886.

Reprinted by G. Olms, Hildesheim, Germany, in 1970.

A dictionary by an early advocate of public music libraries, international in scope and British in emphasis. Brown later joined with Stephen Stratton to produce a similar work concentrating solely on British subjects (**1.162**).

1.67 Carlson, Effie B. *A Bio-Bibliographical Dictionary of Twelve-Tone and Serial Composers.* 233 pp. Metuchen, N.J.: Scarecrow Press, 1970.

Entries for 80 twelve-tone and serial composers, from Gilbert Amy to Bernd Alois Zimmermann, with a bibliography (pp. 212–33).

1.68 Choron, Alexandre Étienne, and **François Joseph Marie Fayolle.** *Dictionnaire historique des musiciens, artistes et amateurs, morts ou vivans, qui se sont illustrés en une partie quelconque de la musique et des arts qui y sont relatifs. Précédé d'un sommaire de l'histoire de la musique.* 2 vols. Paris: Valade, 1810–11.

Reprinted in 1817. The 1810–11 ed. was reprinted in 1971 by G. Olms, Hildesheim, Germany.

The first important French biographical music dictionary. It is international in scope, with partial works lists for major composers, and serves as a valuable guide to early 19th-century French musical opinion. The work is by Fayolle, assisted to such an extent by the writings of Gerber (**1.78**), Forkel (**4.25**), and Burney (**2.7**) that Fétis labeled him a plagiarist. Choron contributed the historical introduction and a few of the articles. "Additions et corrections" are on pp. 451–70, Vol. 2. This dictionary was expanded, in English trans., in *A Dictionary of Musicians* (**1.71**).

1.69 Cohen, Aaron I. *International Encyclopedia of Women Composers.* 2nd ed., revised and enlarged. 2 vols. 1,151 pp. New York: Books & Music USA, 1987.

The 1st ed. was published in New York by Bowker, 1981 (597 pp.).

Brief biographical coverage, with lists of compositions, for 6,196 women composers. There are an appendix listing composers by country and century, an extensive bibliography of works about women composers (pp. 783–816), and a sizable discography (pp. 1068–1142).

The 1st ed. is reviewed by Carol Neuls-Bates in *Notes* 40 (1983): 53–55 and by Adrienne Fried Block in *AM* 3 (1985): 107–10; the 2nd ed. by Ann P. Basart in *CNV* 122 (1988): 23–24, with a table comparing the works list coverage of the relevant *New Grove* title with Cohen, by Nicola LeFanu in *M&L* 71 (1990): 74–75, by Robert Skinner in *ARBA* 20 (1989): no. 1199, and by Judy Tsou in *Notes* 46 (1990): 633–35.

1.70 Cummings, David M. *International Who's Who in Music and Musicians' Directory (in the Classical and Light Classical Fields).* 14th ed. 1,296 pp. Cambridge, England: International Who's Who in Music, 1994.

13th ed., 1992 (1,357 pp.).

The next ed. will include a 2nd vol. covering popular music (jazz, pop, rock, blues, country, folk, dance, and world music), planned to contain over 5,000 entries.

Over 8,000 entries on rising and established figures in classical music. The focus is primarily on living musicians, composers, conductors, music critics, publishers, educators, musicologists, and librarians. The biographies, many of which were supplied by the subjects, are listed alphabetically and include personal information, education and career details, recordings, and addresses, with emphasis on European and Western figures. The appendixes include international lists (with addresses) of orchestras, opera companies, music organizations, major competitions and awards, music libraries, and conservatories.

The 1962 ed. is reviewed by Fred Blum in *Notes* 19 (1962): 442–43. The 9th ed. is reviewed by Carole Franklin Vidali in *ARBA* 13 (1982): no. 1079. The 10th ed. is reviewed by Robert Palmieri in *ARBA* 17 (1986): 1233. The 12th ed. is reviewed by Barbara Jeskallian in *Notes* 47 (1991): 797–98. The 13th edition is reviewed by Robert Skinner in *ARBA* 25 (1994): no. 1346.

1.71 *A Dictionary of Musicians from the Earliest Ages to the Present Time, Comprising the Most Important Biographical Contents of the Works of Gerber, Choron and Fayolle, Count Orloff, Dr. Burney, Sir John Hawkins, etc., Together with More than 100 Original Memoirs of the Most Eminent Living Musicians and a Summary of the History of Music.* 2 vols. London: Sainsbury, 1824.

Reprinted in 1827. A later reprint by Da Capo Press, New York, 1966, contains an essay on the work by H. G. Farmer from *M&L* 12 (1931): 384–92.

The first major biographical dictionary of musicians in English. Although its tone is popular and anecdotal, the work furnishes an excellent picture of contemporary British taste and opinion. Although the compiler is not identified, the work has been attributed to its publisher, John Sainsbury, and has been shown to have been copied and paraphrased from Bingley (**1.65**) and other contemporaneous English publications. See Lawrence I. Ritchey's "The Untimely Death of Samuel Wesley, or The Perils of Plagiarism," in *M&L* 60 (1984): 45–59.

The reprint ed. is reviewed by Vincent Duckles in *Notes* 23 (1967): 737–39.

1.72 Ewen, David. *Composers since 1900: A Biographical and Critical Guide.* 639 pp. New York: H.W. Wilson, 1969.

A *First Supplement* was issued in 1981, 328 pp.

This vol. replaces the author's *Composers of Today* (1934), *American Composers Today* (1949), and *European Composers Today* (1954).

A guide with portraits, lists of major works, and short bibliographies of writings about the composers under consideration.

Reviewed in *Booklist* 66 (1970): 1290–91.

1.73* Ewen, David. *Great Composers, 1300–1900: A Biographical and Critical Guide.* 429 pp. New York: H.W. Wilson, 1966.

Supersedes *Composers of Yesterday,* 1937.

An account of about 200 composers. Each entry has a short works list and a brief bibliography. Appendixes give a chronological list of composers covered, also broken down by nationality.

1.74 Ewen, David. *Musicians since 1900: Performers in Concert and Opera.* 974 pp. New York: H.W. Wilson, 1978.

Supersedes Ewen's *Living Musicians* (1940) and its supplement (1957) with a work wider in scope.

Coverage of 432 "performers, living or dead, whose art has left a permanent impress upon the musical culture of the twentieth century" [Introduction]. This dictionary, international in scope, has entries that include an account of the subject's background and early life, musical training and career, honors, and extra-musical interests. There is a classified list of musicians, arranged by occupation.

1.75 Fétis, François-Joseph. *Biographie universelle des musiciens et bibliographie générale de la musique.* 2nd ed. 8 vols. Paris: Librairie de Firmin-Didot et cie., 1875–78.

Supplément et complément, published under the direction of Arthur Pougin, 2 vols., 1878–80. The 2nd ed. was reprinted by Culture et Civilisation in Brussels, 1972, in 10 vols. First published 1835–44.

A work that set the standard for modern biographical research in music, called *Fétis.* A significant achievement for its time, it contains biographical and bibliographical information (much of which modern scholarship has shown to be less than accurate), lists of major works, and, occasionally, annotated lists of books about composers. Although outdated and marred by the author's personal critical bias, it has been a starting point for research.

1.76* Fuller, Sophie. *Pandora Guide to Women Composers: Britain and the United States, 1629–Present.* 368 pp. London; San Francisco, Calif.: Pandora, 1994.

An illustrated biographical dictionary with 104 entries for composers who have "lived and worked in Britain, Ireland or the United States," selected not by their quality but to present "as wide a picture as possible of women from different backgrounds with different career patterns writing different kinds of music." There are a chronological list of composers, a classified bibliography (pp. 354–64), and an annotated list of organizations and resource centers for further study.

1.77* Gammond, Peter. *An Illustrated Guide to Composers of Classical Music.* 240 pp. London: Salamander Books, 1980.

Over a hundred composers alphabetically covered in a guide intended for the amateur musician, with portraits furnished for most and manuscript facsimiles for a few. The name–title index omits the main composer entries. No source material is cited.

1.78 Gerber, Ernst Ludwig. *Historisch-biographisches Lexikon der Tonkünstler, welches Nachrichten von dem Leben und Werken musikalischer Schriftsteller, berühmter Componisten, Sänger, usw. . . . enthält.* 2 vols. Leipzig: J.G.I. Breitkopf, 1790–92.

Gerber, Ernst Ludwig. *Neues historisch-biographisches Lexikon der Tonkünstler.* 4 vols. Leipzig: A. Kühnel, 1812–14.

A reprint of the two lexica was published in 4 vols. by Akademische Druck- und Verlagsanstalt, Graz, Austria, 1966–69, as *Historisch-biographisches Lexikon der Tonkünstler (1790–92) und Neues historisch-biographisches Lexikon der Tonkünstler (1812–14). Mit den in den Jahren 1792 bis 1834 veröffentlichen Ergänzungen sowie der Erstveröffentlichung handschriftlicher Berichtigungen und Nachträge,* edited by Othmar Wessely. Included therein is a supplementary volume containing additions and corrections made by Gerber's contemporaries and published in the *Leipzig Allgemeine Musikalische Zeitung* and other journals, as well as the author's own manuscript revisions.

Early biographical dictionaries of great historical importance. The compiler extended the biographical content of Walther's *Lexicon* (**1.59**) and produced the first major self-contained dictionary of musical biography. The 4-vol. ed. of 1812 supplements but does not supersede the earlier 2-vol. ed. For complete coverage, both compilations must be used.

1.79 Gilder, Eric. *The Dictionary of Composers and Their Music: A Listener's Companion.* New, revised ed. 592 pp. New York: Holt, Rinehart & Winston, 1986.

First published in 1978, 406 pp.; 2nd ed., 1985.

Brief biographical entries for 426 composers, including those the editor has judged most likely to be encountered on programs of classical music. The works lists are arranged chronologically for each composer; there is also an inclusive chronological list of all included composers' works, as well as time-lines for cited composers, showing with whom each was contemporaneous.

Reviewed by Ann Basart in *Fontes* 35 (1988): 208–9 and by John E. Druesedow, Jr., in *ARBA* 18 (1987): 1229.

1.80 Greene, David Mason. *Greene's Biographical Encyclopedia of Composers.* 1,348 pp. Garden City, N.Y.: Doubleday, 1985.

A biographical dictionary written for the informed amateur and limited to 2,433 composers of art music. There is an alphabetical list of composers cited, but the entries themselves are listed chronologically by composer's birthdate.

Reviewed by Richard Koprowski in *Notes* 42 (1985): 787 and by John E. Druesedow, Jr., in *ARBA* 18 (1987): 1223.

1.81* Handy, D. Antoinette. *Black Conductors.* 557 pp. Metuchen, N.J.: Scarecrow Press, 1994.

Profiles of 114 19th- and 20th-century Black conductors. The range of Western music—art, popular, and jazz—is represented. There is thorough documentation of information for the most familiar names, and a single, comprehensive index is supplied.

Reviewed by Dena J. Epstein in *Notes* 52 (1996): 1182–83.

1.82* Heister, Hanns-Werner, and **Walter-Wolfgang Sparrer.** *Komponisten der Gegenwart.* 2 vols. Munich: Edition Text and Kritik, 1992– .

A loose-leaf biographical dictionary of contemporary composers, issued serially. Its first issue lists over 250 composers, with each entry including a biography, musical examples, works lists, analyses, and selected bibliography and discography. Each entry starts on a separate leaf to ease interfiling. It is a subscription publication, scheduled to be updated twice annually.

1.83* Holly, Ellistine Perkins. *Biographies of Black Composers and Songwriters: A Supplementary Text Book.* 92 pp. Dubuque, Iowa: William C. Brown Publishers, 1990.

A supplement for introductory music courses, with 103 short biographies of African-American composers, including information submitted by the subjects.

1.84* Holmes, John L. *Conductors on Record.* 734 pp. Westport, Conn.: Greenwood Press, 1982.

A shorter, related title, updated, with information on compact discs, was published as *Conductors: A Record Collector's Guide* (London: V. Gollancz, 1988, 336 pp.).

A biographical dictionary of musicians, international in scope, concentrating on their work as conductors of classical music, choral or instrumental. Much of each entry is on the subject's recordings, although that coverage is at times quite selective because the standard discographical information is not supplied.

Reviewed by William C. Rorick in *Notes* 39 (1983): 857–58 and by Dean Tudor in *ARBA* 14 (1983): no. 947.

1.85 Hughes, Rupert. *The Biographical Dictionary of Musicians.* Completely revised and newly edited by Deems Taylor and Russell Kerr. Over 8,500 entries, together with a pronunciation dictionary of given names and titles and a key to the pronunciation of 16 languages. 481 pp. New York: Blue Ribbon Books, 1940.

A separate issue of the dictionary was included in Hughes's *Music Lovers' Encyclopedia*, New York, 1939. Reprinted by the Scholarly Press, St. Clair Shores, Mich., 1972.

One of the most popular music reference works of its day in the U.S., intended for concert-going music lovers. There are brief entries, with representative works cited for composers. It is useful for its abundant citations of obscure performers.

1.86 "Index to Music Obituaries." In *Notes* (**4.63**).

Formerly titled "Index to Music Necrology."

An index to the death of musicians that began with coverage of the year 1965. The index gradually added more indexing sources while becoming more selective in the inclusion of names. References to music dictionaries and encyclopedias in which biographical information may be found are cited, thereby assisting their revision. (See also **12.24**).

1.87* Jacobs, Arthur. *The Penguin Dictionary of Musical Performers: A Biographical Guide to Significant Interpreters of Classical Music—Singers, Solo Instrumentalists, Conductors, Orchestras and String Quartets—Ranging from the Seventeenth Century to the Present Day.* 250 pp. London: Viking, 1990.

A dictionary of musicians that includes persons omitted from *The New Grove* (**1.48**), with brief accounts of career and recording history (if appropriate). Although it omits many current small vocal ensembles (Quink, King's Singers, Hilliard Ensemble), instrumental ones (Academy of Ancient Music) are included.

1.88 Kutsch, K. J., and **Leo Riemens.** *Grosses Sängerlexikon.* 2 vols., 3,452 cols. Bern, Switzerland: Francke Verlag, 1991.

Earlier eds. were issued in 1962, 1975, 1979, and 1982 as *Unvergängliche Stimmen: Sängerlexikon* in Bern and Munich by Francke Verlag. The 1987 ed. became *Grosses Sängerlexikon.* An English trans. of the 1st ed., expanded and annotated by Harry Earl Jones, was published as *A Concise Biographical Dictionary of Singers from the Beginning of Recorded Sound to the Present* (Philadelphia, Pa.: Chilton Book Company, 1969, 487 pp.).

Brief biographies of great singers who have flourished since the invention of sound recording, with entries including information on the singers' principal roles, the character of the voices, and the labels under which recordings were made. There are no detailed discographies. There is an appendix, a selective catalog of opera and operetta.

The 1987 edition is reviewed by Ann P. Basart in *CNV* 120 (1988): 13 and by Elizabeth Forbes in *M&L* 69 (1988): 538–40, with errata.

1.89* LaBlanc, Michael L. *Contemporary Musicians: Profiles of the People in Music.* 14 vols. to date. Detroit, Mich.: Gale Research, Inc., 1989– .

An illustrated biographical dictionary, issued serially, including discographies and indexes. The *contemporary* in the title seems to mean "20th-century" because some of the entries are on musicians who have been dead for decades. The coverage includes a wide range of musicians, primarily from popular fields (Broadway, country, folk, gospel, pop–rock, rhythm and blues, and soul, for example), although classical and performance artists are included, as well as ensembles in a variety of the areas. Each entry gives a brief biography, a detailed career overview, a list of compositions (if relevant), with a selected discography and a bibliography subdivided by books and periodicals. Each vol. has cumulative name and subject indexes. This is also available in electronic format through NEXIS (Mead Data Control) in NEXIS, PEOPLE, and SPORTS libraries in the GALBIO file.

Reviewed by Linda M. Fidler in *Notes* 47 (1990): 390 and by Robert Skinner in *ARBA* 21 (1990): no. 1221.

1.90 Laurence, Anya. *Women of Notes: 1,000 Women Composers Born before 1900.* 101 pp. New York: B. Rosen Press, 1978. (The theatre student)

An extensive bio-bibliography of women composers active before 1900, arranged alphabetically under the country of origin. There are a short bibliography of sources and a discography.

Reviewed by Sam Dennison in *AM* 3 (1985): 479–82 and by Dominique-René de Lerma in *ARBA* 11 (1980): no. 999.

1.91 LePage, Jane Weiner. *Women Composers, Conductors, and Musicians of the Twentieth Century: Selected Biographies.* 3 vols. Metuchen, N.J.: Scarecrow Press, 1980–88.

Extensive articles on significant women engaged in various aspects of making music. Discographies, lists of compositions, and many quotations about each person are included. Each volume has an index with both corporate and personal names. Discographies and works lists for each composer are included, as well as a variety of indexes.

The 1st vol. is reviewed by Jeannie Pool in *Fontes* 37 (1990): 310–11, by Carole Franklin in *ARBA* 12 (1981): no. 1038, and by Edith Borroff in *SSN* 11 (Fall 1985): 87. Vol. 2 is reviewed by Carole Franklin Vidali in *ARBA* 15 (1984): no. 884. Vol. 3 is reviewed by Judy Tsou in *Notes* 47 (1990): 380–81.

1.92* Manén Planas, Juan. *Diccionario de celebridades musicales.* 669 pp. Barcelona: Editorial Ramón Sopena, S.A., 1978. (Biblioteca hispania)

An illustrated collection of 323 biographies of composers, conductors, performers, and writers on music, with some facsimiles of signatures, and occasionally with condensed works lists. There are no bibliographies. The selection of subjects is international, but entries emphasize the subjects' Spanish connection.

1.93 Mattheson, Johann. *Grundlage einer Ehren-Pforte, woran die tüchtigsten Capellmeister, Componisten, Musikgelehrten, Tonkünstler, etc., erscheinen sollen. Zum fernern Ausbau angegeben von Mattheson, Hamburg, 1740. Vollständiger, originalgetreuer Neudruck mit gelegentlichen bibliographischen Hinweisen und Matthesons Nachträgen,* edited by Max Schneider. 428 pp. with *Anhang,* 51 pp. Berlin: Leo Liepmannssohn, 1910.

Reprints were issued in 1969 by Bärenreiter, Kassel, and by Die Akademische Druck- und Verlagsanstalt, Graz.

Strictly speaking, a volume of 140 collected biographies rather than a biographical dictionary. But this volume stands first, chronologically, among all the self-contained works of musical biography, establishing the precedent for Gerber's *Lexikon* (**1.78**) and subsequent dictionaries of musical biography. Most of the essays were contributed by the subjects themselves.

1.94 Mirkin, Mikhail Iur´evich. *Kratkiĭ Biograficheskiĭ slovar´ zarubezhnykh Kompositorov / Brief Biographical Dictionary of Foreign Composers.* 265 pp. Moscow: Sovetskii Kompozitor, 1969.

A biographical dictionary covering about 2,500 composers, excluding those from the former Soviet Union.

1.95* Mize, J. T. H. *The International Who is Who in Music.* 5th (mid-century) ed. 576 pp. Chicago, Ill.: Who is Who in Music, Inc., Ltd., 1951.

Approximately 5,000 entries for living musicians include some with small photographs and many with physical description (hair and eye color, height, weight) of the subject. Errata abound.

Reviewed by Charles Warren Fox in *Notes* 9 (1951): 124–25.

1.96* Morton, Brian, and **Pamela Collins.** *Contemporary Composers.* 1,019 pp. Chicago, Ill.: St. James' Press, 1992.

A dictionary of composers, including for each entry a biography, a works list, and an evaluation of works; there are 494 entries by over 160 contributors. The works lists include information on instrumentation, date of composition, publisher, discography, other publications, critical assessment and an analysis of the subject's major works, and composers' own statements. The intended scope of coverage is international, with Africa and Asia covered; women are strongly represented.

Reviewed by Arnold Whittall in *M&L* 74 (1993): 312–14 and by Kathleen A. Abromeit in *Choice* 30 (1992): 598.

1.97* Olivier, Antje, and **Karin Weingartz-Perschel.** *Komponistinnen von A–Z.* 363 pp. Düsseldorf: Tokkata Verlag für Frauenforschung, 1988.

A biographical dictionary, international in scope, listing 279 women composers, both current and historical. Each listing has a brief biographical paragraph on the subject, a classified works list, and, when relevant, a discography; most listings are accompanied by an illustration: a portrait of the composer, an excerpt from a published work, a title-page reproduction, or a music manuscript facsimile. Among the more unexpected entries is one for Anne Boleyn. There is a brief bibliography (pp. 360–62).

1.98* Osborne, Charles. *The Dictionary of Composers.* 380 pp. New York: Taplinger Publishing Co., 1977.

First published in London by The Bodley Head, 1977.

A biographical dictionary designed for the music enthusiast. The editor, with 25 additional contributors, covers 179 composers, although without works lists or bibliographies.

Kenyon C. Rosenberg gives this a strongly negative review in *ARBA* 11 (1980): no. 1000.

1.99 Paris, Alain. *Dictionnaire des interprètes et de l'interprétation musicale au XXe siècle.* New edition. 1,278 pp. Paris: R. Laffont, 1995. (Bouquins)

First ed., 1982, 874 pp. A German ed., *Lexikon der Interpreten klassischer Musik im 20. Jahrhundert,* was edited by Rudolf Kimmis and Peter Gülke and published by Deutscher Taschenbuch Verlag in Munich and by Bärenreiter Verlag in Kassel, 1992 (1,032 pp.).

A useful biographical dictionary of performing musicians. A collection of essays on the situation and evolution of musical interpretation in the 20th century precedes the biographical section on individual artists and another section covering musical ensembles. The indexes are arranged by performance medium.

1.100 Parker, John R. *A Musical Biography: or, Sketches of the Lives and Writings of Eminent Musical Characters, Interspersed with an Epitome of Interesting Musical Matter.* With a new introduction by Frederick Freedman. 250 pp. Detroit, Mich.: Information Coordinators, 1975.

A reprint of the 1825 ed. published by Stone & Fovell in Boston, Mass.

The first biographical music dictionary published in the U.S., headed by biographies of Handel and Haydn, in honor of the Handel and Haydn Society, the venerable Boston musical institution to which it was dedicated. Some articles on musical terminology are also included.

Reviewed by Alan C. Buechner in *Notes* 33 (1976): 303–4.

1.101 Pedigo, Alan. *International Encyclopedia of Violin–Keyboard Sonatas and Composer Biographies.* 2nd ed., revised and enlarged. 341 pp. Booneville, Ark.: Arriaga Publications, 1995.

First ed., 1979, 135 pp.

A work most useful for the national lists of composers and the brief composer biographies. The first ed. is reviewed by Frederic Schoettler in *ARBA* 11 (1980): no. 974.

1.102 Ricart Matas, José. *Diccionario biográfico de la música.* 3rd ed. 1,143 pp. Barcelona: Editorial Iberia, 1980.

The 2nd ed. was published in 1962 (1,143 pp.).

A dictionary of musical biography, international in scope, with brief biographical entries that have lists of works for major composers together with bibliographical references.

1.103* Sadie, Julie Anne, and **Rhian Samuel.** *The New Grove Dictionary of Women Composers.* xliii + 548 pp. London: Macmillan, 1994.

The American ed. was published in New York by W.W. Norton as *The Norton/Grove Dictionary of Women Composers.*

A dictionary of 875 women composers of Western classical music with truly international representation; the foreword announces it to be the "last of the subject dictionaries related" to the *New Grove* (**1.48**), although also conceding that the relationship between it and the parent volumes is, because of the evolving intellectual climate, more tenuous than that between the *New Grove* and its other offspring. The cutoff birthdate for inclusion is generally 1955 and inclusion is a "record of achievement, not of promise." The contributors are the usual international body of experts. The signed entries, in the *New Grove* style, include a biography and an examination of the composer's work, although there are no musical examples; almost all entries include a works list (classed if the length requires) with unpublished material and a bibliography, and many entries are illustrated. There is a chronology (pp. xx–xxxii) of women's musical achievements.

Reviewed by members of Susan Wollenberg's women composers seminar at the Faculty of Music, Oxford University, in *MT* 136 (1995): 194–96 and by Judy Tsou in *Notes* 53 (1996): 423–25.

1.104 Saerchinger, César. *International Who's Who in Music and Musical Gazetteer: A Contemporary Biographical Dictionary and a Record of the World's Musical Activity.* 861 pp. New York: Current Literature Publishing Company, 1918.

A geographical index and directory of schools and organizations now only of historical interest. The biographical section is still useful for minor figures of the first two decades of the century. Composers, performers, critics, musicologists, and teachers are included, with the entries recounting their education, field of activity, principal works, and addresses.

1.105 Sakka, Keisei. *Meikyoku jiten / Dictionary of Famous Music and Musicians.* 702 pp. Tokyo: Ongaku no Tomosha, 1969.

A general bio-bibliography in Japanese on Western music and musicians.

1.106 Schaal, Richard. *Musiker-Monogramme: Ein Verzeichnis mit einem Quellen-Anhang, Kataloge und Literatur.* 122 pp. Wilhelmshaven, Germany: Heinrichshofen, 1976. (Taschenbücher zur Musikwissenschaft, 27)

A reference work in two parts: an index of monograms with their explanations, and an index of persons with the monograms associated with them. The appendix lists library catalogs (national and international), dictionaries of anonymous and pseudonymous works, and representative source studies.

1.107 Schäffer, Bogusław. *Leksykon kompozytorów XX wieku.* 2 vols. Cracow: Polskie Wydawn. Muzyczne, 1963–65.

A Polish-language dictionary of 20th-century composers, international in scope, but particularly strong in its coverage of Slavic musicians. Entries include bibliographies and some portraits.

1.108 Schmidl, Carlo. *Dizionario universale dei musicisti.* 2 vols. Milan: Sonzogno, 1928?–29. *Supplemento,* 1938 (806 pp.).

First published 1888–89 in 1 vol.

A major Italian bio-bibliography, a good general biographical source for obscure Italian musicians. Its emphasis is on native composers, librettists, and performers, with full articles on well-known persons and brief accounts of minor ones. The dates are given for the first publication of dramatic works. Works lists are included, citing modern editions. It is particularly valuable for its articles on Italian literary figures and their relation to music. All forenames are Italianized.

1.109 Seeger, Horst. *Musiklexikon: Personen A–Z.* 860 pp. Leipzig: Deutscher Verlag für Musik, 1981.

Updated and extracted from the editor's *Musiklexikon in zwei Bänden* (**1.52**), 1966.

Very brief biographical entries with classified lists of the composers' major works. The scope is international, with subjects from the Eastern bloc receiving the best coverage.

1.110 Simpson, Harold. *Singers to Remember.* 223 pp. Lingfield, England: Oakwood Press, 1973.

A collection of biographies of 98 singers, with selective contemporary discographies, intended for "younger collectors of vocal recordings."

1.111 Southern, Eileen. *Biographical Dictionary of Afro-American and African Musicians.* 478 pp. Westport, Conn.: Greenwood Press, 1982. (Greenwood Encyclopedia of Black Music)

A dictionary that examines its subjects from historical perspective, using some previously published sources. The biographies include citations of sources. There are lists by periods, by birthplace, and by musical occupation, as well as a selective bibliography and a general index.

Reviewed by Doris McGinty in *BPM* 11 (1987): 79–82 and by Dominique-René de Lerma in *Ethnomusicology* 27 (1983): 543–44.

1.112 Stern, Susan. *Women Composers: A Handbook.* 191 pp. Metuchen, N.J.: Scarecrow Press, 1978.

A reference work whose entries provide very brief data and sources of further information. The sources are separately listed. Cross-references are provided for women who have used more than one form of their names. There are a supplementary list of women composers for whom no information could be found and a supplementary bibliography of works that provide information on women composers.

Reviewed by Judith Tick in *Notes* 36 (1979): 99–100 and by A. F. Leighton Thomas in *MR* 42 (1981): 62–67.

1.113* Walser, Paul L. *The Music World Obituary Digest: A Quick Reference Book Covering All Categories of Music.* Updated 2nd ed. 65 pp. Bakersfield, Calif.: P.L. Walser, 1995.

An eccentrically organized necrology of recording artists. Neither the date of death nor the source of information is given. The subject's professional name, age, cause of death, and a brief career description are supplied. The subjects are organized in four categories according to principal type of music performed. Although not cumulated, the information supplied in *Notes*'s "Index to Music Obituaries" each June is more dependable (**1.86**).

NATIONALLY ORIENTED DICTIONARIES

Any dictionary of musical biography may be expected to be strongest in names within its own language group. There are numerous specialized dictionaries of biography devoted specifically to the musicians of particular countries; occasionally these books also have information on other musical details of the country under consideration. Only the most important and representative of such dictionaries are listed below, with the emphasis on recent publications. Entries are arranged by country or, occasionally, by region or ethnic group (e.g., Arabic countries or Latin America).

ARABIC COUNTRIES

1.114* Budhaynah, Muhammad. *al-Mamsuah al-Musiqiyah.* 517 pp. Tunis: The author, 1991.

An illustrated dictionary of musicians from Arab countries, with a brief bibliography and indexes.

ARGENTINA

1.115 Arizaga, Rodolfo. *Enciclopedia de la música Argentina.* 371 pp. Buenos Aires: Fondo Nacional de las Artes, 1971.

Chiefly a biographical dictionary of Argentine musicians, which also includes terms for dance forms, musical institutions, and the like. The biographical entries have partial lists of the composers' works. There are also chronological tables covering the history of Argentine music from 1901 to 1970.

1.116* Kurucz, Ladislao. *Vademecum musical argentino.* 142 pp. Buenos Aires: Edición Vamuca, 1983.

A handbook of Argentine music. The biographical section (pp. 13–92) is the largest chapter, with some illustrations. Entries are classified by the subject's principal talent (composer, singer, pianist). A number of entries provide only an address. The listing of orchestras gives the names of the first-desk players and is divided into two alphabets: symphony orchestras and chamber ensembles. Entries for choral ensembles and musical organizations are divided by location: in Buenos Aires or in the provinces. Other categories are too short to classify.

1.117 Senillosa, Mabel. *Compositores argentinos.* 2nd ed., augmented. 451 pp. Buenos Aires: Casa Lottermosser, 1956.

The 1st ed. was issued as *Homenaje al artista argentinos, músicos,* 1948.

A dictionary of Argentine composers, with some entries supplied by the composers themselves.

AUSTRALIA

1.118 Mackenzie, Barbara, and **Findlay Mackenzie.** *Singers of Australia, from Melba to Sutherland.* 309 pp. Melbourne: Lansdowne, 1967.

Also published in London by Newnes, 1968.

A collection of biographies with a liberal selection of portraits; entries include a bibliography. The authors have compiled data on the results of vocal competitions in Australia.

1.119 Murdoch, James. *Australia's Contemporary Composers.* 223 pp. + 18 plates. Melbourne: Macmillan, 1972.

Reissued in 1975 by Sun Books, Melbourne.

A collection of extended biographical essays, with discographies and index.

AUSTRIA

1.120* Goertz, Harald. *Österreichische Komponisten der Gegenwart: Ein Handbuch.* 96 pp. Vienna; Munich: Doblinger, 1979.

Biographies of 116 Austrian composers, including a classified works list in each entry.

1.121 Knaus, Herwig. *Die Musiker im Archivbestand des kaiserlichen Obersthofmeisteramtes (1637–1705).* 3 vols. Vienna: Hermann Böhlaus Nachf., 1967–69. (Österreichische Akademie der Wissenschaften. Philosophisch-Historische Klasse, 254/1, 259/1, 264/1) (Veröffentlichungen der Kommission für Musikforschung, 7–8, 10)

An archival study of early Austrian musicians, composed of transcriptions of documents pertaining to musical activities in Austrian courts, chapels, and municipalities. Each volume has an index of names. Madeleine Jurgens's *Documents du Minutier Central concernant l'histoire de la musique (1600–1650)* is a similar study, based on the French national archives (**7.385**).

1.122* Lang, Siegfried. *Lexikon österreichischer U-Musik-Komponisten im 20. Jahrhundert.* 248 pp. Vienna: im Auftrag des Österreichischen Komponistenbundes (ÖKB) / Arbeitskreis U-Musik, 1986.

A biographical lexicon that supplies each subject's dates and current address, with an account of the professional career and a condensed works list for most. There is a detailed name index.

1.123 Suppan, Wolfgang. *Steirisches Musiklexikon: Im Auftrage des Steirischen Tonkünstlerbundes unter Benützung der "Sammlung Wamlek."* 7 vols. in 5. 676 pp. + 56 plates. Graz, Austria: Akademische Druck- und Verlagsanstalt, 1962–66. (Musik aus der Steiermark, 4; Beiträge zur steirischen Musikforschung, 1)

A biographical dictionary of musicians associated with Graz and other parts of Styria, comprehensive for pre-1800 names and selective for post-1800, with good bibliographical coverage for composers' works and for writings on the musicians.

Reviewed by Fritz Racek in *Die Musikforschung* 22 (1969): 388–89.

BELGIUM

1.124 Centre Belge de Documentation Musicale. *Music in Belgium: Contemporary Belgian Composers.* 158 pp. Brussels: Published in cooperation with the CeBeDeM, by A. Manteau; Boston: Crescendo Publishing Company, 1964.

A publication designed to stimulate interest in contemporary Belgian music, with biographical sketches of 48 modern Belgian composers, including portraits and lists of their major works. There is an index of names, as well as brief lists of recordings.

1.125* Gregoir, Édouard Georges Jacques. *Les artistes-musiciens belges au XVIIIme et au XIXme siècle.* 486 pp. Brussels: Schott Frères, 1885.

A biographical dictionary of Belgian musicians by a prominent scholar in the field. The author earlier covered the same area in *Galerie biographique des artistes musiciens belges du XVIIIe et XIXe siècle,* 1862 (212 pp.).

1.126 Hemel, Victor van. *Voorname belgische toonkunstenaars uit de 18de, 19de en 20ste eeuw. Beknopt overzicht van hun leven en oeuvre.* 3rd ed. 84 pp. Antwerp: Cupido-uitgave, 1958.

First published in 1933 (59 pp.).

Brief biographies of 101 Belgian musicians from the 18th century to the 1950s.

1.127 Vannes, René, and **André Souris.** *Dictionnaire des musiciens (compositeurs).* 443 pp. Brussels: Larcier, 1947. (Petits dictionnaires des lettres et des arts en Belgique, 4)

Information on Belgian composers from the 15th century to 1830, with comprehensive lists of works, published or in manuscript, and references to other sources of information.

Comments by Richard S. Hill in *Notes* 6 (1949): 607–8.

BOLIVIA

1.128* Messmer, Peter Vásquez. *Compositores bolivianos.* 96 pp. La Paz, Bolivia, 1975.

An illustrated biographical dictionary of Bolivian composers. Enthusiastic commentary and a selected list of compositions are given for each of 35 Bolivian musicians (including 1 woman); most of the subjects are 20th-century figures, arranged geographically by place of birth or most significant activity.

BRAZIL

1.129 Marcondes, Marcos Antônio. *Enciclopédia da música brasileira: Erudita, folclórica, popular.* 2 vols. 1,190 pp. São Paulo: Art Editora, 1977.

A good overview of the Brazilian musical world, including entries on Brazilian musicians, terms, genres, and instruments, with extensive works lists for composers. Many useful appendixes are included: a discography (pp. 835–81) arranged by composer and medium, a chronological list of Brazilian operas, Brazilian music periodicals, Brazilian theaters, and a first-line index of music. There is a general bibliography (pp. 1,163–90).

Two recordings (33-1/3 rpm, stereophonic, 12 in.) accompany these volumes.

Reviewed by Luiz Hector Corrêa de Azevedo in *LAMR* 4 (1983): 271–73.

1.130 Mariz, Vasco. *Dicionário biográfico musical: Compositores, intérpretes e musicólogos.* 3rd ed., revised and enlarged. 249 pp. Belo Horizonte, Brazil: Villa Rica, 1991.

The 2nd ed. was published in 1985 (286 pp.). The 1st ed. was published as *Dicionário bio-bibliográfico musical (brasileiro e internacional)* by Livraria Kosmos in 1948 (246 pp.).

A biographical dictionary containing brief entries for the best-known figures in music since the renaissance, including performers, and especially useful for information on Brazilian musicians.

BULGARIA

1.131 Krŭstev, Venelin. *Entsiklopediia na bŭlgarskata muzikalna kultura.* 465 pp. Sofia: Bŭlgarska Akademiia na Naukite, 1967.

An illustrated Bulgarian bio-bibliographical dictionary of musicians, with additional information on Bulgarian instruments and musical institutions.

CANADA

1.132* Beatty, Carolyn. *Directory of Associate Composers.* 1 vol. Toronto; Montreal; Vancouver; Calgary: CMC (Canadian Music Centre), 1989–91.

French ed. published in the same format as *Répertoire des compositeurs agrées.*

A loose-leaf source for information on 237 Canadian composers, associates of the Canadian Music Centre, each with a classified list of no more than 30 of their works, with entries written by the subjects; the 1989 and 1991 entries should be interfiled.

1.133 Canadian Broadcasting Corporation. *Catalogue of Canadian Composers.* Revised and enlarged ed. Edited by Helmut Kallmann. 254 pp. Ottawa: Canadian Broadcasting Corporation, 1952.

The 1st ed. was published in 1947. The revised ed. was reprinted by the Scholarly Press, St. Clair, Mich., in 1972.

A catalog with 356 brief biographical sketches giving the education, professional activities, and addresses of their subjects. The works lists are as complete as possible, with titles, publication dates, media, durations, and publishers; unpublished works are included. There is a list of Canadian publishers and composers' organizations.

The CBC also published *Thirty-Four Biographies of Canadian Composers* in 1964, reprinted in 1972 by the Scholarly Press, St. Clair, Mich. (110 pp.).

Reviewed by H. Dorothy Tilly in *Notes* 9 (1952): 615.

1.134* Guérin, François. *Les musiques électroacoustiques.* 76 pp. Quebec: Centre de musique canadienne, 1983. (À l'écoute de la musique d'ici, 2)

A brief history and a catalog of Canadian composers of electronic music and their works.

1.135 Kallmann, Helmut, Gilles Potvin, and **Kenneth Winters.** *Encyclopedia of Music in Canada.* 2nd ed. xxxi + 1,524 pp. Toronto; Buffalo, N.Y.: University of Toronto Press, 1992.

French ed. was published in 3 vols. as *Encyclopédie de la musique au Canada* in Saint-Laurent, Quebec, by Fides in 1993 (lv + 3,810 pp.). The 1st ed. was published in 1981, xxix + 1,076 pp.; the French version was published in 1982 as *Encyclopédie de la musique au Canada,* xxxi + 1142 pp.

An exemplary work with 3,162 entries, all of which have a Canadian context, clearly describing Canada's contributions to the world of music. It is truly encyclopedic in scope, with lengthy articles, many illustrations and tables, lists, bibliographies, and superb indexes. Helmut Kallmann recounts his work in "The Making of a One-Country Music Encyclopedia: An Essay after an Encyclopedia," *Fontes* 41 (1994): 3–19.

Reviewed by Kenneth DeLong in *Notes* 50 (1994): 1449–50, by Charlotte Leonard in *Fontes* 40 (1993): 268–69, and by Dean Tudor in *ARBA* 25 (1994): no. 1312. The 1st ed. is reviewed by John E. Druesedow, Jr., in *ARBA* 14 (1983): no. 930, by Gordana Lazarevich in *Notes* 39 (1982): 98–99, by George A. Proctor in *Fontes* 29 (1983): 92, and, in its French version, by François Lesure in *Fontes* 30 (1983): 224–25.

1.136 MacMillan, Keith, and **John Beckwith.** *Contemporary Canadian Composers.* 248 pp. Toronto; New York: Oxford University Press, 1975.

The French ed., revised, was published in 1977 as *Compositeurs canadiens contemporains,* edited by Louise Laplante and trans. by Véronique Robert in Montreal, by Les Presses de l'Université du Québec, 382 pp.

A biographical dictionary with bibliographical references, analyses of the most important works of modern composers, and an index. There are lists of all varieties of Canadian musical organizations.

The French ed. is reviewed by Kathleen Toomey in *Notes* 35 (1978): 86.

CHILE

1.137* Pereira Salas, Eugenio. *Biobibliografía musical de Chile desde los origenes a 1886.* 136 pp. Santiago de Chile: Ediciones de la Universidad de Chile, 1978. (Serie de monografías anexas a los Anales de la Universidad de Chile)

A illustrated dictionary of 199 Chilean composers, with brief biographies and a consecutively numbered works list, as well as a brief appendix of music.

COLOMBIA

1.138 Davidson, Harry C. *Diccionario folclórico de Colombia: Músicos, instrumentos y danzas.* 3 vols. Bogotá: Banco de la República, Departamento de Talleres Gráficos, 1970.

Entries on genres, forms, instruments, and terms of the folk music and dance of Colombia, from *adagio* to *zumba.* Sources are cited in context. Some of the articles are quite extensive (e.g., *El arpa*) and one, on the dance form *bambuco,* occupies 400 pp. There is an index to names, forms, and instruments.

CROATIA

1.139 Kovačević, Krešimir.. *Hrvatski kompozitori i njihova djela.* 553 pp. Zagreb: Naprijed, 1960.

Biographies of 50 generally contemporary Croatian composers, giving descriptive accounts of their principal works. There are summaries in English, a classified index of analyzed works, and a general index.

CUBA

1.140 Orovio, Helio. *Diccionario de la música cubana: Biográfico y técnico.* 2nd ed., corrected and augmented. 516 pp. Havana: Editorial Letras Cubanas, 1992.

First ed., 1981, 441 pp.

Primarily a biographical dictionary, with entries for musical terms, institutions and organizations, and instruments.

1.141 Ramirez, Serafin. *La Habana artista: Apuntes historicos.* 687 pp. Havana: Imp. del E. M. de la Capitania General, 1891.

An early attempt to record activity in 19th-century Cuba that includes notes on 19th-century Cuban dances, a 200-pp. dictionary of composers, and a 100-pp. section on the literature of music, as well as an index of "composiciones musicales."

CZECH REPUBLIC AND SLOVAKIA

1.142* Burjánek, Josef, and **Petar Zapletal.** *Svaz Českých Skladatelů a Koncertních Umělců (SCSKU).* 292 pp. Prague: Supraphon, 1975.

A bio-bibliographical dictionary of Czech musicians.

1.143 Černušák, Gracian, Bohumír Štědron, and **Zdenko Nováček.** *Československý hudební slovník osob a institucí.* 2 vols. Prague: Státní hudební vydavatelství, 1963–65.

A Czech and Slovak bio-bibliographical dictionary including information on places and institutions.

Reviewed by Camillo Schoenbaum in *Die Musikforschung* 18 (1965): 347–49.

1.144 Dlabač, Jan Bohumir. *Allgemeines historisches Künstler-Lexikon für Böhmen und zum Theil auch für Mähren und Schlesien. Auf Kosten der hochlöblichen Herrenstände Böhmens hrsg.* 3 vols. Prague: Gedruckt bei G. Haase, 1815.

Reprinted, including the 1913 *Beiträge und Berichtigungen zu Dlabacz Lexikon böhmischer Künstler* (Prague, K. Andre), by Georg Olms, Hildesheim, Germany, 1973, 4 vols. in 1.

An early dictionary of Czech (Bohemian and Moravian) musicians and artists.

1.145 Gardavský, Čeněk. *Contemporary Czechoslovak Composers.* 562 pp. Prague: Panton, 1965.

Also published in a French ed., *Les compositeurs tchécoslovaques contemporains,* 1966 (560 pp.), with Miroslav Barvík.

An English-language dictionary with biographical and bibliographical information on more than 300 Czech composers.

1.146* Martínková, Alena. *Čeští skladatelé současnosti.* 325 pp. Prague: Panton, 1985.

A dictionary of biographies that includes bibliographies.

FINLAND

1.147* Marvia, Einari. *Suomen säveltäjiä.* 2nd ed. 2 vols. Porvoo, Finland: W. Söderström, 1965–66.

First published in 1 vol. (761 pp.) in 1945, edited by Sulho Ranta, as *Suomen säveltäjiä puolentoista vuosisadan ajalta.*

A multivolume work on Finnish composers.

FRANCE

1.148* Benoit, Marcelle. *Dictionnaire de la musique en France aux XVIIe et XVIIIe siècles.* Publié avec le concours de l'Association Orcofi pour l'Opéra, la Musique et les Arts et du Centre National des Lettres. 811 pp. Paris: Fayard, 1992.

A carefully organized comprehensive dictionary of an important segment of French musical history. An international group of contributors was responsible for the signed articles covering the range of the period (biographies, titles, terminology, and musical instruments), with helpful illustrations and tables adding to the succinct entries. Most articles have references to the classified bibliography (pp. 739–81) of 1,751 items. The index is divided by personal name (further subdivided by nationality and occupation), title, musical terms, and "vie musicale" (institutions, theaters, and cities).

1.149 Benoit, Marcelle. *Musiques de cour: Chapelle, chambre, écurie. Recueil de documents, 1661–1733.* 553 pp. Paris: Éditions A. et J. Picard & Cie., 1971. (Vie musicale en France sous les rois Bourbons, 20)

A rich documentary study of musicians active in the French court from 1661 to 1733, based on material in the national archives and the Bibliothèque Nationale.

Reviewed by Norbert Dufourcq in *Revue de musicologie* 59 (1973): 295–97, and by Ivo Supičič in *IRASM* 17 (1986): 131–36.

1.150 Brossard, Yolande de. *Musiciens de Paris, 1535–1792: Actes d'état civil d'après le fichier Laborde de la Bibliothèque nationale.* 302 pp. Paris: A. et J. Picard & Cie., 1971. (Vie musicale en France sous les rois Bourbons, 11)

A directory of early Parisian musicians based on a file of 6,624 cards listing musicians of all varieties active in Paris during the period covered, compiled by Léon de Laborde (d. 1869). There is an index of musicians, arranged chronologically under their specialties.

1.151 *Tablettes de renommée des musiciens: Auteurs, compositeurs, virtuoses, amateurs, et maîtres de musique vocale et instrumentale, les plus connus en chaque genre.* 125 pp. Paris: Cailleau, 1785.

Reprinted by Minkoff Reprints, Geneva, in 1971.

An early bio-bibliographical work focusing on the musicians of Paris, with brief entries in a classified format.

GERMANY

1.152 Bösken, Franz. *Musik und Musiker am Mittelrhein: Ein biographisches, orts- und landesgeschichtliches Nachschlagewerk in Verbindung mit den Musikwissenschaftlichen Instituten der Universität Frankfurt am Main.* 2 vols. Mainz: Schott, 1974–81. (Beiträge zur mittelrheinischen Musikgeschichte, 20–21)

A biographical work concentrating on musical figures from the Frankfurt area. The 1st vol. was edited by Hubert Unverricht, the 2nd by Kurt Oehl.

1.153* Brand, Bettina. *Komponistinnen in Berlin.* 448 pp. Berlin: Musikfrauen, 1987.

Published to celebrate the 750th anniversary of the founding of Berlin, a collection giving an account of the creative careers of approximately 100 women composers of the last 300 years. The individual entries include reproductions of such previously unpublished archival material as photographs, correspondence, concert programs, contemporary articles and reviews, and music scores. Most entries include lists of composers' works, bibliographies, and discographies.

Reviewed by Judy Tsou in *Notes* 47 (1990): 380–81.

1.154* Bruchhäuser, Wilfried W. *Komponisten der Gegenwart im Deutschen Komponisten-Verband: Ein Handbuch.* 3rd ed. 1,008 + 27 pp. Berlin: Der Verband, 1987.

A supplement to this ed. was published in 1990, 164 pp. First ed., 1985, 851 pp.

A bio-bibliographical directory of composers of the former West Germany.

1.155* Dohr, Christoph. *Musikleben und Komponisten in Krefeld: Das 20. Jahrhundert.* 640 pp. Berlin: Merseburger, 1992. (Beiträge zur rheinischen Musikgeschichte, 144)

A bio-bibliographical dictionary limited to 20th-century composers working in the Krefeld area, with bibliographical references and index.

1.156 Fellerer, Karl G. *Rheinische Musiker.* 9 vols. Cologne: Arno Verlag, 1960–81. (Beiträge zur rheinischen Musikgeschichte, 43, 53, 58, 64, 69, 80, 97, 111, and 129)

A series of vols., giving biographical and bibliographical information on musicians of the Rhineland, issued serially. Each vol. is complete in itself, with cumulative indexing. There were numerous contributors; from Folge 6 (1969) on the editor was Dietrich Kämper. As in Mattheson's *Grundlage einer Ehren-Pforte* (1910) (**1.93**), many of the biographies are self-compiled.

1.157 Kossmaly, Carl, and **C. H. Herzel.** *Schlesisches-Tonkünstler-Lexikon, enthaltend die Biographieen aller schlesischen Tonkünstler, Componisten, Cantoren, Organisten, Tongelehrten, Textdichter, Orgelbauer, Instrumentenmacher.* Edited by Kossmaly and Carlo (pseud.). 332 pp. Breslau, Poland: E. Trewendt, 1846–47.

Reprinted by G. Olms, Hildesheim, Germany, 1982.

Originally issued in four parts, each in a separate alphabet, a lexicon with long articles giving classified lists of compositions, roles for performers, and concert programs.

1.158 Lipowsky, Felix J. *Baierisches Musik-Lexikon.* 338 (438) pp. Munich: Giel, 1811.

Reprint of the original edition by G. Olms, Hildesheim, 1982.

An early dictionary of some historical importance, covering Bavarian performers and composers and listing their major compositions; there are occasional title-page transcriptions.

1.159 Müller von Asow, Hedwig, and **Erich H. Müller von Asow.** *Kürschners deutscher Musiker-Kalender.* 2nd ed. 1,702 cols. Berlin: Walter de Gruyter, 1954.

First published in 1929 as *Deutsches Musiker-Lexikon,* edited by Erich H. Müller (Dresden: W. Limpert, 1929), 1,644 cols.

Entries for living German, Austrian, and Swiss musicians in all categories, and German-born musicians living in foreign countries, giving essential biographical information and detailed lists of works, with excessive use of abbreviations. There are indexes of names by date of birth (1854–1939) and date of death (1929–54).

1.160 Verband deutscher Komponisten und Musikwissenschaftler. *Komponisten und Musikwissenschaftler der Deutschen Demokratischen Republik: Kurzbiographien und Werkverzeichnisse.* 2nd ed., expanded. 239 pp. Berlin: Verlag Neue Musik, 1967.

The 1st ed. was published in 1959, 198 pp.

Brief biographical sketches of composers and musicologists of the former East Germany, with lists of their major works, preceded by a group of essays on music life and institutions in East Germany. Selected portraits of the subjects are included.

GREAT BRITAIN

1.161 Baptie, David. *Musical Scotland, Past and Present: Being a Dictionary of Scottish Musicians from about 1400 till the Present Time, to Which is Added a Bibliography of Musical Publications Connected with Scotland from 1611.* 253 pp. Paisley, Scotland: J. and R. Parlane, 1894.

Reprinted by G. Olms in Hildesheim, Germany, and New York, 1972.

A dictionary of Scottish musicians, with varying levels of information supplied for the subjects. There are a selective bibliography (pp. 243–47) and an appendix of lists covering such topics as "Hereditary Pipers."

1.162 Brown, James Duff, and **Stephen S. Stratton.** *British Musical Biography: A Dictionary of Musical Artists, Authors, and Composers Born in Britain and Its Colonies.* 462 pp. Birmingham, England: Chadfield, 1897.

Reprinted by Da Capo, New York, 1971.

A dictionary emphasizing composers alive at the time of the original publication. Great masters are treated briefly to afford room for the obscure. Included are a number of Britons not noted elsewhere, with excellent bibliographies. Users should also note Brown's international biographical dictionary (**1.66**).

1.163 Highfill, Philip H., Jr., Kalman A. Burnim, and **Edward A. Langhans.** *A Biographical Dictionary of Actors, Actresses, Musicians, Dancers, Managers and Other Stage Personnel in London, 1660–1800.* 16 vols. Carbondale, Ill.: Southern Illinois University Press, 1973–93.

An exhaustively researched multivolume work. Each vol. contains about 1,000 biographical entries detailing facts about the individuals listed.

Vols. 1–2 are reviewed by Neal Zaslaw in *Notes* 31 (1974): 311–12; Vols. 5–6 are reviewed by Stoddard Lincoln in *Notes* 35 (1979): 886–87; Vols. 11–12 are reviewed by David A. Day in *Notes* 48 (1991): 111–12. The completed set is reviewed by Lowell Lindgren in *Notes* 52 (1995): 60–63.

1.164* Leach, Gerald. *British Composer Profiles: A Biographical Dictionary and Chronology of Past British Composers, 1800–1989.* 2nd ed. 127 pp. High Breeches, Gerrards Cross, England: British Music Society, 1989.

The 1st ed. was published in Maidenhead, England, by the British Music Society, 1980 (100 pp.).

A list of British composers of the last two centuries, with brief biographies and a chronological table. No sources are given.

1.165* Matthews, Betty. *The Royal Society of Musicians of Great Britain List of Members, 1739–1984.* 253 pp. London: The Society, 1985.

A list, with biographical details, of the members of Great Britain's foremost professional society for musicians.

1.166 Palmer, Russell. *British Music.* 283 pp. London: Skelton Robinson, 1947.

An illustrated biographical index of contemporary British musicians and musical organizations.

1.167 Pulver, Jeffrey. *A Biographical Dictionary of Old English Music.* 537 pp. London: Kegan Paul, Trench, Trubner & Co.; New York: E.P. Dutton & Co., 1927.

Reprinted by Burt Franklin, New York, 1969, and by the Da Capo Press, New York, 1973, with a new introduction and a bibliography of the writings of Jeffrey Pulver by Gilbert Blount.

Covering English musicians active from about 1200 to the death of Purcell in 1695, with entries citing manuscript sources, contemporary publications, and, occasionally, modern editions. Although somewhat discursive in style, with works lists scattered through the bodies of the articles, this book is useful as a starting point for the study of early English musicians. The author compiled a companion volume covering old English musical terms (**1.318**).

HUNGARY

1.168 Czigány, Gyula. *Contemporary Hungarian Composers.* 4th revised, enlarged ed. 219 pp. Budapest: Editío Musica, 1979.

First ed., 1970, 156 pp.; 3rd ed., 1974, 176 pp.

A bio-bibliography including a discography of works by Hungarian composers.

INDIA

1.169* Dasasarma, Amala. *Musicians of India: Past and Present Gharanas of Hindustani Music and Genealogies.* 348 pp. Calcutta: Naya Prokash, 1993.

A source that includes genealogical tables and bibliographical references.

1.170* Nirmla Devi, Mrs. *Dictionary of Music.* 256 pp. New Delhi: Anmol Publications, 1990.

A source serving as a general dictionary of music, with entries for terms, instruments, and compositions; includes terms and biographies from Indian music.

1.171* Rajagopalan, N. *A Garland: A Biographical Dictionary of Carnatic Composers and Musicians.* 2 vols. Bombay: Bharatiya Vidya Bhavan, 1990–92.

Vol. 2, published in Madras by Carnatic Classicals, is titled *Another Garland.*

A biographical dictionary with over 1,000 entries for composers, musicians, musicologists, and hymnodists. The 2nd vol. has a chronological list of composers and musicians, arranged by birthdate, as well as an alphabetical list, with location, of those covered in the two vols.

1.172 Sambamoorthy, P. *A Dictionary of South Indian Music and Musicians.* 2nd ed. 3 vols. Madras: Indian Music Publishing House, 1984.

The 1st ed., issued from 1952 to 1971 in 3 vols., covered only A–F.

A dictionary with portraits of the composers and performers under discussion.

1.173 *Who's Who of Indian Musicians.* 160 pp. New Delhi: Sangeet Natak Akademi, 1984.

First published in 1968, 100 pp.

Brief biographical entries on living Indian musicians giving date of birth, area of specialization, and addresses.

IRELAND

1.174 Deale, Edgar M. *A Catalogue of Contemporary Irish Composers.* 2nd ed. 108 pp. Dublin: Music Association of Ireland, 1974.

The 1st ed. was published in 1968 (74 pp.).

Data on the works of contemporary Irish composers including brief biographical information and addresses of the composers and full descriptions of their works: titles, media, durations, instrumentation, and availability. There are a list of publishers and a list of abbreviations. This was followed by Harrison's *Catalogue of Contemporary Irish Music,* 1982 (**5.84**).

ISRAEL (AND JEWISH MUSICIANS)

1.175 Gradenwitz, Peter. *Music and Musicians in Israel: A Comprehensive Guide to Modern Israeli Music.* 3rd ed. 227 pp. Tel Aviv: Israeli Music Publications, 1978.

Originally published in Jerusalem, 1952, 107 pp.; subsequently issued in Tel Aviv, 1959 (226 pp.).

Biographies, varying in length, of about 60 composers, grouped by school. The appendix (pp. 133–63) contains an alphabetical list of composers and their works, but without reference to the opening biographical section. Also given is a list of publishers and a group of publishers' catalogs.

1.176 Nulman, Macy. *Concise Encyclopedia of Jewish Music.* 276 pp. New York: McGraw-Hill Book Company, 1975.

A highly selective work whose 500+ entries include musical terms, biographies of both liturgical and concert musicians, Biblical and post-Biblical musical instruments, Jewish musical organizations and movements, musical works on Old Testament subjects, and principal published collections, with information emphasizing current practices. Included are extensive musical examples and a 4-page "Highlights in the History of Jewish Music."

Briefly reviewed by Stephen M. Fry in *Notes* 32 (1976): 556 and by Eric Werner in *Notes* 32 (1976): 771–72.

1.177 Ravina, Menashe, and **Shlomo Skolsky.** *Who is Who in ACUM: Authors, Composers and Music Publishers, Biographical Notes and Principal Works.* 95 pp. Tel Aviv: ACUM Ltd., Société d'auteurs, compositeurs et éditeurs de musique en Israel, 1965.

Addenda and Corrigenda, 1965, 10 pp.

A dictionary giving brief biographies, with lists of works, authors, composers, and publishers affiliated with ACUM, a performing rights organization founded in Israel in 1934.

1.178 Saleski, Gdal. *Famous Musicians of Jewish Origin.* 716 pp. New York: Bloch Publishing Company, 1949.

First published in 1927 as *Famous Musicians of a Wandering Race,* 463 pp.

An illustrated collection of about 400 informal biographies, classified according to type of musical activity (composers, conductors, violinists, etc.). There are no bibliographies, but major works are mentioned in the articles. There is a section on Israeli musicians (pp. 679–716).

1.179 Shalita, Israel, and **Hanan Steinitz.** *Entsiklopedyah le-Musikah / Encyclopedia of Music.* 2 vols. Tel Aviv: Joshua Chachik, 1965.

In Hebrew and international in scope, the 1st vol. is a biographical dictionary of Jewish and world musicians, the 2nd is a dictionary of terms, theory, instruments, forms, and history of Jewish and world music. There are indexes of Hebrew equivalents for English names and terms.

1.180 Stengel, Theophil, and **Herbert Gerigk.** *Lexikon der Juden in der Musik, mit einem Titelverzeichnis jüdischer Werke.* 404 cols. Berlin: B. Hahnefeld, 1943. (Veröffentlichungen des Instituts der NSDAP zur Erforschung der Judenfrage, 2)

First published in 1940, 380 pp.

Among the more shameful publications of German National Socialism, a dictionary of Jewish musicians compiled to further the purposes of anti-Semitism.

ITALY

1.181 Alcari, Cesare. *Parma nella musica.* 259 pp. Parma, Italy: M. Fresching, 1931.

A biographical dictionary of musicians associated with Parma, either by birth or career. Emphasis is placed on 19th-century figures, with extended bibliographies for the most important musicians (Verdi, Pizzetti). Included is the "Bibliografia dal 1913 al 1930 (in continuazione alla 'Bibliographia verdiana' di Carlo Banbianchi)," pp. 218–53.

1.182 Berutto, Guglielmo. *Il Piemonte e la musica, 1800–1984.* 419 pp. + 34 plates. Turin: G. Berutto, 1984.

A bio-bibliographical dictionary of the Italian Piedmont region, arranged in sections by occupation of the subject: *musicisti, cantanti, editori, impresari, registri, scenografi, danzi-bandi musicali, società corali, teatri scomparsi,* and *esistenti.* A final section gives brief historical sketches.

1.183 Damerini, Adelmo, and **Franco Schlitzer.** *Musicisti toscani.* Scritti di G. Barblan et al., Settembre, 1955. 81 pp. Siena, Italy: Ticci, 1955.

A list of Tuscan musicians, published by the Accademia Musicale Chigiana.

1.184 De Angelis, Alberto. *L'Italia musicale d'oggi: Dizionario dei musicisti: Compositori, direttori d'orchestra, concertisti, insegnanti, liutari, cantanti, scrittori musicali, librettisti, editori musicali, ecc.* 3rd ed., with an appendix. 523 + 211 pp. Rome: Ansonia, 1928.

First published in 1918; 2nd ed., 1922.

A dictionary whose entries for then-living Italian composers include comprehensive works lists.

1.185 Masutto, Giovanni. *I maestri di musica italiani del secolo XIX: Notizie biografiche.* 3rd ed., corrected and augmented. 226 pp. Venice: Gio. Cecchini, 1882.

First published in 1880 by Fontana. Includes an appendix dated 1884.

Short biographical entries for composers, educators, and performers, with a thumbnail description of their professional careers and a general description of their work. There are no bibliographical citations.

JAPAN

1.186* *Contemporary Music of Japan '72: Leading Composers and Their Works.* 116 pp. Tokyo: Ongaku no Tomosha, 1972.

A list of contemporary Japanese composers, giving birthdates and a brief account of their professional training and careers, with a detailed description of their major compositions. There is a classified title index.

1.187* Murata, Takeo. *Ensoka daijiten / The Biographical Dictionary of Musicians.* 2 vols. Tokyo: Ongaku Kansho Kyōiku Shinkōkai, 1982.

A major Japanese biographical dictionary, which has a bibliography in the 1st vol. (pp. xi–xv) and an index in Vol. 2.

LATIN AMERICA

1.188 Mayer-Serra, Otto. *Música y músicos de Latinoamérica.* 2 vols. (1,134 pp.) Mexico City: Editorial Atlante, 1947.

A dictionary that is primarily biographical, although entries for some terms, dance forms, and musical instruments are included. The lists of composers' works vary from brief résumés to full tabulations for major composers. Selected portraits of the subjects are included.

1.189 Pan American Union. Music Section. *Composers of the Americas, Biographical Data and Catalogs of Their Works.* Nos. 1–19. Washington, D.C.: Pan American Union, 1955–79.

A serial publication, each issue including 4–16 composers, alphabetically arranged, with brief biographies in English and Spanish and portraits of the subjects. The works of each composer are listed chronologically within the principal media, with date of composition, timing, and publishing and recording information, if applicable.

LITHUANIA

1.190* Gaudrimas, Juozas. *Kompozitory i muzykovedy sovetskoĭ Litvy (1940–1975).* 247 pp. Vilnius: Vaga, 1978.

A bio-bibliography of Soviet Lithuanian musicians.

THE NETHERLANDS

1.191 Gregoir, Édouard Georges Jacques. *Biographie des artistes-musiciens néerlandais des XVIIIe et XIXe siècles et des artistes étrangers résidant ou ayant résidé en Néerlande à la même époque.* 238 pp. Brussels: Schott Frères; Antwerp: L. de la Montagne, 1864.

Based on and supplementing his *Essai historique sur la musique,* Brussels, 1861.

Brief biographies of Dutch musicians, summarizing their careers and mentioning their major works, without full listings.

1.192 Straeten, Edmund S. J. van der. *La musique aux pays-bas avant le XIXe siècle: Documents inédits et annotés: Compositeurs, virtuoses, théoriciens, luthiers, opéras, motets, airs nationaux, académies, maîtrises, livres, portraits, etc.; avec planches de musique et table alphabétique.* 8 vols. Brussels: C. Muquardt, 1867–88.

Vols. 2–7 published by G. A. Van Trigt; Vol. 8 by B. Schott Frères. Reprinted by Dover, New York, 1968, in 4 vols.

Although not strictly a biographical dictionary, nevertheless an invaluable collection of documents, transcripts of records, and biographical and bibliographical notes related to the activities of Flemish musicians (Dutch and Belgian). Vol. 6 is devoted to Flemish musicians in Italy, Vols. 7 and 8 to Flemish musicians in Spain. This is rich in information of great interest to students of early European music. Vol. 9, announced at the end of Vol. 8 as being "En préparation," was never published.

NEW ZEALAND

1.193* Thomson, John Mansfield. *Biographical Dictionary of New Zealand Composers.* 168 pp. Wellington, New Zealand: Victoria University Press, 1990.

A dictionary of over 100 composers who have spent a significant part of their creative careers in New Zealand. Works lists are either complete (if under 30 works) or selected by the composer. The accompanying bibliographies are selective, so that only significant articles are included. Appendixes list musical organizations, publishing companies, and record companies of New Zealand.

PARAGUAY

1.194 Boettner, Juan Max. *Música y músicos del Paraguay.* 294 pp. Asunción, Paraguay: Edición de Autores Paraguayos Asociados, 1956.

A history of Paraguayan music, also including an "Indice biográficos de músicos del Paraguay" (pp. 258–86) and a bibliography (pp. 287–94).

POLAND

1.195 Chomiński, Józef Micha. *Słownik muzyków polskich.* 2 vols. Cracow: Polskie Wydawn. Muzyczne, 1964–67.

At head of title: Instytut Sztuki Polskie Akademii Nauk.

A biographical dictionary of Polish musicians of all periods, including organists, lutenists, and other obscure figures, especially strong in 19th-century musicians. Works lists and brief bibliographies are provided. An addendum to Vol. 1 is given at the end of Vol. 2. There is a list of commonly used reference and research sources.

1.196 Chybiński, Adolf. *Słownik muzyków dawnej Polski do roku 1800.* 163 pp. Cracow: Polskie Wydawn. Muzyczne, 1949.

A biographical dictionary of musicians (composers and performers) active in Poland up to 1800, with brief articles citing principal works and a list of references. The preface discusses such sources of information as Fétis (**1.75**) and Eitner (**5.544**), as well as many Polish publications and archives.

1.197 Sowiński, Wójciech. *Les musiciens polonais et slaves, anciens et modernes: dictionnaire biographique des compositeurs, chanteurs, instrumentistes, luthiers, constructeurs d'orgues, poètes sacrés et lyriques, littérateurs et amateurs de l'art musical. . . . Précédé d'un résumé de l'histoire de la musique en Pologne.* 599 pp. Paris: A. Le Clere et Cie., 1857.

Reprinted by Da Capo Press, New York, in 1971. Another ed., in Polish, was published in 1974.

Preceded by a history of Polish music (pp. 1–44) and an account of old Polish and Slavic musical instruments (pp. 45–58), a dictionary with long biographical articles, and full bibliographies of major composers.

PORTUGAL

1.198 Amorim, Eugénio. *Dicionário biográfico de musicos do norte de Portugal.* 110 pp. Porto: Edições Maranus, 1935.

A list of chiefly 19th- and 20th-century musicians, who are given mostly brief, though some extended, articles, with compositions listed in the body of the text.

1.199 *Catálogo geral da música portuguesa: Repertório contemporâneo.* 1 vol. (loose-leaf) Lisbon: Direcção-Geral do Património Cultural, A Secretaria, 1978– .

Biographical sketches of contemporary Portuguese composers in English, French, and Portuguese. Also included are lists of works, bibliographies, and discographies of each composer.

1.200 Mazza, José. *Dicionário biográfico de músicos portugueses, com prefácio e notas do José Augusto Alegria.* 103 pp. Lisbon, 1945.

"Extraido de revista, Ocidente, 1944–45."

A dictionary compiled around 1790 and preserved in manuscript in the Biblioteca Publica de Evora. The entries are arranged by Christian name; many are members of religious orders. The dictionary (pp. 13–40) is followed by additional biographical information supplied from other sources (pp. 41–103).

1.201 Vasconcellos, Joaquim A. da Fonseca E. *Os musicos portuguezes: Biographia-bibliographia.* 2 vols. Porto, Portugal: Imprensa Portugueza, 1870.

Useful for early names; includes long biographical articles with works lists and discussions of compositions, as well as library locations of manuscripts. The discussions of operas include date and place of first performance.

1.202 Vieira, Ernesto. *Diccionario biographico de musicos portuguezes: Historia e bibliographia da musica em Portugal.* 2 vols. Lisbon: M. Moreira e Pinheiro, 1900–4.

More inclusive than Vasconcellos (**1.201**), a biographical dictionary with comprehensive lists of works for major composers; the 2nd vol. has much supplementary material and a chronological index.

ROMANIA

1.203 Cosma, Viorel. *Muzicieni români, compozitori si muzicologi: Lexicon / Romanian Musicians, Composers and Musicologists: A Dictionary.* 475 pp. Bucharest: Uniunii Compozitorilor, 1970.

An expansion of *Compozitorisi muzicologi români: mic lexicon,* 1965 (386 pp.).

A collection of biographical data and information on the works of the most prominent Romanian composers and musicologists, including musicians of earlier times but stressing the contemporary scene. There are portraits and discographies.

1.204* Sava, Iosif, and Luminita Vartolomei. *Muzica si muzicieni.* 207 pp. Bucharest: Romfel, 1993.

A Romanian dictionary of music and musicians.

RUSSIA

1.205 Bélza, Igor´. *Handbook of Soviet Musicians.* Edited by Alan Bush. 101 pp. London: Pilot Press, 1944.

First published 1943. Reprinted in 1971 by Greenwood Press, Westport, Conn., and in 1972 by Scholarly Press, St. Clair Shores, Mich.

A collection of 40 short biographies with portraits and a separate bibliographical section (pp. 62–101), giving a works list for each composer, with English titles and composition dates, when known.

1.206 Bernandt, Grigoriĭ Borisovich, and **Izrail´ Markovich Iampol´skiĭ.** *Sovetskie kompository i muzykovedy: Spravochnik v trekh tomakh.* 3 vols. Moscow: Vses. izd-vo Sovetskiĭ kompozitor, 1978–82.

The 2nd vol. was edited by Lev. G. Grigor´ev and Ia. M. Plat´ev. First published in 1957, edited by Bernandt and A. Dolzhanskiĭ, 695 pp.

Biographical sketches of over 1,500 Soviet composers, with a full, classified list of their compositions; premiere dates of large works are given. Literary works by the musicians are also listed.

The 1st ed. is reviewed by Fred K. Prieberg in *MA* 78 (July 1958): 28–29.

1.207* Bernandt, Grigoriĭ Borisovich, Izrail´ Markovich Iampol´skiĭ, and Tamara Efimovna Kisileva. *Kto pisal o muzyke: Biobibliograficheskii slovar´ muzykal´nykh kritikov i lits, pisavshikh o muzyke v dorevoliutsionnoi Rossii i SSSR.* 4 vols. Moscow: Sovetskii Kompozitor, 1971–89.

An extensive biographical dictionary of musicians, both in pre-Revolutionary Russia and in the Soviet Union, liberally cross-referenced, with extensive works lists.

1.208* Gerlach, Hannelore. *Fünfzig sowjetische Komponisten der Gegenwart: Fakten und Reflexionen: Eine Dokumentation.* 624 pp. Leipzig: Edition Peters, 1984.

An examination, in dictionary format, of the lives, works, and philosophies of 50 Soviet composers, with an appendix of their portraits.

1.209* Ho, Allan, and **Dmitry Feofanov.** *Biographical Dictionary of Russian/Soviet Composers.* 739 pp. Westport, Conn.: Greenwood Press, 1989.

A list of over 2,000 composers born in Russia, the Soviet Union, or its various provinces or republics, as well as a few foreign-born composers who spent significant time in Russia. The entries give extensive bibliographical and discographical help, and pronunciation of the Russian names is provided.

Reviewed by Margarita Mazo in *Fontes* 39 (1991): 79–81, by Malcolm Barry in *M&L* 72 (1991): 616–18, and by Roy Guenther in *Notes* 47 (1991): 795–96.

SOUTH AFRICA

1.210 Huskisson, Yvonne. *The Bantu Composers of Southern Africa / Die Bantoe-Komponiste van Suider-Afrika.* xxxvi + 335 pp. Johannesburg: South African Broadcasting Corporation, 1969.

A bilingual (English and Afrikaans) dictionary of Bantu composers, giving for each entry brief family and educational background, as well as nonmusical career information, musical works lists, and paraphrases of many of the vocal works. Also included are portraits of the musicians, an index of composers, and a study of the traditional instruments of the Bantu (pp. 301–35).

1.211 Malan, Jacques P. *South African Music Encyclopedia.* 4 vols. Cape Town: Oxford University Press, 1979–86. A publication of the Human Sciences Research Council, Pretoria.

An extended work whose coverage, limited to the period 1652–1960, includes the music of both Europeans and indigenous South Africans. The biographical entries give comprehensive works lists; bibliographies follow many articles.

SPAIN

1.212 Alcahali, José de Lihory, Barón de. *La música en Valencia: Diccionario biográfico y crítico.* 445 pp. Valencia: Domenech, 1903.

A Spanish biographical and topical dictionary. The biographical entries are of widely varying length, with summary works lists for major composers and occasional musical examples. Under "Anónimos" (pp. 39–70) are long literary digressions on liturgical drama, dance music, military music, and other topics.

1.213* Asenjo y Barbieri, Francisco. *Biografías y documentos sobre música y músicos españoles.* Edited by Emilio Casares. 586 pp. Madrid: Fundación Banco Exterior, 1986. (Legado barbieri, 1)

A modern compilation of the previously unpublished research of a distinguished 19th-century Spanish musicologist, from material bequeathed to the Biblioteca Nacional, Madrid, in 1894.

1.214* Blas Vega, José, and **Manuel Ríos Ruiz.** *Diccionario enciclopédia ilustrado del flamenco.* 2 vols. Madrid: Editorial Cinterco, 1990.

First ed., 2 vols. (868 pp.), 1988.

SWEDEN

1.215* Jacobsson, Stig, and **Hans-Gunnar Peterson.** *Swedish Composers of the 20th Century: Members of the Society of Swedish Composers: Biographies.* 2nd ed. 205 pp. Stockholm: Svensk Musik, Swedish Music Information Center, 1990.

A complement to the series of selective catalogs published by the Swedish Music Information Center, intended as "a basis for use as information in concert programs," with some illustrations (portraits and musical excerpts). The entries include biographies and a characterization of the subject's style and personality, but not complete works lists, of all present and former members of the Society of Swedish Composers.

SWITZERLAND

1.216 Refardt, Edgar. *Historisch-biographisches Musikerlexikon der Schweiz.* 355 pp. Leipzig; Zurich: Gebruder Hug & Co., 1928.

Comprehensive biographical coverage for names connected with Swiss music from the middle ages to the end of the 19th century. The contents include musicians and instrument makers of the 17th and 18th centuries, with composers only for the 19th and 20th centuries. There are lists of works.

1.217 Schuh, Willi. *Schweizer Musiker-Lexikon: Dictionnaire des musiciens suisses.* Im Auftrag des Schweizerischen Tonkünstlervereins. 421 pp. Zurich: Atlantis Verlag, 1964.

A 15-page supplement was issued in 1965.

The expansion of a biographical dictionary of Swiss musicians that appeared originally as Vol. 2 of the *Schweizer Musikbuch* (Zurich, 1939). The *Lexikon* covers Swiss musicians of all periods as well as foreign musicians resident in Switzerland or associated with Swiss music. The articles are in French and German, with excellent bibliographical coverage.

1.218 Schweizerischer Tonkünstlerverein. *40 Contemporary Swiss Composers / 40 compositores suizos contemporáneos.* 222 pp. Amriswil, Switzerland: Bodensee-Verlag, 1956.

A collection of brief biographies of composers whose works have been performed at the annual festivals (1930–54) of the Swiss Composers' League or the International Society of Contemporary Music, with critical commentary in English and Spanish. A few representative works are described and a larger selection listed, with imprints and instrumentation given. Portraits and discographies are included.

TURKEY

1.219 Öztuna, T. Yilmaz. *Buyuk türk musikisi ansiklopedisi.* 2 vols. Ankara: Kultur Bakanligi, 1990.

An earlier ed. was published in 2 vols. as *Türk musikisi ansiklopedisi* in Istanbul by M. E. B. Devlet Kitaplari, 1969–74, based on the author's *Türk musikisi lugati.*

A Turkish dictionary of terms and biography. The terms are general musical concepts, but the biographies are restricted to Turkish figures. Bibliographical references are included.

UNITED STATES (NATIONAL)

1.220 Hitchcock, H. Wiley, and **Stanley Sadie.** *The New Grove Dictionary of American Music.* 4 vols. New York: Grove's Dictionaries of Music; London: Macmillan, 1986.

The principal reference work on American music, often called "Amerigrove." This work was compiled using both reworked articles from *The New Grove* (**1.48**) and newly commissioned ones "to reflect the essence of American music" (Preface); the articles are signed. The coverage of American music and musicians is broadly considered, but not without significant flaws and omissions, with concise articles summarizing the works of lesser-known persons and thorough, well-illustrated pieces with works lists and bibliographies for well-known persons. Many of the articles bring bits of information together for the first time. There is detailed coverage of popular styles and genres, including entries for important popular groups, as well as descriptions of uniquely American musical instruments and historical entries for musical publishers. Like *The New Grove,* the dictionary lacks an index. Dominique-René de Lerma and Marsha J. Reisser in their *Black Music and Musicians in The New Grove Dictionary of American Music and The New Harvard Dictionary of Music* (Chicago, Ill.: Center for Black Music Research, Columbia College Chicago, 1989, CBMR monographs, 1) give partial detailed access, as does Robert H. Cowden's *Instrumental Virtuosi: A Bibliography of Biographical Materials* (**1.251**), which lists the instrumentalists who are the subject of Amerigrove articles. The dictionary is copiously illustrated, with excellent illustrations and a list of contributors.

Wiley Hitchcock gave a preview in "On the Path to the US Grove" in *ISAMN* 13 (1983): 1–2 no. 1. Susan Feder, the editorial coordinator, talks about organizing the *Dictionary* in "The American Grove: An Insider's Account" in *ISAMN* 16 (1986): 1–2+ no. 1. An involuntary picture of the team techniques used in compiling the *Dictionary* appeared in correspondence between Leonard Burkat and Stanley Sadie in *AM* 7 (1989): 461–64, 8 (1990): 227–29, and 8 (1990): 229–30. Earlier correspondence on a portion of the same basic subject was initiated by Allen P. Britton's review in *AM* 5 (1987): 194–203, with a response from Stanley Sadie in *AM* 6 (1988): 92.

There are also extensive reviews by Mary Wallace Davidson et al. in *Notes* 44 (1987): 43–47, by Ann P. Basart in *CNV* 109 (1987): 3–4, by Peter Dickinson in *M&L* 70 (1989): 233–36, by Wilfrid Mellers in *TLS* (January 9 1987): 39, and by Richard A. Crawford in *College Music Symposium* 27 (1987): 172–86, and shorter ones by Gary Giddins in *Village Voice* 35 (January 1 1987): 75–76 and by Ross Wood in *ARBA* 19 (1988): no. 1277.

1.221 American Society of Composers, Authors and **Publishers.** *ASCAP Biographical Dictionary.* Compiled for the American Society of Composers, Authors and Publishers by Jaques Cattell Press. 4th ed. 589 pp. New York: R.R. Bowker, 1980.

First ed., *The ASCAP Biographical Dictionary of Composers, Authors and Publishers,* edited by Daniel I. McNamara, published by T.Y. Crowell, 1948 (483 pp.). 2nd ed., edited by Daniel I. McNamara, published by T.Y. Crowell, 1952 (636 pp.). 3rd ed., compiled and edited by the Lynn Farnol Group, Inc., 1966 (845 pp.).

A list of the more prominent members of America's foremost performing rights society. The 1st ed. gives all the present and past members of ASCAP to 1948, together with their biographical data, addresses, and lists of their work. The 4th ed. has brief biographies, including birthplace and date, study and training, career outline, main collaborators, and major published works, of 8,000+ of the 28,000-member ASCAP, both living and deceased, including lyricists and composers of popular and art music. There is a separate, complete list of the 8,000 publisher members.

The 1st ed. is reviewed by Minnie Elmer in *Notes* 5 (1948): 239–40. The 2nd ed. is reviewed by Richard S. Hill in *Notes* 9 (1952): 606–7. The 3rd ed. is reviewed by Ruth Hilton in *Notes* 24 (1967): 46. The 4th ed. is reviewed by Alan Hoffman in *Notes* 39 (1982): 103–4 and by Frederic Schoettler in *ARBA* 13 (1982): no. 1077.

1.222 Anderson, E. Ruth. *Contemporary American Composers: A Biographical Dictionary.* 2nd ed. 578 pp. Boston, Mass.: G.K. Hall, 1980.

First ed., 1976, 513 pp.

A list of approximately 4,500 composers, with career data, selected works lists, and current position and address. Among the criteria for inclusion are a birthdate no earlier than 1870, American citizenship or extended residence in the U.S., and at least one original composition published, commercially recorded, or performed in an urban area. Composers who wrote only teaching pieces, jazz, popular, folk, or rock music are excluded. The entries include a list of representative works.

The 1st ed. is reviewed by Anthony Burton in *Brio* 13 (1976): 52 no. 3, by Paul Griffiths in *MT* 118 (1977): 476–77, and by Stephen M. Fry in *Notes* 32 (1977): 603–4. The 2nd ed. is reviewed by Ned Quist in *AM* 3 (1985): 238–40 and by Avery T. Sharp in *ARBA* 14 (1983): no. 944.

1.223 Berry, Lemuel, Jr. *Biographical Dictionary of Black Musicians and Music Educators,* Vol. 1. 308 pp. Guthrie, Okla.: Educational Book Publishers, 1978.

Entries on individuals and ensembles giving brief biographical data on classical, jazz, and popular music figures, in two alphabetical lists. The second addendum list is about as long as the first and includes more jazz and pop figures. There are many appendixes, as well as indexes to names and specialties.

1.224* Butterworth, Neil. *A Dictionary of American Composers.* 523 pp. New York: Garland Publishing, 1984. (Garland reference library of the humanities, 296)

The first dictionary of American art music composers by a non-American. The professional training and careers of about 500 composers are described in detail, with entries varying in length from a few lines to the 11 pp. given Aaron Copland. When possible, the information included was submitted to the subject for correction. An appendix lists teachers and their pupils.

Reviewed by William J. Dane in *ARBA* 16 (1985): no. 1161, by Ned Quist in *AM* 3 (1985): 238–40, by Peter Dickinson in *M&L* 66 (1985): 58–59, and by Karl Kroeger in *Notes* 41 (1985): 726–27.

1.225 Claghorn, Charles Eugene. *Biographical Dictionary of American Music.* 491 pp. West Nyack, N.Y.: Parker Publishing, 1973.

A list of 5,200 brief entries for musicians (including composers of art music, lyricists, and singers) from colonial times to the 1970s, working with a wide range of styles and genres. There are also entries for ensembles, listing principal members.

Reviewed in *ALA Booklist* (February 1 1975).

1.226 Ewen, David. *American Composers: A Biographical Dictionary.* 793 pp. New York: G.P. Putnam's Sons, 1982.

Biographical information and stylistic characteristics for 300 American composers, ranging in time from William Billings to the present, including a statement on compositional aims by each composer, a list of principal works, and a brief bibliography.

Reviewed by Ned Quist in *AM* 3 (1985): 238–40 and by Frederic Schoettler in *ARBA* 15 (1984): no. 924.

1.227* Grattan, Virginia L. *American Women Songwriters: A Biographical Dictionary.* 279 pp. Westport, Conn.: Greenwood Press, 1993.

Biographies of 181 American-born women, from the wide range of the musical world, classified by type of music created, omitting only art music. Each entry describes the family background, education, and career of the subject and concludes with a brief bibliography. There are a general bibliography, a general index, and a song index.

Reviewed by Karin Pendle in *ARBA* 25 (1994): no. 1325, comparing it with *The New Grove Dictionary of American Music* (**1.220**).

1.228 Jablonski, Edward. *The Encyclopedia of American Music.* 629 pp. Garden City, N.Y.: Doubleday, 1981.

A seven-chapter work organized in roughly chronological order, ending with the 1930s Depression and World War II. Each chapter has a chronological summary before a section of entries defining relevant terms, organizations, composers, works, and publications. There are no bibliographical references. There is no index access to subject matter because the index lists only personal names. The appendix (pp. 579–92) is a discography of American music.

Reviewed by Susan T. Sommer in *Notes* 38 (1982): 607–8.

1.229 Jacobi, Hugh William. *Contemporary American Composers Based at American Colleges and Universities.* 240 pp. Paradise, Calif.: Paradise Arts Publishers, 1975.

Biographies interpolating citations of major works. Quotations from composers follow each alphabetical section.

Briefly reviewed by Stephen M. Fry in *Notes* 32 (1975): 302.

1.230 Jaques Cattell Press. *Who's Who in American Music: Classical.* 2nd ed. 783 pp. New York: R.R. Bowker, 1985.

First ed., 1983, 582 pp.

Brief biographical entries compiled from information provided by the subjects. The 9,028 entries, alphabetically arranged, include résumés of professional careers and mailing addresses. There are indexes by geographical location and by profession.

Reviewed by George Hill in *Notes* 41 (1985): 518–19 and in *ARBA* 18 (1987): no. 1254.

1.231 Reis, Claire R. *Composers in America: Biographical Sketches of Contemporary Composers with a Record of Their Works.* Revised and enlarged ed. 399 pp. New York: Macmillan, 1947.

First published in 1930 as *American Composers of Today* (50 pp.), with a 2nd ed. published as *American Composers: A Record of Works Written between 1912 and 1932* in September 1932 by the International Society for Contemporary Music, United States section, in New York (128 pp.) and as *Composers in America: Biographical Sketches of Living Composers with a Record of Their Works, 1912–1937,* by The Macmillan Company, New York, in 1938, 270 pp.

A survey of music written by American art composers, 1915 to 1947, arranged in dictionary-style format. Included are biographies of 332 composers, with a classified list of their works, both print and manuscript, with date, duration, and publisher (if appropriate) cited. There is a supplementary list of 424 names without biographical data. Carol J. Oja compiled an index, arranged by publisher, to the composers in the 1932 ed., published in *Notes* 45 (1988): 249–50 (**9.113**).

Reviewed by Lee Fairley in *Notes* 4 (1947): 458–59.

1.232 Schiavo, Giovanni Ermenegildo. *Italian-American History.* 2 vols. New York: Vigo Press, 1947–49. (The Italian American experience)

The 2nd vol. is subtitled *The Italian Contribution to the Catholic Church in America.* Reprinted in New York by Arno Press, 1975.

Part of a series of vols. devoted to Italian-American cultural relations. The first volume includes a section on Italian music and musicians in America and a "Dictionary of Musical Biography."

Reviewed by Elio Gianturco in *Notes* 7 (1950): 485–86.

1.233 Thomson, Virgil. *American Music since 1910.* 204 pp. New York: Holt, Rinehart & Winston, 1971. (Twentieth-century composers, 1)

A biographical dictionary of 106 American composers (pp. 118–85), set within a collection of critical essays. The entries are brief, citing principal works and including stimulating commentary.

Reviewed by Hugh Aitken in *Notes* 28 (1971): 244–45.

UNITED STATES (REGIONAL)

Musicians with a primarily local reputation can be challenging to locate in sources covering larger areas. Edward W. Hathaway's "Developing a State Archive of Local Music Materials," in *Notes* 45 (1989): 482–94, has a short appendix of state music histories and musicians' directories, providing titles assisting in more geographically restricted research in American music.

1.234 Bureau of Musical Research series. **Hollywood, Calif.**

Saunders, Richard D. *Music and Dance in California and the West.* 311 pp. 1948. Earlier eds. with slightly varying titles were published in 1933 and 1940.

Includes "Personalities of Music and Dance" (pp. 161–281).

Saunders, Richard D., and **William J. Perlman.** *Music and Dance in the Central States.* 173 pp. 1952.

Includes "Personalities of Music and Dance" (pp. 67–162).

Spaeth, Sigmund, and **William J. Perlman.** *Music and Dance in New York State.* 435 pp. 1951.

Includes "Personalities of Music and Dance" (pp. 159–385).

Spaeth, Sigmund, and **William J. Perlman.** *Music and Dance in Pennsylvania, New Jersey and Delaware.* 339 pp. 1954.

Includes a biographical section (pp. 169–305) and a classified professional directory (pp. 307–24).

Spaeth, Sigmund, and **William J. Perlman.** *Music and Dance in the New England States, Including Maine, New Hampshire, Vermont, Massachusetts, Rhode Island & Connecticut.* 347 pp. 1953.

Includes "Biographical Section" (pp. 157–309) and "Classified Professional Directory" (pp. 311–32).

Spaeth, Sigmund, and **William J. Perlman.** *Music and Dance in the Southeastern States, Including Florida, Georgia, Maryland, North & South Carolina, Virginia & the District of Columbia.* 331 pp. 1952.

Whitlock, E. Clyde, and **Richard D. Saunders.** *Music and Dance in Texas, Oklahoma, and the Southwest.* 256 pp. 1950.

Includes "Personalities of Music and Dance" (pp. 140–232).

A series of 7 regional reference works, with long articles covering the development of music and dance activities in the areas under discussion, and with a pronounced emphasis on the commercial aspects of music. There are biographical entries on composers, performers, conductors, and educators, with some illustrations.

1.235* Degláns, Kerlinda, and **Luis E. Pabón Roca.** *Catálogo de música clásica contemporánea de Puerto Rico / Puerto Rican Contemporary Classical Music Catalogue.* 197 pp. Río Piedras, Puerto Rico: Pro-Arte Contemporáneo, 1989.

A bilingual collection of 25 biographies of Puerto Rican composers, each with a list of works. The works lists include information on instrumentation, publisher, and date of composition; discographical information is included for many of the works. The biographical information was provided by the subjects; the composers included were either born in Puerto Rico or spent much professional time there.

1.236 Edwards, George Thornton. *Music and Musicians of Maine, Being a History of the Progress of Music in the Territory Which Has Come to be Known as the State of Maine, from 1604 to 1928.* xxv + 542 pp. Portland, Me.: The Southworth Press, 1928.

Reprinted in 1970 by AMS Press, New York.

An illustrated history with a "Biographical Section, 1927–28" (pp. 355–477).

1.237* Eichhorn, Hermene Warlick, and **Treva Wilkerson Mathis.** *North Carolina Composers as Represented in the Holograph Collection of the Library of the Women's College of the University of North Carolina.* 39 pp. Greensboro, N.C.: Published by the Women's College of the University of North Carolina, under the auspices of the Women's College Library, 1945.

A short list, with biographies, portraits, works lists, and bibliographies, of composers active in the state before the end of World War II.

1.238* Ferris, William R. *Mississippi Black Folklore: A Research Bibliography and Discography.* 61 pp. Hattiesburg, Miss.: University and College Press of Mississippi, Southern Station, 1971.

A guide to the culture of Mississippi, with a general bibliography on the state and a section of additional bibliographies on such subjects as blues, songs, and a classified discography.

1.239 Granniss, Lewis C. *Connecticut Composers.* 125 pp. New Haven, Conn.: Connecticut State Federation of Music Clubs, 1935.

Brief biographies with lists of major works. There are a list of early tune book writers and a chronological list of composers.

1.240* Kanahele, George S. *Hawaiian Music and Musicians: An Illustrated History.* xxx + 543 pp. Honolulu, Hawaii: University Press of Hawaii, 1979.

An "illustrated history" in dictionary format. The alphabetical section, "Hawaiian Music and Musicians" (pp. 1–416) has often extensive entries for musicians, songs (often with lyrics and melody supplied), terms, organizations, and musical instruments. There are an annotated bibliography by Elizabeth Tatar (pp. 503–19) and a comprehensive index (pp. 523–43).

Reviewed by Mantle Hood in *AM* 1 (1983): 86–87 and by Stephen M. Fry in *ARBA* 11 (1980): no. 943.

1.241* Kaufman, Charles H. *Music in New Jersey, 1655–1860: A Study of Musical Activity and Musicians in New Jersey from Its First Settlement to the Civil War.* 297 pp. Rutherford, N.J.: Fairleigh Dickinson University Press, 1981.

A history, with many helpful lists, including a master index (pp. 202–9) to the 2,695 personal names listed in the work and a helpful bibliography (pp. 273–88).

Reviewed by Karl Kroeger in *AM* 3 (1985): 89–91.

1.242* Knippers, Ottis J. *Who's Who among Southern Singers and Composers.* 168 pp. Hot Springs National Park, Ark.: Knippers Brothers, 1937.

Also published the same year in Lawrenceburg, Tenn., by James D. Vaughan.

A collection of 145 biographies, politically correct for its day, of the lives, musical education, and musical careers of 145 singers and composers of gospel music, including 4 women. Most entries are illustrated. Although the subjects of the entries may not have been born in the South, all spent the majority of their years there.

1.243 Mangler, Joyce Ellen. *Rhode Island Music and Musicians, 1733–1850.* 90 pp. Detroit, Mich.: Information Service, 1965. (Detroit studies in music bibliography, 7)

Primarily a directory of Rhode Island musicians, indexed chronologically as well as by profession. The 1st supplement lists organ builders and installations in Rhode Island churches; the 2nd lists members of the Psallonian Society, 1816–32. There is a bibliography of primary and secondary sources.

Reviewed by Donald W. Krummel in *Notes* 23 (1966): 265.

1.244 North Carolina Federation of Music Clubs. *North Carolina Musicians: A Selective Handbook.* 82 pp. Chapel Hill, N.C.: The University of North Carolina Library, 1956. (University of North Carolina library extension publications, Vol. 21/4)

Biographies of North Carolina musicians (pp. 5–66) and an account of the state's musical organizations, festivals, contests, and clinics.

1.245* Pebworth, James R. *A Directory of 132 Arkansas Composers.* 89 pp. Fayetteville, Ark.: University Library, University of Arkansas, 1979.

A list of composers having a definite link with Arkansas, with entries including birth and death dates, the subject's musical involvement, career, style of composition, and connection with Arkansas. There are a brief bibliography and a representative works list.

BIOGRAPHICAL DICTIONARIES: INDEXES

1.246 Bull, Storm. *Index to Biographies of Contemporary Composers.* 3 vols. New York; Metuchen, N.J.: Scarecrow Press, 1964–87.

An index giving access to a wide range of biographical material in 275 sources. The 1st vol. indexes 69 sources of biographical information (such as dictionaries, who's whos, and publishers' lists) for 5,800 composers; no page references to the sources are given. The 2nd vol. indexes an additional 108 reference works for 8,000 composers, half of whom are new to the collection. The 3rd vol. indexes another 98 reference works and lists more than 13,500 composers, about 5,900 of whom have never been listed before. The composer entries provide name of composer, country of birth or residence, year of birth, and date of death (if known or approximate), with abbreviations indicating the source of biographical information. The list of abbreviations in each vol. provides the basic bibliographical information about the sources.

Vol. 2 is reviewed by Steven Stucky in *Notes* 32 (1975): 296–97. Vol. 3 is reviewed by Ann P. Basart in *CNV* 118 (1987): 11–12 and by Dominique-René de Lerma in *ARBA* 19 (1988): no. 1296.

1.247* Carner, Gary. *Jazz Performers: An Annotated Bibliography of Biographical Materials.* Foreword by John Chilton. 364 pp. New York: Greenwood Press, 1990. (Music reference collection, 26)

An annotated bibliography of 2,927 entries for jazz books, theses, dissertations, and scholarly journal articles "related to jazz lives," organized so that "the reader, at a glance, can see the entire sweep of writings on a given artist." The material ranges from reading material for children to books and articles for "jazz scholars, lecturers, and librarians." There is a "Supplementary bibliography" (pp. 281–350), classified by format, as well as author and subject indexes.

Reviewed by Michael Cogswell in *Notes* 47 (1991): 1161–63.

1.248* Cowden, Robert H. *Classical Singers of the Opera and Recital Stages: A Bibliography of Biographical Materials.* 509 pp. Westport, Conn.: Greenwood Press, 1994. (Music reference collection, 42)

A bibliography of biographical material on 1,532 singers. Appendix II lists singers given an individual entry in *The New Grove Dictionary of Opera* (**1.469**).

Reviewed by George Louis Mayer in *ARBA* 26 (1995): no. 1250.

1.249* Cowden, Robert H. *Concert and Opera Conductors: A Bibliography of Biographical Materials.* 285 pp. New York: Greenwood Press, 1987. (Music reference collection, 14)

A gathering of biographical material from reference works and monographs, with less attention paid to periodical literature. Appendix II (pp. 261–76) is an index to conductors found in *Baker's Biographical Dictionary,* 7th ed., 1984. There is also an author index (pp. 277–85) to the material listed in the main body of work.

Reviewed by George Louis Mayer in *ARBA* 19 (1988): no. 1259, by Ned Quist in *Notes* 47 (1991): 780–81, and by Ann P. Basart in *CNV* 119 (1988): 13.

1.250 Cowden, Robert H. *Concert and Opera Singers: A Bibliography of Biographical Materials.* 278 pp. Westport, Conn.: Greenwood Press, 1985. (Music reference collection, 5)

An annotated, classified bibliography, arranged by subject, treating collective works and separate monographs on singers, and including an index to singers in *The New Grove* (**1.48**) (pp. 251–64).

Reviewed by Ann P. Basart in *Fontes* 33 (1986): 261–62 and in *CNV* 104 (1986): 13, by Dee Baily in *Choice* 23 (1986): 1369, by Robert J. Dennis in *Notes* 43 (1986): 303–4, and by Robert Skinner in *ARBA* 18 (1987): no. 1256.

1.251* Cowden, Robert H. *Instrumental Virtuosi: A Bibliography of Biographical Materials.* 349 pp. New York: Greenwood Press, 1989. (Music reference collection, 18)

A gathering of biographical material on instrumental soloists from reference works and monographs, with less attention paid to periodical literature. Appendix II (pp. 297–312) lists instrumentalists in *Baker's Biographical Dictionary of Musicians,* 7th ed., 1984 (**1.62**). Appendix III (pp. 313–21) lists instrumentalists found in *The New Grove Dictionary of American Music* (**1.220**). Appendix IV is an index of authors, editors, and compilers.

Reviewed by William J. Dane in *ARBA* 21 (1990): no. 1258, and by Ned Quist in *Notes* 47 (1991): 780–81.

1.252 Farkas, Andrew. *Opera and Concert Singers: An Annotated Bibliography of Books and Pamphlets.* 363 pp. New York: Garland Publishing, 1985. (Garland reference library of the humanities, 466)

A bibliography in two major sections. The first is organized by singer, with entries for works devoted to one singer, excluding reviews and criticism; the second contains entries for works about more than one singer, organized by author or title. Most entries are annotated. There are cross-references from the first section on singers to entries in the second. International in scope, the work cites 1,850 titles in 29 languages on 796 singers from a period of 413 years, ending in 1984. Although comprehensiveness was an objective, the work almost entirely excludes periodical articles.

Reviewed by George Louis Mayer in *ARBA* 17 (1986): no. 1273.

1.253* Floyd, Samuel A., Jr., and **Marsha J. Reisser.** *Black Music Biography: An Annotated Bibliography.* xxvi + 302 pp. White Plains, N.Y.: Kraus International Publications, 1987.

A selective and annotated guide to biographical material on 86 Black musicians, each entry with a selective discography.

Reviewed by Ann P. Basart in *CNV* 127 (1988): 20 and by Dominique-René de Lerma in *ARBA* 20 (1989): no. 1224.

1.254* Gray, John. *Blacks in Classical Music: A Bibliographical Guide to Composers, Performers and Ensembles.* 280 pp. New York: Greenwood Press, 1988. (Music reference collection, 15)

A guide to the literature available on 269 musicians and 19 ensembles, from the 18th century to the present and from 14 countries and regions.

Reviewed by Dominique-René de Lerma in *ARBA* 20 (1989): no. 1224, by Marsha J. Reisser in *Notes* 45 (1989): 514–15, and by Ann P. Basart in *CNV* 128 (1988): 8–9.

1.255* Greene, Frank. *Composers on Record: An Index to Biographical Information on 14,000 Composers in 200 Reference Books.* xxxi + 604 pp. Metuchen, N.J.: Scarecrow Press, 1985.

An index to entries for composers of commercially available Western art music. In his preface, the editor describes this book as containing "the names of the 14,000 composers that have appeared in the 66 discographies and record catalogues indexed plus those composers found in the record collection of the Music Library of the University of Toronto." There is a detailed bibliography of the reference sources consulted (pp. xv-xx).

Reviewed by Dominique-René de Lerma in *ARBA* 17 (1986): no. 1248.

1.256 Historical Records Survey. District of Columbia. *Bio-Bibliographical Index of Musicians in the United States of America from Colonial Times.* Sponsored by the Board of Commissioners of the District of Columbia. 2nd ed. 439 pp. Washington, D.C.: Music Section, Pan American Union, 1956.

First ed., 1941. Unaltered reprints, 1971, by the AMS Press, New York, and 1972, by the Scholarly Press, St. Clair Shores, Mich.

An index to biographical information contained in 66 works (such as dictionaries and histories) on American music published between 1846 and 1941, giving the occupation of the subject and page references to the volumes indexed.

1.257 Hixon, Donald L., and **Don A. Hennessee.** *Women in Music: An Encyclopedic Biobibliography.* 2nd ed. 2 vols. Metuchen, N.J.: Scarecrow Press, 1994.

The 1st ed. was published as *Women in Music: A Bio-Bibliography,* 1975 (347 pp.).

An index to the biographical material on women in music and its ancillary disciplines in 169 reference works. The individual entries, listed under the subject's best-known name, include the various names attached to the subject (maiden name, pseudonym, or stage names), the place and dates of birth and death, the fields of musical specialization or activity, and the presence of illustrations. The bio-bibliographical section (pp. 1–1,203) is followed by a list of specializations, subdivided by country and century, and a list of women included in each category.

Reviewed by Karin Pendle in *ARBA* 26 (1995): no. 1254.

1.258* *Internationaler biographischer Index der Musik: Komponisten, Dirigenten, Instrumentalisten, und Sänger / World Biographical Index of Music: Composers, Conductors, Instrumentalists, and Singers.* 2 vols. (xl + 792 pp.) Munich: K.G. Saur, 1995.

An index to 60,000 names of composers, conductors, instrumentalists, and singers derived from 6 biographical archives: German; American; French; Italian; Spanish, Portuguese and Latin American; and British. Each entry is listed alphabetically by name, pseudonym, and name variant, birth and death dates, profession, biographical sources, originating biographical archive, and fiche and frame number in the original biographical archive. The 6 complete biographical archives are available on CD-ROM (**12.5**). The bibliographical references are listed separately (pp. xv-xl).

1.259* Leyser, Brady J., and **Pol Gosset.** *Rock Stars/Pop Stars: A Comprehensive Bibliography, 1955–1994.* 302 pp. Westport, Conn.: Greenwood Press, 1994. (Music reference collection, 43)

A list of over 3,600 books about people associated with rock and pop music (artists, groups, record company executives, producers, managers, and DJs) arranged alphabetically by name of subject. Some entries are divided by type of material: bibliographies, fiction, and discographies. Coverage includes books published in the U.S., Canada, and England, and a few English-language books published elsewhere. There are subject, author, and title indexes, and a list of sources.

1.260* McNeil, Barbara, and **Miranda C. Herbert.** *Performing Arts Biography Master Index.* 2nd ed. Detroit, Mich.: Gale Research Company, 1981. (Gale biographical index series, 5)

A revised ed. of Dennis La Beau's *Theatre, Film, and Television Biographies Master Index,* 1979.

An index to 270,000 citations from 109 biographical reference sources in the performing arts, including 48 music titles such as *The New Grove Dictionary of Music and Musicians* (**1.48**), Ruth Anderson's *Contemporary American Composers* (**1.222**), and Roger Kinkle's *The Complete Encyclopedia of Popular Music and Jazz, 1900–1950* (**1.395**).

1.261* Nishimura, Mari. *The Twentieth-Century Composer Speaks: An Index of Interviews.* xxxii + 189 pp. Berkeley, Calif.: Fallen Leaf Press, in association with the Kunitachi College of Music, Library, 1993. (Fallen Leaf reference books in music, 28)

A index giving access to 1,083 published interviews with 20th-century composers. The entries generally include the name and dates of the composer interviewed, the interviewer, the date and place of the interview, the topics discussed, the language, and a full citation of the source of the interview. The information for entries was gleaned principally from periodicals and works on a single composer, rather than such interview collections as Ulla Colgrass's *For the Love of Music.* There are indexes by interviewers and by subject.

Reviewed by Marjorie Hassen in *Notes* 51 (1994): 225, by Vivian Perlis in *Fontes* 41 (1994): 305–6, by Arthur R. Upgren in *ARBA* 25 (1994): no. 1334, and by Harold J. Diamond in *Choice* 31 (1994): 1304.

1.262* Steinzor, Curt Efram. *American Musicologists, c. 1890–1945: A Bio-Bibliographical Sourcebook to the Formative Period.* 286 pp. New York: Greenwood Press, 1989. (Music reference collection, 17)

Bio-bibliographies of 34 men and 1 woman, including 19 native-born Americans, selected for their prominence in histories of musicology, contributions to early AMS publications, extensive careers, and influence as teachers. Each entry includes brief biographical facts (dates, education, teachers, professional positions), a list of writings (books, articles, musical editions, and reviews, but not liner notes, literary translations, or musical compositions), and sources for further information, published and unpublished. Bibliographies range in length from 6 items for Theodore Baker to 381 items (plus editions and reviews) for Paul Nettl; they were compiled using published and unpublished periodical indexes, including the card index in the Library of Congress Music Division and the sprawling Works Progress Administration index at Northwestern University. Over 200 reviews from Paul Henry Lang and over 100 each from Hugh Leichtentritt and Richard S. Hill are cited. One appendix lists 15 items dealing with the early history of musicology and a second attempts a classified subject list of the musicological writings in the book.

Reviewed by Richard D. Green in *Notes* 47 (1991): 1173–74 and by George Louis Mayer in *ARBA* 21 (1990): no. 1217.

1.263 Toomey, Kathleen M., and **Stephen C. Willis.** *Musicians in Canada: A Bio-Bibliographical Finding List / Musiciens au Canada: Index bio-bibliographique.* 185 pp. Ottawa: Canadian Association of Music Libraries, 1981. (Canadian Association of Music Libraries, Publications, 1; Association Canadienne des bibliothèques musicales, Publications, 1)

Previous ed. was published as *Bio-Bibliographical Finding List of Canadian Musicians and Those Who Have Contributed to Music in Canada,* 1961, 53 pp.

A helpful and thorough index providing access to biographical and bibliographical information on over 1,700 Canadian musicians in 218 sources. There are lists of musicians by specialty. The 1st ed. is reviewed by John Haskins in *Notes* 19 (1961): 78.

TERMS

1.264* Akademyah la-lashon ha-'Ivrit (Jerusalem). *Milon le-munahe ha-musikah / Dictionary of Musical Terms.* 174 pp. Jerusalem, 1955. (Milonim miktso'iyim, 1)

A dictionary of music terminology in Hebrew, Italian, English, French, and German.

1.265 Albina, Diāna. *Muzikas terminu vārdnīca.* 303 pp. Riga, Latvia: Latvijas valsts izdevniecība, 1962.

A Latvian dictionary of musical terms.

1.266* Amarnath, Pandit. *Living Idioms in Hindustani Music: A Dictionary of Terms and Terminology.* 2nd ed. 146 pp. New Delhi: Vikas Publishing House, 1990.

An alphabetical collection of over 600 terms (words, phrases, proverbs, and sayings) from the Hindustani music tradition.

1.267* Ammer, Christine. *The A to Z of Foreign Musical Terms: From Adagio to Zierlich: A Dictionary for Performers and Students: The English Equivalents of 3,000 Foreign Expression Marks and Directions from French, German, Italian, Latin, Portuguese and Spanish Scores.* 123 pp. Boston: E.C. Schirmer, 1989.

The 1st ed. was published in 1971 under the title *Musician's Handbook of Foreign Terms* (71 pp.).

"Virtually all of the terms in this book appear in actual music scores" [Introductory note]. The main exceptions are organ stops, pitch names, and names of instruments in the four principal languages (French, German, Italian, and Spanish). The terms are drawn from more than 30,000 scores and, occasionally, have more than one definition; also included are pronunciation guides for Italian, German, and French, some notational tables, and tables of key signatures, intervals, and ornaments and signs.

1.268* Anderton, Craig. *The Electronic Musician's Dictionary.* 119 pp. New York: Amsco Publications (Music Sales Corporation), 1988.

A collection of clear, concise definitions of over 1,000 terms related to electronically produced music, including complex technical terms as well as jargon. The author supplies generous cross-references and occasional charts and diagrams.

Reviewed by Ann P. Basart in *CNV* 132 (1989): 22.

1.269 Apel, Willi. *Harvard Dictionary of Music.* 2nd ed., revised and enlarged. 935 pp. Cambridge, Mass.: Belknap Press of Harvard University Press, 1969.

First ed. issued in 1944 (824 pp.). Reissued in 1947 (833 pp.). Succeeded by *The New Harvard Dictionary of Music,* edited by Don Michael Randel (**1.320**). A related title is 1978's *Harvard Concise Dictionary of Music* (577 pp.), also edited by Randel (**1.44**).

An influential source that started life as a major one-editor dictionary; its 2nd ed. was the work of one editor and 98 contributors. The entries are restricted to musical topics and compositions, omitting biographical articles, and include bibliographies, line drawings, and many musical examples. The abbreviation guide (pp. xi-xiv) serves as a general bibliography.

The 1st ed. is reviewed by Leonard Burkat in *Notes* 2 (1944): 54–56. The 2nd ed. is reviewed by Vincent H. Duckles in *Notes* 27 (1970): 256–58 and by Charles Rosen in the *New York Review of Books* 14 (February 1970): 11–15.

1.270 Baker, Theodore. *Schirmer Pronouncing Pocket Manual of Musical Terms.* Revised by Laura Kuhn. 5th ed. xxii + 341 pp. New York: Schirmer Books, 1995.

Editions in 1905 and 1947 were published as *Pronouncing Pocket-Manual of Musical Terms, Together with the Elements of Notation and Biographical Dates of Noteworthy Musicians,* 256 pp., edited by Theodore Baker and Nicolas Slonimsky.

Reprinted by AMS Press, New York, in 1970 and 1977.

A similar title by Baker was published as *A Dictionary of Musical Terms, Containing Upwards of 9,000 English, French, German, Italian, Latin, and Greek Words and Phrases Used in the Art and Science of Music . . . with a Supplement Containing an English–Italian Vocabulary for Composers.* 6th ed., thoroughly reviewed and augmented by an appendix of 700 additional words and phrases. New York: G. Schirmer, 1902.

First ed., 257 pp., 1895. Second ed., revised and enlarged, 239 pp., 1896. Third ed., revised and enlarged, 257 pp., 1897. Sixth ed., 257 pp., 1902. Fourteenth ed., thoroughly revised and augmented by an appendix of 700 additional words and phrases, 1912, 257 pp.

As the title attests, a small, useful manual with brief definitions of over 9,000 English and foreign words, especially those used in performance. There are more extended articles on such topics as pitch, notation, and instruments.

1.271 Balter, G. *Fachwörterbuch Musik: Deutsch–russisch/russisch–deutsch.* 484 pp. Leipzig: VEB Deutscher Verlag für Musik; Moscow: Sovetsky Kompozitor, 1976.

Additional title page in Russian.

Basically a bilingual glossary.

Reviewed by Detlef Gojowy in *Melos/NZ* 4 (1978): 357 no. 4.

1.272* Barber, Josephine. *German for Musicians.* 277 pp. Bloomington, Ind.: Indiana University Press; London: Faber, 1985.

More a basic grammar for musicians than a reference source. The offering of a musical German vocabulary (pp. 205–30) and of common abbreviations (pp. 230–33) helpful to the beginning researcher makes this a useful tool.

Reviewed in *Central Opera* 26 (1985–86): 75 no. 3, by Elizabeth Forbes in *MT* 126 (1985): 605, by Kenneth Whitton in *M&L* 67 (1986): 424–25, by Richard Dale Sjoerdsma in *NATS* 44 (1988): 30–31 no. 5, and by Richard Koprowski in *Notes* 42 (1986): 786.

1.273* Bassi, Adriano. *Le parole della musica.* 159 pp. Rome: Gremese Editore, 1992.

A dictionary with brief definitions of musical terminology, instruments (folk and art), and dances, with occasional illustrations.

1.274* Bayoumi, Ahmed. *Dictionary of Music Terms / al-Qamus al-musiqi: English, French, Italian, German, Greek, Arabic, etc., with Illustrations & Photos of Musical Instruments.* 503 pp. Cairo: Ministry of Culture, National Cultural Center, Cairo Opera House, 1992.

A polyglot musical dictionary with definitions in Arabic.

1.275* Bernhard, Michael. *Lexicon musicum latinum medii aevi / Wörterbuch der lateinischen Musikterminologie des Mittelalters bis zum Ausgang des 15. Jahrhunderts / Dictionary of Medieval Latin Music Terminology to the End of the 15th Century.* 1 vol. to date. (106 pp.) Munich: Verlag der Bayerischen Akademie der Wissenschaften in Kommission bei der C.H. Beck'schen Verlagsbuchhandlung, 1992– .

Published in fascicles.

A project whose goal is "to record and investigate the technical Latin musical vocabulary of the Middle Ages." There are a bibliography (pp. xix–lxiii) and an inventory of sources (pp. lxvii–xciv). Reviewed by Christian Meyer in *Revue de musicologie* 79 (1993): 150–51.

1.276 Bobillier, Marie (Michel Brenet, pseud.). *Dictionnaire pratique et historique de la musique: 510 citations musicales, 140 figures.* Edited by Amédée Gastoué. 487 pp. Paris: A. Colin, 1926.

A Spanish ed., *Diccionario de la música: Histórico y técnico,* trans. by José Barberá Humbert, J. Ricart Matas, and Aurelio Capmany, was published in Barcelona by Iberia-J. Gil in 1964 (548 pp.), amended to include Spanish terms and Latin and South American terminology and folklore.

The standard French dictionary of music, including terms from Greek and medieval music theory and historical sketches of musical forms. The articles are fairly long, with excellent small illustrations. There are no bibliographies.

1.277* Bosseur, Jean-Yves. *Vocabulaire de la musique contemporaine.* 194 pp. Paris: Minerve, 1992. (Collection musique ouverte)

Extended quotations from the writings of major figures in and commentators on contemporary music, defining and expanding on words and phrases in common use in the field.

1.278* Braccini, Roberto. *Praktisches Wörterbuch der Musik: Italienisch, englisch, deutsch, französisch.* 431 pp. Mainz: Schott; Munich: Piper, 1992.

An earlier ed., *Vocabolario practico della musica / Practical Vocabulary of Music / Praktisches Wörterbuch der Musik / Vocabulaire pratique de la musique / Vocabulario práctico de la música,* was published by Belwin Mills Publishing Corp., Melville, N.Y., in 1984 (168 pp.).

A classified polyglot dictionary of 3,962 musical terms, "intended for musicians, teachers, students and amateurs who wish to understand and use specialist foreign terms, . . . based on practical experience, derived from the examination of directions given on a large number of orchestral scores, piano pieces and transcriptions, and instrumental parts, . . . as well as contemporary musical terms from the field of jazz, pop, and electronic music." Each section, except the sections for jazz and French-language specialist terms, is arranged alphabetically by the Italian entry. There are special sections for French and for English and American specialist terms. A detailed index (pp. 245–431) locates each term cited for the user.

1.279* Brossard, Sébastien de. *Appendix to Grassineau's Musical Dictionary, Selected from the Dictionnaire de musique of J. J. Rousseau.* 52 pp. London: Printed for J. Robson, 1769.

A reference tool whose contributors were James Grassineau, John Christopher Pepusch, and Jean-Jacques Rousseau (**1.324**). Grassineau's *Musical Dictionary* (**1.298**) was translated, with additions, from the French of Brossard, probably under the supervision of Pepusch. The Appendix was issued with and also separately from the main work.

1.280 Brossard, Sébastien de. *Dictionaire de musique, contenant une explication des termes grecs, latins, italiens, & françois les plus usitez dans la musique. A l'occasion desquels on rapporte ce qu'il y a de plus curieux, & de plus necessaire à sçavoir; Tant pour l'histoire & la theorie, que pour la composition, & la pratique . . . de la musique . . . ensemble, une table alphabetique des termes françois qui sont dans le corps de l'ouvrage. . . . Un traité de la maniere de bien prononcer, sur tout en chantant, les termes italiens, latins, & françois. Et un catalogue de plus de 900 auteurs, qui ont écrit sur la musique.* 388 pp. Amsterdam: Aux depens d'Estienne Roger, 1705.

A preliminary ed., *Dictionnaire des terms grecs, latins, et italiens,* was published in 1701, in octavo format. The 1st ed. was published in 1703, the 2nd in 1705 (380 pp.). An English ed., trans. by James Grassineau, was published by J. Wilcox in London (**1.298**).

The prototype for all modern dictionaries of musical terms, as well as a pioneer work in music bibliography, containing in its 1703 ed. a list of over 900 authors who wrote about music from antiquity to Brossard's time. The most prominent and immediate of Brossard's descendants is by Grassineau.

The 1964 reprint is reviewed by Vincent Duckles in *Notes* 24 (1968): 700–1.

1.281 Carter, Henry Holland. *A Dictionary of Middle English Musical Terms.* 655 pp. Bloomington, Ind.: Indiana University Press, 1961. (Indiana University humanities series, 45)

Reprinted by Kraus International, New York, in 1968.

As the author's introduction states, a book derived from "essentially everything published in Middle English." The terms are not only given traditional statements of definition but also quoted in their original contexts with citation of their sources. There is a bibliography of works quoted (pp. 569–604), as well as an extensive list of works consulted but not quoted (pp. 605–49).

Reviewed by Leonard Ellinwood in *Notes* 19 (1962): 262–63 and by Rossell Hope Robbins in *JAMS* 16 (1963): 75–78.

1.282* Cary, Tristram. *Dictionary of Musical Terminology.* xxxii + 542 pp. New York: Greenwood Press, 1992.

The British ed. was published as *Illustrated Compendium of Musical Technology* (London: Faber & Faber, 1992).

A 1-vol. encyclopedia of music technology, with over 600 copiously illustrated main entries and 200 subsidiary ones, emphasizing electronic instruments and computer music, with some traditional instruments, with helpful quotations from acknowledged experts, detailed enough for the novice.

Reviewed by F. Richard Moore in *Notes* 50 (1994): 1021–23 and by David Ossenkop in *Choice* 30 (1993): 1106. The British ed. is reviewed by Peter Nelson in *M&L* 74 (1993): 470–71.

1.283* Chang, Yao-shui. *Chung-kuo yin yüeh tz'u tien.* 525 pp. Taipei: Ch'ang ch'un shu shu fang; Tsung ching hsiao Chung-kuo yin yüeh shu fang, min kuo 74, 1985.

A Chinese dictionary of music, containing Chinese music terminology, brief biographical information on ancient Chinese musicians, the names and histories of classical songs, and information on Chinese musical instruments. The terms are succinctly defined and the texts clearly printed in traditional Chinese characters. The index is arranged by the number of strokes of the first Chinese character of the entry.

1.284 Chetrikov, Svetoslav. *Muzikalen terminologichen rechnik.* 2nd ed. 448 pp. Sofia: Muzika, 1979.

First ed., 1969.

A Bulgarian dictionary of musical terms.

1.285* *Chung-kuo i shu yen chiu so.* *Chung-kuo yin yüeh tz'u tien. Pei-ching ti 1 pan.* 524 pp. + 48 pp. of plates. Pei-ching, China: Jen min yin yüeh ch'u pan she, 1984.

A Chinese dictionary of music, covering entries in Chinese music theory, composition, and performance, as well as ancient and modern musicians; only a few living musicians are covered. Information on and illustrations of Chinese musical instruments are included. The musical scores and prose are representative of writings before 1949.

The text is printed in simplified characters. The original lyrics of ethnic folk songs are either transliterated into Mandarin Chinese or transliterated with Chu-yin fu hao and Pinyin. A subject index and a character stroke index are appended at the end of the book.

1.286 Clason, W. E. *Elsevier's Dictionary of Cinema, Sound, and Music, in Six Languages: English/American, French, Spanish, Italian, Dutch, and German.* Compiled and arranged on an English alphabetical base. 948 pp. Amsterdam; New York: Elsevier Publishing Company, 1956. (Elsevier's multilingual dictionaries)

One of a series of polyglot technical dictionaries relating to special fields of science and industry. The 3,213 terms offer brief definitions and the equivalent phrases in French, Spanish, Italian, Dutch, and German, arranged under the English term, with indexes in each of the five other languages.

1.287 Dembski, Stephen, Gerard Gusbisch, Jorge Labrouve, and **Patrick Marcland.** *Lexique musical international / International Vocabulary of Music / Lessico musicale internazionale / Internationales Musiklexikon / Vocabulario musical international.* 151 pp. Paris: Éditions Transatlantiques, 1979.

A polyglot dictionary of terms in English, French, Italian, German, and Spanish.

1.288* Dobson, Richard. *A Dictionary of Electronic and Computer Music Technology: Instruments, Terms, Techniques.* 224 pp. Oxford: Oxford University Press, 1992.

A British-oriented technical dictionary, with some charts and diagrams. Entries are limited to issues relevant to products that have been manufactured commercially at some time. There are an index of products and manufacturers, a name index, and a general index.

Reviewed by F. Richard Moore in *Notes* 50 (1994): 1021–23, by John L. Walters in *TLS* 4700 (1993): 6, and by Peter Manning in *M&L* 74 (1993): 318–19.

1.289 Dolzhanskiĭ, Aleksandr Naumovich. *Kratkiĭ muzykal'nyĭ slovar'.* 6th ed. 517 pp. Leningrad: Muzyka, 1966.

First published in Leningrad in 1952.

A standard Russian dictionary of music terminology.

1.290 Eggebrecht, Hans Heinrich. *Handwörterbuch der musikalischen Terminologie.* Im Auftrag der Kommission für Musikwissenschaften und der Literatur zu Mainz. Wiesbaden: F. Steiner, 1972– . Issued in parts.

A work providing the most thorough and scientific treatment of musical terms, with an exhaustive historical and etymological analysis of term families, showing their changes in meaning and citing quotations from the literature. The dictionary is compiled in loose-leaf format, with dividers.

A preliminary notice and discussion is in *Archiv für Musikwissenschaft* 25 (1968): 241–77 and 27 (1970): 214–22.

1.291 Eimert, Herbert, and **Hans Ulrich Humpert.** *Das Lexikon der elektronischen Musik.* 428 pp. Regensburg: Gustav Bosse Verlag, 1973.

Brief terminological articles citing musical works where appropriate. There are a bibliography and an index to persons mentioned.

1.292* al-Faruqi, Lois Ibsen. *An Annotated Glossary of Arabic Musical Terms.* 511 pp. Westport, Conn.: Greenwood Press, 1981.

An index of English musical terms (with the corresponding Arabic), an index of Arabic roots, a guide to pronunciation and translation, and a helpful bibliography.

Reviewed by John Andrus in *Notes* 38 (1982): 847–48 and by Ahmad Gamaluddin in *ARBA* 13 (1982): no. 1023.

1.293 Fink, Robert, and **Robert Ricci.** *The Language of Twentieth Century Music: A Dictionary of Terms.* 125 pp. New York: Schirmer Books; London: Collier-Macmillan, 1975.

Now historic rather than current in coverage of styles and genres in art, film, jazz, and rock music. This dictionary has terms on technical areas of music as well as those connected to instruments, analysis, and performance practice, and an appendix of terms arranged topically by 22 categories.

Reviewed briefly by Stephen M. Fry in *Notes* 32 (1975): 303 and by Steven Stucky in *Notes* 32 (1976): 774–75.

1.294* *Foclóir ceoil / Dictionary of Music.* 71 pp. Dublin: An Gúw, 1985.

An English–Irish dictionary of musical terms.

1.295* Fotine, Larry. *Contemporary Musician's Handbook and Dictionary.* 224 pp. Sepulveda, Calif.: Poly Tone Press, 1984.

A compact dictionary divided into the fundamentals of music theory, the cross-referenced musical dictionary, the musical instrument families, and the singing ranges of human voices. There are no biographical entries.

1.296 Gold, Robert S. *Jazz Talk.* 322 pp. Indianapolis, Ind.: Bobbs-Merrill Co., 1975.

Reprinted in 1982 by Da Capo Press, New York. Successor to Gold's *A Jazz Lexicon* (New York: Alfred A. Knopf, 1964), 363 pp.

A book that describes itself as "a dictionary of the colorful language that has emerged from America's own music." This dictionary of slang terms, based on historical usage, provides definitions, sometimes word origins, and quotations from the literature of jazz, aided by an extensive bibliography.

Briefly reviewed by Stephen M. Fry in *Notes* 32 (1975): 302.

1.297 Grant, Parks. *Handbook of Music Terms.* 476 pp. Metuchen, N.J.: Scarecrow Press, 1967.

A dictionary for the music student and concertgoer.

Reviewed by James W. Pruett in *Notes* 24 (1968): 720–21.

1.298 Grassineau, James. *A Musical Dictionary, Being a Collection of Terms and Characters, Ancient as well as Modern, Including the Historical, Theoretical, and Practical Parts of Music.* 347 pp. London: Printed for J. Wilcox, 1740.

Reprinted by Broude Brothers, New York, in 1966 (Monuments of music and music literature in facsimile, II, 40).

The first important dictionary of music in English, largely an adaptation of Brossard (**1.280**), but with some important additions. The 1769 edition includes an appendix with additional terms from Rousseau's *Dictionnaire* (**1.324**).

1.299 Grigg, Carolyn Doub. *Music Translation Dictionary: An English-Czech-Danish-Dutch-French-German-Hungarian-Italian-Polish-Portuguese-Russian-Spanish-Swedish Vocabulary of Musical Terms.* 336 pp. Westport, Conn.: Greenwood Press, 1978.

A polyglot glossary of 1,300 musical terms with an index of all terms for words in Roman characters and another for those in Cyrillic. Bibliography.

Reviewed by Nanna Schiødt in *Notes* 27 (1980): 122, and, with errata noted, by Natalia Sonovytsky in *ARBA* 11 (1980): no. 949.

1.300* Habela, Jerzy. *Slowniczek muzyczny.* 8th ed. 223 pp. Cracow: Polskie Wydawn. Muzyczne, 1969. (Biblioteka sluchacza koncertomego. Seria wprowadzajaca, 1)

A Polish dictionary of musical terminology.

1.301* Headington, Christopher. *Illustrated Dictionary of Musical Terms.* 159 pp. New York: Harper & Row, 1980.

An English edition was published by Hamlyn in 1983.

As the title suggests, a dictionary supported by musical examples, photographs, prints, and the like. The definitions are brief and no bibliographic support is supplied.

Reviewed by John E. Druesedow, Jr., in *ARBA* 12 (1981): no. 1014.

1.302* Hopf, Helmuth, Walter Heise, and **Siegmund Helms.** *Lexikon der Musikpädagogik.* 362 pp. Regensburg: Gustav Bosse Verlag, 1984. (Bosse Musik paperback, 23)

A dictionary of terms associated with music education, with signed entries and impressive bibliographic backing by the 100 multinational contributors. There are name and subject indexes.

1.303 Janovka, Tomás Baltazar. *Clavis ad thesaurum magnae artis musicae.* 324 pp. Prague: Georgij Labaun, 1701.

Reprinted by Frits Knuf, Amsterdam, in 1973 (Dictionarium musicum, 2). A 2nd ed., *Clavis ad musicam,* was published in 1715.

One of the first modern dictionaries of musical terms, with Brossard (**1.280**). (The two compilers worked simultaneously but independently of each other.) Janovka covers about 170 musical subjects, defining terms in Latin and Italian, as well as a few in German, French, and Czech, with musical examples.

1.304* Johnson, Jeffrey. *Thesaurus of Abstract Musical Properties: A Theoretical and Compositional Resource.* 344 pp. Westport, Conn.: Greenwood Press, 1995. (Music reference collection, 45)

A reference source for composers and theorists who use set-class analysis and need organized information about all set-classes, as well as important references in theoretical information and a strong bibliography. However, a citation for Ann Basert [sic] reduces the reader's confidence in the accuracy of the numbered contents and subsets.

Reviewed by Steven A. Harper in *Notes* 52 (1996): 1,161–62.

1.305 Katayen, Lelia, and Val Telberg. *Russian–English Dictionary of Musical Terms.* 125 ll. New York: Telberg Book Corporation, 1965.

A collection of Russian–English equivalents in musical terminology. No definitions are given, but there is a brief bibliography.

1.306* Kaufmann, Walter. *Selected Musical Terms of Non-Western Cultures: A Notebook-Glossary.* 806 pp. Warren, Mich.: Harmonie Park Press, 1990. (Detroit studies in music bibliography, 65)

A multinational dictionary of terms. The country of origin and the bibliographic source are supplied. There is a bibliography of 321 reference works, monographs, and articles (pp. 791–806). The list includes dialectal features as well as numerous terms encountered only in spoken language.

Reviewed by Carl Rahkonen in *Notes* 48 (1991): 127–28, by Rob van der Bliek in *Fontes* 38 (1991): 342–43, and by Bruno Nettl in *M&L* 73 (1992): 633–34.

1.307 Koch, Heinrich Christoph. *Musikalisches Lexicon: welches die theoretische und praktische Tonkunst, encyclopädisch, bearbeitet, alle alten und neuen Kunstwörter erklärt, und die alten und neuen Instrumente beschrieben, enthält.* 2 vols. Frankfurt am Main: A. Hermann dem Jüngern, 1802.

A 2nd ed. was published in 1817. The 1802 ed. was reprinted by Georg Olms, Hildesheim, Germany, in 1964 and 1975. An abridged ed., *Kurzgefasstes Handwörterbuch der Musik für praktische Tonkünstler und für Dilettanten,* was published in Leipzig in 1807 and was reprinted in Hildesheim by G. Olms, 1981. A revised ed. by Arrey von Dommer, printed in Heidelberg in 1865, bears very little resemblance to the original.

One of the first of a long line of German dictionaries of musical terms, particularly important for definitions and concepts pertaining to late baroque and classical period music and instruments.

1.308* Krolick, Bettye. *Dictionary of Braille Music Signs.* 199 pp. Washington, D.C.: National Service for the Blind and Physically Handicapped, Library of Congress, 1979.

Braille ed., 2 vols., 1979.

A dictionary of braille music notation, ordered by its braille symbol. The dictionary begins with a history of braille music (xi–xvii). Over 400 music signs and 100 literary abbreviations are included, but no definitions are given. (The user is referred to the *Harvard Concise Dictionary of Music* (**1.44**), available in braille.) Because some signs and formats given are not officially approved for music transcription, this dictionary should not be used as a transcription manual.

Reviewed by Robert Skinner in *ARBA* 12 (1981): no. 1015.

1.309* Kruntiaeva, Tat´iana, and Natal´ia Molokova. *Slovar´ inostrannykh muzykal´nykh terminov.* 6th ed. 135 pp. Leningrad: Muzyka, 1987.

An oft-revised dictionary of musical terminology.

1.310 Leuchtmann, Horst. *Dictionary of Terms in Music: English–German, German–English.* 4th ed., revised and enlarged. 411 pp. Munich; New York: K.G. Saur, 1992.

The 1st ed. was published as *Langenscheidts Fachwörterbuch, Musik* by Langenscheidt, Berlin, 1964 (359 pp.), the 2nd by Verlag Dokumentation Saur in Munich, 1977 (493 pp.), and the 3rd, 1981 (560 pp.).

An English–German, German–English dictionary of terms offering no definitions, merely verbal equivalents. Its unusual features include a list of 950 popular titles of musical works and a section devoted to the vocabulary of change ringing.

The 2nd ed. is reviewed by Simone Wallon in *Fontes* 26 (1979): 310–11 and the 3rd ed. is reviewed by Guy A. Marco in *ARBA* 13 (1982): no. 1024.

1.311 Leuchtmann, Horst. *Terminorum musicae index septem linguis radactus: Polyglot Dictionary of Musical Terms: English, German, French, Italian, Spanish, Hungarian, Russian.* 798 pp. Budapest: Akadémiai Kiadó; Kassel, Germany: Bärenreiter Verlag, 1978.

Sponsored by the International Musicological Society and the International Association of Music Libraries, this polyglot dictionary of musical terms uses German as its basic language while indexing all terms cited in all seven languages. Includes introductory material in each of the seven languages and a Cyrillic index; diagrams of musical instruments are used to illustrate specific definitions.

Reviewed by Simone Wallon in *Fontes* 26 (1979): 145–46 and by Michael Ochs in *Notes* 35 (1979): 619–20.

1.312 Levarie, Siegmund, and **Ernst Levy.** *Musical Morphology: A Discourse and a Dictionary.* 344 pp. Kent, Ohio: Kent State University Press, 1983.

An earlier ed. of this work (*A Dictionary of Musical Morphology*) was published by the Institute of Mediaeval Music, Binningen, Switzerland (and Henryville, Pa., 1980), despite the objections of the authors, who maintained that it was unauthorized, incorrect, and not truly representative of their work. The present edition is fully authorized.

A dictionary covering relatively few terms with lengthy philosophical entries and appended illustrations, with an index to composers and works cited in the entries.

Reviewed by Joscelyn Godwin in *Notes* 40 (1984): 551–53 and by John E. Druesedow, Jr., in *ARBA* 15 (1984): no. 892.

1.313 Lichtenthal, Peter. *Dizionario e bibliografia della musica.* 4 vols. Milan: A. Fontana, 1836.

The 1st ed. was published in 1826 in 2 vols. The 1836 ed. was reprinted by Forni in Bologna, 1970 (Bibliotheca musica Bononiensis, I, 6). A French ed. of the dictionary of terms, trans. and augmented by Dominique Mondo, appeared in Paris in 1839.

The first 2 vols. are a dictionary of music; the last 2 are a translation, with additions, of Forkel's *Allgemeine Litteratur der Musik* (**4.25**).

1.314 Limenta, Fernando. *Dizionario lessicografico musicale italiano–tedesco–italiano.* 391 pp. Milan: Hoepli, 1940.

Designed to provide precise Italian equivalents for German technical terms not adequately treated in most dictionaries.

1.315* Marques, Henrique de Oliveira. *Dicionário de termos musicais: Português, francês, italiano, inglês, alemao* / *Dictionnaire de termes musicaux: Français, portugais, italien, anglais, allemand* / *Dizionario di termini musicali (italiano, portoghese, francese, inglese, tedesco)* / *Dictionary of Musical Terms: English, Portuguese, French, Italian, German* / *Lexikon der musikalischen Terminologie (deutsch, portugiesisch, französisch, italienisch, englisch).* 809 pp. Lisbon: Editorial Estampa, 1987. (Imprensa universitária, 47)

A multilingual dictionary of about 4,000 entries. All items are entered in alphabetical order, with each entry giving an equivalent in each of the other four languages.

1.316* Moore, Shirley. *A French–English Dictionary.* Valuable pronunciation guide by John Austin; editorial assistance by Martin Chalifour. 99 pp. Atlanta, Ga.: Leihall Publications, 1985.

Over 4,000 entries, including terms and phrases from orchestral, instrumental, and vocal scores, plus theory and conducting terms.

1.317 Padelford, Frederick Morgan. *Old English Musical Terms.* 112 pp. Bonn: P. Hanstein, 1899. (Bonner Beiträge zur Anglistik, 4)

Reprinted by Milford House, Boston, Mass., 1973, and by Longwood Press, Portland, Me, 1976.

A dictionary of musical terms found in Old English. The entries cite in context each term's appearance in the literature and provide a definition. Appendixes give Latin–Old English and Modern English–Old English equivalents.

1.318 Pulver, Jeffrey. *A Dictionary of Old English Music and Musical Instruments.* 247 pp. London: Kegan Paul, Trench, Trubner; New York: E.P. Dutton, 1923.

Old English here means Tudor and early Stuart; terms from these reigns are discussed in fairly long articles with references to early literary and musical sources for the terms and 10 plates of instruments from the period. This is a companion volume to Pulver's *A Biographical Dictionary of Old English Music* (**1.167**).

1.319* Ranade, Ashok D. *Keywords and Concepts: Hindustani Classical Music.* 160 pp. New Delhi: Promilla & Company, 1990.

A list of terms arranged systematically rather than alphabetically, with an alphabetical index and a bibliography.

1.320 Randel, Don Michael. *The New Harvard Dictionary of Music.* xxi + 942 pp. Cambridge, Mass.: Belknap Press of Harvard University Press, 1986.

A completely revised ed. of the *Harvard Dictionary of Music* by Willi Apel, 2nd ed. (Cambridge, Mass.: Belknap Press, 1969), 935 pp. (**1.269**).

The standard reference work in English for nonbiographical musical information, designed to provide accurate and pertinent information on all musical topics. The emphasis is on the historical approach and on Western art music, but there is coverage of non-Western and popular music. Good basic bibliographies are provided at the end of excellent brief historical articles. The articles are signed, with numerous musical examples and illustrations. The 60 contributors, a mix of young scholars and established authorities in music, are listed, with their contributions (pp. vii–x); those by Harold Samuel are especially valuable for music reference and research. The list of abbreviated titles serves as a general bibliography (pp. xi–xix). Dominique-René de Lerma and Marsha J. Reisser, in their *Black Music and Musicians in The New Grove Dictionary of American Music and The New Harvard Dictionary of Music* (Chicago, Ill.: Center of Black Music Research, Columbia College Chicago, 1989, CBMR monographs, 1), give specialized access to an area of interest.

The editor wrote a thoughtful article on the place of music lexicography in musicology for *Notes* 43 (1987): 751–66.

Reviewed by Ann P. Basart, with a comparison to *The New Oxford Companion to Music* (**1.6**), in *CNV* 107 (1986): 6, by Christopher Wintle in *TLS* (1987): 496, by Guy A. Marco in *Choice* 24 (1987): 748, and by John Caldwell in *M&L* 70 (1989): 72–73.

1.321 Reid, Cornelius L. *A Dictionary of Vocal Terminology: An Analysis.* 457 pp. New York: Joseph Patelson Music House, 1983.

A dictionary defining the principal terms in common use in the vocal profession from the early 17th century to the present. Scientific terms and anatomical illustrations are included. There are cross-references and a bibliography.

Reviewed by Dee Baily in *Notes* 41 (1985): 517–18, by Ann P. Basart in *CNV* 113 (1987): 5, and by Allie Wise Goudy in *ARBA* 16 (1985): no. 1185.

1.322* Rieländer, Michael M. *Reallexikon der Akustik.* 461 pp. Frankfurt am Main: Bochinsky, 1982.

A technical dictionary with numerous diagrams and photographs. The bibliographical citations are drawn almost entirely from German-language sources, and there is a list of principal sources.

1.323* *RILM Abstracts of Music Literature: English-Language Thesaurus for Volumes 16– (1982–).* Issued by Répertoire international de littérature musicale, under the sponsorship of International Association of Music Libraries and the International Musicological Society. 90 pp. New York: RILM Abstracts, 1990.

Previously issued in 1983 as the thesaurus for Vols. 11– (51 pp.).

A compilation of English-language words used in connection with music, presenting the subject headings of *RILM* and cross-reference access to the same. This is an invaluable tool for efficient use of *RILM Abstracts* (**4.90**).

1.324 Rousseau, Jean-Jacques. *Dictionnaire de musique.* 556 pp. Paris: Chez le veuve Duchesne, 1768.

Reprinted by Georg Olms, Hildesheim, Germany, and Johnson Reprint Corp., New York, 1969. Several eds. were published in Paris and Amsterdam during the 18th century. An English ed., trans. by William Waring, was published as *A Complete Dictionary of Music,* 2nd ed., London, 1779; this ed. was reprinted by AMS Press, New York, 1975 (470 pp.). The 1832 ed. (Paris: Aubrée) was reprinted in 2 vols. by Art & Culture, Paris, 1977.

A historically important and widely influential reference work, based on articles written for, but not included in, the Diderot–d'Alembert *Encyclopédie,* reflecting the stimulating and highly personal views of an 18th-century man of letters.

1.325 Schaal, Richard. *Abkürzungen in der Musik-Terminologie: Eine Übersicht.* 165 pp. Wilhelmshaven, Germany: Heinrichshofen's Verlag, 1969. (Taschenbücher zur Musikwissenschaft, 1)

A dictionary of the abbreviations most frequently used to refer to musical practice, bibliography, and institutions. Although this was intended primarily for German music students, it is also of use to non-German researchers.

1.326 Schaal, Richard. *Fremdwörterlexikon Musik: Englisch–französisch–italienisch.* 2 vols. Wilhelmshaven, Germany: Heinrichshofen's Verlag, 1969. (Taschenbücher zur Musikwissenschaft, 2–3)

A polyglot dictionary of over 15,000 English, French, and Italian musical terms, with their German equivalents.

1.327 Seagrave, Barbara Garvey, and **Joel Berman.** *The A.S.T.A. Dictionary of Bowing Terms for String Instruments.* 2nd ed. 53 pp. Urbana, Ill.: American String Teachers Association, 1976.

The 1st ed. was published in 1968.

A dictionary for the performer, with an emphasis on historical practice. Both historical and modern sources are cited, but there is no bibliography.

1.328 Sinzig, Pedro. *Dicionário músical.* 2nd ed. 612 pp. Rio de Janeiro: Livraria Kosmos Editora, 1959.

The first ed. was issued in 1947, 613 pp.; the 2nd was reprinted in 1976.

A Portuguese-language dictionary of terms, based largely on Apel (**1.269**) and Riemann (**1.45**).

1.329* Slonimsky, Nicolas. *Lectionary of Music: An Entertaining Reference and Reader's Companion.* 521 pp. New York: McGraw-Hill, 1989.

Paperback version published in 1990 by Anchor Books, New York.

A reference work intended by its author as "an introduction to extensive reading on the subject of music." The entries include musical terms and many titles (songs, orchestral works, and operas), as well as lengthier discourses on topics such as "Music," "Music Journals," "Music Therapy," and "Program Music" from the author's unique perspective.

Reviewed by Susan T. Sommer in *Notes* 47 (1990): 408, by Ann Basart in *CNV* 136 (1989): 12, and by Kristin Ramsdell in *ARBA* 21 (1990): no. 1232.

1.330* Spiegl, Fritz. *Music through the Looking Glass: A Very Personal Kind of Dictionary of Musicians' Jargon, Shop-talk and Nicknames; and a Mine of Information about Musical Curiosities, Strange Instruments, Word Origins, Odd Facts, Orchestral Players' Lore, and Wicked Stories about the Music Profession.* 325 pp. London: Routledge & Kegan Paul, 1984.

A curious and entertaining mixture of terminology, nicknames, and titles, wittily rather than technically defined.

Reviewed by Dean Tudor in *ARBA* 17 (1986): no. 1246.

1.331 Stainer, Sir John, and **William Alexander Barrett.** *A Dictionary of Musical Terms.* 4th ed. 456 pp. London: Novello, Ewer; Boston, Mass.: O. Ditson, 1889.

The 1889 ed. was reprinted by Scholarly Press, St. Clair Shores, Mich., in 1974. The 2nd ed., 1898, was reprinted by Olms in Hildesheim, Germany, in 1970.

Terms in Italian, French, Latin, German, Hebrew, Greek, Russian, Spanish, and Arabic, with brief English definitions.

1.332* Strahle, Graham. *An Early Music Dictionary: Musical Terms from British Sources, 1500–1740.* xl + 469 pp. Cambridge, England; New York: Cambridge University Press, 1995.

A source with definitions of musical terms listed in chronological order for each term, so that the changes of meaning can be traced. All aspects of music are included, as well as a bibliography.

Reviewed by Christopher D. S. Field in *Galpin Society Journal* 49 (1996): 220–25.

1.333 Thiel, Eberhard. *Sachwörterbuch der Musik.* 4th ed. 739 pp. Stuttgart: Alfred Kröner Verlag, 1984.

1st ed., 1962, 602 pp.; 2nd ed., 1973, 644 pp.; 3rd ed., 1977.

A German dictionary of terms, containing about 2,500 entries.

The 1st ed. is reviewed by Harold Samuel in *Notes* 20 (1963): 658.

1.334* Thomsett, Michael C. *Musical Terms, Symbols, and Theory: An Illustrated Dictionary.* 277 pp. Jefferson, N.C.; London: McFarland & Company, Inc., 1989.

A dictionary of musical terms, giving the original language, the definition, and relevant cross-references. There are numerous musical examples.

Reviewed, with errata, by Gregg S. Geary in *ARBA* 21 (1990): 1233.

1.335 Tinctoris, Johannes (Jean). *Dictionary of Musical Terms: An English Translation of Terminorum Musicae Diffinitorium Together with the Latin Text.* Trans. and annotated by Carl Parrish, with a bibliographical essay by James B. Coover. 108 pp. New York: Free Press of Glencoe, 1963.

Reprinted in 1978 by Da Capo Press, New York, with an introduction by James W. McKinnon. A facsimile edition was published in 1983 by Bärenreiter, Kassel, Germany, with an introduction by Heinrich Bellermann and an afterword by Peter Gülke (Documenta musicologica, I, 37).

A dictionary of 299 musical terms, published in 1495, and one of the first books on music to be printed. It is important for an understanding of renaissance music theory and practice. The cited edition has the Latin and English printed on pages opposite each other. The Latin text was reprinted in Coussemaker's *Scriptorum* (1867), in Forkel's *Allgemeine Literatur der Musik* (1792), and with a German translation in Chrysander's *Jahrbuch der Musikwissenschaft,* I (1963). It appeared in a French translation with introduction and commentary by Armand Machabey (Paris, 1951).

1.336* Tomlyn, Bo, and **Steve Leonard.** *Electronic Music Dictionary: A Glossary of the Specialized Terms Relating to the Music and Sound Technology of Today.* 77 pp. Milwaukee, Wisc.: Hal Leonard Books, 1988.

A practical everyday glossary of the basic elements of synthesizers, amplification, MIDI, computers, and the physics of sound. Each entry has a subheading that indicates the general category or subject area of the term defined.

1.337 Vannes, René. *Essai de terminologie musicale: Dictionnaire universel comprenant plus de 15,000 termes de musique en italien–espagnol–portugais– français–anglais–allemand–latin et grec, disposés en un alphabet unique; précéde de lettres approbatives de T. Dubois–S. Dupuis–I. Strawinsky.* 230 pp. Thann, France: Sté d'édon "Alsatia," 1925.

Reprinted by Da Capo Press, New York, 1970.

An extensive polyglot dictionary with 15,000 entries in 8 languages, describing forms, terms, and instruments in current use. Brief definitions are given in the original or characteristic language, with equivalents in other languages. No explanatory or historical material is given.

1.338* Wadhams, Wayne. *Dictionary of Music Production and Engineering Terminology.* 257 pp. New York: Schirmer Books; London: Collier Macmillan, 1988.

A dictionary that began life as a glossary for the use of music production and engineering students at the Berklee School of Music, Boston, Mass. Terms have been taken from the worlds of advertising, business, computers, digital recordings, engineering, movies, music publishing, the record industry, studio equipment, unions, and video/television. Each term is identified according to the professions or topic areas to which it belongs, including names and acronyms of trade organizations. Standard units and measures are defined, and a select bibliography is included.

Reviewed by Ann P. Basart in *CNV* 121 (1988): 17–18.

1.339 Wallon, Simone. *L'allemand musicologie.* 161 pp. Paris: Beauchesne, 1980. (Guides musicologiques, 2)

A phrase book devoted solely to musicological terms, translating German to French.

1.340* White, Glenn D. *The Audio Dictionary.* 2nd ed., revised and expanded. 413 pp. Seattle, Wash.: University of Washington Press, 1991.

1st ed., 1987, 291 pp.

A dictionary of musical, acoustical, and audio terms, defined for the nonspecialist, with ample cross-references for full access. Bibliographical references are included (pp. 407–13).

Reviewed by Patrick T. Will in *Notes* 49 (1993): 1098–99.

1.341* Whitfield, Charles. *L'anglais musicologie: L'anglais des musiciens.* 149 pp. Paris: Beauchesne, 1989. (Guides musicologiques, 4)

A French–English conversation and phrase book for musicians and music researchers. A thorough index (pp. 122–45) leads the user to the desired word, in context.

1.342* Yarbrough, Julie. *Modern Languages for Musicians.* 499 pp. Stuyvesant, N.Y.: Pendragon Press, 1992.

Access to English, German, French, and Italian. This book gives an introduction to the international phonetic alphabet (IPA).

COUNTRY, JAZZ, POPULAR, AND FOLK MUSIC

Resources for reference and research in the areas of country music, jazz and blues, popular music (including rock), and folk music are perhaps the fastest growing category of 1-vol. music reference tools. Numerous dictionaries, encyclopedias, and other related works are now widely available, although many may lack references to the sources for the information provided.

COUNTRY MUSIC

1.343* Bernard, Russell D. *The Comprehensive Country Music Encyclopedia from the Editors of Country Music Magazine.* 449 pp. New York: Times Books, 1994.

An illustrated dictionary, largely biographical (covering singers, instrument makers, producers, disc jockeys), with occasional entries for musical genres, radio and television programs, publishing companies and record labels, instruments, terms, places (cities, concert halls, etc.), magazines, and organizations.

1.344* Biracree, Tom. *The Country Music Almanac.* 280 pp. New York: Prentice-Hall General Reference, 1993.

A collection of country music biographies and lists (country music lists and Country Music Association awards) of interest to country music researchers and enthusiasts.

1.345 Cackett, Alan, and **Alec Foege.** *The Harmony Illustrated Encyclopedia of Country Music.* 3rd ed., completely revised and updated. 208 pp. New York: Crown Trade Paperbacks, 1994.

Also published in Zurich by Edition Olms Zurich as *The New Illustrated Encyclopedia of Country Music,* 1994. First published, edited by Fred Dellar, Ray Thompson, and Douglas B. Green, as *The Illustrated Encyclopedia of Country Music* (New York: Harmony Books, 1977), 256 pp. Revised as *The Harmony Illustrated Encyclopedia of Country Music* by Fred Dellar, Alan Cackett, Ray Thompson, and Douglas B. Green, 2nd ed., 1987 (208 pp.).

Short biographies of musicians prominent in country music, with members of ensembles listed with the name of their group. An appendix lists less prominent musicians not mentioned in the main text. The musicians' major hits are verified by their inclusion in *Billboard,* and their awards, both for sales and for other achievements, are listed. There is no index.

The 2nd ed. is reviewed by Dean Tudor in *ARBA* 19 (1988): no. 1310.

1.346* Carlin, Richard. *The Big Book of Country Music: A Biographical Encyclopedia.* 526 pp. New York: Penguin, 1995.

Despite the subtitle, this book defines schools of country music (bluegrass, honky-tonk), techniques (yodeling), types of songs (cowboy songs, weepers), and professions (singer/songwriter), and gives an account of more than 500 individuals and ensembles connected with country music. The biographical entries use the subject's stage name, but the real name is given, as well as dates, place of birth, and career, with a mention of the best-known songs associated with the subject. The discography that ends most articles gives album title, label name and number, and, often, an illuminating detail for each title. A bibliography and a personal name index are included.

1.347* Dellar, Fred, and **Richard Wootton.** *The Country Music Book of Lists.* 175 pp. New York: Times Books, 1984.

An eccentrically organized approach to country music trivia, covering such areas as souvenir shops, country music advertising, fan clubs, singing cowboys, trademarks, and previous occupations of country musicians.

1.348 Richards, Tad, and **Melvin B. Shestack.** *The New Country Music Encyclopedia.* 270 pp. + 16 pp. plates. New York: Simon & Schuster, 1993. (A Fireside book)

An update of Shestack's *Country Music Encyclopedia,* published by T.Y. Crowell in 1974 (410 pp.).

Profiles of and interviews with over 200 currently active country music performers. The entries for country soloists and ensembles include birth information, a style synopsis, a list of most memorable songs, and the music awards received. Includes a discography of 101 albums of country music, which gives label names but not numbers, and a title/name/subject index.

1.349* Sakol, Jeannie. *The Wonderful World of Country Music.* 240 pp. New York: Grosset & Dunlap, 1979.

Reprinted by Putnam in 1983.

A generously illustrated encyclopedia, with brief biographical entries and longer topical articles on such varied subjects as "Agencies Booking Country Music," "Fairs and Festivals," "Lingo" (including a section on "Talking Southern"), "Mail Order," and "Zodiac Signs of Country Music Stars." There is an index of names, titles, and subjects.

1.350 Stambler, Irwin, and **Grelun Landon.** *Encyclopedia of Folk, Country, and Western Music.* 2nd ed. 902 pp. + 56 pp. of plates. New York: St. Martin's Press, 1983.

First ed., 1969 (396 pp.).

Chiefly a collection of biographical entries on performers, with coverage of genres. The appendixes include awards lists (pp. 829–96) and a selective discography and bibliography (pp. 897–902).

Reviewed by Robert Skinner in *ARBA* 15 (1984): no. 920 and by Janet R. Ivey in *ARBA* 17 (1986): no. 1288.

FOLK MUSIC

1.351 Baggelaar, Kristin, and **Donald Milton.** *Folk Music: More than a Song.* 419 pp. New York: Crowell, 1976.

Published in London as *The Folk Music Encyclopedia* by Omnibus Press in 1977.

Entries on persons and groups, incorporating biographical, political, social, musical, and discographical information, with illustrations. There are no bibliographies.

Reviewed by Norm Cohen in *JEMFQ* 13 (1977): 42 no. 45 and by Richard Weissman in *MEJ* 64 (December 1977): 75–76.

1.352* Figueroa, Frank M. *Encyclopedia of Latin American Music in New York.* 237 pp. St. Petersburg, Fla.: Pillar Publications, 1994.

An encyclopedia of popular Latin American music, with most entries biographical (individual and ensemble). Other entries explain technical music terms, performing locations, radio stations, and record labels. Included are a discography (pp. 194–204), bibliographical references (pp. 206–13), and a thorough index (pp. 216–37).

1.353 Lawless, Roy McKinley. *Folksingers and Folksongs in America: A Handbook of Biography, Bibliography, and Discography.* New revised ed. with special supplement. 750 pp. New York: Duell, Sloan and Pearce, 1965.

First published in 1960 (662 pp.).

A general book of knowledge for folk song enthusiasts, with information pertaining to singers, song collecting, sources, and recordings. The largest part of this work is devoted to biographical information on American folk singers.

The 1st ed. is reviewed by Rae Korson in *Notes* 18 (1960): 62.

1.354* Leydi, Roberto, and **Sandra Montovani.** *Dizionario della musica popolare europea.* 316 pp. Milan: V. Bompiani Editore, 1970. (Guide culturali Bompiani)

An Italian dictionary of folk music terms, including musical instruments, with illustrations and musical examples. Many entries include a brief supportive discography.

1.355 Paulin, Don. *Das Folk-Musik-Lexikon.* 128 pp. Frankfurt am Main: Fischer-Taschenbuch-Verlag, 1980.

A bio-bibliographical work covering individuals and ensembles, with good coverage of European figures. The entries include discographical information. Includes an index and a bibliography (pp. 117–19).

JAZZ AND BLUES MUSIC

1.356 Bogaert, Karel. *Blues Lexicon: Blues Cajun, Boogie Woogie, Gospel.* 480 pp. Antwerp: Standaard, 1972.

Biographical information including discographies for hundreds of blues performers. The introduction by John Godrich provides a survey of significant blues literature.

1.357* Case, Brian, Stan Britt, and **Chrissie Murray.** *The Harmony Illustrated Encyclopedia of Jazz.* 3rd ed., fully revised and updated. 208 pp. New York: Harmony Books, 1987.

Reprinted in London by Tiger Books International, 1991, as *International Encyclopedia of Jazz;* the 1st ed., with the same title, was published in 1978 (223 pp.). A Spanish ed. was published by Ediciones Jucar, Madrid, 1982 (218 pp.).

A generously illustrated, wide-ranging jazz biographical dictionary, with a list of record albums ending each entry. The appendix gives some briefer entries, without discographies, and the index gives access to all personal name citations.

Reviewed by Paul Baker in *PMS* 11 (Fall 1987): 108–9 and by William Brockman in *ARBA* 19 (1988): no. 1313.

1.358 Charters, Samuel B. *Jazz: New Orleans.* Revised ed. 173 pp. New York: Oak Publications, 1963.

First published in 1958 by Walter C. Allen.

Brief descriptions of musicians and musical groups, arranged by chronological period. Includes a discographical appendix and index to names of musicians and bands, halls, cabarets, and tune titles.

1.359 Chilton, John. *Who's Who of Jazz: Storyville to Swing Street.* 5th ed. 375 pp. London: Papermac, 1989.

First published in London by the Bloomsbury Book Shop, 1970 (447 pp.), and subsequently in Philadelphia, Pa., by the Chilton Book Co., 1972 (419 pp.). The 4th ed. was published by Da Capo Press, London, in 1985, 375 pp. A paperback ed. was issued in London by Papermac, 1989.

Brief biographies of over 1,000 jazz musicians, tracing their affiliations with various ensembles. There is a partial list of bandleaders mentioned in the text (pp. 416–18).

Reviewed by James Patrick in *Notes* 29 (1973): 719–21 and by Diane J. Cimbala in *ARBA* 17 (1986): no. 1269.

1.360* Claghorn, Charles Eugene. *Biographical Dictionary of Jazz.* 377 pp. Englewood Cliffs, N.J.: Prentice-Hall, 1982.

A biographical dictionary of jazz musicians. Though quite brief, most entries include a quotation encapsulating the musical personality and style of the subject.

Reviewed by John P. Schmitt in *ARBA* 15 (1984): no. 923.

1.361* Clayton, Peter, and **Peter Gammond.** *Jazz A–Z.* 262 pp. Enfield, Middlesex, England: Guinness Books, 1986.

Spine title: *The Guinness Jazz A–Z.*

A Spanish trans. by José Ramon Rubio was published as *Jazz A–Z: Guia alphabetica de los nombres, los lugares y la gente del jazz* in Madrid by Altea, Taurus, Alfaguara in 1989.

A dictionary defining the geography, place names, venues, landmarks (both real and metaphysical), shrines, movements, dances, publications, artifacts, and language. Jazz musicians are listed by nickname rather than by surnames (as Bix, or Satchmo). Includes both an occasional selective bibliography and a list of and index to the jazz musicians mentioned.

Reviewed by William Brockman in *ARBA* 19 (1988): no. 1314.

1.362 Feather, Leonard. *The Encyclopedia of Jazz.* Completely enlarged, revised, and brought up to date. 527 pp. New York: Horizon Press, 1960.

First published in 1955; *Supplement,* 1956. Reprinted by Quartet Books, London and New York, 1978, and by Da Capo Press, New York, 1984.

Introductory essays on the history, sociology, and structure of jazz (pp. 13–90), followed by a biographical dictionary of jazz musicians, outlining their careers and summarizing their recording activities (pp. 96–473).

Reviewed by Alan P. Merriam in *Notes* 13 (1956): 288–90.

1.363 Feather, Leonard. *The Encyclopedia of Jazz in the Sixties.* 312 pp. New York: Horizon Press, 1966.

Reprinted in New York by Da Capo Press in 1986.

Similar in content and organization to **1.362,** with numerous portraits. The biographies stress affiliations with recording companies. There are short essays on the state of jazz, the results of jazz polls, and other topics.

1.364 Feather, Leonard, and **Ira Gitler.** *The Encyclopedia of Jazz in the Seventies.* 393 pp. New York: Horizon Press, 1976.

Reprinted in New York by Da Capo Press in 1987. Paperback ed. published by Quartet Books in 1978.

As in **1.362** and **1.363,** a compilation of biographies surrounded with short topical essays, covering events from mid-1966 to mid-1976. An added feature is "A Guide to Available Jazz Films," by Leonard Maltin (pp. 382–86).

Reviewed in *Jazz Podium* 26 (1977): 39 and in *Down Beat* 44 (December 15 1977): 52, 60.

1.365 Harris, Sheldon. *Blues Who's Who: A Biographical Dictionary of Blues Singers.* 775 pp. New Rochelle, N.Y.: Arlington House, 1979.

Reprinted in New York by Da Capo Press in 1981, in an edition supplemented by author emendations in 1991, and in a paperback edition in 1993.

Illustrated coverage of 571 blues singers active from 1900 to 1978, with a bibliography of sources and film, radio, television, theater, song, and names and place indexes.

Reviewed by Raymond F. Kennedy in *Notes* 37 (1980): 327–28 and by Stephen M. Fry in *ARBA* 11 (1980): no. 998.

1.366 Herzhaft, Gérard. *Encyclopedia of the Blues.* Trans. by Brigitte Debord. 513 pp. Fayetteville, Ark.: University of Arkansas Press, 1992.

French ed. published as *Encyclopédie du blues: Étude bio-discographique d'une musique populaire négro-americaine* in Lyons by Fédèrop in 1979, 346 pp.

An encyclopedia of blues artists (pp. 2–298) identifying the main blues figures, with more general entries for those with smaller roles but only an index citation for those briefly involved. The classified selective bibliography (pp. 401–6) includes a variety of source material, and an annotated discography (pp. 407–23) lists 200 compact discs, with label information (from 1990). An annotated alphabetized list of 300 blues standards (pp. 435–78) gives, by title, the recording history of a work, and a section on blues artists and their instruments lists, by instrument, major and secondary musicians, each with the recording most stylistically characteristic. There is a personal name index.

Reviewed by Bruce A. Schuman in *ARBA* 25 (1994): no. 1370.

1.367* Johnson, Bruce. *The Oxford Companion to Australian Jazz.* 320 pp. Melbourne: Oxford University Press, 1987.

An essay on Australian jazz, followed by a biographical dictionary of Australian jazz musicians (pp. 79–298) covering individuals and ensembles. The comprehensive index (pp. 302–20) covers both the essay and the dictionary.

1.368 Kernfeld, Barry. *The New Grove Dictionary of Jazz.* 2 vols. London: Macmillan; New York: Grove's Dictionary of Music, 1988.

Reprinted in a 1-vol. ed. (1,408 pp.) in 1995.

The first fully developed dictionary of jazz, including a comprehensive treatment of terminology and theory, articles on instruments, record labels, festivals, venues, films, institutions, individuals who are not performers, and an extensive bibliography, as well as articles on individual performers, ensembles, and styles of jazz. A model of scholarly breadth and rigorous methodology, this work carries over some entries from *The New Grove Dictionary of Music and Musicians* (**1.48**) and *The New Grove Dictionary of American Music* (**1.220**).

It is the largest dictionary of jazz ever published; it contains the broadest coverage and gives detailed attention to all periods and styles of jazz from many countries in an effort to counteract the factionalism seen in some jazz literature. Although the purpose of an encyclopedic work is to reflect the current understanding of its subject, a large amount of information is published for the first time here, and many of the major articles represent new approaches to jazz. The dictionary includes extensive bibliographies supplemented by references to holdings of oral history collections. Close attention is paid to the music itself; numerous musical examples are precisely defined, musical structures, procedures, and styles are described in detail, and there are informed analytical surveys (with musical examples) of such theoretical topics as forms, harmony, and improvisation.

The work focuses on jazz, not on related popular and commercial music, from the genesis of the music—principally from Black Americans at the turn of the twentieth century—to the mid-1980s. Included are extensive articles on topics such as arrangement and recording. These synthetic and often segmented articles present many examples, facts, and even directories of information. There are bibliographies for virtually every article; the articles on performers and ensembles include selected lists of recordings. There is a substantial general bibliography. The articles are signed by contributors, and there is a list of contributors identifying their articles. This book is well illustrated and handsomely produced, with wide margins.

Reviewed by Alan Rosenthal in *Fanfare* 13 (1989): 559–60 no. 2, by Bruce Cook in *The New Leader* 72 (January 23 1989): 20–21, and by Lee Bash in *Jazz Educators Journal* 21 (1989): 58–60 no. 3.

1.369* Longstreet, Stephen. *Jazz from A to Z: A Graphic Dictionary.* 1 vol. (unpaged). Highland Park, N.J.: Catbird Press / Independent Publishers Group, 1989.

1.370* McRae, Barry. *The Jazz Handbook.* 272 pp. Boston: G.K. Hall, 1989. (G.K. Hall performing arts handbooks)

First published in England by Longman Group UK Limited, 1987.

A chronologically arranged dictionary of 200 jazz musicians, organized to show musical lineage. Following is a databank of additional information showing prominent jazz record labels, a glossary, a bibliography, a list of information sources arranged by country, and a comprehensive index.

1.371* Matzner, Antonín, Ivan Poledňák, and **Igor Wasserberger.** *Encyklopedie jazzu a moderní populární kudby: Část jmenná—Československá scena.* 649 pp. + 40 pp. of plates. Prague: Editio Supraphon, 1990.

A jazz encyclopedia stressing the Czech scene and including bibliographical references.

1.372 Panassié, Hugues, and **Madeleine Gautier.** *Dictionnaire du jazz.* New ed., revised and augmented. 378 pp. Paris: Albin Michel, 1987.

First published by Robert Laffont, Paris, 1954. Subsequently published by Albin Michel, 1971 (360 pp.). The 1980 ed. is a reprint of the 1971 ed. with a supplement of 9 pp. of new entries and a preface. An English trans. by Desmond Flower, edited by A. A. Gurwitch, was published as *Guide to Jazz* (Boston, Mass.: Houghton Mifflin Company, 1956).

A standard sourcebook on jazz. It is chiefly biographical, with portraits of the subjects, but with some terms also included.

The 1956 English translation is reviewed by Alan P. Merriam in *Notes* 14 (1957): 362.

1.373 Rose, Al, and **Edmond Souchen.** *New Orleans Jazz: A Family Album.* 3rd ed., revised and enlarged. 362 pp. Baton Rouge, La.: Louisiana State University Press, 1984.

First published in 1967, 231 pp.; revised ed., 1978, 322 pp.

Copiously illustrated, with many early photographs. There are special sections on musicians, ensembles, and the places where they performed.

Reviewed by Frank Tirro in *Notes* 25 (1968): 33–34.

1.374* Santelli, Robert. *Big Book of Blues: A Biographical Encyclopedia.* 491 pp. New York: Penguin Books, 1993.

Over 600 entries for Black and White American and British blues performers describing each blues artist's life, career, and contributions to the blues. An "essential listening" supplement of recordings lists each artist's significant compact discs, generally reissues. Includes a bibliography (pp. 477–80) and a personal name/ensemble index to the biographical entries.

Reviewed by Dan Bogey in *LJ* 119 (1994): 110.

POPULAR MUSIC

1.375 Bane, Michael. *Who's Who in Rock.* 259 pp. New York: Facts on File, 1981; New York: Everest House, 1982.

Also published in Oxford by Clio Press, 1981.

A biographical dictionary whose 1,200+ rock stars range from Roy Acuff and Joan Baez to Frank Zappa and ZZ Top. The brief entries have descriptions of the subjects' music, but no sources are given and only brief biographical details are provided. There is an index of personal names and album titles (pp. 241–59).

Reviewed by Doris Evans McGinty in *BPM* 11 (1983): 212–14 and by Stephen L. Nugent in *Popular Music* 5 (1985): 235–44.

1.376 Bertoncelli, Riccardo. *Enciclopedia rock anni '50.* 3rd ed. 436 pp. Milan: Arcana, 1989.

Enciclopedia rock anni '60. 3rd ed., revised and corrected. 614 pp. Milan: Arcana, 1988.

Enciclopedia rock anni '70. 4th ed. 833 pp. Milan: Arcana, 1990.

Enciclopedia rock anni '80. 2nd ed. 842 pp. Milan: Arcana, 1989.

A series of Italian dictionaries of rock music covering personalities and events by decade that includes biographical entries with discographical citations. Each has a short general bibliography.

1.377 Bianco, David. *Who's New Wave in Music: An Illustrated Encyclopedia, 1976–1982 (the First Wave).* 430 pp. Ann Arbor, Mich.: Pierian Press, 1985. (Rock & roll reference series, 14)

A directory, with history, personnel, addresses, bibliography (pp. 333–38), and discography, of 854 New Wave groups. The bibliography indexes the relevant sections of seven American rock magazines. A list of record companies and labels gives the names, label numbers, and performer information for their issues. Also included is a glossary of New Wave musical terms, an outline of the eight major New Wave categories, and a list of ensembles grouped by musical style, as well as personal name, record label, song/album title, and geographical indexes.

Reviewed by Mary Larsgaard in *ARBA* 17 (1986): no. 1291.

1.378* Birosik, Patti Jean. *The New Age Music Guide: Profiles and Recordings of 500 Top New Age Musicians.* xxii + 218 pp. New York: Collier/Macmillan, 1989.

A work defining 16 subgenres of New Age music, 500 artists, and about 200 labels producing their music.

Reviewed by Sarah P. Long in *Notes* 48 (1991): 538–39.

1.379 Busby, Roy. *British Music Hall: An Illustrated Who's Who from 1850 to the Present Day.* 191 pp. London: Paul Elek; Salem, N.H.: Merrimack Book Service, 1976.

A biographical dictionary of British popular entertainers.

Reviewed in *Variety* 286 (February 5 1977): 128.

1.380* Claghorn, Charles Eugene. *Popular Bands and Performers.* 467 pp. Lanham, Md.: Scarecrow Press, 1995.

A biographical dictionary with rarely more than one fact provided (beyond name and birth-date) for each entry. It was intended to be used with Patricia Havlice's *Popular Song Index* (**5.386**). The names of members of musical ensembles are not always included. The criteria for inclusion are unclear: Claudio Abbado, for example, is among the unexpected entries.

1.381* Clarke, Donald. *The Penguin Encyclopedia of Popular Music.* 1,378 pp. New York: Viking Penguin, 1989.

An encyclopedia organized by the editor, joined by 15 contributors, gathering nearly 3,000 entries mostly for performers but also for songwriters, producers, and record labels. The entries range in length from a healthy paragraph to 4–5 pp. for such entries as "Rock." Generous cross-references are built into the entries; unfortunately, there is no access to the numerous song titles mentioned, and the sources of information are not provided. An extensive index (pp. 1,287–1,378) includes the names of persons, institutions, and companies.

Reviewed by David Dodd in *Notes* 48 (1992): 923 and by Amanda Maple in *Fontes* 40 (1993): 64–65.

1.382 Clifford, Mike. *The Harmony Illustrated Encyclopedia of Rock.* 7th ed. 208 pp. New York: Harmony Books; London: Salamander Books, 1992.

The 2nd ed. was published as *The Illustrated New Musical Express Encyclopedia of Rock*, 1978; 3rd ed., 1982 (288 pp.), edited by Nick Logan; 4th ed., 1983 (272 pp.); 5th ed., 1983 (272 pp.).

A brief reference work covering performers, support personnel, record companies, and musical instruments important in the rock music world. The entries include a list of hit singles, with both U.S. and U.K. chart positions, and a list of albums in chronological order. An appendix (pp. 198–208) lists the "one-hit wonders, the has-beens, the never-haves, the once-weres, the could-bes, and the you-never-knows in the musical world."

The 4th ed. is reviewed by Richard W. Grefrath in *ARBA* 16 (1985): no. 1215.

1.383* Clifford, Mike. *The Illustrated Encyclopedia of Black Music.* 224 pp. New York: Harmony Books, 1982.

A biographical dictionary with over 650 entries for musicians (both composers and performers) associated with soul music, reggae, rhythm and blues, blues, disco, and jazz-funk, but not mainstream jazz. The coverage, organized by decade, starts with the 1940s and ends with the 1980s. The entries give date and place of birth, musical background and associates, and most prominent songs recorded and albums made; label information, but not label numbers, is provided. There is a detailed index, complete with cross-references.

Reviewed by Robert Skinner in *ARBA* 15 (1984): no. 891.

1.384 Craig, Warren. *The Great Songwriters of Hollywood.* 287 pp. San Diego, Calif.: A.S. Barnes; London: Tantivy Press, 1980.

A biographical work covering composers and librettists. There are lists of songs and song indexes.

1.385 Craig, Warren. *Sweet and Lowdown: America's Popular Song Writers.* 645 pp. Metuchen, N.J.: Scarecrow Press, 1978.

Biographical sketches of 144 Tin Pan Alley composers (no rock, folk, or country), followed by chronological lists of their productions and songs. The author claims to rectify factual errors in other works on the same subject. There are indexes to song titles and productions.

Reviewed by Julian Hodgson in *Brio* 16 (1979): 23–24 and, in a helpful comparative style, by John Shepard in *Notes* 36 (1979): 372–73.

1.386 Ewen, David. *American Songwriters: An H.W. Wilson Biographical Dictionary.* 489 pp. New York: H.W. Wilson, 1987.

A successor to and total reorganization of his *Popular American Composers,* 1962, and its *First Supplement,* 1972.

A biographical dictionary covering 90 composers and 46 lyricists and composer–lyricists, emphasizing biography over criticism and giving a brief history for 5,600 of the composers' songs, which are indexed (pp. 453–89).

Reviewed by John E. Druesedow, Jr., in *ARBA* 19 (1988): no. 1267, with errata.

1.387* Gammond, Peter. *The Oxford Companion to Popular Music.* 739 pp. Oxford; New York: Oxford University Press, 1991.

Successor to the Gammond–Clayton *Guide to Popular Music* (London: Phoenix, 1960), 274 pp. Reprinted with corrections in 1993.

A dictionary of terms, musical instruments, concert halls, titles (song, album, show, and film), and brief biographies, intended for both the student and the professional user in the many international areas of popular music. There are indexes to people and groups (pp. 631–54), shows and films (pp. 655–88), and songs and albums (pp. 689–739).

Reviewed by Amanda Maple in *Fontes* 40 (1993): 64–65.

1.388* Hale, Mark. *HeadBangers: The Worldwide Megabook of Heavy Metal Bands.* xxii + 542 pp. Ann Arbor, Mich.: Popular Culture, 1993. (PCI collector editions) (Rock & roll reference series, 37)

An encyclopedia listing 3,458 heavy metal bands, with bibliographical and discographical information from the 1960s to the 1980s. The preface discusses the subtleties of heavy metal styles. The many helpful indexes include band names, performer names, bands and performers (arranged by country), U.S. bands and performers (arranged by state), band styles and influences, album titles, and album labels and numbers.

Reviewed by B. Lee Cooper in *PMS* 17 (Spring 1993): 119–21 no. 1, by Robert Walser in *Notes* 50 (1993): 631, and by Megan S. Farrell in *ARBA* 25 (1994): no. 1378.

1.389* Hardy, Phil, and **Dave Laing.** *The Da Capo Companion to 20th-Century Popular Music.* Revised and updated ed. 1,211 pp. New York: Da Capo Press, 1995.

First published as The Faber Companion to 20th-Century Popular Music (London; Boston, Mass.: Faber & Faber, 1990), 875 pp.

A biographical dictionary with coverage of almost 2,000 Anglo-American recording artists, selected as being commercially successful, musically influential, and artistically excellent. Sources are not cited. There is a brief glossary of styles and genres.

1.390* Hardy, Phil, and **Dave Laing.** *Encyclopedia of Rock.* Revised by Stephen Barnard and Don Perretta. 480 pp. London: Macdonald Orbis; New York: Schirmer Books, 1987.

First published in 1976 by Panther Books, London (3 vols.).

A heavily illustrated encyclopedia, primarily biographical (with both soloists and ensembles, performing and producing), but with entries for such areas as musical genres and record companies. There is no additional indexing.

Reviewed by Linda M. Fidler in *Notes* 47 (1990): 390.

1.391* Heatley, Michael. *The Ultimate Encyclopedia of Rock: The World's Most Comprehensive Illustrated Rock Reference.* 352 pp. New York: HarperPerennial, 1993.

Also published in 1993 by Olms, Hildesheim, Germany, as *Illustrated Encyclopedia of Rock,* and in Zurich as *The Illustrated Encyclopedia of Rock: The World's Most Comprehensive Illustrated Rock Reference;* the British ed. was published as *The Virgin Encyclopedia of Rock.*

A reference book that, although not quite living up to its title, covers many aspects of rock—the people, arts, performances, venues, labels, producers, studios, culture, and humor, with many color illustrations.

1.392 Helander, Brock. *The Rock Who's Who: A Biographical Dictionary and Critical Discography Including Rhythm-and-Blues, Soul, Rockabilly, Folk, Country, Easy Listening, Punk, and New Wave.* 686 pp. New York: Schirmer Books; London: Collier Macmillan, 1982.

A biographical dictionary, with tabulated discographies in order of recording date and including basic sales information. There are articles on nonmusical figures, with a classified bibliography (pp. 663–77) and index.

Reviewed by Richard W. Grefrath in *ARBA* 15 (1984): no. 925.

1.393* Jakubowski, Maxim. *MTV Music Television, Who's Who in Rock Video.* 190 pp. London: Zomba Books, 1983.

A heavily illustrated dictionary celebration of the establishment of the video music channel, with 100 biographical entries for performers, concentrating on the video segments of their musical careers. Each entry includes a video list.

Reviewed by Barbara A. Kemp in *ARBA* 17 (1986): no. 1300.

1.394 Jasper, Tony, and **Derek Oliver.** *The International Encyclopedia of Hard Rock and Heavy Metal.* Fully revised and updated. 448 pp. London: Sidgwick & Jackson, 1991.

First ed., New York: Facts on File, 1985 (400 pp.). A revised ed. was published in London, 1986, by Sidgwick & Jackson (388 pp.).

A biographical dictionary, international in scope, with entries for almost 1,500 groups and individual musicians. The individual entries include basic biographical facts, some attempts at critical analysis, and a selective discography.

The 1983 ed. is reviewed by Dean Tudor in *ARBA* 17 (1986): no. 1301.

1.395 Kinkle, Roger D. *The Complete Encyclopedia of Popular Music and Jazz, 1900–1950.* 4 vols. New Rochelle, N.Y.: Arlington House, 1974.

Contents: Vol. 1, *Music Year by Year, 1900–1950;* Vol. 2, *Biographies, A–K;* Vol. 3, *Biographies, L–Z;* Vol. 4, *Indexes and Appendixes.*

An essential reference source for the genre and the period it covers. Despite the limitations of the title, this work covers musicians (vocalists, instrumentalists, conductors, composers, arrangers, and lyricists) whose careers began before 1950 and therefore includes some works written up to the early 1970s. Vol. 1 has lists of significant works organized by year of appearance (Broadway musicals, popular songs, movie musicals, representative recordings), 1900–50. The next 2 vols. have 2,006 short biographies with works and recording lists, but no bibliographic citations. Vol. 4 contains lists of poll and prize winners, indexes of names, titles, and popular songs, and numerical lists of principal record labels.

Reviewed by Felicity Howlett in *Notes* 32 (1975): 44–46.

1.396 Lacombe, Alain, and **Claude Rode.** *La musique du film.* 516 pp. Paris: Éditions Francis Van de Velde, 1979.

Preceded by five chapters on the nature of film music, a collection of biographical entries on composers, each with lists of films for which music was provided. There are lists of 20th-century composers whose music has been adapted to film, and indexes of names and titles.

1.397* Larkin, Colin. *The Guinness Encyclopedia of Popular Music.* 2nd ed. 6 vols. 4,991 pp. Enfield, Middlesex, England; New York: Guinness Publishers, Stockton Press, 1995.

The 1st ed. was published in 4 vols. by Guinness Publishing, London, and in Chester, Conn., by New England Publishing Associates, 1992.

Also continues to be updated in such series as the Guinness Encyclopedia of Popular Music and the Guinness Who's Who in Popular Music by separately issued paperback titles such as *The Guinness Who's Who of Blues* (2nd ed., 1995, 414 pp.), *The Guinness Who's Who of Country Music* (1993, 473 pp.), *The Guinness Who's Who of Fifties Music* (1993, 351 pp.), *The Guinness Who's Who of Film Musicals and Musical Films* (1994, 351 pp.), *The Guinness Who's Who of Folk Music* (1993, 320 pp.), *The Guinness Who's Who of Heavy Metal* (1995, 2nd ed., 416 pp.), *The Guinness Who's Who of Indie and New Wave Music* (2nd ed., 1995, 416 pp.), *The Guinness Who's Who of Jazz* (1995, 508 pp.), *The Guinness Who's Who of Rap, Dance & Techno* (1994, 348 pp.), *The Guinness Who's Who of Reggae* (1994, 318 pp.), *The Guinness Who's Who of Seventies Music* (1993, 457 pp.), *The Guinness Who's Who of Sixties Music* (1992, 349 pp.), *The Guinness Who's Who of Soul Music* (1993, 315 pp.), and *The Guinness Book of Stage Musicals* (1994, 382 pp.).

An encyclopedia, chiefly biographical, covering a wide international range of popular music, with 14,500 entries.

The first edition is reviewed by Louis G. Zelenka in *ARBA* 25 (1994): no. 1363.

1.398* Leduc, Jean Marie, and **Jean-Noël Ogouz.** *Le rock de A à Z: Dictionnaire illustré.* 4th ed. 550 pp. Paris: Albin Michel, 1990.

3rd ed., 1984 (511 pp.).

An illustrated dictionary of rock, international in scope, principally biographical, but also including terminology and record companies. There are entries both for individual musicians and for their ensembles. Most entries conclude with a discography giving album title and label but omitting label number. There is no index but there is a "sommaire" of entries.

1.399* Lissauer, Robert. *Lissauer's Encyclopedia of Popular Music in America: 1888 to the Present.* xxi + 1,687 pp. New York: Paragon House, 1991.

A new ed. was anticipated in 1996.

A three-part reference work on popular music in the United States. The principal section (pp. 1–1,005) is an alphabetical list of songs, giving for each the writers, date of introduction, and date of revival (if relevant); following is a chronology (pp. 1,009–1,256), listing by year the songs cited in the first part. The 3rd section lists alphabetically the creators of the songs, citing their creations. There is a brief bibliography (pp. 1,685–87).

1.400 Nite, Norm N. *Rock On: The Illustrated History of Rock 'n' Roll.* 3 vols. New York: Harper & Row, 1982–85.

Contents: Vol. 1, *The Solid Gold Years* (originally published in 1974 by T.Y. Crowell, 1982), 722 pp.; Vol. 2, *The Years of Change, 1964–1978* (originally *The Modern Years, 1964–Present,* T.Y. Crowell, 1978), 590 pp.; 2nd ed., 1984, 749 pp.; Vol. 3, *The Video Revolution, 1978–Present* (with Charles Crespo, 1985), 444 pp.

Brief biographical entries on individuals and groups active in rock and roll as related genres. The entries include chronological lists of principal recordings. There are indexes of song titles.

1.401* Noyer, Alain-Pierre. *Dictionnaire des chanteurs francophones de 1900 à nos jours: 900 biographies d'interprètes, 6000 titres de chansons.* 210 pp. Paris: Conseil International de la Langue Française, 1989.

Includes both soloists and ensembles (Swingle Singers), listing popular singers who have given 20th-century performances in French. The brief entries include the subject's birthplace and, often, year of birth, as well as titles of songs from the subject's repertoire. There is an index of singers.

1.402* Perboni, Elia. *Dizionario della musica pop-leggera italiana.* 320 pp. Milan: Gammalibri, 1984.

A biographical dictionary of performers of popular Italian music, giving for each a brief discography, without label information.

1.403 Rice, Edward le Roy. *Monarchs of Minstrelsy, from "Daddy" Rice to Date.* 366 pp. New York: Kenny Publishing Company, 1911.

Colorful, illustrated biographical sketches of leading performers in late-19th-century American minstrel shows. The information is arranged in roughly chronological order.

1.404 Romanowski, Patricia, Holly George-Warren, and **Jon Pareles.** *The New Rolling Stone Encyclopedia of Rock & Roll.* Completely revised and updated. 1,120 pp. New York: Fireside, 1995.

The first ed., by Pareles and Romanowski, was published as *The Rolling Stone Encyclopedia of Rock & Roll* in 1983, by Rolling Stone Press/Summit Books, 615 pp.

A collection of 2,200 entries (including 500 new ones) on significant and insignificant persons, groups, terms (including dance styles), record companies, and other influences contributing to the rock industry. The entries on performers include chronological lists of recordings, giving brief titles and manufacturers' names, omitting catalog numbers. The entries for groups list backup personnel, who often also have individual entries.

1.405 Roxon, Lillian, and **Ed Naha.** *Lillian Roxon's Rock Encyclopedia.* Revised ed. 565 pp. New York: Grosset & Dunlap, 1978.

An Australian ed. published in Sydney by Angus & Robertson, 1980. First ed. published 1969, 611 pp.; reissued in 1969 by Grosset as no. 255 of The universal library.

An updated version of the pioneering original edition, covering the growth of the industry and the eclectic branching of the genre. There are lists of albums and single titles, as well as an index.

The 1st ed. is reviewed by Gilbert Chase in *Notes* 28 (1972): 694–97. The 2nd ed. is reviewed by Stephen M. Fry in *ARBA* 11 (1980): no. 983.

1.406 Schmidt-Joos, Siegfried, Barry Graves, and **Bernie Sigg.** *Das neue Rock-Lexikon.* New ed. 2 vols. 1,048 pp. Reinbeck bei Hamburg: Rowohlt, 1990. (Rororo-Handbuch)

First published in 1973 (350 pp.); 2nd ed., 1975 (445 pp.).

Biographical dictionary of rock performers, both individual and group. The entries are brief, with cross-references and selective discographies. Includes an appendix of entries on terms and recording companies, an extensive bibliography, and an index to names cited in articles.

1.407 Sevran, Pascal. *Dictionnaire de la chanson française.* 379 pp. Paris: M. Lafron, 1986.

Successor to an ed. by France Vernillat and Jacques Charpentreau, published by Larousse, Paris, 1968 (256 pp.), as part of the series Les dictionnaires de l'homme du XXe siècle, D27.

An illustrated biographical dictionary of French popular song. The coverage extends from the 13th century to the present day, with emphasis on singers of the 19th and 20th centuries. The dictionary includes both terms and biographies, with no citation of sources, and is preceded by a "petite histoire de la chanson française."

1.408 Shaw, Arnold. *Dictionary of American Pop/Rock: Rock, Pop, Rhythm and Blues, Folk, Country, Blues, Gospel, Jazz Films, Musical Theater, Recordings and Music Business.* 440 pp. New York: Schirmer Books; London: Collier Macmillan, 1982.

Brief entries, with cross-references, on the terminology of the field and on the important individuals in it. The biographical entries discuss style characteristics and contributions; there are also entries on important clubs and locations. There is an index to names and terms.

Reviewed by Dean Tudor in *ARBA* 15 (1984): no. 894.

1.409 Stambler, Irwin. *Encyclopedia of Pop, Rock & Soul.* Revised ed. 881 pp. + 48 pp. of plates. New York: St. Martin's Press; London: Macmillan, 1989.

Printed by Papermac, London, in a paperback ed., 1992. First ed., 1974 (609 pp.).

Biographical entries of both performing groups and individuals (pp. 1–768). The appendixes give lists of the winners of various prizes: the Recording Industry Association of America's gold (from 1958) and platinum (from 1974) records; in selected categories, the Grammys, from the National Academy of Recording Arts and Sciences (from 1958), and the musical Oscar winners and nominations from 1958. There is a bibliography (pp. 875–81).

Reviewed by David Dodd in *Notes* 48 (1992): 923 and by Ann P. Basart in *CNV* 135 (1989): 27.

1.410 Walker, Leo. *The Big Band Almanac.* Revised ed. 466 pp. New York: Da Capo Press, 1989. (A Da Capo paperback)

Corrected reprint of the 1st ed. by Ward Ritchie Press in Pasadena, Calif., and Vinewood Enterprises, Inc., Hollywood, both 1978.

An illustrated biographical dictionary principally of band leaders flourishing from the early 1920s to the mid-1950s in the United States. Each entry includes information on band origin and affiliation, sidemen, principal vocalists, theme songs, and recording company contracts. There is an index of names and ensembles.

Reviewed by Dean Tudor in *ARBA* 11 (1980): no. 990.

1.411* Warner, Jay. *The Billboard Book of American Singing Groups: A History, 1940–1990.* 542 pp. New York: Billboard Books, 1992.

A dictionary of popular American singing groups, both well known and obscure but interesting, with three or more people singing in harmony, divided by decade according to each group's greatest musical activity. An essay on the period begins each decade, and each entry ends with a chronologically arranged discography of singles and albums, citing label, label number, and date of release.

Reviewed by Daphne Fallieros Potter in *ARBA* 25 (1994): no. 1359.

1.412* Weiss, Wiesław, and **Roman Rogowiecki.** *Rock encyklopedia.* 646 pp. + 48 pp. of plates. Warsaw: Iskry, 1994.

Rock music defined from a Polish perspective.

1.413 York, William. *Who's Who in Rock Music.* Revised ed. 413 pp. New York: Scribner; London: Arthur Barker, 1982.

First published by Atomic, Seattle, Wash., 1978 (260 pp.).

A collation of information gleaned from rock album covers, discussing sidemen broadly, if with dubious authority.

OPERA, THEATER, AND FILM MUSIC

Dictionaries of opera and theater music are of two principal kinds: compilations of fact related to the history or the production of musical dramatic works, which are cited as dictionaries or handbooks of opera; and lists of operatic works, often in chronological order, associated with a particular place (region, country, city, or opera house). Works of the latter type that deal with geographic units smaller than a country can properly be described as bibliographies of music, and are found in Chapter 5's subdivision "Regional and Local Opera Repertoires" (**5.467–5.502**). Collections solely giving opera plots are excluded.

1.414* Adam, Nicky. *Who's Who in British Opera.* 339 pp. Aldershot, England: Scholar Press; Brookfield, Vt.: Ashgate Publishing Company, 1993.

A concentration on people currently active in the United Kingdom's operatic world, including almost 500 singers, composers, conductors, directors, designers, administrators, editors, librettists, teachers, translators, critics, and writers. Each entry succinctly describes the subject's career and includes listings for recordings, videos, and publications, when relevant. The information came from questionnaires, supplemented by research, when necessary; the proofs of the entries were submitted to the subjects for correction and approval. The three appendixes list the subjects cited, classified by principal profession; operas arranged alphabetically by title, with composer; and the record labels cited, with the acronym used.

Reviewed by Phillip P. Powell in *ARBA* 26 (1995): no. 1283.

1.415* Alier Aixala, Roger, Xose Aviñoa, and **F. X. Mata.** *Diccionario de la zarzuela: Biografías de compositores, argumentos y comentarios musicales sobre las principales zarzuelas del repertorio actual.* 386 pp. Madrid: Ediciones Daimon Manuel Tamayo, 1986.

A dictionary with entries for 111 zarzuela composers and their work. The "Discografia de la zarzuela" (pp. 351–68) includes 30 composers and 111 of their zarzuelas, some with multiple performances.

1.416 Altmann, Wilhelm. *Katalog der seit 1861 in den Handel gekommenen theatralischen Musik (Opern, Operetten, Possen, Musik zu Schauspielen usw.): Ein musikbibliographischer Versuch.* 384 pp. Wolfenbüttel, Germany: Verlag für musikalische Kultur und Wissenschaft, 1935–39. (Incomplete)

This work was published in *Lieferungen,* of which four appeared, carrying the entries through "Siegmund, Josef."

Entries for operas, ballets, and incidental music since 1861, arranged under the name of the composer, with cross-references from the librettist and others connected with the work. The *Katalog* gives brief titles of works, type, librettist, date of first performance (if known), type of score, language of text, and publisher. Although there is no key to the abbreviations of publishers' names, most can be readily identified.

1.417* Anderson, James. *The Harper Dictionary of Opera and Operetta.* 691 pp. New York: HarperCollins, 1990.

First published in England as the *Bloomsbury Dictionary of Opera and Operetta* by Bloomsbury Publishing Limited, 1989. Reprinted by Wings Books, New York, as *The Complete Dictionary of Opera and Operetta,* 1993. A 2nd ed., *Dictionary of Opera and Operetta,* was published in London by Bloomsbury, 1995, 656 pp.

More than 4,500 entries describe many areas of the operatic world: opera festivals, companies, opera houses, instruments especially related to opera (as the *Aida* trumpet), literary sources, operatic themes (artists in opera, writers as librettists), operas (plot summary, premiere information, and libretto author and source), arias (location in the work and character singing it), operatic characters (role description and vocal range), and personal names (composers, singers, conductors, administrators, stage designers, etc.). There are approximately 100 panels of charted information, listing such areas as individual vocal ranges and literary derivatives. The 1st appendix gives a chronology of operatic history, charted by country; a 2nd lists 760 commercially recorded operas by composer.

The 1st ed. is reviewed by James Miller in *Fanfare* 14 (1991): 416–17 no. 6 and by David Ossenkop in *Choice* 28 (1991): 909; the English ed. is reviewed by Alison Hall in *Fontes* 37 (1990): 316–17 and by Julian Budden in *M&L* 74 (1993): 579–81.

1.418* Bagnoli, Giorgio. *The La Scala Encyclopedia of the Opera.* Trans. by Graham Fawcett. 398 pp. New York: Simon & Schuster, 1993.

First published in Italian as *Opera* (Milan: A. Mondadori, 1993), 383 pp.

A generously illustrated opera dictionary, with no clear connection to La Scala. There are alphabetized entries for 468 operas, 186 composers, 441 singers, 143 conductors, and 43 librettists, a brief discography, and 17 single-page opera-related essays.

1.419 Bernandt, Grigoriĭ Borisovich. *Slovarʹ oper: Vpervye postavlennykh ili iz dannykh v Dorevoliutsionnoi Rossii I v SSSR, 1736–1959.* 554 pp. Moscow: Sovetskii Kompozitor, 1962.

A dictionary of operas first performed or first published in Russia 1736–1959. The entries are arranged alphabetically by title and include the work's genre, composer, first performance, librettist, literary source, and many production details. The dictionary is indexed by composer, librettist, and author of the original literary source.

1.420* Blanchard, Roger, and **Roland de Candé.** *Dieux et divas de l'opéra.* 2 vols. Paris: Plon, 1986–87.

Contents: Vol. 1, *Des origines à la Malibran;* Vol. 2, *De 1820 à 1950: Grandeur et décadence du bel canto.*

Topically grouped biographies of prominent singers throughout the history of opera, with some illustrations. Includes an appendix of major operas and one of principal roles.

1.421 Bloom, Ken. *American Song: The Complete Musical Theatre Companion, 1900–1984.* 2 vols. New York: Facts on File, 1985.

Information on over 5,000 productions, on and off Broadway. The 2nd vol. is an index to the individual songs in each production.

Reviewed by Doris Evans McGinty in *BPM* 13 (1985): 124–26 and by Ed Glazier in *Notes* 43 (1986): 301–3.

1.422* Bloom, Ken. *Hollywood Song: The Complete Film & Musical Companion.* 3 vols. 1,504 pp. New York: Facts on File, 1995.

A collection of data on songs from almost 7,000 American and foreign films. The first 2 vols. list all movies alphabetically by title, giving releasing studio and year of release, composer, director, screenwriter, source, cast, song, and notes on the songs. Films produced for video are excluded, as are films containing only a vocal of a public domain tune. Vol. 3 lists the films chronologically and has indexes to personnel (giving the connection to each film) and songs.

1.423 Bordman, Gerald. *The American Musical Theatre: A Chronicle.* 2nd ed. 821 pp. New York: Oxford University Press, 1992.

The 1st ed. was published in 1978 (749 pp.) and an expanded ed. (782 pp.) in 1986.

Information on American musicals that includes opening date and theater, plot synopsis, characters and originators of the roles, and critical comments based on contemporary reviews. Includes a title index and an index to literary sources of shows, to persons, and to songs mentioned (but not all songs from the shows covered). There is no bibliography.

The 1st ed. is reviewed by Doris E. McGinty in *BPM* 7 (1979): 255–56. The 2nd ed. is reviewed by Thomas Riis in *Notes* 50 (1994): 985–88.

1.424 Brockpähler, Renate. *Handbuch zur Geschichte der Barockoper im Deutschland.* 394 pp. Emsdetten, Germany: Verlag Lechte, 1964. (Die Schaubühne: Quellen und Forschungen zur Theatergeschichte, 62)

A handbook of historical information related to German baroque opera. Organized by place (47 municipalities), each entry includes a bibliography of relevant literature, sections devoted to the history of music or opera in that place, and a list of the works performed. There are indexes by place, musicians, poets, and dancing masters.

1.425 Burton, Jack. *The Blue Book of Hollywood Musicals: Songs from the Sound Tracks and the Stars Who Sang Them since the Birth of the Talkies a Quarter-Century Ago.* 296 pp. Watkins Glen, N.Y.: Century House, 1953.

Complementing the *Blue Book of Tin Pan Alley,* 1951 (**5.444**), and *The Blue Book of Broadway Musicals,* 1952 (**1.426**), an anthology completing a trilogy on popular music. Helpful access to this trilogy is through *The Index of American Popular Music* (**5.443**).

1.426 Burton, Jack, and **Larry Freeman.** *The Blue Book of Broadway Musicals.* 335 pp. Watkins Glen, N.Y.: Century House, 1975.

The 2nd book in a trilogy on popular music, the 1st of which is *The Blue Book of Tin Pan Alley* (**5.444**) and the 3rd is *The Blue Book of Hollywood Musicals* (**1.425**). The 1st ed., edited by Jack Burton, was published in 1952 (320 pp.).

A list of entries, including title, composer, author, principals, and musical numbers, for more than 1,500 operettas, musical comedies, and revues from the 1890s to 1951. The arrangement is by decade, with a general introduction to each period.

1.427 Caselli, Aldo. *Catalogo delle opere liriche pubblicate in Italia.* 891 pp. Florence: Leo S. Olschki, 1969. (Historiae musiciae cultores, Biblioteca, 27)

An ambitious attempt to cover all operas produced in Italy from 1600 to the 1960s. Organized to permit approaches through composer, city and theater, title, and librettist. The effort to achieve comprehensiveness led to some sacrifice of accuracy.

Reviewed by Thomas Walker in *Notes* 26 (1970): 758–59.

1.428 Clément, Félix, Pierre Larousse, and **Arthur Pougin.** *Dictionnaire des opéras: Dictionnaire lyrique, contenant l'analyse et la nomenclature de tous les opéras et opéras-comiques représentés en France et à l'étranger depuis l'origine de ce genre d'ouvrages jusqu'à nos jours: complété par des suppléments périodiques maintenant à cet ouvrage un caractère d'actualité.* 1,203 pp. Paris: Librairie Larousse, 1905.

A reprint of the 1905 ed. was published in 1969 by Da Capo, New York, in 2 vols., omitting the index of composers in the original ed. The 1st ed. was published in 1869 as *Dictionnaire lyrique,* and was revised and published in Paris by the Administration du Grand Dictionnaire Universal in 1881 as *Dictionnaire des opéras.*

A comprehensive work listing by title (often under the French form, with reference to other forms) operas and comic operas presented in France and elsewhere from opera's first days to the publication date of this tool. The information in each entry includes the language of the text, the number of acts, the authors of the words and music, the place and date of the first performance, and a brief sketch of the plot, with occasional criticism. There is a composer index.

1.429 Comuzio, Ermanno. *Film Music Lexicon.* 304 pp. Pavia, Italy: Amministrazione Provinciale de Pavia, 1980.

International in scope, providing information on 500 musicians, listing the motion pictures for which they were composed. The "Filmografia" has entries from 1906 to 1980 on films with original music judged of particular value, films of a musical character (with subjects on symphonies, operas, ballets, or biographies of great musicians), musicals, and films featuring jazz, pop, and rock music. Includes a name index and a bibliography.

1.430 Dahlhaus, Carl, and **Sieghart Döhring.** *Pipers Enzyklopädie des Musiktheaters: Oper, Operette, Musical, Ballett.* 5 vols. to date. Munich; Zurich: Piper, 1986– .

A beautifully produced multivolume encyclopedia of opera, generously illustrated with detailed labels. The range of theatrical productions covered gives a wide view of many composers' total dramatic work. The entries include information on the location of autographs and the identity of the early editions, as well as bibliographies. The entries are signed. Performer entries are not included.

The first 2 vols. are reviewed by Ann P. Basart in *CNV* 124 (1988): 5.

1.431 Dassori, Carlo. *Opere e operisti (Dizionario lirico 1541–1902): Elenco nominativo univer-sale dei maestri compositori di opere teatrali, col prospetto cronologico dei loro principali lavori e catalogo alfabetico generale dall'origine delle opere serie, semiserie, buffe, comiche e simili rappre-sentate . . . dall'origine dell'opera in musica fino ai d'i nostri, coll'indicazione di data e di luogo della prima rappresentazione, avuto speciale riguardo al repertorio italiano.* 977 pp. Genoa: Tipografia Editrice R. Istituto Sordomuti, 1903.

Reprinted by A. Forni in Bologna in 1979 (Bibliotheca musica Bononiensis, III, 64).

A dictionary listing 15,406 operas by 3,628 composers, with author and title lists only, with-out descriptive or critical matter. The 1st part is an alphabetical list of composers, with birth and death dates and, under each name, a chronological list of operas, with dates and places of first performances. The 2nd part is a title list of all operas that have been performed in Italy.

1.432 *Directory of American and Foreign Contemporary Operas and American Opera Premieres, 1967–1975.* 66 pp. New York: Central Opera Service, 1975.

An issue of the *Central Opera Service Bulletin,* Vol. 17, no. 2 (Winter 1975).

A list of operas by American composers premiered and operas by foreign contemporary composers presented in the period 1967–75.

There is a brief review by Stephen M. Fry in *Notes* 32 (1976): 555.

1.433 Drone, Jeanette Marie. *Index to Opera, Operetta, and Musical Comedy Synopses in Collections and Periodicals.* 171 pp. Metuchen, N.J.: Scarecrow Press, 1978.

An index to 78 anthologies and 4 American periodicals, giving access to the plots of 1,605 works by 627 composers. A bibliography of biographies and general opera dictionaries and encyclopedias, not indexed by the editor, is included. Similar titles were produced by Waldemar Rieck (**1.466**) and William Studwell (**1.479**).

Reviewed by Stephen M. Fry in *Notes* 35 (1978): 93 and by Frits Noske in *Fontes* 26 (1979): 92–93.

1.434 Eaton, Quaintance. *Opera Production: A Handbook.* 2 vols. Minneapolis, Minn.: University of Minnesota Press, 1961–74.

The 1st vol. was reprinted by Da Capo Press, New York, 1974, as *Opera Production I: A Handbook,* 266 pp.

A dictionary of operas available for performance, with the basic data needed for a staged production. The 1st vol. contains useful information on 224 long and 148 short operas, including for each work the timing, ranges of the leading roles, instrumentation, source and cost of scores and parts, an index to photographs of productions (in *ON,* unless otherwise specified), and lists of opera companies that have produced that work. The 2nd vol. treats 368 lesser-known operas in similar fashion and includes "Production Problems of Handel's Operas," by Randolph Mickelson.

The 1st ed. of the 1st vol. is reviewed by Edward N. Waters in *Notes* 19 (1962): 258–59. The 2nd vol. is reviewed by Boris Goldovsky in *Notes* 32 (1975): 53–54.

1.435 Ewen, David. *New Complete Book of the American Musical Theater.* xxv + 800 pp. New York: Holt, Rinehart & Winston, 1970.

First issued as the *Complete Book of the American Musical Theater,* 1958.

A sourcebook of information about American musical comedies and revues.

Reviewed by Edward N. Waters in *Notes* 16 (1955): 255.

1.436 Ewen, David. *The New Encyclopedia of the Opera.* 759 pp. New York: Hill & Wang, 1971.

The 1st ed. was published in 1955 as *Encyclopedia of the Opera* (594 pp.) and was reissued, with a supplement, in 1963. The British version of the 1971 ed. was published in London by Vision in 1973.

A list in one alphabet of composers, text incipits, terms, plots, singers, librettists, and theaters. The plot summaries show the position of major arias in the dramatic action.

Reviewed by Piero Weiss in *Notes* 28 (1972): 679–80; the London ed. is reviewed by Jack A. Westrup in *M&L* 55 (1974): 242–43.

1.437 Forbes, Elizabeth. *Opera from A to Z.* 153 pp. London: Kaye & Ward; South Brunswick, N.J.: A.S. Barnes, 1977.

A dictionary of opera including bibliographical references.

1.438 Gänzl, Kurt. *The British Musical Theatre.* 2 vols. London: Macmillan Press; New York: Oxford University Press, 1986.

A substantial survey of the British light musical theater, excluding opera, confining itself to works with words and music written particularly for the show in question. Organized chronologically, each year's entries are preceded by a brief essay on the character of the times. Entries provide performance information and history, including references to TV/video productions. Characters and players are cited. There are appendixes listing printed and recorded works. There is an index of names, titles, theaters, and titles of journals or newspapers cited.

Reviewed by George Rowell in *TLS* (November 7 1986): 1245.

1.439* Gänzl, Kurt. *The Encyclopedia of the Musical Theatre.* American ed. 2 vols. New York: Schirmer Books; Toronto: Maxwell Macmillan Canada, 1994.

Published in Oxford, England, by Blackwell Publishers in 1994.

A dictionary of composers for the musical theater and of those associated with their productions; there are also entries by production title. Information is given on international productions and on recordings issued. The entries concentrate on the history of the work rather than on just a synopsis of the plot. There are no definitions of terms and the songs mentioned are not indexed.

Reviewed by Stephen Banfield in *MT* 136 (1995): 156 and by Jon P. Cobes in *LJ* 119 (June 1 1994): 98.

1.440* Gourret, Jean. *Dictionnaire des cantatrices de l'Opéra de Paris.* With the collaboration of Simon Ferdinand et al. 319 pp. + 40 plates. Paris: Albatros, 1987.

An earlier ed., *Encyclopédie des cantatrices de l'Opéra de Paris,* compiled with the collaboration of Jean Giraudeau, was published by Mengès in 1981, 316 pp.

A dictionary of women singers, with the entries arranged in chronological order by the date of their first Paris Opéra appearance. There is an index of personal names.

1.441* Gourret, Jean. *Dictionnaire des chanteurs de l'Opéra de Paris.* With the collaboration of Jean Giraudeau. 331 pp. + 32 pp. of plates. Paris: Albatros, 1982.

A dictionary of the male singers who appeared at the Paris Opéra from 1671 to 1980, arranged chronologically by date of debut. For the more important singers basic dates are also given, with career information, principal roles, and a characterization of their voice and art. There were many foreign guest singers and the coverage is international.

1.442 Green, Stanley. *Broadway Musicals, Show by Show.* 4th ed., revised and updated by Kay Green. 372 pp. Milwaukee, Wisc.: Hal Leonard Publishing Co., 1994.

The 3rd ed. was published in 1990, 373 pp., by Hal Leonard; the 2nd ed. in 1987 by Hal Leonard in Milwaukee, 368 pp., and by Faber in London, 361 pp.; and the 1st ed. in Milwaukee, Wisc., by H. Leonard Books, 1985, 361 pp.

A chronological source with 300 entries providing brief histories, information on each production, and photographs. There are indexes to titles, composers, lyricists, librettists, directors, choreographers, principal members of casts, and theaters.

The 1st ed. is reviewed by Eric W. Johnson in *LJ* 111 (February 15 1986): 173.

1.443 Green, Stanley. *Encyclopaedia of the Musical Film.* 344 pp. New York: Oxford University Press, 1981.

A companion to the author's *Encyclopedia of the Musical Theatre* (**1.444**) sharing its format and containing succinct information on the musical screen's most prominent individuals, productions, and songs. Emphasis is on Hollywood output, including feature-length cartoons, but British musical films and selected original television musicals are also covered. Western musicals (those of the singing cowboys, such as Gene Autry and Roy Rogers), short subjects, documentary musicals, foreign-language musicals, and silent films with accompanying scores are all excluded, as are composers known for their film music who did not compose for musicals.

Entries for individuals contain year-by-year lists of every production with which they were associated. Production entries include major performers and their roles, songs, and singers, as well as songs intended for the film but cut. Song entries include those primarily written for or first introduced in films. Some entries include bibliographic references. Includes a list of Academy Award nominations and prize winners, a classified bibliography of biographies (classical and popular composers), a list of title changes for British and American versions of the same productions, a general bibliography, and a discography arranged by title.

Reviewed by Alan Hoffman in *Notes* 38 (1982): 846–47.

1.444 Green, Stanley. *Encyclopedia of the Musical Theatre: An Updated Reference Guide to over 2,000 Performers, Writers, Directors, Productions, and Songs of the Musical Stage, Both in New York and London.* 492 pp. New York: Da Capo Press, 1984.

A reprint of the ed. published as the *Encyclopaedia of the Musical Theatre* by Dodd, Mead,

New York, in 1976 (488 pp.), supplemented with photographs and addenda. Published as *Encyclopedia of the Musical* in London by Cassell, 1977, 488 pp. Published in a paperback ed. by Oxford University Press, New York, in 1988.

Descriptions of almost all 20th-century productions in New York and London, with a bibliography and discography (pp. 471–88), as well as a supplementary list of awards and prizes and runs of over 1,000 performances.

Reviewed by Stephen M. Fry in *Notes* 38 (1977): 848–49.

1.445* Green, Stanley. *Hollywood Musicals, Year by Year.* 351 pp. Milwaukee, Wisc.: Hal Leonard Books, 1990.

A companion to the author's *Broadway Musicals, Show by Show* (**1.442**), presenting commentary on 285 popular American musical films, including animated feature films, chronologically arranged from 1927 to 1989. Excluded are operas (except *Porgy and Bess*), westerns with singing cowboys, foreign-language films, documentaries, and silent films with accompanying scores. Each entry lists credits (including cast), featured songs, date of release, length, and an indication of whether a commercially released soundtrack recording or videocassette was made. Most entries are illustrated with studio stills. Paragraph- to page-length commentaries give for each film a plot summary, details of production history, and remarks on its success.

1.446* Griffel, Margaret Ross. *Operas in German: A Dictionary.* Adrienne Fried Block, advisory editor. xxviii + 735 pp. New York: Greenwood Press, 1990.

A dictionary of 380 operas written with a German text. The entries give a plot synopsis and information on published editions of both score and libretto, a discography (with discographic information), and a bibliography. Appendixes list 1,250 additional opera titles, composers (with opera titles), librettists, authors of the original book on which the libretto is based, a selected list of literary sources (by title), a chronological list, a classified bibliography, a character index, a performer index, and a general opera title index.

Reviewed by Winfried Kirsch in *Fontes* 39 (1992): 366–68, by Paula Morgan in *Notes* 49 (1992): 168–69, and by David Ossenkop in *Choice* 28 (1991): 1289.

1.447 Gruber, Clemens M. *Opern-Uraufführungen: Ein internationales Verzeichnis von der Renaissance bis zur Gegenwart.* 3 vols. Vienna: Österreichische Verlagsanstalt, 1978–94.

Contents: Vol. 1, *Uraufführungen von Opern deutscher, österreicher und schweizer Komponisten vor 1800, sowie ein Nachtrag und ein Korrekturverzeichnis zu den Bänden 2 und 3,* 1994; Vol. 2, *Komponisten aus Deutschland, Österreich und der Schweiz, 1800–1899* (397 pp.), 1987; Vol. 3, *Komponisten aus Deutschland (der BRD und der DDR), Österreich und der Schweiz, 1900–1907* (319 pp.), 1978.

A dictionary with entries by composer, giving dates and places of world premieres, the numbers of acts, and names of librettists, with title and location indexes, *Anhang,* and supplement.

1.448* Hamilton, David. *The Metropolitan Opera Encyclopedia: A Comprehensive Guide to the World of Opera.* 415 pp. New York: Simon & Schuster; London: Thames & Hudson, 1987.

A 1-vol. opera encyclopedia that includes opera terminology.

Reviewed by Arthur Jacobs in *M&L* 69 (1988): 541–42, by Winton Dean in *TLS* (February 26 1988): 222, and by Ann P. Basart in *CNV* 124 (1988): 5.

1.449* Hischak, Thomas S. *Stage It with Music: An Encyclopedic Guide to the Musical Theatre.* 341 pp. Westport, Conn.: Greenwood Press, 1993.

A list of persons (producers, performers, authors, composers, costume designers, etc.), terms, subjects, musicals, genres, and musical series, in one alphabet. The index gives personal names, titles of musicals and songs, and subjects.

Reviewed by Thomas E. Luddy in *LJ* 118 (June 15 1993): 62.

1.450* Holden, Amanda, Nicholas Kenyon, and **Stephen Walsh.** *The Viking Opera Guide.* xxii + 1,305 pp. + CD-ROM. London; New York: Viking, 1993.

Coverage by 104 authorities of 1,587 works, arranged alphabetically by composer, from monodies and masques to all types of opera, operettas, and major musicals. There are biographical entries for composers. The information given for the individual operas includes the date of composition, premieres, casts, orchestration, plot synopsis, background, musical highlights, recordings, and editions.

Reviewed as one of the works covered by David Littlejohn's "Everything You Ever Wanted to Know about Opera: A Review-Essay of Recent Reference Works" in *Notes* 51 (1995): 854–58, and by Andrew Porter in *TLS* 4728 (November 12 1993): 9.

1.451 Johnson, H. Earle. *Operas on American Subjects.* 125 pp. New York: Coleman-Ross Company, 1964. (Coleman-Ross books on music)

An alphabetical list, by composer, of operas from the 17th century to the 1960s, based on American subject matter or involving American characters. The entries supply much interesting information related to plot, performance, and estimates by contemporary critics. There are topical, title, and general indexes.

Reviewed by Klaus Speer in *Notes* 22 (1962): 913–14.

1.452* Kornick, Rebecca Hodell. *Recent American Opera: A Production Guide.* 352 pp. New York: Columbia University Press, 1990.

A list of over 200 operas of the past 20 years by 125 American composers, including for each entry its type of drama, its style of music, its length, the author and source of its libretto, its performances and recordings, the plot, the vocal ranges of its roles, and critical appraisals of the work.

Reviewed by William J. Waters in *LJ* 115 (1990): 67.

1.453* LaRue, C. Steven. *International Dictionary of Opera.* 2 vols. Detroit, Mich.: St. James Press, 1993.

Over 200 contributors combining to write a 1,100-entry source on opera, covering individual operas, composers, librettists, producers, designers, performers, and conductors.

Reviewed by Koraljka Lockhart in *ARBA* 25 (1994): no. 1353, by Guy A. Marco in *Choice* 31 (1993): 267, and as one of the works covered by David Littlejohn's "Everything You Ever Wanted to Know about Opera: A Review-Essay of Recent Reference Works," in *Notes* 51 (1995): 858–61.

1.454 Lessing, Gotthold E. *Handbuch des Opern-Repertoires.* New ed. 393 pp. London; New York: Boosey & Hawkes, 1952.

An organized compilation of facts related to the performance of 392 operas in the current repertoire, with an emphasis on German titles. The entries include information on casts of characters, locales of action, instrumentation, duration of acts, dates of first performance, and publishers of music. Intended for use by theatrical managers, conductors, and dramatists and in libraries.

1.455 Loewenberg, Alfred. *Annals of Opera, 1597–1940, Compiled from the Original Sources.* 3rd ed., revised and corrected by Harold Rosenthal. xxv pp. + 1,756 cols. Totowa, N.J.: Rowman and Littlefield; London: J. Calder, 1978.

First ed., 1943, by W. Heffer, Cambridge, England, 879 pp., and subsequently published in a 2nd revised and corrected ed. by Societas Bibliographica, Geneva, 1955, in 2 vols. The 1955 ed. was reprinted by Rowman and Littlefield, New York, 1970, and by the Scholarly Press, St. Clair Shores, Mich., 1972.

A strictly chronological approach to opera research. Part 1 is a chronological list of over 4,000 operas by date of first performance, including (with a few exceptions) only works known to have been produced. The list is limited to older operas that are extant and modern ones that have created interest outside their country of origin. Each entry includes the composer's name, the original title of the work, and English translation for all languages except German, French, and Italian. The librettist is identified and the place and date of the first performance are given. Part 2 is an index by title, composer, and librettist, with a general index for other names, places, and subjects. This is a work of distinguished scholarship, essential for the historical study of opera.

The 2nd ed. is reviewed by Edward N. Waters in *Notes* 13 (1956): 285–86. The 3rd ed. is reviewed by Margaret Ross Griffel in *CM* 31 (1981): 75–77, by George Louis Mayer in *ARBA* 11 (1980): no. 976, and by Andrew Porter in *Notes* 36 (1979): 358–59.

1.456 Manferrari, Umberto. *Dizionario universale delle opere melodramatiche.* 3 vols. Florence: Sansoni, 1954–55. (Contributi alla biblioteca bibliografica italica, 4, 8, 10)

One of the most comprehensive lists of opera before Stieger's work (**1.476**). The entries are arranged by composer, giving title, librettist, and place and date of first performance in other opera houses. There is a typescript index of librettists cited in entries composed before 1801 that was prepared in Venice in 1966.

1.457 Mezzanotte, Riccardo. *The Simon and Schuster Book of the Opera: A Complete Reference Guide—1597 to the Present.* Trans. from Italian by Catherine Atthill et al. 512 pp. New York: Simon & Schuster, 1978.

A translation of *L'opera: Repertorio della lirica dal 1597,* published in Milan, 1977, by A. Mondadori. The German version, *Oper: Eine illustrierte Darstellung der Oper von 1597 bis zur Gegenwart,* trans. by Brigitte de Grandis Grossmann and Sigrid Oswald, was published in Laaber, Germany, by Laaber-Verlag and in Wiesbaden by Drei Lilien Verlag in 1981 (508 pp.). A Spanish ed., *La opera: Enciclopedia del arte lírico,* trans. by Juan Novella Domingo, was published by Aguilar, Madrid, in 1981 (518 pp.). The British ed. was titled *Phaidon Book of the Opera: A Survey of 780 Operas from 1597,* published in Oxford by Phaidon in 1979 (511 pp.).

A copiously illustrated, chronologically arranged collection of descriptions and synopses, with the first cast cited if known. There are indexes of titles and composers, librettists, and sources.

1.458 Moore, Frank L. *Crowell's Handbook of World Opera.* 683 pp. New York: Thomas Y. Crowell, 1961.

Reprinted by Greenwood Press, Westport, Conn., in 1974. The English ed. was published as *The Handbook of World Opera,* by Arthur Baker, London, in 1962.

A rich accumulation of facts under such headings as opera titles, opera characters, first lines and titles of famous musical numbers, opera chronology, glossary, and melodic themes of the most famous numbers, with numerous indexes.

Reviewed by Edward N. Waters in *Notes* (1962): 258–59.

1.459 Northouse, Cameron. *Twentieth Century Opera in England and the United States.* 400 pp. Boston, Mass.: G.K. Hall, 1976.

A chronological list of first performances, 1900–74, with another list of operas with unknown premiere dates, organized by composer. The appendixes include a list of operas based on literary works and a list of published operas. There are indexes to composers, librettists, opera titles, literary titles, and literary authors.

Reviewed by Irwin Kraus in *Notes* 34 (1977): 340–42.

1.460 Orrey, Leslie. *The Encyclopedia of Opera.* 376 pp. London: Pitman; New York: Scribner's, 1976.

Brief signed articles on people, characters, titles, terms, places, plots, and subjects, including musical comedies in its scope. The main body of the work is preceded by a short history of the bibliography of opera. Gilbert Chase served as advisory editor.

Reviewed by Irwin Kraus in *Notes* 34 (1977): 340–42.

1.461 Osborne, Charles. *The Dictionary of the Opera.* 382 pp. New York: Simon & Schuster, 1983.

A convenient, illustrated source for the opera enthusiast, it provides brief entries on over 300 composers, 800 singers, designers, conductors, and directors, as well as brief synopses of over 570 operas, including place and date of first performances. No bibliographical references are provided. A separate section is devoted to short histories of leading opera houses.

Reviewed by Allie Wise Goudy in *ARBA* 15 (1984): no. 893.

1.462* Peterson, Bernard L., Jr. *A Century of Musicals in Black and White: An Encyclopedia of Musical Stage Works, by, about, or involving African Americans.* 529 pp. Westport, Conn.: Greenwood Press, 1993.

A reference work designed to represent the collaboration between White and Black artists, including composers, librettists, musicians, producers, and performers, covering the period from 1873 to 1992. There is a strong list of bibliographical references (pp. 420–29).

Reviewed by Suzanne Flandreau in *Notes* 52 (1996): 797–99 and by John E. Druesedow in *Choice* 31 (1994): 1562.

1.463 Regler-Bellinger, Brigitte, Wolfgang Schenck, and **Hans Winking.** *Knaurs grosser Opernführer.* 672 pp. Munich: Droemer Knaur, 1983.

An earlier ed., *Knaurs Opernführer,* edited by Gerhart von Westermann and Karl Schumann, was published by Droemer/Knaur in Munich and Zurich, 1969, 511 pp. An English ed., *Opera Guide,* edited and introduced by Harold D. Rosenthal and trans. by Anne Ross, was adapted from an earlier ed. and published by E.P. Dutton, New York, 1965, 584 pp.

A dictionary, known as *Opernführer,* including bibliographical references, a discography (pp. 633–50), and indexes.

1.464 Rich, Maria F. *Directory of American Contemporary Operas.* 79 pp. New York: Central Opera Service, 1967.

A special issue of the *Central Opera Bulletin* 10 (December 1967): no. 2.

A list of operas by American composers premiered since 1930, arranged alphabetically by composer, with place of performance, librettist, cast, number of acts, and availability.

1.465 Rich, Maria F. *Who's Who in Opera: An International Biographical Directory of Singers, Conductors, Directors, Designers, and Administrators, also Including Profiles of 101 Opera Companies.* 684 pp. New York: Arno Press, 1976.

Information on 2,300 artists in 144 opera companies. The profiles of opera companies include recent repertoires and budgets. There is also a directory of international agents.

Reviewed by Kären Nagy in *Notes* 34 (1977): 91 and by Irwin Kraus in *Notes* 34 (1977): 340–42.

1.466 Rieck, Waldemar. *Opera Plots: An Index to the Stories of Operas, Operettas, etc., from the Sixteenth to the Twentieth Century.* 102 pp. New York: New York Public Library, 1927.

Reprinted in 1927 from four issues of the *Bulletin of the New York Public Library,* January–April, 1926.

Over 200 books and editions published in English, French, German, and Danish in the past 80 years have been indexed; 998 composers are represented by more than 2,775 operatic works.

Two more recent titles along these lines are by Jeanette Drone (**1.433**) and William Studwell (**1.479**).

1.467 Riemann, Hugo. *Opern-Handbuch, Repertorium der dramatisch-musikalischen Litteratur (Opern, Operetten, Ballette, Melodramen, Pantomimen, Oratorien, dramatische Kantaten u.s.w.).* 862 pp. Leipzig: C.A. Koch, 1887.

Originally published in fascicles, including a concluding supplement by C. A. Koch, 1881–86. Published by Koch in one volume, including the first supplement, in 1887. Intended as an opera supplement to Riemann's *Lexikon* (**1.45**). The 1892 ed., which includes the 2nd supplement, 1892, was reprinted by Olms, Hildesheim, Germany, in 1979 (862 pp.).

Title articles give genre, number of acts, composer, librettist, and first performance; the composer articles include dates and a chronological operas list, and the librettist entries have dates and chief activity.

1.468 Ross, Anne. *The Opera Directory.* 566 pp. London: John Calder; New York: Sterling Publishing Co., 1961.

Issued with various titles under the imprints of publishers in Paris, Geneva, and Berlin.

An international sourcebook of opera facts and figures, with introductions and headings in six languages (English, French, German, Italian, Spanish, and Russian). The material is organized under 13 headings, including opera singers, conductors, producers and designers, technical staff, theaters and producing organizations, festivals, living composers, works by living composers, librettists, colleges and schools of music, casting index, and glossary.

1.469* Sadie, Stanley, and Christine Bashford. *The New Grove Dictionary of Opera.* 4 vols. London: Macmillan; New York: Grove's Dictionaries of Music, 1992.

An almost comprehensive opera reference work, with 80 to 90% of its contents written specifically for this edition by 1,300 contributors. There is strong coverage of persons (especially composers and singers, but also including conductors, librettists, designers, producers, directors, dancers, choreographers, patrons, and impresarios). Other entries include operas (listed by title in the original language), opera houses, national opera traditions, and opera-related terms (allegory, censorship, rehearsals, seating, sociology, and versifications). The "Libretto" entry includes an extensive bibliography. Also included are indexes of role names and of incipits of arias and ensembles.

Robert Cowden, in Appendix II of his *Classical Singers of the Opera and Recital Stages: A Bibliography of Biographical Materials,* indexes the singers given individual entries.

Reviewed by Robert Craft in *TLS* 4699 (1993): 16, by George Louis Mayer in *ARBA* 25 (1994): no. 1356, by John Simon in *National Review* 45 (April 26 1993): 50, by Paul Griffiths in *The New Yorker* 69 (March 8 1993): 108–10, by Charles Rosen in *The New York Review of Books* 40 (April 22 1993): 10, by Susan T. Sommer in *Fontes* 41 (1994): 223–24, by Matthew Gurewitsch in *The Yale Review* 82 (January 1994): 126–27, and by Neil Zaslaw in *MQ* 78 (1994): 149–58, and as one of the works covered by David Littlejohn's "Everything You Ever Wanted to Know about Opera: A Review-Essay of Recent Reference Works," in *Notes* 51 (1995): 843–54.

1.470* Salem, James. *A Guide to Critical Reviews, Part II: The Musical, 1909–1989.* 3rd ed. 820 pp. Metuchen, N.J.: The Scarecrow Press, 1991.

First ed., 1967, 353 pp. Second ed., 1976.

A list of sources for reviews of musical plays on the New York stage, covering general circulation American and Canadian periodicals and the *New York Times.* The musicals are listed alphabetically by title and include Broadway musicals, some off-Broadway and off-off-Broadway shows, and some musicals that closed during pre-Broadway tryouts. Operas (except *Porgy and Bess* and some works by Marc Blitzstein and Gian Carlo Menotti) and many operettas are excluded. Each entry gives author, composer, lyricist, and often staging and production credits, along with the opening date, number of performances, and citations to critical reviews. There are three indexes: authors, composers, and lyricists; directors, designers, and choreographers; and original works and authors (sources for stories of musical plays). Appendixes list long-running musicals, Pulitzer Prize musicals, New York Drama Critics' Circle Award musicals, and Tony Award musicals.

The first ed. is reviewed by Ellen Kenny in *Notes* 25 (1968): 245–46.

1.471 Seeger, Horst. *Opern-Lexikon.* 3rd enlarged ed. 702 pp. Wilhelmshaven, Germany: Noetzel Verlag, Heinrichshofen Bücher, 1987.

The 1st ed. was published as *Opernlexikon* by Henschelverlag Kunst und Ges., Berlin, 1978, 598 pp. A 2-vol. 3rd ed. was published in 1979 by Rowohlt in Reinbek bei Hamburg as part of the series Rororo Handbuch.

A fact-packed opera dictionary with about 10,000 entries, covering operas and their composers, performers and members of the production staff, opera characters and opera companies, opera terminology, and first-line access to opera selections, with emphasis on the repertoire of Eastern Europe and the former Soviet Union.

The 1979 ed. is reviewed by Egon Voss in *Neue Zeitschrift* 40 (1979): 422; the 1987 ed. is reviewed by Ruth W. Tucker in *Notes* 47 (1991): 785–87.

1.472 Sharp, Harold S., and **Marjorie Z. Sharp.** *Index to Characters in the Performing Arts.* 4 vols. in 6. New York: Scarecrow Press, 1966–73.

Partial contents: Part 2, *Opera and Musical Productions* (2 vols.); Part 3, *Ballets.*

An index of which the 2nd part (1969) identifies characters in operas, ballad operas, operettas, musical comedies, and plays in which music is introduced; the coverage ranges from the 13th century to the 1965–66 Broadway season and includes 2,542 musical productions and approximately 20,000 of their characters. There are lists of both the characters covered and the productions from which the characters are derived. Part 3 (1972) is a finding list for approximately 3,000 characters from 818 ballets with plots, with a list of ballets covered.

1.473* Simas, Rick. *The Musicals No One Came to See: A Guidebook to Four Decades of Musical-Comedy Casualties on Broadway, Off-Broadway and in Out-of-Town Try-Out, 1943–1983.* 639 pp. New York: Garland, 1987. (Garland reference library of the humanities, 563)

A comprehensive reference documenting four decades of musical shows premiering in New York between 1943 and 1983 that ran for fewer than 300 performances or that closed on tryout. Among these are such gems as *Pal Joey, Porgy and Bess,* and *Candide,* which were flops until their later revivals. Also included is an appendix of opening dates and three indexes listing show titles, sources of adaptations, and source authors, librettists, and composers and lyricists.

Reviewed by Ann P. Basart in *CNV* 122 (1988): 20–21.

1.474* Smith, Eric Ledell. *Blacks in Opera: An Encyclopedia of People and Companies.* 236 pp. Jefferson, N.C.: McFarland, 1994.

Photographs, bibliography, and indexes. Lists of performers, directors, and production personnel note musical education, repertoire, companies and orchestras performed with, birth and death dates, recordings, and videos.

1.475 Smith, William C. *The Italian Opera and Contemporary Ballet in London, 1789–1820: A Record of Performances and Players with Reports from the Journals of the Time.* 191 pp. London: Society for Theatre Research, 1955. (Society for Theatre Research. Annual publication, 1953–54)

Cites 618 works produced in London theaters during the period under consideration, with commentary by the author and quotations from contemporary sources. There are indexes of operas, burlettas, cantatas; ballets and divertissements; and singers, ballet personnel, composers, and instrumentalists.

Reviewed by Michael M. Winesanker in *Notes* 12 (1955): 587–98.

1.476 Stieger, Franz. *Opernlexikon / Opera Catalogue / Lexique des opéras / Dizionario operistico.* Edited by Franz Grasberger. 4 parts in 11 vols. Tutzing, Germany: Schneider, 1975–83.

Contents: *Title Catalog,* 3 vols.; *Composers,* 3 vols.; *Librettists,* 3 vols.; *Appendix,* 2 vols.

A thorough approach to the bibliography of opera. Each of the main vols. presents permutations of the same information: opera title, composer, librettist, premiere date and place, genre, or opus number. All information is taken from the sources. 50,000 titles of theatrical works are listed, as well as 3,200 ballets and 3,400 oratorios. Only premieres are listed; revisions of a work are not included. The appendixes provide various chronological lists: operas composed before composers who were also librettists, an index to composers with additional full entries included, German opera and Singspiel by period, and Italian opera in Italy and elsewhere, by period.

Reviewed by Sven Hansell in *Fontes* 23 (1976): 199–201.

1.477* Stockdale, F. M., and **M. R. Dreyer.** *The International Opera Guide.* 342 pp. North Pomfret, Vt.: Trafalgar Square, 1989.

A reference work in two parts: the first on opera houses and their companies, the second on operas and their composers.

Reviewed by Norma Jean Lamb in *Notes* 48 (1991): 537–38.

1.478* Studwell, William E., and **David A. Hamilton.** *Ballet Plot Index: A Guide to Locating Plots and Descriptions of Ballets and Associated Material.* 466 pp. New York: Garland Publishing, 1987. (Garland reference library of the humanities, 756)

Access to the plots in 53 collections, international in scope, juvenile and adult, published 1926–82. Around 1,600 titles are located, both directly composed and derived.

Reviewed by Marlene M. Wong in *Notes* 47 (1990): 402–4.

1.479* Studwell, William E., and **David A. Hamilton.** *Opera Plot Index: A Guide to Locating Plots and Descriptions of Opera, Operettas, and Other Works of the Musical Theater, and Associated Material.* 466 pp. New York: Garland Publishing, 1990. (Garland reference library of the humanities, 1099)

An index of opera synopses in collection, similar to those by Drone (**1.433**) and Rieck (**1.466**).

Reviewed by Ray Reeder in *Notes* 47 (1991): 406–7 and by J.S. Sauer in *Choice* 28 (1990): 288.

1.480 Suskind, Steven. *Show Tunes, 1905–1991: The Songs, Shows, and Careers of Broadway's Major Composers.* xxviii + 769 pp. Revised and expanded ed. New York: Limelight Editions, 1992.

First published by Dodd, Mead in New York, 1986, xxii + 728 pp.

A study of 30 composers with a section on notable Broadway scores by other composers, a chronological list of productions, a collaborator reference list, and a bibliography. There are indexes to song titles, show titles, and persons.

The first ed. is reviewed by Ann P. Basart in *CNV* 128 (1998): 9.

1.481 Towers, John. *Dictionary-Catalogue of Operas and Operettas Which Have Been Performed on the Public Stage.* 1,045 pp. Morgantown, W.V.: Acme Publishing Company, 1910.

Reprinted in 2 vols. by Da Capo Press, New York, 1967.

A list, arranged by title, of 28,015 operas, giving for each composer his or her nationality and dates and supplying alternative and transliterated titles as needed. There is a composer index, but no information on librettists or historical and descriptive material is supplied.

Reviewed by Donald Krummel in *Notes* 24 (1968): 502–3.

1.482 Vallance, Tom. *The American Musical.* 192 pp. London: A. Zwemmer; New York: Castle Books, 1970.

An illustrated biographical dictionary with brief entries and more lengthy lists of credits for persons connected with staged or filmed musicals, including composers, authors, performers, and directors. No sources are cited. There is an index to shows listed in the entries.

1.483 Várnai, Péter. *Operalexikon.* 533 pp. Budapest: Zenemukiadó, 1975.

A Hungarian dictionary of opera, especially strong on Eastern European opera.

1.484 Wallace, Mary Elaine, and **Robert Wallace.** *Opera Scenes for Class and Stage.* xlviii + 260 pp. Carbondale, Ill.: Southern Illinois University Press, 1979. *More Opera Scenes for Class and*

Stage from One Hundred Selected Operas. xli + 201 pp. Carbondale, Ill.: Southern Illinois University Press, 1990.

A ready-reference, 2-vol. source to excerpts from over 200 operas, arranged by voice category and including a guide to opera ensembles, for opera workshop use. The entries give an identification of excerpts, duration, and a summary of the dramatic situation. There is a bibliography and indexes of operas, composers, arias and ensembles, and editions of piano–vocal scores.

The 1st vol. is reviewed by Richard Le Sueur in *Notes* 36 (1980): 651–52.

1.485 Warrack, John, and **Ewan West.** *The Oxford Dictionary of Opera.* 782 pp. Oxford: Oxford University Press, 1992.

An updating of the *Concise Oxford Dictionary of Opera,* 1986, whose 1st ed. was published in 1964, with the 2nd following in 1979. A further update appeared in 1994. A 1996 ed., *The Concise Oxford Dictionary of Opera,* was anticipated.

A dictionary covering such topics as synopses, famous arias, singers, places, styles, technical terms, bibliographies, and opera history.

Reviewed in *M&L* 74 (1993): 579–81 by Julian Budden, and as one of the works covered by David Littlejohn's "Everything You Ever Wanted to Know about Opera: A Review-Essay of Recent Reference Works," in *Notes* 51 (1995): 861–64. The 1979 2nd ed. is reviewed by Koraljka Lockhart in *ARBA* 25 (1994): no. 1357 and by Susan T. Sommer in *Notes* 36 (1980): 660.

1.486 White, Eric Walter. *A Register of First Performances of English Operas and Semi-Operas from the 16th Century to 1980.* 130 pp. London: Society for Theatre Research, 1983.

A chronological list of first public performances of English operas (defined as those by British composers with English librettos) and "semi-operas" (masques, farce jigs, pasticcios, burlettas, dramatic operas, and operettas). Works with no spoken dialogue are identified. The earliest entry is "1517 or somewhat after" and the last is for September 2, 1980. Each entry gives composer name, title of work, name of librettist, type of work, number of acts, and place of first performance, where known. Some entries are annotated. There are also cross-references to later adaptions and a title index.

1.487* Wild, Nicole. *Dictionnaire des théâtres parisiens au XIXe siècle: Les théâtres et la musique.* 509 pp. Paris: Aux Amateurs de livres, 1989. (Domaine musicologique, 4 [i.e., 6])

A dictionary of Parisian theaters, including opera houses. Despite the title, coverage of some houses begins before the 19th century. Each entry gives a brief history, the various names by which the theater has been known, repertoire produced, and a roll of the various production personnel on the staff. The bibliographical references (pp. 457–80) include both manuscript and print sources. There is a name index (pp. 483–505), giving the subject's profession (directeur, copiste, chef d'orchestre) as well as page citations.

Reviewed by David A. Day in *Notes* 48 (1991): 111–12.

MUSICAL INSTRUMENTS: MAKERS, PERFORMERS, AND TERMINOLOGY

There is a substantial group of reference books concerned with the construction, performance, terminology, and iconography of musical instruments. A great deal of work has been done with respect to the violin, and an increasing number of reference tools are devoted to keyboard and wind instruments. For specific descriptions, prices, and illustrations of individual instruments, particularly those of the string family, the researcher should not neglect the catalogs of various dealers (Hamma, Herrmann, Hill, Lyon and Healy, Wurlitzer, etc.). These are not included in the list below. For the iconography of musical instruments, see Buchner (**1.496**), Besseler (**2.41**), Kinsky (**2.52**), and Komma (**2.53**), as well as Chapter 8.

GENERAL WORKS

1.488 Sadie, Stanley. *The New Grove Dictionary of Musical Instruments.* 3 vols. London: Macmillan Press; New York: Grove's Dictionaries of Music, 1984.

A copiously illustrated dictionary of musical instruments based on modern scholarship, unique in its genre. The *Dictionary* is composed of articles on Western and non-Western musical instruments, historical and modern, their makers, and performance practices, many derived but largely rewritten from articles in *The New Grove* (**1.48**), with good bibliographical support. There is extensive coverage of folk and ethnic instruments by experts in the regions in which the instruments are located. The numerous cross-references linking articles and terms make up for the lack of an index by culture or region.

Reviewed by Mary Rasmussen in *Notes* 42 (1986): 529–32, by André P. Larsen in *JAMS* 41 (1988): 375–82, by John E. Druesedow in *Choice* 22 (1985): 1478, by William Malm in *Ethnomusicology* 30 (1986): 337–38, and by George Lewis Mayer in *ARBA* 17 (1986): no. 1252.

1.489* Acht, Rob van. *Checklist of Technical Drawings of Musical Instruments in Public Collections of the World.* 185 pp. Celle, Germany: Moeck; The Hague: Haags Gemeentemuseum, 1992.

A well-organized guide to a historically wide range of instruments and their construction, including bibliographical references and an index.

1.490 Ames, David W., and Anthony V. King. *Glossary of Hausa Music and Its Social Contexts.* 184 pp. Evanston, Ill.: Northwestern University Press, 1971.

A technical glossary of musical instruments and sound production providing indicators of the sociocultural context of musical performance of the sub-Saharan Hausa culture. There are indexes of Hausa terms and English equivalents.

Reviewed by Charlotte J. Frisbie in the *Yearbook of the International Folk Music Council* 7 (1975): 159–60.

1.491* Anoyanakis, Fivos, Fivi Caramerou, and Christopher N. W. Klint. *Greek Popular Musical Instruments.* Trans. from the Greek by Christopher N. W. Klint. 2nd ed. 414 pp. Athens: Melissa Publishing House, 1991.

The 1st ed. was published in Athens by the National Bank of Greece in 1979, 414 pp.

Detailed descriptions and illustrations of musical instruments that are an important part of Greek musical performances, both folk and more commercially based. Also included are a bibliography (pp. 380–82) and a discography (pp. 383–84).

Reviewed by Anthony Baines in the *Galpin Society Journal* 34 (1981): 153–54, by Helen Myers in *MT* 122 (1981): 315, and by Margaret Anne Downie in *AMISN* 90 (1983): 118–21.

1.492 Baines, Anthony. *European and American Musical Instruments.* 174 pp. + 112 plates. London: Batsford; New York: Viking Press, 1966.

Reprinted in London by Chancellor in 1983.

A "pictorial museum" of musical instruments selected from American and European collections. The instruments are grouped by families: string, woodwind, brass, and percussion. Much precise technical information on the individual instruments is included, as well as historical background. The present location of all instruments is given.

Reviewed by Albert Protz in *Die Musikforschung* 21 (1968): 388–89.

1.493* Baines, Anthony. *The Oxford Companion to Musical Instruments.* 404 pp. Oxford; New York: Oxford University Press, 1992.

A generously illustrated dictionary of Western and non-Western musical instruments, aimed at the musical amateur. Electronic instruments are omitted. There are musical examples, an index of instrument makers, and a bibliography.

Reviewed, with errata, by Laurence Libin in *M&L* 74 (1993): 565–66 and by Richard H. Swain in *ARBA* 25 (1994): no. 1338.

1.494 Bragard, Roger, and **Ferdinand J. de Hen.** *Musical Instruments in Art and History.* Trans. by Bill Hopkins. 281 pp. + 119 plates. New York: Viking Press, 1968. (A studio book)

Originally published as *Les instruments de musique dans l'art et l'histoire* by the Société française du livre in Paris, 1967 (258 pp.). A 2nd ed. was published in Brussels by A. deVisscher in 1973 (270 pp.). A German ed., *Musikinstrumente aus zwei Jahrtausenden,* was trans. by Dieter Krickeberg (Stuttgart: Belser Verlag, 1968). An Italian ed., *Strumenti musicali nell'arte e nella storia,* was published in Milan by Bramante in 1967 (257 pp.), and a Spanish ed., *Instrumentos de música,* was published in Barcelona by Ediciones Daimon, Manuel Tamayo, 1975 (270 pp.).

An attractive picture book of early instruments, with popular commentary.

Reviewed by Edmund A. Bowles in *Notes* 25 (1969): 735–36 and by Mary Remnant in *M&L* 50 (1969): 301–3. The German ed. is reviewed by J. H. van der Meer in *Die Musikforschung* 24 (1971): 481–83.

1.495* Bruni, Antonio Bartolomeo. *Un inventaire sous la terreur: État des instruments de musique relevé chez les émigrés et condamnés.* Introduction, biographical notices, and notes by Jules Gallay. xxxiv + 238 pp. Paris: G. Chamerot, 1890.

Reprinted by Minkoff in 1984.

Official inventories of musical instruments seized from the homes of emigrants and those condemned during the French Revolution, with the names of the makers and, occasionally, the date.

1.496 Buchner, Alexandr. *Musical Instruments: An Illustrated History.* Trans. by Borek Vancura. 274 pp. New York: Crown, 1973.

Previously issued as *Musical Instruments through the Ages,* with an earlier trans. by Iris Urwin (37 pp. + 323 plates), London, by Spring Books, 1956. First published in Czech by Artia, Prague. The German ed. was published as *Musikinstrumente im Wandel der Zeiten.*

Not a dictionary or encyclopedia, but important as a collection of 323 beautifully reproduced plates of musical instruments and their representations of musical performance in painting, engraving, and sculpture.

1.497 Buchner, Alexandr. *Musikinstrumente der Völker.* Trans. into German by O. Guth. 295 pp. Hanau/Main, Germany: Dausien, 1968.

Published at the same time as *Hudební nástroje národů* in Prague by Artia. Published in English as *Folk Music Instruments* by Crown, New York, in 1972.

A pictorial work with focus on European folk music instruments.

1.498 Crane, Frederick. *Extant Medieval Musical Instruments: A Provisional Catalogue by Types.* 105 pp. Iowa City, Iowa: University of Iowa Press, 1972.

Over 550 brief descriptions of the surviving medieval musical instruments in art and archeological museums throughout the world, as well as of instruments known to exist in modern times and now lost. The instruments are classified according to the Hornbostel–Sachs system (idiophones, chordophones, and aerophones). There are 30 pen sketches of instruments and a bibliography (pp. 91–105).

Reviewed by Howard Mayer Brown in *EM* 1 (1973): 239–41, by Edward M. Ripin in *AMISJ* 1 (1975): 131–33, and by Bruce Bellingham in *Notes* 30 (1973): 280.

1.499* Curtis, Tony. *Musical Instruments.* 128 pp. Glenmayne, England; Galashiels, Scotland: Lyle Publications, 1978. (Antiques and their values)

A classified list of antique musical instruments and their then-current market value.

Reviewed by Hermann Moeck in *Tibia* 1 (1980): 53.

1.500 The Diagram Group. *Musical Instruments of the World: An Illustrated Encyclopedia.* 320 pp. London: Paddington Press/Two Continents Publishing Group; New York: Facts on File, 1976. Reprinted in New York by Bantam Books, 1978. Excerpts were published as *Scribner Guide to Orchestral Instruments* (New York: C. Scribner's Sons, 1983), 121 pp.

Drawings of instruments (orchestra, folk, non-Western, and ancient), some with diagrams showing details of construction or methods of sound production and music making. For orchestral instruments, the information given includes pitch range, works featuring the instrument, its position in the orchestra, and musical excerpts. Drawings are accompanied by brief prose explications, and there are definitions of related terms. There are an index and a bibliography.

Reviewed by Stephen M. Fry in *Notes* 33 (1977): 847, by Laurence Libin in *Notes* 34 (1977): 336–40, and by Charles D. Patterson in *ARBA* 11 (1980): no. 973.

1.501* Groce, Nancy. *Musical Instrument Makers of New York: A Directory of Eighteenth- and Nineteenth-Century Urban Craftsmen.* xxi + 200 pp. Stuyvesant, N.Y.: Pendragon Press, 1991. (Annotated reference tools in music, 4)

A directory of New York instrument makers active before 1890. The entries supply addresses and dates and give information on the noncraft elements of the subjects' careers.

Reviewed by Robert E. Eliason in *Notes* 49 (1993): 1,091–92.

1.502* Haine, Malou. *Les facteurs d'instruments de musique à Paris au XIXe siècle: Des artisans face à l'industrialisation.* 472 pp. Brussels: Éditions de l'Université de Bruxelles, 1985. (Faculté de philosophie et lettres, 94)

A liberally illustrated study of 19th-century Parisian musical instrument makers.

Reviewed by Tula Giannini in *Notes* 49 (1992): 108–10 and by Theodore Zeldin in *M&L* 69 (1988): 279–80.

1.503 *Handbuch der europäischen Volksmusikinstrumente.* Edited by the Institut für Deutsche Volkskunde Berlin in conjunction with the Musikhistorischen Museum Stockholm by Ernst Emsheimer and Erich Stockmann. 4 vols. in 5 (to date). Leipzig: Deutscher Verlag für Musik, 1968–86.

Contents of Series I: Band 1. Sárosi, Bálint. *Die Volksmusikinstrumente Ungarns,* 1968, 148 pp. Band 2. Kunz, Ludvík. *Die Volksmusikinstrumente der Tschechoslowakei,* 1974, 2 vols. Band 4. Bachmann-Geiser, Barbara. *Die Volksmusikinstrumente der Schweiz,* 1981, 131 pp. Band 5. Kumer, Zmaga. *Die Volksmusikinstrumente im Slowenien,* Ljubljana, Slovenia: Slovenska akademija znanosti in umetnosti, Znastvenoraziskovalni center SAZU, Institut za slovensko narodopisje, 1986, 107 pp.

A series projected to describe folk instruments in the Czech Republic, Slovakia, Bulgaria, the nations of the former Soviet Union, Greece, Portugal, Switzerland, Turkey, and Norway.

Band 4 is reviewed by Thomas Vennum, Jr., in *Ethnomusicology* 29 (1985): 517–20.

1.504 Haupt, Helga. "Wiener Instrumentenbauer von 1791 bis 1815." In *Studien zur Musikwissenschaft, Beihefte der Denkmäler der Tonkunst in Österreich,* Bd. 24, pp. 120–84. Graz, Austria: Hermann Böhlau, 1960.

A well-documented study, alphabetically listing Viennese instrument makers in all categories, with addresses and dates of activity for each entry.

1.505* Kartomi, Margaret J. *On Concepts and Classifications of Musical Instruments.* 329 pp. Chicago, Ill.: University of Chicago Press, 1990. (Chicago studies in ethnomusicology)

Not a dictionary or encyclopedia but a solid examination of the various approaches to labeling musical instruments by classification.

Reviewed by Jay Weitz in *Fontes* 39 (1992): 363–64, by Andrew Kaye in *Notes* 48 (1992): 915, and by Jeremy Montagu in the *Galpin Society Journal* 49 (1996): 214.

1.506* Maersch, Klaus. *Bildwörterbuch Musikinstrumente: Gliederung, Baugruppen, Bauteile, Bauelemente.* 218 pp. Mainz; New York: Schott, 1987.

A collection of line drawings of Western musical instruments. Each instrument is labeled with the German technical terms for the instrument's various parts.

1.507 Marcuse, Sibyl. *Musical Instruments: A Comprehensive Dictionary.* Corrected ed. 608 pp. New York: W.W. Norton, 1975. (The Norton library)

First published in Garden City, N.Y., by Doubleday. Reprinted in London by Country Life in 1966 (608 pp.).

Intended to serve English language readers as Sachs's *Real-Lexikon* (**1.510**) does German. The coverage is historical and international in scope, although gaps in its non-European and folk instrument listings are acknowledged. There is a list of sources about musical instruments (pp. 603–8).

Reviewed by Stephen M. Fry in *Notes* 32 (1976): 556.

1.508* Rasof, Henry. *The Folk, Country and Bluegrass Musician's Catalogue: A Complete Sourcebook for Guitar, Banjo, Fiddle, Bass, Dulcimer, Mandolin, Autoharp, Harmonica, and More.* 192 pp. New York: St. Martin's Press, 1982.

A compilation of information on American folk instruments, including their construction, price range, dealers, discography, and bibliography for instruction and repair.

1.509 Sachs, Curt. *Handbuch der Musikinstrumentenkunde.* 2nd ed. 419 pp. Leipzig: Breitkopf & Härtel, 1930. (Kleine Handbücher der Musikgeschichte nach Gattungen, 12)

First ed., 1920. Reprinted in Germany by G. Olms, Hildesheim, and Breitkopf & Härtel, Wiesbaden, both in 1967.

Not precisely a dictionary but a systematic and historical description of musical instruments classified according to their methods of sound production: idiophones, membranophones, chordophones, and aerophones. Much of the same ground is covered in Sachs's *The History of Musical Instruments* (New York: W.W. Norton, 1940), in which the approach is chronological and by cultural area.

1.510 Sachs, Curt. *Real-Lexikon der Musikinstrumente.* Revised and enlarged ed. xxiii + 451 pp. New York: Dover Publications, 1964. (American Musicological Society Music Library Association. Reprint series)

First published in Berlin by G. Olms in 1913, 442 pp. Reprinted in Hildesheim, Germany, by G. Olms in 1962.

The standard technical and historical dictionary of instruments of all periods and countries. The entries include the names of instruments and parts of instruments in some 120 languages and dialects of Europe, Africa, and Asia, with illustrations and locations of examples in instrument collections. Some bibliographies are provided. This is Sachs's great work in this field and for decades was one of the best sources of information on instruments.

Reviewed by Guy Oldham in *MT* 107 (1966): 1064–66 and by J. A. Westrup in *M&L* 43 (1966): 277–78.

1.511 Stiller, Andrew. *Handbook of Instrumentation.* 2nd ed. xxii + 533 pp. Philadelphia, Pa.: Kallisti Music Press, 1994.

The 1st ed. was published in Berkeley by the University of California Press, 1985.

A thorough, well-illustrated compendium of information about a wide range of instruments, planned to be "a guide to the potentials and limitations of every instrument currently in use for the performance of classical and popular music in North America." There are 5 appendixes and a bibliography of works consulted.

1.512 Tintori, Giampiero. *Gli strumenti musicali: Con circa 1,000 esempli musicali e 138 tavole fuori testo.* Ricerca iconografia di Alberto Basso. 2 vols. 138 plates. Turin: Unione Tipografico-Editrice Torinese, 1971.

A generously illustrated book on musical instruments whose main organization is geographical, with subdivisions covering the various types of instruments. There are numerous musical examples, a comprehensive bibliography and glossary, and a general index.

1.513 Valdrighi, Luigi Francesco. *Nomocheliurgografía antica e moderna, ossia elenco di fabbricatori di strumenti armonici con note espicative a documenti estratti dall'Archivio di Stato in Modena.* 436 pp. Bologna: Forni, 1967. (Bibliotheca musica Bononiensis, I, 3)

Reprint of the Modena ed. of 1884, with 5 supplements originally published 1888–94.

An alphabetical list of musical instrument makers. The 1st section has 3,536 entries, which give name, nationality, birth and death dates, the names of any special instruments, and the school, style, or system. The 2nd section gives fuller biographical treatment of many names mentioned in the first section.

1.514 Winternitz, Emanuel. *Musical Instruments of the Western World.* 259 pp. + 100 plates. London: Thames and Hudson; New York; Toronto: McGraw-Hill Book Co., 1966.

Published in German as *Die schönsten Musikinstrumente des Abendlandes* in Munich by Keyser in 1966 (267 pp.).

A magnificent picture book of music.

Reviewed by Howard Mayer Brown in *Notes* 25 (1968): 223–25.

1.515 Wright, Rowland. *Dictionnaire des instruments de musique: Étude de lexicologie.* 192 pp. London: Battley Bros., 1941.

An etymological dictionary of names for musical instruments mentioned in French writings from ancient times to the end of the 19th century. This is extremely well documented, with precise bibliographical references, and is one of the few dictionaries of terms to use a thoroughly etymological approach.

AUTOMATIC INSTRUMENTS

1.516 Boston, Noel, and **Lyndesay G. Langwill.** *Church and Chamber Barrel-Organs; Their Origin, Makers, Music and Location: A Chapter in English Church Music.* 2nd ed., revised and enlarged. 125 pp. Edinburgh: L.G. Langwill, 1970.

The 1st ed. was published in 1967, 120 pp.

A history and description of the mechanical English barrel organ, with tune lists (secular and sacred), a directory of barrel organ builders, and a directory of churches connected (past and present) with this specialized instrument.

1.517 Bowers, Q. David. *Encyclopedia of Automatic Musical Instruments: Cylinder Music Boxes, Disc Music Boxes, Piano Players and Player Pianos, Coin-Operating Pianos, Orchestrions, Photoplayers, Organettes, Fairground Organs, Calliopes, and Other Self-Playing Instruments Mainly of the 1750–1940 Era; Including a Dictionary of Automatic Musical Instrument Terms.* 1,008 pp. Vestal, N.Y.: Vestal Press, 1972.

A book for collectors of automatic musical instruments, profusely illustrated, with much documentary information.

1.518* Bulleid, H. A. V. *Cylinder Musical Box Technology: Including Makers, Types, Dating and Music.* 292 pp. Vestal, N.Y.: Almar Press, 1994.

An exhaustive, well-illustrated study for cylinder musical box enthusiasts, with a dictionary of makers and dealers, help on dating of boxes, and information on tune sheets and other accessories, as well as on the composers whose works are used and on the appearance of these boxes in film and print. Clear, detailed repair instruction is provided. Includes a brief bibliography and detailed index.

KEYBOARD INSTRUMENTS

1.519* Alink, Gustav A. *International Piano Competitions.* 3 vols. The Hague: G.A. Alink, 1990.

An exhaustive survey of the world of piano competitions. The 1st vol. tells of the methodology used in gathering the information in the 2nd and 3rd volumes. The 2nd vol. lists 15,000 pianists, and the 3rd volume lists the competition results. There are various indexes.

Reviewed by Dean Elder in *Clavier* 46 (1993): 24–26 no. 7.

1.520 Boalch, Donald H. *Makers of the Harpsichord and Clavichord, 1440–1840.* Edited by Charles Mould, with an index of technical terms in seven languages by Andreas H. Roth. 3rd ed. xxxii + 788 pp. Oxford: Clarendon Press/Oxford University Press, 1995.

The 1st ed. was published by G. Ronald, London, 1956, 169 pp.; the 2nd by Oxford University Press in 1974, 225 pp.

An illustrated directory list of makers of early keyboard instruments (pp. 1–214), followed by a directory describing their surviving instruments (pp. 217–690), giving dates, registers, compasses, histories, and present ownership, identifying information from the 2 earlier eds., and a bibliography (pp. 749–80).

The 1st ed. is reviewed by Frank Hubbard in *Notes* 14 (1957): 572–73 and in the *TLS* (December 21 1956); the 2nd ed. is reviewed by Howard Schott in *EM* 3 (1975): 83–85, by Peter Williams in *MT* 115 (1974): 1,049, and by Liliane Omnès in *Revue de Musicologie* 61 (1975): 342–44 no. 2.

1.521* Bonavia-Hunt, Noel A. *Modern Organ Stops: A Practical Guide to Their Nomenclature, Construction, Voicing, Artistic Use with a Glossary of Technical Terms Relating to the Science of Tone Production from Organ Pipes.* 112 pp. London: Musical Opinion, 1923.

Reprinted in Braintree, Mass., by the Organ Literature Foundation, 1975.

A guide whose descriptions are occasionally illustrated, with a glossary (pp. 91–112).

1.522* Clinkscale, Martha Novak. *Makers of the Piano, 1700–1820.* 403 pp. Oxford: Oxford University Press, 1993.

A work useful as an index to hundreds of sources and instruments.

Reviewed by John Koster in *Notes* 51 (1994): 569–73, by Michael Latcham in *AMISN* 23 (February 1994): 5–6, by Nicholas Renouf in *EKJ* 12 (1994): 118–21, by Cyril Ehrlich in *TLS* 4727 (November 5 1993): 7, by Harold J. Diamond in *Choice* 31 (1994): 911, and by Dorothy de Val in *M&L* 76 (1995): 289–91.

1.523* Colt, C. F., and **Antony Miall.** *The Early Piano.* 160 pp. London: Stainer & Bell, 1981.

A description of 36 instruments from Colt's collection of 130 fortepianos. The ones included date from 1775 to 1868, each with a historical introduction and splendid photographs. (The many illustrations include color plates.) There is a brief introductory historical summary and a translation of Hummel's "Elementary Instructions" (1827), plus miscellaneous related information.

1.524* Dubal, David. *The Art of the Piano: Its Performers, Literature, and Recordings.* 476 pp. New York: Summit Books, 1989.

The English ed. was published in London by Tauris in 1990.

A 2-part reference work for the piano-loving amateur. Part 1 (pp. 29–276) is an alphabetical assessment of history's best-known concert pianists; the 2nd part lists, by composer, significant works in the piano repertoire, with occasional recommended performances, although without complete discographic information.

Reviewed by Susan Kagan in *LJ* 114 (September 1 1989): 182 and by Cyril Ehrlich in *TLS* (January 25 1991): 18.

1.525* Fine, Larry. *The Piano Book: Buying and Owning a New or Used Piano.* 3rd ed. 194 pp. Boston, Mass.: Brookside Press; Chicago, Ill.: Independent Publishers Group, 1994.

An evaluation of every brand of piano sold in the U.S. over the preceding 10 years, with current prices. Chapters on piano moving and storage, tuning and servicing, inspecting, Steinways, and the tricks of the trade.

Reviewed by Robert Palmieri in *ARBA* 20 (1989): no. 1215.

1.526* Gellerman, Robert F. *The American Reed Organ: Its History; How It Works, How to Rebuild It: A Treatise on Its History, Restoration and Tuning, with Descriptions of Some Outstanding Collections, Including a Stop Dictionary and a Directory of Reed Organs.* 173 pp. Vestal, N.Y.: Vestal Press, 1973.

A combination of historical study and repair manual, with relevant addresses.

1.527* Gellerman, Robert F. *Gellerman's International Reed Organ Atlas: Some Account of the Various Manufacturers of Reed Organs of Divers Kinds Including Seraphines, Melodeons, Harmoniums, Cabinet Organs, Parlor Organs, Cottage Organs, Organettes, and Player Organs.* 169 pp. Vestal, N.Y.: Vestal Press, 1985.

A dictionary of manufacturers and their model names, with varying amounts of information provided and liberal cross-references. There are occasional illustrations of advertisements and trademarks. The geographical index (pp. 157–69), generally arranged by country, subdivides the U.S. by state. Manufacturers of reed organ components are so indicated.

Reviewed by Robert Skinner in *ARBA* 18 (1987): no. 1242.

1.528* Gillespie, John, and **Anna Gillespie.** *Notable Twentieth-Century Pianists: A Bio-Critical Sourcebook.* 2 vols. xxviii + 910 pp. Westport, Conn.: Greenwood Press, 1995. (Bio-critical sourcebooks on musical performance)

A biographical dictionary with extensive information on 100 pianists, whose entries include commentary on the subject's life, training, career, and style, reviews, selective discographical information, and bibliographical references. The abbreviations for periodicals and newspapers (pp. xv–xix) and the general bibliography (pp. xxi–xxviii) serve the user as a detailed bibliography. There is a thorough name index, with the names of the featured pianists distinguished by boldface.

1.529 Herzog, Hans Kurt. *European Piano Atlas: I. Piano-Nummern deutscher, europäischer und überseeischer Instrumente: Klaviere, Flügel, Cembali, Harmonien bis 1988 / Piano Serial Numbers of German, European and Foreign Instruments: Uprights, Grands, Harpsichords, Harmoniums untill [!] 1988. II, 1400 Klavierbauer, 1600–1925 / Piano Makers.* 7th ed. 159 pp. Frankfurt am Main: E. Bochinsky, 1989. (Schriftenreihe der Musikinstrument, 2)

The 1st ed. was published as *Taschenbuch der Piano-Nummern deutscher, europäischer und überseeischer Instrumente.*

A guide to dating keyboard instruments made in Europe, with text in English, German, French, Italian, and Swedish.

1.530 Hirt, Franz Josef. *Meisterwerke des Klavierbaus / Stringed Keyboard Instruments: Geschichte der Saitenklaviere von 1440 bis 1880.* 235 pp. Olten, Switzerland: Urs Graf Verlag, 1981.

The first German ed. was published in 1955 (521 pp.) and, trans. by M. Boehme-Brown, was published with parallel text in English and German as *Stringed Keyboard Instruments* by Boston Nook and Art Shop, 1968 (465 pp.).

A beautifully illustrated book with full-page photographs and useful information about the history, design, construction, and makers of keyboard instruments.

1.531* Husarik, Stephen. *American Keyboard Artists.* 2nd (1992–93) ed. 488 pp. Chicago, Ill.: Chicago Biographical Center, 1992.

Earlier ed. published in 1989, 538 pp.

A collection of nearly 2,000 entries for keyboard professionals. The entries include information about the principal instrument played, birthplace and date, education, career, performances, broadcasts, repertoire, recordings, competition, publications, bibliography, management, and mailing address. Foreigners appearing frequently in the United States are included. There is a geographic index and another by instrument, with the specialties indicated by number; a numerical translation table follows. Most information was provided by the subjects, with an asterisk at the head of the entry indicating it to be written by the dictionary's staff.

1.532 Irwin, Stevens. *Dictionary of Pipe Organ Stops.* 2nd ed. 422 pp. New York: Schirmer Books; London: Collier Macmillan, 1983.

The 1st ed., 1962. 264 pp. The revised ed. was published in 1965. 276 pp.

A dictionary containing detailed descriptions of more than 600 stops, together with definitions of many other terms connected with the organ and an examination of the acoustic properties of many types of pipes and the various divisions of the organ. The author also compiled the *Dictionary of Hammond-Organ Stops: An Introduction to Playing the Hammond Electric Organ and a Translation of Pipe-Organ Stops into Hammond-Organ Number-Arrangements* (New York: G. Schirmer, 1939), 89 pp.

Reviewed by Roger Fisher in *Organ* 62 (1983): 186–87, by Charles D. Patterson in *ARBA* 16 (1985): no. 1173, and by Klaus Speer in *Notes* 20 (1983): 477–78.

1.533 Lunelli, Renato. "Dizionario degli organari Veneti o attivi nel Veneto." In *Studi e documenti di storia organaria Veneta,* pp. 145–236. Florence: Leo S. Olschki, 1973. (Studi di musica Veneta, 3)

Following the dictionary is a bibliography of sources (pp. 237–51).

1.534 Lyle, Wilson. *A Dictionary of Pianists.* 343 pp. New York: Schirmer Books; London: Hale, 1984.

International in scope, covering 4,000 concert pianists, with brief biographical sketches mentioning instructors and pupils, prizes won, and stylistic characteristics. Also cited are the individual's principal recordings and compositions, if any. There is less coverage of performers on historical instruments. An appendix lists winners of international piano competitions and medalists of conservatories and music schools. There is a list of addresses of competition organizers. No sources are cited.

Reviewed by Marjorie E. Bloss in *ARBA* 17 (1986): no. 1256.

1.535 Michel, Norman Elwood. *Historical Pianos, Harpsichords and Clavichords.* 236 pp. Pico Rivera, Calif.: N. Michel, 1970.

1963 ed., 209 pp., with supplements published in 1963 (8 pp.) and 1966 (10 pp.).

A photograph volume of pianos connected to U.S. presidents, statesmen, and actors, as well as pianos from libraries, historical societies, museums, and other institutions from countries around the world.

1.536 Michel, Norman Elwood. *Michel's Organ Atlas; Organs, Melodeons, Harmoniums, Church Organs, Lap Organs, Barrel Organs.* 128 pp. Pico Rivera, Calif.: N.E. Michel, 1969.

A directory containing 141 photographs and 869 names of organs.

1.537* Palmieri, Robert, and **Margaret W. Palmieri.** *The Piano.* 536 pp. New York: Garland Publishing, Inc., 1993. (Encyclopedia of keyboard instruments, 1; Garland reference library of the humanities, 1131)

The first of a three-volume concentration on the makeup and historical background of the piano, organ, and clavichord and harpsichord. Articles by 76 scholars, each with bibliographies citing source material, are accessible through a generous name/subject index.

Reviewed by Martha Novak Clinkscale in *Notes* 51 (1995): 1,303 and by C. Michael Phillips in *ARBA* 26 (1995): no. 1278.

1.538 *Pierce Piano Atlas.* 8th ed. 416 pp. Long Beach, Calif.: B. Pierce, 1982. Published from 1947 to 1961 as *Michel's Piano Atlas,* edited by Norman Elwood Michel.

A listing of the known American piano manufacturers, with varying amounts of information in each entry. For some companies, no information is cited other than name; for others, there are addresses, a brief business history, and a dated list of serial numbers.

1.539 Samoyault-Verlet, Colombe. *Les facteurs de clavecins parisiens, notices biographiques et documents, 1550–1793.* 191 pp. Paris: Société Française de Musicologie/Heugel et Cie., 1966. (Publications de la Société Française de Musicologie, Ser. 2, 11)

Biographies of 140 Parisian makers of keyboard instruments, from information found large-ly in archival documents.

Reviewed by Maurice A. Byrne in the *Galpin Society Journal* 25 (July 1972): 136–37.

1.540 Schimmel, Klaus. *Piano-Nomenclatur: Ein Bildwörterbuch der Teile von Klavier und Flügel: Deutsch, englisch, französisch, italienisch und norwegisch.* 2nd ed. 127 pp. Frankfurt am Main: Verlag Bochinsky/Das Musikinstrument, 1983. (Fachbuchreihe das Musikinstrument, 14)

Terms connected with piano construction in German, English, French, Italian, Norwegian, and Spanish.

1.541* Shaw, H. Watkins. *The Succession of Organists of the Chapel Royal and the Cathedrals of England and Wales from c. 1538: Also of the Organists of the Collegiate Churches of Westminster and Windsor, Certain Academic Choral Foundations, and the Cathedrals of Armagh and Dublin.* 480 pp. Oxford: Clarendon Press, 1991. (Oxford studies in British church music)

A detailed directory of English organists, listed chronologically under place of appointment (the Chapel Royal, the forty-eight cathedrals of England and Wales, the two collegiate church-es, the seven academic choral foundations, and the three Irish cathedrals), with brief histories of the foundations served. There is a bibliography (pp. 427–33) and a name index (pp. 435–45). A complement is Enid Bird's *20th Century English Cathedral Organists* (1990), which is illustrated and includes some appointments Shaw omits.

Reviewed by John Morehen in *M&L* 74 (1993): 71–72 and by Andrew Ashbee in *Notes* 49 (1993): 980–82.

1.542 Shead, Herbert A. *The Anatomy of the Piano.* 177 pp. Old Woking, England: Unwin Brothers Ltd.; London: Heckscher, 1978.

An illustrated dictionary of the piano.

1.543* Taylor, S. N. *The Musician's Piano Atlas.* 216 pp. Macclesfield, Cheshire, England: Omicron Publishing, 1984.

A serial begun in 1984, covering the history of piano manufacturing in England and supply-ing dated manufacturer numbers.

PERCUSSION INSTRUMENTS

1.544* Adato, Joseph, and **George Judy.** *The Percussionist's Dictionary: Translations, Descriptions, and Photographs of Percussion Instruments from around the World.* 95 pp. Melville, N.Y.: Belwin-Mills Publishing Corporation, 1984.

A description of percussion instruments commonly used in Western music, with precise, well-worded definitions. Especially useful is the section of foreign terms and their translations (pp. 65–94), covering 26 languages.

Reviewed by Larry White in *Percussion Notes* 24 (1985): 76 no. 1.

1.545 Avgerinos, Gerassimos. *Lexikon der Pauke.* 105 pp. Frankfurt am Main: Verlag Das Musikinstrument, 1964.

A dictionary of terms, chiefly German, connected with drums and drum playing.

1.546* Beck, John. *Encyclopedia of Percussion.* 436 pp. New York: Garland Publishing, 1995. (Garland reference library of the humanities, 947)

A dictionary of over 3,000 percussion-related terms, a glossary of percussion terms in four languages, a biographical list of noted percussionists, and a bibliography of percussion methods.

Reviewed by Kathleen Kastner in *Notes* 52 (1996): 799–801.

1.547* Cohan, Jon. *Star Sets: Vintage and Custom Drum Kits of the Great Drummers.* 128 pp. Milwaukee, Wisc.: Hal Leonard, 1994.

Descriptions of over forty outstanding drum kits of rock-n-roll, jazz, rhythm and blues, and country drummers of the last seven decades, with diagrams detailing brands, sizes, colors, and related details.

1.548* Lang, Morris, and **Larry Spivack.** *Dictionary of Percussion Terms as Found in the Symphonic Repertoire.* 132 pp. New York: Lang Percussion Company; Bethesda, Md.: Drums Unlimited, 1988.

First ed., 1977, 124 pp.

A dictionary with terms from France, Italy, Germany, Japan, Africa, Spain, Latin America, and Russia.

STRINGS

1.549 Bachmann, Alberto A. *An Encyclopedia of the Violin.* Trans. by Frederick H. Martens; edited by Albert E. Wier. 470 pp. New York; London: D. Appleton Century Company, 1937.

First published by D. Appleton and Company in 1925 and 1929. Reprinted, with a new preface by Stuart Canin, by Da Capo Press, New York, 1966.

A sourcebook on the violin, its history, construction, literature, and performers. The organization is by chapters, many of which have lexicons and bibliographies.

The reprint ed. is reviewed by David Montagu in *Notes* 23 (1966): 59.

1.550 Bachmann, Alberto A. *Les grands violinists du passé.* 468 pp. Paris: Fischbacher, 1913.

Biographies of 40 violinist-composers, varying in length but with lists of works and a numbers of full or partial thematic catalogs (Corelli, Kreutzer, Leclair, Rode, Sarasate, Tartini, Viotti, and Vivaldi).

1.551 Bone, Philip James. *The Guitar and Mandolin: Biographies of Celebrated Players and Composers.* 2nd ed., enlarged. 388 pp. London; New York: Schott, 1954.

The 1st ed. was published in 1914. The 2nd ed. was reprinted in London in 1972.

A bio-bibliography listing both performers and composers, including standard composers who have written for guitar or mandolin. Major works are mentioned, but there are no complete works lists. Some portraits are included.

1.552 Brinser, Marlin. *Dictionary of Twentieth-Century Italian Violin Makers.* 111 pp. Irvington, N.J.: American Graphic, 1978.

A useful list of 600+ violin makers active in Italy 1900–75, reproduced from typescript. The entries give birth and death dates, location of shop, and occasional comments on the quality of instruments by the makers. An appendix includes label facsimiles. Brinser was an American importer of Italian violins.

1.553 Carfagna, Carlo, and **Mario Gangi.** *Dizionario chitarristico italiano (chitarristi, liutisti, tiorbisti, compositori, liutai ed editori).* 97 pp. Ancona, Italy: Bèrben, 1968.

In two alphabetical lists: the first devoted to guitarists, lutenists, theorbo players, and composers, the second to instrument makers and editors.

1.554 Clarke, A. Mason. *A Biographical Dictionary of Fiddlers, Including Performers on the Violoncello and Double Bass, Past and Present, Containing a Sketch of Their Artistic Career, Together with Notes of Their Compositions.* 390 pp. London: W. Reeves, 1895.

Reprinted by Scholarly Press, St. Clair Shores, Mich., in 1972.

A compilation of anecdotal accounts.

1.555 Evans, Tom, and **Mary Anne Evans.** *Guitars: Music, History, Construction and Players from the Renaissance to Rock.* 479 pp. New York: Facts on File, 1982.

Previously published by Paddington Press (Grosset & Dunlap). Reprinted by Oxford

University Press, London, in 1984. A French ed., *Le grand livre de la guitare, de la renaissance au rock: Musique, histoire, facture, artistes,* was published by A. Michel in Paris, 1979 (354 pp.).

A sourcebook including biographical information.

1.556 Fairfield, John H. *Known Violin Makers.* 5th ed. 225 pp. Cape Coral, Fla.: Virtuoso Press, 1983.

First published by Bradford Press, New York, 1942 (192 pp.). Reprinted with supplements in 1973 and 1980. 4th ed., 1983 (218 pp.).

Separate listings of European makers from the 16th century and of American makers. Each entry includes a brief biography, description of works, and the then-current price range of instruments.

1.557 Fuchs, Albert. *Taxe der Streichinstrumente: Anleitung zur Einschätzung von Geigen, Violen, Violoncelli, Kontrabässe usw. nach Herkunft und Wert.* 13th ed. 230 pp. Hofheim, Germany: Hofmeister, 1991.

First published in 1906. 7th ed., 1970 (206 pp.); 9th ed., 1975 (202 pp.); 12th ed., 1985 (206 pp.).

A handbook for appraising the origins and values of string instruments, with brief entries on luthiers and a geographic index.

1.558* Gregory, Hugh. *1000 Great Guitarists.* 164 pp. London: Balafon; San Francisco, Calif.: GPI Books/Publishers Group West, 1994.

An illustrated biographical dictionary of performers associated with the guitar.

Reviewed by James M. Murray in *ARBA* 26 (1995): no. 1276.

1.559 Hamma, Fridolin. *German Violin Makers: A Critical Dictionary of German Violin Makers with a Series of Plates Illustrating Characteristic and Fine Examples of Their Work.* 49 pp. + 61 plates. London: William Reeves, 1961.

Translated by Walter Stewart from the 1948 German ed., *Meister deutscher Geigenbaukunst* (Stuttgart: Schuler-Verlag, 1948).

An alphabetical list of 550 names of important German makers, with plates illustrating their work.

Reviewed by Cynthia L. Adams in *Notes* 19 (1962): 261–62.

1.560 Hamma, Walter. *Geigenbauer der deutschen Schule des 17. bis 19. Jahrhunderts / Violin Makers of the German School from the 17th to the 19th Century / Luthiers de l'École Allemande du 17e au 19e Siècle.* 2 vols. Tutzing, Germany: H. Schneider, 1986.

A list of early German string instrument makers, with parallel texts in German, English, and French.

1.561 Hamma, Walter. *Meister italienischer Geigenbaukunst.* 8th revised and enlarged ed. by Stefan Blum. 808 pp. Wilhelmshaven, Germany: Noetzel Verlag, 1993.

Revision and expansion of a work first published in 1931; later editions include ones published in Stuttgart by Schuler, 1965 (728 pp.) and in Munich by Schuler in 1976 (727 pp.).

A description of over 300 instruments made by Italian makers. The descriptive entries are arranged alphabetically by maker and include biographical information, c. 1400 illustrations showing details of the instruments, and a geographical index.

1.562* Harvey, Brian W. *The Violin Family and Its Makers in the British Isles: An Illustrated History and Directory.* 432 pp. + 100 plates. Oxford: Clarendon Press; New York: Oxford University Press, 1995.

A history of violin making in Britain from 1647 to the present, including its social and economic background. There is a directory of makers (pp. 313–401), arranged alphabetically by name, occasionally with auction prices. There is a geographic index (pp. 401–6) and a short section of label reproductions (pp. 407–11).

Reviewed by Michael Fleming in the *Galpin Society Journal* 49 (1996): 240–44, by Peter Holman in *Notes* 53 (1996): 442–44, and by Robert Stowell in *M&L* 77 (1996): 269–71.

1.563 Henley, William, and **Cyril Woodcock.** *Universal Dictionary of Violin and Bow Makers.* 2nd ed. 1,268 pp. Brighton, England: Amati Publishing Company, 1973.

The 1st ed. was published from 1959 to 1969 in 7 vols.

A biographical dictionary and price guide with a subjective and literary tone. The biographies are of varying length, with long accounts of important figures, including descriptions of famous instruments. The price guide gives listings for English and American dealers.

1.564 Jahnel, Franz. *Manual of Guitar Technology: The History and Technology of Plucked String Instruments.* English trans. by J. C. Harvey. 229 pp. Frankfurt am Main: Verlag Das Musikinstrument, 1981.

Original ed. published as *Die Gitarre und ihr Bau: Technologie von Gitarre, Laute, Mandoline, Sistern, Tanbur und Saite.* 3rd ed., 1977 (240 pp.).

A compendium of information on the construction of the guitar and other fretted instruments. The bibliography, numerous tables and lists, and detailed plans provide much valuable technical data. This is a handsomely designed and printed volume, especially helpful to the musical instrument maker or interested performer.

1.565 Jalovec, Karel. *Encyclopedia of Violin-Makers.* Trans. by J. B. Kozak; edited by Patrick Hanks. 2 vols. London: Paul Hamlyn, 1968.

Originally published in 2 vols. as *Enzyklopädie des Geigenbaues* (Leiden, The Netherlands: E.J. Brill, 1965).

The 1st vol. includes 24 colored plates (with 51 illustrations); the 2nd has 3,000 reproductions of violin makers' labels. The author has also written in Czech three titles on German and Austrian, Czechoslovakian, and Italian violin makers; their English translations were published as *German and Austrian Violin Makers* (London: Paul Hamlyn, 1964, 439 pp.), *The Violin Makers of Bohemia, Including Craftsmen of Moravia and Slovakia* (London: Anglo-Italian Publications, 1959, 129 pp.), and *Italian Violin Makers* (London: Paul Hamlyn, 1958 and 1964, 445 pp.).

1.566* Kaiser, Rolf. *Gitarrenlexikon.* 286 pp. Reinbek bei Hamburg: Rowohlt, 1987.

A dictionary of the guitar including a bibliography on the guitar, a bibliography of 20th-century guitar music, and a directory of guitar manufacturers.

1.567 Kienzle, Rich. *Great Guitarists.* 246 pp. New York: Facts on File, 1986.

Extensive biographies of over 60 performers in blues, country, jazz, and rock. Discographies (with general label information), occasional suggested readings, and an index are included.

1.568 Lütgendorff, Willibald Leo, Freiherr von. *Die Geigen- und Lautenmacher vom Mittelalter bis zur Gegenwart.* 4th ed. 2 vols. Frankfurt am Main: Frankfurter-Verlags-Anstalt, 1922.

First published in 1904 in 1 vol., with a 2nd ed. in 2 vols. issued in 1913. The 1922 ed. was reprinted in Nendeln, Liechtenstein, by Kraus Reprint in 1968 and in Tutzing, Germany by Hans Schneider in 1975. Thomas Drescher produced a 3rd vol., *Ergänzungsband* (Tutzing, Germany: Hans Schneider, 1990, xxxi + 948 pp.), with a bibliography (pp. 771–813) and various indexes.

The history of the making of stringed instruments, arranged by country, with helpful illustrations. The 1st vol. has an index of manufacturers by city, with birth and death dates, and a bibliography (pp. 403–20). The 2nd vol. is a biographical dictionary of stringed-instrument makers, with facsimiles of trademarks and labels (pp. 583–668).

1.569* Marcan, Peter. *British Professional Violinists of Today: A Directory of Achievements, Current Activity and Their Related Ensembles.* 102 pp. London: Peter Marcan Publications, 1994. (String players library series, 2)

An illustrated biographical dictionary of about 1,000 violinists.

Reviewed by Michael Perl in *Brio* 32 (1995): 52–53.

1.570 Möller, Max. *The Violin-Makers of the Low Countries (Belgium and Holland).* 185 pp. Amsterdam: M. Möller, 1955.

A historical survey of violin making in Belgium and Holland. There are detailed photographs of the violins (pp. 23–129) and an "Alphabetical Register" that gives brief critical comments on the makers and their work. There is a glossary of terms in English, French, German, and Flemish.

1.571 Morris, W. Meredith. *British Violin Makers: A Biographical Dictionary of British Makers of Stringed Instruments and Bows and a Critical Description of Their Work.* 2nd ed., revised and enlarged. 318 pp. London: R. Scott, 1920.

First published in 1904.

An alphabetical dictionary of violin and bow makers (pp. 87–259), with some labels in facsimile. There is also "A List of Present-Day Makers, and a Few Old Makers Recently Discovered" (pp. 261–94).

1.572 Norlind, Tobias. *Systematik der Saiteninstrumente.* 2 vols. Stockholm: Emil Kihlströms Tryckeri, 1936–39.

At head of title: Musikhistorisches Museum, Stockholm.

Contents: Vol. 1, *Geschichte der Zither* (1936); Vol. 2, *Geschichte des Klaviers* (1939).

Detailed classification and description of stringed instruments based on the archive in the Musikhistorisches Museum in Stockholm, where records of some 40,000 instruments are maintained. Illustrations, bibliographical references, and locations are given for specific instruments in European and American collections. The work was projected in four parts, only two of which were completed.

1.573 Poidras, Henri. *Critical and Documentary Dictionary of Violin Makers Old and Modern.* Trans. by Arnold Sewell. 2 vols. Rouen: Imprimerie de la Vicomté, 1928–30.

Originally published in French, 1924, with a 2nd ed. in 1930. There is also a 1-vol. English ed., 1928. Reprinted by Scholarly Press, St. Clair Shores, Mich., in 1978.

Brief biographical notices with critical comments, arranged alphabetically under national schools (including Italian, French, and German). Photographic plates of the instruments and facsimiles of the labels are included.

1.574 Powroźniak, Józef. *Gitarren-Lexikon.* Trans. from Polish by Bernd Haag. 165 pp. Berlin: Verlag Neue Musik, 1979.

Originally issued in Polish as *Leksykon gitary* in Cracow by Polskie Wydawn. Muzyczne in 1979, 212 pp.

A dictionary of terms and biography devoted to the guitar and its practitioners.

Reviewed by Thomas F. Heck in *Notes* 37 (1981): 588–89.

1.575 Prat Marsal, Domingo. *Diccionario biográfico, bibliográfico, histórico: critico de guitarras (instrumentos afines), guitaristas (profesores, compositores, concertistas, lahudistas, amateurs), guitarreros (luthiers), danzas y cantos, terminología.* 468 pp. Buenos Aires: Casa Romero y Fernandez, 1934.

Reprinted as *A Biographical, Bibliographical, Historical, Critical Dictionary of Guitars (Related Instruments), Guitarists (Teachers, Composers, Performers, Lutenists, Amateurs), Guitar-Makers (Luthiers), Dances and Songs, Terminology,* by Éditions Orphee, Columbus, Ohio, 1986.

Known also as the *Dictionary of Guitarists.*

A dictionary whose main body contains biographies and lists of compositions, with information on dance forms (pp. 423–52) and terminology (pp. 453–64).

1.576 Riley, Maurice W. *The History of the Viola.* 2 vols. Ann Arbor, Mich.: Braun-Brumfield, 1980–91.

The 1st vol. is a reprint of the original ed., published in Ypsilanti, Mich., by the author in 1980. Vol. 2 is a supplement to the original 1st vol.

There are brief biographies of violists in Vol. 1 (pp. 312–76) and Vol. 2 (pp. 355–447). Bibliographical references and indexes are included in each volume.

Reviewed by Marion Korda in *Notes* 37 (1981): 855–56.

1.577 Roda, Joseph. *Bows for Musical Instruments of the Violin Family.* 335 pp. Chicago, Ill.: W. Lewis and Son, 1959.

A brief history and description of the bow, including statistics on dimensions and weight. Also included is a biographical list of bow makers, with 47 excellent plates of their work (pp. 119–325).

1.578 Roth, Henry. *Great Violinists in Performance: Critical Evaluations of over 100 Twentieth-Century Virtuosi.* 266 pp. Los Angeles, Calif.: Panjandrum Books, 1986.

Surveys of Russian, American, and Chinese violinists are preceded by essays on Kreisler, Francescatti, Milstein, Oistrakh, Stern, and Kogan. Entries in the surveys are short, providing basic biographical information and critical comments on performance style and recordings featuring each artist. There are no bibliographical references cited in the entries, but there is a general bibliography and index.

1.579 Stainer, Cecilia. *A Dictionary of Violin Makers, Compiled from the Best Authorities.* Revised ed. 102 pp. London: Novello, 1909.

The 1st ed. was published in 1896, 102 pp. Reprinted by Milford House, Boston, Mass., in 1973, and by Longwood Press, Boston, in 1977.

A useful biographical dictionary of violin makers with critical evaluations of their work, with a bibliography of literature on violin making.

1.580 Straeten, Edmund S. J. van der. *The History of the Violin: Its Ancestors and Collateral Instruments from Earliest Times, with 48 Plates and Numerous Illustrations in the Text.* 2 vols. London: Cassell, 1933.

Reprinted by Da Capo Press, New York, in 1968.

In large part a biographical dictionary, grouped by period and subgrouped by country. It includes many obscure violinist-composers not easily accessible elsewhere, with lists of works, arranged by category.

1.581 Straeten, Edmund S. J. van der. *The History of the Violoncello, the Viola da Gamba, Their Precursors and Collateral Instruments, with Biographies of All the Most Eminent Players of Every Country.* 2 vols. London: William Reeves, 1915.

Reprints published by W. Reeves, London, in 1971 (700 pp.) and by AMS Press, New York, in 1976.

More a history than a dictionary or encyclopedia, but thoroughly indexed (pp. 661–700), so many individuals can be accessed.

1.582 Vannes, René. *Dictionnaire universel des luthiers.* 2 vols. in 1. Brussels: Les Amis de la Musique, 1979.

Reprint of the 2nd ed. (1951–59) and the 3rd ed. (1971–75). First published in Paris by Fischbacher, 1932, as *Essai d'un dictionnaire universel.*

Most comprehensive of all dictionaries of violin makers. Each vol. has its own list of biographical entries, with bibliographical references. Includes 3,400 facsimiles of makers' labels, as well as an index of makers by birthplace or center of activity.

The earlier vol. is reviewed by Doris Commander in *Violins and Violinists* 12 (1951): 326; the latter by Albert van der Linden in *Revue belge de musicologie* 14 (1960): 144 and by William Lichtenwanger in *Notes* 17 (1960): 577.

1.583* Wenberg, Thomas James. *The Violin Makers of the United States: Biographical Documentation of the Violin and Bow Makers Who Have Worked in the United States.* 399 pp. Mt. Hood, Ore.: Mt. Hood Publishing Company, 1986.

The author also wrote *Violin & Bow Makers of Minnesota* (St. Paul, Minn.: Schubert Club Museum, 1988), 82 pp.

Reviewed by Dominique-René de Lerma in *ARBA* 19 (1989): no. 1297.

1.584 Zingel, Hans Joachim. *Lexikon der Harfe: Ein biographisches, bibliographisches, geographisches und historisches Nachschlagewerke von A–Z.* 207 pp. Laaber, Germany: Laaber-Verlag H. Müller-Buscher, 1977.

A dictionary for the harp that does not cite works. There is a bibliography of sources (pp. 203–7).

1.585 Zuth, Josef. *Handbuch der Laute und Gitarre.* 296 pp. Vienna: Verlag der Zeitschrift für die Gitarre, A. Goll, 1926.

Reprints published by Olms, Hildesheim, Germany, 1972 and 1978.

A scholarly work with supported statements and bibliographical references. The contents include terms and biographies (performers, instrument makers, and composers, with composition titles, dates, and publishers); the coverage is international for all periods, with many early names.

WINDS

1.586 Bechler, Leo, and **Bernhardt Rahm.** *Die Oboe und die ihr verwandten Instrumente, nebst biographischen Skizzen der bedeutendsten ihrer Meister.* Anhang: *Musikliteratur für Oboe und englisch Horn.* Edited by Dr. Phillip Losch. 98 + 32 pp. Leipzig: C. Merseburger, 1914.

Reprint of the 1914 ed. by Sändig in Wiesbaden, Germany, 1972, and by Knuf in Buren, The Netherlands, 1978.

A history of the oboe and related instruments, with brief biographical sketches of famous players. Included is a supplementary list of works for oboe and English horn, solo and with other instruments.

1.587 Gorgerat, Gérald. *Encyclopédie de la musique pour instruments à vent.* 3 vols. 2nd ed. Lausanne: Éditions Rencontre, 1955.

An ambitious work that attempts to cover all information pertaining to the making and performance of wind instruments. There are useful fingering charts for all winds. The 3rd vol. has special lists, including principal works for wind instruments, solo and ensemble (pp. 243–83), a dictionary of composers cited in the text, with brief identifications (pp. 285–340), and a table of French terms, with equivalents in Italian, German, English, and Spanish (pp. 341–524).

1.588 Jansen, Will. *The Bassoon: Its History, Construction, Makers, Players and Music.* 6 vols. Buren, The Netherlands: Frits Knuf, 1992.

The 1st ed. was published in 1978, 5 vols.

An extensive work on all aspects of the bassoon and the contrabassoon, including a dictionary of over 630 bassoon makers; a chapter on Heckel, the principal modern firm; bibliographic studies of bassoon literature; bibliographic data on lesser-known composers for the instrument; and lists of music for bassoon. There are a biographical dictionary of bassoonists of the past and present, a bibliography, and a discography of 1,450 records.

1.589* Meckna, Michael. *Twentieth-Century Brass Soloists.* 291 pp. Westport, Conn.: Greenwood Press, 1994. (Bio-critical sourcebooks on musical performance)

A biographical dictionary, international (though largely American) in scope, of 99 musicians who have had brass solo careers in either the popular or classical world. Each entry includes a brief biography (discussing training, career highlights, and awards received), a description of the subject's technique and style, and a selective bibliography and discography.

Reviewed by Steven J. Squires in *ARBA* 26 (1995): no. 1274.

1.590* Mende, Emilie. *Brass Instruments: Dictionary in 3 Languages, English–French–German /
Instruments de cuivre: Dictionnaire en 3 langues, français–allemand–anglais / Blechblasinstrumente:
Fachwörterbuch in 3 Sprachen: Deutsch–englisch–französisch.* 101 pp. Bulle, Switzerland: Éditions
BIM, 1983.

A polyglot glossary of the most important terms in current use in the brass world. In most
instances, the only definition is the foreign equivalent, although occasionally some amplification
is offered.

1.591 Suppan, Wolfgang. *Das neue Lexikon des Blasmusikwesens.* 4th ed. 690 pp. Freiburg-
Tiengen: Blasmusikverlag Schulz, 1994.

First published in 1973 as *Lexikon des Blasmusikwesens* (306 pp.), with the 2nd (1976, 342
pp.) and 3rd (*Das neue Lexikon des Blasmusikwesens,* 1988, 385 pp.) eds. following.

Extensive introductory chapters on the history, supporting organizations, arrangements,
repertoire, conducting, and bibliography of wind bands. There are biographies of composers,
conductors, and performers, each accompanied by a brief bibliography. Its most extensive coverage is of the German-speaking areas of Europe.

The 2nd ed. is reviewed by Georg Karstädt in *Die Musikforschung* 32 (1979): 193–94; the 3rd
ed. by Paul Bryan in the *Journal of Band Research* 26 (1991): 72–75 no. 2.

1.592 Waterhouse, William. *The New Langwill Index: A Dictionary of Musical Wind-Instrument
Makers and Inventors.* xxxvii + 518 pp. London: Tony Bingham, 1993.

The earlier editions, by Lyndesay Graham Langwill, were published as *An Index of Musical
Wind-Instrument Makers.* 6th ed., revised, enlarged, and illustrated. 331 pp. (Edinburgh: L. G.
Langwill, 1980). First published in 1960; 2nd ed., 1962; 3rd ed., 1972; 4th ed., 1974 (272 pp.); 5th
ed., 1977 (308 pp.).

A much-expanded improvement of this standard source, with an index of approximately
6,400 musical wind instrument makers with accompanying maker's mark (if relevant), bibliographical references, and locations of examples of early instruments in museum and private
collections. Some names from earlier editions, not meeting the standards of inclusion, have been
omitted. The liners are a map of central Europe, showing workplaces of 17th- to 19th-century
wind instrument makers. An essay, "Maker's Marks on Wind Instruments," by Herbert Heyde
(pp. xiii–xxxiii), is included. Includes a geographical index of makers' workplaces, a list of collections and libraries cited, a glossary, and a bibliography (pp. 503–18).

The 1st ed. is reviewed by Josef Marx in *Notes* 18 (1961): 234–36; the 2nd by Georg Karstadt
in *Die Musikforschung* 18 (1965): 90–91; the 3rd ed. by Anthony Baines in the *Galpin Society
Journal* 25 (1975): 134–35; and the 4th ed. by Anthony Baines in *M&L* 56 (1975): 413. *The New
Langwill* is reviewed by Jeremy Montagu in *Notes* 52 (1995): 449–50 and by Massimo Gentili-
Tedeschi in *Fontes* 43 (1995): 376–77.

1.593 Worthmuller, Willi. "Die Nürnberger Trompeten- und Posaunenmacher des 17. und 18.
Jahrhunderts." In *Mitteilungen des Vereins für Geschichte der Stadt Nürnberg,* 46 (1955): 372–480.

A musicological study, the major portion of which is a dictionary of 40 Nuremberg brass
instrument makers of the baroque period, with a list of their surviving instruments and tracing
of monograms and other makers' devices.

1.594 Young, Phillip T. *4900 Historical Woodwind Instruments: An Inventory of 200 Makers in
International Collections.* 304 pp. London: Tony Bingham, 1994.

The 1st ed. was published as *Twenty-five Hundred Historical Woodwind Instruments: An
Inventory of the Major Collections.* 155 pp. New York: Pendragon Press, 1982.

A catalog, organized alphabetically by the makers' surnames, listing instruments in orchestral score order. There are appendixes of museums and collections represented and a bibliography of the sources of illustrations, as well as an extensive general bibliography.

The 1st ed. is reviewed by William Waterhouse in the *Galpin Society Journal* 38 (1985):

158–59, by James R. Russell in *Notes* 39 (1983): 844–46, and by Malou Haine in *Fontes* 30 (1983): 225–27. The 2nd ed. is reviewed by Barra Boydell in *EM* 23 (1995): 152–53.

SACRED MUSIC

This section begins with dictionaries on various areas of sacred music. Then Robin Leaver's article on reference sources for specific hymnals (**1.617**) heads a list of handbooks on the hymnology of various Protestant groups, organized by denominations represented. Such handbooks are essentially selective bibliographies of sacred music, but most of them contain enough biographical and factual information to justify listing them among the encyclopedias and dictionaries of music.

1.595 Anderson, Robert, and **Gail North.** *Gospel Music Encyclopedia.* 320 pp. New York: Sterling Publishing Co., 1979.

An illustrated popular biographical dictionary with variable quantities of data presented for over 170 musicians. The useful lists include Dove Award winners, members of the Gospel Music Hall of Fame, and country music radio and television stations. The discography (pp. 271–313) is arranged by performer and there is an index of personal names, titles, ensembles, and institutions.

Reviewed by Frances Farrell in *JEMFQ* 18 (1982): 98 no. 65–66, by Doris E. McGinty in *BPM* 9 (1981): 229–31 no. 2, and by Dean Tudor in *ARBA* 12 (1981): no. 1054.

1.596 Carroll, J. Robert. *Compendium of Liturgical Music Terms.* 86 pp. Toledo, Ohio: Gregorian Institute of America, 1964.

An attempt to provide a single source of information most often requested by students and church musicians.

1.597 Claghorn, Gene. *Women Composers and Hymnists: A Concise Biographical Dictionary.* 272 pp. Metuchen, N.J.: Scarecrow Press, 1984.

A self-described "comprehensive biographical dictionary" listing 755 women hymnists and composers of church and sacred music covering all leading Protestant denominations and including many Roman Catholics and a few Jewish composers. There is a short bibliography.

Reviewed by Gillian Anderson in *Fontes* 32 (1985): 221–22, by Paula Morgan in *Notes* 42 (1986): 552–53, and by Avery T. Sharp in *ARBA* 16 (1985): no. 1162.

1.598 Davidson, James Robert. *A Dictionary of Protestant Church Music.* 349 pp. Metuchen, N.J.: Scarecrow Press, 1975.

Bibliographies connected with the brief entries for terms and subjects, giving this work's approach a new focus. The concentration is generally on terms connected to American and British Protestant movements.

Briefly reviewed by Stephen M. Fry in *Notes* 32 (1975): 301; Leonard Ellinwood gives a lengthier review, with errata, in *Notes* 33 (1976): 769–70.

1.599* DuPree, Sherry Sherrod, and **Herbert C. DuPree.** *African-American Good News (Gospel) Music.* 156 pp. Washington, D.C.: Middle Atlantic Regional Press, 1993.

Biographical sketches and photographs of Black gospel singers, composers, and instrumentalists, with discography (pp. 1–23).

1.600 Frost, Maurice. *English and Scottish Psalm and Hymn Tunes, c. 1543–1677.* 531 pp. London: Oxford University Press, 1953.

An ed. of 457 psalm tunes or harmonized versions thereof. There is a bibliography (pp. 3–50) of English–Scottish "Old Version" psalters from 1556 to 1677, with full descriptions and lists of contents. This work was indexed by Kirby Rogers's *Index to Maurice Frost's English and Scottish Psalm and Hymn Tunes* (MLA Index and Bibliography Series, 8), 1967.

Reviewed by Irving Lowens in *Notes* 11 (1953): 100–1.

1.601 Hayden, Andrew J., and **Robert F. Newton.** *British Hymn Writers and Composers: A Check-List Giving Their Dates and Places of Birth and Death [with Appendix of Revisions].* 98 pp. Croydon, England: Hymn Society of Great Britain and Ireland, 1979.

First ed., 1977, 94 pp.

A list to assist editors of British church bulletins.

1.602 Hughes, Anselm. *Liturgical Terms for Music Students: A Dictionary.* 40 pp. Boston, Mass.: McLaughlin & Reilly, 1940.

Reprinted by Scholarly Press in St. Clair Shores, Mich., 1972.

Concise definitions of terms used in the literature of ancient ecclesiastical music of the West. Tables give the structure of the Mass and the Office. Included are terms from the church calendar, notational terms, and texts with explanations of their place in the liturgy.

1.603 Julian, John. *A Dictionary of Hymnology, Setting forth the Origin and History of Christian Hymns of All Ages and Nations.* Revised ed. with new supplement. 2 vols. 1,768 pp. London: John Murray, 1907.

Reprinted by Dover Publications in New York, 1957, and by Kregel Publications in Grand Rapids, Mich., 1985. The 1st ed. was published in 1892.

A vast amount of information on musical and literary aspects of Christian hymnology. Entries are under authors, titles, and subjects of hymn texts, as well as brief biographical notices. There are long articles on American, English, and Latin hymnology. The entries on individual hymns give information on the original publication and their location in other hymnals.

The 1985 reprint ed. is reviewed by John E. Druesedow, Jr., in *ARBA* 17 (1986): no. 1238.

1.604 Kornmüller, P. Utto. *Lexikon der kirchlichen Tonkunst.* 2nd ed. 2 vols. in 1. Regensburg: A. Coppenrath, 1891–95.

First published in 1870. Reprinted by Olms, Hildesheim, Germany, in 1975.

An encyclopedia of Roman Catholic terminology. The 1st vol. is a dictionary of subjects, terms, and instruments connected with Catholic church music, with a subject index of topics discussed in extended articles. The 2nd vol. is a biographical dictionary of church musicians. The entries for early names cite published works; those for recent names cite categories of compositions.

1.605 Kümmerle, Salomon. *Encyklopädie der evangelischen Kirchenmusik.* 4 vols. Gütersloh, Germany: Druck und Verlag von E. Bertelsmann, 1888–95.

Originally published in *Lieferungen,* 1883–95. The 2nd ed. was reprinted by Georg Olms in Hildesheim, Germany, and New York in 1974.

Terms and biographies related to Protestant church music. There are entries for chorale titles, with full musical quotations of the melodies.

The 1st vol. of the original ed. is reviewed by Friedrich Spitta in *Vierteljahrschrift für Musikwissenschaft* 1 (1885): 235–38.

1.606* Lercaro, Giacomo. *A Small Liturgical Dictionary.* Edited by J. B. O'Connell. Trans. from Italian by J. F. Harwood-Tregear. 248 pp. London: Burns & Oates; Collegeville, Minn.: Liturgical Press, 1959.

Originally published in Italian as *Piccola dizionario liturgico.*

A dictionary of terms connected with the Roman Catholic liturgy and its parts: the Mass, the Divine Office, the sacraments and sacramentals, and the liturgical year. Before the dictionary proper (pp. 33–248) are an explanation and an outline of the structure of the Mass.

1.607 McCutchan, Robert G. *Hymn Tune Names, Their Sources and Significance.* 206 pp. Nashville, Tenn.: Abingdon Press, 1957.

Reprinted by Scholarly Press, St. Clair Shores, Mich., 1976.

An alphabetical list of some 2,000 tunes, giving their musical structures and thematic incipits in letter notation, with commentary related to authors, composers, and sources and numerous cross-references. Includes a melodic index and a first-line index of texts, with author, translator, and tune name.

Reviewed by Irving Lowens in *Notes* 15 (1958): 218–19.

1.608 Mizgalski, Gerard. *Podreczna encyklopedia muzyki kościelnej.* 566 pp. Warsaw: Ksiegarnia Sw. Wojciecha, 1959.

An illustrated Polish dictionary of sacred music, with biographical articles stressing contributions to church music.

1.609 Ortigue, Joseph Louis d'. *Dictionnaire liturgique, historique et théoretique de plain chant et de musique d'église, au moyen âge et dans les temps modernes.* 1,563 pp. Paris: J.P. Migne, 1853.

Reprinted by Da Capo Press, New York, in 1971.

A pioneer reference work on liturgical music, documented with frequent references to the works of the leading 18th- and 19-century specialists in church music.

1.610 Porte, Jacques. *Encyclopédie des musiques sacrées.* 4 vols. Paris: Éditions Labergerie, 1968–70.

Contents: Vol. 1, *L'expression du sacré en Orient, Afrique, Amérique du Sud;* Vol. 2, *Traditions chrétiennes, des premiers siècles aux cultes révolutionnaires;* Vol. 3, *Traditions chrétiennes (suite et fin), essence, nature et moyens de la musique chrétienne;* Vol. 4, *Documents sonores* (Commentaires [16 pp.] and phonodiscs [8 7(records]).

A handsomely designed publication with numerous mounted, full-color plates. The editor is assisted by a large group of authorities, chiefly French. The entries are extended articles; there are no definitions of terms.

1.611* Poultney, David. *Dictionary of Western Church Music.* xxii + 252 pp. Chicago, Ill.: American Library Association, 1991.

A dictionary of 400 entries with cross-references, whose picture of the Western church is primarily Christian. There are 80 essays on composers of church music, ranging from over 4 pages on Bach to a fraction of a page on John Wesley and Healey Willan. There is a chart of composers, arranged chronologically by genre (Mass, motet, Magnificat, Passion, anthem/service, church cantata, oratorio, and organ music).

Reviewed by Robin A. Leaver in *Notes* 49 (1992): 170, by Bonnie Jo Dopp in *LJ* 116 (1991): 182, and by Gregg Geary in *Choice* 29 (1992): 1374.

1.612 Richter, Gottfried Lebrecht. *Allgemeines biographisches Lexikon alter und neuer geistlicher Liederdichter.* 487 pp. Leipzig: Martini, 1804.

Reprinted in Leipzig by Zentralantiquariat der Deutschen Demokratischen Republik, 1970.

A collection of brief biographies, generally with dates and the subject's most familiar and popular titles supplied, for the writers of hymn texts.

1.613 Schalk, Carl. *Key Words in Church Music; Definition Essays on Concepts, Practices, and Movements of Thought in Church Music.* 365 pp. St. Louis, Mo.: Concordia Publishing House, 1978.

A dictionary of ideas, intended for the practicing church musician, that relate to the history and use of music in the Christian church, compiled by the editor and 29 other contributors. Focuses principally on Lutheran practices but provides general historic context for contemporary practice. Bibliographical references are included.

Reviewed by Richard T. French in *Notes* 35 (1979): 631 and by John E. Druesedow, Jr., in *ARBA* 11 (1980): no. 970.

1.614 Stubbings, George W. *A Dictionary of Church Music.* 128 pp. London: Epworth Press, 1949; New York: Philosophical Library, 1950.

A practical reference book for church music and liturgy, written by an Anglican church musician. It is useful for church organists and choir directors supporting other denominations as well. There are short explanations of technical terms and concise articles on topics related to church music.

Briefly reviewed by Leonard Ellinwood in *Notes* 8 (1950): 180.

1.615 Thomson, Ronald W. *Who's Who of Hymn Writers.* 104 pp. London: Epworth Press, 1967.

Brief biographies of the principal Protestant hymn text writers with a representative selection of their hymns.

1.616 Weissenbäck, Andreas. *Sacra Musica: Lexikon der katholischen Kirchenmusik.* 419 pp. Klosterneuburg bei Wien, Austria: Verlag der Augustinus-Druckerei, 1937.

A dictionary with biography, terms, and subjects in one alphabet, with articles on religious organizations and music publishing houses. This is more comprehensive than Kornmüller (**1.604**), but the articles are briefer.

HANDBOOKS ON HYMNOLOGY

1.617 Leaver, Robin A. "Hymnals, Hymnal Collections and Collection Development." In *Notes* 47 (1990): 331–54.

A discussion of some of the principal bibliographical resources relating to hymnals, together with a list of hymnal-based reference materials. Citing numerous general reference sources of use in identifying hymnals and related works, this basic bibliography of hymnals, hymnal companions, and handbooks is arranged in three broad sections: North America, arranged by denomination; the English-speaking world outside North America, arranged by denomination; and non–English-language traditions, arranged by language. The last section is very selective.

Anglican/Episcopal

1.618* Barrett, James E. *The Hymnary II: A Table for Service Planning.* 2nd ed. 84 pp. Missoula, Mont.: Hymnary Press, 1987.

An expansion and revision of a work that originally appeared in *The Maryland Diocesan Resonator,* 1977–79. First compiled and published by the author as *The Hymnary* in 1980, 89 pp. The present ed. was prepared after extensive study of *The Hymnal 1982.* Released in a loose-leaf format.

The first ed. is reviewed by Charles Huddleston Heaton in *The American Organist* 15 (1981): 8 no. 6.

1.619* Dearmer, Percy *Songs of Praise Discussed; A Handbook to the Best-Known Hymns and to Others Recently Introduced; with Notes on the Music by Archibald Jacob.* xxxii + 559 pp. London: Oxford University Press, H. Milford, 1933.

Reprinted in 1952.

A very useful handbook on Anglican hymnody.

1.620 Frost, Maurice. *Historical Companion to Hymns Ancient and Modern.* 716 pp. London: Printed for the Proprietors by William Clewes and Sons, 1962.

The latest revision of a work compiled in 1909 by W. H. Frere as *Historical Edition of Hymns Ancient and Modern;* revised in 1950.

Texts and commentary for 636 hymns, including the language of the original. There are a first-line index, brief biographies of hymn writers, a chronological list of authors and translators, an alphabetical index of tunes, and an index of plainsong, in which all usages are listed. There are notes on the composers, with chronology, list of publications and tunes, and a metrical index.

1.621* Hatchett, Marion J. *A Liturgical Index to The Hymnal 1982.* 338 pp. New York: Church Hymnal Corp., 1986. (Hymnal studies, 5)

An index designed to help in the selection of hymns for the various rites and for different days and seasons of the liturgical year. The approach is that of *The Book of Common Prayer*, beginning with the first Sunday of Advent and ending with hymns supporting *The Book of Occasional Services.*

1.622* Hatchett, Marion J. *Music for the Church Year: A Handbook for Clergymen, Organists, and Choir Directors.* 138 pp. New York: Seabury Press, 1964.

A discussion based on the *Hymnal 1940* of the Episcopal church and on the Episcopal church calendar.

1.623 *The Hymnal 1940 Companion.* Prepared by the Joint Commission on the Revision of the Hymnal of the Protestant Episcopal Church. 3rd ed., revised. 741 pp. New York: Church Pension Fund (Church Hymnal Corp.), 1956.

First published in 1949 (732 pp.).

Historical essays on each text and tune, as well as the original texts of many foreign hymns, especially those in Latin and German. There are brief biographies of authors, composers, translators, and arrangers, as well as a variety of lists and indexes: organ works based on hymns tunes, with publishers; scriptural texts; melodies; tunes; first line of text; and general. The 1st vol. of *The Hymnal 1982 Companion,* edited by Raymond F. Glover, has been issued (New York: The Church Hymnal Corporation, 1990); the 2nd vol. is awaited.

The 1st ed. is reviewed in *Notes* 7 (1949): 115–16 by J. Murray Barbour. *The Hymnal 1982 Companion* is reviewed by Alice M. Caldwell in *Notes* 29 (1993): 1088–90.

1.624* Klepper, Robert F. *A Concordance of The Hymnal 1982: According to the Use of the Episcopal Church.* 888 pp. Metuchen, N.J.: Scarecrow Press, 1989.

A concordance covering the verbal text of hymns in *The Hymnal 1982,* locating alphabetically the keywords used in the *Hymnal* and showing each word in context.

Congregational

1.625* Klepper, Robert F. *A Concordance of The Pilgrim Hymnal.* 784 pp. Metuchen, N.J.: Scarecrow Press, 1989.

A concordance covering the verbal text of hymns in *The Pilgrim Hymnal.*

Reviewed by Nicholas Temperley in *Notes* 47 (1990): 401–2.

1.626 Parry, Kenneth Lloyd. *Companion to Congregational Praise.* With notes on the music by Erik Routley. 580 pp. London: Independent Press, 1953.

An English hymnal companion with a bibliography, notes on the texts and music for 884 hymns and chants, biographical notes, and a chronological list of 396 sources cited in the musical notes. There are an index of tune names and a first-line index of hymns.

Evangelical and Reformed

1.627 Haeussler, Armin. *The Story of Our Hymns: The Handbook to the Hymnal of the Evangelical and Reformed Church.* 1,088 pp. Saint Louis, Mo.: Published by the authority of the General Synod of the Evangelical and Reformed Church by Eden Publishing House, 1952.

Commentary on 561 hymns and other liturgical works, with biographical and historical notes on hymn writers and notes on sources. There are indexes to scriptural texts, first lines of text, topical indexes, metrical indexes, indexes of hymn tunes, composers, arrangers, and sources.

Lutheran

1.628 Mahrenholz, Christhard, and **Oskar Söhngen.** *Handbuch zum evangelischen Kirchengesangbuch.* 3 vols. in 5. Göttingen: Vandenhoeck & Ruprecht, 1953–70.

A supplementary vol., *Die Lieder unserer Kirche,* by Johannes Kulp, Göttingen, 1958.

A compendium of information related to the German Lutheran hymnal, including a word and subject concordance, the Biblical sources of hymns, biographical sketches of the poets and composers, the history of the hymns, and studies of the individual hymns and their melodies.

1.629 Polack, William G. *The Handbook of the Lutheran Hymnal.* 3rd and revised ed. 681 pp. St. Louis, Mo.: Concordia, 1958.

Reprinted by the Northwestern Publishing House, Milwaukee, Wisc., 1975.

Texts of and commentary on 660 Lutheran hymns, with biographical and historical notes on the authors and composers. Includes an index of Biblical reference, a table of hymns for feasts and festivals, a first-line index (including stanzas of hymns), a tune index, a metrical index, a topical index, and an index of authors and translators. Daniel Werning's index (**5.240**) gives additional background information on the melodies included.

1.630* Precht, Fred L. *Lutheran Worship Hymnal Companion.* 891 pp. St. Louis, Mo.: Concordia, 1992.

A source providing background information to *Lutheran Worship* (St. Louis, Mo.: Concordia, 1982).

1.631 Stulken, Marilyn Kay. *Hymnal Companion to the Lutheran Book of Worship.* xxiii + 647 pp. Philadelphia, Pa.: Fortress Press, 1981.

Commentary on the hymns in the *Lutheran Book of Worship* (1978). The bulk of the book consists of entries on individual hymns arranged by first line of text. Each entry discusses sources, translators, tunes, and substantial biographical information on the author (and translator, if applicable) of the text. The extensive appendixes include a bibliography, a calendar of the church year (with appropriate hymns), a chronological list of tunes, and a chronological list of first lines by original language. There are indexes to authors, composers, and sources; tunes; first lines of canticles; and first lines of hymns in original languages and translations.

Mennonite

1.632 Hostetler, Lester. *Handbook to the Mennonite Hymnary.* 425 pp. Newton, Kans.: General Conference of the Mennonite Church of North America, 1949.

A commentary on 623 Mennonite hymns and other liturgical pieces with bibliography and indexes.

Methodist

1.633 Gealy, Fred D., Austin C. Lovelace, and **Carlton R. Young.** *Companion to the Hymnal: A Handbook to the United Methodist Book of Hymns.* 766 pp. Nashville, Tenn.: Abingdon Press, 1970.

Background material to the hymnal published in 1964.

1.634* Ingram, Robert D. *Scriptural and Seasonal Indexes of The United Methodist Hymnal.* 112 pp. Nashville, Tenn.: Abingdon Press, 1991.

A scriptural index listing hymns in Biblical order. The seasonal index begins with a list of the topics covered, including the major days from the Christian liturgy, services with special functions (such as baptisms, funerals, and weddings), and days designated for specific celebration by the United Methodist Church (such as Bible Sunday or Scout Sunday). Also includes the Revised Common Lectionary (1992), a calendar and table of suggested scripture readings (generally Old Testament, Gospel, and Epistle) for a three-year cycle, based on the New Revised Standard Version of the Bible.

1.635* Klepper, Robert F. *Methodist Hymnal Concordance.* 794 pp. Metuchen, N.J.: Scarecrow Press, 1987.

A concordance covering the verbal text of the hymns in *The Book of Hymns,* 1966.
Reviewed by Carol June Bradley in *ARBA* 19 (1988): no. 1291 and by Nicholas Temperley in *Notes* 47 (1990): 401–2.

1.636 McCutchan, Robert Guy. *Our Hymnody, a Manual of the Methodist Hymnal.* Index of scriptural texts by Fitzgerald Sale Parker. 619 pp. New York: Abingdon Press, 1942.
First published in New York by The Methodist Book Concern in 1937.
Commentary on 664 hymns and other liturgical pieces, with a hymn calendar, bibliography, and nine special indexes.

1.637* Rogal, Samuel J. *Guide to the Hymns and Tunes of American Methodism.* xxii + 318 pp. Westport, Conn.: Greenwood Press, 1986. (Music reference collection, 7)
Access to the six major hymnals of American Methodism from 1878 to 1966. There are separate alphabetical lists of writers of the music and of the texts, as well as an index to the first line of the texts.
Reviewed by Paul Cors in *ARBA* 18 (1987): no. 1250.

1.638* Young, Carlton R. *Companion to the United Methodist Hymnal.* 940 pp. Nashville, Tenn.: Abingdon Press, 1993.
The background of hymns included in the *United Methodist Hymnal* of 1989.

Moravian

1.639* Adams, Charles B. *Our Moravian Hymn Heritage: Chronological Listing of Hymns and Tunes of Moravian Origin in the American Moravian Hymnal of 1969.* 144 pp. Bethlehem, Pa.: Moravian Church in America, 1984.
Covering the hymns in the *American Moravian Hymnal* with text or tune by a member of the Moravian Church (Unitas Fratrum), a handbook listing 219 texts and 89 tunes in all. There are indexes of authors and translators, of composers, arrangers, and sources of tunes of the Moravian original; of tune names; and of first line of hymn texts.
Reviewed in *Hymn* 39 (1988): 34 no. 4.

Mormon

1.640 Cornwall, J. Spencer. *Stories of Our Mormon Hymns.* 4th enlarged printing. 304 pp. Salt Lake City, Utah: Deseret Book Company, 1975.
A popular companion to the Mormon hymnal, giving information on composers and writers of approximately 311 hymns used in the Mormon church.

Presbyterian

1.641 Covert, William Chalmers, and **Calvin Weiss Laufer.** *Handbook to the Hymnal.* lxi + 566 pp. Philadelphia, Pa.: Presbyterian Board of Christian Education, 1935.
A companion to *The Hymnal,* adopted for the Presbyterian Church in the U.S.A. in 1933.

1.642* McKim, LindaJo H. *The Presbyterian Hymnal Companion.* 427 pp. Louisville, Ky.: Westminster/John Knox Press, 1993.
A handbook to the most recent Presbyterian hymnal.

United Church of Christ

1.643 Ronander, Albert C., and **Ethel K. Porter.** *Guide to the Pilgrim Hymnal.* 456 pp. Philadelphia, Pa.: United Church Press, 1966.

INDEXES TO HYMNALS

1.644 Diehl, Katharine Smith. *Hymns and Tunes: An Index*. 1,242 pp. New York: The Scarecrow Press, Inc., 1966.

A comprehensive tool for locating or identifying a Protestant hymn or hymn tune. Approaches are offered through the first lines of text (almost all in English), authors, tune names, composers, and by melodies given in alphabetical notation. Appendixes include a glossary and a chronological list of the 78 (generally 20th-century) hymnals indexed.

1.645 Ellinwood, Leonard W. *Dictionary of American Hymnology: First Line Index: A Project of the Hymn Society of America.* 179 reels of microfilm, with printed guide. New York: University Music Editions, 1984.

An index to about 5,000 American hymnals published through 1978, including over 1 million first lines of hymn texts. The printed guide has the front matter and pp. 1–26 of the introduction (Reel 001), which provide the detail needed to use the index. Includes "Essays on Hymns with Confused Authorship" (pp. 27–118, Reel 001). The index gives access by title and composer.

1.646 Parks, Edna D. *Early English Hymns: An Index.* 168 pp. Metuchen, N.J.: Scarecrow Press, 1972.

A list of 1,157 hymns from some 51 hymnals and psalters and other sources. No music is given, but the tune names are identified and metrical structure is given.

1.647 Perry, David W. *Hymns and Tunes Indexed by First Lines, Tune Names, and Metres Compiled from Current English Hymnbooks.* 310 pp. Croydon, England: Hymn Society of Great Britain and Ireland; Royal School of Church Music, 1980.

Access to 37 20th-century English hymnals representing a variety of denominations. There are indexes to first lines (pp. 1–121), to tunes (pp. 123–229), and to meters (arranged metrically).

DICTIONARIES OF QUOTATIONS

MUSICAL

1.648 Barlow, Harold, and **Sam Morgenstern.** *A Dictionary of Musical Themes.* Revised ed. 642 pp. New York: Crown Publishers, 1975.

First published in 1948, 656 pp., with reissues in 1957 and 1966. This ed. was also published by E. Benn, London.

A thematic catalog whose 10,000 themes from the instrumental works of the concert repertoire are arranged alphabetically by composer. The themes are indexed by scale degree in letter notation, with all themes transposed to C major or minor. There is a title index.

Reviewed by Eric Blom in *M&L* 30 (1949): 271–73 and by Charles Seeger and Richard S. Hill in *Notes* 5 (1948): 375–76.

1.649 Barlow, Harold, and **Sam Morgenstern.** *A Dictionary of Opera and Song Themes, including Cantatas, Oratorios, Lieder and Art Songs.* Revised ed. 642 pp. New York: Crown Publishers; London: E. Benn, 1976.

Originally published as *A Dictionary of Vocal Themes,* 1950, 547 pp. Reissued in 1960.

A collection of vocal themes arranged alphabetically by composer. The themes are indexed by scale degrees in letter notation; there is also a title and first-line index.

The original ed. is reviewed by Harold Spivacke in *Notes* 8 (1951): 334–35.

1.650 Burrows, Raymond, and **Bessie Carroll Redmond.** *Concerto Themes.* 296 pp. New York: Simon & Schuster, 1951.

A thematic catalog limited to coverage of the concerto, more inclusive than Barlow–Morgenstern (**1.648**) for this format. The catalog is arranged alphabetically by composer and indexed by concerto titles, keys, and solo instruments.

1.651 Burrows, Raymond, and **Bessie Carroll Redmond.** *Symphony Themes.* 295 pp. New York: Simon & Schuster, 1942.

A thematic catalog of symphonies in the standard concert repertoire, arranged alphabetically by composer. The table of contents includes references to scores, to analyses, and to printed program notes for each symphony cited in the catalog. Thematic incipits are the opening measures and principal subjects of each movement. There are indexes by key and by title of symphony.

1.652 Parsons, Denys. *The Directory of Tunes and Musical Themes.* 288 pp. Cambridge, England: Spencer Brown, 1975.

Organized identification of about 15,000 vocal and instrumental themes, giving the pitch direction of the first 16 notes in each theme. Included is a directory of popular tunes and a section on national anthems in musical notation coded to demonstrate this accessible identification scheme.

Briefly reviewed by Stephen M. Fry in *Notes* 32 (1976): 556–57 and by Marsha Berman in *Notes* 33 (1977): 601.

PROSE

1.653* Amis, John, and **Michael Rose.** *Words about Music: An Anthology.* 440 pp. London: Faber & Faber, 1989.

Reprinted in New York by Paragon House, 1989.

A selection of literary writings on music.

1.654 Crofton, Ian, and **Donald Frasier.** *A Dictionary of Musical Quotations.* 191 pp. London; Sydney: Croom Helm; New York: Schirmer Books, 1985.

More than 3,000 notable utterances by and about musicians, some of them quite extensive. The entries are multilingual, but principally originally in English, with all foreign quotations translated to English, and are arranged in a single alphabetical sequence of topics and composers, with some cross-references. In each topic or under each composer, the quotations are listed chronologically. Sources of quotations and dates of sources are provided. There is an index of authors and speakers of quoted material. A subject index of significant keywords, each linked to a short identifying phrase from the quotations, is provided.

Reviewed by William Brockman in *ARBA* 17 (1986): no. 1250, by Ross Wood in *LJ* 110 (October 1 1985): 91, and by Harold J. Diamond in *Choice* 23 (1986): 724.

1.655* Kimball, Kathleen, Robin Peterson, and **Kathleen Johnson.** *The Music Lover's Quotation Book: A Lyrical Companion.* 118 pp. Toronto: Sound and Vision, 1990.

1.656 Shapiro, Nat. *Encyclopedia of Quotations about Music.* 418 pp. Garden City, N.Y.: Doubleday, 1978.

Over 2,000 quotations, all originally in or translated into English, arranged in subject categories, with indexes to persons and sources and to keywords and phrases. There are diverse musical statements, poems, anecdotes, book titles, and graffiti, from sources ranging from the Bible to the works of George Bernard Shaw to Frank Zappa.

1.657* Watson, Derek. *Chambers' Music Quotations.* 423 pp. Edinburgh: Chambers, 1991.

Later reissued in Ware, England, by Wordsworth Reference, 1994.

A classified collection of quotations concerning music, with index.

COMPOSITIONAL DEVICES

1.658* Bartel, Dietrich. *Handbuch der musikalischen Figurenlehre.* 307 pp. Laaber, Germany: Laaber-Verlag, 1985.

An organized catalog of musical rhetoric figures commonly used in the baroque.

Reviewed by Gregory S. Johnston in *Notes* 44 (1987): 62–64.

1.659 Read, Gardner. *Music Notation: A Manual of Modern Practice.* 2nd ed. 482 pp. Boston, Mass.: Allyn & Bacon, 1969.

First published in 1964 (452 pp.). The 2nd ed. was reprinted by Taplinger Publishing Company, New York, in 1979.

A practitioner's guide to contemporary conventions of musical notation, which includes some discussion of radical solutions.

Reviewed by Paul A. Pisk in *Notes* 22 (1966): 109.

1.660 Read, Gardner. *Thesaurus of Orchestral Devices.* xxi + 631 pp. New York: Pitman Publishing Corporation, 1953.

Reprinted in Westport, Conn., by Greenwood Press, 1969.

A lexicon of instrumentation intended for students and professional orchestrators. Known familiarly as *Orchestral Devices,* this collection of nomenclature in English, Italian, French, and German includes ranges of instruments and lists of devices, with reference to the page and measure number of the score. There is an index of nomenclature and terminology.

Reviewed by Lawrence Morton in *Notes* 11 (1954): 463–64.

1.661 Risatti, Howard. *New Music Vocabulary: A Guide to Notational Signs for Contemporary Music.* 219 pp. Urbana, Ill.: University of Illinois Press, 1975.

Organized into six chapters: The first surveys general material pertinent to many instruments, succeeding chapters deal with the instrumental groups, and the sixth deals with the voice. All of the signs are graphically displayed, with explanation of their meanings. There is a list of composers cited, a bibliography, and a general index listing musical instruments and specific terms.

Reviewed briefly by Stephen M. Fry in *Notes* 32 (1975): 303 and by Steven Stucky in *Notes* 32 (1976): 774–75.

1.662 Schillinger, Joseph. *Encyclopedia of Rhythms: Instrumental Forms of Harmony; A Massive Collection of Rhythm Patterns (Evolved According to the Schillinger Theory of Interference) Arranged According to Instrumental Form.* 250 pp. New York: C. Colin, 1966.

Reprinted by Da Capo Press, New York, in 1976.

This practical handbook of rhythm patterns presents the entire range of rhythm resources, from the simplest to the most complex.

The book is arranged in two sections: rhythmic resultants and analyzing rhythmic resultants with fractioning.

1.663 Slonimsky, Nicolas. *Thesaurus of Scales and Melodic Patterns.* 243 pp. New York: Coleman-Ross; Scribner's, 1947.

Reprinted in London by Duckworth, 1975, and by Macmillan, New York, and by Collier Macmillan, London, in 1986.

A reference book for composers seeking new materials, containing nearly 1,000 scales, both traditional and contrived.

Reviewed by Henry Cowell in *Notes* 4 (1947): 171–73.

LISTS AND HANDBOOKS

1.664 Dearling, Robert, Celia Dearling, and **Brian Rust.** *The Guinness Book of Music Facts and Feats.* 3rd ed. 288 pp. Enfield, Middlesex, England: Guinness Superlatives, 1986.

The 1st ed., edited by the Dearlings, was published in 1976 (278 pp.). Published in a Dutch translation by Charles Fabius in Haarlem by De Haan, 1978, and in an American ed., *Music Facts and Feats,* by Sterling in 1980. The 2nd ed. was published in 1981.

A list of curious musical information and feats in a format well designed for reference use, including a bibliography of 50 titles, as well as a good index.

Reviewed by Dominique-René de Lerma in *ARBA* 18 (1987): no. 1235. The 2nd ed. is reviewed by Robert Palmieri in *ARBA* 13 (1982): no. 1039.

1.665 Heinzel, Erwin. *Lexikon historische Ereignisse und Personen, in Kunst, Literatur und Musik.* xxvi + 782 pp. + 9 pp. of plates. Vienna: Brüder Hollinek, 1956.

Supplemented by his *Lexikon der Kulturgeschichte in Literatur, Bildender, Kunst und Musik.* 493 pp. Vienna: Brüder Hollinek, 1962.

A dictionary of artistic, literary, and musical works based on the lives of historical persons or events, related in spirit to **1.667.** Entries are arranged alphabetically, with persons and events interfiled, and include a historical summary followed by a classified list of the works in which the person or event is represented.

1.666 Kupferberg, Herbert. *The Book of Classical Music Lists.* 244 pp. New York: Facts on File, 1985.

A paperback ed. was published by Penguin Books, New York, in 1988.

A collection of statistics and other information, serious and trivial, unlikely to be found easily elsewhere.

Reviewed by Ann P. Basart in *CNV* 111 (1987): 14, by William Shank in *LJ* 111 (March 1 1986): 88, by Guy Marco in *Choice* 23 (1986): 1196, and by George Lewis Mayer in *ARBA* 17 (1986): no. 1267.

1.667 Leipoldt, Friedrich, and **Clemens M. Gruber.** *Lexikon der musischen Künste: Begriffe, Namen, Themen aus Musik, Malerei und Dichtung.* 382 pp. Wilhelmshaven, Germany: Florian Noetzel Verlag, 1986.

A fascinating attempt to provide access to musical works by theme or reference to extra-musical ideas, related to **1.665.** A collection of brief biographical entries for composers and librettists, as well as those with a more tenuous music connection (such as John Calvin), joined by entries for musical works, musical themes, and literary sources. The personal entries give nationality, occupation, dates, and an abbreviated works list. There are many cross-references.

<img — decorative flourish — 2 — decorative flourish>

2

HISTORIES AND CHRONOLOGIES

The abundance of music histories published in the last quarter century makes this section particularly selective. The titles include only standard general histories of music in the major European languages together with some of the more recent outline histories. Excluded are all histories devoted to the music of a particular national group and most early histories (pre-1850) unless, like Burney (**2.7**), Hawkins (**2.19**), Forkel (**2.14**), or Martini (**2.25**), they are of extraordinary interest and are currently available. Also excluded are histories of special periods and forms, except when part of a comprehensive series. Music histories come and go, and few of those designed for the general reader or music student may be expected to outlive their time. This explains the loss of Ferguson and Finney from this list.

Warren Allen's *Philosophies of Music History* (**2.1**) heads this chapter, although it is not a history of music, because it provides a "bibliography of literature concerning the general history of music in chronological order." It covers works from 1600 to 1939 and, supplemented by S. T. Worsthorne's article "Histories" in the *Grove Dictionary of Music and Musicians,* 5th ed. (1954), provides chronological and systematic lists of histories of music to mid-century.

HISTORIES

2.1 Allen, Warren D. "Bibliography of Literature Concerning the General History of Music in Chronological Order." In his *Philosophies of Music History: A Study of General Histories of Music, 1600–1939.* New York; Boston, Mass.: American Book Company, 1939, pp. 343–65.

Reprinted by Dover Publications, New York, 1962 (Dover books on music).

A chronological list of 317 titles, 1600–1939. Although not all can be described as histories in the modern sense, all bear on the development of music historiography.

2.2 Abbiati, Franco. *Storia della musica.* 3rd ed. 4 vols. Milan: Garzanti, 1967–69.

Contents: Vol. 1, *Dal origini al Cinquecento;* Vol. 2, *Il Seicento e il Settecento;* Vol. 3, *L'Ottocento;* Vol. 4, *Il Novecento.*

The 1st ed. was published in 5 vols., 1939–49; the 2nd ed., 1944–54. A 1-vol. abridgment of the 2nd ed. was published by Garzanti in 1955 (282 pp.) and updated from the 3rd ed. in 1971. A Spanish ed., *Historia de la música,* was published in Mexico City by Union Tipografica Editorial Hispano Americana, 1958–60, 5 vols.

A general history of music for Italian readers, by a single author, with numerous pictorial and musical illustrations. Each major section is followed by an anthology of excerpts from the writings of modern authorities on the period under consideration. There is a bibliography at the end of each volume.

2.3 Abraham, Gerald. *The Concise Oxford History of Music.* 968 pp. London; New York: Oxford University Press, 1979.

A German ed. was trans. by K. L. Nicol as *Geschichte der Musik* (Freiburg im Breisgau: Herder, 1983. 2 vols., 742 pp.) (Das grosse Lexikon der Musik, 9–10) (**1.21**).

A work by the general editor of the *New Oxford History of Music* (**2.27**) that extends far beyond a condensation of that series. It is one of the most informative of all 1-vol. histories, Western-oriented but giving informed glimpses of other cultures' music. There are 314 musical examples, 64 plates, and many informative footnotes, as well as an extensive, though necessarily selective, bibliography compiled by experts in the area under examination (pp. 864–912) and a thorough index. Listing the publishers of the cited scores would have been useful for the reader's further study.

Reviews by Clifford Bartlett in *Brio* 16 (1979): 50–52, by Anthony Milner in *EM* 8 (1980): 233–34, by Paul Henry Lang in *Notes* 37 (1980): 42–43, and by Kurt von Fischer in *M&L* 62 (1981): 68–71. The German ed. is reviewed in *Neue Zeitschrift* 10 (October 1984): 49–50.

2.4 Adler, Guido. *Handbuch der Musikgeschichte.* 2nd ed. 2 vols. Berlin-Wilmersdorf: H. Keller, 1930.

Contents: Bd. 1, *Die Musik der Natur- und orientalischen Kulturvölker. Antike. Erste Stilperiode. Zweite Stilperiode;* Bd. 2, *Dritte Stilperiode.*

Reprinted by Hans Schneider in Tutzing, Germany, 1961, and by Deutscher Taschenbuch-Verlag in Munich, 1975. First ed., in 1 vol., published in Frankfurt, 1924.

A standard compendium of music history, representing the accomplishments of German musicological scholarship in its early period of expansion and influence. Major articles were contributed by such authorities as Alfred Einstein, Wilhelm Fischer, Robert Haas, Friedrich Ludwig, Curt Sachs, Arnold Schering, Peter Wagner, and Egon Wellesz.

2.5 Ambros, August Wilhelm. *Geschichte der Musik: Mit zahlreichen Notenbeispielen und Musikbeilagen.* 3rd ed. 5 vols. Leipzig: F.E.C. Leuckart, 1887–1911.

Reprinted by Olms, Hildesheim, Germany, in 1968. First published 1862–82.

One of the last major one-person histories of music. The coverage starts with music in ancient civilizations. The author did not live to carry the 4th vol. past the beginning of the 17th century; that volume was edited from the manuscript by Gustav Nottebohm and Carl Ferdinand Becker. A 2-vol. continuation by Wilhelm Langhans appeared in 1882–87 as *Die Geschichte der Musik des 17., 18. und 19. Jahrhunderts in chronologischem Anschlusse.* Based on original research, Ambros's work is particularly important for its coverage of the sources of medieval and renaissance music.

2.6 Bourdelot, Pierre, and **Pierre Bonnet.** *Histoire de la musique, et de ses effets, depuis son origine jusqu'à présent.* 487 pp. Paris: Chez Jean Cochart, 1715.

Editions were also published in Amsterdam (1725) and The Hague (1743). The Paris ed. was reprinted in Geneva by Slatkine in 1969; the Amsterdam ed. was reprinted by Akademische Druck- und Verlagsanstalt in Graz, Austria, 1966 (*Die grossen Darstellungen der Musikgeschichte in Barock und Aufklärung,* 2).

One of the first general histories of music. It was begun by Abbé Pierre Bourdelot, continued by his nephew Pierre Bonnet, and completed and published by Pierre's brother Jacques.

2.7 Burney, Charles. *A General History of Music: From the Earliest Times to the Present Period.* 4 vols. London: The author, 1776–89.

Reprinted in 2 vols., with critical and historical notes by Frank Mercer, by G.T. Foulis in London, and Harcourt, Brace in New York (1935). The Mercer ed. was reprinted by Dover Publications, New York, in 1965, and by the Folio Society, London, in 1969 and Eulenburg, London, in 1974.

A monumental work of its day, setting the standard for future efforts. Burney shares with Sir John Hawkins (**2.19**) credit for the emergence of music historiography in England in the latter part of the 18th century. He financed the publication of his *History* himself and, perhaps for fiscal recovery, made it accessible to the literate public of his day, musicians and nonmusicians. He also left published documentation of the expeditions he made for his historical research: *The Present State of Music in France and Italy* (1771; 2nd corrected ed., 1773) and *The Present State of Music in Germany, the Netherlands, and United Provinces* (1773, 2nd corrected ed., 1775); that these travelogues needed more than 1 ed. testifies to their public reception and their effectiveness as a preview of the *General History*. In addition to its merits as a source of musical information, Burney's work is marked by high literary quality.

2.8 Chailley, Jacques. *40,000 Years of Music.* Trans. from French by Rollo Myers, with a preface by Virgil Thomson. 229 pp. London: Macdonald; New York: Farrar, Straus & Giroux, 1964.

Reprinted by Da Capo Press, New York, 1975. Originally published by Libraries Plan, Paris, as *40,000 ans de musique,* 1961. Spanish ed., *40,000 anos de música (El hombre al descubrimiento de la música),* Caralt, 1970 (296 pp.).

A provocative approach to music history, treating the subject within the framework of sociology and the history of ideas.

2.9 Corte, Andrea della, and **Guido Pannain.** *Storia della musica.* 4th revised and enlarged ed. 3 vols. Turin: Unione Tipografico-Editrice Torinese, 1964.

Contents: Vol. 1, *Dal medioevo al Seicento;* Vol. 2, *Il Settecento;* Vol. 3, *L'Ottocento e il Novecento.*

First published in 1935; 2nd ed., 1942; reprinted, 1944; 3rd ed., 1952.

A standard general history of music for Italian readers.

2.10 Crocker, Richard. *A History of Musical Style.* 573 pp. New York: McGraw-Hill, 1966.

Reprinted by Dover, New York, in 1986.

One of the few histories of music to focus consistently on musical style.

There is a detailed critical discussion by Leo Treitler in "The Present as History," in *PNM* 7 (1969): 1–58. Reviewed by Martin Chusid in *Notes* 23 (1967): 732–33, by Gwynn McPeek in *JRME* 15 (1967): 333–36, and by Henry Leland Clarke in *JAMS* 21 (1968): 103–5.

2.11 Dahlhaus, Carl. *Neues Handbuch der Musikwissenschaft.* 14 vols. Wiesbaden: Akademische Verlagsgesellschaft Athenaion; Laaber, Germany: Laaber-Verlag Müller-Buscher, 1980–92.

Contents: Vol. 1, *Die Musik des Altertums,* edited by Albrecht Riethmüller and Frieder Zaminer (1989, 358 pp.); Vol. 2, *Die Musik des Mittelalters,* edited by Hartmut Möller and Rudolf Stephan (1991, 464 pp.); Vol. 3, *Die Musik des 15. und 16. Jahrhunderts,* edited by Ludwig Finscher (1989–90, 2 vols.); Vol. 4, *Die Musik des 17. Jahrhunderts,* edited by Werner Braun (1981, 385 pp.); Vol. 5, *Die Musik des 18. Jahrhunderts,* edited by Carl Dahlhaus (1985, 434 pp.); Vol. 6, *Die Musik des 19. Jahrhunderts,* edited by Carl Dahlhaus (1980, 360 pp.); English ed., *Nineteenth-Century Music,* trans. by J. Bradford Robinson (Berkeley, Calif.: University of California Press, 1989, 417 pp.) (Calif. studies in 19th century music, 5); Vol. 7, *Die Musik des 20. Jahrhunderts,* edited by Hermann Danuser (1984, 465 pp.); Vols. 8–9, *Aussereuropäische Musik,* edited by Hans Oesch (1984–87, 2 vols.); Vol. 10, *Systematische Musikwissenschaft,* edited by Carl Dahlhaus and Helga de la Motte-Haber (1982, 367 pp.); Vol. 11, *Musikalische Interpretation,* edited by Hermann Danuser and Thomas Binkley (1992, 469 pp.); Vol. 12, *Volks- und Popularmusik in Europa,* edited by Doris Stockmann, Andreas Michel, and Philip Vilas Bohlman (1992, 506 pp.); Vol. 13, *Register,* edited by Hans-Joachim Hinrichsen (1995, 408 pp.).

A multivolume history of music, each vol. serving as a guide to a specific historical period or realm of musicology, with individual chapters prepared by an expert or team of experts in the specialty. In addition to discussions of methodology, problems, and directions, there are bibliographies, maps, discographies, tables of pertinent information, and indexes.

Vol. 1 is reviewed by David Wulstan in *M&L* 73 (1992): 268–69. Vol. 7 is reviewed by

Douglas Jarman in *M&L* 66 (1985): 172–73. Vol. 8 is reviewed by René T. A. Lysloff in *Ethnomusicology* 30 (1986): 360–62. Vol. 9 is reviewed by Bruno Nettl in *Ethnomusicology* 33 (1989): 147–49. Vol. 10 is reviewed by Bojan Bujić in *M&L* 66 (1985): 135–37.

2.12 De la Fage, J. Adrien. *Histoire générale de la musique ancienne et de la danse.* 2 vols. 1080 pp. Paris: Antiquité Comptoir des Imprimeurs unis, 1844.

Reprinted by Forni Editore in Bologna, 1971 (Bibliotheca musica Bononiensis, III/84), and by Olms, Hildesheim, Germany, 1978.

A history noteworthy for its wide range of interest in the music of other cultures, a forerunner of ethnomusicology. The 2nd vol. contains musical examples (30 pp.) and 29 plates of illustrations.

2.13 Einstein, Alfred. *A Short History of Music.* 4th American ed., revised. 438 pp. New York: Knopf, 1947.

Third ed., 1938 (New York: Dorset Press, 438 pp.). Also issued as a paperback (New York: Vintage Books, 1956). Originally published in German, 1918, as *Geschichte der Musik.*

One of the most perceptive and authoritative concise histories of music, published in numerous editions and translations. Most editions incorporate a useful anthology of 39 musical examples, indexed in Hilton (**5.437**); originally issued in 1917 as "Beispielsammlung zur älteren Musikgeschichte." The handsomely illustrated ed., edited by A. Hyatt King (London: Cassell, 1953), does not contain the musical supplement.

2.14 Forkel, Johann Nikolaus. *Allgemeine Geschichte der Musik.* 2 vols. Leipzig: im Schwikertschen Verlag, 1788–1801.

Reprinted by Olms, Hildesheim, Germany, 1962, and by the Akademische Druck- und Verlagsanstalt in Graz, Austria, 1967, edited by Othmar Wessely (*Die grossen Darstellungen der Musikgeschichte in Barock und Aufklärung,* 8).

The first full-scale history of music in German, by the scholar who has been called the father of modern musicology. The work covers through the early 16th century.

2.15 Grout, Donald Jay, and **Claude V. Palisca.** *A History of Western Music.* 4th ed. 910 pp. New York: W.W. Norton, 1988.

First ed., 1960 (742 pp.); revised ed., 1973 (818 pp.); 3rd ed., the first under joint authorship, 1980 (910 pp.). The 1st 3 eds. were also published in abridged form in 1964, 1973, and 1981. A music collection, *The Norton Anthology of Western Music,* intended to accompany this title and edited by Claude V. Palisca, was first issued in 1980, with a 2nd ed. in 1988. 5th ed. anticipated, 1996.

Intended for undergraduate music students or for the general reader, based on a stylistic approach. An elementary knowledge of musical terms and harmony is assumed. The history contains numerous musical and pictorial illustrations, with an annotated bibliography for further reading, a chronology of musical and historical events, and a glossary of terms.

The 1st ed. is reviewed by Albert T. Luper in *Notes* 18 (1960): 47–48, by Warren Allen in *JRME* 8 (1960): 124–26, and by Alec Harman in *MT* 103 (1962): 845–47.

2.16 Gruber, Roman Il´ich. *Vseobshchaia istoriia muzykal'noi kul´tury.* 3rd ed. 2 vols. Moscow: Gosudarstvennoe muzykal´noe izdatel´stvo, 1965– .

First ed., 1941–52. Second ed., 1956–60. A Romanian trans. by Tatiana Nichitin was issued in Bucharest, 1963.

A general history of music from antiquity to the beginning of the 17th century.

2.17 Handschin, Jacques. *Musikgeschichte im Überblick.* 2nd revised ed. Edited by Franz Brenn. 442 pp. Lucerne: Räber, 1964.

First ed., 1948 (432 pp.). Reprinted by Heinrichshofen, Wilhelmshaven, Germany, 1981 (450 pp.).

A stimulating short history weighted in the direction of medieval and renaissance music, with chronological tables and a classified bibliography.

2.18 Harman, Alec, Anthony Milner, and **Wilfrid Mellers.** *Man and His Music: The Story of Musical Experience in the West.* New ed. 1,245 pp. London: Barrie & Jenkins, 1988.

First published by Rockliff, 1957–59, in 4 vols. Published by Oxford University Press, 1962, 1,172 pp. Reprinted in London by Barrie & Rockliff, 1969, and by Barrie and Jenkins, 1977 and 1980.

A history designed for a lay audience, stressing music's social and cultural background, with a comparative chronology and a list of recommended books and music.

The 1st vol. of the 1st ed. is reviewed by William G. Waite in *Notes* 16 (1958): 49–50; Vol. 2 is reviewed by J. Merrill Knapp in *Notes* 17 (1960): 569–70; Vols. 3 and 4 are reviewed by William S. Newman in *Notes* 15 (1957): 99–101. The composite vol. is reviewed by Jack A. Westrup in *M&L* 43 (1962): 265–66.

2.19 Hawkins, Sir John. *A General History of the Science and Practice of Music.* 5 vols. London: Payne and Son, 1776.

A new ed., "with the author's posthumous notes," published by Novello, 1853, 3 vols., with 3rd vol. an atlas of portraits; 3 vols. reprinted by Novello, 1875. The 1853 ed., with a new introduction by Charles Cudworth, was reprinted by Dover Publications, New York, in 1963, and by Akademische Druck- und Verlagsanstalt in Graz, Austria, 1969.

Hawkins's history of music appeared in the same year that the first volume of Burney's history (**2.7**) was published. The two works invite comparison, largely to Hawkins's disadvantage, although his history has much to recommend it. It contains extensive translations of excerpts from early theoretical works and many examples of early music.

The Dover reprint is reviewed by Bernard E. Wilson in *Notes* 22 (1966): 1026–27.

2.20 Honolka, Kurt. *Knaurs Weltgeschichte der Musik.* 640 pp. Munich; Zurich: Th. Knaur Nachf., 1968.

Reprinted in Eltville am Rhein, Germany, by Rheingauer Verlagsgesellschaft, 1976, and by Droemer-Knaur, Munich and Zurich, in 1979. A Spanish ed., *Historia de la música,* was published in Madrid, 1979, 486 pp.

A general, generously illustrated history, with contributions by Hans Engel, Paul Nettl, Kurt Reinhard, Lukas Richter, and Bruno Stäblein.

2.21* Hughes, Andrew. *Style and Symbol: Medieval Music, 800–1453.* xxxi + 587 pp. Ottawa: Institute of Medieval Music, 1989. (Wissenschaftliche Abhandlungen / Musicological studies, 51)

A work in 2,027 numbered paragraphs, organized into 20 chapters. This textbook on medieval music, with numerous musical examples, is so meticulously indexed that it can serve as a reference work to terms, names, styles, and pieces. There is a bibliography of 114 items.

Reviewed by Mark Everist in *M&L* 74 (1993): 44–53.

2.22 Knepler, Georg. *Geschichte als Weg zum Musikverständnis: zur Theorie, Methode und Geschichte der Musikgeschichtsschreibung.* 2nd ed. 664 pp. Leipzig: Reclam, 1982.

First ed., 1977.

A thoroughly Marxist view of musical scholarship, with an extensive bibliography.

2.23 Laborde, Jean-Benjamin de. *Essai sur la musique ancienne et moderne.* 4 vols. Paris: Impr. de P.-D. Pierres, et se vend chez E. Onfroy, 1780.

Reprinted by Akademische Druck- und Verlagsanstalt, Graz, Austria, and by the AMS Press, New York, 1978.

The major French contribution to music historiography of the 18th century. Because it is not chronological, however, it suffers by comparison to Burney (**2.7**) and Hawkins (**2.19**). The *Essai* is a vast assemblage of information on musical ethnology, iconography, organology, history, biography, and other humanistic concerns, including French lyric poetry and the chanson.

2.24 Lang, Paul Henry. *Music in Western Civilization.* 1,107 pp. New York: W.W. Norton & Company, Inc., 1941.

An account of music in the context of the social, political, and cultural currents of Western civilization. One of the most influential music histories produced in America (and translated into German, Spanish, Portuguese, Czech, and Japanese), it coincided with and contributed to the general acceptance of music history in American higher education.

2.25 Martini, Giovanni Battista. *Storia della musica.* 3 vols. Bologna: Lelio dalla Volpe, 1757–81.

Reprinted by Akademische Druck- und Verlagsanstalt, Graz, Austria, 1967, edited by Othmar Wessely, with index.

An influential work and sourcebook for later historians, despite its archaic methodology and coverage extending only to the music of the ancients.

The 1967 ed. is reviewed by Jack A. Westrup in *M&L* 49 (1968): 55–57 and by Werner Kümmel in *Die Musikforschung* 22 (1969): 238–39.

2.26 Nef, Karl. *An Outline of the History of Music.* Trans. by Carl F. Pfatteicher. 400 pp. New York: Columbia University Press, 1935.

Originally *Einführung in die Musikgeschichte,* 1920, with many reprint editions. An augmented French ed. by Yvonne Rokseth was published in 1931.

An excellent outline history for use in college or university courses, brief yet comprehensive, readable yet scholarly, rich in bibliographical information and musical examples in the text.

2.27 *The New Oxford History of Music.* 10 vols. London; New York: Oxford University Press, 1954–90.

Contents: Vol. 1, *Ancient and Oriental Music,* edited by Egon Wellesz, 1957 (530 pp.); Vol. 2, *The Early Middle Ages to 1300,* edited by Richard Crocker and David Hiley, 2nd ed. (795 pp.) (The 1st ed. of Vol. 2 was *Early Medieval Music up to 1300,* edited by Anselm Hughes, 1955, 434 pp.); Vol. 3, *Ars Nova and the Renaissance,* edited by Dom Anselm Hughes and Gerald Abraham, 1960 (565 pp.) (reprinted with corrections in 1986); Vol. 4, *The Age of Humanism, 1540–1630,* edited by Gerald Abraham, 1968 (978 pp.); Vol. 5, *Opera and Church Music, 1630–1750,* edited by Anthony Lewis and Nigel Fortune, 1975 (869 pp.) (reprinted with corrections and revised bibliography, 1986); Vol. 6, *Concert Music (1630–1750),* edited by Gerald Abraham, 1986 (786 pp.); Vol. 7, *The Age of Enlightenment (1745–1900),* edited by Egon Wellesz and Frederick Sternfeld, 1973 (724 pp.); Vol. 8, *The Age of Beethoven, 1790–1830,* edited by Gerald Abraham, 1982 (747 pp.) (reprinted, with corrections, 1988); Vol. 9, *Romanticism (1830–1890),* edited by Gerald Abraham, 1990 (935 pp.); Vol. 10, *The Modern Age (1890–1960),* edited by Martin Cooper, 1974 (764 pp.).

A multivolume history of music, each volume of which is a composite work made up of contributions by scholars of international repute, edited by a specialist in the period and usually containing an extensive bibliography. The set was planned in 10 vols., plus a vol. of chronological tables and a general index; plans for that final vol. are incomplete.

An accompanying set of LP recordings, *The History of Music in Sound* (RCA Victor LM 6015–6016, 6029–6031, 6037, 6057, 6092, 6146, and 6153, 22 discs in 10 vols.) was issued 1954–57, accompanied by 10 vols. of extensive notes in pamphlet form, thoroughly documenting the works performed. No attempt has been made to update this release and bring it up to modern technical or performance practice standards.

The 1st vol. is reviewed by Curt Sachs in *Notes* 15 (1957): 97–99, by Roy Jesson in *MQ* 44 (1958): 245–53, and by Charles Seeger in *Ethnomusicology* 3 (1959): 96–97. The 1st ed. of Vol. 2 is reviewed by Charles Warren Fox in *MQ* 41 (1955): 534–47 and by Jeremy Noble in *M&L* 36

(1955): 65–70; the 2nd ed. of Vol. 2 is reviewed by Mark Everist in *M&L* 74 (1993): 44–53 and by Isobel Woods Preece in *Notes* 48 (1991): 477–79. Vol. 3 is reviewed by Richard H. Hoppin in *MQ* 47 (1961): 116–25 and by Thurston Dart in *M&L* 42 (1961): 57–60. Vol. 4 is reviewed by Howard M. Brown in *Notes* 26 (1969): 133–36, by Paul Doe in *M&L* 51 (1970): 66–69, and by Claude V. Palisca in *JAMS* 23 (1970): 133–36. Vol. 6 is reviewed by Michael Tilmouth in *EM* 15 (1987): 83 and by H. Diack Johnstone in *M&L* 69 (1988): 70–74. Vol. 7 is reviewed by Daniel Heartz in *MT* 115 (1974): 295–301, by William S. Newman in *JAMS* 28 (1975): 384–85, and by Arthur Hutchings in *M&L* 55 (1979): 465–71. Vol. 8 is reviewed by David Kirley in *Brio* 20 (1983): 23–25 no. 1, by Julian Rushton in *M&L* 65 (1984): 51–55, by Leon Botstein in *MQ* 70 (1984): 146–53, by Philip Gossett in *MT* 127 (1986): 149–51, by William S. Newman in *Notes* 40 (1983): 47–49, and by Nick Rossi in *OQ* 1 (1983): 170–72. Vol. 9 is reviewed by Stephen Town in *Choral Journal* 32 (1991): 51+ no. 3, by David Johnson in *Fanfare* 14 (1991): 413–15 no. 6, by David Allenby in *MT* 132 (1991): 345, by Susan Youens in *College Music Symposium* 31 (1991): 136–40, and by John Williamson in *M&L* 73 (1992): 291–96. Vol. 10 is reviewed by Peter S. Odegard in *JAMS* 29 (1976): 153–56.

2.28 [*Norton History of Music*]. 6 vols. New York: W.W. Norton, 1940–66.
A well-regarded publisher's series of independent works on different periods in the history of music. The volumes by Reese, Bukofzer, and Austin are particularly rich in bibliographical content; Reese's Middle Ages bibliography at one time was the most influential list of its type available to students of early music.
Sachs, Curt. *The Rise of Music in the Ancient World, East and West.* 1943, 324 pp.
Translated into German, 1968 (323 pp.), Japanese, 1969 (413 pp.), and Italian, 1992 (338 pp.).
Reese, Gustave. *Music in the Middle Ages: with an Introduction on the Music of Ancient Times.* 1940, 502 pp.
Also published in an Italian ed. as *La musica nel medioevo* (Florence: Sansoni, 1964. 642 pp.). Much new illustrative material is added to this ed. A Spanish ed., *La música en la Edad Media,* was published in Madrid by Alianza, 1989 (576 pp.).
Reese, Gustave. *Music in the Renaissance.* Revised ed. 1959, 1,022 pp.
First ed., 1954.
A Spanish ed. was published in 2 vols. as *La música en el Renacimiento,* 1988, by Alianza, Madrid.
The 1st ed. is reviewed by Denis Stevens in *M&L* 36 (1955): 70–73, by Charles van den Borren in *JAMS* 8 (1955): 123–31, and by J. A. Westrup in *Notes* 11 (1954): 547–48; the revised ed. is reviewed by Edgar H. Sparks in *Notes* 17 (1960): 569.
Bukofzer, Manfred F. *Music in the Baroque Era, from Monteverdi to Bach.* 1947, 489 pp.
A French translation, *La musique baroque,* was published in Paris by J.C. Lattes, 1982, 490 pp.
Reviewed by Otto Kinkeldey in *Notes* 5 (1949): 224–25.
Einstein, Alfred. *Music in the Romantic Era.* 1947, 371 pp.
Published in French in Paris by Gallimard, 1959 (485 pp.), and in Slovak in Bratislava by OPUS, 1989 (503 pp.).
Reviewed by Richard S. Hill in *Notes* 4 (1947): 461–63.
Austin, William W. *Music in the 20th Century, from Debussy through Stravinsky.* 1966, 708 pp.
Also published by Dent in London, 1967.
Reviewed by Peter Evans in *M&L* 49 (1968): 43–47, by H. Wiley Hitchcock in *Notes* 23 (1966): 254–57, and by Henry Leland Clarke in *JRME* 15 (1967): 174–76.

2.29 *Norton Introduction to Music History.* 8 vols. New York: W.W. Norton, 1978–92.
Hoppin, Richard. *Medieval Music.* 1978, 566 pp. *The Anthology of Medieval Music* (1978, 177 pp.) is the score supplement.

Reviewed by Rebecca Baltzer in *Notes* 35 (1979): 869–70.

Downs, Philip G. *Classical Music: The Era of Haydn, Mozart, and Beethoven.* 1992, 697 pp. *The Anthology of Classical Music* (1992, 554 pp.) is the score supplement.

Reviewed by Andrea Lanza in *Il saggiatore musicale* 2 (1995): 357–61.

Plantinga, Leon. *Romantic Music: A History of Musical Style in Nineteenth-Century Europe.* 1984, 523 pp. *The Anthology of Romantic Music* (1984, 637 pp.) is the score supplement.

Morgan, Robert P. *Twentieth-Century Music: A History of Musical Style in Modern Europe and America.* 1991, 554 pp. *The Anthology of Twentieth-Century Music* (1991, 452 pp.) is the score supplement.

Reviewed by John Thow in *Notes* 49 (1992): 122–24 and by Arnold Whittall in *M&L* 73 (1992): 468–71.

These titles were designed to expand, update, and replace the original *Norton History of Music* (**2.28**).

2.30 *The Oxford History of Music.* 2nd ed. 8 vols. London: Oxford University Press, 1929–38.

First ed., 1901–5, in 6 vols. Vols. 4–6 of the 2nd ed. are reprints of the original vols.

Introductory vol., edited by Percy C. Buck (1929, 239 pp.). A symposium by nine scholars covering Greek and Hebrew music, notation, musical instruments, theory to 1400, plainsong, folk song, and social aspects of music in the middle ages. Bibliographies are provided for the individual chapters (pp. 233–39).

Vols. 1–2: *The Polyphonic Period,* edited by H. E. Wooldridge; 2nd revised ed. by Percy C. Buck (1928–32, 334 + 500 pp.). Vol. 3: *The Music of the Seventeenth Century,* edited by Charles Hubert H. Parry (1902, 474 pp.); 2nd revised ed. by E. J. Dent, 1938. Vol. 4: *The Age of Bach and Handel,* edited by J. A. Fuller Maitland; 2nd ed. (1931, 362 pp.). Vol. 5: *The Viennese Period,* edited by W. H. Hadow (1931, 350 pp.). Vol. 6: *The Romantic Period,* edited by Edward Dannreuther (1931, 374 pp.). Vol. 7: *Symphony and Drama,* edited by H. C. Colles (1934, 504 pp.).

A series still valuable but succeeded by the *New Oxford History of Music* (**2.27**).

2.31 *The Prentice-Hall History of Music Series.* H. Wiley Hitchcock, general editor. Englewood Cliffs, N.J.: Prentice-Hall, 1965– .

Yudkin, Jeremy. *Music in Medieval Europe.* 1989, xxi + 612 pp. Issued with 2 90-min. audio cassettes.

The successor to Albert Seay's *Music in the Medieval World* (1st ed., 1965, 182 pp.; 2nd ed., 1975, 182 pp.).

The Yudkin ed. is reviewed by Mark Everist in *M&L* 74 (1993): 44–53.

Brown, Howard Mayer. *Music in the Renaissance.* 1976, 384 pp.

Palisca, Claude V. *Baroque Music.* 3rd ed. 1991, 336 pp.

First ed., 1968, 230 pp.; 2nd ed., 1981, 300 pp.

The 1st ed. is reviewed by David Burrows in *Notes* 25 (1969): 717–18.

Pauly, Reinhard G. *Music in the Classic Period.* 3rd ed. 1988, 265 pp.

First ed., 1965, 214 pp.; 2nd ed., 1973, 206 pp.

The 1st ed. is reviewed by Eugene Helm in *Notes* 25 (1968): 40–41.

Longyear, Rey M. *Nineteenth-Century Romanticism in Music.* 3rd ed. 1988, 367 pp.

First ed., 1969, 220 pp.; 2nd ed., 1973, 289 pp.

Salzman, Eric. *Twentieth-Century Music: An Introduction.* 3rd ed. 1988, 330 pp.

First ed., 1967, 196 pp.; 2nd ed., 1974, 242 pp.

The 2nd ed. is reviewed by John Graziano in *Notes* 31 (1975): 574–75.

Nettl, Bruno. *Folk and Traditional Music of the Western Continents,* with chapters on Latin America by Gérard Béhague. 3rd ed., revised and edited by Valerie Woodring Goertzen, 1990, 286 pp.

First ed., 1965, 213 pp.; 2nd ed., 1973, 258 pp.

Reviewed by Alfred W. Humphreys in *JRME* 13 (1965): 259–60, by Fritz Bose in *Die*

Musikforschung 21 (1968): 107–8, and by Wolfgang Suppan in *Jahrbuch für Volksliedforschung* 12 (1967): 217–18.

Malm, William P. *Music Cultures of the Pacific, the Near East, and Asia.* 2nd ed. 1977, 236 pp. First ed., 1967, 169 pp.; 3rd ed., 1996, with 2 audio cassettes, is anticipated.

Hitchcock, H. Wiley. *Music in the United States: A Historical Introduction.* 3rd ed. 1988, 365 pp.

First ed., 1969, 270 pp.; 2nd ed., 1974, 286 pp.

The 1st ed. is reviewed by Ross Lee Finney in *Notes* 26 (1969): 271–72. The 3rd ed. is reviewed by J. Bunker Clark in *AM* 7 (1989): 465–67.

Béhague, Gérard. *Music in Latin America: An Introduction.* 1979, 369 pp.

Published in Spanish as *La música en America Latina, una introduccion,* trans. by Miguel Castillo Didier (Caracas: Monte Avila, 1983), 502 pp.

Reviewed by Gerald R. Benjamin in *Ethnomusicology* 25 (1981): 144–45, by Dominique-René de Lerma in *BPM* 9 (1991): 99–100, and by Simon Collier in *M&L* 64 (1983): 89–91.

Wade, Bonnie C. *Music in India: The Classical Traditions.* 1979, 252 pp.

Reprinted by Riverdale Co., Riverdale, Md., 1987, by Sangam Books in London, 1988, and by Manohar in New Delhi, 1987 and 1994.

An unnumbered publisher's series of short, 1-vol. surveys by leading American scholars, covering the major historical periods as well as folk and non-Western music. The individual volumes are frequently revised.

2.32 Printz, Wolfgang Caspar. *Historische Beschreibung der edelen Sing- und Kling-Kunst.* 240 pp. Dresden: J.C. Mieth, 1690.

Reprinted by Akademische Druck- und Verlagsanstalt, Graz, Austria 1964, edited and indexed by Othmar Wessely, as the 1st vol. in the series *Die grossen Darstellungen der Musikgeschichte in Barock und Aufklärung.*

A work often called the first history of music. The author's observations are based largely on Biblical authority and legend, but his work exercised considerable influence on 18th-century lexicographers and historians.

2.33 Riemann, Hugo. *Handbuch der Musikgeschichte.* Edited by Alfred Einstein. 2nd ed. 2 vols. in 4. Leipzig: Breitkopf & Härtel, 1920–23.

First ed., 1904–13. Reprinted by Johnson Reprint Corporation, New York, 1972.

A product of one of the most vigorous and stimulating minds in German musicology, always provocative, often misleading. There are extensive chapter bibliographies and sections devoted to brief biographies of musicians, although the emphasis is on musical styles and forms. The numerous transcriptions of early music must be viewed in light of the author's unorthodox editorial methods.

2.34 Roland-Manuel. *Histoire de la musique.* New ed. 2 vols. Paris: Gallimard, 1982. (Encyclopédie de la Pléiade, 9 and 16)

Contents: Vol. 1, *Des origines à Jean-Sebastien Bach,* 2,238 pp.; Vol. 2, *Du XVIIIe siècle à nos jours,* 1,878 pp.

First ed., 1960–63; reprinted 1977.

An important work. The approach is international, with contributions by specialists from many different countries. Vol. 1 begins with a chapter on "Éléments et genèses," followed by surveys of the music of non-Western cultures, including ancient and Oriental music and the music of the Muslim world. Thereafter the organization is chronological within individual countries. At the end of Vol. 2 are chapters on contemporary music and the history of musicology and criticism. Each volume has a chronological table, index, and analytical table of contents.

2.35* *Storia della musica.* New ed., enlarged, revised, and corrected. 12 vols. Turin: EDT, 1991–93. (Biblioteca di cultura musicale, 1)

Contents: Vol. 1, Comotti, Giovanni. *La musica nella cultura greca e romana* (180 pp.); Vol. 2, Cattin, Giulio. *La monodia nel medioevo* (310 pp.); Vol. 3, Gallo, F. Alberto. *La polifonia nel medioevo* (172 pp.); Vol. 4, Gallico, Claudio. *L'eta dell'Umanesimo e del Rinascimento* (197 pp.); Vol. 5, Bianconi, Lorenzo. *Il Seicento;* Vol. 6, Basso, Alberto. *L'eta di Bach e di Haendel;* Vol. 7, Di Benedetto, Renato. *L'Ottocento* (283 pp.); Vol. 8, Di Benedetto, Renato. *Romanticismo e scuole nazionali nell'Ottocento* (311 pp.); Vol. 9, Della Seta, Fabrizio. *Italia e Francia nell'Ottocento* (409 pp.); Vol. 10, Salvetti, Guido. *La nascita del Novecento* (379 pp.); Vol. 11, Vinay, Gianfranco. *Il Novecento nell'Europa orientale e negli Stati Uniti* (229 pp.); Vol. 12, Lanza, Andrea. *Il secondo Novecento II* (293 pp.). (Biblioteca di cultura musicale, 1)

First edition published 1976–82, 10 vols. in 12. English translation of the 1st ed. of Vol. 2 was published as *Music of the Middle Ages,* trans. by Steven Botterill (Vol. 1) and Karen Eales (Vol. 2), 2 vols. (Cambridge, England; New York: Cambridge University Press, 1984–85), with an extensive bibliography (Vol. 1, pp. 231–45; ,Vol. 2, pp. 141–48).

Music of the Middle Ages is reviewed by John Caldwell in *M&L* 66 (1985): 403–5 and by James W. McKinnon in *Notes* 42 (1985): 280–81.

2.36 Subirá, José. *Historia de la música.* 3rd ed. 4 vols. Barcelona: Editorial Salvat, 1958.
First ed., 1947; 2nd ed., 1951.
Handsomely printed and illustrated, musically and pictorially, with some emphasis on ethnomusicology. The approach is generally chronological, but with chapters on the development of notation, 17th-century theory, and performance practice.

2.37 Ulrich, Homer, and **Paul A. Pisk.** *A History of Music and Musical Style.* 696 pp. New York: Harcourt, Brace & World, 1963.
A history of music that offers a clear, straightforward presentation of historical developments in musical style.
Reviewed by Susan Thiemann in *Notes* 20 (1963): 638–42.

2.38 Wiora, Walter. *The Four Ages of Music.* Trans. by M. D. Herter Norton. 233 pp. New York: Norton, 1965.
Originally published by W. Kohlhammer Verlag in Stuttgart, 1961, as *Die vier Weltalter der Musik* (Urban-Bücher, 56); also published in France as *Les quatres ages de la musique, de la préhistoire à l'éra de la technique.*
An original approach to music history and its periodization, treating the subject in the context of universal history and anthropology.
Reviewed by Johannes Riedel in *JRME* 13 (1965): 260–61 and by Rose Brandel in *Notes* 24 (1968): 695–97.

2.39 Wörner, Karl Heinrich. *History of Music: A Book for Study and Reference.* Trans. and supplemented by Willis Wager. 5th ed. 712 pp. New York: Free Press, 1973.
First published as *Geschichte der Musik,* 1954; 2nd ed., 1956; 3rd ed., 1961; 4th ed., 1965; 5th ed., 1972; 6th ed., 1975; 7th ed., 1980, 692 pp.; 8th ed., 1993, 694 pp.
A well-organized outline history of music with excellent bibliographical information that uses a variety of approaches: stylistic, national, and biographical. Paragraphs are numbered for easy reference.

MUSICAL ICONOGRAPHY

Musical iconography has become a branch of scholarship with its own principles, methodologies, and literature. At the same time, writers of histories of music have become more conscious of the value of including numerous well-chosen images in their texts. The tradition, begun by George Kinsky in his *Geschichte der Musik in Bildern* (**2.52**), is very much alive and flourishing. Meanwhile, other scholars and publishers have compiled anthologies of images incorporating some reference to music as important adjuncts to the study of music by period, place, and genre; the extensive series *Musikgeschichte in Bildern* (**2.41**) is an example of this practice.

There is an international body devoted to all aspects of musical iconography, the Répertoire Internationale d'Iconographie Musicale, with headquarters at the Graduate Center of the City University of New York; an article by Barry S. Brook, "RIdIM: A New International Venture in Musical Iconography" in *Notes* 28 (1972): 652–63, provides background. RIdIM produces a *Newsletter* that publishes important articles on the subject, relates the activities of the organization, and reports on scholarship in musical iconography that is under way or published elsewhere. The series RIdIM/RCMI (Research Center for Music Iconography) Inventory of Music Iconography organizes by holding institution art relating to music. Additional independent references of this type may be found in Chapter 7 (see Florence, Galleria degli Uffizi, for example).

2.40 Bernard, Robert. *Histoire de la musique.* 5 vols. Paris: F. Nathan, 1969–71.

First published in 3 vols., 1961–63.

A history of music distinguished for its fine printing and rich illustrative material, including numerous plates in full color. The work lacks a bibliography or other documentation. Vol. 1 treats the history of European music to the end of the 18th century; Vols. 2 and 3 cover 19th- and 20th-century developments in Europe and the Americas, with brief discussions of Oriental music. The 5th vol., *Complément à l'histoire de la musique*, containing indexes and a glossary, was published in 1971.

2.41 Besseler, Heinrich, and **Max Schneider.** *Musikgeschichte in Bildern,* Band 1– . Leipzig: Deutscher Verlag für Musik, 1961– .

A multivolume work projected to cover all periods in the history of music as well as some of the systematic branches. The publication of the volumes and their respective subsections (*Lieferungen*) has not followed in chronological order. Each issue contains numerous plates, with commentary, a bibliography, chronological tables, and indexes. The released issues include the following:

Band I: *Musikethnologie.*

Lief. 1: **Collaer, Paul.** *Ozeanien.* 1965, 232 pp.

Reviewed by Dieter Christensen in *Die Musikforschung* 20 (1967): 339–41, by Bruno Nettl in *Notes* 23 (1966): 276, and by Wolfgang Suppan in *Jahrbuch für Volksliedforschung* 16 (1971): 262–64.

Lief. 2: **Collaer, Paul.** *Amerika: Eskimo und indianische Bevölkerung.* 1967, 210 pp.

Reviewed by Fritz Bose in *Die Musikforschung* 22 (1969): 522–23 and by Bruno Nettl in *Notes* 24 (1968): 717–18.

Lief. 3: **Collaer, Paul,** and **Emmy Bernatzik.** *Südostasien.* 1979, 180 pp.

Lief. 4: **Daniélou, Alain.** *Südasien: Die indische Musik und ihre Traditionen.* Trans. by Fritz Bose. 1978, 146 pp.

Lief. 8: **Collaer, Paul,** and **Jürgen Elsner.** *Nordafrika.* 1983, 205 pp.

Lief. 9: **Gansemans, Jos, Barbara Schmidt-Wrenger,** and **Simha Arom.** *Zentralafrika.* 1986, 211 pp.

Reviewed by V. Kofi Agawu in *M&L* 70 (1989): 74–76.

Lief. 10: **Kubik, Gerhard.** *Ostafrika.* 1982, 250 pp.

Lief. 11: **Kubik, Gerhard.** *Westafrika.* 1989, 221 pp.

Band II: *Musik des Altertums.*

Lief. 1: **Hickmann, Hans.** *Ägypten.* 2nd ed., 1961, 185 pp.

Reviewed by Caldwell Titcomb in *JAMS* 17 (1964): 386–91 and by Fritz Bose in *Die Musikforschung* 17 (1964): 184–85.

Lief. 2: **Rashid Subhi Anwar.** *Mesopotamien.* 1984, 182 pp.

Lief. 4: **Wegner, Max.** *Griechenland.* 1964, 143 pp.

Reviewed by Emanuel Winternitz in *JAMS* 19 (1966): 412–15.

Lief. 5: **Fleischhauer, Günter.** *Etrurien und Rom.* 1965, 193 pp. 2nd revised ed., 1977.

Lief. 7: **Martí, Samuel.** *Alt-Amerika: Musik der Indianer in präkolumbischer Zeit.* 1970, 193 pp.

Lief. 8: **Kaufmann, Walter.** *Altindien.* 208 pp., 1981.

Reviewed by Wolfgang Suppan in *Jahrbuch für Volksliedforschung* 16 (1971): 262–64 and by Josef Kuckertz in *Ethnomusicology* 30 (1986): 351–52.

Lief. 9: **Karomatov, Faizulla Muzaffarovich.** *Mittelasien.* 1987, 178 pp.

Band III: *Musik des Mittelalters und der Renaissance.*

Lief. 2: **Farmer, Henry George.** *Islam.* 1966, 205 pp.

Reviewed by Egon Wellesz in *M&L* 49 (1968): 73–74 and by Ella Zonis in *JAMS* 22 (1969): 193–96.

Lief. 3: **Smits van Waesberghe, Joseph.** *Musikerziehung: Lehre und Theorie der Musik im Mittelalter.* 1969, 213 pp.

The section "Chronologische Übersicht der Musiktraktate, und Literaturverzeichnis" (pp. 195–202) provides a bibliographical key to the historical study of music education, citing the most important treatises devoted to music theory and instruction from the 5th to the 15th centuries, as well as an extensive bibliography of books and articles on medieval music instruction.

Lief. 4: **Stäblein, Bruno.** *Schriftbild der einstimmigen Musik.* 1975, 257 pp.

Lief. 5: **Besseler, Heinrich,** and **Peter Gülke.** *Schriftbild der mehrstimmigen Musik.* 1973, 183 pp. 2nd ed., 1981.

Lief. 8: **Bowles, Edmund A.** *Musikleben im 15. Jahrhundert.* 1977, 189 pp.

Lief. 9: **Salmen, Walter.** *Musikleben im 16. Jahrhundert.* 1976, 205 pp.

Reviewed by Mary Rassmussen in *Notes* 34 (1978): 592–94.

Band IV: *Musik der Neuzeit.*

Lief. 1: **Wolff, Hellmuth Christian.** *Oper, Szene und Darstellung von 1600 bis 1900.* 1968, 212 pp.

Reviewed by Elvidio Surian in *JAMS* 24 (1971): 306–8.

Lief. 2: **Schwab, Heinrich W.** *Konzert: Öffentliche Musikdarbietung vom 17. bis 19. Jahrhundert.* 1971, 228 pp.

Lief. 3: **Salmen, Walter.** *Haus- und Kammermusik; Privates Musizieren im gesellschaftlichen Wandel zwischen 1600 und 1900.* 1969, 203 pp.

Japanese ed. published by Ongakunotomosha, Tokyo, 1985.

Lief. 4: **Salmen, Walter.** *Tanz im 17. und 18. Jahrhundert.* 1988, 206 pp.

Lief. 5: **Salmen, Walter.** *Tanz im 19. Jahrhundert.* 1989, 178 pp.

2.42* Bowles, Edmund A. *Musical Ensembles in Festival Books, 1500–1800: An Iconographical & Documentary Survey.* xxii + 583 pp. Ann Arbor, Mich.: UMI Research Press, 1989. (Studies in music, 103)

A presentation and examination of 101 festival books published between 1519 and 1790. The author offers a representatively selective rather than comprehensive array, with an annotated bibliography (pp. 547–71) and translations from the books; the original texts, however, are not supplied.

Reviewed in Margaret Downie Banks in *AMISJ* 16 (1990): 180–85.

2.43 Brown, Howard Mayer, and **Joan Lascelle.** *Musical Iconography: A Manual for Cataloguing Musical Subjects in Western Art before 1800.* 220 pp. Cambridge, Mass.: Harvard University Press, 1972.

A workable cataloging scheme addressing problems of providing access to images on musical subjects and promoting standardization of cataloging in an effort to increase cooperation among scholars of musical iconography. There is an introductory essay on what works of art teach us about music, followed by rules and guidelines for cataloging works of art. Appendixes include a list of common names of instruments, with cross-references, and subject entries gathered to date, as well as bibliographical references.

Reviewed by Mary Rasmussen in *JAMS* 27 (1974): 353–60 and by Jeremy Montagu in *EM* 2 (1974): 41–43.

2.44 Cohen, H. Robert, Sylvia L'Écuyer Lacroix, and **Jacques Léveillé.** *Les gravures musicales dans L'Illustration, 1843–1899.* 3 vols. Quebec: Les Presses de l'Université Laval; New York: Pendragon Press, 1982–83. (La vie musicale en France au dix-neuvième siècle, 1)

A catalog of 3,360 music-related engravings from the French periodical *L'Illustration,* with a thesaurus to direct the user to appropriate images, providing a treasure of 19th-century French musical life. This was published under the auspices of Répertoire International d'Iconographie Musicale (RIdIM).

Reviewed by Clifford Bartlett in *Brio* 21 (1984): 57 and by François Lesure in *Fontes* 31 (1984): 242.

2.45 Collaer, Paul, Albert Van der Linden, and **F. van den Bremt.** *Historical Atlas of Music: A Comprehensive Study of the World's Music, Past and Present.* Trans. by Allan Miller. 175 pp. Cleveland, Ohio: World Publishing Company, 1968.

Also issued by Harrap in London and Toronto, 1968. Originally published as *Atlas historique de la musique* by Elsevier in Paris, 1960.

An illustrated survey of music history, with 15 full-page maps and over 700 illustrations.

Reviewed by Robert E. Wolf in *MQ* 47 (1961): 413–16.

2.46 Crane, Frederick. *A Bibliography of the Iconography of Music.* 41 pp. New York: Printed by the Research Center for Musical Iconography, Graduate Center of CUNY, 1971.

A compilation of articles, catalogs, illustrated histories, and other studies, organized for the planning sessions for the Repertory of Musical Iconography, St. Gall, August 1971.

2.47* Duffin, Ross. *The Cleveland Museum of Art.* 49 pp. New York: Research Center for Music Iconography, 1991. (RIdIM/RCMI inventory of music iconography, 8)

A catalog of art held by the Cleveland Museum of Art; all art cited has musical references.

Reviewed by Laurence Libin in *JAMS* 46 (1993): 144–52.

2.48 Dufourcq, Norbert. *La musique, les hommes, les instruments, les oeuvres.* 2 vols. Paris: Larousse, 1965.

A fine, visually oriented history of music, an expansion of Dufourcq's *La musique des origines à nos jours,* which was first published in 1946, appearing in 7 eds. The contributors, leading authorities in the field, are chiefly French. This work in turn served as the basis for the *Larousse Encyclopedia of Music,* edited by Geoffrey Hindley. (New York: World Publishing Company, 1971, 576 pp.).

2.49* Ford, Terence, and **Andrew Green.** *National Gallery of Art, Washington.* In collaboration with Emilio Ros-Fábregas. 11 pp. New York: Research Center for Musical Iconography, 1986. (RIdIM/RCMI inventory of music iconography, 1)

The first of a series of inventories listing art with musical content.

2.50* Ford, Terence, and **Andrew Green.** *The Pierpont Morgan Library: Medieval and Renaissance Manuscripts.* In collaboration with Emilio Ros-Fábregas and Elizabeth Wright. 144 pp. New York: Research Center for Musical Iconography, 1988. (RIdIM/RCMI inventory of music iconography, 3)

An inventory of early manuscripts with musical references, organized to enhance further iconographic study.

Reviewed by Ann P. Basart in *CNV* 130 (1989): 10–11.

2.51* Hurwitt, Elliott, and **Terence Ford.** *The Frick Collection, New York.* 26 pp. New York: Research Center for Musical Iconography, 1987. (RIdIM/RCMI inventory of music iconography, 7)

An inventory of art with musical references held by the Frick Collection.

2.52 Kinsky, Georg. *A History of Music in Pictures.* 363 pp. New York: Dutton, 1937.

Reprinted in New York by Dover Publications in 1951. Originally published as *Geschichte der Musik in Bildern,* 1929; the first English ed. was published in 1930. There is also a French ed.

A classic collection. The pictures include musicians' portraits; music in painting, drawing, and sculpture; facsimile pages of early musical and theoretical works; and early instruments. They are arranged chronologically from antiquity to the early 20th century. There is an index to instruments, place names, and personal names.

The reprint is reviewed by William Lichtenwanger in *Notes* 9 (1952): 422.

2.53 Komma, Karl Michael. *Musikgeschichte in Bildern.* 332 pp. Stuttgart: Alfred Kröner, 1961.

A collection of 743 well-reproduced illustrations covering the history of music from ancient times to the present, with detailed commentary on each illustration.

Reviewed by Hans Engel in *Die Musikforschung* 18 (1965): 440–41.

2.54 Leppert, Richard D. *The Theme of Music in Flemish Painting of the Seventeenth Century.* 2 vols. Munich; Salzburg: E. Katzbichler, 1977.

A catalog of 770 paintings with indexes to instruments and themes as well as a plethora of ancillary data.

Reviewed by François Lesure in *Fontes* 25 (1978): 197.

2.55 Lesure, François. *Musik und Gesellschaft im Bild: Zeugnisse der Malerei aus sechs Jahrhunderten.* Trans. from French by Anna Martina Gottschalk. 245 pp. + 105 plates. Kassel, Germany: Bärenreiter, 1966.

Skillful use of pictorial materials to illuminate the musical-social structure of European culture from the 14th through the 19th centuries.

Reviewed by Steven J. Ledbetter in *Notes* 24 (1968): 702–4.

2.56 Michels, Ulrich. *DTV-Atlas zur Musik: Tafeln und Texte.* 2 vols. Munich: Deutscher Taschenbuch-Verlag; Kassel, Germany: Bärenreiter, 1980–85.

First published, 1977. Also published by Alianza, Madrid (1982–) as *Atlas de música,* and in France by Fayard as *Guide illustré de la musique,* trans. by Jean Gribenski, Gilles Leothaud, and Michele Dujany.

A music dictionary, with each page of text faced by one of musical examples, charts, and diagrams, in which the details, relationships, and forms are clarified by color.

2.57* Owens, Margaret Boyer, and **Terence Ford.** *Art Institute of Chicago.* 26 pp. New York: Research Center for Musical Iconography, 1987. (RIdIM/RCMI inventory of music iconography, 2)

Another in the series inventorying the major art collections and their music-connected holdings.

2.58 Parigi, Luigi. *La musica nelle gallerie di Milano. Con 21 illustrazioni in tavole fuori testo.* 71 pp. + 21 plates. Milan: Perrella, 1935.

A catalog of paintings with musical subjects to be found in the art galleries of Milan. There are descriptions of each work and its subject matter.

2.59 Pincherle, Marc. *An Illustrated History of Music.* Revised ed. Edited by Georges and Rosamund Bernier. Trans. by Rollo Myers. 230 pp. New York: Reynal; London: Macmillan, 1962.

Published in France as *Histoire illustrée de la musique* (Paris: Gallimard, 1959).

A beautifully designed volume, with 240 illustrations. The text is planned as an introduction to music history but maintains a high standard of accuracy and critical comment, while lacking a bibliography or any other documentation.

Reviewed by Denis Stevens in *MT* 101 (1960): 493, by Emanuel Winternitz in *Notes* 18 (1960): 48–50, and by Jack A. Westrup in *M&L* 41 (1960): 388.

2.60 Seebass, Tillman, and **Tilden Russell.** *Imago musicae: International Yearbook of Musical Iconography; Official Organ of the International Repertory of Musical Iconography.* Basel: Bärenreiter; Durham, N.C.: Duke University Press, 1985–90.

Vols. 1–5. Lucca: Libreria Musicale Italiana Editrice, 1991– . Vol. 6– .

Articles on specific artistic works and collections of works, music and the visual arts in cultural life, catalogs and inventories of collections (real and synthetic) of art works that incorporate musical images, and bibliography of writings on musical iconography since 1975.

2.61 Vorreiter, Leopold. "Musikikonographie des Altertums im Schrifttum 1850–1949 und 1950–1974." In *AM* 46 (1974): 1–42.

A bibliographic essay of 532 titles providing information on the iconography of ancient music and general ethnic music.

CHRONOLOGIES AND CALENDARS

2.62* Adkins Chiti, Patricia. *Almanacco delle virtuose, primedonne, compositrici e musiciste d'italia dall'A.D. 177 ai giorni nostri.* 331 pp. and compact disc. Novara: Istituto Geografico de Agostini, 1991.

Featuring Italian women in music, a day-by-day almanac, from 177 A.D. to the present: important births, deaths, important performances, commentaries, letters, poems, and reviews. Also included are four short articles for each calendar month on historical, biographical, and other musical subjects. There are many illustrations, a bibliography, discography, and a detailed name index.

2.63* Boydell, Brian. *A Dublin Musical Calendar, 1700–1760.* 320 pp. Dublin: Irish Academic Press, 1988.

A tool, more than a calendar, giving through helpful indexes access to information on music life in Dublin, 1700–1760.

Reviewed by Graydon Beeks in *Notes* 47 (1990): 372–74.

2.64 Burbank, Richard. *Twentieth-Century Music.* xxi + 485 pp. New York: Facts on File, 1984. British ed., Thames and Hudson, London, 1984.

A musical chronology giving the events of each year from 1900 to 1979, arranged in five basic categories, listed separately under each year: opera; dance; instrumental and vocal music; births, deaths, and debuts; and related events. The entries are written in the present tense and quotes from the newspapers of the day abound. There is an index of names and titles (pp. 429–85).

Reviewed by Raymond McGill in *Brio* 21 (1984): 77–78 and by Frederic Schoettler in *ARBA* 16 (1985): no. 1164.

2.65 Cullen, Marion Elizabeth. *Memorable Days in Music.* 233 pp. Metuchen, N.J.: Scarecrow Press, 1970.

A calendar of musical events by day of year with popular quotations about music inserted for each day, and notes of important persons' birth and death days, premieres, and other musically significant days.

2.66 Dufourcq, Norbert, Marcelle Benoit, and **Bernard Gagnepain.** *Les grandes dates de l'histoire de la musique.* 2nd ed. 127 pp. Paris: Presses Universitaires de France, 1976.

Dates of events, with historical commentary, from the first century A.D. to 1960, organized by periods: middle ages, renaissance, and 17th, 18th, 19th, and 20th centuries.

2.67 Eisler, Paul E. *World Chronology of Music History.* 6 vols. to date. Dobbs Ferry, N.Y.: Oceana Publications, 1972– .

Contents: Vol. 1, *4000 B.C. to 1594 A.D.;* Vol. 2, *1594 to 1684;* Vol. 3, *1685–1735;* Vol. 4, *Name Index, Volumes 1–3;* Vol. 5, *1736–1786;* Vol. 6, *1771–1796.*

An ambitious multivolume survey of the chronology of music, to be 8–10 vols. at completion. The publisher plans for the series to contain over 100,000 entries, covering all significant dates in music history: composers, compositions, performers, premieres, and other pertinent dates.

The 5th vol. is reviewed by George Louis Mayer in *ARBA* 11 (1980): no. 941.

2.68 Gangwere, Blanche M. *Music History from the Late Roman through the Gothic Periods, 313–1425: A Documented Chronology.* 247 pp. Westport, Conn.: Greenwood Press, 1986. (Music reference collection, no. 6)

A synopsis of important topics arranged chronologically and in outline form. For each topic, references are provided to sources and secondary works in the principal bibliography. Maps and supplemental sources are provided for each period. A general bibliography (pp. 195–213), a discography (pp. 214–15), an author-composer index, and a subject index are included; the bibliographies cite primarily English-language sources. This is an interesting concept, and potentially useful in providing an overview for nonspecialists or a foil for specialists. Poor production standards make the text occasionally difficult to read.

Reviewed by Marion S. Gushee in *Notes* 45 (1989): 517–18, by George Louis Mayer in *ARBA* 18 (1887): no. 1226, and by Ann P. Basart in *CNV* 102 (1986): 22.

2.69 Gangwere, Blanche M. *Music History during the Renaissance Period, 1425–1520: A Documented Chronology.* 492 pp. New York: Greenwood Press, 1991. (Music reference collection, 28)

Organized much like the author's earlier chronology (**2.68**), again stressing English-language sources.

Reviewed by Keith E. Mixter in *Fontes* 39 (1992): 364–66.

2.70* Hall, Charles J. *Eighteenth-Century Musical Chronicle: Events 1750–1799.* 177 pp. New York: Greenwood Press, 1990. (Music reference collection, 25)

A chronology listing primarily musical events, with a brief summary of the events in the other arts, society, and politics, originating as an aid for the production of a series of radio programs. Perhaps because of program requirements, this account of the last half of the 18th century ignores the years traditionally labeled as the end of the baroque.

Reviewed by George R. Hill in *Notes* 48 (1991): 84–85.

2.71* Hall, Charles J. *Nineteenth-Century Musical Chronicle: Events, 1800–1899.* 374 pp. New York: Greenwood Press, 1989. (Music reference collection, 21b)

A chronology formatted like the author's 18th-century compilation.

Reviewed by Horst Leuchtmann in *Fontes* 38 (1991): 246–47 and by Theodore Albrecht in *Notes* 48 (1991): 91–93.

2.72 Hall, Charles J. *Twentieth-Century Musical Chronicle: Events, 1900–1988.* New York: Greenwood Press, 1989. (Music reference collection, 20)

An earlier version was published in 1980 by Opus, Northbrook, Ill., as *Hall's Musical Years, the Twentieth Century, 1900–1979: A Comprehensive Year-by-Year Survey of the Fine Arts.*

2.73 Hendler, Herb. *Year by Year in the Rock Era: Events and Conditions Shaping the Rock Generations that Reshaped America.* xxv + 350 pp. Westport, Conn.: Greenwood Press, 1983.

A chronicle of political, social, and popular musical events, with bibliography (pp. 339–50) but no index.

Reviewed by Barbara E. Kemp in *ARBA* 16 (1985): no. 1216.

2.74* Holland, Ted. *This Day in Afro-American Music.* 164 pp. San Francisco, Calif.: Pomegranate Artbooks, 1993.

A calendar rather than a chronology, a source arranged by day rather than by year, with a chronologically arranged event (generally birth or death dates rather than career highlights), followed by a brief account of the subject's professional history. The African-American musicians covered range from Paula Abdul and Cannonball Adderley to Andre Watts and Lester Young.

2.75* Kendall, Alan. *Chronicle of Classical Music: An Intimate Diary of the Lives and Music of the Great Composers.* 288 pp. London; New York: Thames and Hudson, 1994.

A French ed., *Chronique de la musique: L'histoire de la musique classique et de compositeurs année par année* (288 pp.), was published in Paris by Éditions de la Martiniere in 1995.

A chronology of musical events over the last four centuries, nicely illustrated.

Reviewed by Nicky Hind in *Brio* 32 (1995): 49–50 and by Timothy J. McGee in *LJ* 119 (1994): 84.

2.76* Kraus, Gottfried. *Musik in Österreich: Eine Chronik in Daten, Dokumenten, Essays und Bildern: Klassische Musik, Oper, Operette, Volksmusik, Unterhaltungsmusik, Avantgardemusik, Komponisten, Dirigenten, Virtuosen, Sänger, Musikstätten, Festspiele, Instrumentenbau.* 518 pp. Vienna: C. Brandstätter, 1989.

A chronology covering the range of Austrian music.

2.77 La Grange, Henri Louis de. *Documents du demi-siècle: Tableau chronologique des principales oeuvres musicales de 1900 à 1950, établi par genre et par année.* 153 pp. Paris: Richard-Masse, 1952. (Revue musicale, 216)

A year-by-year list of the important musical works, 1900–50, with miscellaneous information on music for each year. Catalogs of six publishers, with the significant work issued by them in this period: Heugel, Costallat, Amphion, Ricordi, Choudens, and Ouvrières. Minimal bibliographic information is supplied.

2.78 Lahee, Henry Charles. *Annals of Music in America; A Chronological Record of Significant Musical Events, from 1640 to the Present Day, with Comments on the Various Periods into which the Work is Divided.* 298 pp. Boston, Mass.: Marshall Jones Company, 1922.

Reprinted in New York by AMS Press, 1969, and in Freeport, N.Y., by Books for Libraries Press in 1970.

A chronology of musical events in the part of North America that became the U.S. There is an index of compositions (pp. 193–279) and their first American performance, given chronologically under the composer's name, as well as a section of miscellaneous events (conductors' appointments, debuts by performance category, choral and instrumental societies, and the like).

2.79 Manson, Adele P. *Calendar of Music and Musicians.* 462 pp. Metuchen, N.J.: Scarecrow Press, 1981.

A day-by-day list of important musical events, with indexes to personal and corporate names and to titles.

Reviewed by John E. Druesedow, Jr., in *ARBA* 13 (1982): no. 1014, with errata, and by Michael Ochs in *Notes* 38 (1982): 612–13.

2.80 Mattfeld, Julius. *Variety Music Cavalcade, 1621–1969: A Chronology of Vocal and Instrumental Music Popular in the United States.* 3rd ed. 766 pp. Englewood Cliffs, N.J.: Prentice-Hall, 1971.

A concept originally appearing in a modified form as *Variety Radio Directory, 1938–39,* supplemented in weekly issues of *Variety.* In its present form, it was first issued as *Variety Music Cavalcade, 1620–1950,* in 1952, 637 pp.; the revised ed. (xxiii + 713 pp.), increasing coverage through 1961, appeared in 1962.

A chronological bibliography of American popular music, with parallel social, cultural, and historical events listed for each year. There is a title index to musical works, with dates of first publication.

The 1st ed. is reviewed by Margaret Mott in *Notes* 9 (1952): 608–9; the 3rd ed. is reviewed by Irving Lowens in *Notes* 20 (1963): 233–34.

2.81* Millard, Bob. *Country Music: 70 Years of America's Favorite Music.* xxiv + 328 pp. New York: HarperPerennial, 1993.

From the 1920s to 1992, a list of the highlights of American country music, stressing various awards, with indexes by personal name and song title.

2.82* Nite, Norm N. *Rock On Almanac: The First Four Decades of Rock 'n' Roll: A Chronology.* 2nd ed. 581 pp. New York: HarperPerennial, 1992.

First ed., 1989, by the Perennial Library, 532 pp.

A chronology much in format like Julius Mattfeld's *Variety Music Cavalcade* (**2.80**), covering the years from 1954 to 1992, with some preliminary coverage of the 1940s through 1953. Each year's survey includes the top news stories of the year, the year's top sports winners, and the year's popular music highlights; the debut artists of the year and their respective debut albums are given, as well as a monthly list of hit records and their performers, with indication given when they received gold record or number-one status. Also listed annually are top singles, top albums, notable births and deaths, top movies, Academy Award winners, and top television shows. There is a glossary of terms, as well as indexes of performers and song titles.

2.83 Schäffer, Bogus̆ťaw. *Maly informator muzyli XX mieku.* 4th ed. 412 pp. Cracow: Polskie Wydaw. Muzyczne, 1987.

First ed., 1958 (142 pp.); 2nd ed., 1967 (184 pp.); 3rd ed., 1975 (384 pp.).

A chronology of musical events of the 20th century, including a bibliography (pp. 377–82) and indexes.

2.84 Slonimsky, Nicolas. *Music since 1900.* 5th ed. 1,260 pp. New York: Schirmer Books; Toronto: Maxwell Macmillan Canada, 1994.

First published by Norton, New York, in 1937; the 2nd ed. was published in 1938; the 3rd ed. in New York by Coleman-Ross in 1949 (759 pp.); the 4th in New York by Scribner's in 1971 (1,595 pp.), with a supplement in 1986 (390 pp.).

A daily account of significant events in music history, extended to 1991. Categories covered include the dates of composition and first performance, the founding of institutions and societies, and the births and deaths of contemporary musicians. Although the contents are international in scope, the emphasis is on events in the United States since 1950. There is a dictionary of new terms.

The 3rd ed. is reviewed by Edward N. Waters in *Notes* 6 (1949): 616–17. The 5th ed. is reviewed by Joy Haslam Calico in *Fontes* 42 (1995): 383–87 and by Robert Skinner in *ARBA* 26 (1995): no. 1262.

SOURCE READINGS

2.85* Barker, Andrew. *Greek Musical Writings.* 2 vols. Cambridge, England; New York: Cambridge University Press, 1984–89. (Cambridge readings in the literature of music)

Contents: Vol. 1, *The Musician and His Art;* Vol. 2, *Harmonic and Acoustic Theory.*

The first paperback ed. was published in 1989.

Newly translated excerpts from classic Greek writings on music, some in English for the first time.

Vol. 1 is reviewed by Clifford Barlett in *Brio* 21 (1984): 53–54, by John Caldwell in *EM* 13 (1985): 93, by J. Solomon in *M&L* 67 (1986): 80–82, by T. A. Szlezak in *Die Musikforschung* 41 (1988): 288–90, and by J. G. Landels in *MT* 127 (1986): 153–54. Vol. 2 is reviewed by E. Kerr Borthwick in *M&L* 72 (1991): 69–71 and by Edward Lippman in *Notes* 47 (1991): 727–29.

2.86* Barzun, Jacques. *Pleasures of Music: A Reader's Choice of Great Writings about Music and Musicians from Cellini to Bernard Shaw.* 624 pp. New York: The Viking Press, 1951.

Second ed., *Pleasures of Music: An Anthology of Writings about Music and Musicians from Cellini to Bernard Shaw,* published by University of Chicago Press, 1977 (371 pp.); the fiction chapter is omitted.

An anthology of writings organized by category. Chapter topics include fiction, criticism, musical life, fantasies and confessions, correspondence, maxims, and good stories. A list of sources and a bibliography are included.

Reviewed by Richard V. Lindabury in *Notes* 9 (1952): 280–81.

2.87* Becker, Judith O., and **Alan H. Feinstein.** *Karawitan: Source Readings in Javanese Gamelan and Vocal Music.* 3 vols. Ann Arbor, Mich.: Center for South and Southeast Asian Studies, University of Michigan, 1984–88. (Michigan papers on South and Southeast Asia, 23, 30–31)

Contents: Vol. 1, *Writings by Martopangrawit, Sumarsam, Sastrapusyaka, Gitosaprodjo, Sindoesawarno, Poerbapangrawit, and Prohobohardjono;* Vol. 2, *Writings by Warsodiningrat, Sumarsam, Gitosaprodjo, Purbodiningrat, Poerbatjaraka, Sindoesawarno, and Paku Buwana X;* Vol. 3, Appendix 1, *Glossary and index of technical terms mentioned in the texts;* Appendix 2, *Javanese cipher notation (titilaras kepatihan) of musical pieces mentioned in the texts;* Appendix 3, *Bibliographies of authors and of sources mentioned by authors, translators, editors, and consultants.*

An anthology of articles and monographs on Javanese music written from c. 1930–75.

The 1st vol. is reviewed by Neil Sorrell in *M&L* 67 (1986): 172, by R. Schumacher in *World of Music* 27 (1985): 83–84, and by R. Vetter in *Asian Music* 16 (1985): 186–89 no. 2. The 2nd vol. is reviewed by Margaret Sarkissian in *Notes* 45 (1989): 512–14, by R. Schumacher in *World of Music* 30 (1988): 88–90, and by Neil Sorrell in *M&L* 69 (1988): 502–3. The 3rd vol. is reviewed by Neil Sorell in *M&L* 70 (1989): 525–26, by B. Brinner in *Ethnomusicology* 34 (1990): 140–47, and by R. Schumacher in *World of Music* 31 (1989): 113–15.

2.88* Bent, Ian. *Music Analysis in the Nineteenth Century.* 2 vols. Cambridge, England; New York: Cambridge University Press, 1994. (Cambridge readings in the literature of music)

Contents: Vol. 1, *Fugue, Form and Style;* Vol. 2, *Hermeneutic Approaches.*

Two vols. differing from the others in this Cambridge series, with the readings dealing with specific works or a certain repertoire rather than more philosophical issues, as found in Bujić (**2.90**) and Le Huray and Day (**2.107**). The 1st vol. includes newly translated analyses of writings on fugue, style, and form, and on the works of specific composers, including Palestrina, Bach, Handel, and Mozart. The 2nd vol. emphasizes analyses written from a more metaphoric style. Both volumes include bibliographic essays and extensive indexes.

The 1st vol. is reviewed by Lydia D. Rohmer in *Brio* 32 (1995): 54–55; the 2nd is reviewed by Diether de la Motte in *Die Musikforschung* 48 (1995): 334.

2.89* Blackburn, Bonnie, Edward E. Lowinsky, and **Clement A. Miller.** *A Correspondence of Renaissance Musicians.* xliv + 1,067 pp. Oxford: Clarendon Press; Oxford University Press, 1991.

The correspondence of renaissance musicians Giovanni Spataro, Marc'Antonio Cavazzoni, Giovanni del Lago, and Pietro Aaron, impeccably edited. Included are 110 letters they wrote to one another and to other musicians. The majority of the letters are from Spataro, collected by del Lago. Offered here is a more personal type of source reading, providing a look at the musical world of the renaissance not found in the theoretical writings of the day.

Reviewed by John Kmetz in *Notes* 50 (1993): 111, by Anna Maria Busse Berger in *Early Music History* 12 (1993): 191–203, by J. Dean in *M&L* 75 (1994): 435–37, by Jessie Ann Owens in *JAMS* 46 (1993): 313–18, and by P. Urquhart in *JMR* 14 (1994): 93–97.

2.90* Bujić, Bojan. *Music in European Thought, 1851–1912.* 414 pp. Cambridge, England; New York: Cambridge University Press, 1988. (Cambridge readings in the literature of music)

In a sense, a continuation of the Le Huray–Day collection (**2.107**). The writings cover the middle years of the 19th century to the early years of the 20th. Musical aesthetics is the primary area of interest of this vol., and German writers are heavily represented. Included are an extensive bibliography and an index.

Reviewed by Rey M. Longyear in *Notes* 47 (1991): 749–50, by Leon Botstein in *NCM* 13 (1989): 168–78, by Roger Hollinrake in *M&L* 70 (1989): 423–25, and by Peter Kivy in *JMR* 9 (1989): 43–45.

2.91* Campbell, Stuart. *Russians on Russian Music, 1830–1880: An Anthology.* xxi + 295 pp. Cambridge, England: Cambridge University Press, 1994.

A collection of writings on music by leading Russian composers and music critics, with editorial commentary.

Reviewed by David Brown in *M&L* 76 (1995): 627–29.

2.92* Chase, Gilbert. *The American Composer Speaks: A Historical Anthology, 1770–1965.* 318 pp. Baton Rouge, La.: Louisiana State University Press, 1966.

Representative writings by 30 American composers from William Billings to Earle Brown, with bibliography.

Reviewed by Paul Turok in *Music Journal* 25 (1967): 91.

2.93 Chiu, Lien-k'ang. *Ch'un ch'iu chan kuo yin yüeh shih liao.* 104 pp. Hong Kong: 1980.

A selection of source readings on music from various Chinese classics of the Spring and Autumn period (722–481 B.C.) and the Warring States period (404–221 B.C.), with a bibliography of sources.

2.94 Corte, Andrea della. *Antologia della storia della musica.* 4th ed., revised in 1 vol. 491 pp. Turin: G.B. Paravia, 1945.

First published in 2 vols., 1927, with subsequent editions in 1929 and 1937.

A mixture of writings by modern European scholars, but with some early documents (by Zarlino, Caccini, and Peri) represented.

2.95* Coussemaker, Charles Edmond Henri de. *Scriptorum de musica medii aevi novam seriem a Gerbertina alteram collegit nuncque primum.* 4 vols. Paris: A. Durand, 1864–76.

Later printings in Milan (Bollettino Bibliografico Musicale, 1931 and 1973) and Hildesheim, Germany, by Georg Olms Verlag, 1963.

Designed as a supplement to Gerbert's *Scriptores ecclesiastici de musica* (**2.99**). In light of modern scholarship, these vols. are full of errors, yet Coussemaker provides a starting place for subsequent research in this area.

2.96 Dahlhaus, Carl, and **Ruth Katz.** *Contemplating Music: Source Readings in the Aesthetics of Music.* 4 vols. to date. New York: Pendragon Press, 1986–94. (Aesthetics in music, 5)

Contents: Vol. 1, *Substance* (1986); Vol. 2, *Import* (1989); Vol. 3, *Essence* (1992); Vol. 4, *Community of discourse* (1994).

Readings arranged first by broad philosophical concept and then, within each concept, chronologically, enabling the reader to experience the progression and changes in these concepts over time. Almost 100 essays are included, ranging from writings by Plato and Boethius to Schoenberg and Ligeti. There are introductory essays for each broad section and short introductions for each author. Many entries appear in English translation for the first time.

Vol. 1 is reviewed by R. Sparshott in *MT* 129 (1988): 131–33, by Roger Hollinrake in *M&L* 73 (1992): 270–71, by Leon Botstein in *NCM* 13 (1989): 168–78, and by Donald Burrows in *Notes* 49 (1992): 592–96. Vol. 2 is reviewed by William McClellan in *Fontes* 38 (1991): 248–49, by Roger Hollinrake in *M&L* 73 (1992): 270–71, by Donald Burrows in *Notes* 49 (1992): 592–96, by Ivan Supičić in *IRASM* 24 (1993): 175–77 no. 2, and by G. Falcone in *Nuova rivista musicale italiana* 28 (1994): 111–13. Vol. 3 is reviewed by T. Schipperges in *Die Musikforschung* 46 (1993): 336, by P. Franklin in *MT* 134 (1993): 392–93, and by Roger Hollinrake in *M&L* 75 (1994): 69–70. Vol. 4 is reviewed by L. Rohmer in *Brio* 31 (1994): 58–59.

2.97* Demuth, Norman. *An Anthology of Musical Criticism from the 15th to the 20th Century.* xxvii + 397 pp. London: Eyre & Spottiswoode, 1947.

A collection of musical criticism dating from the 15th century to "living memory." The acknowledgments section includes names of writers (Ernest Newman, George Bernard Shaw, and Donald Tovey) not included in this volume. There is a bibliography of sources (pp. 383–97). This is a good and gentler companion volume to Slonimsky's *Lexicon of Musical Invective* (**2.122**).

Reviewed by Abraham Veinus in *JAMS* 4 (1951): 55–56 and by W. McNaught in *MT* 90 (1949): 281.

2.98* Fubini, Enrico. *Music and Culture in Eighteenth-Century Europe: A Source Book.* Trans. from the original sources by Wolfgang Freis, Lisa Gasbarrone, and Michael Louis Leone; trans. edited by Bonnie J. Blackburn. 421 pp. Chicago, Ill.: University of Chicago Press, 1994.

The original ed. was published in Turin by EDT/Musica in 1986 as *Musica e cultura nel Settecento europeo,* 349 pp.

One of the most comprehensive collections of key writings about 18th-century music. Included in the English translation is a new chapter on the revaluation of instrumental music, as well as new selections in Chapters 4 and 6. A biographical dictionary, a bibliography (pp. 413–14), and an index are included.

The English trans. is reviewed by Raymond Monelle in *M&L* 76 (1995): 431–32 and by G. Cook Kimball in *OQ* 11 (1995): 119–22.

2.99* Gerbert, Martin. *Scriptores ecclesiastici de musica sacra potissimum: Ex variis Italiae, Galliae & Germaniae codicibus manuscriptis collecti et nunc primum publica luce donati.* 3 vols. St. Blasian, 1784.

One of the oldest anthologies of writings on music. Although by current standards Gerbert's collection of original documents would appear faulty, this is still one of the most significant collections of its kind. This work was continued by Coussemaker's anthology (**2.95**).

2.100* Godwin, Joscelyn. *The Harmony of the Spheres: A Sourcebook of the Pythagorean Tradition in Music.* 495 pp. Rochester, Vt.: Inner Traditions International, 1993.

An anthology of 52 excerpts, dating from the 5th century B.C. to the 19th century.

Reviewed by Jon Barlow in *Notes* 50 (1994): 1422–25.

2.101* Godwin, Joscelyn. *Music, Mysticism and Magic: A Sourcebook.* 349 pp. London; New York: Routledge & Kegan Paul, 1986.

Another edition was published in New York by Arcana, 1987.

A collection of 61 excerpts, with authors ranging in time from Plato to Stockhausen. There are a bibliography of cited works, an *index nominum,* and an *index rerum.*

Reviewed by M. McMullin in *MR* 47 (1986): 126–27, by P. Gouk in *M&L* 68 (1987): 263–64, and by Jonathan Harvey in *MT* 128 (1987): 441.

2.102* Guthie, Kenneth Sylvan. *The Pythagorean Sourcebook and Library: An Anthology of Ancient Writings which Relate to Pythagoras and Pythagorean Philosophy.* Edited by Davis R. Fideler. 361 pp. Grand Rapids, Mich.: Phanes Press, 1987.

The first ed. was published in Yonkers, N.Y., by The Platonist Press in 1919 as *Pythagoras: Source Book and Library.*

A collection containing all authoritative material available at that time about Pythagoras and a complete collection of writings of his disciples. The new ed. contains the texts from the original ed., with some illustrations, a bibliography, an index, and a glossary of Pythagorean terminology.

Reviewed by Douglas Leedy in *Notes* 47 (1991): 729–30.

2.103 Harrison, Frank. *Time, Place and Music: An Anthology of Ethnomusicological Observations c. 1550 to c. 1800.* 221 pp. Amsterdam: Frits Knuf, 1973. (Source materials and studies in ethnomusicology, 1)

A compendium of observations by travelers on non-Western musical cultures.

Reviewed by Lucy Durán in *M&L* 55 (1974): 485–86, by Bruno Nettl in *Notes* 31 (1975): 553–60, by T. Lowe Dworsky in *Ethnomusicology* 19 (1975): 308–10, and by Raymond Firth in *EM* 3 (1975): 401–5.

2.104 Hermand, Jost, and **James Steakley.** *Writings by German Composers.* 303 pp. New York: Continuum, 1984. (The German library, 51)

Translated texts by 45 composers whose native language was German, from Johann Walther to Hans Werner Henze. The selections are arranged chronologically, first by composer and then in the order written. The concluding acknowledgments provide a list of modern sources from which these texts were reprinted and credits for translators.

2.105* Jan, Karl von. *Musici scriptores graeci: Aristoteles, Euclides, Nicomachus, Bacchius, Gaudentius, Alypius et melodiarum veterum quidquid exstat.* xciii + 503 pp. Leipzig: B.G. Teubner, 1895. (Bibliotheca scriptorum graecorum et romanorum Teubneriana)

"Supplementum, Melodiarum religuiae" published in 1899. Facsimile ed. published by G. Olms, Hildesheim, Germany, 1962.

One of the early standard compilations of Greek theoretical treatises.

2.106* Langer, Suzanne K. *Reflections on Art: A Source Book of Writings by Artists, Critics, and Philosophers.* 364 pp. Baltimore, Md.: Johns Hopkins University Press, 1958.

Subsequently reprinted by Johns Hopkins (1959), Oxford University Press (1961, 1968, and 1972), and Arno Press (1979).

An anthology dealing not only with readings that pertain to music, but also to other arts: Writings deal with artistic creation, artistic expression, and the role of art in society.

Reviewed by Frank Howes in *M&L* 40 (1959): 385 and by Fred Blum in *Notes* 16 (1959): 391–93.

2.107 Le Huray, Peter, and **James Day.** *Music and Aesthetics in the Eighteenth and Early Nineteenth Centuries.* 597 pp. Cambridge, England; New York: Cambridge University Press, 1981. (Cambridge readings in the literature of music)

Published in an abridged ed., 1988, 399 pp.

Almost 100 source readings by about 80 writers, designed to illustrate some of the main aesthetic issues hotly and continuously debated during the 18th and early 19th centuries, arranged in chronological order. Each reading begins with an introduction that sets the context and gives suggestions for further reading. Sources are cited. There are a bibliography and an index of names, titles, and places, as well as a general index.

Reviewed by Elaine R. Sisman in *JAMS* 35 (1982): 565–77, by Margaret Ross Griffel in *Notes* 38 (1982): 838–39, by Howard Serwer in *M&L* 63 (1982): 316–19, by William Weber in *MT* 128 (1987): 141–42, by Philippe Autexier in *Revue de musicologie* 67 (1981): 256–57, and by Rudolf Flotzinger in *Die Musikforschung* 37 (1984): 321–22.

2.108* Lippman, Edward A. *Musical Aesthetics: A Historical Reader.* 3 vols. New York: Pendragon Press, 1986–90. (Aesthetics in music, 4)

Contents: Vol. 1, *From Antiquity to the Eighteenth Century;* Vol. 2, *The Nineteenth Century;* Vol. 3, *The Twentieth Century.*

A broad variety of source readings on the philosophies and aesthetics of music. Each vol. includes lists for additional reading and brief bibliographies.

Vol. 1 is reviewed by Philip Alperson in *Notes* 44 (1987): 269–70, by F. Sparshott in *MT* 128 (1987): 332–33, and by Bojan Bujić in *M&L* 69 (1988): 496–98. Vol. 2 is reviewed by G. Lenz in *Die Musikforschung* 44 (1991): 180–81 and by Leon Botstein in *NCM* 13 (1989): 168–78. Vol. 3 is reviewed by Jay Rahn in *Notes* 48 (1991): 508–10 and by Bojan Bujić in *M&L* 74 (1993): 458–59.

2.109* Lockspeiser, Edward. *The Literary Clef: An Anthology of Letters and Writings by French Composers.* 186 pp. London: J. Calder, 1958.

Correspondence from nine French composers—Berlioz, Bizet, Chabrier, Debussy, Fauré, Lalo, Ravel, Saint-Saëns, and Satie—as well as Harriet Smithson. There is a brief bibliography.

Reviewed by Hans Redlich in *MR* 20 (1959): 167–73 no. 2.

2.110 MacClintock, Carol. *Readings in the History of Music in Performance.* 432 pp. Bloomington, Ind.: Indiana University Press, 1979.

First Midland Book ed., 1982.

Selected sources on the history of performance practice from the late middle ages to the mid-19th century. There is no index.

Reviewed by James W. Pruett in *Notes* 36 (1980): 892–93, by Robert Donington in *EM* 8 (1980): 383–87, and by G. Paine in *Choral Journal* 22 (1982): 35–38 no. 5.

2.111 McKinnon, James. *Music in Early Christian Literature.* 180 pp. Cambridge, England; New York: Cambridge University Press, 1987. (Cambridge readings in the literature of music)

First paperback ed., 1989.

Translations of writings about music from the Patristic period, with bibliography and index.

Reviewed by Albert C. Rotola in *Notes* 47 (1990): 368–70, by Helmet Hucke in *Die Musikforschung* 43 (1990): 391–92, by J. A. Smith in *M&L* 69 (1988): 244–46, by Marie-Noël Colette in *Fontes* 35 (1988): 73, and by Geoffrey Chew in *MT* 128 (1987): 405.

2.112* Mark, Michael L. *Source Readings in Music Education History.* 274 pp. New York: Schirmer Books; London: Collier Macmillan, 1982.

A collection of writings tracing the significance of music education in western culture from antiquity through the 20th century. The writings are by philosophers, educators, psychologists, and political figures. The statements of belief of some professional organizations are included. There is no index.

Reviewed by Carroll Gonzo in *MEJ* 70 (April 1984): 26–27.

2.113* Morgenstern, Sam. *Composers on Music: An Anthology of Composers' Writings from Palestrina to Copland.* xxiii + 584 pp. New York: Pantheon, 1956.

The writings of 88 composers, chronologically arranged, with a list of sources (pp. 557–69).

Reviewed by D. Cox in *MT* 98 (1957): 134–35 and by Edward Waters in *Notes* 14 (1957): 571–72.

2.114* Nettl, Paul. *The Book of Musical Documents.* 381 pp. New York: Philosophical Library, 1948.

An anthology of quotations from letters, memoirs, articles, and theoretical writings, arranged chronologically in 17 chapters, ending with a chapter, "Music in a Degenerate World," that includes passages on the role of music in Nazi Germany. The preface is by Carleton Sprague Smith.

Reviewed by Arthur Jacobs in *MT* 90 (1949): 154 and by Leonard Burkat in *Notes* 6 (1949): 312–13.

2.115 Neuls-Bates, Carol. *Women in Music: An Anthology of Source Readings from the Middle Ages to the Present.* 351 pp. New York: Harper & Row, 1982.

A new ed. was anticipated for 1996, to be published by Northeastern University Press, Boston.

A collection dating from the 4th century, although most selections date from the mid-19th century to the present. Each excerpt includes background information; there is a bibliography.

Reviewed by Pamela Bristah in *Notes* 40 (1983): 302–3 and by Henry Raynor in *MR* 46 (1985): 148–50 no. 2.

2.116* Palisca, Claude V. *The Florentine Camerata: Documentary Studies and Translations.* 234 pp. New Haven, Conn.: Yale University Library, 1989. (Music theory translation series)

An anthology of documents, with excerpts by members of the circle of Giovanni Bardi and the Florentine Camerata. This collection was published to provide English translations of important sources previously not available. Included are translations and, when no others are available, critical editions of the sources.

Reviewed by E. Thomas Glasgow in *OQ* 7 (1990–91): 146–48, by Georgie Durosoir in *Revue de musicologie* 76 (1990): 249–52, and by H. Wiley Hitchcock in *Performance Practice Review* 3 (1990): 78–81.

2.117* Paynter, John, Tim Howell, Richard Orton, and **Peter Seymour.** *Companion to Contemporary Musical Thought.* 2 vols. xxxviii + 1,208 pp. New York: Routledge, 1992.

An anthology of writings on musical scholarship of the late 1980s and early 1990s, divided into four sections: people and music, the technology of music, the structure of music, and the interpretation of music. The "Notes on contributors" in the prefatory section provides useful information on the authors; there is an extensive index.

Reviewed by David Wright in *MT* 135 (1994): 153–55, by Roger Scruton in *TLS* 4766 (1994): 14–15, and by Nicholas Cook in *M&L* 75 (1994): 115–20.

2.118* Prod'homme, Jacques Gabriel. *Écrits de musiciens (XVe–XVIIIe siècles).* 3rd ed. 455 pp. New York: Da Capo Press, 1985. (Da Capo Press music reprint series)

First published in Paris, 1912, by Mercure de France, 455 pp.

The forerunner of similar anthologies including *Antologia della storia della musica* (**2.94**), *The Book of Musical Documents* (**2.114**), and *Source Readings in Music History* (**2.126**). Included are writings by Dufay, Goudimel, Palestrina, Caccini, and J. S. Bach.

2.119 Rogova, Aleksandr Ivanovich. *Muzykal´naia éstetika Rossii odinadtsatogo-vosemnadtsato-go vekov. [Dokumenty i materialy].* Sost. tekstov, perevody i obshchaia vstupit. stat´ia. 245 pp. Moscow: Muzyka, 1973. (Pamiatniki muzykalno-ésteticheskoi mysli)

A collection of source documents on Russian musical aesthetics in the 11th–18th centuries. Bibliographical references are included.

2.120 Rowen, Ruth Halle. *Music through Sources and Documents.* 386 pp. Englewood Cliffs, N.J.: Prentice-Hall, 1979.

In the tradition of Strunk (**2.126**), chronologically ordered translations of excerpts of 103 source documents, each provided with historical and bibliographical background. There is an index of names and subjects.

Reviewed by James W. Pruett in *Notes* 36 (1980): 892–93, by Iain Fenlon in *MT* 122 (1981): 386, by Don Hixon in *Fontes* 26 (1979): 243–44, and by Henry Raynor in *MR* 48 (1988): 71–72.

2.121* Schwartz, Elliott, and **Barney Childs.** *Contemporary Composers on Contemporary Music.* xxi + 375 pp. New York: Holt, Rinehart & Winston, 1967.

Reprinted in 1978 by Da Capo Press, New York.

The writings of 33 composers, divided into 2 sections: European music before 1945 and experimental music and recent American developments.

2.122 Slonimsky, Nicolas. *Lexicon of Musical Invective: Critical Assaults on Composers since Beethoven's Time.* 2nd ed. 325 pp. New York: Coleman-Ross, 1965.

First ed. published by Coleman-Ross, New York, in 1953, 296 pp. Second ed. was reprinted by the University of Washington Press, Seattle, in various formats, 1969–84.

A collection of 669 verbal assaults, arranged alphabetically by name of the composer discussed and aimed quite squarely at 50 composers by critics of their day as well as by contemporary composers. Excerpts appear in their original language, accompanied by English translations. The opening essay, "Non-Acceptance of the Unfamiliar: Prelude to a Lexicon" (pp. 3–33), sets the scene, and an alphabetical "Invecticon" (pp. 253–83), an index of vituperative, pejorative, and deprecatory words and phrases, shows the range of composers able to share an insulting description; among the more vivid are "goddess of ugliness," "Appalachian Cossacks," "Communist travelling salesman," and examples of animal life from *amoeba* to *woodpeckers.* There is also an index of names and titles.

The 1st ed. is reviewed by Jacques Barzun in *Notes* 10 (1953): 272–73.

2.123* Song, Bang-song. *Source Readings in Korean Music.* 263 pp. Seoul: Korean National Commission for UNESCO, 1980.

Translations, with annotations, of 45 excerpts from source readings on Korean music, dating from the 12th century to the latter half of the 19th. The text is in English and Korean, with notes in English. A glossary and bibliography (pp. 197–208) are included.

Reviewed by R. Provine in *Ethnomusicology* 26 (1982): 486–88 and by H. D. Reese in *World of Music* 26 (1984): 104–5 no. 2.

2.124* Southern, Eileen. *Readings in Black American Music.* 2nd ed. 338 pp. New York: W.W. Norton, 1983.

First ed., 1971, 302 pp.

Readings that illustrate the history of Black American music from the 17th century forward in 41 passages, touching on the African musical heritage. The arrangement is chronological and by historical topics.

2.125 Stepanova, Svetlana Romanova. *Muzykal´naia zhizn´ Moskvy v pervye gody posle oktiabria: Oktiabr´ 1917–1920: Khonika, dokumenty, materialy.* 336 pp. + 16 ll. of illustrations. Moscow: Sov. Kompozitor, 1972.

A collection of source materials concerning musical life in Moscow in the first years after the October Revolution.

2.126 Strunk, W. Oliver. *Source Readings in Music History from Classical Antiquity through the Romantic Era.* 919 pp. New York: W.W. Norton and Company, 1950.

Reissued in a 5-vol. paperback ed., 1965. A revised ed., edited by Leo Treitler and seven collaborators, was expected to appear soon.

A collection of 87 selections from the writings of theorists, composers, teachers, critics, and musicians, arranged chronologically by topic; each item has a concise and illuminating introduction. The translations are excellent and the editorial work exemplary. This is an indispensable volume in any library of music history.

Reviewed by Manfred F. Bukofzer in *Notes* 8 (1951): 517–18, by Erich Hertzmann in *MQ* 37 (1951): 430–32, by Leo Schrade in *JAMS* 4 (1951): 249–51, and by Wilfrid Mellers in *MT* 93 (1951): 450–51.

2.127* Sullivan, Jack. *Words on Music: From Addison to Barzun.* 438 pp. Athens, Ohio: Ohio University Press, 1990.

An anthology of 67 selections, arranged chronologically. Included is a section of "Suggestions for further reading," but no index.

Reviewed by Thomas Wendel in the *Beethoven Newsletter* 7 (1992): 17–18.

2.128* Swan, John C. *Music in Boston: Readings from the First Three Centuries.* 99 pp. Boston: Trustees of the Public Library of the City of Boston, 1977. (National Endowment for the Humanities learning library program. Boston Public Library, 3)

A collection of 20 selections dating from the *Bay Psalm Book* to Henry Taylor Parker, including writings by Cotton Mather, William Billings, Lowell Mason, and John Sullivan Dwight.

2.129 Weiss, Piero, and **Richard Taruskin.** *Music in the Western World: A History in Documents.* 556 pp. New York: Schirmer Books; London: Collier Macmillan, 1984.

A collection of source readings arranged chronologically, intended for undergraduate students of Western music history. The sources are noted and each has an introduction establishing historical context. Includes a glossary and an index of names, works, and subjects.

Reviewed by S. Hegberg in *AMT* 34 (1985): 51.

2.130* Weisstein, Ulrich. *The Essence of Opera.* 372 pp. New York: The Free Press of Glencoe, 1964.

An anthology representing over 50 writers, mostly composers, but also including such notable figures as Dryden, Voltaire, Goethe, Kierkegaard, and Auden.

Reviewed by J. Browning in *Music Journal* 27 (1969): 96.

3

GUIDES TO MUSICOLOGY

This chapter cites works that discuss the methods, materials, and philosophies of musicological research, as well as studies that examine issues and trends in the subdisciplines. Musicology is understood here in the broadest, most inclusive sense of the term, defined by Mantle Hood in the inaugural issue of the *Journal of Musicology* (**3.26**) as "the study of music in terms of itself and within the context of its society." Grouped within this definition may be found a remarkable variety of types of works, including practical guides to research and writing about music; works that survey the content and historical development of musicology, many organized according to Guido Adler's classic division of the discipline into historical and systematic branches; works that consider musicology within the broader context of humanistic scholarship; and works that explore new or newly defined subdisciplines such as performance practice, criticism, and analysis. In recent years, inspired in part by Joseph Kerman's influential *Contemplating Music* (**3.29**), musicologists have become increasingly preoccupied with ideological and methodological issues and with developments in fields such as literary theory and the social sciences, leading to new approaches to the discipline known collectively as the New Musicology.

In order to reflect the increasing wealth and variety of musicological literature, and to accommodate the new approaches to the discipline that have emerged in recent years, the present chapter has been substantially revised from earlier editions. The title has been broadened from the earlier "Guides to Historical and Systematic Musicology" to the more general "Guides to Musicology." In addition, the chapter has been divided into three sections. The first and largest section, "General Works," includes studies that survey musicology as a field of study, including classic works such as Guido Adler's *Methode der Musikgeschichte* (**3.1**) and *Musicology* by Frank L. Harrison, Mantle Hood, and Claude V. Palisca (**3.22**); studies that offer a critical self-assessment of the discipline, such as *Musicology in the 1980s: Methods, Goals, Opportunities* by D. Kern Holoman and Claude V. Palisca (**3.24**); studies outlining the New Musicology, such as *Disciplining Music: Musicology and Its Canons* (**3.4**) by Katherine Bergeron and Philip V. Bohlman and Ruth A. Solie's *Musicology and Difference: Gender and Sexuality in Music Scholarship* (**3.40**); and studies that focus on recent developments in the subdisciplines, such as the volumes on musical analysis by Ian Bent (**3.3**), Nicholas Cook (**3.10**), and Jonathan Dunsby and Arnold Whittall (**3.17**). The second section, "Research Methods, Editing, and Writing," includes guides to musicological research and works that discuss the practices of editing and writing about music. The third section, "Performance Practice," focuses on works that consider the relationship between scholarship and the performance of early music.

GENERAL WORKS

3.1 Adler, Guido. *Methode der Musikgeschichte.* 222 pp. Leipzig: Breitkopf & Härtel, 1919.
Reprinted by Gregg International in 1971.
A study, with Adler's *Der Stil in der Musik* (1911; 2nd ed., 1929), presenting a classic formulation of the content and methods of historical musicology. The work is in two parts: a "General

Section" outlining the nature and scope of the discipline, and a section on Adler's notion of "Style Criticism." The classified bibliographical supplement by Wilhelm Fischer, "Verzeichnis von bibliographischen Hilfswerken für musikhistorische Arbeiten" (pp. 200–22), is outdated but remains valuable as a list of musical reference works before World War I; included are general bibliographical works, general music works, and bibliographies of selective aspects of music history. There are some inaccurate dates and incomplete titles for French and English works, which are less well covered than those in German. An earlier, more succinct presentation of Adler's ideas on musicology is found in his "Umfang, Methode und Ziel der Musikwissenschaft," in *Vierteljahrsschrift für Musikwissenschaft* 1 (1885): 5–8, 15–20, trans. by Martin Cooper as "The Scope, Method and Aim of Musicology," in *Music in European Thought, 1851–1912* (**2.90**), pp. 348–55.

3.2 Bengtsson, Ingmar. *Musikvetenskap: En översikt.* Rev. ed. 448 pp. Stockholm: Esselte Studium, 1977.

First ed., 1973, 448 pp.

A survey of the content and methods of musicology geared toward the Swedish university student. Included are discussions of the historical and systematic branches of musicology, the aesthetic foundations of the discipline, and its relation to other humanistic fields. The bibliography (pp. 412–32) is classified by chapter and includes sources in modern scholarly languages, including Swedish. A brief summary of Bengtsson's views on musicological research and its relationship to literary studies, with particular emphasis on the Nordic countries, is found in his "Funderinger kring litteratur- och musikvetenskap," in *Tidskrift för litteraturvetenskap* 2 (1973–74): 134–39.

Reviewed by Hampus Huld-Nystrom in *Svensk tidskrift för musikforskning* 55 (1973): 71–72 and by Friedhelm Krummacher in *Die Musikforschung* 30 (1977): 502–5.

3.3* Bent, Ian. *Analysis.* Glossary by William Drabkin. 184 pp. New York: W.W. Norton; London: Macmillan, 1987. (The Norton/Grove handbooks in music)

Also trans. into Italian by Claudio Annibaldi and published in Turin by EDT, 1990, as *Analisi musicale* (377 pp.).

A revised and expanded version of Bent's article on analysis in *The New Grove* (**1.48**), hailed by Carl Dahlhaus in *M&L* 62 (1981): 255, as "without a doubt one of the [dictionary's] most outstanding contributions." Bent's monograph offers a broad survey of issues, methods, and writings related to the practice of analyzing music. Its main subdivisions include an introductory chapter on the place and nature of music analysis, chapters surveying the history of analysis from the middle ages to the present day, a chapter surveying eight different analytical approaches (including Schenkerian analysis, pitch-class set theory, semiotics, and information theory), and Drabkin's excellent, well-illustrated glossary of analytical terms (pp. 109–42). The vol. concludes with an extensive bibliography (pp. 143–76), considerably updated from the original article and revised to include topical entries, and an index (pp. 177–83).

Bent's original article is reviewed by Bryan R. Simms in *Music Analysis* 2 (1983): 105–7. The 1987 book is reviewed by Arnold Whittall in *M&L* 69 (1988): 503–5, by Jonathan Dunsby in *MT* 129 (1988): 81, by Esther Cavett-Dunsby in *Journal of the RMA* 115 (1990): 111–22, by Judith Lochhead in *College Music Symposium* 28 (1988): 121–29, by Michael Miller in *Tempo* 163 (1987): 31–33, and by Michael Musgrave in *Music Analysis* 8 (1989): 177–86.

3.4* Bergeron, Katherine, and **Philip V. Bohlman.** *Disciplining Music: Musicology and Its Canons.* 220 pp. Chicago, Ill.: University of Chicago Press, 1992.

A collection of highly diverse, polemically charged essays that grew out of a 1986 conference at Cornell University and the 1987 New Orleans meeting of the AMS. Devoted to "the study of the study of music" [Editor's preface, p. ix], the essays have been widely understood as a response to Kerman's challenges to the discipline in *Contemplating Music* (**3.29**). In his subsequent essay "American Musicology in the 1990s" (*JM* 9 [1991]: 135), Kerman describes the collection as "an explicitly deconstructive critique of the force of canonic works and canonic texts in the various disciplines of music study." The collection as a whole criticizes both the positivist orientation of historical musicology and the types of repertoires and methodologies with which the discipline has traditionally been engaged, arguing for greater attention to "music on the margins" [Editor's prologue, p. 5] and the incorporation of ideas and methodologies from areas such as literary theory, cultural anthropology, and gender studies. Contributions by Don Michael Randel, Ruth A. Solie, Robert P. Morgan, Gary Tomlinson, Philip Gossett, Philip V. Bohlman, Bruno Nettl, Katherine Bergeron, Richard Cohn, and Douglas Dempster are framed by Bergeron's brief prologue and Bohlman's more expansive epilogue, concluding with a brief index (pp. 213–20).

Reviewed by Giulio Ongaro in *AMT* 43 (October/November 1993): 47–48, by Mary Anne Long in *AWC News/Forum* 11 (1993): 17–19, by Josef Kuckertz in *World of Music* 35 (1993): 128–30, by Alan Street in *JMT* 37 (1993): 169–76, by Robert Walser in *M&L* 74 (1993): 569–72, by Lawrence Kramer in *Journal of the RMA* 119 (1994): 130–40, by Leon Botstein in *JAMS* 47 (1994): 340–47, and by David Wright in *MT* 135 (1994): 153–55.

3.5* Bowers, Jane M. "Feminist Scholarship and the Field of Musicology," and **Susan C. Cook,** "Women, Women's Studies, Music and Musicology: Issues of Pedagogy and Scholarship," in *College Music Symposium* 29 (1989): 81–92 and 93–100.

Two articles from the 1988 annual AMS meeting in Baltimore, surveying scholarship on women and music and tracing the emergence of the field of feminist musicology. The authors provide historical and critical perspectives on feminist musical scholarship, with ample citation of recent literature. Cook's article, a synopsis of a panel discussion, includes a list of suggested readings.

3.6* Brett, Philip, Gary C. Thomas, and **Elizabeth Wood.** *Queering the Pitch: The New Gay and Lesbian Musicology.* 357 pp. New York: Routledge, 1994.

Announced as "the first collection of gay and lesbian musicology" [Editors' preface, p. vii], a volume assembling articles by musicologists and interdisciplinary scholars exploring the relationship between music, society, and gay and lesbian sexuality. The authors cover a wide range of subjects, including analysis, criticism, biography, and autobiography, and use approaches that are cross-disciplinary and extremely diverse methodologically. Contributors include Wayne Koestenbaum, Philip Brett, Elizabeth Wood, Suzanne G. Cusick, Lawrence D. Moss, Lydia Hamessley, Joke Dame, Gary C. Thomas, Susan McClary, Martha Mockus, Jennifer Rycenga, Karen Pegley and Virginia Caputo, and Paul Attinello. There is a brief index (pp. 347–55). A useful introduction to both the volume and the subject of gay and lesbian musicology is offered by Brett in "Are You Musical?" (*MT* 135 [1994]: 370–76).

Reviewed by Edward Miller in *TDR (The Drama Review): A Journal of Performance Studies* 38 (1994): 191–94, by Charles Rosen in *The New York Review of Books* (June 23 1994): 55–62, by B. Holsinger in *Nation* 259 (June 4 1994): 22–25, by Mary Ann Smart in *Notes* 51 (1995): 1280–83, by Ruth A. Solie in *JAMS* 48 (1995): 311–23, and by Bruce Holsinger in *Nation* 259 (1994): 22–25.

3.7 Brook, Barry S., Edward O. D. Downes, and **Sherman Van Solkema.** *Perspectives in Musicology: The Inaugural Lectures of the Ph.D. Program in Music at the City University of New York.* 363 pp. New York: W.W. Norton, 1972.

Reprinted by Pendragon Press, New York, 1985.

Based on a lecture/seminar series at CUNY during the 1968–69 academic year, an essay collection offering an expansive view of musicology, defined by Brook "in the broadest terms—historical, systematic, ethnological" [Introduction, p. x]. The 15 speakers/essayists discuss the state of musicology, defining the scope of the discipline and projecting its future. Topics include lacunae, archival research, iconology, musicology's relationship with other musical fields (such as composition and theory) and with related disciplines (such as humanistic studies, religious studies, and the social sciences), and the state of research on the music of various cultures. Most essays conclude with summaries of both the discussions following the lectures and the seminars held the following day, and a selective reading list. The volume includes Brook's "Musicology as a Discipline: A Selected Bibliography" (pp. 335–46).

An unsigned review appears in *MEJ* 59/5 (1973): 90; reviews by Lawrence Gushee in *Yearbook for Inter-American Musical Research* 9 (1973): 162–74, by Ivo Supičić in *IRASM* 5 (1974): 338–40, and by Hans Oesch in *Die Musikforschung* 28 (1975): 111–12; and an unsigned editorial response in *M&L* 54 (1973): 129–32.

3.8* Bukofzer, Manfred. *The Place of Musicology in American Institutions of Higher Learning.* 52 pp. New York: Liberal Arts Press, 1957. (Library of liberal arts)

Written under the auspices of the Committee on Music and Musicology of the American Council of Learned Societies, a short brochure assessing the status of musicology and the state of musicological research in institutions of higher learning at mid-century. Like the companion vol. by Arthur Mendel, Curt Sachs, and Carroll C. Pratt, *Some Aspects of Musicology* (**3.35**), Bukofzer's study was written for the purpose of "advancing the cause of musicology in the United States and . . . attracting increased support for it" [Foreword, p. v]. Included are chapters on "The Aims of Musicology," "Music Scholarship and 'Science,'" "Musicology and the Other Humanistic Disciplines," and "The Study of Non-Western Music."

Reviewed by Glen Haydon in *Notes* 15 (1958): 392–93 and by Carl Allan-Moberg in *Svensk tidskrift för musikforskning* 38 (1956): 195–98.

3.9 Chailley, Jacques. *Précis de Musicologie.* New ed., revised. 496 pp. Paris: Presses Universitaires de France, 1984.

First ed., 1958, 431 pp.

A substantially revised and updated version of Chailley's syllabus for French university students, published under the auspices of the Institute of Musicology of the University of Paris. The text consists largely of annotated bibliographies on different aspects of musical research by leading European musicologists. The coverage of non-French sources is inconsistent. Included are chapters on general reference works, ethnomusicology, various historical periods (subdivided by topic), analysis, aesthetics, pedagogy, psychology and perception, instruments, and dance; there is a brief general index (pp. 494–96).

The 1st ed. is reviewed by Nancy Van Der Elst in *Mens en melodie* 13 (1958): 283–84 and by Hans Engel in *Die Musikforschung* 12 (1959): 500. The revised ed. is reviewed by David Fallows in *EM* 13 (1984): 578, by David Charlton in *MT* 126 (1985): 537–38, and by Michael Stegemann in *Neue Zeitschrift für Musikwissenschaft* 146 (1985): 59 and in *Revue musicale de Suisse Romande* 39 (1986): 39–41.

3.10* Cook, Nicholas. *A Guide to Musical Analysis.* 376 pp. New York: George Braziller, 1987; London: Dent, 1987.

Published by Guerini, Milan, 1991 (284 pp.) in an Italian trans. edited by Guido Salvetti and trans. by Donatella Gulli and Maria Grazia Sità, *Guida all' analisi musicale.*

Designed as a practical introduction to the techniques of musical analysis, with an emphasis on analytical approaches commonly in use. Of particular concern to Cook is the importance of psychological and phenomenological experience to the analyst. Part 1, "Analytical Methods," discusses representative analytical approaches, including traditional approaches (e.g., Donald Francis Tovey, Adolf Bernhard Marx, Charles Rosen), Schenkerian analysis, psychological approaches (e.g., Leonard Meyer and rhythmic process, Rudolph Réti and thematic process), formal approaches (e.g., Allen Forte and set theory, Jean-Jacques Nattiez and semiotics), and analytical approaches developed by ethnomusicologists (e.g., Alan Lomax and cantiometrics, Charles Adams and contour design in Native American repertoires, John Blacking on Venda repertoires). Part 2, "Worked Examples of Analysis," offers model analyses of compositions drawn largely from 19th- and 20th-century art music repertoires. Included is a brief index (pp. 372–76).

Reviewed by Arnold Whittall in *MR* 47 (1986/87): 128–30, by John Wagstaff in *Brio* 24 (1987): 38–39, by V. Kofi Agawu in *M&L* 68 (1987): 375–77, by Thomas Janson in *MEJ* 74 (1987): 13–14, by Matthew G. Brown and Douglas J. Dempster in *JMT* 32 (1988): 148–58, by Michael R. Rogers in *Journal of Music Theory Pedagogy* 2 (1988): 297–310, by Taylor A. Greer in *Theory and Practice* 13 (1988): 133–50, by William Drabkin in *MT* 129 (1988): 81–82, by Malcolm Miller in *Tempo* 163 (1987): 31–33, by Lora L. Gingrich in *Music Theory Spectrum* 14 (1992): 99–102, by Michael D. Green in *JMR* 9 (1989): 174–97, and by Michael Musgrave in *Music Analysis* 8 (1989): 177–86. The Italian ed. is reviewed by Giorgio Sanguinetti in *Nuova rivista musicale italiana* 27 (1993): 104–8 and by Marina Toffetti in *Rivista italiana di musicologia* 29 (1994): 635–39.

3.11* Cook, Susan C., and **Judy S. Tsou.** *Cecilia Reclaimed: Feminist Perspectives on Gender and Music.* 241 pp. Urbana, Ill.: University of Illinois Press, 1994.

A collection of 10 interdisciplinary essays demonstrating feminist approaches to and perspectives on musical research. The foreword by Susan McClary, introduction by Susan C. Cook and Judy S. Tsou, and opening essays by Marcia Citron and Jennifer C. Post establish a conceptual and historical framework for the volume. The ensuing essays discuss subjects ranging from renaissance music to 20th-century classical and popular repertoires and the performance traditions of various cultures. Contributors include Marcia J. Citron, Jennifer C. Post, Linda Phyllis Austern, Patricia Howard, Catherine Parsons Smith, Adrienne Fried Block, Jane L. Baldauf-Berdes, Bonny H. Miller, Venise T. Berry, and Susan C. Cook. Advance notice for the volume and a helpful overview of the field of feminist musicology are offered by Susan McClary in "Of Patriarchs . . . and Matriarchs, Too" (*MT* 135 [1994]: 364–69).

Reviewed by Bonnie Jo Dopp in *LJ* 119 (March 1994): 89, by Susan Key in *AM* 13 (1995): 375–78, and by Claudia MacDonald in *Notes* 52 (1995): 430–33.

3.12* *Current Musicology* 53 (1993).

A special issue of *Current Musicology,* subtitled "Approaches to the Discipline," edited by Edmund J. Goehring, featuring essays examining late-20th-century trends in musicology, music theory, and ethnomusicology. Areas discussed include gender studies, cultural studies, criticism, postmodernism, analysis, and popular culture. Contributors include Harold S. Powers, Gary Tomlinson, Lawrence Kramer, Stephen Blum, Ruth A. Solie, Marcia J. Citron, Scott Burnham, Kofi Agawu, Sandra Pinegar, Paula Higgins, and Leon Botstein.

3.13 Dahlhaus, Carl. *Einführung in die systematische Musikwissenschaft.* With Tibor Kneif, Helga de la Motte-Haber, and Hans-Peter Reinecke. 3rd ed. 201 pp. Laaber, Germany: Laaber-Verlag, 1988. (Musik-Taschen-Bücher. Theoretica, 10)

First published in Cologne by Musikverlag Hans Gerig, 1971, 201 pp., with a 2nd ed. appearing in 1975.

A collection of essays on the various subdivisions of systematic musicology, outlining current ideas, problems, and conditions and concluding with bibliographies.

3.14 Dahlhaus, Carl. *Foundations of Music History.* Trans. by J. B. Robinson. 177 pp. Cambridge, England: Cambridge University Press, 1983.

A translation of Dahlhaus's *Grundlagen der Musikgeschichte,* published initially by Musikverlag Hans Gerig, Cologne, 1977 (263 pp.), and subsequently by Laaber-Verlag, Laaber, Germany, 1982. Published in an Italian trans. by Discanto Edizioni in Florence as *Fondamenti di Storiografia Musicale,* 1980 (212 pp.).

A collection of 10 different "historiographic reflections" [Foreword, p. 1] proposing a philosophical foundation, strongly Germanic in orientation, for the study of musicology; includes a brief bibliography (pp. 166–72).

The German ed. is reviewed by Albrecht Riethmüller in *Melos/NZ* 3 (1977): 457–58, by Wulf Konold in *Musica* 31 (1977): 352–53, by Wilhelm Matejka in *Österreichische Musikzeitschrift* 33 (1978): 319, by Miroslav K. Černý in *Hudebni Veda* 16 (1979): 316–25, by Georg Knepler and Peter Wicke in *Beiträge zur Musikwissenschaft* 21 (1979) 222–28, and by Jürgen Schläder in *Tibia* 9 (1984): 134–36. The English translation is reviewed by Frederick W. Sternfeld in *TLS* 4201 (1983), by Francis Sparshott in *MT* 125 (1984): 45–46, by Henry B. Raynor in *MR* 45 (1984): 147–49, and by Keith Falconer in *RMA Journal* 112 (1986–87): 141–55. The Italian translation is reviewed by Anna Maria Morazzoni in *Rivista italiana di musicologia* 16 (1981): 15–27 and by Antonio Serravezza in *Nuova rivista musicale italiana* 15 (1981): 464–66.

3.15 Duckles, Vincent H., Howard Mayer Brown, George S. Buelow, Mark Lindley, Lewis Lockwood, Milos Velimirovic, and **Ian D. Bent.** "Musicology." In *The New Grove Dictionary of Music and Musicians* (**1.48**).

An extended essay on the nature, subdisciplines, and national traditions of musicology, with discussion of both historical and systematic branches and notation of important achievements; a chronologically arranged bibliography is included.

3.16* Dunsby, Jonathan. *Models of Musical Analysis: Early Twentieth-Century Music.* 153 pp. Oxford: Blackwell Reference, 1993.

A highly diverse collection of essays by different authors, designed to illustrate current trends in the analysis of 20th-century music. The authors address topical issues as well as the works of individual composers and consider both tonal and post-tonal repertoires. Each essay is organized according to the categories of orientation, method, model, and summary, and concludes with a brief bibliography. The contributors include Arnold Whittall, James M. Baker, Malcolm Gillies, Martha Hyde, Craig Ayrey, Bryan R. Simms, and Allan Forte.

Reviewed by Anthony Pople in *MT* 135 (1994): 32–35, by Raymond Monelle in *M&L* 75 (1994): 487–90, and by John Thow in *Notes* 51 (1995): 1338–40.

3.17* Dunsby, Jonathan, and **Arnold Whittall.** *Music Analysis in Theory and Practice.* 250 pp. New Haven, Conn.: Yale University Press; London: Faber, 1988.

An introduction to musical analysis focusing on modern analytical methods while stressing the historical and philosophical context of analysis as a field of study. Although practical in orientation and intended for the general reader as well as the specialist, the volume's concentrated format and the authors' tendency to assume a familiarity with specialized concepts and terminology make for challenging reading. A brief survey of the history of theory introduces the volume's two main sections, devoted to analytical approaches to tonal and atonal repertoires. Primary emphasis is on the analytical methods developed by Heinrich Schenker and Allen Forte, but the authors discuss techniques and strategies associated with various theorists, composers, and analysts, including Arnold Schoenberg, Paul Hindemith, Leonard Meyer, Adele Katz, Felix Salzer, Donald Francis Tovey, and Rudolph Réti. Part 4 offers an overview of semiotics and semiology, emphasizing the ideas of Jean-Jacques Nattiez. There are an extensive bibliography (pp. 233–40) and index (pp. 241–50).

Reviewed by Colin Watts in *International Journal of Music Education* 12 (1988): 82, by William Drabkin in *MT* 129 (1988): 247–48, by John Wagstaff in *Brio* 25 (1988): 70–71, by Taylor A. Greer in *Theory and Practice* 13 (1988): 133–50, by Michael R. Rogers in *Journal of Music Theory Pedagogy* 2 (1988): 297–310, by Anthony Pople in *M&L* 70 (1989): 76–78, by Gregory Proctor in *Fontes* 36 (1989): 243–44, by Alicyn Warren in *Notes* 49 (1992): 154–56, by Michael D. Green in *JMR* 9 (1989): 174–79, by Lora L. Gingrich in *Music Theory Spectrum* 14 (1992): 99–102, by Judith Lochhead in *College Music Symposium* 28 (1988): 121–29, and by Michael Musgrave in *Music Analysis* 8 (1989): 77–186. There is an extended response, referring to Bent's *Analysis* (**3.3**) and Cook's *A Guide to Musical Analysis* (**3.10**), by Pieter C. van den Toorn in "What Price Analysis," *JMT* 33 (1989): 165–89.

3.18 Eggebrecht, Hans Heinrich. *Reflexionen über Musikwissenschaft Heute: Ein Symposium.* 80 pp. Kassel, Germany: Bärenreiter, 1972.

First printed in the proceedings of the International Congress of the Gesellschaft für Musikforschung, Bonn, 1970.

Statements on the state of the discipline by 11 leading musicologists, with discussion from the floor. Topics covered include historical and systematic musicology, tradition in music, musicology as sociology, and musicology and sacred music.

Reviewed by Hans Oesch, *Die Musikforschung* 25 (1972): 508–10 and by Hellmut Kühn in *Musica* 27 (1973): 617.

3.19* Everist, Mark. *Models of Musical Analysis: Music before 1600.* 240 pp. Oxford: Basil Blackwell, 1992.

A diverse collection of essays by different authors, intended to illustrate recent trends in the analysis of medieval and early modern repertoires. In their discussions of individual compositions and groups of works, the authors embrace a wide range of systematic and historical approaches, including Schenkerian analysis, semiotics, text-musical analysis, and cultural-contextual interpretation. Each essay includes a newly prepared or revised ed. of the main composition discussed and concludes with a brief bibliography. Contributors include Leo Treitler, Norman E. Smith, Sarah Fuller, David Lidov, Saul Novak, Cristle Collins Judd, James Haar, Jean-Michel Vaccaro, and David Stern.

Reviewed by Annie Coeurdevey in *Revue de musicologie* 79 (1993): 383–86, by Anthony Pryer in *MT* 134 (1993): 396–97, by David Fallows in *EM* 22 (1994): 321–22, by Tim Carter in *M&L* 75 (1994): 63–66, and by Peter Schubert in *Notes* 50 (1994): 1425.

3.20 Fellerer, Karl G. *Einführung in die Musikwissenschaft.* 2nd, revised and enlarged ed. 190 pp. Münchberg, Germany: Bernhard Hahnefeld, 1953.

Reprinted by Hans Sikorski, Hamburg, 1956.

First published in Berlin by Bernhard Hahnefeld, 1942, 152 pp.

A brief and somewhat dated survey of the content of musical knowledge. Historical musicology plays a minor role. Emphasis is on the systematic areas of acoustics, aesthetics, psychology, sociology, and pedagogy. Each chapter includes extensive bibliographies.

Reviewed by Glen Haydon in *Notes* 11 (1953): 11–12 and, anonymously, in *Die Musikforschung* 8 (1955): 96–97.

3.21 Grubbs, John W., Rebecca A. Baltzer, Gilbert L. Blount, and **Leeman Perkins.** *Current Thought in Musicology.* 313 pp. Austin, Tex.: University of Texas Press, 1976. (Symposia in the arts and the humanities, 4)

Essays by nine of the distinguished scholars, performers, and composers invited to participate in the "Current Thought in Musicology" seminars at the University of Texas at Austin from 1968 through 1971. Topics range from historical musicology, systematic musicology, and ethnomusicology to performance and composition. Contributors are Charles Seeger, Charles Hamm, Elliott Carter, Howard Mayer Brown, Lewis Lockwood, Daniel Heartz, Gilbert Chase, Gilbert Reaney, and Vincent Duckles. The concluding essay is Duckles's "The Library of the Mind: Observations on the Relationship between Musical Scholarship and Bibliography" (pp. 277–96).

Reviewed by Denis Arnold in *M&L* 58 (1977): 356–48, by David Z. Kushner in *AMT* 27 (1977): 40, by Jan LaRue in *Ethnomusicology* 22 (1978): 347–50, and by Clement Calder in *Zeitschrift für Musiktheorie* 9 (1978): 52–53.

3.22 Harrison, Frank L., Mantle Hood, and **Claude V. Palisca.** *Musicology.* 337 pp. Englewood Cliffs, N.J.: Prentice-Hall, 1963. (The Princeton studies: Humanistic scholarship in America)

Reprinted by Greenwood Press, Westport, Conn., in 1974.

Three expansive, thoughtful essays on the place of musicology in the world of learning that represent a milestone in the history of the discipline. Commissioned by the Ford Humanities

Project under the direction of the Council of the Humanities of Princeton University, the vol. has helped to frame discussions of the nature and purposes of musical scholarship in America. Included are essays by Harrison on "American Musicology and the European Tradition," Palisca on "American Scholarship in Western Music," and Hood on "Music, the Unknown." The early impact of the volume can be found in Joseph Kerman's 1964 address to AMS, published as "A Profile for American Musicology," *JAMS* 18 (1965): 61–69, the response by Edward Lowinsky, "Character and Purposes of American Musicology: A Reply to Joseph Kerman," *JAMS* 18 (1965): 222–34, and Kerman's subsequent "Communication," *JAMS* 19 (1965): 426–27.

Reviewed by Jan LaRue in *JAMS* 17 (1964): 209–14, by Louis Lockwood in *PNM* 3 (1964): 119–27, by Vincent Duckles in *Notes* 21 (1964): 368–69, by Paul Henry Lang in a review editorial in *MQ* 50 (1964): 215–26, by Martin Picker in *College Music Symposium* 4 (1964): 83–87, by Alan P. Merriam in *Ethnomusicology* 8 (1964): 179–85, by Jack A. Westrup in *M&L* 45 (1964): 284–85, by Denis Stevens in *MT* 105 (1964): 112–13, by Charles Seeger in *Anuario, Inter-American Institute for Musical Research Yearbook* 1 (1965): 112–18, and by Melva Peterson in *Pan Pipes* 57 (1965): 35.

3.23 Haydon, Glen. *Introduction to Musicology: A Survey of the Fields, Systematic and Historical, of Musical Knowledge and Research.* 329 pp. New York: Prentice-Hall, 1941. (Prentice-Hall music series)

Reissued in 1946, and again in 1947.

Unaltered reprints were published by the University of North Carolina Press, Chapel Hill, 1959, and Greenwood Press, Westport, Conn., 1978.

One of the earliest and most widely circulated English-language studies of the field of musicology. Now dated, the volume remains useful as a synopsis of the issues and problems encountered by the musical researcher. Systematic musicology (acoustics, psychology, aesthetics, theory, pedagogy, and comparative musicology) receives the major emphasis, with historical musicology treated only in the final 54 pages. There are chapter bibliographies and a concluding general bibliography (pp. 301–13), with an index (pp. 315–29).

3.24 Holoman, D. Kern, and **Claude V. Palisca.** *Musicology in the 1980s: Methods, Goals, Opportunities.* 160 pp. New York: Da Capo Press, 1982.

Proceedings of two panel discussions held at the 1981 Boston meeting of the AMS, designed as a review of the current state and trends of musicology as a discipline. The "Musicology I: Current Methodology, Opportunities and Limitations" panel included Claude V. Palisca, Jeremy Noble, Maria Rika Maniates, Joseph Kerman, Leo Treitler, and James McKinnon; the "Musicology II: The Musicologist Today and in the Future" panel included D. Kern Holoman, Richard Taruskin, Anne V. Hallmark, and Rose Rosengard Subotnik. Topics of discussion include archival research, sketch studies, structural and critical analysis, iconography, the musicologist as performer, musicology and criticism, and teaching music history in different environments.

Reviewed by Ingmar Bengtsson in *Svensk tidskrift för musikforskning* 65 (1983): 142–44, by Edith Weber in *Revue historique* 548 (1983): 513–14, and by Christopher Hatch in *Notes* 41 (1984): 51–53.

3.25 Husmann, Heinrich. *Einführung in die Musikwissenschaft.* 2nd, expanded ed. 291 pp. Wilhelmshaven, Germany: Heinrichshovens Verlag, 1975. (Taschenbücher zur Musikwissenschaft, 40)

First published in Heidelberg by Quelle und Meyer, 1958, 268 pp.

An introduction to musicology, emphasizing the systematic branches of acoustics and psychological phenomena; historical musicology plays a minor role. An extensive bibliography (pp. 235–55) is organized by chapter headings.

The 1st ed. is reviewed by Werner Korte in *Die Musikforschung* 13 (1960): 340–42. The 2nd ed. is reviewed by Othmar Wessley in *Österreichische Musikzeitschrift* 31 (1976): 458, by Eberhard Würzl in *Musikerziehung* 31 (1977): 46–47, by Rudolf Stephan in *Melos/NZ* 3 (1977): 280, by Hans G. Schürmann in *Musica* 31 (1977): 446–48, by August Gerstmeier in *Neue Musikzeitung* 26 (1977): 16, and by Helmut Rösing in *Die Musikforschung* 32 (1979): 87.

3.26* *Journal of Musicology: A Quarterly Review of Music History, Criticism, Analysis, and Performance Practice* 1 (1982).

The inaugural issue of the *Journal of Musicology,* featuring a series of topical essays collected under the rubric "Musicology in the 1980s: Points of Arrival and Goals" (pp. 1–66). Paul Henry Lang's opening essay introduces 11 short contributions by leading scholars who contemplate the state of various branches of musicological research. Topics include the place of musicology as a humanistic discipline, the relationship between musicology and areas such as theory, analysis, criticism, and performance, trends in bibliography, and the current state of research in various topical and chronological subfields.

3.27 Karbusicky, Vladimir. *Systematische Musikwissenschaft: Eine Einführung in Grundbegriffe, Methoden und Arbeitstechniken.* 250 pp. Munich: Wilhelm Fink Verlag, 1979. (Uni-Taschenbücher, 911)

A practical guide to systematic musicology designed for use at the University of Hamburg. The introduction and first chapter provide a definition and historical overview of systematic musicology, with additional chapters devoted to various aspects of the field. The chapters conclude with brief bibliographies.

Reviewed by Helga de la Motte-Haber in *Musica* 34 (1980): 294, in *Musik und Bildung* 13 (1981): 52–53, and in *Die Musikforschung* 36 (1983): 103, and by Franz Födermayr in *Österreichische Musikzeitschrift* 37 (1982): 715.

3.28* Kelly, Stephen K. *Fact and Value in Contemporary Musical Scholarship.* 49 pp. Boulder, Colo.: The College Music Society, 1986.

These four essays grew out of a plenary session titled "Fact and Value in Contemporary Musical Scholarship," held in Vancouver in 1985 and sponsored jointly by the annual meetings of the AMS, the SMT, The College Music Society, and the Society for Ethnomusicology. The session was designed "to speak . . . broadly to the place of the respective disciplines in the context of the whole field of music scholarship" [Editor's preface, p. v]. The vol. includes contributions by Margaret Bent, Wallace Berry, Phillip Rhodes, and Carol Robertson, then-presidents of the respective societies, with comments by society members and responses by the four speakers.

3.29 Kerman, Joseph. *Contemplating Music: Challenges to Musicology.* 255 pp. Cambridge, Mass.: Harvard University Press, 1985.

Published simultaneously in London by Fontana Press as *Musicology.*

A provocative and influential critique of musicology, its evolution as a discipline, and its relationship to other musical and humanistic developments. Kerman offers a highly personal response to recent trends in Anglo-American musical scholarship and advocates an aesthetic-based approach he defines as "music criticism" (Chapter 4), with a bibliography of major works cited (pp. 243–48).

The volume as a whole expands on themes Kerman explored in a series of earlier, equally influential articles, including "Music Criticism in America," *Hudson Review* 1 (1949): 557–60, "How We Got into Analysis, and How to Get Out," *Critical Inquiry* 7 (1980): 311–31, and "A Few Canonic Variations," *Critical Inquiry* 10 (1983): 107–25, reprinted in *Canons,* ed. Robert von Halberg (Chicago, Ill.: University of Chicago Press, 1984); he develops these themes further in "American Musicology in the 1900s," *JM* 9 (1991): 131–44.

Reviewed by Julie E. Cumming in *CNV* 88 (1984): 7–11, by Erich Leinsdorf in the *New York Times Book Review* (May 26 1985): 19, by Robert Winter in *The New York Review of Books* (July 18 1985): 23–27, by Christopher Wintle in the *TLS* (May 10 1985): 525, by Susan Haase Derett in *Dansk årborg för musikforskning* 16 (1985): 133–37, by David Fallows in *EM* 13 (1985): 573–75, by Julian Rushton in *M&L* 67 (1985): 195–96, by Christopher Gibbs in *CM* 39 (1985): 66–74, by William H. Youngren in *Yale Review* 75 (1986): 437–44, by Margaret Murata in *Queens Quarterly* 93 (1986): 209–11, by Curtis Price in *MT* 127 (1986): 26–28, by Michael Cherlin in *Theory and Practice* 11 (1986): 53–74, by Peter Evans in *Music Analysis* 5 (1986): 97–103, by John Harbison in *MQ* 72 (1986): 416–18, by Renée Cox in *Southern Humanities Review* 22 (1988): 86–87, by Jerrold Levinson in *Journal of Aesthetic Education* 23 (1989): 113–17, by F. J. Smith in *JMR* 9 (1989): 147–57, by Leo Treitler in *JAMS* 42 (1989): 375–402, by James Porter in *Ethnomusicology* 33 (1989): 531–35, and by Maciej Jablonski in *Muzyka* 37 (1992): 87–90, with an extended response by Margaret Bent in *Fact and Value in Contemporary Musical Scholarship* (**3.28**).

3.30* Kimmey, John A., Jr. *A Critique of Musicology: Clarifying the Scope, Limits, and Purposes of Musicology.* 308 pp. Lewiston, N.Y.; Queenston, Ontario: The Edwin Mellen Press, 1988. (Studies in the history and interpretation of music, 12)

A critique consisting of a broad history of the field of musicology, covering the period from antiquity through the end of the 19th century. Emphasis is weighted toward historical musicology. The introduction defines the practical and philosophical scope of the discussion, followed by chapters devoted to historical retrospectives of musicology from Pythagoras through Hugo Riemann and Guido Adler, and concluding with a phenomenological critique of musicological knowledge, with a bibliography (pp. 253–73), appendixes (pp. 276–89), and a general index (pp. 291–308).

3.31 Kreft, Ekkehard, and **Erhard Johannes Bücker.** *Lehrbuch der Musikwissenschaft.* 699 pp. Düsseldorf: Schwann, 1985.

A compendium of essential and representative facts on music, music theory, music history, and systematic musicology, presented in essay form with copious musical examples. Strongly Germanic in orientation, the vol. is designed to provide basic background information for music professionals or informed amateurs. Each section concludes with a list of musical examples and a bibliography of relevant literature.

Reviewed by A. Schneider in *Literature, Music, Fine Arts* 20 (1987): 46–47.

3.32 Kretzschmar, Hermann. *Einführung in die Musikgeschichte.* 82 pp. Leipzig: Breitkopf & Härtel, 1920. (Kleine Handbücher der Musikgeschichte nach Gattungen, 7)

Reprinted by M. Sändig, Wiesbaden, 1970.

A brief, narrative account of the content and sources for the historical study of music. Relevant literature is mentioned in context. Chapter 1 traces the development of music historiography through the 19th century.

3.33 Lissa, Zofia. *Wstep do muzykologii.* 277 pp. Warsaw: Panstwowe Wydawn. Naukowe, 1974.

First published in 1970, 227 pp.

A guide to musicological research by a leading Polish musicologist. Coverage includes both historical and systematic musicology, with extensive chapter bibliographies valuable for their inclusion of Slavic-language sources.

3.34 Madsen, Clifford K., and **Charles H. Madsen, Jr.** *Experimental Research in Music.* 116 pp. Englewood Cliffs, N.J.: Prentice-Hall, 1970.

Reprinted by Contemporary Pub. Co., Raleigh, N.C., 1978.

A research manual that explores concepts and techniques basic to experimental research in music, emphasizing quantitative and descriptive aspects of scholarship. The 1st part offers a broad classification of experimental topics in music; the 2nd introduces a terminology, rationale, and methodology for experimentation in music. Appendixes include a list of selected periodicals, selected statistics references, and a glossary of statistical terms and tests.

Reviewed by Sherman D. Verder Ark in *Journal of Music Therapy* 8 (1971): 36–37, by Richard L. Wink in *MEJ* 57 (1971): 61, and by Eric Sams in *MT* 112 (1971): 447–48.

3.35* Mendel, Arthur, Curt Sachs, and **Carroll C. Pratt.** *Some Aspects of Musicology: Three Essays.* 88 pp. New York: Liberal Arts Press, 1957.

Written under the auspices on the Committee on Music and Musicology of the American Council of Learned Societies, three essays offering a broad, mid-century view of musicology. Included are Mendel, "The Services of Musicology to the Practical Musician," Sachs, "The Lore of Non-Western Music," and Pratt, "Musicology and Related Disciplines."

Reviewed by Gilman Chase in *The American Organist* 40 (1957): 413–14, by Carl Allan-Moberg in *Svensk tidskrift för musikforskning* 39 (1957): 195–98, and by Glen Haydon in *Notes* 15 (1958): 392–93.

3.36 Pruett, James W., and **Thomas P. Slavens.** *Research Guide to Musicology.* 175 pp. Chicago, Ill.: American Library Association, 1985. (Sources of information in the humanities, 4)

A clear and informative exposition of the development of the discipline, with each of the 14 chapters followed by a substantial bibliography. Emphasis is on trends in historical musicology, music theory and performance practices, and current research in different historical periods. Slavens's bibliography of the research literature, covering about 150 titles, is limited almost entirely to English-language publications.

Reviewed by Lenore Coral in *Notes* 43 (1986): 42–44 and by James Scholter in *MEJ* 72 (1986): 69–71.

3.37* Rieger, Eva. "'Gender Studies' und Musikwissenschaft—ein Forschungsbericht." In *Die Musikforschung* 48 (1995): 235–50.

A survey of useful article citations of over 100 recent studies that explore the relationship between gender, music, and the arts.

3.38 Rosand, Ellen. *The Garland Library of the History of Western Music.* 14 vols. New York; London: Garland Publishing, 1985.

Reprint ed. of articles originally published between 1940 and 1982, chiefly in English but including articles in French, German, and Italian, with bibliographical references.

Contents: Vol. 1, *Medieval Music I, Monophony;* Vol. 2, *Medieval Music II, Polyphony;* Vol. 3, *Renaissance Music, Part I;* Vol. 4, *Renaissance Music, Part II;* Vol. 5, *Baroque Music I, Seventeenth Century;* Vol. 6, *Baroque Music II, Eighteenth Century;* Vol. 7, *Classic Music;* Vol. 8, *Eighteenth- and Nineteenth-Century Sources Studies;* Vol. 9, *Nineteenth-Century Music;* Vol. 10, *Twentieth-Century Music;* Vol. 11, *Opera I, Up to Mozart;* Vol. 12, *Opera II, Mozart and After;* Vol. 13, *Criticism and Analysis;* Vol. 14, *Approaches to Tonal Analysis.*

A compendium of modern musicological writings that is neither a history nor a guide to the practice of musicology, but rather a useful anthology for the practicing scholar and a repertoire of exemplars for the student. This set was given a brief index by Ann P. Basart in *CNV* 109 (1987): 11–28.

3.39* Seeger, Charles. *Studies in Musicology: 1935–1975.* 357 pp. Berkeley: University of California Press, 1977; and *Studies in Musicology II: 1929–1979.* 438 pp. Berkeley: University of California Press, 1994.

Vol. II edited by Anne M. Pescatello.

Two companion studies featuring essays by a pioneer and elder statesman of American musicology. Covering a span of 50 years, the essays include revised or rewritten versions of earlier articles and some essays appearing in print for the first time. Topics range from music theory, historical and systematic musicology, and ethnomusicology to American musical traditions. Vol. I includes an extensive bibliography of the author's writings (pp. 345–53).

The 1st vol. is reviewed by Stephen Blum in *Ethnomusicology* 27 (1983): 360–64, by Mildred

Parker in *Journal of Aesthetics and Art Criticism* 37 (1978): 114–16, by Gerald Abraham in *MT* 119 (1978): 679–80, by Christopher Longuet-Higgins in *M&L* 60 (1979): 354–57, and by Albrecht Riethmüller in *Die Musikforschung* 33 (1980): 496–97. The 2nd vol. is reviewed by David Nicholls in *M&L* 77 (1996): 140–43.

3.40* Solie, Ruth A. *Musicology and Difference: Gender and Sexuality in Music Scholarship.* 355 pp. Berkeley, Los Angeles, and London: University of California Press, 1993.

A collection of 15 essays influenced by recent developments in literary theory, cultural anthropology, and feminist criticism by scholars who explore the impact of gender and sexuality on music, musicians, and musical scholarship. The collection centers around postmodernist notions of diversity and difference. The individual essays, wide-ranging in subject matter and interdisciplinary in scope, are grouped according to the following broad categories: systems of difference, cultural contexts of difference, interpretive strategies, and critical readings. Contributors include Ruth A. Solie, Leo Treitler, John Shepherd, Barbara Engh, Judith Tick, Carol E. Robertson, Nancy B. Reich, Ellen Koskoff, Elizabeth Wood, Mitchell Morris, Gretchen Wheelock, Carolyn Abbate, Philip Brett, Suzanne Cusik, Lawrence Kramer, and Susan McClary.

Reviewed by Charles Rosen in *The New York Review of Books* 41 (June 23 1994): 55–62, by Mary Ann Smart in *JAMS* 47 (1994): 541–49, by Steve Sweeny-Turner in *MT* 135 (1994): 636–37, by John Daverio in *CM* 56 (1994): 86–101, by Ellie M. Hisama in *JM* 12 (1994): 219–32, by Renée Cox Lorraine in *NCM* 19 (1995): 96–111, by Peter Franklin in *M&L* 76 (1995): 135–39, by Gary C. Thomas in *Journal of the History of Sexuality* 5 (1995): 477–80, and by Bruce Holsinger in *The Nation* 259 (July 4 1994): 22–25.

3.41 Stevens, Denis. *Musicology: A Practical Guide.* 224 pp. London: Macdonald Futura, 1980. (Yehudi Menuhin music guides)

The American ed. was published by Schirmer Books, New York, 1981.

A basic introduction to musicological research geared toward the general reader. Part 1 offers a brief explanation and history of the discipline; Part 2 discusses research materials; Part 3 addresses areas of applied musicology, including early music, form, ornamentation, instrumentation, and textual underlay. The volume as a whole reflects the author's background as a conductor of early choral music.

Reviewed by Clifford Bartlett in *Brio* 17 (1980): 67–68 and by David Fallows in *EM* 9 (1981): 243–44.

3.42 Weber, Édith. *La recherche musicologique: Objet, méthodologie, normes de présentation.* 171 pp. Paris: Beauchesne, 1980. (Guides musicologiques, 1)

An introduction to the field of musicology prepared by a leading French musicologist and designed for use at the University of Paris–Sorbonne, including chapters on the aims of musicology and its relationship to other scholarly disciplines, different methods used in musicological research, various types of musical sources, and writing and publishing in musicology, concluding with chapter bibliographies (pp. 151–60) and a brief index (pp. 161–63).

3.43 Westrup, Jack A. *An Introduction to Musical History.* 2nd ed. 176 pp. London: Hutchinson's University Library, 1973.

Published first in London in 1955, as a vol. in the Hutchinson University Library, and subsequently in New York by Harper & Row, 1964 (174 pp.).

Intended as a lay guide to music history and offering one of the clearest and most concise treatments of the problems of music historiography in English. Chapters include "The Scope of Musical History," "The Sources," "The Influence of the Church," "Patronage," and "The Study of Musical History." Included is a brief list of recommended books.

Reviewed by Allen P. Britton in *JRME* 3 (1955): 154.

3.44 Wiora, Walter. *Historische und systematische Musikwissenschaft: Ausgewählte Aufsätze von Walter Wiora.* Edited by Hellmut Kühn and Christoph-Hellmut Mahling. 480 pp. Tutzing, Germany: H. Schneider, 1972.

A collection of writings on musicology by a leading exponent of the systematic approach to musical scholarship, with a bibliography of his later writings.

Reviewed by Carl Dahlhaus in *Die Musikforschung* 26 (1973): 256, by Gino Stefani in *Nuova rivista italiana di musicologia* 8 (1974): 151–54, and by Albrecht Schneider-Klement in *Musica sacra* 93 (1973): 51–53.

3.45 Wiora, Walter. "Musikwissenschaft," in *MGG* (**1.9**), Vol. 9 (1961): 1,192–1,220.

An extended and dated article on the nature, history, and methodologies of musicology. A general overview is followed by discussions of systematic and historical musicology, the history of musicology, and folk music and ethnomusicology and regional traditions, concluding with section bibliographies.

RESEARCH METHODS, EDITING, AND WRITING

3.46* Caldwell, John. *Editing Early Music.* 2nd ed. 135 pp. Oxford: Clarendon Press, 1985. (Early music series, 5)

First ed. published in 1985, 125 pp.; reprinted with corrections in 1987.

A practical discussion of the principles, procedures, and philosophy of editing early music, of value to both scholar and performer. Based in part on the earlier pamphlet by Thurston Dart, Walter Emory, and Christopher Morris, *Editing Early Music: Notes on the Preparation of the Printer's Copy* (Novello, 1963, 22 pp.), it includes general chapters on the principles of transcribing, editing, and preparing copy, with additional chapters on medieval, early renaissance, baroque, and classical music. Appendixes include "Special Signs and Conventions," "Suggested Standardized Part-Names and Abbreviations," "Sample Score Layouts," and "Editorial Treatment of Accidentals." The 2nd ed. includes a postscript about recent developments in early music editing and a revised bibliography.

Reviewed by Clifford Bartlett in *Brio* 22 (1985): 22–25, by David Fallows in *TLS* 4280 (1985): 415, by Helmut Hucke in *Neue Zeitschrift für Musik* 146 (1985): 55–56 no. 10, by Bruno Turner in *EM* 13 (1985): 421–23, by Neal Zaslaw in *MT* 127 (1986): 31, by Judith Blezzard in *MR* 47 (1986–87): 49–52, by Barbara Przybyzewska-Jarminska in *Muzyka* 33 (1988): 137–41, and by Richard Taruskin in *Notes* 42 (1986): 775–79.

3.47 Druesedow, John E., Jr. *Library Research Guide to Music: Illustrated Search Strategy and Sources.* 86 pp. Ann Arbor, Mich.: Pierian Press, 1982. (Library research guides series, 6)

A dated but useful introduction to resource materials and research strategies for the under-graduate music student. Using a case study approach, Druesedow demonstrates the necessary steps to prepare an in-depth research assignment in music. The volume includes clearly illustrated discussions of the card catalog, periodical indexes, primary source materials, foreign language sources, and audiovisual aids. OCLC (**12.1**) is discussed only briefly, with other online databases and computer reference tools predicted as coming "in the not-too-distant future." Appendixes consist of a library use quiz and a list of 303 basic reference sources in music. In *CNV* 62 (1982): 13, Ann P. Basart describes this work as "the first book on library research strategy and sources designed for music undergraduates."

Reviewed by Ann P. Basart in *Notes* 39 (1982): 353–54 and by Homer Ulrich in *AMT* 32 (1982): 56.

3.48* Harder, Paul O. *Music Manuscript Techniques: A Programmed Approach.* 2 vols. Boston, Mass.: Allyn & Bacon, 1984.

A systematic presentation of the techniques and principles of music manuscript preparation, with sufficient drill to ensure their mastery.

3.49 Helm, E. Eugene, and **Albert T. Luper.** *Words and Music: Form and Procedure in Theses, Dissertations, Research Papers, Book Reports, Programs, Theses in Composition.* Revised ed. 91 pp. Totowa, N.J.: European American Music, 1982.

The 1st ed. was published by Joseph Boonin, Hackensack, N.J., 1971 (78 pp.), and reprinted by European American Music Corporation, Clifton, N.J., in 1978.

A practical guide to writing about music, resulting from the authors' experience in teaching music at the college level. Their manual identifies 543 technical and procedural problems encountered by the student writer and offers useful advice on how to research, organize, and prepare various types of written assignments on music. The introduction includes brief bibliographies of general and specialized writing guides.

3.50* Heussenstamm, George. *The Norton Manual of Musical Notation.* 168 pp. New York: W.W. Norton, 1987.

A clear, concise, well-organized manual, meant to be a workbook as well as a textbook; blank staves for drill fill half of some pages. Simple directions are given for pencil-drawing complicated figures and for notating complex rhythms, chords with multiple accidentals, and notes beamed together, with examples supplied showing "correct" (or "preferred") and "incorrect" (or "not recommended") alternatives. Two long examples (one for text overlay) present errors for spotting. Scoring practices are given. Appendixes cover tools, techniques for using ink, reproduction and binding, and popular music notation. Includes a bibliography, a list of companies specializing in music score materials, and an index.

3.51* Holoman, D. Kern. *Writing about Music: A Style Sheet from the Editors of 19th-Century Music.* 61 pp. Berkeley: University of California Press, 1988.

An expanded version of the style sheet used by the California-based journal *Nineteenth-Century Music,* offering solutions to common problems of translation, citation, and general editorial consistency encountered by American authors who wrote about music. Based on the 13th ed. of the *Chicago Manual of Style* (University of Chicago Press, 1982), the book includes chapters on "Music Terminology," "Narrative Text," "Citations," "Musical Examples," "Tables and Illustrations," "The Printed Program," and "Preparing Copy to Submit Electronically," with an appendix listing "Problem Words."

Reviewed by D. W. Krummel in *Notes* 45 (1989): 518–20 and by John Wiser in *Fanfare* 12 (1989): 460.

3.52 Irvine, Demar B. *Writing about Music: A Style Book for Reports and Theses.* 2nd ed., revised and enlarged. 211 pp. Seattle, Wash.; London: University of Washington Press, 1968.

Reissued in 1979. A much expanded ed. of a work first published in 1956 (78 pp.)

A general guide to the preparation of reports and larger writing assignments in music, giving 227 rules for the student writer. The 2nd ed. has been considerably revised and expanded from the earlier edition. Part I, "Style in the Typescript," considers practical problems relating to such issues as spelling, punctuation, abbreviations, foreign words, and footnotes. Part II, "Writing Skills," addresses more general issues of preparation, writing style, and intended audience, concluding with a sample paper and brief bibliography.

Reviewed by Charles Leonard in *JRME* 5 (Spring 1957): 59, by Stanley Sadie in *MT* 11 (1970): 46, and by Judith Duerk in *NATS Bulletin* 26 (1970): 33, 39.

3.53 Karkoschka, Erhard. *Notation in New Music: A Critical Guide to Interpretation and Realisation.* Trans. from German by Ruth Koenig. 183 pp. New York: Praeger, 1972.

Originally published in German by Moeck as *Das Schriftbild der Neuen Musik,* 1966. Also published in London by Universal Editions in 1972.

A summary of notational problems and solutions with a method for looking up specific notational symbols. There is an extensive section of examples of new notations with annotations, as well as indexes to subjects and to names and works.

3.54* LaRue, Jan. *Guidelines for Style Analysis.* 2nd ed. 286 pp. Warren, Mich.: Harmonie Park Press, 1992.

First published in New York by W.W. Norton, 1970, 244 pp.

A practical manual offering suggestions for individual discussions of musical elements (sound, harmony, timbre).

The 1st ed. is reviewed by Eric Sams in *MT* 122 (1981): 243 and by Leonard Duck in *MR* 45 (1984): 150–51. The 2nd ed. is reviewed by Floyd K. Grave in *JM* 11 (1993): 269–76, by Bathia Churgin in *Notes* 50 (1994): 1,429–30, and by Konrad Küster in *Die Musikforschung* 47 (1994): 109.

3.55* Mender, Mona. *Music Manuscript Preparation: A Concise Guide.* 222 pp. Metuchen, N.J.: Scarecrow Press, 1991.

A concise textbook, showing in detail how to prepare a music manuscript, with bibliographical references (pp. 188–91) and an index. The guide is directed to composers who wish to prepare music manuscripts for publication. It assumes familiarity with notation, and more than half the book deals with contemporary music notation, giving samples from 10 living composers.

3.56 Mixter, Keith E. *General Bibliography for Music Research.* 2nd ed. 135 pp. Detroit, Mich.: Information Coordinators, 1975. (Detroit studies in music bibliography, 75)

First published in Detroit by Information Service, 1962, 38 pp. (Detroit studies in music bibliography, 4). Third ed. was anticipated to be published by Harmonie Park Press in Warren, Mich., 1996.

An excellent but dated introduction to nonmusical reference works, listing general bibliographical tools for those engaged in music research. Emphasis is on books from North America and Europe. The book is organized according to reference genres and contains indexes to names and titles.

The 1st ed. is reviewed by Fred Blum in *Notes* 20 (1963): 225–27, by Frank J. Gillis in *Ethnomusicology* 8 (1964): 202, by Richard Browne in *JMT* 8 (1964): 129, by Richard Schaal in *Die Musikforschung* 17 (1964): 295, by John S. Weissmann in *Tempo* 76 (1966): 31–32, and by Lillian M. Ruff in *Consort* 23 (1966): 193. The 2nd ed. is reviewed by François Lesure in *Fontes* 23 (1976): 95, by Peter Ward Jones in *M&L* 57 (1976–77): 176–77, by Guy Marco in *ARBA* 7 (1976): 473–74, and by Stephen M. Fry in *Notes* 32 (1976): 781–82.

3.57 Poultney, David. *Studying Music History: Learning, Reasoning, and Writing about Music History and Literature.* 253 pp. Englewood Cliffs, N.J.: Prentice-Hall, 1983.

A book combining in a single volume elements of a music history survey, a writing manual, a sourcebook, and an annotated bibliography. The volume is cross-referenced to many of the standard anthologies of music, as indexed in Hilton (**5.437**) and Murray (**5.438**). The first six chapters, organized chronologically by historical period, offer selective and superficial overviews of genres, composers, and compositions. Each chapter concludes with a glossary and some have comparative style tables, musical examples, and unidentified historical sources. Chapter 7, "Writing about Music," offers a general discussion of types of written projects and advice for writers. The volume concludes with four appendixes: "Criticism of Writing Samples," "Bibliographies," "For Further Study," and "Scores and Historical Sources Identified."

3.58 Rosecranz, Glen R. *Music Notation Primer.* 59 pp. New York: Passantino, 1979.

A guide to the tools, materials, and techniques of music calligraphy.

3.59 Spiess, Lincoln Bunce. *Historical Musicology: A Reference Manual for Research in Music.* With articles by Ernst C. Krohn, Lloyd Hibberd, Luther A. Dittmer, Tsang-houei Shu, Tatsuo Mingawa, and Zdeněk Nováček. 294 pp. Brooklyn, N.Y.: Institute of Medieval Music, 1963. (Musicological studies, 4).

Reprinted by Greenwood Press, Westport, Conn., 1980.

A dated but informative introduction to the problems of research in the various epochs of Western musical culture. Part I includes a chapter on basic research problems, followed by chapters on individual style periods organized according to "Class Research Problems" and "Individual Research Problems." Part II is an extensive series of bibliographies organized topically, chronologically, and geographically. Appendixes include Krohn's essay "The Development of Modern Musicology" (pp. 153–72), which provides a broad overview of the field and a useful but dated bibliography of the history of the discipline; Lloyd Hibberd's essay "The Doctoral Dissertation in Music"; and Luther Dittmer's essay "Language and the Musicologist," with addenda on Chinese musical terminology by Tsang-houei Shu, on Japanese musical terminology by Tatsuo Mingawa, and on Slavic musicology by Zdeněk Nováček.

Reviewed by Vincent Duckles in *Notes* 20 (1963): 469–71, by Glen Haydon in *College Music Symposium* 3 (1963): 96–98, and by Bruno Nettl in *Ethnomusicology* 8 (1964): 202.

3.60 Wallon, Simone. *La documentation musicologique.* 142 pp. Paris: Beauchesne, 1984. (Guides musicologiques, 3)

A brief handbook on the practice of musicology, including bibliographies and indexes.

3.61 Watanabe, Ruth T. *Introduction to Music Research.* 237 pp. Englewood Cliffs, N.J.: Prentice-Hall, 1967. (Prentice-Hall history of music series)

A general handbook outlining the procedures, resources, and techniques of musical research. The main subdivisions are library orientation, the research paper, and a survey of research materials. Included are indexes of names, titles, and subjects (pp. 213–37).

Reviewed by Donald W. Krummel in *Notes* 24 (1968): 481–82, by Ruth Steiner in *MEJ* 54 (1968): 99, by Joe B. Buttram in *Journal of Music Therapy* 6 (1969): 29, and by Scott Goldthwaite in *JRME* 17 (1969): 258–59.

3.62* Wingell, Richard J. *Writing about Music: An Introductory Guide.* 146 pp. Englewood Cliffs, N.J.: Prentice-Hall, 1990.

A well-organized and eminently useful handbook on writing and research methods, of use to both undergraduate and graduate music students. The main subdivisions include "Words and Music," "Writing a Research Paper on a Musical Topic," and "Other Kinds of Writing about Music." Chapter 3, "Getting Started: Research," provides a practical overview of research strategies that regrettably ignores online databases. The volume offers valuable, no-nonsense advice on stylistic, technical, and mechanical issues for the student writer. The book concludes with a sample paper (pp. 127–42) and an index (143–46).

Reviewed by Glenn L. Glasow in *Notes* 48 (1991): 534–35.

PERFORMANCE PRACTICE

3.63* Berger, Karol. *Musica Ficta: Theories of Accidental Inflections in Vocal Polyphony from Marchetto da Padova to Gioseffo Zarlino.* 266 pp. Cambridge, England: Cambridge University Press, 1987.

A magisterial discussion of implied accidentals, divided into three sections: the relationship of *musica ficta* to the hand; horizontal and vertical considerations in the application of *ficta;* and a discussion of written versus applied accidentals, drawing generously on theory treatises of the era. The bibliography (pp. 246–62) is equally generous in the areas of sources and literature, providing access to the literature on *ficta* through 1984.

Reviewed by Jan Herlinger in *JAMS* 42 (1989): 640–47, by James Haar in *JMR* 10 (1990): 96–102, by John Anthony Caldwell in *RMA Research Chronicle* 23 (1990): 177–81, by Peter Urquhart in *Historical Performance* 2 (1989): 35–38, by Don Harrán in *Performance Practice Review* 3 (1990): 73–77, and by Peter N. Schubert in *CM* 44 (1990): 99–105.

3.64* Brown, Howard Mayer, and **Stanley Sadie.** *Performance Practice.* 2 vols. Basingstoke, England: Macmillan; New York and London: W.W. Norton, 1990. (New Grove Handbooks in Music) (The Norton/Grove handbooks in music)

A pair of volumes, in part from *The New Grove* (**1.48**), drawing on the expertise of a variety of scholars to cover topics in the performance of earlier musics. The 1st vol., "Music before 1600," separates the middle ages from the renaissance, with several chapters within each section on sacred and secular traditions. An interlude on *musica ficta* and on tempo and proportions links the two parts of the book. The 2nd vol., "Music after 1600," also separates the chronological periods, but the chapters themselves focus on the various media—keyboards, strings, woodwinds and brass, and voices—with extra chapters on issues of particular importance for that era (tuning and intonation, improvisation, and cadenzas). Footnotes are generously supplied, but the bibliographies are confined to primary source material.

The 1st vol. is reviewed by Ross W. Duffin in *Historical Performance* 4 (1990): 61–64 and by Timothy J. McGee in *Performance Practice Review* 4 (1991): 64–70. The 2nd vol. is reviewed by John Butt in *Historical Performance* 4 (1991): 118–22, by George Houle in *Performance Practice Review* 4 (1991): 71–75, and by Albert R. Rice in *Performance Practice Review* 4 (1991): 76–79. The set is reviewed by Stanley Boorman in *EM* 18 (1990): 641–45 and by John Kmetz in *Notes* 49 (1992–93): 626–28.

3.65* Cohen, Albert. "The Performance of French Baroque Music: A Report on the State of Current Research." In *Performance Practice Review* 1 (1988): 10–24.

The first part of the article offers a survey of the literature from 1978 to 1988, organized by medium; full citations for the approximately 100 items discussed are provided in the alphabetical bibliography that follows.

3.66* Cyr, Mary. *Performing Baroque Music.* 254 pp. with accompanying audio cassette. Portland, Ore.: Amadeus Press, 1992.

British ed. published by Scolar, Aldershot, 1992.

A concise guide to baroque performance practice, organized by subject matter (tempo, dynamics, pitch, continuo). Bibliographical notes accompany each of the eight chapters, and an appendix provides scores of the principal pieces discussed.

Reviewed by George Houle in *Historical Performance* 7 (1994): 118–19, by Neal Zaslaw in *Notes* 50 (1994): 946–48, and, with a number of cautionary remarks, by Keith Elcombe in *EM* 22 (1994): 499–500.

3.67 Donington, Robert. *The Interpretation of Early Music.* 4th ed., revised. 768 pp. London; Boston, Mass.: Faber & Faber; New York: W.W. Norton, 1989.

Originally published in London by Faber & Faber, 1963, and in New York by St. Martin's Press, 1963, 608 pp. Revised ed., New York, St. Martin's Press, 1965, 608 pp. "New version" published in London, Faber, 1974, 1975, and 1977, and New York, St. Martin's Press, 1974 and 1979, 766 pp. Reprinted in London, Faber & Faber, 1982.

A standard text on the performance of baroque music, including extensive quotations from contemporary sources. The alphabetical bibliography (pp. 673–729) lists facsimiles of primary source materials within the main entry and provides pithy comments for some of the secondary sources.

William S. Newman reviews the 1963 and 1974 eds. from a pianist's perspective in *Piano Quarterly* 49 (1964): 26–31 and *Piano Quarterly* 23 (1975): 40–43 no. 90; J. A. Westrup points to weaknesses in the 1963 and 1974 eds. in *M&L* 44 (1963): 381–85 and *M&L* 56 (1975): 202–4; Albert Cohen lists omissions of the 1963 ed. in *Notes* 22 (1965): 711–14. Gilbert L. Blount reviews the 1974 ed. in *Notes* 34 (1977): 351–52.

3.68* Drescher, Thomas. "Auswahl-bibliographie zum Thema 'Orchesterpraxis' (17. bis Mitte des 19. Jahrhundert)." In *Basler Jahrbuch für historische Musikpraxis* 17 (1993): 191–224.

An international bibliography of approximately 375 items, including both primary sources to c. 1850 and secondary sources with a topical index. The bibliography ends in November 1993.

3.69* Gutknecht, Dieter. *Studien zur Geschichte der Aufführungspraxis alter Musik: Ein Überblick vom Beginn des 19. Jahrhunderts bis zum Zweiten Weltkrieg.* 270 pp. Cologne: Concerto, 1993.

A source that, after a useful survey of the terminological debate, places historically oriented performance in the context of the development of music history as a discipline, discussing the role of the Gesamtausgaben. Concentrating almost entirely on European developments on the continent, Gutknecht emphasizes the importance of the individuals and groups who brought early music to life on original instruments. There are generous footnotes and a substantial bibliography.

3.70* Haskell, Harry. *The Early Music Revival: A History.* 232 pp. London; New York: Thames & Hudson, 1988.

A useful history of the early music movement from the early 19th century to the mid-1970s, with glances at more recent developments. The focus is on the individuals and groups that made up the revival rather than on the music revived. See Gutknecht (**3.69**) for a survey of continental performers.

Reviewed by Denis Stevens in *Historical Performance* 2 (1989): 39–42 and by Elizabeth Roche in *M&L* 70 (1989): 382–84.

3.71* Hefling, Stephen E. *Rhythmic Alteration in Seventeenth- and Eighteenth-Century Music: 'Notes Inégales' and Overdotting.* 232 pp. New York: Schirmer Books; Toronto: Maxwell Macmillan International, 1993.

An even-handed account of the issues involved, based on a rereading both of the theoretical sources discussing rhythmic alteration and the often polemic secondary literature. Nonexperts may want to skip to Chapter 7, which summarizes the argument, although they should examine Table 5-1 on overdotting to see Hefling's theoretical evidence, particularly in light of Neumann's review. The bibliography separates materials on *notes inégales,* those on overdotting, and those on related issues.

A negative review by Frederick Neumann is in *Historical Performance* 7 (1994): 13–26, with a response by Hefling, pp. 85–94; there is a positive review with extensive discussion by David Fuller in *Performance Practice Review* 7 (1994): 120–32, with a response by Hefling, pp. 133–45, and a more traditional review by Erich Schwandt, pp. 146–49.

3.72* Hoffmann-Axthelm, Dagmar. *Schriftenverzeichnis zum Arbeitsbereich historischer Musikpraxis 1974/1975.* 134 pp. Winterthur, Switzerland: Amadeus-Verlag, 1976. (Schola Cantorum Basiliensis)

Subsequent annual list by Hoffmann-Axthelm as "Schriftenverzeichnis zum Arbeitsbereich historischer Musikpraxis" in *Basler Jahrbuch für historische Musikpraxis* 1 (1977) to 15 (1991), continued in 16 (1992) as "Bibliographie der Neuerscheinungen zur historischen Musikpraxis."

A broadly conceived annual bibliography of performance practice items. The author includes works that relate only tangentially to performance practice, including many items of general musicological interest, so each annual list covers approximately 1,000 items. Organized into numerous categories, the bibliography includes reference materials, source studies, notation, music theory, music history, genre studies, dance, performance practice per se, rhythm and tempo, song, instruments, iconography, text and music, and music and society. Each topic is further subdivided. A remarkable endeavor, in both its scope and its completeness.

3.73* Houle, George. *Meter in Music, 1600–1800: Performance, Perception, and Notation.* 174 pp., with accompanying cassette. Bloomington and Indianapolis: Indiana University Press, 1987. (Music: Scholarship and performance)

A survey of meter during the 17th and 18th centuries that draws extensively on theoretical treatises of the era. Includes a discussion of parallels between musical and poetic meters, a comparison of metrical innovations with mensural practice, and a focus on time signatures, tempo, *notes inégales,* and the role of articulation in defining meter. The bibliography is strong, although primary and secondary sources are intermingled.

Reviewed by Eva Linfield in *JMT* 33 (1989): 222–27, by Robert Donington in *EM* 16 (1988): 423–27, and by Alexander Silbiger in *Performance Practice Review* 2 (1989): 89–92.

3.74 Jackson, Roland. *Performance Practice, Medieval to Contemporary: A Bibliographic Guide.* xxix + 518 pp. New York: Garland Publishing, 1988. (Music research and information guides, 9) (Garland reference library of the humanities, 790)

Supplemented by annual updates by Jackson in *Performance Practice Review* in the second issue of each volume.

A bibliography arranged in order by historical periods and then by categories. The 1,392 entries complement *Performance Practice: A Bibliography* (**3.90**), covering works published from 1960 to 1986. Includes an introductory section on the general literature on performance practice and a concluding "Reflections on Performance Practice." Unlike the earlier work, which deals with pre-1900 music, this also includes the performance of 20th-century music. Works on the sociology of music performance are omitted, as are works by performers concerning their lives or interpretation of musical works. There are indexes to theorists, authors, and subjects. The use of indexes is particularly important because each work is cited only once, even though multiple subjects or time periods might apply.

Reviewed by Clifford Bartlett in *Brio* 25 (1988): 31–32, by Pamela C. Poulin in *Notes* 47 (1991): 1174, by Peter Holman in *M&L* 70 (1989): 245–47, and by Cynthia Cyrus in *Fontes* 38 (1991): 147–48.

3.75* Kenyon, Nicholas. *Authenticity and Early Music: A Symposium.* 219 pp. Oxford: Oxford University Press, 1988.

Reprinted 1994.

A seminal collection of essays on the nature of authenticity that grew out of a symposium on the same topic. The authors explore the origins of the early music movement, the origins of the term *authenticity* itself, and the relationship of the historically informed performance to the past and to the present. The contributions by Philip Brett, Howard Mayer Brown, Will Crutchfield, Nicholas Kenyon, Robert P. Morgan, Gary Tomlinson, and Richard Taruskin form modern-day reference points for one side of the "authenticity debate," as does the extensive and provocative response by Rosen.

Reviewed by Charles Rosen in "The Shock of the Old," *The New York Review of Books* 37 (July 19 1990): 46–52, by David Schulenberg in *CM* 48 (1991): 78–87, by Robert Garis in *Historical Performance* 2 (1989): 31–34, and by Robert Donington in *M&L* 70 (1989): 386–91. An extensive review aimed at legal academics draws parallels between legal interpretation and musical interpretation; the authors make a number of telling observations about the Kenyon collection and Rosen's response, as well as about the authenticity movement in general; see Sanford Levinson and J. M. Balkin in "Law, Music and Other Performing Arts," *University of Pennsylvania Law Review* 139 (1991): 1,597–1,658.

3.76* Kite-Powell, Jeffery T. *A Performer's Guide to Renaissance Music.* 379 pp. New York: Schirmer Books; Toronto: Maxwell Macmillan International, 1994. (Performer's guides to early music)

Originally issued as *A Practical Guide to Historical Performance: The Renaissance* (Cleveland, Ohio: Early Music America, 1989; reprinted 1990, 236 pp.).

A collection of essays addressing practical performance issues. The essays on various instruments (such as recorder, crumhorn, and cornett), though uneven in length, will be particularly useful to the novice or intermediate player, providing brief bibliographies and suggested listening.

Additional sections on theoretical and organizational topics are aimed at the collegium director. Complemented by McGee (**3.82**), which provides information on editions and instrumentation.

The Early Music America edition is reviewed by Honey Meconi in *EM* 18 (1990): 137–38, and by Richard Taruskin in *Notes* 47 (1990): 392–94; the Schirmer ed. is reviewed briefly by Jeffrey Nussbaum in *Historic Brass Journal* 6 (1994): 385–87.

3.77* Kivy, Peter. *Authenticities: Philosophical Reflections on Musical Performance.* 299 pp. Ithaca and London: Cornell University Press, 1995.

A discussion of the desirability of using or recreating historical practices in performance. Kivy introduces and evaluates four kinds of authenticity: authorial intention, contemporary sound, contemporary practice, and personal authenticity.

Reviewed by Renée Cox Lorraine in *Notes* 52 (1996): 1151–53.

3.78* Kottick, Edward L. *The Collegium: A Handbook.* 127 pp. Stonington, Conn.: October House, 1977.

A readable, straightforward guide to the collegium, focused in particular on the role of the director and the tasks he or she must undertake. More in-depth information on the various instruments can be found in Kite-Powell (**3.76**), and information on musical issues is available in McGee (**3.82**).

Reviewed by David Fallows in *EM* 7 (1979): 261–63.

3.79* Koury, Daniel J. *Orchestral Performance Practices in the Nineteenth Century: Size, Proportions, and Seating.* 409 pp. Ann Arbor, Mich.: UMI Research Press, 1986. (Studies in musicology, 85).

A revision of the author's dissertation (Boston University, 1981).

An examination of the size and seating plans for orchestras from the 18th and 19th century, also discussing the role of the conductor. The importance of seating is overemphasized, but the access to primary source information of interest, especially in the many tables and figures, is useful.

Reviewed by Nicholas Temperley in *Performance Practice Review* 2 (1989): 170–72; reviewed negatively by John B. Dick in *Galpin Society Journal* 42 (1989): 166–67.

3.80* Le Huray, Peter. *Authenticity in Performance: Eighteenth-Century Case Studies.* 202 pp. Cambridge, England; New York: Cambridge University Press, 1990.

The organization of a discussion of performance issues around selected compositions makes this collection a model of performance-practice investigation from the performer's perspective. The subject index provides access to topics such as overdotting and articulation. This is an interesting contribution.

Reviewed by Thomas Binkley in *Notes* 48 (1992): 866–67, by David Montgomery in *MQ* 76 (1992): 264–82, and by George Houle in *Performance Practice Review* 4 (1991): 208–10.

3.81* Lindley, Mark. *Lutes, Viols, and Temperaments.* 134 pp., with accompanying cassette. Cambridge, England; New York: Cambridge University Press, 1984.

A lavishly illustrated book whose individual chapters discuss pythagorean intonation, equal temperament, mean tone temperament, just intonation, and other tuning schemes in relation to fretting.

Reviewed by Penelope Gouk in *M&L* 67 (1986): 313–16 and, with some corrections, by Jean Bosquet in *Revue belge de musicologie* 41 (1987): 156–58.

3.82* McGee, Timothy J. *Medieval and Renaissance Music: A Performer's Guide.* 273 pp. Toronto; Buffalo, N.Y.: University of Toronto Press, 1985.

First ed. reprinted by the University of Toronto Press in 1988, and by Scolar Press, London, in 1990, 303 pp.

A performer's handbook focused on the music rather than the mechanics of performing early music. See Kite-Powell (**3.76**) for basic instruction in the various media for the renaissance. There are useful discussions on "reading the edition" and on choosing instruments suitable for a particular repertoire, complemented by presentations on ornamentation and improvisation. The many tables and charts give concise overviews of chronological developments. The final chapter lists sources of literature and editions by region and period.

Reviewed by Edward L. Kottick in *Historical Performance* 1 (1988): 80–83 and by Anthony Pryer in *EM* 15 (1987): 79–83.

3.83* Neumann, Frederick. *Performance Practices of the Seventeenth and Eighteenth Centuries.* 605 pp. New York: Schirmer Books; Toronto: Maxwell Macmillan International, 1993.

An attempt at a broad and summary view that is perhaps the *summa* of Neumann's oeuvre, as well as the author's last published book. Like its predecessors, this book challenges received wisdom. The discussion is divided into six large sections: tempo, rhythm, dynamics, articulation, phrasing, and ornamentation.

Reviewed by Albert Cohen in *Performance Practice Review* 7 (1994): 116–19. A bibliography of Neumann's many contributions to performance practice studies can be found at the end of Roland Jackson's laudatory essay in *Performance Practice Review* 7 (1994): 108–15.

3.84* Page, Christopher. *Voices and Instruments of the Middle Ages: Instrumental Practice and Songs in France, 1100–1300.* 316 pp. Berkeley: University of California Press, 1986; London: Dent, 1987.

An investigation of the role of instruments in the songs of troubadours and trouvères, demonstrating the importance of genre in the selection of an appropriate ensemble, with "high style" songs intended for solo voice. Page gives parallel translations for the many excerpts from primary sources, a feature that makes the book especially useful. The appendixes gather information on the terminology of musical instruments, a typology of musical references in French narrative fiction of the period, literary references to stringed instruments, and string materials in the middle ages. The generous bibliography separates primary and secondary sources, and the latter section provides access to both literary and musical studies.

Reviewed by Daniel Leech-Wilkinson in *RMA Journal* 113 (1988): 129–31, by Mark Everist in *M&L* 69 (1988): 246–8, by Mary Remnant in the *Galpin Society Journal* 43 (1990): 175–77, by Lawrence Rosenwald in *Historical Performance* 1 (1988): 75–79, and by Warwick Edwards in *EM* 15 (1987): 393–97.

3.85* Polk, Keith. *German Instrumental Music of the Late Middle Ages: Players, Patrons and Performance Practice.* 272 pp. New York: Cambridge University Press, 1992. (Cambridge musical texts and monographs)

An account of instrumental music investigating the common instruments and ensemble types from 1350 to 1520. Placing instrumental music in its sociocultural context, Polk examines patronage and repertoires. The book ends with a chapter on performance practice that is devoted chiefly to improvisation. A compelling text that reevaluates the importance of instrumental music generally and German instrumental music specifically.

One of the strengths of this book is the reaction it has provoked from reviewers. Reviewed by John Kmetz in the *RMA Journal* 119 (1994): 298–302, by Douglas Kirk in *Historical Performance* 7 (1994): 120–22, and by Beth Bullard in *Notes* 50 (1994): 1,381–84. See also the mostly negative review article by Joan Rimmer in *M&L* 75 (1994): 47–57.

3.86* Rosenblum, Sandra P. *Performance Practices in Classic Piano Music: Their Principles and Applications.* 544 pp. Bloomington, Ind.; Indianapolis: Indiana University Press, 1988. (Music: Scholarship & applications series)

A study addressing both performers and scholars with equal success. It focuses on the performance conventions of the classic era, drawing heavily on both theoretical sources and notational conventions of the composers. After tracing aspects of performance techniques such as dynamics and accentuation, and use of the pedals, Rosenblum ends with a chapter applying these concepts to Beethoven's *Bagatelle,* Op. 126, no. 5.

Reviewed by A. Peter Brown in *Performance Practice Review* 3 (1990): 90–96, by Seth Carlin in *Historical Performance* 2 (1989): 85–87, and by David Fanning in *EM* 17 (1989): 245–47.

3.87* Stowell, Robin. *Violin Technique and Performance Practice in the Late Eighteenth and Early Nineteenth Centuries.* 411 pp. Cambridge, England; New York: Cambridge University Press, 1985. (Cambridge musical texts and monographs)

Reprinted 1990.

An investigation of the violin teaching manuals and the technical issues they discuss, covering the period from 1760 to 1840, following on the contributions of David D. Boyden's *The History of Violin Playing from its Origins to 1761 and its Relationship to the Violin and Violin Music* (London: Oxford University Press, 1965). Individual chapters focus on particular technical problems such as posture, holding the bow, and double stopping. The appendix lists instruction books for the violin in chronological order by country.

Reviewed by Marcus Bennett in *Galpin Society Journal* 41 (1988): 156–59 and by Sonya Monosoff in *Notes* 44 (1987): 261–63.

3.88* Taruskin, Richard. "The Spin Doctors of Early Music." *New York Times,* July 29 1990, Arts and Leisure, pp. 1 and 21. Reprinted under Taruskin's preferred title "The Modern Sound of Early Music" with a postscript from 1994 in his *Text and Act,* pp. 164–72 (**3.89**).

The most widely disseminated of the salvos in the authenticity debate summarizes Taruskin's position that authenticity is a modern ideal that "remakes the music of the past in the image of the present."

3.89* Taruskin, Richard. *Text and Act: Essays on Music and Performance.* 382 pp. New York; Oxford: Oxford University Press, 1995.

A collection of 20 of Taruskin's trenchant essays on historical (and not so historical) performance, with a newly written introductory essay (pp. 3–47) summarizing his position, responding to his detractors, and explaining the origins of some of his essays; brief postscripts with similar material follow each of the reprinted essays. Taruskin challenges the term *authenticity* and argues that the early music movement follows a modernist aesthetic.

Reviewed by John Butt in *EM* 24 (1996): 323–32, with graphic support, and by Sanford V. Levinson and J. M. Balkin in *Notes* 53 (1996): 419–23.

3.90 Vinquist, Mary, and **Neal Zaslaw.** *Performance Practice: A Bibliography.* 114 pp. New York: W.W. Norton, 1971.

First published in issue 8 (1969) of *CM.* Supplemented in *CM* 10 (1970): 144–72, 12 (1971): 129–49, and 15 (1973): 126–33. Book is drawn from issues 8 and 10.

A bibliography, international in scope, whose main section has about 1,200 entries, both primary and secondary sources. The focus is on Western art music between 1100 and 1900; chant is omitted, as are *musica ficta,* instrument construction, and aesthetics. The index provides access to writings on major subtopics; there is a bibliography of chiefly unpublished performance practice bibliographies.

3.91* Wolf, Uwe. *Notation und Aufführungspraxis: Studien zum Wandel von Notenschrift und Notenbild in italienischen Musikdrucken der Jahre 1571–1630.* 2 vols. Kassel, Germany: Merseberger, 1992.

Originally presented as the author's doctoral thesis, Universität Göttingen, 1991.

A description and documentation of the changes in the performance meaning of older signs and the introduction of new signs in Italian prints around 1600, with many musical examples.

Reviewed by Rainer Heyink in *Die Musikforschung* 47 (1994): 183–84.

4

BIBLIOGRAPHIES OF MUSIC LITERATURE

The term *music literature* is used in this chapter for writings on music, a contrast to bibliographies of music, which list musical scores. Such writings may appear as periodical articles or monographs, may be cited in complete, self-contained bibliographical works or in serial publications, and can be organized in terms of a variety of subject fields. They may be arranged in a strict alphabetical order, in chronological order, or in an intricately classified format, grouped in a variety of approaches. Nearly every dissertation or research study has an appended bibliography of relevant literature, and most of the authoritative dictionaries or encyclopedias have subject bibliographies connected with their articles. It would be impossible to cite all of these resources, but the titles selected for inclusion in this chapter are numerous and varied enough to form a substantial sample of the available titles. The subdivisions used are listed in the Table of Contents. Chapters 6 and 7 also include bibliographies of music literature among their entries: It is not unusual for researchers to compile a bibliography of the works and activities of a composer, and many of the published catalogs of major libraries contain separate volumes or sections devoted to their holdings of books on music.

GENERAL WORKS

4.1 Aber, Adolf. *Handbuch der Musikliteratur in systematisch-chronologischer Anordnung.* 696 numbered cols. 350 pp. Leipzig: Breitkopf & Härtel, 1922. (Kleine Handbücher der Musikgeschichte nach Gattungen, 13)

Reprinted in Germany by Olms, Hildesheim, and Breitkopf & Härtel, Wiesbaden, in 1967 and 1983.

An early classified bibliography by a productive and influential editor, intended for students of music history. Its classification system is quite detailed, although the citations are not: In the European fashion, publisher names and pagination are omitted from the entries. Coverage is international, although strongest in German materials. Entries from many important continental and British musicological journals, as well as from *Musical America* and *The Musician* (Boston), are included. There are subject/personal name and author indexes.

4.2 Adlung, Jakob. *Anleitung zu der musikalischen Gelahrtheit.* 816 pp. Erfurt, Germany: J.D. Jungnicol, 1758.

Reprinted in 1953 in Kassel, Germany, by Bärenreiter, 1953, in an ed. supervised by Hans Joachim Moser (Documenta musicologica. 1. Reihe: Druckschriften-Faksimiles, 4). The 2nd ed. was revised by Johann Adam Hiller (Dresden; Leipzig: In der breitkopfischen Buchhandlung, 1782), 976 pp. Both editions were reprinted on microcards by Falls City Microcards, Louisville, Ky., in 1957, and on microfiche by Brookhaven Press, La Crosse, Wisc., 1983.

Chronologically, one of the first important critical bibliographies of music literature. Adlung proposed to list all works on music subjects necessary to "educated music lovers, and particularly to lovers of keyboard music," as well as builders of organs and other instruments.

There is a description of this work in Reese's *Fourscore Classics of Music Literature* (**4.384**), pp. 74–75.

4.3 Baily, Dee. *A Checklist of Music Bibliographies and Indexes in Progress and Unpublished.* 4th ed. 104 pp. Philadelphia, Pa.: Music Library Association, 1982. (MLA index and bibliography series, 3)

The 1st ed., compiled by MLA's Publications Committee in 1963 (6 pp.); the 2nd revised ed. compiled by James W. Pruett, 1969 (25 pp.); and the 3rd ed. compiled by Linda Solow, 1974 (40 pp.).

A list in two sections, giving the results of a survey sponsored by MLA, with 533 entries. The 1st section is organized by researcher's name, with each entry describing the work and its state of completion; addresses are provided. The 2nd is an index to entries, with access to subjects, proper and place names, and titles mentioned with entries. The entries are also listed under broad subjects (such as renaissance era). All projects were unpublished as of July 1981.

4.4 Bayne, Pauline S. *A Basic Music Library: Essential Scores and Books.* 2nd ed. Compiled by the Music Library Association Committee on Basic Music Collection under the direction of Pauline S. Bayne. Edited by Robert Michael Fling. 357 pp. Chicago, Ill.: American Library Association, 1983.

First ed., 1978, 173 pp. Third ed. anticipated, 1997.

Designed to serve as a buying guide and collection evaluator for small- and medium-sized public and academic libraries, 2,262 citations classified by format, medium, and subject are arranged alphabetically by composer or author, with the title given in the accepted uniform title format (and with a good explanation given in the preface of how uniform titles are formed). Included is the Committee's list of the best available editions of score anthologies, choral and dramatic music study and vocal scores (including musicals), and works for piano and organ, orchestra, various chamber combinations, instrumental solos and duos, and concertos in piano reduction. Music periodicals and English-language books on music theory, reference, and history are also listed. The full bibliographic citations include prices (as of 1981) and, when relevant, publishers' numbers and ISBN (or ISSN). Information on sound recordings is not included.

The 1st ed. is reviewed by Margaret Lospinuso in *Notes* 36 (1979): 94–95 and by Olga Buth in *ARBA* 11 (1980): no. 945.

4.5 Becker, Carl Ferdinand. *Systematisch-chronologische Darstellung der musikalischen Literatur von der frühesten bis auf die neueste Zeit.* 572 col. + 34 pp. Leipzig: R. Friese, 1836.

The 1839 ed. was published with an appendix, *Choralsammlungen aus dem 16., 17. und 18. Jahrhundert,* 1839.

Reprinted by Frits A.M. Knuf in Amsterdam, 1964, and on microfiche by Brookhaven Press, Washington, D.C., 1976.

A classified bibliography of many now-obscure works, including newspaper and periodical articles. Becker's work fills the gap, chronologically, between Lichtenthal (**1.313**) and Eitner's *Bücherverzeichnis,* 1885 (**4.23**). The entries provide the date and place of publication and the pagination, with brief annotations. There is a 33-page index by author and title or catchword title of anonymous works.

4.6* Birnbaum, Clemens, and **Horst Albert Scholz.** *Einführung in die Musikliteratur: eine kommentierte Bibliographie.* 2nd ed. 257 pp. Berlin: 1991.

An annotated list of about 1,000 basic music reference sources, classified by format (dictionaries and encyclopedias) and subject (music theory). Each classification has an opening essay. The bibliographic citations omit the publisher's name. There is a name index.

4.7 Blechschmidt, Eva Renate. "Bibliographie der Schriften über Musik aus der Deutschen Demokratischen Republik, 1945–1959." In *Beiträge zur Musikwissenschaft,* Jahrg. 1 (1959), Heft 3, pp. 51–75; Jahrg. 2 (1960), Heft 1, pp. 50–68, and Heft 2, pp. 64–78.

A classified list covering the writings on music produced in East Germany from 1945 to 1959. Complemented by Knepler (**4.31**).

4.8 Blom, Eric. *A General Index to Modern Musical Literature in the English Language, Including Periodicals for the Years 1915–1926.* 159 pp. London; Philadelphia, Pa.: Curwen, 1927.

Reprinted by Da Capo Press, New York, in 1970 (Da Capo Press music reprint series).

A list with entries for books arranged by author and for parts of books arranged by subject's keyword, in one alphabet.

4.9 Blum, Fred. *Music Monographs in Series: A Bibliography of Numbered Monograph Series in the Field of Music Current since 1945.* 197 pp. New York: Scarecrow Press, 1964.

A list of the contents of more than 259 monographic series active after World War II, from some 30 countries. The list includes author, title, and date for each publication, alphabetically arranged by series title or sponsoring organization. Over one-third of the series are broadly musicological in content; others, ranging in tone from academic to popular, cover the gamut of musical subject matter.

Later German-language series are covered by Hermann Walther in his *Bibliographie der Musikbuchreihen: 1886–1990* (**4.44**).

Reviewed by Thomas Watkins in *CM* (Fall 1965): 227–29 and by Richard Schaal in *Die Musikforschung* 22 (1969): 521.

4.10 Bobillier, Marie (Michel Brenet, pseud.). "Bibliographie des bibliographies musicales." In *L'année musicale* 3 (1913): 1–152.

Reprinted by Da Capo Press, New York, 1971.

One of the first bibliographies of music bibliography, dated but still useful, listing general works, including periodical articles, by author; individual bibliographies; catalogs of libraries; and catalogs of dealers and publishers.

4.11 Briquet, Marie. *La musique dans les congrès internationaux, 1835–1939.* 124 pp. Paris: Heugel, 1961. (Publications de la Société française de musicologie, sér. 2, 10)

A bibliographical survey of the contributions in music made at international congresses, 1835–1939, with a classified list of 164 congress reports, itemizing papers on music. The survey is indexed by meeting place, chronology, author, and subject, and is chronologically followed in coverage by Tyrrell and Wise (**4.43**).

Reviewed by Richard Schaal in *Die Musikforschung* 17 (1964): 183.

4.12* Brockman, William S. *Music: A Guide to the Reference Literature.* 254 pp. Littleton, Colo.: Libraries Unlimited, Inc., 1987. (Reference sources in the humanities series)

A new ed., edited by Brockman and Leslie Troutman, recently announced, is anticipated.

Classified, thoughtfully evaluative annotations for 558 music reference works, principally in English, giving a well-balanced, current look at the field. The bibliographic citations list the most recent edition, as well as the LC card number, the ISBN (or ISSN), and reprint information, if relevant. Following are similarly annotated listings for 109 current music periodicals and 172 music organizations and associations (composer societies, musical instrument societies, research centers and institutes, service organizations, trade and business associations, and membership societies and associations, both professional and amateur). There are detailed author/title and subject indexes.

Reviewed by Ann P. Basart in *CNV* 123 (1988): 18–19, by Charles Lindahl in *Notes* 47 (1990): 405–6, by George Louis Mayer in *ARBA* 20 (1989): 1167, by Keith E. Mixter in *Fontes* 36 (1989): 62–63, and by John Wagstaff in *M&L* 70 (1989): 394–95.

4.13 Brook, Barry S. *Thematic Catalogues in Music, an Annotated Bibliography: Including Printed, Manuscript, and In-Preparation Catalogues; Related Literature and Reviews; An Essay on the Definitions, History, Functions, Historiography, and Future of the Thematic Catalogue.* xxxvi + 347 pp. Hillsdale, N.Y.: Pendragon Press, 1972. (*RILM* retrospectives, 1)

Published under joint sponsorship of the Music Library Association and *RILM* Abstracts of Music Literature. This work supersedes *A Checklist of Thematic Catalogues,* edited by MLA's Committee on Thematic Indexes (1954), and its *Supplement,* issued by Queens College (1966). A new ed. of this bibliography has been expected for some time.

A list of some 1,500 entries, including a number of 18th-century manuscript catalogs, a great many unpublished catalogs, and some large-scale national projects in progress. The editor's overview of thematic catalogs is found in "A Tale of Thematic Catalogues," in *Notes* 29 (1973): 407–15, updated and amplified in his article "Thematic Catalogue" in *The New Grove* (**1.48**). See also Wettstein's bibliography (**6.6**).

Reviewed by Lenore Coral in *JAMS* 26 (1973): 332–33 and by Neal Zaslaw in *Notes* 29 (1973): 444–45.

4.14 Browne, Richmond. "Index of Music Theory in the United States, 1955–1970." In *In Theory Only, Journal of the Michigan Music Theory Society* 3 (1978): nos. 7–11.

An index of articles, books, dissertations, and reviews published from 1955 to 1970 on music theory, terms and concepts, analyses, and technical music theory (such as notation and orchestration), and also including some works on ethnomusicology, musicology, aesthetics, philosophy, and theory pedagogy. There are author and subject indexes, as well as indexes of musical compositions analyzed and of historical theorists whose work is treated as a subject.

4.15 Büchting, Adolf. *Bibliotheca musica: Verzeichnis aller in Bezug auf die Musik, 1847–66, im deutschen Buchhandel erschienenen Bücher und Zeitschriften.* Nebst Fortsetzung 1: die Jahre 1867–71 umfassend. 2 vols. Nordhausen, Germany: A. Büchting, 1867–72.

A bibliography of music literature covering German publications from 1847 to 1871, taking its place chronologically after Becker (**4.5**) in the history of music bibliography. The eight-year gap in coverage between the two was filled by Robert Eitner (**4.23**).

4.16 Carl Gregor, Duke of Mecklenburg. *Bibliographie einiger Grenzgebiete der Musikwissenschaft.* 197 pp. Baden-Baden: Librarie Heitz, 1962. (Bibliotheca bibliographica Aureliana, 6)

A bibliography devoted to areas peripheral to the traditional emphasis on historical musicology, including books and periodical articles on aesthetics, psychology, sociology of music, the relationship between music and the other arts, and the musical interests of poets, writers, and philosophers. There are 3,519 entries, arranged alphabetically by author, with indexes of subjects and persons.

Reviewed by Wolfgang Schmieder in *Die Musikforschung* 20 (1967): 461–62.

4.17 Coover, James B. *Antiquarian Catalogues of Musical Interest.* xxxi + 372 pp. London; New York: Mansell Pub., 1988.

A preliminary ed. was issued as *Provisional Checklist of Priced Antiquarians' Catalogues* by the Music Library, SUNY, Buffalo, in 1981 (150 ll.).

A bibliography with 5,531 entries arranged alphabetically by 640 dealers' names. The entries describe and date each catalog, giving the dealer's catalog number and the number of items offered. The indexes list the entries by place and by subject, including named collections offered for sale.

Reviewed by Lenore Coral in *Fontes* 36 (1989): 333–34 and by Ann P. Basart in *CNV* 133 (1989): 15.

4.18* Crabtree, Phillip D., and **Donald H. Foster.** *Sourcebook for Research in Music.* 236 pp. Bloomington, Ind.: Indiana University Press, 1993.

A carefully classified, minimally annotated bibliography of resources for music research and of more basic sources for general research, intended as an introduction to a variety of information formats. Despite the occasional bursts of wishful thinking (for example, the 2nd ed. of

Brook's *Thematic Catalogues in Music* has not been published to date), a generally accurate list of music reference works and of the plans of a number of music reference series.

Reviewed by John Wagstaff in *M&L* 76 (1995): 274–75, by Richard Turbet in *Brio* 32 (1995): 57, by D. W. Krummel in *Choice* 31 (1994): 1268, and by Thomas F. Heck in *Fontes* 41 (1994): 392–94.

4.19* Damschroder, David, and David Russell Williams. *Music Theory from Zarlino to Schenker: A Bibliography and Guide.* xliii + 522 pp. Stuyvesant, N.Y.: Pendragon Press, 1990. (Harmonologia, 4)

A thorough, carefully wrought bibliographic handbook whose main section is a "Dictionary of Theorists," 396 pp., covering over 225 theorists from the 16th to the 20th century, each with an account of life and work, a list of writings (published and unpublished), and a bibliography of works on the theorist. There are indexes by subject, chronology, title, and name.

Reviewed by Burdette L. Green in *Fontes* 38 (1991): 340–41, by Nicholas Marston in *M&L* 73 (1992): 436–37, and by Thomas Christensen in *Notes* 48 (1992): 1,306–7.

4.20 Davies, J. H. *Musicalia: Sources of Information in Music.* 2nd ed., revised and enlarged. 184 pp. Oxford; New York: Pergamon Press, 1969. (The commonwealth and international library. Libraries and technical information division)

First ed., 1966, 218 pp.

A practical guide listing performing and study editions of music anthologies, reference works, and histories of various musical formats, as well as important periodical articles, with the individual lists divided by user category: ordinary listeners, choral conductors, chamber musicians and solo instrumentalists, and musicologists. Appendixes include principal music collections, formerly in private hands, now in institutions and libraries of Great Britain; music publishers and agents; music publishers' organizations; and performing rights and collecting societies. The index covers titles, authors, and subjects. Most helpful to students are the 48 full-page reprints from a variety of major music reference tools.

Reviewed by François Lesure in *Fontes* 17 (1970): 55.

4.21 De Lerma, Dominique-René. *A Bibliography of Black Music.* 4 vols. Westport, Conn.: Greenwood Press, 1981–84. (The Greenwood encyclopedia of Black music)

Contents: Vol. 1, *Reference Materials,* 1981 (124 pp.); Vol. 2, *Afro-American Idioms,* 1981 (220 pp.); Vol. 3, *Geographical Studies,* 1982 (297 pp.); Vol. 4, *Theory, Education, and Related Studies,* 1984 (254 pp.).

An annotated bibliography, international in scope but emphasizing the United States. The bibliography includes books, articles, graduate student papers, and journals on many areas of Black musical life, a total of 19,397 entries. The citations and their arrangement are based on the *RILM* model (**4.90**), with coverage particularly intense up to 1975. Vol. 3 includes an extensive bibliography on acculturation and an index to authors and editors in that volume. Vol. 4, combining a variety of subjects, has an author index to its contents. De Lerma began his compilation with the publication of *The Black-American Musical Heritage: A Preliminary Bibliography,* published by Kent State University in 1969 (MLA, Midwest Chapter, Explorations in music librarianship, 3). An earlier, related publication by De Lerma is *A Name List of Black Composers* (Minneapolis, Minn.: AAMOA, 1973), 27 pp. (Afro-American Music Opportunities Association, Resource papers, 2)

The 1st vol. of the *Bibliography* is reviewed by Deane Root in *Notes* 38 (1982): 832–33, by Sam Dennison in *AM* 2 (1984): 103–5 no. 2, by Doris McGinty in *BPM* 9 (1982): 229–31, by Robert Skinner in *ARBA* 13 (1982): no. 1017, and by Barbara L. Hampton in *Ethnomusicology* 27 (1983): 382–84. The 2nd vol. is reviewed by Doris Evans McGinty in *BPM* 9 (1981): 114–15, by Dean Tudor in *ARBA* 14 (1983): no. 920, and by Barbara L. Hampton in *Ethnomusicology* 27 (1983): 382–84. The 3rd vol. is reviewed by Doris Evans McGinty in *BPM* 11 (1981): 79–82 no. 1

and by Robert Skinner in *ARBA* 14 (1983): no. 921. The 4th vol. is reviewed by Willie Collins in *Ethnomusicology* 29 (1985): 384–85 and by Robert Skinner in *ARBA* 16 (1985): no. 1211.

4.22 Duckles, Vincent H., and **Michael A. Keller.** *Music Reference and Research Materials: An Annotated Bibliography.* 4th ed., revised. 740 pp. New York: Schirmer Books; Toronto: Maxwell Macmillan Canada, 1994.

Originating with Duckles's *A Guide to Reference Materials on Music,* first published as a class syllabus in Berkeley by the University of Calif. Press, 1949; revised ed., 1952 (48 pp.); 3rd ed., 1955 (69 pp. and *Supplement*). The 1st ed. of *Music Reference and Research Materials* was published in New York and London by Free Press of Glencoe in 1964 (331 pp.); the 2nd was published in New York by the Free Press in 1967 (335 pp.); the 3rd in New York by the Free Press, 1974 (526 pp.); the 4th ed., with Michael A. Keller, in New York by Schirmer Books (Collier Macmillan) in 1988 (714 pp.).

An annotated, classified list of 3,074 reference sources (books, periodical articles, and databases), with personal name (authors, editors, and reviewers), selected music bibliographical series, title (including names of institutions), and subject indexes. Detailed bibliographic citations are given, including reprint information. The editors include current and historical works, in English and European languages, with a smattering of Asian titles as well. Reviews are cited. The written contributions of Vincent Duckles to music bibliography and librarianship are noted in "Vincent Duckles (1913–1985): A Bibliography of His Publications," by Patricia Elliott and Mark S. Roosa in *Notes* 44 (1987): 252–58, with addenda listed in *Notes* 44 (1988): 856.

The 1952 ed. of the syllabus is reviewed by Glen Haydon in *Notes* 10 (1953): 281–82. The 1st ed. is reviewed by Jan LaRue in *JAMS* 19 (1966): 257–61, and by Klaus Speer in *Notes* 21 (1964): 375. The 2nd ed. is reviewed by William S. Newman in *Notes* 24 (1967): 265–66. The 3rd ed. is reviewed in *ALA Reference and Subscription Book Review* (December 1 1974): 83–84. The 4th ed. is reviewed by D. W. Krummel in *Notes* 46 (1989): 64–66, by Ann P. Basart in *CNV* 129 (1989): 9–10, and by Daniel Zager in *Fontes* 36 (1989): 239–40. The 4th ed., revised, is briefly reviewed by Marjorie Hassen in *Notes* 51 (1994): 226–27, by Paul Cauthen in *RQ* 34 (1994): 253–54, and by Karl Kroeger in *Fontes* 42 (1995): 191–92.

4.23 Eitner, Robert. *Bücherverzeichnis der Musikliteratur aus den Jahren 1839 bis 1846 im Anschluss an Becker und Büchting.* 89 pp. Leipzig: Breitkopf & Härtel, 1885. (Monatshefte für Musikgeschichte. Beilage. 17. Jahrgang)

A bibliography intended to bridge the gap between Becker (**4.5**) and Büchting (**4.15**).

4.24 Elste, Martin. *Verzeichnis deutschsprachiger Musiksoziologie 1848–1973.* 2 vols. Hamburg: Verlag der Musikalienhandlung Karl Dieter Wagner, 1975. (Schriftenreihe zur Musik, 7)

A classified bibliography with indexes to names and periodicals, as well as keywords in context (KWIC) to titles.

4.25 Forkel, Johann Nikolaus. *Allgemeine Litteratur der Musik, oder, Anleitung zur Kenntniss musikalischer Bücher: Welche von den ältesten bis auf die neusten Zeiten bey den Griechen, Römern und den meisten neuern europäischen Nationen sind geschrieben worden.* 540 pp. Leipzig: Schwickert, 1792.

Reprinted by Olms, Hildesheim, Germany, in 1962, with a reprint of Tinctoris's *Terminorum musicae diffinitiorum.*

The first comprehensive bibliography of music literature, still a work of great utility, presenting a classified list of some 3,000 works on all aspects of musical knowledge, with brief biographical notices on all the authors and descriptive annotations. Complete tables of contents are given for the most important books. Forkel's classification system has served as a model for many subsequent bibliographies; see Scott Goldthwaite's "Classification Problems, Bibliographies of Literature about Music," in *LQ* (October 1948): 255 ff. Forkel's work was expanded and translated into Italian by Pietro Lichtenthal in 1822 (**1.313**).

4.26 Gardeton, César. *Bibliographie musicale de la France et de l'étranger, ou Répertoire général systématique de tous les traités et oeuvres de musique vocale et instrumentale, imprimés ou gravés en Europe jusqu'à ce jour avec l'indication de lieux de l'impression, des marchands et des prix.* 608 pp. Paris: Chez Niogret, 1822.

Reprinted by Minkoff, Geneva, 1978 (Archives de l'édition musicale française, 6).

An early 19th-century bibliography of music and music literature, chiefly French, although listing titles from other European countries. A section is devoted to reviews, biographies, analyses, and musical news, and a directory of Parisian musicians of all kinds.

4.27 Gerboth, Walter. *An Index to Musical Festschriften and Similar Publications.* 188 pp. New York: W.W. Norton, 1969.

An index expanded from a preliminary version originally published in *Aspects of Medieval and Renaissance Music: A Birthday Offering to Gustave Reese* (New York: W.W. Norton, 1966), pp. 183–307, giving users of the 1969 ed. the most comprehensive treatment of music Festschriften available to that time. The first section is a list of more than 400 musical Festschriften, arranged under the name of the individual or institution honored, with each entry having a full bibliographic citation; the second section is a classified subject list of more than 2,700 articles contained in the aforementioned Festschriften; and the third is an author and subject index. An earlier article by Ernst C. Krohn, "Musical Festschriften and Related Publications," in *Notes* 21 (1964): 94–108, was a pioneering work in this area. *RILM* (**4.90**) provides coverage of musical Festschriften published after 1967.

Reviewed by Donald Seibert in *Notes* 26 (1970): 760–61.

4.28 Heussner, Horst, and **Ingo Schultz.** *Collectio musica: Musikbibliographie in Deutschland bis 1625.* xl + 254 pp. Kassel, Germany: Internationale Vereinigung der Musikbibliotheken / Internationale Gesellschaft für Musikwissenschaft, 1973. (Catalogus musicus, 6)

A classified bibliography of music and music literature published in Germany before 1625, arranged in two language groups, Latin and German. There are indexes to names of composers; authors of texts, editors, and collectors; printers, publishers, and dealers; names of presses; and titles appearing twice. There are bibliographies of contemporaneous bibliographies and of modern secondary literature, as well as lists of corrigenda and addenda.

4.29* *International Basic List of Literature on Music.* Compiled by the Public Libraries Commission of the International Association of Music Libraries. 41 pp. The Hague: Nederlands Bibliotheek en Lectuur Centrum, 1975.

The first basic list of standard literature on music, intended primarily as a guide for public music libraries, containing about 500 titles and excluding periodicals and libretti, consisting mainly of titles printed since 1945, and derived from six basic lists compiled in Denmark, England, Germany, Holland, Hungary, and the U.S.

Reviewed by Pauline Shaw Bayne in *Notes* 34 (1977): 80–81.

4.30 Kahl, Willi, and **Wilhelm-Martin Luther.** *Repertorium der Musikwissenschaft, Musikschrifttum, Denkmäler, und Gesamtausgaben in Auswahl (1800–1950) mit Besitzvermerken deutscher Bibliotheken und Musikwissenschaftlicher Institute.* 271 pp. Kassel, Germany: Bärenreiter, 1953.

A comprehensive bibliography of music literature, broadly classified, prepared to serve as a union list of musicological holdings in postwar German libraries. The contents, international in scope, number 2,785 entries and include useful lists of Festschriften, conference reports, and critical editions. There are indexes by person, subject, and geographical location.

Reviewed by Otto E. Albrecht in *Notes* 11 (1954): 468–69 and by Vincent Duckles in *JAMS* 7 (1954): 242–45.

4.31 Knepler, Georg. *Beiträge zur Musikwissenschaft. Sonderreihe: Bibliographien, musikwissenschaftliche Literatur sozialistischer Länder.* 4 vols. Berlin: Verlag neue Musik, 1966–76.

Contents: Band I, *SR Rumänien (1945–1965)* (66 pp.); Band II, *VR Polen (1945–65)* (192 pp.); Band III, *Deutsche Demokratische Republik, 1945–1970* (334 pp.); Band IV, *Sowjetunion, 1945–1970* (1976, 312 pp.); *Anhang: Verzeichnis der Autoren und der publizierten Titel in russischer Sprache* (1976, 166 pp.).

A bibliography of musicological writings from Eastern Europe. The 3rd vol. is a classified, indexed bibliography of 3,495 published writings on musicology by German and foreign authors. The 4th vol. is a classified bibliography of 4,007 entries, transliterated from Cyrillic. The *Anhang* is an index of authors included, with the titles in Cyrillic characters.

4.32 Kramer, Jonathan D. "Studies in Time and Music: A Bibliography." In *Music Theory Spectrum* 7 (1985): 72–106.

A classified bibliography listing post-1900, primarily English-language articles on time in music, including relevant articles from the fields of psychology, sociology, philosophy, criticism of other temporal arts, and anthropology.

4.33* Krummel, Donald W. *Bibliotheca Bolduaniana: A Renaissance Music Bibliography.* 191 pp. Detroit, Mich.: Information Coordinators, 1972. (Detroit studies in music bibliography, 22)

Paulus Bolduan's 80-page section on music, in the Bibliotheca philosophicam with 1,299 titles, is reproduced in facsimile with annotations and a supporting bibliography (pp. 15–18).

Reviewed by Samuel Pogue in *JAMS* 27 (1974): 142–44.

4.34* Lewis, Thomas. *The Pro/Am Guide to U.S. Books about Music: Annotated Subject Guide to Current & Backlist Titles.* 212 pp. White Plains, N.Y.: Pro/Am Music Resources, Inc., 1986.

A classified list of books on musical topics available for purchase. The first annual supplement was published in 1988 (90 pp.), including titles reviewed in 1987 and earlier titles omitted from the 1986 edition, with an 18,000-entry cumulative index.

Reviewed by William Brockman in *ARBA* 19 (1988): no. 1263.

4.35 Marco, Guy A., and **Sharon Paugh Ferris.** *Information on Music: A Handbook of Reference Sources in European Languages.* 3 vols. Littleton, Colo.: Libraries Unlimited, 1975–84.

Contents: Vol. 1, *Basic and Universal Sources,* 1975 (164 pp.); Vol. 2, *The Americas* (with Ann M. Garfield), 1977 (296 pp.); Vol. 3, *Europe* (with Ann G. Olszewski), 1984 (519 pp.).

An annotated guide to music reference works in a variety of formats, designed to give comprehensive access to music information, published and unpublished. Although a 6-vol. work was projected, the project has been halted, temporarily at least, with 3 vols. Each of the 3,700 entries provides complete bibliographic information, an LC classification, and references to other guides for music reference and research materials. Each volume has indexes to names and titles and to subjects (in the LC Subject Headings format). The index to Vol. 2 covers entries in the first 2 vols. Vol. 3 has an update to Vol. 2 and an appendix of revisions to Vols. 1 and 2.

Marlene Wehrle updated the Canadian section (pp. 22–35) in "Reference Sources on Canadian Music: A Supplement to Guy Marco *Information on Music,* Volume II," in *Fontes* 41 (1994): 40–52.

Vol. 1 is reviewed by Tony Hodges in *Brio* 12 (1975): 44–45, by Stephen M. Fry in *Notes* 32 (1975): 303, by Gordon S. Rowley in *Fontes* 23 (1976): 202–5, and by Peter Ward Jones in *M&L* 58 (1977): 454–55. Vol. 2 is reviewed by Joan Kunselman in *Notes* 34 (1978): 881, by Gordon S. Rowley in *Fontes* 26 (1979): 62–63, and by Robert Follet in *LAMR* 5 (1984): 106–8. Vol. 3 is reviewed by George R. Hill in *ARBA* 16 (1985): no. 1159 and, briefly, by Richard Andrewes in *MT* 128 (1987): 270.

4.36 Mathiesen, Thomas J. *A Bibliography of Sources for the Study of Ancient Greek Music.* 59 pp. Hackensack, N.J.: Joseph Boonin, 1974. (Music indexes and bibliographies, 10)

A bibliography of "all the myriad sources dealing with ancient Greek music theory." The 949 entries are arranged alphabetically by author and theorist and include books, articles, dissertations, and translations. The various editions of each theorist's work are listed chronologically under the theorist's name and then by the work's title. The entries give the author's name, title, imprint information, and pagination. Further evidence of the compiler's interest and expertise in this subject area is his *Ancient Greek Music Theory: A Catalogue Raisonné of Manuscripts* (**4.383**).

4.37 Matthew, James E. *The Literature of Music.* 281 pp. London: E. Stock, 1896. (The book-lover's library)

Reprinted by Da Capo Press, New York, 1969.

Essays on the literature of music in historical sequence to the 18th century and thereafter by topics: histories, biographies, dictionaries, sacred music, opera, instruments of music, music as a science, and bibliography. Although dated, this is a useful survey of the earlier literature of music.

4.38 Ogawa, Takashi. *Hompô Yôgaku Bunken Mokuroku / A List of Books about Foreign Music in the Japanese Language.* 3rd ed. 267 pp. Tokyo: Ongaku no Tomosha, 1965.

First ed., 1952 (307 pp.); 2nd ed., 1957 (425 pp.).

A comprehensive bibliography, by the music librarian of the Japan Broadcasting Corporation, in Japanese on non-Japanese music, including both translations and many original works.

The 1st ed. is reviewed by Edwin G. Beal, Jr., in *Notes* 10 (1952): 106–7; the 2nd ed. is reviewed by Beal in *Notes* 16 (1958): 62–63.

4.39 *Performing Arts Books, 1876–1981, Including an International Index of Current Serial Publications.* 1,656 pp. New York; London: R. R. Bowker, 1981.

An extensive but seemingly mechanically compiled retrospective bibliography whose entries have been given LC classification and are works published or distributed in the United States; the entries are derived from the *American Book Publishing Record.* About one-third of the works are books about music. The indexes, which cover both books and serials, are to subjects, authors, and titles.

Reviewed by Susan T. Sommer in *Notes* 39 (1982):104–5.

4.40 Riemann, Hugo. *Geschichte der Musiktheorie im IX.-XIX. Jahrhunderts.* 2nd ed. xxiii + 550 pp. Berlin: M. Hesse, 1921.

Reprinted by Olms in Hildesheim, Germany, 1961, edited by Gustav Becking (541 pp.), and 1990 (xxiii + 550 pp.). The 1st ed. was published in Leipzig by M. Hesse, 1898 (529 pp.). An English-language ed., *History of Music Theory, Books 1 and 2: Polyphonic Theory to the Sixteenth Century,* was trans. by Raymond H. Haggh (Lincoln, Neb.: University of Nebraska Press, 1966; New York: Da Capo Press, 1974, xxii + 435 pp.).

A convenient list of early primary sources on music theory from the 9th to the 19th centuries, with each entry citing the author's name, brief title, and the approximate date. The English translation updates Riemann's bibliography with entries for modern editions, annotations (including a few references to modern secondary literature), and fuller bibliographic information.

4.41 Sheehy, Eugene P. "Music." In his *Guide to Reference Books* (pp. 599–628). 10th ed. Chicago, Ill.; London: American Library Association, 1986.

The 11th ed., to be edited by Robert Balay, is anticipated for publication in 1996.

An annotated bibliography of 353 titles likely to be found in general libraries, supplemented by "Music" in his *Guide to Reference Books Covering Materials from 1985 to 1990: Supplement to the Tenth Edition* (Chicago, Ill.; London: American Library Association, 1992), pp. 186–201. The *Guide* is a vast annotated bibliography of reference tools in every major discipline. Previous generations of scholars knew the work as "Mudge," and then "Winchell." A new edition is being directed by Robert Balay. Through each edition one is guided to literature and reference works in unfamiliar territories. Although not comprehensive, its coverage of subjects is very broad. There is a single index to authors and titles.

4.42 *Sovetskaia literatura o muzyke.* 8 vols. Moscow: Sovetskii Kompozitor, 1955–84.

A bibliographical series, issued irregularly, covering the period from 1918 to 1970, providing a classified list of books and periodical articles in Russian, published in the former Soviet Union. The title, imprint, and editor vary. Includes a list of periodicals covered and a name index.

4.43 Tyrrell, John, and **Rosemary Wise.** *A Guide to International Congress Reports in Musicology, 1900–1975.* 353 pp. New York: Garland Publishing, 1979. (Garland reference library of the humanities, 118)

A bibliographical guide locating and identifying published congress reports of music and related areas and indexing the papers published in those reports. The organization is chronological, indexed by place, by titles, by series and sponsors, by authors and editors, and by subject. This work is complemented by Briquet (**4.11**).

Reviewed by Walter Gerboth in *Notes* 36 (1980): 902–3, and by Rita Benton in *Fontes* 27 (1980): 121.

4.44* Walther, Hermann. *Bibliographie der Musikbuchreihen: 1886–1990.* 352 pp. Kassel, Germany: Bärenreiter, 1991. (Catalogus musicus, 12)

A bibliography of 520 numbered, music-related monographic series, published in German-speaking countries, containing several thousand titles. The subject index is particularly useful; name and place indexes are also included. Fred Blum's *Music Monographs in Series* (**4.9**) lists over 259 series titles from 30 countries.

Reviewed by Daniel Zager in *Fontes* 39 (1992): 191–92.

4.45 Wescott, Steven D. *A Comprehensive Bibliography of Music for Film and Television.* xxi + 432 pp. Detroit. Mich.: Information Coordinators, 1985. (Detroit studies in music bibliography, 54)

An extensive, broadly classified international bibliography of 6,340 entries, many with brief annotations, including articles and a wide variety of other sources on the subject. There is an index to names and subjects.

"Additions to Steven D. Wescott, *A Comprehensive Bibliography of Music for Film and Television,*" by Gillian B. Anderson, arranged in accordance with Wescott's classification scheme, was published in 1986 by the Library of Congress (68 pp.) and reprinted in *Foundations in Music Bibliography* (**13.19**), pp. 77–99, followed there by her "Supplement to Steven D. Wescott, *A Comprehensive Bibliography of Music for Film and Television*" (pp. 109–44).

Reviewed by Ann P. Basart in *CNV* 104 (1986): 13–14.

4.46 Williams, David Russell. *A Bibliography of the History of Music Theory.* 2nd ed. 58 pp. Fairport, N.Y.: Rochester Music Publishers, 1971.

First published by Rochester Music Publishers, Rochester, N.Y., in 1970 (53 pp.).

A selective bibliography of music theory works and the writings devoted to them, organized chronologically in study units, as in a syllabus. There are indexes of treatises and names. This work is superseded by Damschroder and Williams's *Music Theory from Zarlino to Schenker: A Bibliography and Guide,* 1990 (xliii + 522 pp.) (**4.19**).

4.47 Winick, Steven. *Rhythm: An Annotated Bibliography.* 157 pp. Metuchen, N.J.: Scarecrow Press, 1974.

A list of about 500 English-language sources written from 1900 to 1972, divided into three categories, focusing on music education: general background, psychology of rhythm, and the pedagogy of rhythm. There is an index of authors, editors, and reviewers.

CURRENT OR ANNUAL PUBLICATIONS, INCLUDING PERIODICALS LISTING MUSIC LITERATURE

Many periodicals of a more scholarly bent include as a regular feature a list of new publications in the field covered. A sampling of some of the more influential music periodicals is included in the following list.

4.48 *Acta Musicologica.* Internationale Gesellschaft für Musikwissenschaft, 1928–52. Vols. 1–24.

The journal of the Internationale Gesellschaft für Musikwissenschaft. "Index novorum librarum," a department appearing in most issues of this journal through 1952, is one of the best sources of bibliographical information for 1930–50, giving a classified list of books on music in all languages. The early years of *Acta* itself are accessible through the index prepared by Cecil Adkins and Alis Dickinson, *Acta Musicologica: An Index, Fall 1928–Spring 1967* (Basel: Bärenreiter-Verlag, 70 pp.). There is an author and subject index. A list of bibliographies of new books, crediting their individual compilers, is on p. 70.

4.49 *Bibliographia Musicologica: A Bibliography of Musical Literature, 1968–76.* 9 vols. Utrecht: Joachimsthal, 1970–80.

An international bibliography of books on music, listed alphabetically by author or title, with a subject index, covering the period 1968–76. Each entry gives publishing information, pagination, and price; entries include current reprints, facsimile and revised editions, and dissertations. There is a name/subject index.

Vol. 3 (1970) is reviewed by Stephen M. Fry in *Notes* 32 (1975): 301.

4.50 *Bibliographic Guide to Music.* Boston, Mass.: G.K. Hall, 1975– .

The 1st vol. of this series was published as the *Music Book Guide: 1974* (Boston, Mass.: G.K. Hall, 1974).

An annual list of music publications (books, serials, scores, libretti, and recordings) cataloged by the staff of the Research Libraries of the New York Public Library, as well as similar items from the Library of Congress's MARC tapes. Although in the *Guide* only the main entry gives a full bibliographic citation, listings appear under author or composer, title, and LC subject heading. The *Guide* supplements the New York Public Library's *Dictionary Catalog of the Music Collection* (**7.362**).

The 1975 ed. is reviewed by Stephen M. Fry in *Notes* 33 (1976): 305, by Miriam Miller in *Brio* 14 (1977): 22, and, briefly, by Paul R. Lehman in *JRME* 24 (1976): 212. The 1980 ed. is reviewed by George R. Hill in *ARBA* 13 (1982): no. 1016.

4.51 *Bibliographie des Musikschrifttums.* Jahrgang 1936–38; 1950– . Leipzig; Frankfurt am Main: Friedrich Hofmeister, 1936–38; Mainz: Schott: 1950– .

A reprint edition, published in Nendeln, Liechtenstein by Kraus Reprint.

A bibliographic study, with a decidedly academic slant, listing 6,000–7,000 entries annually and including both books and an index to periodical literature in all European languages, from both musical and nonmusical journals. The citations are classified in approximately 50 broad subject areas, with an index of names (author and subject) and places. The emphasis is on "serious" music and follows in direct line of descent the listings in the Peters *Jahrbuch* (**4.55**).

Jahrbuch 1950–51 is reviewed by Richard Schaal in *Die Musikforschung* 8 (1955): 371–72, by Richard S. Hill in *Notes* 11 (1954): 555–57, and by Scott Goldthwaite in *JAMS* 8 (1955): 55–57.

4.52 *Deutsche Musikbibliographie.* Leipzig: F. Hofmeister, 1829– . Jahrgang 1– .

Title varies: 1829–1942, *Hofmeisters musikalisch-literarischer Monatsbericht.*

A monthly list of German, Swiss, and Austrian music and music literature publications, useful chiefly for the music titles contained. The arrangement is alphabetical by author or composer, with publication date and place, pagination, and price given. The entries are cumulated in Hofmeister's *Jahresverzeichnis* (**4.58**).

4.53 *Ethnomusicology; Journal of the Society for Ethnomusicology.* Middletown, Conn.: Wesleyan University Press, 1953– . Vol. 1– .

Title varies: 1953–57, *Ethno-Musicology Newsletter.* Imprint varies: after January 1972, published by the Society for Ethnomusicology.

A journal that includes in each issue a section of current bibliography listing books, dissertations, films, exchange publications, and periodical articles related to the field, organized by geographical areas and special topics (such as dance), a comprehensive survey of ethnomusicological literature, in all formats. From 1967, the lists have included discography and, later, film and videos. The journal also publishes occasional special bibliographies on the work of leading ethnomusicologists and musically notable geographical regions; see **4.153**, **4.155**, **4.165**, **4.176**, and **4.177**.

4.54 *Hofmeisters Handbuch der Musikliteratur.* Leipzig: F. Hofmeister, 1844–1943. Bd. 1–19.

A cumulation of *Jahresverzeichnis der deutsche Musikalien und Musikschriften* (**4.58**), preceded by a similar work compiled by C. F. Whistling and published in Leipzig by Anton Maysel, 1817, listing music and music literature through 1815, updated through 1827 by 10 supplements published by Maysel (no. 1), Hofmeister (nos. 2–8), and Whistling (nos. 9–10). This 1817 vol., with supplements, was reprinted in 1975 by Garland Publishing, New York, with an introduction by Neil Ratliff explicating the history and relationships of these important bibliographies. Vienna House, New York, published in 1972 a 2-vol. reprint as *Handbuch der musikalischen Literatur.*

Title varies: Vols. 1–3 (to 1844), C. F. Whistling's *Handbuch der musicalischen Literatur;* Vols. 4–6 (1844–67), *Handbuch der musikalischen Literatur;* Vols. 4–18 (1844–1933) also called *Ergänzungsbande* 1–15. There is an Olms reprint (1975, 1,298 pp.) of the first three *Ergänzungsbande* (originally published 1828–39) of the Whistling *Handbuch* up to 1838. Publication in Vol. 19 (1943) for the years 1934–40 was interrupted after the letter *L* in the alphabet.

The *Handbuch* is of greatest importance for its listings of published music, an invaluable dating assistance; each vol. also contains an *Anhang* of books and writings on music. The long life of the series and the leading position occupied by German music publishing houses during the period covered make it a major reference tool.

For a detailed description of the organization of this complex trade bibliography, see "A Survey of the Music Catalogues of Whistling and Hofmeister," by Rudolf Elvers and Cecil Hopkinson, in *Fontes* 19 (1972): 1–7, and Ann Basart's "Whistling in the Dark No Longer," in *CNV* 8 (1976): 5–6. The Ratliff ed. of the Whistling *Handbuch* is reviewed by François Lesure in *Fontes* 24 (1977): 102.

4.55 *Jahrbuch der Musikbibliothek Peters.* Leipzig: C.F. Peters, 1895–1941. Vols. 1–47.

A yearbook with most issues containing a section "Verzeichnis der in allen Kulturländern erschienenen Bücher und Schriften über Musik," which omitted periodical articles but included a regular section listing new periodicals and other serial publications issued during the year under examination. It was this section, expanded to include periodical articles, that was broken out and continued as the *Bibliographie des Musikschrifttums* (**4.51**).

4.56 *Jahrbuch für Liturgik und Hymnologie.* Kassel, Germany: Johannes Stauda-Verlag, 1955– . Bd. 1– .

A yearbook with each issue containing an extensive "Literaturbericht," classified, frequently annotated, and covering all aspects of liturgics and hymnology.

4.57 *Jahrbuch für Volksliedforschung; im Austrag des Deutschen Volksliedarchivs.* Berlin; Leipzig: Walter de Gruyter, 1928– . Erster Jahrgang– .

Publication suspended between 1951 and 1964.

A yearbook that from 1965 has carried an extensive section of reviews ("Besprechungen") of the important literature in the field of folk song research.

4.58 *Jahresverzeichnis der deutschen Musikalien und Musikschriften.* 128 vols. Leipzig: VEP Friedrich Hofmeister-Musikverlag, 1852–1985. Jahrgang 1–128.

Title varies: Vols. 1–77 (1852–1928), *Verzeichnis der im Jahre . . . erschienenen Musikalien;* Vols. 78–91 (1929–42), *Hofmeisters Jahresverzeichnis;* Vols. 92–118, (1943–68); Vols. 119–28 (1969–85), *Jahresverzeichnis der deutschen Musikalien und Musikschriften.*

An annual list, with index, that cumulates the material in the *Deutsche Musikbibliographie* (**4.52**) and is, in turn, cumulated in *Hofmeisters Handbuch der Musikliteratur* (**4.54**).

4.59 *Journal of Music Theory.* New Haven, Conn.: Yale School of Music, 1957– . Vols. 1– .

A journal with each issue containing a "Bibliography of Current Periodical Literature" covering articles related to music theory.

4.60 *Musica Disciplina: A Yearbook of the History of Music.* Rome: American Institute of Musicology, 1946– . Vols. 1– .

Title and publisher vary: Vol. 1, 1948, *Journal of Renaissance and Baroque Music.*

A yearbook including until 1976 a bibliography of books, periodical articles, doctoral dissertations, and editions related to early music.

4.61 *Musica / Realtà; Rivista Quadrimestale.* Milan: Edizioni Unicoplo, 1979– . Vol. 1– .

A journal containing an annual "Supplemento libri: Libri d'interesse musicale stampati in Italia" with brief, classified reviews prepared by musicologists associated with the Dipartimento di Musica e Spettacolo dell'Università di Bologna. A list of books published but not reviewed is appended to each category ("Analisi musicale," "Cataloghi," "Musica antica," "Musica del '900").

4.62 *Musik-Information: Bibliographische Titelübersicht.* Berlin: Leitstelle für Information und Dokumentation "Musik" an der Deutschen Hochschule für Musik "Hanns Eisler." 1971– . Jahrg. 1– .

An introductory number, Jahrg. 0, Heft A, was issued in 1970.

A monthly publication covering important international books and journals in musicology, with subject and author indexes.

4.63 *Notes, the Quarterly Journal of the Music Library Association,* 1948– . 2nd series. Vol. 1– .

Title varies: initially, *Music Library Association Notes, a Magazine Devoted to Music and Its Literature.*

An American journal providing the largest available source of reviews of music and its literature, as well as substantial listings of the same. *Notes*'s "Books Received" section, currently edited by Stephen Yusko, since 1950 has been international in scope, classified by language, and for a time included American dissertations on music. The section "Music Received," edited for many years by Ruth Watanabe, is one of the most extensive classified lists of newly published scores. The column "New Periodicals," currently edited by Suzanne Eggleston, twice a year offers reviews of new music periodicals and recounts events of interest in the music periodical world.

Two ruminative surveys by Donald W. Krummel shed light on the general trends of *Notes* in its first 40 years: "Twenty Years of *Notes*: A Retrospective" in *Notes* 21 (1964): 56–82 and "The Second Twenty Volumes of *Notes*: A Retrospective Re-cast" in *Notes* 40 (1985): 7–25. Karen R. Little recently compiled an index for the second series's first 50 years (**4.111**).

4.64 *Periodica Musica: Newsletter of the Répertoire International de la Presse Musicale du XIXe Siècle, Centres Internationaux de Recherche sur la Presse Musicale.* College Park, Md.: University of Maryland, Center for Studies in 19th-Century Music, 1983– . Vol. 1– .

First published in Vancouver at the University of British Columbia by the Centre for Studies in Nineteenth-Century Music.

An annual newsletter for an association that has as its goal the provision of access to the enormous volume of periodical literature about music published in the 19th century. The newsletter covers research and publications relating to the music periodicals of the 19th century. See also *Répertoire International de la Presse Musicale: A Retrospective Index Series (RIPM)* (**4.123**).

4.65 *Svensk tidskrift för musikforskning / Swedish Journal of Musicology.* Stockholm, 1919– . Vol. 1– .

A journal that since 1927 has maintained a broadly classified, annual list of "Svensk musikhistorisk bibliografi," which also indexes Swedish periodicals.

LISTS OF MUSIC PERIODICALS

The most comprehensive list of music periodicals is found in Imogen Fellinger's article "Periodicals" (**4.66**) in *The New Grove* (**1.48**), while her bibliography of 19th-century music periodicals (**4.72**) gives that century virtually complete coverage. Wilhelm Freystätter offered the best chronological survey of the early music periodicals (**4.75**), supplemented and expanded by the historical study of Eckart Rohlfs (**4.82**). Music researchers should also be aware of the information provided by general reference works on periodicals, accessible through Sheehy (**4.41**), such as Ulrich's *International Periodicals Directory* and the *Union List of Serials*.

4.66 Fellinger, Imogen. "Periodicals." In *The New Grove Dictionary of Music and Musicians* (**1.48**).

A general account of the historical development of music periodicals, with a comprehensive and accessible list, arranged chronologically by continent and country, with an alphabetical index and an excellent bibliography that includes brief but essential annotations; included in the bibliography are citations for indexes to periodicals.

4.67 Basart, Ann Phillips. *Writing about Music: A Guide to Publishing Opportunities for Authors and Reviewers.* xxiv + 588 pp. Berkeley, Calif.: Fallen Leaf Press, 1989. (Fallen Leaf reference books on music, 11)

A substantial expansion of Basart's article "Editorial Practice and Publishing Opportunities in Serious English-Language Music Journals: A Survey," *CNV* 79 (1984): 9–51.

Detailed information on over 430 current periodicals, from 21 countries, that publish music-related articles and reviews in English. Only periodicals that consider unsolicited material are included. This book gives a good overall picture of editorial practices in music periodicals in the late 1980s.

Forty monographic series in music are listed and described. Extensive information from the editors of the journals and series is provided. There are indexes to titles and organizations, subjects, locations, and type of material reviewed. Creative use of the indexes will reveal periodicals on subjects of interest but little visibility (such as reggae). There is a list of dropped titles.

Reviewed by Albert La Blanc in *CRME* 109 (1991): 81–84, by Deborah Coclanis in *Notes* 47 (1991): 799–800, by Claire Brook in *Fontes* 37 (1990): 281–82, by Robert Palmieri in *ARBA* 21 (1990): no. 1237, and by Robert Hansen in *OJ* 24 (1991): 50 no. 2.

4.68 *Bibliografia muzyczna polskich czasopism niemuzycznych.* 6 vols. Cracow: Polskie Wydawn. Muzyczne, 1962–79.

Contents: Vol. 1, *Muzyka w polskich czasopismach niemuzycznych w latach 1800–1830,* opracomal Stanislaw Papierz (349 pp., 1962); Vol. 2, *Muzyka w polskich czasopismach literackichi spolecznych, 1831–1863* (169 pp., 1973), opracomal Sylwester Dziki; Vol. 3, *Muzyka w polskich czasopismach literackich i spolecznych, 1864–1900,* opracomala Elżbieta Szczawinska (399 pp., 1964); Vol. 4, *Muzyka w polskich czasopismach literackich i artystycznych, 1901–1918,* opracomala Elżbieta Szczawinska (1971, 364 pp.); Vol. 5, *Muzyka w czasopismach polskich, 1919–1939,* opracomal Kornel Michałowski (2 vols., 1979).

Bibliographies of periodical literature about music, covering 1800–1939. Each vol. includes an index.

4.69 Coover, James B. "A Bibliography of East European Music Periodicals." In *Fontes* 3 (1956): 219–26; 4 (1957): 97–102; 5 (1958): 44–45 and 93–99; 6 (1959): 27–28; 7 (1960): 16–21 and 69–70; 8 (1961): 75–90; 9 (1962): 78–80.

An attempt at a comprehensive and authoritative list of all music periodicals that have been and are being published in Bulgaria, Czechoslovakia, Estonia, Finland, Hungary, Latvia, Lithuania, Poland, Romania, the USSR, and Yugoslavia.

4.70 Fairley, Lee. "A Check-List of Recent Latin American Music Periodicals." In *Notes* 2 (1945): 120–23.

A list of 23 periodicals from the collections of the Library of Congress and the Pan American Union, with brief comments on each. The coverage is of publications between 1940 and 1947.

4.71 Fellinger, Imogen. "List of Union Catalogues of (Music) Periodicals." In *Fontes* 28 (1981): 323–27.

A bibliography of 54 lists from 30 countries, arranged by country, of union lists of serials, most of them general with a music section or with music entries scattered. Full bibliographic information is provided.

4.72 Fellinger, Imogen. *Verzeichnis der Musikzeitschriften des 19. Jahrhunderts.* 557 pp. Regensburg: Gustav Bosse, 1969. (Studien zur Musikgeschichte des 19. Jahrhunderts, 10)

A bibliography that locates and lists chronologically over 2,300 music periodicals, some established as late as 1918, with a rich supply of bibliographical information. Includes a historical survey of 19th-century music periodicals (pp. 10–28) and a bibliography of literature on periodicals (pp. 33–37). Indexes give access by title, editor, place of publication, printer and publisher, and subject.

Since the initial publication, a series of supplements has appeared in *Fontes:* Nachträge, Folge 1, 17 (1970): 2–8; Folge 2, 18 (1971): 59–62; Folge 3, 19 (1972): 41–44; Folge 4, 20 (1973): 108–11; Folge 5, 21 (1974): 36–38; Folge 6, 17 (1971): 62–66.

Reviewed by J. A. Westrup in *M&L* 50 (1969): 400–3 and by Philip Gossett in *Notes* 26 (1970): 740–41.

4.73* Fidler, Linda M., and **Richard S. James.** *International Music Journals.* 544 pp. New York: Greenwood Press, 1990. (Historical guides to the world's periodicals and newspapers)

A collection of 1- to 2-page signed evaluations and summary histories by 48 contributors of 181 major music journals on music scholarship, performance, composition, discography, and librarianship from six continents. The arrangement is alphabetical by title, with cross-references provided from the various other forms of the title. For each item, a narrative history, publication highlights, a description, and an evaluation are given, along with information on where the publication is indexed and its publication history and editors. Chronological, geographic, and subject access is provided via lists, along with separate chapters on journals begun in the 1980s and music periodical indexes. There is a selected bibliography.

Reviewed by Imogen Fellinger in *Fontes* 43 (1996): 213–14.

4.74 Fredricks, Jessica. "Music Magazines of Britain and the U.S." In *Notes* 6 (1949): 239–63 and 457–59; 7 (1950): 372–76.

A list of 200 music periodicals arranged alphabetically by title, indexed by subject and type, with brief descriptions of character and contents.

4.75 Freystätter, Wilhelm. *Die musikalischen Zeitschriften seit ihrer Entstehung bis zur Gegenwart; chronologisches Verzeichniss der periodischen Schriften über Musik.* 139 pp. Munich: T. Riedel, 1884.

Reprinted by Frits A.M. Knuf in Amsterdam, 1963 and 1971.

Based on Eduard Gregoir's *Recherches historiques concernant les journaux de musique depuis les temps les plus reculés jusqu'à nos jours,* Antwerp, 1872.

A chronological list, 1722 to 1844, with extensive annotations on content, editors, and contributors, still valuable as a convenient source of information on early music periodicals.

4.76* Henkel, David K. *The Official Identification and Price Guide to Rock and Roll Magazines, Posters, and Memorabilia.* 614 pp. New York: House of Collectibles / Ballantine Books, 1992. (The official price guide)

4.77 Hodges, Anthony. *The British Union Catalogue of Music Periodicals.* Edited by Raymond McGill. xxiv + 145 pp. London: Library Association Publishing, in association with the International Association of Music Libraries, Archives, and Documentation Centres, United Kingdom Branch, 1985.

A catalog of music periodical holdings of 292 institutions in the United Kingdom and of 10 institutions in the Republic of Ireland. Periodicals are listed by title, with cross-references from subsequent or alternative titles. The entries give the name of the sponsoring organization or publisher, country and city of origin, dates of publication, other miscellaneous information, and years, volumes, or issues held at institutions, providing full names, addresses, and telephone numbers. The titles originally in non-Roman alphabets are transliterated.

Reviewed by Nigel Simeone in *Brio* 22 (1985): 18–19 and by George R. Hill in *ARBA* 17 (1986): no. 1236.

4.78 Michałowski, Kornel. *Bibliografia polskich czasopism muzycznych.* Cracow: Polskie Wydawn. Muzyczne, 1955– . (Materialy do bibliografii muzyki polskiej, 4 and 5)

A bibliography of Polish music periodicals, with classified lists of their contents.

4.79 *Ongaku kankei chikuji kankōbutsu shozai mokuroku / Union List of Periodicals in Music* (Ongaku Toshokan Kyogikai). 1979 ed. 129 pp. Tokyo, 1980.

Supplements the 3rd ed., 1969.

A list of 970 periodicals in 25 Japanese music libraries, with separate lists for Japanese-language titles and Western titles. Japanese and Russian titles are romanized. Library locations and extent of holdings are noted.

4.80 Riedel, A. *Répertoire des périodiques musicaux belges.* 48 pp. Brussels: Commission belge de bibliographie, 1954. (Bibliographia belgica, 8)

A list of 330 entries; the first 130 are music serials and the remainder are periodicals in the usual sense.

4.81* Robinson, Doris. *Music and Dance Periodicals: An International Directory and Guidebook.* 382 pp. Voorheesville, N.Y.: Peri Press, 1989.

A classified annotated guide to 1,867 music and dance periodicals. The information provided varies greatly from one title to another. The fullest entries contain title; beginning date; the language of the text; the name, address, and phone numbers of issuing body and editor; circulation and subscription rates; availability in microform; the ISSN and the OCLC (**12.1**) number; the Dewey and LC classifications; the length of an average issue; the types of reviews and articles carried; information about ads; and where indexed.

Reviewed by Ann P. Basart in *Fontes* 36 (1989): 242–43 and in *CNV* 129 (1989): 11–12.

4.82 Rohlfs, Eckart. *Die deutschsprachigen Musikperiodica, 1945–57.* 108 pp. Regensburg: G. Bosse, 1961. (Forschungsbeiträge zur Musikwissenschaft, 11)

A sourcebook of information about German-language music periodicals, their history, coverage, distribution, and subject emphasis. The systematic bibliographic "Anhang" (pp. 5–64) lists 589 periodicals in 12 categories. There are indexes by chronology, place, and title.

Reviewed by Fred Blum in *Notes* 19 (1961): 77–78 and by Wolfgang Schmieder in *Die Musikforschung* 21 (1968): 105–7.

4.83 Solow, Linda I. "Index to 'Music Periodicals' Reviewed in *Notes* (1976–1982)." In *Notes* 39 (1983): 585–90.

A title index to music periodicals reviewed, principally by Charles Lindahl, in a series of articles.

4.84 Svobodová, Marie. "Music Journals in Bohemia and Moravia 1796–1970." In *Fontes* 19 (1972): 22–41.

An alphabetical title list of 259 journals, with a chronological index. The Czech titles are translated into English or the subjects covered are indicated, with the number supplied from Fellinger's *Verzeichnis* (**4.72**), where applicable. The author also wrote, with Juraj Potúček, "Music Journals in Slovakia, 1871–1970," in *Fontes* 21 (1974): 32–36, which lists 27 titles, with a chronological index, title translations into English, and a brief description of contents.

4.85 Thoumin, Jean-Adrien. *Bibliographie rétrospective des périodiques françaises de littérature musicale 1870–1954.* 179 pp. Paris: Éditions documentaires industrielles et techniques, 1957.

An alphabetical list of 504 French music periodicals, with a chronological index, an index of persons, and an index of places of publication. Errata given, pp. 175–79.

4.86 Weichlein, William J. *A Checklist of American Periodicals, 1850–1900.* 103 pp. Detroit, Mich.: Information Coordinators, 1970. (Detroit studies in music bibliography, 16)

A concise source of information on American music periodicals, giving title, place and dates of publication, frequency of issue, and representative library holdings. Also includes a chronological list, a table showing the geographic origins, a publisher–editor index, and a bibliography.

Reviewed by Dena J. Epstein in *Notes* 27 (1971): 489.

4.87 Wunderlich, Charles. *A History and Bibliography of Early American Musical Periodicals, 1782–1852.* 783 ll. Ann Arbor, Mich.: University Microfilms, 1962.

A doctoral dissertation written for the University of Michigan, Ann Arbor, 1962.

A chronological and descriptive bibliography of 69 periodicals (ll. 304–655), providing variant titles, dates and numbers of publication, imprint, subscription rates, related titles, editors' names with biographical information, principal authors, notes on content, lists of music published in each periodical, and information about libraries holding copies. Includes an appendix with entries on 800 publishers, printers, engravers, and others, title and geographic indexes, and a list of references (ll. 288–303). This is a complement to Weichlein's *Checklist* (**4.86**).

4.88 Zecca-Laterza, Agostina. *Catalogo dei periodici musicali delle biblioteche lombarde.* 50 pp. Milan: Biblioteca del Conservatorio Giuseppe Verdi, 1979.

A union list of music periodicals held in libraries in Lombardy, arranged alphabetically by title, including in each entry a list of libraries where copies are held. The periodicals published in Lombardy are cited in a chronological index, arranged in alphabetical order by city.

Reviewed by Gisella de Caro in *Associazione italiana bibliotechna bollettino* 19 (1979): 234.

INDEXES OF MUSIC PERIODICALS AND PERIODICAL LITERATURE ABOUT MUSIC

Access to the contents of music periodicals is a research problem not dealt with until the 20th century. *Music Index* (**4.89**) was the first large-scale attempt to provide the needed access, and a scattering of retrospective title indexes have begun to provide approaches to pre-1949 journal contents. *RILM* **(4.90)** supplied an even more far-flung approach while sacrificing timeliness; machine-readable indexing **(12.9** and **12.13)** has helped make the project accessible to those lacking the earlier, paper subscription.

4.89 *The Music Index; A Subject–Author Guide to Current Music Periodical Literature.* Detroit, Mich.: Information Service, Inc., January 1949– . Vol. 1, no. 1– .

Issued monthly with annual or, occasionally, 2-year cumulations. A list of subject headings used is issued annually in a separate vol. Originally subtitled *The Key to Current Music Periodical Literature.*

The principal index to more than 500 music periodicals, with access by author and subject. Founded by Florence Kretschmar, *Music Index* has from its beginning met a long-felt need of the community of music researchers, although its path has not been straight. The first annual issue cumulated the indexing of 81 periodicals, including 26 foreign titles. When an established title is added to the list of periodicals indexed, there is occasionally retrospective indexing. There is selective indexing of nonmusic journals containing occasional music articles. Each issue of the *Index* gives full listings, including publisher, address, and price, for each periodical title covered. Composer and subject entries, from the first year arranged in one alphabet, were in later years joined by author entries. Reviews of books are gathered together under "Book Reviews" and then alphabetically by the author's or editor's name; concert and publication reviews for art music (and orchestra program notes) are indexed under the composer's name (with an asterisk noting a premiere). Popular concert reviews are indexed under the name of the performing artist or group; sound recordings are not usually indexed. There are generous cross-references.

The demands of careful indexing for a long time made publication lag time a characteristic of *Music Index,* although the gap has closed in recent years. The appearance of *Music Index* on CD-ROM **(12.11)** is discussed elsewhere.

The 1st annual cumulation is reviewed by Irene Millen in *Notes* 7 (1950): 570–71; the 2nd by George Hanson in *Notes* 9 (1952): 282–83; the 3rd by Frank C. Campbell in *Notes* 10 (1953): 447–48; the 1954 cumulation by Richard Appel in *Notes* 14 (1957): 364–65; and the following two by James B. Coover in *Notes* 16 (1958): 45–46.

4.90 Répertoire international de littérature musicale / International Repertory of Music Literature / Internationales Repertorium der Musikliteratur. *RILM Abstracts of Music Literature.* New York: International *RILM* Center, 1967– . Vol. 1– .

An international quarterly journal of abstracts in English of current scholarly literature on music in all languages (including books, articles, commentaries, prefaces to editions, dissertations, and reviews), published under the aegis of the International Musicological Society, the International Association of Music Libraries, and the American Council of Learned Societies, a source for keyword access to these abstracts, arranged in a clear classification. Each issue contains an author index and every 4th issue includes a name, title, and subject index to the year's entries, with a cumulation every 5 years.

Barry S. Brook fully discusses the *RILM* project and its initial implications in his "Music Literature and Modern Communication: Revolutionary Potential of the ACLS/CUNY/*RILM* Project," in *College Music Symposium* 9 (1969): 48–59.

Also available online through OCLC's FirstSearch, and on CD-ROM under the title MUSE **(12.9)**.

✍

4.91 Allorto, Riccardo. *La rassegna musicale: Indice generale delle annate 1928–52.* Vols. 1–22. 174 pp. Turin: Roggero & Tortia, 1953.

An index including coverage of articles and reviews of musical performances, books, and recordings, continued by Francesco Degrada's *Indici de "La rassegna musicale" (annate XXIII–XXXII, 1953–1962) e dei "Quaderni della Rassegna musicale" (n. 1, 2, 3, 1964–1965)* (Florence: Leo S. Olschki, 1968), 81 pp. (Quaderni della Rivista italiana di musicologia, 2)

4.92 Anderson, Gillian B. *Music in New York during the American Revolution: An Inventory of Musical References in Rivington's New York Gazette.* With the editorial assistance of Neil Ratliff. xxix + 135 pp. Bloomington, Ind.: Music Library Association, 1987. (MLA index and bibliography series, 24)

An inventory bringing together all references to music, musicians, musical instruments, and musical events found in the loyalist *New York Gazette* between 1773 and 1783, with an analysis of its findings in the introduction. Arranged alphabetically by name, title, and subject, the inventory includes not only *New York Gazette* articles but also notices and advertisements, with extensive cross-references. The citations for compositions (none by native-born Americans) provide references to *RISM* (**5.590**) when possible. The author's introduction analyzes the data contained in the index.

Reviewed by Karl Kroeger in *Notes* 47 (1990): 384–85.

4.93 Anderson, Gillian. "Unpublished Periodical Indexes at the Library of Congress and Elsewhere in the United States of America." In *Fontes* 31 (1984): 54–60.

Coverage of card files at the Library of Congress and the Boston Public Library, as well as the Works Progress Administration index now at Northwestern University. This resource lists periodicals and periods of publications indexed. There are also citations for indexes at Washington University in St. Louis, Howard University in Washington, D.C., and the Sibley Music Library in Rochester, N.Y. Dena J. Epstein's "The Mysterious WPA Music Periodical Index," in *Notes* 45 (1989): 463–82, gives an accompanying clear and helpful overview of the underused and potentially helpful indexes, with detailed appendixes of periodicals indexed, of periodicals listed by the WPA as not indexed, and of the number of journals in the WPA project by language.

4.94* Arneson, Arne Jon. *The Music Educators Journal: Cumulative Index, 1914–1987, Including the Music Supervisor's Bulletin and the Music Supervisor's Journal.* 380 pp. Stevens Point, Wisc.: Index House, 1987.

An index to 73 years of an important American music education periodical. Includes an author/title index, a subject index (with generous cross-references), and an index to book reviews.

Reviewed by Ann P. Basart in *CNV* 121 (1988): 17 and in *Fontes* 35 (1988): 289, and by William J. Dane in *ARBA* 20 (1989): no. 1187.

4.95 Arroyo, Flora. *Artículos sobre música en revistas españolas de humanidades.* Editor-coordinator, Jacinto Torres. Madrid: Instituto de Bibliografía Musical, 1982– . Vol. 1– .

A bibliography of articles about music appearing in major intellectual Spanish journals published from the end of the 19th century to 1980, including indexes.

4.96 *Arts and Humanities Citation Index.* Philadelphia, Pa.: Institute for Scientific Information, 1977– .

The print version issued three times a year, with the last issue an annual cumulation.

A complex bibliographic tool providing a kind of access new to musical studies. The "Source Index" lists by author articles published during the period covered; the "Citation Index" lists by author, composer, or artist works referred to in the source articles (whether in footnotes, endnotes, or the body of the article); the "Permuterm Index" arranges meaningful words in the titles of the source articles to allow access by pairing such words; and the "Corporate Index" lists source article authors by institutional affiliation. About 60 music periodicals are regularly indexed, as well as numerous essays in conference reports and other anthologies. This source is also available as an online file through the publisher (**12.3**) and the First Search complex.

Thomas F. Heck has written an illustrated introduction to the opportunities and pitfalls of the *Index* as a reference work, "The Relevance of the *Arts and Humanities* Data Base to

Musicological Research," in *Fontes* 28 (1981): 81–87. A review and explanation by Michael A. Keller and Carol A. Lawrence appear in *Notes* 36 (1980): 575–600.

4.97 Ascherson, F. "Musikalische Bibliographie." In *Vierteljahrschrift für Musikwissenschaft.* Edited by Friedrich Chrysander and Philipp Spitta. Vols. 1–10. Leipzig, 1885–94.

A section included in each volume, usually including a list of scholarly music books, critical editions, and the contents of current scholarly periodicals in all European languages.

4.98 Basart, Ann Phillips. *Perspectives of New Music: An Index, 1962–1982.* 127 pp. Berkeley, Calif.: Fallen Leaf Press, 1984. (Fallen Leaf reference books in music, 1)

A thoughtfully designed access to the first 20 years of this solid journal.

Reviewed by Charles G. Eubanks in *Notes* 41 (1984): 294 and by Allie Wise Goudy in *ARBA* 16 (1985): no. 1170.

4.99 Belknap, Sara Y. *The Guide to the Performing Arts, 1957–68.* New York: Scarecrow Press, 1960–72. Vols. 1–11.

An annual periodical index to the performing arts, begun as a supplement to the compiler's *Guide to the Musical Arts: An Analytical Index of Articles and Illustrations, 1953–56* (New York: Scarecrow Press, 1957). The *Guide* contains "general" and "television arts" sections. There are references to performing groups and performers as well as general subject headings.

4.100 Blom, Eric, and **Jack A. Westrup.** *Music and Letters: Index to Volumes 1–40, 1920–1959.* 140 pp. London: Oxford University Press, 1962.

An index with two major sections—articles and reviews—with access by author and subject.

4.101 Clark, Chris, and **Andy Linehan.** *POMPI: Popular Music Periodicals Index.* Nos. 1–2, October 1984–September 1986. 212 pp. London: British Library National Sound Archive, 1988.

Devoted exclusively to the indexing of periodical articles on the performance and production of popular music and jazz.

Selective indexing of over 6,500 entries covering 60 periodical titles. The focus is on interviews, feature articles, obituaries, and shorter informative items. No reviews of recordings, live performances, or books are indexed. Periodicals originating in the United Kingdom are especially well represented in the list of titles indexed.

Clark describes the *Index* in *Fontes* 38 (1991): 32–37.

Reviewed by Linda M. Fidler in *Notes* 47 (1990): 390–91.

4.102 Daugherty, Donald Hayes. *A Bibliography of Periodical Literature in Musicology and Allied Fields and a Record of Graduate Theses Accepted, October 1938–September 1940.* 2 vols. Washington, D.C.: American Council of Learned Societies, 1940–43.

Vol. 2 was compiled by Daugherty, Leonard Ellinwood, and Richard S. Hill.

A bibliography that indexes about 240 music and nonmusic periodicals in all European languages, with signed abstracts or annotations for most of the articles. The 1st vol. has a list of musicology-related graduate theses accepted in American colleges.

4.103 Erichsen, Jörgen Poul. *Indeks til danske periodiske musikpublikationer 1795–1841: Kumuleret og annoteret indeks til Apollo, Nordens Apollo, Nye Apollo, Odeon, Musikalsk Theater Journal [og] Vaudeville Journal.* 132 pp. (Århus, Denmark: Statsbiblioteksforlaget, 1975.

Access to early Danish music-connected periodicals, with index.

4.104* Gatten, Jeffrey N. *The Rolling Stone Index: Twenty-Five Years of Popular Culture, 1967–1991.* 1,096 pp. Ann Arbor, Mich.: Popular Culture, Ink., 1993. (PCI collector editions)

A compilation of indexes to minor yet culturally relevant elements in *Rolling Stone.* The citations for book reviews, concert reviews, record reviews, and cover appearances are some of the nine main approaches to *Rolling Stone* access. There are over 73,000 entries and the total information on a subject can be gained only by consulting a combination of the indexes.

Reviewed by Ina Wise in *LJ* 118 (1993): 83.

4.105 Goodkind, Herbert K. *The Musical Quarterly: Cumulative Index, 1915 thru 1959* [Vols. 1–45]. 204 pp. New York: Goodkind Indexes, 1960. *Supplement, 1960–1962.* New York, 1963.

An index whose main volume indexes by author and subject in separate alphabets, whereas the *Supplement* does the same in one alphabet. The index material includes book reviews and the "Current Chronicle," as well as articles. Hazel G. Kinscella's "Americana Index to *The Musical Quarterly,* 1915–1957," published in *JRME* 6 (1958) no. 2 (144 pp.), indexes all articles related to American music and musical events.

4.106* Griffin, Thomas. *Musical References in the Gazzetta di Napoli, 1681–1725.* xxxv + 140 pp., with computer disk. Berkeley, Calif.: Fallen Leaf Press, 1993. (Fallen Leaf reference books in music, 17)

A list of the events the *Gazzetta* covered in detail, which include the many festivals and celebrations held in Naples during the period in question. The computer disk includes search software.

Reviewed by Lowell Lindgren in *Notes* 50 (1994): 950–51 and by Silvia Di Pietro Liti in *Fontes* 42 (1995): 376–77.

4.107* Gruber, Clemens M. *Bibliographie der österreichischen Musikzeitschriften 1930–1938.* 113 pp. Vienna: VWGÖ, 1992.

The lists of contents of 12 music periodicals published in Vienna in the 1930s, with several indexes.

4.108* Höslinger, Clemens. *Musik-Index zur "Wiener Zeitschrift für Kunst, Literatur, Theater und Mode," 1816–1848.* 186 pp. Munich; Salzburg: Musikverlag Emil Katzbichler, 1980. (Publikationen der Sammlungen der Gesellschaft der Musikfreunde in Wien, 4)

A classified index to the musical contents of the 19th-century *Wiener Zeitschrift für Kunst, Literatur, Theater und Mode,* giving information on a work's place of performance and identifying the major performers, as well as issue and year of the article describing that performance.

4.109 Kast, Paul, and **Ernst-Ludwig Berz.** "Bibliographie der Aufsätze zur Musik in ausser-musikalischen italienischen Zeitschriften." In *Analecta Musicologica,* Veröffentlichungen der Musikteilung des Deutschen Historischen Instituts in Rom, 1 (1963): 90–112; 2 (1965): 144–228.

A bibliography of writings on music in Italian nonmusical journals. The two installments are organized somewhat differently and indexed independently. The first has 237 entries, the second, 1,074.

4.110 Krohn, Ernst C. *The History of Music: An Index to the Literature Available in a Selected Group of Musicological Publications.* 463 pp. St. Louis, Mo.: Washington University, 1952. (Washington University Library studies, 3)

Reissued, with slight corrections, by Baton Music Co., 1958.

A classified index of articles on music history in 39 leading musicological publications, chiefly German and English. A number of important music periodicals (*MQ, M&L,* and others) are indexed from each title's first volume, thus covering access to their contents before the beginning of *Music Index* (**4.89**) in 1949. The entries are chronologically arranged, with subdivisions by subject. Book reviews are included.

Reviewed by Richard G. Appel in *Notes* 10 (1952): 105–6, by Scott Goldthwaite in *JAMS* 6 (1953): 250–51, and by Wolfgang Schmieder in *Die Musikforschung* 6 (1953): 278–80.

4.111* Little, Karen R. *Notes: An Index to Volumes 1–50.* 444 pp. Canton, Mass.: Music Library Association, 1995.

A meticulously produced index to the first 50 years of the second series of *Notes,* the quarterly journal of the Music Library Association. The compiler in her preface writes that the "index is meant to help those who want to reach back to *Notes* to find that elusive quotation, article, or review," and to help them "understand more fully the breadth and depth of coverage to this venerable journal."

4.112 Loewenberg, Alfred, and **Rupert Erlebach.** *Royal Musical Association: Index to Papers Read before the Members, 1874–1944.* 56 pp. Leeds: Printed by Whitehead & Miller for the Royal Association, 1948.

A subject and an author guide to the Musical Association's first 70 years.

4.113 Matthews, Betty. *Index to The Organ, 1921–1970, from the First Issue to Date.* 133 pp. Bournemouth: D. Mummery Ltd., 1970. *Supplement to Index to The Organ, 1970–1982.* 38 pp. Bournemouth: K. Mummery with the cooperation of the English Organ Archive, University of Keele, 1982.

A complete index to all articles through 1982, in 2 vols.

4.114 Meggett, Joan M. *Music Periodical Literature: An Annotated Bibliography.* 116 pp. Metuchen, N.J.: Scarecrow Press, 1978.

A valuable annotated guide to periodical access with 335 entries (including some duplication), covering more than 250 indexes to music periodicals in general works and in works devoted to the subject of music. It provides a bibliography of lists of periodicals and a guide to the literature of the history of music periodicals. Includes an index to authors, compilers, and editors, as well as indexes to subjects and to titles.

Reviewed by Patricia Felch in *Notes* 35 (1979): 637–38 and by Rita Benton in *Fontes* 25 (1978): 417–18.

4.115* Michałowski, Kornel. *Muzyka, 1924–38. Indeks.* 2 vols. Cracow: Polskie Wydawn. Muzycne, 1967. (Bibliografia polskich czasopism muzycznych, 9)

An index to the Polish music periodical, published monthly from 1924 to 1939, edited by M. Glinski.

4.116 *Music Article Guide: A Comprehensive Quarterly Reference Guide to Significant Signed Feature Articles in American Music Periodicals.* Philadelphia, Pa.: Music Article Guide, 1966–76; Information Services, 1977– .

Published quarterly in 10 categories, one of which is "Musicology." Until 1972 there was also a separate *Annotated Guide to Periodical Literature on Church Music.*

Access to over 200 music periodicals, with few titles duplicated by *Music Index* (**4.89**), including many of local or highly specialized interest. The entries, briefly annotated, are grouped by subject and numbered consecutively within each issue.

Reviewed by Bennet Ludden in *Notes* 24 (1967): 719–20 and anonymously in *ALA Booklist* 65 (1969): 1239–41.

4.117 Parigi, Luigi. *Rivista Musicale Italiana*: *Indici dei volumi I a XX (1894–1913).* 256 pp. Turin: Fratelli Bocca, 1917.

Reprinted by Forni Editori, 1961.

Salvatori, A., and **G. Concina.** *Rivista Musicale Italiana*: *Indici dei volumi XXI a XXXV (1914–1928).* 195 pp. Turin: Fratelli Bocca, 1931.

Degrada, Francesco. *Indici dei volumi XXVI a LVII (1929–1955).* 144 pp. Florence: Leo S. Olschki, 1966. (Quaderni della Rivista Italiana di Musicologia, 1)

Cecchi, Paolo. *Nuova revista musicale Italiana: Indici cumulativi (Indice alfabetico e soggettario) delle prime diciotto annate 1967–1984.* 157 pp. Turin: ERI Edizioni Rai, 1986.

A series of indexes providing access to this venerable journal.

The Degrada index is reviewed by Ludwig Finscher in *Die Musikforschung* 21 (1968): 365–66.

4.118* Piombini, Giorgio, Alberto Basso, and **Francesco Luisi.** *Indici della rivista Note d'archivio per la storia musicale: 1924–1943.* 369 pp. Venice: Edizioni Fondazione Levi, 1983. (Note d'archivio per la storia musicale, nuova serie, anno 1, 1983. Supplement)

An index to the first 20 years of *Note d'archivio per la storia musicale.*

4.119* Prodan, James C. *Index of Articles in I.D.R.S. Publications, 1969–1991.* 14 pp. 1991.

An index of International Double Reed Society publications: *Double Reed, the Journal of the International Double Reed Society; To the World's Bassoonists;* and *To the World's Oboists.*

4.120 *Recording Industry Index.* Vols. 1–3. Cherry Hill, N.J.: National Association of Recording Manufacturers, 1977–79.

A cumulative subject index of U.S. trade and consumer publications. The main body consists of a subject index arranged alphabetically. The 20 sources indexed complement the indexing in the *Music Article Guide* (**4.116**), *Music Index* (**4.89**), *RILM Abstracts of Music Literature* (**4.90**), and *Popular Music Periodicals Index* (**4.101**).

4.121* Rees-Davies, Jo. *Clarinet & Saxophone Periodicals Index.* 116 ll. England: Clarinet and Saxophone Society, 1986.

An index giving access to the articles on the clarinet and saxophone in an international array of both music and general periodicals, with entries classified by 44 subject headings. Reviews of books and music are not included.

4.122 Refardt, Edgar. *Verzeichnis der Aufsätze zur Musik in den nicht-musikalischen Zeitschriften der Universitätsbibliothek Basel.* 105 pp. Leipzig: Breitkopf & Härtel, 1925.

A classified list of writings on music in over 500 nonmusical newspapers and periodicals, arranged alphabetically by author. One of the few efforts to compile a bibliography of musical literature in journals outside the field. As a partial update, *CM* in Spring and Fall 1965: 121–27 and 221–26 published "Articles Concerning Music in Non-Music Journals 1949–64." The 1st installment stressed articles on historical subjects; the 2nd stressed articles under various systematic headings (acoustics, philosophy and aesthetics, music in literature, psychology, and sociology).

4.123* *Répertoire International de la Presse Musicale: A Retrospective Index Series (RIPM).* H. Robert Cohen, general editor. Ann Arbor, Mich.: UMI Center for Studies in Nineteenth-Century Music, University of Maryland, 1988– .

A series organized to provide access to major 18th- through early-20th-century periodical literature dealing with music by indexing music periodicals and, occasionally, reprinting on microfilm the titles so indexed. The established structure of each title is a detailed introductory guide explaining how to use the publication, a calendar or annotated title catalog providing the contents of each issue, and a keyword/author index, usually generated by computer. The editors and the titles indexed so far include the following:

Ballerini, Graziano. *I teatri, 1827–1831.* 2 vols. lx + 511 pp. (1992, Microfilm issued of the original periodical).

Capra, Marco. *L'Armonia, 1856–1859.* lii + 367 pp. (1989).

Capra, Marco. *Gazzetta musicale di Firenze, 1853–1855.* lii + 314 pp. (1989, Microfilm issued of the original).

Clinkscale, Edward H. *The Musical Times, 1844–1900.* 7 vols. to date (1994–).

Cloutier, Diane. *Revue musicale, 1827–1835.* 2 vols. liii + 593 pp. (1991).

Colombo, Paola. *La musica popolare, 1882–1885.* lii + 222 pp. (1993).

Conati, Marcello. *L'Italia musicale, 1847–1859.* 5 vols. (1992).

Conati, Marcello. *Strenna teatrale europea, 1838–1848.* xlviii + 182 pp. (1989, Microfilm issued of the original).

Day, David A. *The Message Bird, 1849–1852.* xxx + 292 pp. (1992).

Day, David A. *The New York Musical World, 1852–1860.* 4 vols. xxxii + 1,221 pp. (1993).

Deaville, James Andrew, and **Beverly J. Sing.** *Allgemeine Wiener Musik-Zeitung, 1841–1848.* 4 vols. lvi + 1,325 pp. (1990).

Feurzeig, Lisa. *Eutonia, 1829–1833, 1835, 1837.* lii + 244 pp. (1990).

Gíslason, Donald G. *La Chronique musicale, 1873–1876.* xli + 217 pp. (1988).

Heyter-Rauland, Christine. *Cäcilia 1824–1837, 1839, 1842–1848.* 2 vols. lx + 493 pp. (1994).

Hoedmaeker, Liesbeth. *Nederlandsch muzikaal tijdschrift 1839–1848.* lvi + 226 pp. (1994).

Kamphuis, Elisabeth. *Het Muziekcollege.* lvi + 133 pp. (1993).

Kitson, Richard. *Dwight's Journal of Music, 1852–1881.* 6 vols. xxxii + 2,041 pp. (1991).

Kitson, Richard. *The Quarterly Musical Magazine and Review, 1818–1828.* 2 vols. xxviii + 486 pp. (1989, Microfilm issued of the original).

Kugle, Karl. *Allgemeine musikalische Zeitung, 1863–1882.* 7 vols. lx + 2,296 pp. (1995).

Lang, Martina. *Berlinische musikalische Zeitung, 1805–1806.* lii + 142 pp. (1990).

Lang, Martina, and **Martina Wurzel.** *Berlinische musikalische Zeitung, 1824–1830.* 2 vols. lii + 461 pp. (1994).

Marino, Marina, and Marcello Conati. *La musica, 1855, 1857–1859.* lii + 210 pp. (1989, Microfilm issued of the original).

Marino, Marina. *La musica, 1876–1878, 1883–1885.* lii + 282 pp. (1989, Microfilm issued of the original).

Mazzucchelli, Giovanni, and **Marcello Capra.** *Il teatro illustrato, 1880–1886.* 4 vols. lvi + 1,060 pp. (1993).

Menardi Noguera, Flavio, and **Marcello Capra.** *Paganini, 1887–1891.* lvi + 252 pp. (1993, Microfilm issued of the original periodical).

Sing, Beverly J. *Allgemeine musikalische Zeitung, mit besonder Rücksicht auf den österreichischen Kaiserstaat, 1817–1824.* 2 vols. lx + 563 pp. (1992).

Sing, Beverly J. *Deutsche Musik-Zeitung, 1860–1862.* liv + 276 pp. (1994).

Sing, Beverly J. *Monatschrift für Theater und Musik, 1855–1865.* 3 vols. lii + 1,045 pp. (1993).

Snigurowicz, Diana, and **Diane Cloutier.** *L'art musical, 1860–1870, 1872–1894.* 5 vols. xlix + 2,020 pp. (1988).

Snigurowicz, Diana. *The Harmonicon, 1823–1833.* 4 vols. xxviii + 1,437 pp. (1989).

Snigurowicz, Diana. *The Musical Examiner, 1842–1844.* xxx + 228 pp. (1992).

Snigurowicz, Diana. *The Musical Standard, 1862–1871* (first series). 3 vols. xxxii + 932 pp. (1991).

Stalb, Claudia. *Musik-Welt, 1880–1882.* lvi + 171 pp. (1992).

Vosteen, Annette. *Berliner musikalische Zeitung, 1844–1847.* lvi + 195 pp. (1994).

4.124 Ruecker, Norbert, and **C. Reggentin-Scheidt.** *Jazz Index; Bibliographie unselbständiger Jazzliteratur / Bibliography of Jazz Literature in Periodicals and Collections.* Frankfurt: N. Ruecker, 1977–83. Vols. 1–7.

First vol. published quarterly; Vols. 2–5 published semiannually; Vols. 6–7 published annually.

An index to about 50 jazz periodicals and anthologies of essays, with access by author and subject. From 1978, there was a blues section; there is an especially useful "list of unconventional literature" at the end of each issue.

Reviewed by Roger Cottrell in *Jazz Forum* 12 (1978): 52, by Carl Gregor Herzog zu Mecklenburg in *Jazz Podium* 27 (1978): 44, and by Harold Rauter in *Jazzforschung* 9 (1977): 183.

4.125 Shirley, Wayne D. *Modern Music, Published by the League of Composers, 1924–1946: An Analytic Index.* Edited by William Lichtenwanger and Carolyn Lichtenwanger. 246 pp. New York: AMS Press, 1976.

A valuable subject index to the 23 vols. of an important 20th-century American music periodical. The stylish preface is a model essay on music indexing, comparable in wit and intelligence to Nicolas Slonimsky's essay on music lexicography in the 6th–8th editions of *Baker's Biographical Dictionary* (**1.62**). Constructed from a perspective of more than 50 years and with historians' needs in mind, this is a superb example of its genre.

Briefly reviewed by Stephen M. Fry in *Notes* 33 (1976): 306–307.

4.126 Tilmouth, Michael. "A Calendar of References to Music in Newspapers Published in London and the Provinces (1660–1719)." In *RMA Research Chronicle* 1 (1962): 1–107.

An index to English newspapers with an informative introduction, a list of titles indexed. The calendar is arranged chronologically and cites advertisements, lists, notices, availability of music, and concerts. The index was published in the following vol. (pp. 1–15).

4.127 Tudor, Dean. *Popular Music Periodicals Index, 1973–1976.* 4 vols. Metuchen, N.J.: Scarecrow Press, 1974–77.

The author was assisted by Nancy Tudor (Vol. 1), Andrew D. Armitage (Vols. 2–3), and Linda Biesenthal (Vol. 4)

Planned as a complement to the author's *Annual Index to Popular Music Record Reviews* (**10.208**) to provide popular music coverage, both thorough and selective, to about 80 generally English-language titles, published primarily in the United States, Canada, and Great Britain. The subject and author sections each provide full bibliographic information for citations.

4.128* Vann, Kimberly R., and **David Martin.** *Black Music in Ebony: An Annotated Guide to the Articles on Music in Ebony Magazine, 1945–1985.* 119 pp. Chicago, Ill.: Center for Black Music Research, Columbia College, 1990. (CBMR monographs, 2)

A chronologically arranged bibliography prepared by students in a Black music history course at Columbia College, Chicago, in 1986. *Ebony Magazine* is a general-interest publication aimed at an African-American readership, and most of the articles on music feature popular and jazz music and musicians, although all musical genres and persons are included. There are five indexes: authors, genres, performing media, subjects, and titles.

4.129 Williams, Michael D. *Source: Music of the Avant Garde: Annotated List of Contents and Cumulative Indices.* 52 pp. Ann Arbor, Mich.: Music Library Association, 1978. (MLA index and bibliography series, 19)

A tool accessing the works in the highly individualistic periodical.

Reviewed by Ann Basart in *Notes* 35 (1979): 893–94.

4.130 Wolff, Arthur S. *Speculum: An Index of Musically Related Articles and Book Reviews.* 2nd ed. 64 pp. Philadelphia, Pa.: Music Library Association, 1981. (MLA index and bibliography series, 9)

First ed. published in 1970, Ann Arbor, Mich., 31 pp. (MLA index series, 9).

Originally published as *"Speculum": A Journal of Mediaeval Studies, 1926–1962: A Checklist of Articles and Book Reviews Pertaining to Music* by North Texas State University, Denton, Tex., 1965.

4.131 *Zeitschrift der Internationalen Musikwissenschaft.* Vols. 1–15. Leipzig: 1899/1900–1913/14.

Most issues contain departments under the headings "Kritische Bücherschau" and "Zeitschriftenschau." The latter indexes approximately 84 periodicals, chiefly musical, in a variety of languages. The first 11 vols. are indexed by author only, but Vols. 12–15 are indexed by subject, with cross-references from the author.

4.132 *Zeitschrift für Musikwissenschaft.* Vols. 1–17. Leipzig, 1918–35.

A source that indexed annually the periodical literature on music in some 200 journals, in a variety of languages. The period 1914–18 is covered in the 1918 index, thus joining neatly with **4.131**.

SPECIAL AND SUBJECT BIBLIOGRAPHIES

ANALYSES AND NOTES

4.133 Diamond, Harold J. *Music Analyses: An Annotated Guide to the Literature.* 716 pp. New York: Schirmer Books, 1991.

The 1st ed. was published as *Music Criticism: An Annotated Guide to the Literature* by Scarecrow Press, Metuchen, N.J., in 1979 (316 pp.).

Over 4,600 citations and accompanying descriptions of analytical literature from English-language books, periodicals, and dissertations on Western art music. The citations are arranged alphabetically by composer and then by work, except for general analytical works. The annotations indicate the nature and level of the analysis, and full citations for the sources are given in each entry, including, for dissertations, *Dissertation Abstracts* numbers. Includes an index of distinctive titles and a classified bibliography of sources.

The 1st ed. is reviewed by Barbara Henry in *Notes* 37 (1980): 64–65 and by George R. Hill in *ARBA* 12 (1981): no. 1011. *Music Analyses* is reviewed by Arthur B. Wenk in *Notes* 48 (1992): 1307–8.

4.134 Voorhees, Anna Tipton. *Index to Symphonic Program Notes in Books.* 136 pp. Kent, Ohio: School of Library Science, Kent State University, 1970. (Keys to music bibliography, 1)

An annotated list of 57 books in English, dating from 1879 to 1967, containing programs for orchestral music, and a composer/title index to the contents of the same. Excluded from consideration are volumes of printed programs of individual concerts.

Reviewed by Richard H. Hunter in *Notes* 29 (1972): 254–55.

4.135 Wenk, Arthur. *Analyses of Nineteenth- and Twentieth-Century Music, 1940–1985.* xxvii + 370 pp. Boston: Music Library Association, 1987. (MLA index and bibliography series, 25)

Cumulates and updates the indexes originally published as nos. 13, 14, and 15 in the MLA series as *Analyses of Twentieth-Century Music: 1940–1970* (1975), *Analyses of Twentieth-Century Music: Supplement, 1970–1975* (1975), and *Analyses of Nineteenth-Century Music: 1940–1980* (1980).

An index put together "to provide rapid access to technical materials of an analytical nature contained in periodicals, monographs, *Festschriften,* and dissertations." There are 5,664 entries by 2,400 authors, arranged alphabetically by composer covered and subdivided by genre for composers having over 10 entries. The entries contain the composer's name, the title, and the author and the source of the analysis. The list of abbreviations is, in effect, the bibliography of sources for the analyses. There is an author index. This approach is much like that of Diamond (**4.133**), but with more technically complex analyses.

Reviewed by Charles Lindahl in *Notes* 47 (1990): 405–6, by Phillip P. Powell in *ARBA* 20 (1989): no. 1173, and by Ann P. Basart in *CNV* 118 (1987): 11–12.

DISSERTATIONS

Doctoral dissertations, along with articles in scholarly periodicals and collections of essays, represent the growing edge of research in any field. Bibliographies of doctoral studies in music are available for the United States (**4.136**), Germany and other German-speaking countries (**4.142, 4.146,** and **4.147**), France (**4.140**), and Great Britain (**4.137**), but studies produced in other countries are less easy to locate. Included here are reference tools concerned exclusively with studies in music. There are also a number of comprehensive national bibliographies of dissertations from which music titles can be extracted. For these, the user should consult the *Guide to Reference Books* (**4.41**) and Keith Mixter's *General Bibliography for Music Research* (**3.56**). Chief among the general bibliographies is *Dissertation Abstracts International* (**12.4**), available both in print and electronic format, which began in 1938 as an American list and from 1969 included dissertations from a number of European institutions.

4.136 Adkins, Cecil, and **Alis Dickinson.** *Doctoral Dissertations in Musicology.* 2nd series, 1st cumulative ed. 545 pp. Philadelphia, Pa.: American Musicological Society; Basel: International Musicological Society, 1990. Supplements, 1991– .

Earlier eds. had the same editors and similar title. The 1st ed. was issued by the Joint Committee of the Music Teachers National Association and the American Musicological Society, 1951; the 2nd–4th eds. were compiled by Helen Hewitt, who also edited supplements that appeared in *JAMS* and *AMT.* The 5th ed. was compiled by Cecil Adkins as *Doctoral Dissertations in Musicology* (Philadelphia, Pa.: American Musicological Society, 1971), 203 pp. The 6th ed. (the first combined publication of *Doctoral Dissertations in Musicology* [6th cumulative ed.] and *Musicological Works in Progress* [1st cumulative ed.]), *International Index of Dissertations and Works in Progress,* was compiled by Adkins and Alis Dickinson (Philadelphia, Pa.: American Musicological Society, 1977), 423 pp. The 7th ed., Philadelphia, Pa.: American Musicological Society; Basel: International Musicological Society, 1984, 545 pp. Various supplements provide updates until the next cumulation.

A source listing both completed dissertations and, indicated by asterisk, those in progress. Through the first 4 eds., entries are grouped by historical periods under the institutions where the degrees were completed. The 5th and following eds. abandon listings under institution and instead organize the entries into broad historical periods. The section "Works in Progress," which was included through the 6th ed., now is an annual feature in *Acta Musicologica*; see Adkins's report in *Acta Musicologica* 43 (1971): 103–6. The list from 1984 on is international, covering dissertations from 32 countries, but all those begun or completed before 1972 are American or Canadian. Earlier non-American dissertations are covered by Schaal's *Verzeichnis musikwissenschaftlicher Dissertationen* (**4.146** and **4.147**) and annual lists in *Die Musikforschung* for German-language dissertations. For earlier British dissertations, see the lists in the Royal Musical Association's *Research Chronicle* beginning with no. 3 (1963) *et passim*. French dissertations are covered by Gribenski's *Thèses de doctorat* (**4.140**).

4.137* Bartlett, Ian, and **Benedict Sarnaker.** *Register of Dissertations and Theses on Music in Britain and Ireland: Cumulative List of Accepted Dissertations and Theses to 1991 Together with Supplement 1.* 156 pp. London: The Royal Musical Association, 1992. (R.M.A. research chronicle, 25)

A revised and enlarged ed. of *Register of Theses on Music Accepted for Higher Degrees in Britain and Ireland,* 1979.

4.138 De Lerma, Dominique-René. *A Selective List of Masters' Theses in Musicology.* Compiled for the American Musicological Society. 42 pp. Bloomington, Ind.: Denia Press, 1976.

Entries for 257 titles submitted by 36 institutions. The entries give information on availability for copying or interlibrary loan. There are indexes by personal name, topic, or participating institution.

4.139 Dundes, Alan. *Folklore Theses and Dissertations in the United States.* 610 pp. Austin, Tex.: Published for the American Folklore Society by the University of Texas Press, 1976. (Publications of the American Folklore Society, Bibliographical and special series, 27)

A chronological list of theses and dissertations that includes many music-related titles difficult to access through traditional music reference sources. Indexes to subjects, authors, and institutions are provided.

4.140 Gribenski, Jean. *Thèses de doctorat en langue française relatives à la musique: Bibliographie commentée / French Language Dissertations in Music: An Annotated Bibliography.* xxxix + 270 pp. New York: Pendragon Press, 1979. (*RILM* retrospectives, 2)

A classified list of doctoral dissertations in French (1883–1976) on music and closely related disciplines, and defended at universities in Belgium, Canada, France, and Switzerland. Each entry is extensively annotated in French. There are indexes to authors, subjects, dates, and universities.

Reviewed by Geraldine Ostrove in *Notes* 36 (1979): 377–78 and by François Lesure in *Fontes* 27 (1980): 230–31.

4.141 *International Directory of Approved Music Education Doctoral Dissertations in Progress.* Urbana, Ill.: Published by the Council for Research in Music Education, University of Illinois, in behalf of the Graduate Program in Music Education, 1989– .

Also known as *Approved Doctoral Dissertations in Progress in Music Education, International Directory of Approved Music Education Dissertations in Progress* (1984–86), *Doctoral Dissertations in Progress, Directory of International Music Education Dissertations in Progress,* and *International Institutional Directory of Approved Music Education Doctoral Dissertations in Progress.*

A classified directory with entries giving name and address of candidate, institution, and title of dissertation. There are indexes to names and to institutions.

4.142 Landmann, Ortrun. "Verzeichnis der im Berichtsjahr . . . bei der deutschen Bücherei zu Leipzig registrierten musikwissenschaftlichen Dissertationen und Habilitationsschriften." In *Deutsches Jahrbuch der Musikwissenschaft.* Leipzig: Peters, 1957– .

A continuation of the bibliography of dissertations, completed primarily in the former East Germany, originally begun in the *Peters Jahrbuch* (**4.55**).

4.143 Larson, William S. *Bibliography of Research Studies in Music Education, 1932–48.* 119 pp. Chicago, Ill.: Music Educators National Conference, 1949.

An earlier ed., compiled by Arnold M. Small, was published in 1944 by the State University of Iowa Press. Supplements to the 1949 ed. appear in *JRME.*

A bibliography whose main purpose, according to its Foreword, is to "provide an inventory of completed research studies in music education that will save much duplication of effort in the interest of economy and progress."

Reviewed by George R. Henderson in *Notes* 7 (1949): 121.

4.144* Maranto, Cheryl Dileo, and **Kenneth E. Bruscia.** *Master's Theses in Music Therapy: Index and Abstracts.* 149 pp. Philadelphia, Pa.: Esther Boyer College of Music, Temple University, 1988.

Reviewed by Richard M. Graham in *Notes* 48 (1991): 539–40.

4.145 Meadows, Eddie S. *Theses and Dissertations on Black American Music.* 19 pp. Beverly Hills, Calif.: Theodore Front Musical Literature, 1980. (Front music publications, 1)

A classified and briefly annotated bibliography of 119 doctoral dissertations, 120 master's theses, and a few variously classified works, lacking both references to *Dissertation Abstracts* and indexes.

4.146 Schaal, Richard. *Verzeichnis deutschsprachiger musikwissenschaftlicher Dissertationen, 1861–1960.* 167 pp. Kassel, Germany: Bärenreiter, 1963. (Musikwissenschaftliche Arbeiten, 19)

A list, arranged alphabetically by author, of 2,819 German-language music dissertations, with publication data given for relevant titles. There is a subject index.

Reviewed by Erich Schenk in *Die Musikforschung* 17 (1964): 421–23, with numerous additional entries supplied.

4.147 Schaal, Richard. *Verzeichnis deutschsprachiger musikwissenschaftlicher Dissertationen, 1961–1970, mit Ergänzungen zum Verzeichnis 1861–1960.* 91 pp. Kassel, Germany: Bärenreiter, 1974.

A supplement to **4.146** of 1,271 dissertations, most written between 1961 and 1970, listed alphabetically by author, with publication dates indicated for work subsequently published. There is a subject index.

4.148* Slawska, Maria. *Bibliografia prac magisterskich i doktorskich, napisanych na kierunkach wychomania muzycznego, myzszych uczelni i instytutom w latach 1974–1981.* 306 pp. Katowice,

Poland: Centrum Informacji i Dokumentacji Wychomania Muzycznego Polshiej Sekcji ISME przy Biblioteca Glomnej Akademii Muzycznej w Katowicach, 1986.

4.149* Slawska, Maria. *Bibliografia prac magisterskich i doktorskich z zakresu wychomania muzycznego, napisanych w myzszych uczelniach i instytutach w latach 1982–1986.* 221 pp. Katowice, Poland: Centrum Informacji i Dokumentacji Wychomania Muzycznego Polshiej Sekcji ISME przy Biblioteca Glomnej Akademii Muzycznej w Katowicach, 1987.

4.150 Texas Music Educators Association. *A Bibliography of Master's Theses and Doctoral Dissertations in Music Completed at Texas Colleges and Universities, 1919–1972.* Revised ed. 152 pp. Houston, Tex.: Texas Music Educators Association, 1974.

The 1st ed., 1964, covered to 1962.

A list, arranged chronologically by institution, of research studies in music education completed in 14 Texas colleges and universities. There are subject and author indexes.

4.151 University Microfilms International. *Music and the Performing Arts: Citations to 2,014 Doctoral Dissertations and Masters Theses Published between 1986 and 1988.* 56 pp. Ann Arbor, Mich.: University Microfilms International, 1989.

Earlier editions include *Melange of Dissertations in Music* (22 pp., 1977), a list of doctoral dissertations and master's theses accepted from 1974 to 1977; *Music, a Dissertation Bibliography* (1979, 36 pp.), listing 58 master's theses and 1,791 doctoral dissertations accepted from 1974 through 1978; *Recent Studies in Music: A Catalog of Doctoral Dissertations* (1983, 36 pp.), containing citations for over 1,800 doctoral dissertations and master's theses accepted between 1978 and 1982; and *Music, a Catalog of Selected Doctoral Dissertation Research* (1987, 50 pp.), with citations to 1,765 dissertations and master's theses published between 1983 and 1986.

A list of graduate research in music that includes selected British dissertations, beginning July 1988.

ETHNOMUSICOLOGY

Ethnomusicology is a field of study that has come into its own in recent years. Its growth is steady, and with the growth comes literature requiring bibliographic control. The increase in the number of bibliographies has called for special selectivity in this section: Some of the older sources from earlier editions of this work have been omitted, to make room for the new. As in previous editions, no attempts have been made to include the many useful bibliographies appended to monographs, periodical articles, or encyclopedia articles, nor were general bibliographies on folklore or cultural anthropology included, even though many have significant musical citations.

4.152 Aning, B. A. *An Annotated Bibliography of Music and Dance in English-Speaking Africa.* 47 pp. Legon, Ghana: Institute of African Studies, University of Ghana, 1967.

An annotated bibliography of 132 items concentrating especially on the relationship between music and dance. Coverage is limited to countries south of the Sahara where English is spoken. The work is divided generally by region and country, and includes an author index.

Reviewed by Alan P. Merriam in *Ethnomusicology* 16 (1972): 544–45.

4.153* Barnett, Elise. "Special Bibliography: Art Music of India." In *Ethnomusicology* 14 (1970): 278–312.

An unannotated bibliography of 741 books and articles published 1959–70. Only works or translations in European languages are listed, but recent reports of older books and selected items from earlier years are included. A very useful subject classification index is appended.

4.154 Baumann, Max Peter. *Bibliographie zur ethnomusicologischen Literatur der Schweiz: mit einem Beitrag zu Geschichte, Gegenstand und Problemen der Volksliedforschung.* 312 pp. Winterthur, Switzerland: Amadeus, 1981.

An extensive unannotated bibliography of more than 2,783 items that follows the general discussion of the history of and problems in the study of Swiss folk music. Indexes to names, places, subjects, and songs are also included.

Reviewed by Christine Burkhardt-Seebass in *Schweizerische Musikzeitung* 122 (1982): 39–40 and by Dieter Christensen in the *Traditional Music Yearbook* 14 (1982): 138.

4.155 Cavanagh, Beverly. "Annotated Bibliography: Eskimo Music." In *Ethnomusicology* 16 (1972): 479–87 no. 3.

Well-annotated entries on tribal musics of the circumpolar region (Greenland, the Canadian Arctic, and Alaska), including many more obscure sources in such languages as Danish and Russian. Although it concentrates specifically on sources related to music, help is also provided to those wishing to pursue aspects of these cultures that are not directly related to music.

4.156* Davis, Martha Ellen. *Music and Dance in Latin American Urban Contexts: A Selective Bibliography.* 20 pp. Brockport, N.Y.: State University of New York, 1973. (Urban anthropology bibliography, 1)

A bibliography of works published in the 1960s. Materials in Spanish and Portuguese from South and Central America, Mexico, the Caribbean, and the southwestern United States are included.

4.157* Emezi, H. O. "A Bibliography of African Music and Dance: The Nigerian Experience, 1930–1980." In *Current Bibliography on African Affairs* 18 (1985–86): 117–47 no. 2.

An unannotated list of 375 books, articles, and dissertations. Although there are a few general sources, most of the citations concentrate on Nigerian music and musical culture. A helpful 3-page introduction is provided.

4.158 Emsheimer, Ernst. "Musikethnographische Bibliographie der nichtslavischen Völker in Russland." In *Acta Musicologica* 15 (1943): 77–86.

An unannotated bibliography of 433 items (primarily books and articles) covering the music of the non-Slavic peoples of Russia. An author index, classified by ethnic type, is also included.

4.159* Endo, Hirosi. *Bibliography of Oriental and Primitive Music.* 62 pp. Tokyo: Nanki Music Library, 1929.

An old work, but one especially strong in materials on Asian music in Asian languages. As Bruno Nettl points out (**4.182**), this list is historically one of the most significant contributions to the field of ethnomusicology by a non-Westerner.

4.160* Frisbie, Charlotte Johnson. *Music and Dance Research of Southwestern United States Indians: Past Trends, Present Activities, and Suggestions for Future Research.* 109 pp. Detroit: Information Coordinators, 1977. (Detroit studies in music bibliography, 36)

A bibliographic essay chronicling research from 1880 through 1976. Though written in narrative form, the text is keyed to full citations at the end of the text. Also included are discographies, lists of pertinent recording companies and archives, and suggestions for future research.

Reviewed by Stephen M. Fry in *Notes* 34 (1977): 357–58.

4.161 Gaskin, Lionel J. P. *A Select Bibliography of Music in Africa.* Compiled at the International African Institute by Lionel J. P. Gaskin under the direction of Prof. K. P. Wachsmann. 83 pp. London: International African Institute, 1965. (African bibliography series, 8)

An unannotated bibliography of more than 3,370 items, including reference works, general studies of African and tribal musics, books and articles on the music of specific countries, musical instruments, and dance. Catalogs, bibliographies, and periodicals are also included, and there are indexes to authors and geographical and ethnic classifications.

Reviewed by Leonard Vohs in *Die Musikforschung* 22 (1969): 390–91 and by Douglas Varley and Alan Taylor in *Ethnomusicology* 11 (1967): 125–28.

4.162 Gillis, Frank, and **Alan E. Merriam.** *Ethnomusicology and Folk Music: An International Bibliography of Dissertations and Theses.* 148 pp. Middletown, Conn.: Published for the Society of Ethnomusicology by the Wesleyan University Press, 1966. (Special series, 1)

A compilation and updating of earlier lists published in *Ethnomusicology* in 1960 by Merriam and in 1962 by Gillis.

An international bibliography of 897 entries arranged by author, giving title, degree, institution, and date of dissertation. Works from a number of academic disciplines are included. Folk music, jazz, education in non-Western music, the sociology and psychology of music, the computer in music research, and other subjects are considered along with the more traditional spheres of the music of nonliterate and Near and Far Eastern peoples. Subjects and institutions are indexed.

Reviewed by Barbara Smith in *Ethnomusicology* 12 (1968): 453–54.

4.163* Gourlay, Kenneth A. *A Bibliography of Traditional Music in Papua New Guinea.* 176 pp. Port Moresby, Australia: Institute of Papua New Guinea Studies, 1974.

An annotated bibliography of some 275 sources organized alphabetically by author, which covers Papua New Guinea, Torres Strait islands, parts of Java, and the Solomon Islands. The book includes references to reviews and a comprehensive index, arranged by subject.

Reviewed by Virginia Marion in *Ethnomusicology* 20 (1976): 386 and by Steven Feld in *Ethnomusicology* 23 (1979): 327–28.

4.164 Guédon, Marie-Françoise. "Canadian Indian Ethnomusicology: Selected Bibliography and Discography." In *Ethnomusicology* 16 (1972): 465–79 no. 3.

A list covering ethnomusicological source materials on Canadian Indians (non-Eskimos), including published sources, films and sound recordings, and selected unpublished theses. The arrangement is by cultural area: Eastern Woodland/Great Lakes, Plains, Yukon–Mackenzie Basin, Plateau, and Northwest Coast. Information on dance is also included.

4.165* Han Kuo-Huang. "Three Chinese Musicologists: Yang Yinliu, Yin Falu, Li Chunyi." In *Ethnomusicology* 24 (1980): 483–529 no. 3.

One of the few attempts to compile the work of non-Western musical scholars. The article is part of a larger project initiated in 1968 to include entries of important Chinese musical figures in Riemann (**1.45**) and *MGG* (**1.9**).

4.166* Haroon, Mohammed. *Indian Music Literature.* 144 pp. Delhi: Indian Bibliographies Bureau, 1991.

An unannotated bibliography of literature on Indian music including both Western and Indian scholarship. Broad topics are covered, such as general and comparative studies, biography, musicology, philosophical and scientific studies, the sociology of music, organology, vocal music, religion and music, nonclassical idioms such as film and folk musics, and music education. A name index is included.

4.167 Haywood, Charles. *A Bibliography of North American Folklore and Folksong.* 2nd revised ed. 2 vols. New York: Dover Publications, 1961.

First published in 1 vol. (1,292 pp.) by Greenberg, New York, 1951.

A massive bibliography selectively annotated. The 1st vol. covers the U.S. and Canada and is divided into five sections: general works, bibliography by region, bibliography by ethnic grouping, bibliography by occupation (such as cowboy and lumberjack songs), and a miscellaneous section (for songs based on American characters, war songs, White spirituals, and songs of the Shakers). The 2nd vol. covers "the American Indian north of Mexico, including the Eskimos" and is divided into two sections: general works and bibliographies of cultural areas. A comprehensive index is provided, as well as an index supplement for composers, arrangers, and performers. The endpapers of both vols. have maps of regional and cultural areas.

There is a review of the 1st ed. by Duncan Emrich in *Notes* 8 (1951): 700–1.

4.168* Heisley, Michael. *An Annotated Bibliography of Chicano Folklore from the Southwestern United States, III: Singing, Dancing and Musicmaking.* Los Angeles, Calif.: University of California, 1977.

An annotated bibliography of works (including theses and dissertations) covering the musical lives of Chicanos and Chicanas in five southwestern states.

4.169 Kendadamath, G. C. *Indian Music and Dance: A Select Bibliography.* 261 pp. Varanasi, India: Indian Bibliographic Centre, 1986.

An unannotated bibliography of 2,434 books and articles in English. Although the occasional Western scholar is included, the majority of writings are by Indian scholars. The bibliography is arranged by general classifications: Chapters 1–5 are on music and Chapters 6–14 are on dance. Author and subject indexes are appended.

4.170* Koch, G. E. "A Bibliography of Publications on Australian Aboriginal Music: 1975–1985." In *Musicology Australia* 10 (1987): 58–71.

4.171 Kunst, Jaap. *Ethnomusicology: A Study of Its Nature, Its Problems, Methods and Representative Personalities to Which is Added a Bibliography.* 3rd, much enlarged ed. of *Musicologica.* 303 + 46 pp. The Hague: Martinus Nijhoff, 1959.

The *Supplement to the Third Edition of Ethnomusicology,* published by M. Nijhoff in 1960, 45 pp., with a 2nd supplement in 1969, 46 pp. The 3rd ed., with its 2nd supplement (1969), was reprinted in 1969 and 1974 by M. Nijhoff.

The 1st ed. of *Musicologica: A Study of the Nature of Ethnomusicology, Its Problems, Methods, and Representative Personalities,* was published in Amsterdam by Indisch Institut in 1950, 77 pp. The 2nd ed. was published in 1955 by M. Nijhoff, 158 pp.; the 3rd ed. in 1959, 303 pp., with the *Supplement to the Third Edition of Ethnomusicology* published by M. Nijhoff in 1960, 45 pp.

A significant resource and a fundamental work with an extensive bibliography (pp. 79–215) based on Kunst's own collection of materials. The bibliography includes more than the 5,079 numbered sources. Its coverage is extremely good through the 1950s and is strong on Asian and tribal musics. The "Current Bibliography" section of the journal *Ethnomusicology* continues to publish bibliographies, discographies, and filmographies even today, based on Kunst's work.

The 1st ed. is reviewed by Manfred F. Bukofzer in *Notes* 9 (1952): 421–22. The 2nd ed. is reviewed by Josef Brozek in *Notes* 13 (1955): 57–58. There is a review of the 3rd ed. by Bruno Nettl in *Notes* 16 (1959): 560–61 and of the *Supplement* by William Lichtenwanger in *Notes* 19 (1961): 79.

4.172 Kuppuswamy, Gowry, and **M. Hariharan.** *Indian Dance and Music Literature: A Select Bibliography.* 156 pp. New Delhi: Biblia Impex, 1981.

An unannotated bibliography of 800 books and 3,000 articles on the classical and folk musics of India. The vast majority of material documented is written by Indian scholars. Indian musicology is a large field, virtually unknown in the West, and this book demonstrates its vitality. A subject index is included.

Reviewed by R. C. Mehta in the *Journal of the Indian Musicological Society* 16 (1985): 77–78.

4.173 Laade, Wolfgang. *Gegenwartsfragen der Musik in Afrika und Asien: Eine grundlegende Bibliographie.* 110 pp. Baden-Baden: V. Koerner, 1971. (Sammlung musikwissenschaftlichen Abhandlungen, 51)

An unannotated list of 898 book and periodical citations relating to the music of Africa (including Christian church music) and Asia. The section on Asia is classified by country. The book includes a compilation of institutions and societies, a list of radio stations, and a classified subject index.

Reviewed by Alfons M. Dauer in *Jahrbuch für Volksliedforschung* 18 (1973): 194–95 and by Inge Skog in *Svensk tidskrift för musikforskning* 60 (1978): 77–79.

4.174 McLean, Mervyn. *An Annotated Bibliography of Oceanic Music and Dance.* Revised and enlarged 2nd ed. 502 pp. Warren, Mich.: Harmonie Park Press, 1995. (Detroit studies in music bibliography, 74)

First ed. and *Supplement* published by the Polynesian Society (Wellington and Auckland, New Zealand), in 1977 and 1981.

Coverage of Pacific islands, together with New Guinea and nearby islands including Torres Strait. Australia, Malaysia, the Philippines, and Indonesia are excluded. Entries are from books, articles, reviews, record liner notes, and manuscript collections in major European languages. Sources in Dutch, Japanese, and Indonesian are for the most part excluded.

The 1st ed. is reviewed by Adrienne Kaeppler in *Ethnomusicology* 23 (1979): 142–43; the *Supplement* is reviewed by Elizabeth Tatar in *Ethnomusicology* 27 (1983): 388.

4.175 Marks, Paul F. *Bibliography of Literature Concerning Yemenite-Jewish Music.* 50 pp. Detroit, Mich.: Information Coordinators, 1973. (Detroit studies in music bibliography, 27)

A selectively annotated bibliography on the unique contributions to music of Jews in the Islamic culture of Yemen, and their subsequent assimilation into Palestine. Literature on music is combined with historical, sociological, and anthropological studies. A short discography is also included.

4.176 Maultsby, Portia K. "Selective Bibliography: U.S. Black Music." In *Ethnomusicology* 19 (1975): 421–49 no. 3.

An attempt to list articles and books that "are the result of serious study and an understanding of the concept of the 'black aesthetic'" and "to include sources by writers from diverse ethnic backgrounds whose approaches to and concepts of black music vary." Though unannotated, the bibliography is organized according to broad topic, genre and style, and performer, and includes folk, jazz, blues, and classical traditions.

4.177* Moyle, Alice M. "Source Materials: Aboriginal Music of Australia and New Guinea." In *Ethnomusicology* 15 (1971): 81–93.

A combined bibliography/discography of materials relating to aboriginal music in Australia and the western half of New Guinea. The list is unannotated, but each item is keyed to specific geographic areas.

4.178 *Musikethnologische Jahresbibliographie Europas / Annual Bibliography of European Ethnomusicology.* 10 vols. Bratislava: Slovenske Narodne Museum, 1966–75.

An annual bibliography of traditional and folk musics in Europe. Each vol. is arranged by country and contains approximately 400 to 600 citations. The introductions to each vol. are in German and English, and the citations are in the original languages.

The 1st vol. is reviewed by Rolf W. Brednich in *Jahrbuch für Volksliedforschung* 15 (1970): 182–83 and by Frank J. Gillis in *Ethnomusicology* 16 (1972): 138–39. Vols. 4–7 are reviewed by Barbara J. Krader in *Ethnomusicology* 21 (1977): 147–48.

4.179* Myers, Helen. *Ethnomusicology: An Introduction.* xxiv + 487 pp. New York: W.W. Norton, 1992. (The Norton/Grove handbooks in music)

A very complete overview of the current state of ethnomusicology. After a historical overview of the field, the 2nd part provides topical discussions on theory and method, including Myers on fieldwork, Anthony Seeger on the ethnography of music, Stephen Blum on analysis, and John Blacking on the biology of music making. Part 3 contains discussions on the ethics of fieldwork, gender, the music industry, preservation of world musics, and Bruno Nettl's survey of recent directions in the field. Part 4 includes 5 reference aids, including an essay with a bibliography of 85 items by Jennifer C. Post titled "Recent Resources in Ethnomusicology."

Reviewed by Carl Rahkonen in *Notes* 50 (1994): 1435–37.

4.180* Myers, Helen. *Ethnomusicology: Historical and Regional Studies.* xxviii + 541 pp. New York: W.W. Norton, 1993. (The Norton/Grove handbooks in music)

A companion vol. to *Ethnomusicology: An Introduction* (**4.179**). After an introduction by Myers, part 2 has a lengthy historical survey of ethnomusicological research by geographic location. Part 3 has regional studies of Europe, Africa, West Asia, South Asia, Western Central Asia and the Caucasus, Eastern Central Asia, East Asia, Southeast Asia, Oceania, North America, the West Indies, and Latin America. These 2 vols. in the Norton/Grove series are recent attempts at an overview of the entire field of ethnomusicology. Each vol. deals with particular issues or geographical regions through individual essays by distinguished scholars. They both include up-to-date bibliographies and excellent indexes.

Reviewed by Carl Rahkonen in *Notes* 50 (1994): 1435–37.

4.181* Nelson, S. G. *Documentary Sources of Japanese Music.* 41 pp. Tokyo: Research Archives for Japanese Music, Ueno Gakuen College, 1986.

A bibliographic guide to a manuscript collection of traditional Japanese music.

4.182 Nettl, Bruno. *Reference Materials in Ethnomusicology: A Bibliographic Essay.* 2nd ed., revised. 40 pp. Detroit: Information Coordinators, 1967. (Detroit studies in music bibliography, no. 1)

First published in 1961.

An older standard guide to the reference literature intended to help users find and evaluate general information in the field of ethnomusicology. In addition to an introduction to the field, the essay covers a survey of the field, research methods, the elements of music, organology, collections, periodicals, directories, and bibliographies, as well as a section outlining various special approaches to the field. A list of publications cited is appended. Nettl attempts to cover such collateral areas as anthropology, folklore, linguistics, psychology, geography, and travel, but he does not, for the most part, cover European and American folk idioms. Emphasis is on the music of nonliterate or primitive cultures and Eastern high cultures.

Reviewed by William Lichtenwanger in *Notes* 19 (1962): 428–30 and by Marius Schneider in *Die Musikforschung* 19 (1964): 88–89.

4.183 Nettl, Bruno. *Theory and Method in Ethnomusicology.* 306 pp. New York: Free Press of Glencoe, 1964.

A basic guidebook intended for those entering the field. Chapter 2 discusses aspects of library research and covers bibliographical resources. The theory and discussion of the field has been updated in Nettl's 1983 *The Study of Ethnomusicology: Twenty-Nine Issues and Concepts* (Urbana, Ill.: University of Illinois Press, 1983, 410 pp.), which includes a 33-page bibliography.

Reviewed by David P. McAllester in *MQ* 51 (1965): 425–28.

4.184* Rahkonen, Carl. *World Music in Music Libraries.* 77 pp. Canton, Mass.: Music Library Association, 1994. (MLA technical reports, 24)

The proceedings of a plenary session at the Music Library Association meeting in 1992, with specialized essays of interest to librarians and archivists on collecting and processing ethnomusicological materials, doing reference work in ethnomusicology and world music, ethnomusicological sound archives, and world music in public libraries. The essays on reference and collection development include bibliographies.

Reviewed by John Wagstaff in *Brio* 32 (1995): 144–45.

4.185* Rakotomalala, M. M. *Bibliographie critique d'intérêt ethnomusicologique sur la musique malagasy.* 107 pp. Antananarivo, Madagascar: Musée d'art et d'archéologie de l'Université de Madagascar, 1986. (Travaux et documents / Musée d'Art et d'Archéologie de l'Université de Madagascar, 23)

An annotated bibliography on the traditional music of Madagascar.

4.186* **Rehnberg, Mats.** *Folkmusik i Sverige; Bibliografisk hjälpreda.* 133 pp. Stockholm: Institutet for folklivsforskning, 1981.

A classified unannotated bibliography of literature on Swedish folk music, as well as Swedish folk song collections. Both sections are divided by region. The bibliography includes other sections on instruments, choral music, and sound archives. There are no indexes; arrangement is alphabetical by author. Most of the materials are in Swedish.

4.187* **Rhodes, Willard.** "North American Indian Music: A Bibliographic Survey of Anthropological Theory." In *Notes* 10 (1952): 33–45.

A bibliographic essay surveying scholarly literature from the 1880s to the 1950s.

4.188* **Richmond, W. Edson.** *Ballad Scholarship: An Annotated Bibliography.* xxvii + 356 pp. New York: Garland, 1989. (Garland folklore bibliographies, 14) (Garland reference library of the humanities, 499)

A selectively annotated bibliography, divided into 13 topical sections. Section K, Ballad Music, is the shortest in the bibliography, with only 54 citations. However, there is a useful section on ballads in collections. Author and subject indexes are included.

4.189* **Schuursma, Ann Briegleb.** *Ethnomusicology Research: A Select Annotated Bibliography.* xxvii + 173 pp. New York: Garland Publishing, 1992. (Garland library of musical ethnology, 1) (Garland reference library of the humanities, 1136) (Garland bibliographies in ethnomusicology, 3)

A classified annotated bibliography surveying ethnomusicological literature in English, French, and German published after 1960 (although foreign language coverage is very slight). It does not cover specific geographical regions unless the particular research has added something theoretically significant to the field as a whole. It does cover topics such as the history of ethnomusicology, theory and method, fieldwork techniques, analysis, and sources from related fields. The introductory remarks provide a brief state of the field. Name and subject indexes are provided.

Reviewed by Philip Vandermeer in *Fontes* 39 (1992): 371–72.

4.190 **Smith, Donna Ridley.** *Non-Western Music: A Selected Bibliography of Materials in the California State University, Sacramento, Library.* 3rd ed. 45 pp. Sacramento, Calif.: California State University Library, 1982. (Bibliographic series / The Library, California State University, Sacramento, 10)

The 2nd ed., by Sheila J. Johnson, was published in 1973, 40 pp.

A bibliography of works on African, Asian, and Oceanic musics held by the California University, Sacramento, Library.

4.191 **Song, Bang-song.** *An Annotated Bibliography of Korean Music.* 250 pp. Providence, R.I.: Asian Music Publications, Brown University, 1971. (Asian music publications, A, 2)

A list of more than 1,300 books, articles, reviews, and other publications (with annotations in English) on all aspects of Korean music and music in Korea. It covers works in many languages including Korean, and includes indexes to names, subjects, books, journals, and Festschriften.

Reviewed by Barbara B. Smith in *Ethnomusicology* 19 (1975): 318–19.

4.192* **Southern, Eileen,** and **Josephine Wright.** *African-American Traditions in Song, Sermon, Tale and Dance, 1600s-1920: An Annotated Bibliography of Literature, Collections, and Artworks.* xlv + 365 pp. New York: Greenwood Press, 1990. (The Greenwood encyclopedia of Black music)

An annotated and classified bibliography of primary materials that seeks to integrate the various folk arts of African Americans into a greater whole. It includes 2,328 entries divided into four broad historical eras. There are indexes to names, subjects, and songs, and a bibliography of sources consulted in the compilation of the work.

Reviewed by D. Antoinette Handy in *Notes* 48 (1991): 117–18 and by Dena J. Epstein in *AM* 10 (1992): 217–19.

4.193 Thieme, Darius L. *African Music: A Briefly Annotated Bibliography.* xxii + 55 pp. Westport, Conn.: Greenwood Press, 1978.

An earlier ed. was a typescript from the Library of Congress, 1964.

A general bibliography of 597 articles, books, and other items on the music of sub-Saharan Africa. The coverage ranges from 1950 to 1963 and includes indexes for authors, tribal names, and linguistic areas.

The earlier ed. is reviewed by Alan P. Merriam in *Ethnomusicology* 9 (1965): 178–80.

4.194 Varley, Douglas H. *African Native Music: An Annotated Bibliography.* 1st ed. reprinted, with additional note. 116 pp. Folkestone, England: Dawsons, 1970.

First ed., Royal Empire Society, London, 1936.

Selective coverage of African music south of the Sahara. Chapters include music and musical instruments in Africa generally and by country, African music in the Americas, African music and the church, and drum languages. Also included are lists of works on bibliography, discography, and classification. The annotations are very brief.

4.195 Vetterl, Karel. *A Select Bibliography of European Folk Music.* 144 pp. Prague: Institute for Ethnography and Folklore of the Czechoslovak Academy of Sciences, in cooperation with the International Folk Music Council, 1966.

A bibliography particularly useful for materials from the former Soviet Union. The work is in two sections: "Publications of General Interest" includes encyclopedias, bibliographies, and general monographs, and "Publications Concerning Individual Countries" has listings arranged by country, from Albania to Yugoslavia, and including Turkey and Greenland.

Reviewed by Ann Briegleb in *Ethnomusicology* 12 (1968): 161–62, by Rolf Wilhelm Brednich in *Jahrbuch für Volksliedforschung* 14 (1969): 175, and by Erik Dial in *Svensk tidskrift for musikforskning* 54 (1972): 144–45.

4.196 Waterman, Richard A., William Lichtenwanger, Virginia Hitchcock Hermann, Horace I. Poleman, and **Cecil Hobbs.** "Bibliography of Asiatic Musics." In *Notes* 5 (1947): 21–35; 25 (1948): 178–86; 5 (1948): 354–62, 549–62; 6 (1948): 122–36, 281–96; 6 (1949): 419–36, 570–83; 7 (1949): 84–98; 7 (1950): 265–79, 415–23; 8 (1950): 100–18; 8 (1951): 322–29, 683–92.

Originally published as *Bibliography of Music of the Middle East and Far East* for the Subcommittee on Musical Information of the Music Advisory Committee of the Department of State, 1944.

A classified, partially annotated bibliography in all European languages, including Russian and romanized Turkish, published serially, of 3,488 books, articles, sections of larger works, texts, transcriptions, and recordings, arranged geographically and ethnologically. The 15-part list of printed matter also includes 72 sources of Asiatic recordings and an index to ethnic groups.

4.197* Wolff, Jürgen B., and **Erik Kross.** *Bibliographie der Literatur zum deutschen Volkslied: mit Standortangaben an den wichtigsten Archiven und Bibliotheken der DDR.* 232 pp. Leipzig: Zentralhaus-Publikation, 1987. (Kleine Reihe deutsche Volkslieder, 7–8)

A bibliography of about 16,000 entries, including both literature about German folk music and catalogs of folk songs collections.

MUSIC HISTORY

Medieval and Renaissance Music

4.198* Barker, John W. *The Use of Music and Recordings for Teaching about the Middle Ages: A Practical Guide, with Comprehensive Discography and Selective Bibliography.* 230 pp. Kalamazoo, Mich.: Medieval Institute Publications, 1988.

A discography (pp. 148–89) among the most thorough currently available for this repertoire, with a detailed bibliography (pp. 190–230).

Reviewed by Kenneth Kreitner in *Notes* 47 (1990): 73 and by Daniel Leech-Wilkinson in *EM* 17 (1989): 573.

4.199 Gallo, F. Alberto. "Philological Works on Musical Treatises of the Middle Ages: A Bibliographical Report." In *Acta Musicologica* 44 (1972): 78–101.

A narrative bibliography treating the work accomplished in the editing and description of medieval treatises. The material is discussed chronologically and by country, with copious notes.

4.200 Gleason, Harold. *Music Literature Outline.* Series 1–5. 2nd ed. 5 vols. Bloomington, Ind.: Frangipani Press, 1981.

First published in Rochester, N.Y., by Levis Music Stores, 1949–55.

Contents: Ser. 1, *Music in the Middle Ages and Renaissance* (2nd ed., 1951); Ser. 2, *Music in the Baroque;* Ser. 3, *Early American Music from 1620 to 1920;* Ser. 4, *Contemporary American Music;* Ser. 5, *Chamber Music from Haydn to Bartok.*

Historical outlines, or syllabi, with copious bibliographical references, books, periodical articles, scores, and recordings. The organization of Series 1 and 2 follows closely that of the corresponding works by Reese and Bukofzer in the *Norton History of Music Series* (**2.29**).

4.201 Hughes, Andrew. *Medieval Music: The Sixth Liberal Art.* Revised ed. 360 pp. Toronto: University of Toronto Press in association with the Center for Medieval Studies, University of Toronto, 1980. (Toronto medieval bibliographies, 4)

First published in 1974, 326 pp. Also published in London by E. Benn.

A classified, succinctly annotated bibliography of the literature on medieval music, giving varied access to over 2,000 entries through indexes of authors and editors and a separate subject index. The preface is a guide to the bibliographical conventions adopted and a "Key to the Bibliography" provides a useful guide to the subject matter. The 1980 revision has both alterations to the original text and a supplemental section at the end of the volume.

The later ed. is reviewed by Richard Crocker in *CNV* 66 (1982): 7–8 and by John E. Druesedow, Jr., in *ARBA* 12 (1981): no. 1012. The earlier ed. is reviewed by John Caldwell in *M&L* 56 (1975): 401–3 and by Howard Mayer Brown in *EM* 4 (1976): 67.

4.202 Smith, Carleton Sprague, and **William Dinneen.** "Recent Work on Music in the Renaissance." In *Modern Philology* 42 (1944): 41–58 no. 1.

A bibliographical article in narrative style citing and evaluating research and editorial activity in Renaissance music from about 1900 to 1944.

4.203 Smits van Waesberghe, Joseph. "Das gegenwärtige Geschichtsbild der mittelalterlichen Musik." In *Kirchenmusikalisches Jahrbuch* 46–49 (1962–65).

A narrative survey and discussion, arranged by major topics, of the contributions on medieval music in 19 current musicological and historical journals, from 1957 to 1964.

4.204 Suñol, Grégorio Maria. "Bibliographie générale." In his *Introduction à la paléographie musicale Grégorienne,* pp. 511–65. Paris: Desclée, 1935.

A bibliography first appearing in the original 1925 ed. of the author's work on Gregorian paleography. The entries are broadly classified and listed in the order of publication.

4.205 Velimirović, Miloš. "Present State of Research in Byzantine Music." In *Acta Musicologica* 43 (1971): 1–20.

A narrative bibliography citing the important work accomplished in this area since 1950.

Baroque and Classical Music

4.206* Baron, John H. *Baroque Music: A Research and Information Guide.* 587 pp. New York:

Garland, 1993. (Music research and information guides, 16) (Garland reference library of the humanities, 871)

An annotated bibliography of 1,412 items (books, dissertations, essays in anthologies, and periodical articles) written from 1960 to 1991. The historic period covered is 1580–1730, with the bulk of the items discussing music from 1600 to 1720. The entries are organized by topic: general, musicians, national studies, theory, instrumental music, vocal music, opera incidental music, patronage, pedagogy, music printing, music iconography, the "modern revival," and performance practice. Numbered entries give author, title, pagination, LC call number or other identifying number (ISBN, Dewey class number, *RILM* number, or UMI number), and a short description, sometimes evaluative. There are indexes of authors, names, and subjects.

Reviewed by Karin Pendle in *ARBA* 25 (1994): no. 1306.

4.207 Hill, George R. *A Preliminary Checklist of Research on the Classic Symphony and Concerto to the Time of Beethoven (excluding Haydn and Mozart).* 58 pp. Hackensack, N.J.: J. Boonin, 1970. (Music indexes and bibliographies, 2)

A list of 450 items—books, dissertations, and articles—in major European languages. After general items on the symphony and concerto, the arrangement is geographic (England, France, Italy, Mannheim, North Germany and Scandinavia, and Vienna), with separate lists of composers and bibliographic entries for symphonies and concertos. There is a composer index. Bibliographic items were compiled by students in graduate courses taught by Jan LaRue at New York University. Composer lists are compiled from the works of Barry Brook, Adam Carse, Charles Cudworth, and Jan LaRue.

4.208* Sadie, Julie Ann. *Companion to Baroque Music.* 549 pp. New York: Schirmer Books, 1990.

A geographically classified, biographical dictionary and guide to national traditions, with each area headed by a short essay on the region, written by an authority for that area. Includes a chronology of persons and events (pp. 449–504), a selective, classified, European-style (without publisher given) bibliography of recent books in English, and a detailed index (pp. 510–49) of names and places.

Reviewed by Carolyn Gianturco in *Notes* 49 (1993): 1431–33 and by Donald J. Burrows in *EM* 19 (1991): 635–36.

4.209 Schwartz, Judith L., and **Christena L. Schlundt.** *French Court Dance and Dance Music: A Guide to Primary Source Writings, 1643–1789.* 386 pp. Stuyvesant, N.Y.: Pendragon Press, 1987. (Dance and music series, 1)

A work designed to "facilitate reconstruction of French court dancing in the 17th and 18th centuries in its contemporary setting." The authors gathered printed sources from the reigns of Louis XIV–XVI that concern French court dance and its music, both in France and abroad. The guide is in three sections: information on dance and dancing in social and theatrical contexts, selected writings about music and other subjects relevant to dance music in the French style, and tangentially related writings on physical, social, or cultural settings and aesthetic matters. The foreword to each section refers to modern secondary literature. Includes a single short-title list in chronological order and an index to subjects, names, and titles. Each entry includes a lengthy annotation. There is a useful summary of subject headings. This is a groundbreaking bibliographic effort of great merit.

Reviewed by Shirley Wynne in *Notes* 47 (1991): 789–90 and by Erich Schwandt in *M&L* 70 (1989): 72–73.

4.210 Stedman, Preston. *The Symphony: A Research and Information Guide, Vol. I: The Eighteenth Century.* 343 pp. New York: Garland Publishing, 1990– . (Music research and information guides, 14) (Garland reference library of the humanities, 862)

An annotated bibliography of 931 books, articles, theses, and dissertations. After short sections on general resources and subjects, the bulk of the book is arranged alphabetically by country. No criteria for inclusion are given. There are indexes by author, title, composer, and subject.

Reviewed by A. Peter Brown in *M&L* 72 (1991): 593–95.

4.211* Ziffer, Agnes. *Kleinmeister zur Zeit der Wiener Klassik: Versuch einer übersichtlichen Darstellung sogenannter "Kleinmeister" im Umkreis von Haydn, Mozart, Beethoven und Schubert sowie Studien zur Quellensicherung ihrer Werke.* 277 pp. + 26 pp. plates. Tutzing, Germany: Verlegt bei Hans Schneider, 1984. (Publikationen des Instituts für Österreichische Musikdokumentation, 10)

An organized overview of the manuscripts left by members of the circles surrounding Joseph Haydn, Mozart, Beethoven, and Schubert. There are many samples from the circle members' autograph manuscripts, to show for identification purposes the characteristics of each composer's musical handwriting: dynamic markings, clef signs, stems, and cross-beams.

Reviewed by H. C. Robbins Landon in the *Haydn Yearbook* 16 (1985): 275.

Romantic Music

4.212 Baumgartner, Alfred. *Musik der Romantik.* 744 pp. Henndorf, Germany: Kiesel, 1983. (Der Grosse Musikführer)

One vol. from a series of five by the author (*Alte Musik*, 1981, 755 pp.; *Barock Musik*, 1981, 664 pp.; *Musik der Klassik*, 1983, 744 pp.; and *Musik des 20. Jahrhunderts* (**4.215**)), giving brief entries on the life and works of composers of the designated period, arranged chronologically by date of birth, with an occasional illustration, a lexicon of terms used in music of the period, a bibliography, and an index.

4.213* Seaton, Douglass. *The Art Song: A Research and Information Guide.* xxvii + 273 pp. New York: Garland Publishing, 1987. (Music research and information guide, 6) (Garland reference library of the humanities, 673)

Headed by an introductory essay defining the art-song, which also explains criteria for inclusion in this annotated bibliography of 970 articles, books, theses, and dissertations in English, German, and several Romance languages. Organized by broad categories with the bulk of the material under the heading "Studies of Individual Composers and Works." There are a list of sources, an index of authors, editors, translators, and compilers, and a subject index.

Reviewed by Kevin A. Freeman in *Notes* 48 (1991): 512–14, by Ian Ledsham in *M&L* 70 (1989): 528–30, by Ann P. Basart in *CNV* 123 (1988): 17–18, and by Robert Skinner in *ARBA* 19 (1988): no. 1264.

Contemporary Art Music

4.214 Basart, Ann Phillips. *Serial Music: A Classified Bibliography of Writings on Twelve-Tone and Electronic Music.* 151 pp. Berkeley; Los Angeles, Calif.: University of California Press, 1961. (University of California bibliographic guides)

A classified bibliography of 823 items treating the literature of 12-tone music, electronic music, the second Viennese school (Schoenberg, Berg, and Webern), and 29 other contemporary composers using serial techniques. There are author and subject indexes.

Reviewed by Dika Newlin in *Notes* 19 (1961): 256–57, by James B. Coover in *JMT* 6 (1962): 316–17, by Donald Mitchell in *Tempo* 63 (1962–63): 46–48, and by Josef Rufer in *Die Musikforschung* 17 (1964): 315–16.

4.215* Baumgartner, Alfred. *Musik des 20. Jahrhunderts.* 744 pp. Henndorf, Germany: Kiesel, 1985. (Der Grosse Musikführer)

Part of a series designed to cover Western art music, including bibliographical references and index. See **4.212.**

4.216 Cross, Lowell M. *A Bibliography of Electronic Music.* 126 pp. Toronto: University of Toronto Press, 1967.

A bibliography of writings on electronic music, including articles covering developments in the field between 1948 and 1966. Arranged by author, with a subject index.

Reviewed, with addenda, by Otto Luening in *Notes* 25 (1969): 502–3.

4.217 Tjepkema, Sandra L. *A Bibliography of Computer Music: A Reference for Composers.* 276 pp. Iowa City, Iowa: University of Iowa Press, 1981.

A comprehensive list of books, articles, dissertations, and papers relating to the use of computers by composers. There are indexes to subjects, to names not appearing in the alphabetical array of authors' names, and to studios or centers of activity.

Reviewed by Ann P. Basart in *Notes* 38 (1982): 848–49.

4.218 Warfield, Gerald. *Writings on Contemporary Music Notation: An Annotated Bibliography.* 93 pp. Ann Arbor, Mich.: Music Library Association, 1976. (MLA index and bibliography series, 16)

A comprehensive bibliography of books and articles on new music published between 1950 and 1975, selectively including works published earlier in the century and works referring to new notation but not entirely devoted to the subject. Brief annotations and complete bibliographic information are included, with citations of printing techniques. The list is arranged alphabetically by author, with a brief subject index.

MUSICAL INSTRUMENTS

The literature on musical instruments can be found in a variety of reference works. The reader in search of further information should look in Chapter 1 under Musical Instruments: Makers, Performers, and Terminology (**1.488–1.594**) and in Chapter 8, Catalogs of Musical Instrument Collections. Many of the reference tools cited contain appended bibliographies on the subject. This section is subdivided in part by category of instrument.

4.219* Baron, John H. *Chamber Music: A Research and Information Guide.* 500 pp. New York: Garland Publishing, 1987. (Music research and information guides, 8) (Garland reference library of the humanities, 704)

A classified and annotated bibliography of 1,600 entries.

Reviewed by Clifford Bartlett in *Brio* 25 (1988): 32–33, by Ann P. Basart in *CNV* 119 (1988): 14–15, by James Dack in *M&L* 69 (1988): 524–26, and by Allie Wise Goudy in *ARBA* 19 (1988): no. 1300.

4.220* Cingolani, Sergio. *Acustica degli strumenti musicali: bibliografia 1840–1990 / Acoustics of Musical Instruments: Bibliography 1840–1990.* 327 pp. Cremona, Italy: Editrice Turris, 1992. (Collana di liuteria e cultura musicale, 3)

A bibliography concentrating on literature covering the acoustical properties of music and individual instruments.

4.221 Meer, John Henry van der. "Ältere und neuere Literatur zur Musikinstrumentenkunde." In *Acta Musicologica* 51 (1979): 1–50.

An extensive discussion of the literature of musical instruments, citing 415 titles and ranging from important catalogs of exhibitions to monographs on the development of individual instruments.

4.222 Oberkogler, Friedrich. *Vom Wesen und Werden der Musikinstrumente.* 2nd ed. 175 pp. Schaffhausen, Switzerland: Novalis, 1985.

First published in 1976.

A narrative bibliography on the nature and development of musical instruments.

Keyboard

4.223 Graaf, G. A. C. de. *Literatuur over het orgel / Literature on the Organ.* 71 pp. Amsterdam: G.A.C. de Graaf; Utrecht: F. Knuf, 1957. (Bibliotheca organologica, 51)

A list of over 1,250 titles of books, brochures, and reprints concerning the use, history, and construction of organs. Books on the technique of organ playing are not included. The introduction and title page are in Dutch, English, German, French, Spanish, and Italian.

4.224* Hinson, Maurice. *The Pianist's Reference Guide: A Bibliographical Survey.* 336 pp. Los Angeles, Calif.: Alfred Publishing Co., 1987.

An annotated bibliography of nearly 100 books, theses, and dissertations, most in English. All books were in print in 1985. The annotations are mainly descriptive; those for theses and dissertations are edited abstracts taken from *Master's Abstracts* and *Dissertation Abstracts.* The 15 subject indexes provide access to items on accompanying, aesthetics, analysis, biographies, construction and design, group piano, history and criticism, lists of piano music, ornamentation, pedagogy, performance anxiety, performance technique, piano duets, transcriptions, and two or more pianos. There are a composer index and a list of publishers.

Reviewed by Robert Skinner in *ARBA* 19 (1988): no. 1296.

4.225 Hinson, Maurice. *The Piano Teacher's Source Book: An Annotated Bibliography of Books Related to the Piano and Piano Music.* 2nd ed. 187 pp. Melville, N.Y.: Belwin Mills Publishing Corporation, 1980.

First published in 1974, with a 1976 supplement.

A classified bibliography of English-language books, stressing the easily obtainable, with indexes to authors and composers.

The 2nd ed. is reviewed by Marsha Berman in *ARBA* 12 (1981): no. 1042. The 1st ed. is reviewed by Stewart Gordon in *AMT* 24 (1975): 59 no. 6 and by William J. Connor in *MT* 116 (1975): 1068–69.

4.226 Liebenow, Walther M. *Rank on Rank: A Bibliography of the History and Construction of Organs.* 171 pp. Minneapolis, Minn.: Martin Press, 1973.

A bibliography whose brief entries are arranged geographically, with separate sections on history and construction.

Reviewed by Walter Hilse in *Notes* 31 (1975): 572–74.

4.227* Palmieri, Robert. *Piano Information Guide: An Aid to Research.* 329 pp. New York; London: Garland Publishing, 1989. (Garland reference library of the humanities, 806) (Music research and information guides, 10)

A selective annotated bibliography of information on the piano in its various forms, the music written for it, and the composers writing that music. An appendix gives a classified chronology of important events in the development of the piano; another provides piano terminology in five languages (English, French, German, Italian, and Spanish). Includes an author/title index and a name/subject index.

Reviewed by Thelma C. Diercks in *Notes* 47 (1991): 777–79 and by Robert Kosovsky in *Fontes* 39 (1992): 74–75.

4.228 Reuter, Rudolf. *Bibliographie der Orgel; Literatur zur Geschichte der Orgel bis 1968.* 256 pp. Kassel, Germany: Bärenreiter, 1973. (Veröffentlichungen der Orgelwissenschaftlichen im Musikwissenschaftlichen Seminar der Westfälischen Wilhelms-Universität, 3)

A bibliography of 8,574 books and articles, not including works about organists or reviews of performances; American sources are generally omitted. The arrangement is alphabetical by author; there are indexes by location, names of persons, and subjects. There is a list of periodicals devoted to literature on the organ.

Reviewed by Walter Hilse in *Notes* 31 (1975): 572–74 and by Peter Williams in *M&L* 56 (1975): 77–78.

4.229 Schulz, Ferdinand F. *Pianographie: Klavierbibliographie der lieferbaren Bücher und Periodica sowie der Dissertationen in deutscher, englischer, französischer und italienischer Sprache.* 2nd ed., revised and enlarged. 458 pp. Recklinghausen, Germany: Piano-Verlag, 1982.

First published in 1978, 148 pp.

A classified bibliography of 2,000 publications about pianos, music for pianos, and composers of piano music. Includes a short Nachtrag, extensive lists of addresses of publishers, libraries, piano competitions, and music societies. There is no subject or title index.

4.230* Wallmann, James L. "Organ Bibliographies, Real and Imaginary." In *CNV* 127 (1988): 1– .

A bibliographical essay on the organ and related matters.

4.231* Wettstein, Hermann. *Die Orgelbauerfamilie Silbermann: Bibliographie zu ihrem Leben und Werken / Silbermann, a Family of Organ Builders: A Bibliography of Their Life and Work.* 2nd ed. 139 pp. Buren, the Netherlands: F. Knuf, 1989. (Bibliotheca organologica, 81)

First ed. published by the Universitätsbibliothek at Freiburg im Breisgau, 1983, 89 pp. (Schriften der Universitätsbibliothek Freiburg im Breisgau, 6).

Percussion

4.232 Bajzek, Dieter. *Percussion: An Annotated Bibliography with Special Emphasis on Contemporary Notation and Performance.* 185 pp. Metuchen, N.J.: Scarecrow Press, 1988.

An annotated, classified bibliography of 1,400+ items, concentrating on English-language material published from 1968, with some earlier works of interest and major publications in foreign languages. Largely excluded from the list are works for percussion, bibliographical material, and works on bells and other "mechanical" instruments. The appendixes include a selected list of percussion music, transcriptions, and analyses; relevant bibliographies, indexes, and reviews; and a list of percussion magazines and musical journals with regular features on percussion.

Reviewed by Dominique-René de Lerma in *ARBA* 20 (1989): no. 1214.

Strings

4.233 Bakus, Gerald J. *The Spanish Guitar: A Comprehensive Reference to the Classical and Flamenco Guitar.* 204 pp. Los Angeles, Calif.: Gothic Press, 1977.

Includes bibliography and index.

4.234 Chou, Ch'ing-yün. *Ch'in shih pu / History of the Ch'in, Supplement.* 5 vol. China: Meng-p'o shih ts'ang pan, 1919.

On double leaves, Oriental style, in case. In Chinese.

A collection of quotations from various Chinese texts in which people connected with the ch'in, a zitherlike instrument, such as musicians and ch'in makers are mentioned. The selections are arranged chronologically by the person's name, beginning with legendary times and continuing into the 10th century, totaling over 100 names. Each person is identified briefly, the quotation is cited, and the source is named.

Another two titles are included in this publication. The first is *Ch'in Shih Hsü / Continuation of the History of the Ch'in,* a 3-vol. work containing the names of another 400 people associated with the ch'in who lived in the Sung dynasty (from A.D. 960) to the 19th century. There are appendixes devoted to Buddhists and women. The second is *Ch'in Shu Pieh Lu / Bibliography of Works on the Ch'in,* a 1-vol. annotated list of 200 books and manuscripts on the ch'in from the Chou (1122 B.C.) to the Ch'ing (1655–1911) dynasties.

4.235 Hermann, Judy. "Violin Makers: A Selective Bibliography." In *CNV* 96 (1985): 5–9.

Published in an abbreviated version in *Metrodata, the Newsletter of the Los Angeles Metropolitan Cooperative Library System,* November–December 1984.

An annotated bibliography.

4.236 Heron-Allen, Edward. *De Fidiculis Bibliographia: Being the Basis of a Bibliography of the Violin.* 2 vols. lxxviii + 416 pp. London; Sydney: Griffith, Farran, Okeden & Welsh, 1890–94.

Reprinted by Holland Press, London, in 1961.

A classified bibliography of literature on the violin in all its aspects. Full bibliographical data is given, with copious annotations. The work was issued in parts, printed on the recto only, and concludes with four supplements.

4.237 Lyons, David. *Lute, Vihuela, Guitar to 1800: A Bibliography.* 214 pp. Detroit, Mich.: Information Coordinators, 1978. (Detroit studies in music bibliography, 40)

A bibliography of music for and articles and books on the instruments in the title, as well as the theorbo, orpharion, bandora, and mandolin, including a list of editions featuring tablature, with cross-references and an author index. An addendum of 231 sources is separately indexed.

Reviewed by Thomas F. Heck in *Notes* 36 (1979): 107–8, by François Lesure in *Fontes* 26 (1979): 297, and by Joseph F. Chouinard in *ARBA* 11 (1980): no. 972.

4.238* McCutcheon, Meredith Alice. *Guitar and Vihuela: An Annotated Bibliography.* xlv + 353 pp. New York: Pendragon Press, 1985. (*RILM* retrospective, 3)

A bibliography of 1000+ books and articles on composers, performers, music and analysis, iconography, design, and construction.

Reviewed by Ann P. Basart in *CNV* 104 (1986): 14 and by William Brockman in *ARBA* 17 (1986): no. 1253.

4.239 Pohlmann, Ernst. *Laute, Theorbe, Chitarrone: Die Lauten-Instrumente, ihre Musik und Literatur von 1500 bis zur Gegenwart.* 2nd ed. 416 pp. Bremen: Edition Eres, 1972.

The 1st ed. was published in Bremen by Deutsche Musikpflege in 1968, 297 pp.

A sourcebook of information about instruments of the lute family, including sources, composers, literature, descriptions of tablatures, locations of existing instruments, and makers.

Reviewed by Stanley Buetens in *JLSA* 5 (1972): 114–16 and by Anthony Rooley in *EM* 3 (1975): 157 no. 2.

4.240 Schwarz, Werner, and **Monika Haringer.** *Guitar Bibliography: An International Listing of Theoretical Literature on Classical Guitar from the Beginning to the Present.* xxxii + 257 pp. Munich; New York: K.G. Saur, 1984.

A bilingual classified bibliography of 4,705 entries.

Reviewed by William Brockman in *ARBA* 17 (1986): no. 1254.

4.241 Sollinger, Charles. *String Class Publications in the United States, 1851–1951.* 71 pp. Detroit, Mich.: Information Coordinators, 1974. (Detroit studies in music bibliographies, 30)

Headed by a five-part essay on the history of instrumental music instruction in U.S. classrooms, the 2nd part is a five-part annotated bibliography of all string class method books in the Library of Congress published from 1851 to 1951, supplemented by other materials included to show the effect of the class teaching idea on music publishing. Annotations quote from descriptions provided by the authors or publishers themselves. Each section of the bibliography is organized alphabetically by author. There are no indexes.

Winds

4.242* Fasman, Mark J. *Brass Bibliography: Sources on the History, Literature, Pedagogy, Performance, and Acoustics of Brass Instruments.* 452 pp. Bloomington, Ind.: Indiana University Press, 1990.

A classified bibliography listing over 6,000 books, journal articles, and dissertations on brass instruments.

Reviewed by John Bewley in *Notes* 48 (1992): 1309–11 and by Greg Notess in *Fontes* 39 (1992): 77–78.

4.243* Griscom, Richard, and **David Lasocki.** *The Recorder: A Guide to Writings about the Instrument for Players and Researchers.* 504 pp. New York: Garland Publishers, 1994. (Music research and information guides, 19) (Garland reference library of the humanities, 1026)

An annotated and classified bibliography of about 1,500 items, meticulously constructed, with preference given to sources in English.

Reviewed by John Turner in *M&L* 76 (1995): 615–16 and by William E. Hettrick in *Notes* 52 (1996): 796–97.

4.244 Miller, Dayton C. *Catalogue of Books and Library Material Relating to the Flute and Other Musical Instruments, with Annotations.* 120 pp. Cleveland, Ohio: Privately printed by the Judson Company, 1935.

The catalog, briefly annotated, of the literary portion of one of the largest collections ever assembled on the flute and related instruments, now housed in the Music Division of the Library of Congress. The collection includes material on all wind instruments, in the form of books, pamphlets, periodical articles, newspaper clippings, concert programs, makers' catalogs, and price lists.

4.245 Skei, Allen B. *Woodwind, Brass, and Percussion Instruments of the Orchestra: A Bibliographic Guide.* 271 pp. New York: Garland Publishing, 1985. (Garland library of the humanities, 458)

A selective, classified, annotated bibliography of 1,195 items, compiled as a guide for a professional audience. There is an index of names and subjects.

Reviewed by Arnold Myers in the *Galpin Society Journal* 42 (1989): 151–52 and by Ross Wood in *ARBA* 17 (1986): no. 1266.

4.246 Warner, Thomas E. *An Annotated Bibliography of Woodwind Instruction Books, 1600–1830.* 138 pp. Detroit, Mich.: Information Coordinators, 1967. (Detroit studies in music bibliography, 11)

A chronological bibliography of 450 items, including a number of unlocated titles. There is a list of modern works cited, indexed by author and anonymous titles and by type of instrument.

JAZZ AND POPULAR MUSIC

Jazz

4.247* Agostinelli, Anthony J. *The Newport Jazz Festival: Rhode Island, 1954–1971: A Bibliography, Discography and Filmography.* 64 pp. Providence, R.I.: The author (Oak Lawn, 176 Everett Avenue, 02906), 1977.

A detailed, narrowly focused but useful source for Festival research, this typescript-reproduced source includes two appendixes: a list of the Voice of America broadcasts, giving the principal performers, and a list of the Festival's dates.

4.248 Carl Gregor, Duke of Mecklenburg. *International Bibliography of Jazz Books, Volumes I–II.* Compiled with the assistance of Norbert Rücker. 2 vols. Baden-Baden: Valentin Koerner, 1983. (Collections d'Études Musicologiques, 67, 76) (Sammlung musikwissenschaftlicher Abhandlunge, 67, 76)

The first 2 of a projected 4 vols. intended to revise and expand the author's earlier bibliography and its two supplements (**4.249**).

A bibliography including brief transcriptions of tables of contents and arranged alphabetically. Includes a list of phantom titles as well as indexes to collaborators, keywords and persons named in titles, subjects, collections and series, and countries of publication. There is a chronological survey of years of publication.

4.249 Carl Gregor, Duke of Mecklenburg. *International Jazz Bibliography: Jazz Books from 1919 to 1968.* 198 pp. Strasbourg: P.H. Heitz, 1969. (Sammlung musikwissenschaftlicher Abhandlunge, 49)

1970 Supplement to International Jazz Bibliography & International Drum and Percussion Bibliography. 59 + 43 pp. Graz, Austria: Universal Edition, 1971. (Studies in jazz research, 3) (Beiträge zur Jazzforschung, 3)

1971/72/73 Supplement to International Jazz Bibliography (IJB) & Selective Bibliography of Some Jazz Background Literature & Bibliography of Two Subjects Previously Excluded. 246 pp. Vienna: Universal Edition, 1975. (Beiträge zur Jazzforschung, 6)

A pioneering attempt to compile a truly international list of jazz research material.

The 1969 ed. is reviewed by Ekkehard Jost in *Die Musikforschung* 24 (1971): 330–31 and by Alan Merriam in *Ethnomusicology* 14 (1970): 177. The first supplement is reviewed by James Patrick in *Notes* 29 (1972): 236–39 and the 2nd in *Jazz Podium* 24 (1975): 34 no. 3.

4.250* Gray, John. *Fire Music: A Bibliography of the New Jazz, 1959–1990.* 515 pp. New York: Greenwood Press, 1991. (Music reference collection, 31)

A comprehensive bibliography (7,105 entries) of information in books, dissertations, articles, films, videos, and audio tapes on avant-garde jazz. The materials cited are in English, French, German, Italian, Dutch, and Swedish. A chronology lists events in both jazz and politics, 1954–88. Chapters cover African-American cultural history and the arts, New Jazz (broadly and regionally), jazz collectives, the New York loft and club scene, biographical and critical studies (the bulk of the book), reference works, and archives and research centers. Appendixes list performers geographically and by instrument. Includes an artist index and an author index.

Reviewed by Ingrid Monson in *Notes* 49 (1993): 1072–73.

4.251 Hefele, Bernhard. *Jazz Bibliography: International Literature on Jazz, Blues, Spirituals, Gospel and Ragtime Music with a Selected List of Works on the Social and Cultural Background from the Beginning to the Present.* 368 pp. Munich; New York: K.G. Saur, 1981.

A superb bibliography including 6,000 entries arranged by topic, some citing reviews. There is a name index.

Reviewed by Nina Davis-Millis in *Notes* 39 (1982): 102–3 and by William Brockman in *ARBA* 13 (1982): no. 1067.

4.252 Kennington, Donald, and **Danny L. Read.** *The Literature of Jazz: A Critical Guide.* 2nd ed., revised. 282 pp. Chicago, Ill.: American Library Association, 1980.

The 1st ed. was published in 1970 in England by the Library Association, followed by an American edition in 1971.

Organized access to jazz literature. Nine short chapters arrange works by topic, with each discussing an aspect of jazz documentation, and each followed by an annotated bibliography. There are indexes by names and by title.

There is an unfavorable review by Eileen Southern of the 1st American ed. in *Notes* 29 (1972): 35–36. The 2nd ed. is reviewed by Brian Redfern in *Brio* 18 (1981): 36–37, by Dean Tudor in *ARBA* 13 (1982): no. 1070, by William H. Tallmadge in *AM* 2 (1984): 94 no. 2, and by George L. Starks in *BPM* 11 (1983): 215.

4.253 Meadows, Eddie S. *Jazz Reference and Performance Materials: A Select Annotated Bibliography.* xliii + 806 pp. New York: Garland Publishing, 1995. (Garland library of music ethnology, 4) (Garland reference library of the humanities, 1471)

The 1st ed. was issued as *Jazz Reference and Research Materials: A Bibliography.* xxi + 300 pp. New York: Garland Publishing, 1981. (Critical studies on Black life and culture, 22) (Garland reference library of the humanities, 251)

A bibliography arranged in two sections: "Jazz and Its Genres" and "Reference Materials," with the latter organized by reference and research genre (bibliographies, histories, discographies, etc.). Each section is separately indexed by name and subject.

The 1st ed. is reviewed by William Tallmadge in *AM* 2 (1984): 92–94, with many corrections, and by Dominique-René de Lerma in *ARBA* 13 (1982): no. 1073.

4.254 Meeker, David. *Jazz in the Movies.* New enlarged ed. Unpaged (c. 350 pp.). New York: Da Capo Press, 1982. (Roots of jazz)

This ed. was first published by Talisman Books, London, 1981. The original ed. was published by the British Film Institute, London, 1972, as *Jazz in the Movies: A Tentative Index to the Work of Jazz Musicians for the Cinema* (89 pp.). A 1977 ed., *Jazz in the Movies: A Guide to Jazz Musicians 1917–1977* (286 pp.) was published in New Rochelle, N.Y., by Arlington House and by Talisman Books, London.

A list that cites and describes 3,724 films, including television films, mentioning jazz musicians responsible for the musical elements of the soundtrack. There is a name index.

Reviewed by Charles Miller in *Notes* 35 (1979): 636.

4.255 Merriam, Alan P. *A Bibliography of Jazz.* With the assistance of Robert J. Benford. 145 pp. Philadelphia, Pa.: American Folklore Society, 1954. (Publications of the American Folklore Society, bibliographical series, 4)

Reprinted by Da Capo Press and by Krause Reprint Company, both in New York, 1970.

A list of 3,324 numbered entries, arranged alphabetically by author, with subject emphasis indicated by a code system. Includes a list of 113 jazz periodicals and a subject index.

Reviewed by Marshall W. Stearns in *Notes* 12 (1955): 436–37; the Da Capo Press reprint is reviewed by Eileen Southern in *Notes* 29 (1972): 34–38.

Popular Music

4.256 Booth, Mark W. *American Popular Music: A Reference Guide.* 212 pp. Westport, Conn.: Greenwood Press, 1983. (American popular culture series)

A collection of bibliographic essays that starts with an overview of American popular music and then deals, chapter by chapter, with a variety of popular genres, from pre–20th-century music to rock, ending each chapter with a substantial bibliography of books. Over 1,100 works are described in the essays, which show each title's relevance to the beginning researcher. The appendixes list "Some Significant Dates in the History of American Popular Music [1814–1982]" and "Addresses of Selected Reference Collections." There is an extensive name and subject index that guides the reader by author (though not by title) to a discussion of each author's work.

Reviewed by Michael Meckna in *AM* 4 (1986): 358–69, by Dean Tudor in *ARBA* 15 (1984): no. 915, and by Diane Parr Walker in *Notes* 41 (1985): 722–23.

4.257 Cooper, B. Lee. *The Popular Music Handbook: A Resource Guide for Teachers, Librarians and Media Specialists.* xxvi + 415 pp. Littleton, Colo.: Libraries Unlimited, 1984.

A guide giving recommended teaching topics on popular music; a classified bibliography of popular music resources, occasionally annotated; popular music discographies; and a basic popular music collection for libraries. There are indexes to artists and performers and to subjects, and a selective general bibliography (pp. 361–406).

Reviewed by George Louis Mayer in *ARBA* 16 (1985): no. 1205.

4.258* Cooper, B. Lee, and **Wayne S. Haney.** *Rockabilly: A Bibliographic Resource Guide.* 372 pp. Metuchen, N.J.: Scarecrow Press, 1990.

Extensive lists of printed resources on 35 years of rockabilly performers. More than 220 rockabilly singers and instrumentalists are included, with author index and bibliography.

Reviewed by Don Cusic in *PMS* 17 (Spring 1993): 118–19 and by Kip Lornell in *Notes* 48 (1992): 911–12.

4.259 Dimmick, Mary L. *The Rolling Stones: An Annotated Bibliography.* Revised and enlarged ed. 159 pp. Pittsburgh, Pa.: University of Pittsburgh Press, 1979.

Originally issued in 1973, 73 pp.

A bibliography with liberal annotations, some critical and some descriptive. As a collection of documentation and commentary, this is a model of its kind.

The 1979 ed. is reviewed by Marsha Berman in *ARBA* 11 (1980): no. 982.

4.260* Figuerosa, Rafael. *Salsa and Related Genres: A Bibliographical Guide.* 109 pp. Westport, Conn.: Greenwood Press, 1992. (Music reference collection, 38)

A guide to salsa, the "Afro-Hispanic music of the Antilles," including information on related genres, listing books, articles, dissertations, encyclopedia entries, videos, recordings, liner notes, and reviews.

Reviewed by Ted Solís in *Notes* 50 (1993): 625–26 and by Gregg S. Geary in *ARBA* 25 (1994): no. 1381.

4.261* García, Florencio Oscar. *Samba: A Bibliography with Introduction: History, People, Lyrics, Recordings.* 110 pp. Albuquerque, N.M.: FOG Publications, 1992.

4.262* Gatten, Jeffrey N. *Rock Music Scholarship: An Interdisciplinary Bibliography.* 294 pp. Westport, Conn.: Greenwood Press, 1995. (Music reference collection, 50)

4.263* Haggerty, Gary. *A Guide to Popular Music Reference Books: An Annotated Bibliography.* 210 pp. Westport, Conn.: Greenwood Press, 1995. (Music reference collection, 47)

A book containing 427 annotations organized into 13 categories (including biographies, dictionaries of terms, and yearbooks). Only books in print at the time of compilation or considered standard were included. Popular music is defined as commercially successful music, so gospel music is included but most folk and art music is not. Also excluded are iconographic works and record price guides. There is one index combining authors, titles, and subjects.

Reviewed by J. A. Badics in *Choice* 33 (1996): 1096.

4.264* Hart, Mary L., Brenda M. Eagles, and **Lisa N. Howorth.** *The Blues: A Bibliographical Guide.* 636 pp. New York: Garland Publishing, 1989. (Music research and reference guides, 7) (Garland reference library of the humanities, 565)

A classified bibliographical guide of 4,700+ citations, with contributions by seven prominent scholars in the field. The largest section is that of blues biographies, with over 2,700 entries.

Reviewed by David Dodd in *Notes* 47 (1990): 387 and by Mark Tucker in *M&L* 72 (1991): 317–18.

4.265* Hefele, Bernhard. *Bibliographie Jazz, Rock, Pop, 1990: Ein Verzeichnis der deutschsprachigen Literatur.* 357 pp. Pullach, Germany: Verlag W. Gorzny, 1993.

An earlier ed. was published as *Jazz, Rock, Pop: eine Bibliographie der deutschsprachigen Literatur von 1988 bis 1989* in Munich and New York by K.G. Saur, 1991 (457 pp.).

A bibliography of recent German-language writings on popular music, with access through an index.

Reviewed by Bob Rusch in *Cadence* 17 (September 1991): 17.

4.266 Hoffmann, Frank W. *The Literature of Rock, 1954–1978.* 337 pp. Metuchen, N.J.: Scarecrow Press, 1981. Supplements: *The Literature of Rock II, 1979–1983.* With B. Lee Cooper and Lee Ann Hoffmann. 1986, 2 vols. *The Literature of Rock III, 1984–1990, with Additional Material for the Period 1954–1983.* With B. Lee Cooper. 1995, 1,003 pp.

A classified, annotated bibliography with a brief historical survey of the literature and an annotated list of popular music periodicals. The first vol. has a basic stock list of rock recordings and a bibliography and index to persons and groups. The supplements are selective bibliographies arranged according to a historical outline of the genre. There are additional categories for materials not fitting into the historical framework. Also included are lists of books cited in the bibliographies, a basic stock list of rock recordings arranged according to the historical outline, a list of periodicals covering the genre, and an index of artists, groups, genres, concepts, and trends.

Vol. I is reviewed by Nina Davis-Millis in *Notes* 38 (1981): 318–19 and by Dean Tudor in *ARBA* 13 (1982): no. 1068; Vol. III is reviewed by B. Lee Cooper in *LJ* 120 (March 1 1995): 62.

4.267 Iwaschkin, Roman. *Popular Music: A Reference Guide.* 658 pp. New York: Garland Publishing, 1986. (Garland reference library of the humanities, 642) (Music research and information guides, 4)

A classified, annotated bibliography of 5,276 works covering the broadest range of popular music styles and genres, and including a bibliography of bibliographies and a list of popular music periodicals. There are indexes of names, groups, and, selectively, titles.

Reviewed by Paul F. Wells in *AM* 7 (1989): 346–48 and by Dominique-René de Lerma in *ARBA* 18 (1987): no. 1262.

4.268 Kuhnke, Klaus, Manfred Miller, and **Peter Schulze.** *Schriften zur populären Musik: Eine Auswahl-Bibliographie.* 2 vols. Bremen: Archiv für Populäre Musik, 1975–77. (Archiv für Populäre Musik. Schriften, 1–2)

A classified list of titles about a broad range of popular musics. There are indexes by author and translator, subject, and period.

4.269 Lowe, Leslie. *Directory of Popular Music 1900–1980.* 1,440 pp. Droitwich, England: Peterson Publishing Co., Ltd., 1986.

The 1st ed. was published in 1975 and covered 1900–65 (1,034 pp.).

A work designed to be a standard reference book for popular music in Great Britain. A chronological section gives recording information about popular songs, including the citation of recordings. Following sections treat stage songs, films, music publishers, award-winning songs, and theme songs. There is an index to song titles.

4.270* McCoy, Judy. *Rap Music in the 1980s: A Reference Guide.* 261 pp. Metuchen, N.J.: Scarecrow Press, 1992.

An annotated bibliography of 1,000 articles (from general as well as music magazines), reviews, news stories, and books. Also included is a discography of albums that contributed to the evolution of rap music, as well as indexes by date, subject, personal name, and title.

4.271 Macken, Bob, Peter Fornatale, and **Bill Ayres.** *The Rock Music Source Book.* 644 pp. Garden City, N.Y.: Anchor Books, 1980.

A book written to "unearth the varied treasures, both of music and meaning, that are buried in the history of rock music." The 1st part is a subject guide to rock music, using 50 personal, social, and political themes as the organized headings. With each theme is an epigrammatic definition of the theme, cross-references to other themes, and lists of "classic," "definitive," and "reference" songs (the explanations of these characterizations are on pp. 29–33). Songs are cited with performing artist and recording company as the only identifiers. The 2nd part has 5 sections: a discography, a filmography, a section on rock history with important dates and deaths, a directory of record companies, and a bibliography of rock magazines and books.

Reviewed by Robert Palmieri in *ARBA* 13 (1982): no. 1071.

4.272 MacPhail, Jessica Holman Whitehead. *Yesterday's Papers: The Rolling Stones in Print, 1963–1984.* 216 pp. Ann Arbor, Mich.: Pierian Press, 1986. (Rock & roll reference series, 19)

A bibliography of writings about the Rolling Stones found in primarily American newspapers and magazines from 1963 to 1984. The entries are grouped according to type—such as books, magazine articles, newspaper articles, and recordings reviews—with separate indexes by author, title, subject date, and title of source publication (primarily newspapers and magazines).

4.273* Pruett, Barbara J. *Marty Robbins: Fast Cars and Country Music.* 601 pp. Metuchen, N.J.: Scarecrow Press, 1990.

A documentary approach, with a chronology, a classified bibliography, a discography (pp. 386–475), and an interview with the subject.

Reviewed by B. Lee Cooper in *PMS* 17 (Spring 1993): 116–17.

4.274 Sandberg, Larry, and **Dick Weissman.** *The Folk Music Sourcebook.* New, updated ed. 272 pp. New York: Da Capo Press, 1989.

First ed., Knopf, 1976, 260 pp.

A book treating North American folk music in both the popular and the ethnic sense. The new ed., while leaving much unchanged, has updated the book's directory features. There is information on blues and on North American Indian music. Styles and genres are discussed, each with a discography. There are biographical entries, an annotated list of songbooks and instructional materials, and a list of reference works. Includes a list of periodicals and a directory of organizations, centers, archives, and festivals, with substantial discographical material, including videos.

Reviewed by David Dodd in *Notes* 47 (1991): 790–91.

4.275* Sonnier, Austin M., Jr. *A Guide to the Blues: History, Who's Who, Research Sources.* 287 pp. Westport, Conn.: Greenwood Press, 1994.

A basic research guide. Part 1 comprises six essays on the history, development, and influence of blues music, each with an extensive bibliography. Part 2 contains a biographical dictionary of 300+ blues musicians (listing some recordings for most), 30 pages of black-and-white photos of musicians in action, a selected filmography, a compilation of the bibliographies from the essays, and a discography arranged first by recording medium, then by recording company. There is a subject index.

Reviewed by Laura Dankner in *Notes* 52 (1995): 119–20.

4.276 Tamm, Eric. "Materials of Rock Music Research." In *CNV* 90–94 (1985).

A thoughtful annotated bibliography arranged in classified order. The introductory comments to each section of the classified arrangement describe some of the issues and the quandaries in which scholars of rock find themselves.

4.277 Taylor, Paul. *Popular Music since 1955: A Critical Guide to the Literature.* 533 pp. London; New York: Mansell; Boston, Mass.: G. K. Hall, 1985.

A critical bibliographical guide to the literature of popular music published in England between 1955 and 1983. The book focuses principally on rock music. An annotated, categorized bibliography of 1,800 entries gives full bibliographic citations and publishing history: generalia, social aspects, artistic aspects, business, genres, individual lives and works, fiction, and periodicals. Includes a glossary (pp. 479–96), and author, title, and subject indexes.

Reviewed by Andy Linehan in *Brio* 22 (1985): 32–33; by B. Lee Cooper in the *Sonneck Society* 13 (1987): 28–29, and by Dominique-René de Lerma in *ARBA* 17 (1986): no. 1283.

4.278 Terry, Carol B. *Here, There & Everywhere: The First International Beatles Bibliography, 1962–1982.* 282 pp. Ann Arbor, Mich.: Pierian Press. 1985. (Rock & roll reference series, 11)

A bibliography classified by form (books, book chapters, fan magazines) and including sections on reviews of books, films, and recordings, with numbered entries arranged alphabetically by author. There are indexes by author, title, and subject.

Reviewed by Richard W. Grefrath in *ARBA* 17 (1986): no. 1304.

4.279* Wolter, Stephen, and **Karen Kimber.** *The Who in Print: An Annotated Bibliography, 1965 through 1990.* 154 pp. Jefferson, N.C.: McFarland and Co., 1992.

MUSIC EDUCATION

4.280 Brookhart, Edward. *Music in American Higher Education: An Annotated Bibliography.* 245 pp. Warren, Mich.: Harmonie Park Press, 1988. (Bibliographies in American music, 10)

A bibliography of 1,300 classified entries on the place and function of music in American institutions of higher education, c. 1830 to 1985. There are no entries for archival materials; readers are referred to the *National Union Catalog of Manuscripts* and *Resources of American*

Music History (**4.355**). There are descriptive annotations with some critical commentary, and author and subject indexes.

Reviewed by Robert Skinner in *ARBA* 20 (1989): no. 1168.

4.281 Harris, Ernest E. *Music Education: A Guide to Information Sources.* 566 pp. Detroit, Mich.: Gale Research Co., 1978. (Education information guide series, 1) (Gale information guide library)

A work citing both historical and current titles, including many not found in standard bibliographies. Arranged in 74 sections, the titles are divided into 5 main categories: general reference sources, music in education, subject matter areas, special uses of music, and multimedia and equipment. There are appendixes listing library holdings and music periodicals, as well as author, title, and subject indexes.

Reviewed by Stephen M. Fry in *Notes* 35 (1978): 93–94 and by Gerald B. Olson in *JRME* 27 (1979): 192–95.

4.282 Larson, William S. *Bibliography of Research Studies in Music Education, 1932–48.* 119 pp. Chicago, Ill.: Music Educators National Conference, 1949.

An earlier ed., compiled by Arnold M. Small, was published in 1944 by the State University of Iowa Press. Supplements to the 1949 ed. were in *JRME* in 1957, 1964, 1968, and 1972.

A bibliography whose main purpose, according to its Foreword, is to "provide an inventory of completed research studies in music education that will save much duplication of effort in the interest of economy and progress."

Reviewed by George R. Henderson in *Notes* 7 (1949): 121.

4.283* Lescat, Philippe. *Méthodes & traités musicaux en France 1660–1800: Réflexions sur l'écriture de la pédagogie musicale en France suivies de catalogues systématiques et chronologiques, de repères biographiques et bibliographiques.* 239 pp. La Villette, Paris: Institut de Pédagogie Musicale et Choréographique, 1991.

A survey of late-17th- and 18th-century French music theory treatises, with a "catalogue systematique" (pp. 139–89) and a "catalogue chronologique" (pp. 191–202).

4.284 Music Educators National Conference. Music in American Education Committee. *Music in American Education.* Edited by Hazel N. Morgan. 365 pp. Chicago, Ill.: Music Educators National Conference, 1955. (Music education source book, 2)

Brief bibliographies to various chapters and subchapters concerned with aspects of American public school music.

4.285 Phelps, Roger P., Lawrence Ferrara, and **Thomas W. Goolsby.** *A Guide to Research in Music Education.* 4th ed. 367 pp. Metuchen, N.J.: Scarecrow Press, 1993.

The 1st ed. was published by W. C. Brown Co. in Dubuque, Iowa, in 1969 (239 pp.), the 2nd ed. by Scarecrow Press in 1980 (385 pp.), and the 3rd ed. by Scarecrow in 1986 (368 pp.); all were edited by Roger P. Phelps.

Intended for the graduate student in music education, covering bibliography and research procedures and techniques, including bibliographical references (pp. 333–58) and index.

4.286* Rainbow, Edward L., and **Hildegard C. Froehlich.** *Research in Music Education: An Introduction to Systematic Inquiry.* 330 pp. New York: Schirmer Books, 1987.

How to do research in music education.

NATIONAL MUSICOLOGICAL COVERAGE

Since 1957, a series of articles has appeared in *Acta Musicologica,* the journal of the International Musicological Society, surveying the bibliographical and research activities in music in various countries since the end of World War II. Most of them cite major scholarly publications, dissertations, and important music reference works. The countries and areas covered, their chroniclers, and the date of publication in *Acta* include Australia (1984, Margaret Kartomi), Austria (1975, Othmar Wesseley; 1979, Rudolf Flotzinger), Belgium (1958, Suzanne Clercx-Lejeune; 1989, Henri Vanhulst), Canada (1981, Maria Rika Maniates; 1988, Zoltan Roman), China (1989, Jin Jingyan), Croatia (1991, Stanislav Tuksar), the Czech Republic (1977, Theodora Strakova), Denmark (1972, Torben Schousboe), Finland (1959, Nils-Eric Ringbom), France (1958, François Lesure; 1991, Jean Gribenski and François Lesure), Germany (1957, Harald Heckmann), Great Britain (1980, David Fallows, Nigel Fortune, Arnold Whittall, and John Blacking; 1983, David Fallows; 1986, Barry Cooper), Iran (1980, Mohammad Tagli Massoudieh), Iraq (1980, Scheherazade Qassim Hassan), Ireland (1988, Harry White), Israel (1958, Edith Gerson-Kiwi; 1981, Edith Gerson-Kiwi and Amnon Shiloah; 1991, Don Harrán and Edwin Seroussi), Italy (1959, Riccardo Allorto and Claudio Sartori; 1982, F. Alberto Gallo, Agostino Ziino, Giulio Cattin, Lorenzo Bianconi, Elvidio Surian, Antonio Serravezza, and Tullia Magrini), Japan (1963, Francesca Yosio Namura; 1982, Wolfgang Suppan and Hachirō Sakarishi), Korea (1985, Bang-Song Song), Latin America (1959, Daniel Devoto), the Netherlands (1960, Eduard Reeser; 1983, Albert Dunning), Norway (1972 and 1980, Dag Ebbe-Schjelderup), the Philippines (1982, Corazon C. Diaquino), Portugal (1960, Macario Santiago Kastner; 1984, Manuel Carlos De Brito), Russia (1974, Boris Jarustovsky), Scandinavia (1958, Berbert Rosenberg), South Africa (1986, Socrates Paxinos), South America (1957, Fritz Bose), Spain (1980, Manuel Querol; 1990, Juan José Carreras), Sweden (1972, Anders Lonn; 1975, Erik Kjellberg), Switzerland (1958, Hans Peter Schanzlin; 1989, Ernst Lichtenhahn), United States of America (1961, Scott Goldthwaite; 1975, Claude Palisca; 1979 and 1980, James Haar; 1983, George S. Buelow; 1981, Ruth Steiner), Vietnam (1977, Tran Van Khe), and Yugoslavia, including Bosnia-Herzegovina, Croatia, and Slovenia (1958 and 1979, Dragotin Cvetko).

Africa

4.287* Gray, John. *African Music: A Bibliographical Guide to the Traditional, Popular, Art, and Liturgical Musics of Sub-Saharan Africa.* 499 pp. Westport, Conn.: Greenwood Press, 1991. (African special bibliographical series, 14)

A classified bibliography with sources as early as 1732, although most are from 1890 to the present. Both print (books, dissertations, unpublished papers, and newspaper and magazine articles) and nonprint (films, videotapes, and audio tapes) are included, in the major Western languages as well as in several African ones. The basic areas of classification are cultural history and the performing arts (entries 1–224), ethnomusicology (225–317), general and regional studies of traditional local village or rural music (318–3,203), popular music and musicians (3,204–4,967), art music (4,968–5,060), and church music (5,061–5,105). The appendixes include reference works, archives and research centers (giving both books listing such and names, addresses, and material about individual centers), and a selective discography (giving record albums, with label information and the names and addresses of record retail outlets and record companies). There are indexes for ethnic groups, subjects, artists, and authors.

Reviewed by Christopher A. Waterman in *Notes* 51 (1994): 213–15 and by Kofi Agawu in the *Traditional Music Yearbook* 24 (1992): 169.

4.288* Lems-Dworkin, Carol. *African Music: A Pan-African Annotated Bibliography.* 328 pp. London; New York: Hans Zell, 1991.

An attempt not only to update earlier works, but also to broaden their scope. The book covers all of Africa (not just sub-Saharan) and African-influenced musics in the Western hemisphere. Annotated for the most part, it includes subject and author indexes.

Arabia

4.289 Farmer, Henry George. *The Sources of Arabian Music: An Annotated Bibliography of Arabic Manuscripts Which Deal with the Theory, Practice, and History of Arabian Music from the Eighth to the Seventeenth Century.* 71 pp. Leiden: E.J. Brill, 1965.

First published in Bearsden, Scotland, issued privately by the author in 1940 as a reprint from the *Records of the Glasgow Bibliographical Society,* Vol. 13 (97 pp.).

Entries arranged chronologically by century, preceded by a brief general discussion of Arabian music and its sources.

4.290* Krüger-Wust, Wilhelm J. *Arabische Musik in europäischen Sprachen: Eine Bibliographie.* 124 pp. Wiesbaden: Harrassowitz, 1983.

A list by author of 2,100 books and articles in European languages, dating from the mid-19th century to the end of the 1970s. There are a selective discography and a classified subject index.

Argentina

4.291 Suarez Urturbey, Pola. *La Música en revistas Argentinas.* 70 pp. Buenos Aires: Fondo Nacional de las Artes, 1969.

A bibliography of 652 entries for articles on music in four Argentine periodicals: *La Geceta musical* (1874–87), *La Moda* (1837–38), *Revista de estudios musicales* (1949–54), and *La Revista de musica* (1927–30). There is an index of names.

Australia

4.292* Crisp, Deborah. *Bibliography of Australian Music: An Index to Monographs, Journal Articles, and Theses.* 260 pp. Armidale, New South Wales: Australian Music Studies Project, 1982. (Australian music studies, 1).

A bibliography of 2,218 entries, dating from 1790 to 1981 and covering the spectrum of Australian music, with subject index.

Brazil

4.293* Antônio, Irati. *Bibliografía de Música Brasileira: 1977–1984.* Projeto e organização, Irati Antônio, Rita de Cássia Rodrigues, Heloísa Helena Bauab. 275 pp. São Paulo: Universidade de São Paulo, Escola de Comunicações e Artes, Serviço de Biblioteca e Documentação: Centro Cultural São Paulo, Divisão de Pesquisas, 1988.

A bibliography of 2,239 books, book chapters, pamphlets, dissertations, theses, and periodical articles on Brazilian music. Holdings information for the collection is given for seven Brazilian libraries. Indexes include both subject and name, as well as an alphabetical list of periodicals indexed. Future volumes planned for this series include a retrospective volume covering works up to 1977, and volumes covering works from 1985 on.

Reviewed by Edward A. Riedinger in *Fontes* 38 (1991): 242–43.

4.294 Azevedo, Luiz H. Corrêa de. *Bibliografia Musical Brasileira (1820–1950).* 252 pp. Rio de Janeiro: 1952. (Ministério da educaçao e saude. Instituto nacional do livro, Col. Bl. Bibliografia, 9)

A bibliography of 1,639 titles under 13 subject sections. Included are writings by Brazilian authors on non-Brazilian music. Publications including only music are omitted.

Reviewed by A. Hyatt King in *M&L* 35 (1954): 67–68 and by Charles Seeger in *Notes* 11 (1954): 551–52.

Canada

4.295 Bradley, Ian L. *A Selected Bibliography of Musical Canadiana.* Revised ed. 177 pp. Victoria, B.C.: University of Victoria, 1976.

First published in 1974.

A bibliography whose classified contents include bibliographies, theses, biographies, compositions, education, ethnomusicology, histories, and a miscellaneous category. The list of theses written at Canadian academic institutions is of particular interest.

China

4.296 Chung-yang yin yüeh hsüeh yüan. Chung-kuo yin yüeh yen chiu so. *Chung-kuo ku-tai yin-yüeh shu-mu.* 142 pp. Pei-ching, China: Yin yüeh ch'u pan she, 1962.

A bibliography of works about ancient Chinese music divided into three parts: commonly available books on music, books known to be in existence but not seen by the author, and known lost works. Works on histories, theatrical music, instruments, religious and ceremonial music, ch'in, and musical technique are covered. Each entry provides titles, author or editor, imprint information, and call numbers in the Library of Musical Research in the Central Music Conservatory in Pei-ching.

4.297 *Chung-kuo yin yüeh shu p'u chih.* 200 pp. Pei-ching, China: Jen min yin yüeh ch'u pan she, 1984.

A union catalog of holdings of Chinese music titles in 37 Chinese libraries, covering the period from 722 B.C. to 1949. It is a classified catalog in two parts: one for the period from 722 B.C. to 1911 and another for 1912–49. There is an index to all titles.

4.298* Kaufmann, Walter. *Musical References in the Chinese Classics.* 265 pp. Detroit, Mich.: Information Coordinators, 1976. (Detroit monographs in musicology, 5)

The literary references to a lost body of music.

Reviewed by Stephen M. Fry in *Notes* 34 (1977): 358–59.

4.299 Lieberman, Fredric. *Chinese Music: An Annotated Bibliography.* 2nd ed., revised and enlarged. 257 pp. New York: Garland Publishing, 1979. (Garland reference library of the humanities, 75) (Garland bibliographies in ethnomusicology, 1)

First ed. published by the Society for Asian Music, 1970 (157 pp.) and supplemented in 1973 (Asian music publications. Series A: Bibliographies and research aids, 1).

An annotated bibliography of 2,441 items, attempting exhaustive coverage of publications in Western languages. Although no Asian-language articles are included, the coverage of works by native scholars writing in English is particularly strong. The entries are arranged alphabetically by author. There are also indexes to serials and other names, as well as a selective topical guide designed to offer starting points for the study of Chinese music, also touching on drama and dance.

Reviewed by Judith J. Johnson in *Notes* 36 (1979): 370–71, by François Lesure in *Fontes* 27 (1980): 58–59, by K. H. Han in *Ethnomusicology* 26 (1982): 484–86, and by Frederic Schoettler in *ARBA* 11 (1980): no. 948. The 1st ed. is reviewed by Rulan Chao Pian in *Notes* 28 (1971): 227–29.

Czech Republic

4.300 Muzíková, Ruzena. *Selective Bibliography of Literature on Czech and Slovak Music.* 124 pp. Prague: Czechoslovak Music Information Centre, 1969.

A useful bibliography of Czechoslovakian music literature for English readers. The Czech titles are given in English translation, with brief descriptions of content and bibliographical features, and are classified in nine major sections: bibliography, catalogs, dictionaries, periodical publications, history of Czech and Slovak music, monographs, anthologies, instruments, and notation.

4.301 Vyborny, Zdeněk. "Czech Music Literature since World War II." In *Notes* 16 (1959): 539–46.

Trans. from German by William Lichtenwanger.

A classified bibliography, each section preceded by a brief descriptive statement, with titles given in Czech and English.

France

4.302 Cohen, Albert, and **Leta E. Miller.** *Music in the Paris Academy of Sciences, 1666–1793: A Source Archive in Photocopy at Stanford University: An Index.* 69 pp. Detroit, Mich.: Information Coordinators, 1979. (Detroit studies in music bibliography, 43)

An index of connections with music in the proceedings of the Académie Royale des Sciences. A study by Cohen, based on these documents, was published as *Music in the French Royal Academy of Sciences: A Study in the Evolution of Musical Thought* (Princeton, N.J.: Princeton University Press, 1981).

Reviewed by Catherine Massip in *Fontes* 29 (1982): 149, by Robert Skinner in *ARBA* 11 (1980): no. 967, and by Leonard Duck in *MR* 45 (1984): 149–50.

4.303 Leguy, Jean. *Répertoire bibliographique des ouvrages en français sur la musique: 1975.* 3rd ed. 175 pp. Tours, France: Librairie musicale Ars Musicae, 1989.

Supplement: Janvier 1975–debut 1990 (Tours, France: Librairie musicale Ars Musicae, 1990, 207 pp.). Earlier, less comprehensive supplemental volumes were also issued. The series was begun by Leguy as *Catalogue bibliographique des livres de langue française sur la musique* (Paris: E. Ploix, 1954), 59 pp.

A classified list of works about music, arranged by author in each section, with most titles published in France in the mid-20th century. Although this series was designed as sales catalogs, it has a practical bibliographic application.

4.304* Pistone, Danièle. *Répertoire international des travaux universitaires relatifs à la musique française du moyen age à nos jours (thèses et mémoires).* 414 pp. Paris: Honoré Champion, 1992. (Observatoire musical français, 1)

A bibliography, international in scope, listing theses and dissertations on French music, arranged chronologically by subject.

Germany

4.305 Krautwurst, Franz. *Das Schrifttum zur Musikgeschichte der Stadt Nürnberg.* 68 pp. Nuremberg: Stadtbibliothek Nürnberg, 1964. (Veröffentlichungen der Stadtbibliothek Nürnberg, 7)

A bibliography of writings about music in the city of Nuremberg.

4.306 Zentralinstitut für Musikforschung. *Bericht über die musikwissenschaftlichen Arbeiten in der Deutschen Demokratischen Republik, 1968– .* Berlin: Verlag Neue Musik, 1969– .

Abstracts of scholarly papers and dissertations by East German musicologists.

Great Britain

4.307* Ashbee, Andrew. *Records of English Court Music.* 9 vols. Brookfield, Vt.: Scolar Press, 1986– .

Contents: Vol. 1, 1660–85 (286 pp.); Vol. 2, 1685–1714 (246 pp.); Vol. 3, 1625–49 (285 pp.); Vol. 4, 1603–25 (258 pp.); Vol. 5, 1625–1714 (355 pp.); Vol. 6, 1558–1603 (268 pp.); Vol. 7, 1485–1588 (xxiv + 467 pp.); Vol. 8, 1485–1714 (xxiv + 326 pp.); Vol. 9, Index (267 pp.).

Some vols. originally published in Snodlands, Kent, by the author.

A successor to a work by Lafontaine (1909) and to Stokes's *The Musical Antiquary* (1903–13), as well as Ashbee's earlier *Lists of Payments to the King's Musick in the Reign of Charles II (1660–1685)* (1981). Ashbee has compiled a list from English court records of documents relating to music and provided current access information. Samples are also provided from the records of the Lord Steward. The index vol. includes a list of primary sources consulted, as well as indexes of subjects and names of persons and places.

Vols. 1–5 are reviewed by Robert Ford in *Notes* 50 (1993): 127–29. Vol. 1 is reviewed by Kenneth Fincham in *M&L* 68 (1987): 290, by Peter Holman in *MT* 128 (1987): 439, and by David Hunter in *Notes* 44 (1987): 273. Vol. 2 is reviewed by Irena Cholij in *M&L* 70 (1989): 95–96 and by Peter Holman in *MT* 129 (1988): 25. Vol. 3 is reviewed by Ian Spink in *M&L* 71 (1990): 242–43. Vol. 4 is reviewed by Lynn Hulse in *M&L* 73 (1992): 101–3, with detailed information on omissions (sources not covered). Vol. 5 is reviewed by Ian Spink in *M&L* 73 (1992): 440–41. Vol. 6 is reviewed by Lynn Hulse in *M&L* 75 (1994): 258–59. Ashbee's *Lists* is reviewed by Peter Holman in *MT* 123 (1982): 334, by Watkins Shaw in *M&L* 65 (1984): 81, and by Gordon Standford in *VdGSAJ* 26 (1989): 104–6.

4.308 Ford, Wyn Kelson. *Music in England before 1800: A Select Bibliography.* 128 pp. London: The Library Association, 1967. (Librarians Association bibliographies, 7)

A classified bibliography, confined to literature published in the 20th century in English, French, and German, in two major divisions: music and its environment and persons. The major critical editions of composers' works are cited in the second part.

4.309 Kassler, Jamie Croy. *The Science of Music in Britain, 1714–1830: A Catalogue of Writings, Lectures, and Inventions.* 2 vols. lxii + 1,339 pp. New York: Garland Publishing, 1979. (Garland reference library of the humanities, 79)

An extensively annotated bibliography, arranged by author of English-language writings, on four areas of musical knowledge: technical, mathematical, critical, and physical. Works on sacred and theatrical music, singing, and playing are omitted. The location of sources and a supporting bibliography are supplied for each source. Three appendixes cover genres of publication issued in Britain 1714–1830, encyclopedias and dictionaries, and musical periodicals. There are indexes of names, tradesmen, places, and genres and subjects.

Reviewed by Kerry S. Grant in *Notes* 37 (1980): 43–44 and by Frederic Schoettler in *ARBA* 11 (1980): no. 944.

4.310* Miller, Leta E., and **Albert Cohen.** *Music in the Royal Society of London, 1660–1806.* 264 pp. Detroit, Mich.: Information Coordinators, 1987. (Detroit studies in music bibliography, 56)

An annotated bibliography to references on music found in the archives of the Royal Society, with an introductory essay on the collection and indexes to ease access.

Reviewed by Grayson Beeks in *Notes* 47 (1990): 372–74 and by George Louis Mayer in *ARBA* 19 (1988): no. 1272.

4.311* Porter, James. *The Traditional Music of Britain and Ireland.* xxix + 408 pp. New York: Garland Publishing, 1989. (Music research and information guides, 11) (Garland reference library of the humanities, 807)

A selective annotated bibliography citing 1,739 works published between 1700 and 1989 in such fields as history, composition, belles lettres, medieval studies, archaeology, and social theory. There are four broad divisions: reference works, journals, collections of music transcriptions, and research publications. Indexes are given to geographical areas and subjects, as well as names.

Reviewed by Rob van der Bliek in *Fontes* 38 (1991): 243–44, by Ann Buckley in the *Traditional Music Yearbook* 22 (1990): 151–53, and by David Dodd in *Notes* 47 (1990): 391–92.

4.312* Turbet, Richard B. *Tudor Music: A Research and Information Guide.* With an appendix updating *William Byrd: A Guide to Research.* 247 pp. New York: Garland Publishing, 1994. (Music research and information guides, 18) (Garland reference library of the humanities, 1122)

A selective bibliography organized to help musicians in the area of performance practice, arranged in 12 subject categories. There are no subject or works indexes, but there are selective ones for authors and musicians.

Reviewed by Milton H. Crouch in *ARBA* 26 (1995): no. 1253.

4.313 Woodfill, Walter L. "Bibliography." In his *Musicians in English Society,* pp. 315–61. Princeton, N.J.: Princeton University Press, 1953.

Unabridged reprint by Da Capo Press, New York, 1959.

A substantial list of the primary and secondary sources for the study of English music of the late 16th and early 17th centuries. The list is divided into sections covering the periods before and after 1700.

Reviewed by Joseph Kerman in *JAMS* 7 (1954): 145–46 and by Vincent Duckles in *Notes* 11 (1953): 100–1.

Greece

4.314 Ratliff, Neil. "Resources for Music Research in Greece: An Overview." In *Notes* 36 (1980): 50–64.

A review of music collections in Greece.

Hungary

4.315* Lengyel, Vera Zimane. *A Magyar Zenei Szakirodalom bibliografiaja / Bibliographia-musicologiae Hungaricae, 1980– .* Budapest: MTA Zenetudományi Intézet, 1982– .

A bibliography of books on music published in Hungary, books on music by Hungarian authors, and books on Hungarian music, arranged by subject.

4.316 Rajeczky, B. "Musikforschung in Ungarn 1936–1960 (Bibliographischer Bericht)." In *Studia Musicologica* 1 (1961): 225–49.

A brief survey of Hungarian musical scholarship, with a classified bibliography of music literature. The Hungarian titles are given with German translations. There are sections on folk music, Hungarian music history, general music history, and collective works.

Israel and Jewish Music

4.317 Heskes, Irene. *The Resource Book of Jewish Music: A Bibliographical and Topical Guide to the Book and Journal Literature and Program Material.* 302 pp. Westport, Conn.: Greenwood Press, 1985. (Music reference collection, 3)

An annotated bibliography of 1,200 published English-language books, periodicals, instruction manuals, music collections, and dance materials on Jewish music, classified by type of publication, but with a topical index. Includes an author index and a glossary of Judaica.

Reviewed by Allie Wise Goudy in *ARBA* 17 (1986): no. 1229.

4.318 Weisser, Albert. *Bibliography of Publications and Other Resources on Jewish Music.* 117 pp. New York: National Jewish Music Council, 1969.

Revised and enlarged edition based in part on *The Bibliography of Books and Articles on Jewish Music* prepared by Joseph Yasser and published in 1955.

Italy

4.319* Biagi Ravenni, Gabriella. *Diva panthera: Musica e musicisti al servizio della stato lucchese.* 215 pp. Lucca, Italy: Accademia luccese di scienze, lettere ed arti, 1993. (Studie e testi, 33)

A musical history of 18th-century Lucca, with a bibliography (pp. 171–83) and indexes.

4.320* Gamberini, Leopoldo. *La vita musicale europea del 1800: Archivio Musicale Genovese.* 11 vols. Siena, Italy: Università, Facoltá di magistero in Arezzo, Istituto di storia dell'arte, Cattedra di storia della musica, 1978–89. (La vita musicale europea del 1800)

Access to 19th-century musical events in Genoa through transcriptions of excerpts from the general Genoese newspapers, arranged chronologically, with an index to the contents.

Reviewed by Thomas F. Heck in *Fontes* 38 (1991): 337–38.

Japan

4.321 Fukuda, Naomi. *Bibliography of Reference Works for Japanese Studies / Nihon no sanko tosho.* 210 pp. Ann Arbor, Mich.: Center for Japanese Studies, University of Michigan, 1979.

A bibliography that includes annotated entries on Japanese music (pp. 48–50). Reference works, dictionaries, handbooks, directories, chronologies, annuals, and books on instruments and folk music are covered.

4.322 *Nihon no Sankō Tosho / Guide to Japanese Reference Books.* 2 vols. Chicago, Ill.: American Library Association, 1966–79.

The 2nd vol. was a supplement published by the Library of Congress, Washington, D.C.

A bibliography that includes 29 annotated entries on Japanese music (pp. 49–52). Titles are given in kanji, romanized and translated. The annotations are in English. The types of reference works covered include bibliography, dictionaries, biographies, chronologies, yearbooks, illustrations, recorded music, and folk music.

4.323 Tsuge, Gen'ichi. *Japanese Music: An Annotated Bibliography.* 161 pp. New York: Garland Publishing, 1986. (Garland bibliographies in ethnomusicology, 2) (Garland reference library of the humanities, 472)

Includes publications on Japanese music in Western languages that appeared through 1983. Although its scope is limited primarily to publications dealing with traditional Japanese music, some writings concerning dance, drama, and performing arts of a ritualistic nature are included.

A collection of 881 annotated entries (from formats including scholarly books and articles) arranged in three lists: bibliographies and discographies, directories and periodicals, and books and articles on Japanese music. (The last section is by far the longest.) The index is in three sections: subject (subdivided by fields of study), names, and formats (such as collections with staff notation, dissertations, encyclopedia and dictionary entries, and iconography).

Reviewed by Ann P. Basart in *CNV* 105 (1986): 11, by George R. Hill in *ARBA* 18 (1987): no. 1222, and by H. D. Reese in *The World of Music* 29 (1987): 75–77.

Latin America

4.324 Druesedow, John. "Music . . . Bibliography." In *Latin America and the Caribbean: A Critical Guide to Research Sources,* pp. 575–88. Edited by Paula H. Covington. Westport, Conn.: Greenwood Press, 1992. (Bibliographies and indexes in Latin America and Caribbean studies, 2)

An annotated bibliography of 151 books and articles on music of all genres and styles in Latin America and the Caribbean. The first section is devoted to works covering music of the region and is arranged by type of publication (guides, bibliographies, biographies, catalogs, dictionaries and encyclopedias, dissertations, guides to archives, histories, and surveys). Subsequent entries are devoted to the same publication types, but are presented for each country, from Argentina to Venezuela. There are concluding sections on current periodicals and descriptions of distinguished special collections of musical materials in North American universities. There is an excellent introductory essay by Gérard Béhague on the history of scholarship on music from Latin America and the Caribbean.

4.325 Kuss, Marlena. "Current State of Bibliographic Research in Latin American Music." In *Fontes* 31 (1964): 206–28.

An extensive prose bibliography with bibliographical supplements, invaluable for the information conveyed.

4.326 "Music Section." In *Handbook of Latin American Studies.* Cambridge, Mass.: Harvard University Press, 1936–50; Gainesville, Fla.: University of Florida Press, 1951–78; Austin, Tex.: University of Texas Press, 1979– .

Vols. for 1936–50 reprinted by the University of Florida Press; those for 1936–94 were published on CD-ROM by the Hispanic Division of the Library of Congress.

The first issue to include a mention of music was for 1937, in which Irma Goebel Labastille published "The Music of Mexico and Central America." In 1939, William Berrien prepared the bibliography. In 1940–42, Gilbert Chase was responsible. From 1943–52, Charles Seeger prepared the section; Richard A. Waterman compiled the bibliography from 1954 to 1959, Bruno Nettl was editor 1959–63, Gilbert Chase returned to active duty from 1964 to 1968, Gérard Béhague took over from 1970 to 1974, and Robert Stevenson has been responsible since 1975.

From 1939, the *Handbook* has included a brief introductory essay and a classified bibliography of practically everything having to do with Latin American music. Includes a section for generalia and entries arranged by country or region. Anthologies are analyzed and periodical articles cited. Each volume indexes titles, subjects, and authors; lists of journals indexed are supplied. Since 1965, the *Handbook* has been divided, with social sciences being covered in odd-numbered years and the humanities in even-numbered years.

4.327 Stevenson, Robert Murrell. "The Americas in European Music Encyclopedias; Part I: England, France, Portugal." In *Inter-American Music Review* 3 (1981): 159–207.

A review of the lexicographical coverage of Latin America, including an extensive discussion of the *New Grove* (**1.48**).

Mexico

4.328 Young Osorio, Sylvana. "Guia Bibliografica." In *La Música de México 2,* Vol. 2. Mexico City: Instituto de Investigaciones Estéticas, Universidad Nacional Autónoma de México, 1984.

A bibliography of the history of music in Mexico.

New Zealand

4.329* Harvey, D. R. *A Bibliography of Writings about New Zealand Music Published to the End of 1983.* 222 pp. Wellington: Victoria University Press, 1985.

A comprehensive list of monographs, dissertations, and periodical articles on music and music-making in New Zealand, omitting newspaper articles, concert reviews, and coverage of recent popular and Maori music.

Poland

4.330 Lissa, Zofia. "Die Musikwissenschaft in Volkspolen (1945–56)." In *Die Musikforschung* 10 (1957): 531–47.

Trans. from Polish by Werner Kaupert.

A bibliographical essay, with many titles cited, discussing the state and organization of Polish musicology since World War II.

4.331* Michałowski, Kornel, and **Gillian Olechno-Huszcza.** *Polish Music Literature (1515–1990): A Selected Annotated Bibliography.* 243 pp. Los Angeles, Calif.: University of Southern California, Friends of Polish Music, 1991. (Polish music history series, 4)

Includes bibliographical references and index.

4.332 Mrygon, Adam, and **Eva Mrygon** (also known as **Adam** and **Eva Mrygoniowie).** *Bibliografia polskiego pismiennictwa muzykologicznego (1945–1970).* 208 pp. Warsaw: Panstwowe Wydawn. Naukowe, 1972.

A classified bibliography of 3,398 items, covering all aspects of Polish musicology.

4.333* Smialek, William. *Polish Music: A Research and Information Guide.* 260 pp. New York: Garland Publishing, 1989. (Music research and information guides, 12) (Garland reference library of the humanities, 1093)

A resource for all types of Polish music. There is a selective annotated bibliography of 600 items, with a discography of over 400 sound recordings (pp. 181–222), as well as a section on ethnomusicology, covering Polish folk music, jazz in Poland, and the music of ethnic Poles in North America. A subject/author index is included.

Reviewed by Cindy Bylander in *Fontes* 38 (1991): 246–47.

4.334 Strumillo, Tadeusz. *Materialy do bibliografii muzyki polskiej.* 5 vols. Cracow: Polskie Wydawn. Muzyczne, 1954–78.

A series of bibliographies on Polish music and music literature.

Vol. 1: Michałowski, Kornel. *Opery polski.* 1954, 227 pp.

Polish operas and foreign operas with Polish settings, listed by title, with composer, librettist, date, and place of first performance.

Vol. 2: Nowaczyk, Erwin. *Pieśni solowe S. Moniuszki, katalog tematyczny.* 1954, 332 pp.

A thematic catalog of 304 songs by Moniuszki, giving authors of text and lists of editions.

Vol. 3: Michałowski, Kornel. *Bibliografia polskiego pismiennictwa muzycznego.* 1955, 280 pp.

A classified bibliography of books on music in Polish and lists of theses and dissertations, 1917–54.

A supplement to Vol. 3 was published in 1964 as Vol. 4, with classified lists of new Polish books on music published between 1955 and 1963, with some addenda from earlier years. A second supplement to Vol. 3, published as Vol. 5, was published in 1978, covering the period from 1964 to 1974.

Portugal

4.335 Guimarães, Bertino Daviano Rocha da Silva. *Primeiro esboço duma bibliografia musical portuguesa, com uma breve notícia histórica da música no nosso país.* 174 pp. Porto, Portugal: 1947.

A bibliography of music-related writings by Portuguese authors, writings on music in Portugal by native or foreign authors, old Portuguese pedagogical works, special bibliographies, and music periodicals, preceded by a "breve notíce histórica."

Russia

4.336 Koltypina, Galina, and **N. G. Pavlova.** *Sovetskaia literatura o muzyke: Bibliograficheskii ukazatel knig, khurnalnykh statei i retsenzii za 1968–1970.* 2 vols. Moscow: Sovetskii Kompozitor, 1979–84.

A bibliography of Soviet music literature that includes periodical articles.

4.337 Moldon, David. *A Bibliography of Russian Composers.* 364 pp. London: White Lion Publishers, 1976.

A bibliography covering English-language books on Russian music and Russian composers. Includes indexes of authors, editors, and composers; translators and illustrators; and subjects.

4.338* Mooser, Robert-Aloys. *Annales de la musique et des musiciens en Russie au XVIIIme siècle.* 3 vols. Geneva: Mont-Blanc, 1948–50.

Contents: I, *Des origines à la mort de Pierre III (1762);* II, *L'époque glorieuse de Catherine II (1762–1796);* III, *La règne de Paul Ier (1796–1801), Appendices.*

A chronological list of the music (vocal and instrumental) and musicians in the various fields of Russian music.

The 1st vol. is reviewed by Donald Jay Grout in *Notes* 6 (1948): 158–59; Vols. 2–3 are reviewed by Judah A. Joffe in *Notes* 9 (1952): 412–14.

Serbia

4.339 Đorđević, Vladimir R. *Ogled srpske musike bibliografije do 1914. Godine / Essay on Serbian Musical Bibliography until 1914.* 281 pp. Belgrade: Nolit, 1969.

An annotated bibliography of 2,350 items in Serbo-Croatian, with separate sections for printed music, musical literature, and manuscripts. There are indexes of authors and titles, and summaries in French and English.

Slovakia

4.340 Potúček, Juraj. *Súpis slovenských hodobnín a literatúry o hudobníkoch / Catalog of Slovak Printed Music and Books on Musicians.* 435 pp. Bratislava: Nakl. Slovenská akadémie věd a umění, 1952.

A list of musicians active in Slovakia to 1949 or mentioned in Slovak periodical literature. There are bibliographies of works with Slovak texts, 1881 to 1949. There are chronological, classified, and name indexes.

4.341 Potúček, Juraj. *Súpis slovenských hodobno-teoretických prá. / Catalog of Slovak Musico-Theoretical Works.* 467 pp. Bratislava: Slovenská akadémie věd, 1955.

A multifaceted look at Slovak music, including a classified bibliography of literary and theoretical works, including periodical articles (pp. 15–216); a list of theoretical works from 1519 to 1853, in chronological order (pp. 219–25); a biographical section including, under composers' names, both publications of music and critical articles (pp. 223–380); and a classified list of music published (pp. 383–403).

4.342 Potúček, Juraj. *Výberofá bibliografia zo slovenskej hudobnovednej literatúry 1862–1962 / Selective Bibliography of Slovak Musicological Literature 1862–1962.* 116 pp. Bratislava: Slovenská akadémie věd, 1963.

Spain

4.343 *Libros de música.* 2nd ed. 327 pp. Madrid: Instituto Nacional del Libro Español, Ministerio del Cultura, 1982.

First ed., 1981, 302 pp.

The Spanish national bibliography of music, a classified bibliography of books in Spanish, including sections on pedagogy, folklore, and popular music, as well as scholarly topics. There are indexes to names, subjects, and institutions.

Sweden

4.344 Davidsson, Åke. *Bibliografi över svensk musiklitteratur 1800–1945.* 2nd ed., with updated supplement. 267 pp. Stockholm: Almqvist & Wiksell International, 1980. (Acta bibliothecae R. Universitatis Upsaliensis, 22)

First published in Uppsala, 1948, 215 pp.

A classified bibliography of 5,423 items, listing general works, general music histories, histories of music in Sweden, works on musicians of all nationalities, and theoretical works, restricted to writings by Swedish authors and subjects connected with Swedish music.

United States of America

4.345* Bonin, Jean M. *Piano-Beds and Music by Steam: An Index with Abstracts to Music-Related United States Patent Records, 1790–1874.* 236 pp. Berkeley, Calif.: Fallen Leaf Press, 1993. (Fallen Leaf reference books in music, 24)

A compilation of abstracts of U.S. music patents with almost 1,100 entries culled from the 156,000 entries in an 1874 federal publication, *Subject-Matter Index of Patents Issued by the U.S.*

Patent Office from 1790 to 1873, Inclusive. There are 1,056 utility patents, 36 design patents, and 6 trademark patents. The entries include the original specifications, a title statement, the editor's abstract of the specific contribution, the name and address of the inventor, the date of the patent award, the official patent number, and the editor's number; there are indexes by name, geographic location, and subject.

Reviewed by Cynthia Adams Hoover in the *ISAMN* 23 (Spring 1994): 11, by John E. Druesedow, Jr., in *ARBA* 25 (1994): no. 1318, and by Bart Hopkin in *Notes* 51 (1995): 936.

4.346* Feintuch, Burt. *Kentucky Folkmusic: An Annotated Bibliography.* 105 pp. Lexington, Ky.: University Press of Kentucky, 1985.

A classified bibliography of 709 books and articles on community-based musicians (excluding those connected to the mass media) through 1983. The entries are arranged in eight broad subject categories: collections and anthologies; fieldworkers, collectors, and scholars; singers, musicians, and other performers; text-centered studies; studies of history, context, and style; festivals; dance; and discographies, checklists, and other specialized reference tools), with indexes for authors, subjects, and periodicals cited.

Reviewed by Norman D. Stevens in *ARBA* 17 (1986): no. 1285.

4.347 Floyd, Samuel A., Jr., and **Marsha J. Reisser.** *Black Music in the United States: An Annotated Bibliography of Selected Reference and Research Materials.* 234 pp. Millwood, N.Y.: Kraus International Publications, 1983.

A bibliography written to provide guidance, stimulate additional research, and promote Black music scholarship. This reference survey and its appendix cite 411 bibliographies and indexes, catalogs, discographies, biographical dictionaries, and anthologies, all on Black music, with extensive annotations and review sources. Also included are a directory, with access information, of archives holding material relevant to the subject, and indexes to personal names, titles (in English), and subjects.

Reviewed by Dominique-René de Lerma in *ARBA* 15 (1984): no. 883, by Eileen Southern in *BPM* 12 (1984): 137–39, and by D. Antoinette Handy in *AM* 4 (1986): 357–58.

4.348* Fry, Stephen M. *California's Musical Wealth: Sources for the Study of Music in California.* 130 pp. Santa Barbara, Calif.: The Southern California Chapter, Music Library Association, 1988.

A collection of papers on access to research areas in the history of music in California, given at a joint meeting of the Northern and Southern California Chapters of the Music Library Association in 1985.

Reviewed by David Dodd in *Notes* 48 (1991): 120–21.

4.349 Heard, Priscilla S. *American Music, 1698–1800: An Annotated Bibliography.* 246 pp. Waco, Tex.: Baylor University Press, Markham Press Fund, 1981.

A bibliography that includes all entries pertaining to music from the *American Bibliography* by Evans and Shipton, and the supplement by the American Antiquarian Society, which covers the addenda of Bristol. The list is arranged by imprint date and the coverage includes works about music as well as printed music. There is a related work, concentrating on the printed music in Evans, by Donald L. Hixon (**5.135**).

4.350 Heintze, James R. *American Music Studies: A Classified Bibliography of Master's Theses.* xxvi + 311 pp. Detroit, Mich.: Information Coordinators; Published for the College Music Society, 1984. (Bibliographies in American music, 8)

A list of 2,370 theses on music and related areas, a complement to Mead's bibliography (**4.356**). There are indexes to authors, places, and subjects.

Reviewed by Ann P. Basart in *Notes* 42 (1986): 553–54 and by George Louis Mayer in *ARBA* 16 (1985): no. 1158.

4.351* Heintze, James R. *Early American Music: A Research and Information Guide.* 511 pp. New York: Garland Publishing, 1990. (Music research and information guides, 13) (Garland reference library of the humanities, 1007)

Annotations for books, articles, dissertations, papers, published sermons and discourses, catalogs, lists, directories, and other materials, 1,957 entries in all, arranged in broad classifications. Master's theses are omitted, included instead in Heintze's *American Music Studies: A Classified Bibliography of Master's Theses* (**4.350**). There are author/title and subject indexes.

Reviewed by John Druesedow in *Notes* 47 (1990): 383–84, by Karl Kroeger in *Fontes* 38 (1991): 148–49, and by Carol J. Oja in *M&L* 73 (1992): 597–98.

4.352 Horn, David. *The Literature of American Music in Books and Folk Music Collections: A Fully Annotated Bibliography.* 556 pp. Metuchen, N.J.: Scarecrow Press, 1977.

First published as *The Literature of American Music: A Fully Annotated Catalogue of the Books and Song Collections in Exeter University Library* (Exeter, 1972), 172 pp. With the collaboration of Richard Jackson, a supplement to the 1977 ed. was published in 1988 by Scarecrow Press, Metuchen, N.J. (570 pp.).

A classified and chronologically arranged work, organized on historical and cultural bases, giving detailed descriptions and informed evaluations of almost 1,400 titles published through the mid-1970s. The 1st vol. has an index to names and titles, and an unannotated appendix of 302 works discovered while the book was in preparation. The *Supplement* includes books published through 1980, as well as some titles omitted from the earlier volume; there are 996 annotated titles and 323 unannotated ones. Most of the entries in both volumes describe folk and popular music; omitted are entries for magazine and journal articles, fiction, dissertations, popular song collections, art music scores, general reference works, and standard music reference works.

The 1st vol. is reviewed by Dan Morgenstern in the *Journal of Jazz Studies* 5 (1979): 93–95, by Eileen Southern in *BPM* 6 (1978): 94–96, by Irving Lowens in *Fontes* 25 (1978): 112–13, and by Stephen M. Fry in *Notes* 34 (1977): 89–90; the *Supplement* is reviewed by Ann P. Basart in *CNV* no. 126 (1986): 19 and by John Druesedow in *Notes* 47 (1990): 383–84.

4.353 Johnson, H. Earle. *First Performances in America to 1900: Works with Orchestra.* 446 pp. Detroit, Mich.: Published for the College Music Society by Information Coordinators, 1979. (Bibliographies in American music, 4)

A sourcebook for statistics and information on first American performances of orchestral music. The 1,140 musical works by 200+ composers are arranged in alphabetical order by composer, giving title and date of first performance in major American cities. Choral performances with orchestra as well as some chamber music performances are included. The annotations often are derived from contemporary reviews.

Reviewed by Mary Jane Corry in *Notes* 36 (1980): 653–54, by Marilyn Strong-Norosha in *ARBA* 11 (1980): no. 942, and by Himie Voxman in *Fontes* 27 (1980): 56–57.

4.354 Krummel, Donald W. *Bibliographical Handbook of American Music.* 269 pp. Urbana, Ill.: University of Illinois Press, 1987. (Music in American life)

An overview of 750+ reference sources on the subject of American music, broadly defined, organized in four major sections: chronological perspectives, contextual perspectives, musical mediums and genres, and bibliographical forms. Each chapter and most sections begin with introductory remarks and follow with citations, often in a classified array, then in chronological order. There is much statistical information, demonstrating the author's thorough familiarity with the titles cited. Name and subject indexes conclude the volume.

Reviewed by Ann P. Basart in *CNV* 126 (1988): 19–20 and in *Notes* 45 (1989): 507–8, by William Brockman in *ARBA* 20 (1989): no. 1171, by Richard Crawford in *Ethnomusicology* 33 (1989): 324–25, and by David Nicholls in *M&L* 70 (1989): 121.

4.355 Krummel, D. W., Jean Geil, Doris J. Dyen, and **Deane L. Root.** *Resources of American Music History: A Directory of Source Materials from Colonial Times to World War II.* 463 pp. Urbana, Ill.: University of Illinois, 1981. (Music in American life)

A geographically organized list of source materials, including printed and manuscript music, programs and catalogs, institutional and personal papers, pictures, and sound recordings, indispensable for the study of American music. It emphasizes collections in the United States in both public institutions and in private hands, as well as a few important ones in other countries. The inventories give the size and profile of the individual collections, with the more specialized holdings described in considerable detail. This was an American Bicentennial project, with hundreds of local correspondents. Includes a bibliography of reference works and a detailed index to names, titles, and subjects.

D. W. Krummel's "Little RAMH, Who Made Thee?," in *Notes* 37 (1980): 227–38, explains its genesis.

Reviewed by Thomas F. Heck in *Fontes* 29 (1982): 198–99, by Charles Hamm in *AM* 3 (1985): 232–35, by George R. Hill in *ARBA* 13 (1982): no. 1027, by H. Wiley Hitchcock in *ISAMN* 10 (1981): 15 no. 2, and by Richard Jackson in *Notes* 38 (1982): 595–96.

4.356 Mead, Rita H. *Doctoral Dissertations in American Music: A Classified Bibliography.* 155 pp. Brooklyn, N.Y.: Institute for Studies in American Music, Brooklyn College, CUNY, 1974. (I.S.A.M. monographs, 3)

A classified bibliography of 1,226 entries covering dissertations on American music, but in many cases written within disciplines other than music (such as sociology, theater, anthropology, history, American studies, theology, literature, and education). The entries include the University Microfilm and Library of Congress microfilm numbers, as well as references to *Dissertation Abstracts.* There are author and subject indexes.

Reviewed by Geoffrey C. Weston in *Notes* 32 (1976): 548.

4.357* Miller, Terry E. *Folk Music in America: A Reference Guide.* New York: Garland Publishing, 1986. (Garland reference library of the humanities, 496) (Music research and information guides, 6)

A selective, annotated, classified bibliography with nearly 2,000 entries, covering the range of print material: books, dissertations, *Festschriften.* and scholarly journal articles, among others, generally dating from the 20th century. The *Guide* is divided into nine topical sections The sparse indexing gives limited access.

Reviewed by Jennifer C. Post in *Ethnomusicology* 31 (1987): 452–53 and by Doris Evans McGinty in *BPM* 15 (1987): 233–34.

4.358 Skowronski, JoAnn. *Black Music in America: A Bibliography.* 723 pp. Metuchen, N.J.: Scarecrow Press, 1981.

A list of books and articles about Black music and musicians in the United States from colonial times through 1979, in three sections. The first, on selected musicians and singers, lists 97 names and writings about them; the second has 2,145 citations for books and articles on Black music, grouped according to publication date; the third has citations for 93 reference works in a variety of formats (dictionaries, encyclopedias, discographies, catalogs, etc.), arranged chronologically by date of publication.

Reviewed by Deane Root in *Notes* 38 (1982): 832–36, by Edward Berlett in *ARBA* 14 (1983): no. 924, and by Samuel A. Floyd, Jr., in *AM* 3 (1985): 102–3.

4.359* Spencer, Jon Michael. *As the Black School Sings: Black Music Collections at Black Universities and Colleges, with a Union List of Book Holdings.* 185 pp. New York: Greenwood Press, 1987. (Music reference collection, 13)

The results of a survey of the music collections of 17 historically Black American colleges and universities, carefully indexed.

Reviewed by Dominique-René de Lerma in *ARBA* 19 (1988): no. 1274 and by Dena J. Epstein in *Notes* 45 (1988): 66–68.

4.360 Stoneburner, Bryan C. *Hawaiian Music: An Annotated Bibliography.* 100 pp. New York: Greenwood Press, 1986. (Music reference collection, 10)

A list of 564 historical and critical writings on Hawaiian music, musicians, and musical life from 1831 to 1980, limited to sources in English, German, French, and Spanish. The arrangement is by author. There is a glossary of Hawaiian terms and locations are given for the periodicals cited. There is a subject index.

Reviewed by Amy K. Stillman in *SSB* 3 (1987): 75–76, by Ann P. Basart in *CNV* 109 (1987): 4, and by Elizabeth Tatar in *Ethnomusicology* 33 (1989): 342–43.

4.361* Thompson, Donald, and **Annie F. Thompson.** *Music and Dance in Puerto Rico from the Age of Columbus to Modern Times: An Annotated Bibliography.* 339 pp. Metuchen, N.J.: Scarecrow Press, 1991. (Studies in Latin American music, 1)

Annie Thompson earlier compiled *An Annotated Bibliography of Writings about Music in Puerto Rico* (Ann Arbor, Mich.: Music Library Association, 1974, 34 pp.) (MLA index and bibliography series, 12), which is superseded by the new title.

An annotated bibliography of 995 books and periodicals, the first in a series intended to expand the range of scholarly resources available in English for the study of Latin American music. It provides a bibliographic basis for a broader comprehensive history of Puerto Rican performance.

Reviewed by Catherine Dower in *LAMR* 13 (1992): 247–50 and by Dena J. Epstein in *Fontes* 41 (1994): 303.

4.362 Warner, Thomas E. *Periodical Literature on American Music, 1620–1920: A Classified Bibliography with Annotations.* xli + 644 pp. Warren, Mich.: Harmonie Park Press, for the College Music Society, 1988. (Bibliographies in American music, 12)

A classified bibliography of 5,348 entries, compiled from over 600 periodicals, both musical and nonmusical. There is no coverage of folk or Native American music. There are author and subject indexes.

Reviewed by John Druesedow in *Notes* 47 (1990): 383–84 and by Linda Pohly in *Fontes* 37 (1990): 72–73.

Yugoslavia (including Bosnia/Herzegovina, Croatia, and Slovenia)

4.363 Pruett, Lilian. "Music Research in Yugoslavia." In *Notes* 36 (1980): 23–49.

A knowledgeable view of resources available to scholars before the disruptions of the early 1990s.

OPERA AND THEATER MUSIC

4.364 Bustico, Guido. *Bibliografia della storia e cronistorie dei teatri italiani: Il Teatro musicale italiano.* 83 pp. Milan: Bollettino Bibliografici Musicale, 1929.

First published in Rome by the Fondazione Leonardo per la Cultura Italiana in 1924 (Guide bibliografiche, 22).

A two-part bibliography, including periodical articles, with occasional brief annotations. The first part is a general bibliography of Italian musical theater (pp. 19–27); the second is a bibliography of musical theater in specific Italian cities, arranged alphabetically by place.

4.365 Cohen, H. Robert, and **Marie-Odile Gigou.** *Cent ans de mise en scène lyrique en France (env. 1830–1930): Catalogue descriptif des livrets de mise en scène, des libretti annotés et des partitions annotées dans la Bibliothèque de l'Association de la Régie Théâtrale (Paris) / One Hundred*

Years of Operatic Staging in France. lviii + 334 pp. New York: Pendragon Press, 1986. (Musical life in 19th-century France / La vie musicale en France au XIX siècle, 2)

A catalog of documents in the Bibliothèque de l'Association (the central depository for staging manuals), intended to provide a base on which later investigations of other collections can build. The catalog, arranged by title of staged work, supplies the names of the composer and librettist, the dates of the work's premiere, and a description of the livret de mise en scène. There are indexes to composers, librettists, and other names, and to theaters by country and city.

4.366 Fuld, James J. *The Book of World-Famous Libretti: The Musical Theater from 1598 to Today.* Rev. ed. xxxvii + 363 pp. New York: Pendragon Press, 1994.

First ed., 1984. xxxviii + 365 pp.

A collection of extensive descriptions of the original libretti of 168 operas and other works for the musical theater, included either for their importance in the current international repertoire or for their historical stature. The works are arranged by title in alphabetical order in their original language; each entry includes a facsimile of the original libretto's title page and library location. Appendixes include librettist, composer, and chronological arrangements of the works under examination.

The 1st ed. is reviewed by Marita McClymonds in *Fontes* 32 (1985): 140–41.

4.367* Giovine, Alfredo. *Bibliografia di teatri musicali italiani (storia e cronologie).* 67 pp. Bari, Italy: Edizioni Fratelli Laterza, 1982. (Biblioteca dell'Archivio delle tradizioni poplari baresi)

A bibliography of histories and chronologies of Italian theaters used for staged musical events, including opera.

4.368 Grout, Donald Jay, and **Hermine Weigel Williams.** "Bibliographies, Lexicons, Guides, Histories, and Other Works Dealing with Opera." In their *A Short History of Opera,* 3rd ed., pp. 731–825. New York: Columbia University Press, 1988.

An earlier version of this bibliography appeared in the 2nd ed. (pp. 585–768), 1965.

One of the most comprehensive bibliographies of literature on opera, including books and articles in leading European and American periodicals, arranged alphabetically by author.

4.369 Marco, Guy A. *Opera: A Research and Information Guide.* 373 pp. New York: Garland Publishing, 1984. (Garland reference library of the humanities, 468)

A classified annotated bibliography, with extensive editorial opinion, listing 704 core titles on opera. Works about operetta and Singspiel are included selectively; works on the American musical theater are omitted. All items included are in western European languages. This guide is especially good for studies of individual operas and opera in specific countries and regions. Bibliographies of individuals are excluded, but a checklist of opera composers and 1,051 of their major works is included as an appendix. There are substantial author/title and subject indexes.

Reviewed by George Jellinek in *OQ* 3 (1985–86): 144–46 no. 4, by George Louis Mayer in *ARBA* 16 (1985): no. 1201, and by Valencia Williams in *LJ* 110 (1985): 87.

4.370 Osthoff, Wolfgang, Herbert Schneider, and **Hellmuth Christian Wolff.** *Quellentexte zur Konzeption der europäischen Oper im 17. Jahrhundert.* 200 pp. Basel; Kassel, Germany; London: Bärenreiter, 1981. (Musikwissenschaftliche Arbeiten, 27)

Source documents on the first century of opera, with text in French, German, and Italian.

4.371* Sampson, Henry T. *Blacks in Blackface: A Source Book on Early Black Musical Shows.* 552 pp. Metuchen, N.J.: Scarecrow Press, 1980.

A guide that includes synopses of Black musicals and biographies of musicians, with supporting essays.

4.372 Sartori, Claudio. *I libretti italiani a stampa dalle origini al 1800: Catalogo analitico con 16 indici.* 6 vols. in 7. Cuneo, Italy: Bertola & Locatelli, 1990–94.

Supersedes his photocopied *Primo tenativo di catalogo unico dei libretti italiani* (Milan: Biblioteca Nazionale Braidense & Ufficio Ricerca Fondi Musicali, 1973–81), issued in unnumbered leaves.

This catalog is intended to be as complete a list as possible of Italian and Latin texts for music and any translation published through 1800. Handwritten librettos have been omitted.

Some 25,000 texts for operas, serenades, cantatas, prologues, choral works, intermezzi, dances, oratorios, and other forms of literary works with incidental musical settings or musical works with incidental texts set to music, arranged alphabetically. Complete title page transcriptions with annotations and locations of extant copies are given, as well as citations of corresponding musical scores, with cross-references from alternative titles. The 16 indexes include places of performance; authors of text; composers; impresarios; designers, architects, and painters; choreographers; costume makers; sword masters; scene shifters and property and stage managers; orchestra conductors; harpsichordists; violinists; other musicians; singers; teachers; and dancers. There are lists of bibliographical references, principal abbreviations, and *RISM* sigla (corresponding to those found in the last volume of *RISM* A).

Reviewed by Eleanor Selfridge-Field in *Notes* 51 (1994): 575–78.

4.373 Senelick, Laurence, David F. Cheshire, and **Ulrich Schneider.** *British Music-Hall, 1840–1923: A Bibliography and Guide to Sources, with a Supplement on European Music-Hall.* 361 pp. Hamden, Conn.: Archon Books, 1981. (Archon books on popular entertainments)

A bibliography of 3,863 items in 12 parts, including a directory of collections in Ireland, the United Kingdom, and the United States, with entries describing resources available on the subject and a bibliography of reference works. The subject areas covered include periodicals with news and information on music halls and the entertainment presented; general studies on the music hall, including picture books and memoirs; the architecture of music halls; legislation and regulations affecting music halls and their entertainments, including morality and censorship; performances by genre; individual performers; performance materials (joke books, song books, etc.); a selective list of literary and artistic works in which music halls or their entertainments are themes or prominent locations; and a discography of music hall entertainment on LP. Supplements present bibliographies on selected entertainments and music halls in European (East and West), Russian, African, and Asian locations. There are addenda, an index of authors, and a cross-index of London music halls.

4.374 Surian, Elvidio. *A Checklist of Writings on 18th-Century French and Italian Opera (Excluding Mozart).* 121 pp. Hackensack, N.J.: Joseph Boonin, 1970. (Music indexes and bibliographies, 3)

A list of 1,501 citations in 10 classifications on the subject, including librettists and theatrical production and excluding Mozart, Singspiel, ballad opera, and Russian opera.

4.375 Wildbihler, Hubert, and **Sonja Volklein.** *The Musical: An International Annotated Bibliography: Eine internationale annotierte Bibliographie.* xxiv + 320 pp. Munich; New York: K.G. Saur, 1986.

An overview of the entire theoretical literature on the stage and film musical from its beginnings to 1986, consisting of 3,629 entries arranged in a classified order. Included are sections on general references, predecessors, history and development, production, musicals and the public, musicals outside North America, the film musical, and people associated with musicals, with annotations only for the most important works. Excluded are citations for libretti, scores, and reviews of performances. Includes lists of sources and periodicals consulted and an author and subject index.

PRIMARY SOURCES: EARLY MUSIC LITERATURE

The entries in this section are concerned with writings on music that appeared before 1800. For further listings of early music literature, consult the general bibliographies compiled before 1840, such as Becker (**4.5**), Forkel (**4.25**), and Lichtenthal (**1.313**). See also the narrative bibliography by James E. Matthew (**4.37**) and the catalogs of libraries with noteworthy holdings in early music theory, such as the U.S. Library of Congress (**7.577**), the collection of Alfred Cortot (**7.620**), and the Paul Hirsch Library in the British Library (**7.259**). The *RISM* volume *Écrits imprimés concernant la musique* (**4.381**) is the international union catalog covering early separate publications on music.

4.376 Adler, Israel. *Hebrew Writings Concerning Music, in Manuscripts and Printed Books from Geonic Times up to 1800.* 389 pp. Munich: G. Henle Verlag, 1975. (Répertoire international des sources musicales, B IX, 2)

A bibliography supplying the actual texts of 66 Hebrew writings concerning music, dating from the 12th to the 16th centuries, as well as a catalog of these sources. English summaries of all texts are given. The entries for the 276 manuscripts and 384 books are arranged alphabetically by author. There are indexes of quotations and reference works citing both Hebrew and Arabic titles, a bibliography, and a general name, title, and subject index, approachable through Hebrew and English.

Reviewed by Michael Ochs in *Notes* 33 (1976): 56–57, by Joseph Smits van Waesberghe in *Fontes* 24 (1977): 53, and by Eric Werner in *JAMS* 30 (1970): 529–31.

4.377 Coover, James B. "Music Theory in Translation: A Bibliography." In *JMT* 3 (1959): 70–96 and 13 (1969): 230–49.

A list of English translations of early theory works, arranged alphabetically, by author, with titles ranging in time from antiquity to the present day.

4.378 Davidsson, Åke. *Bibliographie der musiktheorietischen Drucke des 16. Jahrhunderts.* 99 pp. + 25 facsimile plates. Baden-Baden: Heitz, 1962. (Bibliotheca bibliographica aureliana, 9)

A bibliography of 16th-century theory works, more than 600 titles, arranged alphabetically by author, with bibliographical reference to literature on the sources. Includes an index of persons (printers, editors, etc.) and a bibliography (pp. 85–88).

4.379 Davidsson, Åke. *Catalogue critique et descriptif des ouvrages théoriques sur la musique imprimés au XVIe et XVIIe siècles et conservés dans les bibliothèques suédoises.* 83 pp. Uppsala: Almqvist & Wiksell, 1953 (Studia musicologica upsaliensia, 2)

A union catalog of early works on music theory in Swedish libraries. The 108 works are fully described, with locations and references to relevant literature. There is a bibliography of works cited (pp. 77–83).

Reviewed by Catherine Brooks in *Notes* 11 (1954): 476–77.

4.380 Farmer, Henry George. *The Sources of Arabian Music: An Annotated Bibliography of Arabic Manuscripts Which Deal with the Theory, Practice, and History of Arabian Music from the Eighth to the Seventeenth Century.* 71 pp. Leiden, The Netherlands: E. J. Brill, 1965.

First published in Bearsden, Scotland, issued privately by the author in 1940 as a reprint from the *Records of the Glasgow Bibliographical Society,* Vol. 13 (97 pp.).

Entries arranged chronologically by century, preceded by a brief general discussion of Arabian music and its sources.

4.381 Lesure, François. *Écrits imprimés concernant la musique.* 2 vols. 1,069 pp. Munich: G. Henle, 1971. (Répertoire international des sources musicales, B VI)

A comprehensive bibliography of writings on music printed before 1800, comprising all theoretical, historical, aesthetic, or technical literature. Location symbols identify copies held in European and American libraries. Includes a brief introduction, a list of the institutions contributing information on their holdings, an index of printers, and a chronological index. Anonymous works are listed by title in a separate section and there is an addendum. For supplementary information, see Lesure's "*Écrits imprimés concernant la musique*; addenda et corrigenda," in *Fontes* 26 (1979): 1–4.

4.382 Mandyczewski, Eusebius. "Bücher und Schriften über Musik. Druckwerke und Handschriften aus der Zeit bis zum Jahre 1800." In *Geschichte der K.K. Gesellschaft der Musikfreunde in Wien,* pp. 55–84. Vienna: Druck von A. Holzhausen, 1912.

An extremely useful list of the pre-1800 writings on music in the library of the Gesellschaft der Musikfreunde in Vienna.

4.383* Mathiesen, Thomas J. *Ancient Greek Music Theory: A Catalogue Raisonné of Manuscripts.* xc + 828 pp. Munich: G. Henle, 1988. (Répertoire international des sources musicales, B XI)

A list of 299 sources dealing specifically with music and omitting Byzantine sources unless they preserve the Greek philosophical doctrine and appear with the ancient treatises.

Reviewed by Oliver B. Ellsworth in *Notes* 48 (1991): 468–71.

4.384 Reese, Gustave. *Fourscore Classics of Music Literature: A Guide to Selected Original Sources on Theory and Other Writings on Music Not Available in English, with Descriptive Sketches and Bibliographical References.* 91 pp. New York: Liberal Arts Press, 1957.

Reprinted by Da Capo Press, New York, in 1970.

A list of 80 works, in chronological order, with illuminating commentary. This bibliography, sponsored by the American Council of Learned Societies, was intended to stimulate new English editions and translations of important early theory works. There is a title index.

Reviewed by Glen Haydon in *Notes* 15 (1958): 392–93.

4.385 Shiloah, Amnon. *The Theory of Music in Arabic Writings (c. 900–1900): Descriptive Catalogue of Manuscripts in Libraries of Europe and the U.S.A.* xxviii + 512 pp. Munich: G. Henle, 1979. (Répertoire international des sources musicales, B X)

Preceded by a historical introduction and classification of the manuscripts, 341 sources arranged by author, analyzed, and described, with text in English or Arabic. Each entry includes an incipit, an explicit, and bibliographical references. Includes a bibliography of library catalogs, a general bibliography, and an Arabic bibliography, as well as a general index to names, titles, terms, and subjects.

Reviewed by Charles Burnett in *Early Music History* 1 (1981): 378–81.

4.386 Smits van Waesberghe, Joseph, Peter Fischer, and **Christian Haas.** *The Theory of Music from the Carolingian Era up to 1400: Descriptive Catalogue of Manuscripts.* 4 vols. to date. Munich: G. Henle, 1961– . (Répertoire international des sources musicales, B III, 1–4)

Contents: Vol. 1, *Austria, Belgium, Switzerland, Denmark, France, Luxembourg, and the Netherlands,* 1961, 155 pp. Vol. 2, *Italy,* edited by Peter Fischer, 1968, 148 pp. Vol. 3, *Manuscripts from the Carolingian Era up to c. 1500 in the Federal Republic of Germany,* edited by Michel Huglo and Christian Meyer, 1986, xxx + 232 pp. Vol. 4, *Manuscripts from the Carolingian Era up to c. 1500 in Great Britain and in the United States,* edited by Christian Meyer, Michel Huglo, and Nancy C. Phillips, 1992, 211 pp.

A description of all manuscripts in which are preserved Latin treatises dealing with the theory of music in use from the Carolingian era to 1400. The ultimate list of theoretical texts on music. Each volume includes an index of libraries and an index of authors and of incipits of anonymous treatises. The initial criteria were relaxed to include manuscripts dating from the 15th and even the 16th century when these are sole surviving sources of the earlier tradition.

The 1st vol. is reviewed by James B. Coover in *JMT* 6 (1962): 314–15. The 3rd vol. is reviewed by Lawrence Gushee in *Notes* 45 (1988): 282–83.

4.387* *Thesaurus Musicarum Latinarum: TML: Canon of Data Files, Including General Information on the Thesaurus Musicarum Latinarum, the TML Introduction, the Principles of Orthography, and the Tables of Codes.* 6th ed. xxvi + 229 pp. Bloomington, Ind.: Thesaurus Musicarum Latinarum, School of Music, Indiana University, 1995.

The account of an evolving database (**12.38**), directed by Thomas J. Mathiesen, that will eventually contain the entire corpus of Latin music theory written during the Middle Ages and early Renaissance, updated as needed to list the texts currently available as data files through TML.

4.388 Vivell, Cölestin. *Initia tractatuum musices ex codicibus editorum; collegit et ordine alphabetico disposuit.* 352 pp. Graz, Austria: J. Meyerhoff, 1912.

Reprinted by Minkoff in Geneva, 1979.

An index to the first lines of each chapter in each treatise in Martin Gerbert's *Scriptores ecclesiastici de musica sacra* (**2.99**) and in Edmond Coussemaker's *Scriptorum de musica medii aevi* (**2.95**) and to musical treatises in 11 other 19th-century collections. Included are analytical indexes to sources indexed, an index to authors of treatises (and to titles of anonymous treatises), and a chronological index to treatises.

SACRED MUSIC

Bibliographies of writings on sacred music are surprisingly few. Additional references can be found in the various handbooks to hymnology (**1.617–1.647**) and in the current listings in the *Jahrbuch für Liturgik und Hymnologie* (**4.56**) and Grégorio Suñol's bibliography of works related to Gregorian chant (**4.204**). Kenneth Hartley's *Bibliography of Theses and Dissertations in Sacred Music* (**4.391**) provides information on academic works to the mid-1960s, with extensive bibliographies.

4.389* Gambassi, Osvaldo. *La Cappella musicale di S. Petronio: Maestri, organisti, cantori e strumentisti dal 1436 al 1920.* 512 pp. Florence: L.S. Olschki, 1987. (Programma di studi e ricerche sulla cultura e la vita civile del Settecento in Emilia-Romagna promosso dalla Regione. Settore musica e teatro, 2) ("Historiae musicae cultores" biblioteca, 44)

A documentary history of the Capella Musicale di S. Petronio in Bologna, from the surviving church records.

Reviewed by Anne Schnoebelen in *M&L* 69 (1988): 369–71.

4.390* Harper, John. *The Forms and Orders of Western Liturgy from the Tenth to the Eighteenth Century: A Historical Introduction and Guide for Students and Musicians.* 337 pp. Oxford: Clarendon Press, 1991.

A concise, well-organized guide to the liturgy of the Western Christian Church, both pre- and post-Reformation, and to the liturgical use made of specific surviving sources, predominantly English in origin. Appendixes include tables showing the important features of the liturgical calendar, Psalter organization and use, frequently used choral texts in Latin and English, a select bibliography, and a glossary of ecclesiastical and liturgical terms.

Reviewed by David Hiley in *Notes* 49 (1993): 1423–29.

4.391 Hartley, Kenneth R. *Bibliography of Theses and Dissertations in Sacred Music.* 127 pp. Detroit, Mich.: Information Coordinators, 1967. (Detroit studies in music bibliography, 9)

An earlier ed. was published by the New Orleans Baptist Theological Seminary in 1963.

Entries covering 20th-century American master's theses and Ph.D. dissertations to the mid-1960s, arranged by degree-granting institutions and then alphabetically by author, with author and subject indexes.

4.392 Jackson, Irene V. *Afro-American Religious Music: A Bibliography and Catalogue of Gospel Music.* 210 pp. Westport, Conn.: Greenwood Press, 1979.

A bibliography of 873 books, essays, magazine and newspaper articles, and dissertations covering "music of the established Black churches or denominations in the United States and the Caribbean as well as Afro-American cults in the Caribbean and South America." Religious music indigenous to West Africa is covered as well. There is a subject index. The catalog of gospel music is arranged by composer and covers music by African Americans written 1938–65; it is based on the collections and catalogs of the Library of Congress.

Reviewed in the *Journal of Negro History* 65 (1980): 89–90, by Dominique-René de Lerma in *ARBA* 11 (1980): no. 947, and by Portia K. Maultsby in *Ethnomusicology* 25 (1981): 147–48.

4.393 Lütolf, Max. *Analecta Hymnica Medii Aevi: Register.* Edited in cooperation with Dorothea Baumann, Ernst Meier, Markus Römer, and Andreas Wernli. 2 vols. in 3. Bern; Munich: Franke Verlag, 1978. (Musikwissenchaftliches Seminar der Universität Zürich, 1)

An index to the massive *Analecta Hymnica Medii Aevi* by G. M. Dreves, Clemens Blume, and H. M. Bannister, organized in four sections: incipits, literary genres, liturgical feasts, and authors (presumed or attributed).

Reviewed by Marie-Noëlle Colette in *Fontes* 26 (1979): 246–47 and by James W. McKinnon in *Notes* 36 (1979): 378–79.

4.394 Powell, Martha C., and **Deborah C. Loftis.** *A Selected Bibliography of Church Music and Music Reference Materials.* 95 pp. Louisville, Ky.: Southern Baptist Theological Seminary, 1977.

A supplement, 10 pp., is bound in at the end.

A list of writings on the church music of American Protestant denominations. The bibliographic entries are annotated, giving the contents and the work's use.

Reviewed by Stephen M. Fry in *Notes* 35 (1978): 94–95.

4.395 Szövérffy, Joseph, and **Eva C. Topping.** *A Guide to Byzantine Hymnography: A Classified Bibliography of Texts and Studies.* 2 vols. to date. Brookline, Mass.: Classical Folia Editions; Leyden: E. J. Brill, 1979– . (Medieval classicals: texts and studies, 11–12)

A classified analytical guide to over 6,000 entries and 2,000 separate titles, the latter cited in both Roman and Cyrillic characters. An announced 3rd vol., which will complete the bibliography and index the whole project, has yet to be published.

4.396 Von Ende, Richard C. *Church Music: An International Bibliography.* 453 pp. Metuchen, N.J.: Scarecrow Press, 1980.

A classified list, international in scope, of 5,445 works focused almost entirely on works about Christian church music. Some anthologies of music are cited. There is an index to authors, editors, and compilers.

Reviewed by Richard French in *Notes* 37 (1981): 590–91.

4.397 Yeats-Edwards, Paul. *English Church Music: A Bibliography.* 217 pp. London; New York: White Lion, 1975.

A selective bibliography of books, pamphlets, and tracts published in England on English church music, listed under subject headings. There is a general index to the 1,220 entries.

Reviewed by Peter Le Huray in *M&L* 57 (1976): 418–19, with errata, and by Alan Pope in *Brio* 13 (1976): 25.

WOMEN

4.398 Block, Adrienne Fried, and **Carol Neuls-Bates.** *Women in American Music: A Bibliography of Music and Literature.* xxvii + 302 pp. Westport, Conn.: Greenwood Press, 1979.

A classified, thoroughly annotated and indexed collection of over 5,000 bibliographic citations organized with abstracts on the *RILM* model (**4.90**), with an author/subject index to the literature and a composer/author index to music. The music entries have timings and performance data supplied and were selected for their current value as performance pieces. The coverage is comprehensive for art music and for popular music through 1920. Includes a helpful historical introduction and an index to recordings.

Reviewed by Carolyn Raney in *AM* 1 (1983): 80–83, by Dominique-René de Lerma in *ARBA* 11 (1980): no. 946, by Rita H. Mead in *Notes* 36 (1980): 642–44, by Léonie Rosenstiel in *CM* 31 (1981): 71–74, and by Doris E. McGinty in *BPM* 8 (1980): 256–59.

4.399 Skowronski, JoAnn. *Women in American Music: A Bibliography.* 183 pp. Metuchen, N.J.: Scarecrow Press, 1978.

A partially annotated list of books, periodicals, and articles, arranged in four sections covering periods of American history, beginning with the American Revolution, and containing two genre bibliographies: general history and reference works. There is a name index.

Reviewed by Carol Neuls-Bates in *Notes* 35 (1979): 635–36.

❦ 5 ❦

BIBLIOGRAPHIES OF MUSIC

In this chapter are bibliographies of musical scores rather than lists of writings about music. There are fewer basic subdivisions than in Chapter 4, with the major approaches being for the performer or researcher in search of music appropriate to a particular instrument or ensemble combination, and, on the other hand, for the student of early music. There are also substantial music bibliographies listed in other chapters of this book. Many bibliographies and thematic catalogs covering the works of individual composers are included in Chapter 6. The two significant online catalogs are in Chapter 12 (**12.5** and **12.6**). Also omitted are the catalogs of individual music publishing firms, except where their coverage extends beyond the output of a single business house, such as Hofmeister (**4.54**) or Pazdirek (**5.11**). Bibliographies of the work of early music publishers are in Chapter 9.

GENERAL WORKS

5.1* Arnold, Ben. *Music and War: A Research and Information Guide.* xxvi + 431 pp. New York: Garland Publishing, 1992. (Garland reference library of the humanities, 1581) (Music research and information guides, 17)

A selective bibliography of war-related music, chronologically arranged by subject covered, with bibliographical references (pp. 363–80) and indexes.

Reviewed by Scott Messing in *Notes* 51 (1994): 574–75.

5.2 Aronowsky, Solomon. *Performing Times of Orchestral Works.* xxix + 802 pp. London: E. Benn, 1959.

A work covering both standard and minor composers of all countries and periods, with some emphasis on British names. Arrangements are listed under both the composer and the arranger. Works others than the purely orchestral (operas, orchestral versions of solo songs, and opera excerpts, for example) appear frequently. No precise indication of edition or publisher is given, but there are lists of publishers and publishers' organizations. Other bibliographies of orchestral music (**5.132** and **5.268**) include timings as but a part of information offered. The format of Reddick's *The Standard Musical Repertoire, with Accurate Timings* (**5.10**) is much more compact.

Reviewed by Howard Mitchell in *Notes* 17 (1960): 237–39.

5.3 *Bonner Katalog: Verzeichnis reversgebundener musikalischer Aufführungsmateriale.* Edited by the Deutsche Musikarchiv of the Deutsche Bibliothek with the Deutsche Musikverleger-Verband. 2nd revised ed. 530 pp. Munich; New York: K.G. Saur, 1982.

First published in Bonn by Musikhandel-Verlagsgesellschaft, 1959 (326 pp.).

Not a catalog of German music, strictly speaking, but a list by composer of musical works marketed in Germany and protected by international copyright under the Bern Convention. Copyright editions of works by early composers are included. The types of works are indicated by symbols, and durations and publishers are given. This is an excellent source of information on published contemporary art music. There are entries under authors of texts, editors, arrangers, and translators.

Reviewed by Allie Wise Goudy in *ARBA* 14 (1983): no. 919.

5.4 Cudworth, Charles. "Ye Olde Spuriosity Shoppe, or, Put It in the Anhang." In *Notes* 12 (1954–55): 25–40, 533–53.

A lively discussion of the problems of plagiarism, hoaxes, misattribution, and the use of pseudonyms in the field of music. There are three useful supplements: spuriosities, listed under their supposed composers; nicknames and falsely titled compositions; and pseudonyms, altered forms of names, and nicknames.

For a work covering similar material, see **7.479**.

5.5 Fuld, James J. *The Book of World-Famous Music: Classical, Popular and Folk.* 4th ed., revised and enlarged. 718 pp. + 8 pp. plates. New York: Dover Publications, 1995.

First ed., Crown Publishers, New York, 1966, 564 pp. 2nd ed., 1971, 688 pp. 3rd ed., Dover Publications, 1985, 714 pp. A successor to the author's *American Popular Music (Reference Book)*, 1955, a selected list of first or early editions of American popular songs.

A work that traces the lineage, print or manuscript, of many of the most familiar compositions of the Western world, including much documentary information. The entries are alphabetically arranged, with musical incipits and detailed commentary on the sources, composers, and history. This is an admirable exercise in bibliography.

The 1966 ed. is reviewed by Ruth Hilton in *Notes* 23 (1966): 56–57; the 1971 ed. is reviewed by Nyal Williams in *Notes* 29 (1973): 448–49. The 3rd ed. is reviewed by Ann P. Basart in *CNV* 104 (1986): 15, with a reply and explanation by the author in *CNV* 111 (1987): 2, and by Dominique-René de Lerma in *ARBA* 18 (1987): no. 1236.

5.6* Goodenberger, Jennifer. *Subject Guide to Classical Instrumental Music.* 163 pp. Metuchen, N.J.: Scarecrow Press, 1989.

Topical access to the standard repertoire. The musical works are from the standard body of post-1600 instrumental music; the editor has designated 208 categories for subject-related music, with many cross-references.

Reviewed by Jean M. Bonin in *Notes* 47 (1990): 70–71, by Ann P. Basart in *CNV* 135 (1989): 26–27, and by Barry J. Zazslow in *Fontes* 37 (1990): 278–80, with errata.

5.7 *Music in Print Annual Supplement, 1979–86.* 8 vols. Philadelphia, Pa.: Musicdata, 1980–86. (Music in print)

An annual publication that supplemented the various individual titles of the Music in Print series in choral music (secular, **5.202**; sacred, **5.204**), guitar music (**5.282**), organ music (**5.232**), classical vocal music (**5.340**), orchestra music (**5.269**), and string music (**5.293**).

Reviewed by Stephen M. Fry in *ARBA* 11 (1980): no. 994.

5.8* *Music in Print Master Composer Index, 1995.* 2 vols. Philadelphia, Pa.: Musicdata, 1995. (Music in print series, XC) *Music in Print Master Title Index, 1995.* 2 vols. Philadelphia, Pa.: Musicdata, 1990. (Music in print series, XT)

The master indexes were first published in 1988: *Composer Index,* 824 pp., and *Title Index,* 581 pp.

Two volumes that bring together the data presented in the basic Music in Print volumes and their supplements (see **5.7**), making access to the information therein much easier. Because of the varying titles used and reported by the publishers to Musicdata, the title index contains many entries difficult to interpret.

The 1988 editions are reviewed by Charles A. Lindahl in *Notes* 47 (1990): 406 and by Kathleen Abromeit in *Choice* 28 (1990): 286.

5.9 Ogawa, Takashi. *Yogaku sakuin: Sakkyokusha to gendai to yakudai o hikidasu tameno / Music Index: For Reference to Original Composers, Foreign Titles and Japanese Titles.* 2 vols. Tokyo: Min'on Ongaku Shiryokan, 1975–81.

Text in English and Japanese characters.

A three-part list of musical works: entries arranged alphabetically by composer (pp. 1–294), entries arranged alphabetically by title in Western languages (pp. 297–503), and entries arranged by title in Japanese (pp. 507–765).

5.10 Reddick, William J. *The Standard Musical Repertoire, with Accurate Timings.* 192 pp. Garden City, N.Y.: Doubleday, 1947.

Reprinted in New York by Greenwood Press, 1969.

A classified list of orchestral music, works for piano and for violin, songs, and choral compositions, with timings, to the nearest 5 seconds, designed primarily for program directors of radio stations. See also Aronowsky **(5.2).**

Reviewed by Donald L. Engle in *Notes* 5 (1948): 240–41.

5.11 *Universal-Handbuch der Musikliteratur aller Zeiten und Völker; Als Nachschlagewerke und Studienquelle der Welt-Musikliteratur.* 14 vols. Vienna: Pazdirek & Co., 1904–10.

Reprinted by Knuf, Hilversum, in 1966, 14 vols. in 12.

Known as Pazdirek, the nearest thing to a comprehensive list of music in print ever published. This source is useful primarily for the 19th-century material in establishing the existence and dates of editions. The arrangement is under composer by opus number, if known; otherwise, entries are arranged by title.

5.12* Walker-Hill, Helen. *Music by Black Women Composers: A Bibliography of Available Scores.* 110 pp. Chicago, Ill.: Center of Black Music Research, Columbia College, 1995. (CBMR monographs, 5)

A classified list of works by Black women composers, both currently in print and held in libraries and archives. The relevant addresses are supplied and background information (including performances and recordings) is often present. The index of composers includes vital dates, if known.

RECENT WORKS

The music bibliographies listed here, most of them currently issued, generally restrict their entries to musical scores. For a full coverage, one should consult the various national bibliographies in which music appears along with listings from other fields. An excellent introduction to the use of then-current major bibliographical tools is given by Donald W. Krummel and James B. Coover in "Current National Bibliographies: Their Music Coverage," in *Notes* 17 (1960): 375–88 **(5.13).** A more general current list of national bibliographies can be found in the *Guide to Reference Books* **(4.41).** See also the current lists and reviews in such periodicals as *Notes, Music Review, JAMS,* and *Music and Letters.*

5.13 Krummel, Donald W., and **James B. Coover.** "Current National Bibliographies: Their Music Coverage." In *Notes* 17 (1960): 375–88.

A survey of music coverage in the national bibliographies of the Western Hemisphere, Europe, Africa, Asia, and Oceania.

5.14 *British Catalogue of Music.* London: The Council of the British National Bibliography, Limited, 1957–73; British Library Bibliographic Services Division, 1974– .

Published quarterly, with the last issue of each year cumulating that year's titles.

A national musical bibliography, organized in two parts: a classified and an alphabetical section. There are lists of music publishers with their British agents specified. The classification scheme was published as *The British Catalogue of Music Classification,* compiled by E. J. Coates (London: The Council of the British National Bibliography, Limited, 1960), 56 pp.

The 1982 ed. is reviewed by Clifford Bartlett in *Brio* 20 (1983): 13–14; the 1983 ed. is reviewed by Richard Andrewes in *MT* 126 (1985): 467.

5.15 Bulling, Burchard, and **Helmut Fosner.** *Deutscher Büchereiverband Arbeitsstelle für das Büchereiwesen; Musikbibliographischer Dienst MD), 1.-13. Jahrgang.* Berlin: Deutscher Büchereiverband, 1970–82.

A periodical publication issued six times a year, the sixth issue being a cumulation of all the current publications of serious music. The list is international in scope but German in practice because it is compiled from information reported by 12 German public libraries. The entries are printed in catalog card format on one side of the page, so they could be cut and filed in a card tray; the publication was also available in loose sheets for this purpose.

5.16 Cunning, Carol. *Composium Directory of New Music: Annual Index of Contemporary Compositions, 1970–1982/83.* Los Angeles, Calif.: Crystal Record Company, 1971–83.

An annual compilation of *Composium: A Quarterly Index of Contemporary Compositions,* a list of recent works by living American composers, including both published and currently unpublished compositions; although all the composers listed are American, this is not specified. The works are indexed by instrumentation and by composer. There is also a brief bibliographical sketch of each composer listed.

Reviewed by Melva Peterson in *AM* 2 (1984): 100–1 no. 2.

5.17* *Deutsche Nationalbibliographie und Bibliographie der im Ausland erschienenen deutschsprachigen Veröffentlichungen: Reihe M, Musikalien und Musikschriften; Monatliches Verzeichnis. Bearbeiter und Herausgeber, Die Deutsche Bibliothek. Jan. 1991– .* Frankfurt am Main: Buchhändler-Vereinigung, 1991– .

A monthly catalog of new publications of printed music and music literature in separate sections. The music is classified by form or performing force. There are both composer and name/title indexes. The books on music are taken from other sections of the *Bibliographie;* there is a concluding index covering names, titles, and subjects.

5.18 *Fontes Artis Musicae; Review of the International Association of Music Libraries.* Vol. 1– , 1954– .

Until 1976, each issue contains a "Liste internationale sélective," largely devoted to listings of current music publications by country, compiled by a series of national editors. Thereafter, there is an occasional shorter, annotated list, "Publications à caractère bibliographique."

5.19* *International Directory of Contemporary Music, 1990– .* New York: Contemporary Music International Information Service, 1991– .

The 1994 edition was titled *International Directory of Contemporary Music 1994 and 1995: Instrumentation* (464 pp.).

An annual directory of contemporary music, classified by instrumentation, based on the holdings of the Contemporary Music Service in New York and the Bibliothèque International de Musique Contemporaire, Paris, with over 12,000 works by 2,100+ composers from 50 countries.

Reviewed by Richard N. Burke in *Notes* 50 (1993): 630–31.

5.20 *Letopis´ muzykal´noi literatury.* Izdtsia s 1931 Goda; Vykhodit 4 raza v god. Moscow: Izdatel´stvo vsesoiuznoi knizhnoi palaty. 1931– .

A quarterly publication whose organization and content may vary slightly. In 1960 it was a classified list of publications in musical notation, including literary works with musical supplements or extensive musical illustration, and music issued periodically. Each issue has an index by composer, with separate lists of books, magazines, and newspapers containing music. There is an annual index of vocal works by title and first line, and by language of text. The entries give full bibliographical information, including complete contents, price, and size of edition.

5.21 *National Union Catalog: Music and Phonorecords, 1953–57 to 1968–72: A Cumulative List of Works Represented by Library of Congress Printed Cards and Titles Reported by Other American Libraries.* 11 vols. Ann Arbor, Mich.: J.W. Edwards, 1958–73. (Library of Congress catalogs)

The quinquennial cumulation of the LC *Music and Phonorecords,* continued by the National Union Catalog's *Music, Books on Music and Sound Recordings* (**5.22**). The 1953–57 cumulation was issued as Vol. 27 of the *National Union Catalog* in 1958. The 1958–62 catalog was published in Totowa, N.J., by Rowman and Littlefield in 1963 as Vols. 51–52 of the *National Union Catalog.* Neither the 1963–67 cumulation (3 vols.) nor the 1968–72 cumulation (5 vols.) was issued as a vol. of the *National Union Catalog.*

A list, issued semiannually and cumulated annually, of currently cataloged materials—music accessions, print (scores, libretti, and books on music and musicians), manuscript (generally scores), and sound recordings (musical and otherwise)—most of which are recent acquisitions of the Library of Congress and of libraries participating in its cooperative cataloging program. Included are purchased current or retrospective materials and a selection of recent copyright deposits. The entries were reproduced from the Library's printed cards, with a name and subject index. A related title containing cataloging issued during that period is **5.25**.

5.22 *National Union Catalog: Music, Books on Music, and Sound Recordings.* Washington, D.C.: Library of Congress, 1973– . (Library of Congress catalogs)

A semiannual publication, with an annual vol. published as the 2nd issue of each year and quinquennial cumulations published by Rowman and Littlefield, Totowa, N.J., 8 vols. covering 1973–77, 7 vols. covering 1978–82, and 10 vols. covering 1983–89. No cumulation was issued of the final set. This is a continuation of **5.21**.

A bibliography containing cataloging records created by the Library of Congress and by participating libraries whose collection efforts are sufficiently broad and whose cataloging standards are sufficiently worthy.

5.23 *National Union Catalog: Pre-1956 Imprints: A Cumulative Author List Representing Library of Congress Printed Cards and Titles Reported by Other American Libraries.* 685 vols. London: Mansell, 1968–81.

A 68-vol. supplement was published 1980–81, for a total of 754 vols.

A list of holdings of selected portions of the collections of the major research libraries of the U.S. and Canada, plus more rare items in the collections of selected smaller, specialized libraries. There are over 10 million entries for materials in over 700 libraries, including books, pamphlets, maps, atlases, and music. Works in non-Roman alphabets are included only if there is a printed LC card for them. Cross-references are provided sparingly and there are few added entries. The supplement includes over 3 million entries for new titles and corrected entries accumulated over the publication of the original volumes. A separate section at the end of each supplementary volume reports additional locations for items already located.

Naturally, numerous entries are for books falling into the music literature and music theory classifications, as well as for scores. However, entries representing the holdings of many of North America's most distinguished music collections are not represented for a variety of reasons. Score entries are particularly sparse in number relative to the great strengths of American and Canadian libraries. Krummel gives a thumbnail sketch of the situation in his *Bibliographical Handbook of American Music* (pp. 158–59) (**4.354**).

5.24 *The New Music Repertoire Directory.* 2 vols. to date. New York: American Music Center and Chamber Music America, 1983– .

A list of interesting or successful new music solicited from a number of ensembles and composers' organizations. Each entry supplies title, instrumentation, source of score and performance materials, and the name of the ensemble recommending it. The arrangement is by composer with lists of participating ensembles and resource organizations.

5.25 Olmsted, Elizabeth H. *Music Library Association Catalog of Cards for Printed Music, 1953–1972: A Supplement to the Library of Congress Catalogs.* 2 vols. Totowa, N.J.: Rowman and Littlefield, 1974.

Entries for printed music reported to the National Union Catalog for the period 1953–72, complementing the cataloging in the LC catalogs covering music (**5.21** and **5.22**). The body of the work is photocopies of the cards supplied, with attendant reproduction difficulties. The name of the library holding each title is not included.

5.26 *Prírustky hudebnin v Ceskych a Slovenskych knihovnach.* Brno, Moravia: Moravska zewska knihona v Brne, 1992– .

First issued in 1955 (Vols. 1–37) as *Prírustky hudebnin v Ceskoslovenskych knihovnach.*

The joint accession list of the principal music libraries in Slovakia and the Czech Republic, generally listing 2,000–3,000 items annually, classified by medium, without index.

5.27 U.S. Copyright Office. *Catalog of Copyright Entries, volumes 1–41. New Ser., Musical Compositions.* Washington, D.C.: Government Printing Office, 1906–46.

U.S. Copyright Office. *Catalog of Copyright Entries. 3rd Ser.: Music.* Washington, D.C.: Government Printing Office, 1947–77. Vols. 1–31.

U.S. Copyright Office. *Catalog of Copyright Entries. 4th Ser., pt. 3: Performing Arts.* Washington, D.C.: Government Printing Office, 1978– .

From 1891 to 1906, the quarterly copyright index issued by the Treasury Department, with musical compositions included as part of the general series. From 1906 to 1945, music (published or not) was entered by title in each monthly issue, followed by renewals, with an annual index. In 1947 this arrangement was succeeded by a division into unpublished music, published music, and renewals; a title index was added to the first two sections. This section of the *Catalog of Copyright Entries,* including some entries covering registrations beginning in 1891, was issued in 65 reels of microfilm by the Library of Congress Photoduplication Service in 1980. Reels 1–13 consist of a copy of every index (weekly, quarterly, and annual) covering the years 1898–1946, to facilitate copyright searches. The actual entries for 1891–1946 begin with reel 14.

The format of the third series was changed in Vol. 11 (1958), when the list was grouped under current registrations and renewal registrations, with the title as main entry and a name index for composers, authors, editors, compilers, claimants, and so forth. The third series cites all music deposited for copyright in the U.S., whether published in the U.S. or elsewhere. This is the most comprehensive catalog of music of its time. With the implementation of the Copyright Act of 1976, a fourth series, published in microfiche format, began in 1978, with music entries included in two sections: part 3, *Performing Arts,* issued quarterly, for music scores; and part 7, *Sound Recordings,* issued semiannually. Each part is provided with an index of names. The citations include basic bibliographic information.

5.28 Zaimont, Judith Lang, and **Karen Famera.** *Contemporary Concert Music by Women: A Directory of the Composers and Their Works.* A project of the International League of Women Composers, Inc. 355 pp. Westport, Conn.: Greenwood Press, 1981.

A directory of contemporary women composers. The connection of this volume with the International League of Women Composers, which clearly made possible its production, seemed also to serve as a limiting factor in its scope.

Reviewed by Judith Kaufman in *Notes* 38 (1982): 611–12.

MUSIC IN PERIODICALS

5.29* Borucki, William Carl. *Guide to the Musical Supplements of La revue musicale.* 49 pp. Huntsville, Tex.: Recital Publications, 1992.

An index to the musical supplements of *La revue musicale,* published in Paris from 1920.

5.30 Fellinger, Imogen. *Periodica Musicalia (1789–1830); im Auftrag des Staatlichen Instituts für Musikforschung Preussischer Kulturbesitz.* 1 + 1,259 pp. Regensburg: Gustav Bosse, 1986. (Studien zur Musikgeschichte des 19. Jahrhunderts, 55)

An index to and bibliography of music published in periodicals from 1789 to 1830, including lists of contents and multiple indexes.

Reviewed by Thomas F. Heck in *CNV* 125 (1988): 16–17.

5.31 *Hand-List of Music Published in Some British and Foreign Periodicals between 1787 and 1848, Now in the British Museum.* 80 pp. London: Trustees of the British Museum, 1962.

An index to the music, chiefly songs, in 12 periodicals: 1,855 entries arranged by composer. The contents are printed from slips prepared for entry in the British Museum catalog. See also Imogen Fellinger's *Periodica Musicalia* (**5.30**).

Reviewed by Richard Schaal in *Die Musikforschung* 17 (1964): 423.

NATIONAL MUSIC BIBLIOGRAPHIES

In this section are bibliographies of music (scores), concerned with the music of particular nations. Many of these bibliographies originate in the various national music centers that promote the work of native composers. Keith MacMillan compiled an account of 19 of these centers in his "Directory of National Music Centers," in *Notes* 27 (1971): 680–93. Several of the works in the National Musicological section of Chapter 4 (**4.287–4.363**) also include lists of composers' works.

AUSTRALIA

5.32 Australasian Performing Rights Association. *Catalogue of Major Musical Compositions by Australian and New Zealand Composers.* 52 pp. Sydney: Australasian Performing Rights Association, 1967.

Supplemental catalog of New Zealand composers (9 pp.) inserted.

5.33 Australia Music Centre. *Catalogue of Australian Choral Music.* 130 pp. Sydney: Australia Music Centre, 1985. (Catalogues of Australian compositions, 4)

A bibliography that updates and replaces the choral entries in the Australia Music Centre's 1976 *Vocal and Choral Music* (**5.38**).

5.34 Australia Music Centre. *Catalogue of Instrumental and Chamber Music.* 142 pp. Sydney: Australia Music Centre, 1976. (Catalogues of Australian compositions, 2)

A bibliography that includes Australian music for solo instruments and chamber ensembles.

5.35 Australia Music Centre. *Catalogue of Orchestral Music.* 109 pp. Sydney: Australia Music Centre, 1976.

A list of orchestral music by Australian composers.

5.36 Australia Music Centre. *Electronic Music.* 65 pp. Sydney: Australia Music Centre, 1977. (Catalogues of Australian compositions, 7)

Catalog of Australian electronic music, with bibliography (pp. 61–64).

5.37 Australia Music Centre. *Jazz.* 280 pp. Sydney: Australia Music Centre, 1978. (Catalogues of Australian compositions, 8)

Catalog of Australian jazz compositions.

5.38 Australia Music Centre. *Vocal and Choral Music.* 264 pp. Sydney: Australia Music Centre, 1976. (Catalogues of Australian compositions, 4)

Followed in part by *Catalogue of Australian Choral Music*, 1985 (**5.33**).

A list of music for solo voices, vocal ensembles, and choruses by Australian composers.

5.39* Broadstock, Brenton. *Sound Ideas: Australian Composers Born since 1950: A Guide to Their Music and Ideas.* 344 pp. The Rocks, New South Wales: Australian Music Centre, 1995.

A history of Australian music, with lists of composers' works, bibliographical references, and discography.

5.40 Burcher, Suellen. *Dramatic Music.* 212 pp. Sydney: Australia Music Centre, 1977. (Catalogues of Australian compositions, 5)

A list of Australian operas and other staged dramatic works.

5.41 Green, Anthony. *Catalogue of Australian Brass Music in the Collection of the Australian Music Centre.* 3rd ed. 32 pp. Ultimo, New South Wales: Australian Music Centre, 1988.

Replaces the Centre's 1985 *Brass and Concert Band Music.* The first ed. was published as *Military and Brass Band Music,* 1977 (28 pp.).

Music for band and brass ensembles.

5.42 Green, Anthony. *Catalogue of Australian Keyboard Music in the Australian Music Centre Collection.* 2nd ed. 98 pp. Ultimo, New South Wales: Australian Music Centre, 1988.

The first ed. was published as *Catalogue of Keyboard Music,* 1976, 90 pp.

Music for organ, harpsichord, and piano.

AUSTRIA

5.43 *Österreichische Musikbibliographie: Verzeichnis der österreichischen Neuerscheinungen auf der Gebiete der Musik.* 5 vols. Vienna: Verein der österreichische Buch-, Kunst-, Musikalien-, Zeitungs- und Zeitschriftenhändler, March 1949–December 1953, Jahrg. 1–5.

A publication consisting of two quarterly lists of publications newly issued in Austria, one for music literature and another for printed music. Each is arranged alphabetically by author or composer (or by title), and presents a short title, imprint information, collation, and price. The issues conclude with an index of editors and another of titles, first lines of text, and keywords.

BELGIUM

5.44 Centre Belge de Documentation Musicale. *Catalogus van werken van belgische componisten.* Brussels: Centre Belge de Documentation Musicale, 1953–57.

An irregularly published series of catalogs, in French or Flemish, averaging 20 pages each, devoted to contemporary Belgian composers and their works.

CANADA

5.45* Bergeron, Chantel. *Répertoire bibliographique de textes de présentation générale et d'analyse d'oeuvres musicales canadiennes (1900–1980) / Canadian Musical Works, 1900–1980: A Bibliography of General and Analytical Sources.* 96 pp. Ottawa: Canadian Association of Music Libraries, 1983. (Publications; Canadian Association of Music Libraries / Publications; Association canadienne des bibliothèques musicales, 3)

A bibliography whose preface describes it as a "checklist of nearly 2,000 references from 82 secondary sources which mention close to 1,500 serious works" by over 165 Canadian composers from 1900 to 1980.

5.46* Canadian Music Centre. *Brass Chamber Music in the Library of the Canadian Music Centre.* 12 ll. Toronto: The Centre, 1990.

The most recent editions of lists on other topics include *Acquisitions, 1986* (1987, 35 pp.), *Music for Accordion* (1982, 14 pp.), *Music for Bassoon* (1982, 27 pp.), *Music for Chamber Music*

(1980, c. 800 pp.), *Music for Clarinet* (1981, 45 pp.), *Solo French Horn Music* (1990, 75 pp.), *Music for Guitar* (1980, 18 pp.), *Music for Keyboard* (1971, 91 pp.), *Music for Saxophone* (1981, 20 pp.), *Music for Viola* (1981, 38 pp.), *Operas, Including Operettas & Stage Works* (1982, 20 pp.), and *Vocal Music* (3rd ed., 1976, 108 ll.). John Adaskin described the Canadian Music Centre in *Notes* 19 (1962): 601–2.

5.47* Canadian Music Library Association. *Musical Canadiana: A Subject Index, A Preliminary Edition in Which will be Found Listed Some 800 Vocal and Instrumental Pieces of Music Published ... up to 1921.* 62 pp. Ottawa: Canadian Library Association, 1967.

5.48 Jarman, Lynne. *Canadian Music, a Selected Checklist, 1950–73 / La musique canadienne, une liste selective, 1950–73: A Selective Listing of Canadian Music for Fontes Artis Musicae, 1954–73, Based on the Catalogued Entries of Canadiana from 1950.* 170 pp. Toronto; Buffalo, N.Y.: University of Toronto Press, 1976.

A project of the Canadian Music Library Association, which arranged the *Fontes* entries of Canadian music in a classified format. There is an index to composers and authors.

5.49 King, Sam D., and **Mark Hand.** *Canadian Orchestral Music Catalogue / Catalogue, musique orchestrale canadienne.* New ed. 247 pp. Toronto: Canadian Music Centre, 1994.

A list of Canadian orchestral music including full orchestra, chamber orchestra, string orchestra, symphonic wind ensemble, and band available from the libraries of the Canadian Music Centre.

5.50 Kitz, Mitchell, and **Mark Hand.** *Canadian Choral Music Catalogue.* 4th ed. 271 pp. Toronto: Canadian Music Centre / Centre de musique canadienne, 1993.

First published as *Catalogue of Canadian Choral Music, Available for Perusal from the Library of the Canadian Music Centre* (Toronto: CMC, 1966), 195 ll.; Supplement (1983, 35 pp.).

A list of Canadian choral music available from the libraries of the CMC.

5.51* MacInnis, Peggy. *Guidelist of Canadian Solo Free Bass Accordion Music Suitable for Student Performers.* 92 pp. Toronto: Canadian Music Centre, 1991.

5.52* Shand, Patricia Martin. *A Guide to Published Canadian Violin Music Suitable for Student Performers.* 101 pp. Toronto: Canadian Music Centre in cooperation with the Canadian Music Educators' Association, 1993.

A list of 33 solo violin and violin and piano works by 12 Canadian composers.

Reviewed by Richard Watts in *ARBA* 26 (1995): no. 1279.

5.53* Walter, Cameron. *A Guide to Unpublished Canadian Jazz Ensemble Music Suitable for Student Performers.* 76 pp. Toronto: Canadian Music Centre in co-operation with the Canadian Music Educator's Association, 1994.

CZECH REPUBLIC AND SLOVAKIA

5.54 Hošek, Miroslav. *Katalog der Oboeliteratur, tschechischer und slowakischer Autoren.* 89 pp. Prague: Czech Music Information Center, 1969.

An alphabetical list by composer of chamber works for oboe and 13 other instruments. Concertos and other orchestral works featuring the oboe are also included. There are indexes of libraries, publishers, and instrumental combinations.

DENMARK

5.55* *Dansk musikførtegnelse,* Vol. 1– . Copenhagen: Musikhandlerforeningen, 1931– .

An annual publication of the Danish National Bibliography's music section.

5.56 Malmgren, Jens-Ole. *Danske komponister af i dag; en vaerkfortegnelse / Danish Composers of Today: A Catalogue of Works / Danische Komponisten von Heute: Ein Werkverzeichnis.* 2 vols. (loose-leaf). Copenhagen: Dansk Komponistførening, 1980– .

A list of works, including information on publisher and performing forces necessary, cited in chronological order. Members of the Dansk Komponistførening are listed separately, with addresses and telephone numbers but without biographies.

The catalog will be constantly updated with new works and new composers. Revised pages will be sent automatically to those who own a copy of the catalog.

5.57 *Samfundet til udgivelse af Dansk musik: Catalogue, 1871–1971. The Society for Publishing Danish Music.* 155 pp. Copenhagen: Dan Fog, 1972.

A similar list was published in 1956 by Knud Larsen Musikforlag, with a *Supplement* in 1968.

A reference tool giving brief biographies of Danish composers (pp. 20–38); the catalog, arranged alphabetically by composer (pp. 39–85); chronological and systematic lists of publications; a list of recordings issued by the Society; a general index; and a 1972 price list.

FINLAND

5.58 *Suomalaista musiikkia: Suomalainen orkesterimusiikki, orkesterisaestyksellinen vokaalimusiikki, oopperamusiikki, balettimusiikki / Finnish Music: Finnish Orchestral Works, Vocal Works with Orchestra, Operas, Ballets.* 282 pp. Helsinki: Luovan Saveltaiteen Edistamissaatio, 1973.

A bibliography, in Finnish and English, of works by Finnish composers.

FRANCE

5.59 *Le bibliographe musical: Paraissant tous les deux mois avec le concours d'une réunion d'artistes et d'érudites.* Première Année (1872)–Cinquième Année (1876), Numéro 1–29, 499 pp. (continuous pagination). Paris: Pottier de Lalaine, 1872–76.

Reprinted in Scarsdale, N.Y., by Annemarie Schnase, 1969, 2 vols.

A bibliographical journal issued bimonthly by a group of scholars, librarians, and musicians. A typical issue contains short articles of bibliographical interest, reports of auction sales, reviews, and descriptions of music institutions. The most frequent contributor is Arthur Pougin. Superseded by **5.60**.

5.60 *Bibliographie musicale française: Catalogue des nouvelles oeuvres musicales françaises.* Année 1–26, Numéro 1–192. 47 vols. in 23. Paris: La Chambre Syndicale des Éditeurs de Musique, 1875–1920.

Reprinted by Annemarie Schnase, Scarsdale, N.Y., 1968.

A monthly trade list of music issued by the major French publishers over a period of 45 years. The lists are classified by performing media. Some of the publishers represented are Brandus, Colombier, Choudens, Durand, Gauthier, Grus, Le Bailly, Leduc, Lemoine, and E. Mathieu. Supersedes **5.59**.

Reviewed by Rita Benton in *Fontes* 26 (1979): 313.

5.61* *Bibliographie nationale française: Bibliographie établié par la Bibliothèque nationale a partir des documents deposés au titre du dépôt légal. Supplement III, Musique, Vol. 1– .* Paris: La Bibliothèque, 1992– .

Earlier titles include *Bibliographie de la France: Notices établies par la Bibliothèque nationale, 1977–1989* (13 vols.). From 1990 to 1991, published as *Bibliographie nationale française, notices établiés par la Bibliothèque nationale.* 2 vols. Paris: Bibliothèque Nationale, Office Général du Livre, 1990–91.

Issued three times a year.

5.62 Pierreuse, Bernard. *Catalogue général de l'édition musicale en France: Livres, méthodes et partitions de musique sérieuse en vente / General Catalog of Music Publishing in France: Books, Methods, and Scores of Serious Music on Sale.* 476 pp. Paris: Éditions Jobert; Distribution, Éditions Musicales Transatlantiques, 1984.

A classified list of available works arranged by composer or author. Title, version, publisher, and, occasionally, date of composition are indicated. There is an index to composers. In the choral and band sections, only classical works are listed.

5.63* Switten, Margaret Louise. *Music and Poetry in the Middle Ages: A Guide to Research on French and Occitan Song, 1100–1400.* xxvi + 452 pp. New York: Garland, 1995. (Garland medieval bibliographies, 19) (Garland reference library of the humanities, 1102)

GERMANY

5.64 Dupont, Wilhelm. *Werkausgaben Nürnberger Komponisten in Vergangenheit und Gegenwart.* 378 pp. Nuremberg: Selbstverlag der Stadtbibliothek, 1971. (Beträge zur Geschichte und Kultur der Stadt Nürnberg, 18)

A list of editions of music by composers from Nuremberg.

5.65 Simbriger, Heinrich. *Werkkatalog zeitgenossischer Komponisten aus den deutschen Ostgebieten.* Esslingen, Germany: Künstlergilde, 1961– .

A classified bibliography of works of East German composers. The entries give the title of work, instrumentation, the publisher (if any), and timing. A preliminary section is devoted to biographical sketches of the composers.

5.66 *Was wir singen: Katalog des in der Deutschen Demokratischen Republik erschienenen weltlichen Lied- und Chormaterials, Band I: 1945–58 Auswahl.* Edited by the Zentralhaus für Volkskunst. 255 pp. Leipzig: Friedrich Hofmeister, 1959.

A title list of 6,582 entries, supplemented by lists of collections and of cantatas and oratorios. There are indexes by subtitles or working titles, by voice combination and affective theme, and by national character; there are further indexes by text writers and composers.

GREAT BRITAIN

5.67 *British Catalogue of Music, 1957–1985.* Edited by Michael D. Chapman and Elizabeth Robinson. 10 vols. London; New York: K.G. Saur, 1988.

A cumulative ed. of the national musical bibliography, arranged much like the serial title (**5.14**).

5.68* Bryant, Michael, Marc Naylor, and **Jo Rees-Davies.** *Clarinet and Saxophone Music in the British Music Information Centre.* 85 pp. Brighton: Clarinet and Saxophone Society of Great Britain; London: The Centre, 1989.

Reviewed by Ian Ledsham in *Brio* 23 (1986): 84–85.

5.69 *Catalogue of Printed and Manuscript Music.* 2nd ed. 179 pp. Glasgow: Scottish Music Archive, 1979.

First ed., 1970, 74 pp., with a *Supplement,* 1972.

A classified list of music by contemporary Scottish composers giving instrumentation, duration, publisher, and availability of the material. The archive is centered at the University of Glasgow, but its policies are dictated by a committee of members from a number of Scottish musical institutions.

Reviewed by Richard Andrewes in *MT* 122 (1981): 675–76.

5.70 Composers' Guild of Great Britain. *Catalogue of Works by Members. Volume 1: British Orchestra Music.* 2 vols. London: The Guild; British Music Information Centre, 1958–72.

The guild has also published brief catalogs of works by living composers of chamber music (1969, 42 pp.), instrumental solos and duets (1972, 96 pp.), and keyboard solos and duets (1974, 63 pp.).

5.71 Cudworth, Charles. "Thematic Index of English Eighteenth-Century Overtures and Symphonies." In the Appendix to *Proceedings of the Royal Musical Association* 78 (1953): 9.

The appendix to his paper "The English Symphonists of the Eighteenth Century."

5.72* Gore, Charles. *The Scottish Fiddle Music Index: Tune Titles from the 18th & 19th Century Printed Instrumental Music Collections, List of Indexed and Related Collections and Where to Find Them.* 477 pp. Musselburgh, Scotland: Amaising Publishing House, 1994.

5.73 Griffiths, Paul. *British Music Catalogue, 1945–1981; Vol. 1: Works for Piano.* 39 pp. London: Warwick Arts Trust, 1983– .

A classified catalog restricted to British published music and music by British composers, some of whose works are published, including educational material.

5.74* Harley, John. *British Harpsichord Music.* 347 pp. Aldershot, England: Scolar Press; Brookfield, Vt.: Gower, 1992–94.

Contents: Vol. 1, Sources; Vol. 2, History.

A list of over 300 manuscripts and 1,500 printed sources. The manuscripts are in three groups: publicly owned, privately owned, and missing. Within each group they are arranged alphabetically by location. The printed works are listed chronologically and, within each year, alphabetically by composer or title; later editions, including 20th-century works, are covered. There is an extensive classified bibliography.

The 1st vol. is reviewed by Barry Cooper, with addenda and errata, in *M&L* 74 (1993): 281–83. The set is reviewed by V. J. Panetta in *Notes* 52 (1995): 457–58.

5.75 Swanekamp, Joan. *English Ayres: A Selectively Annotated Bibliography and Discography.* 141 pp. Westport, Conn.: Greenwood Press, 1984.

"In 1926 Philip Heseltine under the pseudonym of Peter Warlock published *The English Ayre,* a slim volume with a brief two-page bibliography. Since that time articles and books focusing on the ayre composers have appeared with increasing frequency, as have editions and recordings of their works. This bibliography strives to bring these materials together as a companion volume to the Warlock book. It includes the composers mentioned by Warlock, as well as eight additional composers from E. H. Fellowes' *English School of Lutenist Song Writers* and *English Lute Songs*" [Introductory remarks].

There are 903 entries, arranged by composer and subdivided by literature, music, and recordings categories. Literary works are arranged alphabetically by author. No reviews are cited. Collections are listed by title. There are author and title indexes.

Reviewed by Linda Phyllis Austern in *Notes* 41 (1985): 728–29 and by Avery T. Sharp in *ARBA* 16 (1985): no. 1180.

HUNGARY

5.76 *Bibliographia Hungarica 1945–1960: Catalogus systematicus notarum musicarum in Hungaria editarum. Edidit Bibliotheca nationalis Hungariae a Francisco Széchényi fundata.* 361 pp. Budapest: Országos Széchényi Könyvtár, 1969.

A classified list of all Hungarian music publications between 1945 and 1960, indexed by composer and by first line of text.

5.77 Dedinsky, Izabella K. *Zeneművek, 1936–1940.* 286 pp. Budapest: Kiadja az országos széchényi könyvtár, 1944.

A classified bibliography of music, popular and serious, published in Hungary, 1936–40.

5.78 *Magyar Nemzeti Bibliográfia: Zeneművek bibliográfiája.* 8. évf., 3.-füzet; szept. 30, 1977– . Budapest: Országos Széchényi Könyvtár.

Continues *Magyar zeneművek bibliográfiája, 1970–1977.*

The current Hungarian national bibliography on music, a quarterly supplement to *Magyar nemzeti bibliográfia: Könyvek bibliográfiája.*

5.79* *Országos Széchényi Könyvtár. Magyar könyvészet, 1945–1960: A Magyarországon nyomtatott zeneművek szakositott jegyzéke.* 360 pp. Budapest, 1969.

A classified bibliography of music published in Hungary, 1945–60.

ICELAND

5.80 Burt, Amanda. *Iceland's Twentieth-Century Composers and a Listing of Their Works.* 71 pp. Annandale, Va.: Charles Baptie Studios, 1977.

First ed., 1975, 30 pp.

INDIA

5.81* Bhagyalekshmy, S. *Carnatic Music Compositions: An Index.* 162 pp. Trivandrum, India: CBH Publications; Madras: Karnatic Music Book Center, 1994.

An index to classical music of southern India.

5.82 Kaufmann, Walter. *The Ragas of North India.* 625 pp. Bloomington, Ind.: Indiana University Press, 1968. (Asian Studies Research Institute. Oriental series, 1)

Reprinted by Da Capo Press, New York, in 1984, and by Asia Publishing in Sittingbourne, England 1993.

Kaufmann, Walter. *The Ragas of South India: A Catalogue of Scalar Material.* xxxiv + 732 pp. Bloomington, Ind.: Indiana University Press, 1976.

Simultaneously published in New Delhi, India, by Oxford and IBH Pub. Co.; reprinted by them and by Asia Publishing, Sittingbourne, in 1991.

Both a historical work and a thematic catalog.

5.83 Kuppuswamy, Gomri, and **Muthuswamy Hariharan.** *Index of Songs in South Indian Music.* 970 pp. Delhi; New Delhi: B. R. Publishing Corporation, Distributed by D. K. Publishers' Distributors, 1981.

The general introduction gives the beginning, raga, tala, language, composer, and details of availability for each song. There are separate indexes for raga, tala, language, and composer.

The source of each song is given.

IRELAND

5.84* Harrison, Bernard. *Catalogue of Contemporary Irish Music.* 221 pp. Dublin: Irish Composers' Centre, 1982.

ISRAEL/JEWISH

5.85 Goldberg, Ira S. *Bibliography of Instrumental Music of Jewish Interest; Part 1: Orchestra and Band; Part 2: Ensemble and Solo.* Revised and enlarged ed. 2 vols. New York: National Jewish Music Council, 1970.

5.86 Sendrey, Alfred. *Bibliography of Jewish Music.* 404 pp. New York: Columbia University Press, 1951.

Reprinted by Kraus Reprint Company in 1969.

A classified bibliography of 5,854 items on Jewish music and musicians. There follows a classified list of about 4,000 pieces of Jewish music, alphabetical by composer within classifications, giving scoring, author, and language of text and the publisher and date of publication; recordings and some manuscripts are also included.

Reviewed by Milton Feist in *MQ* 37 (1951): 432–35, by Ernst C. Krohn in *JAMS* 7 (1954): 150–52, and by Eric Werner in *Notes* 8 (1951): 352–54.

5.87* Tischler, Alice. *A Descriptive Bibliography of Art Music by Israeli Composers.* xxiii + 424 pp. Warren, Mich.: Harmonie Park Press, 1988. (Detroit studies in music bibliography, 62)

A bibliography of some 3,200 alphabetically arranged musical works by the 63 Israeli composers covered, with generously detailed descriptions of individual works and useful indexes. Excluded are composers born after 1947 and Israelis living permanently in other countries.

Reviewed by Israel J. Katz in *Notes* 47 (1991): 754–55 and by Ann P. Basart in *CNV* 134 (1989): 9.

ITALY

5.88 Bowers, Jane. "The Emergence of Women Composers in Italy, 1566–1700." In *Women Making Music; The Western Art Tradition, 1150–1950,* pp. 116–67. Edited by Jane Bowers and Judith Tick. Urbana, Ill.: University of Illinois Press, 1986.

An article including a bibliography of 65 compositions by Italian women published 1566–1700 (pp. 162–67), 48 of which are not in *RISM*.

Reviewed by Jane Gottlieb in *Notes* 47 (1991): 56–59.

5.89* Brumana, Biancamaria, and **Galliano Ciliberti.** *Musica e musicisti nella Cattedrale di S. Lorenzo a Perugia (XIV-XVIII Secolo).* 228 pp. Florence: L. S. Olschki, 1991. (Biblioteca / Historiae Musicae Cultores, 62)

The musical history of the cathedral of San Lorenzo in Perugia from the 14th to the 18th centuries, from surviving documents.

5.90* Cook, Susan C., and **Thomasin K. LeMay.** *Virtuose in Italy, 1600–1640: A Reference Guide.* 163 pp. New York: Garland, 1984.

A guide to the sources dealing with women singers of madrigals in 17th-century Italy, with an annotated bibliography of musical sources (pp. 89–129).

Reviewed by Allie Wise Goudy in *ARBA* 16 (1985): no. 1183.

5.91* Whittemore, Joan. *Music of the Venetian Ospedali Composers: A Thematic Catalogue.* 184 pp. Stuyvesant, N.Y.: Pendragon Press, 1995. (Thematic catalogs, 21)

A thematic catalog of 1,289 manuscripts, including for the first time nearly 700 manuscripts from the archives of St. Mark's. There are indexes to archives and to composers, and a bibliography.

JAPAN

5.92* Matsushita, Hitoshi. *A Checklist of Published Instrumental Music by Japanese Composers.* 181 pp. Tokyo: Academia Music, 1989.

A list, intended for international use, of works published from 1868 to 1987 in Japan.

Reviewed by Mari Nishimura in *Notes* 48 (1991): 103–4.

5.93* Narazaki, Yoko. *Nihon no Kangengaku sakuhihyo 1912–1992 / Orchestral Works by Japanese Composers 1912–1992.* 375 pp. Tokyo: Nihon Kokyogaku Shinko Zaidan, 1994.

LATIN AMERICA

5.94 Chase, Gilbert. *A Guide to the Music of Latin America.* A joint publication of the Pan American Union and the Library of Congress. 2nd ed., revised and enlarged. 411 pp. Washington, D.C.: Pan American Union, 1962.

The 1st ed. was published as *Guide to Latin American Music,* 1945, and was reprinted by the AMS Press, New York, in 1962. A reprint of the 2nd ed. was published by AMS Press, New York, in 1972.

The general classified and annotated bibliography of Latin American music with listings for each country or region, preceded by a brief discussion of the area under discussion and followed by listings related to individual composers of the area as well as regional folk music. (Latin America includes Central and South America, the Caribbean, and the southwestern United States.) There is an index of authors, names, and subjects.

Reviewed by Bruno Nettl in *Ethnomusicology* 9 (1965): 167–68.

5.95* Tiemstra, Suzanne Spicer. *The Choral Music of Latin America: A Guide to Compositions and Research.* 317 pp. New York: Greenwood Press, 1992. (Music reference collection, 36)

Headed by a "Brief History of Art Music in Latin America" (pp. 1–28) and "A Practical Guide to Research," a catalog of Latin American choral works (pp. 37–166), including bibliographic and location information. Appendixes give lists of anthologies and collections of music, series of music, music publishers, a selected discography and list of recording companies, music archives, periodicals, and a selected bibliography.

Reviewed by Paul R. Laird in *Fontes* 40 (1993): 168–69, by James R. Heintze in *Choice* 30 (1992): 451, and by Nick Strimple in *Notes* 50 (1995): 629.

MEXICO

5.96 Huerta, Jorge A. *A Bibliography of Chicano and Mexican Dance, Drama, and Music.* 59 pp. Oxnard, Calif.: Colegio Quetzalcoatl, 1972.

A bibliography whose three main subdivisions cover dance, drama, and music, subdivided into pre-Columbian, Mexican, and Aztlan sections.

THE NETHERLANDS

5.97* Vester, Frans, and **Rein de Reede.** *Catalogus van de Nederlandse fluitliteratuur / Catalogue of Dutch Flute Literature.* 294 pp. Buren, The Netherlands: F. Knuf, 1988. (Flute library, 12)

A list of works featuring the flute by Dutch composers or composers active in Dutch musical life. Includes a chronological index, an index arranged by instrumentation, and a bibliography.

Reviewed by Ann P. Basart in *CNV* 135 (1989): 23–24.

NORWAY

5.98* *Norsk Musikkfortegnelse / Norwegian National Bibliography of Printed Music, 1993– .* Oslo: Universitetsbibliotek, Oslo, 1993– .

A new national bibliography of music, issued annually and arranged alphabetically by composer or title.

5.99* *Norwegian Chamber Music: Woodwinds.* 94 pp. Oslo: Norsk musikkinformasjon, 1985.

One of a series of lists, with bibliographical and discographical information, compiled by Norway's Music Information Centre. Other lists are on such areas of chamber music as accordion, brass, organ, percussion, piano, and strings.

5.100* *Norwegian Orchestral Music: 2000 Norwegian Orchestral Works from the Baroque Era to the Present / Norsk orkestermusick: 2000 Norske orkesterwerker fra barokken til var egen tid*. 94 pp. Oslo: Norwegian Music Information Centre, 1993.

PAPUA NEW GUINEA

5.101 Gourlay, K. A. *A Bibliography of Traditional Music in Papua New Guinea*. 176 pp. Port Moresby, Australia: Institute of Papua New Guinea Studies, 1974.

A list that covers Papua New Guinea, Torres Strait islands, parts of Java, and the Solomon Islands. There is a comprehensive index.

POLAND

5.102 Hordyński, Władysław. *Katalog polskich druków muzycznych 1800–1863 / Catalogue des imprimés musicaux polonais de 1800–1863, volume 1– .* Cracow: Polskie Wydawn. Muzyczne, 1968– .

Contents: Vol. 1, *Biblioteka Uniwersytecka w Poznaniu u Biblioteka Kórnicka Polskiej Akademii Nauk.*

A bibliography planned as the first volume in a series of bibliographies of Polish music.

5.103* **Tomaszewski, Wojciech.** *Bibliografia Warszawskich druków muzycznych, 1801–1850.* 463 pp. Warsaw: Biblioteka Narodowa, 1992.

A detailed bibliography of music published in Warsaw during the first half of the 19th century.

ROMANIA

5.104* *Bibliografia nationale Romana.* Bucharest: Biblioteca Nationala a Romaniei, 1993– .

A quarterly catalog of Romanian scores and sound recordings.

RUSSIA

5.105 Hofmeister, Friedrich (Firm). *Verzeichnis der in Deutschland seit 1868 erchienenen Werke russischer Komponisten.* 253 pp. Leipzig: Druck der Buchdruckerei Frankenstein, 1949.

An alphabetical list of Russian composers, with their works given in opus number order. The detailed bibliographical information includes the price but lacks the date of publication.

SCANDINAVIA

5.106* **Lammers, Mark Edward.** *Nordic Instrumental Music for Colleges and Universities.* 210 pp. Stockholm: MOMUS; St. Peter, Minn.: Gustavus Adolphus College, 1991.

A selective, annotated list, arranged by instrument, with entries including country, publishing information, and level of difficulty, of primarily original instrumental compositions from Denmark, Iceland, Finland, Norway, and Sweden, playable by college and university students. Most works were published between 1970 and 1990.

SOUTH AFRICA

5.107* **Levy, M. S.** *Catalogue of Serious Music, Original Works, Arrangements and Orchestrations, Published and in Manuscript, by Southern African Composers and Arrangers.* 2nd ed. 3 vols. Johannesburg: SAMRO, 1992.

A catalog of works by members of SAMRO, Southern African Music Rights Organization, 1962–92.

5.108 Van der Merwe, F. Z. *Suid-Afrikaanse musiekbibliografie 1787–1952.* 410 pp. Pretoria: J. L. Van Schaik, 1958.

Supplemented by *En 1953–1972 bygewerk vir die Raad vir geesteswetenskaplike Navorsing deur Jan van de Graaf* (Cape Town: Tafelberg-uitgewers vir die Instituut vir Taal. Lettere en Kuns. Raad vir Geestesweten-skaplike Navorsing, 1974), 297 pp.

A comprehensive bibliography of music related to South Africa (works by South African composers, wherever published, and writings on South African themes or subject matter). The largest part of the citations refers to songs, marches, or dance music of a popular nature, although a few studies and monographs are interfiled. Entries are unclassified, arranged alphabetically by composer or author. There is an index of South African composers and musicians. The language is Afrikaans.

SPAIN

5.109* *Bibliografia española: Suplemento de musica impresa, 1985– .* Madrid: Ministerio de Cultura, Direccio General del Libro y Bibliotecas, 1990– .

A supplement of Spanish printed music.

5.110* Garcia Estefania, Alvaro. *Piano y otros instrumentos de Espana.* 266 pp. Madrid: Sociedad General de Autores de Espana, 1995. (Ediciones musicales)

A bibliography of keyboard music principally by Spanish composers, including non-Spanish composers in editions by Spanish arrangers and editors, restricted to Spanish publishers. In addition to solo repertory, music for two pianos, two organs, piano duet, and eight-hand piano is included.

SWEDEN

5.111 Kallstenius, Edwin. *Swedish Orchestral Works: Annotated Catalogue.* 85 pp. Stockholm: Nordiska Musikförlaget, 1948.

A compact compilation containing portraits, biographical sketches, and annotated lists of works (including playing time and instrumentation) of 25 Swedish composers, intended for conductors, members of program committees, and other music lovers.

5.112 Nisser, Carl M. *Svensk instrumentalkomposition, 1770–1830: Nominalkatalog.* 467 pp. Stockholm: Bökforlaget Gothia, 1943.

A list of Swedish instrumental music by native composers or composers living in Sweden. The entries are arranged alphabetically by composer, with detailed bibliographical and analytical descriptions, including key, movements, time signature, and measure count. There are bibliographical references and an index of names and places.

5.113 *Svensk musik för orkester (Hyresmaterial) / Swedish Music for Orchestra (Hire Material), 1985.* 150 pp. Stockholm: STIMS Informationscentral för Svensk Musik, 1985.

A catalog produced by the Swedish music information service covering rental scores and parts for orchestra by Swedish composers.

5.114* *Swedish Choral Music: A Selective Catalogue.* 2nd ed. 60 pp. Stockholm: Svensk Musik, Swedish Music Information Center, 1988.

In English and Swedish, with indexes.

UNITED STATES OF AMERICA

5.115 American Society of Composers, Authors and Publishers. *ASCAP Index of Performed Compositions.* 1,423 pp. New York: American Society of Composers, Authors, and Publishers, 1978.

First issued in 1942 as the *ASCAP Index*, for the use of radio broadcasting stations, with subsequent editions in 1952, 1954, and 1963, under the present title. *Supplement* published in 1981, 99 pp.

A minimally edited alphabetical list of compositions in the ASCAP repertoire that have appeared in the society's survey of radio, television, and wired-music performances, including easy listening, soul, country, religious, children's, gospel, rock, pop, film, folk, educational, classical, jazz, and musical theater genres. The works are listed alphabetically by title, with citations of composer and publisher. The *ASCAP Symphonic Catalog* (**5.116**) gives more complete coverage of the ASCAP classical repertory.

5.116 American Society of Composers, Authors, and Publishers. *ASCAP Symphonic Catalog.* 3rd ed. 511 pp. New York: R.R. Bowker, 1977.

Previous editions, 1959, 375 pp., and 1966, 754 pp.

An alphabetical list, by composers and arrangers, of 26,000 pieces of symphonic literature controlled by ASCAP and its 40 foreign affiliates. The entries give instrumentation, duration, and publisher. There is a list of publishers' addresses and U.S. agents.

Reviewed by Stephen M. Fry in *Notes* 34 (1977): 619.

5.117 Anderson, Gillian B. *Freedom's Voice in Poetry and Song.* 888 pp. Wilmington, Del.: Scholarly Resources Inc., 1977.

An anthology of political and patriotic prose and music. The first part gives an inventory of topical lyrics in colonial American newspapers from 1773 to 1783; the second is a songbook of works from the period. Bibliographical references and indexes are included.

5.118 Board of Music Trade of the United States of America. *Complete Catalogue of Sheet Music and Musical Works.* xxvi + 575 pp. New York: Board of Music Trade, 1870.

Reprinted by Da Capo Press, New York, in 1973.

A classified catalog of music and books about music published by members of the board and in print at the time of publication. There is little bibliographic information and no index. Dena Epstein's revision of the introduction to the reprint of the *Catalog* is in *Notes* 31 (1974): 7–29.

Reviewed by Don Hixon in *ARBA* (1975): no. 1121.

5.119* Bottje, Will Gay. *A Catalog of Representative Works by Resident, Living Composers of Illinois: Containing Also Brief Biographical Sketches and List of Publishers.* 28 ll. Carbondale, Ill.: Southern Illinois University, 1960.

5.120* Britton, Allen Perdue, and **Irving Lowens.** *American Sacred Imprints, 1698–1810: A Bibliography.* Completed by Richard Crawford. 798 pp. Worcester, Mass.: American Antiquarian Society/University of Virginia Press, 1990.

A bibliography of 677 printed collections of sacred music, alphabetically arranged. The introduction, by Richard Crawford, gives a historical perspective. Includes a list of bibliographic references (pp. 61–75) and a variety of indexes. This is a complement to Sonneck's *A Bibliography of Early Secular American Music (18th Century)* (**5.601**), Richard J. Wolfe's *Secular Music in America, 1801–1825: A Bibliography* (**5.151**), and Irving Lowens's *A Bibliography of Songsters Printed in America before 1821* (**5.142**). Britton and Lowens chronicled their early research in "Unlocated Titles in Early Sacred American Music," *Notes* 11 (1953): 33–48.

Reviewed by David P. McKay in *AM* 10 (1992): 370–73, by Nicholas Temperley in *JAMS* 45 (1992): 123–31, and by Karl Kroeger in *Notes* 48 (1991): 54–58, with errata.

5.121 Broadcast Music, Inc. *Symphonic Catalogue.* 375 pp. Revised ed. New York: Broadcast Music, Inc., 1971.

First ed., 1963, 132 pp. *Supplement No. 1* to the revised ed. was published in 1978, 138 pp.

An alphabetical list, by composer, of symphonic works whose performing rights are controlled by Broadcast Music, Inc. (BMI). Each entry gives the duration, instrumentation, and publisher of the work.

5.122* Camus, Raoul F. *The National Tune Index: Early American Wind and Ceremonial Music, 1636–1836.* 29 microfiche and printed user's guide (36 pp.).New York: University Music Editions, 1987.

A computer-generated index of 20,733 citations from 298 collections and 1,077 pieces of sheet music found in the U.S., Canada, U.K., Ireland, Germany, Belgium, Sweden, and France, emphasizing the roots of early American wind band, field, percussion, and ceremonial music largely from Hessian, French, and British sources. Seven helpful indexes make the information accessible to the user. An account is given of Phase 2 of the *Index* by Camus in *Notes* 52 (1996): 723–43.

5.123* Carter, Madison H. *An Annotated Catalog of Composers of African Ancestry.* 145 pp. New York: Vantage Press, 1986.

A list of African-American composers, each entry with a brief, classified works list and the library locations of these compositions, compiled by an amateur enthusiast.

Reviewed by Ann P. Basart in *CNV* 121 (1988): 16–17 and by Dominique-René de Lerma in *ARBA* 19 (1988): no. 1270.

5.124 *Catalog of the American Music Center Library: Music for Orchestra, Band and Large Ensemble.* 196 pp. New York: The Center, 1982. (Catalog of the American Music Center, 3)

A catalog of the holdings of music for large instrumental ensemble by American composers in the American equivalent of a national music information center.

5.125* De Lerma, Dominique-René. *Black Concert and Recital Music: A Provisional Repertoire List.* 40 pp. Bloomington, Ind.: Afro-American Music Opportunities Association, 1975.

A list of 245 works by 40 composers.

Briefly reviewed by Stephen M. Fry in *Notes* 32 (1975): 301–2.

5.126* DeVenney, David P. *American Choral Music since 1920: An Annotated Guide.* 278 pp. Berkeley, Calif.: Fallen Leaf Press, 1993. (Fallen Leaf reference books in music, 27)

A bibliography covering nearly 2,000 works by 76 composers from around 1920 to the present. The entries give dates, performing forces required, text author, duration, and publisher. There is also an annotated bibliography (pp. 193–216) on the history and performance practice of this music.

Reviewed by Lori N. White in *SSB* 21 (1995): 26 no. 1, by Paul B. Cors in *ARBA* 26 (1995): no. 1280, by John Wagstaff in *Brio* 32 (1995): 134–35, and by Tinsley Silcox in *Fontes* 42 (1995): 195–96.

5.127* DeVenney, David P. *American Masses and Requiems: A Descriptive Guide.* 210 pp. Berkeley, Calif.: Fallen Leaf Press, 1990. (Fallen Leaf reference books in music, 15)

A description of about 700 works (including performance forces, duration, and publisher), dating from the early 19th century to the present day. The editor also describes in detail 28 of this repertoire's most important pieces and includes bibliographical references and indexes.

Reviewed by Ralph Hartsock in *Fontes* 39 (1992): 195–96.

5.128* DeVenney, David P. *Early American Choral Music: An Annotated Guide.* 149 pp. Berkeley, Calif.: Fallen Leaf Press, 1988. (Fallen Leaf reference books in music, 10)

A bibliography listing 32 composers, with entries for each known choral work (excluding stage works, hymns, liturgical chants, psalm tunes, fuguing tunes, works for solo ensembles, and nonart music), dating from around 1670 to 1820. The entries give opus number, the date of composition, the performing forces required, the text sources, the duration (if more than 10 minutes), the publisher and date of publication, the manuscript location, and the name of collection. There is a bibliography of writings about the music.

Reviewed by Susan Ross in *Fontes* 36 (1989): 157 and by Paul B. Cors in *ARBA* 20 (1989): no. 1218.

5.129 DeVenney, David P. *Nineteenth-Century American Choral Music: An Annotated Guide.* xxi + 182 pp. Berkeley, Calif.: Fallen Leaf Press, 1987. (Fallen Leaf reference books in music, 8)

There is an extensive bibliography (pp. 97–116).

5.130 Dichter, Harry, and **Elliott Shapiro.** *Handbook of Early American Sheet Music, 1768–1889.* 297 pp. New York: Dover Publications, 1979.

A reprint, with corrections, of *Early American Sheet Music, Its Lure and Lore, Including a Directory of Early American Music Publishers* (New York: R.R. Bowker, 1941), 287 pp.

A bibliographic catalog arranged by periods and by types within periods, with directories of publishers and of lithographers and artists.

5.131* Dox, Thurston J. *American Oratorios and Cantatas: A Catalog of Works Written in the United States from Colonial Times to 1985.* 2 vols. Metuchen, N.J.: Scarecrow Press, 1986.

A major list of 3,450 extended choral works.

Reviewed by George Louis Mayer in *ARBA* 18 (1987): no. 1249.

5.132 Eagon, Angelo. *Catalog of Published Concert Music by American Composers.* 2nd ed. 348 pp. Metuchen, N.J.: Scarecrow Press, 1969.

The 1st ed. was published by the Music Branch, Information Center, U.S. Information Agency, in 1964, with a supplement issued in 1965. The 1st supplement to the 2nd ed. was published in 1971 (150 pp.), with a 2nd supplement following in 1974 (148 pp.).

A useful, well-organized bibliography of works entered alphabetically by composer and classified as vocal solo, instrumental solo, instrumental ensemble, concert jazz, percussion, orchestra, etc. Includes a key to publishers and an author index. Information given includes duration of orchestral works and authors of text for vocal compositions.

The 1964 ed. is reviewed by Karl Kroeger in *Notes* 22 (1966): 1032–33, the 2nd ed. by Richard Hunter in *Notes* 26 (1970): 759–60, and the 2nd supplement by Deane L. Root in *MT* 116 (1975): 627.

5.133* Hedges, Bonnie, and **Bonlyn Hall.** *Twentieth-Century Composers in the Chesapeake Region: A Bio-Bibliography and Guide to Library Holdings.* 168 pp. United States: Chesapeake Chapter, Music Library Association, 1994.

A survey of composers born or active in Delaware, Maryland, Virginia, West Virginia, and the District of Columbia during the 20th century.

5.134 Heintze, James R. *American Music before 1865 in Print and on Record: A Biblio-Discography.* Revised ed. 248 pp. Brooklyn, N.Y. Institute for Studies in American Music, Conservatory of Music, Brooklyn College of CUNY, 1990. (ISAM monographs, 30)

First ed., *American Music before 1865 in Print and on Record: A Biblio-Discography* (Brooklyn, N.Y.: Institute for Studies in American Music, Brooklyn College, 1976. 113 pp., ISAM monographs, 6), supplemented by articles in *Notes* 37 (1978): 571–80 and 39 (1981): 31–36.

A work with origins in the musical flurry heralding the American Bicentennial, listing, with indexes, "Music in Performance and Other Editions" (items 1–172, arranged by anthology title or composer, classified by medium), "Music in Facsimile Editions" (items 173–330, similarly arranged but unclassified), and a discography (items 331–1310, arranged by composer or title). There are indexes of record manufacturers, giving a description of each album cited (pp. 145–214), and of composers, compilers, and titles

The 1st ed. is reviewed by the current author in *Notes* 33 (1977): 842–43. The 2nd ed. is reviewed by John Druesedow in *Notes* 47 (1991):700.

5.135 Hixon, Donald L. *Music in Early America: A Bibliography of Music in Evans.* 607 pp. Metuchen, N.J.: Scarecrow Press, 1970.

An index to the music published in 17th- and 18th-century America as represented by Charles Evans's *American Bibliography* and the Readex Corporation's microprint edition of *Early American Imprints, 1639–1800*. The major part of the work is devoted to entries for the music under composer, editor, or compiler. There is also a valuable section of bibliographical sketches, followed by indexes of names of composers and compilers, titles, and Evans's serial numbers. Priscilla Heard's bibliography (**4.349**) gives other musical access to Evans's work.

5.136 Jackson, Richard. *United States Bicentennial Music.* 20 pp. Brooklyn, N.Y.: Institute for Studies in American Music, School of Performing Arts, Brooklyn College of CUNY, 1977. (ISAM special publications, 1)

470 entries for music composed or reprinted for the American Bicentennial.

Reviewed by Kären Nagy in *Notes* 34 (1978): 880.

5.137 Jackson, Richard. *United States Music: Sources of Bibliography and Collection Biography.* 80 pp. Brooklyn, N.Y.: Institute for Studies in American Music, Department of Music, Brooklyn College of CUNY, 1973. (ISAM monographs, 1)

A generic bibliography (reference works, historical studies, regional studies) with a topical section. Each entry is extensively annotated and evaluated. There is an author/compiler index.

5.138 Kirk, Elise K. "Sheet Music Related to the United States War with Mexico (1846–1848) in the Jenkins Garrett Library, University of Texas at Arlington." In *Notes* 37 (1981): 15–30.

An inventory arranged by composer, also providing information on other copies at the Beinecke Library of Yale University, the Lilly Library of Indiana University, and the Library of Congress.

5.139* Koshgarian, Richard. *American Orchestral Music: A Performance Catalog.* 761 pp. Metuchen, N.J.: Scarecrow Press, 1992.

A catalog of the orchestral works of approximately 900 American composers born within the last 100 years, listing over 7,000 works, including concertos, orchestral works with chorus or vocal solos, and chamber orchestral works.

Reviewed by Clifford Bartlett in *Brio* 30 (1993): 118–19, by Evan Feldman in *Fontes* 41 (1994): 228–30, by Allie Wise Goudy in *ARBA* 25 (1994): no. 1347, and by William K. Kearns in *Notes* 50 (1994): 1451–53.

5.140* Kroeger, Karl. *American Fuguing Tunes, 1770–1820: A Descriptive Catalog.* 220 pp. Westport, Conn.: Greenwood Press, 1994. (Music reference collection, 41)

A list of almost 1,300 fuguing tunes.

Reviewed by Gregg S. Geary in *ARBA* 26 (1995): no. 1281.

5.141 Lawrence, Vera Brodsky. *Music for Patriots, Politicians, and Presidents: Harmonies and Discords of the First Hundred Years.* 480 pp. New York: Macmillan, 1975.

A well-organized and illustrated sourcebook for information related to early American music, especially that connected with national political campaigns. Numerous facsimiles of title pages and excerpts for texts are included, as well as bibliographical references and index. See also **5.143**.

5.142 Lowens, Irving. *A Bibliography of Songsters Printed in America before 1821.* xxxviii + 229 pp. Worcester, Mass.: American Antiquarian Society, 1976.

A bibliography of collections of secular poems or song lyrics intended to be sung. There is an introductory essay on the songster. Detailed bibliographical descriptions with extensive annotations in chronological order are provided. There is a geographic directory of printers, publishers, booksellers, and engravers, as well as an index of compilers, editors, proprietors, and authors, and an index to titles of songsters.

Reviewed by Richard Crawford in *Fontes* 24 (1977): 299–303.

5.143* Miles, William J. *Songs, Odes, Glees and Ballads: A Bibliography of American Presidential Campaign Songsters.* lii + 200 pp. New York: Greenwood Press, 1990. (Music reference collection, 27)

5.144 Phemister, William. *American Piano Concertos: A Bibliography.* 323 pp. Detroit, Mich.: Published for the College Music Society by Information Coordinators, 1985. (Bibliographies in American music, 9)

A sourcebook of information on over 1,100 concertos composed in the United States. There is no index.

Reviewed by Ann P. Basart in *CNV* 104 (1986): 14–15 and by Allie Wise Goudy in *ARBA* 17 (1986): no. 1258.

5.145 Rabson, Carolyn, and **Kate Van Winkle Keller.** *The National Tune Index: 18th-Century Secular Music* (and *User's Guide*). 80 microfiche and 96 pp. New York: University Music Editions, 1980.

An extensive list of representative sources of American secular music, consisting of cross-referenced indexes of source contents, sorted by text, and by music incipits represented in scale degrees, stressed notes, and interval sequences.

A source derived from the National Tune Index databank, which contains about 40,000 examples of Anglo-American, 18th-century secular tunes. There are source indexes by genre. The *User's Guide* includes a short title index, a bibliography of sources, and an index to the various elements of the bibliography of sources. See also Keller's *Popular Secular Music in America through 1800* (**5.570**).

Reviewed by Gary W. Chapman in *Notes* 38 (1982): 608.

5.146 Rogal, Samuel J. "A Bibliographical Survey of American Hymnody 1640–1800." In *Bulletin of the New York Public Library* (Winter 1975): 231–52.

5.147 Solow, Linda. *The Boston Composers Project: A Bibliography of Contemporary Music.* Compiled by the Boston Area Music Libraries: Mary Wallace Davidson, Brenda Chasen Goldman, Geraldine Ostrove, associate editors. 775 pp. Cambridge, Mass.: MIT Press, 1983.

The Boston Area Music Libraries issued a supplement covering 1982–86 in 1987 (112 ll.).

A list of compositions by art music and jazz composers in the Boston area during the latter half of the 1970s, arranged alphabetically by composer. There is an index to names and titles. Geraldine Ostrove describes the methodology of the project in *Fontes* 30 (1983): 36–39.

Reviewed by Margaret Jory in *Notes* 42 (1985): 62–63 and by Charles Ellis in *AM* 3 (1985): 62–63.

5.148* Stillman, Amy K. "Published Hawaiian Songbooks." In *Notes* 44 (1987): 221–39.

A definition and analysis of the song types in Hawaiian vocal anthologies, with a checklist of major published Hawaiian songbooks.

5.149* Villamil, Victoria Etnier. *A Singer's Guide to the American Art Song, 1870–1980.* xxi + 452 pp. Metuchen, N.J.: Scarecrow Press, 1993.

A collection of 146 composer biographies, with discussions of their vocal compositions, including recording and publishing information.

Reviewed by Lori N. White in *SSB* 21 (1995): 26 no. 1 and by George Louis Mayer in *ARBA* 26 (1995): no. 1272.

5.150 White, Evelyn Davidson. *Choral Music by Afro-American Composers: A Selected, Annotated Bibliography.* 167 pp. Metuchen, N.J.: Scarecrow Press, 1981.

A 2nd ed., *Choral Music by African-American Composers: A Selected Annotated Bibliography,* is anticipated.

A bibliography arranged by composer whose entries cite title, copyright date, voicing, range, degree of difficulty, performing forces, publisher, and publisher's catalog number. There is an index to titles.

5.151 Wolfe, Richard J. *Secular Music in America, 1801–1825: A Bibliography.* 3 vols. New York: New York Public Library, Astor, Lenox and Tilden Foundations, 1964.

A major work of bibliography in the field of early American music, continuing the Sonneck–Upton *Bibliography* (**5.601**) and complemented by the Fuld–Davidson *18th-Century American Secular Music Manuscripts* (**5.551**) and the Britton–Lowens–Crawford *American Sacred Imprints, 1698–1810: A Bibliography* (**5.120**). The entries are arranged alphabetically by composer, with brief biographies and full bibliographical descriptions and locations of copies in American libraries and private collections.

The appendixes include "Unrecorded 18th-Century Imprints Located during the Course of This Work," "A List of Works in the Sonneck–Upton *Bibliography* Which Have Been Redated into 19th-Century," and "Locations of Newly Discovered Copies of Works in the Sonneck–Upton Bibliography." There are indexes of titles; first lines; publishers, engravers and printers; and numbering systems, as well as a general index.

Reviewed by James C. Downey in *Anuario, Inter-American Institute for Musical Research* 1 (1965): 122–24.

MUSIC FOR INSTRUCTION AND PERFORMANCE

The reference tools here are designed for the musician needing to locate and select musical material for performance, whether for solo or ensemble use. The need for such tools, incorporating the latest publications, is a perpetual one that has encouraged a continuing procession of resources. The following titles are classified, organized (with few exceptions) by instrument, although there are bibliographies focusing primarily on one instrument that include listings for another and bibliographies for instrumental ensembles, of course. The index gives access to additional titles containing works in a distinctive format by a single nationality.

5.152 Brüchle, Bernhard. *Musik-Bibliographien für alle Instrumente / Music Bibliographies for All Instruments.* English trans. by Colleen Gruban. 96 pp. Munich: Bernhard Brüchle Edition, 1976.

A bilingual list of 297 bibliographies of music for instruments, both solo and in chamber ensemble. There is a list of music publishers, followed by lists of special journals and societies devoted to instruments, of bibliographic tools, and of information centers, as well as an index of instruments covered.

Reviewed by Stephen Fry in *Notes* 34 (1977): 87.

ACCORDION

5.153* Maurer, Walter. *Akkordeon-Bibliographie: Schulen, Etüden, Literatur zum Solo-, Duo-, Orchesterspiel, Kammermusik, und Konzerte.* 398 pp. Trossingen, Austria: Hohner, 1990.

A classified bibliography of accordion music.

BAGPIPES

5.154 Bagpipe Music Index. *Current Alphabetical Tune Listing.* Unpaged. Glen Ridge, N.J.: Bagpipe Music Index, 1966.

An index, reproduced from typescript, containing 2,430 entries from 35 tune books. The tunes are listed alphabetically by title, with the tune's composer, location in the book, tune type, meter, and number of parts.

5.155* Bain, Harry. *Bain's Directory of Bag-Pipe Tunes.* 143 pp. Edinburgh: Albyn Press, 1983.

5.156 Cannon, Roderick D. *A Bibliography of Bagpipe Music.* 295 pp. Edinburgh: John Donald, 1980.

A descriptive bibliography of all the music printed for each type of bagpipe played in the British Isles, to distinguish the various editions of each book, to ascertain dates and authorship, and to collect background information of interest to players and music historians. There are descriptions of 133 titles from the literature and music of the bagpipe in its various local styles, with four sections devoted to different pipe practices: Union pipes (both Irish and Scottish publications, 18 entries), Northumbrian bagpipes (small and half-long pipes, 8 entries), Scots Highland pipes (99 entries), and Irish warpipes and Brien Boru pipes (8 entries). Unfortunately, the contents of anthologies are not analyzed.

Reviewed by Amy Aaron in *Notes* 37 (1980): 60–61 and by Howard Weiss in *Ethnomusicology* 27 (1983): 549–50.

5.157* Chalmers, Donald. *The New Melody Directory: Highland Bagpipe.* 2 vols. Coburg, Victoria, Australia: Melodex, 1986.

An index and thematic catalog of bagpipe music.

5.158* MacRaonuill, Alasdair. *Eachdraidh a' cuil soir / History of the Music Great.* 2nd ed. Unpaged. Austin, Tex.: The author, 1989.

The 1st ed., 1988, has c. 300 pp., and is a detailed index of 313 tunes for bagpipes from 34 tune books and tutors, with details about each tune.

An index to bagpipe tunes in various collections, including historical commentary.

5.159* Pekaar, Robert L. *An Encyclopedia of Tunes of the Great Highland Bagpipe.* 3rd ed. 336 pp. London, Ontario: Scott's Highland Services, 1994.

The vol. cited covers entries A–O.

5.160* Seanair. *Gaelic Names of Pipe Tunes: Pronunciations, English Translations, the Gaelic Songs.* 64 pp. Kingston, Ontario: Iolair Pub., 1994.

A bibliography of bagpipe music and Gaelic songs.

BAND/WIND ENSEMBLES

5.161* Anesa, Marino, and **Roberto Leydi.** *Dizionario della musica italiana per banda: Biografie dei compositori e catalogo delle opere dal 1800 al 1945.* 515 pp. Bergamo, Italy: Tipolitografia Secomandi, 1993.

A reference work listing the Italian composers of band music and their composition, 1800–1945.

5.162 *Band Music Guide: Alphabetical Listing of Titles and Composers of All Band Music Materials of All Publishers.* 9th ed. 354 pp. Northfield, Ill.: Instrumentalist Company, 1989.

First published as Kenneth Berger's *Band Music, a Listing of Band Music by All Publishers* (Evansville, Ind.: Berger Band, 1953), 152 pp. Revised ed., published 1956 (200 pp.). *Band Music Guide: A Directory of Published Band Music* (Evanston, Ill.: Instrumentalist Company, 1959). 3rd ed., 1962 (342 pp.), by Instrumentalist Company, Evanston, Ill. 5th ed., *Band Music Guide: Alphabetical Listing of Titles of All Band Music and all Composers of Band Music* (Evanston, Ill.: Instrumentalist Company, 1970), 377 pp., with *Addendum* (1973, 78 pp.). 6th ed., 1975 (360 pp.); 7th ed., 1978 (367 pp.); 8th ed., 1982 (408 pp.). Berger's name was dropped as editor with the 6th ed. in 1975.

An attempt at a comprehensive list of band music, intended to aid school band directors in the U.S. in their program preparation. Works are listed by title, with separate sections for anthologies, solos and ensembles with band, method books, and marching routines.

5.163 Berger, Kenneth W. *Band Encyclopedia.* 604 pp. Evansville, Ind.: Distributed by Band Associates, 1960.

A compendium of information useful to band directors, including revisions of the author's earlier *Band Bibliography, Band Discography,* and *Bandsman,* a biographical dictionary of band musicians.

Reviewed by Keith Polk in *Notes* 18 (1961): 424–26 and by J. M. Lundahl in *JRME* 10 (1962): 81–82.

5.164 Heller, George N. *Ensemble Music for Wind and Percussion Instruments: A Catalog.* 142 pp. Washington, D.C.: Music Educators National Conference, 1970.

5.165* Rehrig, William H. *The Heritage Encyclopedia of Band Music: Composers and Their Music.* Edited by Paul E. Bierley. 2 vols. Westerville, Ohio: Integrity Press, 1991.

An attempt to document all editions of all music ever published (and some unpublished) for concert and military bands, an outgrowth of the research begun by Robert Hoe, Jr., whose Heritage of the March series of recordings made available to American libraries much previously unrecorded band music, *gratis.* The entries are arranged by composer, with bibliographical information often included. There are many unique entries.

Reviewed by Donald Morris in *Notes* 51 (1994): 217–18 and by Leslie Bennett in *Fontes* 39 (1992): 378–79.

5.166* Renshaw, Jeffrey H. *The American Wind Symphony Commissioning Project: A Descriptive Catalog of Published Editions, 1957–1991.* 383 pp. Westport, Conn.: Greenwood Press, 1991. (Music reference collection, 34)

A catalog of the 150+ works sponsored by the Pittsburgh, Pa.-based wind ensemble, including detailed data on the compositions, biographical information on their composers, and facsimiles, as well as a selective discography.

Reviewed by Evan Feldman in *Fontes* 41 (1994): 228–30 and by William K. Kearns in *Notes* 50 (1994): 1,451–53.

5.167 Reynolds, H. Robert. *Wind Ensemble Literature.* 2nd revised ed. 174 pp. in various pagings. Madison, Wisc.: University of Wisconsin Bands, 1975.

A repertoire list in four parts: compositions for wind ensemble/symphonic band; compositions for solo instruments, voice, or narrator with wind ensemble/symphonic band; chorus or choruses with wind ensemble/symphonic band; and addendum, including works for which the editor had incomplete information. Each section is organized alphabetically by composer and includes a code for instrumentation, publication information, and references to selected recorded information.

5.168 *Selective Music List for Bands.* Revision. 57 pp. Nashville, Tenn.: National Band Association, 1990.

1986 list, 71 pp.

A bibliography of band music, graded by level of difficulty.

5.169 Suppan, Armin. *Repertorium der Märsche für Blasorchester.* 2 vols. to date. Tutzing, Germany: Hans Schneider, 1982– . (Alta musica, 6, 13)

A list of marches arranged alphabetically by composer, giving titles and publishing information. There is an index to titles.

5.170 Wallace, David, and **Eugene Corporon.** *Wind Ensemble/Band Repertoire.* 248 pp. Greeley, Colo.: University of Northern Colorado, 1984.

A broadly classified list of works for wind ensemble, citing composer, title, instrumentation, and, by reference, publisher. Works for voice and wind ensemble are included. There is no index.

5.171 Whitwell, David. *Band Music of the French Revolution.* 212 pp. Tutzing, Germany: Schneider, 1979. (Alta musica, 5)

A history with an extensive bibliography and a thematic catalog.

5.172 Whitwell, David. *The History and Literature of the Wind Band and Wind Ensemble.* 9 vols. Northridge, Calif.: Winds, 1982–84.

Contents: Vol. 1, *The Wind Band and Wind Ensemble before 1500;* Vol. 2, *The Renaissance Wind Band and Wind Ensemble;* Vol. 3, *The Baroque Wind Band and Wind Ensemble;* Vol. 4, *The Wind Band and Wind Ensemble of the Classic Period, 1750–1800;* Vol. 5, *The Nineteenth-Century Wind Band and Wind Ensemble in Western Europe;* Vol. 6, *A Catalog of Multi-Part Instrumental Music for Wind Instruments or for Undesignated Instrumentation before 1600;* Vol. 7, *A Catalog of Multi-Part Instrumental Music for Wind Instruments or for Undesignated Instrumentation;* Vol. 8, *Wind Band and Wind Ensemble Literature of the Classic Period;* Vol. 9, *Wind Band and Wind Ensemble Music of the Nineteenth Century.*

A monumental history and bibliography.

Reviewed by Kerry S. Grant in *Notes* 41 (1984): 61–62 and by Clifford Bartlett in *Brio* 22 (1985): 25–27.

BRASS

5.173 Anderson, Paul G., and **Larry Bruce Campbell.** *Brass Music Guide: Solo and Study Guide Material in Print.* 345 pp. Northfield, Ill.: Instrumentalist Co., 1987. (Music guide series, 4)

First published as *Brass Solo and Study Material Music Guide,* 1976, 237 pp. *Brass Music Guide: Solo and Study Guide Material in Print, 1985,* published in 1984, 294 pp.

A bibliography of classified lists divided by instrument, with each entry citing a brief title and a publisher code; there is a composer index.

The 1976 ed. is reviewed by Kim Dunnick in *ITGJ* 2 (1977): 38–39.

5.174 Rasmussen, Mary. *A Teacher's Guide to the Literature of Brass Instruments.* 84 pp. Durham, N.H.: Brass Quarterly, 1964.

A general discussion of music available for brass ensembles and solos, with extensive listings giving publisher, price, instrumentation, and grade level of the works cited.

5.175* Thompson, J. Mark, and **Jeffrey Jon Lemke.** *French Music for Low Brass Instruments: An Annotated Bibliography.* 178 pp. Bloomington, Ind.; Indianapolis, Ind.: Indiana University Press, 1994.

An annotated list of solo pieces and pedagogical materials for tenor trombone, bass trombone, tuba, and bass saxhorn. Each entry gives date, publisher, length, range, level of difficulty and an indication of its use as a competition solo at the Paris Conservatory, and a description of its musical style or character. A discography (pp. 152–64) is included.

French Horn

5.176 Brüchle, Bernhard. *Horn Bibliographie.* 3 vols. Wilhelmshaven, Germany: Heinrichshofen, 1970–83.

The 1st vol. was published with a 14-page supplement of plates. The 3rd vol. was written with D. Leinhard.

A bibliography with entries classified according to ensembles: horn solo, horn and keyboard, various duo combinations, trios, quartets, etc. The work contains a bibliography of literature on the instrument, list of publishers, and index of names.

5.177 Gregory, Robin. *The Horn: A Comprehensive Guide to the Modern Instrument and Its Music.* 2nd ed. 410 pp. London: Faber; New York: Praeger, 1969.

First ed., 1961, published as *The Horn: A Guide to the Modern Instrument,* by Faber & Faber, London.

A book on the horn whose third appendix (pp. 181–303) is a classified list of horn music, solo and in combination with various ensembles, instrumental or vocal. The entries have composer, title, ensemble, or publisher.

Trombone

5.178 Arling, Harry J. *Trombone Chamber Music: An Annotated Bibliography.* 2nd ed. 43 pp. Nashville, Tenn.: Brass Press, 1983.

1st ed., 1978, 48 pp.

A guide with the majority of works cited composed in the 20th century. Most involve the trombone as the only brass instrument.

The 1st ed. is reviewed by Peter B. Brown in *Notes* 36 (1979): 103–4, the 2nd by Andreas Sprinz in *Brass Bulletin* 50 (1985): 101.

5.179 Everett, Thomas G. *Annotated Guide to Bass Trombone Literature.* 3rd ed., revised and enlarged. 94 pp. Nashville, Tenn.: The Brass Press, 1985. (Brass research series, 6)

The 1st ed. was published in 1973, the 2nd in 1978.

A list with 726 entries of published and manuscript music, with a bibliography, discography, and composer index.

The 2nd ed. is reviewed by Peter B. Brown in *Notes* 36 (1979): 103–4, and the 3rd by Robert Skinner in *ARBA* 17 (1986): no. 1264.

Trumpet

5.180 Cansler, Philip T. *Twentieth Century Music for Trumpet and Organ: An Annotated Bibliography.* 46 pp. Nashville, Tenn.: Brass Press, 1984. (Brass research series, 11)

A catalog and description of 83 compositions, giving for each entry a short biography of the composer and a critical interpretation of the work. There are also lists of pieces arranged by composer's nationality, as well as a bibliography of sources consulted.

Reviewed by Anne F. Hardin in *ITGJ* 10 (1985): 57 no. 1 and by Ann P. Basart in *CNV* 104 (1986): 16.

5.181 Carnovale, Norbert, and **Paul F. Doerksen.** *Twentieth-Century Music for Trumpet and Orchestra.* 64 pp. Nashville, Tenn.: Brass Press, 1994. (Brass research series, 13)

First issued in 1975, 55 pp.

A guide to 329 works with imprint information, duration, range, and reviews cited.

The 1st ed. is reviewed by Stephen Fry in *Notes* 32 (1976): 780 and by Charles Decker in *ITGJ* 2 (1977): 39.

5.182* Hiller, Albert. *Music for Trumpets from Three Centuries (c. 1600–after 1900): Compositions for 1–24 (Natural) Trumpets with and without Timpani.* 257 pp. Cologne: Wolfgang G. Haas, 1993. (Cologne music series, pts. 1–3)

A source including both bibliographical and discographical indexes.

Tuba/Euphonium

5.183 Bell, William J., and **R. Winston Morris.** *Encyclopedia of Literature for the Tuba.* 161 pp. New York: C. Colin, 1967.

A bibliography of music for the tuba.

5.184* Bird, Gary. *Program Notes for the Solo Tuba.* 146 pp. Bloomington, Ind.: Indiana University Press, 1994.

A collection of program notes, written by the composers, for 88 works for tuba, tuba and piano, and tuba with other accompaniment. Each entry gives a complete bibliographic citation, a history of the piece, its instrumentation and movements, and a description of its musical structure and characteristics.

5.185* Louder, Earl, and **David R. Corbin, Jr.** *Euphonium Music Guide.* 46 pp. Evanston, Ill.: Instrumentalist Co., 1978.

An annotated list of works, original and arranged, featuring the euphonium.

5.186 Morris, R. Winston. *Tuba Music Guide.* 60 pp. Evanston, Ill.: Instrumentalist Co., 1973.
A classified and annotated bibliography of solo and chamber music for the tuba.

BRASS ENSEMBLES

5.187 Anderson, Paul G., and **Lisa Ormston Bontrager.** *Brass Music Guide: Ensemble Music in Print.* 345 pp. Northfield, Ill.: Instrumentalist Co., 1987. (Music guide series, 5)
First published in 1978, 259 pp.
Classified lists with brief titles and publisher code and a composer index.

5.188* Bundesakademie für Musikalische Jugendbildung. *Literatur für zwei und mehr verschiedene Blechblasinstrumente.* 224 pp. Trossingen, Germany: Bundesakademie für Musikalische Jugendbildung, 1994. (Repertoireverzeichnis, 1)
A classified bibliography of music for two or more brass instruments.

5.189 Devol, John. *Brass Music for the Church: A Bibliography of Music Appropriate for Church Use.* 103 pp. New York: Harold Branch, 1974.
A list of 1,309 works, including brass parts for 1 trumpet up to a 20-piece brass choir.
Reviewed in *Instrumentalist* 30 (December 1975): 26.

CHAMBER ENSEMBLES

5.190 Altmann, Wilhelm. *Kammermusik-Katalog: Ein Verzeichnis von seit 1841 veröffentlichten Kammerwerken.* 6th ed. 400 pp. Leipzig: F. Hofmeister, 1945.
Reprinted in 1967 by F. Hofmeister in Hofheim am Taunus. First published in Leipzig, 1910. The 4th ed. was published in Leipzig by C. Merseburger in 1931, 251 pp., with a *Supplement* published by F. Hofmeister in 1936, 73 pp.
Succeeded by Richter's *Kammermusik-Katalog* (**5.198**).
A international bibliography of chamber music published since 1841, including both separate works and works in collections, classified by medium, with composer indexes.

5.191 Aulich, Bruno. *Alte Musik für Liebhaber.* 3rd ed. 320 pp. + 16 pp. of plates. Munich: Artemis Verlag, 1981.
Previously published as *Alte Musik für Hausmusikanten* (Munich: Heimeran, 1968), 288 pp.
An extensive introduction to the performance factors and genres of early instrumental music. Bio-bibliographical section listing modern editions of music originally intended for or arranged as chamber music. There is an index to names and terms.

5.192 Cobbett, Walter Willson. *Cyclopedic Survey of Chamber Music.* With supplementary material edited by Colin Mason. 2nd ed. 3 vols. London; New York: Oxford University Press, 1963.
First published in 2 vols., 1929–30. The 2nd ed. is a reissue of the original 2 vols. with minor corrections, plus a 3rd vol., which selectively updates the information in the 1st two.
A biographical and subject dictionary of chamber music (for three to nine solo instruments), encompassing instruments, performing ensembles, and competitions, giving under the composer's name a full list of works in this category, excluding solo works and piano compositions. The main emphases are critical, historical, and analytical. The excellent critical and bibliographical material includes signed articles by such authorities as Eric Blom and Percy Scholes. Colin Mason for Vol. 3 wrote extended articles surveying chamber music since 1929 in Europe and Great Britain; the survey also includes "Chamber Music in America" by Nicolas Slonimsky and "Soviet Chamber Music" by I. I. Martinov. There are a classified bibliography on chamber music and an index of composers.

The 2nd ed. is reviewed by Homer Ulrich in *Notes* 21 (1963): 124–26.

5.193 Forsyth, Ella Marie. *Building a Chamber Music Collection: A Descriptive Guide to Published Scores.* 191 pp. Metuchen, N.J.: Scarecrow Press, 1979.

Descriptions of formal and stylistic traits of over 300 works from the basic chamber music repertoire, arranged in classified format, with a bibliography and indexes.

Reviewed by Frederic Schoettler in *ARBA* 11 (1980): no. 992 and by Karl Van Ausdal in *Notes* 36 (1980): 658–59.

5.194 Hinson, Maurice. *The Piano in Chamber Ensemble: An Annotated Guide.* xxxiii + 570 pp. Bloomington, Ind.: Indiana University Press, 1978.

A classified bibliography covering music from c. 1700 to the present, with considerable attention to contemporary music. Includes a brief annotated bibliography (pp. 545–49) of suggested readings on the subject and an index of composers.

Reviewed by Bennett Ludden in *Notes* 35 (1979): 891–92 and by Peter Ward Jones in *M&L* 60 (1979): 335.

5.195 Lemacher, Heinrich. *Handbuch der Hausmusik.* 454 pp. Graz, Austria: A. Pustet, 1948.

A handbook on more accessible, less technically demanding music. The book from p. 219 on lists works for solo instruments and various chamber ensembles. Many lesser-known works are included. The arrangement is alphabetically by composer, within the various categories. Each citation gives the publisher and brief description.

5.196* Ping-Robbins, Nancy R. *The Piano Trio in the Twentieth Century: A Partially Annotated Bibliography with Introduction and Appended Lists of Commissioned Works and Performing Trios.* 153 pp. Raleigh, N.C.: Regan Press, 1984.

A bibliography with the publishing information occasionally omitted.

5.197* Rangel-Ribeiro, Victor, and **Robert Markel.** *Chamber Music: An International Guide to Works and Their Instrumentation.* 271 pp. New York: Facts on File, 1993.

A bibliography in chart form, listing 8,000 works with up to 20 instruments. The list is in two parts: "Composers to the Time of Haydn and Mozart" and "Composers from Beethoven to Our Time," with a "Master Quick-Reference Index" (pp. 229–67).

Reviewed by Harold J. Diamond in *Choice* 31 (1993): 590 and by George Louis Mayer in *ARBA* 25 (1994): no. 1349.

5.198 Richter, Johannes. *Kammermusik-Katalog; Verzeichnis der von 1944 bis 1958 veröffentlichten Werke für Kammermusik und für Klavier vier- und sechshändig sowie für zwei und mehr Klaviere.* 318 pp. Leipzig: F. Hofmeister, 1960.

Successor to Wilhelm Altmann's work of the same title (**5.190**), covering chamber music from 1945 through 1958. The entries are classified and include chamber music with voice and piano duet. Includes an index of composers and collection titles and a list of publishers.

5.199* Scott, William. *A Conductor's Repertory of Chamber Music: Compositions for Nine to Fifteen Solo Instruments.* xli + 383 pp. Westport, Conn.: Greenwood Press, 1993. (Music reference collection, 39)

Headed by "A Historical Survey of Conducting Chamber Music," a list of about 1,000 works for 9 to 15 instruments, arranged alphabetically by composers, followed by "The Repertory Classified" (pp. 83–138) and a title index (pp. 139–59). Neither the composers' dates nor the dates of composition are given. There is a brief bibliography (pp. 161–63).

Reviewed by Evan Feldman in *Fontes* 41 (1994): 228–30, by C. Michael Phillips in *ARBA* 25 (1994): no. 1350, and by Harold J. Diamond in *Choice* 31 (1993): 590.

CHORAL MUSIC

5.200* Anderson, Kenneth H. *Catalogue of Sets of Vocal Music Available for Loan in the Public Libraries of Greater London and the Counties of Bedfordshire, Berkshire, Birminghamshire, East Sussex, Essex, Hertfordshire, Kent, Surrey, West Sussex.* 2 vols. London: London and South Eastern Library Region, 1989.

First ed. published in London: Laser, 1979, 314 pp.

A source giving access to British interlibrary loan possibilities. The 1st vol. lists entries in classified order (operas, oratorios, etc.); the 2nd has both a composer and a title index, giving access to choral anthologies as well as single titles.

A related title by the author, *Music for Choirs: Sets of Choral Works in the Public Libraries of Cambridgeshire, Northamptonshire, Nottinghamshire and Suffolk: Catalogue* (Nottingham: East Midlands Regional Library System, 1984), 359 pp., gives access to another body of library holdings.

The 1st ed. is reviewed by Richard Andrewes in *MT* 122 (1981): 675–76, the 2nd ed. by Stuart Waumsley in *Brio* 27 (1990): 233–34.

5.201 Burnsworth, Charles C. *Choral Music for Women's Voices: An Annotated Bibliography of Recommended Works.* 180 pp. Metuchen, N.J.: Scarecrow Press, 1968.

Detailed critical and descriptive annotations for some 135 choral works for women's voices and a like number of arrangements. The works are indexed by title, number of vocal parts, grade of difficulty, extended compositions, and collections.

5.202 Daugherty, F. Mark, and **Susan H. Simon.** *Secular Choral Music in Print.* 2nd ed. 2 vols. 1,190 pp. Philadelphia, Pa.: Musicdata, 1987. (Music in print series, 2)

1991 Supplement arranged by Daugherty and Simon, 188 pp. *1993 Supplement,* with the same editors, 223 pp. A *Master Index* was published by Musicdata in 1993, 365 pp. An *Arranger Index* was published in 1987, 128 pp.

A revised ed. of the 1st, 1974 ed. was edited by Thomas R. Nardone, James H. Nye, and Mark Resnick, as was the 1982 supplement.

A list, arranged alphabetically by composer and then by title, of editions of secular choral music reported by their publishers as being in print. No attempt was made to put variant titles of the same work together. Prices are sometimes given.

The 1974 ed. is reviewed by Barbara A. Petersen in *Notes* 31 (1975): 773–74. The 1987 ed. and the *Arranger Index* are reviewed by Paul B. Cors in *ARBA* 20 (1989): nos. 1219 and 1220.

5.203* DeVenney, David P., and **Craig R. Johnson.** *The Chorus in Opera: A Guide to the Repertory.* 203 pp. Metuchen, N.J.: Scarecrow Press, 1993.

A list of choral works able to be performed independently of their parent work, based on the repertoire listed in the 10th ed. of *Kobbé's Complete Opera Book.*

Reviewed by Ruthann Boles McTyre in *Fontes* 41 (1994): 133–34 and by Karin Pendle in *ARBA* 25 (1994): no. 1353.

5.204 Eslinger, Gary S., and **F. Mark Daugherty.** *Sacred Choral Music in Print.* 2nd ed. 2 vols. Philadelphia, Pa.: Musicdata, 1985. (Music in print series, 1)

1988 Supplement, edited by Susan H. Simon, 277 pp. *1992 Supplement,* edited by F. Mark Daugherty and Susan H. Simon, 304 pp.

The 2nd ed. is an update of the 1st vol. of *Choral Music in Print,* 1974, edited by Thomas R. Nardone, James H. Nye, and Mark Resnick, the 1976 supplement to *Choral Music in Print,* edited by Thomas R. Nardone, and the 1981 supplement, edited by Nancy K. Nardone.

A list, arranged alphabetically by composer and then by title, of editions reported by their publishers as being in print. No attempt was made to put variant titles of the same work together. Prices are sometimes given.

The 1st ed. is reviewed by Barbara Peterson in *Notes* 31 (1975): 773–75 and by Malcolm Jones in *Brio* 12 (1975): 17–18. The 2nd ed. is reviewed by Ann P. Basart in *CNV* 101 (1986): 12 and by Avery T. Sharp in *ARBA* 18 (1987): no. 1251.

5.205* Evans, Margaret R. *Sacred Cantatas: An Annotated Bibliography, 1960–1979.* 188 pp. Jefferson, N.C.: McFarland, 1982.

A list of 465 18th- to 20th-century sacred cantatas published with English texts, original or translated.

Reviewed by Avery T. Sharp in *ARBA* 14 (1983): 922.

5.206* Green, Jonathan D. *A Conductor's Guide to Choral–Orchestral Works.* 322 pp. Metuchen, N.J.: Scarecrow Press, 1994.

A guide to 89 major 20th-century works, with some English text, for full chorus and orchestra, by 49 composers. Each entry has a composer biography, instrumentation, origin of the text, editions published, availability of performance material, special performance needs, a discography, and a brief bibliography of the composer and the work.

5.207 Knapp, J. Merrill. *Selected List of Music for Men's Voices.* 165 pp. Princeton, N.J.: Princeton University Press, 1952.

A bibliography of original and arranged works for male chorus, both published and unpublished. The arrangement is alphabetical by composer within the main classification scheme. Each entry includes the birth and death dates of composers, the scoring, language, publisher and editor, and the degree of difficulty. There is an index of composers.

Reviewed by Archibald T. Davison in *Notes* 10 (1952): 104–5.

5.208 Locke, Arthur Ware, and **Charles K. Fassett.** *Selected List of Choruses of Women's Voices.* 3rd ed., revised and enlarged. xxiii + 253 pp. Northampton, Mass.: Smith College, 1964.

First published in 1927; 2nd ed., 1946, edited by A. W. Locke, 237 pp.

A bibliography whose principal section is a catalog arranged alphabetically by composer, with titles of choruses, vocal combinations, publishers, or source in a collection. The foreign titles are usually translated. Collections are listed separately and their contents given. The indexes include a chronological list of composers, compositions by categories, authors and sources of texts, and first lines and titles.

5.209 May, James D. *Avant-Garde Choral Music: An Annotated Selected Bibliography.* 258 pp. Metuchen, N.J.: Scarecrow Press, 1977.

A bibliography of music readily available in the United States, giving extensive information on musical characteristics. The indexes are classified by performing forces required.

Reviewed by Stephen M. Fry in *Notes* 34 (1977): 359.

5.210 Roberts, Kenneth. *A Checklist of Twentieth-Century Choral Music for Male Voices.* 32 pp. Detroit, Mich.: Information Coordinators, 1970. (Detroit studies in music bibliography, 17)

A list compiled to update Knapp (**5.207**), arranged alphabetically by composer. Supplying the composers' dates and indexing the various characteristics of the works (intended function, instrumentation, etc.) would contribute to this work's usefulness.

5.211* Sharp, Avery T. *Choral Music Reviews Index* (I: *1983–1985;* II: *1986–1988*). 2 vols. New York: Garland Publishing, 1986–90. (Garland reference library of the humanities, 674 and 962)

A descriptive, multireferenced index. The 1st vol. covers more than 2,400 reviews in 16 English-language journals, divided into three sections, each listing works alphabetically by title. Section I lists octavos (brief choral works); Section II, collections of choral works; and Section III, extended choral works. Each entry gives all bibliographic information provided by the reviewing journal, a citation to the journal issue, and a review outline summarizing the reviewer's comments. Indexes provide access to choral title by composer, editor/arranger/compiler, choral voicing, solo voicing, recommended level or type of choir, accompanying instruments, use or special purpose, and recommendations for small chorus.

The 2nd vol. brings to date the published reviews of 2,000 choral works in 15 English-language journals.

The 1st vol. is reviewed by Ann P. Basart in *CNV* 110 (1987): 11 and by Paul B. Cors in *ARBA* 18 (1987): 1239. The 2nd vol. is reviewed by David P. DeVenney in *Notes* 47 (1990): 406–7 and by Lorna Young in *Fontes* 37 (1990): 280–81.

5.212 Temperley, Nicholas, and **Charles G. Manns.** *Fuguing Tunes in the Eighteenth-Century.* 493 pp. Detroit, Mich.: Information Coordinators, 1983. (Detroit studies in music bibliography, no. 49)

An analytical census of 1,239 tunes, with a historical introduction and a list of sources. The indexes include texts, tune names, and persons. There is also a list of modern editions.

Reviewed by Allen P. Britton in *Fontes* 32 (1985): 88–89, by Karl Kroeger in *Notes* 41 (1984): 58–61, and by Carole Franklin Vidali in *ARBA* 16 (1985): no. 1160.

5.213 Tortolano, William. *Original Music for Men's Voices: A Selected Bibliography.* 2nd ed. 201 pp. Metuchen, N.J.: Scarecrow Press, 1981.

First published in 1973, 123 pp.

A bibliography of entries, arranged by composer, providing information on performing forces and duration. There is a section on music found in collections. There are six essays on the subject, and there are indexes of authors and sources of text and of first lines and titles.

Reviewed by George Louis Mayer in *ARBA* 13 (1982): no. 1020.

5.214* White, J. Perry. *Twentieth Century Choral Music: An Annotated Bibliography of Music Suitable for Use by High School Choirs.* 2nd ed. 214 pp. Metuchen, N.J.: Scarecrow Press, 1990.

First ed., 1982, 143 pp.

A list of 367 works, with entries giving composer, title, vocal requirements, accompaniment, range, level of difficulty, style, publisher, duration, usage, and date, classified by vocal combination. There are composer and title indexes.

Reviewed by Avery T. Sharp in *ARBA* 14 (1983): no. 925.

ELECTRONIC AND COMPUTER MUSIC

5.215 Davies, Hugh. *Répertoire international des musiques electroacoustiques / International Electronic Music Catalog: A Cooperative Publication of le Groupe de recherches musicales de l'O.R.T.F., Paris and the Independent Electronic Music Center, New York.* xxx + 330 pp. Cambridge, Mass.: Distributed by MIT Press, 1968.

A catalog of some 5,000 works, intended to document all the electronic music ever composed. The main alphabet is by country, subdivided by city (and, in the U.S., by state). Data is given on composers, titles of works, functions, composition dates, durations, and number of tracks involved. Appendixes include a discography, a directory of permanent studies, and an index of composers.

Reviewed by Jon Appleton in *Notes* 25 (1968): 34–35.

5.216* Wallace, David E. *A Second Listing of Multi-Media Works Available from Composers at Colleges and Universities.* 138 pp. Monmouth, Ore.: Oregon College of Education, 1973.

A list that includes biographical sketches (pp. 118–34).

KEYBOARD MUSIC

5.217 Alker, Hugo. *Literatur für alte Tasteninstrumente; Versuch einer Bibliographie für die Praxis.* 2nd ed. 79 pp. Vienna: Wissenschaftliches Antiquariat H. Geyer, 1967. (Wiener Abhandlungen zur Musikwissenschaft und Instrumentenkunde, 2)

First published in Vienna, 1962, by H. Geyer (82 pp.).

A keyboard bibliography whose main division is between music for harpsichord and music for organ (without pedals); the entries are brief, with information given for publishers and editors. The collections are entered by title and are filed in the same alphabet with composers. The emphasis was on music then available in practical editions.

5.218* Burhardt, Stefan. *Polonez: Katalog Tematyczny / Polonaise: Thematic Catalogue, volume 2: 1792–1830; volume 3: 1831–1981.* Edited by M. Prokopowicz and A. Spoz. 3 vols. Cracow: Polskie Wydawn. Muzyczne, 1976.

5.219* *Classical Keyboard Music in Print, 1993.* Inaugural ed. 690 pp. Palo Alto, Calif.: Accolade Press, 1993.

5.220* Heinrich, Adel. *Organ and Harpsichord Music by Women Composers: An Annotated Catalog.* 373 pp. New York: Greenwood Press, 1991. (Music reference collection, 30)

A bibliography of organ and harpsichord works, most of which are by 20th-century women composers. The citations in the main section are listed alphabetically by composer and generally include year of completion, the source, the playing time, the degree of difficulty, the publisher and date of publication or library source, and recording information. Indexes include an instrumentation index (pp. 139–87), a title index (pp. 189–227), coded lists of publishers, libraries, record companies, and composers' biographies (pp. 241–342), a chronological list of composers by country, and a coded bibliography of 56 items.

Reviewed by Brian Doherty in *Notes* 49 (1993): 1,485–86 and by Claudia Macdonald in *Fontes* 39 (1992): 383–84, with a response by the author.

5.221 Meggett, Joan. *Keyboard Music by Women Composers: A Catalog and Bibliography.* 210 pp. Westport, Conn.: Greenwood Press, 1981.

A catalog of the harpsichord, piano, and organ works of 290 composers, including brief biographies and lists of sources. Includes an extensive annotated bibliography of sources referring to more than one woman composer (pp. 3–19) and a discography (pp. 203–10).

5.222 Sartorius, Richard H. *Bibliography of Concertos for Organ and Orchestra.* 68 pp. Evanston, Ill.: Instrumentalist Company, 1961.

A list that includes primary sources as well as modern publications, with extensive annotations, biographical and descriptive. The locations of the original material are given. The list includes much material not exclusively for organ.

5.223* Sloane, Sally Jo. *Music for Two or More Players at Clavichord, Harpsichord, Organ: An Annotated Bibliography.* 104 pp. New York: Greenwood Press, 1991. (Music reference collection, 29)

A list arranged alphabetically by composer, with brief annotations and publisher information. Information on recordings, when available, is included.

Harpsichord

5.224 Arneson, Arne Jon, and **Stacie Williams.** *The Harpsichord Booke, Being a Plaine and Simple Index to Printed Collections of Musick by Different Masters for the Harpsichord, Spinnet, Clavichord and Virginall.* xliii + 119 pp. Madison, Wisc.: Index House, 1986.

An index to multicomposer anthologies of compositions that include early music (to 1800) for harpsichord and its kindred instruments, excluding works for organ or pianoforte. Includes a bibliography of anthologies indexed (pp. xviii–xliii), as well as indexes of composers, titles, and editors.

Reviewed by Ann P. Basart in *CNV* 106 (1986): 25–26 and by Robert Skinner in *ARBA* 19 (1988): no. 1294.

5.225 Bedford, Frances. *Harpsichord and Clavichord Music of the Twentieth Century.* liv + 609 pp. Berkeley, Calif.: Fallen Leaf Press, 1993. (Fallen Leaf reference books in music, 22)

Earlier ed. issued as *Twentieth-Century Harpsichord Music: A Classified Catalog,* by Frances Bedford and Robert Conant. xxi + 95 pp. Hackensack, N.J.: Joseph Boonin, 1974. (Music indexes and bibliographies, 8)

An exhaustive list, international in scope, with entries for solo and multiple harpsichord music, classified by type of ensemble: harpsichord and string instrument, harpsichord and one other keyboard instrument, etc. Over 5,000 harpsichord works and 174 clavichord works by over 2,600 composers are cited, with entries including background information and degree of difficulty. There are composer and title indexes and a list of publishers. Appendixes include lists of helpful addresses and of libraries holding related print and sound collections.

Reviewed by Robert Palmieri in *ARBA* 25 (1994): no. 1355, by Keith Paulson-Thorp in *EKJ* 12 (1994): 126–29, by John Wagstaff in *Brio* 32 (1995): 134–35, and by Barbara Harbach in *Notes* 51 (1995): 1335. The 1st ed. is reviewed by Jo Ann Smith in *AMT* 24 (1975): 49–50 and by Peter Williams in *Organ Yearbook* 7 (1976): 170.

5.226* Gustafson, Bruce, and **David Fuller.** *A Catalogue of French Harpsichord Music, 1699–1780.* xxi + 446 pp. Oxford; New York: Clarendon Press, 1990.

A guide to manuscript and printed sources of French harpsichord music, including bibliographical references and indexes, concluding the work begun with **5.227.**

Reviewed by Carol Henry Bates in *EKJ* 12 (1994): 121–22, by George Lucktenberg in *Notes* 49 (1992): 544–46, by Howard Schott in *MT* 132 (1991): 395, and by Ross Wood in *Fontes* 39 (1992): 75–76.

5.227 Gustafson, Bruce. *French Harpsichord Music of the 17th Century: A Thematic Catalog of the Sources, with Commentary.* 3 vols. Ann Arbor, Mich.: UMI Research Press, 1979.

An impressive bibliographic survey with descriptions of and commentary on each manuscript arranged by present location and, in Vols. 2–3, with detailed bibliographic descriptions, thematic entries, and concordances to other manuscripts. The complex thematic catalog and the index to all 3 vols. are not well explained, but once understood are quite useful.

5.228 Silbiger, Alexander. *Italian Manuscript Sources of 17th-Century Keyboard Music.* xxiv + 219 pp. Ann Arbor, Mich.: UMI Research Press, 1980. (Studies in musicology, 18)

Inter alia, an annotated catalog of about 75 manuscripts. Each manuscript is described, but individual works are not listed. Includes an extensive bibliography, an extended essay on the sources, and short studies on seven of the most important composers.

Reviewed by Georgie Durosoir in *Fontes* 28 (1981): 330.

Organ

5.229 Arnold, Corliss Richard. *Organ Literature: A Comprehensive Survey.* 3rd ed., revised, enlarged and updated. 2 vols. 915 pp. Metuchen, N.J.: Scarecrow Press, 1995.

First ed. published in 1973 (656 pp.); 2nd ed., 1984, 2 vols.

A bibliography of organ music, with historical background. The historical survey (Vol. 1) has accompanying bibliographies. The biographical catalog (Vol. 2) provides basic information about composers and editions of their published works, while incidentally supplying a convenient (and often overlooked) index to the organ music anthologies cited in the bibliography. There is a helpful index to J. S. Bach's organ works, tabulated to show their location in the major modern collected editions.

The 3rd ed. is reviewed by Jayson Rod Engquist in *The American Organist* 30 (January 1996): 67–68. The 2nd ed. is reviewed by Kurt Dorfmüller in *Fontes* 32 (1985): 218–20, by John E. Druesedow, Jr., in *ARBA* 16 (1985): no. 1174, by Nathan A. Randall in *Notes* 42 (1985): 58–59, and by R. John Specht in *SSN* 12 (1986): 17–18. The 1st ed. is reviewed by Walter Hilse in *Notes* 31 (1975): 572–74.

5.230* **Beckmann, Klaus.** *Repertorium Orgelmusik: Orgel solo, Orgel + Instrument/e: 1150–1992, 25 Länder: Komponisten, Werke, Editionen: Eine Auswahl.* 656 pp. Moos am Bodensee, Germany: Bodensee-Musikversand, 1994. (Veröffentlichung der Gesellschaft der Orgelfreunde, 143)

A bio-bibliographic dictionary, arranged by country, listing composers and their works for organ.

5.231 **Edson, Jean Slater.** *Organ-Preludes: An Index to Compositions on Hymn Tunes, Chorales, Plainsong Melodies, Gregorian Tunes and Carols.* 2 vols. 1,169 pp. Metuchen, N.J.: Scarecrow Press, 1970.

In 1974, her *Organ-Preludes: Supplement* was published, 315 pp., which included corrections and additions to the first 2 vols.

A list of preludes for organ, with access according to origin. The 1st vol. is a composer index, with settings listed alphabetically under the composer's name and publisher identified. The 2nd vol. is an index of tune names, identified by thematic incipits. Each tune name is followed by a list of the composers who have set it.

The *Supplement* is reviewed by Ann Bond in *MT* 115 (1974): 1048–49.

5.232 **Frankel, Walter A.,** and **Nancy K. Nardone.** *Organ Music in Print.* 2nd ed. 354 pp. Philadelphia, Pa.: Musicdata, 1984. (Music in print series, 3)

1990 *Supplement,* edited by F. Mark Daugherty, 297 pp. First ed., 1975, 262 pp.

A list of organ music currently available for purchase.

5.233 **Kratzenstein, Marilou.** *Survey of Organ Literature and Editions.* 246 pp. Ames, Iowa: Iowa State University Press, 1980.

A survey of organ music, arranged by country, with essays on the development of the instrument, major composers, and each national school. Each essay precedes a bibliography of editions arranged by composer or, in the case of anthologies, by title. This was originally published as a series of articles in the American organ magazine *Diapason,* 1971–77.

Reviewed by Pierre Hardouin in *Fontes* 28 (1981): 149–50 and by Stephen M. Fry in *ARBA* 12 (1981): no. 1043.

5.234* **Lawrence, Joy E.** *The Organist's Shortcut to Service Music: A Guide to Finding Intonations, Organ Compositions, and Free Accompaniments Based on Traditional Hymn Tunes.* 2nd ed. xxxii + 439 pp. Cleveland, Ohio: Ludwig Music Publishing Company, 1989.

First ed., 1986.

A bibliography of hymn settings, hymn accompaniments, and hymn introductions for organ.

5.235 **Lohmann, Heinz.** *Handbuch der Orgelliteratur.* 206 pp. Wiesbaden: Breitkopf & Härtel, 1975.

A work in three parts: an index to settings of chorale melodies, both German and others, arranged alphabetically by the "name" of the chorale; an index of editions of works for organ; and a series of indexes to chorale tunes, melody names, and first lines. Though international in scope, this stresses the German Protestant tradition much more strongly than does Edson (**5.231**).

5.236 **Lukas, Viktor.** *Reclams Orgelmusikführer.* 5th ed., revised and enlarged. 461 pp. Stuttgart: Philipp Reclam, 1986. (Universal-Bibliothek, 8880)

The 1st ed. was published as *Orgelmusikführer,* 1963, 271 pp. An English-language ed. from the 5th ed., *A Guide to Organ Music,* was trans. by Anne Wyburd with addenda by Lee Garrett (Portland, Ore.: Amadeus Press, 1989), 272 pp.

A listener's guide to concert organ literature, quite selective and confined to the European repertoire, with brief biographies of the composers and numerous thematic quotations. Includes a section on the organ with other instruments, a glossary of organ terms, and a description of the mechanics of the instruments, plus an index of composers and works.

5.237 Spelman, Leslie P. *Organ Plus: A Catalogue of Ensemble Music for Organ and Instruments.* 4th ed. Edited by Jayson Rod Engquist. 67 pp. New York: American Guild of Organists, 1992.

An *Addendum* of 12 pp. was also issued in 1981. The 1st ed. was issued in 1975 (35 pp.), the 2nd in 1977 (37 pp.), the 3rd in 1981 (46 pp.).

A classified catalog of over 1,000 entries, citing composer, title, collation, level of difficulty, publisher, and dates of publication. The list omits most music for organ with orchestra, relying on Richard Sartorius's 1961 *Bibliography of Concertos for Organ and Orchestra* (**5.222**), organ with piano, organ with handbells, or voices with organ. There is no index.

Reviewed by Leonard Raver in *Notes* 41 (1981): 293.

5.238 Stellhorn, Martin H. *Index to Hymn Preludes, Voluntaries, Paraphrases, Variations and Other Organ Compositions, Based on Hymns, Chorales and Carols.* 151 pp. St. Louis, Mo.: Concordia Publishing House, 1948.

An alphabetical list of 2,200 compositions based on hymn tunes in general use in the Lutheran church, drawn from 75 anthologies and publishers' lists of sheet music. Each entry gives the key, technical difficulty, and length.

5.239 Weigl, Bruno. *Handbuch der Orgelliteratur: Vollständige Umarbeitung des Führers durch die Orgelliteratur.* Edited by Bernhard Kothe and Theophil Forchhammer. 318 pp. Leipzig: F.E.C. Leuckart, 1931.

A detailed, classified list of organ compositions, international in coverage, with both solo works and categories for works with orchestra, instruments, or voices. Original works and transcriptions are listed separately, and works are graded by difficulty.

5.240 Werning, Daniel. *A Selected Source Index for Hymn and Chorale Tunes in Lutheran Worship Books.* 234 pp. St. Louis, Mo.: Concordia Publishing House, 1985.

An index organized alphabetically by tune name of the hymns and chorales contained in the four major Lutheran hymnals produced in the United States between 1941 and 1982. Under each tune name, selected organ settings and choral settings are listed in separate sequences, by composer or by title of anthology.

Piano

5.241 Altmann, Wilhelm. *Verzeichnis von Werken für Klavier vier- und sechshändig sowie für zwei und mehr Klaviere.* 133 pp. Leipzig: F. Hofmeister, 1943.

A classified catalog of works for piano, four and six hands, and for two or more pianos, with and without other instruments. Both original works and arrangements are included. The entries are alphabetical by composer within each classification. Indexed by composer.

5.242 Basart, Ann P. "Guides to Piano Music: A Check-List." In *CNV* 53 (1981): 13–21.

An annotated, indexed checklist of bibliographies of piano music for performance.

5.243 Chang, Frederic Ming, and **Albert Faurot.** *Team Piano Repertoire: A Manual of Music for Multiple Players at One or More Pianos.* 184 pp. Metuchen, N.J.: Scarecrow Press, 1976.

A classified, annotated list of music with cryptic bibliographical information. Arrangements and transcriptions are listed, as well as some recordings.

Reviewed by Stephen M. Fry in *Notes* 34 (1977): 87 and by J. M. Nectoux in *Fontes* 24 (1977): 100.

5.244* Edel, Theodore. *Piano Music for One Hand.* 121 pp. Bloomington, Ind.: Indiana University Press, 1994.

A bibliography of piano music for one hand, both solo and ensemble (chamber works) and concertos for piano. The entries give the publication, the work's length, and level of difficulty.

5.245* Faurot, Albert. *Concert Piano Repertoire: A Manual of Solo Literature for Artists and Performers.* 338 pp. Metuchen, N.J.: Scarecrow Press, 1974.

Reviewed by Saul Dorfman in *Piano Quarterly* 23 (1974–75): 41–42.

5.246* Friskin, James, and **Irwin Freundlich.** *Music for the Piano: A Handbook of Concert and Teaching Material from 1580 to 1952.* 432 pp. New York: Rinehart & Co., 1954. (Field of music, 5)

Reissued in 1960 and reprinted by Dover Publications, New York, in 1954.

Reviewed by Arthur Loesser in *Notes* 11 (1954): 470–71.

5.247 Fuszek, Rita M. *Piano Music in Collections: An Index.* 895 pp. Detroit, Mich.: Information Coordinators, 1982.

A reference work that covers 496 collections in two sections: an index to the collections, arranged by composer, and a list of the contents of the collections. There are lists of editors, catalogs, and editions of composers' works and a title index.

Reviewed by François Lesure in *Fontes* 20 (1983): 78, by Carol June Bradley in *ARBA* 14 (1983): no. 951, by Dominique-René de Lerma in *LJ* 107 (1982): 1646, and by Dale L. Hudson in *Notes* 39 (1983): 855.

5.248 Gillespie, John, and **Anna Gillespie.** *A Bibliography of Nineteenth-Century American Piano Music with Location Sources and Composer Biography-Index.* 358 pp. Westport, Conn.: Greenwood Press, 1984. (Music reference collection, 2)

A selective, classified bibliography including some 2,000 works of music from the late 18th century and extending into the first part of the 20th century, by 253 composers, with bibliographic information, library location, and an occasional commentary on the music supplied.

Reviewed by Robert Palmieri in *ARBA* 19 (1988): no. 1295 and by John Stroud in *Notes* 41 (1985): 520–21.

5.249 Hinson, Maurice. *Guide to the Pianist's Repertoire.* 2nd, revised and enlarged ed. xxxiii + 856 pp. Bloomington, Ind.: Indiana University Press, 1987.

The 1st ed. was published in 1973 (xlv + 831 pp.), with a *Supplement* (xliii + 413 pp.) from 1979.

A sizable bibliography of piano music that attempts to grade representative works of each composer cited, some 1,800 in all. Specifically related bibliographic entries of book and periodical articles have been incorporated into the main body of the text. The indexes include composers by national designations, Black composers, women composers, compositions for tape and piano, compositions for prepared piano, and titles in anthologies and collections.

The 1st ed. is reviewed by Malcolm Bilson in *Notes* 30 (1973): 287–88 and by Howard Ferguson in *M&L* 55 (1974): 107–8. The *Supplement* is reviewed by Marsha Berman in *ARBA* 12 (1981): no. 1041. The 2nd ed. is reviewed by Thelma C. Diercks in *Notes* 47 (1991): 777–79 and by Robert Palmieri in *ARBA* 19 (1988): no. 1295.

5.250 Hinson, Maurice. *Music for More than One Piano: An Annotated Guide.* xxvii + 218 pp. Bloomington, Ind.: Indiana University Press, 1983.

A bibliography that includes works originally written for piano and other forces, if arranged by the composer, as well as transcriptions of important composers. Critical comments and publisher information are provided, as well as indexes of special ensembles.

Reviewed by John E. Druesedow, Jr., in *ARBA* 15 (1984): no. 913, by Paula Morgan in *Notes* 40 (1984): 554, and by Ross Wood in *LJ* 108 (1983): 1697.

5.251 Hinson, Maurice. *Music for Piano and Orchestra: An Annotated Guide.* Enlarged ed. xxiv + 359 pp. Bloomington, Ind.: Indiana University Press, 1993.

The 1st ed. was published in 1981 (xxiii + 327 pp.).

A source providing cryptic bibliographic information, as well as more extensive analytical reports on the works cited, including not only the standard repertoire but also numerous contemporary works. The entries are arranged alphabetically by composer, with works in chronological order. The works listed are for nine or more instruments, generally post-1700, including a few transcriptions, and accessed by a classified index. A helpful feature is the list of many of the cadenzas written for the Beethoven and Mozart concertos.

Reviewed by Joy Haslam Calico in *Fontes* 42 (1995): 384–87. The 1st ed. is reviewed by Judith Kaufman in *Notes* 38 (1982): 611–12.

5.252* Hinson, Maurice. *The Pianist's Guide to Transcriptions, Arrangements, and Paraphrases.* xxi + 159 pp. Bloomington, Ind.: Indiana University Press, 1990.

Reviewed by Thelma C. Diercks in *Notes* 47 (1991): 777–79, by Patricia Elliott in *Beethoven Newsletter* 5 (1990): 45, and by Harold J. Diamond in *Choice* 27 (1990): 1656.

5.253* Horne, Aaron. *Keyboard Music of Black Composers: A Bibliography.* 331 pp. Westport, Conn.: Greenwood Press, 1992. (Music reference collection, 37)

A list of art and popular keyboard solos and music for various instrumental combinations including keyboard.

Reviewed by Suzanne Flandreau in *Notes* 50 (1993): 207.

5.254* International Piano Archives at Maryland. *Catalog of the Reproducing Piano Roll Collection, International Piano Archives at Maryland.* 281 pp. College Park, Md.: Music Library, University of Maryland, 1983. (Publications of the Music Library, University of Maryland at College Park, 2)

A catalog arranged alphabetically by performer. Each entry includes the company, composer, arranger, title, IPA call number, date, and a variety of additional information. There are indexes by composers, company numbers, and master rolls.

5.255* Kehler, George. *The Piano in Concert.* 2 vols. 1,467 pp. Metuchen, N.J.: Scarecrow Press, 1982.

A collection of over 17,000 concert programs by some 2,000 pianists.

Reviewed by Frederic Schoettler in *ARBA* 14 (1983): no. 952.

5.256 Kennard, Daphne. "Music for One-Handed Pianists." In *Fontes* 30 (1983): 117–31.

Revision of a list first published in *Brio* 13 (1976): 39–42 no. 2.

A comprehensive list of music for one-handed pianists, with short lists of duets for one and two pianos, references to anthologies, an article, and a thesis.

5.257 McGraw, Cameron. *Piano Duet Repertoire: Music Originally Written for One Piano, Four Hands.* 334 pp. Bloomington, Ind.: Indiana University Press, 1981.

A bibliography whose listings exclude transcriptions from other media except in "rare cases where composers themselves have made the transcriptions or where such adaptations have long been considered part of the standard four-hand repertoire." Indexes of music publishers and library locations are provided.

Reviewed by Albert Seay in *Notes* 38 (1981): 316.

5.258* Maxwell, Grant L. *Music for Three or More Pianists: An Historical Survey and Catalogue.* 467 pp. Metuchen, N.J.: Scarecrow Press, 1993.

A history starting with J. S. Bach's keyboard music for three or more players, c. 1730. By the early 20th century, a body of transcriptions and arrangements had accumulated, and many of these are included in a comprehensive bibliography (pp. 413–42) with an illustrative, detailed guide to the catalog. A discography and an index conclude the book.

Reviewed by C. Michael Phillips in *ARBA* 25 (1994): no. 1337.

5.259 Moldenhauer, Hans. *Duo-Pianism: A Dissertation.* 400 pp. Chicago, Ill.: Chicago Musical College Press, 1951.

A work containing a list of original two-piano music, arranged alphabetically by composer, with publishers given. The main part of the dissertation is on the practical rather than the historical aspects of the subject.

5.260 Rezits, Joseph, and **Gerald Deatsman.** *The Pianist's Resource Guide: Piano Music in Print and Literature on the Pianistic Art, 1978–79.* 1,491 pp. Park Ridge, Ill.: Pallma Music Co.; San Diego, Calif.: Kjos West, 1978.

A guide composed of three major sections: a classified and computer-generated list of music for piano with a title index, a classified list of books on the subject of pianos with an author index, and a piano reader's guide, consisting of reviews of 118 books and a topical index to books. Publisher information is provided.

5.261 Ruthardt, Adolf. *Wegweiser durch die Klavier-Literatur.* 10th ed. 398 pp. Leipzig; Zurich: Hug & Co., 1925.

First published in 1888.

A selective list of keyboard music, including works for four or more hands, from the renaissance to the early 20th century, classified according to genre and degree of difficulty. There are brief descriptions of lesser-known works, as well as a bibliography of writings on keyboard music (pp. 359–76).

5.262* Walker-Hill, Helen. *Piano Music by Black Women Composers: A Catalog of Solo and Ensemble Works.* 143 pp. New York: Greenwood Press, 1992. (Music reference collection, 35)

Arranged by composer, a list of 55 Black women composers (53 American and 2 British) with brief biographies and a list of works with piano, both published and unpublished.

5.263 Wolters, Klaus. *Handbuch der Klavierliteratur: Klaviermusik zu zwei Händen.* 4th ed., revised and enlarged. 699 pp. Zurich: Atlantis Musikbuch-Verlag, 1994.

First published in 1967; 2nd ed., 1977, 660 pp.

Intended as a guide and aid to piano teachers, an extensive bibliography of editions interspersed with commentaries on the editions, composers, and works. Arrangements for piano are included, especially from earlier periods. The section on contemporary music treats jazz, modern dance, avant-garde music, and other national musics. The only index is to names.

ORCHESTRA

5.264 Altmann, Wilhelm. *Orchester-Literatur-Katalog; Verzeichnis von seit 1850 erschienenen Orchester-Werken.* 2 vols. Leipzig: F.E.C. Leuckart, 1926–36.

Reprinted by M. Sändig, Walluf bei Wiesbaden, 1972.

A bibliography of orchestral music published since 1850 listing full and study scores, instrumental parts, and arrangements. The 2nd vol., covering compositions from 1926 to 1935, gives instrumentations and timings and contains a composer index to both volumes. Thematic quotations are given for groups of works whose numbers are often confused (such as Mozart's and Joseph Haydn's symphonies, and Handel's concertos). Titles are arranged alphabetically under 20 different classifications (symphonies, variations, etc.).

5.265 American Society of Composers, Authors, and Publishers. *ASCAP Symphonic Catalog.* 3rd ed. 511 pp. New York: R.R. Bowker, 1977.

Previous editions, 1959, 375 pp., and 1966, 754 pp.

An alphabetical list, by composers and arrangers, of 26,000 pieces of symphonic literature controlled by ASCAP and its 40 foreign affiliates. The entries give instrumentation, duration, and publisher. There is a list of publishers' addresses and U.S. agents.

Reviewed by Stephen M. Fry in *Notes* 34 (1978): 619.

5.266 Basart, Ann P. "Finding Orchestral Music." In *CNV* 59 (1982): 14–24.

An annotated, indexed checklist of bibliographies of orchestral music for performance, including a section on finding orchestral program notes.

5.267 Brook, Barry S. *The Symphony, 1720–1840: Reference Volume: Contents of the Set and Collected Thematic Indices.* lvi + 627 pp. New York: Garland Publishing, 1986.

The thematic catalog of the 549 works of 244 composers in the collection *The Symphony, 1720–1840,* which includes 13 thematic indexes not in the individual volumes when originally published. There are also thousands of incipits, with copious information on each symphony and its sources, organized by composer but not indexed, with a bibliography of catalog references.

5.268 Daniels, David. *Orchestral Music: A Handbook.* 2nd ed. 413 pp. Metuchen, N.J.: Scarecrow Press, 1982.

First ed., *Orchestral Music: A Source Book,* 1972, 301 pp.

Gathers in one vol. the information about orchestral works needed to plan programs and organize rehearsals, instrumentation, duration, and source of performance materials. The entries are arranged by composer. Particularly useful are the list of works by performing forces, the list of orchestra works by duration, and the list of composers by nationality or ethnic group.

5.269 Farish, Margaret K. *Orchestral Music in Print.* 1,029 pp. Philadelphia, Pa.: Musicdata, 1979. (Music in print series, 5)

1983 Supplement, 237 pp. *1994 Supplement,* 427 pp. *Master Index 1994,* 447 pp.

A list, arranged alphabetically by composer and then by title, of editions of orchestral music reported by their publishers as being in print. No attempt was made to put variant titles of the same work together. Prices and publishers' numbers are sometimes given.

Reviewed by Dominique-René de Lerma in *ARBA* 12 (1981): no. 1049.

5.270* LaRue, Jan. *A Catalogue of 18th-Century Symphonies, Vol. 1: Thematic Identifier.* 352 pp. Bloomington, Ind.: Indiana University Press, 1989.

A source giving thematic access to 16,558 incipits of symphonies and similar works used in concert from c. 1720 to c. 1810. A 2nd vol. containing composers' works lists is planned.

Reviewed by Richard Andrewes in *Fontes* 37 (1990): 277–78, by Sterling Murray in *Notes* 47 (1991): 1,122–24, and by Ann P. Basart in *CNV* 133 (1989): 13–14.

5.271 Müller-Reuter, Theodor. *Lexikon der deutschen Konzertliteratur: Ein Ratgeber für Dirigenten, Konzertveranstalter, Musikschriftsteller, und Musikfreunde.* xxii + 625 pp. Leipzig: G.F. Kahnt Nachf., 1909.

The *Nachtrag zu Band I* was published in 1921, 232 pp. The 1909 vol. was reprinted by Da Capo Press, New York, in 1972.

The standard guide to orchestral and chamber music by the major composers of the romantic period, with detailed information on the date of composition, first performance, duration, instrumentation, and relation to the composer's other works. The 1909 vol. covers the work of Schubert, Mendelssohn, Schumann, Berlioz, Liszt, Raff, Wagner, Draeseke, Reinecke, Bruch, Gernsheim, and Richard Strauss. The *Nachtrag* is devoted to the symphonies of Beethoven, Brahms, and Haydn.

5.272* Rabson, Carolyn. *Orchestral Excerpts: A Comprehensive Index.* 221 pp. Berkeley, Calif.: Fallen Leaf Press, 1993. (Fallen Leaf reference books in music, 25)

Reviewed by George Louis Mayer in *ARBA* 25 (1994): no. 1348.

5.273* Reed, Tony. *British Union Catalogue of Orchestral Sets.* 2nd ed. xxxvii + 380 pp. England: British Library Document Supply Centre in cooperation with IAML (UK), 1989.

2nd ed. *Supplement,* edited by Pat Dye and Tony Reed, 1995 (xxxiv + 68 pp.).

A list of 9,682 entries from 68 libraries, arranged alphabetically by composer. A title index gives additional access.

The 2nd ed. is reviewed by Frederick James Kent in *Notes* 47 (1991): 798–99 and by Dorothy Freed in *Fontes* 38 (1991): 336–37.

5.274 Saltonstall, Cecilia Drinker, and **Henry Saltonstall.** *A New Catalog of Music for Small Orchestra.* 323 pp. Clifton, N.J.: European American Music Corporation, 1978. (Music indexes and bibliographies, 14)

Supersedes the *Catalogue of Music for Small Orchestra,* compiled by Cecilia Drinker Saltonstall and Hannah Coffin Smith; edited by Otto E. Albrecht. (Washington, D.C.: Music Library Association, 1947), 267 pp.

A catalog whose compilers defined a small orchestra as one having at least 10 parts, with a minimum of 3 string parts and a wind section of 2–12 parts. The 6,380 entries, arranged alphabetically by composer, were gathered from the most recent catalogs of music publishers, catalogs of national music information centers, and lists of music available in lending libraries. The entries include detailed instrumentation and duration. There is a list of publishers' and agents' addresses. The earlier edition, which included 998 entries, had an index of works for distinctive titles and a classified index of wind instrument requirements; the 1978 ed. has no indexes.

The 1978 ed. is reviewed by James N. Berdahl in *Notes* 36 (1979): 374–75; the earlier ed. is reviewed by Thor Johnson in *Notes* 4 (1947): 457–58.

5.275* Schönherr, Max. *Lanner, Strauss, Ziehrer: Synoptisches Handbuch der Tänze und Märsche.* 525 pp. Vienna: Doblinger, 1982.

A thematic catalog of Viennese dance music and marches.

PERCUSSION

5.276 Combs, F. Michael. *Solo and Ensemble Literature for Percussion.* 93 ll. Knoxville, Tenn.: Percussive Arts Society, 1978.

First ed., 1967; reissued in enlarged form, 1972 (66 pp.), and supplemented in 1976.

A classified list of music for various percussion instruments, with information on publishers and sources.

5.277* Siwe, Thomas. *Percussion Solo Literature.* 519 pp. Champaign, Ill.: Media Press, 1995.

The 1st vol. of a replacement for the author's previous *Percussion Solo and Ensemble Literature.*

A bibliography with an extensive list, annotated where possible, of unaccompanied and accompanied solo literature, indexed by category (mallet instruments, timpani, etc.).

PLECTORAL INSTRUMENTS (GUITAR, HARP, LUTE, MANDOLIN, ETC.)

5.278* Bell, Joshua. *Mandolin Music in America: 3800 Pieces for Mandolin and Where to Find Them.* 67 pp. Arlington, Va.: Plucked String, 1993.

5.279 Gilmore, George, Mark Pereira, and **Peter Kun Frary.** *Guitar Music Index: A Cross-Indexed and Graded Listing of Music in Print for Classical Guitar and Lute.* 2 vols. to date. Honolulu, Hawaii: Galliard Press, 1976– .

The 1st vol. is reviewed by Stephen M. Fry in *Notes* 34 (1978): 620–21.

5.280* Helleu, Laurence. *La guitare en concert: Catalogue des oeuvres avec guitare du XXe siècle (duos, trios, musique de chambre, orchestre, concertos).* 189 pp. Paris: Éditions Musicales Transatlantiques, 1985.

A bibliography, international in scope, of 20th-century chamber music including guitar.

Reviewed by Ann P. Basart in *CNV* 111 (1987): 15.

5.281 International Music Service. *A Catalog of Music for the Harp—& Sundry Items.* 95 pp. + 24 pp. of music. New York: International Music Service, 1986.

Earlier version, loose-leaf, was distributed from 1981.

A distributor's catalog.

5.282* Jape, Mijndert. *Classical Guitar Music in Print.* 443 pp. Philadelphia, Pa.: Musicdata Inc., 1989. (Music in print series, 7)

A classified list of works currently in print, both solo and chamber, which include guitar. Other features include thematic indexes of the preludes, studies, and exercises for guitar by Francisco Tárraga (pp. 138–71), of the works by Johann Sebastian Bach arranged for guitar (pp. 178–94), and composer–title, instrumentation, and series indexes.

Reviewed by Dorman H. Smith in *Notes* 47 (1991): 1,153–54.

5.283* MacAuslan, Janna. *A Catalog of Compositions for Guitar by Women Composers.* 45 pp. Portland, Ore.: DearHorse Publications, 1984.

5.284* Michel, Catherine, and **François Lesure.** *Répertoire de la musique pour harp publiée du XVIIe au début du XIXe siècle: Bibliographie.* 285 pp. Paris: Aux Amateurs de Livres International: Diffusion, Klincksieck, 1990.

5.285 Moser, Wolf. *Gitarre-Musik: Ein internationaler Katalog.* Hamburg: Joachim Trekel, Der Volksmusikverlag, 1973–77.

The 1st vol. was revised in 1975 and 1979. A 2nd ed., covering A–F, was begun in 1985.

A classified list arranged by performing forces, with sections for etudes, collections, books about the guitar, and flamenco guitar music. There is a composer index. Vol. 2 supplements Vol. 1.

5.286* Nordstrom, Lyle. *The Bandora: Its Music and Sources.* 147 pp. Warren, Mich.: Harmonie Park Press, 1992. (Detroit studies in music bibliography, 66)

An investigation of music including the bandora, a plucked string instrument invented in England by John Rose in 1562. The bandora's use peaked in the late 16th and 17th centuries.

Reviewed by Calvin Elliker in *Fontes* 40 (1993): 342–43, by Katharine Hogg in *Brio* 30 (1993): 114–15, and by James Tyler in *Notes* 51 (1994): 582–84.

5.287* Palkovic, Mark. *Harp Music Bibliography: Compositions for Solo Harp and Harp Ensemble.* 352 pp. Bloomington, Ind.: Indiana University Press, 1995.

A list of 3,300 works, including method books and orchestra studies. The solo and chamber works are divided into original works for harp and arrangements. Includes an index of composers' names and works and a separate index for works playable on the nonpedal harp.

5.288 Rensch, Roslyn. *The Harp: Its History, Technique and Repertoire.* 246 pp. New York: Praeger Publishers, 1969.

A historical monograph with bibliographies and discographies.

5.289 Rezits, Joseph. *The Guitarist's Resource Guide: Guitar Music in Print and Books on the Art of the Guitar.* 574 pp. San Diego, Calif.: Pallma Music Co., distributed by N.A. Kjos Music Co., 1983.

A resource that includes sections on lute, mandolin, and vihuela music. Each section has a composer and title index, eccentrically alphabetized. The guitar section is further subdivided by performing forces.

Reviewed by William Brockman in *ARBA* 16 (1985): no. 1179.

5.290 Rudén, Jan Olof. *Music in Tablature: A Thematic Index with Source Descriptions of Music in Tablature Notation in Sweden.* 257 pp. Stockholm: Svenskt Musikhistoriskt Arkiv, 1981. (Musik i Sverige / Music in Sweden, 5)

One of the first national catalogs of music in tablature, which includes bibliographical references and an index.

5.291* **Smith, Dorman H.,** and **Laurie Eagleson.** *Guitar and Lute Music in Periodicals: An Index.* 104 pp. Berkeley, Calif.: Fallen Leaf Press, 1990. (Fallen Leaf reference books in music, 13)
Reviewed by Calvin Elliker in *Fontes* 39 (1992): 379–80.

STRINGS

5.292 **Basart, Ann P.** "Finding String Music." In *CNV* 57 (1981): 6–16.
An annotated, indexed checklist to bibliographies of string music for performance.

5.293 **Farish, Margaret K.** *String Music in Print.* 2nd ed. 464 pp. New York; London: R.R. Bowker Co., 1973.
A 1984 supplement, 269 pp., was published by Musicdata, Philadelphia, Pa., as part of the Music in print series. A preliminary ed. appeared in 1963. First ed., 1964, by Bowker, 420 pp., with a 1968 supplement (204 pp.). The 2nd ed. was reprinted in 1980 by Musicdata (Music in print, 6).
A list, divided by instrumentation, of solo and chamber works including at least one string instrument, reported by their publishers as being in print. Prices are not given, but publisher numbers are occasionally included.
The preliminary ed. is reviewed by Joel H. Berman in *Notes* 20 (1963): 229; the 1964 ed. is reviewed by Katherine Holum in *JRME* 13 (1965): 190–91; the 1968 supplement is reviewed by Dena J. Epstein in *Notes* 25 (1969): 746; and the 2nd ed. is reviewed by Boris Schwarz in *Notes* 30 (1974): 60–61.

5.294 **Feinland, Alexander.** *The Combination of Violin and Violoncello without Accompaniment.* 117 pp. Calvert Independent, 1947.
The 1st ed. was published as *The Combination Violin and Violoncello without Accompaniment* in Paramaribo, Surinam, by J.H. Oliviera in 1944, 121 pp.
A classified catalog, including manuscripts, of music from the baroque to the present, with the original publisher or manuscript location given (pp. 67–108). There is also a section of biographical sketches of the composers represented.

5.295* **Horne, Aaron.** *String Music of Black Composers: A Bibliography.* 327 pp. New York: Greenwood Press, 1991. (Music reference collection, 33)

5.296 **Iotti, Oscar Raoul.** *Violin and Violoncello in Duo without Accompaniment.* 73 pp. Detroit, Mich.: Information Coordinators, 1972. (Detroit studies in music bibliography, 25)
A bibliography based on Feinland's *The Combination of Violin and Violoncello without Accompaniment* (**5.294**), containing 987 entries.

5.297 **Letz, Hans.** *Music for the Violin and Viola.* 107 pp. New York: Rinehart, 1948. (The field of music, 2)
A selected graded list of music for unaccompanied violin or violin with piano (pp. 1–94), followed by a similar list of music for the viola (pp. 96–107).

5.298 **Toskey, Burnett R.** *Concertos for Violin and Viola: A Comprehensive Encyclopedia.* 992 pp. Seattle, Wash.: B.R. Toskey, 1983.
A list of more than 8,400 concertos for solo violin or viola. In addition to information on the composer and the music, a descriptive review is provided for each work. There are numerous indexes and a bibliography.

Double Bass

5.299 **Grodner, Murray.** *Comprehensive Catalogue of Available Literature for the Double Bass.* 3rd ed. 169 pp. Bloomington, Ind.: Lemur Musical Research, 1974.

First published in 1958, 50 pp. 2nd ed., 1964, 84 pp.

A list of works in print in 1974, with solos and ensembles for 2 to 14 instruments, using double bass. Each entry gives composer, title, instrumentation, grade of difficulty, and price, with occasional notes on availability. Also includes a short bibliography of works about the double bass and bass playing, as well as an index of names.

The first ed. is reviewed by Darius Thieme in *Notes* 16 (1959): 258.

5.300 Planyavsky, Alfred. *Geschichte des Kontrabasses.* 2nd ed. 917 pp. Tutzing, Germany: H. Schneider, 1984.

First ed., 1970, 537 pp.

Primarily a historical study of the string bass from the 16th century to the present—its construction, technique, and repertoire. Relevant to this chapter is a classified catalog of double bass music, with the instrument both as soloist and as a member of an ensemble (pp. 713–851). The work also contains a bibliography (pp. 689–712), a discography (pp. 853–78), and an index of names and subjects.

Viol

5.301 De Smets, Robin. *Published Music for the Viola da Gamba and Other Viols.* 105 pp. Detroit, Mich.: Information Coordinators, 1971. (Detroit studies in music bibliography, 18)

Classified lists of works for viols alone and with other instruments. The entries show instrumentation, editor, publisher, and publisher's number. There is a bibliography of collected works for viols and of sources consulted.

Reviewed by Richard Taruskin in *Notes* 28 (1972): 444–45.

5.302 Dodd, Gordon. *Thematic Index of Music for Viols.* 1 vol. (loose-leaf). London: Viola da Gamba Society of Great Britain, 1980– .

Kept up-to-date by installment.

A service organized to provide thematic incipits, and locations in the case of manuscript sources, of music for viols by British composers or found mainly in British sources. Each installment includes a list of entries, a bibliography, and, for each composer, a brief essay on style. There are frequent remarks on the sources. Gordon Dodd wrote on the genesis of the *Index* in *Fontes* 25 (1978): 239–42.

Viola/Viola d'Amore

5.303 Altmann, Wilhelm, and **Wadim Borissowsky.** *Literaturverzeichnis für Bratsche und Viola d'amore.* 148 pp. Woffenbüttel, Germany: Verlag für Musikalische Kultur und Wissenschaft, 1937.

A classified catalog including solo works, duos, and other combinations in which the viola has the leading role. It lists some works in manuscript and all known editions of published works, with dates. Transcriptions as well as original works are included.

5.304* Berck, Heinz. *Viola d'amore Bibliographie: Verzeichnis gedruckter und ungedruckter Werke mit Viola d'amore als Soloinstrument, in Duos, Trios, Quartetten, Quintetten usw., als Soloinstrument in Konzerten, in Werken mit Singstimmen sowie Schul- und Studienwerke: dazu eine Bibliographie des Musikschrifttums zur Viola d'amore.* New ed. 338 pp. Hofheim, Germany: F. Hofmeister, 1994.

First ed. was published in Kassel by Bärenreiter, 1986 (215 pp.).

5.305 Drüner, Ulrich. "Das Viola-Konzert vor 1840." In *Fontes* 28 (1981): 153–76.

A bibliography documenting the development of the viola concerto in its first stage. The works of 141 composers are listed and locations of the sources are given.

5.306 Ewald, Konrad. *Musik für Bratsche, Führer durch die heute zugängliche Literatur für Viola.* 153 pp. Liestal, Switzerland: Printed for the author, 1975.

A bibliography arranged by composer in three broad chronological sections. Each chronological division has a section in which the music is discussed and another in which it is just listed, with publication information. Includes a classified index to performing forces and an index to composers.

5.307 Williams, Michael D. *Music for Viola.* 362 pp. Detroit, Mich.: Information Coordinators, 1979. (Detroit studies in music bibliography, 42)

A classified bibliography attempting to be comprehensive, providing complete bibliographic information for each work cited.

Reviewed by Ann M. Woodward in *Fontes* 27 (1980): 237–38 and by Linda Solow in *Notes* 36 (1980): 900–1.

5.308 Zeyringer, Franz. *Literatur für Viola: Verzeichnis der Werke für Viola-Solo, Duos mit Viola, Trios mit Viola, Viola-Solo mit Begleitung, Blockflöte mit Viola, Gesang mit Viola und der Schul- und Studienwerke für Viola / Literature for Viola: Catalogue of Works for Viola Solo, Duos with Viola, Trios with Viola, Solo Viola with Accompaniment, Recorder with Viola, Voice with Viola, and Methods, Etudes and Exercises for Viola.* New, revised ed. 446 pp. Hartberg, Austria: J. Schönwetter Jun., 1985.

First published in 1963, 151 pp. Supplement, 1965, 82 pp. 2nd ed., 1976, 418 pp.

An extensive classified bibliography with publisher and composer indexes.

Violin

5.309* Johnson, Rose-Marie. *Violin Music by Women Composers: A Bio-Bibliographic Guide.* 253 pp. New York: Greenwood Press, 1989. (Music reference collection, 22)

A list of solo recital, concerto, and chamber music for violin by 158 women, providing a short bibliography for each composer. Biographies are organized by style period, music by genre. Many of the music entries are annotated. Includes an index of composers, a discography (pp. 203–35), and a bibliography (pp. 237–53).

Reviewed by Judy Tsou in *Notes* 47 (1990): 396–97.

5.310 Loft, Abram. *Violin and Keyboard: The Duo Repertoire.* 2 vols. New York: Grossman Publishers, 1973.

Reprinted by Amadeus Press, Portland, Ore., 1991.

Not a bibliography but rather extensive critical commentary on the corpus of violin sonata music. Includes a bibliography at the end of the 1st vol. and a list of editions used at the end of the 2nd.

Reviewed by Sonya Monosoff in *Notes* 31 (1974): 56–59.

Violoncello

5.311* Homuth, Donald. *Cello Music since 1960: A Bibliography of Solo, Chamber, and Orchestra Works for the Solo Cellist.* 451 pp. Berkeley, Calif.: Fallen Leaf Press, 1994. (Fallen Leaf reference books in music, 26)

A list of more than 5,200 works by 3,100 composers. Each entry includes the date of composition, duration, publisher or source, first performances, recordings, instrumentation, new performance techniques used, and level of difficulty. There are indexes of cellists and composers.

Reviewed by Helga Wingold in *Notes* 52 (1995): 491–92 and by Sarah Dorsey in *Fontes* 42 (1995): 381–82.

5.312 Kenneson, Claude. *Bibliography of Cello Ensemble Music.* 59 pp. Detroit, Mich.: Information Coordinators, 1974. (Detroit studies in music bibliography, 31)

Classified citations of cello music ranging from cello duets to orchestral music, including works with piano.

Reviewed by Lynda Lloyd Rees in *MT* 116 (1975): 711.

5.313* Markevitch, Dimitry. *The Solo Cello: A Bibliography of the Unaccompanied Violoncello Literature.* 113 pp. Berkeley, Calif.: Fallen Leaf Press, 1989. (Fallen Leaf reference books in music, 12)

Reviewed by Robert Skinner in *ARBA* 21 (1990): no. 1260.

5.314 Nogué, Édouard. *La littérature du violoncello: Choix de morceau classés et annotés.* With the assistance of a group of cellists. 151 pp. Paris: Delagrave, 1925.

A classified and graded list of nearly 2,000 works for violoncello, solo or with other instruments. There are short descriptions of the works and the publishers are indicated.

5.315 Weigl, Bruno. *Handbuch der Violoncell-Literatur; systematisch geordnetes Verzeichnis der Solo- und instruktiven Werke für das Violoncell.* 3rd ed. 257 pp. Vienna: Universal Edition, 1929.

A classified list of compositions for cello and orchestra, cello and piano, cello solo, or cello accompanied by other instruments. This is comparable in arrangement to the author's *Handbuch der Orgelliteratur* (**5.239**).

VOCAL MUSIC (SOLO AND CHAMBER)

5.316 Basart, Ann P. "Finding Vocal Music." In *CNV* 55 (1981): 5–15 and 56 (1981): 14–22.

An annotated, indexed checklist to bibliographies providing information on vocal music and choral music for performance.

5.317 Berry, Corre. *Vocal Chamber Duets: An Annotated Bibliography.* 71 pp. National Association of Teachers of Singing, 1981.

With indexes to voice combinations, poets, and titles and first lines.

Reviewed by Irvin Bushman in *NATS* 38 (1982): 53 no. 3.

5.318* Boldrey, Richard. *Guide to Operatic Duets.* 130 pp. Dallas, Tex.: Pst . . . Inc., 1995.

A list of all duets from the "significant repertory" listed by role, title, and vocal category, with additional cross-references for opera and composer.

Reviewed by Carol Kimball in *OJ* 28 (1995): 66–67.

5.319* Boldrey, Richard. *Guide to Operatic Roles and Arias.* 554 pp. Dallas, Tex.: Pst . . . Inc., 1995.

A list of the roles and arias from over 1,000 operas, cross-referenced by voice category, composer, and opera.

Reviewed by Carol Kimball in *OJ* 28 (1995): 66–67.

5.320* Brusse, Corre Berry. *Sacred Vocal Duets: An Annotated Bibliography.* 82 pp. Jacksonville, Fla.: National Association of Teachers of Singing, 1987.

A list of 475 original duets with sacred texts. There are indexes to nonkeyboard accompaniments, vocal combinations, composers, poets, and titles and first lines.

Reviewed by Richard Dale Sjoerdsma in *NATS* 45 (1988): 35 no. 1 and by Ann P. Basart in *CNV* 133 (1989): 14.

5.321 Carman, Judith E., William K. Gaeddert, and **Rita M. Resch.** *Art-Song in the United States, 1801–1987: An Annotated Bibliography.* With a special section, "Art-song in the United States, 1759–1810," by Gordon Myers. 2nd ed., revised and enlarged. 371 pp. Jacksonville, Fla.: National Association of Teachers of Singing, 1987.

First ed., 1976.

A practical tool for teachers of singing. Arranged by composer, the bibliography is limited to music for a single solo voice with English text, commercially available at the time of compilation. Extensive information on each publication is provided. Includes an index to broad subjects and poets and indexes to composers and titles.

Reviewed by Richard Dale Sjoersdma in *NATS* 45 (1988): 34–35 no. 1.

5.322 Coffin, Berton. *Singer's Repertoire.* 2nd ed. 5 vols. New York: Scarecrow Press, 1960–62.
The 1st ed. was published in 1 vol., 1956.

A classified catalog of art songs from the solo vocal repertoire, with each vol. devoted to a particular vocal range: coloratura, lyric and dramatic soprano, mezzo and contralto, lyric and dramatic tenor, and baritone and bass. Information is given on song subject, accompaniment, and publisher. Vol. 5 is program notes for *The Singer's Repertoire,* written with Werner Singer.

Reviewed by Arnold Caswell in *JRME* 9 (1961): 76.

5.323 Dunlap, Kay, and **Barbara Winchester.** *Vocal Chamber Music: A Catalog.* 140 pp. New York: Garland Publishing, 1985. (Garland reference library of the humanities, 465)

A list of music written from 1650 to 1980 for at least 1 voice and 1 instrument other than guitar and up to 12 solo voices and 12 solo instruments. There is an index by performing forces.

Reviewed by Ann Basart in *CNV* 102 (1986): 21–22 and by Allie Wise Goudy in *ARBA* 18 (1997): no. 1247.

5.324 Edwards, J. Michele. *Literature for Voices in Combination with Electronic and Tape Music: An Annotated Bibliography.* 194 pp. Ann Arbor, Mich.: Music Library Association, 1977. (MLA index and bibliography series, 7)

A historical list to 1975 and a finding aid, with extensive information about each composition. There are appendixes covering publishers, music information centers, foreign and hard-to-find record labels, studios, and bibliography. There is also an index to the entries by medium.

Reviewed by Peter Ward Jones in *M&L* 60 (1969): 229 and by Stephen M. Fry in *Notes* 34 (1978): 879.

5.325 Espina, Noni. *Repertoire for the Solo Voice: A Fully Annotated Guide to Works for the Solo Voice Published in Modern Editions and Covering Material from the 13th Century to the Present.* 2 vols. 1,290 pp. Metuchen, N.J.: Scarecrow Press, 1977.

A classified, annotated bibliography of art songs, arranged by the nationality of the composer. There are also sections of opera arias, florid display songs, and traditional songs. The entries provide information on the source of text, the degree of difficulty, the accompaniment, the publisher of modern editions, and location in collections. Remarks are made on the general style and musical and vocal requirements of each song. There are indexes to sources of texts (poets and literary titles) and composers.

Reviewed by Stephen M. Fry in *Notes* 34 (1978): 620.

5.326 Espina, Noni. *Vocal Solos for Christian Churches: A Descriptive Reference of Solo Music for the Church Year, Including a Bibliographical Supplement of Choral Works.* 3rd ed. 241 pp. Metuchen, N.J.: Scarecrow Press, 1984.

First published as *Vocal Solos for Protestant Services* in 1965 (197 pp.) and 1974 (218 pp.).

There are indexes of occasions, voice types, titles, and composers.

5.327* Evans, May Garrettson. *Music and Edgar Allan Poe: A Bibliographical Study.* 97 pp. Baltimore, Md.: Johns Hopkins Press, 1939.

Reprinted by Greenwood Press, New York, 1968.

A study with generous bibliographical lists, pp. 29–90.

5.328* Fitch, Donald. *Blake Set to Music: A Bibliography of Musical Settings of the Poems and Prose of William Blake.* xxix + 281 pp. Berkeley, Calif.: University of California Press, 1989. (University of California publications. Catalogs and bibliographies, 5)

A list of 1,412 works, arranged alphabetically by composer.

Reviewed by Bryan N. S. Gooch in *Notes* 48 (1991): 107–8.

5.329 Gooch, Bryan N. S., David S. Thatcher, and **Odean Long.** *Musical Settings of British Romantic Literature: A Catalogue.* 2 vols. 1,768 pp. New York: Garland Publishing, 1982. (Garland reference library of the humanities, 326)

    A list of published and unpublished compositions setting British romantic texts by authors born after 1750 who lived to 1800 or later, organized by author and literary title, with information on composers and their settings following. Bibliographical information on poetry and settings is provided. There is an index of authors, first lines and titles, and composers.

5.330 Gooch, Bryan N. S., David S. Thatcher, and **Odean Long.** *Musical Settings of Early and Mid-Victorian Literature: A Catalogue.* xxxvi + 946 pp. New York: Garland Publishing, 1979. (Garland reference library of the humanities, 149)

    A list by author of published and unpublished musical settings of prominent British authors born after 1800 who lived to 1850 or later, excluding writers associated with the romantic movements. Provides information on performing forces and publication details both for the poetry and the musical settings. There are indexes by composer, title, and first line.

5.331 Gooch, Bryan N. S., David S. Thatcher, and **Odean Long.** *Musical Settings of Late Victorian and Modern British Literature: A Catalogue.* xxiii + 1,112 pp. New York; London: Garland Publishing, 1979. (Garland reference library of the humanities, 149)

    Reviewed by Stephen Fry in *Notes* 34 (1977): 88–89.

5.332* Gooch, Bryan N. S., and **David Thatcher.** *A Shakespeare Music Catalogue.* 5 vols. 2,847 pp. Oxford: Clarendon Press, 1991.

    A list of 21,362 musical works and collections, with an annotated bibliography of 2,323 entries. The indexes include Shakespeare's titles and lines; titles of musical works; composers, arrangers, and editors; and librettists and other writers. Supplementary lists include publishers. Bryan N. S. Gooch wrote of this project in "A Shakespearean Music Catalogue: The Path and the Progress," *Fontes* 37 (1990): 121–24.

    Reviewed by Linda Phyllis Austern in *Fontes* 40 (1993): 59–60, by David Greer in *M&L* 74 (1993): 425–26, and by Edward Hotaling in *Notes* 49 (1992): 628.

5.333* Honegger, Marc, and **Paul Prévost.** *Dictionnaire des oeuvres de l'art vocal.* 3 vols. 2,367 pp. Paris: Bordas, 1991–92.

    Includes bibliographical references and indexes.

5.334 Hovland, Michael. *Musical Settings of American Poetry: A Bibliography.* xli + 531 pp. Westport, Conn.: Greenwood Press, 1986. (Music reference collection, 8)

    A list of 5,800 settings of 99 American authors by 2,100 composers, providing bibliographical information as well as brief remarks on performing forces. Recordings are occasionally cited. The citations are arranged by author, indexed by composers and titles of literary works.

    Reviewed by Ann P. Basart in *CNV* 106 (1986): 21 and by Allie Wise Goudy in *ARBA* 18 (1987): no. 1248.

5.335 Kagan, Sergius. *Music for the Voice: A Descriptive List of Concert and Teaching Material.* Revised ed. 780 pp. Bloomington, Ind.: Indiana University Press, 1968.

    First published in New York by Rinehart & Co., 1949, 507 pp., as no. 3 in the Field of music series.

    An annotated bibliography of art song. Songs are listed alphabetically by composer and nationality within four large categories: pre–19th-century songs and airs, 19th- and 20th-century songs, folk songs, and operatic excerpts. Each section has its own bibliography, and there are numerous biographical sketches of songwriters. The data given for each song includes title, vocal compass, tessitura, and type, with descriptive and evaluative comments.

    The 1st ed. is briefly reviewed by Paul Hue in *Notes* (1949): 316.

5.336* Klaus, Kenneth S. *Chamber Music for Solo Voice and Instruments, 1960–1989: An Annotated Guide.* 222 pp. Berkeley, Calif.: Fallen Leaf Press, 1994. (Fallen Leaf reference books in music, 29)

A list of 705 works by over 500 composers for voice and small instrumental ensemble. The main section is arranged by vocal range, with each selection entered alphabetically by composer; each listing includes the date of composition, names of the individual movements, the publisher, the source and language of text, the instrumentation, the vocal range, and the level of difficulty. There are indexes by performing media (instrumentation), composers, sources of text, and publisher.

Reviewed by Nancy L. Walker in *Notes* 52 (1996): 801–2.

5.337* Lowenberg, Carlton. *Musicians Wrestle Everywhere: Emily Dickinson and Music.* xxviii + 210 pp. Berkeley, Calif.: Fallen Leaf Press, 1992. (Fallen Leaf reference books in music, 19)

A detailed list citing over 1,600 musical settings, both solo and ensemble, of Dickinson's texts (poems and letters) by 276 composers.

Reviewed by Marjorie E. Bloss in *ARBA* 25 (1994): no. 1308.

5.338 Lust, Patricia D. *American Vocal Chamber Music, 1945–1980: An Annotated Bibliography.* 273 pp. Westport, Conn.: Greenwood Press, 1985. (Music reference collections, 4)

A bibliography of 544 entries, listing music written for 1 or 2 voices and 1 to 15 instruments, excluding voice and piano, arranged alphabetically by composer, with annotations describing their unusual features, including nontraditional notation. Appendixes classify the works by performing forces; there are indexes to titles and to names of persons and ensembles.

Reviewed by Paula Morgan in *Notes* 42 (1986): 551–53 and by Frederic Schoettler in *ARBA* 17 (1986): no. 1265.

5.339* Manning, Jane. *New Vocal Repertory: An Introduction.* 284 pp. Oxford, England: Clarendon Press, 1994.

Originally published by Macmillan, London, 1986.

A list and description of over 70 English-language songs, graded in 6 classifications, with performance advice, programming suggestions, information on available editions, and a bibliography (pp. 277–82).

Reviewed by Peter Dickinson in *M&L* 69 (1988): 115–16.

5.340 Nardone, Thomas R. *Classical Vocal Music in Print.* 650 pp. Philadelphia, Pa.: Musicdata, 1976. (Music in print series, 4)

1985 Supplement, edited by Gary S. Eslinger, was published in 1986, 253 pp. *1995 Supplement*, edited by F. Mark Daugherty, was published in 1995, 287 pp., and the *Master Index 1995,* 287 pp., was published in the same year.

A list, arranged alphabetically by composer and then by title, of editions reported by their publishers as being in print. No attempt was made to put variant titles of the same work together. Prices and publishers' numbers are sometimes given.

The *1985 Supplement* is reviewed by Allie Wise Goudy in *ARBA* 18 (1987): no. 1252.

5.341* O'Brien, Robert F. *School Songs of America's Colleges and Universities: A Directory.* 197 pp. New York: Greenwood Press, 1991.

An alphabetical list, arranged by state and then by institution, with information on sources, composers, and publishers.

5.342* Ord, Alan J. *Songs for Bass Voice: An Annotated Guide to Works for Bass Voice.* 217 pp. Metuchen, N.J.: Scarecrow Press, 1994.

Texts and Translations

5.343* Alton, Jeannine, and **Brian Jeffery.** *Bele buche e bele parleure: A Guide to the Pronunciation of Medieval and Renaissance French for Singers and Others.* 79 pp. London: Tecla Editions, 1976.

Pronunciations for French vowels and consonants from 1100 to 1600, presented in text and chart forms. Regional variations are covered (Provençal, Picard, and Norman). Twelve poems of varying date are presented, with commentary on pronunciation; all are spoken on an accompanying cassette, and six of them are sung in musical settings from their era. A brief bibliography is supplied (p. 30).

Reviewed by Nigel Wilkins in *French Studies* 34 (1980): 118–19 and by C. A. Robson in *M&L* 62 (1981): 417.

5.344* Bernac, Pierre. *The Interpretation of French Song.* Translations of song texts by Winifred Radford. 326 pp. New York; Washington: Praeger Publishers, 1970.

British ed. published by Cassell in London.

Texts, poetic translations, and suggestions for interpretation of selected songs by Berlioz, Gounod, Franck, Saint-Saëns, Delibes, Bizet, Duparc, Chabrier, Chausson, Fauré, Debussy, Satie, Caplet, Roussel, Ravel, and Poulenc. Additional composers are listed with selections of their songs, not described in detail due to space limitations. The introductory chapters cover the performance and interpretation of French vocal music. There are separate indexes for titles, first lines, and composers.

Reviewed by Astra Desmond in *M&L* 51 (1970): 310–11.

5.345* Drinker, Henry S. *Texts of the Choral Works of Johann Sebastian Bach in English Translation.* 4 vols. New York: Privately printed and distributed by the Association of American Colleges Arts Program, 1943.

Contents: Vols. 1–2, *Cantatas.* Vol. 3, *Passions, Oratorios, Motets, Secular and Unpublished Cantatas and Songs.* Vol. 4, *Index and Concordance to the English Texts of the Complete Choral Works of Johann Sebastian Bach.*

A collection of the original vocal texts, with English translations. This is one of a series of translations by Drinker: *The Bach Chorale Texts in English Translation, with Annotations Showing the Use of the Melodies Elsewhere by Bach in His Vocal and Organ Works, and a Musical Index to the Melodies* (1941, 105 pp.) fills out his Bach translations, with additional access to the chorales. The vocal works of other composers are covered by his *English Texts for the Songs by Modeste Mussorgsky (1835–1881)* (1950, 22 pp.), *English Texts of Thirty Beethoven Solo Songs* (1952, 15 pp.), *English Texts to the Vocal Works of Heinrich Schütz* (1952, 182 pp.), *Hugo Wolf: The Texts of the Solo Songs* (1949, 98 pp.), *Texts of the Solo Songs of Franz Schubert in English Translation* (1951, 255 pp.), *Texts of the Vocal Works of Johannes Brahms in English Translation* (1946, 210 pp.), and *Texts of the Vocal Works of Robert Schumann in English Translation* (1947, 145 pp.).

The Mussorgsky and Schubert translations are reviewed by Philip L. Miller in *Notes* 8 (1951): 716, and the collection of Schumann translations is reviewed by Richard V. Lindabury in *Notes* 5 (1947): 110–11.

5.346* Challis, Natalia. *The Singer's Rachmaninoff.* 258 pp. New York: Pelion Press, 1989.

Reviewed by Kevin A. Freeman in *Notes* 47 (1990): 399–400.

5.347* Cockburn, Jacqueline, and **Richard Stokes.** *The Spanish Song Companion.* 268 pp. London: Victor Gollancz Ltd., 1992.

A survey of Spanish song from the medieval period to the 20th century. There are chapters on monody and polyphony, the beginnings of solo song, and song in the theater (tonadilla and zarzuela). Each chapter, after an introduction, gives texts, with a brief biographical sketch of each composer covered. Chronologically arranged chapters on individual composers follow. In translation, the Spanish word order is observed closely; the translators attempt to convey the poet's meaning "without any slavish adherence to the original rhymes and rhythm." An afterword lists works by living Spanish composers that are not yet well known outside Spain, and an appendix contains texts and translations relevant to the text but not included therein. "Notes on the Poets" has 45 biographical sketches. A select discography follows the chronological format of the book. There are indexes of composers, poets and translators, and titles and first lines.

5.348* Coffin, Berton, Pierre Delattre, Ralph Errole, and **Werner Singer.** *Phonetic Readings of Songs and Arias.* 361 pp. Boulder, Colo.: Pruett Press, 1963.

Reprinted by Metuchen, N.J., and London: Scarecrow Press, 1981.

IPA transcriptions of 413 Italian, German, and French songs included in Coffin's *The Singer's Repertoire* (2nd ed.; New York: Scarecrow Press, 1960). For each language section, assisted by a specialist in the language, Coffin gives an outline of that language's transcription and problems associated with diction. Texts are arranged alphabetically by composer, in a two-line format with IPA pronunciation under the original text. An index of titles and first lines is provided, as well as a brief bibliography covering singing diction in general and for each of the languages included.

Reviewed by Philip L. Miller in *Notes* 21 (1964): 374–75.

5.349* Coffin, Berton, Werner Singer, and **Pierre Delattre.** *Word-by-Word Translations of Songs and Arias Part I—German and French.* 620 pp. New York: Scarecrow Press, 1966.

Schoep, Arthur, and Daniel Harris. *Word-by-Word Translations of Songs and Arias Part II—Italian.* 563 pp. Metuchen, N.J.: Scarecrow Press, 1972.

Companion vols. to Coffin's *The Singer's Repertoire* (2nd ed.; New York: Scarecrow Press, 1960), with a two-line bilingual format: the first line in the original language, and the second a word-by-word translation intended to provide "the synchronization of meaning with the text." An explanatory third line is added when the meaning of the word-by-word translation is unclear. Texts are listed alphabetically by composer. An index of first lines and titles is provided for each volume.

Reviewed by Harvey Ringel in *NATS* 23 (1966): 16 no. 2 and 29 (1972): 31 no. 1.

5.350* Fischer-Dieskau, Dietrich. *The Fischer-Dieskau Book of Lieder: The Original Texts of Over Seven Hundred and Fifty Songs.* With English trans. by George Bird and Richard Stokes. 437 pp. New York: Alfred A. Knopf, 1977.

First published as *Texte deutscher Lieder,* 1976; a paperback ed. was published by Limelight Editions, New York, in 1984.

A collection of originally German poetry with English translation on facing page. The translators attempt to retain the "full sense, and much as possible of the tone" of the original poetry; thus the translations are neither precisely literal nor so poetic as to distort the poet's words. Texts are arranged alphabetically by German title; poet's name and lists of musical settings are provided for each text. Nearly 50 composers are represented, from the early 18th to the late 20th century. Alphabetical indexes are included for composers, poets and translators, and titles and first lines. Includes an informative philosophical/historical essay by Fischer-Dieskau on German art song.

Reviewed by Richard Dale Sjoerdsma in *NATS* 41 (1985): 39 no. 5.

5.351* Harrison, Donna Esselstyn. *Poetry in Song Literature: A Handbook for Students of Singing.* 254 pp. Sister Bay, Wisc.; Evanston, Ill.: William Caxton Ltd., 1989.

Texts, word-by-word translations, and background for selected German, French, Italian, and English poems set to music. English texts are provided for works from other languages (Hebrew, Latin, and Greek) as well. For each text, the poet's name and dates and a selective list of settings are included. The emphasis is on the songs' poets and settings in their historic eras. The work is chronologically arranged by poet, beginning with poems from classical antiquity through the middle ages, renaissance, baroque, classical, and romantic periods up to the modern era. There are some inaccuracies in dates and names of composers listed. A selected bibliography covers historical, musical, and literary aspects of the texts, although its most recent entry is dated 1977. An index of poets and titles of poems is provided.

Reviewed by Richard Dale Sjoerdsma in *NATS* 47 (September/October 1990): 42 no. 1.

5.352* Hines, Robert S. *Singer's Manual of Latin Diction and Phonetics.* 86 pp. New York: Schirmer Books, 1975.

A more technical approach than that of *The Choral Director's Latin* (**5.369**). Diction rules are provided, including an alphabetical chart of Latin spellings with IPA symbols, and a glossary of phonetic terms. Selected liturgical Latin texts (including but not limited to the Ordinary of the Mass, Stabat Mater, Te Deum, and Magnificat) are presented in a three-line format, the original divided by syllables and marked for accents, with IPA version and poetic translation following. The far-from-literal translations are taken from various liturgical publications. A brief bibliography (pp. 85–86) is included.

Reviewed by Elizabeth Forbes in *MT* 118 (1977): 563.

5.353* Jeffers, Ron. *Translations and Annotations of Choral Repertoire.* Vol. 1, *Sacred Latin Texts.* Corvallis, Ore.: Earthsongs, 1988.

Word-by-word translations and explanations of liturgical context for sacred texts. An introductory section provides basic information on the liturgical year and the hours of the Divine Office; a glossary of terms and pronunciation guide (both Roman and Austro-German) follow. The text section is divided into three parts: the Roman Mass, the Requiem Mass, and numerous other sacred texts; a detailed discussion of liturgical context accompanies each text. A word-by-word translation appears under each line of Latin text; side by side with this is a prose translation that "restores syntactical order and clarifies meaning." An appendix lists selected settings of the sacred texts found in the book, listing composer and voices or instruments required for performance. The title and first-line index is arranged alphabetically in the Latin text; each title or line is accompanied by a brief English translation.

Reviewed by Floyd Slotterback in *Choral Journal* 29 (1988–89): 37–38.

5.354* LeVan, Timothy. *Masters of the French Art Song: Translations of the Complete Songs of Chausson, Debussy, Duparc, Fauré and Ravel.* 445 pp. Metuchen, N.J.: Scarecrow Press, 1991.

A companion to the author's *Masters of the Italian Art Song* (**5.355**), containing texts and translations, arranged alphabetically by composer, in the three-line format of original-language text; word-by-word translation; and reconstruction of the second line in more standard English, although not always idiomatically sensitive. Not all of the named composers' songs are included, nor is information on poets and dates of composition. There are indexes of song titles and first lines.

Reviewed by Richard Dale Sjoerdsma in *NATS* 49 (1992): 34 no. 1 and by James R. Briscoe in *Fontes* 39 (1992): 382–83.

5.355* LeVan, Timothy. *Masters of the Italian Art Song: Word-by-Word and Poetic Translations of the Complete Songs for Voice and Piano.* 321 pp. Metuchen, N.J.: Scarecrow Press, 1990.

A collection including texts set by Bellini, Donaudy, Donizetti, Puccini, Rossini, Tosti, and Verdi. Texts are in a three-line format: original-language text, a word-by-word translation in the original word order, and a reconstruction of the second line in more standard English. Some translations may be inaccurate. Indexes are provided for song titles and first lines.

5.356* Magner, Candace A. *Phonetic Readings of Brahms Lieder.* 412 pp. Metuchen, N.J.: Scarecrow Press, 1987.

A comprehensive pronunciation guide to all German songs of Johannes Brahms, presenting each line of German text with its pronunciation clearly spelled in IPA directly below. Included with the texts of Lieder are four appendixes cross-referencing the poems by opus numbers, title, first line, and poet. The index locates each song by title and first line.

Reviewed by Kevin A. Freeman in *Notes* 47 (1990): 399–400.

5.357* Magner, Candace A. *Phonetic Readings of Schubert's Lieder.* 2 vols. Metuchen, N.J.: Scarecrow Press, 1994.

A comprehensive pronunciation guide to all German songs of Franz Schubert, presenting each line of German text with pronunciation clearly spelled in IPA directly below. Included are nearly 600 texts of Schubert Lieder, along with four appendixes cross-referencing the poems by Deutsch catalog numbers (**6.308**), title, first line, and poet. The index locates each song by title and first line.

5.358* Metzner, Günter. *Heine in der Musik: Bibliographie der Heine-Vertonungen.* 12 vols. Tutzing, Germany: H. Schneider, 1989–94.

A bibliography of every reference to every Heine setting, classical and popular. The works, arranged by composer, are listed in Vols. 1–8; Vols. 9–10 have a list by poem-incipit; Vol. 11 is the index and Vol. 12 the bibliography.

Vols. 3–4 are reviewed by Ewan West in *M&L* 72 (1991): 301–2 and by Lawrence D. Snyder in *Notes* 47 (1990): 399.

5.359* Miller, Philip L. *German Lieder.* 336 pp. New York: Continuum, 1990. (The German library, 42)

A collection of German Lieder texts, arranged by the most prominent composer of a setting, with English translations that attempt to "convey as nearly as possible the meaning of the original poems." Some alternative settings are listed. There are indexes of composers, poets, and titles and first lines. The foreword by Hermann Hesse is a translation of a letter he wrote to a singer.

Reviewed by Helene M. Kastinger Riley in *Colloquia Germanica* 24 (1991): 251–52.

5.360 Miller, Philip L. *The Ring of Words: An Anthology of Song Texts.* 200 pp. Garden City, N.Y.: Doubleday, 1963.

Paperback ed. published 1966. Reprinted by W.W. Norton, 1973 (xxviii + 518 pp.).

An anthology of poems set as art songs that have become part of the standard repertoire, in German, French, Italian, Spanish, Russian, Norwegian, and Swedish, with English translations of the texts. The texts are arranged by language and composer. The translations facing the original text are as close to the original poems as possible while retaining English readability and attempting to make the meaning of the original words reasonably clear. Indexes are provided for composers as well as for titles and first lines.

Reviewed by Jan LaRue in *Notes* 20 (1963): 474 and by Bernard E. Wilson in *Notes* 23 (1966): 267–68.

5.361* Paquin, Marie-Thérèse. *Airs et mélodies Mozart, Schubert, classiques italiens; traduction mot à mot, accent tonique / translation word-for-word, stress.* 122 pp. Montreal: Presses de l'Université de Montréal, 1983.

A line-by-line text with literal translations into French and English, with "literary" translations side-by-side. There are selected Italian songs by Mozart and Schubert, as well as Italian songs written in the classical period and a few others; in all, 66 song texts are treated. Analytical notes accompany each text, providing brief information about the composer and the song.

5.362* Paquin, Marie Thérèse. *Dix cycles de Lieder / 10 cycles of Lieder: Traduction mot à mot et juxtalinéaire / Word for word and juxtalinear translation.* 277 pp. Montreal: Les Presses de Université de Montréal, 1977.

Line-by-line text with word-for-word translations into French and English, with poetic translations side-by-side. Contains "An die ferne Geliebte" by Beethoven; "Vier ernste Gesänge" by Brahms; "Kindertotenlieder" and "Lieder eines fahrenden Gesellen" by Mahler; "Die Schöne Müllerin," "Winterreise," and "Schwanengesang" by Schubert; and "Frauenliebe- und Leben," "Dichterliebe," and "Der arme Peter" by Robert Schumann. There is an index of German titles.

5.363* Peters, Erskine. *Lyrics of the Afro-American Spiritual: A Documentary Collection.* xxxi + 463 pp. Westport, Conn.: Greenwood Press, 1993. (The Greenwood encyclopedia of Black music)

5.364 Phillips, Lois. *Lieder Line by Line, and Word for Word.* 365 pp. New York: C. Scribner's Sons, 1980.

Also published in London by Duckworth in 1979.

A collection of Lieder texts that presents the original German lyrics with a literal English translation below each word, and, alongside, an English prose version for Lieder by Beethoven, Brahms, Mahler, Schubert, Robert Schumann, Richard Strauss, Wagner, and Wolf. Composers appear in chronological order. Within the composer groupings, texts are also arranged chronologically, although the date of each text is not included; this can make use somewhat frustrating. An index to German titles and first lines is provided.

Reviewed by Richard Dale Sjoerdsma in *NATS* 38 (1982): 46 no. 3, by Suzanne Thorin-Perlongo in *Notes* 37 (1980): 57, and by Eric Sams in *MT* 121 (1980): 103.

5.365* Piatak, Jean, and **Regina Avrashov.** *Russian Songs and Arias, Phonetic Readings, Word-by-Word Translations, and a Concise Guide to Russian Diction.* 206 pp. Dallas, Tex.: Pst . . . Inc., 1991.

A two-part guide for singing Russian songs. Part 1covers Russian diction, including the alphabet, sounds, and special features; much of this information has been criticized as inaccurate or misleading. Part 2 offers text, phonetic readings (often inaccurate), and word-by-word translations of songs and arias, alphabetically arranged by composer, including Arensky, Balakirev, Borodin, Dargomizhsky, Glinka, Medtner, Mussorgsky, Prokofiev, Rachmaninoff, Rimsky-Korsakov, Rubinstein, Shostakovich, and Tchaikovsky. A brief bibliography is included; there are indexes for Russian titles and first lines as well as English titles and first lines. Spelling errors abound. Although this may prove helpful for the beginner, it is not a scholarly source.

Reviewed by Laurence R. Richter in *Slavic and East European Journal* 38 (1994): 401–4.

5.366 Prawer, S. S. *The Penguin Book of Lieder.* 208 pp. Baltimore, Md.: Penguin Books, 1964. Reprint ed., 1979.

Texts and poetic translations for selected Lieder of Haydn, Mozart, Beethoven, Loewe, Schubert, Mendelssohn, Schumann, Liszt, Wagner, Franz, Brahms, Wolf, Mahler, Strauss, Schoenberg, Webern, Berg, and Hindemith. Each section is introduced with a brief description of the composer's works. "Notes on the Poets" provides biographical information for more than 70 poets whose works are included in the book, with page numbers where their work may be found. A "Select Bibliography" lists general works on Lieder, plus references for specific composers, all in English. This is now somewhat outdated, as is the "Discography and Suggestions for a Basic Collection of Lieder Recordings." The introductory essay discusses the relationship of music and poetry in German song. An index of titles and first lines is provided.

Review by Walter Allen Stults in *NATS* 21 (October 1964): 29–30 no. 2, by Bernard E. Wilson in *Notes* 23 (1966): 267–68, and by Andrew Porter in *MT* 105 (1964): 433.

5.367* Richardson, Dorothy, and **Tina Ruta.** *Arie Antiche.* 147 pp. Orleans, Mass.: Paraclete Press, 1990.

Word-by-word and poetic translations from Alessandro Parisotti's collection of arias and songs, *Arie antiche, ad una voce per canto e pianoforte* (Milan: Ricordi, 1885–1900, 3 vols.). The two-line format texts (original language and word-by-word translations) are followed by a nonsinging poetic translation that endeavors to retain the style and sense of the Italian poems. Composer and title indexes identify the Ricordi vol. in which the song is found.

5.368* Rohinsky, Marie-Claire. *The Singer's Debussy.* 317 pp. New York: Pelion Press, 1987.

Reviewed by Kevin A. Freeman in *Notes* 47 (1990): 399–400.

5.369* Trusler, Ivan. *The Choral Director's Latin.* 102 pp. Lanham, Md.: University Press of America, 1987.

A handbook of pronunciation for church Latin, including chapters on diction for vowels, consonants, and compound sounds. Texts, simple phonetic English spellings, and somewhat poetic English translations for the Latin texts most often set to music make the Latin text accessible to those unfamiliar with the language. Unfortunately, the texts, pronunciations, and translations are not on facing pages, or in a line-by-line format, but on separate pages, one following the other. There is a "Textual Comparison of Requiems" (pp. 48–52) in chart form for the requiems of Mozart, Berlioz, Verdi, and Fauré.

5.370* **Wigmore, Richard.** *Schubert—the Complete Song Texts: Texts of the Lieder and Italian Songs,* with English trans. by Richard Wigmore. 380 pp. New York: Schirmer Books, 1988.
Reviewed by Kevin A. Freeman in *Notes* 48 (1991): 512–14.

Indexes

5.371 Bayne, Pauline Shaw, and **Patricia Barkelow.** *Song Index: University of Tennessee, Knoxville.* 30 microfiche and accompanying booklet. Knoxville, Tenn.: University of Tennessee Library, 1981.

An index to songs in 554 songbooks and anthologies, many indexed in other works, with indexes to song titles, composers, genres, language of texts, authors, geographic or ethnic sources, and performance forces. Some of the songbooks are the work of a single composer, generally not included in such indexes, thus giving helpful title access to the individual songs in song cycles and such. There is up-to-date access to this index through the Internet.

5.372 Brunnings, Florence E. *Folk Song Index: A Comprehensive Guide to the Florence E. Brunnings Collection.* lxxxi + 357 pp. New York: Garland Publishing, 1981. (Garland reference library of the humanities, 252)

A title index to the 49,399 songs in print and sound anthologies in the Brunnings Collection, North Weymouth, Mass., with references from the first lines to titles. There is a list of the 1,305 anthologies indexed.
Reviewed by Norm Cohen in *JEMFQ* 17 (1981): 109 no. 62 and by Anthony G. Barrand in *AM* 3 (1985): 91–93.

5.373* **Cleveland Public Library.** *Index to Negro Spirituals.* 84 pp. Chicago, Ill.: Center for Black Music Research, Columbia College, 1991. (CBMR monographs, 3)
Originally published by the Library in 1937 with the sponsorship of the Works Progress Administration.

An index to 31 collections originally published 1867–1933; 7 of these anthologies are only partially indexed.

5.374* **Cook, James Ballou.** *Finding List of Vocal Music, 1949–1969.* 21 vols. Rochester, N.H.: James Ballou Cook & Co., 1948–69.

An index to then-available anthologies of popular song collections published in the United States. The introduction of the first issue stated that "this is a service book, aimed particularly at the retail music trade, and has been sold as a leased service. . . . We plan to publish a new edition annually." Copies were sold outright to libraries, however, rather than issued on a lease basis, as they were to individual subscribers.
Reviewed by Philip L. Miller in *Notes* 25 (1968): 246–47.

5.375 Day, Cyrus L., and **Eleanore Boswell Murrie.** *English Song-Books, 1651–1702: A Bibliography with a First-Line Index of Songs.* xxi + 439 pp. London: Bibliographical Society, 1940.

A list, with full bibliographic description, including contents, of 252 secular songbooks published in England and Scotland. The arrangement is chronological, with nonextant works included. The first-line index has 4,150 songs by about 250 composers; there are also indexes by composer, author of text, performer, tunes and airs, sources, titles of collections, printers, publishers, and booksellers. This is a model of descriptive bibliography, particularly valuable for its coverage of the publishing Playfords and their contemporaries. The authors also wrote "English Song-Books, 1651–1702, and Their Publishers," in *Library,* ser. 4, 16 (March 1936): no. 4.

5.376 Dean-Smith, Margaret. *A Guide to English Folk Song Collections, 1822–1952, with an Index to Their Contents, Historical Annotations, and an Introduction.* 120 pp. Liverpool: University Press of Liverpool in association with The English Folk Dance & Song Society, 1954.

An index to 56 collections, some in multivolume sets, of English folk songs published from 1822 to 1952. The main entry is by song title, with cross-references from the text incipit. There is a chronological list of collections, with detailed annotations.

Reviewed by Bertrand H. Bronson in *JAMS* 8 (1955): 57–58 and by Rae Korson in *Notes* 11 (1954): 570.

5.377 De Charms, Desirée, and **Paul F. Breed.** *Songs in Collections: An Index.* xxxix + 588 pp. Detroit, Mich.: Information Services, Inc., 1966.

An index to 411 collections of solo songs published between 1940 and 1957, with entries for more than 9,493 songs, planned to coordinate with Sears (**5.390**). Composed songs are entered under composer; anonymous and folk songs are entered alphabetically by title under nationality. The emphasis, however, is on art songs and operatic arias. No collections of songs by a single composer are included. There are separate sections for carols, divided by nationality, and for sea chanteys, and a complete title and first-line index.

Reviewed by Donald Ivey in *JRME* 15 (1967): 169–70, by Imogen Fellinger in *Die Musikforschung* 23 (1970): 96–97, and by Ellen Kenny in *Notes* 23 (1966): 269–70.

5.378* *Dover Popular Music Index and Catalog: Over 1200 Songs and Popular Piano Pieces Located for You in Inexpensive Dover Collections.* 15 pp. New York: Dover Publications, 1994.

An index to Dover Publications's collections of song reprints and anthologies of popular piano music.

5.379* Ferguson, Gary Lynn. *Song Finder: A Title Index to 32,000 Popular Songs in Collections, 1854–1992.* 344 pp. Westport, Conn.: Greenwood Press, 1995. (Music reference collection, no. 46)

A index to anthologies of popular American songs, compiled from collections held by the State Library of Louisiana.

Reviewed by Michael Colby in *LJ* 120 (1995): 74.

5.380 *Folio-Dex.* 1 vol. (Loose-leaf, unpaged.) Loomis, Calif.; Salt Lake City, Utah: Folio-Dex Co., 1970–86.

A title index to songs in collections of printed music, commercially available when the index was published. Indication was made of the accompaniment (organ, piano, guitar). This subscription service was published in loose-leaf format for easy updating. The publisher also produced in a similar format *Folio-Dex II,* an index of different types of music (popular, classical, sacred, etc.) listing songs published in a format appropriate for choir, band, and orchestra.

5.381 Gargan, William, and **Sue Sharma.** *Find That Tune: An Index to Rock, Folk-Rock, Disco and Soul in Collections.* 303 pp. New York: Neal Schumann, 1984.

Gargan, William, and Sue Sharma. *Find That Tune: An Index to Rock, Folk-Rock, Disco and Soul in Collections.* 387 pp. New York: Neal Schumann, 1988.

A 2-vol. index whose 1st vol. gives access to over 4,000 songs in 203 collections published 1950–81. Includes a list of collections indexed, as well as a title index that includes information on composer and lyricist, performers, publisher, and copyright date. There is an index to first lines, composers and lyricists, and performers. The 1988 ed. indexes 4,000 songs in collections published from 1950 to 1985 not indexed in the earlier ed.

Reviewed by Norma Jean Lamb in *Notes* 41 (1984): 286–87 and by Richard W. Grefrath in *ARBA* 16 (1985): no. 1206.

5.382* Goleeke, Thomas. *Literature for Voice: An Index of Songs in Collections and Source Book for Teachers of Singing.* 223 pp. Metuchen, N.J.: Scarecrow Press, 1984.

Access to 60 secular art song anthology vols. often used for teaching, with a bibliography (pp. 159–72).

Reviewed by George Louis Mayer in *ARBA* 16 (1985): no. 1185 and by Paula Morgan in *Notes* 41 (1985): 521–22.

5.383* Goodfellow, William D. *SongCite: An Index to Popular Songs.* 433 pp. New York: Garland, 1995. (Garland reference library of the humanities, 1918)

An index to 248 collections, containing over 7,000 songs.

5.384* Goodfellow, William D. *Wedding Music: An Index to Collections.* 197 pp. Metuchen, N.J.: Scarecrow Press, 1992.

An index to over 190 collections of wedding music, with several thousand different titles. In addition to traditional wedding compositions, many modern love songs are also included. Most works are for some combination of voice, piano, or organ, but some music for guitar and other instruments is also indexed.

5.385* Goodfellow, William D. *Where's That Tune?: An Index to Songs in Fakebooks.* 449 pp. Metuchen, N.J.: Scarecrow Press, 1990.

An index to 64 fakebooks, with an annotated list.

Reviewed by Anthony Lis in *Fontes* 40 (1993): 65–68.

5.386 Havlice, Patricia. *Popular Song Index.* 933 pp. Metuchen, N.J.: Scarecrow Press, 1975.

First supplement, indexing 72 collections dating between 1970 and 1975, was published in 1978 (386 pp.). Second supplement, indexing 156 collections from 1974 to 1981, was published in 1984 (530 pp.). Third supplement, indexing 181 collections from 1979 to 1987, was published in 1989 (875 pp.).

A multivolume song index, whose 1st vol. indexes 301 collections published between 1940 and 1972. The 4 volumes index folk songs, popular songs, spirituals, hymns, children's songs, sea chanteys, and blues in 710 song anthologies published since 1940. Each vol. has a bibliography of sources and indexes to titles, first lines, first lines of choruses, and composers and lyricists.

There is a brief review of the 1st vol. by Stephen M. Fry in *Notes* 32 (1976): 781, and of the 1st supplement by Cheryl Sprague in *Notes* 35 (1978): 94 and by Patricia Felch in *Notes* 35 (1979): 637–38. The 3rd supplement is reviewed by Linda M. Fidler in *Notes* 47 (1990): 390–91.

5.387 Lammel, Inge. *Bibliographie der deutschen Arbeiterliederbücher, 1933–1945.* 2nd revised ed. 106 pp. Leipzig: Deutscher Verlag für Musik, 1977. (Veröffentlichung der Akademie der Künste der Deutschen Demokratischen Republik, Sektion Musik, Abteilung Arbeiterleiderarchiv)

A bibliography, including indexes to collections, of songs of working persons in Germany, 1844–1945.

5.388 Leigh, Robert. *Index to Song Books: A Title Index to Over 11,000 Copies of Almost 6,900 Songs in 111 Song Books Published between 1933 and 1962.* 273 pp. Stockton, Calif.: Robert Leigh, 1964.

A reprint was published by Da Capo Press, New York in 1973.

An index whose coverage and approach make clear that it was intended to supplement the Sears *Song Index* (**5.390**), although, as the title states, access is only by title, so the aims were not fully realized.

5.389* Peterson, Carolyn Sue, and **Ann D. Fenton.** *Index to Children's Songs: A Title, First Line, and Subject Index.* 318 pp. New York: H.W. Wilson, 1979.

An index to 298 songbooks, published 1909–77, containing over 5,000 songs, with generous cross-references.

5.390 Sears, Minnie E. *Song Index: An Index to More than 12,000 Songs in 177 Song Collections.* 650 pp. New York: H.W. Wilson, 1926.

Supplement: An Index to More than 7,000 Songs in 104 Collections was published in 1934, 366 pp. The reprint ed., which contains both the original and supplement vols., was published by the Shoe String Press, Hamden, Conn., 1966.

An index containing titles, first lines, authors' names, and composers' names in one alphabet. Each song is listed under title, with added entries under composer and author and cross-references for first lines and variant or translated titles. There are both classified and alphabetical lists of the song collections indexed, with full bibliographical citations. The work of Sears was continued by De Charms and Breed (**5.377**) and Leigh (**5.388**).

5.391* Snyder, Lawrence D. *German Poetry in Song: An Index of Lieder.* 730 pp. Berkeley, Calif.: Fallen Leaf Press, 1995. (Fallen Leaf reference books in music, 30)

Snyder, Lawrence D. *Index of Composers' Titles: Supplement to German Poetry in Song: An Index of Lieder.* 197 pp. Berkeley, Calif.: Fallen Leaf Press, 1995.

An index of over 9,800 Lieder composed after 1770, arranged by poet. There is a list of 7,450 poems by more than 1,100 poets set to music by 370 composers; information is given on first lines, composers, dates of compositions, opus numbers, instrumentation, translators, and cycles. There is a separate 200-pp. title, composer, and first-line index, with score sources. The decision to include the title index came too late for the first printing, but future printings will include it.

5.392 Studwell, William E. *Christmas Carols: A Reference Guide.* Indexes by David A. Hamilton. 278 pp. New York: Garland Publishers, 1985.

The book has four sections: general background material on the carol; a bibliography (pp. xvii–xxxiii); a historical dictionary that lists 789 carols and Christmas songs, providing historical and other information about them and in most cases locating them in one or more anthologies; and, finally, title, persons and group, and place indexes to the historical dictionary.

Entries for the carols are arranged alphabetically, but in their original language. The title index brings together all versions and languages; there are no cross-references. There is also a carol chronology.

Reviewed by Ann P. Basart in *CNV* 102 (1986): 22–23.

WIND INSTRUMENTS (SOLO AND CHAMBER)

5.393 Basart, Ann P. "Bibliographies of Wind Music: A Check-List." In *CNV* 37 (1979): 10–13 and 39 (1980): 9–13.

An annotated checklist to bibliographies providing information on music for wind instruments.

5.394 Chapman, James, Sheldon Fine, and **Mary Rasmussen.** "Music for Wind Instruments in Historical Editions, Collected Works, and Numbered Series: A Bibliography." In *Brass and Woodwind Quarterly* 1 (1968): 115–49 and 2 (1969): 17–58.

A bibliography indexing 42 collected editions of early music and series containing music, without voices, for specified instrumentation with basso continuo; music, with voices, for specified instrumentation; music, without voices, for unspecified instrumentation; and music, with voices, for unspecified instrumentation.

5.395 Helm, Sanford Marion. *Catalog of Chamber Music for Wind Instruments.* Revised reprint. 85 pp. New York: Da Capo Press, 1969.

First published in 1952 by the author in Ann Arbor at the University of Michigan's School of Music as National Association of College Wind and Percussion Instrument Instructors, Publication no. 1.

A list of chamber music ranging from 3 to 12 instruments and using at least 1 wind instrument, classified according to ensemble size and instrumentation. The entries give publisher, date, and the American agent for then–available editions. There is a composer index.

The 1952 ed. is reviewed by Josef Marx in *Notes* 10 (1952): 450–51.

WOODWIND INSTRUMENTS

5.396 Gillespie, James E. *The Reed Trio: An Annotated Bibliography of Original Published Works.* 84 pp. Detroit, Mich.: Information Coordinators, 1971. (Detroit studies in music bibliography, 20)

5.397* Horne, Aaron. *Woodwind Music of Black Composers.* 145 pp. New York: Greenwood Press, 1990. (Music reference collection, 24)

5.398 Hošek, Miroslav. *Das Bläserquintett / The Woodwind Quintet.* English trans. by Colleen Gruban. 234 pp. Grünwald, Germany: B. Brühle, 1979.

A bibliography of woodwind quintets by categories, with essays on origin, acoustics, and performance practice. Also provided are lists of personnel in professional woodwind quintets and a bibliography.

5.399 Houser, Roy. *Catalogue of Chamber Music for Woodwind Instruments.* 2nd ed. 158 ll. Bloomington, Ind.: Indiana University Press, 1960.

Reprinted by Da Capo Press, New York, in 1973. Supplement: *Woodwind Ensembles Bibliography.*

A bibliography of material for 3 to 10 instruments, classified according to ensemble.

5.400 Peters, Harry B. *The Literature of the Woodwind Quintet.* 174 pp. Metuchen, N.J.: Scarecrow, 1971.

A basic list of woodwind quintet music, followed by a section on the quintet with one, two, three, four, or five additional performers.

5.401 Rasmussen, Mary. *A Teacher's Guide to the Literature of Woodwind Instruments.* 226 pp. Durham, N.H.: Brass and Woodwind Quarterly, 1968.

Bibliographies of woodwind music for solos or ensembles.

5.402* Voxman, Himie, and **Lyle Merriman.** *Woodwind Music Guide: Ensemble Music.* 498 pp. Evanston, Ill.: Instrumentalist Company, 1982. (Music guide series, 2)

1973 ed., 280 pp.

A classified list, arranged by format, with minimal bibliographic information.

5.403 Voxman, Himie, and **Lyle Merriman.** *Woodwind Music Guide: Solo and Study Material in Print.* 499 pp. Evanston, Ill.: Instrumentalist Company, 1984. (Music guide series, 3)

Earlier ed. published as *Woodwind Solo and Study Material Music Guide,* 1975.

A classified list with brief titles and publisher codes.

Bassoon

5.404* Bartholomäus, Helge. *Das Fagottensemble: Kleines Handbuch zur Musikpraxis.* 107 pp. Berlin: Musik- und Buchverlag W. Feja, 1992.

A bibliography that includes lists of works for two or more bassoons, bassoons with other instruments, and bassoons with orchestra.

5.405* Beebe, Jon P. *Music for Unaccompanied Solo Bassoon: An Annotated Bibliography.* 99 pp. Jefferson, N.C.: McFarland and Company, 1990.

A bibliography of 159 entries, including transcriptions and works for unspecified instrument thought suitable for bassoon.

Reviewed by Kristine K. Fletcher in *Notes* 48 (1991): 102–3.

5.406* Bulling, Burchard. *Fagott Bibliographie.* 520 pp. Wilhelmshaven, Germany: Florian Noetzel Verlag, 1989.

A classified list of 13,000 works for bassoon and contrabassoon, both solo and with other instruments.

Reviewed by Kristine K. Fletcher in *Notes* 48 (1991): 102–3.

5.407* Fletcher, Kristine Klopfenstein. *The Paris Conservatoire and the Contest Solos for Bassoon.* 142 pp. Bloomington, Ind.: Indiana University Press, 1988.

A history of the Conservatoire's contests, including an annotated bibliography of commissioned works for bassoon, 1898–1984.

Reviewed by Edward Blakeman in *M&L* 70 (1989): 273–74.

5.408* Königsbeck, Bodo. *Bassoon Bibliography.* 500 pp. Monteux, France: Musica Rara, 1994.

A list of 21,000 titles, including 1,000 concerti and 4,000 wind quintets. Each entry includes the year of composition and first performance, the duration, publisher, publication date, plate number, and the location of manuscripts and early and current editions.

5.409 Wilkins, Wayne. *The Index of Bassoon Music including the Index of Baroque Trio Sonatas.* 76 + 11 pp. Magnolia, Ark.: Music Register, 1976.

Supplements published in 1976–77 and 1978.

Classified lists of works citing composer and publisher.

Clarinet

5.410 Brixel, Eugen. *Klarinetten-Bibliographie.* 2nd ed. 493 pp. Wilhelmshaven, Germany: Heinrichshofens Verlag, 1978.

A classified list, international in scope, citing composer, title, and publisher of music for solo clarinet and for clarinet as part of an ensemble. Includes a short bibliography of literature about the clarinet and an index to composers listed.

5.411 Gee, Harry R. *Clarinet Solos de Concours, 1897–1980: An Annotated Bibliography.* 118 pp. Bloomington, Ind.: Indiana University Press, 1981.

An annotated bibliography of the clarinet music approved by the Paris Conservatory as repertoire for its annual clarinet competition.

Reviewed by Carl E. Hane, Jr., in *Notes* 39 (1982): 101–2.

5.412 Gillespie, James E., Jr. *Solos for Unaccompanied Clarinet: An Annotated Bibliography of Published Works.* 79 pp. Detroit, Mich.: Information Coordinators, 1973. (Detroit studies in music bibliography, 28)

A bibliography whose annotations feature composers' comments on performance and include biographical information.

5.413* International Clarinet Society. Research Center. *Catalog of the International Clarinet Society Score Collection.* 2nd ed. 188 pp. College Park, Md.: Music Library of the University of Maryland, 1990. (Publications of the Music Library of the University of Maryland at College Park, 1)

The 1st ed. was published in 1982, 139 pp., with a 1987 supplement (16 pp.).

A catalog arranged alphabetically by composer. Each entry has title, imprint, instrumentation, collation, and ICS number. There is an instrumentation index.

5.414* Newhill, John P. *The Basset-Horn and Its Music.* 2nd ed. 128 pp. Sale, Cheshire: The author, 1986.

A book whose largest section is its classified repertoire list.

Reviewed by Ann P. Basart in *CNV* 106 (1986): 25.

5.415 Tuthill, Burnet C. "The Concertos for Clarinet." In *JRME* 10 (1962): 47–58.

A brief introduction to the history of the clarinet concerto and its literature, followed by an annotated list of such concertos from the 18th century to the present. This list was supplemented by Robert A. Titus in *JRME* 13 (1965): 169–76.

5.416* Wilkins, Wayne. *The Index of Clarinet Music.* 143 pp. Magnolia, Ark.: Music Register, 1975.

Classified lists of works, citing composer and publisher.

Crumhorn

5.417* Meyer, Kenton Terry. *The Crumhorn: Its History, Design, Repertory, and Technique.* 273 pp. Ann Arbor, Mich.: UMI Research Press, 1983. (Studies in musicology, 66)

Reviewed by Anthony Baines in *Galpin Society Journal* 40 (1987): 77–78.

Flute and Recorder

5.418 Alker, Hugo. *Blockflöten-Bibliographie.* New ed. 2 vols. Wilhelmshaven, Germany: Heinrichshofen's Verlag; New York: C.F. Peters, 1985.

Contents: Band I, *Systematischer Teil;* Band II, *Alphabetischer Teil,* 3 vols. (Wilhelmshaven, Germany: Heinrichshofen's Verlag).

First ed., 1960–61, 2 vols. (Vienna: Universitätsbibliothek); 2nd ed., 1966–75, (Wilhelmshaven, Germany: Heinrichshofen's Verlag) includes as its 3rd vol. a supplement covering works issued 1970–74.

The premier bibliography of recorder music. The 1st vol. of the unlabeled 3rd ed. includes a classified list of music for recorder, arranged by composer and title, with publisher's imprint; there is a section devoted to articles about performance practice and other works relating to the recorder. Band II contains an alphabetical index to the composers contained in the 1st vol., with a list of publishers' names and addresses.

5.419* Boenke, Heidi M. *Flute Music by Women Composers: An Annotated Catalog.* 201 pp. New York: Greenwood Press, 1988. (Music reference collection, 16)

Based on the 1st ed. of **1.69**, a bibliography of flute works by women, each entry with a brief biography and list of works including flute, with OCLC numbers, LC card number, or call number given. There are occasional annotations of works and indexes by instrumentation, title, publisher, and composer.

Reviewed by Judy Tsou in *Notes* 47 (1990): 396–97 and by Allie Wise Goudy in *ARBA* 20 (1989): no. 1196.

5.420 Bowers, Jane. "A Catalogue of French Works for the Transverse Flute, 1692–1761." In *Recherches sur la musique française classique* 18 (1978): 89–125. Paris: Éditions A. et J. Picard. 1978.

5.421* Gronefeld, Ingo. *Die Flötekonzerte bis 1850: Ein thematisches Verzeichnis.* 3 vols. Tutzing, Germany: H. Schneider, 1992–94.

5.422 McGowan, Richard A. *Italian Baroque Solo Sonatas for the Recorder and the Flute.* 70 pp. Detroit, Mich.: Information Coordinators, 1978. (Detroit studies in music bibliography, 37)

A bibliography in two sections: the first listing and describing 18th-century manuscripts and editions, and the second giving modern editions.

5.423 Pellerite, James J. *A Handbook of Literature for the Flute: Compilation of Graded Method Materials, Solos, and Ensemble Music for Flutes.* Revised 3rd ed. xxii + 408 pp. Bloomington, Ind.: Zalo Publications, 1978.

First published, 1963, 96 pp.

A graded and annotated bibliography of flute literature currently available. Reviewed by Martin Silver in *Notes* 35 (1979): 636–37.

5.424 Pierreuse, Bernard. *Flûte littérature: Catalogue général des oeuvres édités et inédités par formations instrumentales / General Catalog of Published and Unpublished Works by Instrumental Category.* 670 pp. Paris: Société des Éditions Jobert / Éditions Musicales Transatlantiques, 1982.

An international catalog with a composer index, a list of publishers, and a list of major libraries.

5.425 Vester, Frans. *Flute Music of the 18th Century: An Annotated Bibliography.* 573 pp. Monteux, France: Musica Rara, 1985.

A classified list whose 10,000+ entries include information on the location of works, when known, as well as title, instrumentation, and publisher (both original and modern). As with Vester's *Flute Repertoire Catalogue* (**5.426**), there are indexes of the contents by composer. This work omits music including voice, studies, method and instruction books, literature about the flute, and a list of publishers, although it does include a list of libraries holding printed sources.

Reviewed by Ann P. Basart in *CNV* 122 (1988): 21–22.

5.426 Vester, Frans. *Flute Repertoire Catalogue: 10,000 Titles.* 383 pp. London: Musica Rara, 1967.

A list of music for flute alphabetically by composer, with indexes directing the user to music for flute in combination with other instruments and with orchestra and voice. Includes a short bibliography of literature on the flute and a list of publishers of flute music.

5.427 Wilkins, Wayne. *The Index of Flute Music including the Index of Baroque Trio Sonatas.* 131 pp. Magnolia, Ark.: Music Register, 1974.

Supplements published in 1975 (25 pp.) and 1978 (14 pp.).

Classified lists of works, citing composer and publisher.

Oboe and English Horn

5.428 Gifford, Virginia Snodgrass. *Music for Oboe, Oboe d'Amore, and English Horn: A Bibliography of Materials at the Library of Congress.* xli + 431 pp. Westport, Conn.: Greenwood Press, 1983. (Music reference collection, 1)

A bibliography of cataloged and uncataloged holdings at the Library of Congress, essentially a locating device for the Library's holdings in specified classes. It includes a detailed table of contents and indexes of publishers, instruments, and composers.

Reviewed by William J. Dane in *ARBA* 15 (1984): no. 912.

5.429* Haynes, Bruce. *Catalogue of Chamber Music for the Oboe, 1654–c. 1825.* 4th ed., rev. and corrected. 86 pp. The Hague: B. Haynes, 1980.

5.430 Haynes, Bruce. *Music for Oboe, 1650 to 1800: A Bibliography.* 2nd ed., revised and expanded. 432 pp. Berkeley, Calif.: Fallen Leaf Press, 1992. (Fallen Leaf reference books in music, 16)

First issued in 1982 as *Music for Oboe to 1800;* issued in 1985 as *Music for Oboe, 1650–1800: A Bibliography* (394 pp.).

A list of over 10,000 works for the oboe, English horn, oboe da caccia, and the like. Each entry includes the title, opus or register number, date, exact instrumentation, location of the original work, existing modern editions, and historical notes of interest.

Reviewed by Giuseppe Cattaneo in *Fontes* 39 (1992): 382 and by Janet K. Page in *Notes* 50 (1993): 186. The first ed. is reviewed by Robert Skinner in *ARBA* 18 (1987): no. 1241.

5.431 Hošek, Miroslav. *Oboen-Bibliographie.* 2nd ed., edited by Rudolf H. Führer. 403 pp. Wilhelmshaven, Germany: Heinrichshofen, 1984.

Essentially a reprint of the 1975 ed.

A bibliography of modern, published oboe music, international in scope, arranged alphabetically by composer. There is a separate bibliography of oboe methods. Includes an index by instrumentation, a list of publishers, and a short bibliography of works about the oboe.

The 1976 ed. is reviewed by Peter Bloom in *Notes* 33 (1976): 76–77.

5.432* McMullen, William Wallace. *Soloistic English Horn Literature from 1736–1984.* 257 pp. Stuyvesant, N.Y.: Pendragon Press, 1994. (Juilliard performance guides, 4)
Reviewed by Ian Fairclough in *ARBA* 26 (1995): no. 1275.

5.433 Wilkins, Wayne. *The Index of Oboe Music including the Index of Baroque Trio Sonatas.* 96 + 11 pp. Magnolia, Ark.: Music Register, 1976.
Supplements published in 1977 (9 pp.) and 1978.
Classified lists of works for solo oboe and oboe in ensemble, citing composer and publisher.

Saxophone

5.434* Gee, Harry R. *Saxophone Soloists and Their Music, 1844–1985: An Annotated Bibliography.* 300 pp. Bloomington, Ind.: Indiana University Press, 1986.
Reviewed by Marilyn Strong Noronha in *ARBA* 18 (1987): no. 1246.

5.435 Londeix, Jean-Marie, and **Bruce Ronkin.** *150 Years of Music for Saxophone: Bibliographical Index of Music and Educational Literature for the Saxophone, 1844–1994 / 150 ans de musique pour saxophone : Répertoire général des oeuvres et des ouvrages d'enseignement pour le saxophone, 1844–1994.* 438 pp. Cherry Hill, N.J.: Roncorp, 1994.

The 1st ed. was published as *125 ans de musique pour saxophone,* Alphonse Leduc, Paris, 1971.

A bilingual general list, arranged by composer, of works involving saxophone, followed by indexes under individual instruments (soprano, alto, tenor, baritone) and by ensembles. Composers are identified, and full biographical information, with critical quotations, is given for major composers. Supplementary lists of addresses for composers and publishers of saxophone music are given.

5.436* Wilkins, Wayne. *The Index of Saxophone Music.* 59 pp. Magnolia, Ark.: Music Register, 1979.
Classified lists of works for saxophone and for saxophone in ensembles, citing composer and publisher.

INDEXES TO GENERAL ANTHOLOGIES OF MUSIC

5.437 Hilton, Ruth. *An Index to Early Music in Selected Anthologies.* 127 pp. Clifton, N.J.: European American Music Corp., 1978. (Music indexes and bibliographies, 13)

An index to 1,633 pieces of music dating from antiquity to the end of the baroque in 19 anthologies. Part I cites entries for composers and titles; each entry provides information about the type of work, the country of origin, the date of composition or first publication, performing medium, text, source, "school," and thematic catalog number. Chants and anonymous works are entered by title, except for dances, which are entered by form (such as estampie). Part II is a subject (form and genre) index. Includes a list of the thematic catalogs used in the index and another of the anthologies treated.

Reviewed by Susan T. Sommer in *Notes* 35 (1979): 641–42.

5.438* Murray, Sterling E. *Anthologies of Music: An Annotated Index.* 2nd ed. xxiii + 215 pp. Warren, Mich.: Harmonie Park Press, 1992. (Detroit studies in music bibliography, 68)

The 1st ed. was published by Information Coordinators, Detroit, Mich., in 1987 (xxiii + 178 pp.) (Detroit studies in music bibliography, 55).

An index to 40 anthologies of music published between 1942 and 1991, totaling 66 volumes containing 4,670 musical works by 600 composers. The works can be accessed by composer or by genre, but not by title.

Reviewed by Clifford Bartlett in *Brio* 30 (1993): 110–11, by Joy Haslam Calico in *Fontes* 42 (1995): 384–87, by John E. Druesedow, Jr., in *ARBA* 25 (1994): no. 1319, and by Holly E. Mockovak in *Notes* 51 (1994): 573–74. The 1st ed. is reviewed by Ann P. Basart in *CNV* 131 (1988): 15–16 and by Carol June Bradley in *ARBA* 19 (1988): no. 1292.

5.439* Perone, James E. *Musical Anthologies for Analytical Study: A Bibliography.* 182 pp. Westport, Conn.: Greenwood Press, 1995. (Music reference collection, 48)

Detailed information about and access to 14 standard anthologies, with an index of composers, works, and the type of score used.

JAZZ AND POPULAR MUSIC

The study of jazz and popular music (including film music) has permeated the academic curricula. Nevertheless, a sizable percentage of books in the field continue to be the work of dedicated amateurs. In the 20th century, popular music has come to mean mass-disseminated music and is really distinct from folk music and other music of the people. Jazz is even more established as a fully accepted scholarly specialty and bibliographical resources have expanded concomitantly. Some of the principal items in this area are listed below. Others are spread throughout this volume, accessible through the index.

5.440 Anderson, Gillian B. *Music for Silent Films, 1894–1929: A Guide.* 182 pp. Washington, D.C.: Library of Congress, 1988.

A guide organized alphabetically by film title. The approximately 1,060 entries include information on the author or literary source, producer, director, film company, composer, publisher and imprint of music, instrumentation, pagination, size, copyright data, projection time and film footage, LC or Museum of Modern Art (MOMA) call number, collation, and microfilm and item numbers.

The purpose of this work is to provide a guide for locating scores and musical cue sheets made for films of the silent era, 1894–1929. An essay about the nature, history, and presentation of the musical accompaniments for silent films provides the context for these artifacts. All the entries are for microfilmed items in the LC and the MOMA music collections. MOMA's collection is on permanent loan to the LC Music Division.

Appendixes list materials found at the Kleiner Collection at the University of Minnesota, the Eastman House in Rochester, N.Y., and the Fédération International des Archives du Film in Brussels, Belgium. The index is to names and titles found on the LC and MOMA scores and cue sheets. There is an extensive bibliography.

Reviewed by Ann P. Basart in *CNV* 133 (1989): 14–15, by Alfred W. Cochran in *Notes* 46 (1990): 636–37, by Donald Hunsberger in *AM* 11 (1993): 254–55, and by H. Stephen Wright in *Fontes* 37 (1990): 204–5.

5.441* Benjamin, Ruth, and **Arthur Rosenblatt.** *Movie Song Catalog: Performers and Supporting Crew for the Songs Sung in 1460 Musical and Non-Musical Films, 1920–1988.* 352 pp. Jefferson, N.C.: McFarland & Co., 1993.

Reviewed by Louis G. Zelenka in *ARBA* 25 (1994): no. 1309.

5.442 Brooks, Elston. *I've Heard Those Songs Before: The Weekly Top Ten Tunes for the Past Fifty Years.* 444 pp. New York: Morrow Quill Paperbacks, 1981.

Titles of the most played popular songs on American radio from 1930 to 1980 in chronological order, with notes on the events of the year and an index to titles cited.

Reviewed by Kenyon C. Rosenberg in *ARBA* 14 (1983): no. 954.

5.443 Burton, Jack. *The Index of American Popular Music: Thousands of Titles Cross-Referenced to Our Basic Anthologies of Popular Songs.* Unpaged. Watkins Glen, N.Y.: Century House, 1957.

The index to *The Blue Book of Tin Pan Alley* (**5.444**), *The Blue Book of Broadway Musicals* (**1.426**), *The Blue Book of Hollywood Musicals* (**1.425**), and *The Melodies Linger On* by Larry Freeman (Watkins Glen, N.Y.: Century House, 1951), 212 pp., a short history of American popular song.

5.444 Burton, Jack, and **Larry Freeman.** *The Blue Book of Tin Pan Alley: A Human Interest Encyclopedia [of] American Popular Music.* Expanded new ed. 2 vols. Watkins Glen, N.Y.: Century House, 1962–65.

First published in 1951 (520 pp.), edited by Jack Burton. Complementing *The Blue Book of Broadway Musicals,* 1952 (**1.426**), and *The Blue Book of Hollywood Musicals,* 1953 (**1.425**), an anthology completing a trilogy on popular music.

A compilation of song lists. The approach is chronological, with detailed lists of songs by the principal American popular composers of the period, covering jazz and its musicians as well as popular music.

Reviewed by Armine Dikijian in *Notes* 9 (1951): 130–31.

5.445 Chipman, John H. *Index to Top-Hit Tunes (1900–1950).* 249 pp. Boston, Mass.: Bruce Humphries, 1962.

An alphabetical index, by title, of some 3,000 of the most popular American songs of the first half of the 20th century. The entries supply key, composer and author, publisher and original publication date, and the film or musical comedy origin (if applicable). Includes a chronological index and a short bibliography.

5.446 *80 Years of American Song Hits, 1892–1972: A Comprehensive Yearly Reference Book Listing America's Major Hit Songs and Their Writers.* 106 pp. New York: Chappell, 1973.

A chronological list of song hits as generally determined by radio exposure, citing authors and composers or performers. The list has only 2 songs for the first year and more than 60 for the last.

5.447 Ewen, David. *American Popular Songs: From the Revolutionary War to the Present.* 507 pp. New York: Random House, 1966.

Information on more than 3,600 songs popular in America from 1775 to 1966. The entries, arranged alphabetically by title, cite composer, lyricist, place, medium, and date, and include the performer who made the song popular.

Reviewed by Ruth Hilton in *Notes* 24 (1968): 501.

5.448* Green, Jeff. *The Green Book of Songs by Subject: The Thematic Guide to Popular Music.* 4th ed., updated and expanded. 730 pp. Nashville, Tenn.: Professional Desk References, 1995.

Third ed., *The Green Book: Songs Classified by Subject,* was published in Smyrna, Tenn., by Professional Desk References in 1989. The 2nd ed., *1987 Green Book,* was published in Altadena, Calif., by Professional Desk References in 1986, 400 pp. First ed., *The Green Book: Catalog of Songs Categorized by Subject,* was published as a loose-leaf ed. in Los Angeles, Calif., 1982.

A list of over 21,000 popular songs from 1900 to the present, arranged by subject and including popular standards, top hits, album rock, country hits, Black hits, jazz vocals, big band classics, motion picture soundtracks, and Broadway musicals. Compiled from recorded titles, with each entry including label, format, and performer information. See also Stecheson (**5.464**).

5.449 Hasse, John Edward. *Ragtime: Its History, Composers and Music.* 400 pp. New York: Schirmer Books, 1985.

A ragtime handbook, with a brief history and essays on its principal figures and the use of ragtime elements in other genres. There are lists of compositions, ragtime folios and method books, and ragtime music by women. Includes a thorough bibliography (pp. 318–47) and discography (pp. 348–67).

5.450* Heskes, Irene. *Yiddish American Popular Songs, 1895 to 1950: A Catalog Based on the Lawrence Warwick Roster of Copyright Entries.* xlv + 527 pp. Washington, D.C.: Library of Congress, 1992.

A list and description of 3,427 Yiddish songs, with each entry giving the Yiddish and English titles, composer, lyricist, arranger, publisher, and a description of the song.

Reviewed by S. Robert Waxman in *SSB* 21 (1995): 27 no. 1.

5.451* Hischak, Thomas. S. *The American Musical Theatre Song Encyclopedia.* 568 pp. Westport, Conn.: Greenwood Press, 1995.

A list, with commentary, of over 1,800 songs from more than 500 Broadway musicals. Includes a list of alternative song titles (pp. 413–15), a list of the musicals contributing songs to the list (pp. 417–89), a bibliography (pp. 491–99), and a detailed index (pp. 501–43).

5.452* Krasker, Tommy, and **Robert Kimball.** *Catalog of the American Musical: Musicals of Irving Berlin, George & Ira Gershwin, Cole Porter, Richard Rodgers & Lorenz Hart.* 442 pp. Washington, D.C.: National Institute for Opera and Musical Theater, 1988.

A book documenting the primary sources for 75 classic works of the American musical theater: holograph sketches, original manuscripts, and first editions.

Reviewed by Larry Stumpel in *AM* 8 (1990): 363–65.

5.453* Larson, Randall D. *Musique Fantastique: A Survey of Film Music in the Fantastic Cinema.* 592 pp. Metuchen, N.J.: Scarecrow Press, 1985.

A history of the music in the very special area of films, with discography (pp. 360–437) and filmography (pp. 438–567).

5.454 Lax, Roger, and **Frederick Smith.** *The Great Song Thesaurus.* 2nd ed., updated and expanded. 774 pp. New York: Oxford University Press, 1989.

First ed., 1984, 665 pp.

A sectional reference work whose main section covers about 11,000 best-known American and British popular songs, from the 13th century's "Sumer is icumen in" to 1986's popular works. The selection makes clear the authors' moderate tastes. Other lists include award-winning songs; "trademark" theme and signature songs; song titles; British titles; "elegant plagiarisms," songs based on other sources; a thesaurus of titles by subject, keyword, and category; and lyric key lines, an index to first lines of choruses, refrains, or verses. To locate copies of the songs, a song index such as that by Havlice (**5.386**) must be consulted.

The 1st ed. is reviewed by Norma Jean Lamb in *Notes* 41 (1985): 709–11 (giving errata not corrected in the 2nd ed.) and by Dean Tudor in *ARBA* 16 (1985): no. 1173. The 2nd ed. is reviewed by David Dodd in *Notes* 47 (1990): 389–90 and by Ann P. Basart in *CNV* 134 (1989): 7–9.

5.455 Lewine, Richard, and **Alfred Simon.** *Songs of the Theater.* 897 pp. New York: H.W. Wilson Co., 1984.

Earlier editions appeared as *Encyclopedia of Theatre Music: A Comprehensive Listing of More than 4000 Songs from Broadway and Hollywood, 1900–1960* (New York: Random House, 1961), 248 pp., and *Songs of the American Theater: A Comprehensive Listing of More than 12,000 Songs, including Selected Titles from Film and Television Productions* (New York: Dodd, Mead, 1973), 820 pp.

A title list of songs from virtually all the musical productions appearing on and off Broadway, 1891 to 1983. Each entry includes names of composers and lyricists, authors, and name and dates of the show. There are indexes to names, titles of shows, and film and television productions, and a chronological list of shows citing all songs with references to sources and adaptations.

Reviewed by Ed Glazer in *Notes* 43 (1986): 301–3 and by George R. Hill in *ARBA* 17 (1986): no. 1249.

5.456 Limbacher, James L. *Film Music: From Violins to Video.* 835 pp. Metuchen, N.J.: Scarecrow Press, 1974.

An anthology of essays on the subject, with a bibliography (Part 1) and a second part, divided into four sections, listing various approaches to film music: film titles and dates, films and their composers, composers and their films, and a discography of recorded movie music. There is a name and title index to Part 1.

Reviewed by Clifford McCarty in *Notes* 31 (1974): 48–50.

5.457 Limbacher, James L., and **H. Stephen Wright.** *Keeping Score: Film Music 1972–1979.* 510 pp. Metuchen, N.J.: Scarecrow Press, 1981.

Continued by *Keeping Score: Film and Television Music, 1980–1988: With Additional Coverage of 1921–1979* (Metuchen, N.J.: Scarecrow Press, 1991), 916 pp.

A continuation of *Film Music: From Violins to Video* (**5.456**), superseding some of its individual entries with corrected information. This is a book of lists: winners of Academy Awards for the best original film scores 1935–79, a necrology of film music composers, a bibliography of recent books on film music, film music titles and dates, films and their composers/adapters, composers and their films, and recorded musical scores.

Reviewed by Gillian B. Anderson in *AM* 3 (1985): 354–55.

5.458 Lynch, Richard Chigley. *Musicals: A Complete Selection Guide for Local Productions.* 2nd ed. 404 pp. Chicago, Ill.: American Library Association, 1994.

First ed., *Musicals: A Directory of Musical Properties Available for Production.* 1984, 197 pp.

5.459 McCarty, Clifford. *Film Composers in America: A Check List of Their Work.* 193 pp. Glendale, Calif.: John Valentine, 1953.

Reprinted by Da Capo Press, New York, 1972.

A listing of 163 composers working in America (though not all American), with film scores for each arranged chronologically by film release date. There are indexes of film titles and orchestrators.

Reviewed by Frederick W. Sternfeld in *Notes* 11 (1953): 105.

5.460* Miletich, Leo N. *Broadway's Prize-Winning Musicals: An Annotated Guide for Libraries and Audio Collectors.* 255 pp. New York: Haworth Press, 1993. (Haworth library and information science)

A checklist of titles, record labels, and inventory numbers; plot summaries, cast lists, key song titles, reviews, composer information; background and film versions; finding out-of-print recordings; a bibliography; and recorded anthologies.

5.461* Mott, Margaret M. "A Bibliography of Song Sheets: Sports and Recreations in American Popular Songs." In *Notes* 6 (1949): 379–418, 7 (1950): 522–61, and 9 (1951): 33–62.

A topically arranged bibliography, with classifications ranging from the standard sports to drinking songs.

5.462* Paymer, Marvin E. *Facts behind the Songs: A Handbook of American Popular Music from the Nineties to the '90s.* 564 pp. New York: Garland Publishing, 1993. (Garland reference library of the humanities, 1300)

A selective collection of anecdotal information on American popular songs, intended as an overview of the last century.

Reviewed by Kathleen Abromeit in *Choice* 31 (1994): 1,094.

5.463 Shapiro, Nat, and **Bruce Pollock.** *Popular Music, 1920–1979: A Revised Cumulation.* 3 vols. Detroit, Mich.: Gale Research Co., 1985.

Supersedes *Popular Music: An Annotated Index of American Popular Songs* by Shapiro alone, an 8-vol. 1st ed. published 1964–79 by the Adrian Press, New York. Supplemented by Barbara Cohen-Stratyner's *Popular Music, 1900–1919: An Annotated Guide to American Popular Songs, including Introductory Essay, Lyricists and Composers Index, Important Chronological Index, and List of Publishers* (Detroit, Mich.: Gale Research, 1988), xxx + 656 pp., and by Bruce Pollock's *Popular Music, 1980–1989: An Annotated Guide to American Popular Songs, including Introductory Essay, Lyricists and Composers Index, Important Performance Index, Chronological Index, Awards Index, and List of Publishers* (Detroit, Mich.: Gale Research, Inc., 1995), lxvi + 911 pp. Pollock is also editing Vols. 15–18, 1990–93, each containing a list of a single year's songs.

An annotated index of 18,000+ American popular songs, part of a series intended as a selective annotated list of the significant popular songs of the 20th century. In the first ed., songs are listed alphabetically by title under each year of the decade. Each vol. has its own index of titles and list of publishers.

The early editions are reviewed by Ruth Hilton in *Notes* 25 (1968): 247–48 and 27 (1970): 60–61 and by Michael D. Williams in *Notes* 31 (1974): 307–8. The cumulative ed. is reviewed by George R. Hill in *ARBA* 17 (1986): no. 1281.

5.464 Stecheson, Anthony, and **Anne Stecheson.** *The Stecheson Classified Song Directory.* 504 pp. Hollywood, Calif.: Music Industries Press, 1961.

Supplement issued 1978, 69 pp.

About 100,000 songs popular in the United States, arranged under 400 topics or catchwords. Composers, titles, publishers, and, sometimes, dates are cited. There is no title index. See also Green (**5.448**).

5.465 Voigt, John. *Jazz Music in Print and Jazz Books in Print.* 3rd ed. 195 pp. Boston, Mass.: Hornpipe Music Publishing Co., 1982.

The 1st and 2nd editions were released in 1975 and 1978 as *Jazz Music in Print.*

A catalog organized by individual artist, providing the contents of anthologies, with publisher and catalog distribution numbers cited. There is a list of publishers.

The 2nd ed. is reviewed by Lewis Porter in *BPM* 7 (1979): 121–23 and by Dan Morgenstern in *Journal of Jazz Studies* 5 (1979): 97–98.

5.466 Woll, Allen L. *Songs from Hollywood Musical Comedies, 1927 to the Present: A Dictionary.* 251 pp. New York: Garland Publishing, 1976. (Garland reference library of the humanities, 44)

A dictionary covering American musical films as well as foreign films of musicals that appeared on Broadway. There is an alphabetical list of song titles with references to the films for which they were written. Only musicals produced after 1950 with soundtrack recordings are included. Includes a chronological list of shows and an index of composers and lyricists. No single entry presents all the information given on a particular film.

Reviewed by Neil Ratliff in *Fontes* 23 (1976): 202.

REGIONAL AND LOCAL OPERA REPERTOIRES

A useful type of reference work is one that traces the chronology of opera as it has been performed in a particular region, city, or theater. Many of the leading opera companies of the world have been provided with such chronicles, which often include valuable data about first productions, the original cast of singers and dancers, the frequency of performance, etc. Strictly speaking, these works are bibliographies of music, and they can be distinguished from other reference tools devoted to the musical theater, namely, dictionaries of opera and theater music (Chapter 1), special catalogs of related library collections (Chapter 7), and bibliographies of music literature devoted to the same subject. All can be accessed through the index.

5.467* **Achberger, Karen.** *Literatur als Libretto: Das deutsche Opernbuch seit 1945; mit einem Verzeichnis der neuen Opern.* 288 pp. Heidelberg: Carl Winter Universitätsverlag, 1980. (Reihe Siegen, 21)

A study of the contemporary opera libretto, with Anhang B (pp. 242–88) giving a list of operas written with German libretti that opened from 1945 to 1976, arranged chronologically and giving both text source and premiere information.

5.468 **Allacci, Leone.** *Drammaturgia di Lione Allacci, accresciuta e continuata fino all'anno MDCCLV.* Revised and continued by Giovanni Cendoni, Apostolo Zeno, Giovanni degli Apostoli, and others. 1,016 cols. Venice: Presso G. Pasquali, 1755.

First ed., Rome, 1666. The 1755 ed. was reprinted by Bottega d'Erasmo, Turin, in 1966, with an introduction by Francesco Bernadelli.

A list, alphabetical by title, of dramatic works produced in the Italian theater from the late 15th century to 1755. The contents include more than musical titles, and there are many operas and oratorios. The degree of accuracy is high.

5.469 **Bauer, Anton.** *Opern und Operetten in Wien: Verzeichnis ihrer Erstaufführungen in der Zeit von 1629 bis zur Gegenwart.* 156 pp. Graz-Cologne: Hermann Böhlaus Nachf., 1955. (Wiener musikwissenschaftliche Beiträge, 2)

Arranged by title, a list of 4,856 stage works, with indexes by composer, author, and chronology.

5.470 **Bignami, Luigi.** *Cronologia di tutti gli spettacoli rappresentati al Teatro Comunale di Bologna della sua apertura 14 maggio 1763 a tutto l'autunno 1881.* 248 pp. Bologna: Mattiuzzi, 1882.

A list of transcriptions of theater bills for the designated period. All types of dramatic works are included, but by far the largest part of the repertoire is opera. There are indexes of performers, composers, authors, and other categories of theater personnel.

5.471 **Bolongaro-Crevenna, Hubertus.** *L'Arpa festante: Die Münchner Oper, 1651–1825, von den Anfängen bis zum Freyschützen.* 272 pp. Munich: Callwey, 1963.

A cultural history of the Munich Opera from its beginning to 1825. There is a chronological list of the repertoire (pp. 209–72), with factual information drawn from the Munich theater archives.

5.472* **Borroff, Edith.** *American Operas: A Checklist.* Edited by J. Bunker Clark. xxiv + 334 pp. Warren, Mich.: Harmonie Park Press, 1992. (Detroit studies in music bibliography, 69)

A list of over 4,000 operas by more than 2,000 composers.

Reviewed by Paula Morgan in *Notes* 50 (1994): 1,453–54 and by Michael Pisani in *SSB* 20 (1994): 29–30 no. 3.

5.473 **Brenner, Clarence D.** *A Bibliographical List of Plays in the French Language 1700–1789.* With a new foreword and an index by Michael Keller and Neal Zaslaw. 229 pp. + an index of 43 unnumbered pp. New York: AMS Press, 1979.

Reprint of the 1st ed., published by the University of California, Berkeley, 1947.

A bibliography of "plays," which Brenner construed as all stage works, including operas, ballets, and divertissements as well as *opéras-comiques*. The *List* of 1947 includes all information on the sources' title pages, libretti in Parisian libraries, archives, and published collections. The reprint provides a composer index.

5.474* **Columbro, Marta.** *La raccolta di libretti d'opera del Teatro San Carlo di Napoli.* 107 pp. Lucca, Italy: Libreria Musicale Italiana, 1992. (Ancilla musicae, 3)

Published under the sponsorship of Società italiana di musicologia.

5.475* *Dreissig Jahre Deutsche Oper Berlin, 1961–1991.* 519 pp. Berlin: Deutsche Oper Berlin, 1992. (Beiträge zum Musiktheater, 10)

5.476 Falk, Marguerite. *Les parodies du Nouveau Théâtre Italien (1731); Répertoire systématique des timbres.* 213 pp. Bilthoven, The Netherlands: A.B. Creyghton, 1974.

An index to vocal music in the 25 vaudevilles in the source volumes and a concordance to nine other 18th-century collections. The arrangement is by first line of text with an alphabetical representation of the melody, followed by a thematic index to the music arranged as in Barlow–Morgenstern (**1.648** and **1.649**). There are also appendixes of extracts of the "Parodies," showing the placement of the airs and of the musical incipits in order of appearance.

5.477 Filippis, Felice de, and **Raffaele Arnese.** *Cronache del Teatro di S. Carlo.* 2 vols. Naples: Edizioni Politica Popolare, 1961–63.

A generously illustrated work documenting the history of the San Carlo Opera, Naples, with a chronological list, by year from 1737 to 1960, of first performances of operas given, a biographical dictionary of opera composers, lists of their major works, and indexes of librettists and singers. There is a summary of the seasons in which each work was performed.

5.478* Fitzgerald, Gerald. *Annals of the Metropolitan Opera: The Complete Chronicle of Performances and Artists.* 2 vols. New York: Metropolitan Opera Guild; Boston: G.K. Hall, 1989.

The successor to William Seltsam's *Metropolitan Opera Annals* and its three supplements (1947–78), giving a chronological arrangement of the casts of each Metropolitan Opera performance.

Reviewed by David Breckbill in *Notes* 47 (1991): 1,159–60.

5.479 Florimo, Francesca. *La Scuola Musicale di Napoli e i suoi conservatorii, con uno sguardo sulla storia della musica in Italia.* 4 vols. Bologna: Forni editore, 1969. (Bibliotheca musica Bononiensis, III/9)

Contents: Vol. I, *Come venne la musica in Italia;* Vols. II–III, *Cenno storico sulla scuola musicale di Napoli e suoi conservatorii, con le biografie dei maetri useiti dai medesimi;* Vol. IV, *Elenco di tutte le opere in musica rappresentate nei teatri di Napoli.*

Reprint of the ed. published by Stabilimento Tipografico di Vinc. Moreno, Naples, 1881–83. An earlier version was published as *Cenna storico sulla scuola musicale di Napoli,* 2 vols., 1869–71.

A history of Neapolitan music. Vol. IV organizes information under the name of the individual theater, citing title of opera, poet, composer, performers, and general observations.

5.480 Fog, Dan. *The Royal Danish Ballet, 1769–1958, and August Bournonville: A Chronological Catalogue of the Ballets and Ballet-Divertissements Performed at the Royal Theatres of Copenhagen, and a Catalogue of August Bournonville's works.* 79 pp. Copenhagen: Dan Fog, 1961.

A list of the 516 ballet works performed by the Royal Danish Ballet, citing the choreographer, composer, and publisher of the music, if available. There are indexes of titles and of persons, as well as facsimile plates of music title pages.

5.481 Gatti, Carlo. *Il Teatro alla Scala, nella storia e nell'arte (1778–1963).* 2 vols. Milan: Ricordi, 1963.

A handsome set, the 2nd vol. of which contains the chronicles of La Scala—complete inventories of the opera, ballet, and concert performances from 1778 to 1960, with an analytical index. The chronologies were compiled by Giampietro Tintori.

5.482* Girardi, Michele, and **Franco Rossi.** *Il Teatro la Fenice: Cronologia degli spettacoli, 1792–1936.* xxxi + 491 pp. Venice: Albrizzi editore, 1989.

Girardi, Michele, and Franco Rossi. *Il Teatro la Fenice: Cronologia degli spettacoli, 1938–1991.* xxiii + 650 pp. Venice: Albrizzi editore, 1992.

A detailed account of concerts, ballets, and operas taking place at Venice's most prominent theater.

The 1st vol. is reviewed by Julian Budden in *M&L* 72 (1991): 448–50.

5.483* **Grandini, Alfredo.** *Cronache musicali del Teatro Petrarca di Arezzo: Il primo cinquanten-nio (1833–1882).* 377 pp. Florence: L.S. Olschki, 1995. ("Historiae musicae cultores" biblioteca, 76)

The musical history of Arezzo's Teatro Petrarca from 1833 to 1882.

5.484 **Groppo, Antonio.** "Catalogo di tutti i drammi per musica recitati ne'Teatri di Venezia dall'anno 1637, in cui ebbere principio le pubbliche rapresentazioni de'medesimi fin all'anno presente 1745." In *Bollettino Bibliografico Musicale,* Nuovo serie, Milan, 1952.

Published serially, in four installments.

A list of 811 operas performed in Venice between 1637 and 1745, in chronological order, with title, librettist, composer, theater, and date of performance. There is an index of titles.

5.485* **Hill, Laura Callegari, Gabriella Sartini,** and **Gabriele Bersani Berselli.** *La librettistica bolognese nei secoli XVII e XVIII: Catalogo ed indici.* xliii + 350 pp. Rome: Torre d'Orfeo, 1989. (Società e cultura del settecento in Emilia Romagna. Studi e ricerche) (Biblioteca musicologica, 1)

A computer-accessible, chronological list of 1,327 librettos of operas, oratorios, dramatic cantatas, and serenatas, with indexes by title, genre, place of performance, composer, librettist, singer, choreographer, dancer, and dedicatee.

Reviewed by Eleanor Selfridge-Field in *Notes* 48 (1991): 112–13.

5.486 **Lajarte, Théodore de.** *Bibliothèque musicale du Théâtre de l'Opéra: Catalogue historique, chronologique, anecdotique.* Published under the auspices of the Ministère de l'Instruction Publique et des Beaux-arts. 2 vols. Paris: Libraire des Bibliophiles, 1878.

Reprinted by Olms, Hildesheim, Germany, 1969.

A descriptive list of 594 stage works, arranged in order of their first production at the Opéra, 1671–1876, classified by Périodes: Époque de Lully (1671–97), Époque de Campra (1697–1733), Époque de Rameau (1733–74); Époque de Gluck (1774–1807), Époque de Spontini (1807–26), and Époque de Rossini and Meyerbeer (1826–76). There are Notices biographiques at the end of each Période. There is a composer and title index to works in the repertoire, with many helpful appendixes.

Reviewed by Thomas Walker in *Notes* 36 (1979): 90–92.

5.487 **La Vallière, Louis César de la Baume La Blanc, duc de.** *Ballets, opéra, et autres ouvrages lyriques, par ordre chronologique depuis leur origine; avec une table alphabétique des ouvrages et des auteurs.* 298 pp. Paris: Cl. J. Baptiste Bauche, 1760.

An unaltered reprint was published by H. Baron, 1967.

A chronological list, preceded by catalogs of poets and composers.

5.488 **Mattfeld, Julius.** *A Handbook of American Operatic Premieres, 1731–1962.* 142 pp. Detroit, Mich.: Information Service, 1963. (Detroit studies in music bibliography, 5)

A list of nearly 2,000 premieres of operas and related works from 1731 through 1962. Included are operas by both native and naturalized composers that have been performed outside the country. The works are listed alphabetically by title, with a composer index.

5.489 **Mooser, Robert-Aloys.** *Opéras, intermezzos, ballets, cantates, oratorios joués en Russie durant le XVIIIe siècle, avec l'indication des oeuvres de compositeurs russe parues en occident, à la même: Essai d'un répertoire alphabétique et chronologique.* 177 pp. 3rd ed., revised and completed. Basel: Bärenreiter, 1964.

First published in 1945 by Imprimerie A. Kundig, Geneva (173 pp.); 2nd ed., R. Kister, Geneva, 1955 (169 pp.).

A bibliography in each entry cites the librettist, translators, date and place of first performance, language of performance, date of libretto publication, and other information. The sources of information are well documented. Indexes.

The 2nd ed. is reviewed by Anna A. Abert in *Die Musikforschung* 9 (1956): 106.

5.490* Neef, Sigrid. *Handbuch der russischer und sowjetischen Oper.* 760 pp. Kassel, Germany: Bärenreiter, 1989.

First published in Berlin by Henschelverlag Kunst und Gesellschaft, 1985.

An account of 64 composers and 152 operas, covering all of Russian opera and representing all 15 republics of the former USSR. Each opera entry has the title translated to German, the original title in a German-based transliteration, title-page information including subtitles, the number of acts and scenes, and information on the libretto, the year of composition, the premiere date and place, principal roles, instrumentation, performance timings, versions, plot synopsis, the reception of the work, the location of the autograph, the publication data, and bibliography.

Reviewed by Malcolm Hamrick Brown in *Notes* 47 (1990): 68–69.

5.491 Pitou, Spire. *The Paris Opéra: An Encyclopedia of Operas, Ballets, Composers, and Performers.* 3 vols. in 4. Westport, Conn.: Greenwood Press, 1983–90.

Contents: Vol. 1, *Genesis and Glory, 1671–1715;* Vol. 2, *Ròcoco and Romantic, 1715–1815;* Vol. 3, *Growth and Grandeur, 1815–1914* (2 vols.).

A reference work with many details of the Paris Opéra's history. The 1st vol. includes a list of leading singers and dancers from 1671 to 1982. The entries for the staged productions have a plot synopsis. There are repertoire lists and a general index.

Vol. 1 is reviewed by Carl B. Schmidt in *JAMS* 38 (1985): 385–93, by George Louis Mayer in *ARBA* 16 (1985): no. 1202, and by Laurie Shulman in *Notes* 41 (1985): 730–31. Vol. 3 is reviewed by Carl B. Schmidt in *Notes* 48 (1992): 1,273–74.

5.492* Porter, Susan L. *With an Air Debonair: Musical Theatre in America, 1785–1815.* 631 pp. Washington, D.C.; London: Smithsonian Institution Press, 1991.

Early American musical theater history documented in two useful appendixes: "A Preliminary Checklist of Musical Entertainments Performed in the United States, 1785–1815" (pp. 425–500) and "Musical Theatre Performances in Five American Cities (New York, Philadelphia, Boston, Baltimore and Charleston), 1801–15" (pp. 501–42).

Reviewed by Wayne Schneider in *AM* 11 (1993): 112–14 and by Victor Fell Yellin in *Notes* 49 (1993): 1,061–64.

5.493* Price, Curtis A. *Music in the Restoration Theatre: With a Catalogue of Instrumental Music in the Plays, 1665–1713.* 291 pp. Ann Arbor, Mich.: UMI Research Press, 1979. (Studies in musicology, 4)

A book planned as a companion reference tool to the Day–Murrie *English Song-Books* (**5.375**). About 450 plays are covered. This is an admirably thorough source that relies on established reference works.

Reviewed by Stoddard Lincoln in *Notes* 37 (1981): 585–86 and by Joseph J. Chouinard in *ARBA* 12 (1981): no. 1053.

5.494 Radiciotti, Giuseppe. *Teatro e musica in Roma nel secondo quarto del secolo XIX (1825–50).* 166 pp. Rome: Tip. della R. Accademia dei Lincei, 1905.

A chronicle of the musical-dramatic productions given in the three major theaters in Rome during the early 19th century: Teatro Valle, Teatro Argentina, and Teatro Apollo.

5.495 Salvioli, Giovanni. *I teatri musicali di Venezia nel secolo XVII (1637–1700): Memorie storiche e bibliografiche di Livio Niso Galvani* [pseud.]. 193 pp. Milan: Ricordi, 1878.

Reprinted by A. Forni, Bologna, 1969 (Biblioteca musica Bononiensis, III/32).

A chronological list of operas performed in Venice during the 17th century, arranged under 16 different theaters or opera houses. The entries are listed by title, with composer, librettist, publication date of libretto, dedicatee, and other useful information. There are indexes of names, titles, librettists, and composers.

5.496 Shteinpress, Boris S. *Opernye premery XX veka: slovar´.* 469 pp. Moscow: Sovetskii Kompozitor, 1983.

A list of first performances of 20th-century operas in the former USSR, with indexes.

5.497 Trezzini, Lamberto. *Due secoli di vita musicale: Storia del Teatro Comunale di Bologna.* 2 vols. Bologna: Edizioni ALFA, 1966.

A musical history of Bologna. The 1st vol. is a collection of essays. The 2nd consists of a *Repertorio critico degli spettacoli e delle esecuzioni musicali dal 1763 al 1966,* by Sergio Paganelli, a chronological list of opera, oratorio, and symphony productions, giving the names of cast members, soloists, and conductors.

5.498* Weaver, Robert Lamar, and **Norma Wright Weaver.** *A Chronology of Music in the Florentine Theater, 1590–1750: Operas, Prologues, Finales, Intermezzos, and Plays with Incidental Music.* 421 pp. Detroit, Mich.: Information Coordinators, 1978. (Detroit studies in music bibliography, 38)

A list chronologically arranged by performance or the occasion for the performances of operas and other theatrical forms of fundamental interest. There are indexes to librettists, composers, singers and actors, other persons engaged in producing these events, theaters, sponsoring organizations and performing groups, and titles. Includes a general index and a bibliography. Most of the sources of information are libretti, but some information is drawn from diaries and archival sources. This is a remarkable sourcebook on the birth of opera.

Reviewed by Thomas Walker in *Notes* 36 (1979): 90–92.

5.499* Weaver, Robert Lamar, and **Norma Wright Weaver.** *A Chronology of Music in the Florentine Theater, 1751–1800: Operas, Prologues, Farces, Intermezzos, Concerts, and Plays with Incidental Music.* xxxvii + 996 pp. Warren, Mich.: Harmonie Park Press, 1993. (Detroit studies in music bibliography, 70)

Reviewed by Evan Baker in *Fontes* 41 (1994): 225–27.

5.500 Wiel, Taddeo. *I teatri musicali veneziani del settecento: Catalogo delle opere in musica rappresentate nel secolo XVIII in Venezia (1701–1800).* lxxx + 635 pp. New ed., with an introduction and an updated bibliography by Reinhard Stohm. Leipzig: Peters, 1979.

First published in Venice, 1897, by Fratelli Visentini, lxxx + 600 pp. Reprinted by A. Forni, Bologna, in 1978 (Biblioteca musica Bononiensis, 3/51).

A chronological list of 1,274 operas performed in Venice in the 18th century. The entries give librettist, composer, place of performance, cast (if known), and ballet (if included). There are indexes of titles, librettists, composers, singers, and dancers.

5.501 Wolff, Stephane. *Un demi-siècle d'Opéra comique (1900–50).* 2 vols. Paris: Éditions André Bonne, 1953.

A history of the Opéra-comique, Paris. Includes a list of the works arranged alphabetically by title, with much detailed information on the cast and the production (pp. 15–231), and a series of bibliographical sections treating the singers, dancers, conductors, and other personnel involved in Opéra-comique production (pp. 233–339).

5.502 Wolff, Stephane. *L'Opéra au Palais Garnier, 1875–1962: Les oeuvres, les interprètes.* 565 pp. Paris: "L'Entr'acte," 1963.

Reprinted by Slatkine, Paris, 1983 (Collection ressources, 145).

A book of facts related to the Paris Opéra and its productions from 1875 to 1962.

EARLY MUSIC IN MODERN EDITIONS (INCLUDING COLLECTIONS AND MONUMENTS)

The purpose of the bibliographies in this section is to direct the user to new editions of old music—one of the most pressing needs of performers, teachers, and music historians. Some of the titles listed focus on the contents of the major critical editions (*Denkmäler, Gesamtausgaben*);

others emphasize practical, performing editions of early music. In either case, listings of this kind are soon out of date. To keep abreast of new publications in this area, one should consult the music review sections of a variety of current publications: *Notes, Music and Letters, Early Music, Die Musikforschung,* and the *Journal of the American Musicological Society,* as well as such regular listings as may be found in *Fontes Artis Musicae.* Though dated, by far the most useful guide to the contents of the historical sets and critical editions is Heyer (**5.511**). The publication by Fallen Leaf Press of George Hill's *Collected Editions, Historical Sets, and Monuments of Music: A Bibliography,* due to be released in the near future, will update coverage of such sources and provide increased access.

5.503 Abravanel, Claude. "A Checklist of Music Manuscripts in Facsimile Edition." In *Notes* 34 (1978): 557–70.

A selected bibliography of facsimiles of entire works, substantially supplemented by James B. Coover in "Music Manuscripts in Facsimile Edition: Supplement," in *Notes* 37 (1981): 533–56 and "Composite Music Manuscripts in Facsimile," in *Notes* 38 (1981): 275–95. Coover's earlier article has a helpful section on facsimile series included in his bibliography, whereas his later article lists only complete manuscripts, mostly medieval and renaissance, reproduced in facsimile, arranged by location of manuscript, with cross-references from the names of the manuscripts and an index to personal names, as well as to items in series. The *RISM* items in the list are identified and sigla noted.

These articles have been expanded and kept current by the catalogs and updates issued by OMI (Original Manuscripts and Incunabula), a specialized music company owned by Steven and Olga Immel that concentrates on sales of such facsimiles; their catalogs, though meticulously edited and excellent for noting published facsimile editions, lack the full information necessary for a complete bibliographic citation.

5.504 Charles, Sydney Robinson. "Editions, Historical." In *The New Grove Dictionary of Music and Musicians* (**1.48**), vol. 5, pp. 848–69. Julie Woodward assisted with the bibliography.

Extensive bibliographies of single-composer complete editions, other collected editions, editions of theoretical works, anthologies (extended, small vocal, small instrumental, and small general), and a short bibliography on the subject.

5.505 Charles, Sydney Robinson. *A Handbook of Music and Music Literature in Sets and Series.* 497 pp. New York: Free Press; London: Collier-Macmillan, 1972.

A useful but dated guide to the contents of critical editions, both collective sets and those devoted to the work of individual composers, designed to complement rather than replace Heyer (**5.511**) and Blum (**4.9**). Two further sections treat monographs and facsimile series and music periodicals and yearbooks.

Reviewed by Dale Good in *Notes* 30 (1974): 789–90.

5.506 *Composers' Collected Editions from Europe.* 8th revised ed. 322 pp. Wiesbaden: Otto Harrassowitz, 1995. (Special music catalog, 18)

A music dealer's catalog of composers' complete works published in Europe and the British Isles, ranging from Albinoni to Zajc, valuable for its currency and completeness of coverage. Harrassowitz also publishes *Monuments of Music from Europe* in its *Special music catalog* series.

5.507 "Editions et rééditions de musique ancienne (avant 1800)." In *Fontes* 1–22 (1954–75).

A list of early music, with international coverage. Full bibliographical information, including price, is given.

5.508 Eitner, Robert. *Verzeichniss neuer Ausgaben alter Musikwerke aus der frühesten Zeit bis zum Jahre 1800.* 208 pp. Berlin: Trautwein, 1871. (Monatshefte für Musikgeschichte. Beilage. 1871)

Nachträgen, published in *Monatshefte* 9 (1877); "Register zu den Nachträgen" as its *Beilage,* 1877; and 10 (1878).

Reprinted by Anne-Marie Schnase, Scarsdale, N.Y., 1960.

A catalog still useful as a guide to the contents of early historical collections, including music in histories. *Abtheilung I* is an annotated list of collections and literary works containing music. *Abtheilung II* is an index of composers and their works, with separate lists of anonymous works and of German secular song through the 16th century.

5.509 Hagopian, Viola L. *Italian Ars Nova Music: A Bibliographic Guide to Modern Editions and Related Literature.* 2nd ed., revised and expanded. 175 pp. Berkeley and Los Angeles, Calif.: University of California Press, 1973.

First ed., 1964, 75 pp.

An organized, annotated bibliography treating the work done by scholars in the field of 14th-century Italian music.

The 1st ed. is reviewed by Ursula Günther in *Die Musikforschung* 20 (1967): 83–84; the 2nd is reviewed by David Fallows in *EM* 4 (1976): 475.

5.510 Hall, Alison. *E.H. Fellowes, an Index to The English Madrigalists and The English School of Lutenist Song Writers.* 100 pp. Boston, Mass.: Music Library Association, 1984. (MLA index and bibliography series, 23)

An analytical index to E. H. Fellowes's multivolume collections: *The English Madrigalists* and *The English School of Lutenist Song Writers.*

5.511 Heyer, Anna Harriet. *Historical Sets, Collected Editions, and Monuments of Music: A Guide to Their Contents.* 3rd ed. 2 vols. Chicago, Ill.: American Library Association, 1980.

First published in 1957 (485 pp.); 2nd ed., 1969 (573 pp.).

An indispensable guide to the contents of the principal anthologies of music, citing approximately 1,300 anthologies, ranging from 1-vol. works to the extended national monuments and complete works of prolific composers. There are detailed lists of the contents of sets, including such publisher's series as Bärenreiter's *Hortus Musicus,* Nagel's *Musik-Archiv,* and Kistner and Siegel's *Organum.* Without recourse to Heyer, access to tens of thousands of works would be tedious at best and, occasionally, impossible.

The entries provide full bibliographic information and list specific contents of individual volumes, with numerous cross-references. An index of composers, editors, and titles provides access to the anthologies' contents. A team of scholar-bibliographers under the direction of George R. Hill is preparing a continuation of this work, to be published by Fallen Leaf Press, with a more thorough index, using electronic access to ease the approach to detailed information contained herein.

The 1st ed. is reviewed by Irene Millen in *Notes* 15 (1958): 390–91 and by Harriet Nicewonger in *LJ* (September 1958): 2,380. The 2nd ed. is reviewed by Lenore Coral in *JAMS* 24 (1971): 308–9 and by Richard H. Hunter in *Notes* 26 (1969): 275–77. The 3rd ed. is reviewed by George R. Hill in *Notes* 38 (1982): 594.

5.512 "Novae editiones musicae classicae." In *Acta Musicologica,* 3–24 (1931–52).

A regular list of new editions of early music, arranged alphabetically by composer, giving title, scoring, editor, place, publisher, date, and price.

5.513 Ochs, Michael. *An Index to Das Chorwerk, Vols. 1–110.* 38 pp. Ann Arbor, Mich.: Music Library Association, 1970. (MLA index series, 10)

Composer index and title index. The information given for each entry includes volume, page, type of composition, and vocal ensemble required.

5.514 Petrov, Stoian V., and **Khristo Kodov.** *Starobulgarski muzikalni pametnitsi.* [*Old Bulgarian Musical Documents.*] 360 pp. Sofia: Nauka i izkustvo, 1973.

Facsimiles of most of the musical notation preserved in Bulgarian manuscripts.

Reviewed by Miloš Velimirović in *Notes* 32 (1976): 531–33.

5.515 Samuel, Harold E. "Editions, Historical." In Don M. Randel's *The New Harvard Dictionary of Music* (**1.320**), pp. 264–76.

A list of 427 important serial publications of early music, from plainsong through the 18th century. The list is in three sections: collected works, *Denkmäler,* and series of performing editions.

PRIMARY SOURCES OF EARLY MUSIC: MANUSCRIPTS AND PRINTED BOOKS

This section lists bibliographies of original source materials, chiefly those with contents written before 1800. The list is highly selective. Nearly every dissertation or research study on early music contains its bibliography of primary sources. Some of these bibliographies are of great value, but any attempt to cite them all would extend far beyond the scope of the present work. The major reference works such as *The New Grove* (**1.48**), *MGG* (**1.9**), or Riemann's *Lexikon* (**1.45**) contain abundant lists of primary sources. See, for example, the *MGG* articles under "Ars antiqua," "Ars nova," or "Chanson," and the "Sources" article in *The New Grove.*

In the past two decades, the characteristics of the various series of *Répertoire International des Sources Musicales* (*RISM*) have become well defined and important progress has been made in each series toward the goal of providing international union catalogs of the primary and early secondary sources for the study of music written before 1800. *RISM* series A part I concerns the works of individual composers; the *Einzeldrucke* vols. (**5.599**) provide citations of editions of printed music by individual composers. *RISM* series A part II, the music manuscripts 1600–1800 (**5.582** and **12.14**), is under way in its mission to prepare an international union list of manuscripts of music attributable to single composers; this series is newly available in electronic format: CD-ROM (published by K.G. Saur) and in an active database housed at Harvard University. *RISM* series B (**4.376**, **4.381**, **4.383**, **4.385**, **4.386**, **5.516**, **5.520**, **5.526**, **5.546**, **5.565**, **5.571**, **5.572**, **5.589**, **5.608**, **5.622**) concerns a variety of collective works, including a 2-vol. bibliography of writings about music published before 1800. *RISM* series C (**7.1**) is a multivolume international directory of music research libraries and collections.

One of the most direct approaches to primary sources is found in Chapter 7, "Catalogs of Music Libraries and Collections." Another useful approach, although not extensively used here, is through catalogs of such antiquarian music and book dealers as Lisa Cox and J.&J. Lubrano, following the earlier Martin Breslauer publications (**5.525**). Chapter 9, "Histories and Bibliographies of Music Printing and Publishing," includes bibliographies of the output from some of the major music publishing houses from the 16th through the 18th centuries.

5.516* Adler, Israel, and **Lea Shalem.** *Hebrew Notated Manuscript Sources up to circa 1840: A Descriptive and Thematic Catalogue with a Checklist of Printed Sources.* 2 vols. lxxix + 899 pp. Munich: G. Henle Verlag, 1989. (Répertoire international des sources musicales, B IX, 1)

Vol. 1 is a catalog; Vol. 2, the index.

Restricted to sources with notated music, a bibliography whose entries include musical incipits, given in staff notation with accompanying text, as found in 212 manuscripts described in the main body of the bibliography, with an additional 18 manuscripts cited in the appendixes. These manuscripts are scattered in 22 libraries in 9 countries.

Reviewed by Jay Weitz in *Fontes* 39 (1991): 144–45 and by Macy Nulman in *Notes* 47 (1991): 1,176–77.

5.517 Anderson, Gordon A. "Notre Dame and Related Conductus: A Catalogue Raisonné." In *Miscellanea Musicologica. Adelaide Studies in Musicology* 6 (1972): 153–229 and 7 (1975): 1–81.

A work in progress designed to give systematic coverage to all pieces that may be designated conductus and issue from c. 1170 to the end of the 13th century. The sources are identified and bibliographic references are cited.

5.518 Becker, Carl Ferdinand. *Die Tonwerke des XVI. und XVII. Jahrhunderts, oder, Systematisch-chronologische Zusammenstellung der in diesen zwei Jahrhunderten gedruckten Musikalien.* 2nd ed. 358 cols. Leipzig: E. Fleischer, 1855.

First ed., 1847. The 2nd ed. was reprinted by Olms, Hildesheim, Germany, 1969.

An early classified bibliography of musical source materials, chronologically arranged under categories, with an index of composers and a general index to the whole. The bibliography attempts to list all musical compositions published in the 16th and 17th centuries to which actual or approximate dates could be assigned. An abridgment of Rimbault's *Bibliotheca Madrigaliana* (**5.592**) is included as a supplement.

5.519 Besseler, Heinrich. "Studien zur Musik des Mittelalters: 1. Neue Quellen des 14. und beginnenden 15. Jahrhunderts; 2. Die Motette von Franko von Köln bis Philipp von Vitry." In *Archiv für Musikwissenschaft* 7 (1925): 167–252 and 9 (1927): 137–258.

Two articles that are basic source studies for the music of the late medieval period, containing numerous inventories and descriptions of *ars nova* manuscripts. They supplement the work of Friedrich Ludwig covering the *ars antiqua* sources (**5.576**).

5.520 Boetticher, Wolfgang. *Handschriftlich überlieferte Lauten- und Gitarrentabulaturen des 15. bis 18. Jahrhunderts: beschreibender Katalog.* 82 + 374 pp. Munich: Henle, 1978. (Répertoire international des sources musicales, B VII)

A descriptive catalog of 726 manuscripts containing lute and guitar music in tablature within the *RISM* time span (until c. 1820). Included are manuscripts containing music for other plectoral instruments (e.g., theorbo and chitarrone), organized by country, city, and library. *RISM* issued a separate supplement by Christian Meyer, *Register der Tablaturgattungen und Namen zusammengestellt,* a classified register of the tablatures and an index to names in the catalogs. There is supplemental information in "Zur inhaltlichen Bestimmung des für Laute intavolierten Handschriftenbestands," by Wolfgang Boetticher in *Acta Musicologica* 51 (1979): 193–203. Dinko Fabris provides a supplement of 18 previously unknown lute tablatures from 11 Italian cities in "Primie aggiunte Italiane al volume *RISM* B/VII" in *Fontes* 29 (1982): 103–21.

Reviewed by Hans Lenneberg in *Notes* 36 (1979): 108, by Jörg Wagner in *Musica* 33 (1979): 74–75, and by Arthur Ness in *JAMS* 34 (1981): 339–45.

5.521 Böker-Heil, Norbert, Harald Heckman, and **Ilse Kindermann.** *Das Tenorlied: Mehrstimmige Lieder in deutschen Quellen 1450–1580.* Edited for the Deutsche Musikgeschichtlichen Archiv and the Staatlichen Institut für Musikforschung Preussischer Kulturbesitz Berlin. 3 vols. Kassel, Germany: Bärenreiter, 1979. (Catalogus musicus, 9–11) (RISM Sonderband)

A thematic catalog with incipits for each voice, arranged by source (both print and manuscript) with indexes to text incipits and musical incipits. This most significant achievement was made possible through the application of automated data processing techniques. The 3rd vol. indexes composers and their works (pp. 7–50), text incipits (pp. 51–126), and melodic incipits, arranged by intervallic structure (pp. 127–554).

Reviewed by Wolfgang Steinbeck in *Die Musikforschung* 34 (1981): 490–91 and by Christian Meyer in *Revue de musicologie* 66 (1980): 97–99; Vol. 3 is reviewed by Clifford Bartlett in *Brio* 24 (1987): 80–81 and by Christian Meyer in *Fontes* 34 (1987): 69.

5.522 Bohn, Emil. "Bibliothek des gedruckten mehrstimmigen weltlichen deutschen Liedes vom Anfange des 16. Jahrhunderts bis c. 1640." In his *Fünfzig historische Concerte in Breslau, 1881–1892,* pp. 77–188. Breslau, Poland: Hainauer, 1893.

A bibliography of printed German secular polyphonic song. The collections are listed chronologically to 1625; the vols. containing works by individual composers are listed alphabetically. Detailed bibliographical information is provided, but contents are not given. This is a useful guide to the printed sources of early German song.

5.523 Boorman, Stanley, John A. Emerson, David Fallows, David Hiley, Ernest H. Sanders, Ursula Günther, Gilbert Reaney, Kurt von Fischer, Charles Hamm, Jerry Call, and **Herbert Kellman.** "Sources, MS." In *The New Grove Dictionary of Music and Musicians* (**1.48**), Vol. 17, pp. 590–702.

A comprehensive guide to early music manuscripts. After an introduction to the nature, function, preparation, history, and study of musical manuscripts, there are eight extensive bibliographies of manuscript sources of Western music: Western plainchant, secular monophony, organum and discant, early motet, English polyphony 1270–1400, French polyphony 1300–1420, Italian polyphony c. 1325–c. 1430, and renaissance polyphony. Each section presents and describes manuscripts, citing modern editions and secondary literature for each source. The introductory sections are followed by a brief bibliography.

Ann P. Basart compiled an "Index to the Manuscripts in the *New Grove* Articles on 'Sources'" in *CNV* 117–34 (1987–89). The index covers citations of manuscripts in the articles "Sources, Manuscripts," "Sources of Instrumental Ensemble Music to 1630," "Sources of Keyboard Music to 1660," and "Sources of Lute Music" in *The New Grove*. The filing is word by word, rather than letter by letter, arranged alphabetically with entries and cross-references in one alphabet. The entries are arranged by country, city, library or archive, name of collection, and manuscript shelf mark. This is a substantial aid to readers of *The New Grove* seeking information on a specific manuscript. Entries also mention topics within the "Source" articles where the citation is located, and there are helpful explanatory notes.

5.524 Borren, Charles van den. "Inventaire des manuscrits de musique polyphonique qui se trouvent en Belgique." In *Acta Musicologica* 5 (1933): 66–71, 120–27, and 177–83, and 6 (1934): 23–29, 65–73, and 116–21.

An inventory of the manuscript sources of early polyphony in Belgian libraries. There are detailed descriptions, listing the contents of manuscripts in the libraries in Brussels, Ghent, Liège, Louvain, Mechlin, and Tournai.

5.525 Breslauer, Martin. *Das deutsche Lied, geistlich und weltlich bis zum 18. Jahrhundert.* 304 pp. Berlin: M. Breslauer, 1908. (Documente frühen deutschen Lebens, Reihe 1)

Reprinted by Olms, Hildesheim, Germany, 1966.

An important music dealer's catalog listing 556 items in the field of early German song. The entries have full bibliographic descriptions with descriptive annotations and numerous title-page facsimiles. Prices are given. There is an index of first lines of song texts, melodies, and persons.

5.526* Bridgman, Nanie. *Manuscrits de musique polyphonique, XVe et XVIe siècles: Italie: Catalogue.* 97 + 681 pp. Munich: G. Henle, 1991. (Répertoire internationale des sources musicales, B IV, 5)

A catalog with descriptions of 169 polyphonic music manuscripts of the 15th and 16th centuries housed in Italian libraries, with a full contents list; the bibliography is representative only after 1979. Previous vols. in Series B, Part IV, have appeared under the title *Manuscripts of Polyphonic Music* (**5.546** and **5.589**).

Reviewed by Allan Atlas in *Notes* 49 (1992): 64–67, by Martin Staehelin in *Fontes* 40 (1993): 164–66, and, with comparisons to the *Census-Catalogue* (**5.531**), by Margaret Bent in *JAMS* 48 (1995): 272–83.

5.527 Bridgman, Nanie. "Musique profane italienne des 16e et 17e siècles dans les bibliothèques françaises." In *Fontes* 2 (1955): 40–59.

Full bibliographic descriptions of 32 16th- and 17th-century prints of Italian secular music in French libraries.

5.528 Brook, Barry S. *La symphonie française dans la seconde moitié du XVIIIe siècle.* 3 vols. Paris: Publications de l'Institut de Musicologie de l'Université de Paris, 1962.

A landmark study of the French symphony. Vol. 1 looks at the French symphony from 1750, with important bibliographical supplements: Annexe IV, "Index thématique arrangé par tonalités et temps" (pp. 511–73); Annexe V, "Index alphabetique des incipits transposés en do majeur ou do mineur et indiqués par les lettres" (pp. 574–84); Annexe VI, "Inventaire sommaire de la symphonie et de la symphonie concertante française" (pp. 585–633); Annexe VII, "Rééditions et enregistrements" (pp. 634–39), with a bibliography and a general index. Vol. 2, "Catalogue thématique et bibliographique," has full descriptions of the works, locations of sources, and short biographies of each composer represented. The 3rd vol. has scores of 6 previously unedited symphonies. The works treats some 1,200 symphonies by 150 composers.

Reviewed by Marc Pincherle in *Revue de musicologie* 49 (1963): 131–33, by H. C. Robbins Landon in *Die Musikforschung* 17 (1964): 435–39, and by Jan LaRue in *MQ* 24 (1963): 384–88.

5.529 Brown, Howard Mayer. *Instrumental Music Printed before 1600: A Bibliography.* 559 pp. Cambridge, Mass.: Harvard University Press, 1965.

A bibliography of the greatest importance for students of early instrumental music, chronologically arranged, beginning with Michel de Toulouze's *L'art et instruction de bien dancer* (c. 1480) and ending with works printed in 1599. The full bibliographic descriptions incorporate much valuable commentary. Included are references to works now lost. The supporting material includes a list of works cited (pp. 441–69) and indexes to relevant libraries and their holdings; the volumes described, arranged by type of notation; the volumes described, arranged by performing medium; names; and first lines and titles.

Reviewed, with addenda, by Claudio Sartori in *Notes* 22 (1966): 1,209–12, by Jack A. Westrup in *M&L* 47 (1966): 354–55, by Jeremy Noble in *JAMS* 19 (1966): 415–17, by Ingrid Brainard in *Die Musikforschung* 20 (1967): 465–70, by Martin Picker in *MQ* 28 (1967): 136–39, and by A. Hyatt King in *Library,* ser. 5, 22 (June 1969): 154–58.

5.530 Caldwell, John. "Sources of Keyboard Music to 1660." In *The New Grove Dictionary of Music and Musicians* (**1.48**).

An article that includes sources up to 1660, divided into broad geographic areas and further divided within those areas into manuscript and printed sources, arranged geographically. The sources are described and the contents analyzed, though incompletely; modern editions and secondary literature are cited.

5.531 Call, Jerry, and **Herbert Kellman.** *Census-Catalogue of Manuscript Sources of Polyphonic Music, 1400–1550.* Compiled by the University of Illinois, Musicological Archives for Renaissance Manuscript Studies. 5 vols. Rome: American Institute of Musicology; Neuhausen-Stuttgart: Hänssler-Verlag, 1979–88. (Renaissance manuscript studies, 1)

The 1st vol. was edited by Charles Hamm with Herbert Kellman; Vols. 2–5 were edited by Herbert Kellman.

An exceptional catalog with extensive descriptions and analyses of sources of renaissance polyphony; virtually all sources are in microfilm copies in the Illinois Archives. It is called a census-catalog because the intention of the compiler and editors was to gather in one publication information on all sources, whether obtainable by the archive or not. The entries are arranged alphabetically by location of the institution holding the original. Each entry provides a summary of the source's contents, a contents list in order of appearance, an extensive description of the source (including information on provenance), and citations of literature about the source. Includes an extended bibliography of secondary sources cited, an index of composers, and a general index of persons, places, *RISM* numbers, and watermarks in each of Vols. 1–3; each vol. also includes an index of informal names and designations for manuscripts and a key to sigla. The 4th vol. lacks these indexes and lists but describes additional A–U manuscripts in a 263-page supplement. The supplement also has revisions for previously described manuscripts. The 5th vol. has a cumulative bibliography and cumulative indexes, as well as statistics on distribution of manuscripts by country, city, and library. There is also an index to provenance by country and period of origin. Finally, there is a general index.

Charles Hamm and Herbert Kellman present their vision of the Archive in "The Musicological Archive for Renaissance Manuscript Studies" in *Fontes* 16 (1969): 148–49. The five vols. are reviewed by Reinhard Strohm in *JAMS* 48 (1995): 485–90. The 1st vol. is reviewed by John Caldwell in *M&L* 61 (1980): 394–95 and by Thomas Noblitt in *Tijdschrift van der verenig-ing voor Nederlandse muziekgeschiedenis* 42 (1982): 156–65. Vols. 4 and 5 are reviewed by David Fallows in *EM* 12 (1989): 89–90 and by Daniel Zager in *Notes* 47 (1991): 734–36.

5.532* Coelho, Victor. *The Manuscript Sources of Seventeenth-Century Italian Lute Music: A Catalogue Raisonné.* xxix + 711 pp. New York: Garland Publishing Co., 1995.

A complete thematic catalog with extensive supportive apparatus.

Reviewed by James Tyler in *Notes* 52 (1992): 1,158–60.

5.533 Corbin, Solange. *Répertoire de manuscrits médievaux contenant des notations musicales.* 3 vols. Paris: Éditions du Centre National de la Recherche Scientifique, 1965–74.

Contents: Vol. 1, *Bibliothèque Sainte-Geneviève,* 1965 (147 pp. + 27 plates); Vol. 2, *Bibliothèque Mazarine,* edited by Madeleine Bernard, 1966 (176 pp. + 16 plates); Vol. 3, *Bibliothèques: Arsenal, Nationale (musique), Universitaire, École des Beaux-Arts, et fonds privés,* edited by Madelaine Bernard, 1974 (246 pp.).

A series designed to provide descriptions and inventories of all the manuscripts containing medieval chant notation. Each vol. includes bibliographies and facsimiles. The 1st vol. has tables of the origins of notation (describing types of books and their notations), provenance of each manuscript, the contents of the manuscripts by musico-liturgical genres, neumes, and pictorial images of instruments. There is a map outlining the notational styles in northern France. There are similar tables in the other vols. The 3rd vol. includes a table of text incipits.

The first 2 vols. are reviewed by John A. Emerson in *JAMS* 22 (1969): 119–22 and by Ewald Jammers in *Die Musikforschung* 21 (1968): 103–4. The 3rd vol. is reviewed by Michel Huglo in *Revue de musicologie* 62 (1976): 297–300.

5.534 Crane, Frederick. *Materials for the Study of the Fifteenth Century Basse Danse.* 131 pp. Brooklyn, N.Y.: Institute of Mediaeval Music, 1968. (Wissenschaftliche Abhandlungen, 16)

A focused view of a narrowly defined area of study, with a bibliography (pp. 118–28).

Reviewed by Peter Gülke in *Die Musikforschung* 24 (1971): 339–40.

5.535 Daniel, Ralph T., and Peter Le Huray. *The Sources of English Church Music, 1549–1660.* 2 vols. London: Published for the British Academy by Stainer and Bell, 1972. (Early English church music, supplementary vol., 1)

A complete inventory of sources from the early reformation to the restoration. Part I is a list of the sources, printed or in manuscript, a thematic catalog of all anonymous works, and a first-line index of anthems. Part II has services and anthems arranged alphabetically by composer, with data on the sources and their location.

Reviewed by Bradford R. DeVos in *Notes* 31 (1974): 305–7.

5.536 Danner, Peter. "Bibliography of Guitar Tablatures, 1546–1764." In *Journal of the Lute Society of America* 5 (1972): 40–51.

A bibliography of 165 printed and 50 manuscript sources, with brief descriptive annotations.

5.537 Daschner, Hubert. *Die gedruckten mehrstimmigen Chansons von 1500–1600: Literarische Quellen und Bibliographie.* lxx + 195 pp. Bonn: Rheinische Friedrich-Wilhelms-Universität, 1962.

A dissertation whose largest part is a first-line index of 4,273 polyphonic chansons from the printed collections of the 16th century.

5.538 Davidsson, Åke. *Catalogue critique et descriptif des imprimés de musique des XVIe et XVIIe siècles, conservés dans les bibliothèques suédoises (excepté la Bibliothèque de l'Université royale d'Upsala).* 471 pp. Uppsala: Almquist et Wiksells, 1952. (Studia musicologica Upsalliensia, 1)

A union catalog of early music in 18 Swedish libraries, excluding the University of Uppsala, which is treated elsewhere (**7.518**). Full descriptions, contents, and references are provided, as well as a bibliography of works cited (pp. 455–71).

5.539* Doni, Anton Francesco. *La Libraria.* 192 pp. Venice: A. Salicato, 1580. Reprinted in Bologna by A. Forni, 1979 (Bibliotheca musica Bononiensis, I, 13).

A bibliographical study whose musical value is in its descriptions of the printed music anthologies known to the author, many of which have not survived to the present.

5.540 Duckles, Vincent H. "The Music for the Lyrics in Early Seventeenth-Century English Drama: A Bibliography of the Primary Sources." In *Music in English Renaissance Drama,* pp. 117–60. Edited by John H. Long. Lexington, Ky.: University of Kentucky Press, 1968.

A bibliography of the manuscript and early printed sources for the songs introduced into English drama from 1603 to 1642, citing modern editions when available.

5.541 Duyse, Florimond van. *Het oude Nederlandsche lied: wereldlijke en geestelijke liederen uit croegerem tijd, teksten en melodieën, verzameld en toegelicht door Fl. van Durse.* 4 vols. The Hague: M. Nijhoff, 1903–08.

First issued in parts, 1900–08; unaltered reprint by Frits A.M. Knuf, Hilversum, The Netherlands, 1965.

The standard reference book for the study of early Dutch song, an edition of 714 melodies given with their variants and with an abundance of related information on texts and music. Sacred song is treated in Vol. 3; Vol. 4 contains indexes of names, song titles, and first lines of texts.

5.542 Edwards, Warwick. "Sources of Instrumental Ensemble Music to 1630." In *The New Grove Dictionary of Music and Musicians* (**1.48**).

An article concerned with music for two or more instruments (excluding keyboards, lutes, and other chordal instruments), without voice. "An attempt has been made to identify music originally conceived for instruments." Organized geographically, the entries give locations, manuscript numbers or titles (and if titles, then imprint information), and a description of contents, citing any modern editions or secondary literature.

5.543 Eitner, Robert. *Bibliographie der Musik-Sammelwerke des XVI. und XVII. Jahrhunderts.* With Franz Xavier Haberl, A. Lagerberg, and C. F. Pohl. 964 pp. Berlin: L. Liepmannssohn, 1877.

Supplemented by additions and corrections published in Eitner's *Monatshefte für Musikgeschichte* 14 (1882): 152–55, 161–64.

The original ed. was reprinted by Olms, Hildesheim, Germany, 1963.

The chronological bibliography of some 795 collections of music published between 1501 and 1700, with full descriptions, a summary of contents, lists of composers represented, and library locations of individual copies. The second part of the work (pp. 297–938) is a first-line index of the vocal texts, arranged alphabetically by composer. Eitner's *Sammelwerke* is one of the major bibliographical tools for historical research in music, although it has been superseded, in part, by the first *RISM* vol. to appear (**5.571**).

5.544 Eitner, Robert. *Biographisch-bibliographisches Quellen-Lexikon der Musiker und Musikgelehrten der christlichen Zeitrechnung bis zur Mitte des neunzehnten Jahrhunderts.* 10 vols. Leipzig: Breitkopf & Härtel, 1898–1904.

Supplemented by the *Miscellanea Musicae Bio-bibliographica,* which gives additions and corrections, and by Giuseppe Radiciotti's "Aggiunte e correzioni ai dizionari biografici dei musicali" in *Sammelbände der Internationalen Musikgesellschaft* 14 (1914): 551–67 and 15 (1915): 566–86; Radiciotti pays special attention to Italian composers.

Reprinted with the supplements by Musurgia, New York, in 1947. A new ed. was published by Breitkopf & Härtel in Wiesbaden, 1959–60. The "2. verbesserte Auflage" was published in Graz, Austria, by Akademische Druck- und Verlagsanstalt, 1959–60.

Until the advent of the *Répertoire internationale des sources musicales* (**5.590**), Eitner's *Quellen-Lexikon* was the basic tool for locating primary sources of music by composers born before 1771, including many obscure names. Both printed music and manuscripts are included, with locations in European libraries. Although the work is badly out of date, with much of the information (particularly about locations) no longer correct, Eitner is still valuable, especially to identify works no longer extant, as it precedes the two major multinational conflagrations that resulted in so much damage to European library collections.

Michel Brenet's (Marie Bobillier's) review in *La revue musicale* (1905): 480–89 has corrections. Stephen A. Willier's article, "The Present Location of Libraries Listed in Robert Eitner's *Biographisch-bibliographisches Quellen-Lexikon*" in *Fontes* 28 (1981): 220–39, documents the present location of most of the collections mentioned in the "Verzeichnis der Bibliotheks-Abkürzungen" in the *Quellen-Lexikon*'s 1st vol. Michael Och's "In Eitner's Footsteps," in *Notes* 48 (1992): 1,216–24, gives a concise yet eloquent account of Eitner's life and philosophy, largely in Eitner's own words.

5.545 Fernández de la Cuesta, Ismael. *Manuscritos y fuentes en España: Edad media.* 397 pp. Madrid: Editorial Alpuerto, D.L., 1980. (Colección O.O.)

An international inventory of medieval Spanish music manuscripts and other sources arranged in order of collection. Annotations include physical description, notation style, contents analytics, references to related manuscripts, and bibliographical references. There are indexes to first lines of Visigothic and Mozarabic chants, Gregorian chants, Latin monody, polyphony, romances, and locations, and a general bibliography (pp. 22–32).

5.546 Fischer, Kurt von. *Handschriften mit mehrstimmiger Musik des 14., 15., und 16. Jahrhunderts: Mehrstimmige Musik italienischen, polnischen, und tschechischen Quellen des 14. Jahrhunderts. Mehrstimmige Stücke in Handschriften aller Länder aus der Zeit um 1400–1425/30. Organale Sätze im älteren Stil und mehrstimmige Stücke in Choralhandschriften des 15. und 16. Jahrhunderts.* 2 vols. 1,221 pp. Munich-Duisburg: G. Henle, 1972. (Répertoire international des sources musicales, B IV, 3–4)

A bibliography of polyphonic music of the 14th–16th centuries. The first group, the manuscripts of polyphonic music of the 14th–16th centuries, follows *RISM* B IV, 1–2 (**5.589**). It covers sources of the Italian Trecento and Polish and Czech sources of the 14th century. Group 2, the sources of 14th-century polyphonic music in manuscripts from all countries dating from 1400 to 1425, links *RISM* B IV, 2 to the present vol. Group 3 is sources of organ polyphony of the 15th and 16th centuries and of choral manuscripts of these centuries in which polyphonic pieces in black notation occur next to liturgical, monodic ones. The manuscripts are arranged by country, city, and library in each of the groups described above. There are indexes of text incipits and composers.

5.547 Fischer, Kurt von. *Studien zur italienischen Musik des Trecento und frühen Quattrocento.* 132 pp. Bern: P. Haupt, 1956. (Publikationen der Schweizerischen Musik Musikforschenden Gesellschaft, 2/5)

A bibliography of Italian secular music of the 14th and early 15th centuries. Text incipits are arranged alphabetically for 177 madrigals, 25 caccie, and 423 ballate, with information on sources and modern editions.

Reviewed by Hans Tischler in *Notes* 15 (1958): 405–6.

5.548 Fortune, Nigel. "A Handlist of Printed Italian Secular Monody Books, 1602–1635." In *RMA Research Chronicle* 3 (1963): 27–50.

A list of all Italian publications from 1602 to 1635 containing at least one secular monody, with locations given for the rare titles. The notes indicate contemporary reprints and modern editions where they exist.

5.549 Frere, W. H. *Bibliotheca Musico-Liturgica: A Descriptive Handlist of the Musical and Latin-Liturgical MSS. of the Middle Ages Preserved in the Libraries of Great Britain and Ireland.* Printed for the members of the Plainsong and Mediaeval Music Society. 2 vols. London: Quaritch, 1901–32.

Reprinted by Georg Olms, Hildesheim, Germany, 1967.

A union list of manuscript sources of early music in Great Britain. The 1st vol. (nos. 1–545) lists manuscripts at Lambeth and Oxford. The 2nd vol. (nos. 546–1,031) lists manuscripts in cathedral chapter libraries and at Manchester, Dublin, Cambridge, and other places. There are full descriptions of the manuscripts and indexes of service books, places, persons, and Oxford Bodleian and Cambridge University manuscripts.

5.550 Friedlaender, Max. *Das deutsche Lied im 18. Jahrhundert, Quellen und Studien.* 2 vols. in 3. Stuttgart; Berlin: Cotta, 1902.

Reprinted by Georg Olms, Hildesheim, Germany, 1962.

A bibliography of German songbooks, 1689–1799, with detailed commentary on and musical excerpts from the most important examples. The 2nd vol. provides a discussion of the poets, with indexes of names and text incipits.

5.551 Fuld, James J., and **Mary Wallace Davidson.** *18th-Century American Secular Music Manuscripts: An Inventory.* 225 pp. Philadelphia, Pa.: Music Library Association, 1980. (MLA index and bibliography series, 20)

A thorough description and analysis of 85 18th-century secular musical manuscripts owned by 20 libraries and private individuals. There are full descriptions, analyses, and indexes.

Reviewed by Geraldine Ostrove in *Fontes* 28 (1981): 195 and by Irving Lowens in *Notes* 37 (1981): 594–95.

5.552 Geck, Martin. *Deutsche Oratorien, 1800 bis 1840; Verzeichnis der Quellen und Aufführungen.* 105 pp. Wilhelmshaven, Germany: Heinrichshofen's Verlag, 1971. (Quellen-Kataloge zur Musikgeschichte, 4)

A bibliography of German oratorios, in three major parts: an alphabetical list of oratorios arranged by composer, a list of performance by place, and a chronological list. Some reviews and notices in contemporary periodicals are indicated. Oratorios by some 100 composers are cited.

5.553 Geering, Arnold. *Die Organa und mehrstimmigen Conductus in den Handschriften des deutschen Sprachgebietes vom 13. bis 16. Jahrhundert.* 99 pp. Bern: P. Haupt, 1952. (Publikationen der Schweizerischen Musik Musikforschenden Gesellschaft, 2/1)

A study of the sources of early polyphony in the German-speaking countries, with a list of the relevant manuscripts and an inventory of the organum and conductus settings they contain.

5.554 Gennrich, Friedrich. *Bibliographie der ältesten französischen und lateinischen Motetten.* 124 pp. Darmstadt: Selbstverlag, 1957. (Summa musicae medii aevi, 2)

A bibliography of the 13th-century motet with a guide to the manuscript sources and a record of scholarly work done in this field, expanding Friedrich Ludwig's beginning in his *Repertorium* (**5.576**). Motets are grouped under their respective tenors, with references to all known concordances and modern editions. There are supplementary bibliographies of literature and scripts, indexes of Latin and French tenors, and incipits to motettus and triplum parts.

Reviewed by Hans Tischler in *Notes* 16 (1959): 561–62.

5.555 Gennrich, Friedrich. *Der musikalische Nachlass der Troubadours: Kommentar.* 176 pp. Darmstadt: Selbstverlag, 1960. (Summa musicae medii aevi, 4)

A complete bibliography of the 302 surviving musical settings of troubadour songs, with information on sources, editions of text and music, verse forms, and use of melody as a contrafactum. The songs are numbered consecutively but grouped under composer, with bibliographical references to work done on the individual musicians; 25 manuscript sources are described and discussed. *Summa musicae medii aevi* 3 (1958) is a musical edition of the surviving troubadour melodies.

5.556 Gerstenberg, Walter, and **Martin Hürlimann.** *Composers' Autographs.* Trans. from German with a new preface by Ernst Roth. 2 vols. London: Cassell, 1968.

The 1st vol. was originally issued as *Musikerhandschriften von Palestrina bis Beethoven,* edited by Walter Gerstenberg (Zurich: Atlantis Verlag, 1960), 173 pp.; the 2nd vol. was originally *Musikerhandschriften von Schubert bis Strawinsky,* edited by Martin Hürlimann (Zurich: Atlantis-Verlag, 1969), 80 pp., both of which were based on *Musikerhandschriften von Bach bis Schumann,* by Georg Schünemann (Berlin; Zurich: Atlantis Verlag, 1936, 106 pp. + 3 ll. music).

Two handsome vols. of facsimiles made chiefly from composers' autographs in the Berlin State Library. Vol. 1 contains 159 plates; Vol. 2, 140 plates, with brief descriptive commentaries and identification of the sources.

Reviewed by Werner Neumann in *Die Musikforschung* 17 (1964): 454–55.

5.557* Gillingham, Bryan. *Indices to the Notre-Dame Facsimiles.* 75 pp. Ottawa: Institute of Medieval Music, 1994. (Musicological studies, 63)

A quick reference to the facsimile editions, with indexes to the four basic Notre Dame manuscripts: Firenze, Biblioteca Medicea-Laurenziana, Pluto 29, 1; Madrid 20486; Wolfenbüttel, Herzog-August-Bibliothek 677 (*olim* Helmstedt, 628); and Wolfenbüttel 1206 (*olim* Helmstedt, 1099), with a cumulative index and a bibliography.

5.558 Göhler, Albert. *Verzeichnis der in den Frankfurter und Leipziger Messkatalog der Jahre 1564 bis 1759 angezeigten Musikalien.* 20 + 64 + 96 + 34 pp. (4 parts in 1 vol.) Leipzig: im Kommision bei C.F. Kahnt nachf., 1902.

Unaltered reprint by Frits A.M. Knuf, Hilversum, The Netherlands, 1965.

A bibliography of the music listed in the Frankfurt and Leipzig catalogs from 1564 to 1759, separately listed by century, under composer and identified by type.

5.559* Goy, François-Pierre, Christian Meyer, and **Monique Rollin.** *Sources manuscrites en tablature, luth et theorbe (c. 1500–c. 1800): Catalogue descriptif, Vol. 1: Conföderatio Helvetica (CH), France (F).* 170 pp. + 1 microfiche. Baden-Baden: Editions V. Koerner, 1991. (Collection d'études musicologiques, Sammlung musikwissenschaftlicher Abhandlungen, 82)

The indexes are on microfiche, to be cumulated in a future vol.

Reviewed by Victor Coelho in *Notes* 51 (1994): 112–15.

5.560 Gröninger, Eduard. *Repertoire-Untersuchungen zum mehrstimmigen Notre-Dame-Conductus.* 163 pp. Regensburg: Bosse, 1939. (Kölner Beiträge zur Musikforschung, 2)

An introductory essay of 59 pages, followed by tabulations, with concordances, of the polyphonic conductus compositions found in the four major Notre Dame sources. (See also **5.517**.)

5.561* Hofman, May, and **John Morehan.** *Latin Music in British Sources, c1485–1610.* 176 pp. London: Stainer and Bell for the British Academy, 1987. (Early English church music, Suppl. 2)

A comprehensive index of Latin music copied and printed in England between the late 15th and early 17th centuries. The list of Latin works by British composers, arranged alphabetically by composer, includes title, number of voices, liturgical function, cantus firmus source, modern editions, and printed sources. Less information is given in the section "Latin Compositions by Foreign Composers in British Sources." Also includes a thematic catalog of anonymous compositions in these sources and a first-line index of all works in all three sections.

Reviewed by Kenneth Kreitner in *Notes* 47 (1990): 72 and by Hugh Benham in *M&L* 70 (1989): 249–52, with addenda.

5.562* Honegger, Genevieve. *Alsace: Catalogue des imprimés anciens: Musique polyphonique XVIe–XVIIIe siècles.* 146 pp. Strasbourg: Bibliothèque nationale et Universitaire de Strasbourg; Association regionale pour le developpement de l'action musicale, 1993. (Patrimoine musical regional)

A union list of early polyphonic printed editions held in the Alsace region.

5.563 Hughes, Andrew. *Medieval Manuscripts for Mass and Office: A Guide to Their Organization and Terminology.* 470 pp. Toronto; Buffalo, N.Y.: University of Toronto Press, 1982.

A book organizing surviving medieval manuscripts on the liturgy of the Roman Catholic Church. After an extensive introduction on history and context, music, order and content of services in general terms, and terminology of the liturgies and source manuscripts, there are chapters on liturgical time, textual and musical form, Offices and the Mass, and the content and form of liturgical books. There are specific sections on individual feasts and rites appropriate for them. The book provides instruction on reading and using texts and chants in liturgical manuscripts dating from c. 1300 to c. 1600.

The extensive outline of the book printed on the recto of the frontispiece should be consulted. There are many appendixes, including facsimiles of manuscript pages, a bibliography of secondary sources, and a list of primary sources, as well as indexes of sources and other manuscripts, manuscripts by location, incipits, and a general index. A useful key to symbols used is printed on the flyleaves.

Reviewed by David G. Hughes in *JAMS* 37 (1984), by Jeremy Noble in *Early Music History* 9 (1984): 356–62, and by Anne Walters Robertson in *JM* 4 (1985–86): 350–54.

5.564 Huglo, Michel. *Les tonaires: Inventaire, analyse, comparison.* 487 pp. Paris: Société Française de Musicologie, 1971.

An extended bibliographical and historical work on the medieval tonaries. Huglo describes and discusses each manuscript, analyzes its contents, and compares it to others. The manuscripts are classed by date, region, and musical and liturgical characteristics. Includes an index of books discussed, arranged by city, library, and manuscript name and number, as well as bibliographies of printed tonaries (facsimiles and originals) and of secondary literature. There is a table of incipits and mnemonic formulas.

5.565 Husmann, Heinrich. *Tropen- und Sequenzenhandschriften.* 236 pp. Munich-Duisburg: G. Henle, 1964. (Répertoire international des sources musicales, B V, l)

A vol. devoted to the manuscript sources of tropes and sequences, with the sources grouped by country. Each entry gives information on the signature, provenance, type of liturgical book, notation, structure of the source, contents, and related literature. There are indexes of manuscripts arranged by libraries and by places of origin, and further indexes of places and subjects, names of saints, and names of persons.

Reviewed by Edward H. Roesner in *JAMS* 21 (1968): 212–15.

5.566 *Index to Early American Periodicals to 1850: E. Songs* (Cards E1 to E11). New York: Readex Microfilm Corp., 1965. (Bibliographic aids in microprint)

The microprint edition of the entries under "Songs" from an index of some 650,000 cards compiled by members of the English department of Washington Square College, New York University, with the aid of the Works Project Administration, indexing some 340 early American magazines by authors, composers, anonymous titles, and first lines.

5.567* Jackson, Barbara Garvey. *Say Can You Deny Me: A Guide to Surviving Music by Women from the 16th through the 18th Centuries.* xxi + 486 pp. Fayetteville, Ark.: University of Arkansas Press, 1994.

A union list of the holdings of works by women composers in over 400 libraries worldwide. It covers the renaissance, baroque, classical, and early romantic periods; the entries give title, publication or manuscript information, and medium. Includes an appendix of modern editions and facsimiles and a media index.

Reviewed by Deborah Hayes in *Notes* 52 (1995): 455–56.

5.568* Jeffery, Peter. *A Bibliography for Medieval and Renaissance Musical Manuscript Research Secondary Materials at the Alcuin Library and the Hill Monastic Manuscript Library.* 68 pp. Collegeville, Minn.: St. John's University Press for the Hill Monastic Manuscript Library, 1980.

A handy, pocket-size, annotated bibliography with sections on musical paleography, musical iconography, catalogs, music texts and studies, and reference materials. There is an index to names and titles.

5.569* Johnson, Cleveland. *Vocal Compositions in German Organ Tabulatures, 1500–1650: A Catalogue and Commentary.* 2 vols. in 1. New York: Garland Publishing, 1989. (Outstanding dissertations in music from British universities)
Reviewed by Robert Judd in *M&L* 74 (1993): 136–37.

5.570 Keller, Kate Van Winkle. *Popular Secular Music in America through 1800: A Preliminary Checklist of Manuscripts in North American Collections.* 140 pp. Philadelphia, Pa.: Music Library Association, 1981. (MLA index and bibliography series, 21)
An exploration of a little-known area of scholarship.

5.571 Lesure, François. *Recueils imprimés, XVIe–XVIIe siècles.* 639 pp. Munich: G. Henle, 1960. (Répertoire international de sources musicales, B I)
The first part of the systematic-chronological section of a comprehensive bibliography of music sources currently being compiled under the joint auspices of the International Musicological Society and the International Association of Music Libraries. The present vol. supersedes Eitner's *Bibliographie der Musik-Sammelwerke* (**5.543**) and, when complete, the entire *RISM* project will replace his *Quellen-Lexikon* (**5.544**) as a modern, comprehensive reference tool for locating primary source materials for musical research. This vol. lists collections of music published between 1501 and 1700, with a summary of their contents and with locations of copies in major European and American libraries. There are indexes of editors and printers and of titles and authors. There is also a "Supplement" by Lesure in *Notes* 28 (1972): 397–418.
Reviewed by Vincent H. Duckles in *Notes* 18 (1961): 225–27, by Jack A. Westrup in *M&L* 42 (1961): 76, by Daniel Heartz in *JAMS* 14 (1961): 268–73, and by Gustave Reese in *Fontes* 8 (1961): 4–7.

5.572 Lesure, François. *Recueils imprimés, XVIIIe siècle.* 461 pp. Munich-Duisburg: G. Henle, 1964. (Répertoire international des sources musicales, B II)
A bibliography citing about 1,800 collections printed between 1701 and 1801, giving basic bibliographic descriptions, composers represented, and locations of copies throughout the world. This vol. is organized alphabetically by title rather than chronologically, as in *Recueils imprimés, XVIe–XVIIe siècles* (**5.571**). There are indexes of publishers and printers and of composers' names.

5.573* Lincoln, Harry B. *The Italian Madrigal and Related Repertories: Indexes to Printed Collections, 1500–1600.* 1,139 pp. New Haven, Conn.; London: Yale University Press, 1988.
A source providing access to anthologies of madrigals, with a composer index with incipits. There are indexes to first lines and to sources, as well as a thematic locator index.
Reviewed by Michael A. Keller in *Fontes* 37 (1990): 276–77.

5.574* Lincoln, Harry B. *The Latin Motet: Indexes to Printed Collections, 1500–1600.* 835 pp. Ottawa: Institute of Mediaeval Music, 1993. (Wissenschaftliche Abhandlungen, 59)
A composer-based index with incipits, an index to first lines, a thematic locator index, an index to sources, and a bibliography of modern editions. Omitted from the survey are single-composer publications and manuscript sources.
Reviewed by Bonnie J. Blackburn in *M&L* 76 (1995): 411–13.

5.575 Linker, Robert W. *Music of the Minnesinger and Early Meistersinger: A Bibliography.* 79 pp. Chapel Hill, N.C.: University of North Carolina Press, 1961.
A bibliography of German medieval song arranged alphabetically under the composers' names. A preliminary list gives 40 manuscript sources and 41 modern publications of literary history, music, and text editions.
Reviewed by Walter Salmen in *Die Musikforschung* 17 (1964): 432.

5.576 Ludwig, Friedrich. *Repertorium organorum recentioris et motetorum vetustissimi stili.* 2 vols. in 3. Halle, Germany; Langen dei Frankfurt: M. Niemeyer, 1910–62. (Summa musicae medii aevi, Bd. 7–8)

Contents: Band 1, *Catalogue raisonné der Quellen.* Abteilung 1, *Handschriften in Quadrat-Notation,* 344 pp. Abteilung 2, *Handschriften in Mensuralnotation,* Besorgt von Friedrich Gennrich. Band 2, *Musikalisches Anfangs-Verzeichnis des nach Tenores Geordneten Repertorium.*

Band 1, Abteilung 2, and Band 2 were edited from Ludwig's proof sheets (unpublished during his lifetime) by Friedrich Gennrich. Band 1, Abteilung 2 contains a reprint of Ludwig's "Die Quellen der Motetten ältesten Stils," first published in *Archiv für Musikwissenschaft* 5 (1923). A 2nd ed., edited by Luther A. Dittmer, appeared in 1964–78 as a joint publication of the Institute of Medieval Music, New York, and Georg Olms, Hildesheim, Germany (Wissenschaftliches Abhandlungen, 7, 17, 26).

Since 1910, the starting point for studies in the music of the *ars antiqua,* a thematic catalog of 515 motets based on 50 tenors taken from the liturgy of the Mass. The *Repertorium* is essentially an inventory, with concordances, of the contents of the major manuscripts of the Notre Dame repertoire. Band 1, Abteilung 2 is chiefly inventories of two major sources of the 13th-century motet: the *Montpellier Codex* and the *Clayette MS.* "Die Quellen der Motetten ältesten Stils" is a basic source study of medieval polyphony, with complete or partial inventories for some 50 manuscripts with motets of the ars antiqua.

5.577 Meyer, Ernst Hermann. "Quellennachweise." In his *Die mehrstimmige Spielmusik des 17. Jahrhunderts in Nord- und Mittel-Europa, mit einem Verzeichnis der deutschen Kammer- und Orchestermusikwerke des 17. Jahrhunderts.* 258 pp. Kassel, Germany: Bärenreiter-Verlag, 1932. (Heidelberger Studien zur Musikwissenschaft, 2)

A bibliography of the sources of 17th-century chamber music of the Northern European school.

5.578 Mischiati, Oscar. *Bibliografia delle opere dei musicisti bresciani pubblicate a stampa dal 1497 al 1740.* Editio minor. 205 pp. Brescia: Centro di Studi Musicali "Luca Marenzio," 1982. (Pubblicazioni del Centro di Studi Musicali "Luca Marenzio," presso la Civica biblioteca queriniana di Brescia)

Also known as the *Bibliografia dei musicisti bresciani.*

Including 7 titles in the Addenda, a bibliography of 817 works written by Brescian composers, entered under composer and then chronologically. There are title page transcriptions and references to *RISM* (**5.590**), to Eitner (**5.544**), and to *Il Nuovo Vogel* (**5.605**). Library locations are given; there are lists of holding libraries and private collections cited. A section describes anthologies in which Brescian composers' music appears, with references from the main bibliography. There is a classified index.

5.579* Mischiati, Oscar. *Bibliografia delle opere pubblicate a stampa dai musicisti Veronesi nei secoli XVI–XVIII.* 362 pp. Rome: Torre d'Orfeo, 1993. (Biblioteca musicologica, 2)

5.580 Mischiati, Oscar. *La prassi musicale presso i Canonici regolari del Ss. Salvatore: nei secoli XVI e XVII e i manoscritti polifonici della Biblioteca musicale "G. B. Martini" di Bologna.* 157 pp. Rome: Edizioni Torre d'Orfeo, 1985. (Documenta. Istituto di paleografia musicale, 1)

A study of musical practices with bibliographic references.

5.581* Mischiati, Oscar, Mariella Sala, and **Ernesto Meli.** *Bibliografia delle opere dei musicisti bresciani pubblicate a stampa dal 1497 al 1740.* 2 vols. xxii + 909 pp. Florence: L.S. Olschki, 1992. (Biblioteca di bibliografia italiana, 126)

An updating and expansion of the work first released in 1982 (**5.578**).

Reviewed by Marcoemilio Camera in *Fontes* 42 (1995): 287–89.

5.582 *Musikhandshriften 1600–1800: Datenbank-Index / Music Manuscripts 1600–1800: Database Index / Manuscrits musicaux 1600–1800: banque de donné: index.* 2 microfiches and a 16-pp. pamphlet. Kassel, Germany: Bärenreiter, 1986. (Répertoire international des sources musicales, A/II)
  First issued 1983, microfiche.
  Series A/II could not be published in book form, as originally planned, and can never be published as a self-contained catalog because of the enormous number of items in it. The Commission Mixte and The Advisory Research Committee decided to publish indexes only, on microfiche.
  The index to a database of music manuscripts written between 1600 and 1800. *RISM* A/II is the part of the international union catalog of music devoted to music attributable to a single composer and preserved in manuscripts dating between 1580 and 1850. The bibliographic approach here is based on individual musical works rather than bibliographic entries or documents. Includes a principal entry describing each manuscript and then as many analytic entries as are needed to describe the individual works in each manuscript.
  RISM A/II is a database and the microfiche indexes distributed by the *RISM* Sekretariat in Frankfurt are intended to provide the most commonly needed access points to fuller information in the database. However, it is possible to query the database by other access points and to combine searches. Among the available possibilities are names (composer, librettist, former owners, dedicatee, and copyist), musical information (instrumentation, key or mode, genre, and musical incipits), text (title, text incipit, and text language), physical attributes (type of manuscript, size, format, collation, and watermark), provenance, dates, and opus or thematic catalog number. For example, it should be possible to extract entries for works involving a single librettist from a particular geographical region or location; it should be equally possible to discover works written in the 18th century for flute in the key of B minor. Indeed, it is the specific intention of the *RISM* Commission Mixte that national organizing bodies will produce catalogs of holdings based on the *RISM* database. One such is Gertraut Haberkamp's *Die Musikhandschriften der Benediktiner-Abtei Ottobeuren: Thematischer Katalog* (**7.369**).
  Of the hundreds of thousands of worksheets describing European-held manuscripts sent for entry to the *RISM* Sekretariat for entry into the database, less than 20% have been entered. The U.S. Music Manuscript Inventory, based in the Isham Memorial Library of the Loeb Music Library, Harvard University, catalogs and analyzes the nearly 12,000 manuscripts in America qualifying for inclusion in *RISM* A/II. Queries are accepted by the staffs of the *RISM* Sekretariat in Kassel, Germany, and the United States for interrogations of the files in their hands. Remote access is available to the U.S. file (**12.36**).
  The microfiche index provides access by composers' names, uniform title, medium of performance, thematic catalog number, opus number, key, location and shelf mark, and *RISM* control number. Entries in the microfiche index do not include music or text incipits.
  The following articles describe the development and principles of *RISM* A/II:
  Böker-Heil, Norbert. "Computer-Einsatz bei der Serie A/II RISM: Möglichkeiten, Bedingungen, Vorschläge." In *Fontes* 22 (1975): 86–89.
  Dorfmüller, Kurt. "The changing face of RISM." In *Fontes* 25 (1978): 285–89.
  Rösing, Helmut. "Zur Katalogisierung von Musikdrucken und Musikhandschriften der Serie A: Konzept und Realisation der Serie A II des Internationalen Quellenlexikon der Musik." In *Acta Musicologica* 51 (1979): 184.
  Rösing, Helmut. "RISM-Handschriftenkatalogisierung und elektronische Datenverarbeitung (EDV)." In *Fontes* 26 (1979): 107–9.
  Rösing, Helmut. "Sinn und Nutzen des Versuchs einer weltweiten Erfassung von Quellen zur Musik." In *Quellenforschung in der Musikwissenschaft,* ed. by Georg Feder (Wolfenbutteler Forschungen, 15), 1982.

5.583 Ness, Arthur J. "Sources of Lute Music." In *The New Grove Dictionary of Music and Musicians* (**1.48**).

An introduction to the sources, with descriptions and analysis of each source. The source citations are arranged chronologically by country. Modern editions and secondary literature are cited with each source.

5.584 Newman, Joel. *An Index to Capoversi and Titles Cited in Einstein's The Italian Madrigal.* 39 pp. New York: Publications of the Renaissance Society of America, 1967. (Indexes and bibliographies, 3)

Incorporated into the 1971 ed. of *The Italian Madrigal.*

An index to more than 2,000 madrigal titles cited in Einstein's work. The composer and poet are cited where known. Those with musical settings in the Einstein book are identified.

5.585 Page, Christopher. "A Catalogue and Bibliography of English Song from Its Beginnings to c. 1300." In *RMA Research Chronicle* 13 (1978): 67–83.

A catalog listing "all the 12th- and 13th-century songs with English words known to exist," with 19 items arranged in chronological order, indicating first line and source, with extensive descriptions and lists of modern editions.

5.586 Pillet, Alfred. *Bibliographie der Troubadours.* Edited by Dr. Henry Carstens. xliv + 518 pp. Halle, Germany: M. Niemeyer, 1933. (Schriften der Königsberger Gelehrten Gesellschaft. Sonderreihe, 2)

Reprint by Burt Franklin, New York, 1968.

A list based on a bibliography of troubadour songs compiled by Karl Bartsch in 1872. The songs are arranged alphabetically by first word of text, with inclusive numeration and subseries of numbers for works by individual authors. The emphasis is on literary rather than musical scholarship.

5.587 Preston, Michael James. *A Complete Concordance to the Songs of the Early Tudor Court.* 433 pp. Leeds: W.S. Maney and Son, 1972. (Compendia, computer-generated aids to literary and linguistic research, 4)

An index and concordance to the poetry in the three British Library manuscripts containing virtually all that is known of early Tudor song: BL Add. Ms. 5665 (Ritson's ms.), BL Add. Ms. 5465 (The Fayrfax ms.), and BL Add. Ms. 31922 (Henry VIII's ms.). This concordance treats the works edited by John Stevens in *Music and Poetry of the Early Tudor Court* (London: Methuen, 1961). In addition to a first-line index are keyword out-of-context concordances for English and foreign words, reverse indexes to English and foreign words, an index to rhymes, and ranking lists of the frequency of appearance of English words and foreign words.

5.588 Raynaud, Gaston. *Bibliographie des altfranzösischen Liedes, Erster Teil.* Newly edited and expanded by Hans Spanke. 386 pp. Leiden, The Netherlands: E.J. Brill, 1955.

Reprinted by Brill in 1980, with a discography and an index to chansons by A. Bahat, 348 pp.

The first part of a projected revision of Raynaud's *Bibliographie des chansonniers français des XIIIe et XIVe siècles* (Paris, 1884, 2 vols.). This work serves as a guide to trouvère songs, similar to that offered by Pillet (**5.586**) or Gennrich (**5.555**) for the troubadour repertory. The bibliography lists more than 2,130 songs, arranged according to the rhyme word of the first stanza, with references to the manuscript source and to literary and musical studies concerned with the item. There is a bibliography of the manuscript sources, modern editions, and studies (pp. 1–32).

5.589 Reaney, Gilbert. *Manuscripts of Polyphonic Music.* 2 vols. 876 + 427 pp. Munich-Duisburg: Henle, 1966–69. (Répertoire international des sources musicales, B IV, 1–2)

Contents: Vol. 1, *11th–14th century;* Vol. 2, *C. 1320–1400.*

A bibliography of manuscripts of polyphonic music, grouped by nationality of location and described individually, with detailed bibliographical references. There are thematic incipits in square notation. Vol. 2 includes a supplement to Vol. 1, in alphabetical order by country, town, and library, with its own indexes to composers and text incipits.

The 2nd vol. is reviewed by Ernest Sanders in *M&L* 51 (1970): 458–59.

5.590 *Répertoire international des sources musicales [RISM],* 1960– .

An internationally organized reference tool. The early organizational stages of this monumental international research tool are found in Manfred F. Bukofzer's "Toward a New Inventory of Musical Sources," in *Notes* 8 (1951): 265–78; and in an account of the first joint meeting of the two sponsoring organizations (the International Musicological Society and the International Association of Music Libraries) in *Notes* 9 (1952): 213–35.

For documentation on the U.S. response to *RISM,* see *"RISM:* A Report on U.S. Activities," by Wayne D. Shirley in *Notes* 23 (1967): 477–97.

Entries herein that are part of *RISM* include **4.376, 4.381, 4.383, 4.385, 4.386, 5.516, 5.520, 5.526, 5.546, 5.565, 5.571, 5.572, 5.582, 5.589, 5.599, 5.608, 5.622,** and **7.1.**

5.591 Riedel, Friedrich W. *Quellenkundliche Beiträge zur Geschichte der Musik für Tasteninstrumente in der zweiten Hälfte des 17. Jahrhunderts (vornehmlich in Deutschland).* 224 pp. Kassel, Germany; Basel: Bärenreiter, 1960. (Schriften des Landesinstituts für Musikforschung Kiel, 10)

A source study concerned with late-17th-century prints and manuscripts of keyboard music, with emphasis on the German school. Numerous useful lists and inventories are incorporated into the work (such as "Verzeichnis der 1648–1700 im Druck veröffentlichten Musik für Tasteninstrumente," pp. 57–72). There is a "Quellenregister" (Handschriften), pp. 219–24.

5.592 Rimbault, Edward F. *Bibliotheca Madrigaliana; A Bibliographical Account of the Musical and Poetical Works Published in England during the 16th and 17th Centuries under the Titles of Madrigals, Ballets, Ayres, Canzonets, etc.* 88 pp. London: J. Smith, 1847.

Reprinted by B. Franklin, New York, in the 1960s.

An early, and rather faulty, chronological list of vocal music published in England, 1588–1638, giving bibliographic descriptions, contents, and source references. Includes a first-line index of madrigals and songs and a composer index.

An abridgment is included as a supplement in Becker's *Tonwerke* (**5.518**).

5.593 Samuel, Harold E. "Sources, Musical (Pre-1500)." In *The New Harvard Dictionary of Music* (**1.320**).

A brief but useful list of some of the major sources of Gregorian chant and secular monophonic and polyphonic music to 1500. Each entry includes citation of more recent literature about the source. Locations of the sources are given with references to modern editions, if any.

5.594 Sartori, Claudio. *Bibliografia della musica strumentale italiana stampata in Italia fino al 1700.* 2 vols. Florence: Leo S. Olschki, 1952–68. (Biblioteca di bibliografia italiana, 23, 56)

A chronological list of instrumental music, collections of vocal music containing one or more instrumental pieces, or vocal music with one or more instrumental parts, published in Italy to 1700. Also included are a few works by Italian composers published outside Italy. Excluded are lute music and dramatic music. Complete bibliographical data is provided, including dedications, prefaces, and tables of contents. There is a composer index.

The 1st vol. is reviewed by Dragan Plamenac in *Notes* 10 (1953): 616–19, by Harvey Olnick in *MQ* 40 (1954): 98–102, by Willi Apel in *JAMS* 7 (1954): 84–86, and by Richard Schaal in *Die Musikforschung* 7 (1954): 342. The 2nd vol. is reviewed by Owen Jander in *Notes* 26 (1970): 738–39 and by Howard M. Brown in *JAMS* 23 (1970): 531–33.

5.595 Sartori, Claudio. "Finalmente svelati i misteri delle biblioteche italiane." In *Fontes* 2 (1955): 15–37 and 3 (1956): 192–202.

A product of the work on *RISM* in Italy, an article containing a summary report of the holdings of 40 Italian libraries and an alphabetical list of early printed music newly discovered in these collections.

5.596 Schanzlin, Hans Peter. "Musik-Sammeldrucke des 16. und 17. Jahrhunderts in schweizerischen Bibliotheken." In *Fontes* 4 (1957): 38–42.

Schanzlin, Hans Peter. "Musik-Sammeldrucke des 18. Jahrhunderts in schweizerischen Bibliotheken." In *Fontes* 6 (1959): 20–26 and 8 (1961): 26–29.

Preliminary reports prepared by the Swiss office of *RISM*.

5.597 Scheurleer, Daniel F. *Nederlandsche liedboeken; lijst der in Nederland tot het jaar 1800, uitgegevan liedboeken.* 321 pp. The Hague: M. Nijhoff, 1912. Erstes Supplement, 1923.

A bibliography of songbooks published in the Netherlands from 1487 to 1800, with or without music, arranged chronologically under main headings of sacred and secular music, with index by author, editor, publisher, and main word of title. There are 3,887 titles in the main work, 660 in the supplement.

5.598 Schierning, Lydia. *Die Überlieferung der deutschen Orgel- und Klaviermusik aus der 1. Hälfte des 17. Jahrhunderts: Eine quellenkundliche Studie.* 147 pp. Kassel, Germany: Bärenreiter, 1961. (Schriften des Landesinstituts für Musikforschung Kiel, 12)

A source study devoted to the manuscripts of German organ and keyboard music of the first half of the 17th century. Each manuscript is described and the contents inventoried.

5.599 Schlager, Karlheinz. *Einzeldrucke vor 1800.* 12 vols. Kassel, Germany: Bärenreiter-Verlag, 1971– . (Répertoire international des sources musicales, A I, 1–9, 11–12, and Supplements)

Otto Albrecht joined Schlager for the editing of Vols. 8 and 9; Gertraut Haberkamp and Helmut Rösing were responsible for *Anhänge* 1 and 2. Vols. 11 and 12 and their continuations, the *Addenda et Corrigenda,* were edited by Ilse and Jürgen Kindermann.

An alphabetical catalog citing individual editions of music printed between 1500 and 1800 under the name of a single composer, intended to supersede the list of works in Eitner's *Quellen-Lexikon* (**5.544**). Each entry includes as much of the title as is needed to distinguish the edition and imprint, as well as a unique *RISM* identifier and the location of each surviving exemplar known. Each vol. contains a list of contributing libraries, arranged by country and city. The 9th vol. includes an appendix devoted to printed editions with composers' attributions by initial and another appendix including anonymous printed editions. The *Anhänge* exclude entries in the *British Union Catalogue of Early Music* (**5.600**) and *Das Deutsche Kirchenlied* (**5.622**, *RISM* B VIII "DKL"). Rösing and Haberkamp prepared "Text- und Musikincipit-Register zu den Anhängen 1 und 2 in *RISM* A/I Band 9," for *Fontes* 28 (1981): 259–306; this is an index to the text incipits appearing as part of a title in either of the appendixes and an index to the music incipits cited in the appendixes. In the two indexes, asterisks are used to denote the existence of music incipits. The *Addenda et Corrigenda,* from Vol. 11, incorporate new rules for inclusion, allowing entries for all editions by composers born before 1770 published before 1830, and by composers born after 1770 who died before 1810. "Works by these composers published by 1830 and 1850 (the final terminus) are also included if no earlier editions of these works are recorded."

Additional documentation on Series A was provided by "*RISM:* zur Katalogisierung von Musikdrucken und Musikhandschriften der Serie A," by Karlheinz Schlager, Jürgen Kindermann, and Helmut Rösing in *Acta Musicologica* 51 (1979): 173–92.

Vols. 1–3 are reviewed by Neal Zaslaw in *Notes* 31 (1974): 42–45. Vol. 6 is reviewed by François Lesure in *Fontes* 24 (1977): 193. Vol. 7 is reviewed by Richard Schaal in *Die Musikforschung* 32 (1979): 86–87 and by François Lesure in *Fontes* 26 (1979): 145. Vol. 8 is reviewed by A. Hyatt King in *Fontes* 30 (1983): 78–80.

5.600 Schnapper, Edith B. *British Union Catalogue of Early Music Printed before the Year 1801: A Record of the Holdings of over One Hundred Libraries throughout the British Isles.* 2 vols. London: Butterworths Scientific Publications, 1957.

A major reference tool for work with early printed sources of music. These volumes provide the key to sources in British libraries. There are brief bibliographical entries, which include locations established in more than 100 British libraries.

Reviewed by A. Hyatt King in *M&L* 39 (1958): 77–79, by Richard S. Hill in *Notes* 15 (1958): 565–68, and by Richard Schaal in *Die Musikforschung* 12 (1959): 367–69.

5.601 Sonneck, Oscar George Theodore. *A Bibliography of Early Secular American Music (18th Century).* Revised and enlarged by William Treat Upton. 617 pp. Washington, D.C.: The Library of Congress, Music Division, 1945.

First published in 1905. Reprinted, with a new preface by Irving Lowens, by Da Capo Press, New York, 1964.

A list by title, with full bibliographical descriptions, including first line of text, and completely indexed, with additional lists of composers, songsters, American patriotic music, first lines, opera librettos, and publishers, printers, and engravers provided. The Britton–Lowens *American Sacred Music Imprints, 1698–1810* (**5.120**) complements this source.

The 1945 ed. was given an advance review by John Tasker Howard in *Notes* 2 (1944): 59–62. The 1964 reprint is reviewed by Harry Eskew in *Anuario, Inter-American Journal for Musical Research* 1 (1965): 134.

5.602 Stevenson, Robert. *Renaissance and Baroque Musical Sources in the Americas.* 346 pp. + 73 pp. of music. Washington, D.C.: General Secretariat, Organization of American States, 1970.

Typescript catalog of printed and manuscript works seen in Bogota, Cuzco, Guatemala City, La Paz, Lima, Mexico City, Montevideo, Morelia, Oaxaca, Puebla Sucre, Buenos Aires, Rio de Janeiro, and Santiago. Music cited from the last three locations exceeds the chronological limits into the 20th century. The catalog is almost completely lacking in description, although each source is analyzed and many individual works are described. The bibliography is not indexed or cross-referenced, and some of the commentary is idiosyncratic. Corrigenda are provided on a separate page.

Reviewed by Samuel Claro Valdédes in *Revista musical chilena* 31 (1977): 123–24.

5.603 Stevenson, Robert M. "Sixteenth and Seventeenth Century Resources in Mexico." In *Fontes* 1 (1954): 69–78 and 2 (1955): 10–15.

A list, arranged alphabetically by composer, of the manuscript resources of the Puebla Cathedral music archive, some 365 sacred works by 36 composers. There is also a description of a 16th-century manuscript of sacred music in the library of Canon Octaviano Valdes of Mexico City. Continued by **7.420**.

5.604 Thibault, Geneviève, and Louis Perceau. *Bibliographie des poésies de P. de Ronsard mises en musique au XVIe siècle.* 121 pp. Paris: E. Droz, 1941. (Publications de la Société Française de Musicologie, 2/8)

Chronological bibliography, 1552–1629, of some 146 collections containing musical settings of lyrics by Ronsard. There are full bibliographical citations of the collections, with Ronsard settings listed for each and an index of text incipits, collections, and names.

5.605 Vogel, Emil, Alfred Einstein, François Lesure, and Claudio Sartori. *Bibliografia della musica italiana vocale profana pubblicata dal 1500 al 1700.* New ed. 3 vols. Pomezia, Italy: Staderini-Minkoff, 1977.

A major revision of Vogel's *Bibliothek der gedruckten weltlichen Vocalmusik italiens aus den Jahren 1500–1700,* published in Berlin by A. Haack in 1892. Subsequently issued in a partially revised and enlarged ed. including Alfred Einstein's corrections and additions originally published in *Notes* 2–5 (1945–48), by Olms in Hildesheim, Germany, 1962, in 2 vols.

The basic source of information concerning early printed Italian secular vocal music, often called "Il Nuovo Vogel." The works cited are editions attributed to a single composer between

1500 and 1700. Anthologies are not cited; the reader is instead referred to appropriate *RISM* vols. The editors claim that this ed. supersedes information present in the *Einzeldrucke* vols. (**5.599**) issued before it. Of course, some eds. published with the name of a single composer on the title page include works by other composers. These are included in the bibliography.

Arranged alphabetically by composer, each entry gives full title-page transcription, describes the publication, and lists the works in order of the original ed. Poets are suggested when such attribution is possible. Locations for each publication or partbooks from it are cited. Reissued eds. are cross-referenced. There is an appendix of five additional publications at the end of Vol. 2, and after the indexes in Vol. 3 are more additions and corrections. Cross-references are provided for alternative forms of composers' names. The indexes to composers not cited on the title pages, poets, singers cited on the title pages or in dedications, other persons cited in the publications, and most especially the capoversi of each work make the vast body in this work accessible. The index to capoversi includes numerous and invaluable see references, but the reader must understand that the Italian language was by no means standardized in the period during which these works were written. Thus, for instance, seeking first lines beginning with *Lacrime* as well as *Lagrime* is necessary.

The preface discusses the need for a new Vogel–Einstein and cites the many eds., revisions, and contributing articles that have supplemented the original ed. of 1892 and Alfred Einstein's own considerable revisions.

This ed. is reviewed by Don Harrán in *Fontes* 26 (1979): 67–69, by Francesco Luisi in *Nuova rivista musicale italiana* 13 (1979): 703–5, by Stephen M. Fry in *Notes* 35 (1978): 95, and by Howard Mayer Brown in *JAMS* 36 (1983): 142–50.

5.606 Walther, Hans. *Initia carminum ac versuum medii aevi posterioris latinorum: Alphabetisches Verzeichnis der Versanfange mittellateinischer Dichtungen.* 1,186 pp. Göttingen: Vandenhoeck & Ruprecht, 1959. (Carmina medii aevi posterioris latina, 1)

Not a music bibliography but a valuable reference tool for musicologists working in the field of medieval studies. There is an alphabetical index of text incipits for more than 20,000 medieval Latin lyrics, with references to manuscript sources and modern editions. A bibliography of literature and an index of names and subjects are provided.

5.607 Ward, Tom R. *The Polyphonic Office Hymn 1450–1520; A Descriptive Catalogue.* 315 pp. Neuhausen, Germany: American Institute of Musicology; Stuttgart: Hanssler-Verlag, 1980.

Primarily an annotated catalog of a small segment of the repertory of polyphonic liturgical music of the early Renaissance. The information given here provides bibliographic control over the polyphonic office hymns. Examining new sources and new examination of known ones may increase the size of the repertory, but the inventory provides a context in which to view these works. Finally, this inventory removes 755 works from the vague category *motet*.

Musical incipits are given for each voice in every composition. Entries are in order by first line of text. Sources for each incipit are cited and there are comments on stylistic aspects, especially the presence of cantus firmi. Indexes are provided to texts found in settings in the inventory, cantus firmi used in settings in the inventory, settings by composer, sources for the repertory, and inventory entries for all compositions in each source.

Reviewed by Giulio Cattin in *Rivista italiana di musicologia* 15 (1980): 276–85.

5.608* Wathey, Andrew. *Manuscripts of Polyphonic Music: Supplement 1 to RISM B IV(1–2); The British Isles, 1100–1400.* 38 + 138 pp. Munich: Henle, 1993. (Répertoire international des sources musicales, B/IV, 1–2, Suppl. 1)

5.609* Werf, Henrik van der. *Integrated Directory of Organa, Clausulae and Motets of the Thirteenth Century.* 188 pp. Rochester, N.Y.: H. van der Werf, 1989.

Reviewed by Jeremy Yudkin in *Notes* 47 (1991): 731 and by Darwin Scott in *CNV* 135 (1989): 21–23.

5.610 Winternitz, Emanuel. *Musical Autographs: From Monteverdi to Hindemith.* 2 vols. Princeton, N.J.: Princeton University Press, 1955.

An enlarged and corrected ed. was issued by Dover Publications, New York, in 1965.

A facsimile collection of music manuscripts in the composers' hands. The 1st vol. has commentary on the plates; the 2nd has 196 full-page plates of autograph scores.

Reviewed by Otto E. Albrecht in *Notes* 13 (1956): 279–80 and by Denis Stevens in *JAMS* 11 (1958): 243–44.

5.611 Wolf, Johannes. *Handbuch der Notationskunde. I. Teil: Tonschriften des Altertums und des Mittelalters. II. Teil: Tonschriften der Neuzeit, Tabulaturen, Partitur, Generalbass und Reformversuche.* 2 vols. Leipzig: Breitkopf & Härtel, 1913–19. (Kleine Handbucher der Musikgeschichte, 8)

Reprinted by Olms, Hildesheim, Germany, 1963.

Useful lists of early manuscript sources connected with the author's discussion of notational practices, including "Quellen der Ars antiqua" (Vol. 1, pp. 258–63), "Die Ars nova" (vol. 1, pp. 351–54), "Handschriftliche Quellen des 15. und 16. Jahrhunderts" (Vol. 1, pp. 444–65), "Verzeichnis einiger wichtigen deutschen Lautentabulaturen" (Vol. 2, pp. 47–59), "Italienische Lautentabulaturen" (Vol. 2, pp. 66–71), "Quellen französischer Lautentabulatur" (Vol. 2, pp. 95–106), "Guitarretabulaturen" (Vol. 2, pp. 209–18).

5.612 Wotquenne, Alfred. *Table alphabétique des morceaux mesurés contenus dans les oeuvres dramatiques de Zeno, Metastasio, et Goldoni.* 77 pp. Leipzig: Breitkopf & Härtel, 1905.

An alphabetical first-line index of aria and ensemble texts by Zeno, Metastasio, and Goldoni, citing volume and page numbers in the standard editions of their works and title of the work from which the incipit is derived. There is a table of librettos by the three authors.

FOLK SONG AND BALLAD

This section should be used in conjunction with the section "Bibliographies of Music Literature: Ethnomusicology" (**4.152–4.197**), which lists studies and monographs pertaining to folk song and ballad. Here, the emphasis is on the music itself. The user should bear in mind, however, that a work such as Haywood's *Bibliography of North American Folklore and Folksong* (**4.167**) contains numerous entries for music, both printed and on sound recordings. Also relevant in certain respects are such bibliographies as Sears' *Song Index* (**5.390**), Fuld's *Book of World-Famous Music* (**5.5**), and the bibliographies by Sonneck–Upton (**5.601**) and Wolfe (**5.151**), which bridge the uncertain gap between folk and popular song.

5.613 Bronson, Bertrand H. *The Traditional Tunes of the Child Ballads, with Their Texts, According to the Extant Records of Great Britain and America.* 4 vols. Princeton, N.J.: Princeton University Press, 1959–72.

Contents: Vol. 1, *Ballads 1–53;* Vol. 2, *Ballads 54–113;* Vol. 3, *Ballads 114–243;* Vol. 4 includes addenda and various bibliographies and indexes.

A monumental work of scholarship in the field of English–Scottish ballads, based on the work of Francis J. Child, but far exceeding it in scope and authority. The literary and musical traditions of each ballad are discussed, together with a printing of all known variants, both literary and musical.

Reviewed by Klaus Roth in *Jahrbuch für Volksliedforschung* 13 (1968): 228–29. Vol. 1 is reviewed by Claude Simpson in *JAMS* 12 (1959): 88–90 and by Charles Seeger in *Notes* 16 (1959): 384–85; Vol. 4 is reviewed by Claude Simpson in *JAMS* 26 (1973): 159–61.

5.614 Chappell, William. *Popular Music of the Olden Time: A History of the Ancient Songs, Ballads, and of the Dance Tunes of England.* Reprint by Dover Publications, Inc., of the original London publication of 1855–59. 2 vols. New York: Dover, 1965.

A revision of this work, by H. Ellis Wooldridge, appeared in 1893. This ed. was, in turn, reprinted by Jack Brussel, New York, 1961.

The classic work on English popular song. It is the basis for the expanded work by Claude Simpson on *The British Broadside Ballad* (**5.620**).

5.615* Davis, Arthur Kyle, Jr *Folk Songs of Virginia: A Descriptive Index and Classification of Material Collected under the Auspices of the Virginia Folklore Society.* lxiii + 389 pp. Durham, N.C.: Duke University Press, 1949.

Reviewed by Duncan Emrich in *Notes* 7 (1949): 112–13.

5.616 Laws, George Malcolm. *American Balladry from British Broadsides: A Guide for Students and Collectors of Traditional Songs.* 315 pp. Philadelphia, Pa.: American Folklore Society, 1957. (Publications of the American Folklore Society. Bibliographical and special series, 8)

A discussion of the British broadside and its function as a source for American ballads precedes a bibliographic appendix of ballads in classified order, giving texts and citing sources. There is a brief list of British and American printers of ballads in the 19th century and a short discography of British broadside ballads. Includes a general bibliography and a title index to ballads.

5.617* Livingston, Carole Rose. *British Broadside Ballads of the Sixteenth Century: A Catalogue of the Extant Sheets and an Essay.* 911 pp. New York: Garland Publishing, 1991. (Garland reference library of the humanities, 1390)

5.618* Moore, Ethel, and **Chauncey O. Moore.** *Ballads and Folk Songs of the Southwest: More than 600 Titles, Melodies, and Texts Collected in Oklahoma.* 414 pp. Norman, Okla.: University of Oklahoma Press, 1964.

5.619 Sidel´nikov, Viktor M. *Russkaia narodnaia pesnia: bibliograficheskii ukazatel´ 1735–1945.* 169 pp. Moscow: Izd. Akademii Nauk SSSR, 1962.

At head of title: Akademia Nauk SSSR, Institut Mirovoi Literatury im. A. M. Gor´kogo.

A guide to Russian folk song. Part I has texts of folk poetry and folk songs, published in such places as journals and newspapers, with or without music. The 2nd part lists books and articles on Russian folk song. There is an index of names.

5.620 Simpson, Claude M. *The British Broadside Ballad and Its Music.* 919 pp. New Brunswick, N.J.: Rutgers University Press, 1966.

An indispensable reference tool for students of English popular song from the 16th through the 18th centuries, giving the music for 540 broadside ballads and tracing each melody from its earliest printed and manuscript sources. No ballad texts are printed. The work takes William Chappell's *Popular Music of the Olden Time* (1855–59, 2 vols.; **5.614**) as its point of departure but far exceeds Chappell in coverage.

Reviewed by Bertrand H. Bronson in *MQ* 52 (1966): 384–87, by John Ward in *JAMS* 20 (1967): 131–34, by Walter Woodfill in *JRME* 14 (1955): 238–39, by Walter Suppan in *Jahrbuch für Volksliedforschung* 13 (1968): 229–31, and by Charles Haywood in *Ethnomusicology* 11 (1967): 133–34. See also Ward's extended commentary, "Apropos the British Broadside Ballad and Its Music," in *JAMS* 20 (1967): 28–86.

5.621 Sonkin, Annabelle B. *Jewish Folk-Song Resources; An Annotated Bibliography.* 24 ll. New York: National Jewish Music Council, 1957.

Somewhat dated, but still useful.

SACRED MUSIC

Many of the items in this section are actually editions of Protestant or Catholic liturgical music. At the same time, they qualify as reference books because of the scope and authority of their documentation.

5.622 Ameln, Konrad, Markus Jenny, and **Walther Lipphardt.** *Das Deutsche Kirchenlied, DKL: Kritische Gesamtausgabe der Melodien.* 2 vols. Kassel, Germany: Bärenreiter, 1975–80. (Répertoire International des Sources Musicales, B/VIII, 1–2)

The catalog of all traceable printed sources of German hymns, of all denominations, that contain at least one melody in musical notation. The entries are arranged in chronological order and give title-page transcriptions, including imprint, format and dimensions, and bibliographical references, when necessary. The 2nd vol. includes indexes to titles, personal names, place names, printers, publishers, and DKL symbols. Also includes an afterword and corrigenda.

Reviewed by Pierre Pidoux in *Fontes* 23 (1975): 98–99.

5.623 Bäumker, Wilhelm. *Das katholische deutsche Kirchenlied in seinen Singweisen, von den frühesten Zeiten bis gegen Ende des 17. Jahrhunderts.* 4 vols. Freiburg: Herder'sche Verlagshandlung, 1883–1911.

Reprinted from the original by Georg Olms, Hildesheim, Germany, 1962.

The basic study of the German Catholic church song. The main body of the work is quotations and discussion of the individual melodies, classified according to the church year or liturgical use. Each vol. contains an extensive bibliography, arranged chronologically, of early printed song collections. Entries cover the period from 1470 to 1800. Transcriptions from the prefaces of early song collections are given.

5.624 Becker, Carl F. *Die Choralsammlungen der verschiedenen christlichen Kirchen.* 220 pp. Hildesheim, Germany: H.A. Gerstenberg, 1972.

Reprint of the edition published by F. Fleischer, Leipzig, 1845.

A bibliography of sources for sacred choral music in collections classified by a variety of Christian denominations. Within each section, chronologically arranged, are entries outlining the contents of each title cited, and there are references to related works and modern sources. For some, locations of copies are shown in public and private libraries. There is a section on manuscripts showing no locations. Indexes to the collections in chronological order and to names are provided.

5.625 Bryden, John R., and **David G. Hughes.** *An Index of Gregorian Chant.* 2 vols. Cambridge, Mass.: Harvard University Press, 1969.

Contents: Vol. 1, *Alphabetical Index;* Vol. 2, *Thematic Index.*

A practical index of Gregorian chants found chiefly in modern service books, supplemented with a few medieval manuscripts available in facsimile editions. The 1st vol. gives text incipits; Vol. 2 gives melodic incipits in number notation. This is a useful tool for identifying chants used in polyphonic composition.

Reviewed by Don M. Randel in *Notes* 27 (1971): 477–78 and by Andrew Hughes in *M&L* 51 (1970): 317–19.

5.626 Chevalier, Ulysse. *Repertorium hymnologicum: Catalogue de chants, hymnes, proses, séquences, tropes en usage dans l'église latine depuis les origines jusqu'à nos jours.* 6 vols. Louvain, Belgium: Société des Bollandistes, 1892–1920.

The standard bibliography of Latin rhymed poetic texts for liturgical use, identifying saints and feasts with which each incipit is associated. There are references to author (if known), dates of composition, and sources. A 315-pp. vol. of additions and emendations, *Repertorium repertorii,* was prepared by Clemens Blume, Leipzig, 1901. The *Repertorium* has been reprinted by Bollandistes, 1959; the Blume supplement by Olms, Hildesheim, Germany, 1971. This has been corrected and supplemented by Joseph Szövérffy (**5.646**).

5.627* *Comprehensive Guide to LDS Music in Print.* 148 pp. Orem, Utah: Musicart West, 1984.

A catalog of published music of Mormon composers and arrangers, with all relevant bibliographic information for each work, classified by format.

5.628 Ellinwood, Leonard W., and **Elizabeth Lockwood.** *Bibliography of American Hymnals Compiled from the Files of the Dictionary of American Hymnology, a Project of the Hymn Society of America.* 27 microfiches. New York: University Music Editions, 1983.

A list of 7,500 entries for hymnals in all languages using the Roman alphabet, including nondenominational collections. Printed contents guides on sheets in pockets are included with microfiches in binder.

5.629 Foster, Myles S. *Anthems and Anthem Composers: An Essay upon the Development of the Anthem from the Time of the Reformation to the End of the 19th Century, with a Complete List of Anthems (in Alphabetical Order) Belonging to Each of the Four Centuries.* 225 pp. London: Novello, 1901.

Reprinted by Da Capo Press, New York, 1970.

5.630 *The Gregorian Missal for Sundays, Notated in Gregorian Chant by the Monks of Solesmes.* 717 pp. Solesmes, France: Abbaye de Saint-Pierre, 1990.

Latin and English Mass texts for all Sundays, solemnities, and feasts. Chant melodies appear in traditional square Gregorian notation. The notated Gregorian chant pieces are followed by translations intended to facilitate comprehension of the sung Latin text but are not intended for use in the liturgy. Latin prayers are placed side-by-side on the page with vernacular English translations, the official liturgical translation for English-speaking countries. The alphabetical index of chants is separated into categories of Introits, Alleluia verses, Sequences, Offertories, Communions, Antiphons, Hymns, and Responsories.

5.631 Guentert, Kenneth. *The Christian Music Directories.* 1,296 pp. San Jose, Calif.: Resource Publications, 1993.

The first ed. was published in 1976 as *The Music Locator,* edited by W. Patrick Cunningham (187 pp.). A companion publication, *Christian Music Directories: Recorded Music,* makes related resources available.

5.632 Higginson, J. Vincent. *Handbook for American Catholic Hymnals.* 334 pp. New York: Hymn Society of America, 1976.

A complex work presenting information (text, themes, sources, composers, authors, and bibliography) in several sections arranged by use in the church year. There are indexes to composers, authors, tune names, and first lines.

5.633* Hiley, David. *Western Plainchant: A Handbook.* 661 pp. Oxford: Clarendon Press; New York: Oxford University Press, 1993.

An introduction to plainchant designed to serve as both a beginning text and a reference work for advanced studies. It describes the liturgies the plainchant served, as well as the chief genres of chant, different types of liturgical books, manuscript sources, and plainchant notation. An index of text and music incipits, an index of names and terms, and a substantial bibliography (pp. xxxiii–xciii) are included.

Reviewed by Mary Berry in *M&L* 135 (1994): 38–39, by Rosemary Dubowchik in *Notes* 51 (1994): 555–58, by Peter Phillips in *The New Republic* 210 (February 7 1994): 31, and by Ruth Steiner in *Plainsong and Medieval Music* 3 (1994): 212–17.

5.634 Kirsch, Winfried. *Die Quellen der mehrstimmigen Magnificat- und Te Deum-Vertonungen bis zur Mitte des 16. Jahrhunderts.* 588 pp. Tutzing, Germany: Hans Schneider, 1966.

Reviewed by James Erb in *JAMS* 22 (1969): 122–25 and by Martin Just in *Die Musikforschung* 21 (1968): 523–24.

5.635 Laster, James H. *Catalogue of Choral Music Arranged in Biblical Order.* 261 pp. Metuchen, N.J.: Scarecrow Press, 1983.

A new ed. is anticipated, 1996.

A list of anthems, arranged from Genesis to Revelation and including texts from the Apocrypha. The citations include information about necessary performing forces, publisher, and date of publication. There is a composer index.

5.636 Laster, James H. *Catalogue of Vocal Solos and Duets Arranged in Biblical Order.* 204 pp. Metuchen, N.J.: Scarecrow Press, 1984.

A list of vocal works, with each entry including a Biblical reference, the author of the text (if paraphrased), translator, composer, arranger, editor, title, language (if not in English), vocal range, publisher, date, and edition number. A 2nd ed. is anticipated.

5.637 Metcalf, Frank Johnson. *American Psalmody, or Titles of Books Containing Tunes Printed in America from 1721 to 1820.* New introduction by Harry Eskew. New York: Da Capo Press, 1968.

An unabridged republication of the 1st ed. published in New York in 1917.

A checklist of psalm, hymn, and anthem collections; psalm and hymn collections for children; single hymns and anthems; musical collections; and prose tracts on hymnody and sacred music. Each entry identifies first and successive imprints as well as libraries holding copies. There is a key to the location of collections.

Reviewed by Richard A. Crawford in *Notes* 26 (1969): 42–43.

5.638* Meyer, Christian. *Les mélodies des églises protestantes de langue allemande: Catalogue descriptif des sources et édition critique des mélodies.* 1 vol. to date. Baden-Baden: V. Koerner, 1987– . (Collection d'études musicologiques / Sammlung musikwissenschaftlicher Abhandlungen, 74)

Contents: Vol. 1, *Les mélodies publiées à Strasbourg (1524–1547).*

5.639 Randel, Don M. *An Index to the Chants of the Mozarabic Rite.* 670 pp. Princeton, N.J.: Princeton University Press, 1973.

A comprehensive bibliography of the manuscript sources of Mozarabic chant, indicating the parts of the office for which each chant would have been used.

Reviewed by Christian Meyer in *Revue de musicologie* 59 (1973): 285–86.

5.640 Reich, Wolfgang. *Threnodiae sacrae: Katalog der gedruckten Kompositionen des 16.–18. Jahrhunderts in Leichenpredigtsammlungen innerhalb der Deutschen Demokratischen Republik.* 75 pp. Dresden: Sächsische Landesbibliothek, 1966. (Veröffentlichungen der Sächsischen Landesbibliothek, 7)

A catalog of 434 funereal compositions of the 16th through the 18th centuries, found in collections of the former East Germany, chiefly Gotha, Dresden, East Berlin, and Zwickau.

Reviewed by Martin Geck in *Die Musikforschung* 22 (1969): 389–90.

5.641* Schlager, Karl-Heinz. *Thematischer Katalog der ältesten Alleluia-Melodien aus Handschriften des 10. und 11. Jahrhunderts, ausgenommen das ambrosianische, alt-römische und alt-spanische Repertoire.* 270 pp. Munich: W. Ricke, 1965. (Erlanger Arbeiten zur Musikwissenschaft, 2)

5.642 Schreiber, Max. *Kirchenmusik von 1500–1600, Originaldrucke und Manuskripte chronologisch zusammengestellt.* 88 pp. Regensburg: Druckerei St. Georgsheim Birkeneck, 1932.

A chronological list of 16th-century sacred music from both print and manuscript sources. The entries are arranged alphabetically by composer under year of issue, brief titles, and locations in British and continental libraries. Includes an index of composers and a classified index of forms.

5.643 Schreiber, Max. *Kirchenmusik von 1600–1700, Originaldrucke und Manuskripte chronologisch zusammengestellt.* 184 pp. Regensburg: Druckerei St. Georgsheim Birkeneck, 1934.

A list that treats 17th-century sacred music as in **5.642.**

5.644 Spencer, Donald Amos. *Hymn and Scripture Selection Guide: A Cross-Reference of Scripture and Hymns with over 12,000 References for 380 Hymns and Gospel Songs.* 176 pp. Valley Forge, Pa.: Judson Press, 1977.

An index relating Biblical text to hymns.

5.645* Stanislaw, Richard J. *A Checklist of Four-Shape Shape-Note Tunebooks.* 61 pp. Brooklyn, N.Y.: Institute for Studies in American Music, Department of Music, School of Performing Arts, Brooklyn College of CUNY, 1978. (ISAM monographs, 10)

5.646 Szövérffy, Joseph. *Repertorium hymnologicum novum.* Berlin: Classical Folia Editions, 1983– . (Publications of the archives for medieval poetry, 1–).

Contents: T. 1, Bd. 1. *Einführung und alphabetisches Verzeichnis. Religiöse Dichtung als Kulturphänomen und Kulturleistung.*

"*Das Repertorium novum* will Chevaliers altes Werk (*Repertorium hymnologicum*) ersetzen und mit neuem Material bereichern" [Introduction]. This work corrects and supplements Chevalier's *Repertorium Hymnologicum* and Blume's *Repertorium repertorii* (**5.626**).

5.647 Thuner, O. E. *Dansk Salme-Leksikon: Haandbog i dansk Salmesang. En hymnologisk Sammenstilling af Ord og Toner med historiske og bibliografiske Oplysninger.* 592 pp. Copenhagen: O. Lohse, 1930.

A list of 1,108 Danish psalm settings, with detailed information on sources of texts and music. There is an index of melody groups, personal names, and first lines of texts.

5.648 Wackernagel, Philipp. *Bibliographie zur Geschichte des deutschen Kirchenliedes im XVI. Jahrhundert.* 718 pp. Frankfurt am Main, 1855.

Unaltered reprint of the original ed. by Georg Olms, Hildesheim, Germany 1961.

A chronological list of 1,050 editions of German sacred song published in the 16th century; the list has detailed bibliographical descriptions, with annotations. Transcriptions are given of the introductions to 110 of the collections.

5.649 Wackernagel, Philipp. *Das deutsche Kirchenlied von der ältesten Zeit bis zu Anfang des 17. Jahrhunderts.* Mit Berücksichtigung der deutschen kirchlichen Liederdichtung im weiteren Sinne und der lateinischen von Hilarius bis Georg Fabricius und Wolfgang Ammonius. 5 vols. Leipzig: Teubner, 1864–77.

Reprinted by Olms, Hildesheim, Germany, 1964.

The fundamental research tool for the sources of the texts to German church music. Vol. 1 provides in chronological order the full texts of Latin hymns and sequences from sources ranging from Hilarius of Poitiers to 1579. There is an alphabetical index to the hymns and sequences in mid-volume. The second half of the vol. is an extensive bibliography of German sources of hymns and sequences with complete, almost diplomatic transcriptions of title pages and analytic annotations. There is an index to hymn incipits. Vol. 2 provides texts of German hymns from the time of Otfrid to that of Hans Sachs (roughly to the beginnings of the reformation), citing manuscript and printed sources. There are indexes to text incipits and to authors of the texts. Vol. 3 has information on hymns from the genesis of the reformation, from Martin Luther to Nicholas Herman (1523–53). There are author and text incipit indexes as well as an index to the sources of the themes in the texts. Vol. 4 presents texts from the later reformation, from Paulus Eber to Bartolomaus Ringwaldt (1554–84). The apparatus is as in Vol. 3.

Vol. 5 contains texts from the time of Bartolomaus Ringwaldt to the beginning of the 17th century; in this volume, the foreword is signed by Otto Wackernagel and Ernst Wackernagel. The apparatus is as in Vol. 3.

5.650* Walker, Diane Parr, and **Paul Walker.** *German Sacred Polyphonic Vocal Music between Schütz and Bach: Sources and Critical Editions.* 434 pp. Warren, Mich.: Harmonie Park Press, 1992. (Detroit studies in music bibliography, 67)

A bibliography of both published and manuscript music from the end of the Thirty Years War to 1700, representing both German and Latin texts.

Reviewed by Katharine Hogg in *Brio* 30 (1993): 114–15 and by Eva Linfield in *Notes* 50 (1993): 563–64.

5.651* Wenk, Arthur. *Musical Resources for the Revised Common Lectionary.* 614 pp. Metuchen, N.J.: Scarecrow Press, 1994.

A suggested repertory suitable for the three-year cycle of liturgy in common use in the Christian church; hymns, anthems, and organ music are suggested.

5.652 Zahn, Johannes. *Die Melodien der deutschen evangelischen Kirchen-lieder aus den Quellen geschopft und mitgeteilt.* 6 vols. Gutersloh, Germany: Bertelsmann, 1889–93.

Reprint of the original edition by Olms, Hildesheim, Germany, 1963.

An edition of 8,806 melodies, derived from the earliest sources, for the German Protestant liturgy. These melodies are classified according to metrical form. There are biographical notices of 463 chorale composers or editors of chorale collections (Vol. 5, pp. 307–494). An index of composers and a first-line index of texts are provided. Vol. 6 is a bibliography of 1,408 items listing the sources of the melodies, arranged chronologically from 1507 to 1892, with locations given of copies in the principal European libraries. Further supplements give non-German sources and manuscript sources.

MUSICAL TITLES

5.653 Berkowitz, Freda Pastor. *Popular Titles and Subtitles of Musical Compositions.* 2nd ed. 209 pp. Metuchen, N.J.: Scarecrow Press, 1975.

First ed., 1962, 182 pp.

An alphabetical list of 740 musical works, both well-known and obscure, arranged by title nickname, generally in English, with brief anecdotal accounts of the origins of these popular titles. Includes a bibliography (pp. 181–90) and a composer index.

The 2nd ed. is reviewed by Stephen M. Fry in *Notes* 32 (1976): 554, by François Lesure in *Fontes* 23 (1976): 147, and by John Horton in *MR* 42 (1981): 64 no. 1.

5.654 Hodgson, Julian. *Music Titles in Translation: A Checklist of Musical Compositions.* 370 pp. London: Clive Bingley; Hamden, Conn.: Linnet Books, 1976.

A list of over 14,000 titles from 7,000+ works in one alphabetical sequence giving the original or the English translation, followed by the translation or the original, of titles. The last name of the composer is included for each title, with excerpts cited by their connection to the larger work.

Briefly reviewed by Stephen M. Fry in *Notes* 33 (1976): 82.

5.655 Mies, Paul. *Volkstümliche Namen musikalischer Werke.* 32 pp. Bonn: Musihandel-Verlag, 1960.

Nicknames and popular titles for musical compositions listed under composers, with an alphabetical index of titles.

5.656* Pallay, Steven G. *Cross Index Title Guide to Classical Music.* 206 pp. New York: Greenwood Press, 1987. (Music reference collection, 12)

Title access to 6,000 works from 220 composers.

Reviewed by Ray Reeder in *Notes* 47 (1990): 407–8 and by Ann P. Basart in *CNV* 112 (1987): 13–14.

5.657* Pallay, Steven G. *Cross Index Title Guide to Opera and Operetta.* 214 pp. New York: Greenwood Press, 1989. (Music reference collection, 19)

Access to 5,500 excerpts from over 1,400 operas, operettas, and other vocal works by 535 composers.

Reviewed by Ray Reeder in *Notes* 47 (1990): 407–8.

5.658* Ranson, Phil. *By Any Other Name: A Guide to the Popular Names and Nicknames of Classical Music and to Theme Music in Films, Radio, Television and Broadcast Advertisements.* 5th ed. 65 pp. Newcastle upon Tyne, England: Northern Regional Library System, Central Library, 1984.

A British view of the musical nickname.

Reviewed by Ann P. Basart in *CNV* 112 (1987): 13–14.

6

REFERENCE WORKS ON INDIVIDUAL
COMPOSERS AND THEIR MUSIC

A large number of tools have been created to serve as guides to the music of individual composers; works lists, bio-bibliographies, and thematic catalogs exist in abundance. To cite them all would extend the present work beyond reasonable limits, but an assortment of some of the more important ones, as well as a selection of productions of the last 10 years, is given. The most extensive list of thematic catalogs, both published and unpublished, was compiled by Barry S. Brook (**4.13**). Important nonthematic inventories, generally providing access to scholarly editions of the composers' compositions, are to be found under the individual composers' names in major encyclopedias, such as *The New Grove* (**1.48**) and *MGG* (**1.9**). There has been also a proliferation of bio-bibliographies, especially from the Garland and Greenwood series, the Garland composer resource series and Bio-bibliographies in music. Although most are certainly helpful to the beginning researcher, they are generally predictable in format and hence have received minimal or no annotation here unless the contents demand otherwise.

GENERAL WORKS

6.1 Adams, John L. *Musicians' Autobiographies: An Annotated Bibliography of Writings Available in English, 1800–1980.* 126 pp. Jefferson, N.C.: McFarland & Company, 1982.

A bibliography gathering citations for autobiographies of people working in music, be they composers, performers, critics, impresarios, or those with some musical connection who are best known for other talents. The list is arranged alphabetically by author and excludes letters, histories, diaries, and articles in reference works. There are title, chronological, and subject indexes.

Reviewed by William J. Dane in *ARBA* 15 (1984): no. 882 and by Paula Beversdorf Gabbard in *Notes* 40 (1983): 299–300.

6.2 Basart, Ann P. "Serials Devoted to Individual Composers and Musicians: A Checklist." In *CNV* 83 (1984): 14–22.

The latest compilation of this genre, gathering titles concentrating on individual musicians' life, work, and influence. Earlier work in this area was published by John R. Douglas as "Publications Devoted to Individual Musicians: A Checklist," in *Bulletin of Bibliography and Magazine Notes* 33 (1976): 135–39.

6.3* Douglas, John R. "Musician and Composer Society Directory." In *Notes* 34 (1977): 39–51.

An update by Douglas, "Societies Devoted to Individual Musicians and Composers: A World Directory: 1989 Supplement to the 1977 List," is in *CNV* 132 (1989): 11–17.

6.4 Green, Richard D. *Index to Composer Bibliographies.* 76 pp. Detroit, Mich.: Information Coordinators, 1985. (Detroit studies in music bibliography, 53)

An annotated index of bibliographies on 74 composers, both separately published works and as articles related to the individual composers in periodicals. Bibliographies of composers' works published as part of a biography are excluded. There is an index of authors, compilers, and editors.

Reviewed by A. F. Leighton Thomas in *MR* 47 (1987/88): 146, by Dominique-René de Lerma in *ARBA* 17 (1986): no. 1227, and by Richard Andrewes in *MT* 128 (1987): 270.

6.5 *Thematic Indices / Werkverzeichnisse: Music.* 44 pp. Wiesbaden: Otto Harrassowitz, 1994. (Special issue, 1994)

A music dealer's catalog of composers' thematic catalogs, emphasizing European publications and ordered alphabetically by subject, with full bibliographical citations, giving current prices, valuable for currency and completeness of coverage.

6.6 Wettstein, Hermann. *Bibliographie musikalischer thematischer Werkverzeichnisse.* 408 pp. Laaber, Germany: Laaber-Verlag, 1978.

A bibliography of thematic catalogs, alphabetical by composer. The content and organizational structure of each catalog are described. See also Brook's bibliography (**4.13**).

6.7 Wettstein, Hermann. *Thematische Sammelverzeichnisse der Musik: Ein bibliographischer Führer durch Musikbibliotheken und -Archive.* 268 pp. Laaber, Germany: Laaber-Verlag, 1982.

A highly selective bibliography providing references to thematic indexes of collections and individual volumes in some of the major music libraries and archives. Given are the composers whose works can be found in the collections or volumes listed. A brief index of composers and places is appended.

WORKS ON INDIVIDUAL MUSICIANS

Abel, Karl Friedrich

6.8 Knape, Walter. *Bibliographisch-thematisches Verzeichnis der Kompositionen von Karl Friedrich Abel (1723–1787).* 299 pp. Cuxhaven, Germany: Verlag des Herausgebers Walter Knape, 1972.

A thematic catalog including timing for each movement and date of first publication, if relevant.

Adam, Adolphe

6.9* Studwell, William W. *Adolphe Adam and Léo Delibes: A Guide to Research.* 248 pp. New York: Garland Publishing, 1987. (Garland composer resource manuals, 5) (Garland reference library of the humanities, 681)

For Adam, a biographical overview (pp. 5–10), an annotated list of musical works (pp. 15–28) omitting his 200 light piano works, and an annotated 402-item bibliography. For Delibes, the same basic structure is furnished. There are detailed author, title, and subject indexes.

Reviewed by William J. Dane in *ARBA* 19 (1988): no. 1265 and by A. F. Leighton Thomas in *MR* 50 (1989): 66–68.

Albéniz, Isaac

6.10* Baytelman, Pola. *Isaac Albéniz: Chronological List and Thematic Catalog of His Piano Works.* 124 pp. Warren, Mich.: Harmonie Park Press, 1993. (Detroit studies in music bibliography, 72)

A long-needed thematic catalog for Albéniz, leaving room for expanded and corrected coverage. Included is a brief discography of long-playing records.

Reviewed by Frances Barulich in *Notes* 51 (1995): 939–42 and by Gertraut Haberkamp in *Die Musikforschung* 48 (1995): 93.

Albrechtsberger, Johann Georg

6.11* Weinmann, Alexander. *Johann Georg Albrechtsberger: Thematischer Katalog seiner weltlichen Kompositionen.* 141 pp. Vienna: Musikverlag Ludwig Krenn, 1987. (Beiträge zur Geschichte des Alt-Wiener Musikverlages, 1/5)

A catalog of the secular works of Albrechtsberger, both with and without opus numbers, noting locations of manuscript copies. Dorothea Schröder compiled in 1987 a thematic catalog of the sacred vocal works, and Andreas Weissenbäck in 1914 published a pioneering thematic catalog of Albrechtsberger's church music.

Alwyn, William

6.12* Craggs, Stewart R., and **Alan Poulton.** *William Alwyn: A Catalogue of His Music.* 127 pp. + 17 pp. plates. Hindhead, England: Bravura Publications, 1985. (Bravura studies, 4)

A brief biographical profile by Trevor Hold, a classified catalog of works (pp. 11–99), a discography of 78 and 33 1/3 rpm recordings, both archival and commercially produced (pp. 100–19), and a selective bibliography of the English film and concert composer.

Reviewed by Richard Andrewes in *MT* 128 (1987): 271 and by Malcolm Hayes, with errata, in *Tempo* 159 (1986): 37–38.

Ansermet, Ernest

6.13* Matthey, Jean-Louis, and **Dominique Décosterd.** *Ernest Ansermet: Catalogue de l'oeuvre.* Discography supervised by François Hudry. xxii + 289 pp. Lausanne: Bibliothèque Cantonale et Universitaire, 1983.

The catalog of one of the most profound thinkers among modern conductors and the subject of the Ansermet Archive in Lausanne's library: program notes, articles, and prefaces by Ansermet; articles and other writings about Ansermet; material for his books; letters to and by Ansermet; compositions and orchestrations by Ansermet; and concert programs of his performances. Includes a discography (pp. 257–81) and a bibliography (pp. 286–88).

Arne, Thomas Augustine and Michael

6.14 Parkinson, John A. *An Index to the Vocal Works of Thomas Augustine Arne and Michael Arne.* 82 pp. Detroit, Mich.: Information Coordinators, 1972. (Detroit studies in music bibliography, 21)

A list of all Arne songs published in the 18th century, as well as songs surviving in manuscript. Included is an appendix of lost works and corrections to the *British Union Catalogue of Early Music* (**5.600**) and *Grove's Dictionary of Music and Musicians,* 5th ed. (**1.48**).

Arnold, Malcolm

6.15* Poulton, Alan. *The Music of Malcolm Arnold: A Catalogue.* 224 pp. London; Boston, Mass.: Faber Music in association with Faber & Faber, 1986.

A catalog of works and arrangements, with an excellent discography. The works list includes a chronology, a classified list of works, and a catalog with timings, completion date, location of autograph manuscript, and publisher information, if relevant.

Auber, Daniel François Esprit

6.16* Schneider, Herbert. *Chronologisch-thematisches Verzeichnis sämtlicher Werke von Daniel François Esprit Auber (AWV).* 2 vols. 1,708 pp. Hildesheim, Germany; New York: Georg Olms Verlag, 1994. (Musikwissenschaftliche Publikationen, 1)

A classified thematic catalog, generously supplied with publication and performance details of Auber's dramatic works (pp. 7–1,470).

Aumann, Franz Joseph

6.17* Dormann, Peter. *Franz Joseph Aumann (1728–1797): Ein Meister in St. Florian vor Anton Bruckner, mit thematischem Katalog der Werke.* 481 + 9 ll. plates. Munich: Musikverlag E. Katzbichler, 1985. (Studien zur Landes- und Socialgeschichte der Musik, 6)

Bacarisse, Salvador

6.18* Heine, Christiane. *Catálogo de obras de Salvador Bacarisse.* 354 pp. Madrid: Fundación Juan March, 1990. (Biblioteca de música española contemporánea)

Bach, Carl Philipp Emanuel

6.19* Helm, E. Eugene. *Thematic Catalogue of the Works of Carl Philipp Emanuel Bach.* xxvii + 271 pp. New Haven, Conn.: Yale University Press, 1989.

A long-awaited, well-received catalog. The classified approach by format is further subdivided with works labeled "possibly authentic," "doubtful," and "spurious." Included is a list, by Rachel W. Wade, of works not included in Alfred Wotquenne's *Thematische Verzeichnis der Werke von Carl Philipp Emanuel Bach,* 1905. Other helpful lists include corrections to C. P. E. Bach's works list in *The New Grove* (**1.48**) (pp. 247–49), a concordance of Wotquenne and Helm numbers (pp. 250–53), and an annotated bibliography (pp. 255–71).

Reviewed by Horst Leuchtmann in *Fontes* 38 (1991): 78–79 and by Leta E. Miller in *Notes* 47 (1991): 743–47.

Bach, Johann Sebastian

6.20* Beisswenger, Kirsten. *Johann Sebastian Bachs Notenbibliothek.* 451 pp. Kassel, Germany: Bärenreiter, 1992. (Catalogus musicus, 13)

An attempt to reconstruct the contents of Bach's library, including musical works by other composers.

Reviewed by George B. Stauffer in *Notes* 50 (1994): 1388–90 and by Richard D. P. Jones in *M&L* 74 (1993): 587–88.

6.21* Bullock, William J. *Bach Cantatas Requiring Limited Resources: A Guide to Editions.* 49 pp. Lanham, Md.: University Press of America, 1984.

The description of the available editions of 47 cantatas, with an appendix giving various access points to the cantatas, including by solo vocal requirements.

Reviewed by Malcolm Boyd in *MR* 47 (1986): 130–33.

6.22* Butt, Richard. *The Cantatas of J. S. Bach: A Performers' Index.* 56 pp. Twickenham, England: Editio Abbas, 1984.

A numerical list of cantatas, with durations, soloists, chorus, and orchestra, followed by lists of cantatas arranged by their various instrumental combinations.

6.23* Herz, Gerhard. *Bach-Quellen in Amerika / Bach Sources in America.* 434 pp. Kassel, Germany; New York: Bärenreiter; Ann Arbor, Mich.: UMI Research Press, 1984.

Parallel German and English texts offering information on the primary Bach sources found in the United States, generously illustrated (pp. 314–434).

Reviewed by David Fallows in *EM* 13 (1985): 579.

6.24 Kast, Paul. *Die Bach-Handschriften der Berliner Staatsbibliothek.* 150 pp. Trossingen, Germany: Hohner-Verlag, 1958. (Tübinger Bach-Studien, 2/3)

A catalog of manuscripts of music by members of the Bach family, once a part of the Prussian State Library and later distributed between the two Deutsche Staatsbibliotheken (East and West) and the University Library at Tübingen. This is essentially a finding list for one of the world's great collections of Bach sources, now dispersed. The entries are brief, with indexes of composers, scribes, and former owners of the manuscripts.

6.25* Neumann, Werner, and **Christine Fröde.** *Die Bach-Handschriften der Thomasschule Leipzig: Katalog.* 87 pp. Leipzig: Nationale Forschungs- und Gedenkstätten Johann Sebastian Bach der DDR, 1986. (Beiträge zur Bachforschung, 5)

A brief description of the autograph manuscripts of cantatas held by the Thomasschule.

6.26* Payne, May de Forest. *Melodic Index to the Works of Johann Sebastian Bach.* 101 pp. New York: G. Schirmer, 1938.

Reprinted by AMS Press, New York, 1979.

A methodical approach to the melodies in Bach's works. Stephen C. Bryant and Gary W. Chapman did the same for Joseph Haydn in *Melodic Index to Haydn's Instrumental Music* (**6.178**), and Mozart was similarly served by George R. Hill and Murray Gould in *A Thematic Locator for Mozart's Works, as Listed in Koechel's Chronologisch-thematisches Verzeichnis* (**6.249**).

6.27* Reeder, Ray. *The Bach English-Title Index.* 184 pp. Berkeley, Calif.: Fallen Leaf Press, 1993. (Fallen Leaf reference books in music, 20)

An index of about 14,000 entries representing more than 16,000 titles and textual chorale and chorale preludes from which they were derived. These titles were gathered from scores, libretti (including those in recordings), and critical works. This index was designed to be used with both the 1st and 2nd eds. of Schmieder's catalog (**6.28**). A concordance identifies numbers from the 2nd ed. that differ from those of the 1st.

Reviewed by Mark Y. Herring in *ARBA* 25 (1994): no. 1331.

6.28 Schmieder, Wolfgang. *Thematisch-systematisches Verzeichnis der musikalischen Werke von Johann Sebastian Bach: Bach-Werke-Verzeichnis (BWV).* 2nd, revised and enlarged ed. xlvi + 1,014 pp. Wiesbaden: Breitkopf & Härtel, 1990.

The 1st ed. was published in Leipzig, 1950 (747 pp.); there were numerous unaltered reprints, 1958–80.

The essential reference for Bach scholars and students, a classified thematic catalog providing information on sources of text, instrumentation, early and authoritative publications of the music, manuscript sources, and secondary literature. Each entry includes extensive thematic quotations. The prefaces and remarks are essential aids to the proper use of the catalog. Among the useful appendixes are a chronology of the creation of the compositions, a calendar for the cantatas arranged by liturgical year, a thematic index to the instrumental works, an index to the first lines of text, and an index to names and terms.

The 1st ed. is reviewed by Arthur Mendel in *Notes* 8 (1950): 156–59. The 2nd ed. is reviewed by Joshua Rifkin in *EM* 20 (1992): 336 and by Christoph Wolff in *Notes* 49 (1992): 543–44.

6.29 Schulze, Hans-Joachim, and **Christoph Wolff.** *Bach Compendium: Analytisch-bibliographisches Repertorium der Werke Johann Sebastian Bachs (BC).* 4 vols. to date. Frankfurt; New York: C.F. Peters, 1985– .

Anticipated as a 7-vol. set in 3 parts: Vocal works, instrumental works, and miscellanea. The 1st part is complete and other sections are expected.

A source identifying and documenting the music of Bach. The Foreword states that the purpose of the *Compendium* is to "provide reliable information, both bibliographical and analytical, on Bach's entire output," both from new research and from a reexamination of all relevant sources, although the *Compendium* was not designed to replace Schmieder's catalog (**6.28**).

Reviewed by Lothar Hoffmann-Erbrecht in *Die Musikforschung* 41 (1988): 175–76, by Stephen Dow in *M&L* 69 (1988): 254–55, by Ann Basart in *CNV* 133 (1989): 13, by Joshua Rifkin in *EM* 17 (1989): 79–88, and by John Butt in *Notes* 47 (1990): 361–68.

6.30 Whaples, Miriam K. *Bach Aria Index.* 88 pp. Ann Arbor, Mich.: Music Library Association, 1971. (MLA index series, 11)

An index classifying Bach's arias by performing forces. The works are identified by text incipit, the location in Schmieder's catalog (**6.28**), and in the principal editions. There is an alphabetical index of first lines and instruments.

6.31* Wolff, Christoph. *Bach-Bibliographie: Nachdruck der Verzeichnisse des Schrifttums über Johann Sebastian Bach (Bach-Jahrbuch 1905–1984) mit einem Supplement und Register.* 464 pp. Kassel, Germany: Merseberger, 1985.

A reprint of the nine classified bibliographies in the *Bach-Jahrbuch*, with an index of names and subjects.

6.32* Wutta, Eva Renate. *Quellen der Bach-Tradition in der Berliner Amalien Bibliothek: Mit zahlreichen Abbildungen von Handschriften nebst Briefen der Anna Amalia von Preussen (1723–1787).* 321 pp. Tutzing, Germany: H. Schneider, 1989.

A catalog including facsimile pages from 18th-century manuscript copies of the works of several composers (pp. 73–201), in particular J. S. Bach. Bibliographical references are given (pp. 55–58). The editor published earlier works on Anna Amalia as Eva Renate Blechschmidt.

Badings, Henk

6.33* Klemme, Paul T. *Henk Badings, 1907–87: Catalog of Works.* 201 pp. Warren, Mich.: Harmonie Park Press, 1993. (Detroit studies in music bibliography, 71)

A catalog including a discography (pp. 97–107), a classified works catalog, and an annotated and selected list of bibliographical references (pp. 115–29).

Reviewed by Robert Skinner in *ARBA* 25 (1994): no. 1328.

Banchieri, Adriano

6.34 Mischiati, Oscar. *Adriano Banchieri (1568–1634): Profilo biografico e bibliografia delle opere.* 170 pp. Bologna: Casa Editrice Patron, 1971.

Also published in *Annuario 1965–1970 del Conservatorio di Musica "G. B. Martini" di Bologna*, 1971.

A model bibliographical study of one of the most versatile composers and theorists of the early-17th-century Bolognese school. A preliminary biographical essay is followed by a systematic bibliography of Banchieri's writings. Locations of the works in the major European libraries and in the Library of Congress are given.

Bantock, Sir Granville

6.35* Brock, David. *Sir Granville Bantock: Printed Music in Selected British Libraries.* Compiled for the Bantock Society. 60 pp. West Hagley, West Midlands, England: Lynwood Music (Book Division), 1987.

Barber, Samuel

6.36 Hennessee, Don A. *Samuel Barber: A Bio-Bibliography.* 404 pp. Westport, Conn.: Greenwood Press, 1985. (Bio-bibliographies in music, 3)

One of the first bio-bibliographies in the Greenwood series, bringing together a short biography with long lists (works list, bibliography of works on the composer, and a discography of the composer's works).

Reviewed by John E. Druesedow, Jr., in *ARBA* 17 (1986): no. 1228.

Bartók, Béla

6.37* Antokoletz, Elliott. *Béla Bartók: A Guide to Research.* xxxi + 356 pp. New York: Garland Publishing, Inc., 1988. 356 pp. (Garland composer resource manuals, 11) (Garland reference library of the humanities, 691)

Compiled to provide a variety of users with both scholarly and general works on Bartók, a list of Bartók's works, arranged by format, both musical and prose, followed by a classified bibliography of material on the composer. Both the citations for Bartók's prose and for the works on the composer are annotated. An author–title index is included, as well as an index of Bartók's compositions, an index of proper names, and a subject index.

Reviewed by Philippe A. Autexier in *Revue de musicologie* 75 (1989): 119, by Malcolm Gillies in *M&L* 70 (1989): 428–30, by David Clegg, with corrections, in *MR* 51 (1990): 234–35, by Vera Lampert in *Notes* 46 (1990): 949–50, by George Louis Mayer in *ARBA* 20 (1989): no. 1193, and by Lewis Foreman in *Tempo* 175 (1990): 32.

6.38 Bator, Victor. *The Béla Bartók Archives: History and Catalogue.* 39 pp. New York: Bartók Archives Publication, 1963.

A description of the Archives and of their founding, with summary inventories of materials in such categories as letters, books, articles, clippings, concert programs, printed music, photographs, and recordings as well as autograph manuscripts. This collection has been virtually inaccessible because of legal complications involving its ownership. Two reports by Fritz A. Kuttner in *Die Musikforschung* help clarify its status: "Der Katalog des Bartók-Archives in New York City," 21 (1969): 61–63 and "Das Bartok Archiv in New York City, ein Nachtrag," 22 (1969): 75–76. Further information on access is available in entry no. 215 in *RISM* Series C, *Directory of Music Research Libraries,* Vol. 1 (United States) **(7.1)**.

6.39* Dille, Denis. *Thematisches Verzeichnis der Jugendwerke Béla Bartóks, 1890–1904.* Trans. from French by Raymonde Berthoud. 295 pp. Kassel, Germany: Bärenreiter, 1974.

A thematic catalog covering the composer's youthful work.

Bassett, Leslie

6.40* Johnson, Ellen S. *Leslie Bassett: A Bio-Bibliography.* 171 pp. Westport, Conn.: Greenwood Press, 1994. (Bio-bibliographies in music, 52)

Reviewed by Robert Skinner in *ARBA* 26 (1995): no. 1266.

Beethoven, Ludwig Van

6.41 Bartlitz, Eveline. *Die Beethoven-Sammlung in der Musikabteilung der Deutschen Staatsbibliothek: Verzeichnis Autographe, Abschriften, Dokumente, Briefe.* 229 pp. Berlin: Deutsche Staatsbibliothek, 1970.

A well-organized bibliography of all types of materials in the extensive Beethoven collections of the former East German State Library, which includes manuscripts, sketches, first editions, letters, and items from Beethoven's library. There are numerous bibliographical references.

Reviewed by William Drabkin in *Notes* 28 (1972): 692–94.

6.42 Dorfmüller, Kurt. *Beiträge zur Beethoven-Bibliographie: Studien und Materialien zum Werkverzeichnis von Kinsky-Halm.* 452 pp. Munich: G. Henle Verlag, 1978.

An indispensable adjunct to the Kinsky–Halm *Verzeichnis* **(6.44)**, bringing entries on each work up to date.

Reviewed by Lewis Lockwood in *Fontes* 28 (1981): 22–53 and by Robert Winter in *Notes* 36 (1980): 884–86.

6.43 Hess, Willy. *Verzeichnis der nicht in der Gesamtausgabe veröffentlichten Werke Ludwig van Beethovens, zusammengestellt für die Ergänzung der Beethoven-Gesamtausgabe.* 116 pp. Wiesbaden: Breitkopf & Härtel, 1957.

Citations for 335 works not included in the complete ed., plus 66 doubtful works.

6.44 Kinsky, Georg, and **Hans Halm.** *Das Werk Beethovens: Thematisch-bibliographisches Verzeichnis seiner sämtlichen vollendeten Kompositionen.* xxii + 808 pp. Munich: G. Henle Verlag, 1955.

A thematic catalog in three major sections: works with opus numbers, without opus numbers, and of doubtful or false attribution. Each entry has a thematic incipit, a citation for its location in the *Gesamtausgabe,* information on the creation of the work, manuscript sources, early printed versions, information on the sources and version of the text (if any), and references to discussions of the work in the standard Beethoven biographies and to other secondary literature. There are numerous helpful appendixes.

Reviewed by Donald W. MacArdle in *Notes* 13 (1956): 280–82.

6.45 Klein, Hans-Günter. *Ludwig van Beethoven: Autographe und Abschriften.* 344 pp. Berlin: Merseberger, 1975. (Kataloge der Musikabteilung, Staatsbibliothek Preussischer Kulturbesitz; Reihe 1: Handschriften, 2)

A catalog of the holdings in the Staatsbibliothek der Stiftung Preussischer Kulturbesitz of Beethoven autographs (including sketches and sketchbooks) and copyists' manuscripts in opus-number order, with extensive descriptions. There are indexes to copyists and names, a list of works appearing in the eight sketchbooks, and a bibliography of works consulted (pp. 334–36).

6.46 MacArdle, Donald. *Beethoven Abstracts.* 432 pp. Detroit, Mich.: Information Coordinators, 1973. (Detroit studies in music bibliography, 3)

Abstracts of articles about Beethoven from the 18th century through 1964, divided by format: primary periodicals, secondary periodicals, newspapers, and catalogs.

Reviewed by Douglas Johnson in *Notes* 20 (1974): 513–17.

6.47* MacArdle, Donald W. *An Index to Beethoven's Conversation Books.* 46 pp. Detroit, Mich.: Information Service, 1962. (Detroit studies in music bibliography, 3)

Access to the conversation books published at that time.

Reviewed by Fred Blum in *Notes* 20 (1963): 225–27.

6.48* Meredith, William R., and **Patricia Elliott.** *The Beethoven Bibliography Database: User's Guide and Subject Thesaurus.* 3rd ed. 1 vol. (Various pagings). San Jose, Calif.: Ira F. Brilliant Center for Beethoven Studies, San Jose State University, 1995.

The guide for users of the Beethoven Bibliography Database (**12.17**).

6.49 Schmidt, Hans. "Die Beethovenhandschriften des Beethovenhauses in Bonn." In *Beethoven-Jahrbuch,* Jahrgang 1969–70, pp. 1–443. Bonn: Beethovenhaus, 1971.

A catalog of 776 items. Major sections are letters (489 items), documents partially or wholly in Beethoven's hand (29 items), works (76 items), copies by Beethoven of other composers' works (9 items), sketches (106 items), copyists' works (31 items), and early printed music with annotations by the composer (11 items). There are detailed indexes.

6.50 Tyson, Alan. *The Authentic English Editions of Beethoven.* 152 pp. London: Faber & Faber, 1963.

An important work, one of the first to apply detailed bibliographical analysis to early 19th-century music printing. The author is able to make significant revisions in the chronology of Beethoven's works.

Reviewed by Dagmar von Busch-Weise in *Die Musikforschung* 17 (1964): 443–44, by Albi Rosenthal in *M&L* 45 (1964): 256–58, and by Donald W. MacArdle in *Notes* 22 (1966): 920.

6.51 Unger, Max. *Eine Schweizer Beethovensammlung.* 235 pp. Zurich: Verlag der Corona, 1939. (Schriften der Corona, 24)

A catalog of the Bodmer collection, perhaps the world's greatest accumulation of Beethoven documents, once in private hands but now part of the archive of the Beethoven Haus in Bonn. The catalog is organized in 12 categories, the most important of which are 389 letters, including those of the composer's contemporaries; 108 manuscripts of music; 43 early or first editions; and 17 pictures. There is an index of names.

6.52 Willetts, Pamela J. *Beethoven and England: An Account of Sources in the British Museum.* 76 pp. + 16 plates. London: Trustees of the British Museum, 1970.

A catalog of an exhibit organized to celebrate the 200th anniversary of the composer's birth. Reviewed by William Drabkin in *Notes* 28 (1972): 692–94.

Benda, Franz

6.53* Lee, Douglas A. *Franz Benda (1709–1786): A Thematic Catalogue of His Works.* xxii + 221 pp. New York: Pendragon Press, 1984. (Thematic catalogues, 10)

A list of all works, surviving in both print and manuscript editions, attributed to Benda, with detailed information on copyists and watermarks. Reviewed by Robert Skinner in *ARBA* 16 (1985): no. 1188.

Bennett, Richard Rodney

6.54* Craggs, Stewart R. *Richard Rodney Bennett: A Bio-Bibliography.* 249 pp. New York: Greenwood Press, 1990. (Bio-bibliographies in music, 24)

A list, classified by format, giving information on works and performance (pp. 9–130), discography, and bibliography, reproduced in typescript. Reviewed by John R. Douglas in *Notes* 47 (1991): 762–63.

Bennett, Robert Russell

6.55* Ferencz, George J. *Robert Russell Bennett: A Bio-Bibliography.* 215 pp. New York: Greenwood Press, 1990. (Bio-bibliographies in music, 29)

A works list including selected performances, good cross-references, and commentaries.

Berg, Alban

6.56* Hilmar, Rosemary. *Katalog der Musikhandschriften, Schriften und Studien Alban Bergs im Fond Alban Berg und der weiteren handschriftlichen Quellen im Besitz der Österreichischen Nationalbibliothek.* 212 pp. Vienna: Veröffentlichung der Alban Berg Stiftung in der Universal Edition, 1981. (Alban Berg Studien, 1)

A catalog of the Berg manuscripts in the music collection of the Österreichischen Nationalbibliothek.

6.57* Hilmar, Rosemary. *Katalog der Schriftstücke von der Hand Alban Bergs, der fremd-schriftlichen und gedruckten Dokumente zur Lebensgeschichte und zu seinem Werk.* 161 pp. Vienna: Universal Edition, 1985. (Alban Berg Studien, 1/2)

A well-indexed catalog with transcriptions of 650 letters with Berg connections in the Öster-reichische Nationalbibliothek.

Berlin, Irving

6.58 Jay, Dave. *The Irving Berlin Songography: 1907–1966.* 172 pp. New Rochelle, N.Y.: Arlington House, 1969.

A chronological list of Berlin's songs with annotations and lists of recordings, not including songs recorded in anthologies, separately analyzed. There are no indexes.

Berlioz, Hector

6.59 Holoman, D. Kern. *Catalogue of the Works of Hector Berlioz.* xlv + 527 pp. Kassel, Germany; New York: Bärenreiter, 1987. (New edition of the complete works / Hector Berlioz, 25)

A catalog arranged in several sections: musical works, works contemplated but not composed, and prose works. There is a table of works by oeuvre numbers; the composer's own catalog of his works is included. There are indexes of names and of titles and first lines. The entries provide references to the *Hector Berlioz New Edition of the Complete Works* and to selected secondary sources. This is a model of clarity, completeness, and simplicity.

Reviewed by D. W. Krummel in *JAMS* 43 (1990): 367–75, by François Lesure in *Revue de musicologie* 75 (1989): 301–2, by Julian Rushton in *M&L* 70 (1989): 108–9, with errata and addenda, and by Charles Suttoni in *Notes* 47 (1991): 753–56.

6.60 Hopkinson, Cecil. *A Bibliography of the Musical and Literary Works of Hector Berlioz, 1803–1869, with Histories of the French Music Publishers Concerned.* 2nd ed. Edited by Richard Macnutt. 230 pp. Tunbridge Wells, England: Richard Macnutt, 1980.

First published in Edinburgh in a limited ed. by the Edinburgh Bibliographical Society, 1951 (205 pp.). The 2nd ed. incorporates the author's corrections and additions.

Reviewed by Christopher Rouse in *Notes* 37 (1981): 849–50. The 1st ed. is reviewed by Otto E. Albrecht in *Notes* 9 (1951): 120–22, with included errata and omissions.

6.61* Langford, Jeffrey, and **Jane Denker Graves.** *Hector Berlioz: A Guide to Research.* xxi + 307 pp. New York: Garland Publishing, 1989. (Garland reference library of the humanities, 1025) (Garland composer resource manuals, 22)

Reviewed by Charles Suttoni in *Notes* 47 (1991): 753–56, by Julian Rushton in *M&L* 72 (1991): 123–25, and by Robert Skinner in *ARBA* 21 (1990): no. 1247.

6.62* Wright, Michael G. H. *A Berlioz Bibliography: Critical Writing on Hector Berlioz from 1825 to 1986.* 408 pp. Farnborough, Hampshire, England: Saint Michael's Abbey Press, 1988.

A revised ed. of *A Bibliography of Critical Writings on Hector Berlioz,* 1967.

A bibliography that includes a list of "Berlioz's Own Writings" (pp. 345–53).

Bernstein, Leonard

6.63* Gottlieb, Jack *.Leonard Bernstein: A Complete Catalogue of His Works: Celebrating His 70th Birthday, August 25, 1988.* 95 pp. New York: Jalni Publications; Boosey & Hawkes, 1988.

First published in New York by Amberson Enterprises in 1978 (68 pp.) to celebrate Bernstein's 60th birthday.

Billings, William

6.64* Kroeger, Karl. *Catalog of the Musical Works of William Billings.* 160 pp. New York: Greenwood Press, 1991. (Music reference collection, 32)

A thematic catalog, compiled by the editor of William Billings's *Complete Works,* listing 288 psalm and hymn tunes, as well as 50 anthems. Each entry includes the work's published location (both original and in the *Complete Works*), the source of the text, a musical description of the work (number of measures, key, time signature, directive words, melodic incipit, and timing), and reprints, both by the composer and by others. There is a classified list of works cited in the catalog: American tune books (180 titles), British tune books (8), collections of hymns and poems (19), books and articles, manuscripts, and recordings. The indexes include first-line (of text) index, anthem title index, text source index, index of type of tune (plain tune, fuguing chorus, etc.), and an incipit index, a numerical list of the incipit listings.

6.65 Nathan, Hans. *William Billings, Data and Documents.* 69 pp. Detroit, Mich.: Information Coordinators, 1976. (Bibliographies in American music, 2)
    A bio-bibliographical study covering Billings's life and his musical and literary works.

Bliss, Arthur

6.66* Craggs, Stewart R. *Arthur Bliss: A Bio-Bibliography.* 183 pp. New York: Greenwood Press, 1988. (Bio-bibliographies in music, 13)
    Reviewed by John R. Douglas in *Notes* 47 (1991): 762–63 and by George Louis Mayer in *ARBA* 20 (1989): no. 1200.

6.67* Foreman, Lewis. *Arthur Bliss, Catalogue of the Complete Works.* 159 pp. Sevenoaks, England: Novello, 1980.
    In 1982, a Supplement, prepared by Giles Easterbrook and Trudy Bliss, was published (12 pp.).
    Includes a bibliography (pp. 119–26) and a discography (pp. 127–38).

Bloch, Ernest

6.68 Bloch, Suzanne, and **Irene Heskes.** *Ernest Bloch, Creative Spirit: A Program Source Book.* 146 pp. New York: Jewish Music Council of the National Jewish Welfare Board, 1976.
    A compilation of information related to Ernest Bloch and his music, with a catalog of his published works (pp. 121–34), a brief bibliography, reviews and descriptions of his works, and a discography.
    Reviewed by Alexander Knapp in *M&L* 60 (1979): 461–63 and by Hans Tischler in *Notes* 35 (1979): 890.

6.69* Kushner, David Z. *Ernest Bloch: A Guide to Research.* 345 pp. New York: Garland Publishing, 1988. (Garland composer resource manuals, 14) (Garland reference library of the humanities, 796)
    Reviewed by Ann P. Basart in *CNV* 128 (1988): 8–9 and by William S. Brockman in *ARBA* 20 (1989): no. 1206.

6.70 Sills, David L. "Bloch Manuscripts at the Library of Congress." In *Notes* 42 (1986): 727–53.
    A survey of the collection of music manuscripts, complementing the author's catalog of the Bloch music manuscripts at Berkeley's Music Library (**6.71**).

6.71 Sills, David L. "Ernest Bloch Manuscripts at the University of California." In *Notes* 42 (1986): 7–21.
    A new catalog of Berkeley's Bloch holdings that corrects and expands the one prepared by Minnie Elmer in 1962 and that supplements the one by the author on the Bloch holdings of the Library of Congress (**6.70**).

Boccherini, Luigi

6.72 Gérard, Yves. *Thematic, Bibliographical, and Critical Catalogue of the Works of Luigi Boccherini.* Trans. by Andreas Mayor. 716 pp. London; New York: Oxford University Press, 1969.
    Reviewed by Ellen Amsterdam in *JAMS* 24 (1971): 131–33 and by Eugene K. Wolf in *Notes* 28 (1972): 682–84.

Brahms, Johannes

6.73 Bozarth, George S. "Brahms's Lieder Inventory of 1859–60 and Other Documents of His Life and Work." In *Fontes* 30 (1983): 98–117.

A catalog of documents, including Brahms's index of his works and personal library, an inventory of Lieder in Brahms's hand from 1859–60, his appointment books for the last 30 years of his life, his notebooks, and some musical sketches.

6.74 Bozarth, George S. "The First Generation of Brahms Manuscript Collections." In *Notes* 40 (1984): 239–62.

A biographical study intended to "reassemble . . . sources (at least in catalog format and on microfilm), to establish the 'source situations' of individual compositions, and to ascertain the value of the various manuscripts in source-critical studies. The appendix to this article details the contents of these large collections, as well as many of the smaller private holdings" [From the introductory remarks].

6.75 Bozarth, George S., Elizabeth H. Auman, and **William C. Parsons.** *The Musical Manuscripts and Letters of Johannes Brahms (1833–1897) in the Collections of the Music Division, Library of Congress.* 22 pp. Washington, D.C.: The Library, 1983.

6.76 Dedel, Peter. *Johannes Brahms: A Guide to His Autographs in Facsimile.* 86 pp. Ann Arbor, Mich.: Music Library Association, 1978. (MLA index and bibliography series, 18)

A bibliography of facsimile reproductions of Brahms manuscripts, both prose and musical.

Reviewed by Robert Pascal in *M&L* 60 (1979): 226–27, by Michael T. Roeder in *MR* 40 (1979): 218–20, and by Otto E. Albrecht in *Notes* 35 (1979): 892, with addenda.

6.77 Hofmann, Kurt. *Die Erstdrucke der Werke von Johannes Brahms: Bibliographie mit Wiedergabe von 209 Titelblättern.* xl + 414 pp. Tutzing, Germany: Schneider, 1975. (Musikbibliographische Arbeiten, 2)

An earlier work along the same lines was published by Otto Erich Deutsch as "The First Editions of Brahms," in *MR* 1 (1940): 123–43 and 255–78.

Reviewed by Donald M. McCorkle in *Notes* 32 (1976): 528–30.

6.78* Kross, Siegfried. *Brahms-Bibliographie.* 285 pp. Tutzing, Germany: H. Schneider, 1983.

6.79 McCorkle, Margit, and **Donald M. McCorkle.** *Johannes Brahms, thematisch-bibliographisches Werkverzeichnis.* lxxvii + 841 pp. Munich: G. Henle Verlag, 1984.

The first Brahms thematic catalog to satisfy the demands of modern musicology, similar in intent to the monumental catalogs for Bach (**6.26**), Beethoven (**6.41**), and Mozart (**6.251**). The first thematic catalog for the composer was prepared and published by the firm N. Simrock, Berlin, in 1897, 175 pp., reissued in a new ed. in 1910 and reprinted in 1973 by Da Capo Press, New York, with addenda, corrigenda and a bibliography (xliii–l) by Donald M. McCorkle (1 + 175 pp.).

Reviewed by Karl Geiringer in *Notes* 42 (1985): 289–90 and by David Brodbeck in *JAMS* 42 (1989): 418–31.

6.80* Quigley, Thomas. *Johannes Brahms: An Annotated Bibliography of the Literature through 1982.* xxxix + 721 pp. Metuchen, N.J.: Scarecrow Press, 1990.

Worldwide in coverage, a bibliography providing access to literature written from 1848 to 1982 inclusive. (A supplement is in progress.)

Reviewed by Michael Musgrave in *M&L* 74 (1993): 601–6 and by Horst Leuchtmann in *Fontes* 39 (1992): 72–74.

Bridge, Frank

6.81* Hindmarsh, Paul. *Frank Bridge: A Thematic Catalogue, 1900–1941.* xxxiv + 185 pp. London: Faber Music in association with Faber & Faber, 1983.

A catalog including a bibliography (pp. 169–71) and a discography (pp. 172–76).
Reviewed by Ann P. Basart in *CNV* 101 (1986): 12–13.

6.82* Little, Karen R. *Frank Bridge: A Bio-Bibliography.* 263 pp. Westport, Conn.: Greenwood Press, 1991. (Bio-bibliographies in music, 36)
A tool made especially useful by its indexes, appendixes, and coordination with Hindmarsh's thematic catalog for Bridge (**6.81**).
Reviewed by William A. Everett in *Notes* 51 (1994): 611–13.

Britten, Benjamin

6.83 *Benjamin Britten: A Complete Catalogue of His Published Works.* Revised ed. 53 pp. + supplement and addenda, 4 pp. London: Boosey & Hawkes, 1973.
First published as *Benjamin Britten: A Complete Catalogue of His Works,* 1963, 47 pp.
The catalog produced by his major publisher, with index.

6.84* Evans, John, Philip Reed, and **Paul Wilson.** *A Britten Source Book.* Rev. ed. 328 pp. Aldeburgh, England: Published for the Britten-Pears Library, Aldeburgh, by the Britten Estate, 1987.
A collection of information on the composer, including a chronology, discography (pp. 169–82), and bibliography (pp. 184–308).

Bruckner, Anton

6.85 Grasberger, Renate. *Bruckner-Bibliographie (bis 1974).* 296 pp. Graz, Austria: Akademische Druck- und Verlagsanstalt, 1985. (Anton Bruckner Dokumente und Studien, 4)
Reviewed by Paul Banks in *M&L* 69 (1988): 95.

6.86 Grasberger, Renate. *Werkverzeichnis Anton Bruckner (WAB).* 309 pp. Tutzing, Germany: H. Schneider, 1977. (Instituts für Österreichische Musikdokumentation. Publikationen, 7)
Reproductions of title pages of Bruckner first editions (pp. 171–243).
Reviewed by Stephen M. Fry in *Notes* 34 (1978): 879–80 and by Robert Winter in *Notes* 35 (1979): 640–41.

6.87* Lovallo, Lee T. *Anton Bruckner: A Discography.* 200 pp. Berkeley, Calif.: Fallen Leaf Press, 1991. (Fallen Leaf reference books in music, 6)
Reviewed by David R. Phillips in *MR* 53 (1992): 149–50.

Busoni, Ferruccio

6.88* Kindermann, Jürgen. *Thematisch-chronologisches Verzeichnis der musikalischen Werke von Ferruccio B. Busoni.* 518 pp. Regensburg: G. Bosse, 1980. (Studien zur Musikgeschichte des 19. Jahrhunderts, 19)

6.89* Roberge, Marc-André. *Ferruccio Busoni: A Bio-Bibliography.* xxix + 400 pp. Westport, Conn.: Greenwood Press, 1991. (Bio-bibliographies in music, 34)
Reviewed by Larry Sitsky in *Notes* 48 (1992): 1,265.

Buxtehude, Dietrich

6.90 Karstädt, Georg. *Thematisch-systematisches Verzeichnis der musikalischen Werke von Dietrich Buxtehude: Buxtehude-Werke-Verzeichnis (BuxWV).* 2nd ed. 246 pp. Wiesbaden: Breitkopf & Härtel, 1974.
The 1st ed. was published in 1974 (245 pp.).
The 1st ed. is reviewed by Kerala J. Snyder in *Fontes* 23 (1976): 148–49, by J. A. Westrup in *M&L* 56 (1975): 408–9, and by Rosemary Roberts in *MT* 116 (1975): 341.

6.91 Wettstein, Hermann. *Dietrich Buxtehude (1637–1707): Bibliographie zu seinen Leben und Werk / Bibliography of His Life and Work.* 2nd ed. 109 pp. Munich; New York: K.G. Saur, 1989.

The first ed. was published as *Dietrich Buxtehude (1637–1707): Eine Bibliographie,* in 1979 (98 pp.) (Schriften der Universitätsbibliothek Freiburg, 2).

A bibliography of 519 entries in a classified list in German, with English translations of introductory matter, chapter headings, and bibliographical categories.

Reviewed by Kerala J. Snyder in *Fontes* 37 (1990): 200–1.

Byrd, William

6.92* Turbet, Richard. *William Byrd: A Guide to Research.* 342 pp. New York: Garland Publishing, 1987. (Garland composer resource manuals, 7) (Garland reference library of the humanities, 759)

A bio-bibliography updated in the editor's *Tudor Music: A Research and Information Guide* (**4.312**).

Reviewed by Philip Brett in *CNV* 122 (1988): 17–18.

Carissimi, Giacomo

6.93 Buff, Iva M. *A Thematic Catalog of the Sacred Works of Giacomo Carissimi.* 159 pp. Clifton, N.J.: European American Music Corp., 1979. (Music indexes and bibliographies, 15)

Reviewed by Andrew V. Jones in *Notes* 38 (1981): 66–67.

6.94 Sartori, Claudio. *Giacomo Carissimi: Catalogo delle opere attribuite.* 143 pp. Milan: Finarte, 1975.

A union list of early print and manuscript sources, cited with minimal bibliographic information.

Reviewed by Stephen Fry in *Notes* 33 (1976): 83 and by Iva M. Buff in *Notes* 33 (1977): 584–86.

Carpenter, John Alden

6.95* O'Connor, Joan. *John Alden Carpenter: A Bio-Bibliography.* 248 pp. Westport, Conn.: Greenwood Press, 1994. (Bio-bibliographies in music, 54)

Carter, Elliott

6.96* Doering, William T. *Elliott Carter: A Bio-Bibliography.* 190 pp. Westport, Conn.: Greenwood Press, 1993. (Bio-bibliographies in music, 51)

Carulli, Ferdinando

6.97* Torta, Mario. *Catalogo tematico delle opere di Ferdinando Carulli.* 2 vols. Lucca, Italy: Libreria Musicale Italiana, 1993. (Musicalia, 3)

Castelnuovo-Tedesco, Mario

6.98* Rossi, Nick. *Catalogue of Works by Mario Castelnuovo-Tedesco.* 147 pp. New York: International Castelnuovo-Tedesco Society, 1977.

Chaminade, Cécile

6.99* Citron, Marcia J. *Cécile Chaminade: A Bio-Bibliography.* 243 pp. New York: Greenwood Press, 1988. (Bio-bibliographies in music, 15)

Reviewed by John E. Druesedow, Jr., in *ARBA* 20 (1989): no. 1398 and by Kay Norton in *Notes* 47 (1991): 760–62.

Charpentier, Marc-Antoine

6.100* Hitchcock, H. Wiley. *Les oeuvres de Marc-Antoine Charpentier: Catalogue raisonné / The Works of Marc-Antoine Charpentier.* 419 pp. Paris: Picard, 1982. (La vie musicale en France sous les rois Bourbons)

Chopin, Frédéric

6.101* Brown, Maurice J. E. *Chopin: An Index of His Works in Chronological Order.* 2nd revised ed. 214 pp. London: Macmillan, 1972.
  Reviewed by Frank Zagiba in *Die Musikforschung* 28 (1975): 113 no. 1.

6.102* Chominski, Józef Micha, and **Teresa Dalila Turlo.** *Katalog dziel Fryderyka Chopina / A Catalogue of the Works of Frederic Chopin.* 517 pp. + 80 plates. Cracow: Polskie Wydawn. Muzyczne, 1990. (Documenta Chopiniana, 4)
  A thematic catalog arranged in alphabetical order, with a chronological works list and a list by opus number. The 80 plates are reproductions of title pages. There is a classified chronology of works in the pocket.

6.103* Kobylansk, Krystyna. *Frédéric Chopin: Thematisch-bibliographisches Werkverzeichnis.* 362 pp. Munich: G. Henle. 1979.
  Published previously in Polish as *Rekopisy utworów Chopina: Katalog / Manuscripts of Chopin's Works: Catalog* by Polskie Wydawn. Muzyczne Cracovia, 1977, 2 vols.
  Reviewed by Jean-Jacques Eigeldinger in *Fontes* 29 (1982): 142–45, with a bibliographic addendum to the Chopin thematic catalog; there was an earlier review by Eigeldinger in *Fontes* 26 (1979): 142–44. Also reviewed by Jeffrey Kallberg in *JAMS* 34 (1981): 357–65 and by L. Michael Griffel in *Notes* 37 (1981): 847–49.

6.104 Michałowski, Kornel. *Bibliografia Chopinowska, 1849–1969: Chopin Bibliography.* 267 pp. Cracow: Polskie Wydawn. Muzyczne, 1970.
  A well-organized bibliography of 3,970 items of literature about Chopin, covering documentary evidence, life, works, interpretation, studies of Chopin's reception, and bibliographical publications, with texts in Polish and English and indexes of subjects, Chopin's works, and authors.

Clarke, Jeremiah

6.105 Taylor, Thomas. *Thematic Catalog of the Works of Jeremiah Clarke.* 134 pp. Detroit, Mich.: Information Coordinators, 1977. (Detroit studies in music bibliography, 35)
  The works list of the first organist of the present St. Paul's Cathedral, London.
  Reviewed by Stephen M. Fry in *Notes* 34 (1977): 360.

Clementi, Muzio

6.106 Tyson, Alan. *Thematic Catalogue of the Works of Muzio Clementi.* 136 pp. Tutzing, Germany: H. Schneider, 1967.

Coperario, John

6.107* Charteris, Richard. *John Coprario: A Thematic Catalogue of His Music with a Biographical Introduction.* 113 pp. New York: Pendragon Press, 1977. (Thematic catalogues, 3)

Copland, Aaron

6.108 Skowronski, JoAnn. *Aaron Copland: A Bio-Bibliography.* 273 pp. Westport, Conn.: Greenwood Press, 1985. (Bio-bibliographies in music, 2)

Reviewed by Karl Kroeger in *Notes* 43 (1986): 47–48 and by Robert Palmieri in *ARBA* 17 (1986): no. 1231.

Cornelius, Peter

6.109* Wagner, Günter. *Peter Cornelius: Verzeichnis seiner musikalischen und literarischen Werke.* 532 pp. Tutzing, Germany: H. Schneider, 1986. (Mainzer Studien zur Musikwissenschaft, 13)

Cowell, Henry

6.110* Lichtenwanger, William. *The Music of Henry Cowell: A Descriptive Catalog.* xxxviii + 365 pp. Brooklyn, N.Y.: Institute for Studies in American Music, Conservatory of Music, Brooklyn College of CUNY, 1986. (ISAM monographs, 23)

A catalog of the music of a pioneering composer, chronologically arranged, supplying the date and circumstances of composition, instrumentation, text sources, premiere details, manuscript locations and descriptions, and publication information of almost 1,000 works.

Reviewed by William Brooks in *Notes* 45 (1989): 751–53, by Peter Dickinson in *M&L* 69 (1988): 292–93, and by Ross Wood in *ARBA* 19 (1988): no. 1271.

6.111 Manion, Martha L. *Writings about Henry Cowell: An Annotated Bibliography.* 368 pp. Brooklyn, N.Y.: Institute for Studies in American Music, Conservatory of Music, Brooklyn College of CUNY, 1982. (ISAM monographs, 16)

An annotated list of 1,359 articles tracing Cowell's career.

Reviewed by George R. Hill in *ARBA* 14 (1983): no. 948.

6.112* Saylor, Bruce. *The Writings of Henry Cowell: A Descriptive Bibliography.* 42 pp. Brooklyn, N.Y.: Institute for Studies in American Music, Department of Music, School of Performing Arts, Brooklyn College of CUNY, 1977. (ISAM monographs, 7)

Reviewed by Kären Nagy in *Notes* 34 (1978): 881–82.

Cramer, Johann Baptist

6.113* Milligan, Thomas B. *Johann Baptist Cramer (1771–1858): A Thematic Catalogue of His Works, Based on the Foundation Laid by Jerald C. Graue.* 209 pp. Stuyvesant, N.Y.: Pendragon Press, 1992. (Thematic catalogues, 19)

Reviewed by Steven J. Squires in *ARBA* 26 (1995): no. 1269.

Creston, Paul

6.114* Slomski, Monica J. *Paul Creston: A Bio-Bibliography.* 205 pp. Westport, Conn.: Greenwood Press, 1994. (Bio-bibliographies in music, 55)

Crumb, George

6.115* Gillespie, Don. *George Crumb, Profile of a Composer.* 113 pp. New York: C.F. Peters, 1986. (Composer profiles, 2)

A collection of 12 contributions about the man and his music, with interview, bibliography, discography, reviews, and annotated chronological works list.

Dallapiccola, Luigi

6.116* *Luigi Dallapiccola: Catalogo delle Opere.* 17 pp. Milan: Edizioni Suvini Zerboni, 1979.

Davies, Peter Maxwell

6.117* Bayliss, Colin. *The Music of Sir Peter Maxwell Davies: An Annotated Catalogue.* 300 pp. Beverley, England: Highgate Publications, 1991.

6.118* Smith, Carolyn J. *Peter Maxwell Davies: A Bio-Bibliography.* 343 pp. Westport, Conn.: Greenwood Press, 1995. (Bio-bibliographies in music, 57)

Biographical sketch, annotated alphabetical list of works and first performances, annotated discography, annotated bibliography of 966 items, filmography, and a chronological list of works and first performances (pp. 319–30).

Debussy, Claude

6.119 Abravanel, Claude. *Claude Debussy: A Bibliography.* Detroit, Mich.: Information Coordinators, Inc., 1974. 214 pp. (Detroit studies in music bibliography, 29)

A bibliography assembling books and articles on Debussy and his music. This broad survey of the literature about Debussy, listing 854 works, includes indexes to authors (including editors and translators), reviewers, and other personal names mentioned in the annotation text; personal names in Debussy's critical and literary works; and the periodicals indexed in the bibliography.

Reviewed by François Lesure in *Notes* 31 (1974): 290–91, by Clifford Bartlett in *Brio* 14 (1977): 52–53, and by Rollo Myers in *M&L* 55 (1974): 485–86.

6.120* Briscoe, James R. *Claude Debussy: A Guide to Research.* 504 pp. New York: Garland Publishing, 1990. (Garland composer resource manuals, 27) (Garland reference library of the humanities, 771)

A work whose bibliography emphasizes scholarship since 1972, the stopping point for Abravanel (**6.119**).

Reviewed by Richard Langham Smith in *M&L* 72 (1991): 469–70, by François Lesure in *Fontes* 38 (1991): 83–84, with a reply by the author, and by Kay Norton in *Notes* 47 (1991): 1,137–39.

6.121 Cobb, Margaret G. *Discographie de l'Oeuvre de Claude Debussy.* 128 pp. Geneva: Éditions Minkoff, 1975. (Publications du Centre de Documentation Claude Debussy, 1)

There is a brief review by Stephen M. Fry in *Notes* 32 (1975): 301 and longer ones by James Briscoe in *Notes* 34 (1978): 862–65 and by Jean-Michel Nectoux in *Fontes* 22 (1975): 159–60.

6.122 Lesure, François. *Catalogue de l'oeuvre de Claude Debussy.* 167 pp. Geneva: Minkoff, 1977. (Publications du Centre de Documentation Claude Debussy, 3)

A catalogue raisonné, arranged in chronological order, without thematic incipits and citing dates of composition, providing poet and the source of texts, references to standard secondary literature, and various remarks. The appendixes include Debussy student compositions; works with a domestic character or written for friends; editions, transcriptions, and orchestrations; and unfinished compositions. The indexes include one for dedicatees, a classified index, an index of text incipits, and a title index.

Reviewed by Stephen M. Fry in *Notes* 34 (1977): 359, by James Briscoe in *Notes* 34 (1978): 862–65, and by William W. Austin in *Fontes* 24 (1977): 298–99.

Delibes, Léo

See Adam, Adolphe.

Delius, Frederick

6.123 Lowe, Rachel. *A Descriptive Catalogue with Checklists of the Letters and Related Documents in the Delius Collection of the Grainger Museum, University of Melbourne, Australia.* 233 pp. London: Delius Trust, 1981.

6.124 Lowe, Rachel. *Frederick Delius, 1862–1934: A Reprint of the Catalogue of the Music Archive of the Delius Trust, 1974, with Minor Corrections.* 183 pp. London: Delius Trust, 1986.

First published, 1974.

A list of the printed music held by the Delius Trust as part of the original accession (pp. 177–79).

The 1974 ed. is reviewed by Don Gillespie in *Notes* 32 (1976): 547–58, by Clifford Bartlett in *Brio* 12 (1975): 19–20, and by J. A. Westrup in *M&L* 56 (1975): 407.

6.125* Threlfall, Robert. *A Catalogue of the Compositions of Frederick Delius: Sources and References.* 206 pp. London: Delius Trust/Boosey & Hawkes, 1977.

6.126* Threlfall, Robert. *Frederick Delius: A Supplementary Catalogue.* 252 pp. London: Delius Trust/Boosey & Hawkes, 1986.

Reviewed by Ann P. Basart in *CNV* 135 (1989): 27 and by Stephen Banfield in *M&L* 69 (1988): 292–93.

Diamond, David

6.127* Kimberling, Victoria J. *David Diamond: A Bio-Bibliography.* 192 pp. Metuchen, N.J.: Scarecrow Press, 1987.

Reviewed by Bonnie Jo Dopp in *Notes* 47 (1990): 386 and by Jay Weitz in *Fontes* 36 (1984): 246–47.

Donizetti, Gaetano

6.128 *Il Museo Donizettiano: Catalogo.* 273 pp. Bergamo: Centro di Studi Donizettiana, 1970.

First published in 1936.

A description of an important collection of Donizettiana. The present ed. gives a brief historical introduction, followed by a table of important Donizetti performances between 1946 and 1969. The *Catalogo* proper (pp. 53–273) is subdivided into six parts: autographs and manuscripts, musical publications, theatrical publications, letters and documents, iconography, and artifacts.

Dvořák, Antonín

6.129* Cervinková, Blanká. *Antonín Dvořák (8.9.1841–1.5.1904): bibiograficky katalog / bibliographical catalogue.* 187 pp. Prague: Mestská knihovna, 1991.

A catalog in Czech and English of the printed Dvořák editions, sound recordings, and literature in the Lestske knihovny (City Library) and the Narodni knihovny (National Library) in Prague.

6.130* Yoell, John H. *Antonín Dvořák on Record.* 152 pp. New York: Greenwood Press, 1991. (Discographies, 46)

A selective discography of recordings of Dvořák's work on record, inspired by the deletion of the discography feature from the new Dvořák thematic catalog (**6.129**). The introduction gives an overview of historical Dvořák recordings, from 1901 to the years just following World War II. The discography is organized by basic format (stage works, large-scale choral works, orchestra works, chamber music, keyboard works, solo songs and vocal duets, choral songs, part-songs, and arrangements). There are works and performer indexes.

Elgar, Edward

6.131* Craggs, Stewart R. *Edward Elgar: A Source Book.* Aldershot, England: Scholar Press; Brookfield, Vt.: Ashgate Pub. Co., 1995.

A biographical outline and chronology of the composer's life is combined with a comprehensive bibliography, arranged chronologically by work.

6.132* Kent, Christopher. *Edward Elgar: A Guide to Research.* 523 pp. New York: Garland Publishing, 1993. 523 pp. (Garland reference library of the humanities, 1017) (Garland composer resource manuals, 37)

Falla, Manuel De

6.133 Chase, Gilbert, and **Andrew Budwig.** *Manuel de Falla: A Bibliography and Research Guide.* 145 pp. New York: Garland Publishing, 1986. (Garland composer resource manuals, 4) (Garland reference library of the humanities, 561)

Reviewed by A. F. Leighton Thomas in *MR* 47 (1987–88): 147, by Ronald Crichton in *MT* 128 (1987): 26, by William Brockman in *ARBA* 18 (1987): no. 1220, and by Ann P. Basart in *CNV* 105 (1986): 11.

6.134* Gallego Gallego, Antonio. *Catálogo de obras de Manuel de Falla.* 293 pp. Madrid: Ministerio de Cultura, Dirección General de Bellas Artes y Archivos, 1987.

Farwell, Arthur

6.135* Farwell, Brice. *A Guide to the Music of Arthur Farwell and to the Microfilm Collection of His Work.* 138 pp. Briarcliff Manor, N.Y.: Issued by Brice Farwell for the estate of Arthur Farwell, 1972.
First issued 1971, 130 pp.
Reviewed by H. Wiley Hitchcock in *Notes* 28 (1972): 450–51.

Fauré, Gabriel

6.136 Nectoux, Jean Michel. *Gabriel Fauré: 1900–1977.* 262 pp. Paris: Bibliothèque Nationale, Département de la Phonothèque Nationale et de l'Audiovisuel, 1979. (Phonographies, 1)
A discography whose preface provides Fauré's recording history.
Reviewed by Michael H. Gray in *Fontes* 32 (1985): 150–51, by David Hamilton in *Notes* 37 (1980): 324–26, and by J. F. Weber in *ARSCJ* 12 (1980): 270–72.

Ferrabosco, Alfonso

6.137* Charteris, Richard. *Alfonso Ferrabosco the Elder (1543–1588): A Thematic Catalogue of His Music: With a Biographical Calendar.* 227 pp. New York: Pendragon Press, 1984. (Thematic catalogues, 11)
Reviewed by David Butchart in *EM* 14 (1986): 419–20 and by Patrick Macey in *JAMS* 39 (1986): 650–53.

Field, John

6.138 Hopkinson, Cecil. *A Bibliographical Thematic Catalogue of the Works of John Field.* xxiii + 175 pp. London: The author, 1961.

Foote, Arthur

6.139 Cipolla, Wilma Reid. *A Catalog of the Works of Arthur Foote, 1853–1937.* xxi + 193 pp. Detroit, Mich.: Published for the College Music Society by Information Coordinators, 1980. (Bibliographies in American music, 6)
A thorough bibliography of the published and unpublished compositions, also documenting some of the work of the Boston publisher A.P. Schmidt.
Reviewed by Robert Skinner in *ARBA* 12 (1981): no. 1036.

Foss, Lukas

6.140* Perone, Karen L. *Lukas Foss: A Bio-Bibliography.* 282 pp. Westport, Conn.: Greenwood Press, 1991. (Bio-bibliographies in music, 37)
Reviewed by Byron Adams in *Notes* 48 (1992): 1,299–1,301.

Foster, Stephen Collins

6.141* Elliker, Calvin. *Stephen Collins Foster: A Guide to Research.* 197 pp. New York: Garland Publishing, 1988. (Garland composer resource manuals, 10) (Garland reference library of the humanities, 782)
Reviewed by Tim Cherubini in *Fontes* 36 (1989): 244–46.

6.142* Fuld, James J. *A Pictorial Bibliography of the First Editions of Stephen C. Foster.* 28 pp. + 179 facsimile pp. Philadelphia, Pa.: Musical Americana, 1957.
A bibliography of 204 numbered entries, selected to establish Foster's first editions.
Reviewed by Richard S. Hill in *Notes* 15 (1957): 105–6.

6.143 Whittlesey, Walter R., and **O. G. Sonneck.** *Catalogue of First Editions of Stephen C. Foster (1826–1864).* 79 pp. Washington, D.C.: Government Printing Office, 1915.
A pioneering bibliographic study of the composer. Works are arranged by title and indexed by authors of text, publishers, and first lines. There are detailed annotations. As recounted by Calvin Elliker in the Krummel Festschrift (**13.15**), Josiah Lilly depended on this bibliography to establish the collection in his Stephen Foster Memorial, Pittsburgh.

Franz, Robert

6.144 Boonin, Joseph M. *An Index to the Solo Songs of Robert Franz.* 19 pp. Hackensack, N.J.: J. Boonin, 1970.
A list of Franz's songs by opus numbers; a brief survey of their publishing history, including the various collections issued in the late 19th century; a title and first-line index; and a list of the poets whose work was set by Franz.

Frescobaldi, Girolamo

6.145 Hammond, Frederick. *Girolamo Frescobaldi: A Guide to Research.* 412 pp. New York: Garland Publishing, 1988. (Garland reference library of the humanities, 672) (Garland composer resource manuals, 9)
Reviewed by John E. Druesedow, Jr., in *ARBA* 20 (1989): no. 1204.

6.146 Mischiati, Oscar. "Catalogo delle Edizioni Originali delle Opere di Girolamo Frescobaldi." In *Frescobaldi e il suo tempo,* pp. 45–72. Venice: Marsilio, 1983.
The first systematic bibliographic descriptions, organized chronologically, of the early printed editions of Frescobaldi, including transcriptions of the title pages, dedications, and notices to the reader. There are lists of contents for each publication.

Gade, Niels W.

6.147 Fog, Dan. *N. W. Gade-katalog: En fortegnelse over Niels W. Gades trykte kompositioner / Verzeichnis der im Druck erschienenen Kompositionen von Niels W. Gade (1817–1890).* 96 pp. Copenhagen: D. Fog, 1986.

Gassmann, Florian Leopold

6.148 Hill, George R. *A Thematic Catalog of the Instrumental Music of Florian Leopold Gassmann.* 171 pp. Hackensack, N.J.: J. Boonin, 1976. (Music indexes and bibliographies, 12)

Reviewed by Malcolm S. Cole in *Notes* 34 (1977): 596–97.

Geminiani, Francesco

6.149* Careri, Enrico. *Francesco Geminiani (1687–1762): Part I, Life and Works; Part 2: Thematic Catalogue.* 300 pp. Oxford: Oxford University Press, 1993.
Reviewed by Sandra Mangsen in *M&L* 76 (1995): 100–3.

Gershwin, George

6.150* Rimler, Walter. *A Gershwin Companion: A Critical Inventory & a Discography, 1916–1984.* 498 pp. Ann Arbor, Mich.: Popular Culture, 1991. (PCI collector editions)
A list of the composer's works, with a discography provided for each title.

6.151 Schwartz, Charles. *George Gershwin: A Selective Bibliography and Discography.* 118 pp. Detroit, Mich.: Information Coordinators for the College Music Society, 1974. (Bibliographies in American music, 1)
A bibliography that includes a chronology. The discography covers concert and operatic works, song collections, and musicals.

Glanville-Hicks, Peggy

6.152* Hayes, Deborah. *Peggy Glanville-Hicks: A Bio-Bibliography.* 274 pp. New York: Greenwood Press, 1990. (Bio-bibliographies in music, 27)
Reviewed by James R. Briscoe in *Notes* 48 (1991): 535–37.

Gluck, Christoph Willibald Von

6.153 Hopkinson, Cecil. *A Bibliography of the Printed Works of C. W. von Gluck, 1714–1787.* 2nd revised and augmented ed. New York: Broude, 1967.
The 1st ed. was published in London as *A Bibliography of the Works of C. W. von Gluck, 1714–1787,* 79 pp.

6.154* Howard, Patricia. *Christoph Willibald Gluck: A Guide to Research.* xxiii + 178 pp. New York: Garland Publishing, 1987. (Garland composer resource manuals, 8) (Garland reference library of the humanities, 716)
Reviewed by Jeremy Hayes in *M&L* 70 (1989): 94–95 and by George Louis Mayer in *ARBA* 20 (1989): no. 1205.

Godowsky, Leopold

6.155* Saxe, Leonard S. "The Published Music of Leopold Godowsky." In *Notes* 14 (1957): 165–83.
A thorough works list including original compositions, paraphrases, and educational materials.

Gottschalk, Louis Moreau

6.156 Doyle, John G. *Louis Moreau Gottschalk, 1829–1869: A Bibliographical Study and Catalog of Works.* 386 pp. Detroit, Mich.: Published for the College Music Society by Information Coordinators, 1982. (Bibliographies in American music, 7)
A works list, with an extensive bibliography of literature about the composer.
Reviewed by H. Wiley Hitchcock in *Fontes* 30 (1983): 168–70, by John Kirkpatrick in *AM* 3 (1985): 359–60, and by Guy A. Marco in *ARBA* 15 (1984): no. 909.

6.157 Offergeld, Robert. *The Centennial Catalogue of the Published and Unpublished Compositions of Louis Moreau Gottschalk: Prepared for Stereo Review.* 34 pp. New York: Ziff-Davis Publishing Company, 1970.

A catalog whose introduction discusses Gottschalk's output and the state of research based on the source materials, followed by an annotated list of 298 compositions. The annotations are entertaining and informative. This is a model of bibliographic technique.

Reviewed by Alan Mandel in *Notes* 28 (1971): 42–43.

Grainger, Percy

6.158* Balough, Teresa. *A Complete Catalogue of the Works of Percy Grainger.* 255 pp. Nedlands, Australia: Department of Music, University of Western Australia, 1975. (Music monograph, 2)

Reviewed by Clifford Bartlett in *Brio* 13 (1976): 56 and by Stephen M. Fry in *Notes* 33 (1977): 604.

6.159* Lewis, Thomas P. *A Source Guide to the Music of Percy Grainger.* 339 pp. White Plains, N.Y.: Pro/Am Music Resources, Inc., 1991. (Pro/Am general music series, GMS 7)

Granados, Enrique

6.160* Hess, Carol A. *Enrique Granados: A Bio-Bibliography.* 192 pp. New York: Greenwood Press, 1991. (Bio-bibliographies in music, 42)

Griffes, Charles Tomlinson

6.161 Anderson, Donna K. *Charles T. Griffes: An Annotated Bibliography-Discography.* 255 pp. Detroit, Mich.: Information Coordinators, 1977. (Bibliographies in American music, 3)

A bibliography of 525 items, including books, dissertations, theses, and program notes, "selected, but rather complete," listing reviews of important performances; over half the entries are pre-1925. There are chronologies of Griffes's life and works, a complete list of published works and first performances, and an index of performers. The discography is arranged first by record number and then by title.

Reviewed by Peter Dickinson in *MT* 120 (1979): 489–90, by A. F. Leighton Thomas in *MR* 42 (1981): 61–62, by Himie Voxman in *Fontes* 25 (1978): 275–76, and by Stephen M. Fry in *Notes* 34 (1978): 878.

6.162* Anderson, Donna K. *The Works of Charles T. Griffes: A Descriptive Catalogue.* 566 pp. Ann Arbor, Mich.: UMI Research Press, 1983. (Studies in musicology, 68)

A thorough, meticulously documented list of the short-lived composer's output, classified by format, with accompanying essays on each format covered (songs, piano music, etc.) and detailed descriptions of Griffes's sketchbooks and unfinished works, the latter also classified. The seven appendixes include chronological lists of completed work and of fragments, a list of poets and texts, and works available for rental.

Reviews by Peter Dickinson in *MT* 126 (1985): 349 and by Robert Kenselaar in *Notes* 43 (1985): 519–20.

Guido d'Arezzo

6.163* Waelther, Ernst Ludwig. *Wortindex zu den echten Schriften Guidos von Arezzo.* Edited by Michael Bernhard. 174 pp. Munich: Verlag der Bayerischen Akademie; C.H. Beck, 1979. (Veröffentlichungen der Musikhistorischen Kommission, 2)

Reviewed by Christian Meyer in *Revue de musicologie* 66 (1980): 96–97 no. 1.

Guillaume de Machaut

6.164* Earp, Lawrence. *Guillaume de Machaut: A Guide to Research.* 669 pp. New York: Garland Publishing, 1995. (Garland composer resource manuals, 36) (Garland reference library of the humanities, 996)

The standard bio-bibliographical format, superbly done, with a discography (pp. 389–445), bibliography (pp. 447–620), and indexes.

Handel, George Frideric

6.165 Bell, A. Craig. *Handel: A Chronological Thematic Catalogue.* 452 pp. Darley, England: Grian-Aig Press, 1972.

First published as *Chronological Catalogue of Handel's Work,* 1969.

A catalog containing some 3,000 thematic incipits. The appendixes list spurious and doubtful works, unpublished and lost works, and works with opus numbers. There are indexes by librettists, instrumental and vocal titles, and instrumental interludes. Includes a classified index and a first-line index.

6.166* Best, Terence. *Handel Collections and Their History.* 252 pp. Oxford: Clarendon Press; New York: Oxford University Press, 1993.

A conference proceedings.

Reviewed by Richard G. King in *M&L* 76 (1995): 427–31 and by Richard Luckett in *MT* 135 (1994): 292–93.

6.167* Burrows, Donald, and **Martha J. Ronish.** *A Catalogue of Handel's Musical Autographs.* xxxviii + 332 pp. Oxford: Clarendon Press; New York: Oxford University Press, 1994.

A full description of the physical characteristics and musical contents of about 7,800 leaves. The text section is followed by about 200 pages of watermark reproductions. The resulting datings should also be helpful in the study of other composers.

Reviewed by Winton Dean in *M&L* 76 (1995): 619–20 and by Katharine Hogg in *Brio* 32 (1995): 39–40.

6.168* Clausen, Hans Dieter. *Händels Direktionspartituren (Handexemplare).* 281 pp. Hamburg: Verlag der Musikalienhandlung, 1972. (Hamburger Beiträge zur Musikwissenschaft, 7)

A catalog of the autograph conducting scores used by Handel, almost all now housed in the Stadt- und Universitätsbibliothek, Hamburg, listing each manuscript's contents, describing the watermarks, copyists, and performance changes and designations. These scores were used by Chrysander for his Handel *Gesamtausgabe.*

Reviewed by Winton Dean in *MT* 116 (1975): 45–48.

6.169 Eisen, Walter, and **Margret Eisen.** *Händel-Handbuch.* 4 vols. Kassel, Germany: Bärenreiter, 1978–85.

Contents: Vol. 1, *Lebens- und Schaffensdaten* by Siegfried Flesch and *Thematisch-systematisches Verzeichnis, Bühnenwerke* by Bernd Baselt; Vol. 2, *Thematisch-systematisches Verzeichnis: Oratorische Werke; Vokale Kammermusik; Kirchenmusik* (1984, 800 pp.) by Bernd Baselt; Vol. 3, *Thematisch-systematisches Verzeichnis: Instrumentalmusik, Pasticci und Fragmente* (1986, 442 pp.) by Bernd Baselt; Vol. 4, *Dokumente zu Leben und Schaffen* by Otto Erich Deutsch.

The 1st vol. is reviewed by Hugh Cobbe in *Notes* 36 (1980): 883–84. The 2nd vol. is reviewed by Clifford Bartlett in *Brio* 22 (1985): 60–62 and by Mary Ann Parker-Hale in *JAMS* 39 (1986): 655–63. The 3rd vol. is reviewed by Clifford Bartlett in *Brio* 24 (1987): 73–76 and by Terence Best in *M&L* 69 (1988): 66–67.

6.170* Parker-Hale, Mary Ann. *G. F. Handel: A Guide to Research.* 294 pp. New York: Garland Publishing, 1988. (Garland composer resource manuals, 19) (Garland reference library of the humanities, 717)

Reviewed by C. Steven LaRue in *Notes* 48 (1992): 867–68 and by George Louis Mayer in *ARBA* 21 (1990): no. 1250.

6.171 Sasse, Konrad. *Händel Bibliographie: Zusammendt unter Verwendung des im Händel-Jahrbuch 1933 von Kurt Taut veröffentlichten Verzeichnisses des Schrifttums über Georg Friedrich*

Händel, Abgeschlossen im Jahre 1961. 2nd ed., with a supplement for the years 1962–65. 432 pp. Leipzig: Deutscher Verlag für Musik, 1967.

The 1st ed., 352 pp., was published in 1963.

The expansion of a bibliography compiled by Kurt Taut for the 1933 *Händel-Jahrbuch,* with a supplement by Sasse from the 1955 *Jahrbuch.* A highly organized work citing literature on every aspect of the composer's life and work. There is an author index.

Reviewed by Willi Reich in *Literature, Music, Fine Arts* 1 (1968): 87–89.

6.172 Smith, William C. *Handel: A Descriptive Catalogue of the Early Editions.* 2nd ed. with supplement. 378 pp. Oxford: B. Blackwell, 1970.

First published by Cassell, London, in 1960, 366 pp.

A revised ed. whose Supplement, pp. 331–40, brings the information up to date.

Hanson, Howard

6.173* Perone, James E. *Howard Hanson: A Bio-Bibliography.* 327 pp. Westport, Conn.: Greenwood Press. (Bio-bibliographies in music, 47)

Reviewed by Robert Palmieri in *ARBA* 25 (1994): no. 1330.

Harris, Roy

6.174* Stehman, Dan. *Roy Harris: A Bio-Bibliography.* 475 pp. Westport, Conn.: Greenwood Press, 1991. (Bio-bibliographies in music, 40)

Reviewed by Bill F. Faucett in *Notes* 49 (1991): 612–13.

Hartmann, Karl Amadeus

6.175 McCredie, Andrew D. *Karl Amadeus Hartmann: Thematic Catalogue of His Works.* 227 pp. Wilhelmshaven, Germany: Edition Heinrichshofen; New York: C.F. Peters, 1982. (Catalogues of musical sources / Quellenkataloge zur Musikgeschichte, 18)

Hasse, Johann Adolph

6.176 Hansell, Sven Hostrup. *Works for Solo Voice of Johann Adolph Hasse, 1699–1783.* 110 pp. Detroit, Mich.: Information Coordinators, 1968. (Detroit studies in music bibliography, 12)

Reviewed by Robert L. Marshall in *Die Musikforschung* 24 (1971): 463–64 and by Owen Jander in *Notes* 25 (1969): 722–23.

Haydn, Joseph

6.177* Brown, A. Peter, James T. Berkenstock, and **Carol Vanderbilt Brown.** *Joseph Haydn in Literature: A Bibliography.* 180 pp. (pp. 173–352). Munich: G. Henle, 1974. (Haydn-Studien, 3, 3–4)

Reviewed by J. A. Westrup in *M&L* 56 (1975): 78–79.

6.178 Bryant, Stephen C., and **Gary W. Chapman.** *Melodic Index to Haydn's Instrumental Music: A Thematic Locator for Anthony van Hoboken's Thematisch-bibliographisches Werkverzeichnis, Volumes I and III.* 100 pp. New York: Pendragon Press, 1982. (Thematic catalogues, 8)

A source easing the user's access to Hoboken's monumental thematic catalog (**6.181**).

Reviewed by Catherine Massip in *Fontes* 31 (1984): 134 and by Karl Geiringer in *Notes* 41 (1984): 70–71.

6.179 Fuchs, Aloys. *Joseph Haydn: Thematisches Verzeichnis sämtlichen Kompositionen: Facsimile-Ausgabe.* Edited by Richard Schaal. 204 pp. Wilhelmshaven, Germany: Heinrichshofen's Verlag, 1968. (Quellenkataloge zur Musikgeschichte, 2)

A thematic catalog of Haydn's works, compiled by Viennese collector Aloys Fuchs and published in 1839, reproduced in facsimile.

Reviewed by H. C. Robbins Landon in the *Haydn Yearbook* 6 (1969): 217–18.

6.180* Grave, Floyd K., and **Margaret G. Grave.** *Franz Joseph Haydn: A Guide to Research.* 451 pp. New York: Garland Publishing, 1990. (Garland reference library of the humanities, 740) (Garland composer resource manuals, 31)

Reviewed by Hollace A. Schafer in *Notes* 48 (1992): 1,256–58, by A. Peter Brown in *M&L* 72 (1991): 595, and by Denis McCaldin in *MT* 132 (1991): 349–50.

6.181 Hoboken, Anthony van. *Joseph Haydn: Thematisch-Bibliographisches Werkverzeichnis.* 3 vols. Mainz: B. Schott's Söhne, 1957–78.

Also issued separately were *Beilage zu Band I* and *Beilage zu Band I und II.*

Contents: Band I, *Instrumentalwerke* (xxi + 848 pp.). Band II, *Vocalwerke*. Band III, *Register; Addenda und Corrigenda.*

The standard classified thematic catalog organizing the works of Joseph Haydn, with information on autographs, manuscripts, and early printed editions. There are extensive appendixes: an analysis of early printed collections and "complete" works, a concordance from the opus numbering scheme to the Hoboken *Gruppe* and item numbers, an index to publishers, an index to common or local names for various Haydn works, a list of institutions holding manuscripts, a list by *Gruppe* and item number to the autographs, a title and text incipit index to vocal music, and an index to persons, institutions, and works. The editor gives a preliminary report on his project in "The First Thematic Catalog of Haydn's Works," *Notes* 9 (1952): 226–27.

The 1st vol. is reviewed by Otto Erich Deutsch in *MR* 18 (1957): 330–36, by Karl Geiringer in *Notes* 14 (1957): 565–66, and by Rosemary Hughes in *M&L* 39 (1958): 86–90. The 2nd vol. is reviewed by H. C. Robbins Landon in *Haydn Yearbook* 9 (1975): 361–64, by Karl Geiringer in *JAMS* 25 (1972): 471–73, by James Webster in *Notes* 29 (1972): 234–36, and by Alan Tyson in *MT* 115 (1974): 657–58. The 3rd vol. is reviewed by George Hill in *Notes* 36 (1979): 102–3 and by David Wyn Jones in *Haydn Yearbook* 11 (1980): 199–204.

6.182* Jaenecke, Joachim. *Joseph und Michael Haydn: Autographe und Abschriften: Katalog.* 401 pp. Munich: G. Henle, 1990. (Staatsbibliothek Preussischer Kulturbesitz Kataloge der Musikabteilung. Reihe 1, Handschriften, 4)

6.183 Lowens, Irving. *Haydn in America*, with *Haydn Autographs in the United States,* by Otto B. Albrecht. 134 pp. Detroit, Mich.: Published for the College Music Society by Information Coordinators, 1979. (Bibliographies in American music, 5)

A dual effort documenting performances and publications in the United States of Joseph Haydn's works, as well as listing American locations of Haydn's autograph manuscripts.

Reviewed by Jens Peter Larsen in *AM* 2 (1984): 82–86 and by John E. Druesedow, Jr., in *ARBA* 12 (1981): no. 1039.

6.184 Vecsay, Jeno. *Haydn Compositions in the Music Collection of the National Széchényi, Budapest; Published on the Occasion of the 150th Anniversary of Haydn's Death (1809–1959).* 167 pp. Budapest: Publishing House of the Hungarian Academy of Sciences, 1960.

Also published in Hungarian and German.

A classified list of 372 items, 72 of which are Haydn autographs. There are also 42 facsimiles of manuscripts, prints, and other documents related to the composer's career.

Haydn, Michael

6.185* Sherman, Charles H., and **T. Donley Thomas.** *Johann Michael Haydn (1737–1806): A Chronological Thematic Catalogue of His Works.* 385 pp. Stuyvesant, N.Y.: Pendragon Press, 1992. (Thematic catalogues, 17)

The first modern catalog of Michael Haydn's works, omitting spurious compositions. Reviewed by James B. Beston in *ARBA* 25 (1994): no. 1332 and by Heikki Poroila in *Fontes* 42 (1995): 189–90.

Hensel, Fanny Mendelssohn

6.186* Klein, Hans-Günter. *Die Kompositionen Fanny Hensels in Autographen und Abschriften aus dem Besitz der Staatsbibliothek zu Berlin, Preussischer Kulturbesitz.* 146 pp. Tutzing, Germany: H. Schneider, 1995. (Musikbibliographische Arbeiten, 13)

Henze, Hans Werner

6.187 Rexroth, Dieter. *Der Komponist Hans Werner Henze: Ein Buch der Alten Oper Frankfurt, Frankfurt Feste '86.* 382 pp. Mainz; New York: Schott, 1986.

A handbook that includes material by Henze, a Henze Werkverzeichnis (pp. 341–82), and bibliographical references.

Hewitt, John Hill

6.188 Hoogerwerf, Frank W. *John Hill Hewitt: Sources and Bibliography.* 42 pp. Atlanta, Ga.: Emory General Libraries, 1981.

A guide giving a clear overview to the collection on Hewitt, a 19th-century American composer of songs and ballads who was active in all aspects of the popular theater; the collection is housed in the Woodruff Library, Emory University.

Reviewed by John W. Wagner in *AM* 3 (1985): 93–94.

Hill, Edward Burlingame

6.189* Tyler, Linda L. *Edward Burlingame Hill: A Bio-Bibliography.* 168 pp. New York: Greenwood Press, 1989. (Bio-bibliographies in music, 21)

Reviewed by John E. Druesedow, Jr., in *ARBA* 21 (1990): no. 1255 and by Bill F. Faucett in *Notes* 48 (1991): 493–95.

Hindemith, Paul

6.190* Miller, Carl S. *The Paul Hindemith Collection: Yale University Music Library Archival Collection Mss 47.* 162 ll. New Haven, Conn.: Yale University Music Library, 1994

An inventory, with index, of the collection.

6.191* *Paul Hindemith: Werkverzeichnis / List of Works.* 75 pp. Mainz; New York: Schott, 1985.

A catalog of Hindemith's works, by his main publisher.

Holst, Gustav

6.192 Holst, Imogen. *A Thematic Catalogue of Gustav Holst's Music.* 285 pp. London: Faber Music Ltd., in association with G. and I. Holst, 1974.

Reviewed by J. A. Westrup in *M&L* 56 (1975): 88.

Howells, Herbert

6.193* *Herbert Howells: The Music Manuscripts in the Royal College of Music Library.* 79 pp. London: Royal College of Music, 1992.

"A detailed shelf finding guide to the largest single source of Howells manuscripts." Reviewed by William A. Everett in *Notes* 51 (1994): 611–13.

Husa, Karel

6.194* Hitchens, Susan Hayes. *Karel Husa: A Bio-Bibliography.* 166 pp. Westport, Conn.: Greenwood Press, 1991. (Bio-bibliographies in music, 31)
Reviewed by Bonna J. Boettcher in *Notes* 48 (1992): 886–87.

Ireland, John

6.195* Craggs, Stewart R. *John Ireland: A Catalogue, Discography and Bibliography.* 161 pp. Oxford: Oxford University Press, 1993.
Published in association with the John Ireland Trust, a chronological list of all of Ireland's compositions from 1895 to 1961, giving full details of composition dates, dedication or commissioning, instrumentation, duration, first performance, publication, location of the autograph manuscript, critical commentaries in the bibliography, and significant recordings, as well as notes in the form of commentaries on the work's background, lost works, commissions that did not come to fruition, and biographical information about the composer and dedicatees.
Reviewed by Michael Hurd in *M&L* 75 (1994): 308–9, by William A. Everett in *Notes* 51 (1994): 611–13, and by Heikki Poroila in *Fontes* 42 (1995): 189–90.

Isaac, Heinrich

6.196* Picker, Martin. *Henricus Isaac: A Guide to Research.* 308 pp. New York: Garland, 1991. (Garland composer resource manuals, 35) (Garland reference library of the humanities, 897)
A research guide in the established format. The 3rd section is on Isaac sources and lists about 300 renaissance manuscripts and print with at least one Isaac work. The discography has almost 100 albums, dating from 1951 to 1990; most entries are long-playing records, but audio cassettes and compact discs are also included.
Reviewed by Thomas Noblitt in *Notes* 49 (1992): 538–39, by Christian Meyer in *Revue de musicologie* 78 (1992): 334–35, and by Allan W. Atlas, with addenda, in *M&L* 73 (1992): 568–69.

Ives, Charles

6.197* Block, Geoffrey. *Charles Ives: A Bio-Bibliography.* 422 pp. New York: Greenwood Press, 1988. (Bio-bibliographies in music, 14)
Reviewed by Dominique-René de Lerma in *ARBA* 20 (1989): no. 1195, by Thomas Winters in *Notes* 49 (1992): 133–34, and by Ann P. Basart in *CNV* 130 (1989): 9–10.

6.198* De Lerma, Dominique-René. *Charles Edward Ives, 1874–1954: A Bibliography of His Music.* 212 pp. Kent, Ohio: Kent State University Press, 1970.
A bibliography with a works list, arranged alphabetically. There are indexes of publishers, medium, chronology, arrangers, poets and librettists, phonorecords, and performers.

6.199* Henderson, Clayton W. *The Charles Ives Tunebook.* 292 pp. Warren, Mich.: Published for the College Music Society by Harmonie Park Press, 1990. (Bibliographies in American music, 14)
A classified list (hymns, patriotic songs, etc.) of the tunes used by Ives.
Reviewed by Peter Dickinson in *M&L* 74 (1993): 116–17, by Harriette Hemmasi in *Fontes* 39 (1992): 196–97, and by Geoffrey Block in *Notes* 49 (1992): 134–36.

6.200 Kirkpatrick, John. *A Temporary Mimeographed Catalog of the Music Manuscripts and Related Materials of Charles Edward Ives.* 279 pp. New Haven, Conn.: Yale School of Music, 1960.
A catalog, typescript-reproduced, compiled 1954–60, of the Ives collection housed in Yale's library.

6.201 Warren, Richard, Jr *Charles E. Ives: Discography.* 124 pp. New Haven, Conn.: Yale University Library, 1972. (Historical sound recordings publication series, 1)

A discography of every recording in the Charles E. Ives Collection, Jackson Music Library, Yale University, including all known commercial recordings. The arrangement is alphabetical order by title of work; the entries include Kirkpatrick's numbers for the works of Ives, the names of performers, and recording information. Includes a supplement listing radio and TV broadcasts about Ives and another listing recorded interviews and comments on Ives and his music. There is an index of performers.

Reviewed by Michael H. Gray in *Notes* 31 (1974): 63–66.

Janáček, Leoš

6.202* Simeone, Nigel. *The First Editions of Leos Janácek: A Bibliographical Catalogue with Reproductions of Title Pages.* 316 pp. Tutzing, Germany: H. Schneider, 1991. (Musikbibliographische Arbeiten, 11)

A record of first publications, with half-sized reproductions of the title pages of each work listed.

Reviewed by Damjana Bratuz in *Notes* 49 (1993): 1,029–30 and by John Tyrrell in *M&L* 74 (1993): 109–10.

Josquin des Prez

6.203 Charles, Sydney Robinson. *Josquin des Prez: A Guide to Research.* 235 pp. New York: Garland Publishing, 1983. (Garland composer resource manuals, 2) (Garland reference library of the humanities, 330)

An introduction to research on Josquin, presenting a summary of the sources documenting Josquin's life, with references to the literature discussing each document. It provides a categorical list of works about Josquin's music with two tables (pp. 18–19) showing the organization of the *Collected Works,* and a list of compositions showing sources, bibliography, recordings, and modern editions of each work. Includes a list of sources with modern editions and literature about each cited, a discography with title index, a bibliography of works cited, and an index to names of persons, places, and titles.

Reviewed by Allie Wise Goudy in *ARBA* 16 (1985): no. 1187, by John Milsom in *M&L* 66 (1985): 276–77, by A. F. Leighton Thomas in *MR* 47 (1986–87): 146+, by Richard Andrewes in *MT* 126 (1985): 467, and by Richard Taruskin in *Notes* 42 (1985): 39–41.

Kaye, Ulysses

6.204* Hobson, Constance Tibbs, and **Deborra A. Richardson.** *Ulysses Kay: A Bio-Bibliography.* 216 pp. Westport, Conn.: Greenwood Press, 1994. (Bio-bibliographies in music, 53)

The biography, chronological works list, bibliography, and discography of an active African-American composer of over 135 works for a variety of formats.

Reviewed by Dominique-René de Lerma in *ARBA* 26 (1995): no. 1266.

Koechlin, Charles

6.205* *Catalogue des oeuvres de Charles Koechlin.* Introduction by Henri Sauguet. liv + 109 pp. Paris: Max Eschig, 1975.

Reviewed by Elise K. Kirk in *Notes* 34 (1978): 613–14.

Krenek, Ernst

6.206* Bowles, Garrett H. *Ernst Krenek: A Bio-Bibliography.* 428 pp. New York: Greenwood Press, 1989. (Bio-bibliographies in music, 22)

Reviewed by Milton H. Crouch in *ARBA* 21 (1990): no. 1240, by Glenn Glasow in *Notes* 47 (1990): 377–79, and by Ann P. Basart in *CNV* 135 (1989): 25–26.

Kuhlau, Friedrich

6.207 Fog, Dan. *Kompositionen von Fridr. Kuhlau: Thematisch-Bibliographischer Katalog.* 203 pp. Copenhagen: Dan Fog Musikverlag, 1976.

The first complete catalog of Kuhlau's works, listing 233 items, with an index of titles and text incipits and an index to personal names.

Reviewed by June C. Ottenberg in *Notes* 35 (1978): 84–85 and by François Lesure in *Fontes* 24 (1977): 193–94.

Langlais, Jean

6.208* Thomerson, Kathleen. *Jean Langlais: A Bio-Bibliography.* 191 pp. New York: Greenwood Press, 1988. (Bio-bibliographies in music, 10)

Discography, pp. 57–96; bibliography, pp. 97–160.

Reviewed by George Louis Mayer in *ARBA* 20 (1989): no. 1212 and by Kay Norton in *Notes* 47 (1991): 760–62.

Lanner, Joseph

6.209 Weinmann, Alexander. *Verzeichnis der im Druck erschienenen Werke von Joseph Lanner, sowie Listen der Plattennummern der Originalausgaben für alle Besetzungen.* 31 pp. Vienna: Leuen, 1948. (Beiträge zur Geschichte des Alt-Wiener Musikverlages, 1/1)

Tables listing the work of Lanner (1801–43) in opus number order, with plate numbers of the first editions. There is an alphabetical index of works by title.

Lasso, Orlando di

6.210 Erb, James. *Orlando di Lasso: A Guide to Research.* xxxiv + 357 pp. New York: Garland Publishing, 1990. (Garland reference library of the humanities, 982) (Garland composer resource manuals, 25)

A composer research guide including a brief biography, works lists, bibliography (most thorough 1978), and discography, with guides to the two incomplete collected editions.

Reviewed by Tim Carter in *EM* 20 (1992): 154–57, by Noel O'Regan in *M&L* 74 (1993): 63–65, and by David Crook in *Notes* 49 (1992): 86–87.

Ligeti, György

6.211* Richart, Robert. *György Ligeti: A Bio-Bibliography.* 188 pp. Westport, Conn: Greenwood Press, 1991. (Bio-bibliographies in music, 30)

Reviewed by Alan Green in *Notes* 48 (1992): 885–86.

Liszt, Franz

6.212* Auman, Elizabeth, and **Raymond A. White.** *The Music Manuscripts, First Editions, and Correspondence of Franz Liszt (1811–1886) in the Collections of the Music Division, Library of Congress.* 126 pp. Washington, D.C.: Library of Congress, 1991.

6.213 Eckhardt, Mária P. *Liszt's Music Manuscripts in the National Széchényi Library, Budapest.* Trans. by Erzsébet Mészáros, revised by Rena Mueller. 252 pp. Budapest: Akadémiai Kiado; Stuyvesant, N.Y.: Pendragon Press, 1986. (Studies in Central and Eastern European music, 2)

6.214* Saffle, Michael. *Franz Liszt: A Guide to Research.* 407 pp. New York: Garland Publishing, 1991. (Composer resource manuals, 29) (Garland reference library of the humanities, 754)

An examination of Liszt research from the 1830s to the present, including a biographical sketch of Liszt's activities, a brief summary of his compositions and literary works, a study of lacunae in Liszt studies, a list of important Liszt archives, a description of Liszt societies and their publications, a short Liszt dictionary, a chapter on important performances and festivals dating from 1986 (the international Liszt year), an essay on Liszt in film, a selected discography, and index. The bibliography cites hundreds of secondary sources in English, German, French, Italian, Hungarian, Romanian, Russian, Spanish, and Portuguese. References are also included to such primary sources as Liszt's compositions, literary works, and letters.

Reviewed by Dolores Pesce in *Notes* 49 (1992): 111–12.

6.215 Suttoni, Charles. "Franz Liszt's Published Correspondence: An Annotated Bibliography." In *Fontes* 26 (1979): 191–234.

A good example of focused bibliographical research on the letters of many important composers. There are indexes of correspondence and to authors and editors.

Locke, Matthew

6.216 Harding, Rosemary. *A Thematic Catalogue of the Works of Matthew Locke, with a Calendar of the Main Events of His Life.* 177 pp. Oxford: R.E.M. Harding; distributed by Blackwell, 1971.

Reviewed by Jack A. Westrup in *M&L* 53 (1972): 442–44, reviewed anonymously in *TLS* 3,658 (1972): 387, by Michael Tilmouth in *MT* 113 (1972): 561–62, and by Gloria Rose in *Notes* 29 (1973): 457.

Luening, Otto

6.217* Hartsock, Ralph. *Otto Luening: A Bio-Bibliography.* 272 pp. Westport, Conn.: Greenwood Press, 1991. (Bio-bibliographies in music, 35)

Reviewed by Byron Adams in *Notes* 48 (1992): 1,299–1,301 and by Carl Rahkonen in *Fontes* 29 (1992): 385.

Lully, Jean-Baptiste

6.218* Cohen, Albert. "The Lully Archive at Stanford University." In *Notes* 44 (1987): 5–6.

A short history and description.

6.219* Schmidt, Carl B. *The Livrets of Jean-Baptiste Lully's Tragédies Lyriques: A Catalogue Raisonné.* xli + 633 pp. New York: Performers' Editions, 1995.

6.220 Schneider, Herbert. *Chronologisch-Thematisches Verzeichnis sämtlicher Werke von Jean-Baptiste Lully (LWV).* 570 pp. Tutzing, Germany: H. Schneider, 1981. (Mainzer Studien zur Musikwissenschaft, 15)

A splendid catalog covering both print and manuscript sources and identifying false attributions and lost copies. Musical incipits are printed in treble and bass parts. Bruce Gustafson's "The Lully Labyrinth: Cross-References and Misattributions in the *Lully-Werke-Verzeichnis*" in *Notes* 44 (1987): 33–39 updates this work. Carl B. Schmidt's "Newly Identified Manuscript Sources for the Music of Jean-Baptiste Lully," in *Notes* 44 (1987): 7–32, amplifies the post-1981 knowledge of Lully manuscript locations in libraries and private collections throughout the world.

McCabe, John

6.221* Craggs, Stewart R. *John McCabe: A Bio-bibliography.* 276 pp. New York: Greenwood Press, 1991. (Bio-bibliographies in music, 32)

MacDowell, Edward

6.222 Sonneck, Oscar George. *Catalogue of First Editions of Edward MacDowell (1861–1908).* 89 pp. Washington, D.C.: Government Printing Office, 1917.

A catalog including works with and without opus numbers, compositions written under pseudonyms, and works edited by the composer. There is an index of titles, first line of texts, authors and translators, and publishers.

McKinley, William Thomas

6.223* Sposato, Jeffrey S. *William Thomas McKinley: A Bio-Bibliography.* 303 pp. Westport, Conn.: Greenwood Press, 1995. (Bio-bibliographies in music, 56)

Mahler, Gustav

6.224* Filler, Susan M. *Gustav and Alma Mahler: A Guide to Research.* li + 336 pp. New York: Garland Publishing, 1989. (Garland reference library of the humanities, 738) (Garland composer resource manuals, 28)

A guide whose core is an annotated selective bibliography of the literature (with 18 languages represented) on the music and lives of the Mahlers, their social setting, and the history of the publishers of their music. Also included are lists and glossaries on the Mahlers' musical and literary works, the major library and archival sources for the researcher, the societies devoted to their music and lives, and festivals and symposia. There is a section on the ideological controversy over the Mahlers and on the conflict between Jews and anti-Semites as a historical factor in their lives and works. Both primary and secondary sources span the years from the mid-19th century to the present.

Reviewed by Edward R. Reilly in *Fontes* 38 (1991): 84–86, with a response by the author, by David C. Birchler in *Notes* 47 (1991): 750–60, by Allie Wise Goudy in *ARBA* 21 (1990): no. 2141, and by Peter Franklin in *M&L* 72 (1991): 134–36.

6.225* McClatchie, Stephen. "The Gustav Mahler–Alfred Rosé Collection at the University of Western Ontario." In *Notes* 52 (1995): 385–406.

A description of the collection once belonging to Mahler's brother-in-law, especially strong in Mahler family letters and music manuscripts.

6.226* Namenwirth, Simon Michael. *Gustav Mahler: A Critical Bibliography.* 3 vols. Wiesbaden: Otto Harrassowitz, 1987.

A selective bibliography of about 2,000 publications on Mahler, published to 1985, with extensive quotes translated into English from the non-English sources. Works in Eastern European languages were omitted. The 3rd vol. is a complex series of indexes.

Reviewed by Ann P. Basart in *CNV* 122 (1988): 18–19 and by John Williamson in *M&L* 70 (1989): 269–73, with errata.

6.227* Smoley, Lewis M. *The Symphonies of Gustav Mahler: A Critical Discography.* 191 pp. New York: Greenwood Press, 1986. (Discographies, 23)

A discography whose annotations begin to acclimate the reader to the subtleties of this body of Mahler recordings.

Reviewed by George R. Hill in *ARBA* 18 (1987): no. 1253 and by J. M. Perrault in *Notes* 47 (1987): 273–76.

6.228 Vondenhoff, Bruno, and **Eleanore Vondenhoff.** *Gustav Mahler Dokumentation, Sammlung Eleanore Vondenhoff.* xxii + 676 pp. Tutzing, Germany: H. Schneider, 1978. (Publikationen des Instituts für Österreichische Musikdokumentation, 4)

A 4-pp. "Ergänzung des Nachtrags" was issued and has been inserted in many copies.

A catalog of the Vondenhoff collection of documents on the life and works of Gustav Mahler, now housed in the music collection of the Austrian National Library, Vienna.

Reviewed by Robert P. Morgan in *Notes* 35 (1979): 873–74.

Marcello, Benedetto and Alessandro

6.229 Fruchtman, Caroline S. *Checklist of Vocal Chamber Works by Benedetto Marcello.* 37 pp. Detroit, Mich.: Information Coordinators, 1967. (Detroit studies in music bibliography, 10)
    Reviewed by Owen Jander in *Notes* 24 (1968): 491–92.

6.230* Selfridge-Field, Eleanor. *The Works of Benedetto and Alessandro Marcello: A Thematic Catalogue with Commentary on the Composers, Repertory, and Sources.* 517 pp. Oxford: Oxford University Press, 1990.
    Also includes a list of cantatas, with incipits, by Rosanna Scalfi Marcello, Benedetto's wife.
    Reviewed by Graham Dixon in *EM* 19 (1991): 283–85, by Robert M. Cammarota in *Notes* 48 (1992): 868–71, and by John Walter Hill in *M&L* 73 (1992): 441–42.

Martin, Frank

6.231* King, Charles W. *Frank Martin: A Bio-Bibliography.* 251 pp. New York: Greenwood Press, 1990. (Bio-bibliographies in music, 26)
    Reviewed by Jane H. Galante in *Notes* 48 (1991): 95–97 and by Nancy L. Stokes in *Fontes* 39 (1992): 78–79.

Martinů, Bohuslav

6.232* Červinkova, Blanká. *Bohuslav Martinů (8.12.1890–28.8.1959): Bibliografický Katalog.* 206 pp. Prague: Panton, 1990.
    Reviewed by Judith Mabary in *Notes* 49 (1992): 128–30.

Mason, Lowell

6.233 Mason, Henry L. *Hymn-Tunes of Lowell Mason: A Bibliography.* 118 pp. Cambridge, Mass.: University Press, 1944.
    Reprinted by AMS Press, New York, 1976.
    A bibliography of the hymn tunes of the prolific 19th-century American composer classifying Mason's 210 original tunes and 487 arrangements of others' tunes in 14 different ways.
    Reviewed by Frank J. Metcalf in *Notes* 1 (1944): 58–59.

Mason, William Gregory

6.234* Graber, Kenneth. *William Mason (1829–1908): An Annotated Bibliography and Catalog of Works.* xxx + 349 pp. Warren, Mich.: Published for the College Music Society by Harmonie Park Press, 1989. (Bibliographies in American music, 13)
    An annotated bibliography of writing by and about Mason, a thematic catalog of his works, and a selection of concert programs from his professional life.
    Reviewed by Kendall L. Crilly in *Fontes* 38 (1991): 149–51 and by Linda L. Tyler in *Notes* 47 (1991): 771–72.

Mathias, William

6.235* Craggs, Stewart. *William Mathias: A Bio-Bibliography.* 246 pp. Westport, Conn.: Greenwood Press, 1995. (Bio-bibliographies in music, 58)

Mendelssohn-Bartholdy, Felix

6.236 Crum, Margaret. *Catalogue of the Mendelssohn Papers in the Bodleian Library, Oxford.* 3 vols. Tutzing, Germany: H. Schneider, 1980– . (Musikbibliographische Arbeiten, 7)

Contents: Vol. 1, *Correspondence of Felix Mendelssohn-Bartholdy and Others;* Vol. 2, *Music and Papers;* Vol. 3, *Printed Music and Books,* by Peter Ward.
Reviewed by Douglass Seaton in *Notes* 38 (1982): 603–4.

Messager, André

6.237* Wagstaff, John. *André Messager: A Bio-Bibliography.* 188 pp. New York: Greenwood Press, 1991. (Bio-bibliographies in music, 33)
Well-organized access to information on an important Parisian musical figure (1853–1929): composer, conductor, and administrator.
Reviewed by James William Sobaskie in *Notes* 50 (1994): 1,405–7.

Messiaen, Olivier

6.238* Morris, David. *Messiaen: A Comparative Bibliography of Material in the English Language.* 91 pp. Belfast: University of Ulster, 1991.
Arranged work by work, with extensive abstracts from different articles; a compendium of comparative criticism, with index.

Milhaud, Darius

6.239* Bloch, Francine. *Darius Milhaud, 1892–1974.* 281 pp. + 16 plates. Paris: Bibliothèque Nationale, Département de la Phonothèque Nationale et de l'Audiovisuel, 1992. (Phonographies, 3)
An extensive discography of the prolific composer, published by France's national library. An insert lists recordings published in 1992.

Monteverdi, Claudio

6.240* Adams, K. Gary, and **Dyke Kiel.** *Claudio Monteverdi: A Guide to Research.* 273 pp. New York: Garland Publishing, Inc., 1989. (Garland composer resource manuals, 23) (Garland reference library of the humanities, 792)
A selective, annotated guide listing Monteverdi literature (scholarly books, articles, dissertations, and occasional concert reviews) published through 1986. Most items are in English, Italian, German, or French, although representative titles in other languages are also cited. A works list, with references to modern editions, heads the volume; the bibliography itself is divided into works for a general background, Monteverdi's life, studies of his music, and modern Monteverdi performance. Includes an author index, an index of Monteverdi's compositions, and a general index of proper names.
Reviewed by Tim Carter in *EM* 18 (1990): 292–93, by Allie Wise Goudy in *ARBA* 21 (1990): no. 1238, by Denis Stevens, with corrections and additions, in *MT* 131 (1990): 547, and by William V. Porter in *Notes* 47 (1991): 1,117–18. A substantial number of additional secondary sources are cited in the review by Jeffrey Kurtzman in *M&L* 71 (1980): 548–50.

6.241* Stattkus, Manfred H. *Claudio Monteverdi: Verzeichnis der erhaltenen Werke (SV).* Kleine Ausg. 183 pp. Bergkamen, Germany: Musikverlag Stattkus, 1985.
A catalog of Monteverdi's works, without thematic incipits.
Reviewed by Denis Stevens in *EM* 15 (1987): 537 and by Nigel Fortune in *M&L* 69 (1988): 64–65.

6.242* Westerlund, Gunnar, and **Eric Hughes.** *Music of Claudio Monteverdi: A Discography.* 72 pp. London: British Institute of Recorded Sound, 1972.
An index providing access to 325 recordings of Monteverdi's works issued before October 1971. The review by Jeffrey Kurtzman in *Notes* 30 (1974): 532–33 includes a short errata list.

Moscheles, Ignaz

6.243 Kistner, Friedrich, firm. *Thematisches Verzeichnis im Druck erschienener Compositionen von Ignaz Moscheles.* 66 pp. Leipzig: Friedrich Kistner, 1862.

A facsimile of the Kistner ed. was published in London by H. Baron, 1966.

Mozart, Wolfgang Amadeus

6.244 Angermüller, Rudolph, and **Otto Schneider.** *Mozart-Bibliographie (bis 1970): Mozart Jahrbuch 1975.* 362 pp. Kassel, Germany: Bärenreiter, 1976. (Mozart Jahrbuch 1975 des Zentralinstitutes für Mozartförschung der Internationalen Stiftung Mozarteum Salzburg).

Supplemented by *Mozart-Bibliographie 1971–1975 mit Nachträgen zur Mozart-Bibliographie bis 1970,* by the same authors, published by Bärenreiter, 1978, 175 pp., and by similar titles covering 1976–80 (Bärenreiter, 1982, 175 pp.), 1981–85 (Bärenreiter, 1987, 121 pp.), and 1986–91 (Bärenreiter, 1992, 332 pp.).

Over 10,000 entries arranged alphabetically by author and indexed by Köchel number, personal name, places, and subjects. The coverage is best for German-language works, adequate for works in French and Italian, but less than satisfactory for works in English.

Reviewed by A. Hyatt King in *Fontes* 24 (1977): 100–2 and 30 (1983): 170, and by William P. Robinson in *Notes* 34 (1977): 67–70. The 1978 supplement is reviewed by Bernard E. Wilson in *Notes* 35 (1979): 879–80.

6.245* Casaglia, Gherardo. *Il catalogo delle opere di Wolfgang Amadeus Mozart: Nuovo ordinamento e studio comparativo delle classificazioni precedenti.* 444 pp. Bologna: Editrice Compositori, 1976.

Reviewed by A. Hyatt King in *M&L* 58 (1977): 452.

6.246* Clive, Peter. *Mozart and His Circle: A Biographical Dictionary.* 242 pp. New Haven, Conn.: Yale University Press; London: Dent, 1993.

A biographical dictionary with entries stressing the Mozartean connections of some 280 people in Mozart's personal and professional sphere, as well as of some early biographers. There are several additional features: a chronicle of Mozart's life (pp. 1–8), information on the Masonic lodges with Mozartean connections, information on Mozart's operas and the Viennese theater of Mozart's time, a bibliography, an index of Mozart's works, and an index of persons and operas.

Reviewed by Julian Rushton in *MT* 135 (1994): 452–53.

6.247 Haberkamp, Gertraut. *Die Erstdrucke der Werke von Wolfgang Amadeus Mozart.* 2 vols. Tutzing, Germany: H. Schneider, 1986. (Musikbibliographische Arbeiten, 10/1–10/2)

Contents: Vol. 1, *Bibliographie Textband;* Vol. 2, *Bibliographie Bildband.*

Reviewed by Jean Gribenski in *Revue de musicologie* 77 (1991): 349–51.

6.248* Hastings, Baird. *Wolfgang Amadeus Mozart: A Guide to Research.* 411 pp. New York: Garland Publishing, 1989. (Garland composer resource manuals, 16) (Garland reference library of the humanities, 910)

Reviewed by William S. Brockman in *ARBA* 21 (1990): no. 1244 and by John A. Rice in *Notes* 47 (1991): 1,128–30.

6.249 Hill, George R., and **Murray Gould.** *A Thematic Locator for Mozart's Works, as Listed in Koechel's Chronologisch-thematisches Verzeichnis.* 76 pp. Hackensack, N.J.: J. Boonin, 1970. (Music indexes and bibliographies, 1)

A systematic organization of Mozart incipits. The first section arranges the themes by interval size, the second by pitch name.

Reviewed by Neal Zaslaw in *Notes* 28 (1972): 445–46.

6.250 Klein, Hans-Günter. *Wolfgang Amadeus Mozart: Autographe und Abschriften.* Kassel, Germany: Merseberger, 1982. (Staatsbibliothek Preussischer Kulturbesitz; Kataloge der Musikabteilung. Erste Reihe: Handschriften, 6)

The catalog of the Library's rich holdings of Mozart manuscripts and correspondence.

6.251 Köchel, Ludwig, Ritter van. *Chronologisch-thematisches Verzeichnis sämtlicher Tonwerke Wolfgang Amadeus Mozarts, nebst Angabe der verlorengegangen, angefangenen, von fremder Hand bearbeiten, zweifelhaften und unterschobenen Kompositionen.* 6th ed., edited by Franz Giegling, Alexander Weinmann and Gerd Sievers. 1,024 pp. Wiesbaden: Breitkopf & Härtel, 1964.

First published in Leipzig, 1862. The 2nd ed., 1905, was edited by Paul Graf von Waldersee; the 3rd ed., edited by Alfred Einstein, was published in 1937 and reissued with a supplement in 1947 by Edwards Brothers, Ann Arbor, Mich. The 4th and 5th eds. were unaltered reprints of the 3rd, without the supplement.

The monumental thematic catalog of Mozart's works, brought up to modern standards in the 3rd ed. Presented in chronological order, the entries cite references to manuscripts, early editions, and the modern complete works (the *Sämtlicher Werke* of Breitkopf & Härtel as well as the *Neue Ausgabe Sämtlicher Werke* of Bärenreiter through 1964), and provide a classified catalog with brief thematic incipits as an overview of the main chronological catalog. There are numerous appendixes providing information on early "complete" editions and the Hoboken *Photogrammarchiv* in Vienna (**7.570**). Includes an index to vocal titles and first lines and a general index. This is a tour de force of scholarship and a brilliant example of the accretion of musico-bibliographical knowledge by generations of researchers.

The 1964 ed. is reviewed by Ludwig Finscher in *Fontes* 11 (1964): 95–98.

6.252 Mozart, Wolfgang Amadeus. *Mozart's Thematic Catalogue (British Library Stefan Zweig MS 63): A Facsimile Edition.* Introduced and edited by Albi Rosenthal and Alan Tyson. 160 pp. London: British Library; Ithaca, N.Y.: Cornell University Press, 1990.

Mozart's catalog of his musical works, with transcription and other editorial support.

Reviewed by Alec Hyatt King in *M&L* 72 (1991): 597–99, by D. W. Krummel in *Choice* 29 (1992): 906, by Paul Griffiths in *TLS* (November 29 1991): 3, and by John A. Rice in *Notes* 48 (1991): 484–86.

6.253 Schlager, Karl-Heinz. *Wolfgang Amadeus Mozart: Verzeichnis von Erst- und Frühdruck bis etwa 1800.* 2 vols. Kassel, Germany: Bärenreiter, 1978. (RISM, A, 1, supplement)

"Sonderdruck aus Répertoire International des Sources Musicales A/I, Einzeldruck vor 1800. Redaktion Karl-Heinz Schlager. Bd. 6: Montalbano-Pleyel." The second volume includes the directory of sigla of libraries contributing to the catalog.

6.254* Zaslaw, Neal, and **William Cowdery.** *The Compleat Mozart: A Guide to the Musical Works of Wolfgang Amadeus Mozart.* 351 pp. New York: Mozart Bicentennial at Lincoln Center: Norton, 1990.

Reviewed by Malcolm Miller in *MT* 132 (1991): 568–69 and by John A. Rice in *Notes* 48 (1991): 568–69.

6.255* Zaslaw, Neal, and **Fiona Morgan Fein.** *The Mozart Repertory: A Guide for Musicians, Programmers, Researchers.* 157 pp. Ithaca, N.Y.: Cornell University Press, 1991.

A source resolving numbering differences among the various Mozart catalogs, by the editor of the next edition of the Köchel catalog.

Reviewed by Malcolm Miller in *MT* 132 (1991): 568–69.

6.256* Ziegler, Frank. *Wolfgang Amadeus Mozart: Autographenverzeichnis.* 62 pp. Berlin: Deutsche Staatsbibliothek, 1990. (Handschrifteninventare / Deutsche Staatsbibliothek, 12)

Reviewed by John A. Rice in *Notes* 48 (1991): 484–86.

Musgrave, Thea

6.257 Hixon, Donald L. *Thea Musgrave: A Bio-Bibliography.* 187 pp. Westport, Conn.: Greenwood Press, 1984. (Bio-bibliographies in music, 1)

The 1st of a series, each devoted to a single composer. The established format begins with a biography, followed by works list, critical bibliography, and, often, a discography.

Reviewed by Robert Palmieri in *ARBA* 16 (1985): no. 1199.

Nielsen, Carl

6.258* Bjørnum, Birgit, and **Klaus Møllerhøj.** *Carl Nielsens samling*: *A Catalogue of the Composer's Musical Manuscripts in the Royal Library, Copenhagen.* 301 pp. Copenhagen: Det Kongelige Bibliotek, Museum Tusculanum Press, University of Copenhagen, 1992. (Danish humanist texts and studies, 4)

Rösing, Helmut. "RISM-Handschriftenkatalogisierung und elektronische Datenverarbeitung (EDV)." In *Fontes* 26 (1979): 107–9.

6.259* Miller, Mina F. *Carl Nielsen: A Guide to Research.* 245 pp. New York: Garland Publishing, 1987. (Garland composer resource manuals, 6) (Garland reference library of the humanities, 662)

Reviewed by A. F. Leighton Thomas in *MR* 50 (1989): 304–6 and by Allie Wise Goudy in *ARBA* 19 (1988): no. 1262.

Obrecht, Jacob

See Ockeghem, Johannes.

Ockeghem, Johannes

6.260* Picker, Martin. *Johannes Ockeghem and Jacob Obrecht: A Guide to Research.* 203 pp. New York: Garland Publishing, 1988. (Garland composer resource manuals, 13)

Guides to two composers' lives and works, with carefully detailed works lists, bibliographies containing out-of-the way references, and a meticulously compiled discography.

Reviewed, with some addenda, by Richard Taruskin in *Notes* 47 (1990): 358–60, by Robert Skinner in *ARBA* 20 (1989): no. 1210, and by David Fallows in *M&L* 70 (1989): 249–52.

Paisiello, Giovanni

6.261* Robinson, Michael F., and **Ulrike Hofmann.** *Giovanni Paisiello: A Thematic Catalogue of His Works.* 2 vols. Stuyvesant, N.Y.: Pendragon, 1991–94. (Thematic catalogues, 15)

A list of 3,000 items in 191 collections, with a unique numbering system; the 1st vol. contains the dramatic works, the 2nd vol. the rest.

Reviewed by Heikki Poroila in *Fontes* 42 (1995): 189–90.

Palestrina, Giovanni Pierluigi da

6.262 Hall, Alison. *Palestrina: An Index to the Casimiri, Kalmus, and Haberl Editions.* 82 pp. Philadelphia, Pa.: Music Library Association, 1980. (MLA index and bibliography series, 22)

Pallavicino, Benedetto

6.263 Flanders, Peter. *A Thematic Index to the Works of Benedetto Pallavincino.* 85 pp. Hackensack, N.J.: Joseph Boonin, 1974. (Music indexes and bibliographies, 11)

Parker, Horatio

6.264 Rorick, William C. "The Horatio Parker Archives in the Yale University Music Library." In *Fontes* 26 (1979): 298–304.

A description of the papers left by a prominent member of the "Second New England School."

Partch, Harry

6.265* McGeary, Thomas. *The Music of Harry Partch: A Descriptive Catalog.* 185 pp. + 10 plates. Brooklyn, N.Y.: Institute for Studies in American Music, Conservatory of Music, Brooklyn College of CUNY, 1991. (I.S.A.M. monographs, 31)

A list of all extant Partch compositions.

Reviewed by Richard Kassel in *Notes* 49 (1992): 611–12 and by David Nicholls in *M&L* 73 (1992): 477–78.

Pergolesi, Giovanni Battista

6.266 Paymer, Marvin E. *Giovanni Battista Pergolesi, 1710–1736: A Thematic Catalogue of the Opera Omnia with an Appendix Listing Omitted Compositions.* 99 pp. New York: Pendragon Press, 1977. (Thematic catalogues, 1)

Reviewed by Stephen Shearon in *Notes* 48 (1992): 871–74.

6.267* Paymer, Marvin E., and **Hermine W. Williams.** *Giovanni Battista Pergolesi: A Guide to Research.* 190 pp. New York: Garland Publishing, 1989. (Garland reference library of the humanities, 1058) (Garland composer resource manuals, 26)

Reviewed by Michael Talbot in *M&L* 72 (1991): 105–7.

Perle, George

6.268* *George Perle, a Catalog of Works.* 20 pp. Boston, Mass.: E.C. Schirmer, 1991.

A catalog of works, with a brief biographical note in English, French, and German.

Persichetti, Vincent

6.269* Patterson, Donald L., and **Janet L. Patterson.** *Vincent Persichetti: A Bio-Bibliography.* 336 pp. New York: Greenwood Press, 1988. (Bio-bibliographies in music, 16)

Reviewed by Byron Adams in *Notes* 48 (1992): 1,299–1,301, and by George Louis Mayer in *ARBA* 20 (1989): no. 1208.

Pezel, Johann

6.270 Wienandt, Elwyn A. *Johann Pezel, 1639–1694: A Thematic Catalogue of His Instrumental Works.* xxxiii + 102 pp. New York: Pendragon Press, 1983. (Thematic catalogues, 9)

Pinkham, Daniel

6.271 DeBoer, Kee, and **John B. Ahouse.** *Daniel Pinkham: A Bio-Bibliography.* 238 pp. New York: Greenwood Press, 1988. (Bio-bibliographies in music, 12)

Reviewed by Marjorie E. Bloss in *ARBA* 20 (1989): no. 1201.

Pleyel, Ignace

6.272 Benton, Rita. *Ignace Pleyel: A Thematic Catalogue of His Compositions.* 482 pp. New York: Pendragon Press, 1977. (Thematic catalogues, 2)

Exhaustive coverage of the voluminous works of a popular composer of the late 18th and early 19th centuries, with indexes by publisher and title and a thematic locator.

Reviews by Floyd K. Grave in *JAMS* 33 (1980): 204–10, by Stephen M. Fry in *Notes* 34 (1978): 878–79, by Lenore Coral, with additions, in *Notes* 35 (1978): 75–76, and by Alan Tyson in *Fontes* 26 (1979): 139–41.

Poulenc, Francis

6.273 Bloch, Francine. *Francis Poulenc, 1928–1982.* 253 pp. + 16 pp. of plates. Paris: Bibliothèque Nationale, Département de la Phonothèque Nationale et de l'Audiovisuel, 1984. (Phonographies, 2)

An extensive discography arranged by opus with an index to performers' names. A discography of Poulenc as performer, speaker, and interpreter of other composers is included.

Reviewed by J. F. Weber in *ARSCJ* 16 (1984): 55–56 and by Ann P. Basart in *CNV* 101 (1986): 12.

6.274* Keck, George Russell. *Francis Poulenc: A Bio-Bibliography.* 304 pp. New York: Greenwood Press, 1990. (Bio-bibliographies in music, 28)

Reviewed by James Briscoe in *Fontes* 41 (1994): 131–33.

6.275* Schmidt, Carl B. *The Music of Francis Poulenc (1899–1963): A Catalogue.* 608 pp. Oxford; New York: Clarendon Press; Oxford University Press, 1995.

A catalog lacking incipits but little else in its bibliographic listings, with entries including date, dedication, instrumentation, the location of the holograph and the copyist's manuscripts, the printed editions, including revisions, arrangements, and transcriptions, the premiere and other important performances, commentary (general and advertisements), literature, and a discography, as well as information on the text.

Puccini, Giacomo

6.276 Hopkinson, Cecil. *A Bibliography of the Printed Works of Giacomo Puccini, 1858–1924.* 77 pp. New York: Broude Brothers, 1968.

An analytical bibliography.

Purcell, Henry

6.277* Charteris, Richard. "A Checklist of the Manuscript Sources of Henry Purcell's Music in the University of California, William Andrews Clark Memorial Library, Los Angeles." In *Notes* 52 (1995): 407–21.

A description of the 12 sources, which are either manuscript or print with manuscript emendations.

6.278 Zimmerman, Franklin B. *Henry Purcell: A Guide to Research.* 333 pp. New York: Garland Publishing, 1989. (Garland composer resource manuals, 18) (Garland reference library of the humanities, 885)

This manual provides a numbered list of Purcell's complete works, a compilation of his hitherto unpublished prefaces and dedications to his published works, an account of his life and times, information on editions of his music, and a selective bibliography with commentary.

The list by Zimmerman of Purcell's works brings into the fold a number of newly identified titles, discovered after the publication of the compiler's *Analytical Catalogue* (**6.279**). There is also a classified bibliography.

Reviewed by Marjorie E. Bloss in *ARBA* 21 (1990): no. 1257.

6.279* Zimmerman, Franklin B. *Henry Purcell, 1659–1695: An Analytical Catalogue of His Music.* 2nd rev. ed. xxxvi + 473 pp. Philadelphia, Pa.: University of Pennsylvania Press, 1983.

The first ed. was published in 1963 (London: Macmillan; New York: St. Martin's Press, 1963), xxiv + 575 pp. Reprinted in 1990 by P.R.O. Music Publications, Philadelphia, Pa. Bibliography (pp. 427–53).

6.280* Zimmerman, Franklin B. *Henry Purcell, 1659–1695: Melodic and Intervallic Indexes to His Complete Works.* 133 pp. Philadelphia, Pa.: Smith-Edwards-Dunlap, 1975.

Both indexes identify each theme according to the numbers assigned in Zimmerman's *Henry Purcell, 1659–1695: An Analytical Catalogue of His Music* (**6.279**) (London: Macmillan, 1963) and locate each by volume and page number in the Purcell Society's edition of *The Works of Henry Purcell* (London: Novello, 1878–).

Quantz, Johann Joachim

6.281* Augsbach, Horst. *Johann Joachim Quantz, thematisches Verzeichnis der musikalischen Werke: Werkgruppen QV 2 und QV 3.* 59 pp. Dresden: Sächsische Landesbibliothek, 1984. (Studien und Materialen zur Musikgeschichte Dresdens, 5)

Reviewed by Nikolaus Delius in *Tibia* 11 (1986): 48–49.

Rachmaninoff, Sergei

6.282 Palmieri, Robert. *Sergei Vasil´evich Rachmaninoff: A Guide to Research.* 335 pp. New York: Garland Publishing, 1985. (Garland composer resource manuals, 3) (Garland reference library of the humanities, 471)

An extensive list of compositions (pp. 3–66), repertoire list (pp. 67–91), discography (pp. 93–118), and bibliography (pp. 295–97), as well as a variety of indexes.

Reviewed by John E. Druesedow, Jr., in *ARBA* 17 (1986): no. 1230.

Rameau, Jean Philippe

6.283* Foster, Donald H. *Jean-Philippe Rameau: A Guide to Research.* 292 pp. New York: Garland Publishing, 1989. (Garland reference library of the humanities, 895) (Garland composer resource manuals, 20)

A research guide whose primary feature is a comprehensive annotated bibliography of 711 secondary sources, mainly of the last 100 years.

Reviewed by Graham Sadler in *M&L* 72 (1991): 103–5 and by Bruce Gustafson in *Notes* 47 (1991): 739–40.

Reger, Max

6.284* Grim, William E. *Max Reger: A Bio-Bibliography.* 270 pp. Westport, Conn.: Greenwood Press, 1988. (Bio-bibliographies in music, 7)

Reviewed by Allie Wise Goudy in *ARBA* 20 (1989): no. 1203 and by Paul Taylor in *Fontes* 37 (1990): 66–67.

6.285 Rösner, Helmut. *Max-Reger-Bibliographie. Das internationale Schrifttum über Max Reger 1893–1966.* 138 pp. Bonn; Hannover; Munich: Dümmler, 1968. (Veröffentlichungen des Max-Reger-Institutes, 5)

Reviewed by Gerd Sievers in *Die Musikforschung* 24 (1971): 93–95.

6.286* Shigihara, Susanne. *Max-Reger-Bibliographie. Das Internationale Schrifttum über Max Reger von 1967 bis 1981, nebst einem Nachtrag bis 1966 und Materialien des Max-Reger-Institutes.* 109 pp. Bonn: F. Dümmlers Verlag, 1983.(Veröffentlichungen des Max-Reger-Institutes, 9)

A follow-up to the bibliography edited by Rösner (**6.285**).

Respighi, Ottorino

6.287* Adriano. *An International Respighi Discography.* 53 pp. Zurich: Adriano Records, 1981.

A booklet attempting to list, in a tabular format reproduced from notecards, all recordings of Respighi's works, including his transcriptions, issued up to the close of his centenary year by commercial, educational, society, and private labels.

Reviewed by J. F. Weber in *ARSCJ* 13 (1981): 111 no. 2.

Rimsky-Korsakov, Nikolai

6.288* Seaman, Gerald R. *Nikolai Andreevich Rimsky-Korsakov: A Guide to Research.* 377 pp. New York: Garland Publishing, 1988. (Garland composer resource manuals, 17) (Garland reference library of the humanities, 726)

Reviewed by Roy J. Guenther in *Notes* 48 (1991): 491–93 and by Carole Franklin Vidali in *ARBA* 21 (1990): no. 1252.

Rochberg, George

6.289* Dixon, Joan DeVee. *George Rochberg: A Bio-Bibliographic Guide to His Life and Works.* xlvi + 684 pp. Stuyvesant, N.Y.: Pendragon Press, 1992.

Rodgers, Richard

6.290 Green, Stanley. *Rodgers and Hammerstein Fact Book: A Record of Their Works Together and with Other Collaborators.* 762 + 32 pp. New York: Drama Books Specialists, 1981.

Previously published as *The Richard Rodgers Fact Book* in 1965, 582 pp. The 2nd ed. was first published in New York by Lynn Farnol Group in 1980 (762 + 30 pp.).

Information on Richard Rodgers, on Oscar Hammerstein II, and on Rodgers and Hammerstein. The first two sections include information on the subjects' early careers, and then in chronological order with entries for each professional production. Each entry has the names of responsible participants (author, producer, director, etc.), places and dates of out-of-town tryouts, plot synopses, cast, lists of musical numbers by act, and review excerpts. There are indexes to songs and productions; lists of songs by subject citing source musical production, a bibliography (pp. 709–20), and a discography (pp. 721–34), but no personal name index.

Reviewed by Deane L. Root in *AM* 1 (1983): 83–85, with additional biographical sources.

Rolla, Alessandro

6.291* Inzaghi, Luigi, and **Luigi Alberto Bianchi.** *Alessandro Rolla: Catalogo tematico delle opere.* 298 pp. Milan: Nuove Edizioni, 1981.

The introduction, life, and chronology (pp. 11–55) of a composer whose compositions are largely unpublished and who received a brief summary works list even in *The New Grove* (**1.48**).

Rorem, Ned

6.292* McDonald, Arlys L. *Ned Rorem: A Bio-Bibliography.* 284 pp. New York: Greenwood Press, 1989. (Bio-bibliographies in music, 23)

Reviewed by Bonnie Jo Dopp in *Notes* 47 (1990): 368 and by Robert Palmieri in *ARBA* 21 (1990): no. 1248.

Rosbaud, Hans

6.293 Evans, Joan. *Hans Rosbaud: A Bio-Bibliography.* xxiii + 298 pp. Westport, Conn.: Greenwood Press, 1992. (Bio-bibliographies in music, 43)

A leading conductor in the performance of contemporary music.
Reviewed by David Breckbill in *Notes* 50 (1994): 1,013–15.

Rossi, Salamone

6.294 Newman, Joel, and **Fritz Rikko.** *A Thematic Index to the Works of Salamon Rossi.* 143 pp. Hackensack, N.J.: J. Boonin, 1972. (Music indexes and bibliographies, 6)
Reviewed by Neal Zaslaw in *Notes* 31 (1975): 577.

Roussel, Albert

6.295* Follet, Robert. *Albert Roussel: A Bio-Bibliography.* 134 pp. New York: Greenwood Press, 1988. (Bio-bibliographies in music, 19)
Reviewed by Donna A. Buchanan in *Notes* 47 (1990): 375–77 and by Allie Wise Goudy in *ARBA* 21 (1990): no. 1242.

6.296* Labelle, Nicole. *Catalogue raisonné de l'oeuvre d'Albert Roussel.* 159 pp. Louvain-la-Neuve, Belgium: Département d'Archéologie et d'Histoire de l'Art, Collège Érasme, 1992. (Publications d'histoire de l'art et d'archéologie de l'Université Catholique de Louvain, 78) (Musicologica neolovaniensia, Studia 6)
A catalog of the corpus of Roussel's musical works, citing the available bibliographic and location data in a clear, accessible format.
Reviewed by James William Sobaskie in *Notes* 50 (1994): 1,404–5 and by Richard Langham Smith in *M&L* 74 (1993): 461.

Ruggles, Carl

6.297* Green, Jonathan D. *Carl Ruggles: A Bio-Bibliography.* 148 pp. Westport, Conn.: Greenwood Press, 1995. (Bio-bibliographies in music, 59)

Saint-Saëns, Camille

6.298* *Catalogue Général et Thématique des Oeuvres de C. Saint-Saëns.* New ed. 145 pp. Paris: A. Durand et fils, 1908.

Sammartini, Giovanni Battista

6.299 Jenkins, Newell, and **Bathia Churgin.** *Thematic Catalogue of the Works of Giovanni Battista Sammartini: Orchestral and Vocal Music.* 315 pp. Cambridge, Mass.: Published for the American Musicological Society by Harvard University Press, 1976.
Reviewed by Eugene K. Wolf in *Notes* 34 (1978): 850–52 and by Howard Brofsky in *JAMS* 31 (1978): 365–67.

Sauguet, Henri

6.300* Austin, David L. *Henri Sauguet: A Bio-Bibliography.* 271 pp. New York: Greenwood Press, 1991. (Bio-bibliographies in music, 39)
A comprehensive works list, arranged chronologically by genre, including an annotated bibliography of the composer–critic's writings, with an index and discography (pp. 129–38).
Reviewed by James William Sobaskie in *Notes* 50 (1994): 1,405–7 and by James Briscoe in *Fontes* 41 (1994): 131–33.

Scarlatti, Alessandro and Domenico

6.301* Longo, Alessandro. *D. Scarlatti: Indice tematico delle sonate per clavicembalo contenute* *nella raccolta completa / Thematic Index of the Harpsichord Sonatas Included in the Complete Collection.* 36 pp. Milan: Ricordi, 1952.

6.302* Vidali, Carole F. *Alessandro and Domenico Scarlatti: A Guide to Research.* xxi + 253 + xi + 132 pp. New York: Garland Publishing, 1993. (Garland reference library of the humanities, 1125) (Garland composer resource manuals, 34)

A bibliography arranged in two parts that includes discographies (pp. 113–22 and 213–34) and indexes.

Reviewed by George Louis Mayer in *ARBA* 25 (1994): 1334.

Schoenberg, Arnold

6.303* Christensen, Jean. *From Arnold Schoenberg's Literary Legacy: A Catalog of Neglected Items.* 164 pp. Warren, Mich.: Harmonie Park Press, 1988. (Detroit studies in music bibliography, 59)

Reviewed by Carol June Bradley in *ARBA* 20 (1989): no. 1197 and by Irene Heskes in *Notes* 48 (1991): 456–61.

6.304* Glennan, Kathryn P., Jerry L. McBride, and **R. Wayne Shoaf.** *Arnold Schoenberg Institute Archives Preliminary Catalog.* 3 vols. Los Angeles, Calif.: The Institute, 1986.

6.305 Kimmey, John A., Jr. *The Arnold Schoenberg–Hans Nachod Collection.* 119 pp. + 115 ll. of plates. Detroit, Mich.: Information Coordinators, 1979. (Detroit studies in music bibliography, 41)

An annotated catalog of the collection of correspondence, proof sheets, and holographs in the Music Library of North Texas State University, Denton, Texas.

Reviewed by Alexander L. Ringer in *Fontes* 27 (1980): 224–25 and by Frederic Schoettler in *ARBA* 11 (1980): no. 968.

6.306* Rufer, Josef. *The Works of Arnold Schoenberg: A Catalogue of His Compositions, Writings, and Paintings.* Trans. by Dika Newlin. 214 pp. London: Faber & Faber, 1962.

6.307* Shoaf, R. Wayne. *The Schoenberg Discography.* 2nd ed., revised and expanded. 264 pp. Berkeley, Calif.: Fallen Leaf Press, 1994. (Fallen Leaf reference books in music, 18)

First ed., 1986, 200 pp.

The 1st ed. is reviewed by Robert J. Dennis in *Notes* 47 (1991): 762–63 and by George Louis Mayer in *ARBA* 19 (1988): no. 1284. The 2nd ed. is reviewed by Richard Turbet in *Brio* 32 (1995): 56.

Schubert, Franz

6.308 Deutsch, Otto Erich. *Franz Schubert: Thematisches Verzeichnis seiner Werke in chronologischer Folge.* A new ed. in German, revised and edited by the Editorial Board of the Neue Schubert Ausgabe and Wolfgang Aderhold. 718 pp. Kassel, Germany: Bärenreiter, 1978. (Neue Schubert Ausgabe, VIII, 4)

The 1st ed. was published as *Schubert: Thematic Catalogue of All His Works in Chronological Order,* in collaboration with Donald R. Wakeling (New York: W.W. Norton; London: Dent, 1951), 556 pp.

Reviewed by L. Michael Griffel in *Notes* 36 (1979): 83–86 and by Robert Winter in *NCM* 3 (1979): 154–60. The 1st ed. is reviewed by Alfred Einstein in *Notes* 8 (1951): 692–93 and by Helen Joy Sleeper in *JAMS* 6 (1953): 247–49.

6.309 Hilmar, Ernst. *Verzeichnis der Schubert-Handschriften in der Musiksammlung der Wiener Stadt- und Landesbibliothek.* 144 pp. + 68 ll. of plates. Kassel, Germany: Bärenreiter, 1978. (Catalogus musicus, 8)

Reviewed by L. Michael Griffel in *Notes* 36 (1979): 83–86.

6.310* Kahl, Willi. *Verzeichnis des Schrifttums über Franz Schubert, 1828–1928.* 264 pp. Regensburg: Bosse, 1938. (Kölner Beiträge zur Musikforschung, 1)

6.311* *Schubert-Gedenkstatte Schloss Atzenbrugg: Franz Schubert und sein Freundeskreis: Museums-Führer.* Edited by a Committee on Preservation for the Schubert-Gedenkstatte, Schloss Atzenbrugg. 110 pp. Tutzing, Germany: H. Schneider, 1992. (Veröffentlichungen des Internationalen Franz Schubert Instituts, 8)

The catalog of a museum devoted to Schubert and his circle.

Schütz, Heinrich

6.312 Blum, Klaus, and **Martin Elste.** *Internationale Heinrich-Schütz Diskographie 1928–1972.* 232 pp. Bremen: The author, 1972.

A list of all commercial recordings of the music of Schütz recorded through 1928, and background details about these recordings.

Reviewed by Michael H. Gray in *Notes* 31 (1974): 63–66.

6.313 Miller, D. Douglas, and **Anne L. Highsmith.** *Heinrich Schütz: A Bibliography of the Collected Works and Performing Editions.* 278 pp. New York: Greenwood Press, 1986. (Music reference collection, 9)

An annotated guide to the very complex bibliography of modern editions of the works of Schütz. There are source and title indexes, as well as an index to performing forces.

Reviewed by Dominique-René de Lerma in *ARBA* 18 (1987): no. 1221 and by Ellen McDonald in *CNV* 109 (1987): 3.

6.314 Skei, Allen B. *Heinrich Schütz: A Guide to Research.* 186 pp. New York: Garland Publishing, 1981. (Garland composer resource manuals, 1) (Garland reference library of the humanities, 272)

Reviewed by Gregory S. Johnston in *MR* 51 (1990): 61–62 and by François Lesure in *Fontes* 3 (1983): 223.

Schuller, Gunther

6.315* Carnovale, Norbert. *Gunther Schuller: A Bio-Bibliography.* 338 pp. New York: Greenwood Press, 1987. (Bio-bibliographies in music, 6)

Reviewed by Bonnie Jo Dopp in *Notes* 47 (1990): 386, by Richard Jackson in *CNV* 135 (1989): 21, by Robert Palmieri in *ARBA* 19 (1988): no. 1266, and by Paul Robinson in *Fontes* 37 (1990): 74.

Schumann, Robert

6.316* Hofmann, Kurt. *Die Erstdrucke der Werke von Robert Schumann: Bibliographies mit Wiedergabe von 234 Titelblättern.* xlv + 464 pp. Tutzing, Germany: H. Schneider, 1979. (Musikbibliographische Arbeiten, 6)

Reviewed by Susan T. Sommer in *Notes* 37 (1980): 322–23.

6.317* Hofmann, Kurt, and **Siegmar Keil.** *Robert Schumann: Thematisches Verzeichnis sämtlicher im Druck erschienenen musikalischen Werke mit Angabe des Jahres ihres Entstehens und Erscheinens.* 5th revised ed. 175 pp. Hamburg: Schuberth, 1982.

6.318 Munte, Frank. *Verzeichnis des deutschsprachigen Schrifttums über Robert Schumann: 1856–1970: Anh. Schrifttum über Clara Schumann.* 151 pp. Hamburg: Verlag der Musikalienhandlung Wagner, 1972. (Schriftenreihe zur Musik)

A bibliography of writings on Robert and Clara Schumann, confined to writings in German.

Reviewed by Friedheim Krummacher in *Melos/NZ* 1 (1975): 507–8 no. 6.

6.319 Ochs, Michael. *Schumann Index, Part 1: An Alphabetical Index to Robert Schumann: Werke.* 26 pp. Ann Arbor, Mich.: Music Library Association, 1967. (MLA index series, 6)

6.320 Weichlein, William. *Schumann Index, Part 2: An Alphabetical Index to the Solo Songs.* 35 pp. Ann Arbor, Mich.: Music Library Association, 1967. (MLA index series, 7)

Seeger, Ruth Crawford

6.321 Graume, Matilda. "Ruth Crawford Seeger." In *Women Making Music: The Western Art Tradition, 1150–1950,* pp. 370–88. Edited by Jane Bowers and Judith Tick. Urbana: University of Illinois Press, 1986.

An essay that includes a list of compositions by Seeger and a discography of those works.
Reviewed by Jane Gottlieb in *Notes* 47 (1991): 56–59.

Shostakovich, Dmitri

6.322* Hulme, Derek C. *Dmitri Shostakovich: A Catalogue, Bibliography, and Discography.* 2nd ed. 479 pp. Oxford: Clarendon Press, Oxford University Press, 1991.

First published in 1982 as *Shostakovich, Catalogue, Bibliography, & Discography,* by Kyle & Glen Music in Muir of Ord, Ross-shire, Scotland, 1982 (248 pp.).

A catalog beginning to make clear the bibliographical challenges of a definitive and authoritative Shostakovich thematic catalog. Included is an appendix listing BBC broadcasts featuring Shostakovich.

Reviewed by Eric Roseberry in *M&L* 73 (1992): 312–13 and by Laurel A. Fay in *Notes* 49 (1991): 585–86.

6.323 MacDonald, Malcolm. *Dmitri Shostakovich: A Complete Catalogue.* 2nd ed. 56 pp. London: Boosey & Hawkes, 1985.

First ed., 1977.
A chronological list of works, with a classified and an alphabetical index.

Sibelius, Jean

6.324 Blum, Fred. *Jean Sibelius: An International Bibliography on the Occasion of the Centennial Celebrations, 1965.* xxi + 114 pp. Detroit, Mich.: Information Service, 1965. (Detroit studies in music bibliography, 8)

A bibliography including books and dissertations devoted to Sibelius (pp. 1–11), books partially devoted to Sibelius (pp. 13–45), articles in music journals (pp. 47–71), and articles in general journals (pp. 73–94). There is an index of names.

Reviewed by Gerhard Hahne in *Die Musikforschung* 22 (1969): 100 and by Ruth Watanabe in *Notes* 23 (1966): 279.

6.325* Kilpeläinen, Kari. *The Jean Sibelius Musical Manuscripts at Helsinki University Library: A Complete Catalogue.* xxxii + 487 pp. Wiesbaden: Breitkopf & Härtel, 1991.

A catalog of the largest collection of Sibelius music manuscripts (1880s-1957), which includes 1,893 items.

Reviewed by Glenda Dawn Goss in *Notes* 48 (1992): 1,229–30.

Smetana, Bedřich

6.326* Bennett, John R. *Smetana on 3000 Records.* 466 pp. Blandford, England: Oakwood Press, 1974.

Sousa, John Philip

6.327* Bierley, Philip E. *The Works of John Philip Sousa.* New ed. 234 pp. Columbus, Ohio: Integrity Press, 1984.

A revised and enlarged version of the 1st ed., *John Philip Sousa: A Descriptive Catalog of his Works* (Urbana, Ill.: University of Illinois Press, 1973), 177 pp.

A classified, well-illustrated list of all of Sousa's works, both musical and literary, with detailed information. A chronological list is appended.

The 1st ed. is reviewed by Donald W. Stauffer in *JRME* 23 (1975): 155–56. The 2nd ed. is reviewed by Dianna Eiland in *AM* 5 (1987): 458–59, by Jonathan Elkus in *NCM* 9 (1986): 251–52, and by Frederic Schoettler in *ARBA* 17 (1986): no. 1226.

Spohr, Louis

6.328* Göthel, Folker. *Thematisch-bibliographisches Verzeichnis der Werke von Louis Spohr.* xxiv + 576 pp. Tutzing, Germany: H. Schneider, 1981.

Includes bibliographical references and indexes.

Reviewed by Clive Brown in *M&L* 69 (1988): 389–90.

Stradella, Alessandro

6.329 Gianturco, Carolyn, and **Eleanor McCrickard.** *Alessandro Stradella (1639–1682): A Thematic Catalogue of His Compositions.* xxvii + 325 pp. Stuyvesant, N.Y.: Pendragon, 1991. (Thematic catalogues, 16)

A solidly constructed catalog of the work of a legendary composer.

Reviewed by Massimo Gentile Tedeschi in *Fontes* 39 (1992): 76, by John Walter Hill in *M&L* 73 (1992): 441–42, and by Anne Schnoebelen in *Notes* 48 (1992): 1,250–52.

Johann Strauss Family

6.330 Weinmann, Alexander. *Verzeichnis sämtlicher Werke von Johann Strauss, Vater und Sohn.* 171 pp. Vienna: Musikverlag Ludwig Krenn, 1956. (Beiträge zur Geschichte des Alt-Wiener Musikverlages, 1/2)

6.331 Weinmann, Alexander. *Verzeichnis sämtlicher Werke von Josef und Eduard Strauss.* 104 pp. Vienna: Ludwig Krenn, 1967. (Beiträge zur Geschichte des Alt-Wiener Musikverlages, 1/3)

Strauss, Richard

6.332* Brosche, Günther, and **Karl Dachs.** *Richard Strauss: Autographen in München und Wien: Verzeichnis.* 387 pp. Tutzing, Germany: H. Schneider, 1979. (Veröffentlichungen der Richard-Strauss-Gesellschaft, München, 3)

Reviewed by Michael Kennedy in *M&L* 61 (1980): 402 and by Barbara A. Petersen in *Notes* 37 (1980): 324–25.

6.333 Müller von Asow, Erich Hermann. *Richard Strauss: thematisches Verzeichnis.* 3 vols. 1,688 pp. Vienna; Munich: L. Doblinger, 1955–74.

Vol. 3, which deals with the works not assigned opus numbers, after the death of Müller von Asow was edited by Alfons Ott and Franz Trenner; its final 33 pages have corrections and additions.

Reviewed by Neal Zaslaw in *Notes* 31 (1975): 772–73.

6.334 Ortner, Oswald, and **Franz Grasberger.** *Richard-Strauss-Bibliographie.* 2 vols. Vienna: Georg Prachner; Kommission bei Verlag Brüer Hollinek, 1964–73. (Museion, Veröffentlichungen der Österreichischen Nationalbibliothek, neue Folge, dritte Reihe, 2)

Contents: Vol. 1, *1882–1944;* Vol. 2, *1944–1964* (compiled by Günther Brosche).

A bibliography organized in terms of various aspects of Strauss's career. The largest section is devoted to writings related to individual compositions.

6.335 Trenner, Franz. *Richard Strauss: Werkverzeichnis.* 153 pp. Vienna: Doblinger, 1985.

A revised works list to be used in conjunction with the Müller von Asow thematic catalog (**6.333**).

Reviewed by Scott Warfield in *Notes* 42 (1985): 292–93.

Stravinsky, Igor

6.336 De Lerma, Dominique-René, and **Thomas J. Ahrens.** *Igor Fedorovitch Stravinsky, 1882–1971: A Practical Guide to Publications of His Music.* 158 pp. Kent, Ohio: Kent State University Press, 1974.

The purpose of this book is to list alphabetically the published music by Igor Stravinsky, including information beneficial to librarians and students for the identification of the composer's complete works and their publication sources. It is primarily a register of the publications, with supplemental data. Additional access is given by the publisher index, medium/format index, index of proper names (with the identification tied to specific works), and chronological index (1904–68).

6.337* Heintze, James R. *Igor Stravinsky: An International Bibliography of Theses and Dissertations, 1925–87.* 215 pp. Warren, Mich.: Harmonie Park Press, 1988. (Detroit studies in music bibliography, 61)

An annotated bibliography, arranged alphabetically by author, listing 396 doctoral dissertations, master's theses, and bachelor's essays from 138 colleges and universities in 15 countries; the U.S. and Canada are covered more thoroughly than countries outside North America. The introduction lists an additional eight titles. Each entry includes author, title, degree awarded, discipline (if other than music), university, date of degree, and number of pages. There are indexes to colleges and universities represented, as well as subjects (including personal names) and titles.

Reviewed by John Shepard in *Notes* 46 (1990): 623–28, by Ann P. Basart in *CNV* 135 (1989): 25–26, by William S. Brockman in *ARBA* 21 (1990): no. 1245, and by Anthony Pople in *M&L* 72 (1991): 476.

6.338 *Igor Strawinsky (1882–1971) Phonographie: Seine Eigeninterpretation auf Schallplatten und in den europäischen Rundfunkanstalten, zusammen mit einem Verzeichnis der in den deutschen Rundfunkanstalten und im Deutschen Rundfunkarchiv vorhandenen Rundfunkproduktionen und historischen Schallplattenaufnahm en von Strawinsky-Werken.* 216 pp. Frankfurt am Main: Deutsches Rundfunkarchiv, 1972.

A discography of recordings of Stravinsky conducting his own works and the works of others. Also included are citations of other conductors' interpretations of Stravinsky. The discography is in six sections, the most prominent of which lists Stravinsky's works chronologically and cites names of performers and conductors, describes the works, lists recordings, and gives timings. A subsequent section lists Stravinsky as conductor or performer of the works of other composers, in order by composer. There is a small list of recorded interviews with Stravinsky. There are indexes to sound recording archives cited, authors of texts, dedicatees, and performers. There are chronological lists of recordings by date of session and of first performance.

6.339* Lindlar, Heinrich. *Lübbes Strawinsky Lexikon.* 224 pp. Bergisch Gladbach, Germany: G. Lübbes, 1984.

The first in a new type of lexicon devoted to one composer: introduction on the life, articles on individual works, and the important collaborators (poets, choreographers, conductors, performers).

6.340 Shepard, John. "The Stravinsky *Nachlass:* A Provisional Checklist of Music Manuscripts." In *Notes* 40 (1984): 719–50.

An inventory including extensive descriptions of 223 music manuscript items for 98 works by Stravinsky, including arrangements and copies of the works of other composers.

6.341* White, Eric Walter. *Stravinsky: The Composer and His Works.* 2nd ed. London: Faber & Faber; Berkeley, Calif.: University of California Press, 1979.

First ed., 1966, 608 pp.

After an opening sketch of the composer's life, a book listing Stravinsky's compositions, both original works and arrangements of the work of others, giving for each the circumstances of composition or arrangement, its early performance history, and the work's revisions, adaptations, and transcriptions, relating the works both to each other and to Stravinsky's career, giving musical examples as needed. The appendixes contain nine of his prose works (which had been difficult to locate), a list of his arrangements for player piano, and a bibliography of books by and about him.

Reviewed by François Lesure in *Fontes* 27 (1980) 121–22.

Sullivan, Arthur

6.342 Allen, Reginald, and **Gale R. D'Luhy.** *Sir Arthur Sullivan, Composer and Personage.* 215 pp. New York: Pierpont Morgan Library; London: Chappell, 1975.

Variant edition issued as *Presenting in Word and Song, Score and Deed, the Life and Work of Sir Arthur Sullivan, Composer for Victorian England from Onward, Christian Soldiers to Gilbert and Sullivan Opera* (New York: Pierpont Morgan Library; Boston, Mass.: David R. Godine, 1975, 215 pp.).

This volume presents the life of Sir Arthur Sullivan as seen in the archive formed first by his mother and then by Sullivan himself. The original archive is supplemented with dozens of autograph manuscripts and letters, printed scores, librettos, posters, drawings, prints, photographs, and memorabilia that came to the Pierpont Morgan Library before the acquisition of the papers of Sir Arthur Sullivan and afterward, and today form the Gilbert and Sullivan Collection in the Library.

An exhibition catalog of heroic scope, also including items associated with Sir William Gilbert and Richard D'Oyly Carte. See also **12.25.**

Reviewed by Andrew Lamb in *MT* 116 (1975): 792–93 and by Doug Coe in *Notes* 32 (1976): 553.

6.343* Dillard, Philip H. *How Quaint the Ways of Paradox!: An Annotated Gilbert & Sullivan Bibliography.* 208 pp. Metuchen, N.J.: Scarecrow Press, 1991.

6.344* Dixon, Geoffrey. *The Gilbert and Sullivan Concordance: A Word Index to W. S. Gilbert's Libretti for the Fourteen Operas.* 2 vols. New York: Garland Publishing, 1987. (Garland reference library of the humanities, 702)

6.345 Poladian, Sirvart. *Sir Arthur Sullivan: An Index to the Texts of His Vocal Works.* 91 pp. Detroit, Mich.: Information Coordinators, 1961. (Detroit studies in music bibliography, 2)

A comprehensive index of first lines, titles, and refrains to the composer's vocal works, sacred and secular.

Reviewed by William Lichtenwanger in *Notes* 19 (1962): 428–30.

Szymanowski, Karol

6.346* Michałowski, Kornel. *Karol Szymanowski, 1882–1937: Katalog tematyczny dzieł i bibliografia / Thematic Catalogue of Works and Bibliography / Thematisches Werkverzeichnis und Bibliographie.* 348 pp. Cracow: Polskie Wydawn. Muzyczne, 1967.

A multilingual thematic catalog and bibliography (pp. 285–326).

6.347* Michałowski, Kornel. *Karol Szymanowski: Bibliografia 1967–1991, dyskografia 1981–1991.* 162 pp. Cracow: Musica Iagellonica, 1993.
A continuation of **6.346**.

Tailleferre, Germaine

6.348* Shapiro, Robert. *Germaine Tailleferre: A Bio-Bibliography.* 280 pp. Westport, Conn.: Greenwood Press, 1994. (Bio-bibliographies in music, 48)
Reviewed by Carl B. Schmidt in *Notes* 53 (1996): 474–76 and, in scathing tones, by Karin Pendle in *ARBA* 26 (1995): no. 1271.

Tartini, Giuseppe

6.349 Brainard, Paul. *Le sonate per violino di Giuseppe Tartini: Catalogo tematico.* xl + 145 pp. Padua: Accademia Tartiniana, 1975. (Le opere di Giuseppe Tartini, 3. Studi e ricerche di studiosi moderni, 2)
A catalog of works for solo violin.
Reviewed by Sven Hansell, with addenda, in *Fontes* 35 (1978): 270–73.

Tchaikovsky, Peter

6.350* *Systematisches Verzeichnis der Werke von Pjotr Iljitsch Tschaikowsky: Ein Handbuch für die Musikpraxis.* Edited by the Tschaikowsky-Studio Institut International. 112 pp. Hamburg: Musikverlag Hans Sikorski, 1973.
A classified catalog of Tchaikovsky's works, musical and literary. There is also a chronological list.
Reviewed by Boris Schwarz in *Notes* 31 (1974): 61–62.

Telemann, Georg Philipp

6.351* Jaenecke, Joachim. *Georg Philipp Telemann: Autographe und Abschriften: Katalog.* 453 pp. Munich: G. Henle Verlag, 1993. (Staatsbibliothek zu Berlin, Preussischer Kulturbesitz; Kataloge der Musikabteilung. Erste Reihe: Handschriften, 7)
A list of the 99 Telemann autographs and 350 manuscripts containing works, largely vocal, by Telemann and held by the Staatsbibliothek Preussische Kulturbesitz, Berlin. There are illustrations of 52 copyists' hands and a variety of helpful indexes.
Reviewed by Steven Zohn in *M&L* 76 (1995): 96–98 and by Diane Steinhaus Pettit in *Fontes* 42 (1995): 193–94.

6.352 Landmann, Ortrun. *Die Telemann-Quellen der Sächsischen Landesbibliothek.* 156 pp. Dresden: Sächsischen Landesbibliothek, 1983. (Studien und Materialien zur Musikgeschichte Dresdens, 4)

6.353 Menke, Werner. *Thematisches Verzeichnis der Vokalwerke von Georg Philipp Telemann (TWV).* 2 vols. Frankfurt am Main: V. Klostermann, 1982–83.
A 2nd ed. of Bd. 2 was published in 1988.

6.354* Ruhnke, Martin. *Georg Philipp Telemann: Thematisch-Systematisches Verzeichnis seiner Werke: Telemann-Werkverzeichnis (TWV).* 2 vols. Kassel, Germany: Bärenreiter, 1984–94. (Musikalische Werke. Supplement / Georg Philipp Telemann)

6.355* Wettstein, Hermann. *Georg Philipp Telemann: Bibliographischer Versuch zu seinem Leben und Werk, 1681–1767.* 68 pp. Hamburg: K.D. Wagner, 1981. (Veröffentlichungen der Hamburger Telemann-Gesellschaft, 3)

Thompson, Randall

6.356* **Benser, Caroline Cepin,** and **David Francis Urrows.** *Randall Thompson: A Bio-Bibliography.* 230 pp. New York: Greenwood Press, 1991. (Bio-bibliographies in music, 38)

A biography and documentation of the works of Randall Thompson, both musical and prose, including a bibliography and discography. Appendixes include both a chronological and an alphabetical list of compositions, as well as a list of forthcoming publications from E.C. Schirmer. A well-detailed index completes the work.

Reviewed by Marilyn Barnes in *SSN* 17 (1991): 133, by Ralph Hartsock in *Fontes* 39 (1992): 195–96, and by Byron Adams in *Notes* 48 (1992): 1,299–1,301.

Thomson, Virgil

6.357 **Meckna, Michael.** *Virgil Thomson: A Bio-Bibliography.* 203 pp. New York: Greenwood Press, 1986. (Bio-bibliographies in music, 4)

Reviewed by Ann P. Basart in *CNV* 109 (1987): 5 and by John E. Druesedow, Jr., in *ARBA* 19 (1988): no. 1269.

Tippett, Michael

6.358* **Theil, Gordon.** *Michael Tippett: A Bio-Bibliography.* 344 pp. New York: Greenwood Press, 1989. (Music reference collection, 21)

A reference work designed to direct users to all pertinent, substantive, and accessible information about Tippett, with a works list giving all of Tippett's known works in alphabetical order by title; the discography lists all known recordings under the same system. The bibliography includes separate lists of writings by and about Tippett. Appendixes give a list of compositions chronologically arranged, a classified list of published compositions, a list of honors and awards, a list of ballet and television productions, and a short list of other resources (archives, exhibitions, and conferences). This is a model bio-bibliography.

Reviewed by Ian Kemp in *Fontes* 39 (1991): 86 and by John R. Douglas in *Notes* 47 (1991): 762–63.

Vaughan Williams, Ralph

6.359* **Butterworth, Neil.** *Ralph Vaughan Williams: A Guide to Research.* 382 pp. New York: Garland Publishing, 1990. (Garland reference library of the humanities, 779) (Garland composer resource manuals, 21)

Discography, pp. 125–205.

Reviewed by John R. Douglas in *Notes* 47 (1991): 762–63 and by Alain Frogley in *M&L* 72 (1991): 308–10.

6.360* **Kennedy, Michael.** *A Catalogue of the Works of Ralph Vaughan Williams.* Revised ed. 329 pp. London; New York: Oxford University Press, 1982.

A catalog printed in 1964 as part of Kennedy's *The Works of Ralph Vaughan Williams,* issued later separately with corrections and revisions. The bibliography of Vaughan Williams's writings has been expanded and the catalog of his manuscript collection of folk songs is included.

Reviewed by Allie Wise Goudy in *ARBA* 15 (1984): no. 910.

Verdi, Giuseppe ·

6.361 **Chusid, Martin.** *A Catalog of Verdi's Operas.* 201 pp. Hackensack, N.J.: Joseph Boonin, 1974. (Music indexes and bibliographies, 5)

First ed., 1973, 125 pp.

A catalog of Verdi's 26 operas, with information on early performances and autograph manuscripts. There is a bibliography (pp. 184–95).

Reviewed by David Lawton in *JAMS* 29 (1976): 151–53, by Julian Budden in *M&L* 56 (1975): 66–68, by Andrew Porter in *MT* 116 (1975): 879–80, and by David Rosen in *Notes* 31 (1975): 570–72.

6.362 Hopkinson, Cecil. *A Bibliography of the Works of Giuseppe Verdi, 1813–1901.* 2 vols. New York: Broude Brothers, 1973–78.

The 1st vol. contains information on vocal and instrumental works and a list of Verdi's manuscripts and their locations; the 2nd vol. includes operatic works.

The 1st vol. is reviewed, with addenda, by David Rosen in *Notes* 31 (1975): 570–72 and by Julius Budden in *M&L* 55 (1974): 345–47. The 2nd vol. is reviewed by James J. Fuld in *Notes* 35 (1979): 626 and by Andrew Porter in *Fontes* 27 (1980): 55–56.

6.363 Kaufman, Thomas G., and **Marion Kaufman.** *Verdi and His Major Contemporaries: A Selected Chronology of Performance with Casts.* 590 pp. New York: Garland Publishing, 1990. (Garland reference library of the humanities, 1016) (Annals of Italian opera, 1)

Reviewed by Roberta Montemorra Marvin in *Notes* 49 (1992): 113–15.

Victoria, Tomás Luis de

6.364 Bibliography Committee, New York Chapter, Music Library Association. *An Alphabetical Index to Tomás Luis de Victoria, Opera Omnia.* 26 pp. Ann Arbor, Mich.: Music Library Association, 1966. (MLA index series, 5)

One of three similar indexes produced by this committee in the 1960s for this series; the other two are on Berlioz (1964) and Monteverdi (1963).

Villa-Lobos, Heitor

6.365* Appleby, David P. *Heitor Villa-Lobos: A Bio-Bibliography.* 358 pp. Westport, Conn.: Greenwood Press, 1988. (Bio-bibliographies in music, 9)

Reviewed by Carole Franklin Vidali in *ARBA* 20 (1989): no. 1194.

Viotti, Giovanni Battista

6.366* White, Chappell. *Giovanni Battista Viotti (1755–1824): A Thematic Catalogue of His Works.* 175 pp. New York: Pendragon Press, 1985. (Thematic catalogues, 12)

Vivaldi, Antonio

6.367* Bellina, Anna Laura, Bruno Brizi, and **Maria Grazia Pensa.** *I libretti Vivaldiani: Recensione e collazione dei testimoni a stampa.* 243 pp. + 12 plates. Florence: Leo S. Olschki, 1982. (Studi di musica veneta. Quaderni Vivaldiani, 3)

Descriptions of Vivaldi libretti, arranged alphabetically by title. Each entry gives a bibliographical citation, the protagonists, singers, and library holdings. There are indexes of names and arias. Each plate reproduces the title pages of nine libretti.

6.368 Coral, Lenore. *A Concordance of the Thematic Indexes to the Instrumental Works of Antonio Vivaldi.* 40 pp. Ann Arbor, Mich.: Music Library Association, 1972. (MLA index series, 4)

First ed., 1965, 32 pp.

Reviewed by Seymour Kesten in *JAMS* 28 (1975): 153–56.

6.369 Fanna, Antonio. *Opere strumentali di Antonio Vivaldi (1678–1741): Catalogo numerico-tematico, secondo la catalogazione Fanna.* 2nd ed., revised and enlarged. 185 pp. Milan: Ricordi, 1986.

1st ed. published in 1968 as *Antonio Vivaldi (1678–1741): Catalogo numero-tematico delle opere strumentali,* 192 pp.

6.370 Ohmura, Noriko. *A Reference Concordance Table of Vivaldi's Instrumental Works.* 267 pp. Tokyo: Academia Music, 1972.

Reviewed by Seymour Kesten in *JAMS* 28 (1975): 153–56 and by Lenore Coral in *Notes* 30 (1974): 533–34.

6.371 Ryom, Peter. *Répertoire des oeuvres d'Antonio Vivaldi: Les compositions instrumentales,* Vol. 1– . lxiii + 726 pp. Copenhagen: Engstrom & Sodering A.S. Musikforlag, 1986– .

A classified catalog describing the latest and most widely accepted numbering system for the instrumental works of Vivaldi, a complex repertory with numerous identification systems provided from Vivaldi's time to the present. This catalog gives substantial descriptions of autograph sources, references to preceding thematic catalogs, references to the Ricordi edition of the complete instrumental works, and various historical or bibliographical remarks. There are tables of concordances to the Rinaldi *Catalogo,* the Pincherle *Inventaire thématique,* and the Fanna *Catalogo.* Exhaustive lists of known copies of early printed sources are not provided; readers are referred to RISM A/I/9 (**5.599**). The introduction, essay on bibliographic research, and key to the repertoire are essential aids to using the Ryom *Répertoire.* There are indexes to names, titles of vocal works cited, and titles. Ryom's earlier short catalog, *Verzeichnis der Werke Antonio Vivaldis: RV* (Leipzig: Deutscher Verlag für Musik, 1979), 226 pp., gives access to Vivaldi's music including voices.

Reviewed by Eleanor Selfridge-Field in *Notes* 45 (1988): 69–72.

6.372* Talbot, Michael. *Antonio Vivaldi: A Guide to Research.* New York: Garland Publishing, 1988. xlv + 197 pp. (Garland composer resource manuals, 12) (Garland reference library of the humanities, 757)

Reviewed by Carol June Bradley in *ARBA* 20 (1989): no. 1211, and by John Walter Hill in *M&L* 70 (1989): 245–47.

Wagner, Richard

6.373 Barth, Herbert. *Internationale Wagner-Bibliographie / International Wagner Bibliography / Bibliographie internationale de la littérature sur Wagner.* 1945–55. Bayreuth: Edition Musica, 1956.

A bibliography containing selective lists of German, English, and French writings on Wagner. This is the first of a series of similar bibliographies by Barth, subsequently published in 1961, 1968, and 1979, with each offering a special appendix including a Wieland Wagner bibliography, a tabulation of Bayreuth festival casts from 1876 to 1960, and a Wagner discography.

6.374* Bauer, Hans-Joachim. *Richard Wagner-Lexikon.* 608 pp. Bergisch Gladbach, Germany: G. Lübbe, 1988.

6.375* Brown, Jonathan. *Parsifal on Record: A Discography of Complete Recordings, Selections and Excerpts of Wagner's Music Drama.* 192 pp. Westport, Conn: Greenwood Press, 1992. (Discographies, 48)

Commentaries on the recordings in the introduction. Excerpts identified by musical incipits, with date, place of recordings, record numbers, and performers. Indexes for singers and performers.

6.376* Deathridge, John, Martin Geck, and **Egon Voss.** *Wagner Werk-Verzeichnis (WWV): Verzeichnis der musikalischen Werke Richard Wagners und ihrer Quellen.* 607 pp. Mainz: Schott, 1986.

Reviewed by David Breckbill in *Notes* 47 (1991): 718–22, by Barry Millington in *M&L* 69 (1988): 396–98, and by Ann P. Basart in *CNV* 111 (1987): 13–14.

6.377 Hopkinson, Cecil. *Tannhäuser: An Examination of 36 Editions.* 48 pp. Tutzing, Germany: H. Schneider, 1973. (Musikbibliographische Arbeiten, 1)

6.378 Klein, Horst F. G. *Erst- und Frühdrucke der Textbücher von Richard Wagner: Bibliographie.* 63 pp. Tutzing, Germany: H. Schneider, 1983. (Musikbibliographische Arbeiten, 6)

6.379 Klein, Horst F. G. *Erstdrucke der musikalischen Werke von Richard Wagner: Bibliographie.* 236 pp. Tutzing, Germany: H. Schneider, 1983. (Musikbibliographische Arbeiten, 5)

A beginning attempt to note the early publications of Wagner's musical compositions. Reviewed by James J. Fuld in *Notes* 41 (1984): 284–85.

Walton, William

6.380* Craggs, Stewart R. *William Walton: A Catalogue.* 202 pp. Oxford; New York: Oxford University Press, 1990.

A revised ed. of *William Walton: A Thematic Catalogue of His Musical Works,* 1977, 273 pp.

A catalog of the works of Sir William Walton, bestowing C (for "Craggs") numbers on the works. This ed. omits the musical incipits given in the 1st ed. and adds information on the composer's final works.

Reviewed by Peter Ward Jones in *M&L* 73 (1992): 143–44. The 1st ed. is reviewed by Stephen M. Fry in *Notes* 34 (1978): 620 and by Joan Kunselman in *Notes* 34 (1978): 872–74.

6.381* Craggs, Stewart R. *William Walton: A Source Book.* 333 pp. Aldershot, England: Scolar Press; Brookfield, Vt.: Ashgate Publishing Co., 1993.

A chronology and descriptions of Walton manuscripts and first editions join with a bibliography (pp. 265–323) and discography (pp. 249–63).

Reviewed by Richard Turbet in *Brio* 30 (1993): 33–34, by Martin Jenkins in *Fontes* 42 (1995): 102–3, and by Walter Aaron Clark in *Notes* 51 (1994): 153–54.

6.382* Smith, Carolyn J. *William Walton: A Bio-Bibliography.* 246 pp. New York: Greenwood Press, 1988. (Bio-bibliographies in music, 18)

Reviewed by Kristin Ramsdell in *ARBA* 21 (1990): no. 1254.

Ward, Robert

6.383* Kreitner, Kenneth. *Robert Ward: A Bio-Bibliography.* 173 pp. New York: Greenwood Press, 1988. (Bio-bibliographies in music, 17)

Reviewed by John E. Druesedow in *ARBA* 21 (1990): no. 1246.

Weber, Carl Maria von

6.384 Bartlitz, Eveline. *Carl Maria von Weber: Autographenverzeichnis.* 164 pp. Berlin: Deutsche Staatsbibliothek, 1986. (Handschrifteninventare. Deutsche Staatsbibliothek, 9)

A catalog of the autograph manuscripts housed in the Deutsche Staatsbibliothek, Berlin, with helpful indexes.

6.385* Henderson, Donald G., and **Alice H. Henderson.** *Carl Maria von Weber: A Guide to Research.* 385 pp. New York: Garland Publishing, 1990. (Garland composer resource manuals, 2) (Garland reference library of the humanities, 1006)

Webern, Anton von

6.386 Roman, Zoltan. *Anton von Webern: An Annotated Bibliography.* 219 pp. Detroit, Mich.: Information Coordinators, 1983. (Detroit studies in music bibliography, 48)

A record of the writings on Webern, with coverage from over 100 journals in numerous languages.

Reviewed by George R. Hill in *ARBA* 15 (1984): no. 911.

Weill, Kurt

6.387* Farneth, David. *A Guide to the Weill–Lenya Research Center.* 146 pp. New York: Kurt Weill Foundation for Music, 1995.

The guide to a model center for research, with a chronological list of Weill's works, ordered by premiere date (pp. 101–11), a list of Lenya's performances, recordings, films, radio plays, television appearances, and awards (pp. 113–20), and bibliography (pp. 121–24). The Center's home page is **12.39.**

Wilder, Alec

6.388* Demsey, David, Ronald Prather, and **Judith Bell.** *Alec Wilder: A Bio-Bibliography.* 274 pp. Westport, Conn.: Greenwood Press, 1993. (Bio-bibliographies in music, 45)

A short biography, a works list (with information on first performances), a discography, a bibliography of works by and about Wilder, an inventory of unpublished material, and a list of Wilder's publishers.

Reviewed by Gunther Schuller in *Notes* 51 (1994): 81–83.

Wolf, Hugo

6.389* Ossenkop, David. *Hugo Wolf: A Guide to Research.* xxxii + 329 pp. New York: Garland Publishing, 1988. (Garland composer resource manuals, 15) (Garland reference library of the humanities, 747)

A thorough examination of material needed by Wolf researchers, including an annotated bibliography and a detailed works list with publishing history.

Reviewed by Christopher Hatch in *Notes* 47 (1991): 759, by Kirsten Ramsdell in *ARBA* 20 (1989): no. 1207, by John Williamson in *M&L* 70 (1989): 568–69, and by Ann P. Basart in *CNV* 130 (1989): 10.

Wuorinen, Charles

6.390* Burbank, Richard D. *Charles Wuorinen: A Bio-Bibliography.* 330 pp. Westport, Conn.: Greenwood Press, 1994. (Bio-bibliographies in music, 49)

Discography (pp. 95–113).

Reviewed by Koraljka Lockhart in *ARBA* 26 (1995): no. 1265.

Zelenka, Johann Dismas

6.391* Landmann, Ortrun, Wolfgang Reich, Wolfgang Horn, and **Thomas Kohlhase.** *Zelenka-Dokumentation: Quellen und Materialien.* 2 vols. Wiesbaden: Breitkopf & Härtel, 1989.

Zemlinsky, Alexander

6.392* Oncley, Lawrence A. "The Works of Alexander Zemlinsky: A Chronological List." In *Notes* 34 (1977): 291–302.

With brief descriptive notes and location information.

7

CATALOGS OF MUSIC LIBRARIES AND COLLECTIONS

Knowledge of the published catalogs of the major music libraries and collections is essential for locating source materials for research or study. The latest development to ease access to at least some of these collections is that of the various electronic networks. It will be a long time, however, before these networks eliminate the need for print catalogs. The most recent comprehensive survey of music libraries is the article "Libraries" (**7.2**) in *The New Grove* (**1.48**), whereas the most potentially complete overview is the *Directory of Music Research Libraries* (**7.1**), published under the auspices of the International Association of Music Libraries as Series C of *RISM* (**5.590**). The latter supplies international coverage for music libraries in Europe, North America, and other parts of the world. A substantial though dated list (by Alfons Ott) of music libraries is found in *MGG* (**1.9**). The German music libraries are also separately described and their catalogs cited in Richard Schaal's *Führer durch deutsche Musikbibliotheken*, 1971 (**7.187**). In addition, *Fontes* has published numerous special issues on various countries' music libraries and archives, including Belgium (22 [1976]), Canada (34 [1987]) and (41 [1994]), Czechoslovakia (38 [1991]), Denmark (42 [1995]), France (37 [1990]), Great Britain (25 [1978]), Italy (18 [1971]), Japan (34 [1988]), The Netherlands (21 [1974]), New Zealand (39 [1992]), Sweden (11 [1964]) and (33 [1986]), and the United States (16 [1969]). These give valuable descriptive material on the various nations' resources.

This chapter covers the catalogs of the principal music libraries of the world, as well as some important or interesting archival collections. Also included are a few exhibit catalogs and a number of auction or sale catalogs of music collections that have been dispersed, an important category of bibliographical tool that is often overlooked. It goes without saying that many musical source materials have never been cited in special music catalogs. Information must be sought in general library catalogs of early printed books and manuscripts. Descriptions of the music manuscripts in the Bodleian Library at Oxford, for example, must be extracted from the volumes of Madan's *Summary Catalogue of Western Manuscripts in the Bodleian Library at Oxford* (1895–1953). Likewise, Cambridge University music manuscripts are fully described in the series of college library catalogs compiled by Montague Rhodes James. No attempt has been made in this chapter to cite general catalogs of this kind, but the reader's attention may be called to the invaluable guide to Latin manuscript books before 1600, a list of the printed catalogs and unpublished inventories of extant collections by Paul Kristeller, *Latin Manuscript Books before 1600* (revised ed., Fordham University Press, 1960). Of course, the search for music sources has been greatly facilitated by the continuing appearance of volumes in the series *Répertoire international des sources musicales* and related volumes deriving from the large store of information in the offices of the *RISM*-Sekretariat in Frankfurt. In the present list the catalogs have been grouped, as far as possible, by place. Place is ordinarily designated as a city followed by the appropriate country (or state in the case of the United States). Certain national union catalogs or descriptions of the holdings of several libraries within a country are entered under the name of the country. Catalogs of important collections and collections belonging to important and influential persons are grouped in a special category at the end of this chapter (**7.605–7.648**).

The first two entries of this chapter provide substantial information about research music libraries, their holdings, and their catalogs. The first entry is for an international directory of music research libraries issued under the auspices of the International Association of Music Libraries and issued as Series C of *RISM*. The second entry supplements and updates the first.

7.1 Benton, Rita. *Directory of Music Research Libraries.* Kassel, Germany; New York: Bärenreiter, 1967– . (Répertoire international des sources musicales, C)

Parts II and III issued by the Commission on Research Libraries of the International Association of Music Libraries; the remaining vols. were issued as numbers in *RISM,* Series C.

Vol. 1: *Canada; United States.* 2nd revised ed. 282 pp. Kassel, Germany; New York: Bärenreiter, 1983– .

Superseding Part I: *Canada and the United States.* Preliminary ed. Iowa City, Iowa: University of Iowa, 1967. 70 pp.

The Canadian section was edited by Marian Kahn and Helmut Kallmann, the United States section by Charles Lindahl.

Descriptions of music collections in general, special and private libraries. The introduction to the United States section contains valuable information on the revision and the guidelines for including libraries in it. The entries are arranged alphabetically by name of city and then institution. Addresses, telephone numbers, services offered, nature of catalogs, collection size, and public hours are listed, and significant special collections are described. Literature pertinent to each collection is cited and references to more extensive or more specific descriptions in the works cited in the initial bibliography of general literature are provided, as is a general bibliography of literature on library collections in the United States and Canada. There are indexes to host institutions, personal and corporate names of collections, and archives within host institutions. The *RISM* sigla for each library is given in parentheses immediately after the entry number; page headings show country codes in the same fashion. The United States section entries include references to entries in *Resources of American Music History* (**4.355**).

Reviewed by Geraldine Ostrove in *Fontes* 31 (1984): 134–35.

Part II: *Thirteen European Countries.* Preliminary ed. 235 pp. Iowa City, Iowa: University of Iowa, 1970.

A directory arranged by country (Austria, Belgium, Switzerland, the Federal Republic of Germany, the German Democratic Republic, Denmark, Ireland, Great Britain, Luxembourg, Norway, The Netherlands, Sweden, and Finland), and within each country alphabetically by city and then alphabetically by institution. Includes a short bibliography of general literature and, at the beginning of each country's section, a bibliography of works on libraries and collections in that country. For some cities there is also a bibliography of works (e.g., Cologne, p. 79). Libraries cited are primarily those reporting holdings to *RISM*, although some others are included. Generally, the entries have the same kind of information as given in Vol. 1, although some entries are quite brief. The bibliographies of literature on works and collections in each institution are invaluable. The index cites present and former names of libraries and their host institutions and is arranged by country.

There are reviews by Jack A. Westrup in *M&L* 52 (1971): 316, by Vincent H. Duckles in *JRME* 20 (1972): 293–94, by Susan T. Sommer in *Notes* 29 (1972): 259–60, and by François Lesure in *Fontes* 18 (1971): 129.

Part III: *Spain, France, Italy, Portugal.* Preliminary ed. 342 pp. Iowa City, Iowa: University of Iowa, 1972.

4 pp. errata bound in after p. 342.

A directory with organization and content similar to Parts I and II. Some entries note published catalogs of individual collections that are continuously updated and annotated by hand in the home institutions. Supplemental information for Spanish libraries was given by Maurice Esses in "New Information Concerning Some Music Research Libraries in Spain," in *Fontes* 26 (1979): 189–91, and for Spain and Portugal by Eugene Casjen Cramer in "New Information Concerning Some Music Libraries and Archives in Spain and Portugal," in *Notes* 40 (1984): 30–40.

Parts I–III are reviewed by Eugene K. Wolf in *JAMS* 29 (1976): 484–86; Part III is reviewed by Richard Andrewes in *MT* 118 (1977): 304.

Vol. 4: *Australia.* [Edited by Cecil Hill.] *Israel.* [Edited by Katya Manor.] *Japan.* [Edited by James Siddons.] *New Zealand.* [Edited by Dorothy Freed.] 177 pp. Kassel, Germany: Bärenreiter, 1979.

Organized as Parts I–III. The Japanese place names are transliterated, with city names showing the prefecture.

Reviewed by Harold J. Diamond in *Notes* 36 (1980): 660–61 and by Wolfgang Krueger in *Fontes* 27 (1980): 223–24.

Vol. 5: *Czechoslovakia, Hungary, Poland.* [Edited by James B. Moldovan.] *Yugoslavia.* [Edited by Lilian Pruett.]

Organized as above.

7.2 Benton, Rita, Mary Wallace Davidson, Samuel Claro, Catherine Dower, José Ignacio Perdomo Escobar, Norma González, Francesco Curt Lange, Mercedes Reis Pequeno, Robert Stevenson, Pola Suárez Urturbey, Dorothy Freed, Werner Gallusser, Don Harrán, Katharine A. Haslam, and **James Siddons.** "Libraries." In *The New Grove Dictionary of Music and Musicians* (**1.48**).

A description of the history and various functions and types of music libraries, followed by a geographically organized survey of music libraries. There is an introductory paragraph on each country's music libraries that occasionally cites the principal means of access to music bibliographical records for that country. Each entry in the survey describes the library's history and holdings, as well as citing any literature about the library, including catalogs. This survey supplements the *RISM* Series C directories (**7.1**) and provides information about libraries in countries not yet covered by those directories. The article covers only institutional libraries and provides a directory of national music information centers.

The New Grove Dictionary of American Music (**1.220**) updates information on American libraries in "Libraries," by Mary Wallace Davidson.

CATALOGS OF MUSIC LIBRARIES

Århus, Denmark

STATSBIBLIOTEKET

7.3 Clausen, Per Groth. *Dansk musik: Katalog øver Statsbibliotekets samling af trykte musikalier / Danish Music: A Catalogue of Printed Music in the State and University Library, Aarhus.* xxiv + 316 pp. Århus: Universitetsforlaget i Århus, 1977.

A classified catalog of the Danish printed music in the Århus collections in 1975. The entries give publisher and publisher's number, opus number, and number of pages. Includes an index to names cited in the classified catalog, as well as an alphabetical list, by composer, of titles not listed in the classified catalog but available in an unbound collection at the university.

7.4 *Musikalier.* 4 vols. 2nd ed. Århus: Århus Stiftsbogtrykkerie forlaget, 1951–70. (Fagkataloger, 3)
First ed., 1925–29.

The catalog of the music collection at the Statsbiblioteket. The 1st vol. contains collections and music for one instrument; the 2nd vol., chamber and orchestral music; the 3rd vol., vocal, dramatic, and folk music; the 4th vol., a supplement to the first three and an index to composers.

7.5 Winkel, Erling, and **Ingeborg Heilmann.** *Fagkataloger.* 2nd ed. 4 vols. Århus: Århus Stiftsbogtrykkerie, 1946–57. (Fagkataloger, 4)
> First ed., 1925.
> A multivolume music catalog; 3 vols. list music and the fourth lists music literature and has a composer index. The volumes listing music include both anthologies and separate publications, with the contents given for anthologies.

Aberdeen, Scotland

7.6 Cooper, B. A. R. "Catalogue of Early Printed Music in Aberdeen Libraries." In *RMA Research Chronicle* 14 (1978): 2–138.
> A catalog covering holdings of the University Library, the Library of the University Music Department, and the Aberdeen City Public Library. It updates the *British Union Catalogue of Early Music* (**5.600**) and *RISM* (**5.590**), providing 800 entries, of which 100 seem to be unique. The arrangement is alphabetical by main entry (author or title). Entries occasionally provide annotations. Appendixes include writings on music, volumes with plainsong, private collections, and a chronological index. Includes an index to genres and an index of publishers.

Adria, Italy

CATTEDRALE DI ADRIA. ARCHIVIO CAPITOLARE

7.7 Cavallini, Ivano. "Il fondo musicale dell'Archivio della Chiesa Cattedrale di Adria: Elenco." In *Fontes* 27 (1980): 84–91.
> An inventory of early printed editions and manuscripts, most of the 19th century.

7.8* Passadore, Francesco. *Il fondo musicale dell'Archivio Capitolare della Cattedrale di Adria.* xxxi + 335 pp. Rome: Edizioni Torre d'Orfeo, 1989. (Cataloghi di fondi musicali italiani, 11)
> At head of title: Giunta Regionale del Veneto. Fondazione Ugo e Olga Levi. Associazione Veneta per la Ricerca delle Fonti Musicali.
> The catalog of the music holdings of the Archivio of the Cathedral, including musical incipits, bibliographical references, and indexes.
> Reviewed by Graham Dixon in *M&L* 72 (1991): 429 and by D. W. Krummel in *Notes* 48 (1992): 918–21.

Alsace, France

7.9* Honegger, Genevieve. *Alsace: Catalogue des imprimés anciens: Musique polyphonique XVIe–XVIIIe siècles.* 146 pp. Strasbourg: Bibliothèque Nationale et Universitaire de Strasbourg, Association Régionale pour le Développement de l'Action Musicale, 1993. (Patrimoine musical régional)

Altötting, Germany

STIFTSKIRCHE

7.10* Schwindt-Gross, Nicole. *Die Musikhandschriften der Stiftskirche Altötting, des Kollegiatstifts Landshut und der Pfarrkirchen Beuerberg, Schnaitsee und St. Mang in Füssen: Thematischer Katalog.* xl + 331 pp. Munich: G. Henle, 1992. (Kataloge bayerischer Musiksammlungen, 18)
> A catalog including bibliographical references (pp. 290–308) and indexes.

Amsterdam, The Netherlands

NEDERLANDS FILMMUSEUM

7.11* Houten, Theodore van. *Silent Cinema Music in the Netherlands: The Eyl/Van Houten*

Collection of Film and Cinema Music in the Nederlands Filmmuseum. 328 pp. Buren, The Netherlands: F. Knuf, 1992.

Reviewed by David Kershaw in *Notes* 51 (1994): 154–55.

VERENIGING VOOR NEDERLANDSE
MUZIEKGESCHIEDENIS. BIBLIOTHEEK

7.12 *Catalogus van de bibliotheek der Vereniging voor Nederlandse Muziekgeschiedenis.* 274 pp. Amsterdam: G. Alsbach, 1919.

A classified catalog, including both early and recent works, containing a special section of manuscripts. There is an index of names and titles.

Ancona, Italy

7.13* **Salvarani, Marco.** *Catalogo delle opere musicali della Biblioteca Communale "Luciano Benincasa" di Ancona.* 272 pp. Rome: Edizioni Torre d'Orfeo, 1988. (Cataloghi di fondi musicali italiani, 9)

At head of title: Associazione Marchigiana per la Ricerca e Valorizzazione delle Fonti Musicali.

Aosta, Italy

BIBLIOTECA CAPITOLARE

7.14 **Chatrian, Giorgio.** *Il fondo musicale della Biblioteca Capitolare di Aosta.* 252 pp. + 16 pp. plates. Turin: Centro Studi Piemontesi, Fondo "Carlo Felice Bona," 1985. (Il gridelino, 5)

A classified catalog of manuscripts and printed works. Dedications are transcribed in full and anthologies are analyzed. Includes an extensive introductory essay on the cathedral and the collection, and a name index.

Assisi, Italy

BIBLIOTECA COMUNALE

7.15 **Pennacchi, Francesco.** *Catalogo generale delle opere musicali: Città di Assisi: Biblioteca Comunale.* 45 pp. Parma, Italy: Freschig, 1921. (Associazione dei Musicologi Italiani. Catalogo generale delle opere musicali, 11)

Part of a series, later expanded.

7.16 **Sartori, Claudio.** *Catalogo del fondo musicale nella Biblioteca Comunale di Assisi.* 449 pp. Milan: Istituto Editoriale Italiano, 1962. (Bibliotheca musicae, 1)

A catalog that expands the earlier work of Francesco Pennacchi (**7.15**), listing early printed music, books, and manuscripts separately. Most of the material is pre-1800, but a few 19th-century manuscripts are included. The entries give contents of early items and locations for rarities. There are descriptive annotations.

Reviewed by Walther Dürr in *Die Musikforschung* 18 (1965): 83–84 and by Albert Seay in *JAMS* 16 (1963): 269–79.

Astorga, Spain

CATEDRAL DE ASTORGA

7.17* **Álvarez Pérez, José María.** *Catalogo y estudio del Archivo musical de la Catedral de Astorga.* 226 pp. Cuenca, Spain: Instituto de Musica Religiosa de la Diputación Provincial, 1985.

A thematic catalog of music manuscripts in the Catedral de Astorga.

Atlanta, Georgia

EMORY UNIVERSITY. WOODRUFF LIBRARY

7.18 Hoogerwerf, Frank W. "Confederate Sheet Music at Robert W. Woodruff Library, Emory University." In *Notes* 34 (1978): 7–26.

A checklist of Emory's collection of Confederate sheet music, arranged by title.

Augsburg, Germany

KREIS- UND STADTBIBLIOTHEK

7.19 Schletterer, Hans M. *Katalog der in der Kreis- und Stadtbibliothek der Städtischen Archive und der Bibliothek des Historischen Vereins zu Augsburg befindlichen Musikwerke.* 138 pp. Augsburg: Fidelis Butsch Sohn, 1879. (Monatsheft für Musikgeschichte, Beilage, Jahrgang 10–11, 1878–79)

Another ed. was published in 1879 by T. Trautwein, Berlin.

Essentially a classified inventory of 43 manuscripts and several hundred printed works, including 29 early books on music. Entries provide title page transcriptions and information on part books. Includes a name and subject index and an index of publishers and booksellers.

ST. ANNA LUTHERAN CHURCH AND SCHOOL

7.20 Schaal, Richard. *Das Inventar der Kantorei St. Anna in Augsburg: Ein Beitrag zur protestantischen Musikpflege im 16. und beginnenden 17. Jahrhundert.* 107 pp. Kassel, Germany: Bärenreiter, 1965. (Catalogus musicus, 3)

The transcription of an inventory compiled in the early 17th century of the music collection of the Lutheran church and school of St. Anna in Augsburg. The collection itself is no longer intact.

STAATS- UND STADTBIBLIOTHEK

7.21 Gottwald, Clytus. *Handschriften der Staats- und Stadtbibliothek Augsburg. Band I: Die Musikhandschriften der Staats- und Stadtbibliothek Augsburg (einschliesslich der Liturgica mit Notation).* xxxiii + 328 pp. Wiesbaden: Otto Harrassowitz, 1974. (Handschriftenkataloge der Staats- und Stadtbibliothek Augsburg, 1)

A catalog providing extensive descriptions and full analytical entries of musical manuscripts in the state and city library of Augsburg. There are indexes to names, places, and things and to first lines and titles, as well as a list of prior owners.

Austin, Texas

UNIVERSITY OF TEXAS AT AUSTIN. HARRY RANSOM HUMANITIES RESEARCH CENTER

7.22 *Library Chronicle* 25/26 (1984).

Eight articles providing information on French music manuscripts (including Ravel's *Daphnis et Chloé, Rapsodie Espagnole,* and *Ma Mère l'Oye* and works by Debussy, Fauré, Roussel, and Dukas), the Bachmann Collection of 19th-century first and early editions, sacred vocal music from the Cortot Collection, various settings by William Walton of *Façade,* and the Ross Russell Collection of materials on Charlie "Bird" Parker and Dial Records.

Auvergne, France

7.23* Constant, Françoise, and **Jean-Louis Jam.** *Catalogue des fonds musicaux anciens conservés en Auvergne.* 68 pp. Clermont-Ferrand, France: AREPANA; Aix-en-Provence: EDISUD, 1992. (Patrimoine musical régional)

A union catalog of early editions of music held in the Auvergne region.

Avignon, France

BIBLIOTHÈQUE MUNICIPALE LIVRÉE CECCANO

7.24* Castinel, Nathalie. *Catalogue du fonds musical: Avignon, Bibliothèque Municipale Livrée Ceccano, Vol. 1–* . 1 vol. to date. Paris: ARCAM; Aix-en-Provence: EDISUD, 1989– . (Patrimoine musical regional)

Ávila, Spain

CATEDRAL DE ÁVILA

7.25* López Calo, José. *Catálogo del archivo de musica de la Catedral de Ávila.* 306 pp. + 32 pp. plates. Santiago de Compostela: Sociedad Española de Musicología, 1978. (Publicaces de la Sociedad Española de Musicología, B1)
   "Apéndice documental-biográfia" (pp. 211–99).

REAL MONASTERIO DE SANTA ANA

7.26* Vicente Delgado, Alfonso de. *La música en el Monasterio de Santa Ana de Ávila (Siglo XVI–XVII): Catálogo.* 267 pp. Madrid: Sociedad Española de Musicología (Editorial Alpuerto), 1989. (Publicaciones de la Sociedad Española de Musicología, B5)
   A thematic catalog of music manuscripts of the 16th and 17th centuries.

Badajoz, Spain

MONASTERIO DE GUADALUPE

7.27 Barrado, Archangel. *Catálogo del archivo musical del Monasterio de Guadalupe.* 181 pp. Badajoz, Spain: 1945.
   The catalog of a collection of accompanied sacred vocal music, chiefly late 18th century. It includes 947 items, preceded by a historical study of the archive. There are indexes of composers and musical forms.

Baden-Württemberg, Germany

7.28* Günther, Georg. *Musikalien des 18. und 19. Jahrhunderts aus Kloster and Pfarrkirche Ochsenhausen: Katalog.* xxv + 464 pp. Stuttgart: Metzler, 1995. (Quellen und Studien zur Musik in Baden-Württemberg, 1) (Kataloge des Schwabischen Landesmusikarchivs am Musikwissenschaftlichen Institut der Universität Tubingen, 1)

Baltimore, Maryland

JOHNS HOPKINS UNIVERSITY. MILTON S. EISENHOWER LIBRARY

7.29 *Guide to the Lester S. Levy Collection of Sheet Music.* 40 pp. Baltimore, Md.: Milton S. Eisenhower Library, Johns Hopkins University, 1984.
   An introduction to one of the most extensive collections of sheet music in the United States.

Barcelona, Spain

DIPUTACIÓN PROVINCIAL. BIBLIOTECA CENTRAL

7.30 Pedrell, Felipe. *Catàlech de la Biblioteca Musical de la Diputació de Barcelona ab notes* *històriques, biogràfiques y critiques, transcripcions en notació moderna dels principals motius musicals y facsímils dels documents més importants pera la bibliografía espanyola.* 2 vols. Barcelona: Palau de la Diputació, 1908–9.

A classified catalog of 1,271 entries, including theory, history, practical music, with full bibliographical entries, collations, extensive notes, facsimiles, and musical quotations. The items are listed by signature number, with an alphabetical index in Vol. 2.

Barletta, Italy

BIBLIOTECA COMUNALE "SABINO LOFFREDO"

7.31* **Fabris, Dinko.** *Il fondo musicale "Gallo" della Biblioteca Comunale di Barletta.* 232 pp. Barletta, Italy: Città di Barletta, Assessorato alla Cultura, Biblioteca Comunale "Sabino Loffredo," 1983. (Ricerche della biblioteca, 4)

The catalog of the collections of Vincenzo and Antonio Gallo.

Basel, Switzerland

PAUL SACHER STIFTUNG

7.32 Lichtenhahn, Ernst, and **Tilman Seebass.** *Musikhandschriften aus der Sammlung Paul Sacher: Festschrift zu Paul Sachers siebzigstem Geburtstag.* 197 pp. Basel: Editions Roche, 1976.

A catalog that includes, in addition to a number of facsimiles of manuscripts in the Sammlung Sacher, a "Katalog sämtlicher Musikhandschriften der Sammlung Paul Sacher" (pp. 47–79).

UNIVERSITÄT. BIBLIOTHEK

7.33* **Kmetz, John.** *Die Handschriften der Universitätsbibliothek Basel: Katalog der Musikhandschriften des 16. Jahrhunderts: Quellenkritische und historische Untersuchung.* 482 pp. Basel: Verlag der Universitätsbibliothek Basel, 1988.

A description of 49 (or 35, by more conventional standards) manuscripts. The editor looks for "bibliographical and paleographical evidence for each manuscript's production, and offers, whenever possible, archival data [i.e., letters, account books, and various library inventories] concerning their scribes, owners, and composers, in order to establish the repertory's chronology, authorship, or patterns of transmission" (p. 20).

Reviewed by John Emerson in *Notes* 47 (1990): 59–61 and by Christian Meyer in *Revue de musicologie* 76 (1990): 103–4.

7.34 Refardt, Edgar. *Katalog der Musikabteilung der Öffentlichen Bibliothek der Universität Basel und in ihr enthaltenen Schweizerischen Musikbibliothek. Band I: Musikalische Kompositionen.* 141 pp. Basel: Universitäts-Bibliothek, 1925.

A catalog of works listed in alphabetical order by composer, with important collections analyzed. There are separate lists of collections, followed by a summary of the contents of several manuscript collections of music by Swiss composers. There is an index of editors, arrangers, and librettists.

7.35 Refardt, Edgar. *Thematischer Katalog der Instrumentalmusik des 18. Jahrhunderts in den Handschriften der Universitätsbibliothek Basel.* 59 pp. Bern: P. Haupt, 1957. (Publikationen der Schweizerischen Musikforschenden Gesellschaft, 2:6)

A collection whose major part was assembled by the Basel silk manufacturer Lucas Sarasin (1730–1802). Some 473 of the works cited were once part of his library. With these are incorporated the collection of the Basel Collegium Musicum and that of the de Pury family. References are made to 18th-century printings of the works here found in manuscript.

7.36 Richter, Julius. *Katalog der Musik-Sammlung auf der Universitäts-Bibliothek in Basel (Schweiz).* 104 pp. Leipzig: Breitkopf & Härtel, 1892. (Beilage. Monatshefte für Musikgeschichte. Jahrgang 23–24)

A catalog giving full descriptions, contents, musical quotations for manuscripts, and a list of the early printed music in the university library.

Bath, England

BATH REFERENCE LIBRARY

7.37* Gillaspie, Jon A. *The Catalogue of Music in the Bath Reference Library.* 4 vols. + 8 microfiches. London: Saur, 1986.

An analytical catalog of published music, manuscript music, and manuscripts related to the music collection, with emphasis on Bath-related materials. The catalog includes transcriptions of correspondence and music transcriptions. The microfiches serve as an image and data bank comprising all illustrated title pages, as well as plates, frontispieces, pre-1800 music catalogs and advertisements, significant title pages and other items of interest. Indexes are included.

Reviewed by William Brockman in *ARBA* 18 (1987): 1224.

Bavaria, Germany

7.38* Haberkamp, Gertraut, and **Barbara Zuber.** *Die Musikhandschriften Herzog Wilhelms in Bayern, der Grafen zu Toerring-Jettenbach und der Fürsten Fugger von Babenhausen: Thematischer Katalog.* xl + 195 pp. Munich: G. Henle, 1988. (Kataloge bayerischer Musiksammlungen, 13)

The catalog of three collections of music. The Fugger collection, however, was a casualty of war and now exists only in its 1919 thematic catalog.

Reviewed by John Wagstaff in *M&L* 70 (1989): 408–9 and by Lilian P. Pruett in *Fontes* 37 (1990): 165–66.

7.39* Haberkamp, Gertraut, and **Martin Seelkopf.** *Musikhandschriften katholischer Pfarreien in Franken, Bistum Würzburg: Thematischer Katalog.* xlii + 344 pp. Munich: G. Henle, 1990. (Kataloge bayerischer Musiksammlungen, 17)

Reviewed by D. W. Krummel in *Notes* 48 (1992): 918–21 and by Lilian P. Pruett in *Fontes* 40 (1993): 339–42.

7.40 Münster, Robert. "Die Erfassung von Musikhandschriften aus nichtstaatlichem Besitz in Bayern." In *Mitteilungen für die Archivpflege in Bayern* 12 (1966), Heft 2, pp. 45 ff.

A description of the seizure of privately owned collections of musical autographs.

7.41 Münster, Robert, and **Robert Machold.** *Kataloge bayerischer Musiksammlungen. Thematischer Katalog der Musikhandschriften der ehemaligen Klosterkirchen Weyarn, Tegernsee und Benediktbeuern.* Edited by the General Director of the Bavarian State Library. 196 pp. Munich: Henle, 1971.

A record of the holdings of various Bavarian cloisters and abbeys, whose catalogs are maintained in the Bavarian State Library in Munich.

Reviewed by Robert N. Freeman in *Notes* 33 (1976): 72–73 and by Barry S. Brook in *JAMS* 32 (1979): 549–55.

7.42 Münster, Robert, Robert Machold, Ursula Bockholdt, and **Lisbet Thew.** *Thematischer Katalog der Musikhandschriften der Benediktinerinnenabtei Frauenworth und der Pfarrkirchen Indersdorf, Wasserburg am Inn und Bad Tölz.* 211 pp. Munich: G. Henle, 1975. (Kataloge bayerischer Musiksammlungen)

Thematic catalogs of musical manuscripts, largely 18th-century sacred, at the Benedictine abbey Frauenwörth at Wasserburg–St. Jakob and the Pfarrkirchen Indersdorf at Bad Tölz, with full descriptions of sources and indexes to copyists and watermarks, early printed music in the abbeys of Indersdorf and Wasserburg, names, titles, and first lines. There is a bibliography of works consulted.

Reviewed by Robert N. Freeman in *Notes* 33 (1976): 72–73 and by Barry S. Brook in *JAMS* 32 (1979): 549–55.

7.43 Münster, Robert, Hans Schmid, and **Folker Göthel.** *Musik in Bayern.* I. *Bayerische Musikgeschichte, Überblick und Einzeldarstellungen.* II. *Ausstellungskatalog Augsburg, Juli bis Oktober 1972.* 2 vols. Tützing, Germany: H. Schneider, 1972.

An overview of Bavarian music history. Vol. I is a collection of essays on various aspects of Bavarian music history; Vol. II is an exhibition catalog of 850 items illustrative of Bavarian musical history and culture, with numerous facsimile plates.

7.44* Schwindt-Gross, Nicole, and **Barbara Zuber.** *Die Musikhandschriften der Josefskongregation Ursberg, des Cassianeums Donauworth und der Malteser-Studienstiftung Amberg: Thematischer Katalog.* xxxvi + 428 pp. Munich: G. Henle, 1992. (Kataloge bayerischer Musiksammlungen, 15)

Berea, Ohio

BALDWIN-WALLACE COLLEGE.
RIEMENSCHNEIDER MEMORIAL BACH LIBRARY.

7.45 Kenney, Sylvia W. *Catalog of the Emilie and Karl Riemenschneider Memorial Bach Library.* 295 pp. New York: Columbia University Press, 1960.

A numbered catalog of 2,537 items, of which the first 520 are writings on Bach and his time, Nos. 521–31 are music of Bach's sons and contemporaries, and Nos. 532–2,537 are music of J. S. Bach. The principal grouping is by musical forms; manuscripts are listed separately. Includes an index of cantatas as well as a general index.

There are 13 supplemental catalogs, the first 4 compiled by J. B. Winzenburger, which have been issued to members of the Riemenschneider Bach Institute (1970–84). Current acquisitions are reported in the periodical *Bach*, 1970– .

Reviewed by Walter Emery in *M&L* 42 (1961): 376–77.

Bergamo, Italy

BIBLIOTECA CIVICA

7.46 Gazzaniga, Arrigo. *Il fondo musicale Mayr della Biblioteca Civica di Bergamo, nel secondo centenario della nascita di Giovanni Simone Mayr (1763–1963).* 149 pp. Bergamo: Edizioni "Monumenta Bergomensia," 1963. (Monumenta bergomensia, 11)

A classified catalog of works by Simone Mayr and his contemporaries in the Biblioteca Civica in Bergamo. The listings are chiefly manuscripts, including many autographs; the catalog has 24 pp. of facsimiles.

Berkeley, California

UNIVERSITY OF CALIFORNIA AT BERKELEY.
MUSIC LIBRARY

7.47* *A Collection of Sicilian Libretti: Il melodramma in Sicilia.* 304 + 22 ll. in loose-leaf binder. 19– .

A catalog inventorying a collection of Sicilian opera libretti, made by Taddei di Ferrara, dating from 1650 to the 20th century; this collection is thought to have been purchased by Berkeley in the 1960s. The catalog is unpublished and Berkeley has cataloged the photocopy of a carbon copy.

7.48 Curtis, Alan. "Musique classique française à Berkeley: Pièces inedités de Louis Couperin, Lebègue, La Barre, etc." In *Revue de musicologie* 55 (1969): 123–64.

A description and inventory of 14 manuscripts of French music, chiefly keyboard, from the late 17th and early 18th centuries, in the Music Library of the University of California at Berkeley.

7.49 Duckles, Vincent, and **Minnie Elmer.** *Thematic Catalog of a Manuscript Collection of 18th-Century Italian Instrumental Music in the University of California, Berkeley, Music Library.* 403 pp. Berkeley and Los Angeles, Calif.: University of California Press, 1963.

A collection comprising some 990 manuscripts containing works by 82 composers of the Tartini school at Padua. The central figures are Giuseppe Tartini and Michele Stratico. Preliminary chapters discuss the historical background of the collection and tabulate the handwritings and the watermarks represented.

Reviewed by Charles Cudworth in the *Galpin Society Journal* 18 (1965): 140–41, by Denis Stevens in *MT* 105 (1964): 513–14, and by Donald W. Krummel in *Notes* 22 (1966): 1,025–26.

7.50* Emerson, John A. *Catalog of Pre-1900 Vocal Manuscripts in the Music Library, University of California at Berkeley.* xxiii + 348 pp. Berkeley, Calif.: University of California Press, 1988. (University of California publications. Catalogs and bibliographies, 4)

A catalog of a collection containing works both too early and too late to be found in *RISM* (**5.590**), as well as titles so reported. The editor wrote about his project in "On the Making of a Catalog of Music Manuscripts," *CNV* 122 (1988): 5–7.

Reviewed by Marie Louise Göllner in *Notes* 50 (1993): 588–89, by Oliver Neighbour in *M&L* 70 (1989): 395–96, and by Ann P. Basart in *CNV* 120 (1988): 14.

Berlin, Germany

DEUTSCHE STAATSBIBLIOTHEK

7.51 Kast, Paul. *Die Bach-Handschriften der Berliner Staatsbibliothek.* 150 pp. Trossingen, Germany: Hohner-Verlag, 1958. (Tübinger Bach-Studien, 2/3)

A catalog of manuscripts of music by members of the Bach family, once part of the collection of the Prussian State Library, now distributed between the two Deutsche Staatsbibliotheken (West and East) and the University Library at Tübingen. This is essentially a finding list for one of the world's great collections of Bach sources, with brief entries and indexes of composers, scribes, and former owners of the manuscripts.

7.52 Köhler, Karl-Heinz. "Die Musikabteilung." In *Deutsche Staatsbibliothek, 1661–1961.* Redaktion Horst Kunze, Werner Dube, Gunter Froschner. Band I: *Geschichte und Gegenwart,* pp. 241–74. Leipzig: VEB Verlag für Buch- und Bibliothekswesen, 1961.

A narrative account of the founding of the Music Division of the Berlin State Library, the work of its successive directors, and the growth of its collections up to the restoration of the music room after its destruction in World War II. The riches of the collection are summarized, particularly the Bach, Mozart, and Beethoven holdings. The author is director of the Music Division.

7.53 Köhler, Karl-Heinz. "Return of Treasures to the Deutsche Staatsbibliothek." In *Fontes* 26 (1979): 86–87.

A report on the manuscripts moved from Berlin in the closing days of World War II.

7.54 Lewis, Nigel. *Paperchase: Mozart, Beethoven, Bach: The Search for Their Lost Music.* 246 pp. London: Hamish Hamilton, 1981.

A recounting in exposé style of the history of the evacuation—from the Preussische Staatsbibliothek to Schloss Fürstenstein, thereafter to the Benedictine monastery in Grüssen, and eventually to Cracow at the end of World War II—of almost 200 manuscripts by more than 20 composers, including J. S. Bach, W. A. Mozart, Beethoven, Mendelssohn, Schumann, J. Haydn, Brahms, Schubert, C. P. E. Bach, Telemann, E. T. A. Hoffmann, Paganini, and Hugo Wolf. The author provides details, without citing sources or providing footnotes, of the discovery and recovery of some of these works. There are some references in the story to verify the main points, and the involvement of Carleton Smith and the key role of Peter Whitehead in the affair are made clear.

JOACHIMSTHALSCHES GYMNASIUM. BIBLIOTHEK

7.55 Eitner, Robert. *Katalog der Musikalien-Sammlung des Joachimsthalschen Gymnasium zu Berlin.* 106 pp. Berlin: T. Trautwein, 1884. (Beilage, Monatshefte für Musikgeschichte. Jahrgang 16)

A collection incorporating the library of Princess Anna Amalia, sister of Friedrich the Great (**7.611**). It is strong in 18th-century music of the North German school, with 627 numbered items. There is an author–composer index. The collection was partially dispersed and destroyed in World War II.

7.56 Eitner, Robert. *Thematischer Katalog der Von Thulemeier'schen Musikaliensammlung in der Bibliothek des Joachimsthal'schen Gymnasiums zu Berlin.* 110 pp. Leipzig: Breitkopf & Härtel, 1899. (Beilage, Monatshefte für Musikgeschichte. Jahrgang 30–31)

The collection covers the period 1700–1800.

Königliche Hausbibliothek

7.57 Thouret, Georg. *Katalog der Musiksammlung aus der Königlichen Hausbibliothek im Schlosse zu Berlin.* 356 pp. Leipzig: Breitkopf & Härtel, 1895.

Supplemented by *Neue Erwerbungen der Königlichen Hausbibliothek zu Berlin* (Beilage, Monatshefte für Musikgeschichte. Jahrgang 35, 1903).

Brief entries, alphabetical by composer, for 6,836 items, both printed and manuscript, with a special section of works dedicated to members of the royal family and a supplementary section for military music.

STAATSBIBLIOTHEK DER STIFTUNG PREUSSISCHER KULTURBESITZ

7.58 Jaenecke, Joachim. *Die Musikbibliothek des Ludwig Freiherrn von Pretlack, 1716–1781.* 330 pp. Wiesbaden: Breitkopf & Härtel, 1973. (Neue musikgeschichtliche Forschungen, 8)

The Pretlack collection now housed in the Staatsbibliothek der Stiftung Preussischer Kulturbesitz, Berlin.

7.59 Kümmerling, Harald. *Katalog der Sammlung Bokemeyer.* 423 pp. Kassel, Germany: Bärenreiter, 1970. (Kieler Schriften zur Musikwissenschaft, 18)

The reconstruction of an important 18th-century private music library of more than 3,000 manuscripts, printed music, and theoretical works. The collection has been partially dispersed. Parts of the collection surviving in the West Berlin State Library have been identified by Kümmerling and the rest reconstructed.

Reviewed by Richard H. Hunter in *Notes* 28 (1971): 57–58.

Bern, Switzerland

SCHWEIZERISCHE LANDESBIBLIOTHEK

7.60 Joss, K. *Katalog der Schweizerischen Landesbibliothek: Musik-Werke der Mitglieder des Schweizerischen Tonkünstlervereins veröffentlicht von 1848–1925.* 152 pp. Bern-Bumpliz: Buchdruckerei Benteli, 1927.

A catalog of about 5,000 titles, abridged to essential information, in a classified arrangement.

Bethlehem, Pennsylvania

ARCHIVES OF THE MORAVIAN CHURCH

7.61 *A Catalogue of Music by American Moravians, 1724–1842, from the Archives of the Moravian Church at Bethlehem, Pennsylvania.* 118 pp. Bethlehem, Pa.: Moravian Seminary and College for Women, 1938.

Reprinted by AMS Press, New York, 1970.

Short biographies and lists of compositions by 17 Moravian-American composers, with an appendix of 24 plates of selected compositions and sample pages from the original manuscripts.

LITITZ CONGREGATION COLLECTION

7.62 Steelman, Robert. *Catalog of the Lititz Congregation Collection.* 488 pp. Chapel Hill, N.C.: University of North Carolina Press, 1981.

The Lititz Congregation collection is housed at the Moravian Archives in Bethlehem, Pennsylvania. Access to the collection is controlled by the Moravian Church Music Foundation.

A collection of manuscripts of music for Moravian worship and devotional gatherings. There are entries for over 500 manuscripts, each identifying its composer when known and including musical incipits, information on the compositions, an inventory of parts or scoring, and cross-references. There are indexes of composers and of titles and first lines.

Birmingham, England

UNIVERSITY OF BIRMINGHAM. BARBER INSTITUTE OF FINE ARTS. MUSIC LIBRARY

7.63 Fenlon, Iain. *Catalogue of the Printed Music and Music Manuscripts before 1801 in the Music Library of the University of Birmingham, Barber Institute of Fine Arts.* 140 pp. + 7 microfiches. London: Mansell; Munich: Verlag Dokumentation, 1976.

A catalog of printed music, providing complete title page transcription and physical description, and a catalog of music in manuscript, describing and analyzing each manuscript. There are facsimiles of interesting pages as well as indexes to booksellers, printers, and publishers, to artists, designers, and engravers, and to previous owners. Also included is a microfiche of the Library's MS 5001: "Autograph anthems by English composers c. 1665–85."

Bloomington, Indiana

INDIANA UNIVERSITY. ARCHIVES OF TRADITIONAL MUSIC

7.64 Ross, Anne Helen. *Catalog of the Terence R. Bech Nepal Music Research Collection.* Compilation supported by a Research Collections Grant from the National Endowment for the Humanities; project coordinator, Terence R. Bech; project librarian, Anne H. Ross; project director, Frank J. Gillis. 435 pp. Bloomington, Ind.: Archives of Traditional Music, Folklore Institute, Indiana University, 1978.

The catalog of a collection of materials, including musical instruments, on musical culture in Nepal.

INDIANA UNIVERSITY. LATIN AMERICAN MUSIC CENTER

7.65 Lorenz, Ricardo, Luis D. Hernández, and **Gerardo Dirié.** *Scores and Recordings at the Indiana University Latin American Music Center.* 512 pp. Bloomington, Ind.: Indiana University Press, 1994.

A revised, updated ed. of *Music from Latin America Available at Indiana University,* edited by Juan A. Orrego-Salas, 1971, 412 pp.

An updated catalog of one of the most important repositories of Latin American scores and sound recordings in the United States. See also **12.29**.

Reviewed by John E. Druesedow in *Choice* 33 (1996): 758.

INDIANA UNIVERSITY. LILLY LIBRARY

7.66 De Lerma, Dominique-René. *The Fritz Busch Collection: An Acquisition of Indiana University.* 52 pp. Bloomington, Ind.: Indiana University Libraries, 1972. (Indiana University Lilly Library publication, 15)

A description of the Busch collection, which includes a catalog of the annotated scores, a catalog of the phonotapes, a catalog of the manuscripts (scores), and a catalog of the manuscripts (nonmusic).

Bogotá, Colombia

CATEDRAL DE BOGOTÁ

7.67 Perdomo Escobar, José Ignacio. *El Archivio Musical de la Catedral de Bogotá.* 818 pp. Bogotá: Instituto Caro y Cuervo, 1976.

Coverage of the Archivio that includes a dictionary catalog and a bibliography.

Reviewed by Catherine Massip in *Fontes* 26 (1979): 61.

Bologna, Italy

7.68 Bonora, Alfredo, and **Emilio Giani.** *Catalogo delle opere musicali: Città di Bologna: Biblioteca della R. Accademia Filarmonica* [pp. 1–43], *Biblioteca Privata Ambrosini* [pp. 47–66], *e Archivio e museo della Basilica di S. Petronio* [pp. 71–159]. 159 pp. Parma, Italy: Freschig, 1910–38. (Associazione dei Musicologi Italiani. Catalogo delle opere musicali, 2/1)

Reprinted in Bologna by A. Forni, 1989. (Bibliotheca musica Bononiensis, I, 22)

Includes indexes.

ACCADEMIA FILARMONICA

7.69 Masseangeli, Masseangelo. *Catalogo descrittivo degli autografi e ritratti di musicisti lasciati alla Reale Accademia Filarmonica di Bologna.* Compilato a cura degli Accademici Prof. Cav. Federico Parisini e Maestro Ernesto Colombani. 435 pp. Bologna: Regia Tipografia, 1896.

A reprint of the 1881 ed. was published by Forni, Bologna, 1969.

A catalog that first appeared, under a slightly different title, in 1881. The collection includes music manuscripts and portraits of musicians.

7.70 Succi, Emilia. *Catalogo con brevi cenni biografici e succinte discrizioni degli autografi e documenti de' celebri o distinti musicisti.* 179 pp. Bologna: Società Tipografica già Compositori, 1888.

At head of title: Mostra internazionale di musica in Bologna 1888.

A collection of 886 items, chiefly letters by musicians of the 18th and 19th centuries, mostly autographs. The catalog is arranged alphabetically, with brief biographical notices and descriptions of the items.

BIBLIOTECA UNIVERSITARIA

7.71 Frati, Lodovico. "Codici musicali della R. Biblioteca Universitaria di Bologna." In *Rivista musicale italiana* 23 (1916): 219–42.

A general description of the resources of the music collection in the library of the University of Bologna, drawing attention to major holdings in plainchant, early theory, and polyphony.

CIVICO MUSEO BIBLIOGRAFICO MUSICALE

7.72 Gaspari, Gaetano, and **Federico Parisini.** *Catalogo della biblioteca del Liceo Musicale di Bologna.* 5 vols. Bologna: Libreria Romagnoli dall'Acqua, 1890–1943.

Contents: Vol. 1, *Teoria;* Vol. 2, *Practica: Libri liturgici. Musica religiosa* (ed. Luigi Torchi); Vol. 3, *Practica: Musica sacra. Musica vocale profana. Musica vocale moderna da camera e da conserto. Melodrammi* (ed. Luigi Torchi); Vol. 4, *Practica: Musica istrumentale. Appendice* (ed. Raffaele Caldolini); Vol. 5, *Libretti d'opera in musica* (ed. Ugo Sesini).

Vol. 4 originally published by Fratelli Marliani; Vol. 5 by Azzoguidi.

The 5 vols. were reissued by Forni (Bologna, 1961) as *Catalogo della Biblioteca Musicale G. B. Martini di Bologna,* with corrections by Napoleone Fanti, Oscar Mischiati, and Luigi Ferdinando Tagliavini (Studi e testi di musiologia, 1–4) (Bibliotheca musica Bononiensis, I, 12).

A catalog providing access to one of the richest collections of early music in the world, incorporating the library of the 18th-century scholar Padre Giambattista Martini. Full bibliographical descriptions are given, with contents listed for collections; there are transcriptions of numerous prefaces and dedications. The entries are alphabetical within each category. There is a general index of names.

7.73 Schnoebelen, Anne. *Padre Martini's Collection of Letters in the Civico Museo Bibliografico Musicale in Bologna: An Annotated Index.* 721 pp. New York: Pendragon Press, 1979. (Annotated reference tools in music, 2)

An index covering 5,876 letters written by or to 670 correspondents of Giovanni Battista Martini during his 54 years at the monastery of San Francesco, 1730–84. For each letter, the incipit in the original language is supplied along with names of persons and pieces of music cited in the letter. The content of each letter is summarized. There is a name and subject index.

Reviewed by John W. Hill in *Notes* 36 (1980): 893–94, by Vincent H. Duckles in *M&L* 61 (1980): 376–77, and by Pierluigi Petrobelli, with additions, in *Fontes* 27 (1980): 225–27.

7.74* Trovato, Roberto. *Regesto dei manoscritti in lingua francese esistenti presso il Civico Museo Bibliografico Musicale di Bologna.* Presentazione di Liano Petroni. 169 pp. Bologna: Pàtron, 1980. (Regesto dei manoscritti in lingua francese esistenti in biblioteche ed archivi dell'Emilia Romagna, 1)

7.75 Vatielli, Francesco. *La biblioteca del Liceo Musicale di Bologna.* 57 pp. Bologna: Presso M. Zanichelli, 1916. (Biblioteca de "L'Archiginnasio," 2, 14)

Also printed in *L'Archiginnasio* 11 (1916). Reprint published in Sala Bolonese, Arnaldo Forni Editore, 1989 (Bibliotheca musica Bononiensis, III, 54).

CONSERVATORIO DI MUSICA "G. B. MARTINI"
SEE CIVICO MUSEO BIBLIOGRAFICO MUSICALE

IL CONVENTO DI SAN FRANCESCO

7.76* Pollastri, Mariarosa. *Biblioteca del Convento di S. Francesco di Bologna: Catalogo del fondo musicale. Appendice.* 124 pp. Bologna: Forni, 1984. (Bibliotheca musica Bononiensis, I, 20)

A supplement to **7.77.**

7.77 Zanotti, Gino. *Biblioteca del Convento di S. Francesco di Bologna: Catalogo del fondo musicale.* 2 vols. Bologna: Forni, 1970. (Bibliotheca musica Bononiensis, VI, 3)

Contents: Vol. I, *Le edizioni,* 324 pp.; Vol. II, *I manoscritti,* 393 pp.

A set that catalogs the music collection of the Franciscan church where Padre Martini lived and worked during the 18th century. The collection includes a considerable amount of his music. An appendix of music manuscripts, supplied with music incipits and edited by Mariarosa Pollastri, was published by Forni in 1984, 124 pp. (Bibliotheca musica Bononiensis, I, 20).

Bolzano, Italy

PALAZZO TOGGENBURG

7.78 Chini, Tarcisio, and **Giuliano Tonini.** *La raccolta di manoscritti e stampe musicali "Toggenburg" di Bolzano (secc. XVIII–XIX).* xxxii + 307 pp. + 10 ll. of plates. Turin: EDT/Musica, 1986. (Cataloghi di fondi musicali italiani, 5)

The catalog of a collection gathered by a merchant from Menz, containing prints and manuscripts from the last quarter of the 18th century and through the first half of the 19th. The libretto collection is also cataloged.

Bonn, Germany

FRIEDRICH-WILHELMS-UNIVERSITÄT

7.79 Clasen, Theo. "Die musikalischen Autographen der Universitäts-Bibliothek Bonn." In *Festschrift Joseph Schmidt-Görg zum 60. Geburtstag,* pp. 26–65. Bonn: Beethoven-Haus, 1957.

A collection of 567 autographs by 245 musicians, extracted from bequests or autograph books, with a wide representation of musicians and musical scholars of the early 19th century.

7.80* Marx-Weber, Magda. *Katalog der Musikhandschriften im Besitz des Musikwissenschaftlichen Seminars der Rheinischen Friedrich-Wilhelms-Universität zu Bonn.* xxi + 138 pp. Cologne: A. Volk, 1971. (Beiträge zur rheinischen Musikgeschichte, 89)

A catalog of 595 manuscripts, some 550 of which were assembled by organist–cantor Christian Benjamin Klein (1754–1825). Prominent among the composers represented are Benda, Bernabei, Homilius, Reichardt, Weinlig, Wirbach, and Zumsteeg.

Borriana, Spain

7.81* Ros i Pérez, Vicent. *Catáleg de manuscrits musicals de l'Arxiu Històric Parroquial de Borriana (segles XVIII-XX).* 107 pp. Borriana, Spain: Departament d'Investigació Històrica, Museu Arqueològic Municipal, Magnific Ajuntament, 1979. (Papers, 3)

A catalog of music manuscripts.

Boston, Massachusetts

BOSTON PUBLIC LIBRARY

7.82 Boston Public Library. *Dictionary Catalog of the Music Collection of the Boston Public Library.* 20 vols. Boston, Mass.: G.K. Hall, 1972. *First Supplement.* 4 vols. Boston, Mass.: G.K. Hall, 1977.

A photo-offset publication of the dictionary catalog, giving author, title, and subject entries for a collection of some 80,000 volumes covering music, biography, history and criticism, theory and composition, music education, collected editions and monuments, bibliographical works, libretti, and periodicals. This catalog incorporates the Allen A. Brown music collection, which had a separately published catalog issued by the Library in 4 vols., 1910–16 (and reprinted in 1970 by G.K. Hall); excluded are sheet music, clippings and programs, and recordings. The *Supplement* lists musical scores, books, pamphlets, and periodicals cataloged since January 1972.

Brandenburg, Germany

ST. KATHARINENKIRCHE. BIBLIOTHEK

7.83 Taglichsbeck, Johann F. *Die musikalischen Schätze der St. Katherinenkirche zu Brandenburg a.d. Havel: Ein Beitrag zur musikalischen Literatur des 16. und 17. Jahrhunderts.* 50 pp. Brandenburg: A. Müller, 1857.

A catalog of manuscripts and printed works, 1564–1671, chronologically arranged with full bibliographical information and descriptive notes.

Brasov, Romania

HONTERUSGYMNASIUM. BIBLIOTHEK

7.84 Müller von Asow, Erich H. *Die Musiksammlung der Bibliothek zu Kronstadt.* 176 pp. Kronstadt, Romania: J. Gott's Sohn, 1930.

A catalog of manuscripts, printed music and books, with brief biographical sketches of authors or composers, publication dates, and plate numbers.

Brescia, Italy

ARCHIVIO CAPITOLARE DEL DUOMO

7.85* Sala, Mariella. *Catalogo del fondo musicale dell'Archivio Capitolare del Duomo di Brescia.* xxix + 288 pp. Turin: EMT/Musica, 1984. (Catalogo di fondi musicali italiani, 3)

A catalog of printed and manuscript music, mostly from the 16th–18th centuries, including anthologies, with useful histories of the Cappella and the Archivio. There are indexes by composer, text incipits, and musical genre.

Reviewed by Graham Dixon in *EM* 15 (1987): 261–63.

Breslau, Germany and Brieg, Germany

See Wrocław, Poland.

Brno, Slovakia

MORAVSKÉ MUZEUM

7.86 Straková, Theodora, et al. *Průvodce po archívních fondech ústavu dějin hudby Moravského musea v Brně.* 256 pp. + 22 plates. Brno, Slovakia: Ústav degin hudby: Mor. Musea, rozmn., 1971.

With a summary in Russian, German, and English, a catalog of the music holdings of the Moravian Museum in Brno (Brünn).

UNIVERSITÄTSBIBLIOTHEK

7.87 Telec, Vladimir. *Alte Drucke der Werke von tschechischen Komponisten des 18. Jahrhunderts in der Universitätsbibliothek in Brno.* 163 pp. + 8 plates. Prague: Státní Pedagogické Nakladatelství, 1969.

A catalog citing 1,278 works by 42 Czech composers, with a total of 522 bibliographical units; 278 of the items are on microfilm. Full bibliographical descriptions are given, including tempo and metrical indications for the movements of composite works.

Brussels, Belgium

BIBLIOTHÈQUE ROYALE ALBERT IER

7.88 *Catalogue de la bibliothèque de F. J. Fétis, acquisé par l'État belge.* 946 pp. Brussels: C. Muquardt, 1877.

Reprinted by Arnaldo Forni, Bologna, in 1969 (Bibliotheca musica Bononiensis, I, 7).

The catalog of the Fétis library, acquired by the Bibliothèque Royale in 1872 and containing many rarities. 7,325 items are classified under two main headings: "Bibliothèque generale" and "Bibliothèque musicale."

7.89 Huys, Bernard. "Afdeling Muziek (van de Koninklijke Bibliotheek van Belgie)." In *Koninklijke Bibliotheek. Liber memorialis, 1559–1969,* pp. 311–34. Brussels, 1969.

A history of the music collection of the Royal Library at Brussels, including the establishment of a new music division in that library.

7.90 Huys, Bernard. *Catalogue des imprimés musicaux des XVe, XVIe, et XVIIe siècles: Fonds général.* 422 pp. Brussels: Bibliothèque Royale de Belgique, 1965. *Fonds général supplement* by Bernard Huys, 1974.

A catalog of 446 numbered items. The catalog lists works not part of the Fétis collection (**7.88**), although if another copy or a more complete copy is found in Fétis, this information is given. Contents are listed for each item. Of particular interest is the list of music excerpted from theoretical works such as those of Glareanus and Zarlino.

Reviewed by François Lesure in *Revue de musicologie* 51 (1965): 102, by Ute Schwab in *Die Musikforschung* 21 (1968): 104–5, and by Rita Benton in *Fontes* 22 (1975): 155. The *Supplement* is reviewed by François Lesure in *Revue de musicologie* 60 (1974): 217 no. 1–2 and by Giancarlo Rostirolla in *Nuova rivista musicale italiana* 9 (1975): 303–4 no. 2.

7.91 Huys, Bernard. *Catalogue des imprimés musicaux du XVIIIe siècle: Fonds général. Catalogus van de muziek drukken van de XVIIIde eeuw.* 519 pp. Brussels: Bibliothèque Royale Albert Ier, 1974.

A masterful catalog presenting all the musical works and writings about music printed in the 18th century possessed by the Bibliothèque Royale not in the Fétis collection (**7.88**). Complete title page transcriptions, physical descriptions, provenance, references in other catalogs, cross-references, and analysis of collections are provided. There are indexes to authors, composers, and translators, to printers and booksellers, to persons and institutions formerly owning the works, to engravers of music, and to musical genres.

7.92 Huys, Bernard. *Catalogue des partitions musicales éditées en Belgique et acquisés par la Bibliothèque Royale Albert Ier: Fascicule spécial de la Bibliographie de Belgique.* 2 vols. to date. Brussels: La Bibliothèque, 1976– .

Published with an added title page: *Catalogus van de Muziekpartituren in Belgie uitgegeven en verworven door de Koninklijke Bibliotheek Albert 1. Speciale Aflevering van de Belgische Bibliografie.*

Contents: Vol. 1, *1966–1975;* Vol. 2, *1976–80.*

A publication that serves as a catalog of music published in Belgium and acquired by the library.

CONSERVATOIRE ROYAL DE MUSIQUE.

BIBLIOTHÈQUE

7.93 Wotquenne, Alfred. *Catalogue de la bibliothèque.* 4 vols. Brussels: Coosemans, 1898–1912. Annexe I: *Libretti d'operas et d'oratorios italiens du XVIIe siècle.* Brussels: O. Schepens, 1901.

An unaltered reprint was published in 1980 by Éditions Culture et Civilization, Brussels.

A classified catalog to one of the richest European music collections. The printed scores and manuscripts are interfiled.

Budapest, Hungary

ORSZÁGOS SZÉCHÉNYI KÖNYVTÁR

7.94 Bartha, Dénes, and **László Somfai.** "Catalogue raisonnée der Esterházy Opernsammlung, in chronologischer Ordnung der Premièren." In *Haydn als Opernkapellmeister: Die Haydn-Dokumente der Esterházy Opernsammlung,* pp. 179–403. Budapest: Verlag der Ungarischen Akademie der Wissenschaften, 1960.

A chronological list of the operatic works preserved in the Esterházy archive in the National Széchényi Library. Each work is fully described, with special attention given to Haydn's annotations on works performed under his direction. This is an important approach to Haydn research.

7.95 Gombosi, Otto. "Die Musikalien der Pfarrkirche zu St. Aegidi in Bartfa." In *Festschrift für Johannes Wolf,* pp. 38–47. Berlin, 1929.

A description of a collection now in the National Széchényi Library at Budapest. Gombosi discusses some 20 music prints of the 16th century and a number of important 16th- and 17th-century manuscripts.

7.96 Isoz, Kálmán, and **Rezső Lavotta.** *Zenei kéziratok jégyzeke.* 2 vols. 391 + 237 pp. Budapest: Kiadja a Magyar Nemzeti Múzeum Országos Széchényi Könyvtár, 1921–40. (Catalogus bibliothecae musaei nat. hungarici. Musica, I, II)

A description of portions of the library's music collection. The 1st vol. is a catalog of 1,449 autograph letters of musicians, including some of Haydn and Liszt. The 2nd is a catalog of music manuscripts.

7.97* Murányi, Róbert Árpád. *Thematisches Verzeichnis der Musiksammlung von Bartfeld (Bártfa).* xxxv + 446 pp. Bonn: G. Schröder, 1991. (Deutsche Musik im Osten, 2)

A thematic catalog of the Bártfa Collection.

Cádiz, Spain

7.98* Pajares Barón, Máximo. *Archivo de Música de la Catedral de Cádiz.* xxviii + 690 pp. Granada, Spain: Junta de Andalucía, Consejería de Culturay Medio Ambiente, Centro de Documentación Musical de Andalucía, 1993. (La Música en las catedrales andaluzas, I, 4)

A catalog of manuscript and printed sacred polyphony, principally with thematic incipits.

California

7.99 *Catalog of the Opera Collections in the Music Libraries: University of California, Berkeley* [and] *University of California, Los Angeles.* 697 pp. Boston, Mass.: G.K. Hall, 1983.

A catalog produced by the photo-offset duplication of the main entry cards in each library; both have substantial collections of opera scores. Divided into sections for each library; the Berkeley portion is further subdivided into operas and dramatic music for children. Cataloging for the Berkeley collection was subsequently entirely revised to meet contemporary cataloging standards and is in the scores file of the Research Libraries Information Network (RLIN) **(12.2)**.

Reviewed by Evan Baker in *Fontes* 43 (1996): 214–16.

Cambrai, France

7.100 Coussemaker, Charles Edmond Henri de. *Notice sur les collections musicales de la Bibliothèque de Cambrai et des autres villes du Département du Nord.* 180 + 40 pp. Paris: Chez Techener, 1843.

Reprinted by G. Olms, Hildesheim, Germany, in 1975.

A catalog concerned chiefly with 16 manuscripts and 4 printed collections in the Cambrai library. The descriptions are brief, faulty, and outdated.

Cambridge, England

CAMBRIDGE UNIVERSITY

7.101* Bartlett, Clifford. *The Music Collections of the Cambridge Libraries.* 5 vols. Brighton, East Sussex: Harvester Microform, 1987– .

Contents: Pt. 1, Music Manuscripts before 1850 from Cambridge University Library and Ely

Cathedral. Pt. 2, Music Manuscripts from the Rome Music Library, King's College, Cambridge. Pt. 3, Handel Manuscripts from the Fitzwilliam Museum. Pt. 4, English Manuscripts from the Fitzwilliam Museum. Pt. 5, Continental Music Manuscripts before c. 1800 in the Fitzwilliam Museum, sect. A. Pt. 6, Continental Music Manuscripts before c. 1800 in the Fitzwilliam Museum, sect. B.

Parts 3–6 published in Reading, Berkshire, by Research Publications.

The guide to the microfilm collection published by Harvester.

FITZWILLIAM MUSEUM

7.102 Fuller-Maitland, A. J., and **A. H. Mann.** *Catalogue of the Music in the Fitzwilliam Museum, Cambridge.* 298 pp. London: C.J. Clay and Sons, 1893.

A list of 496 titles, including 209 manuscripts, 196 printed books, and an important collection of Handel manuscripts and sketches (pp. 157–227).

7.103* Rumbold, Valerie, and **Iain Fenlon.** *A Short-Title Catalogue of Music Printed before 1825 in the Fitzwilliam Museum, Cambridge.* xxi + 168 pp. Cambridge, England: Cambridge University Press, 1992.

Reviewed by John Wagstaff in *M&L* 75 (1994): 254–55, with a short list of errata.

PETERHOUSE COLLEGE

7.104 Hughes, Anselm. *Catalogue of the Musical Manuscripts at Peterhouse, Cambridge.* 75 pp. Cambridge, England: Cambridge University Press, 1953.

Important source materials for the study of English church music of the 16th and 17th centuries, comprising four Latin part books c. 1540 and two sets of English part books c. 1630–40.

UNIVERSITY LIBRARY

7.105 Fenlon, Iain. *Cambridge Music Manuscripts, 900–1700.* 174 pp. Cambridge, England: Cambridge University Press, 1982.

A catalog, with bibliographical references, of music manuscripts in the various libraries at Cambridge, published to coincide with an exhibition in the Fitzwilliam Museum, July–August 1982.

Reviewed by Christian Meyer in *Fontes* 31 (1984): 133–34.

Cambridge, Massachusetts

HARVARD UNIVERSITY

7.106 *Card Catalog of the Harvard University Music Library to 1985.* 224 negative microfiches. New York: Saur, 1985.

The catalog of one of the great American collections supporting musical research. Part 1 is the dictionary catalog of the book and score holdings of the collections of the Loeb Music Library, the Isham Memorial Library of microforms, the hymnbook collection at the Andover–Harvard Divinity Library, the rare materials in the Houghton Library, and relevant materials from the Widener Library. In Part 1 there are entries of composers, authors, subjects, and series. Part 2 is a shelf list of the Loeb Music Library, providing classified access to the collection as well.

7.107* Wolff, Barbara Mahrenholz. *Music Manuscripts at Harvard: A Catalogue of Music Manuscripts from the 14th to the 20th Centuries in the Houghton Library and the Eda Kuhn Loeb Music Library.* 245 pp. Cambridge, Mass.: Harvard University Library, 1992.

Includes bibliographical references (pp. xvii–xix) and indexes.

Reviewed by Stephen Roe in *Fontes* 40 (1993): 264–65 and by Carl B. Schmidt in *Notes* 50 (1994): 1,018–19.

7.108 Wood, David F. *Music in Harvard Libraries: A Catalogue of Early Printed Music and Books on Music in the Houghton Library and the Eda Kuhn Loeb Music Library.* 306 pp. Cambridge, Mass.: Houghton Library of the Harvard College Library and Harvard University Department of Music, 1980.

Reissued in conjunction with the microfilm collection *History of Music* (Woodbridge, Conn.: Research Publications, 1985).

A catalog describing the music and books on music (1,628 titles) printed before 1801 that had been added to the Harvard Libraries by 1967.

The catalog is arranged by author and composer, with references to principal bibliographic tools. The index to names includes printers, booksellers, and editors. Additions and corrections are cited on p. 282.

Reviewed by Donald W. Krummel in *Notes* 37 (1981): 852–54.

HARVARD UNIVERSITY. ISHAM MEMORIAL
LIBRARY

7.109 Apel, Willi. "The Collection of Photographic Reproductions at the Isham Memorial Library, Harvard University." In *Musica disciplina* 1 (1946): 68–73.

A description of the first stages of the Isham collection of microfilms of musical source materials and other holdings.

Caribbean Islands

7.110 Dower, Catherine A. "Libraries with Music Collections in the Caribbean Islands." In *Notes* 34 (1978): 27–38.

Descriptions of music collections in Aruba, Barbados, Bermuda, Cuba, Curaçao, Haiti, Jamaica, Martinique, Puerto Rico, Trinidad, and the Virgin Islands.

Carpentras, France

BIBLIOTHÈQUE D'INGUIMBERT

7.111 *Catalogue de la collection musicale J. B. Laurens donnée a la ville de Carpentras pour la Bibliothèque d'Inguimbert.* 151 pp. Carpentras, France: J. Seguin, 1901.

Classified catalog of music books and scores; a 19th-century scholar's library. Preceded by a biography of the donor, J. B. Laurens, archeologist, painter, writer, organist, composer, and musicologist.

Casale Monferrato, Italy

ARCHIVIO CAPITOLARE

7.112 Crawford, David. *Sixteenth-Century Choirbooks in the Archivio Capitolare at Casale Monferrato.* 207 pp. American Institute of Musicology, 1975. (Renaissance manuscript studies, 2)

A catalog of seven manuscripts of polyphonic sacred music copied between 1508 and 1518. There are extensive introductory and descriptive remarks, followed by an incipit catalog for each manuscript, ordered as the works appear in each manuscript. Citations for modern editions and secondary literature for all but 90 *unica* are provided. A catalog of compositions (masses, magnificats, hymns, miscellaneous liturgical genres, and motets) and a list of manuscripts cited in the catalog but located elsewhere, as well as a list of early printed music editions containing works in this repertory, are provided. Also includes a similar list of modern editions and a list of liturgical sources quoted, with a general index.

Reviewed by Nicholas Sandon in *EM* 5 (1977): 225–29, by William F. Prizer in *Notes* 34 (1977): 327–29, and by Mary S. Lewis in *JAMS* 31 (1978): 521–29.

Caserta, Italy

BIBLIOTECA PALATINA DI CASERTA

7.113* Massa, Maria Rosa. *Libretti di melodrammi e balli nella Biblioteca palatina di Caserta.* 63 pp. Lucca, Italy: Libreria Musicale Italiana Editrice, 1992. (Ancilla musicae, 5)

The catalog of a collection of 19th-century opera and ballet libretti, with indexes.

Cesena, Italy

BIBLIOTECA COMUNALE

7.114 Paganelli, Sergio. "Catalogo delle opere musicali a stampa dal '500 al '700 conservate presso la Biblioteca Comunale di Cesena." In *Collectanea historiae musicae* 2 (1957): 311–38.

A list of 95 early editions of vocal and instrumental music and 6 theory works.

Charlottesville, Virginia

UNIVERSITY OF VIRGINIA. ALDERMAN LIBRARY

7.115 McRae, Lynn T. *Computer Catalog of Nineteenth-Century American-Imprint Sheet Music.* 12 pp. + 8 microfiches. Charlottesville, Va.: University of Virginia, 1977.

The catalog of a collection in the Rare Book Room, Alderman Library, University of Virginia, that indexes about 7,700 pieces of American sheet music.

UNIVERSITY OF VIRGINIA. MUSIC LIBRARY

7.116* Birch, Courtney. *Russian Literature on Music in the Music Library of the University of Virginia: A Handlist of Holdings to June 1989.* 100 pp. Charlottesville, Va.: University of Virginia, 1989.

Chicago, Illinois

NEWBERRY LIBRARY

7.117 Krummel, Donald W. *Bibliographical Inventory to the Early Music in the Newberry Library, Chicago, Illinois.* 587 pp. Boston, Mass.: G.K. Hall, 1977.

Photo-offset duplication of classified catalog cards from the Newberry Library representing musical items published before 1860 and manuscripts dating from before 1860.

The Newberry Library has one of the most important music collections in the United States, particularly rich in the fields of renaissance music, early theory, and Americana.

Comprehending the introduction is of crucial importance to the efficient use of this work. There are addenda and corrigenda (pp. 527–32), an index to composers, editors, and musical subjects, and an index to printers, engravers, artists, copyists, and publishers.

7.118 Krummel, Donald W. "The Newberry Library, Chicago." In *Fontes* (July–December 1969): 119–24.

A narrative account of the music resources of the Newberry Library in the areas of medieval music, renaissance and baroque music, music of the 18th and 19th centuries, music of master composers, and Americana.

7.119 Wilson, Bernard E. *The Newberry Library Catalog of Early American Printed Sheet Music.* 3 vols. Boston, Mass.: G.K. Hall, 1983.

Photo-offset duplication of cards representing about 6,300 pieces of early American sheet music, including the James Francis Driscoll collection. The catalog covers works printed before 1871. There are sections devoted to main entries, added entries, chronological entries, places, and titles. Approximately 90,000 pieces of American sheet music held by the Newberry are not included in this catalog.

Christchurch, New Zealand

NATIONAL ARCHIVES

7.120* Harvey, Ross. *Music at National Archives: Sources for the Study of Music in New Zealand.* 217 pp. Christchurch, New Zealand: School of Music, University of Canterbury, 1991. (The Canterbury series of bibliographies, catalogues and source documents in music, 5)

Coburg, Germany

7.121* Potyra, Rudolf. *Die Theatermusikalien der Landesbibliothek Coburg: Katalog Rudolf Potyra: Mit einer Abhandlung zur Geschichte des Herzoglichen Hoftheaters Coburg-Gotha und seiner Notensammlung von Jürgen Ergmann.* 2 vols. Munich: G. Henle, 1995. (Kataloge bayerische Musiksammlungen, 20)

Coimbra, Portugal

UNIVERSIDADE. BIBLIOTECA

7.122 *Inventário dos inéditos e impressos musicais (subsidíos par um catálogo).* Fasc. I. 47 + 55 pp. Coimbra, Portugal: Impresso nas Oficinas da "Atlantida," 1937.

A catalog with separate alphabets and pagination for manuscripts and early printed works, and full descriptions of holdings.

7.123* Rees, Owen. *Polyphony in Portugal, c. 1530–c. 1620: Sources from the Monastery of Santa Cruz, Coimbra.* 461 pp. New York: Garland Publishing, 1995. (Outstanding dissertations in music from British universities)

A catalog with descriptions and inventories of approximately 20 music manuscripts originally in the monastery at Santa Cruz and now in the Biblioteca Geral, Universidade de Coimbra.

7.124 Sampayo Ribeiro, Mário de. *Os manuscritos musicais nos. 6 e 12 da Biblioteca Geral da Universidade de Coimbra (Contribuição para um catálogo definitivo).* 112 pp. Coimbra, Portugal, 1941.

A detailed study of two manuscripts of polyphonic music in the university library at Coimbra.

College Park, Maryland

UNIVERSITY OF MARYLAND AT COLLEGE PARK.
MUSIC LIBRARY

7.125 Brundage, Richard, and **Neil Ratliff.** *A Guide to the Jacob Coopersmith Collection of Handeliana at the University of Maryland at College Park.* 18 pp. College Park, Md.: Music Library, University of Maryland, 1986.

Collegeville, Minnesota

ST. JOHN'S ABBEY AND UNIVERSITY. HILL
MONASTIC MANUSCRIPT LIBRARY

7.126 Jeffery, Peter. "Music Manuscripts on Microfilm in the Hill Monastic Manuscript Library at St. John's Abbey and University." In *Notes* 35 (1978): 7–30.

An informative essay surveying the 2,000 music manuscripts gathered from a large number of Roman Catholic European repositories, available on microfilm at the library of the Benedictine house as of August 1977.

7.127 Kreidler, J. Evan. "Austrian Graduals, Antiphoners, and Noted Missals on Microfilm in the Hill Monastic Manuscript Library, St. John's Abbey and University." In *Notes* 36 (1980): 849–63.

7.128 Kreidler, J. Evan. "A Checklist of Spanish Chant Sources at the Hill Monastic Manuscript Library, St. John's Abbey and University." In *Notes* 40 (1984): 7–29.

A tabulation of resources gathered from Spain and elsewhere.

ST. JOHN'S UNIVERSITY. ALCUIN LIBRARY

7.129 Plante, Julian G. "The Monastic Manuscript Microfilm Library." In *Notes* 25 (1968): 12–14.

A description of a microfilm library of nearly 11,000 codices filmed from the monastic libraries in Europe (including Göttweig, Heiligenkreuz, Herzogenburg, Klosterneuburg, Kremsmünster, Lambach, Lilienfeld, and Melk), citing 27 manuscripts of early music theory available for study in the collection.

Cologne, Germany

DOMCAPELLE

7.130 Göller, Gottfried. *Die Leiblsche Sammlung: Katalog der Musikalien der Kölner Domcapelle.* 133 pp. Cologne: Arno Volk-Verlag, 1964. (Beiträge zur rheinischen Musikgeschichte, 57)

The thematic catalog of 291 sacred choral works, chiefly early 19th century, formerly in the chapel of Cologne Cathedral. The collection is now in the Diözesanbibliothek of the Archbishopric of Cologne. A former owner was Carl Leibl, Kapellmeister.

Review by Winfried Kirsch in *Die Musikforschung* 20 (1967): 96.

UNIVERSITÄTS- UND STADTBIBLIOTHEK

7.131 Kahl, Willi. *Katalog der in der Universitäts- und Stadtbibliothek Köln vorhandenen Musikdrucke des 16., 17., und 18. Jahrhunderts.* 20 pp. Cologne, 1958.

A list of 118 items, with bibliographical references.

Cologny, Switzerland

7.132* Seebass, Tilman. *Musikhandschriften der Bodmeriana: Katalog.* 104 pp. Cologny-Geneva: Fondation Martin Bodmer, 1986. (Kataloge / Bibliotheca Bodmeriana, 6)

A catalog of the collection of music manuscripts given by Martin Bodmer in the Bibliotheca Bodmeriana.

Constance, Switzerland

KOLLEGIAT- UND PFARRKIRCHE ST. STEPHAN

7.133 Schuler, Manfred. "Das Noteninventar der Kollegiat- und Pfarrkirche St. Stephan." In *Kirchenmusikalisches Jahrbuch* 58/59 (1974/75): 85–103.

Copenhagen, Denmark

KOMMUNEBIBLIOTEKER

7.134 *Katalog øver musik og musiklitteratur.* 4 vols. Copenhagen: Nordlunde, 1954–58.

Contents: Vol. 1, *Orkestermusik, Kammermusik, Enkelte Instrumenter* (1956, 72 pp.); Vol. 2, *Klaver, Orpel, Harmonium* (1954, 65 pp.); Vol. 3, *Vokalmusik* (1958, 118 pp.); Vol. 4, *Operaer, Operetter, Balletter* (1955, 46 pp.).

A planned 5th vol., devoted to books on music, was never published.

ROYAL LIBRARY

7.135* Bittmann, Inge. *Catalogue of Giedde's Music Collection in the Royal Library of Copenhagen.* 198 pp. Egtved, Denmark: Edition Egtved, 1976.

A catalog of a fairly comprehensive collection, mostly of flute music from the second half of the 18th century, arranged alphabetically by composer with thematic incipits. Includes a classified list of titles, a list of publishers, and a bibliography (pp. 195–98).

Reviewed by Peter Ward Jones in *M&L* 60 (1979): 335–36 and by John Horton in *MR* 40 (1979): 153–54.

7.136* Larsson, Jytte Torpp. *Catalogue of the Rischel and Birket-Smith Collection of Guitar Music in the Royal Library of Copenhagen.* Edited by Peter Danner. 263 pp. Columbus, Ohio: Editions Orphée, 1989.

A catalog of guitar music, printed and manuscript.

Reviewed by Dorman H. Smith in *Notes* 47 (1991): 1,153–55.

Córdoba, Spain

CATEDRAL DE CÓRDOBA

7.137* Nieto Cumplido, Manuel. *La miniatura en la Catedral de Córdoba.* 153 pp. Córdoba: Monte de Piedad y Caja de Ahorros de Córdoba, 1973. (Publicaciones del Monte de Piedad y Caja de Ahorros de Córdoba)

A catalog of illuminated manuscripts in the Biblioteca Capitular and the Archivo Musical.

Cuenca, Spain

SANTA IGLESIA CATEDRAL. ARCHIVO

7.138 Navarro Gonzalo, Restituo. *Catálogo musical del Archivo de la Santa Iglesia Catedral Basilica de Cuenca.* Dirigido por Antonio Iglesias; revisado por Manuel Angulo. 2nd ed., revised and corrected. 376 pp. Cuenca, Spain: Ediciones del Instituto de Música Religiosa, 1973. (Instituto de Musica Religiosa, Publicaciones, 9)

First ed. published as Vol. 1 of the series in 1965, 372 pp.

The catalog of a collection containing extensive holdings of sacred (polyphony, chant, and organ works) and secular (villancicos) music. The identified works are chiefly by Spanish composers, 16th–20th centuries. There are indexes by composer and by century.

Czech Republic and Slovakia

7.139 Fischer, Kurt von. "Repertorium der Quellen tschechischer Mehrstimmigkeit des 14. bis 16. Jahrhunderts." In *Essays in Musicology in Honor of Dragan Plamenac on His 70th Birthday,* pp. 49–60. Pittsburgh, Pa.: University of Pittsburgh Press, 1969.

An article identifying 73 manuscript sources of early Czech polyphony in 23 institutions, chiefly in Czechoslovakia but including the Austrian National Library at Vienna.

7.140 Plamenac, Dragan. "Music Libraries in Eastern Europe: A Visit in the Summer of 1961." In *Notes* 19 (1962): 217–34, 411–20, 584–98.

An illuminating account of conditions in some of the major East European music libraries, including those in the former Czechoslovakia. Locations of important bodies of source materials are indicated.

7.141 Svobodová, Maria. "Musikbuchereien, Archive und Museen in der CSSR." In *AIBM, Landergruppe Deutsche Demokratische Republik: Internationaler Sommerkurs für Musikbibliothekare,* 1964, pp. 48–69. Berlin, 1965.

A descriptive account of the major music archives, libraries, and museums in Czechoslovakia.

7.142 Terrayová, Maria J. "Súpis archívnych hudobných fondov na Slovensku." In *Hudobnovedné študié,* VI, pp. 197–328. Bratislava: Vydavatel´stvo Slovenskej Akadémie, Vied, 1960.

Thematic catalog of the music manuscripts in two hitherto undescribed Czech archives: the archive of the Pfarrkirche of Púchov (on deposit in the Musicological Institute of the Slovakian Academy of Sciences) and the archive of the Príleský Ostrolucky family (on deposit in the Slovakian National Museum in Martin). The manuscripts are chiefly of late-18th-century instrumental and vocal music by Italianate Czech composers of the period.

Dagenham, England

PUBLIC LIBRARIES

7.143 Pugsley, W. C., G. Atkinson, and **C. Tripp.** *Catalogue of Music: A Complete Catalogue of the Scores, Miniature Scores, Recorded Music and Books in the Dagenham Public Libraries.* 2nd ed. 515 pp. Dagenham (Essex): Valence House, 1964.

First ed. published 1958, 299 pp.

Danzig

See Gdansk, Poland.

Darmstadt, Germany

HOFBIBLIOTHEK

7.144 Roth, F. W. E. "Musik-Handschriften der Darmstädter Hofbibliothek." In *Monatshefte für Musikgeschichte* 20 (1888): 64–73, 82–92.

A list of 117 items dating from the 10th to the 19th centuries, with brief descriptions.

7.145 Roth, F. W. E. "Zur Bibliographie der Musikdrucke des XV. bis XVII. Jahrhunderts in der Darmstädter Hofbibliothek." In *Monatshefte für Musikgeschichte* 20 (1888): 118–25, 134–41, 154–61.

A list of 75 printed items, fully described.

INTERNATIONALES MUSIKINSTITUT DARMSTADT

7.146 Internationales Musikinstitut Darmstadt. *Informationszentrum für zeitgenössische Musik: Katalog der Abteilung Noten.* 293 pp. Darmstadt: Internationales Musikinstitut, 1966.

Title varies; began as *Kranichsteiner Musikinstitut.* Various supplements published from 1967.

An international lending library established in 1948 to further the study and performance of contemporary music. The catalog is classified, chiefly of scores, but including a small collection of books.

Reviewed by Karl Kroeger in *Notes* 23 (1967): 531–32.

Denmark

7.147* *Musikalier i danske biblioteker: Accessionskatalog / Music in Danish Libraries: A Union Catalogue, 1970– .* Copenhagen: Bibliotekscentralen, 1970– .

A union catalog of music holdings in Danish libraries.

Detroit, Michigan

DETROIT PUBLIC LIBRARY. HACKLEY COLLECTION

7.148 *Catalog of the E. Azalia Hackley Memorial Collection of Negro Music, Dance and Drama* [in the] *Detroit Public Library.* 510 pp. Boston, Mass.: G.K. Hall, 1979.

Photo-offset duplication of catalog cards representing books, scores, sheet music, broadsides, posters, and photographs in the Hackley Collection.

Dresden, Germany

SÄCHSISCHE LANDESBIBLIOTHEK

7.149 Eitner, Robert, and **Otto Kade.** *Katalog der Musiksammlung der Kgl. öffentlichen Bibliothek zu Dresden (im Japanischen Palais).* 150 pp. Leipzig: Breitkopf & Härtel, 1890. (Monatshefte für Musikgeschichte. Beilage. Jahrgang 21–22)

A catalog of music manuscripts written up to the date of compilation, printed music, and books on music to 1700.

7.150 Kümmerling, Harald, and **Wolfgang Steude.** *Die Musiksammelhandschriften des 16. und 17. Jahrhunderts in der Sächsischen Landesbibliothek zu Dresden.* 315 pp. Wilhelmshaven, Germany: Heinrichhofen's Verlag, 1974. (Quellenkataloge zur Musikgeschichte, 6)

A full description and analysis of 112 manuscripts, with indexes of persons, Latin titles and first lines, and German titles and first lines.

7.151 Reich, Wolfgang. *Klaviermusik der sozialistischen Länder aus der Sächsischen Landesbibliothek.* 79 pp. Dresden: Sächsische Landesbibliothek, 1962.

A list, grouped alphabetically by country, of keyboard music by East European composers. The date, publisher, and pagination are given for each entry.

Dublin, Ireland

7.152 Charteris, Richard. *A Catalogue of the Printed Books on Music, Printed Music, and Music Manuscripts in Archbishop Marsh's Library, Dublin.* 142 pp. Clifden, Co. Kilkenny, Ireland: Boethius Press, 1982. (Boethius editions, 1)

Arranged in three sections, each presenting bibliographical entries for works printed or written before 1800 held by the Archbishop Marsh Library. The catalog includes a page of supplementary references extending the references provided in the catalog. Includes an appendix listing books missing from the library and a name index to collections.

Reviewed by John D. Arnn in *Notes* 39 (1983): 605–6 and by R. Gordon Dodd in *Chelys* 12 (1983): 79–80.

TRINITY COLLEGE LIBRARY

7.153 Ward, John. "The Lute Books of Trinity College, Dublin." In *Lute Society Journal* 9 (1967): 17–40; 10 (1968): 15–32.

Dubrovnik, Croatia

7.154* Blažekovič, Zdravko. *Katalozi muzikalija u Historijskom Arhivu i Muzeju Grada Dubrovnika / Catalogues of Music Manuscripts and Prints of the Collections of the Historical Archives and the Museum of the City of Dubrovnik.* 99 pp. Zagreb: Jugoslavenska Akademija Znanosti i Umjetnosti Zavod za Muzikoloska Istrazivanja, 1988. (Indices collectiorum musicarum tabulariorumque in SR Croatia, 1)

A catalog of the early holdings of the Historical Archives and the Museum, with 193 titles in the former and 30 manuscripts in the latter.

Reviewed by D. W. Krummel in *Notes* 48 (1992): 918–21.

Durango, Mexico

CATEDRAL. CAPILLA DE MÚSICA

7.155 Antúnez, Francisco. *La Capilla de Música de la Catedral de Durango, México, siglo XVII y XVIII.* 47 pp. Aguascalientes, Mexico: 1970.

A history including a short catalog of the music manuscript holdings of the Cathedral.

Durham, England

DURHAM CATHEDRAL

7.156 Crosby, Brian. *A Catalogue of Durham Cathedral Music Manuscripts.* xxxiii + 271 pp. Oxford; New York: Oxford University Press for the Dean and Chapter of Durham, 1986.

The most complete catalog to date of the manuscript music holdings of Durham Cathedral, its monastery, and Bamburgh Castle. There are indexes of composers, dates, dated signatures (for liturgical manuscripts only), copyists, musical genres, titles, and first lines (for Bamburgh Castle manuscripts). The manuscripts are described, but no title analytics are included in the descriptions. The indexes provide the analysis of contents.

Reviewed by David Hunter in *Notes* 44 (1988): 724 and by John Morehen in *M&L* 69 (1988): 371–72.

7.157 Harman, R. Alec. *A Catalogue of the Printed Music and Books on Music in Durham Cathedral Library.* 136 pp. London; New York; Toronto: Oxford University Press, 1968.

Reviewed by Imogen Fellinger in *Die Musikforschung* 25 (1972): 99–100 and by Henry Leland Clarke in *Notes* 25 (1969): 501–2.

Düsseldorf, Germany

GOETHE-MUSEUM. ANTON-UND-KATHARINA-KIPPENBERG-STIFTUNG

7.158* Kähmer, Inge. *Katalog der Musikalien, Goethe-Museum Düsseldorf, Anton-und-Katharina-Kippenberg-Stiftung.* Edited by Jörn Göres. 621 pp. Bonn: Bouvier, 1987. (Schriften des Arbeitskreises Selbständiger Kultur-Institute, 6)

Edinburgh, Scotland

UNIVERSITY OF EDINBURGH. REID LIBRARY

7.159 Gal, Hans. *Catalogue of Manuscripts, Printed Music, and Books on Music up to 1850 in the Library of the Music Department of the University of Edinburgh.* 78 pp. Edinburgh: Oliver and Boyd, 1941.

A catalog of brief entries for a collection important for its holdings in 18th-century music, printed and in manuscript, from the private collection of John Reid, 1721–1807.

Eisenach, Germany

RICHARD WAGNER MUSEUM

7.160 Oesterlein, Nikolaus. *Katalog einer Richard Wagner Bibliothek: Nach den vorliegenden Originalien systematisch-chronologisch geordnetes und mit Citaten und Anmerkungen versehenes* *authentisches Nachschlagebuch durch die gesammte Wagner-Literatur.* 4 vols. Leipzig: Breitkopf & Härtel, 1882–95.

A catalog providing access to a collection of literature on Wagner (Vols. 1–2) as well as a collection of Wagner documents, formerly in Vienna but purchased by the city of Eisenach in 1895 (Vols. 3–4).

Escorial, Spain

MONASTERIO DE SAN LORENZO EL REAL

7.161 Rubio, Samuel, and **J. Sierra.** *Catálogo del Archivio de Música del Monasterio de San Lorenzo El Real de El Escorial.* Préambulo de Antonio Iglesias. 2 vols. xxvii + 668 pp.; 324 pp. Cuenca, Spain: Instituto de Musica Religiosa, 1976–82. (Instituto de Musica Religiosa. Ediciones, 12 and 18)

The catalog of a collection (Vol. 1) with musical incipits (Vol. 2). The collection includes manuscript choirbooks, scores, part books, and unbound sets of parts from the 16th to the 19th century, with descriptions and analyzed contents. Includes an appendix of brief biographies of the principal composers and an index of names.

Essen, Germany

ESSEN STADTBIBLIOTHEK

7.162 Willford, Manfred. *Systematischer Katalog der Musikbibliothek: Verzeichnis des Gesamtbestandes 1973.* 372 pp. Essen, Germany: Stadtbibliothek, 1974.

A classified catalog of books on music.

Ferrara, Italy

BIBLIOTECA COMUNALE

7.163 Davia, Emmanuele, and **Alessandro Lombardi.** *Catalogo generale delle opere musicali: Città di Ferrara: Biblioteca Comunale.* 40 pp. Parma, Italy: Freschig, 1917. (Associazione dei Musicologi Italiani. Catalogo generale delle opere musicali, 9)

Reprinted by Forni, Bologna, 1978.

Florence, Italy

BIBLIOTECA NAZIONALE CENTRALE

7.164 Becherini, Bianca. *Catalogo dei manoscritti musicali della Biblioteca Nazionale di Firenze.* 178 pp. Kassel, Germany: Bärenreiter, 1959.

A catalog with detailed descriptions of 144 numbered items, giving the contents of collections. There are indexes of text incipits, musicians, poets, and names mentioned in the descriptive notes.

Reviewed by Frank L. Harrison in *M&L* 42 (1961): 281, by Nanie Bridgman in *Fontes* 8 (1961): 31–33, and by Walther Dürr in *Die Musikforschung* 14 (1961): 234–35.

7.165* De Angelis, Marcello. *Le Cifre del melodramma: L'archivio inedito dell'impresario teatrale Alessandro Lanari nella Biblioteca Nazionale Centrale di Firenze (1815–1870): Catalogo.* 2 vols. Florence: Giunta Regionale Toscana, La Buova Italia, 1982. (Inventari e cataloghi toscani, 10–11)

A catalog of 19th-century Italian opera forming the collection of impresario Alessandro Lanari.

Reviewed by Gaspare Nello Vetro in *Nuova rivista musicale italiana* 18 (1984): 113–14.

CONSERVATORIO DI MUSICA LUIGI CHERUBINI

7.166* Addamiano, Antonio, and **Jania Sarno.** *Catalogo del Fondo Basevi nella Biblioteca del Conservatorio "Luigi Cherubini" di Firenze: Musica vocale, opere teatrali, manoscritte e a stampa.* xciii + 491 pp. Rome: Edizioni Torre d'Orfeo, 1994. (Cataloghi di fondi musicali italiani, 16)

The catalog of a collection of vocal and dramatic works, collected in the 19th century by Abramo Basevi, a composer, musicologist, and editor for the publishing house of Guidi and of the journals *L'Armonia* (1856–59) and *Il Boccherini.* The collection was earlier described in a brief article by Anna Maria Trivisonno in *Fontes* 32 (1985): 114–16.

7.167 Becherini, Bianca. "I manoscritti e le stampe rare della Biblioteca del Conservatorio 'L. Cherubini' di Firenze." In *La Bibliofilia* 66 (1964): 255–99.

A catalog compiled for the purpose of giving full descriptions of the items in the collection (20 manuscripts and 21 early printed books, "nuova catalogazione e reintegrazione") that are most rare and most interesting to foreign scholars.

7.168 Gandolfi, Riccardo. *Indice di alcuni cimeli esposti appartenenti alla Biblioteca del R. Istituto.* 32 pp. Florence: Tipografia Galletti e Cocci, 1911.

At head of title: "Nella commemorazione cinquantenaria dalla fondazione del R. Istituto Musicale 'Luigi Cherubini' di Firenze."

A catalog with brief descriptive entries for 30 manuscripts and 37 early printed books, 32 theory works, and 4 "curiosita diversi."

7.169 Gandolfi, Riccardo, Carlo Cordara, and **A. Bonaventura.** *Catalogo delle opere musicali teoriche e pratiche di autori vissuti sino ai primi decenni del secolo XIX, Biblioteca del Conservatorio di Musica di Firenze.* 321 pp. Parma, Italy: Freschig, 1929.

A slightly altered reprint of the edition originally published in 1911 as part of the catalog series sponsored by the Associazione dei Musicologi Italiani (IV/1). Reprinted in Bologna by Forni, 1977 (Bibliotheca musica Bononiensis, I, 11).

UFFIZI GALLERY

7.170 Bernardi, Marziano, and **Andrea Della Corte.** *Gli strumenti musicali nei dipinti della Galleria degli Uffizi.* 177 pp. + 51 plates. Turin: Edizioni Radio Italiana, 1952.

A handsome volume with reproductions of musical activity in paintings in the Uffizi Gallery, with commentary on each reproduction and commentary on the artist, its provenance, and related matter. There is an index of artists and instruments depicted.

Reviewed by Albert G. Hess in *Notes* 10 (1953): 452–53.

7.171 Parigi, Luigi. *I disegni musicali del Gabinetto degli "Uffizi" e delle minori collezioni pubbliche a Firenze.* 233 pp. Florence: L.S. Olschki, 1951.

A catalog of prints and drawings with musical content or subject matter showing musicians, musical instruments, and examples of performance practice. The catalog is indexed by instrument and by subject.

France

See also Alsace.

7.172 Bridgman, Nanie. "Musique profane italienne des 16e et 17e siècles dans les bibliothèques françaises." In *Fontes* 2 (1955): 40–59.

Precise descriptions of 32 rarities of the 16th and 17th centuries found in five public or private libraries in France.

7.173 Chaillon, Paule. "Les fonds musicaux de quelques bibliothèques de province." In *Fontes* 2 (1955): 151–63.

The description of a group of source materials found in 24 French provincial libraries, sources that came to light in connection with work done in preparation for the *RISM* vols.

7.174* Guillo, Laurent. *Catalogue de la musique imprimée avant 1801: Conservée dans les bibliothèques de Lyon, Grenoble, et la région.* 156 pp. Grenoble: Agence de Coopération Régionale pour la Documentation des Cahiers de la Pensée Sauvage, 1986.

Frankfurt am Main, Germany

DEUTSCHES RUNDFUNKARCHIV

7.175 Weinbrenner, Hans-Joachim. *Die ersten vier Jahrzehnte unseres Jahrhunderts im Spiegel einer Berliner Schallplattensammlung: Verzeichnis von Musik- und Sprechschallplatten aus der Sammlung des Berliner Theaterwissenschaftlers Martin Günther Sarneck.* 2 vols. Frankfurt am Main: Deutsches Rundfunkarchiv, 1966.

Contents: Bd. 1, *Sänger und Sängerinnen A–S. Nr. 1–1278;* Bd. 2, *Sänger und Sängerinnen T–Z; Instrumentalmusik. Wortaufnahmen.*

Preface signed by Hans-Joachim Weinbrenner.

A catalog of the Sarneck Collection in the Deutsches Rundfunkarchiv. Vol. 2 contains indexes of persons by profession, with a separate composer index.

LESSING-GYMNASIUM. BIBLIOTHEK

7.176 Israël, Carl. *Die musikalischen Schätze der Gymnasialbibliothek und der Peterskirche zu Frankfurt a. M.* 118 pp. Frankfurt am Main: Druck von Mahlau und Waldschmidt, 1872.

A bibliography covering up to about 1800, giving full bibliographical data.

STADT- UND UNIVERSITÄTSBIBLIOTHEK

7.177* Didion, Robert, and Joachim Schlichte. *Thematischer Katalog der Opernsammlung in der Stadt- und Universitätsbibliothek Frankfurt am Main (Signaturengruppe Mus. Hs. Opern).* 565 pp. Frankfurt am Main: Vittorio Klostermann, 1990. (Kataloge der Stadt- und Universitätsbibliothek Frankfurt am Main, 9)

Reviewed by Winfried Kirsch in *Fontes* 39 (1992): 366–68.

7.178 Schlichte, Joachim. *Thematischer Katalog der kirchlichen Musikhandschriften des 17. und 18. Jahrhunderts in der Stadt- und Universitätsbibliothek Frankfurt am Main: (Signaturengruppe Ms. Ff. Mus.).* 500 pp. Frankfurt am Main: Klostermann, 1979. (Kataloge der Stadt- und Universitätsbibliothek Frankfurt am Main, 8)

A catalog focusing mainly on the Telemann holdings (pp. 187–384), but with anonyms and other composers represented. The Telemann works are divided into sacred and secular sections, each organized by Werke numbers. Descriptions include information about copyists and watermarks, with indexes to names and to titles and text incipits. Includes a bibliography of works on watermarks and a general bibliography.

STADTBIBLIOTHEK

7.179 Epstein, Peter. *Kirchliche Musikhandschriften des XVII. und XVIII. Jahrhunderts: Katalog von Carl Süss, im Auftrage der Gesellschaft der Freunde der Stadtbibliothek.* 224 pp. Berlin: Frankfurter Verlags-Anstalt, 1926.

A catalog of music manuscripts that are chiefly cantatas arranged alphabetically under composer, with a separate section of 834 works by G. P. Telemann. Entries give the date if known, title, and instrumentation.

Freiberg, Germany

7.180 Gamber, Klaus. *Codices liturgici latini antiquiores.* 334 pp. Freiberg, Germany: Universitätsverlag, 1963. (Spicilegii friburgensis subsidia, 1)
Liturgical music manuscripts in the library of the University at Freiberg.

7.181 Kade, Otto. *Die älteren Musikalien der Stadt Freiberg in Sachsen.* 32 pp. Leipzig: Breitkopf & Härtel, 1888. (Beilage. Monatshefte für Musikgeschichte. Jahrgang 20)

Freiburg im Breisgau, Germany

7.182 Gottwald, Clytus. *Die Musikhandschriften der Universitätsbibliothek und anderer offentlicher Sammlungen in Freiburg im Breisgau und Umgebung.* 224 pp. Wiesbaden: Otto Harrassowitz, 1979.
A catalog covering music manuscripts in seven institutions, most of them churches or seminaries, in the vicinity of Freiburg im Breisgau. Each manuscript is fully described and analyzed. Some descriptions include thematic incipits. There are indexes to text incipits and to persons, places, and things.

Garden City, New York

7.183* Cantrell, Gary E., and **Madeleine M. Hogan.** *The Stoelzer Collection at Adelphi University: An Inventory.* 73 pp. Garden City, N.Y.: Adelphi University Libraries, 1985.

Gdansk, Poland (formerly Danzig)

7.184 Günther, Otto. *Die musikalischen Handschriften der Stadtbibliothek und in ihrer Verwaltung befindlichen Kirchenbibliotheken von St. Katharinen und St. Johann in Danzig.* 188 pp. Danzig: Saunier, 1911. (Katalog der Handschriften der Danziger Stadtbibliothek, Bd. 4: Handschriften, Teil 4)
The catalog of a war-ravaged collection. The surviving music manuscripts and early printed books of the Danzig Stadtbibliothek have been filmed and are listed in the catalog of music sources published by the Polish National Library in Warsaw (**7.572**). Professor Plamenac in his articles on East European music libraries (**7.140**) gives a summary of the major holdings of this collection.

Genoa, Italy

BIBLIOTECA DELL'ISTITUTO MUSICALE "NICOLÒ PAGANINI"

7.185 Pintacuda, Salvatore. *Catalogo del fondo antico a cura.* 489 pp. Milan: Istituto Editoriale Italiano, 1966. (Bibliotheca musicae, 4)
A catalog of printed and manuscript music, music literature, vocal anthologies, and the rarities by pre-19th-century composers in the Istituto Paganini. Vocal anthologies are analyzed. Information on instrumentation is supplied, and there is a composer index.
Reviewed by Frank A. D'Accone in *Notes* 23 (1967): 530–31.

7.186 Bresciano, Raffaele. *Catalogo generale delle opere musicali: Città di Genova: R. Biblioteca Universitaria.* 21 pp. Parma, Italy: Freschig. (Associazione dei Musicologi Italiani. Catalogo delle opere musicali, 7)

Germany

See also Bavaria.

7.187 Schaal, Richard. *Führer durch deutsche Musikbibliotheken.* 163 pp. Wilhelmshaven, Germany: Heinrichshofen's Verlag, 1971. (Taschenbücher zur Musikwissenschaft, 7)

A list, arranged alphabetically by place, of German libraries, covering all of Germany. For the major libraries there are descriptions of the collection, with some historical information. Bibliographies include catalogs and other publications related to the libraries under consideration.

Germany (formerly Deutsche Demokratische Republik)

DEUTSCHER BIBLIOTHEKSVERBAND. SEKTION MUSIKBIBLIOTHEKEN

7.188 Thuringer, Peter. *Musikbibliotheken und Musikaliensammlungen in der Deutschen Demokratischen Republik.* 62 pp. Halle, Germany: Internat. Vereinigung d. Musikbibliotheken, Landergruppe DDR, 1969.

A publication sponsored by the East German section of the International Association of Music Libraries, describing 91 institutions, with pertinent data concerning their resources and services and citing catalogs and other publications.

Glasgow, Scotland

ANDERSON'S COLLEGE. LIBRARY. EUING COLLECTION

7.189 *The Euing Musical Library: Catalogue of the Musical Library of the Late Wm. Euing, Esq., bequeathed to Anderson's University, Glasgow.* 256 pp. Glasgow: Printed by W.M. Ferguson, 1878.

A classified catalog of a collection strong in theoretical works from 1487 and liturgical music of the Church of England, 16th to 19th centuries.

Göttingen, Germany

NIEDERSÄCHSISCHE STAATS- UND UNIVERSITÄTS-BIBLIOTHEK

7.190 Quantz, Albert. *Die Musikwerke der Kgl. Universitäts-Bibliothek in Göttingen.* 45 pp. Berlin: T. Trautwein, 1883. (Monatshefte für Musikgeschichte. Beilage, Jahrgang 15)

Catalog of 45 theoretical works and some 100 music editions of the 16th and 17th centuries, a good representation of German composers of the period.

Gottweig (Benedictine Abbey), Austria

7.191 Wondratsch, Heinrich. *Der Göttweiger thematische Katalog von 1830 hrsg., kommentiert und mit Registern versehen von Friedrich W. Riedel.* 2 vols. Munich: E. Katzbichler, 1979. (Studien zur Landes- und Sozialgeschichte der Musik, Bds. 2–3)

Edition of a thematic catalog originating in 1830 of a collection of music in the Benedictine Abbey of Gottweig in Austria. The original manuscript title page reads *Katalogus operum musicalium in choro musicali monasterii O.S.P.B. Gottwicensis, R.R.D.D. Altmanno abbate, per R.D. Henricam Wondratsch, p.t. chori regentem, conscriptus. Anno MDCCCXXX. Tom. 1.*

Contents: 1, *Faksimile der Originalhandschrift;* 2, *Historisch-quellenkundliche Bemerkungen, Kommentar und Register.*

Granada, Spain

CAPILLA REAL. ARCHIVO

7.192 López Calo, José. "El Archivo de musica de la Capilla Real de Granada." In *Anuario musical* 13 (1958): 103–28.

The catalog of a small collection of manuscripts, early printed books, and documents, listing full contents for polyphonic sources.

Great Britain

7.193 Penney, Barbara. *Music in British Libraries: A Directory of Resources.* 4th ed. 97 pp. London: Library Association, 1992.

First ed., 1971, and 2nd ed., 1974, 154 pp., edited by Maureen W. Long; 3rd ed., 1981, 452 pp.

The results of a broad survey in Great Britain, including information about services, personnel, and hours of opening. The collections are described in some detail. There are indexes to locations and names of libraries and to composers, names of collections, and the nature of collections.

Greensboro, North Carolina

UNIVERSITY OF NORTH CAROLINA AT GREENSBORO. WALTER CLINTON JACKSON LIBRARY

7.194 Cassell, Barbara B., and **Clifton E. Karnes III.** *Cello Music Collections in the Jackson Library, University of North Carolina at Greensboro. Part I: The Luigi Silva Collection.* 20 pp. Greensboro, N.C.: Walter Clinton Jackson Library, 1978.

Photocopies of catalog cards. The collection is chiefly 20th-century compositions and editions.

Grimma, Germany

KÖNIGLICHE LANDESSCHULE. BIBLIOTHEK

7.195 Petersen, N. M. *Verzeichniss der in der Bibliothek der Königl. Landesschule zu Grimma vorhandenen Musikalien aus dem 16. und 17. Jahrhundert.* 24 pp. Grimma, Germany: G. Gensel, 1861.

A collection whose greater part is now in the Sächsische Landesbibliothek in Dresden.

Grottaferrata, Italy

BIBLIOTECA DELLA BADIA

7.196 Tardo Ieromonaco, D. Lorenzo. "La musica bizantina e i codici di melurgia della biblioteca di Grottaferrata." In *Accademie e biblioteche d'Italia* 4 (1930–31): 355–69.

The library of the principal center of Byzantine musical studies in Italy, with a description of 54 codices.

Gubbio, Italy

CAPPELLA MUSICALE DEL DUOMO

7.197* Clementi, Maria Cecilia. *Cappella Musicale del Duomo di Gubbio nel '500, con il catalogo dei manoscritti coevi.* 137 pp. + 15 plates. Perugia, Italy: Cattedra di Storia della Musica, Universita degli Studi di Perugia: Centro di Studi Musicali in Umbria, 1994. (Quaderni di "Esercizi Musica e Spettacolo," 2)

The catalog of the 16th-century repertoire of the Duomo, with a thematic catalog from the holdings of the Archivio Capitolare.

The Hague, The Netherlands

GEMEENTEMUSEUM

7.198 Charbon, Marie H. *Catalogus van de musiekbibliotheek.* 2 vols. to date. Amsterdam: F. Knuf, 1969–74. (Catalogi van de muziekbibliotheek en de collectie muziekinstrumenten)

Contents: Deel I, *Historische en theoretische werken tot 1800;* Deel II, *Vocale muziek van 1512 tot ca. 1650.*

Simultaneously published by Da Capo, New York, 1969–73.

The first 2 vols. in a series of catalogs projected to cover the resources, printed and in manuscript, of the Music Library of the Gemeentemuseum at The Hague. These catalogs will incorporate the holdings of the Scheurleer collection. A parallel series is devoted to the musical instruments in the Gemeentemuseum (**8.48**). Deel II covers both a cappella and accompanied works. The catalog provides entries for new acquisitions and analyzes contents more extensively than the Scheurleer *Catalogus* (**7.199**) and supplements it. There is an index of text incipits, names, and publishers.

MUZIEKHISTORISCH MUSEUM VAN DR. D. F. SCHEURLEER

7.199 *Catalogus van de muziek-werken en de boeken oven muziek.* 3 vols. The Hague: M. Nijhoff, 1923–25.

The catalog was preceded by two earlier compilations, one in 2 vols., 1885–87, and one in 3 vols., 1893–1910.

A classified catalog. There are numerous facsimiles of early title pages. The Scheurleer collection is both an outstanding working library of musicology and a repository of many rarities. It is now the property of the city of The Hague. The 3rd vol. is a general index.

Halle, Germany

HANDEL-HAUS

7.200 *Katalog zu den Sammlungen des Handel-Hauses in Halle.* 7 vols. to date. Halle an der Saale, Germany: Handel-Haus, 1961– . Vol. 1– .

Contents: Teil 1, *Handschriftensammlung* (1961); Teil 2, *Bildsammlung, Porträts* (1962); Teil 3, *Bildsammlung, Städte- und Gebaudedarstellung* (1964); Teil 4, *Bildsammlung, Hogarth-Graphik;* Teil 5, *Musikinstrumentensammlung, Besaitete Tasteninstrumente* (1966); Teil 6, *Musikinstrumentensammlung, Streich- und Zupfinstrumente* (1972); Teil 7, *Musikinstrumentensammlung, Blasinstrumente, Orgeln, Harmoniums* (1979).

A growing series of catalogs concerned not only with Handel documents but with material on early-19th-century German song, iconography, and musical instruments, with numerous illustrative plates.

Hamburg, Germany

HAMBURGER MUSIKBÜCHEREI

7.201 Eckhoff, Annemarie. *Oper, Operette, Singspiel: Ein Katalog der Hamburger Musikbücherei, 1965.* 207 pp. Hamburg: Hamburger Öffentliche Bücherhallen, 1965.

A catalog of the theater holdings of the Hamburg Musikbücherei, totaling 3,198 vols., 1,590 titles. Full scores and vocal scores are indicated, with publishers and plate numbers. Although the works are chiefly from the 19th- and 20th-centuries, there are some early items. The arrangement is alphabetical by composer, with indexes of Singspiel, full scores, and titles.

Reviewed by Klaus Hortschansky in *Die Musikforschung* 22 (1969): 521–22.

STADT- UND UNIVERSITÄTSBIBLIOTHEK

7.202 Clausen, Hans Dieter. *Händels Direktionspartituren (Handexemplare).* 281 pp. Hamburg: Verlag der Musikalienhandlung, 1972. (Hamburger Beiträge zur Musikwissenschaft, 7)

A catalog of the autograph conducting scores used by Handel, now almost all housed in the Stadt- und Universitätsbibliothek, Hamburg, listing each manuscript's contents and describing the watermarks, copyists, and performance changes and designations. These scores were also used by Chrysander for his *Gesamtausgabe.*

Harburg, Germany

FÜRSTLICH OETTINGEN-WALLERSTEIN'SCHE
BIBLIOTHEK

7.203 Haberkamp, Gertraut. *Thematischer Katalog der Musikhandschriften der Fürstlich Oettingen-Wallerstein'schen Bibliothek Schloss Harburg.* xxxv + 298 pp. Munich: Henle, 1976– . (Kataloge bayerischer Musiksammlungen)

Reviewed by Barry S. Brook in *JAMS* 32 (1979): 549–55, by Stephen M. Fry in *Notes* 34 (1977): 89, and by Catherine Massip in *Fontes* 24 (1977): 295–96.

Heilbronn, Germany

GYMNASIUM. BIBLIOTHEK

7.204 Mayers, Edwin. *Alter Musikschatz.* 82 pp. Heilbronn, Germany: C.F. Schmidt, 1893. (Mitteilungen aus der Bibliothek des Heilbronner Gymnasiums, 2)

STADTARCHIV

7.205 Siegele, Ulrich. *Die Musiksammlung der Stadt Heilbronn: Katalog mit Beiträgen zur Geschichte der Sammlung und zur Quellenkunde des XVI. Jahrhunderts.* 323 pp. Heilbronn, Germany: Stadtarchiv, 1971. (Veröffentlichungen des Archivs der Stadt Heilbronn, 13)

A catalog giving full bibliographical descriptions with contents of collections. *RISM* items are identified. There are 16 plates of early manuscripts, bindings, and editions, with a first-line index and an index of names and subjects.

Hradec Králové (Königgrätz), Czech Republic

MUSEUM

7.206 Černý, Jaromír. *Soupis hudeních rukopisů muzea v. Hraci Králové /Catalog of Music Manuscripts in the Museum at Hradec Králové.* 240 pp. Prague: Universita Karlova, 1966. (Miscellanea musicologica, 19)

A catalog of 56 items, chiefly manuscripts of liturgical music. There is copious indexing by form; the texts are indexed by language, with a bibliography of relevant literature. There are 16 facsimile plates.

Hungary

7.207 Pethos, Iván. "Musikbibliotheken in Ungarn." In *Fontes* 15 (May–December 1968): 114–18.

A description of 15 current Hungarian music libraries, with a table giving comparative statistics on their holdings and services.

Iowa City, Iowa

UNIVERSITY OF IOWA

7.208 Gable, Frederick Kent. *An Annotated Catalog of Rare Musical Items in the Libraries of the University of Iowa.* 130 pp. Iowa City, Iowa: University Libraries, University of Iowa, 1963.

Gordon S. Rowley in 1973 edited a supplemental catalog with additions from 1963 to 1972, 121 pp. Melody Noel Scherubel updated the information on the Library's holdings in 1985, with an emphasis on the theory of music.

A list of rare music-connected items owned by the libraries of the University of Iowa. The first, carefully annotated catalog of 275 items is divided into two parts. The first part lists books on music, the second lists music scores. There is an index of names and selected subjects. The 1973 ed. lists and describes an additional 278 items, identifying the *RISM* items and adding an index of names.

For an account of the history, resources, and services of this music library, see Rita Benton's "The Music Library of the University of Iowa" in *Fontes* 16 (1969): 124–29.

Italy

The first influential series of catalogs of Italian music collection was the 14 vols. published by the Associazione dei Musicologi Italiani as *Catalogo generale delle opere musicali teoriche o pratiche, manoscritti o stampate, di autori vissuti fino ai primi decenni del XIX secolo, esistenti nelle biblioteche e negli archivi d'Italia* (Parma, Italy: Freschig, 1911–38). The Associazione catalogs are of mixed quality and completeness, but in many cases they are the best available lists of the holdings of important Italian libraries. Their coverage is confined to music and theoretical works written or published before 1810. *RISM* should be consulted before these catalogs are approached.

7.209 Rubsamen, Walter H. "Music Research in Italian Libraries." In *Notes* 6 (1948–49): 220–33, 543–69; 8 (1950–51): 70–89, 513.

A narrative account of the author's experiences working in Italian libraries shortly after World War II. There are useful inventories, partially thematic, of manuscripts of early music in Italian libraries. Most of the difficulties described in this article have long since disappeared.

Jena, Germany

UNIVERSITÄTSBIBLIOTHEK

7.210 Roediger, Karl Erich. *Die geistlichen Musikhandschriften der Universitätsbibliothek Jena.* 2 vols. Jena, Germany: Frommansche Buchhandlung Walter Biedermann, 1935.

Contents: Vol. 1, *Textband;* Vol. 2, *Notenverzeichnis.*
Reprinted by Olms, Hildesheim, Germany, 1985.
Primarily a source study with inventories of 18 choirbooks containing music of the Burgundian–Netherland repertory in the University Library at Jena. Vol. 1 treats the sources and their contents, with indexes of liturgical settings, cantus firmi, and composers. There is a list of 63 16th-century prints in the Jena library (pp. 111–14). Vol. 2 is a thematic catalog of the choirbooks.

Jerusalem, Israel

JERUSALEM RUBIN ACADEMY OF MUSIC AND DANCE

7.211* Abravanel, Claude. *The Simeon Bellison Archives at the Jerusalem Rubin Academy of Music and Dance: A Catalogue.* 52 pp. Jerusalem: The Academy, 1993.

The catalog of a collection strong in clarinet music that includes bibliographical references (p. 47) and an index.

JEWISH NATIONAL AND UNIVERSITY LIBRARY

7.212 Adler, Israel, and **Judith Cohen.** *A. Z. Idelsohn Archives at the Jewish National and University Library: Catalogue.* 34 pp. Jerusalem: Magnes Press, Hebrew University, 1976. (Yuval monograph series, 4)

A guide in English and Hebrew to the *Nachlass* of one of the founders of historical and ethnic studies on Jewish music. The collection contains about 950 items, mostly letters and press clippings, dating from 1897 to 1938. Indexes include Idelsohn's works, a chronological index, and a general index.

Reviewed by Simha Arom in *Fontes* 24 (1977): 103.

Jonköping, Sweden

PER BRAHEGYMNASIET

7.213 Ruuth, Gustaf. *Katalog över äldere musikalier i Per Brahegymnasiet i Jonköping /Catalog of the Music Collection in Per Brahegymnasiet, Jonkoping.* 131 pp. Stockholm: Svenskt Musikhistoriskt Arkiv, 1971. (Musik i sverige, 2)

A collection of 18th- and 19th-century music reflecting the repertoires of local musicians.

Kaliningrad, Russia (formerly Königsberg, Germany)

STAATS- UND UNIVERSITÄTS-BIBLIOTHEK.
BIBLIOTHECA GOTTHOLDIANA

7.214 Müller, Joseph. *Die musikalischen Schätze der Königlichen- und Universitäts-Bibliothek zu Königsberg in Preussen: Aus dem Nachlasse Friedrich August Gottholds: Ein Beitrag zur Geschichte und Theorie der Tonkunst.* Im Anhang: Joseph Müller-Blattau, "Die musikalischen Schätze der Staats- und Universitäts-Bibliothek zu Königsberg in Preussen." 731 pp. Hildesheim, Germany; New York: Georg Olms, 1971.

Reprint of the ed. originally published by Adolph Marcus, Bonn, 1870, with an article by Müller-Blattau originally published in the *Zeitschrift für Musikwissenschaft* 6 (1924): 215–39.

An important collection of 55,000 volumes, strong in 17th-century church music, in print and in manuscript, and vocal music from the 16th to the 19th centuries. There are works by various Königsberger Kapellmeistern such as Eccard, Stobaeus, and Sebastini, as well as numerous first editions of Beethoven, Haydn, and Mozart.

Kassel, Germany

DEUTSCHES MUSIKGESCHICHTLICHES ARCHIV

7.215 Heckmann, Harald, and **Jurgen Kindermann.** *Deutsches Musikgeschichtliches Archiv: Katalog der Filmsammlung zusammengestellt und bearbeit.* Kassel, Germany: Bärenreiter, 1955– . Band I, Nr. 1– . Title varies: Nr. 1, *Mitteilungen und Katalog.*

A series of lists documenting the holdings of a microfilm archive of primary source materials, including manuscripts and early printed books, for the study of German music history. For a description of this project and the catalogs, see Heckmann's "Archive of German Music History" in *Notes* 16 (1958): 35–39.

Briefly reviewed by Stephen M. Fry in *Notes* 32 (1976): 781.

LANDESBIBLIOTHEK

7.216 Israel, Carl. *Übersichtlicher Katalog der ständischen Landesbibliothek zu Cassel.* 78 pp. Kassel, Germany: A. Freyschmidt, 1881.

A list of works from the 16th and 17th centuries, both manuscripts and printed books, rich in German and Italian church and chamber music. An unpublished catalog by Wilhelm Lange (**7.217**), available in Kassel, supplements the coverage supplied by Israel's work.

7.217 Lange, Wilhelm. *Katalog der Musikalien der Landesbibliothek, Kassel.* 1 vol. (various pagings). Kassel, Germany, 1920.

An unpublished catalog, available on microfilm from the Deutsches Musikgeschichtliches Archiv, that supplements the printed catalog by Carl Israel (**7.216**), extending the coverage to 18th- and 19th-century materials. The Lange catalog describes 438 folio volumes, 247 quartos, and 53 octavos, with a supplement of 32 items.

Kempten, Germany

PFARRKIRCHE ST. MANG

7.218* Herrmann-Schneider, Hildegard. *Evangelisch-Lutherisches Pfarramt St. Mang: Die Musikhandschriften der evangelisch-lutherischen Pfarrkirche St. Mang in Kempten: Thematischer Katalog.* xxvi + 111 pp. Munich: G. Henle, 1991. (Kataloge bayerischer Musiksammlungen, 19)
Reviewed by Lilian P. Pruett in *Fontes* 40 (1993): 339–42.

Kiel, Germany

7.219 Hortschansky, Klaus. *Katalog der Kieler Musiksammlungen: Die Notendrucke, Handschriften, Libretti und Bücher über Musik aus der Zeit bis 1830.* 270 pp. Kassel, Germany: Bärenreiter, 1963. (Kieler Schriften zur Musikwissenschaft, 14)

A catalog of the music in three libraries in Kiel: the Schleswig-Holsteinische Landesbibliothek, the Bibliothek des Musikwissenschaftlichen Instituts der Universität, and the Universitätsbibliothek.

Knoxville, Tennessee

UNIVERSITY OF TENNESSEE LIBRARY

7.220 Bayne, Pauline Shaw. *The Gottfried Galston Music Collection and the Galston-Busoni Archive.* 297 pp. Knoxville, Tenn.: University of Tennessee Library, 1978.

A catalog of 1,490 numbered items, with multiple indexes, a class index, a title index, and an index of arrangers, editors, and transcribers. The collection is largely miniature scores, books on music, and archival materials.

Königsberg, Germany

See Kaliningrad, Russia.

Kraków, Poland

BIBLIOTEKA JAGIELLONSKA

7.221* Kirch, Dieter, and **Lenz Meierott.** *Berliner Lautentabulaturen in Krakau: Neschreibender Katalog der Handschriften Tabulaturen für Laute und verwandte Instrumente in der Bibliotheka Jagiellońska Kraków aus dem Besitz der ehemaligen Preussischen Staatsbibliothek Berlin.* 432 pp. Mainz: Schott, 1992. (Schriften der Musikhochschule Würzburg, 3)

7.222 Reiss, Josef. *Książki o muzyce w Bibliotece Jagielloński.* 3 vols. Cracow, 1924–38.

Kremsmünster, Austria

BENEDIKTINER-STIFT KREMSMÜNSTER.
BIBLIOTHEK

7.223 *Die Lautentabulaturen des Stiftes Kremsmünster: Thematischer Katalog.* 274 pp. Vienna: Hermann Bohlau, 1965. (Tabulae musicae austriacae, 2)

A description and inventory of a group of nine manuscripts and two early prints of lute music in the library of the Benedictine abbey at Kremsmünster.

Review by Hans Radke in *Die Musikforschung* 21 (1968): 242–44.

Lancaster, England

UNIVERSITY OF LANCASTER. LIBRARY

7.224 Royds, Graham. *Catalogue of the Hans Ferdinand Redlich Collection of Musical Books and Scores, Including Material on the Second Viennese School.* 117 pp. Lancaster, England: University of Lancaster, 1976.

Łancut, Poland

BIBLIOTEKA MUZYCZNA ZAMKU W ŁANCUCIE

7.225 Bieganski, Krzyztof. *Katalog.* 430 pp. Krakow: Polske Wydawn. Muzyczne, 1968.

A library of some 2,637 items, strong in late-18th- and early-19th-century music. The collection is broadly classified as to vocal and instrumental music, theory, and didactic works, with very specific subdivisions. There are indexes of composers, arrangers, publishers (listed by place), ballets, and operas and a first-line index of texts.

Langenburg, Germany

FÜRSTLICH HOHENLOHE-LANGENBURG'SCHE
SCHLOSSBIBLIOTHEK

7.226 Böker-Heil, Norbert, Ursula Böker-Heil, Gertraut Haberkamp, and **Helmut Rösing.** "Fürstlich Hohenlohe-Langenburg'sche Schlossbibliothek. Katalog der Musikhandschriften." In *Fontes* 25 (1978): 205–411.

An experimental printed form of part of the *RISM* A II database covering 249 manuscripts with thematic incipits and brief descriptions. There are indexes to text incipits, titles, genres, names, and the musical incipits.

Lausanne, Switzerland

VAUD. BIBLIOTHÈQUE CANTONALE ET
UNIVERSITAIRE. DÉPARTEMENT DE LA MUSIQUE

7.227 Demont, Micheline. *Inventaire du fonds musical Adrien Bovy.* 63 ll. Lausanne: Bibliothèque Cantonale et Universitaire, 1980. (Inventaire des fonds manuscrits, 11)

7.228* Hefti, Jocelyne. *Inventaire du fonds Paul Piguet.* 181 pp. Lausanne: Bibliothèque Cantonale et Universitaire Lausanne Dorigny, 1993. (Inventaire des fonds manuscrits, 42)

7.229 Matthey, Jean-Louis. *Inventaire du fonds musical Alfred Pochon.* 51 pp. Lausanne: Bibliothèque Cantonale et Universitaire, 1979. (Inventaire des fonds manuscrits, 9)

7.230 Matthey, Jean-Louis. *Inventaire du fonds musical Auguste Sérieyx.* 124 pp. Lausanne: Bibliothèque Cantonale et Universitaire, 1974. (Inventaire des fonds manuscrits, 4)

7.231 Matthey, Jean-Louis. *Inventaire du fonds musical Bernard Reichel.* 101 pp. Lausanne: Bibliothèque Cantonale et Universitaire, 1974. (Inventaire des fonds manuscrits, 5)

7.232 Matthey, Jean-Louis. *Inventaire du fonds musical François Olivier.* 69 pp. Lausanne: Bibliothèque Cantonale et Universitaire, 1971. (Inventaire des fonds manuscrits, 2)

7.233 Matthey, Jean-Louis. *Inventaire du fonds musical George Templeton Strong.* 134 pp. Lausanne: Bibliothèque Cantonale et Universitaire, Département de la Musique, 1973. (Inventaire des fonds manuscrits, 3)

7.234 Matthey, Jean-Louis. *Inventaire du fonds musical Jean Apotheloz.* 35 pp. Lausanne: Bibliothèque Cantonale et Universitaire, 1977. (Inventaire des fonds manuscrits, 8)

7.235 Matthey, Jean-Louis, András Farkas, and **Ferenc Farkas.** *Inventaire du fonds musical Ferenc Farkas: Catalogue des oeuvres.* 49 pp. Lausanne: Bibliothèque Cantonale et Universitaire, 1979. (Inventaire isole: Bibliothèque cantonale et universitaire)

7.236 Matthey, Jean-Louis, and **Rose Hemmerling-Dumur.** *Inventaire du fonds musical Carlo Hemmerling.* 77 pp. Lausanne: Bibliothèque Cantonale et Universitaire, 1976. (Inventaire des fonds manuscrits, 7)

7.237 Matthey, Jean-Louis, and **Louis-Daniel Perret.** *Catalogue de l'oeuvre de Hans Haug.* 83 pp. Lausanne: Bibliothèque Cantonale et Universitaire, 1971. (Inventaire des fonds manuscrits, 1)

7.238 Matthey, Jean-Louis, and **Germaine Schmidt.** *Inventaire du fonds musical Émile-Robert Blanchet.* 71 pp. Lausanne: Bibliothèque Cantonale et Universitaire, Département de la Musique, 1975. (Inventaire des fonds manuscrits, 6)

Legnica, Poland (Formerly Liegnitz, Germany)

OKREGONE MUZEUM

7.239* Kolbuszewska, Aniela, and **Lucja Wojtasnik.** *Bibliotheca Rudolphina: Druki i rekopisy muzyczne z Legnickiej Biblioteki Ksiecia Jerzego Rudolfa: Katalog mustamy.* 36 pp. Legnica: Pazdziernik, 1983.

RITTER-AKADEMIE

7.240 Eitner, Robert. "Katalog der in der Kgl. Ritter-Akademie zu Liegnitz gedruckten und handschriftlichen Musikalien nebst den hymnologischen und musikalisch-theoretischen Werken." In *Monatshefte für Musikgeschichte* 1 (1869): 25–39, 50–56, 70–76 (incomplete).

7.241 Pfudel, Ernst. *Die Musik-Handschriften der Königl. Ritter-Akademie zu Liegnitz.* 74 pp. Leipzig: Breitkopf & Härtel, 1886–89. (Monatshefte für Musikgeschichte. Beilage. Jahrgang 18 u. 21)

Leipzig, Germany

BREITKOPF & HÄRTEL

7.242 Hitzig, Wilhelm. *Katalog des Archivs von Breitkopf & Härtel, Leipzig, im Auftrag der Firma.* 2 vols. in 1. Leipzig: Breitkopf & Härtel, 1925–26.

Vol. 1, *Musik-Autographe;* Vol. 2, *Briefe.*

Full descriptions of 348 autograph scores from Handel to Hindemith, with a composer index. Autograph letters are limited to persons born before 1780. There is a separate index to letters.

KARL-MARX-UNIVERSITÄT LEIPZIG. BIBLIOTHEK

7.243 Orf, Wolfgang. *Die Musikhandschriften Thomaskirche Mss. 49/50 und 51 in der Universitätsbibliothek Leipzig.* 175 pp. Wilhelmshaven, Germany: Heinrichshofen, 1977. (Quellenkataloge zur Musikgeschichte, 13)

MUSIKBIBLIOTHEK DER STADT LEIPZIG

7.244 Krumbiegel, Cornelia, and **Peter Krause.** *Katalog der vor 1800 gedruckten Opernlibretti der Musikbibliothek der Stadt Leipzig.* 2 vols. Leipzig: Musikbibliothek der Stadt Leipzig, 1981–82.

The catalog of an extensive collection, brought together in part from the collection of Carl Ferdinand Becker and the music library of the publishing firm Peters.

Reviewed by Claudio Sartori in *Fontes* 30 (1983): 225.

7.245* Schulze, Hans-Joachim. *Katalog der Sammlung Manfred Gorke: Bachiana und andere Handschr. und Drucke d. 18. und frühe 19. Jh.* 168 pp. Leipzig: Musikbibliothek der Stadt Leipzig, 1977. (Bibliographische Veröffentlichungen der Musikbibliothek der Stadt Leipzig, 8)

MUSIKBIBLIOTHEK PETERS

7.246 Schwartz, Rudolf. *Katalog der Musikbibliothek Peters, Band I: Bucher und Schriften.* 227 pp. Leipzig: C.F. Peters, 1910.

An earlier ed. by Emil Vogel (1894) included both books and music.

The classified catalog of a large reference library of music literature maintained by the firm C.F. Peters before World War I. All publishers are represented. There are many early works, although the chief strength is in 19th-century literature. Entries give the place and date of publication but not the publisher. Major classes include dictionaries, periodicals, music history, biographies and monographs, instruction, instruments, and aesthetics.

Leningrad, Russia

See St. Petersburg, Russia.

Lexington, Kentucky

UNIVERSITY OF KENTUCKY. LIBRARY

7.247 Traficante, Frank. "The Alfred Cortot Collection at the University of Kentucky Libraries." In University of Kentucky Library *Library Notes* 1 (1970): 1–18 no. 3.

A well-illustrated account of the portion of the Cortot collection now resident at the University of Kentucky. Included is an alphabetical list of all the Cortot materials. A shorter version is in *Notes* 26 (1970): 713–17.

Liège, Belgium

CONSERVATOIRE ROYAL DE MUSIQUE. BIBLIOTHÈQUE

7.248* Barthélémy, Maurice. *Catalogue des imprimés musicaux anciens du Conservatoire Royal de Musique de Liège.* 219 pp. Liège: Pierre Mardaga, 1992. (Collection musique / musicologie)

A list of the Conservatoire's early (generally 18th-century) printed music, superseding the editor's 1977 *Inventaire général des manuscrits anciens du Conservatoire Royal de Musique de Liège,* which lists manuscripts in the general collection, as well as holdings from the Debroux and the Terry collections. The entries give basic bibliographic information and (as available) *RISM* numbers.

Reviewed, with a history of earlier catalogs, by Albert Cohen in *Notes* 50 (1994): 1,392–94.

7.249 Barthélémy, Maurice. *Inventaire général des manuscrits anciens du Conservatoire Royal de Musique de Liège.* 128 ll. Liège: DUP, 1977.

A catalog listing manuscripts in the general collection, the Debroux collection, and the Terry collection. There are addenda on p. 119.

7.250 *Catalogue de la Bibliothèque du Conservatoire Royal de Musique de Liège. Fonds Terry: Musique dramatique.* 75 pp. Liège: Conservatoire Royal, 1960.

A 2nd vol. covers "Musique instrumentale," 51 pp.

The catalog of the Terry collection, acquired by the Liège Conservatory in 1882. The dramatic works date chiefly from 1780 to 1880. The collection is broadly classified by full or vocal scores and by language of the libretto (French or foreign). The instrumental music is late-18th- or early-19th-century material, both printed and in manuscript.

Liegnitz, Germany

See Legnica, Poland.

Lille, France

BIBLIOTHÈQUE DE LILLE

7.251 *Catalogue des ouvrages sur la musique et des compositions musicales de la Bibliothèque de Lille.* 752 pp. Lille, France: Imprimerie de Lefebvre-Ducrocq, 1879.

A catalog of 2,721 items. The collection is particularly rich in late-18th- and early-19th-century French operas, which exist here in complete sets of performance materials. There is also a large collection of symphonies, overtures, and chamber music.

Linz, Austria

BUNDESSTAATLICHE STUDIENBIBLIOTHEK

7.252 Smith, William Liddel. "An Inventory of Pre-1600 Manuscripts Pertaining to Music, in the Bundesstaatliche Studienbibliothek (Linz, Austria)." In *Fontes* 27 (1980): 162–71.

An inventory that includes a list of liturgical documents and is based on the microfilm holdings of the Hill Monastic Microfilm Library at St. John's Abbey and University, Collegeville, Minn.

Lisbon, Portugal

BIBLIOTECA DA AJUDA

7.253 Machado-Santos, Mariana Amélia. *Catálogo de música manuscrita.* 9 vols. Lisbon, 1958–69.

A collection of manuscripts, 5,382 items, entered alphabetically by composer and running consecutively through the first 6 vols., with two appendixes in Vols. 7–8 and an index in Vol. 9. The collection is strong in 18th- and early-19th-century music, particularly opera.

LIBRARY OF JOÃO IV, KING OF PORTUGAL

7.254 Crasbeck, Paulo. *Primeira parte do index da livraria de música do muyto alto, e poderoso Rey Dom João o IV.* Edited by J. de Vasconcellos. 525 pp. Porto, 1874–76.

Reprint ed. in Lisbon, 1966, by Academia Portuguesa da História.

The reprinting of a catalog compiled in 1649 by Paul Crasbeck for the royal library in Lisbon, which was destroyed in the earthquake of 1755. The catalog, although of a collection now destroyed, remains an important bibliographical tool for the study of early Spanish and Portuguese music.

Liverpool, England

CENTRAL PUBLIC LIBRARIES

7.255 *Catalogue of the Music Library.* 572 pp. Liverpool: Central Public Libraries, 1954.

An earlier ed. was issued in 1933 as *Catalogue of Music in the Liverpool Public Libraries,* by J. A. Carr under the direction of George H . Parry, published by Liverpool's Libraries, Museums, and Arts Committee, containing all the music and musical literature in the Music Library, the Reference Library, and the Hornby Library.

About 45,000 entries for books and music, most published after 1800.

Reviewed by H. Dorothy Tilly in *Notes* 12 (1955): 237–38.

Łódź, Poland

BIBLIOTEKA UNIWERSYTECKA W ŁÓDZI

7.256 Bielska, Krystyna. *Muzykalia.* 3 vols. Łódź: Uniwersytecka Łódźki, 1975–84.

A catalog of the music holdings of the University Library. Vol. 1 is a catalog of scores in anthologies, collected works, and series published between 1801 and 1945. Vol. 2 is a catalog of opera scores and a discography of operas. Vol. 3 is a catalog of opera libretti; for this volume there was an additional editor, Jerzy K. Andrzejewski.

London, England

BRITISH BROADCASTING CORPORATION.
CENTRAL MUSIC LIBRARY

7.257 Davies, John H. *Catalogues of the BBC, Central Music Library.* 13 vols. London: British Broadcasting Corporation, 1965–82.

Contents: No. 1, *Chamber Music Catalogue: Chamber Music, Violin and Keyboard, Cello and Keyboard* (1 vol., various pagings, 1965); No. 2, *Piano and Organ Catalogue* (2 vols., various pagings, 1965); No. 3, *Song Catalogue* (4 vols.: *Composers,* 1–2; *Titles,* 3–4; 1966); No. 4, *Choral and Opera Catalogue* (2 vols.: *Composers,* 1; *Titles,* 2; 1967); No. 5, *Orchestral Library,* edited by Sheila Compton (4 vols., 1982).

A series of book catalogs recording the holdings of one of the world's great radio music libraries, often called the *BBC Catalogues,* with the set subdivided into five special categories of materials and published under the supervision of the former BBC Music Librarian. Entries include the composer's full name and dates (if known), the work's title, the format (score or parts), duration, and publisher. There are occasional helpful appendixes, as in the *Song Index,* which has lists of national and folk songs by country and song anthologies arranged by nationality and topic (drinking songs, Shakespeare, work songs, etc.); an attempt has also been made to bring together variants (in arrangement or translation) of the same work, under the original title. The chief value of these volumes is in the information offered as a reference tool; the BBC Music Library is not a lending library.

The 1st vol. is reviewed by Donald W. Krummel in *Notes* 23 (1966): 46–48.

BRITISH LIBRARY

7.258 Baillie, Laureen. *The Catalogue of Printed Music in the British Library to 1980.* 62 vols. London; New York: K.G. Saur, 1981–87.

Editor, Vols. 21–62: Robert Balchin.

A bibliographical tool of the first rank, estimated at holding over 1 million records. The collection of printed music forms part of the Department of Printed Books in the British Library Reference Division, to which the Library Departments of the British Museum were transferred in 1973. The introductory "Guide to the Arrangement of Entries" is the essential tool for understanding and using the catalog. A work may appear under the name of the person or body primarily responsible for it, by the name of the compiler, or by title (if anonymous). There are a variety of cross-references leading the user to the principal entry. The arrangement of headings is basically alphabetical, but there is a guide to the arrangement of entries within a heading. Because the catalog was assembled over a long period, the entries vary in fullness of information and, in particular, the rules for entering works in series have varied. This supersedes the *Catalogue of Music. Accessions,* an annual publication of the British Museum begun in 1884, and the 1912 *Catalogue of Printed Music Published between 1487 and 1800 Now in the British Museum,* edited by William Barclay-Squire, 2 vols., with the first *Supplement* included in Vol. 2 and the second, edited by William C. Smith, published separately (1940).

Reviewed by George R. Hill in *ARBA* 18 (1987): no. 1225. Oliver Neighbour addressed "*CPM:* Some Quirks and Caveats," in *Music Publishing and Collecting: Essays in Honor of Donald W. Krummel* (**13.15**), pp. 207–14.

7.259 *Books in the Hirsch Library, with Supplementary List of Music.* 542 pp. London: Trustees of the British Museum, 1959. (Catalogue of printed books in the British Museum. Accessions, 3rd ser., Pt. 291 B)

A collection acquired by the then–British Museum in 1946, including more than 11,500 books on music, particularly strong in German imprints. The brief entries were printed from the slips prepared for the British Museum catalog; entries are quite concise for titles already held by the Museum and periodical titles already held are completely omitted. Many of the important holdings are more fully described in the 4-vol. Hirsch–Meyer catalog (**7.631**), 1928–47; the British Museum's librarians kept the collection's earlier numbering system intact, allowing easy consultation of both. Also included is a supplement to the catalog of the Hirsch Library's music collection, published in 1951.

Reviewed by Richard S. Hill in *Notes* 17 (1960): 225–27.

7.260 Bray, Roger. *The British Library Music Manuscript Collection: A Listing and Guide to [Parts One through Ten of] the Harvester Microfilm Collection.* 4 vols. Brighton: Harvester Press Microform Publications, 1983–86.

Like the other Harvester guides, this includes a list of the contents of each reel in each part and a list of the manuscripts in each part followed by a unified index of names and composers for each vol. Vol. 3 includes a separate index of works by Handel.

7.261 Bray, Roger, and **Oliver Neighbour.** *Printed Music before 1800, Collection One of the Music Collection of the British Library, London.* Series I, *British Printed Music.* Period A, *Music before 1650;* Part One, *Individual Composers;* Part Two, *Anthologies and Tract Volumes.* Introduction by William Pidduck. 108 pp. Brighton: Harvester Press Microform Publications, 1983–86.

For manuscript sources, a list of the contents of each reel in each part and a list of the manuscripts in each part, followed by an index to names and composers in anthologies.

7.262 *Hand-List of Music Published in Some British and Foreign Periodicals between 1787 and 1848, Now in the British Museum.* 80 pp. London: Trustees of the British Museum, 1962.

An index to the music, chiefly songs, in 12 periodicals: 1,855 entries arranged by composer. The contents are printed from slips prepared for entry in the British Museum catalog. See also Imogen Fellinger's *Periodica Musicalia* (**5.30**).

Reviewed by Richard Schaal in *Die Musikforschung* 17 (1964): 423.

7.263 Hughes-Hughes, Augustus. *Catalogue of Manuscript Music in the British Museum.* 3 vols. London: Published for the Trustees of the British Museum, 1906–9.

Contents: Vol. 1, *Sacred Vocal Music;* Vol. 2, *Secular Vocal Music;* Vol. 3, *Instrumental Music, Treatises, Etc.*

Reprint issued in London, 1964.

Entries classified by genre or form, which can cause the contents of a single manuscript to be separated and distributed through the 3 vols. There are indexes to authors, titles, and first lines of songs, both secular and sacred.

7.264 King, Alec Hyatt. *Printed Music in the British Museum: An Account of the Collections, the Catalogues, and Their Formation, up to 1920.* 210 pp. London: C. Bingley; Munich: K.G. Saur, 1979.

A descriptive, historical work of particular use to those making intense use of the collections of printed music in the British Library.

Review by Rita Benton in *Fontes* 27 (1980): 57–58.

7.265* King, Alec Hyatt. *A Wealth of Music in the Collection of the British Library (Reference Division) and the British Museum.* 207 pp. London: C. Bingley, 1983.

A concise tool for locating a complex collection as it was in the early 1980s.

Reviewed by George Louis Mayer in *ARBA* 17 (1986): no. 1237.

7.266 Loewenberg, Alfred. "Early Dutch Librettos and Plays with Music in the British Museum." In *Journal of Documentation* 2 (March 1947): 210–37.

Subsequently published as a separate pamphlet by Aslib, London, 1947, 30 pp.

A catalog of 97 Dutch libretti of the 17th and 18th centuries. The list was projected as the first installment of a complete bibliography of libretti in the British Library, a project yet to be carried out.

7.267 *Music in the Hirsch Library.* London: Trustees of the British Museum, 1951. 458 pp. (British Museum. Department of printed books. Catalogue of printed music in the British Museum. Accessions, Pt. 53)

A catalog listing about 9,000 entries in two sections: "Music Printed before 1800" (pp. 1–112) and "Music Printed since 1800" (pp. 113–438). There is also the "Supplementary List of Music" in the catalog *Books in the Hirsch Library* (**7.259**).

Reviewed by Vincent Duckles in *Notes* 9 (1952): 281–82.

7.268 Squire, William Barclay, Hilda Andrews, and **William Charles Smith.** *Catalogue of the King's Music Library.* 3 vols. London: British Museum, 1927–29.

Contents: Pt. 1, *The Handel Manuscripts;* Pt. 2, *The Miscellaneous Manuscripts,* Hilda Andrews; Pt. 3, *Printed Music and Music Literature.*

The King's Music Library, deposited in the British Museum on permanent loan by King George V in 1911, was originally formed by King George III and Queen Charlotte and added to by purchases and presentations during the following reigns. The 3rd vol. was completed and the whole work arranged and seen through the press by Mr. W. C. Smith, Assistant-Keeper in the Department of Printed Books. The collection is now part of the permanent collection of the British Library and is now generally called the Royal Music Library.

7.269 Turner, Malcolm, and **Arthur Searle.** "The Music Collections of the British Library Reference Division." In *Notes* 38 (1981): 499–549.

A historical résumé of the situation with a description of the services and catalogs of the British Library, followed by descriptions of the Royal Music Library, the Hirsch Library, the general collections of printed music, music in the Department of Manuscripts, and the Music Library in the Department of Printed Books. Includes a chronological survey of music manuscripts in the collections and a bibliography of works about the music holdings in the British Library. A most helpful summary.

7.270 Willetts, Pamela J. *Handlist of Music Manuscripts Acquired 1908–67.* 112 pp. London: Trustees of the British Museum, 1970.

A handlist supplementing the Hughes-Hughes *Catalogue of Manuscript Music* (**7.263**), covering additional manuscripts, Egerton manuscripts, music manuscripts on loan to the Department of Manuscripts, and music manuscripts preserved with printed collections in the Department of Printed Books. There is an index of names.

Review by Gordon Dodd in *Chelys, Journal of the Viola da Gamba Society* 2 (1970): 41–42 and by Jack A. Westrup in *M&L* 52 (1971): 184–85.

ENGLISH FOLK DANCE AND SONG SOCIETY. CECIL SHARP HOUSE. VAUGHAN WILLIAMS MEMORIAL LIBRARY

7.271 *The Vaughan Williams Memorial Library Catalog of the English Folk Dance and Song Society: Acquisitions to the Library of Books, Pamphlets, Periodicals, Sheet Music, and Manuscripts, from its Inception to 1971.* 769 pp. London: Mansell, 1973.

The catalog of a collection focusing primarily, but not exclusively, on folk song and dance of the British Isles. Includes an author catalog, a classified subject catalog, and an index to subjects.

GUILDHALL LIBRARY. GRESHAM MUSIC LIBRARY

7.272 *A Catalogue of the Printed Books and Manuscripts Deposited in Guildhall Library.* 93 pp. London: Corporation of London; Printed by authority of the Library Committee, 1965.

A collection made up chiefly of late-18th-century materials reflecting the collecting activity of Edward Taylor, Gresham Professor from 1837 to 1883. The section on manuscripts was prepared by Margery Anthea Baird. There is an index of names.

MUSICIANS COMPANY

7.273 *An Illustrated Catalogue of the Music Loan Exhibition Held by the Worshipful Company of Musicians at Fishmongers' Hall, June and July 1904.* 353 pp. London: Novello, 1909.

A catalog including early printed music, manuscripts, instruments, portraits, and concert and theater bills, with descriptive annotations, numerous plates, and facsimiles.

Donald W. Krummel's "An Edwardian Gentlemen's Music Exhibition," in *Notes* 32 (1976): 711–18, describes the music exhibition celebrating the 300th anniversary of the royal charter of the Worshipful Company of Musicians.

ROYAL COLLEGE OF MUSIC

7.274 Bray, Roger. *The Music Collection of the Royal College of Music, London: A Listing and Guide to [Parts One through Nine of] the Harvester Microfilm Collection.* 3 vols. Brighton: Harvester Press Microform Publications, 1983–85.

Like the other Harvester guides, this includes a list of the contents of each reel in each part and a list of the manuscripts in each part followed by a unified index of names and composers for each volume.

7.275 Squire, William Barclay. *Catalogue of the Manuscripts in the Royal College of Music.* With additions by Rupert Erlebach. 568 + 216 ll. (typescript). London, 1931.

An unpublished catalog. Typewritten copies are available in the major British libraries, and the catalog may be obtained on microfilm. The Library of the Sacred Harmonic Society forms the nucleus of the holdings, with other additions. "By consent of the council all the manuscripts in this catalog up to and including No. 4105 have been transferred on indefinite loan to the Manuscript Dept. of the British Museum [now Library] (Dec. 1946)." Includes an index of names and complete list of manuscript contents.

7.276 Squire, William Barclay. *Catalogue of the Printed Music in the Library of the Royal College of Music.* 368 pp. London: Printed by order of the Council, 1909.

A collection, rich in sources of early English music, incorporating the holdings of the Sacred Harmonic Society and the library of Sir George Grove.

ROYAL OPERA HOUSE, COVENT GARDEN.
ARCHIVE OFFICE AND MUSIC LIBRARY

7.277* Day, David A. "An Inventory of Manuscript Scores at the Royal Opera House, Covent Garden." In *Notes* 44 (1988): 456–62.

A preliminary list of the scores in the collection, including basic bibliographical and physical descriptions.

SACRED HARMONIC SOCIETY

7.278 *Catalogue of the Library.* New ed., revised and augmented. 399 pp. London: Published by the Society, 1872.

First printed in 1862, with a *Supplement* in 1882.

A classified catalog of printed music, manuscript music, and musical literature, totaling 2,923 numbered items.

WESTMINSTER ABBEY

7.279 Squire, William Barclay. *Musik-Katalog der Bibliothek der Westminster-Abtei in London.* 45 pp. Leipzig: Breitkopf & Härtel, 1903. (Monatshefte für Musikgeschichte, Beilage. Jahrgang 35)

A broadly classified catalog, including both printed and manuscript music, secular and sacred.

London, Ontario, Canada

UNIVERSITY OF WESTERN ONTARIO. MUSIC
LIBRARY

7.280 Neville, Don J. "Opera I. Being the Catalogue of the Collection: Opera 1600–1750 in Contemporary Editions and Manuscripts Now in the Holdings of the Music Library of the University of Western Ontario." In *Studies in Music* 4 (1979): 1–487.

A collection of 220 opera editions and manuscripts sold by Richard Macnutt in 1974, including transcriptions of title pages, bibliographic descriptions, and historical notes.

Opera II covers 1751–1800 and is a reprint of Richard Macnutt's *Music Catalogue 103* with the library's call numbers added. It appeared as the fourth issue of *Studies in Music,* 1979.

Loreto, Italy

SANTA CASA DI LORETO. ARCHIVIO MUSICALE

7.281* Grimaldi, Floriano. *I codici musicali della Cappella di Loreto.* 85 pp. + 12 pp. of plates. Loreto, Italy: Libreria Editrice Lauretana, 1984.

A catalog of music holdings in the library.

7.282 Tebaldini, Giovanni. *L'Archivio musicale della Cappella Lauretana: Catalogo storico-critico.* 198 pp. Loreto, Italy: A cura dell'Amminstrazione di S. Casa, 1921.

A catalog of printed music, 16th–18th centuries, with manuscripts of the same period; an archive of manuscript scores by the Maestri della Cappella as well as anonymous works. There are full descriptions and a detailed history of the chapel, with an index of composers.

Los Angeles, California

7.283 Azhderian, Helen W. *Reference Works in Music and Music Literature in Five Libraries of Los Angeles County.* 313 pp. Los Angeles, Calif.: Published for the Southern California Chapter, Music Library Association, by the University of Southern California, 1953.

Partially updated in 1962 by Joan M. Meggett's *A Partial Supplement of Holdings in the USC Library, January 1952–June 1962,* 13 pp.

A international classified bibliography of musicological literature, with 4,563 entries and full bibliographical citations. There is an author/title index. The libraries are the Henry E. Huntington Library, the William Andrews Clark Library of the University of California at Los Angeles, the Los Angeles Public Library, and the libraries of the University of Southern California and the University of California at Los Angeles.

Reviewed by Otto E. Albrecht in *Notes* 11 (1954): 468–69 and by Vincent Duckles in *JAMS* 7 (1954): 242–45.

UNIVERSITY OF CALIFORNIA, LOS ANGELES

7.284* Alm, Irene. *Catalog of Venetian Librettos at the University of California, Los Angeles.* xxvii + 1,053 pp. Berkeley, Calif.: University of California Press, 1993. (University of California publications. Catalogs and bibliographies, 9)

A collection of some 1,000 libretti, from 1637 to 1767.

Reviewed by Eleanor Selfridge-Field in *Notes* 51 (1994): 575–78.

7.285 Revitt, Paul Joseph. *The George Pullen Jackson Collection of Southern Hymnody: A Bibliography.* 26 pp. Los Angeles, Calif.: UCLA Library, 1964. (UCLA Library occasional papers, 13)

Reviewed by Harry Eskew in *Anuario of the Inter-American Institute for Musical Research* 1 (1965): 135.

7.286* Tusler, Robert L. *Catalog of the Clarence V. Nader Archive, Music Library, University of California at Los Angeles.* 275 pp. Ruth and Clarence Nader Memorial Scholarship Fund, 1980.

A catalog of the collection.

Lucca, Italy

7.287 Bonaccorsi, Alfredo. "Catalogo con notizie biografiche delle musiche dei maestri lucchesi esistenti nelle biblioteche di Lucca." In *Collectanea historiae musicae* 2 (1957): 73–95.

A list of sources from three libraries in Lucca: the Seminario Arcivescovile, the Istituto Musicale "L. Boccherini," and the Biblioteca Governativa.

BIBLIOTECA DEL SEMINARIO ARCIVESCOVILE

7.288 Maggini, Emilio. *Catalogo delle musiche stampate e manoscritte del fondo antico.* 405 pp. Milan: Istituto Editoriale Italiano, 1965. (Bibliotheca musicae; collana di cataloghi e bibliografie, 3)

A catalog of early printed music and manuscripts from the 16th to the early 19th century, with a small collection of writings on music. The contents of collections and locations of other copies are listed. The collection is rich in early-17th-century prints of sacred music.

7.289 Sartori, Claudio. "Il fondo di musiche a stampa della Biblioteca del Seminario di Lucca." In *Fontes* (1955): 134–37.

A list, alphabetical by composer, of the early music editions in the seminary library, including, at the end of the list, five anthologies and three manuscripts.

BIBLIOTECA STATALE

7.290 Paoli, Marco. *I corali della Biblioteca statale di Lucca.* 143 pp. Florence: L.S. Olschki, 1977. (Biblioteca di bibliografia italiana, 83)

A catalog of choirbooks and other manuscripts of choral music in the city library at Lucca, including bibliographical references and indexes.

Lübeck, Germany

STADTBIBLIOTHEK

7.291 Stahl, Wilhelm. *Die Musikabteilung der Lübecker Stadtbibliothek in ihren älteren Beständen: Noten und Bücher aus der Zeit vom 12. bis zum Anfang des 19. Jahrhunderts.* 61 pp. Lübeck, Germany: Verlag der Lübecker Stadtbibliothek, 1931.

A classified author catalog of music literature in Lübeck, with a name and subject index.

7.292 Stahl, Wilhelm. *Musik-Bücher der Lübecker Stadtbibliothek.* 42 pp. Lübeck, Germany: Verlag der Lübecker Stadtbibliothek, 1927.

A classified catalog of 19th- and 20th-century music literature.

7.293 Stiehl, Carl. *Katalog der Musik-Sammlung aus der Stadtbibliothek zu Lübeck.* 59 pp. Lübeck, Germany: Druck von Gebrüder Borchers, 1893.

Updated by Georg Karstädt's *Die Musiksammlung der Stadtbibliothek Lübeck* (Lübeck, Germany: Senat der Hansestadt Lübeck, Amt für Kultur, 1979).

Lüneburg, Germany

RATSBÜCHEREI

7.294 Welter, Friedrich. *Katalog der Musikalien der Ratsbücherei Lüneburg.* 332 pp. Lippstadt, Germany: Kistner & Siegel, 1950.

Music imprints and manuscripts, theoretical and practical music to 1850, and holdings in 17th- and 18th-century instrumental music, particularly in the manuscript collections, which are listed separately, with numerous thematic incipits given.

Lund, Sweden

UNIVERSITETSBIBLIOTEK

7.295 Mühlhauser, Siegfried. *Die Handschriften und Varia der Schubertiana-Sammlung Taussig in der Universitätsbibliothek Lund.* 203 pp. Wilhelmshaven, Germany: Heinrichshofen, 1981. (Quellenkataloge zur Musikgeschichte, 17)

A richly illustrated catalog with facsimile pages of the Otto Taussig collection of Schubertiana in Lund. Included are bibliographical references and index.

Luzern, Switzerland

THEATER- UND MUSIK-LIEBHABERGESELLSCHAFT

7.296 Jerger, Wilhelm. *Die Haydndrucke aus dem Archiv der "Theater- und Musik-Liebhabergesellschaft zu Luzern," nebst Materialien zum Musikleben in Luzern um 1800.* 45 pp. Freiburg in der Schweiz: Universitätsverlag, 1959. (Freiburger Studien zur Musikwissenschaft, 7)

Entries for 64 early Haydn editions, with a table of concordances with the Hoboken *Thematisch-bibliographisches Werkverzeichnis* of Haydn's compositions (**6.181**).

Lyons, France

BIBLIOTHÈQUE MUNICIPALE

7.297* Guillot, Pierre. *Catalogue des manuscrits musicaux de la Bibliothèque Municipale de Lyon.* 150 pp. Bordeaux: Société des Bibliophiles de Guyenne, 1995. (Patrimoine des bibliothèques de France, 1)

Macerata, Italy

BIBLIOTECA COMUNALE "MOZZI-BORGETTI"

7.298 Adversi, Aldo. *Studi sulla Biblioteca Comunale e sui tipografi di Macerata: Miscellanea.* 246 pp. Macerata, Italy: Casa di Risparmio della Provincia di Macerata, 1966.

A catalog of a small collection holding 22 examples of early printed music, 24 items of music literature, and 23 music manuscripts.

Madrid, Spain

AYUNTAMIENTO. BIBLIOTECA MUSICAL CIRCULANTE

7.299 *Catálogo.* Ed. ilus. 610 pp. Madrid: Ayuntamiento, Seccion de Cultura e Informacion, 1946. *Apéndice 1,* 1954, 213 pp.

Music arranged in 16 classes, by instrument and form. Class T, "Bibliografia," contains books on music almost exclusively in Spanish. No publishers or dates are given for entries. There are many light and popular works. There is no index.

BIBLIOTECA MEDINACELI

7.300 Trend, J. B. "Catalogue of the Music in the Biblioteca Medinaceli, Madrid." In *Revue hispanique* 71 (1927): 485–554.

The Medinaceli library holds almost the entire corpus of Spanish (Castilian) madrigals. 34 items are fully described, with inventories of contents and biographical sketches of the composers. The appendix lists musical settings of famous poets.

BIBLIOTECA NACIONAL

7.301 Anglès, Higinio, and **José Subirá.** *Catálogo músical de la Biblioteca Nacional de Madrid.* 3 vols. Barcelona: Consejo de Investigaciones Científicas, Instituto Español de Musicología, 1946–51. (Catálogos de la música antiqua conservada en España, 1–3)

Contents: Vol. 1, *Manuscritos* (490 pp., 27 facsimile plates); Vol. 2, *Impresos: Libros litúrgicos y teóricos musicales* (292 pp., 12 facsimile plates); Vol. 3, *Impresos: Música práctica* (410 pp., 13 facsimile plates).

A catalog by José Janini and José Serrano, with the collaboration of Anscari Mondó, *Manuscritos litúrgicos de la Biblioteca Nacional* (Madrid: Dirección General de Archivo y Bibliotecas, 1969, 332 pp. + 24 plates, supplements the above with extensive information on copyists and miniaturists contributing to the manuscripts.

The Janini–Serrano catalog is reviewed by Don M. Randel in *Notes* 27 (1971): 479.

7.302* *Catálogo de impresos musicales del siglo XVIII en la Biblioteca Nacional.* 140 pp. Madrid: Biblioteca Nacional, Ministerio de Cultura, Dirección General del Libro y Bibliotecas, 1989.

7.303* *Catálogo de villancicos y oratorios en la Biblioteca Nacional, siglos XVIII–XIX.* xxix + 670 pp. Madrid: Biblioteca Nacional, Ministerio de Cultura, Dirección General del Libro y Bibliotecas, 1990.

The 18th- and 19th-century villancicos and oratorios held by the National Library.

7.304* **Sanjurjo de la Fuente, Ana Maria, Maria Isolina Arronte Alonso,** and **Nieves Iglesias Martinez.** *Catálogo del teatro lírico español en la Biblioteca Nacional.* 3 vols. Madrid: Ministerio de Cultura, Dirección General del Libro y Bibliotecas, 1986–91.

A catalog of libretti of operas and zarzuelas.

LA CASA DE ALBA

7.305 Subira, José. "La musique de chambre espagnole et française du XVIIIe siècle dans la bibliothèque du Duc d'Alba." In *Revue de musicologie* 7 (1926): 78–82.

PALACIO REAL. ARCHIVO DE MÚSICA

7.306* **Archivo de Música del Palacio Real de Madrid.** *Catálogo del Archivo de Música de Palacio Real de Madrid.* 807 pp. Madrid: Editorial Patrimonio Nacional, 1993.

A catalog of chiefly 18th-century manuscripts and printed music. Thematic incipits are included.

Mafra, Portugal

PALÁCIO NACIONAL. BIBLIOTECA

7.307* **Azevedo, João M. B. de.** *Biblioteca do Palácio Nacional de Mafra: Catálogo dos fundos musicais.* 205 pp. Lisbon: Foundation Calouste Gulbenkian, 1985.

A catalog of sacred vocal music.

Mainz, Germany

STADTBIBLIOTHEK

7.308 Roth, F. W. E. "Zur Bibliographie der Musikdrucke des XV.–XVIII. Jahrhunderts der Mainzer Stadtbibliothek." In *Monatshefte für Musikgeschichte* 21 (1889): 25–33.

A catalog of 45 early music editions, including both theoretical works and practical music. Full bibliographical citations are given for some items; for other items, there are references to citations in the catalogs of other collections.

Manchester, England

HENRY WATSON MUSIC LIBRARY

7.309* **Cartledge, J. A.** *List of Glees, Madrigals, Part-Songs, Etc., in the Henry Watson Music Library.* 197 pp. Manchester: The Library, 1913.

Reprinted by Burt Franklin, New York, in 1970.

7.310 Walker, Arthur D. *George Frideric Handel: The Newman Flower Collection in the Henry Watson Music Library.* With a foreword by Winton Dean. 134 pp. Manchester: Manchester Public Libraries, 1972.

Melk, Austria

BENEDICTINE ABBEY

7.311* **Weinmann, Alexander.** *Handschriftliche thematische Kataloge aus dem Benediktinerstift Melk.* 228 pp. Vienna: Verlag der Österreichischen Akademie der Wissenschaften, 1984. (Tabulae musicae austriacae, 10)

Facsimiles of a corpus of 20 thematic catalogs dating from 1791 to 1822, from Melk Abbey, Lower Austria, containing about 2,000 incipits of primarily instrumental music from 1750 to 1825.

Reviewed by Robert N. Freeman in *Notes* 42 (1986): 550–51.

Messina, Italy

BIBLIOTECA PAINIANA

7.312* Chirico, Teresa. *Il Fondo Musicale della Biblioteca Painiana di Messina.* 417 pp. Rome: Torre d'Orfeo, 1992. (Cataloghi di fondi musicali italiani, 14)

A catalog including a thematic index and bibliographical references (pp. 51–55).

Mexico

7.313 Spiess, Lincoln, and **Thomas Stanford.** *An Introduction to Certain Mexican Musical Archives.* 184 pp., with 99 unnumbered. Detroit, Mich.: Information Coordinators, 1969. (Detroit studies in music bibliography, 15)

The catalog of musical materials in the archives of the Metropolitan Cathedral of Mexico, the Museo de Virreinato of Tepotzotlán, the Metropolitan Cathedral of Pueblo, the Sánchez Collection in Mexico City now held by the Instituto Nacional de Bellas Artes, the Museo Bello of Puebla, the Collegio de Las Vizcainas in Mexico, Federal District, the Chapultepec Castle in Mexico, Federal District, Huamelula in Oaxaca, the Cathedral of Morelia in Michoacán, and parts of the Biblioteca Nacional in Mexico, Federal District. Includes a bibliography of reference works and an index of composers. A 95-pp. musical supplement is appended. References are made to a fuller and as yet unpublished catalog of these collections.

Reviewed by Henry Cobos in *Notes* 27 (1971): 491–92.

Mexico City, Mexico

BIBLIOTECA NACIONAL DE MEXICO

7.314* Chapa Bezanilla, María de los Ángeles. *Catálogo del Acervo Musical de la Propriedad Literaria de la Biblioteca Nacional de México.* 299 pp. Ciudad Universitaria, México: Universidad Nacional Autónoma de México, 1993.

Middlebury, Vermont

MIDDLEBURY COLLEGE

7.315* Cockrell, Dale. "The Helen Hartness Flanders Ballad Collection, Middlebury College." In *Notes* 39 (1982): 31–42.

A description of the collection specializing in traditional music from the New England states, containing recordings (in a variety of formats), printed music, and unpublished papers, a few from the 18th century.

Milan, Italy

BIBLIOTECA AMBROSIANA

7.316 Cesari, Gaetano. *Catalogo generale delle opere musicali: Città di Milano: Biblioteca Ambrosiana.* 20 pp. (incomplete). Parma, Italy: Freschig, 1910–11. (Associazione dei Musicologi Italiani. Catalogo generale delle opere musicali, 3)

BIBLIOTECA TRIVULZIANA. CIVICA RACCOLTA DELLE STAMPE E DEI DISEGNI

7.317 Arrigoni, Paolo, and **Achille Bertarelli.** *Ritratti di musicisti ed artisti di teatro conservati nella raccolta delle stampe e dei disegni: Catalogo descrittivo.* 454 pp. + 30 plates. Milan: Tipografia del "Popolo d'Italia," 1934.

The catalog of the Bertarelli collection of portraits includes entries for portraits of musicians, singers, comedians, dancers, and other persons connected with the theater. There are separate sections for acrobats, extemporaneous poets, child prodigies, etc. The entries give full names of subjects, descriptions of the pictures, and biographical information. There are numerous indexes, including names, places, and theatrical performances.

Cappella del Duomo. Archivio

7.318 Sartori, Claudio. *La Cappella del Duomo di Milano: Catalogo delle musiche dell'archivio.* 366 pp. Milan: A cura della Ven. Fabbrica del Duomo, 1957.

The catalog of an archive, established in 1394, containing important manuscript holdings of the 15th century and sacred vocal works to the 19th. There are separate sections for manuscripts and printed music, with brief entries and contents given for anthologies.

Conservatorio di Musica "Giuseppe Verdi."
Biblioteca

7.319 *Catalogo della biblioteca: Letteratura musicale e opere teoriche. Parte prima: Manoscritti e stampe fino al 1899.* 151 pp. Milan: Distributed by Casa Editrice Leo S. Olschki, Florence, 1969.

A volume listing 2,458 writings on music published before 1900, with indexes of subjects and of editors, compilers, and translators.

Reviewed by Susan Sommer in *Notes* 27 (1971): 730–31.

7.320* Dorsi, Maria Letizia. *I libretti d'opera dal 1800 al 1825 nella Biblioteca del Conservatorio "G. Verdi" di Milano.* 334 pp. Milan: Edizioni degli Amici della Scala/Messaggerie Libri, 1987. (Musica e teatro, 4–5)

Reviewed by Philip Gossett in *M&L* 69 (1988): 262–63 and by Sylvie Mamy in *Revue de musicologie* 74 (1988): 101–2.

7.321 Grigolato, Gilda. *Catalogo della biblioteca: Fondi speciali 1, Musiche della Cappella di S. Barbara in Mantova.* With indexes by Agostina Zecca Laterza. xliv + 530 pp. Florence: Leo S. Olschki, 1972.

A library catalog, the 2nd of a projected series of 20 vols. directed by Guglielmo Barblan, covering the 16th- and early-17th-century collection of the Cappella di Santa Barbara in Mantua, tranferred to the conservatory in 1854.

Reviewed by Sven H. Hansell in *Notes* 31 (1974): 66–67.

7.322 Guarinoni, Eugenio de'. *Indice generale dell' Archivio Musicale Noseda. Con una breve biografia del fondatore e con alcuni cenni intorno all'archivio stesso ed alla Biblioteca del R. Conservatorio di Musica di Milano.* 419 pp. Milan: E. Reggiani, 1898.

First published in the *Anuario* of the Milan conservatory, 1889–96, with 10,253 titles.

The strength of the collection is centered in late-18th- and early-19th-century music. The index is preceded by a brief historical introduction. Includes an index of composers represented in autographs and an index of operas in full score.

Museo Teatrale alla Scala

7.323 Vittadini, Stefano. *Catalogo del Museo Teatrale alla Scala.* Edito a cura del consiglio direttivo; compilato da Stefano Vittadini. 401 pp. Milan: E. Bestetti, 1940.

An illustrated catalog of the musical-theatrical collection at La Scala. There is a strong bibliography (pp. 375–93).

Modena, Italy

ARCHIVIO DI STATO

7.324 Luin, E. J. "Repertorio dei libri musicali di S. A. S. Francesco II d'Este nell'Archivio di Stato di Modena." In *La Bibliofilia* 38 (1936): 419–45.

A catalog compiled in the late 17th century of the holdings of the music library of Francesco II d'Este, rich in both manuscript and printed editions of late-17th-century opera, oratorios, and cantatas. Much of the material has been incorporated into the collection of the Biblioteca Estense in Modena.

BIBLIOTECA ESTENSE

7.325* Chiarelli, Alessandra. *I codici di musica della raccolta estense: Ricostruzione dall'inventario settecentesco.* 277 pp. Florence: L.S. Olschki, 1987. (Quaderna della rivista italiana di musicologia, 16) (Programma di studi e ricerche sulla cultura e la vita civile del Settecento in Emilia-Romagna. Settore musica e teatro, 3)

7.326 Finzi, Vittorio. "Bibliografia delle stampe musicali della R. Biblioteca Estense." In *Rivista delle biblioteche* (1892–95), Vol. 3, pp. 77–89, 107–14, 162–76; Vol. 4, pp. 16–28, 174–85; Vol. 5, pp. 48–64, 89–142.

Full descriptions of 321 works, with index.

7.327 Lodi, Pio. *Catalogo delle opere musicali: Città di Modena: R. Biblioteca Estense.* 561 pp. Parma, Italy: Freschig, 1916–24. (Associazione dei Musicologi Italiani. Catalogo delle opere musicali, 8)

Reprinted by Forni, Bologna, 1967.

Montecassino, Italy

ARCHIVIO MUSICALE

7.328 Dagnino, Eduardo. "L'Archivio Musicale di Montecassino." In *Casinensia: Miscellanea di studi Cassinesi,* Vol. 1 (1929): 273–96.

A summary account of the music holdings of the Montecassino archive, a collection of some 1,100 items, including more than 100 full scores of 18th-century operas and oratorios.

7.329 Ferretti, Paolo M. "I manoscritti musicali gregoriani dell'archivio di Montecassino." In *Casinensia: Miscellanea di studi Cassinesi,* Vol. 1 (1929): 187–203.

Detailed descriptions of 11 manuscripts of Gregorian chant in the Montecassino archive. The 11th consists of a group of fragments from various sources.

Montecatini Terme, Italy

BIBLIOTECA COMMUNALE

7.330* Kishimoto, Hiroko, Antonio Venturi, and **Alberto Basso.** *Il Fondo Musicale Venturi nella Biblioteca Communale di Montecatini Terme: Catalogo.* 431 pp. Florence: Giunta Regionale Toscana; Milan: Editrice Bibliografica, 1989. (Inventari e cataloghi toscani, 28)

Montserrat, Spain

7.331 Lenaerts, René B. "Niederlandische polyphone Musik in der Bibliothek von Montserrat." In *Festschrift Joseph Schmidt-Görg zum 60. Geburtstag,* pp. 196–201. Bonn: Beethoven-Haus, 1957.

A description of six manuscripts containing Netherlands polyphony: manuscript numbers 765, 766, 769, 771, 772, and 778.

Monza, Italy

DUOMO

7.332 Dalmonte, Rossana. *Catalogo musicale del Duomo di Monza.* xliv + 219 pp. Bologna: Forni, 1969. (Bibliotheca musica Bononiensis, 6/2)

A catalog that includes the holdings of the Archivio Musicale of the Duomo.

Moscow, Russia

LENIN STATE LIBRARY

7.333 *Notnye izdaniia v. fondakh Gosudarstvennoi biblioteki SSSR imeni V. I. Lenina. Katalog / Music Editions in the Collections of the Lenin State Library. Catalog.* 12 vols. to date. Moscow: Gosudarstvennaia Biblioteka SSSR imeni V.I. Lenin, 1976– .

Contents: Part 1, *Monuments of Musical Art: Publications of the 18th Century from the Homeland,* 1979, 100 pp.; Part 2, *Monuments of Musical Art: Foreign Publications of the 16th–19th Centuries and Individually Published Works for Composers (Including Volumes on Haydn and Mozart Scores),* 1982–91, 5 vols.; Part 3, *Russian Musical Folklore Collection, 1917–55, 1956–75,* 1980–85, 2 vols.; Part 4, *Soviet Editions for Accordion, 1956–75,* 1978, 4 vols.; Part 5, *Soviet Editions for Bajan, Concertina, 1956–75,* 1978, 4 vols.; Part 6, *Soviet Editions for Classical Guitar, 1930–75,* 1978; Part 7, *Soviet Editions for Russian (7-String) Guitar, 1923–55, 1956–75,* 1979, 159 pp.; Part 8, *Foreign Publications of Music Written for the Theater,* 1976 and *Soviet Editions of Opera, Ballet, Operetta,* 1978; Part 9, *Soviet Editions of String Music,* 1982, 315 pp.; Part 10, *Works by Haydn,* 1984, 66 pp.; Part 11, *Piano Pedagogical Repertoire, Soviet Scores 1970–80,* 1983; Part 12, *Scores (Including String Music) in the Collection of V. V. Borisovskii,* 1982.

The catalog of a collection of over 300,000 titles in the music collections of the Lenin Library in Moscow, with detailed entries for printed music. There are indexes in each part. The introductions to these catalogs are in Russian, whereas the entries are in the language of the original.

Mount Athos, Greece

7.334 Stathes, Grēgorios Th. *Ta cheirographa vyzantinēs mousikēs. Hagion Oros: Katalogos perigraphikos tōn cheirographōn Kōdikōn vyzantinēs mousikēs tōn apokeimenon en tais vivliothēkais tōn hierōn monōn kai sketon tou Hagiou Orous / The Byzantine Musical Manuscripts of the Athos Monasteries / Les manuscrits de musique byzantine.* 2 vols. Athens: Hidryma Byzantines Mousikologias, 1975–76.

A catalog covering manuscripts in the monasteries Xēropotamou, Docheiariou, Kōnstamonitou, Xenophōntos, Panteleēmonos, Simōnos Petras, Grēgoriou, and Dionysiou.

Münster, Germany

BISCHÖFLICHES PRIESTERSEMINAR. SANTINI BIBLIOTHEK

7.335 Killing, Joseph. *Kirchenmusikalische Schätze der Bibliothek des Abbate Fortunato Santini: Ein Beitrag zur Geschichte der katholischen Kirchenmusik in Italien.* 516 pp. Düsseldorf: L. Schwann, 1910.

A study based on the material in the Santini collection, a library of early music scored from the original part books by Fortunato Santini (1778–1862) and acquired about 1856 by the University Library at Münster. Appendixes include "Verzeichnis der in der Bibliothek Santini enthaltenen Druckwerke" (pp. 455–67) and "Verzeichnis von Musikwerken die in der Santinischen Bibliothek als Handschriften enthalten sind" (pp. 469–516).

7.336 "Verzeichnis der italienischen Messkompositionen aus der Bibliothek des Abbate Fortunato Santini, 18. Jahrhundert," in *Studien über Gebrauch der Instrumente in dem italienischen Kirchenorchester des 18. Jahrhunderts.* Ein Beitrag zur Geschichte der instrumental begleiteten Messe in Italien. (Auf Grund des Materials in der Santini-Bibliothek zu Münster i. W., pp. 45–58.) Quakenbrück, Germany: Robert Kleinert, 1929.

A list of 450 18th-century masses in the Santini library, arranged alphabetically by composer, with descriptions of their instrumentation.

Munich, Germany

BAYERISCHE STAATSBIBLIOTHEK

7.337 Bayerische Staatsbibliothek. *Katalog der Musikdrucke / Catalogue of Printed Music: BSB-Musik.* 17 vols. Munich; New York: K.G. Saur, 1988–90.

The 1st vol. is reviewed by Ann Basart in *CNV* 132 (1989): 19.

7.338 Bayerische Staatsbibliothek. *Katalog der Musikhandschriften: Bayerische Staatsbibliothek.* 3 vols. Munich: G. Henle, 1979–89. (Kataloge bayerischer Musiksammlungen, 5)

A series of catalogs of manuscripts in the Bayerische Staatsbibliothek, Munich.

Contents: Bd 1, *Chorbücher und Handschriften in chorbuchartiger,* edited by Martin Bente et al. (1989, 436 pp.); Bd. 2, Marie Louise Martinez-Göllner, *Tabulaturen und Stimmbücher bis zur Mitte des 17. Jahrhunderts* (1979, 230 pp.); Bd. 3, Bettina Wackernagel, *Collectio Musicalis Maximilianea* (1981, 112 pp.).

Vol. 1 is reviewed by John Wagstaff in *M&L* 72 (1991): 99–100, by Christian Meyer in *Revue de musicologie* 76 (1990): 247 no. 2, and by Lilian P. Pruett in *Fontes* 40 (1993): 339–42.

7.339* Bayerische Staatsbibliothek. *Katalog der Musikzeitschriften: BSB-MuZ / Catalogue of Music Periodicals: Bavarian State Library.* 242 pp. Munich; New York: K.G. Saur, 1990. (Zeitschriften der bayerischen Staatsbibliothek, 1)

7.340 Maier, Julius Joseph. *Die musikalischen Handschriften der K. Hof- und Staatsbibliothek in München.* Erster Theil: *Die Handschriften bis zum Ende des XVII. Jahrhunderts.* 176 pp. Munich: In Commission der Palm'schen Hofbuchhandlung, 1879.

A catalog of 278 items, chiefly anthologies, containing about 6,380 pieces that compose one of the richest collections of 16th-century music, including a notable collection of 74 choirbooks belonging to the original Bavarian court chapel. There is an "Inhalts-Verzeichnis" of anonymous and attributed works.

7.341 Martinez-Göllner, Marie Louise. "Die Augsburger Bibliothek Herwart und ihre Lautentabulaturen: Ein Musikbestand der Bayerischen Staatsbibliothek aus dem 16. Jahrhundert." In *Fontes* (January–June 1969): 29–48.

A study focused primarily on 15 manuscripts of lute tablature acquired in 1586 by the Bavarian State Library with the purchase of the private library of Johann Heinrich Herwart of Augsburg. The article includes the publication of a 16th-century catalog of printed instrumental music in the Herwart collection.

HOFKAPELLE

MUSIKHANDSCHRIFTENSAMMLUNGEN

7.342 Haberkamp, Gertraut, and **Robert Münster.** *Die ehemaligen Musikhandschriftensammlungen der Königlichen Hofkapelle und der Kurfürstin Maria Anna in München: Thematischer Katalog.* xxxiv + 251 pp. Münich: G. Henle, 1982. (Kataloge bayerischer Musiksammlungen, 9)

A catalog of collections held in part at the Bavarian State Library, giving a representation of secular music heard at the Bavarian court from the mid-18th to the mid-19th centuries, as well as operatic works from 1750. Many musical works previously unknown, written by reputable composers, are listed herein.

St. Michaelskirche

7.343 Herrmann-Schneider, Hildegard. *Die Musikhandschriften der St. Michaelskirche in München: Thematischer Katalog.* xxxviii + 392 pp. With *Nachtrag.* 12 pp. Munich: G. Henle, 1985–86. (Kataloge bayerischer Musiksammlungen, 7)

Städtische Musikbücherei

7.344 Krienitz, Willy. *Kataloge der Städtischen Musikbücherei München.* Erster Band: *Klavier.* 407 pp. Munich, 1931.

A catalog of the holdings in keyboard music, some 40,000 items, in one of the major public music libraries in Germany. Included are works for piano solo, piano duet, and two pianos. There is an index of names.

Theatermuseum

7.345 Schaal, Richard. "Die vor 1801 gedruckten Libretti des Theatermuseums Munchen." In *Die Musikforschung* 10 (1957): 388–96, 487–94; 11 (1958): 64–69, 168–77, 321–36, 462–77; 12 (1959): 60–75, 161–77, 299–306, 454–61; 13 (1960): 38–46, 164–72, 299–306, 441–48; 14 (1961): 36–43, 166–83.

Also published separately by Bärenreiter, Kassel, Germany, 1962.

A catalog of 983 librettos listed alphabetically by title, with date and place of first performance and name of composer.

Theatinerkirche Sankt Kajetan

7.346 Gmeinwieser, Siegfried. *Die Musikhandschriften in der Theatinerkirche St. Kajetan in München: Thematischer Katalog.* 208 pp. Munich: Henle, 1979. (Kataloge bayerischer Musiksammlungen, 4)

Universitätsbibliothek

7.347 Gottwald, Clytus. *Die Musikhandschriften der Universitäts-bibliothek München.* 127 pp. Wiesbaden: Harrassowitz, 1968. (Die Handschriften der Universitätsbibliothek München, 2)

Naples, Italy

Biblioteca Nazionale

7.348 Arnese, Raffaele. *I codici notati della Biblioteca Nazionale di Napoli.* 257 pp. Florence: Leo S. Olschki, 1967. (Biblioteca di bibliografia italiana, 47)

Though concerned chiefly with liturgical manuscripts in which musical notation is present, this publication also includes a few sources in mensural notation. There are indexes of types of notation, types of script, chronological arrangement, titles, and names, a bibliography, and "illustrazione dei codici" (pp. 69–233).

Reviewed by Ewald Jammers in *Die Musikforschung* 21 (1968): 504–5.

7.349 Mondolfi, Anna. "Il fondo musicale cinquecentesco della Biblioteca Nazionale di Napoli." In *Collectanea historiae musicae* 2 (1957): 277–90.

A description of 51 16th-century works.

CONSERVATORIO DI MUSICA SAN PIETRO A
MAJELLA. BIBLIOTECA

7.350 Gasparini, Guido, and **Franca Gallo.** *Città di Napoli: Biblioteca del R. Conservatorio di S. Pietro a Majella.* 696 pp. Parma, Italy: Freschig, 1918–34. (Associazione dei Musicologi Italiani. Catalogo generale delle opere musicali, 10/2)

Reprinted by Forni, Bologna, 1988.

7.351* Melisi, Francesco. *Catalogo dei libretti in musica dei secoli XVII e XVIII: Conservatorio di musica "S. Pietro a Majella" di Napoli, Biblioteca.* 295 pp. + 30 ll. of plates. Naples, Italy: The Library, 1986.

A catalog of about 1,500 17th- and 18th-century libretto holdings in the Naples conservatory's library.

7.352* Melisi, Francesco. *Catalogo dei libretti per musica dell'Ottocento, 1800–1860.* 418 pp. Lucca, Italy: Libreria Musicale Italiana Editore, 1990. (Ancilla musicae, 1)

A catalog of 19th-century libretto holdings in the Naples conservatory's library.

7.353 Mondolfi, Anna Bossarelli. "La Biblioteca del Conservatorio di Napoli." In *Accademie e biblioteche d'Italia* 38 (1970): 286–92.

A brief narrative account stressing the important holdings of the library, particularly works related to the opera and cantata and documents of the Bellini-Donizetti period.

7.354 *Il Museo storico musicale di S. Pietro a Majella.* 153 pp. Naples: R. Stabilimento Tipografico Francesco Giannini e Figli, 1930.

A collection of musicians' portraits, busts, autographs, musical instruments, medals, and photographs, 734 items in all. There are special archives of materials related to Vincenzo Bellini and Giuseppe Martucci.

ORATORIO DEI FILIPPINI. ARCHIVIO

7.355 Giacomo, Salvatore di. *Città di Napoli: Archivio dell'Oratorio dei Filippini.* 108 pp. Parma, Italy: Freschig, 1918. (Associazione dei Musicologi Italiani. Catalogo generale delle opere musicali, Vol. 10/1)

New Haven, Connecticut

YALE UNIVERSITY

7.356 Boito, Diane. "Manuscript Music in the James Marshall and Marie-Louise Osborn Collection." In *Notes* 27 (1970): 237–44.

A description of each musical manuscript in the Osborn Collection: 4 from the 16th and 17th centuries; 20 from the 18th century, including 2 Alessandro Scarlatti manuscripts; and 14 from the 20th century, including important works by Britten, Dohnanyi, Holst, Mahler, and Vaughan Williams.

7.357 Brown, Rae Linda. *Music, Printed and Manuscript, in the James Weldon Johnson Memorial Collection of Negro Arts and Letters: An Annotated Catalog.* 322 pp. New York: Garland Publishing, 1982. (Critical studies on Black life and culture, 23) (Garland reference library of the humanities, 277)

A catalog of the 1,057 musical works in the collection established by Carl van Vechten, housed in the Beinecke Rare Book and Manuscript Library.

Reviewed by Janet L. Sims-Wood in *BPM* 11 (1983): 221–22.

7.358 Ford, Robert. "The Filmer Manuscripts: A Handlist." In *Notes* 40 (1978): 814–25.

An inventory of 37 manuscripts of English music from the late 16th through the early 18th centuries, housed in Yale's library.

New York, New York

AMERICAN MUSIC CENTER. LIBRARY

7.359 American Music Center. Library. *Catalog of the American Music Center Library.* 4 vols. New York: American Music Center, 1975–83.

The catalog of the closest institution in the United States to a music information center. The 1st vol., edited by Judith Greenberg Finnell, covers choral and vocal works and is arranged by composer and title. Vol. 2, edited by Karen McNerney Famera, covers chamber music and is classified; there is a composer index. Vol. 3, edited by Karen Famera and others, covers music for orchestra, band, and large ensembles and is composed of bibliographic entries drawn from the New York Public Library's database; the catalog is in a single alphabetical sequence with composer, title, and subject entries as well as cross-references. The 4th vol., edited by Eero Richmond, covers opera and music theater. There are indexes by title, librettist, initial source, subject, and duration. The American Music Center Library collects printed and manuscript works of contemporary American composers and disseminates information about those works.

JUILLIARD SCHOOL

7.360* Gottlieb, Jane. *Guide to the Juilliard School Archives.* 113 pp. New York: Juilliard School, 1992.

NEW YORK PUBLIC LIBRARY. MUSIC DIVISION

7.361 *Catalogue of Jos. W. Drexel's Musical Library. Part I: Musical Writings.* 48 pp. Philadelphia, Pa.: King and Baird, 1869.

The catalog of one of the most important single collections of the Music Division of the New York Public Library. However, the catalog contains only 1,536 of the more than 6,000 items in the Drexel collection. It is especially rich in English printed music and manuscripts of the 16th, 17th, and 18th centuries. The collection contains numerous items from the library of Edward F. Rimbault, English antiquarian and collector.

7.362 *Dictionary Catalog of the Music Collection, New York Public Library.* 2nd ed. 44 vols. Boston, Mass.: G.K. Hall, 1982.

First published in 1965 in 33 vols. Supplemented 1973 and 1976.

Duplication by photo-offset of the card catalog of the holdings of the Music Division, the New York Public Library. Books, pamphlets, and musical scores are arranged in one alphabet. The catalog includes numerous analytics for articles in Festschriften and periodicals. This is a comprehensive reference tool based on the resources of one of the great music libraries of the United States. It is kept current by the *Bibliographic Guide to Music* (**4.50**), an annual supplement published by G.K. Hall beginning in 1976. These vols. include all publications cataloged by the New York Public Library and entries from LC MARC tapes of current cataloging.

PIERPONT MORGAN LIBRARY

7.363 Albrecht, Otto E., Herbert Cahoon, and **Douglas C. Ewing.** *The Mary Flagler Cary Music Collection: Printed Books and Music, Manuscripts, Autograph Letters, Documents, Portraits.* 108 pp., with 49 plates. New York: Pierpont Morgan Library, 1970.

A description of a prominent music collection, with Albrecht providing commentary on music manuscripts, Cahoon on autograph letters and documents, and Ewing on printed books, portraits, and memorabilia. The Cary collection has 64 printed books and 216 manuscripts, as well as a collection of autograph letters and documents and 18 items labeled "portraits and miscellany." Otto Albrecht recounts the growth of the Cary collection and describes related items held by the Library in "Musical Treasures in the Morgan Library," in *Notes* 28 (1972): 643–51.

Reviewed by Susan T. Sommer in *Notes* 28 (1972): 681–82.

7.364 Turner, J. Rigbie. *Nineteenth-Century Autograph Music Manuscripts in the Pierpont Morgan Library: A Check List.* 53 pp. + 17 pp. of plates. New York: The Library, 1982.

An updated revision of an article first published in *NCM* 2 (1980).

Brief descriptive entries on manuscripts dating from 1791 to 1911, including references to sources of further information on the collection and the collectors.

7.365 Turner, J. Rigbie, Robert Kendall, and **James Parsons.** *Four Centuries of Opera: Manuscripts and Printed Editions in the Pierpont Morgan Library.* 132 pp. New York: Pierpont Morgan Library and Dover Publications, 1983.

A volume illustrating the "history of opera through slightly more than 50 examples, from the earliest known opera to one first performed in the past five years." All items described are from the Morgan Library's collection or from collections on deposit there. Each description is extensive and is accompanied by a facsimile of a page from the work in question. Includes a selective checklist of opera manuscripts in the Morgan Library and another of printed operas and opera libretti at the Morgan.

Reviewed by Robert Winter in *Notes* 39 (1983): 851–53.

Northridge, California

7.366* *Guitar Music Collection of Vahdah Olcott-Bickford, Vol. 1: California State University, Northridge.* 344 pp. Northridge, Calif.: Music Library, California State University, Northridge, 1991.

A collection containing over 6,000 titles of 19th- and early-20th-century editions, many printed in 19th-century America, planned in 3 vols.

Oberlin, Ohio

OBERLIN COLLEGE. CONSERVATORY OF MUSIC. MARY M. VIAL MUSIC LIBRARY

7.367 *Mr. and Mrs. C. W. Best Collection of Autographs in the Mary M. Vial Music Library of the Oberlin College Conservatory of Music.* 55 pp. + 10 facsimile plates. Oberlin: Oberlin College Library, 1967.

A collection of 110 autograph letters, signed photographs, and such, chiefly related to 19th- and early-20th-century musicians. Partial translations are given for many of the documents.

Ostiglia, Italy

BIBLIOTECA GREGGIATI

7.368 Sartori, Claudio. *Ostiglia, biblioteca dell'opera Pia Greggiati: Catalogo del fondo musicale.* 655 pp. Milan: Nuovo Istituto Editoriale Italiano, 1983. (Bibliotheca musicae, 7)

A catalog of the printed works of music and music literature gathered from the mid-18th century to the late 19th century by members of the Greggiati family. The entries are arranged in alphabetical order within each section. Another volume covering the manuscripts in the collection is projected. There are no indexes in this volume. Sartori earlier described the collection in "Nascita, letargo e risveglio della Biblioteca Greggiati," *Fontes* 24 (1977): 126–38.

Ottobeuren, Germany

BENEDIKTINER-ABTEI

7.369 Haberkamp, Gertraut. *Die Musikhandschriften der Benediktiner-Abtei Ottobeuren: Thematischer Katalog.* 299 pp. Munich: G. Henle, 1986. (Kataloge bayerischer Musiksammlungen, 12)

Reviewed by Peter Ward Jones in *M&L* 70 (1989): 258–59.

Oxford, England

OXFORD UNIVERSITY. BODLEIAN LIBRARY

7.370 Bray, Roger. *The Bodleian Library Music Collection: A Listing and Guide to Part Two, Part Three, Part Four, and Part Five [and Part Six] of the Harvester Microfilm Collection.* 2 vols. Brighton: Harvester Press Microform Publications, 1984–86.

A guide to the commercially produced film collection. Each vol. lists the contents of the reels in each part of the collection and then lists the manuscripts in each part. There is a unified index of names and composers in each volume.

7.371 [*Catalog, in Manuscript, of the Music Manuscripts in the Bodleian Library: With a List of Books Given to the University by Dr. Heather.*] 1 vol. (unpaged).

An unpublished, handwritten catalog made in the early 19th century, available for study in the Bodleian Library, giving contents for some 303 "Music School" manuscripts dating from the early 17th century.

7.372 Flotzinger, Rudolf. *Choralhandschriften österreichischer Provenienz in der Bodleian Library / Oxford.* 106 pp. Vienna: Verlag der Österreichischen Akademie der Wissenschaft, 1991. (Veröffentlichungen der Kommission für Musikforschung, 26)

A catalog describing all chant sources in the Bodleian with Austrian provenance: 11 books and 5 fragments from the 12th and 13th centuries.

Reviewed by Rob C. Wegman in *M&L* 74 (1993): 59.

7.373 Geil, Jean. "American Sheet Music in the Walter N. H. Harding Collection at the Bodleian Library, Oxford University." In *Notes* 34 (1978): 805–13.

A description of the collection of 60,000 to 70,000 pieces of American sheet music donated to the Bodleian Library.

7.374 Hughes, Anselm. *Medieval Polyphony in the Bodleian Library.* 63 pp. Oxford: Bodleian Library, 1951.

Descriptions and inventories of contents for 51 manuscripts and fragments in the Bodleian, with an index of text incipits, composers, and places of origin.

Reviewed by Manfred Bukofzer in *JAMS* 5 (1952): 53–56.

7.375 *The Oxford Music School Collection at the Bodleian Library, Oxford: A Guide and Index to the Harvester Microfilm Collection.* With an introduction by Margaret Crum. 41 pp. Brighton: Harvester Press Microform Publications, 1979.

A guide to the contents of the 19 reels in the collection, an excellent introduction, and an index of composers and their works. This is a finding aid to a commercial microfilm collection and forms Part One of the Harvester Bodleian Library Music Collection.

7.376 Stevens, Denis. "Seventeenth-Century Italian Instrumental Music in the Bodleian Library." In *Acta musicologica* 26 (1954): 67–74.

A list of some 85 sets of parts of early Italian instrumental music in the Bodleian, arranged by composer in alphabetical order, with essential bibliographical information supplied. In an article in *Collectanea historiae musicae* 2 (1957): 401–12, Stevens discusses nine unica from this collection.

OXFORD UNIVERSITY. CHRIST CHURCH
COLLEGE. LIBRARY

7.377 Arkwright, G. E. P. *Catalogue of Music in the Library of Christ Church, Oxford.* 2 vols. London: H. Milford, Oxford University Press, 1915–23.

The 1st vol. was reprinted by S.R. Publishers, East Ardsley, England, 1971, with a preface by T. B. Strong.

A catalog of the manuscript music preserved in the Christ Church Library, based on that made in 1845–47 by the Rev. H. E. Havergal. The 1st vol. covers works of ascertained authorship. The 2nd vol. describes unattributed vocal and unattributed instrumental works.

7.378 Bray, Roger, and **Tim Carter.** *The Music Collection of Christ Church, Oxford: A Listing and Guide to [Parts One through Three of] the Harvester Microfilm Collection.* 3 vols. Brighton: Harvester Press Microform Publications, 1981–82.

As in the other Harvester guides, a list of the contents of each reel in each part and a list of the manuscripts in each part.

7.379 Hiff, Aloys. A *Catalogue of Printed Music Published Prior to 1801, Now in the Library of Christ Church, Oxford.* 76 pp. London: Oxford University Press, 1919.

A collection rich in Italian and English music of the 16th and 17th centuries, with alphabetical arrangement by composer and with analytics supplied for collections.

Padua, Italy

BASILICA DI SAN' ANTONIO. ARCHIVIO MUSICALE

7.380 Tebaldini, Giovanni. *L'Archivio Musicale della Cappella Antoniana in Padova: Illustrazione storico-critico, con cinque eliotipie.* 175 pp. Padua: Tipografia e Libreria Antoniana, 1895.

A handbook on the Archivio, including a historical essay on the chapel of St. Anthony (pp. 1–92) and a partial catalog of manuscripts and printed editions (pp. 93–149). There are complete lists of works for Vallotti and Sabbatini, and thematic incipits for Tartini concertos.

BIBLIOTECA CAPITOLARE

7.381 Garbelotti, Antonio. "Codici musici della Biblioteca Capitolare di Padova." In *Revista musicale italiana* 53 (1951): 289–314; 54 (1952): 218–30.

A summary description of the manuscript holdings of the Biblioteca Capitolare in Padua. The sources are discussed chronologically by centuries, both plainchant and polyphonic manuscripts considered.

CONSERVATORIO "CESARE POLLINI"

7.382 Durante, Sergio, and **Maria Nevilla Massaro.** *Catalogo dei manoscritti musicali del Conservatorio "Cesare Pollini" di Padova.* xxii + 159 pp. Turin: EDT/Musica, 1982. (Cataloghi di fondi musicali italiani, 1)

The catalog of the musical archives of the Teatro Verdi (formerly the Teatro Nuovo), with scores and parts used for performance from 1773 to 1838.

Reviewed by Graham Dixon in *EM* 15 (1987): 261–63.

Paris, France

7.383 Lesure, François. *Catalogue de la musique imprimée avant 1800 conservée dans les bibliothèques publiques de Paris.* 708 pp. Paris: Bibliothèque Nationale, 1981.

The majority of works cataloged in this source are contained in the Département de la Musique (established in 1942) and in the collections of the Bibliothèques du Conservatoire brought into the Bibliothèque Nationale in 1964.

A catalog by composer generally showing genre or performing forces, imprint, and location, including shelf marks. Unattributed works appear in a separate list by title at the end of the catalog. *RISM* numbers, when appropriate, are supplied. First lines are provided for vocal works. When known, bibliographic announcements in contemporaneous French publications are cited.

ARCHIVES NATIONALES

7.384 Labat-Poussin, Brigitte. *Archives du Théâtre Nationale de l'Opéra (AJ 13 à 1466).* 677 pp. Paris: Archives Nationales, 1977.

A description of the archives of the Opéra, the archives of the Théâtre Italien, the Opéra Comique, and the Théâtre Lyrique, with an index to personnel who served in the Théâtre Nationale de l'Opéra and a general index.

Reviewed by François Lesure in *Fontes* 25 (1978): 195–96.

ARCHIVES NATIONALES. MINUTIER CENTRAL

7.385 Jurgens, Madeleine. *Documents du Minutier Central concernant l'histoire de la musique (1600–1650).* Préface de François Lesure. 2 vols. Paris: S.E.V.P.E.N., 1966–74. (Ministère des Affaires Culturelles. Direction des Archives de France. Archives Nationales)

An organized presentation of documents related to musicians of the first half of the 17th century in the French national archives. Musicians are grouped according to their occupations: musicians of the court, musicians of the city, instrument makers, and music printers. Tome I has a general index (pp. 895–1,038). Tome II presents records of contracts and depositions, giving names and monetary values. The material is arranged chronologically within social categories, as in Tome I, dealing with the Parisian cultural milieu of the first half of the 17th century. Includes a useful introduction and a list of instrument collections. The extensive index (pp. 911–1,086) gives thorough access.

Tome I is reviewed by Albert Cohen in *JAMS* 22 (1969): 126–29 and by James R. Anthony in *Notes* 26 (1970): 126–29. Tome II is reviewed by Margaret Murata in *Notes* 35 (1978): 310.

BIBLIOTHÈQUE DE L'ARSENAL

7.386 Laurencie, Lionel de la, and **Amédée Gastoué.** *Catalogue des livres de musique (manuscrits et imprimés) de la Bibliothèque de l'Arsenal à Paris.* 184 pp. Paris: E. Droz, 1936. (Publications de la Société Française de Musicologie, 2, 7)

Manuscripts and printed music arranged alphabetically by composer, or catchword of title if anonymous, under main divisions of sacred and secular. Included are manuscripts from the 10th century and printed works of the 16th–18th centuries. The collection is exceptionally rich in editions of little-known French composers of the 18th century.

BIBLIOTHÈQUE NATIONALE

7.387 Gastoué, Amédée. *Introduction à la paléographie musicale byzantine: Catalogue des manuscrits de musique byzantine de la Bibliothèque Nationale de Paris et des bibliothèques publiques de France.* 99 pp. Paris: Impressions artistiques L.M. Fortin, 1928. (Publications de la Société Internationale de Musique. Section de Paris)

BIBILOTHÈQUE NATIONALE. COLLECTION
TOULOUSE-PHILIDOR

7.388 Massip, Catherine. "La collection musicale Toulouse-Philidor à la Bibliothèque nationale." In *Fontes* 30 (1983): 184–207.

Following the 1978 sale of the bulk of the collection by St. Michael's College, Tenbury, an inventory of the collection and a concordance to earlier catalogs.

BIBLIOTHÈQUE NATIONALE. DÉPARTEMENT DE
LA MUSIQUE

7.389 Bloch-Michel, Antoine. *Lettres autographes conservées au Département de la Musique: Catalogue sommaire.* 404 pp. Paris: Bibliothèque Nationale, 1984.

A summary description of the collection of 30,000 letters by and to musicians, arranged alphabetically by author, showing the name of the addressee and dates. In addition, other documents are listed in a separate section under author, and there is a supplement of letters entered between 1978 and 1981. A majority of these letters came from the collection in the Bibliothèque du Conservatoire. The listings are simple, without any indication of contents. There is an index of addressees.

7.390 Ecorcheville, Jules. *Catalogue du fonds de musique ancienne de la Bibliothèque Nationale.* 8 vols. Paris, 1910–14.

Reprinted by Da Capo Press, New York, 1972.

A catalog of manuscripts, printed music, and theoretical and literary works on music not included in the general catalog of the library, to 1750, with some thematic incipits. The catalog is arranged alphabetically by composer, with collections analyzed, and brief bibliographical descriptions.

Bibliothèque Sainte-Geneviève

7.391 Garros, Madeleine, and **Simone Wallon.** *Catalogue du fonds musical de la Bibliothèque Sainte-Geneviève de Paris: Manuscrits et imprimés.* 156 pp. Kassel, Germany: Internationale Vereinigung der Musikbibliotheken; Internationale Gesellschaft für Musikwissenschaft, 1967. (Catalogus musicus, 44)

Conservatoire National de Musique et de Déclamation

7.392 Weckerlin, Jean Baptiste. *Catalogue bibliographique, orné de huit gravures, avec notices et reproductions musicales des principaux ouvrages de la réserve.* 512 pp. Paris: Firmin-Didot, 1885.

Reprinted in Hildesheim, Germany, and New York by G. Olms, 1973.

Covering the period to about 1800, a catalog including only part of the early materials in the collection. Following a prefatory history of the library, three sections are given: early treatises, vocal music, and early instrumental music of the French school.

Conservatoire National de Musique et de Déclamation. Fonds Blancheton

7.393 Laurencie, Lionel de la. *Inventaire critique du Fonds Blancheton.* 2 vols. Paris: E. Droz, 1930–31. (Publications de la Société Française de Musicologie, Ser. 2, 2:1–2)

An inventory of the Blancheton collection, 27 vols. containing some 330 instrumental compositions by 104 composers, assembled before 1750. This is an important source material for the history of the symphony, with full descriptions, including critical and biographical notes, on the composers.

Théâtre de l'Opéra

7.394 Lajarte, Théodore de. *Bibliothèque musicale du Théâtre de l'Opéra: Catalogue historique, chronologique, anecdotique.* Published under the auspices of the Ministère de l'Instruction Publique et des Beaux-arts. 2 vols. Paris: Librairie des Bibliophiles, 1878.

Reprinted by Olms, Hildesheim, Germany, in 1969.

A descriptive list of 594 pieces, arranged in order of their first production at the Opéra, 1671–1876, classified by "Périodes": Époque de Lully (1671–97), Époque de Campra (1697–1733), Époque de Rameau (1733–74), Époque de Gluck (1774–1807), Époque de Spontini (1807–26), and Rossini and Meyerbeer (1826–76). There are "Notices biographiques" at the end of each "Période." There is a composer and title index to works in the repertoire, with many helpful appendixes.

Parma, Italy

7.395 Gasparini, Guido, and **Nestore Pellicelli.** *Catalogo generale delle opere musicali: Città di Parma.* 295 pp. Parma, Italy: Freschig, 1909–11. (Associazione dei Musicologi Italiani. Catalogo generale delle opere musicali, 1/1)

Reprinted by Forni, Bologna, 1970.

CONSERVATORIO DI MUSICA "ARRIGO BOITO"

7.396 Allorto, Riccardo. "Biblioteche musicali in Italia: La Biblioteca del Conservatorio di Parma è un fondo di edizioni dei sec. XVI e XVII non comprese nel catalogo a stampa." In *Fontes* 2 (1955): 147–51.

A description of a collection of 31 sets of 16th- and 17th-century part books acquired by the library in 1925.

7.397 Medici, Mario. "Osservazioni sulla Biblioteca Musicale di Parma." In *Avrea Parma* 48 (May–August 1964): 3–49.

A source providing copious data on the library of the Conservatorio. Many of the rare manuscripts and printed books are cited in full, along with an account of the history of the institution and its administrative structure.

Passau, Germany

7.398* Haberkamp, Gertraut, and **Herbert W. Wurster.** *Die Musikhandschriften der Dommusik St. Stephen im Archiv des Bistums Passau: Thematischer Katalog.* 287 pp. Munich: G. Henle, 1993. (Kataloge bayerischer Musiksammlungen, 21)

Philadelphia, Pennsylvania

FREE LIBRARY OF PHILADELPHIA

7.399 Drinker, Henry S. *Drinker Library of Choral Music and the American Choral Foundation Library of the Free Library of Philadelphia: Catalog.* 123 pp. Philadelphia, Pa.: Free Library of Philadelphia, 1971.

First published under the sponsorship of Westminster Choir College, Princeton, N.J., 1947 (81 pp.), with a *Supplement* added in July 1948. Further editions were published in Philadelphia in 1957 and 1965.

A collection of choral materials donated to the Association of American Choruses, housed in the Music Department of the Free Library of Philadelphia, and made available to college, high school, and church choruses and choirs.

7.400 *The Edwin A. Fleisher Collection of Orchestral Music in the Free Library of Philadelphia: A Cumulative Catalog, 1929–1977.* 956 pp. Boston, Mass.: G.K. Hall, 1979.

First published in 1933–45, 2 vols., with a *Supplementary List, 1945–1955,* published in 1956. A revised ed. was published in 1956.

A classified catalog of a loan collection of over 13,000 pieces of orchestra music, much of it unpublished. The individual citations include composer's dates, the title of each work in the original language with English translation, publisher, instrumentation, timing, composition date, and information about the first performance. Occasional thematic incipits are included, and there is an index by performing forces needed. The collection lends performance material at minimum charge, although budgetary problems in recent years have made the loan requirements more stringent.

The 2nd vol. of the 1st ed. is reviewed by Lee Fairley in *Notes* 3 (1946): 177–79. The latest ed. is reviewed by Joseph Boonin in *Notes* 36 (1979): 92–93.

LIBRARY COMPANY

7.401 Wolf, Edwin, II. *American Song Sheets, Slip Ballads and Poetical Broadsides, 1850–1970: A Catalogue of the Collection of the Library Company of Philadelphia.* 205 pp. Philadelphia, Pa.: Library Company of Philadelphia, 1963.

A list, alphabetical by title, of 2,722 American song sheets, ballads, and broadsides, with information on such elements as author, composer, format, and cover design. There is a separate list of 194 Confederate songs. Access to nontitle elements is assisted by the indexes of printers and publishers, authors and composers, and singers. There are reproductions of pictorial covers.

THE MUSICAL FUND SOCIETY

7.402 *Catalog of Orchestral and Choral Compositions Published and in Manuscript between 1790 and 1840 from the Library of the Musical Fund Society of Philadelphia.* 81 pp. Philadelphia, Pa.: Musical Fund Society, 1974.

A list of 299 scores now in the custody of the Music Department, the Free Library of Philadelphia.

UNIVERSITY OF PENNSYLVANIA. VAN PELT
LIBRARY

7.403* Westlake, Neda M., and **Otto Albrecht.** *Marian Anderson: A Catalog of the Collection at the University of Pennsylvania Library.* 89 pp. Philadelphia, Pa.: University of Pennsylvania Press, 1981.

The Philippines

7.404* *Union Catalog on Philippine Culture: Music.* 3 vols. Manila: Cultural Center of the Philippines Library, 1989. (CCP library research guide series, 1)
Contents: Vols. 1–2, *Monographs;* Vol. 3, *Periodical Articles.*

Piacenza, Italy

CATTEDRALE DI PIACENZA. BIBLIOTECA E
ARCHIVIO CAPITOLARE

7.405 Bussi, Francesco. *Archivio del Duomo: Catalogo del fondo musicale.* 209 pp. Milan: Istituto Editoriale Italiano, 1967.

A catalog in four parts: printed music, chiefly of the 16th and 17th centuries; music manuscripts, including anthologies; manuscript and printed liturgical books; and a small collection of books on music. There is an index of names. Claudio Sartori in "L'Archivio del Duomo di Piacenza e il *Liber XIII* di Costanzo Antegnati," *Fontes* 4 (1957): 28–37, describes the collection and its catalog of early printed music, with special attention to a unique copy of the *Liber XIII,* a collection of sacred and secular vocal music by Costanzo Antegnati.

Reviewed by Andreas Wernli in *Die Musikforschung* 30 (1977): 354–56.

Pirna, Germany

7.406 Hoffmann-Erbrecht, Lothar. "Die Chorbücher der Stadtkirche zu Pirna." In *Acta musicologica* 27 (1955): 121–37.

A detailed description of eight mid-16th-century choirbooks of polyphonic music, partially thematic, with summary inventories and two facsimile plates. These manuscripts are now in the Sächsische Landesbibliothek in Dresden.

Pisa, Italy

7.407 Pecchiai, Pietro. *Catalogo generale delle opere musicali: Biblioteche e archivi della Città di Pisa.* 90 pp. Parma, Italy: Freschig, 1932–35. (Associazione dei Musicologi Italiani. Catalogo generale delle opere musicali, 12)

> Reprinted by Forni, Bologna, 1979.

CHIESA CONVENTUALE DEI CAVALIERI DI SANTO STEFANO

7.408* Raffaelli, Paola. *L'Archivio musicale della Chiesa Conventuale dei Cavalieri di Santo Stefano di Pisa: Storia e catalogo.* 315 pp. Florence: Libreria Musicale Italiana, 1994. (Studi musicali toscani, 3)

> Reviewed by David Hiley in *M&L* 77 (1996): 115–16.

Pistoia, Italy

ARCHIVIO CAPITOLARE DELLA CATTEDRALE

7.409 Laugier, Umberto de. *Catalogo generale delle opere musicali: Città di Pistoia: Archivio Capitolare della Cattedrale.* 106 pp. Parma, Italy: Freschig, 1936–37. (Associazione dei Musicologi Italiani. Catalogo generale delle opere musicali, 4/2)

BIBLIOTECA ANTONIO VENTURI

7.410 Meylan, Raymond. "La collection Antonio Venturi, Montecatini-Terme (Pistoia), Italie." In *Fontes* (1958): 21–44.

> A private collection of late-18th-century vocal and instrumental music.

Pittsburgh, Pennsylvania

7.411 Finney, Theodore M. *A Union Catalogue of Music and Books on Music Printed before 1801 in Pittsburgh Libraries.* 2nd ed. 106 ll. (typescript). Pittsburgh, Pa.: University of Pittsburgh, 1963.

> First published, 1959. Supplement to the 2nd ed., 1964, 42 ll.
>
> A list of the holdings in early music in four Pittsburgh-area libraries: the Carnegie Library of Pittsburgh, the University of Pittsburgh library, St. Vincent's College library (Latrobe, Pa.), and the private library of the compiler (now dispersed). There is a strong emphasis on early English music.
>
> Reviewed by Donald W. Krummel in *Notes* 21 (1963–64): 129–31.

7.412 Lotis, Howard. *Latin American Music Materials Available at the University of Pittsburgh and at the Carnegie Library of Pittsburgh.* 145 pp. Pittsburgh, Pa.: Center for Latin American Studies, University of Pittsburgh, 1981.

UNIVERSITY OF PITTSBURGH. MUSIC LIBRARY

7.413 Finney, Theodore M. "A Group of English Manuscript Volumes at the University of Pittsburgh." In *Essays in Musicology in Honor of Dragan Plamenac on His 70th Birthday,* pp. 21–48. Pittsburgh, Pa.: University of Pittsburgh Press, 1969.

> A description of the contents of a collection of 12 17th- and 18th-century manuscripts of English provenance, formerly privately owned and housed in the Music Library of the University of Pittsburgh and later, at the end of his career, sold by Dr. Finney to the Humanities Research Center of the University of Texas at Austin. The study incorporates two indexes, one of composers and the other of initial words and titles.

Plasencia, Spain

CATEDRAL. ARCHIVO

7.414 Rubio, Samuel. "El Archivo de musica en la catedral de Plasencia." In *Anuario musical* 5 (1950): 147–68.

A small collection of early manuscripts and printed music, fully described, with contents listed.

Poland

7.415 Prokopowicz, Maria. "Traditions and Achievements of Music Libraries and Library Science in the Polish People's Republic." In *Fontes* 26 (1979): 36–43.

A brief résumé of activities in Poland since World War II, including a bibliography of pertinent articles on libraries, catalogs of collections, works on music publishing and printing, and works on music bibliography and librarianship.

7.416 Szweykowski, Zygmunt M. *Musicalia vetera: Katalog tematyczny rekopiśmiennych zabytków dawnej muzyki w Polsce / Thematic Catalogue of Early Musical Manuscripts in Poland.* 2 vols. to date. Warsaw: Polskie Wydawn. Muzyczne, 1969– .

The edition will consist of a number of vols. constituting thematic catalogs of individual early manuscripts or their groups. Later vols. will be devoted to the collections from Sandomierz and Lowicz regions.

T. 1, zesz. 6, *Zbiory muzyczne proweniencji wawelskiej / Collections of Music Copied for Use at Wawel.* Edited by Elżbieta Głuszcz-Zwolińska, 1969.

T. 2, zesz. 1, *Zbiory muzyczne proweniencji podkrakowskie / Collections of Music from the Surroundings of Cracow.* Edited by Zofia Surowiak, 1972.

Prague, Czech Republic

CATHEDRAL

7.417 Podlaha, Antonius. *Catalogus collectionis operum artis musicae quae in bibliotheca capituli metropolitani pragensis asservantur.* 87 pp. Prague: Metropolitan Capitulary of Prague, 1926.

NATIONAL MUSEUM

7.418 Buchner, Alexandr. *Hudební sbírka Emiliána Troldy / The Music Library of Emilián Trolda.* 132 pp. Prague: Národní Museum, 1954.

A thematic catalog of the Trolda music collection deposited in the Music Department of the National Museum. The collection contains music dating from c. 1550 to 1820, scored by Trolda from numerous archives, native and foreign.

UNIVERSITY LIBRARY

7.419 Plocek, Václav. *Catalogus codicum notis musicis instructorum qui in bibliotheca publica rei publicae bohemiae socialisticae—in Bibliotheca Universitatis Pragensis servantur / Catalog of Latin Musical Manuscripts in the State Library of the CSSR.* 830 pp. in 2 vols. Prague: University Library, 1971.

Puebla, Mexico

CATEDRAL

7.420 Stevenson, Robert M. "Sixteenth- through Eighteenth-Century Resources in Mexico: Part III." In *Fontes* 25 (1978): 156–87.

A continuation of Stevenson's earlier articles on sources in Mexico (**5.603**). A catalog of 130 sources, arranged by composer.

Pullman, Washington

WASHINGTON STATE UNIVERSITY. ROSBAUD LIBRARY

7.421 Evans, Joan. "The Hans Rosbaud Library at Washington State University, Pullman, Washington, U.S.A." In *Notes* 41 (1985): 26–40.

A description of an extensive collection of correspondence between Rosbaud, a conductor who championed the cause of new music, and composers, performers, conductors, and other persons significant in the history of 20th-century music.

Quebec, Canada

HÔTEL-DIEU AND THE URSULINE CONVENT

7.422 Schwandt, Erich. "The Motet in New France: Some 17th- and 18th-Century Manuscripts in Quebec." In *Fontes* 28 (1981): 194–219.

A thematic catalog for 128 pieces found in 6 manuscript anthologies in the two convents, with an index to titles.

Regensburg, Germany

BISCHÖFLICHE ZENTRALBIBLIOTHEK REGENSBURG

7.423* *Bischöfliche Zentralbibliothek Regensburg: Thematischer Katalog der Musikhandschriften.* 5 vols. Munich: G. Henle, 1989– . (Kataloge bayerischer Musiksammlungen, 14–)

Contents: Vol. 1, *Sammlung Proske, Manuskript des 16. und 17. Jahrhunderts aus den Signaturem A.R., B, C, AN;* Vol. 2, *Sammlung Proske, Manuskripte des 18. und 19. Jahrhunderts aus den Signaturen A.R., C, AN;* Vol. 3, *Sammlunge Proske, Mappenbibliothek;* Vol. 4, *Kollegiatstift Unserer Lieben Frau zur Alten Kapelle, Dom St. Peter und Kollegiatstift zu den Heiligen Johann Baptist und Johann Evangelist in Regensburg;* Vol. 5, *Stadtpfarrkirche St. Jakobus und Tiburtius in Straubing.*

Vols. 2–3 prepared by Gertraut Haberkamp and Jochen Reutter; Vols. 4–5 by Christofer Schweisthal.

The 1st vol. is reviewed by Lilian P. Pruett in *Fontes* 37 (1990): 65–66; Vols. 2–3 are reviewed by Lilian P. Pruett in *Fontes* 40 (1993): 339–42.

FÜRST THURN UND TAXIS HOFBIBLIOTHEK

7.424 Haberkamp, Gertraut, and **Hugo Angerer.** *Die Musikhandschriften der Fürst Thurn und Taxis Hofbibliothek Regensburg: Thematischer Katalog, mit einer Geschichte des Musikalienbestandes.* 500 pp. Munich: Henle, 1981. (Kataloge bayerischer Musiksammlungen, 6)

Reggio-Emilia, Italy

7.425 Gasparini, Guido, and **Nestore Pellicelli.** *Catalogo generale delle opere musicali: Città di Reggio-Emilia.* 24 pp. Parma, Italy: Freschig, 1911. (Associazione dei Musicologi Italiani. Catalogo generale delle opere musicali, 1/2)

Reprinted by Forni, Bologna, 1970.

Rio de Janeiro, Brazil

BIBLIOTECA NACIONAL

7.426 Lange, Francesco Curt. "Estudio Brasilenos I. Manuscritos musicales en la Biblioteca Nacional de Rio de Janeiro." In *Revista de estudios musicales* 1 (April 1950): 98–194.

A list of the chiefly 19th-century composers in the National Library, divided by works of European composers and by works of Brazilian composers or Europeans active in Brazil.

7.427 *Música no Rio de Janeiro imperial 1822–1870.* 100 pp. Rio de Janeiro: Biblioteca Nacional, 1962.

At head of title: "Exposiçao comemorativa do primeiro decénio da seçao de música e arquivo sonore."

A list of 391 items, chiefly Brazilian imprints of the period.

7.428 *Rio musical: Crónica de uma cidade.* 51 pp. Rio de Janeiro: Biblioteca Nacional, 1965.

At head of title: "Exposiçao comemorativa do IV centenário da cidade do Rio de Janeiro."

Riva, Italy

BIBLIOTECA CIVICA DI RIVA DEL GARDA

7.429* Foletto, Angelo, Federica Fanizza, and **Nicola Straffelini.** *Dentro la musica: Itinerari alla scoperta del fondo "Silvio Pozzini" della Biblioteca Civica di Riva del Garda.* 182 pp. Riva, Italy: Commune di Riva del Garda, Biblioteca Civica, 1993.

Catalog, pp. 81–178, and bibliographical references, pp. 179–82.

River Forest, Illinois

CONCORDIA UNIVERSITY. KLINCK MEMORIAL LIBRARY

7.430 Schalk, Carl. *Hymnals and Chorale Books of the Klinck Memorial Library.* 89 pp. River Forest, Ill.: Concordia Teachers College, 1975.

A catalog of a section of the holdings of the then–Concordia Teachers College Library.

Riverside, California

7.431* Lang, Robert, and **JoAn Kunselman.** *Heinrich Schenker, Oswald Jonas, Moriz Violin: A Checklist of Manuscripts and Other Papers in the Oswald Jonas Memorial Collection.* xxvi + 227 pp. Berkeley, Calif.: University of California Press, 1994. (University of California publications. Catalogs and bibliographies, 10)

Rö, Sweden

7.432 Boer, Bertil van, Jr., and **Leif Jonsson.** "The Silverstolpe Music Collection in Rö, Uppland, Sweden: A Preliminary Catalogue." In *Fontes* 29 (1982): 93–103.

An introduction to an extensive collection of 19th-century music in manuscript and printed editions gathered by a family of Swedish nobility and diplomats.

Rome, Italy

For catalogs of music collections in the Vatican, see under Vatican City.

7.433 Kast, Paul. "Römische Handschriften." In *MGG* (**1.9**) 11 (1963): cols. 750–61.

A narrative account citing and describing the principal manuscripts, chiefly polyphonic, in Rome and in the Vatican Library, with a bibliography of writings on Roman libraries and their manuscript sources.

ACCADEMIA DI SANTA CECILIA. BIBLIOTECA

7.434 Andolfi, Otello. *Catalogo generale delle opere musicali . . . Vol. 5: Città di Roma. Biblioteca della R. Accademia di S. Cecilia.* 56 pp. Parma, Italy: Freschig, 1912–13 (incomplete). (Associazione dei Musicologi Italiani. Catalogo generale delle opere musicali, 5)

A catalog of theoretical treatises, with bibliographical description and shelf number.

7.435 Paton, John Glenn. "Cantata and Aria Manuscripts in the Santa Cecilia Library." In *Notes* 36 (1980): 563–74.

An inventory of 36 manuscripts of the 17th and 18th centuries, not indexed, but analyzed and citing modern editions.

BASILICA OF SANTA MARIA

7.436 Cannon, Beekman C. "Music in the Archives of the Basilica of Santa Maria in Trastevere." In *Acta musicologica* 41 (1969): 199–212.

A description and inventory of the music in one of the most renowned Roman churches. Most of the material comes from the latter half of the 17th century. The collection is rich in music by Angelo Berardi, who became Maestro di Cappella in 1693.

BIBLIOTECA CASANATENSE

7.437 Paton, John Glenn. "Cantata Manuscripts in the Casanatense Library." In *Notes* 40 (1988): 826–35.

An analyzed inventory of 32 manuscripts, each consisting mostly of 17th-century Italian cantatas.

BIBLIOTECA CORSINIANA

7.438 Bertini, Argia. *Biblioteca Corsiniana e dell'Accademia Nazionale dei Lincei: Catalogo dei fondi musicali Chiti e Corsiniano.* 109 pp. Milan: Istituto Editoriale Italiano, 1964. (Bibliotheca musicae, 2)

A catalog covering printed music, theoretical works, and manuscripts: 17th- and early-18th-century vocal and instrumental music.

7.439 Reali, Vito. "La collezione Corsini di antichi codici musicali e Girolamo Chiti." In *Rivista musicale italiana* 25 (1918–20).

A description of the founding of the Corsini library and the role played by early-18th-century church musician Girolamo Chiti, friend of Padre Martini.

BIBLIOTECA DORIA PAMPHILJ

7.440 Annibaldi, Claudio. "L'Archivio musicale Doria Pamphilj saggio sulla cultura aristocratica a Roma fra il 16o e 19o secolo." In *Studi musicali* 11 (1982): 91–120.

A discussion of the origin and organization of the Archive citing and describing the catalogs of manuscripts and printed materials, the subject catalog, and the author catalog.

7.441 Holschneider, Andreas. "Die Musiksammlung der Fürsten Doria-Pamphilj in Rom." In *Archiv für Musikwissenschaft* 18 (1961): 248–64.

A description of the collection and an inventory of its contents, classified under five main headings: collections, 16th and 17th centuries; sacred music; oratorios (early manuscripts); operas (early manuscripts); and German instrumental music, chiefly 18th century.

7.442 Lippmann, Friedrich. "Die Sinfonien-Manuskripte der Bibliothek Doria-Pamphilj in Rom." In *Analecta musicologica* 5 (1968): 201–47.

A thematic catalog of 119 symphonies by 36 composers. Many of the works are not known from other sources.

7.443 Lippmann, Friedrich, and **Ludwig Finscher.** "Die Streichquartettmanuskripte der Bibliothek Doria-Pamphilj in Rom." In *Analecta musicologica* 7 (1969): 120–44.

A thematic catalog of the string quartet repertory in the library.

7.444 Lippmann, Friedrich, and **Hubert Unverricht.** "Die Streichtriomanuskripte der Bibliothek Doria-Pamphilj in Rom." In *Analecta musicologica* 9 (1970): 299–335.

A thematic catalog of string trios in the Doria-Pamphilj collection.

CONGREGAZIONE DELL'ORATORIO

7.445 Bertini, Argia *Inventario del fondo musicale dell'Oratorio.* 4 fascicles. Rome, 1968–71.

DEUTSCHES HISTORISCHES INSTITUT

7.446 Fellerer, Karl Gustav. "Die Musikgeschichtliche Abteilung des Deutschen Historischen Instituts in Rom." In *Die Musikforschung* 20 (1967): 410–13.

A brief description of the leading musicological reference library in Italy, calling attention to its major areas of interest, special files, and indexes.

SAN GIROLAMO DELLA CARITÀ

7.447* Simi Bonini, Eleanora. *Il fondo musicale dell'Arciconfraternità di S. Girolamo della Carità.* 229 pp. Rome: Edizioni Torre d'Orfeo, 1992. (Cataloghi di fondi musicali italiani, 15. Pubblicazioni degli Archivi di stato, 69)

An alternative ed. was published in Rome by Ministerio per i Beni Culturali e Ambenientali, Ufficio Centrale per i Beni Archivistici.

The catalog of a collection of manuscript scores of 18th-century oratorios and 19th-century liturgical works held by an institution founded in the early 16th century. The entries give incipits. Musical examples are provided and there are analytical indexes.

SCUOLE PIE A SAN PANTALEO. ARCHIVIO GENERALE

7.448* Careri, Enrico. *Catalogo dei manoscritti musicali dell'Archivio Generale delle Scuole Pie a San Pantaleo.* 122 pp. Rome: Torre d'Orfeo, 1987. (Cataloghi di fondi musicali italiani, 6)

A catalog of the collection of the Collegio Nazareno, Rome, now housed in the Archivio Generale delle Scuole Pie, with sacred and secular vocal and instrumental manuscript music of the late 17th and 18th centuries; the identified composers are Italian. Thematic incipits, bibliographical references, and indexes are included.

Reviewed by Graham Dixon in *M&L* 69 (1988): 510–11.

St. Petersburg, Russia

RIMSKY-KORSAKOV CONSERVATORY. SCIENTIFIC-MUSIC LIBRARY

7.449* *Card Catalog of the Scientific-Music Library of the Rimsky-Korsakov Conservatory, St. Petersburg.* 266 microfiches. New York: Norman Ross Publishing Inc., 1994.

A microform with the holdings of the Manuscript, Book, and Printed Music Divisions.

7.450 Golubovskii, I. V. *Muzykal´nyi Leningrad.* 526 pp. Leningrad: Gosudarstvennoe Muzykalnoe Izdatel´stvo, 1958.

"Biblioteki i muzei," pp. 351–411.

A general description of the musical content of 14 libraries, 2 record libraries, and 12 museums, with lists of manuscripts of Russian composers and offering a few examples of Western manuscripts and early books found in various collections. Details of individual libraries' organization, cataloging, and circulation policies are given.

Salamanca, Spain

CATEDRAL DE SALAMANCA. ARCHIVO DE MUSICA

7.451 García Fraile, Dámaso. *Catálogo archivo de música de la Catedral de Salamanca.* xxiv + 626 pp. Cuenca, Spain: Instituto Música Religiosa de la Diputación Provincial, D.L. 1981. (Instituto de Música Religiosa. Ediciones)

A collection of sacred music in manuscript gathered during the course of events in one of the great cathedrals in Spain. It is rich in manuscripts of music from the 13th to the 18th centuries, particularly in the latter part of that period. There are 10 manuscripts of early polyphony. Catalog entries give titles or first lines, description of the source, dates of copying, key (if relevant), shelf marks, composer (if known), and thematic incipit. Works are arranged by composer after anonymous works and anthologies. There are many indexes: first lines; by composer and then by title; works with various instrumental accompaniments; and by author, showing numbers of works in the catalog.

Salt Lake City, Utah

UNIVERSITY OF UTAH. LIBRARY

7.452 Selby, Carol E. *A Catalogue of Books and Music Acquired from the Library of Hugo Leichtentritt.* 106 pp. Salt Lake City, Utah: University of Utah, 1954. (Bulletin of the University of Utah, 45:10)

A scholar's working library of music books and scores. Although there are a few early editions, the collection is centered in the 19th and 20th centuries. The catalog is divided in two sections: books (pp. 9–46) and music (pp. 49–106).

Salzburg, Austria

DOM ZU SALZBURG

7.453* *Katalog des liturgischen Buch- und Musicalienbestandes am Dom zu Salzburg.* 2 vols. in 1. Salzburg: A. Pustet, 1992. (Veröffentlichungen zur Salzburger Musikgeschichte, 3) (Schriftenreihe des Salzburger Konsistorialarchivs, 1)

Contents: Teil 1, *Die gedruckten und handschriftlichen liturgischen Bücher,* edited by Franz Wasner; Teil 2, *Die Musikhandschriften und Musikdrucke in Chor-Notierung,* edited by Ernst Hintermaier.

A catalog of liturgical music manuscripts.

MOZART-MUSEUM

7.454 *Katalog des Mozart-Museums im Geburts- und Wohnzimmer Mozarts zu Salzburg.* 4th ed. 62 pp. Salzburg: Im Selbstverlage der obengenannten Stiftung, 1906.

The description of a collection of Mozart memorabilia maintained in the composer's birthplace. The collection includes portraits, medals, letters, and music.

MUSEUM CAROLINO AUGUSTEUM

7.455 Gassner, Josef. *Die Musikaliensammlung im Salzburger Museum Carolino Augusteum.* 247 pp. Salzburg, 1962.

Originally published in the Museum's *Jahresschrift,* 1961. Salzburg, 1962, pp. 119–325.

The catalog of a collection, founded in 1834, rich in 19th-century editions, with citations for manuscripts and printed music interfiled. There are full bibliographic citations, with publishers' plate numbers given, as well as a selection of facsimile plates.

ST. PETER'S ABBEY IN SALZBURG. MUSIKARCHIV

7.456 *Katalog. Erster Teil: Leopold und Wolfgang Amadeus Mozart, Joseph und Michael Haydn.* Mit einer Einführung in die Geschichte der Sammlung vorgelegt von Manfred Hermann Schmid. 300 pp. Salzburg, 1970. (Schriftenreihe der Internationalen Stiftung Mozarteum, 3/4) (Zugleich Band I der Publikationen des Instituts für Musikwissenschaft der Universität Salzburg)

Reviewed by Susan T. Sommer in *Notes* 29 (1972): 258.

San Francisco, California

SAN FRANCISCO STATE UNIVERSITY. FRANK V. DE BELLIS COLLECTION

7.457 Jackman, James L. *The Frank V. De Bellis Collection: San Francisco State University (RISM Siglum, US-SFsc), Bound Music Manuscript Miscellanies, Preliminary Survey of Contents with Index of Names.* 92 ll. (photocopy). San Francisco, Calif.: San Francisco State University, 1975.

7.458 *Orchestra Scores and Parts in the Frank V. De Bellis Collection of the California State Colleges.* 24 unnumbered ll. (typescript). San Francisco, Calif.: San Francisco State College, 1964.

A preliminary catalog of the orchestral portion of the De Bellis collection, a collection devoted exclusively to Italian music. The entries are listed alphabetically by composer, with early and modern editions interfiled and parts specified.

San Marino, California

HENRY E. HUNTINGTON LIBRARY AND ART GALLERY

7.459 Backus, Edythe N. *Catalogue of Music in the Huntington Library Printed before 1801.* 773 pp. San Marino, Calif.: The Library, 1949. (Huntington Library lists, 6)

A collection strong in 17th- and 18th-century English music. "Music publications and publications without music notation but of distinct interest to musicians and musicologists" are included in this catalog; excluded are manuscripts, song texts, and opera libretti, but music published in periodicals is included. The entries are arranged by composer, with anonymous works listed under title. There are indexes to composers and editors, a chronological index, and an index to first lines of songs (pp. 380–773), which is a major access point to pre-1800 English song.

Reviewed by Cyrus L. Day in *Notes* 6 (1949): 609–10 and by Harold Spivacke in *MQ* 35 (1949): 640–42.

Santiago, Chile

BIBLIOTECA NACIONAL. SECCIÓN MÚSICA

7.460* Sanhueza Vargas, Pauline. *Catálogo de compositores chilenos: Partituras microfilmadas.* 91 ll. Santiago de Chile: Dirección de Bibliotecas, Archivos y Museos, Biblioteca Nacional de Chile, Sección Música y Medios Múltiples, 1990.

CATEDRAL. ARCHIVO DE MUSICA

7.461 Claro, Samuel. *Catálogo del Archivo musical de la Catedral de Santiago de Chile*. 67 pp. Santiago de Chile: Editorial del Instituto de Extension Musical, Universidad de Chile, 1974.

Santiago, Cuba

7.462 Hernández Balaguer, Pablo. *Catálogo de música de los archivos de la Catedral de Santiago de Cuba y del Museo Bacardí.* 2nd ed. 99 pp. Santiago de Cuba: Editorial Oriente, 1979.

First ed., 1961, 61 pp.

A catalog of works by Cuban composers in the archives of the cathedral at Santiago and in the Bacardi Museum in the same city.

Santiago, Spain

CATEDRAL. ARCHIVO

7.463 López-Calo, José. *La música en la Catedral de Santiago.* 3 vols. to date. La Coruña, Spain: Diputación Provincial de la Coruña, 1992–93.

Contents: Vols. 1–3, *Catálogo del archivo de música.*

Revised ed. of his *Catálogo musical del Archivo de la Santa Iglesia Catedral de Santiago* (Cuenca, Spain: Ediciones del Instituto de Musica Religiosa, 1972, 386 pp.). (Instituto de Musica Religiosa, Publicaciones, 8)

A catalog of one of the richest musical traditions of Spanish cathedrals, arranged by century and then by composer.

Santo Domingo de la Calzada, Spain

7.464* López-Calo, José. *La música en la Catedral de Santo Domingo de la Calzada.* 1 vol. to date. Logroño, Spain: Gobierna de La Rioja, Consejería de Educación, Cultura y Deoirtos, 1988– . (La música en La Rioja, A1–)

A catalog of music manuscripts.

Schotten, Germany

LIEBFRAUENKIRCHE

7.465 Schlichte, Joachim, and **Peter Albrecht.** *Thematischer Katalog der kirchlichen Musikhandschriften in der Liebfrauenkirche zu Schotten, mit einer Geschichte der Kirchenmusik und ihren Notenbeständen.* 375 pp. Tutzing, Germany: H. Schneider, 1985. (Frankfurter Beiträge zur Musikwissenschaft, 19)

Schwerin, Germany

GROSSHERZOGLICHE REGIERUNGSBIBLIOTHEK

7.466 Kade, Otto. *Die Musikalien-Sammlung des Grossherzoglich Mecklenburg-Schweriner Fürstenhauses aus den letzten zwei Jahrhunderten.* 2 vols. Schwerin, Germany: Druck der Sandmeyerschen Hofbuchdruckerei, 1893.

Reprinted by Olms, Hildesheim, Germany, 1974.

A catalog of primarily 18th- and 19th-century manuscripts and printed music. Part I is a thematic catalog, alphabetical by composer, with a classified section under "Anonyma." Part II is libretti. Part III is an index of dedications and autographs.

7.467 Kade, Otto. *Der musikalische Nachlass der Frau Erbgrossherzogin Auguste von Mecklenburg-Schwerin.* 142 pp. Schwerin, Germany: Druck der Sandmeyerschen Hofbuchdruckerei, 1899.

Reprinted by Olms, Hildesheim, Germany, 1974.

Seville, Spain

CATEDRAL DE SEVILLA. BIBLIOTECA COLOMBINA

7.468 Anglès, Higinio. "La musica conservada en la Biblioteca Colombina y en la Catedral de Sevilla." In *Anuario musical* 2 (1947): 3–39.

A list of 88 manuscripts and printed editions from the Colombina library and 9 manuscripts and 22 printed editions from the cathedral archives. There are bibliographical references and notes on all items.

7.469 Chapman, Catherine Weeks. "Printed Collections of Polyphonic Music Owned by Ferdinand Columbus." In *JAMS* 21 (1968): 34–84.

The reconstruction of the 16th-century library of the son of Christopher Columbus, based on a manuscript catalog preserved in that library. The catalog makes reference to a number of editions now lost.

Sheffield, England

UNIVERSITY OF SHEFFIELD. LIBRARY

7.470 Carnell, Peter W. *Broadside Ballads and Song-Sheets from the Herwin MSS. Collection in Sheffield University Library: A Descriptive Catalogue with Indexes and Notes.* 118 pp. Sheffield, England: Sheffield University Library and the Centre for English Cultural Tradition and Language, 1987.

Reviewed by Leslie Shepard in *Folk Music Journal* 5 (1988): 499–500.

Sitten, Switzerland (Valais)

7.471 Stenzl, Jürg. *Repertorium der liturgischen Musikhandschriften der Diozesen Sitten, Lausanne und Genf. Band I: Diozese Sitten.* Freiburg: Universitätsverlag, 1972– . Vol. 1– . (Veröffentlichungen der Gregorianischen Akademie zu Freiburg in der Schweiz neue Folge, 1)

A series devoted to the liturgical music manuscripts in the dioceses of Sitten, Lausanne, and Geneva. Band I has 383 pages, 100 illustrations, 60 facsimiles, and 72 pages of edited music.

Slovakia

See Czech Republic and Slovakia.

Slovenia

7.472 Höfler, J., and **I. Klemenčič.** *Glasbeni rokopisi in tiski na Slovenskem do leta 1800 / Music Manuscripts and Printed Music in Slovenia before 1800: Catalogue.* 105 pp. Compiled by J. Höfler and I. Klemenčič. Ljubljana, Slovenia: Narodna in Univerzitetna knjižnica v Ljubljani, 1967.

An attempt to catalog all surviving early musical material in libraries and archives through-out Slovenia, covering 32 chant manuscripts; 343 general manuscripts, chiefly 18th- and early 19th-century; and an unnumbered section devoted to printed music. Items are located in 17 Slovenian libraries or collections.

Sorau, Germany

See Żary, Poland.

Spain

7.473 Aubry, Pierre. "Iter Hispanicum: Notices et extraits de manuscrits ancienne conservés dans les bibliothèques d'Espagne." In *Sammelbände der Internationalen Musikgesellschaft* 8–9 (1907–8). Also issued separately.

A series of essays treating early Spanish sources of polyphony, Mozarabic chant, the "Cantigas de Santa Maria," and folk music.

7.474* Garrigos i Massana, Joaquin. *Catálogo de manuscritos e impresos musicales de Archivo Historico Nacional y del Archivo de la Corona de Aragon.* 346 pp. Madrid: Dirección General de Bellas Artes y Archivos, Dirección de Archivos Estatales, 1994.

7.475 Riano, Juan F. *Critical and Bibliographical Notes on Early Spanish Music.* 154 pp. London: B. Quaritch, 1887.

Reprinted by Da Capo Press, New York, 1971.

Manuscripts and printed music to 1600, classified, giving descriptions and library locations of manuscripts, with numerous facsimile plates.

Split, Croatia

7.476* Tuksar, Stanislav. *Katalozi muzikalija u Muzeju Grada Split / Catalogue of Music Manuscripts and Prints of the Collections in the City Museum of Split.* 109 pp. Zagreb: Jugoslavenska Akademija Znanosti i Umjetnosti Zavod za Muzikoloska Istrazivanja, 1989. (Indices collectiorum musicarum tabulariorumque in SR Croatia, 2)

A catalog of 185 titles, mostly manuscripts, held by the City Museum of Split, dating from the 18th century.

Reviewed by D. W. Krummel in *Notes* 48 (1992): 918–21.

Springfield, Ohio

WITTENBERG UNIVERSITY. HAMMA SCHOOL OF THEOLOGY. SCHOOL OF MUSIC

7.477 Voigt, Louis, and **Darlene Kalke.** *Hymnbooks at Wittenberg: A Classified Catalog of the Collections of Hamma School of Theology, Wittenberg School of Music, Thomas Library.* 96 unnumbered pp. Springfield, Ohio: Chantry Music Press, 1975.

A list of 1,084 hymnbooks, principally Lutheran, with an index of names.

Stanford, California

STANFORD UNIVERSITY

7.478 Van Patten, Nathan. *Catalogue of the Memorial Library of Music, Stanford University.* 310 pp. Stanford, Calif.: Stanford University Press, 1950.

The 1,226 entries described include manuscripts, printed editions, and inscribed copies of books and scores, with the emphasis on "association items."

Reviewed by Otto E. Albrecht in *Notes* 8 (1951): 706–9.

Stockholm, Sweden

MUSIKALISKA AKADEMIEN

7.479 Bengtsson, Ingmar. *Mr. Roman's Spuriosity Shop: A Thematic Catalogue of 503 Works (1213 Incipits and Other Excerpts) from ca. 1680 to 1750 by More than Sixty Composers.* 95 + 47 pp. Stockholm: Swedish Music History Archive, 1976.

Supplement (December 1976 to March 1980), 1980. 9 pp.

A catalog of more than 1,200 works composed and gathered by Johann Helmich Roman, of which only 250 have supportable attributions.

For another work covering spurious attributions, see **5.4.**

An article from the preface and introduction is in *Fontes* 24 (1977): 121–25.

7.480 Bengtsson, Ingmar, and **Ruben Danielson.** *Handstilar och notpikturer i Kungl. Musikaliska akademiens Roman-samling / Handwriting and Musical Calligraphy in the J. H. Roman Collection of the Swedish Royal Academy of Music.* With an English summary. 74 pp. Uppsala: Almqvist & Wiksells, 1955. (Studia musicologica upsaliensia, 3)

A brief guide to the collection, with some facsimiles.

STIFTELSEN MUSIKKULTURENS FRAMJANDE / FOUNDATION FOR THE PROMOTION OF MUSICAL CULTURE

7.481 *Förtekning över musikhandskrifter: Musikalier, brev och biografica / Catalog of Music Manuscripts, Letters and Biographical Documents.* 51 pp. Stockholm: Svenskt Musikhistoriskt Arkiv, 1972. (Bulletin, 8)

A preliminary catalog, or checklist, of the manuscript collection of Rudolf Nydahl, Stockholm, now owned by the Foundation for Furthering Musical Culture. About 4,500 items in all, including some 1,200 autographs, correspondence, and other documents. The catalog is in two parts: music manuscripts, and letters and other documents. The collection is strong in the work of 19th-century musicians.

Strasbourg, France

ARCHIVES DE LA VILLE

7.482 Kopff, René. "Aperçu général sur les sources dans les Archives de la Ville de Strasbourg." In *Fontes* 26 (1979): 47–54.

An inventory of musical documents in the city archives as well as the archives of St. Thomas Church, the Cathedral, and the musicologist Eugene Wagner.

Stuttgart, Germany

WÜRTTEMBERGISCHE LANDESBIBLIOTHEK

7.483 Gottwald, Clytus. *Die Handschriften der Württembergischen Landesbibliothek Stuttgart. Erste Reihe, erster Band: Codices musici (Cod. Mus. fol. I 1–71).* 184 pp. Wiesbaden: Otto Harrassowitz, 1964.

A description of 53 manuscripts in mensural notation and 18 plainchant sources, giving concordances for texts and music, an index of text incipits, and a thematic catalog for anonymous works, with full bibliographical apparatus. This is an exemplary catalog.

Reviewed by Franz Krautwurst in *Die Musikforschung* 21 (1968): 233–37.

7.484 Gottwald, Clytus. *Die Handschriften der Württembergischen Landesbibliothek Stuttgart. Zweite Reihe: Die Handschriften der ehemaligen königlichen Hofbibliothek. Sechster Band: Codices musici. Erster Teil.* 66 pp. Wiesbaden: Otto Harrassowitz, 1965.

The continuation of the cataloging begun in the preceding vol., covering a different series of manuscripts.

Reviewed by Ute Schwab in *Die Musikforschung* 24 (1971): 210–12.

7.485 Halm, A. *Katalog über die Musik-Codices des 16. und 17. Jahrhunderts auf der K. Landesbibliothek in Stuttgart.* 58 pp. Langensalza, Germany: Beyer, 1902–3. (Monatshefte für Musikgeschichte. Beilage. Jahrgang 34–35)

A catalog citing 70 manuscripts, with lists of contents for each. There is an index to text incipits under individual composers.

Sucre, Bolivia

CATEDRAL PLATENSE

7.486 García Muñoz, Carmen, and **Waldemar Axel Roldán.** *Un archivo musical Americano.* 166 pp. Buenos Aires: Editorial Universitaria de Buenos Aires, 1972.

A manuscript catalog (pp. 51–96) containing 183 numbered items.

Sweden

Swedish bibliographer Åke Davidsson has prepared union catalogs of early printed music and music theory works in Swedish libraries. See his *Catalogue critique et descriptif des ouvrages théoriques sur la musique imprimés au XVIe et au XVIIe siècles et conservés dans les bibliothèques suedoises* (**4.379**) and his *Bibliographie der musiktheoretischen Drucke des 16. Jahrhunderts* (**4.378**).

Syracuse, New York

SYRACUSE UNIVERSITY. GEORGE ARENTS RESEARCH LIBRARY

7.487 Garlington, Aubrey S. *Sources for the Study of 19th-Century Opera in the Syracuse University Libraries: An Annotated Libretti List.* 563 pp. Syracuse, N.Y.: Syracuse University Libraries, 1976.

A catalog of libretti, indexed by composer, librettist, choreographer, etc. Addenda are given, pp. 445–70.

Tenbury Wells, England

ST. MICHAEL'S COLLEGE (TENBURY). LIBRARY

7.488 *Auction Catalogues of the Toulouse-Philidor Collection, the Late Property of St. Michael's College, Tenbury, Eng.: Sold by Auction by Sotheby Parke Bernet & Co., London 26 June 1978 and Pierre Beres, Paris 30 Nov. 1978.* 2 vols. London; Paris: Sotheby Parke Bernet, 1978.

Preauction catalog of a sale that resulted in the dissolution of part of one of England's most distinguished collections. Materials from the St. Michael's College Toulouse-Philidor collection found new homes in the British Library, the Bibliothèque Nationale in Paris, and the University of North Carolina at Chapel Hill, among other institutions. For further information about the holdings that were acquired by the Bibliothèque Nationale, see **7.388.**

7.489 Bray, Roger. *The Music Collection of St. Michael's College, Tenbury: A Listing and Guide to Parts One to Five.* 98 pp. Brighton: Harvester Press Microform Publications, 1983–86.

The *Catalogue of Manuscripts in the Library of St. Michael's College,* compiled by E. H. Fellowes, "has been completely revised" and reproduced in full on the first reel. Like the other Harvester guides, this work includes a list of the contents of each reel in each part and a list of the manuscripts in each part, followed by a unified index of names and composers in the volume. There is also a numerical index to the manuscript volumes in the collection.

7.490 Fellowes, E. H. *The Catalogue of Manuscripts in the Library of St. Michael's College, Tenbury.* 319 pp. Paris: Éditions de l'Oiseau-Lyre, 1934.

Manuscripts in the library bequeathed to the College by Sir Frederick Ouseley. There are 1,386 items, rich in early English music. The Toulouse-Philidor collection, 290 vols. of manuscripts and 67 printed books devoted to the repertory of early 18th-century French opera, was sold in 1978 (**7.488**). The other manuscripts are now at the Bodleian Library, Oxford. There is a composer index.

7.491 Fellowes, E. H. *A Summary Catalogue of the Printed Books and Music in the Library of St. Michael's College, Tenbury.* 143 ll. (unpublished manuscript).

An unpublished catalog of the printed books and music in the library of St. Michael's College, intended as a companion volume to the manuscript catalog (**7.490**) but never printed. The collection of printed materials is now at the Bodleian Library, Oxford, except for duplicates, which have been sold.

Tokyo, Japan

MUSASHINO ACADEMIA MUSICAE. BIBLIOTECA

7.492 *List of Acquisition.* Tokyo: Musashino Academia Musicae, 1957– . No. l– .

Text in Japanese and English.

An annual volume with a classified list of both books and scores acquired from April of one year to March of the next. The first section of each issue is devoted to rare materials.

7.493 *Litterae rarae.* Tokyo: Musashino Academia Musicae, 1962– . Liber primus– .

A catalog of rare music materials added to the collection, published irregularly. Liber Secundus appeared in 1969, 276 pp. This collection is rich in first or early editions of music and music literature from the 16th–19th centuries.

NANKI MUSIC LIBRARY

7.494 *Catalogue of the Nanki Music Library. Part I: Musicology.* 372 pp. Tokyo, 1929.

A reference library for the historical study of Western music. Much of the material came from the collection of W. H. Cummings, an English collector whose library was sold at auction in 1918.

7.495 *Catalogue of Rare Books and Notes: The Ohki Collection, Nanki Music Library.* 60 pp. Tokyo, 1970.

7.496 *Catalogue of the W. H. Cummings Collection in the Nanki Music Library.* 70 pp. Tokyo, 1925.

A catalog focused on the rare materials acquired in the Cummings sale, describing about 450 items, including much important early English music.

Toledo, Ohio

MUSEUM OF ART

7.497 *The Printed Note: 500 Years of Music Printing and Engraving, January 1957.* 144 pp. Toledo, Ohio: Museum of Art, 1957.

Foreword by A. Beverly Barksdale.

The splendidly illustrated catalog of an exhibition devoted to the history of music printing and engraving. Listed are 188 items, on loan from major public and private collections through-out the country, with informative annotations and a bibliography.

Toledo, Spain

BIBLIOTECA CAPITULAR

7.498 Lenaerts, René. "Les manuscrits polyphoniques de la Bibliothèque Capitulaire de Tolede." In *International Society for Musical Research, Fifth Congress, Utrecht, 1952,* pp. 267–81.

Brief descriptions and discussion of about 30 sources of early polyphonic music in the Toledo library.

Toronto, Canada

UNIVERSITY OF TORONTO. THOMAS FISHER
RAREBOOK LIBRARY

7.499 Elliott, Robert, and **Harry M. White.** "A Collection of Oratorio Libretti, 1700–1800, in the Thomas Fisher Rarebook Library, University of Toronto." In *Fontes* 32 (1985): 102–13.

A collection including opera libretti that are not included in this inventory but are included in Beatrice Corrigan's *Catalogue of Italian Plays, 1500–1700, in the University of Toronto* (Toronto: University of Toronto Press, 1961). The arrangement is in chronological order in chart form, with indexes to librettists and composers.

Treviso, Italy

ARCHIVIO MUSICALE DEL DUOMO

7.500 D'Alessi, Giovanni. *La Cappella Musicale del Duomo di Treviso (1300–1633).* 272 pp. Vedelago, Italy: Tipografia "Ars et Religio," 1954.

A historical study of the musical establishment of the cathedral at Treviso. Chapter 15 (pp. 169–218) deals with the musical archive and its resources. Manuscripts are listed briefly; printed works are given greater detail.

BIBLIOTECA CAPITOLARE DEL DUOMO

7.501* Ferrarese, Francesca, and **Cristina Gallo.** *Il fondo musicale della Biblioteca Capitolare del Duomo di Treviso.* xxvii + 395 pp. Rome: Torre d'Orfeo, 1990. (Cataloghi di fondi musicali italiani, 12)

Catalog of the music holdings of the Biblioteca Capitolare of Treviso Cathedral, a collection especially strong in 16th- and 17th-century music, including musical incipits, bibliographical references, and indexes.

Reviewed by Graham Dixon in *M&L* 73 (1992): 98–99.

Trossingen, Germany

BUNDESAKADEMIE FÜR MUSIKALISCHE
JUGENDBILDUNG

7.502* *Literatur für zwei und mehr verschiedene Blechblasinstrumente.* 224 pp. Trossingen, Germany: Bundesakademie für Musikalische Jugendbildung, 1994. (Repertoireverzeichnis, 1)

A list of basic works for brass ensemble, with indexes providing additional access.

7.503* *Literatur für zwei und mehr verschiedene Holzblasinstrumente (auch gemischt mit Blechblasinstrumente).* 161 pp. Trossingen, Germany: Bundesakademie für Musikalische Jugendbildung, 1994. (Repertoireverzeichnis, 2)

A list of basic works for woodwind ensembles, with indexes providing additional access.

Tulln, Austria

PFARRKIRCHE ST. STEPHAN

7.504 Schnürl, Karl. *Das alte Musikarchiv der Pfarrkirche St. Stephan in Tulln.* 88 pp. Vienna: In Kommission bei Hermann Böhlau Nachf., 1964. (Tabulae musicae austriacae, 1)

A catalog, partially thematic, chiefly concerned with manuscripts, although a short section of printed editions is included. The principal composers represented are Albrechtsberger, Diabelli, Eybler, Joseph and Michael Haydn, Mozart, Schubert, and Winter.

Reviewed by Imogene Horsley in *Notes* 24 (1967): 52–53.

Turin, Italy

BIBLIOTECA DI S. M. IL RE

7.505* Fragalà-Data, Isabella. *L'encomio discreto: Catalogo delle musiche encomiastiche e celebrative della Biblioteca Reale di Torino.* xxxi + 475 pp. Turin: Centro Studi Piemontesi, 1991. (Il gridelino, 12)

BIBLIOTECA NAZIONALE

7.506 Cimbro, Attilio, and **Alberto Gentili.** *Catalogo delle opere musicali teoriche e pratiche di autori vissuti sino ai primi decenni del secolo XIX. esistenti nelle biblioteche e negli archivi pubblici e privati d'Italia: Città di Torino: R. Biblioteca Nazionale.* 38 pp. Parma, Italy: Freschig, 1928. (Associazione dei Musicologi Italiani. Catalogo delle opere musicali, 12)

Reprinted by Forni, Bologna, 1978 (Bibliotheca musica Bononiensis, I, 14).

7.507* Fragalà-Data, Isabella, and **Annarita Colturato.** *Biblioteca Nazionale Universitaria di Torino, I: Raccolta Mauro Foà: Raccolta Renzo Giordano.* lxxxvii + 613 pp. Rome: Edizioni Torre d'Orfeo, 1987. (Biblioteca Nazionale Universitaria di Torino, 1) (Cataloghi di fondo musicali italiani, a cura della Società Italiana di Musicologia in collaborazione con il Repertoire International des Sources Musicales, 7)

At head of title: Associazione Piemonte per la Ricerca delle Fonti Musicali.

The catalogs of two 18th-century collections containing many Vivaldi, Stradella, Pallavicino, Legrenzi, Giovanni Gabrieli, and Merulo scores, with other sources dating back to the mid-16th century. Incipits for works not otherwise cataloged in other reference works are supplied, but no incipits for Vivaldi instrumental works are given. Instead, there are references to Ryom (**6.371**). There is an index to text incipits.

Reviewed by Thomas F. Heck in *Fontes* 37 (1990): 202–4, by Eleanor Selfridge-Field in *Notes* 47 (1990): 371–72, and by Michael Talbot in *M&L* 70 (1989): 396–98.

7.508 Gentili, Alberto. "La raccolta di antiche musiche 'Renzo Giordano' alla Biblioteca Nazionale di Torino." In *Accademie e biblioteche d'Italia* 4 (1930–31): 117–25.

A description of the collection of manuscripts of sacred music, instrumental works of Vivaldi and Vanhall, vocal music of Corelli (among others), and operas by Traetta and Vivaldi (among others).

7.509 Gentili, Alberto. "La raccolta di rarità musicali 'Mauro Foà' alla Biblioteca Nazionale di Torino." In *Accademie e biblioteche d'Italia* 1 (1927): 36–50.

A descriptive account of a collection of 95 volumes, both manuscript and prints, founded by Count Giacomo Durazzo, Genoan Ambassador to Venice in 1765. Included are autographs of Vivaldi and Stradella, as well as organ tablatures (**7.510**).

7.510 Mischiati, Oscar. "L'intavolatura d'organo tedesca della Biblioteca Nazionale di Torino: Catalogo ragionato." In *L'Organo, rivista di cultura organaria e organistica* 4 (1963): 1–154.

An inventory of the contents of 16 volumes of German organ tablature in the National Library in Turin, the largest body of source material for German organ music known. The manuscripts contain 1,770 compositions on 2,703 written folios, compiled between 1637 and 1640. Appendixes include paleographical descriptions of the volumes, author lists added by later hands, watermarks, concordant printed editions, manuscripts and modern editions, and an index of composers.

Tuy, Spain

7.511* Trillo, Joám, and **Carlos Villanueva.** *La música en la Catedral de Tui.* xxiii + 555 pp. La Coruña, Spain: Diputación de la Coruña, 1987.

A thematic catalog of manuscripts of sacred vocal music.

Ulm, Germany

7.512* Gottwald, Clytus. *Katalog der Musikalien in der Schermar-Bibliothek Ulm.* xxvi + 185 pp. Wiesbaden: Harrassowitz, 1993. (Veröffentlichungen der Stadtbibliothek Ulm, 17)

A catalog, in part with thematic incipits, of the published and manuscript music of the 16th and early 17th centuries held by the Schermar family library, administered since 1977 by the Stadtbibliothek Ulm.

Umbria, Italy

7.513* Ciliberti, Galliano. *Musica e liturgia nelle chiese e conventi dell'Umbria (secoli X–XV) con un atlante—Repertorio dei piu antichi monumenti musicali Umbri di polifonia sacra.* 164 pp. + 92 pp. plates. Perugia, Italy: Cattedra di Storia della Musica, Universita degli Studi di Perugia, Centro di Studi Musicali in Umbria, 1994. (Quaderni di esercizi. Musica e spettacolo, 3)

A catalog of the musical archives in Orvieto, Perugia, Città di Castello, Todi, Assisi, and Stroncone. The repertory covered is one of the important collections of Umbrian polyphony.

Union of Soviet Socialist Republics

7.514 Rklitskaya, A. D. *Muzykal´nye biblioteki i muzykal´nye fondy v Bibliotekakh SSSR / Music Libraries and Music Holdings in the Libraries of the USSR: A Guide.* Edited by G. P. Koltypina. 175 pp. Moscow: Gos. Biblioteka SSSR imeni Lenina, Otdel Notnykh Izdanii i Zvukozapisei, 1972.

A guide to 335 libraries in the former USSR, arranged geographically and including any library collection containing music. There are indexes by type of library and to the 53 cities included.

Reviewed by Barbara Krader in *Notes* 30 (1974): 529–30.

United States of America

7.515 Albrecht, Otto E. *A Census of Music Manuscripts of European Composers in American Libraries.* 331 pp. Philadelphia, Pa.: University of Pennsylvania Press, 1953.

A list of 2,017 manuscripts in the United States, organized alphabetically by the 571 European composers represented; title, pagination, dimensions, and descriptive notes are supplied, and both the current and the former owners are given. There is an index of owners, present and former (pp. 317–28).

Reviewed by Emanuel Winternitz in *JAMS* 6 (1953): 169–73, by Jack A. Westrup in *MR* 16 (1955): 84–85, and by Barbara Duncan in *Notes* 10 (1953): 443–44.

7.516 Seaton, Douglass. "Important Library Holdings at Forty-One North American Universities." In *CM* 17 (1974): 7–68.

Brief accounts by domestic corresponding editors of the musical rarities in the libraries of Boston, Columbia, Cornell, Harvard, Indiana, Memphis State, New York, Northwestern, Princeton, Rutgers, Stanford, West Virginia, and Yale Universities; Bryn Mawr College; Catholic University of America; CUNY and its Hunter and Queens College campuses; Juilliard School; the Universities of California at Berkeley, Los Angeles, Riverside, and Santa Barbara; and the Universities of Chicago, Colorado, Illinois, Iowa, Kansas, Maryland, Miami, Michigan, Minnesota, North Carolina at Chapel Hill, Oregon, Pennsylvania, Pittsburgh, Rochester (Eastman), Texas, Washington, Western Ontario, and Wyoming.

Unna, Germany

7.517* Olivier, Antje. *Komponistinnen: Bestandsaufnahme: Die Sammlung des Europäischen Frauenmusikarchivs.* 2nd ed., revised and enlarged. 232 pp. Wuppertal, Germany: Tokkata-Verlag für Frauenmusikarchivs, 1994.

The 1st ed., 1990, 165 pp., listed only the holdings of the European Archives of Women Composers (Europäische Frauenmusikarchiv), Düsseldorf, through September 1990.

A descriptive itemization of the collection of the Internationale Komponistinnen-Bibliothek / International Library of Women Composers, Unna, Germany, where the holdings of the former European Archives of Women Composers (Europäische Frauenmusikarchiv), formerly in Düsseldorf, combined with a large private collection, are now housed. The catalog lists scores, sound recordings, and books, and is usefully ornamented with full-page reproductions of title pages and excerpts from compositions by women. There is a name index.

Uppsala, Sweden

UNIVERSITETSBIBLIOTEKET

7.518 Davidsson, Åke. *Catalogue critique et descriptif des imprimés de musique des XVIe et XVIIe siècles conservé à la Bibliothèque de l'Université Royale d'Upsala.* 3 vols. Uppsala: Almqvist et Wiksell, 1911–51.

Contents: Vol. 1, *Musique religieuse, I* (by Rafael Mitjana, 1911); Vol. 2, *Musique religieuse, II; Musique profane, Musique dramatique, Musique instrumentale; Additions au tome I* (1951); Vol. 3, *Recueils de musique religieuse et profane.*

Entries in Vols. 1 and 2 are arranged alphabetically within each category; Vol. 3 is chronological, with an index of the contents of the collections under composer. The 605 bibliographical entries have full citations, including locations of copies in other libraries. Includes an index of printers and publishers and a bibliography of 258 works cited in the catalog's notes.

Reviewed by Otto Kinkeldey in *Notes* 9 (1951): 122–23.

7.519 Davidsson, Åke. *Catalogue of the Gimo Collection of Italian Manuscript Music in the University Library of Uppsala.* 101 pp. Uppsala, 1963. (Acta Bibliothecae R. Universitatis Upsaliensis, 14)

A catalog of 360 items of vocal and instrumental music of the 18th century. An introduction relates the history of the collection. There is a useful bibliography of sources and related literature.

Reviewed by Minnie Elmer in *Notes* 22 (1965): 715–16 and by R. Thurston Dart in *Library,* ser. 5, 20 (June 1965): 166–67.

UNIVERSITETSBIBLIOTEKET. DÜBEN SAMLING

7.520 Grusnick, Bruno. "Die Dubensammlung: Ein Versuch ihrer chronologischen Ordnung." In *Svensk tidskrift för musikforskning* 46 (1964): 27–82; 48 (1966): 63–186.

The collection of music gathered mostly by Gustaf Düben, an organist and composer in Stockholm, 1648–90. The collection consists of approximately 1,500 manuscripts of vocal sacred music, 300 manuscripts of instrumental music, and some printed works. One of the largest collections of 17th-century music extant, it contains many unica and a Buxtehude autograph, as well as numerous contemporaneous copies. The article cites copyists, displays watermarks, and shows the development of the collection chronologically.

Valencia (Region), Spain

7.521 Climent Barber, José. *Fondos musicales de la región valenciana.* 4 vols. to date. Valencia: Instituto de Musicología, Institución Alfonso el Magnánimo, Diputación Provincial, 1979– .

Contents: Vol. 1, *Catedral Metropolitana de Valencia* (471 pp.); Vol. 2, *Real Colegio de Corpus Christi Patriarca* (849 pp.); Vol. 3, *Catedral de Segorbe.*

Vol. 1 covers the manuscripts and printed works in the Catedral Metropolitana de Valencia (1979, 471 pp.), a very large collection. Biographical notes on composers are provided, but only brief bibliographical descriptions of the sources are given. There is an index to names. Vol. 2

covers the manuscripts and printed works in the Archivio Musical of the Real Colegio de Corpus Christi Patriarca, which was an extraordinary musical establishment.

Valladolid, Spain

CATEDRAL. ARCHIVO MUSICAL

7.522 Anglès, Higinio. "El Archivo Musical de la Catedral de Valladolid." In *Anuario musical* 3 (1948): 59–108.

A short catalog listing 20 manuscripts and 97 early printed books. Inventories are given for the contents of the manuscripts and full bibliographic descriptions are given for the prints, with references to Eitner (**5.544**) and other bibliographies.

Vatican City

BIBLIOTECA APOSTOLICA VATICANA

7.523 Bannister, H. M. *Monumenti vaticani di paleografia musicale latina.* 2 vols. 130 plates. Leipzig: Otto Harrassowitz, 1913. (Codices e vaticanis selecti, 12)

Reprinted by the Gregg Press, 1969.

A vol. of commentary and a vol. of plates containing excerpts from Vatican manuscripts, assembled for the purpose of paleographical study. There is a vast amount of information on the manuscript sources of plainchant in the Vatican Library.

7.524* Gialdroni, Giuliana, and **Teresa M. Gialdroni.** *Libretti per musica del Fondo Ferrajoli della Biblioteca Apostolica Vaticana.* 540 pp. Lucca, Italy: Libraria Musicale Italiana; Vatican City: Biblioteca Apostolica Vaticana, 1993. (Ancilla musicae, 4)

7.525 Liess, Andreas. "Die Sammlungen der Oratorienlibretti (1679–1725) und dem restlichen Musikbestand der Fondo San Marcello der Biblioteca Vaticano in Rom." In *Acta musicologica* 31 (1959): 63–80.

A list of 106 oratorio libretti in the Fondo San Marcello of the Biblioteca Vaticana, with information on the entry's citation in Eitner (**5.544**).

7.526* Mori, Elisabetta. *Libretti di melodrammi e balli del secolo XVIII: Fondo Ferraioli della Biblioteca Apostolica Vaticana.* 226 pp. Florence: L.S. Olschki, 1984. (Biblioteconomia e bibliografia, 19)

A catalog of the Ferraioli collection of 18th-century opera libretti.

7.527* Münch, Christoph. *Musikzeugnisse der Reichsabtei Lorsch: Eine Untersuchung der Lorscher musikalischen Handschriften in der Biblioteca Palatina in der Vatikanischen Bibliothek.* 135 pp. Lorsch, Germany: Verlag Laurissa, 1993.

BIBLIOTECA APOSTOLICA VATICANA.
CAPPELLA GIULIA

7.528 Llorens, José M. *Le opere musicali della Cappella Giulia. I: Manoscritti e edizioni fino al '700.* 412 pp. Vatican City: Biblioteca Apostolica Vaticana, 1971. (Studi e testi, 265)

Reviewed by Samuel F. Pogue in *Notes* 29 (1973): 445–48.

BIBLIOTECA APOSTOLICA VATICANA.
CAPPELLA SISTINA

7.529 Haberl, Franz Xaver. *Bibliographischer und thematischer Musikkatalog des Päpstlichen Kapellarchives im Vatikan zu Rom.* 183 pp. Leipzig: Breitkopf & Härtel, 1888. (Monatshefte für Musikgeschichte. Beilage. Jahrgang 19/20)

Descriptions of 269 items, manuscripts and early printed works, with a thematic catalog, by composer, of the early polyphonic sources. There is considerable documentation on the Cappella Sistina and the musicians employed there. The Haberl catalog represents only a small part of the Cappella Sistina collection. See **7.530**.

7.530 Llorens, José M. *Capellae Sixtinae codices musicis notis instructi sive manuscripti sive praelo excussi.* 555 pp. Vatican City: Biblioteca Apostolica Vaticana, 1960.

A catalog of the collection treated by Franz Xaver Haberl (**7.529**) but much more thoroughly (Haberl covered only 269 of the 660 manuscripts and printed volumes present). The volumes are listed by number, with detailed inventories of contents and descriptive Latin annotations. There are thematic lists of anonymous works.

Reviewed by Dragan Plamenac in *Notes* 19 (1961): 251–52, by Peter Peacock in *M&L* 42 (1961): 168–69, and by Glen Haydon in *MQ* 48 (1962): 127–29.

Venice, Italy

7.531 Concina, Giovanni. *Catalogo generale delle opere musicali: Città di Venezia: Biblioteca Querini Stampalia* (pp. 1–25), *Museo Correr* (pp. 29–113), *Pia Casa di Ricovero* (pp. 117–61), and *R. Biblioteca di S. Marco* (compiled by Taddeo Wiel, A. d'Este, R. Fausini) (pp. 169–382). 382 pp. Parma, Italy: Freschig, 1910–38. (Associazione dei Musicologi Italiani. Catalogo delle opere musicali, 6/1)

Reprinted by Forni, Bologna, 1983.

BIBLIOTECA DEL PALAZZO GIUSTINIAN LOLIN

7.532 Cisilino, Siro. *Stampe e manoscritti preziosi e rari della Biblioteca del Palazzo Giustinian Lolin a San Vidal.* 55 pp. Venice: A cura del Fondatore Dott. Ugo Levi sotto gli auspici dell'Ateneo Veneto, 1966.

At head of title: Fondazione Ugo e Olga Levi, Centro di Cultura Musicale Superiore.

The catalog of the library of a musical foundation in Venice, listing 70 items, including printed books and manuscripts from the 16th to the early 19th centuries. Many of the manuscripts are composite in content. The collection contains important source materials for the study of 18th-century instrumental music.

BIBLIOTECA NAZIONALE MARCIANA

7.533 Wiel, Taddeo. *I codici musicali Contariniani del secolo XVII nella R. Biblioteca di San Marco in Venezia.* 121 pp. Venice: F. Ongania, 1888.

Reprinted by Forni, Bologna, 1969.

The catalog of the Contarini collection, a special library of 120 manuscript scores of 17th-century Venetian opera by such composers as Cesti, Cavalli, Pallavicino, and Ziani. The 100 numbered entries give the date of first performance, librettist, cast, and a general description of the work. There is a composer index.

BIBLIOTECA QUERINI-STAMPALIA

7.534* Rossi, Franco. *Le opere musicali della Fondazione "Querini-Stampalia" di Venezia.* xxvii + 279 pp. Turin: EDT/Musica, 1984. (Cataloghi di fondi musicali italiani, 2)

A collection of 18 vols. of late-17th-century opera arias, with generous indexes.

Reviewed by Graham Dixon in *EM* 15 (1987): 261–63 and by Peter Ward Jones in *M&L* 70 (1989): 258–59.

CONSERVATORIO BENEDETTO MARCELLO

7.535* Bianchini, Gigliola, and **Gianni Bosticco.** *Liceo-Società musicale Conservatorio*

"Benedetto Marcello," 1877–1895: *Catalogo dei manoscritti (Prima serie).* li + 335 pp. Florence: L.S. Olschki, 1989. ("Historiae Musicae Cultores." Biblioteca, 48)

> At head of title: Conservatorio Benedetto Marcello, Fondazione Ugo e Olga Levi.
> There are musical incipits (pp. 215–90).
> Reviewed by Michael Talbot in *M&L* 72 (1991): 274–76.

7.536* Bianchini, Gigliola, and **Caterina Manfredi.** *Il fondo Pascolato del Conservatorio "Benedetto Marcello": Catalogo dei manoscritti (prima serie).* xlv + 421 pp. Florence: L.S. Olschki, 1990. (Catalogo dei fondi storici della Biblioteca del Conservatorio di Musica Benedetto Marcello, Venezia, 4) ("Historiae Musicae Cultores." Biblioteca, 52)

> A catalog of the collection that Michele Pascolato donated to the library of the Conservatory, with musical incipits (pp. 299–385).

7.537* De Sanctis, Stefano, and **Nadia Nigris.** *Il fondo musicale dell'I.R.E.: Istituzioni di ricovero e di educazione di Venezia.* xxxvii + 324 pp. Rome: Torre d'Orfeo, 1990. (Cataloghi di fondi musicali italiani, 13)

> The thematic catalog of the music holdings of the Istituzioni, 481 items, including 30 from the Ospedaletto (the Ospedale dei Poveri Derelitti ai SS Giovanni e Paolo, one of the four *ospedali grandi*). A nonthematic catalog of the holdings was published by the Associazione dei Musicologi Italiani in 1914.
> Reviewed by Michael Talbot in *M&L* 73 (1992): 123–25.

7.538* Fabiano, Andrea. *Le stampe musicali antiche del fondo Torrefranca del Conservatorio Benedetto Marcello.* 2 vols. xxiii + 773 pp. Florence: L.S. Olschki, 1992. (Catalogo dei fondi storici della Biblioteca del Conservatorio di Musica Benedetto Marcello, Venezia, 5) ("Historiae Musicae Cultores." Biblioteca, 65)

7.539* Miggiani, Maria Giovanna. *Il fondo giustiniani del Conservatorio "Benedetto Marcello": Catalogo dei manoscritti e delle stampe.* lvi + 613 pp. Florence: L.S. Olschki, 1990. (Catalogo dei fondi storici della Biblioteca del Conservatorio di Musica Benedetto Marcello, Venezia, 3) ("Historiae Musicae Cultores." Biblioteca, 51)

> At head of title: Conservatorio Benedetto Marcello, Fondazione Ugo e Olga Levi.
> There are musical incipits (pp. 435–552).
> Reviewed by Michael Talbot in *M&L* 72 (1991): 274–76.

7.540* Negri, Emanuela, Sabina Corbini, Francesca Gatta, and **Livio Argona.** *Catalogo dei Libretti del Conservatorio Benedetto Marcello.* 4 vols. (to date). Florence: Leo S. Olschki, 1994–95. (Catalogo dei fondo storici della Biblioteca del Conservatorio di Musica Benedetto Marcello, Venezia, 6–9) ("Historiae Musicae Cultores." Biblioteca, 66, 68, 72, 75)

7.541* Rossi, Franco. *I manoscritti del fondo Torrefranca del Conservatorio Benedetto Marcello.* 357 pp. Florence: L.S. Olschki, 1986. (Catalogo dei fondi storici della Biblioteca del Conservatorio di Musica Benedetto Marcello, Venezia, 1) ("Historiae Musicae Cultores." Biblioteca, 45)

> At head of title: Conservatorio Benedetto Marcello, Fondazione Ugo e Olga Levi.
> This alphabetically ordered catalog of manuscripts in the Torrefranca collection also includes anthologies, libretti, treatises, and nonmusical manuscripts. Some thematic incipits are included.

FONDAZIONE CINI

7.542 Bellina, Anna Laura, Bruno Brizi, and **Maria Grazia Pensa.** *La raccolta di libretti d'opera: Catalogo e indici.* 185 pp. Rome: Istituto della Enciclopedia Italiana Fondata da Giovanni Treccani, 1986.

> A catalog of approximately 40,000 libretti in the Rolandi collection. This vol. provides numerous indexes to the multivolume catalog of the collection, which has been in preparation for some time.

La Fondazione Levi

7.543 Rossi, Franco. *La Fondazione Levi di Venezia: Catalogo del fondo musicale.* 347 pp. Venice: Edizioni Fondazione Levi, 1986. (Edizione Fondazione Levi. Serie III, Studi musicologici. C. Cataloghi e bibliografia)

A classified catalog of the substantial collection developed since 1965, covering manuscripts, pictures of musicians, printed music (many already cited in *RISM*), writings about music, and libretti of operas and oratorios. The entries give a full description, contents analysis, medium of performance, composer and title, and author and title. The libretti are entered by title. There are indexes to titles and text incipits, characters in staged works, and names.

Istituzioni di Ricovero e di Educazione

7.544* De Sanctis, Stefano, and **Nadia Nigris.** *Il fondo musicale dell'I.R.E.: Istituzioni di Ricovero e di Educazione di Venezia.* xxxvii + 324 pp. Rome: Torre d'Orfeo, 1990. (Cataloghi di fondi musicali italiani, 13)

The catalog of the music holdings of the Istituzioni.

Vercelli, Italy

Archivio della Cattedrale

7.545 Sartori, Claudio. "Il fondo musicale dell'Archivio della Cattedrale di Vercelli." In *Fontes* 5 (1958): 24–31.

Verona, Italy

Accademica Filarmonica

7.546 Turrini, Giuseppe. *L'Accademia Filarmonica di Verona, dalla fondazione (maggio 1543) al 1600 e il suo patrimonio musicale antico.* 346 pp. Verona: La Tipografica Veronese, 1941.

A detailed history of the Accademia Filarmonica from its beginnings to 1600. Chapter 16 discusses the holdings of the library on the basis of early inventories. Chapter 17 continues the discussion to the first half of the 19th century. Chapter 18 includes a catalog of the existing materials in the "Fondo Musicale Antico," some 217 prints and 21 manuscripts.

7.547 Turrini, Giuseppe. *Catalogo generale delle opere musicali: Città di Verona: Biblioteca della Soc. Accademica Filarmonica di Verona: Fondo musicale antico.* 54 pp. Parma, Italy: Freschig, 1935–36. (Associazione dei Musicologi Italiani. Catalogo generale delle opere musicali, 14)

Reprinted by Forni, Bologna, 1983.

Biblioteca Capitolare

7.548 Piazzi, A., E. Paganuzzi, V. Donella, and **G. Zivelonghi.** *Mille anni di musica nella Biblioteca Capitolare di Verona.* 127 pp. Verona: Stimmatini, 1985.

A handbook with articles on medieval, renaissance, and modern period holdings, lists of items in the Fondi Musicali, and descriptions of the instruments in the Biblioteca Capitolare, with color facsimiles of manuscript pages. There is a bibliography of writings about music in Verona.

7.549 Turrini, Giuseppe. *Il patrimonio musicale della Biblioteca Capitolare di Verona dal sec. XV al XIX.* 83 pp. Verona: "La Tipografica Veronese," 1953. (Estratto dagli Atti dell'Academia di Agricoltura, Scienze e Lettere di Verona, ser. 6, Vol. 2, pp. 95–176)

Versailles, France

7.550* Herlin, Denis. *Catalogue du fonds musical de la Bibliothèque de Versailles.* clxxiv + 778 pp. Paris: Société Française de Musicologie, 1995. (Publications de la Société Française de Musicologie, 2nd series, 14)

Vicenza, Italy

7.551 Rumor, Sebastiano, and **Primo Zanini.** *Catalogo delle opere musicali: Città di Vicenza; Biblioteca bertoliana; Archivio della cattedrale.* 48 pp. Parma, Italy: Freschig, 1923. (Associazione dei Musicologi Italiani. Catalogo delle opere musicali, 6/2)

    Reprinted by A. Forni, 1980 (Bibliotheca musica Bononiensis, I, 17).

ARCHIVIO CAPITOLARE DEL DUOMO

7.552 Bolcato, Vittorio, and **Alberto Zanotelli.** *Il fondo musicale dell'Archivio Capitolare del Duomo di Vicenza.* xxx + 514 pp. Turin: E.D.T./Musica, 1986. (Cataloghi di fondi musicali Italiani, 4)

    The result of collaboration beween the Società Italiana di Musicologia and *RISM,* this catalog treats a corpus of manuscripts and printed music from the 18th century, 15th- and 16th-century printed music, choir and liturgical books, and a few theoretical works. An index is included.

Vienna, Austria

GESELLSCHAFT DER MUSIKFREUNDE

7.553 Deutsch, Walter, Gerlinde Hofer, and **Leopold Schmidt.** *Die Volksmusiksammlung der Gesellschaft der Musikfreunde in Wien (Sonnleithner-Sammlung), 1. Teil.* 1 vol. to date. 186 pp. Vienna: A. Schendl, 1969. (Schriften zur Volksmusik, 2)

    The catalog of a collection of folk music, chiefly Austrian, begun in 1818. The entries are grouped by genre and by region, with a first-line index of songs and indexes of places and names. There are 29 plates duplicating pages from the collection.

    Reviewed by Hartmut Braun in *Jahrbuch für Volksliedforschung* 15 (1970): 159–60.

7.554 *Geschichte der Gesellschaft der Musikfreunde in Wien, 1912–1927* (Fortsetzung der Festschrift zur Jahrhundertfeier vom Jahre 1912). 125 + 42 pp. Vienna: Im Selbstverlage der Gesellschaft der Musikfreunde, 1937.

    A continuation of the documentation given in **7.555.** Of particular interest is Hedwig Kraus's "Die Sammlungen der Musikfreunde, 1912–1937," pp. 1–42.

7.555 Mandyczewski, Eusebius. *Geschichte der K. K. Gesellschaft der Musikfreunde in Wien. In einem Zusatzbande: "Die Sammlungen und Statuten."* 2 vols. Vienna: Adolf Holzhausen, 1912.

    An account of the venerable Viennese musical institution. Vol. 1 is a history of the Gesellschaft from 1812 to 1870 and from 1870 to 1912. Vol. 2, "Zusatz-Band," is not a true catalog but a summary list of the holdings of the archive, library, and museum. Of particular value are Mandyczewski's lists of "Bücher und Schriften über Musik. Druckwerke und Handschriften aus der Zeit bis zum Jahre 1800" (pp. 55–84) and of "Musik-Autographe" (pp. 85–123).

HOFTHEATER

7.556 *Katalog der Portrait-Sammlung der K. V. K. General-Intendanz der K. K. Hoftheater: Zugleich ein biographisches Hilfsbuch auf dem Gebiet von Theater und Musik.* 3 vols. Vienna: Commissions-Verlag von Adolph W. Kunast, 1892–94.

The catalog of a large collection of portraits and other graphic materials related to the theater, classified according to type of theater or kind of entertainment. Gruppe III, Vol. 1 (pp. 119–264) is concerned with pictorial documents on musicians, composers, librettists, concert singers, and writers on music.

INTERNATIONALE AUSSTELLUNG FÜR MUSIK-UND THEATERWESEN

7.557 Adler, Guido. *Fach-Katalog der Musikhistorischen Abteilung von Deutschland und Österreich-Ungarn.* 592 pp. Vienna: Im Selbstverlag der Ausstellungs-Commission, 1892.

The catalog for a large and varied music exhibition held in Vienna in 1892. Included are prints, manuscripts, instruments, portraits, letters, and other documents arranged roughly in chronological order from ancient times to the end of the 19th century.

MINORITENKONVENT

7.558 Riedel, Friedrich Wilhelm. *Das Musikarchiv im Minoritenkonvent zu Wien (Katalog des alteren Bestandes vor 1784).* 139 pp. Kassel, Germany: Bärenreiter, 1963. (Catalogus musicus, 1)

A broadly classified catalog of manuscripts and printed music, chiefly 17th and 18th century, strong in early keyboard music. There are indexes of composers, copyists, and former owners. Reviewed by Othmar Wessely in *Die Musikforschung* 18 (1965): 204–6.

ÖSTERREICHISCHE NATIONALBIBLIOTHEK

7.559* Brosche, Günter. *Beiträge zur musikalische Quellenkunde: Kataloge der Sammlung Hans P. Wertitsch in der Musiksammlung der Österreichischen Nationalbibliothek.* 522 pp. Tutzing, Germany: H. Schneider, 1989. (Publikationen des Instituts für Österreichische Musikdokumentation, 15)

The catalog, with essay-length annotations, of a collection of manuscripts of European composers mainly of the 19th and 20th centuries.

7.560 Grasberger, Franz. *Die Musiksammlung der Österreichischen Nationalbibliothek, Funktion und Benutzung.* 100 pp. Vienna: Österreichische Nationalbibliothek, 1980.

Other editions published in 1978 (70 pp.) and 1970.

A library catalog that includes bibliographical references and an index. Versions were produced in English (1972), Spanish (1971), and French (1971).

7.561 Haas, Robert. *Die Estensischen Musikalien: Thematisches Verzeichnis mit Einleitung.* 232 pp. Regensburg: G. Bosse, 1927.

Reissued as *Forschungsbeiträge zur Musikwissenschaft,* 7 (Regensburg: G. Bosse, 1957).

The catalog, largely thematic, of an important collection of 18th-century instrumental music originating in northern Italy. Included is a small group of cantatas and other vocal works. The catalog is classified with major sections of printed editions and manuscripts, and indexes of names and text incipits.

7.562 Haas, Robert. "Die Musiksammlung der Nationalbibliothek." In *Jahrbuch der Musikbibliothek Peters* 37 (1930): 48–62.

7.563 *Katalog der Handschriften Österreichische Nationalbibliothek, Wien, Musiksammlung.* 106 microfiches with 29-pp. booklet. Vienna: Olms Microform, 1983. (Die Europäische Musik. I, Kataloge, 1)

The photographic reproduction of the music manuscript catalog. Günther Brosche's booklet, *Die Musiksammlung der Österreichischen Nationalbibliothek und ihr Handschriftenkatalog,* accompanies the set.

7.564 Leibnitz, Thomas. *Österreichische Spätromantiker: Studien zu Emil Nikolaus von Reznicek, Joseph Marx, Franz Schmidt und Egon Kornauth: Mit einer Dokumentation der handschriftlichen Quellen in der Musiksammlung der Österreichischen Nationalbibliothek.* 182 pp. Tutzing, Germany: H. Schneider, 1986. (Institut für Österreichische Musikdokumentation, 11)

A monograph on some early-20th-century Viennese composers, with a catalog of the manuscript sources.

7.565 Maier, Elizabeth. *Die Lautentabulaturhandschriften der Österreichischen National-bibliothek (17. und 18. Jahrhundert).* 131 pp. Vienna: Verlag der Österreichischen Akademie der Wissenschaften, 1974. (Tabulae musicae austriacae, 8)

A thematic catalog to the contents of nine manuscripts, with references to modern editions and an extensive introduction. There is an index of names and titles or captions.

7.566 Manuani, Joseph. *Tabulae codicum manuscriptorum praeter graecos et orientales in Bibliotheca Palatina Vindobonensi asservatorum . . . x. LX–X: Codicum musicorum, Pars I–II.* 2 vols. in 1. Vindobonae, Austria: Venum dat. Geroldi Filius, 1897–99.

The catalog of the manuscripts numbered 15,501–19,500, comprising the music manuscript holdings of the Austrian National Library, with an introduction and descriptive notes in Latin. Each volume has an index of names, subjects, and text incipits.

7.567* *Musiksammlung.* 407 negative microfiches. Vienna: Olms Microform, 1983.

Contents: *Katalog der Musikschriften* (106 fiches); *Alter Katalog der Musikdrucke* (249 fiches); and *Katalog der Libretti* (52 fiches).

Microfiche edition of the manuscript and typescript card catalog.

7.568 Nowak, Leopold. "Die Musiksammlung." In *Die Österreichische Nationalbibliothek: Festschrift herausgegeben zum 25. jahrigen Dienstjubiläum des Generaldirektors Prof. Dr. Josef Bick,* pp. 119–38. Vienna: H. Bauer-Verlag, 1948.

7.569 Schaal, Richard. "Die Musikbibliothek von Raimund Fugger d.J.: Ein Beitrag zur Musiküberlieferung des 16. Jahrhunderts." In *Acta musicologica* 29 (1957): 126–37.

The catalog of the Fugger library, from a 16th-century manuscript in the Bavarian State Library, Munich. The bulk of the Fugger family music collection is now in the Austrian National Library.

7.570 Ziffer, Agnes. *Österreichische Nationalbibliothek: Photogrammarchiv: Katalog des Archivs für Photogramme musikalischer Meisterhandschriften, Widmung Anthony van Hoboken.* 1 vol. to date. 482 pp. Wien: Prachner, 1967– . (Museion; neue Folge, 3. Reihe, 3. Veröffentlichungen der Österreichischen Nationalbibliothek)

An archive of photocopies of the autographs of a selected group of great composers, chiefly Viennese, founded in 1927 by Anthony van Hoboken and Heinrich Schenker; there are 2,684 entries, with many references to related literature.

ÖSTERREICHISCHE NATIONALBIBLIOTHEK.
MUSIKSAMMLUNG. SAMMLUNG ANTHONY VAN
HOBOKEN

7.571* Brosche, Günther. *Katalog der Sammlung Anthony van Hoboken in der Musiksammlung der Österreichischen Nationalbibliothek, musicalische Erst- und Fruhdrucke.* Edited for the Institute for Austrian Music Documentation under the direction of Günther Brosche. 11 vols. to date. Tutzing, Germany: H. Schneider, 1983– .

Contents: Bd. 1, *Johann Sebastian Bach und seine Söhne* (edited by Thomas Leibnitz); Bd. 2, *Ludwig van Beethoven* (edited by Karin Breitner and Thomas Leibnitz); Bd. 3, *Ludwig van Beethoven: Werke ohne Opuszahl und Sammelausgaben* (edited by Thomas Leibnitz); Bd. 4,

Johannes Brahms, Frédéric Chopin (edited by Karin Breitner and Thomas Leibnitz); Bd. 5, *Christoph Willibald Gluck, Georg Friedrich Händel* (edited by Karin Breitner); Bd. 6, *Joseph Haydn, Symphonien (Hob. I, Ia)* (edited by Karin Breitner); Bd. 7, *Joseph Haydn Instrumentalmusik (Hob. II–XI)* (edited by Karin Breitner); Bd. 8, *Joseph Haydn Instrumentalmusik (Hob. XIV–XX/1)* (edited by Karin Breitner); Bd. 9, *Joseph Haydn: Vocalmusik (Hob. XX/2–XXXI)* (Edited by Karin Breitner); Bd. 11, *Wolfgang Amadeus Mozart, Werke KV 6–581* (edited by Karin Breitner); Bd. 12, *Wolfgang Amadeus Mozart: Werke KV 585–626a und Anhang* (edited by Karin Breitner).

Catalogs describing the library of first and early editions that once belonged to musicologist and collector Anthony van Hoboken and are now housed in the music section of the Austrian National Library.

Bd. 1 is reviewed by Christoph Wolff in *Notes* 41 (1984): 281–83. Bd. 2 is reviewed by Robert Winter in *Notes* 43 (1986): 41–42. Bde. 7–8 are reviewed by Patricia Elliott in *Notes* 47 (1991): 742–43. Bd. 9 is reviewed by Stephen C. Fisher in *Notes* 50 (1993): 566–68.

Warsaw, Poland

BIBLIOTEKA NARODOWA

7.572 *Katalog mikrofilmów muzycznych (Catalog of Musical Microfilms).* 3 vols. Warsaw: Biblioteka Narodowa, 1956– . Vol. 1– .

A series of catalogs originating in the microfilm archive of the National Library at Warsaw. Three vols.—Vols. 8, 9, and 10—of a larger series (*Katalog mikrofilmów*) are concerned with music. The holdings of numerous Polish libraries are represented.

Vol. 1 (1956) has chiefly manuscripts and printed materials of the 19th century; Vol. 2 (1962), musical documents of the 17th and 18th centuries; and Vol. 3 (1965), historical source materials related to Polish music.

UNIVERSITY LIBRARY

7.573 *Katalog druków muzycznych XVI, XVII e XVIII w. Biblioteki Uniwersytetu warszawskiego. Tom I: Wiek XVI.* 380 pp. Warsaw: Wydawn. Uniwers. Warszawsk, 1970. (Acta bibliothecae universitatis varsoviensis, 7)

Catalog of printed music of the 16th–18th centuries in the University Library at Warsaw. This work is highly praised in a brief description in *Fontes* 19 (1972): 46.

Washington, D.C.

LIBRARY OF CONGRESS. COPYRIGHT OFFICE

7.574 *Dramatic Compositions Copyrighted in the United States, 1870–1916.* 2 vols. Washington, D.C.: Government Printing Office, 1918.

An unaltered reprint was published by Johnson Reprint Corp., New York, 1968.

Reviewed by Lenore Coral in *Notes* 26 (1969): 52–53.

LIBRARY OF CONGRESS. MUSIC DIVISION

7.575 Gewehr, Frances G. *Coolidge Foundation Program for Contemporary Chamber Music: Preliminary Checklist of Works Available for Loan (November 1961).* 38 pp. (typescript). Washington, D.C.: Library of Congress, 1961.

Supplement, April 1963.

A classified list of contemporary chamber music scores and parts that may be borrowed by qualified ensembles for study purposes. Entries give publisher and price; recordings, if available, are also cited.

7.576 Gregory, Julia. *Catalogue of Early Books on Music (before 1800).* 312 pp. Washington, D.C.: Government Printing Office, 1913.

Bartlett, Hazel. *Supplement (Books Acquired by the Library, 1913–42) . . . with a List of Books on Music in Chinese and Japanese.* 143 pp. 1944.

Republication in 1 vol. of the original catalog and its supplement by the Da Capo Press, New York, 1969. The original vol. was "prepared under the direction of O. G. Sonneck."

An early catalog of one of the richest collections of early music theory in the world. The entries conform to the Library's printed catalog cards. The *Supplement* includes "A List of Music in Chinese [by Kuang-ch'ing Wu] and Japanese [by Shiho Sakanishi]" as well as "A List of Books from the Dayton C. Miller Collection."

The reprint ed. is reviewed by Ruth Watanabe in *Notes* 26 (1970): 521–24.

7.577 Library of Congress. *M, ML & MT Shelflist.* 218 microfiches. Ann Arbor, Mich.: University Microfilms International, 1979.

A microfiche edition of the shelf lists of classified materials in the Music Division of the Library of Congress through 1979; thus, a classified catalog.

A study of the LC shelf list was prepared by Michael A. Keller and Holly Rowe and published as "An Analysis of the L.C. Music Shelflist on Microfiche" in *CNV* 78 (1983): 11–18. Additional information on the LC shelf list and its relationship to the actual content of the LC shelves is provided by Robert J. Palian in "Discrepancies between the Keller Shelflist Count and the Contents of the Shelves in the Music Division of the Library of Congress" in *CNV* 83 (June 1984): 43–46.

7.578* *The Music Catalog.* Microfiche. Washington, D.C.: Library of Congress, Cataloging Distribution Service, 1991– .

Issued in two parts: Register and Index.

A serial publication whose first issue was a decennial cumulation; the subsequent quarterly indexes are cumulative for the current year. This is a continuation of *Music, Books on Music, and Sound Recordings* (**5.22**), which was issued in both paper and microfiche editions.

7.579 *The Music Division: A Guide to Its Collections and Services.* 22 pp. Washington, D.C.: Government Printing Office, 1972.

Published in 1960 as *The Music Division in the Library of Congress.*

A brief descriptive account of the work and resources of the Music Division, with illustrations. A later guide including the Music Division was *Library of Congress Music, Theater, Dance: An Illustrated Guide* (Washington, D.C.: The Library, 1993), 80 pp.

7.580 Sonneck, Oscar George Theodore. *Catalogue of Opera Librettos Printed before 1800.* 2 vols. Washington, D.C.: Government Printing Office, 1914.

Reprinted by Johnson Reprint Corp., New York, 1970; and by Burt Franklin, New York, 1967.

The library's collection of libretti began in 1909 with the purchase of the Schatz collection. By 1914 it contained 17,000 items and was particularly strong in first editions of 17th- and 18th-century works. Vol. 1 is a title list, with notes giving date of first performance, place, and name of composer, if known. Vol. 2 is an index by composers, by librettists, and of titles of specific arias mentioned. Mark Evan Bonds's "The Albert Schatz Opera Collections at the Library of Congress: A Guide and a Supplemental Catalogue," in *Notes* 44 (1988): 655–95, describes the Albert Schatz Collection of Opera Librettos and the Albert Schatz Collection of Manuscript Materials.

7.581 Sonneck, Oscar George Theodore. *Dramatic Music: Catalogue of Full Scores.* 170 pp. Washington, D.C.: Government Printing Office, 1908.

Reprinted by Da Capo Press, New York, 1969.

A list of full scores of operas in original editions, with some manuscript copies included, and some photocopies, arranged alphabetically by composer.

The reprint edition is reviewed by Ruth Watanabe in *Notes* 26 (1970): 521–24.

7.582 Sonneck, Oscar George Theodore. *Orchestral Music Catalogue: Scores in the Collection of the Library of Congress.* 663 pp. Washington, D.C.: Government Printing Office, 1912.

Reprinted by Da Capo Press, New York, 1969.

A collection of orchestra scores dating from about 1830 to 1912.

The reprint edition is reviewed by Ruth Watanabe in *Notes* 26 (1970): 521–24.

7.583 Waters, Edward N. *Autograph Musical Scores and Autograph Letters in the Whittall Foundation Collection.* 18 pp. Washington, D.C.: Gertrude Clarke Whittall Foundation, 1953.

WASHINGTON CATHEDRAL. LIBRARY. SEE 7.623

Wasserburg am Inn, Germany

BENEDIKTINERINNENABTEI FRAUENWORTH. SEE 7.42

Wilhering, Austria

CISTERCIAN ABBEY

7.584* Mitterschiffthaler, Gerald Karl. *Das Notenarchiv der Musiksammlung in Zisterzienserstift Wilhering: (Drucke und Handschriften).* 307 pp. Vienna: Verlag d. Österreichische Akademie der Wissenschriften, 1979. (Tabulae musicae austriacae)

Windsor, England

WINDSOR CASTLE. ST. GEORGE'S CHAPEL

7.585 Mould, Clifford. *The Musical Manuscripts of St. George's Chapel, Windsor Castle: A Descriptive Catalogue.* 76 pp. Windsor: Oxley and Son (Windsor) Ltd. for the Dean and Canons of St. George's Chapel in Windsor Castle, 1973. (Historical monographs relating to St. George's Chapel, Windsor Castle, 14)

An index to composers in the 93 manuscripts followed by a table of descriptions of individual manuscripts and groups of manuscripts. There are thematic incipits for anonymous music, with an appendix listing additional early printed music in the collection.

Winston-Salem, North Carolina

COLLEGIUM MUSICUM

7.586 Ingram, Jeannine S. "Repertory and Resources of the Salem Collegium Musicum, 1780–1790." In *Fontes* 26 (1979): 267–81.

A survey of the 100 pieces in printed editions and manuscripts remaining in the Moravian community's musical establishment.

MORAVIAN MUSIC FOUNDATION

7.587 Cumnock, Frances. *Catalog of the Salem Congregation Music.* 682 pp. Chapel Hill, N.C.: University of North Carolina Press, 1980.

An inventory of three sacred choral and solo vocal collections used by the Moravians in 18th- and 19th-century Salem and now housed at the Moravian Music Foundation, Winston-Salem, and at the Moravian Archives in Bethlehem, Pa. There is a lengthy introduction to the 18th- and 19th-century music of the Salem Congregation of the Moravian Church. The thematic catalog entries include attributions to composer, location within the collection, key, and instrumentation and voices required. There are indexes of composers and text incipits.

Reviewed by Karl Kroeger in *Notes* 37 (1981): 854–55 and by Thomas E. Warner in *AM* 1 (1983): 94–96 no. 1.

7.588 Gombosi, Marilyn. *Catalog of the Johannes Herbst Collection.* 255 pp. Chapel Hill, N.C.: University of North Carolina Press, 1970.

A thematic catalog of some 500 manuscripts of sacred music intended for use in the Moravian service. There are about 1,000 anthems and arias in the collection. The catalog is preceded by a historical introduction describing the musical practices of the 18th-century Moravian church. There is an index of composers and titles.

Reviewed by Susan T. Sommer in *Notes* 29 (1972): 258–59.

7.589* John, Robert W. *A Catalogue of the Irving Lowens Collection of Tune Books: Moravian Music Foundation, Winston Salem, North Carolina.* 118 pp. 1971.

A catalog by a professor from the University of Georgia of the collection put together by the prominent American bibliographer and musicologist and now housed in Winston-Salem.

Wolfenbüttel, Germany

HERZOG-AUGUST-BIBLIOTHEK

7.590 Schmieder, Wolfgang. *Musik: Alte Drucke bis etwa 1750.* 2 vols. Frankfurt am Main: V. Klostermann, 1967. (Kataloge der Herzog-August-Bibliothek Wolfenbüttel, 12–13)

Contents: Vol. I, *Textband* (764 pp.); Vol. II, *Registerband* (310 pp.).

A splendid catalog of 1,334 entries, representing the resources of one of the great German libraries, containing early printed music and theoretical treatises.

Reviewed by Harald Heckmann in *Die Musikforschung* 23 (1970): 207–9 and by Donald W. Krummel in *Notes* 26 (1969): 39–40.

7.591 Theil, Eberhard, and **Gisela Rohr.** *Libretti: Verzeichnis der bis 1800 erschienenen Textbücher.* 395 pp. Frankfurt am Main: V. Klostermann, 1970. (Katalog der Herzog-August-Bibliothek Wolfenbüttel, 14)

A catalog of 1,742 listings of pre-1800 libretti of operas, interludes, operettas, musical comedies, burlesques, and ballets. The entire collection was available for purchase on microfiche from Kraus-Thomson, Nendeln, Liechtenstein.

Reviewed by Susan T. Sommer in *Notes* 29 (1972): 259.

7.592 Vogel, Emil. *Die Handschriften nebst den älteren Druckwerken der Musikabteilung.* 280 pp. Wolfenbüttel, Germany: J. Zwissler, 1890. (Die Handschriften der Herzoglichen Bibliothek zu Wolfenbüttel, 8)

A catalog in two sections, one on music manuscripts and another on printed music, each divided into three subsections—works by a single author, works by anonymous authors, and collections—the latter two organized by title. The collection is especially rich in 17th- and 18th-century music. There are no indexes, although anthologies are analyzed.

NIEDERSÄCHSISCHES STAATSARCHIV IN WOLFENBÜTTEL

7.593* Kindler, Klaus. *Findbuch zum Bestand Musikalien des herzoglichen Theaters in Braunschweig, 18.–19. Jh. (46 Alt).* 313 pp. Wolfenbüttel, Germany: Selbstverlag des Niedersächsischen Staatsarchivs, 1990. (Veröffentlichungen der Niedersächsischen Staatsarchivs in Wolfenbüttel, 5)

Wrocław, Poland (formerly Breslau, Germany)

7.594 Bohn, Emil. *Bibliographie der Musik-Druckwerke bis 1700 welche in der Stadtbibliothek, der Bibliothek des Academischen Instituts für Kirchenmusik, und der Königlichen und Universitäts-Bibliothek zu Breslau aufbewahrt werden: Ein Beitrag zur Geschichte der Musik im XV., XVI., und XVII. Jahrhundert.* 450 pp. Berlin: A. Cohn, 1883.

Reprinted by Georg Olms, Hildesheim, Germany, 1969.

The three collections cataloged here are outstanding for their 16th- and 17th-century manuscripts and printed editions, particularly of liturgical and vocal music. Also included are theoretical works (pp. 1–31), practical musical works (pp. 32–351, 374–400), and collections in chronological order (pp. 371–74), with full bibliographical descriptions.

STAATS- UND UNIVERSITÄTS-BIBLIOTHEK

7.595 Kuhn, Friedrich. *Beschreibendes Verzeichnis der alten Musikalien-Handschriften und Druckwerke des Königlichen Gymnasiums zu Brieg.* 98 pp. Leipzig: Breitkopf & Härtel, 1897. (Monatshefte für Musikgeschichte. Beilage, Jahrgang 29)

A collection placed in the library of Breslau University in 1890. There are 54 manuscripts and some 110 printed books, chiefly 16th-century. Contents are given for manuscript anthologies; there are full bibliographical descriptions for printed works.

STADTBIBLIOTHEK

7.596 Bohn, Emil. *Die musikalischen Handschriften des XVI. und XVII. Jahrhunderts in der Stadtbibliothek zu Breslau: Von Beitrag zur Geschichte der Musik in XVI. und XVII. Jahrhundert.* 423 pp. Breslau: Commissions-Verlag von J. Hainauer, 1890.

Reprinted by Georg Olms, Hildesheim, Germany, 1970.

A catalog of 356 items, with full inventories of contents, numerous indexes, and supplementary lists covering first-line incipits of vocal texts, anonymous compositions, and composers.

UNIWERSYTET WROCŁAWSKI

7.597 Kolbuszewska, Aniela. *Katalog muzycznych dziel teoretycznych XVI i XVII wieku. | Catalog of music theory works of the 16th and 17th centuries.* 67 pp. Wrocław: Biblioteka Uniwersytecka, 1973.

A catalog of 102 numbered theoretical works, giving precise bibliographical descriptions with references to descriptive literature. There is information as to provenance, and call numbers are given. There are indexes of printers and publishers, arranged by place, and of names.

Reviewed by Fred Pajerski in *Notes* 31 (1975): 785–86.

York, England

YORK MINSTER. LIBRARY

7.598 Griffiths, David. *A Catalogue of the Music Manuscripts in York Minster Library.* 266 pp. York: University of York Library, 1981.

A catalog of 218 manuscripts in the collection, each described and analyzed, with indexes to composers, first lines and titles, copyists, previous owners, genres and performing forces, and to other names and places.

7.599 Griffiths, David. *A Catalogue of the Printed Music Published before 1850 in York Minster Library.* xxi + 118 pp. York: University of York Library, 1977.

A catalog arranged by composer with brief bibliographic information and references to *RISM* (**5.590**) and to other catalogs. The collection is of sacred music, mainly from the 17th and

18th centuries. There is an extract from the account books in an appendix. Supportive indexes include those to publishers, engravers, music sellers, owners, donors, and dedicatees.

Zamora, Spain

7.600* **López-Calo, José.** *La música en la Catedral de Zamora.* 1 vol. to date. Zamora, Spain: Diputación Provincial, 1985– .
> Contents: Vol. 1, *Catálogo del archivo de música*.

Żary, Poland (formerly Sorau, Germany)

HAUPTKIRCHE

7.601 **Tischler, G.,** and **K. Burchard.** *Musikalienkatalog der Hauptkirche zu Sorau N. L.* 24 pp. Langensalza, Germany: H. Beyer & Sohne, 1902. (Monatshefte für Musikgeschichte. Beilage. Jahrgang 34)
> A collection containing 33 printed editions, chiefly 17th-century, and a small group of manuscripts in which Telemann, Petri, and C. G. Tag are well represented.

Zurich, Switzerland

ALLGEMEINE MUSIKGESELLSCHAFT

7.602 **Walter, Georg.** *Katalog der gedruckten und handschriftlichen Musikalien des 17. bis 19. Jahrhunderts im Besitze der Allgemeinen Musikgesellschaft Zürich.* 145 pp. Zurich: Hug, 1960.
> A collection rich in 17th- and 18th-century instrumental music, supplying thematic incipits for works in manuscript.
>
> Reviewed by Donald W. Krummel in *Notes* 19 (1961): 77 and by Willi Kahl in *Die Musikforschung* 16 (1963): 284.

ZENTRALBIBLIOTHEK

7.603 **Schenk, Erich.** "Die Österreichische Musiküberlieferung der Züricher Zentralbibliothek." In *Die Österreichische Nationalbibliothek: Festschrift hrsg. zum 25. jährigen Dienstjubiläum des Generaldirektors Prof. Dr. Josef Bick,* pp. 576–81. Vienna: H. Bauer-Verlag, 1948.
> Chiefly a list of works by Austrian composers in the Zürich library, giving place, publisher, and library signature. Special attention is given to works not mentioned in Eitner (**5.544**).

Zwickau, Germany

RATSSCHULBIBLIOTHEK

7.604 **Vollhardt, Reinhard.** *Bibliographie der Musikwerke in der Ratsschulbibliothek zu Zwickau.* 299 pp. Leipzig: Breitkopf & Härtel, 1893–96. (Monatshefte für Musikgeschichte. Beilage. Jahrgang 25–28)
> A catalog of 764 numbered items, manuscripts and printed books, including liturgical works, theoretical works, and instrumental and vocal music, chiefly of 16th- and 17th-century materials.

CATALOGS OF PRIVATE MUSIC COLLECTIONS

In this section are cited some of the catalogs of major private music collections. Few of these remain intact. Some, such as the Cortot and Wolffheim collections, have been dispersed; others have changed location in recent years. No attempt has been made here to list all the catalogs issued in connection with auction sales, although some of these are of great bibliographical interest. Some indication of the information to be gained from the study of early music auction catalogs, a field very little explored, can be found in A. Hyatt King's *Some British Collectors of Music, c. 1600–1960* (**7.609**) and in Otto E. Albrecht's article "Collections, Private" (**7.605**) in *The New Grove Dictionary of Music and Musicians*. James B. Coover's *Antiquarian Catalogues of Musical Interest* (**4.17**) will be of use to those interested in private collections. Lenore Coral's work on British book sale catalogs (her thesis, *Music in English Auction Sales, 1676–1750* [University of London, 1974], and, with A. N. L. Munby, *British Book Sale Catalogues, 1676–1800: A Union List* [London: Mansell, 1977]) sheds some light on this subject.

Frits Knuf, Amsterdam, has published a series of reprints of important auction catalogs of music from the collections of Selhof, Burney, Türk, Coussemaker, Novello, and Rimbault. Numerous entries in the preceding section refer to private collections now in institutional custody; there are entries in the index under the names of the previous, private owners of these collections. The first four entries in this section are cited here because they cover numerous collectors.

7.605* Albrecht, Otto. "Collections, Private." In *The New Grove* (**1.48**).

A two-part article describing existing collections still in private hands (listed geographically) and, with bibliographical references, collections once private that are now located within a larger library collection (listed alphabetically with their former owners). An invaluable account of collections' dispersal.

7.606* Coover, James. *Music at Auction: Puttick and Simpson (of London), 1794–1971, Being an Annotated Chronological List of Sales of Musical Materials (by Puttick and Simpson and Their Predecessors), Comprising Music Scores, Manuscripts, Books about Music, Portraits of Musicians, Documents and Letters Relating to Music and Musicians, Musical Instruments (Keyboard, String, Wind, Percussion, and Mechanical), Together with Numerous Sales of Engraved or Stereotyped Music Plates, the Copyrights Attaching Thereto and the Stock, Goodwill, Premises, and Book Debts of Several Businesses, as Well Comprising an Historical Introduction, Numerous Illustrations and Facsimile Excerpts from Various Puttick & Simpson Catalogues.* xxiii + 528 pp. Warren, Mich.: Harmonie Park Press, 1988. (Detroit studies in music bibliography, 60)

The history of the world's most active auction house for music materials, as told through 1,650 of its catalogs, the auctioneers' own copies, now held by the British Library.

Reviewed by David Hunter in *Notes* 46 (1989): 75–77 and by Donald Hixon in *Fontes* 37 (1990): 205–7.

7.607 Folter, Siegrun H. *Private Libraries of Musicians and Musicologists: A Bibliography of Catalogs, with Introduction and Notes.* 261 pp. Buren, The Netherlands: F. Knuf, 1987. (Auction catalogues of music, 7)

This bibliography concentrates on catalogs of private collectors who were or are known to be musicians (composers or performers) or musicologists. Music publishers and dealers as collectors are omitted unless they were active as musicians also.

A list of 392 annotated citations of auction and dealers' catalogs, exhibition catalogs, privately printed and institutional catalogs, and catalogs published in monographs and articles, arranged by name of collector and then chronologically. There are 72 catalogs of private collectors listed; the disposition of these collections is not noted, but there is additional information on the disposition of many collections cited by Folter in Otto Albrecht's "Collections, Private" (**7.605**) in *The New Grove* (**1.48**). Catalogs listed in A. Hyatt King's *Some British Collectors of Music* (**7.609**) are omitted, as are Puttick & Simpson catalogs, studied by James Coover (**7.606**). The citations provide locations of known copies. There are chronological and dealer indexes.

Reviewed by Lenore Coral in *Fontes* 36 (1989): 333–34, by Patricia Elliott in the *Beethoven Newsletter* 5 (1990): 45, and by Ann P. Basart in *CNV* 128 (1988): 7–8.

7.608* Fuld, James J., and **David Hunter.** "Collectors and Music Bibliography: A Preliminary Survey," in the Festschrift David Hunter edited for Donald W. Krummel, *Music Publishing and Collecting: Essays in Honor of Donald W. Krummel* (**13.15**), pp. 215–34.

An introductory essay and a preliminary list of "Collectors Who Have Written Bibliographically of the Subject Area They Collected."

7.609 King, A. Hyatt. *Some British Collectors of Music. c. 1600–1960.* 178 pp. Cambridge, England: Cambridge University Press, 1963. (The Sandars Lectures for 1961)

A pioneering study of the activity of private collectors of music in England, with an appendix containing classified lists of collectors from the mid-17th century to 1960.

Aldrich, Richard

7.610 *A Catalog of Books Relating to Music in the Library of Richard Aldrich.* 435 pp. New York: Printed at the Plimpton Press, Norwood, Mass., 1931.

A classified catalog of music literature, primarily of the 19th and 20th centuries, with a small collection of books printed before 1800 (pp. 35–55). This library has been incorporated into the Harvard University music collection.

Anna Amalia, Princess of Prussia

7.611 Blechschmidt, Eva Renate. *Die Amalien-Bibliothek: Musikbibliothek der Prinzessin Anna Amalia von Preussen (1723–1787): Historische Einordnung und Katalog mit Hinweisen auf die Schreiber der Handschriften.* 346 pp. Berlin: Verlag Merseberger, 1965. (Berliner Studien zur Musikwissenschaft, 8)

The reconstruction of the catalog of an important 18th-century music collection formed by the youngest sister of Friedrich the Great. The bulk of the collection was acquired by the Joachimsthal'sche Gymnasium in the late 18th century. The collection was dispersed for safekeeping in World War II; since then, parts of it have found their way to libraries in Tübingen, Marburg, and the Deutsche Staatsbibliothek in Berlin. Blechschmidt's study treats the history of the collection and describes each item, both print and manuscript, in detail. Special attention is given to identifying the scribes responsible for the manuscript copies. There is a bibliography (pp. 7–12). See also **6.32.**

Reviewed by Peter Williams in the *Organ Yearbook* 7 (1976): 166–67.

Bach, Carl Philipp Emanuel

7.612* Wade, Rachel W. *The Catalog of Carl Philipp Emanuel Bach's Estate: A Facsimile of the Edition by Schneibes, Hamburg, 1790.* xxiii + 194 pp. New York: Garland Publishing, 1981. (Garland reference library of the humanities, 1790)

Reviewed by Darrell M. Byrd in *Notes* 39 (1982): 100–1 and by Frederic Schoettler in *ARBA* 14 (1983): no. 927.

Bach, Johann Sebastian

7.613* Beisswenger, Kirsten. *Johann Sebastian Bachs Notenbibliothek.* 451 pp. Kassel, Germany: Bärenreiter, 1992. (Catalogus musicus, 13)

An attempt to reconstruct the contents of Bach's library, including musical works by other composers.

Reviewed by George B. Stauffer in *Notes* 50 (1994): 1388–90 and by Richard D. P. Jones in *M&L* 74 (1993): 587–88.

Bekker, Paul

7.614 Hailey, Christopher. *Catalogue of the Paul Bekker Collection.* 622 pp. New Haven, Conn.: Yale Music Library, 1993.

Inventory of the Paul Bekker collection in the Music Library, Yale University (MSS 50).

Brahms, Johannes

7.615* Hancock, Virginia. *Brahms's Choral Compositions and His Library of Early Music.* 238 pp. Ann Arbor, Mich.: UMI Research Press, 1983. (Studies in musicology, 76)

A study that includes a descriptive catalog of the early music in Brahms's library. Appendixes include lists of Brahms's manuscript copies of early music and his printed library of early music. The author located "Sources of Brahms's Manuscript Copies of Early Music in the Archiv der Gesellschaft der Musikfreunde in Wien" in *Fontes* 24 (1977): 113–31.

Reviewed by Jane Vial Jaffe in *Notes* 41 (1984): 287–89.

Burney, Charles

7.616 *Catalogue of the Music Library of Charles Burney, Sold in London 8 August 1814.* Introduction by A. Hyatt King. Amsterdam: Frits Knuf, 1973. (Auction catalogues of music, no. 2)

Original ed. published in London, 1814.

A list of the music collection Burney gathered on his travels and in response to his need for sources while writing his *General History of Music* (**2.7**).

Reviewed, with addenda, by Kerry S. Grant in *Notes* 31 (1974): 45–48.

Burrell, Mary

7.617 *The Richard Wagner Collection Formed by . . . Mary Burrell. The Property of the Curtis Institute of Music, Philadelphia; Which will be Sold on Friday, October 27, 1978.* 172 pp. New York: Christie, Manson & Woods, International, 1978.

One of the most distinguished collections of Wagneriana ever in private hands, the collection was sold and largely dispersed.

Canal, Pietro

7.618 *Biblioteca musicale del Prof. Pietro Canal in Crespano Veneto.* 104 pp. Bassano, Italy: Prem. Stabilimento Tipogr. Sante Pezzato, 1885.

A scholar's library of 1,152 items, of which the first 1,034 are books on music; the collection contains many rarities. The owner was a professor at the University of Padua and wrote studies of music in Mantua and Venice.

Caroline, Queen of England, Consort of George II

7.619* Daub, Peggy. "Queen Caroline of England's Music Library," in *Music Publishing and Collecting: Essays in Honor of Donald W. Krummel* (**13.15**), pp. 131–65.

A history of the collection and a list of its musical contents.

Cortot, Alfred

7.620 Goldbeck, Frederik, and **A. Fehr.** *Bibliothèque Alfred Cortot, v. 1: Catalogue établi par Alfred Cortot.* Préface de Henry Prunières. 221 pp. Argentueil, France: Sur les Presses de R. Coulouma, 1936.

Première Partie (all published): *Traités et autres ouvrages théoriques des XVe, XVIe, XVIIe, & XVIIIe siècles.*

The music holdings in the library of Alfred Cortot. Cortot's interests as a collector extended over a wide area of musical practice. The collection passed into the hands of a dealer at the owner's death in 1962. Portions of the Cortot library have since been acquired by the British Library, the Newberry Library in Chicago, the University of California at Berkeley Music Library, the University of Texas at Austin, and the University of Kentucky at Lexington. For an account of this dispersal and a complete list of Kentucky's acquisition of 290 treatises, see Frank Traficante, "The Alfred Cortot Collection at the University of Kentucky Libraries," in *University of Kentucky Library Notes* 1 (Spring 1970): 1–19 no. 3; a shorter version is printed in *Notes* 26 (1970): 713–17. The Cortot materials in the British Library are described by A. Hyatt King and O. W. Neighbour in *British Museum Quarterly* 31 (1966): 8–16. The Cortot materials at the Harry Ransom Humanities Research Center, University of Texas at Austin, are described in *Library Chronicle* 25/26 (1984): 24–49.

Coussemaker, Charles Edmond Henri de

7.621 *Catalogue of the Music Library of Charles Edmond Henri de Coussemaker, Sold at Brussels 1877.* With an introduction by A. Hyatt King. Buren, The Netherlands: Frits Knuf, 1977. (Auction catalogues of music, no. 4)

A facsimile of the classified catalog of the holdings of the pioneering musicologist. Portions of the Coussemaker collection were acquired by Vander Straeten, Weckerlin, the Bibliothèque Royale of Brussels, and the Bibliothèque de Douai.

Dickinson, Edward and June

7.622 **Locke, Ralph P.,** and **Jurgen Thym.** "New Schumann Materials in Upstate New York: A First Report on the Dickinson Collection, with Catalogues of Its Manuscript Holdings." In *Fontes* 27 (1980): 137–61.

An inventory of manuscripts, letters, printed music, books, and miscellaneous items in the collection gathered by Edward and June Dickinson and kept in Livonia, N.Y.

Douglas, Charles Winfred

7.623 **Ellinwood, Leonard,** and **Anne Woodward.** "The Douglas Collection in the Washington Cathedral Library." In *The Life and Work of Charles Winfred Douglas,* pp. 36–72. New York: Hymn Society of America, 1958. (Hymn Society of America, Papers, 23)

A library of hymnology and liturgical music formed by one of the leading authorities in the field.

Feininger, Laurence

7.624 *Repertorium cantus plani.* 2 vols. Tridenti, Italy: Societas Universalis Sanctae Ceciliae, 1969.

The catalog of a private collection of liturgical manuscripts. Vol. I lists antiphonaria; Vol. II, gradualia. Each vol. treats 24 manuscripts. Descriptions are followed by complete inventories of the contents of each source. Indexes of liturgical incipits conclude each volume.

Finzi, Gerald

7.625* **Davie, Cedric Thorp.** *Catalogue of the Finzi Collection in St. Andrews University Library.* 71 pp. St. Andrews, Scotland: University Library, 1982.

Fuchs, Aloys

7.626 **Schaal, Richard.** "The Autographs of the Viennese Music Collections of Aloys Fuchs, Using the Original Catalogues." In *Haydn Yearbook* 6 (1969): 3–191.

The autographs are listed alphabetically by composer, with information as to provenance and destination, if known. The introduction is in German and English.

Fuchs (1799–1853) was the first great collector of musical autographs. Although his collection was dispersed, portions of it can be found in the Berlin Staatsbibliothek, the Staatsbibliothek der Stiftung Preussischer Kulturbesitz, and the Benedictine abbey at Gottweig.

7.627 Schaal, Richard. *Quellen und Forschungen zur Wiener Musiksammlung von Aloys Fuchs.* 151 pp. Vienna: H. Bohlaus Nachf., 1966. (Veröffentlichungen der Kommission für Musikforschung, 5)

A report on the contents of the Fuchs collection, with a bibliography (pp. 135–51).

Gehring, Franz Eduard

7.628 *Katalog der musikalischen Bibliothek des Herrn Dr. F. Gehring . . . die Versteigerung . . . findet am Montag dem 29. November 1880 . . . im Kunst-Auctions-Hause, Berlin.* 143 pp. Berlin: A. Cohn, 1880.

The sale catalog for a collection of 1,671 titles: 317 early works on music history and theory, 191 pieces of instrumental music, 583 opera scores, and other vocal scores. This was a very carefully chosen collection of the most important works available of the time; apparently some of the manuscripts and early printed works came from Otto Jahn. Entries are brief, but additional information on degree of rarity is provided. Manuscripts are mixed in with printed works and can be discovered only by careful reading of the annotations.

Grainger, Percy

7.629* Clifford, Phil. *Grainger's Collection of Music by Other Composers.* 435 pp. Parkville, Victoria: Board of the Grainger Museum, Melbourne University, 1983. (Percy Grainger music collection, part 2) (Catalogue/Grainger Museum, 2)

The Museum, founded by Grainger, was established by donations from Grainger's friends of music manuscripts and published editions of their works. The entries are fully cataloged, with subject, title, and name indexes.

Heyer, Wilhelm

7.630 Kinsky, Georg. *Musikhistorisches Museum von Wilhelm Heyer in Köln: Band 4: Musik-Autographen.* 870 pp. Leipzig: Breitkopf & Härtel, 1916.

The catalog of 1,673 items describing one of the finest collections of musical autographs ever assembled. The collection was dispersed and sold at auction in 1926 by the firm of Henrici and Liepmannssohn. Kinsky's catalogs of the Heyer collection are models of music bibliography, full of biographical and descriptive detail. There are 64 facsimile plates.

For other volumes of the Heyer Katalog, see **8.56** and **8.57**.

Hirsch, Paul

7.631 Hirsch, Paul, and **Kathi Meyer.** *Katalog der Musikbibliothek Paul Hirsch, Frankfort am Main.* 4 vols. Berlin: M. Breslauer, 1928–47. (Vol. 4 has the imprint: Cambridge, England: Cambridge University Press.)

Contents: Vol. 1, *Theoretische Drucke bis 1800;* Vol. 2, *Opern-Partituren;* Vol. 3, *Instrumental und Vocalmusik bis etwa 1830;* Vol. 4, *Erstausgaben, Chorwerke in Partitur, Gesamtausgaben, Nachschlagewerke, etc. Ergänzungen zu Bd. I–III.*

The catalog of the Paul Hirsch library, one of the great private music collections of the world. The collection was removed from Frankfurt to Cambridge, England, just before World War II and was acquired by the British Museum in 1946. For further information, see the articles by P. H. Muir in *MR* 9 (1948): 102–7 and by A. Hyatt King in *Notes* 9 (1952): 381–87, and **7.267**.

The 4th vol. is reviewed by Richard S. Hill in *Notes* 5 (1948): 228–30.

Illing, Robert

7.632* **Illing, Robert.** *Robert Illing Collection: University of Melbourne Library, 1988.* 4 vols. Melbourne: Robert Illing, 1988– .

A catalog, with commentary by Robert Illing, of his collection, most of which is to be given to the University of Melbourne Library.

Indy, Vincent, D'

7.633* *Catalogue des partitions et livres provenant de la bibliothèque de Vincent d'Indy dont la vente, par suite de décès, aura lieu Hôtel des Ventes à Paris, Salle no. 9, les 20 et 21 janvier 1933.* 58 pp. Paris: Lahure, 1933.

The sale catalog of the composer's library.

Jacobi, Erwin R.

7.634 **Puskás, Regula.** *Musikbibliothek Erwin R. Jacobi: Seltene Ausgaben und Manuskripte: Katalog / The Music Library of Erwin R. Jacobi: Rare Editions and Manuscripts.* Allgemeine Musikgesellschaft Zürich. 3rd ed., revised and enlarged. 84 pp. Zurich: Hug, 1973.

The 2nd ed., published in 1970, is titled *Seltene Originalausgaben von Musica Practica und Musica Theoretica aus dem 15.-20. Jahrhundert.*

A private collection of 514 items.

Koch, Louis

7.635* **Kinsky, Georg.** *Manuskripte, Briefe, Dokumente von Scarlatti bis Stravinsky: Katalog der Musikautographen-Sammlung Louis Koch.* xxii + 361 pp. Stuttgart: Hoffmannsche Buchdruckerei Felix Krais, 1953.

The posthumous publication of the catalog of the collection of Louis Koch (1862–1930), generously illustrated with facsimiles.

Reviewed by Richard Hill in *Notes* 11 (1953): 119–20.

La Fage, J. Adrien de

7.636* *Catalogue de la bibliothèque musicale de feu M. J. Adr. de La Fage: Traités generaux et speciaux sur la théorie de biographie: Oeuvres de musique practique de divers genres; partitions, etc.; liturgie et plain chant; ouvrages sur l'art dramatique et la théâtre, etc., etc.* 200 pp. Paris: L. Potier, 1862.

The catalog for a collection offered at auction in Paris, December 15, 1862.

Meyer, André

7.637 **Lesure, François,** and **Nanie Bridgman.** *Collection musicale André Meyer: Manuscrits, autographes, musique imprimée et manuscrite, ouvrages théoriques, historiques et pédagogiques, livrets, iconographie, instruments de musique.* 118 pp. Abbeville, France: F. Paillart, 1960.

A collection of manuscripts and early printed music, particularly noteworthy for its holdings in iconography. The catalog is beautifully illustrated by 292 plates.

Reviewed by Hans Halm in *Die Musikforschung* 17 (1964): 83–84.

Novello, Vincent

7.638 *Catalogue of the Music Library of Vincent Novello, Sold in London 25 June 1852 and 3 September 1862.* With an introduction by A. Hyatt King. Buren, The Netherlands: Frits Knuf, 1975. (Auction catalogues of music, 5)

A facsimile of the list of the collection of Vincent Novello, who had "a remarkable grasp of the functions of a music librarian."

Pincherle, Marc

7.639* *Collection musicale Marc Pincherle dont la vente aux enchères publiques aura lieu Hôtel Drouot, Salle no. 10, les 3, 4, et 5 mars 1975.* c. 150 pp. Paris: Ader, Picard, Tajan, 1975.

Pretlack, Ludwig, Freiherr von

7.640 Jaenecke, Joachim. *Die Musikbibliothek des Ludwig Freiherrn von Pretlack, 1716–1781.* 330 pp. Wiesbaden: Breitkopf & Härtel, 1973. (Neue musikgeschichtliche Forschungen, 8)

The Pretlack collection is now in the Staatsbibliothek der Stiftung Preussischer Kulturbesitz, Berlin.

Rimbault, Edward Francis

7.641 *Catalogue of the Music Library of Edward Francis Rimbault, Sold at London 31 July–7 August 1877, with The Library of Dr. Rainbeau.* With an introduction by A. Hyatt King. Buren, The Netherlands: Frits Knuf, 1975. (Auction catalogues of music, 6)

A facsimile of the list of music and books that supported various of Rimbault's musical studies, such as *Bibliotheca madrigaliana* (**5.592**). Many of the more valuable titles went to Joseph Drexel and thereafter to the New York Public Library (**7.361**). With the actual sale catalog is published the satirical *Catalogue of the Extensive Library of Doctor Rainbeau*, which was previously published as a separate facsimile with an introduction by James B. Coover (Distant Press, 1962).

Schönborn-Wiesentheid Family

7.642 Zobeley, Fritz. *Die Musikalien der Graf von Schönborn-Wiesentheid: Thematisch-Bibliographischer Katalog.* 3 vols. Tutzing, Germany: H. Schneider, 1967–92. (Veröffentlichungen der Gesellschaft für Bayerische Musikgeschichte e.V.)

Contents: I. Teil, *Das Repertoire des Grafen Rudolf Franz Ermein von Schönborn (1677–1754)*; Book 1, *Drucke aus den Jahren 1676 bis 1738;* Book 2, *Handschriften.* II. Teil, *Der Notennachlass der Grafen Hugo Damien Erwein (1738–1817) and Franz Erwein (1776–1840).*

The thematic catalog of a private collection of early vocal and instrumental music assembled by the Counts von Schönborn-Wiesentheid in Schloss Weiler bei Aschaffenburg. Includes 149 items, with full bibliographical descriptions and inventories of contents. There are informative introductory chapters on the history of the collection and its composition. Further catalogs of the manuscript and archive materials are projected.

The 1st vol. is reviewed by W. Gordon Marigold in *Notes* 24 (1968): 715–16.

Selhof, Nicholas

7.643 *Catalogue of the Music Library, Instruments and Other Property of Nicholas Selhof, Sold in The Hague, 1759.* With an introduction by A. Hyatt King. Amsterdam: Frits Knuf, 1973. (Auction catalogues of music, 1)

A facsimile listing about 2,940 works, published and in manuscript.

Stainer, Sir John

7.644 *Catalogue of English Song Books: Forming a Portion of the Library of Sir John Stainer.* 107 pp. Boston, Mass.: Longwood Press, 1977.

Reprint of the Novello, Ewer edition of 1889.

A catalog prepared by Stainer's children on not only songbooks but also books about bells in Stainer's library.

Türk, Daniel Gottlob

7.645 *Catalogue of the Music Library of Daniel Gottlob Türk, Sold in Halle, 13 January 1817.* With an introduction by A. Hyatt King. 72 pp. Amsterdam: Frits Knuf, 1973. (Auction catalogues of music, 3)

A facsimile of the catalog of music and books about music auctioned posthumously, including references to works not sold but in Türk's collection.

Weckerlin, Jean-Baptiste

7.646 Weckerlin, Jean-Baptiste. *Katalog der Musikbibliothek des Herrn J. B. Weckerlin: Music–Tanz–Theater. Versteigerung, 10. bis 12. März 1910.* 172 pp. Leipzig: C.G. Boerner, 1910. (Auktion XCVIII)

The auction catalog of the private library of Weckerlin, a distinguished French 19th-century music librarian and musicologist, illustrated with facsimile pages and descriptive notes, the latter mainly in French. The collection included extensive holdings of vocal music.

Wittgenstein Collection

7.647 Flindell, E. Fred. "Ursprung und Geschichte der Sammlung Wittgenstein im 19. Jahrhundert." In *Die Musikforschung* 22 (1969): 298–314.

A 19th-century collection of musical autographs, including works of Mendelssohn, Brahms, Joachim, Grillparzer, Beethoven, and Schubert. Now largely dispersed, a part is in the Library of Congress.

Wolffheim, Werner J.

7.648 *Versteigerung der Musikbibliothek des Herrn Dr. Werner Wolffheim durch die Firmen: M. Breslauer & L. Liepmannssohn.* 2 vols. in 4. Berlin, 1928–29.

A 2-vol. classified catalog, compiled at the time of sale, of one of the finest collections ever brought together by a private person.

The library included not only rarities but also the standard reference books and editions. There are full bibliographical descriptions with copious notes and numerous facsimile plates.

8

CATALOGS OF MUSICAL INSTRUMENT COLLECTIONS

Collections of musical instruments are often annexed to music libraries. The reader will note that a number of the catalogs in Chapter 7 are concerned, in part, with Western or Asian instruments. In this chapter, the catalogs of some of the major specialized collections of musical instruments are listed along with a few exhibition catalogs emphasizing this area of collecting activity. For a comprehensive and historical view of instrument collections, see Alfred Berner's article, "Instrumentensammlungen," in *MGG* (**1.9**), Vol. 6, cols. 1295–1310. There is also an illuminating paper by Georg Kinsky, "Musikinstrumentensammlungen in Vergangenheit und Gegenwart," in *Jahrbuch Peters* 27 (1920): 47–60.

Four more general surveys of musical instrument collections head this chapter, providing a broad, if occasionally somewhat dated overview of the potential sources for catalogs of musical instruments. Clifford Bevan's survey, *Musical Instrument Collections in the British Isles* (**8.1**), gives an overview of the area's catalogs of individual collections. James B. Coover's *Musical Instrument Collections: Catalogs and Cognate Literature* (**8.2**), cites 2,418 catalogs published up to the late 1970s. Jean Jenkins's *International Directory of Musical Instrument Collections* (**8.3**) gives information, though dated, on a range of collections. A committee of the Music Library Association organized *A Survey of Musical Instrument Collections in the United States and Canada* (**8.4**), a directory describing musical instrument collections, using information gathered through polling done by MLA.

8.1* **Bevan, Clifford.** *Musical Instrument Collections in the British Isles.* 127 pp. Winchester, Hampshire, England: Piccolo Press, 1990.

Includes bibliographical references and index.

Reviewed by Jolyon Fearnley in the *Galpin Society Journal* 44 (1991): 168–69.

8.2 Coover, James. *Musical Instrument Collections: Catalogs and Cognate Literature.* 464 pp. Detroit, Mich.: Information Coordinators, 1981. (Detroit studies in music bibliography, 47)

An annotated bibliography of 2,418 titles arranged first by name of institution or exposition and then by name of private collector. Appendixes list chronologically some early inventories, expositions, and exhibitions. Includes a general index and an index to auctioneers, antiquarians, and firms.

Reviewed by Jeremy Montagu in *EM* 11 (1983): 100–2, by Edgar Hunt in *Galpin Society Journal* 36 (1983): 144–45, by Howard Schott in *M&L* 65 (1984): 370–71, and by Paula Morgan in *Notes* 39 (1982): 360–61.

8.3 Jenkins, Jean. *International Directory of Musical Instrument Collections.* 166 pp. Buren, The Netherlands: Uitgeverij Frits Knuf BV, 1977.

Preceded by *Ethnic Musical Instruments: Identification-Conservation,* edited by Jean Jenkins (London: H. Evelyn for the International Council of Museums, 1970), 59 pp.

Reviewed by Dale Higbee in *AMISJ* 5–6 (1979–80): 213–15, by François Lesure in *Fontes* 25 (1978): 111–12, and by Stephen M. Fry in *Notes* 34 (1978): 880–81.

8.4 Lichtenwanger, William. *A Survey of Musical Instrument Collections in the United States and Canada.* Conducted by a committee of the Music Library Association. 137 pp. Ann Arbor, Mich.: Music Library Association, 1974.

A geographically arranged list with details of 572 collections in institutions. Included is information on historical instruments, modern replicas, ethnic instruments, toy instruments, etc. The directory has addresses, personnel, hours of service, catalogs (if available), and bibliography. There are indexes of instruments and classes of instruments, and of cultural, geographical, and historical origins.

Reviewed by Laurence Libin in *Notes* 33 (1976): 57–59, by Howard Mayer Brown in *AMISJ* 2 (1976): 96–98, and by William Hullfish in *EM* 4 (1976): 203–5.

Amsterdam, The Netherlands

TROPENMUSEUM

8.5* Otter, Elisabeth den. *Pre-Colombian Musical Instruments: Silenced Sounds in the Tropenmuseum Collection.* 47 pp. Amsterdam: KIT-Tropenmuseum, 1994. (Bulletin of the Koninklijk Instituut voor de Tropen, 335)

A description of the Museum's collection of early Latin American instruments.

Ann Arbor, Michigan

UNIVERSITY OF MICHIGAN. STEARNS COLLECTION OF MUSICAL INSTRUMENTS

8.6 Stanley, Albert A. *Catalog of the Stearns Collection of Musical Instruments.* 2nd ed. 276 pp. + 13 plates. Ann Arbor, Mich.: University of Michigan, 1921.

First published in 1918. A supplement, *Stearns Collection of Musical Instruments—1965,* by Robert Austin Warner, was published in 1965 (10 pp.).

A catalog of 1,464 instruments, Western and Asian, with descriptive annotations, a bibliography, and indexes of makers, geographical distribution, and names of instruments. There is a brief, informative survey of the history of the collection, its character, and its present condition.

Antwerp, Belgium

MUSEUM VLEESHUIS

8.7 *Catalogus van de muziekinstrumenten uit de verzameling van het Museum Vleeshuis.* 189 pp. Antwerp: Ruckers Genootschap, 1981.

An illustrated, classified catalog of the 475 early musical instruments in the Museum, with references to maker, city of manufacture, gross measurements, and sources of fuller descriptions for each. Includes an index to names of makers with brief biographical data and a classified bibliography of works consulted.

Basel, Switzerland

HISTORISCHES MUSEUM

8.8 Nef, Karl. *Katalog der Musikinstrumente im Historischen Museum zu Basel.* 74 pp. + 12 plates. Basel: Universitäts-Buchdruckerei von Friedrich Reinhardt, 1906.

Bound with *Festschrift zum zweiten Kongress der Internationalen Musikgesellschaft,* Basel, 1906.

A catalog with 294 instruments listed and described.

Belgium

8.9* Haine, Malou. *Musica: Les instruments de musique dans les collections belges / Musical Instruments in Belgian Collections / Muziek-instrumenten in Belgische verzamelingen.* 214 pp. Liège: Pierre Mardaga, 1989.

A representative sample of European classical and folk instruments, with 167 illustrations, some highly detailed and each with a brief descriptive caption, giving maker, current location, and access number.

Reviewed by Lyn Elder in *Notes* 47 (1991): 773–75, by Albert R. Rice in *AMISJ* 17 (1991): 140–45, by Carl Rahkonen in *Fontes* 38 (1991): 151–52, and by Anthony Baines in *M&L* 72 (1991): 93.

Berkeley, California

UNIVERSITY OF CALIFORNIA. DEPARTMENT OF MUSIC

8.10 Boyden, David. *Catalogue of the Collection of Musical Instruments in the Department of Music, University of California, Berkeley, Part I.* 104 pp. Berkeley, Calif., 1972.

An unpublished catalog describing a collection of 88 instruments, including early originals and modern replicas. There are short essays on the principal instrument forms. Each instrument is introduced historically, followed by its precise dimensions. A second catalog section was projected.

Berlin, Germany

INSTITUT FÜR MUSIKFORSCHUNG

8.11 Berner, Alfred. *Die Berliner Musikinstrumentensammlung: Einführung mit historischen und technischen Erläuterungen.* 58 pp. + 11 plates. Berlin, 1952.

Not strictly a catalog but a guide to the principal types of instruments, with reference to examples in the Berlin collection.

MUSIKINSTRUMENTEN-MUSEUM BERLIN

8.12 Otto, Irmgard. *Musikinstrumenten-Museum Berlin: Ausstellungsverzeichnis mit Personen- und Sachregistern.* 144 pp. Berlin, 1965.

A guide to the Berlin musical instrument collection, with a diagram of the exposition halls, an index of donors, a list of catalog numbers, and 12 pages of photo plates of instruments.

STAATLICHE AKADEMISCHE HOCHSCHULE FÜR MUSIK

8.13 Fleischer, Oskar. *Führer durch die Sammlung alter Musik-Instrumente.* 145 pp. Berlin: A. Haack, 1892.

A classified catalog, chiefly of early Western instruments, with a few Asian.

8.14 Sachs, Curt. *Sammlung alter Musikinstrumente bei der Staatlichen Hochschule für Musik zur Berlin: Beschreibender Katalog.* 384 cols. + 30 plates. Berlin: J. Bard, 1922.

A classified catalog of a collection containing some 3,200 items, of which about 250 are non-European instruments. The entries each give a description of the instrument, information on the maker, and the date and place of manufacture. There is an index of instruments, places, and makers.

8.15 *Das Musikinstrumenten-Museum Berlin: Eine Einführung in Wort und Bild.* 70 pp. Berlin, 1968.

A historical essay, "75 Jahre Musikinstrumenten-Sammlung," by Irmgard Otto, and 56 photo plates of instruments.

Bologna, Italy

8.16* Meer, J. H. van der. *Strumenti musicali europei del Museo civico medievale di Bologna: Con appendici deo fondi strumentali delle Collezioni comunali d'arte, del Museo Davia Bargellini e del Civico museo bibliografico musicale.* 307 pp. Bologna: Nuova Alfa, 1993. (Cataloghi delle collezioni del Museo civico medievale di Bologna)

The catalogs of various Bolognese collections of musical instruments.

TAGLIAVINI COLLEZIONE

8.17 Tagliavini, Luigi Ferdinando, and **John Henry van der Meer.** *Clavicembali e spinette dal XVI al XIX secolo: Collezione L. F. Tagliavini, con i contributi di Wanda Bergamini e Friedemann Hellwig.* 243 pp. Casalecchio di Reno and Bologna: Grafis, 1986.

At head of title: Cassa di risparmio in Bologna; Collezioni d'arte e di documentazione storica. The catalog of an exhibition held at Chiesa di San Giorgio in Poggiale, 1 November–21 December 1986.

The catalog of a remarkable private collection gathered by the distinguished musicologist, organologist, and organist. The collection was exhibited during the 1987 Congress of the International Musicological Society held in Bologna.

Bonn, Germany

8.18* Weber, Rainer. *Zur Restaurierung von Holzblasinstrumenten aus der Sammlung von Dr. Josef Zimmermann im Bonner Beethoven-Haus: Restaurierungsbericht mit Angaben zu Arbeitstechniken.* 200 pp. Celle, Germany: Moeck Verlag, 1993.

The description of the collection of 19 instruments acquired in 1977.

Reviewed by William Waterhouse in *Galpin Society Journal* 48 (1995): 221–22.

Borgentreich, Germany

8.19* Reuter, Hannalore. *Orgelmuseum Borgentreich.* 120 pp. Borgentreich, Germany: Stadt Borgentreich, 1985.

A description of the Museum, founded in 1980.

Reviewed by Irmtraud Krüger in *Galpin Society Journal* 44 (1991): 204.

Boston, Massachusetts

MUSEUM OF FINE ARTS. LESLIE LINDSEY MASON COLLECTION

8.20 Bessaraboff, Nicholas. *Ancient European Musical Instruments.* 503 pp. Cambridge, Mass.: Published for the Museum by the Harvard University Press, 1941.

An authoritative, well-illustrated catalog of 213 items, which provides a wealth of background information for the historical study of instruments, with a bibliography (pp. 453–69) and indexes of names and subjects. There are 16 plates and 72 illustrations in the text. The collection of Canon Francis W. Galpin forms the basis of the Mason collection.

The catalog is reviewed by Curt Sachs in *MQ* (July 1942): 380–83. For an evaluation of the book and a tribute to its author, see David Boyden's article "Nicholas Bessaraboff's *Ancient European Musical Instruments*," in *Notes* 28 (1971): 21–27.

8.21* Koster, John, and **John T. Kirk.** *Keyboard Musical Instruments in the Museum of Fine Arts, Boston.* xl + 368 pp. Boston, Mass.: Museum of Fine Arts, Boston, 1994.

A catalog describing in minute detail (average 5 pages of text) 54 keyboard instruments of all types, with photos and drawings, glossary, bibliography, and index.

Bradford, England

8.22* Myers, Arnold, and **Angela Cartledge.** *Catalogue of the Brass Musical Instruments in the Collections of Bradford Art Galleries and Museums.* 34 pp. Bradford, England: City of Bradford Metropolitan Council, 1991.

Braunschweig, Germany

STÄDTISCHES MUSEUM

8.23 *Verzeichnis der Sammlung alter Musikinstrumente im Städtischen Museum Braunschweig . . . Instrumente, Instrumentenmacher und Instrumentisten in Braunschweig.* 124 pp. Braunschweig: E. Appelhans, 1928. (Werkstücke aus Museum, Archiv und Bibliothek der Stadt Braunschweig, 3)

The catalog, listing 113 European items, occupies pp. 5–34. The remainder of the vol. is devoted to studies of local instrument makers and performers.

Bruges, Belgium

GRUUTHUSEMUSEUM

8.24 Awouters, M., Ignace de Keyser, and **Stefaan Vandenberghe.** *Catalogus van de Muziek-instrumenten: Brugge Gruuthusemuseum.* 120 pp. Bruges: Brugge Gruuthusemuseum, 1985.

Brussels, Belgium

MUSÉE INSTRUMENTAL

8.25 *Catalogue de l'exposition d'instruments de musique des XVIe et XVIIe siècles appartenant au Musée Instrumental de Bruxelles, Chateau de Laarne, Septembre–Novembre 1972.* 184 pp. Buren, The Netherlands: F. Knuf, 1972.

8.26 Mahillon, Victor-Charles. *Catalogue descriptif et analytique du Musée.* 2nd ed. 5 vols. Ghent: A. Hoste, 1893–1922.

A classified catalog for one of the great instrument collections of the world, encompassing more than 3,000 instruments of all cultures. The descriptions include precise indications of each instrument's pitch, tuning, and range.

Bussum, The Netherlands

8.27 Leeuwen Boomkamp, Carel van, and **J. H. van der Meer.** *The Carel van Leeuwen Boomkamp Collection of Musical Instruments.* 188 pp. + 80 plates. Amsterdam: F. Knuf, 1971.

A private collection of 112 items, strongest in its stringed instruments (57) and bows (32), expertly described. Illustrated in photographs, some doctored.

Reviewed by Anthony Baines in *Galpin Society Journal* 25 (1972): 123–35.

Cairo, Egypt

MUSEUM OF EGYPTIAN ANTIQUITIES

8.28 Hickmann, Harald. *Catalogue général des antiquités égyptiennes du Musée du Caire. Nos. 69201–69852: Instruments de musique.* 216 pp. + 116 plates. Cairo: Imprimerie de l'Institut Français d'Archéologie Orientale, 1949.

Classified catalog of 651 ancient Egyptian instruments, or fragments thereof, with detailed descriptions and photo reproductions.

Cambridge, Massachusetts

EDDY COLLECTION

8.29 Good, Edwin M. *The Eddy Collection of Musical Instruments: A Checklist.* 91 pp. Berkeley, Calif.: Fallen Leaf Press, 1985. (Fallen Leaf reference books in music, 3)

An illustrated classified catalog of a private collection of 411 European and American instruments, mostly wind instruments and pianos, from the 18th to the 20th centuries. Each entry provides information on maker, place of manufacture, material, shape, and approximate date of construction. There is a list of manufacturers and dealers with cross-references to entries, but no other indexes, because this was designed as a provisional checklist to be replaced eventually by a fuller catalog of the collection.

Cincinnati, Ohio

CINCINNATI ART MUSEUM

8.30 *Musical Instruments.* 23 pp. Cincinnati, Ohio: Cincinnati Art Museum, 1949.

An illustrated brochure listing 110 instruments, 60 European and 50 non-European.

Clinton, New York

HAMILTON COLLEGE

8.31* Bonta, Stephen. *The Schambach Collection of Musical Instruments.* 64 pp. Clinton, N.Y.: Hamilton College, 1983.

The catalog of a 1983 exhibit held in the Fred L. Emerson Gallery, Hamilton College, of the musical instrument collection of Hans Schambach.

Reviewed by Dale Higbee in *AMISJ* 11 (1985): 176–77.

Cologne, Germany

KÖLNISCHES STADTMUSEUM

8.32* Hoyler, Helmut, Detlef Altenburg, Christoph Dohr, and **Werner Schafke.** *Die Musikinstrumentensammlung des Kölnischen Stadtmuseums.* 310 pp. Berlin: Merseberger, 1993. (Beiträge zur rheinischen Musikgeschichte, 148)

The catalog of Cologne's Stadtmuseum.

Copenhagen, Denmark

CARL CLAUDIUS COLLECTION

8.33 *Carl Claudius' Samling af gamle musikinstrumenter.* 423 pp. Copenhagen: Levin og Munskgaard, 1931.

A rich private collection of musical instruments, now administered by the University of Copenhagen. The catalog describes 757 items.

MUSIKHISTORISK MUSEUM

8.34 Hammerich, Angul. *Das Musikhistorische Museum zu Kopenhagen: Beschreibender Katalog.* Deutsch von Erna Bobe, mit 179 Illustrationen. 172 pp. Copenhagen: G.E.C. Gad, 1909; Leipzig: Kommissionsverlag von Breitkopf & Härtel, 1911.

A classified catalog of 631 items, 582 of which are instruments, Western and Asian, followed by a short list of liturgical manuscripts, printed editions, and miscellany.

Edinburgh, Scotland

EDINBURGH UNIVERSITY

8.35 Blades, James. *A Check-List of Percussion Instruments in the Edinburgh University Collection of Historic Musical Instruments.* 24 pp. Edinburgh: Reid School of Music, Edinburgh University, 1982.

8.36 Melville-Mason, Graham. *An Exhibition of European Musical Instruments. Edinburgh International Festival, 18 Aug.-7 Sept. 1968, Reid School of Music, Edinburgh University.* 99 pp. + 40 plates. Edinburgh, 1968.

The 21st anniversary exhibition of the Galpin Society: an exhibition catalog of 716 items, with bibliography. The instruments are described and their dimensions given. The introductory paragraphs for each group of instruments are supplied by specialists.

8.37* Myers, Arnold. *Historical Musical Instruments in the Edinburgh University Collection: Catalogue of the Edinburgh University Collection of Historic Musical Instruments,* Vols. 1–2 (8 fascicles to date). Edinburgh: The Collection, 1990–93.

Contents: Vol. 1, *The Illustrations* (168 pp.); Vol. 2, pt. A, fascicle 1, *Wind Instruments of Regional Cultures Worldwide* (43 pp.).

A description of the 2,000 instruments of the Edinburgh University collection. Myers had earlier organized a series of 10 checklists (1981–83) of the various sections of the collection. The 2nd vol., issued in fascicles, is also available on e-mail, in ASCII format.

Reviewed by Peter Andreas Kjeldsberg in *Galpin Society Journal* 48 (1995): 216–18.

8.38 Newman, Sidney, and **Peter Williams.** *The Russell Collection and Other Early Keyboard Instruments in Saint Cecilia's Hall, Edinburgh.* 79 pp. Edinburgh: Edinburgh University Press, 1968.

Eisenach, Germany

BACHMUSEUM

8.39 Neue Bach Gesellschaft. *Verzeichnis der Sammlung alter Musikinstrumente im Bachhaus zu Eisenach.* 4th ed. 97 pp. Leipzig: Breitkopf & Härtel, 1964. (Veröffentlichungen der Neuen Bachgesellschaft. Vereinsjahr 50, 1962)

First issued in 1913.

A classified catalog of more than 230 items, illustrated with line drawings.

Erlangen, Germany

8.40* Eschler, Thomas J. *Die Sammlung historischer Musikinstrumente des Musikwissenschaftlichen Instituts der Universität Erlangen-Nürnberg.* 120 pp. Wilhelmshaven, Germany: F. Noetzel, 1993. (Quellenkataloge zur Musikgeschichte, 25)

A description of the musical instrument collection of Friedrich-Alexander-Universität, Erlangen-Nürnberg. The editor also wrote "The Collection of Historical Musical Instruments of the University of Erlangen: A Checklist" in *Galpin Society Journal* 36 (1983): 115–24.

Florence, Italy

CONSERVATORIO DI MUSICA "LUIGI CHERUBINI"

8.41 Bargagna, Leto. *Gli strumenti musicali raccolti nel Museo del R. Istituto L. Cherubini a Firenze.* 70 pp. + 12 plates. Florence: G. Ceccherini, 1911.

A catalog of 146 instruments.

8.42 Gai, Vincio. *Gli strumenti musicali della corte medicea e il Museo del Conservatorio "Luigi Cherubini" di Firenze: Cenni storici e catalogo descrittivo.* 286 pp. Florence: LICOSA, 1969.

An instrumental catalog illustrated by line drawings accompanied by precise measurements and a generous "Bibliografia" (pp. 255–71). An introduction relates the history of the collection.

Frankfurt an der Oder, Germany

BEZIRKSMUSEUM

8.43* Heyde, Herbert. *Historische Musikinstrumente der Staatlichen Reka-Sammlung am Bezirksmuseum Viadrina, Frankfurt (Oder): Katalog.* 208 pp. Leipzig: VEB Deutscher Verlag für Musik, 1989.

Reviewed by Carl Rahkonen in *Fontes* 39 (1991): 151–52.

Gijón, Spain

MUSEO INTERNACIONAL DE LA GAITA

8.44 *Catálogo.* 152 pp. Gijón, Spain: Asturias (España), 1970.

The catalog of a museum devoted to the bagpipe, its history and distribution, organized by country, with numerous color plates and black-and-white illustrations.

Graz, Austria

8.45* Stradner, Gerhard. *Musikinstrumente in Grazer Sammlungen: Grazer öffentliche Sammlungen.* 204 pp. + 48 pp. of plates. Vienna: Verlag der österreichischen Akademie der Wissenschaften, 1986. (Tabulae musicae austriacae, 11)

Gujarat, India

8.46* Bhowmik, S. K. *The Heritage of Musical Instruments: A Catalogue of Musical Instruments in the Museums of Gujarat.* 277 pp. Vadodara, India: Dept. of Museums, Gujarat State, 1990.

The Hague, The Netherlands

HAAGS GEMEENTEMUSEUM

8.47* Acht, Rob van, Vincent van den Ende, and **Hans Schimmel.** *Niederländische Blockflöten des 18. Jahrhunderts / Dutch Recorders of the 18th Century / Sammlung Haags Gemeentemuseum.* 163 pp. Celle, Germany: Moeck-Verlag, 1991.

A compendium of the largest collection of 18th-century Dutch recorders, giving a history of Dutch recorder building, biographies of flute makers, and a detailed description with measurements of each instrument.

Reviewed by Jeremy Montagu in *EM* 19 (1991): 636–41.

8.48 Gleich, Clemens C. J. von. *Catalogi van de muziekbibliotheek en de collectie muziekinstrumenten: Catalogus van de muziekinstrumenten.* Deel I: *Hoorn- en trompetachtige blaasinstrumenten;* door Leo J. Plenckers. 85 pp. + 8 plates. Amsterdam: F. Knuf, 1970.

The first of a series of catalogs projected to cover the musical instrument collections at the Gemeentemuseum. The 1st vol. describes 136 instruments of the horn and trumpet type, arranged by a classified grouping of instrument types, with a glossary and an index of names. This series is paralleled by another devoted to the holdings of the museum's music library (**7.198**).

8.49* Gleich, Clemens von. *A Checklist of Pianos.* 119 pp. The Hague: Haags Gemeentemuseum, 1986. (Checklists of the musical instrument collection of the Haags Gemeentemuseum)

Reviewed by John Cranmer in *Galpin Society Journal* 43 (1990): 194–95.

8.50 Gleich, Clemens von. *Pianofortes from the Low Countries / Pianofortes uit de Lage Landen.* 55 pp. Buren, The Netherlands: Haags Gemeentemuseum; F. Knuf, 1980.

Pianofortes from the 18th and 19th centuries by Dutch makers from the instrument collection of the Haags Gemeentemuseum, described in English and Dutch.

8.51 Ligtvoet, A. W. *Exotische en oude Europese muziekinstrumenten, in de muziekafdeling van het Haagse Gemeentemuseum.* 51 pp. + 25 plates. The Hague: Nijgh & Van Ditmar, 1955.

A general, popular introduction to the collection, with the text in Dutch and English.

8.52 Ligtvoet, A. W., and **W. Lievense.** *Europese muziekinstrumenten in het Haagse Gemeentemuseum.* 160 pp. + 64 pp. illus. The Hague: Gemeentemuseum, 1965.

Halle, Germany

HÄNDEL-HAUS

8.53 *Katalog zu den Sammlungen des Händel-Hauses in Halle.* 3 vols. of 7. Halle, Germany: Händel-Haus, 1966–79.

Contents: 5. Teil, *Musikinstrumentensammlung. Besaitete Tasteninstrumente,* by Konrad Sasse; 6. Teil, *Musikinstrumentensammlung, Streich- und Zupfinstrumente* (1972); 7. Teil, *Musikinstrumentensammlung, Blasinstrumente, Orgeln, Harmoniums* (1979).

One of the largest collections of keyboard instruments in Europe, comprising some 115 items, founded on the collection of J. C. Neupert of Nuremberg, acquired in the 1930s. These are classified catalogs with extensive descriptions, often with photographs of the instruments. There are indexes to makers and bibliographies of the works cited. There is also an index to catalogs by the museum identification number of each instrument, as well as an outline of the cataloging scheme used.

Reviewed by Friedrich Ernst in *Die Musikforschung* 21 (1968): 506–7.

For a catalog of the complete holdings of the Handel House in Halle, see **7.200**.

Holyoke, Massachusetts

MOUNT HOLYOKE COLLEGE

8.54 Skinner, William. *The Belle Skinner Collection of Old Musical Instruments: A Descriptive Catalogue.* 210 pp. Philadelphia; New York: Printed by the Beck Engraving Co., 1933.

An illustrated catalog of 89 instruments, including some particularly fine examples of keyboard instruments, with colored plates. Since 1959 this collection has been on loan to Yale University.

Johannesburg, South Africa

8.55 Lange, Margareet M. de. *Catalogue of the Musical Instruments in the Collection of Percival R. Kirby.* 155 pp. Johannesburg: Africana Museum, 1967.

Leipzig, Germany

HEYER COLLECTION

8.56 Kinsky, Georg. *Kleiner Katalog der Sammlung alter Musikinstrumente.* 250 pp. Cologne, 1913.

An abridgment of the material in **8.57**; valuable because it contains entries for the wind instruments in the Heyer collection, which are not included in **8.57**.

8.57 Kinsky, Georg. *Musikhistorisches Museum von Wilhelm Heyer in Köln.* 2 vols. Leipzig: Breitkopf & Härtel, 1910–16.

The 2 vols. of the catalog concerned with the instrument collection (Vol. 1, *Besaitete Tasteninstrumente. Orgel und orgelartige Instrumente;* Vol. 2, *Zupf- und Streichinstrumente*). The unpublished 3rd vol. was intended to cover the collection's wind instruments. The Heyer instrument collection, one of the finest in the world, was transferred to Leipzig in 1926, where it was destroyed in World War II. Kinsky's catalog is a mine of information for the student of early instruments, as it is copiously illustrated and rich in detail. The print section of the collection is listed as **7.630**.

UNIVERSITÄT. MUSIKINSTRUMENTEN-MUSEUM

8.58 *Kataloge des Musikinstrumenten-Museums der Karl-Marx-Universität zu Leipzig.* Leipzig: Deutscher Verlag für Musik, 1978– . 6 vols. to date.

Contents: Vol. 1, *Flöten* (by Herbert Heyde); Vol. 2, *Kielinstrumente* (by Hubert Henkel); Vol. 3, *Trompeten, Posaunen, Tuben* (by Herbert Heyde); Vol. 4, *Clavichorde* (by Hubert Henkel); Vol. 5, *Hörner und Zinken* (by Herbert Heyde); Vol. 6, *Orgelinstrumente, Harmoniums* (by Klaus Gernhardt, Hubert Henkel, and Winfried Schrammek).

Scientific studies of instruments in the Karl Marx University in Leipzig, with precise measurements provided.

8.59 Rubardt, Paul. *Führer durch das Musikinstrumenten-Museum der Karl-Marx-Universität Leipzig.* 84 pp. + 16 plates. Leipzig: Breitkopf & Härtel, 1955.

8.60 Schultz, Helmut. *Führer durch das Musikwissenschaftliche Instrumenten-Museum der Universität Leipzig.* 85 pp. + 19 plates. Leipzig: Breitkopf & Härtel, 1929.

A classified catalog organized according to the ground plan of the display.

Leningrad, USSR

see Saint Petersburg, Russia.

Linz, Austria

LANDESMUSEUM

8.61 Wessely, Othmar. *Die Musikinstrumentensammlung des Oberösterreichischen Landesmuseums.* 47 pp. Linz, Austria: Demokratische Druck- und Verlags-Gesellschaft. (Kataloge des Oberösterreichischen Landesmuseums, 9)

A collection of 188 items, classified and described briefly.

Liverpool, England

LIVERPOOL MUSEUM

8.62* Rushton, Pauline. *Catalogue of European Musical Instruments in Liverpool Museum.* 182 pp. Liverpool: National Museums & Galleries on Merseyside, 1994.

Reviewed by Darryl Martin and Arnold Myers in *Galpin Society Journal* 48 (1995): 218–20.

London, England

BRITISH MUSEUM

8.63* Anderson, Robert D. *Catalogue of Egyptian Antiquities in the British Museum. Volume 2: Musical Instruments.* 87 pp. + 150 plates. London: British Museum Publications / Oxford University Press, 1976.

An illustrated catalog describing a collection of 111 instruments, with entries including physical descriptions, bibliographic references, date and provenance, measurements, materials used, and the date added to the Museum's collection.

Reviewed by Claudie Marcel Dubois in *Ethnomusicology* 22 (1978): 186–88 and by Jeremy Montagu in *Galpin Society Journal* 31 (1978): 179–85.

8.64 Rimmer, Joan. *Ancient Musical Instruments of Western Asia in the Department of Western Asiatic Antiquities, the British Museum.* 51 pp. + 26 plates. London: British Museum, 1969.

A catalog describing actual instruments as well as replicas. The coverage is of the use of string, wind, and percussion instruments in Sumerian, Babylonian, Anatolian, Assyrian, and Hellenistic Asiatic societies. Several inaccurate reassemblies are corrected. An appendix gives a classified list of instruments and a table of musical references in the Old Testament.

FENTON HOUSE. BENTON FLETCHER COLLECTION

8.65 Russell, Raymond. *Catalogue of the Benton Fletcher Collection of Early Keyboard Instruments at Fenton House, Hampstead.* 26 pp. London: Country Life, Ltd., for the National Trust, 1957.

A descriptive brochure for a collection of early keyboard instruments maintained in playing condition in a late-17th-century house in Hampstead, London.

HORNIMAN MUSEUM AND LIBRARY

8.66 *The Adam Carse Collection of Old Musical Wind Instruments [Now in the Horniman Museum, London].* 88 pp. London: Staple Press for the London County Council, 1951.

A collection of 320 instruments, briefly described and illustrated by drawings, with historical notes for each family.

8.67 Jenkins, Jean L. *Musical Instruments: Handbook to the Museum's Collection.* 2nd ed. 104 pp. + 32 plates. London: Inner London Education Authority, 1970.

First ed. published in 1958.

A catalog that is at the same time a handbook for the study of musical instruments, chiefly non-Western, with a bibliography, discography, and index.

ROYAL COLLEGE OF MUSIC

8.68 *Catalogue of Historical Musical Instruments, Paintings, Sculpture, and Drawings.* 16 pp. London: Royal College of Music, 1952.

Foreword by George Dyson.

A brief inventory including the Donaldson collection of musical instruments, with minimum description.

8.69* Rattray, David. *Masterpieces of Italian Violin Making, 1620–1850: Twenty-six Important Stringed Instruments from the Collection at the Royal Academy of Music.* 72 pp. London: Royal Academy of Music, 1991.

A description of 26 of the 250 stringed instruments belonging to the Royal Academy, by the collection's custodian.

Reviewed by Marcus Bennett in *Galpin Society Journal* 49 (1996): 237–39.

ROYAL MILITARY EXHIBITION, 1890

8.70 Day, Charles Russell. *A Descriptive Catalogue of the Musical Instruments Recently Exhibited at the Royal Military Exhibition, London, 1890.* 253 pp. London: Eyre & Spottiswoode, 1891.

Of this exhibition of wind and percussion instruments, 457 wind instruments are inventoried).

VICTORIA AND ALBERT MUSEUM

8.71 *Catalogue of Musical Instruments.* 2 vols. London: Her Majesty's Stationery Office, 1978–85.

First published in 1968.

Vol. 1, *Keyboard Instruments,* by Raymond Russell (94 pp. + 47 plates). Detailed descriptions of 52 keyboard instruments, including pianos and organs described by Austin Niland. Appendix B, "The Decoration of Keyboard Instruments," by Peter Thornton, with biographical notes on the makers, bibliography, and index.

Vol. 2, *Non-Keyboard Instruments,* by Anthony Baines (121 pp. + 138 plates). The instruments are grouped as stringed instruments and wind instruments, with 16 subgroups of the former, 8 of the latter. Full technical descriptions, with clear plates of details; bibliography and index.

The 1968 ed. is reviewed by Don L. Smithers in *Notes* 26 (1969): 47–48.

8.72 Engel, Carl. *A Descriptive Catalogue of the Musical Instruments of the South Kensington Museum.* 402 pp. London: Printed by G.E. Eyre and W. Spottiswoode for H.M. Stationery Office, 1874.

A catalog preceded by an essay on the history of musical instruments. This museum became the Victoria and Albert Museum.

8.73 *Musical Instruments as Works of Art.* 52 p. London: Her Majesty's Stationery Office, 1982. First ed., 1968, published by the Museum.

A catalog illustrated with more than 100 plates showing details of finely crafted early musical instruments. All examples are from the instrument collection of the Victoria and Albert.

Los Angeles, California

8.74 Lachmann, Erich. *Erich Lachmann Collection of Historical Stringed Musical Instruments.* 53 pp. Los Angeles, Calif.: Allan Hancock Foundation, University of Southern California, 1950.

A handsome catalog of 42 instruments dating from the 17th to the 19th centuries, all in playing condition, noteworthy for photographic illustrations by Irvin Kershner.

Reviewed by Karl Geiringer in *Notes* 8 (1951): 521–22.

Lucerne, Switzerland

Richard Wagner Museum

8.75 Vannes, René. *Katalog der stadtischen Sammlung alter Musikinstrumente im Richard-Wagner-Museum, Tribschen, Luzern.* Erstellt im Auftrag der Museum-Kommission. 40 pp. + 16 plates. Lucerne: Otto Dreyer, 1956.

A catalog of 95 stringed instruments, 46 wind, 11 idiophones, and 37 exotic instruments.

Merano, Italy

8.76* Roos, Wilhelm. *Sammlung historischer Musikinstrumente in der Landesfürstlichen Burg zu Meran.* 55 pp. Merano, Italy: Museum Meran, 1987.

A description of a collection of 33 musical instruments of high caliber, previewed by Roos in *Galpin Society Journal* 32 (1979): 10–23.

Reviewed by William Waterhouse in *Galpin Society Journal* 45 (1992): 142–43.

Merthyr Tydfil, Wales, Great Britain

Cyfarthfa Castle Museum and Art Gallery

8.77* Myers, Arnold, and **Trevor Herbert.** *Catalogue of the European Wind and Percussion Instruments in the Cyfarthfa Castle Museum.* 24 pp. Merthyr Tydfil, Wales: Cyfarthfa Castle Museum and Art Gallery, 1990.

A publication sponsored by the local borough council.

Milan, Italy

CONSERVATORIO DI MUSICA "GIUSEPPE VERDI"

8.78 Guarinoni, E. *Gli strumenti musicali nel Museo del Conservatorio di Milano.* 109 pp. Milan: Hoepli, 1908.

A collection of 278 instruments, 177 European and 91 non-European, with an index of donors and instruments.

MUSEO DEGLI STRUMENTI MUSICALI

8.79 Gallini, Natale, and Franco Gallini. *Catalogo.* 448 pp. Milan: Castello Sforzesco, 1963.

A catalog of the collection of musical instruments. An earlier catalog of the same collection was issued in 1958 as *Civico Museo di Antichi Strumenti Musicali.* The 1963 catalog, completely reorganized, lists 641 items, well described and illustrated in 141 plates.

MUSEO TEATRALE ALLA SCALA

8.80* Bizzi, Guido. *La collezione di strumenti musicali del Museo Teatrale alla Scala: Studio, restauro e restituzione.* 159 pp. Milan: Silvana, 1991.

An illustrated account of the musical instrument collection of the Museum, with a section on the effort spent in restoring and repairing the instruments.

New Haven, Connecticut

YALE UNIVERSITY

8.81 Rephann, Richard. *Checklist: Yale Collection of Musical Instruments.* 43 pp. New Haven, Conn.: Yale University, 1968.

Preface signed by Richard Rephann, curator.

A checklist of 310 instruments, chiefly Western, comprising items from the Morris Steinert, the Belle Skinner (**8.54**), and the Emil Herrmann collections, as well as gifts from private donors and Friends of Music at Yale, with brief descriptions and no bibliography.

8.82 Rephann, Richard T. *The Schambach–Kaston Collection of Musical Instruments.* 87 pp. New Haven, Conn.: Yale University Collection of Musical Instruments, 1988.

New York, New York

METROPOLITAN MUSEUM OF ART

8.83 *Catalog of the Crosby Brown Collection of Musical Instruments of All Nations.* 3 vols. in 4. New York: Metropolitan Museum of Art, 1903–7.

Contents: Vol. 1, *Europe* (1904). Vol. 2, *Asia* (1903). Vol. 3, *Instruments of Savage Tribes and Semicivilized Peoples:* Pt. 1, *Africa* (1907); Pt. 2, *Oceania* (1907); Pt. 3, *Historical Groups* (1905).

See the article by Emanuel Winternitz, "The Crosby Brown Collection of Musical Instruments: Its Origin and Development," in *Metropolitan Museum Journal* 3 (1970). Also printed separately (20 pp.).

8.84 *Catalog of Keyboard Instruments.* 313 pp. New York: Metropolitan Museum of Art, 1903.

8.85* Libin, Lawrence. *American Musical Instruments in the Metropolitan Museum of Art.* 224 pp. New York: Metropolitan Museum; Norton, 1985.

A catalog of a magnificent collection.

8.86 Winternitz, Emanuel. *Keyboard Instruments in the Metropolitan Museum of Art: A Picture Book.* 48 pp. New York: Metropolitan Museum of Art, 1961.

Not a catalog, but a book of photo reproductions of keyboard instruments from the Metropolitan's collection, including details, with commentary by the former curator.

Niedersach, Germany

8.87* Mascher, Ekkehard. *Brauchgebundene Musikinstrumente in Niedersachsen: Studien zu Klanggeräten im Museumsbesitz.* 246 pp. Hildesheim, Germany; New York: Olms, 1986. (Studien und Materialen zur Musikwissenschaft, 4)
Reviewed by William Waterhouse in *Galpin Society Journal* 45 (1992): 142–43.

Nuremberg, Germany

GERMANISCHES NATIONALMUSEUM

8.88* Huber, Renate. *Verzeichnis sämtlicher Musikinstrumente im Germanischen National-museum Nürnberg.* 415 pp. Wilhelmshaven, Germany: F. Noetzel, "Heinrichshofen-Bücher," 1989. (Taschenbücher zur Musikwissenschaft, 109)
A checklist of all 2,500 instruments in the Museum.
Reviewed by Beryl Kenyon de Pascual in *Galpin Society Journal* 45 (1992): 143–44.

8.89 Meer, John Henry van der. *Musikinstrumente von der Antike bis zur Gegenwart.* 301 pp. Munich: Prestel-Verlag, 1983. (Bibliothek des Germanischen Nationalmuseums Nürnberg zur deutschen Kunst- und Kulturgeschichte, 2)
A history of musical instruments based, in large measure, on the collections of the Germanisches Nationalmuseum, Nuremberg.

8.90 Meer, John Henry van der. *Wegweiser durch die Sammlung historischer Musikinstrumente, Germanisches Nationalmuseum Nürnberg.* 2nd ed. 96 pp. Nuremberg: Germanisches Nationalmuseum, 1976.
First published 1971.
A guide to the collections.

8.91* Meer, John Henry van der, and **Martin Kirnbauer.** *Verzeichnis der Europäischen Musikinstrumente im Germanischen Nationalmuseum Nürnberg.* 2 vols. Wilhelmshaven, Germany: Florian Noetzel Verlag, 1978–94. (Instrumentenkataloge des Germanischen Nationalmuseums, Nürnberg, 1) (Quellenkataloge zur Musikgeschichte, 16 and 24)
Contents: Vol. 1, *Horner und Trumpeten, Membranophone, Idiophone*; Vol. 2, *Flöten- und Rohrblattinstrumente bis 1750.*
A catalog with many illustrations and plates, a bibliography, and two indexes. Detailed descriptions are provided. There is a classified index, with a bibliography and index to makers.
Reviewed by Malou Haine in *Fontes* 28 (1981): 255–56.

Oxford, England

ASHMOLEAN MUSEUM

8.92 Boyden, David D. *Catalogue of the Hill Collection of Musical Instruments in the Ashmolean Museum, Oxford.* 54 pp. + 57 plates. London: Oxford University Press, 1969.
Reviewed by Joan Rimmer in *Notes* 26 (1970): 741–44.

OXFORD UNIVERSITY. FACULTY OF MUSIC

8.93* Baines, Anthony. *The Bate Collection of Historical Wind Instruments: Catalogue of the Instruments.* 64 pp. London: Oxford University Press, 1976.
Reviewed by Dale Higbee in *AMISJ* 5–6 (1979–80): 216–17.

Paris, France

CONSERVATOIRE NATIONAL

8.94 Chouquet, Gustave. *Le Musée du Conservatoire National de Musique: Catalogue descriptif et raisonné.* Nouvelle éd. 276 pp. Paris: Firmin-Didot, 1884.

First published in 1875, with supplements by Leon Pillaut in 1894, 1899, and 1903.

A catalog of 1,006 instruments, subdivided into European and non-European sections, with an index of instruments and names. Catalogers of musical instruments owe much to the classification established by Chouquet in this catalog.

Rome, Italy

MUSEO NAZIONALE DELLE ARTI E TRADIZIONI POPOLARI

8.95* Simeoni, Paola Elisabetta, and **Roberta Tucci.** *La collezione degli strumenti musicali.* 502 pp. + 1 sound disc (33 1/3 rpm, 7 in.). (Cataloghi dei musei e gallerie d'Italie. Nuova ser., 4)

A collection of musical instruments connected with Italian folk music, with a selective discography (pp. 375–78) and a variety of indexes.

MUSEO NAZIONALE STRUMENTI MUSICALI

8.96 Cervelli, Luisa. *Antichi strumenti musicali in un moderno museo: Museo nazionale strumenti musicali, Roma.* 2nd ed. 75 pp. Rome: Gela, 1986.

A catalog of the older instruments in the museum, with an index and bibliography.

Saint Petersburg, Russia

8.97 Blagodatov, Georgii Ivanovich. *Katalog sobraniia muzykal´nykh instrumentov (Catalogue of the Musical Instrument Collection, Leningrad Institute of Theatre, Music, and Cinematography).* 127 pp. Leningrad: "Muzyka" Leningr., otd-nie, 1972.

Reviewed by Paul Hailperin in *Galpin Society Journal* 28 (1975): 135–36.

Salzburg, Austria

MUSEUM CAROLINO-AUGUSTEUM

8.98* Birsak, Kurt. *Die Holzblasinstrumente im Salzburger Museum Carolino Augusteum: Verzeichnis und entwicklungsgeschichtliche Untersuchungen.* 211 pp. Salzburg: Salzburger Museum Carolino Augusteum, 1973. (Jahresschrift: Salzburger Museum Carolino Augusteum, 18) (Publikationen des Instituts für Musikwissenschaft der Universität Salzburg, 9)

An illustrated (8 ll. of plates) catalog of a prominent woodwind instrument collection.

8.99 Geiringer, Karl. *Alte Musik-Instrumente im Museum Carolino-Augusteum Salzburg: Führer & beschreibendes Verzeichnis.* 46 pp. Leipzig: Breitkopf & Härtel, 1932.

A catalog of 288 instruments, with an index of makers and 4 photographic plates showing 48 different instruments.

Santa Barbara, California

8.100* Hsu, Dolores M. *The Henry Eichheim Collection of Oriental Instruments: A Western Musician Discovers a New World of Sound.* 88 pp. Santa Barbara, Calif.: University Art Museum, University of California, Santa Barbara, 1984.

The collection of an American composer who was among the early Western connoisseurs of Asian music. This collection is of the finest quality, beautiful in both sound and appearance.

Tokyo, Japan

MUSASHINO ACADEMIA MUSICAE

8.101 *Catalogue, Museum of Musical Instruments: On the 40th Anniversary of the Institute.* 108 pp. Tokyo, 1969.

Text in Japanese and English.

The catalog of a collection established in 1953, classified by national origins of the instruments, with a taxonomy according to method of sound production. Part 2 is a catalog of accessories; Part 3 is a catalog of mechanical devices.

UENO GAKUEN COLLEGE. INSTITUTE FOR THE STUDY OF MUSICAL INSTRUMENTS

8.102 *Catalogue of the European Musical Instruments of the XVIIth, XVIIIth and XIXth Centuries in the Ueno Gakuen Collection.* 243 pp. Tokyo: Ueno Gakuen Educational Foundation, 1980. Supplement: 92 pp. 1990.

Text in Japanese and English.

A book whose main vol. includes 82 pp. of photographs incorporating 3 to 6 views of each of 71 instruments, with text references to photographs by number.

Reviewed by Margaret Birley in *Galpin Society Journal* 44 (1991): 169–71.

Toronto, Canada

ROYAL ONTARIO MUSEUM

8.103 Dselenyi, Ladislav. *Musical Instruments in the Royal Ontario Museum.* 96 pp. Toronto: Royal Ontario Museum, 1971.

A well-illustrated catalog of more than 100 instruments. The instruments come from the bequest of R. S. Williams, beginning in 1913.

Trondheim, Norway

RINGVE MUSEUM

8.104* Kjeldsberg, Peter Andreas. *Musikkinstrumenter ved Ringve Museum / The Collection of Musical Instruments.* 92 pp. Trondheim: Museet, 1976. (Ringve Museums skrifter, 2)

A catalog with brief descriptions of about 600 instruments from all parts of the world, most of which were acquired between 1946 and 1963 by Victoria and Christian Anker Bachle, the Museum's founders. The collection is strong in non–Western European instruments.

Reviewed by Howard Mayer Brown in *EM* 4 (1976): 473.

Verona, Italy

ACCADEMIA FILARMONICO DI VERONA

8.105 Meer, John Henry van der, and **Rainer Weber.** *Catalogo degli strumenti musicali dell'Accademia Filarmonica di Verona.* 146 pp. Verona: Accademia Filarmonica di Verona, 1982.

A catalog of the instrument collections of one of the oldest continuously operating musical organizations in Italy.

Reviewed by Malou Haine in *Fontes* 31 (1984): 135–37.

Vienna, Austria

GESELLSCHAFT DER MUSIKFREUNDE

8.106 Mandyczewski, Eusebius. "Musikinstrumente," in *Zusatz-Band zur Geschichte der KK. Gesellschaft der Musikfreunde in Wien. Sammlung und Statuten*, pp. 154–85. Vienna, 1912.

The catalog of a collection of 355 instruments, of which 221 are of Western origin. The remaining are from Turkey, Africa, Arabia, Persia, Siam, India, China, and Japan.

KUNSTHISTORISCHES MUSEUM

8.107 Luithlen, Victor. *Alte Musikinstrumente: Die Sammlung des Kunsthistorischen Museums in der neuen Burg zu Wien.* 28 pp. Vienna: H. Bauer, 1954.

A brief visitor's guide to the collection described in **8.108** and **8.109**.

8.108 Luithlen, Victor, and **Kurt Wegerer.** *Katalog der Sammlung alter Musikinstrumente.* I. Teil. *Saitenklaviere.* 95 pp. + 32 plates. Vienna: Kunsthistorisches Museum, 1966.

A classified catalog and description of 76 keyboard instruments, full of detailed information on instrument makers, dimensions of the instruments, and bibliographical references. The catalog is the work of the music instrument collection's director and his assistant. This vol. is the first of a projected three that will eventually cover all of the museum's holdings.

Reviewed by Friedrich Ernst in *Die Musikforschung* 21 (1968): 506–7.

8.109 Schlosser, Julius. *Die Sammlung alter Musikinstrumente: Beschreibendes Verzeichnis.* 138 pp. Vienna: Anton Schroll, 1920.

The catalog describes 361 instruments, most of which are illustrated in 57 plates. Included are 31 Asian and folk instruments. Western instruments are entered in chronological order, grouped according to type, with full descriptions and an informative introduction to each major section, such as "Das Orchester des 16. und 17. Jahrhunderts" and "Die Entwicklung des Instrumentenbaus seit dem 18. Jahrhundert." Much useful historical information is given, such as a supplement quoting the descriptions of 20 early instruments from Mattheson's *Neueröffnetes Orchester* (1713).

MUSEUM FÜR VÖLKERKUNDE

8.110 *Aussereuropäische Musikinstrumente.* 89 pp. Vienna: Museum für Völkerkunde, 1961.

Foreword by Alfred Janata.

An illustrated classified catalog of 654 non-European instruments.

Washington, District of Columbia

LIBRARY OF CONGRESS. MUSIC DIVISION

8.111 Herbert, Rembert. *Three Masters: The Stringed Instrument Collection in the Library of Congress.* Additional research by Paula Forrest; photographs by Paula Forrest, Michael Seyfrit, and Dane Penland. 28 pp. Washington, D.C.: Library of Congress, 1983.

A brief guide to the collection.

8.112 *Musical Instruments in the Dayton C. Miller Flute Collection at the Library of Congress: A Catalog.* Washington, D.C.: Library of Congress, 1982– .

Vol. 1: *Recorders, Fifes, and Simple System Transverse Flutes of One Key.* Compiled by Michael Seyfrit.

Planned, when complete, to cover in 7 vols. the 6,000 instruments in the collection. The catalog was preceded by a checklist: *Dayton C. Miller Flute Collection, a Checklist of the Instruments,* by Laura E. Gilliam and William Lichtenwanger, 1961. Vol. 1 treats 273 instruments. There are 56 photographs, and indexes of instrument makers, cities, symbols, and sources. See also Dayton C. Miller's catalog of literature on the flute (**4.244**).

Reviewed by Jane P. Ambrose in *Notes* 39 (1983): 853 and by Edgar Hunt in *Galpin Society Journal* 36 (1983): 145–46.

8.113 Orcutt, William Dana. *The Stradivari Memorial at Washington, the National Capital.* 49 pp. Washington, D.C.: Library of Congress, Gertrude Clarke Whittall Foundation, 1938.

A description of the matched set of Stradivarius instruments donated to the Library of Congress.

SMITHSONIAN INSTITUTION. DIVISION OF
MUSICAL INSTRUMENTS

8.114 *A Checklist of Keyboard Instruments at the Smithsonian Institution.* 79 pp. Washington, D.C.: Smithsonian Institution, 1967.

A catalog that, although lacking full descriptions, is still remarkably rich in information: maker, place of origin, date, type, and compass.

8.115 Densmore, Frances. *Handbook of the Collection of Musical Instruments in the United States National Museum.* 164 pp. + 49 plates. Washington, D.C.: Government Printing Office, 1927. (Smithsonian Institution U.S. National Museum. Bulletin, 136)

8.116 Hoover, Cynthia A. *Harpsichords and Clavichords.* 43 pp. Washington, D.C.: Smithsonian Institution Press, 1969.

A guide to the instruments in the Smithsonian Institution.

Dealers

8.117 Ripin, Edward M. *The Instrument Catalogs of Leopoldo Franciolini.* 201 pp. Hackensack, N.J.: Joseph Boonin, 1974. (Music indexes and bibliographies, 9)

A study of a turn-of-the-century musical instrument dealer and forger through his seven surviving printed catalogs.

Reviewed by Howard Schott in *EM* 3 (1975): 147–48.

9

HISTORIES AND BIBLIOGRAPHIES OF MUSIC PRINTING AND PUBLISHING

Included in this section are bibliographies listing the output from some of the first group of major music printers and publishers, such as Petrucci, Playford, Walsh, and Ballard; studies of music publishing in particular areas (England, Italy, Paris, and Vienna); and a few works concerned with the technical processes of music printing or engraving and historical studies of copyright law; for contemporary law, see "Music Business and Law" (**13.21–13.37**). An extensive but dated bibliography on the history of music printing has been compiled by Åke Davidsson (**9.22**). Alexander Weinmann's series of studies, *Beiträge zur Geschichte des Alt-Wiener Musikverlages* (**9.150**), documents Vienna's music publishing history of the late 18th and early 19th centuries. The titles appear under varied imprints and in two subseries: Reihe 1, *Komponisten;* and Reihe 2, *Verleger.* For the most comprehensive 1-vol., English-language summary, see *Music Printing and Publishing* (**9.1**).

9.1 Krummel, D. W., and **Stanley Sadie.** *Music Printing and Publishing.* 615 pp. New York: W.W. Norton, 1990. (The Norton/Grove handbooks in music)

A vol. incorporating material on the printing and publishing of music that appeared in *The New Grove Dictionary of Music and Musicians* (**1.48**) and *The New Grove Dictionary of American Music* (**1.220**), made current and substantially supplemented. In Part 1, the *New Grove* article "Printing and Publishing of Music," by Krummel and H. Edmund Poole, is a review of the history of music printing from its early stages to modern practices and a survey of publishing practices from 1501 to the present. It has been enlarged by Richard Vendome's account of "Music Printing by Computer." Part 2 is a dictionary of music publishers and printers, based on the roughly 500 entries on music publishers and printers in the two 1980s Grove sets, supplemented by over 150 additional entries. Part 3 is a glossary of music printing and publishing, contributed by Stanley Boorman. Includes an entirely reworked and expanded classified bibliography (pp. 553–63) and a single index (a first in a *New Grove* vol.) of corporate and personal names and cities.

Reviewed by Corey Field in *Notes* 47 (1991): 725–27, by Alec Hyatt King in *M&L* 72 (1991): 413–15, and by John May in *Brio* 28 (1991): 37–38.

9.2* Alaner, Bülent. *Osmanli Imparatorlugu'ndan günümüze belgelerle müzik (nota) y yayinciligi (1876–1986) / Music Publications from Ottoman Empire up [!] Today (1876–1986).* 96 pp. Ankara: Anadol Yavincilik, 1986. (Belgelerle türk müsik tarihi dizisi / A documentary series of history of Turkish music, 1)

A brief history of music publishing in Turkey, in Turkish and an awkward English, which covers the subject from its beginning until the time when it ceased to exist in Turkey.

Reviewed by Mary Kay Duggan in *Notes* 47 (1991): 794–95.

9.3* **Antolini, Bianca Maria,** and **Annalisa Bini.** *Editori e librai musicali a Roma nella prima metà dell'Ottocento.* 235 pp. Rome: Edizioni Torre d'Orfeo, 1988. (Cataloghi di fondi musicali italiani, 8; Serie II: Repertori e bibliografie, 1)

A catalog of 19th-century Roman music publishing, which includes a reprint of a catalog of sacred music published by Pietro Alfieri and a newly compiled catalog of music published by Leopoldo Ratti and Giovanni Battista Concetti.

9.4* **Benton, Rita,** and **Jeanne Halley.** *Pleyel as Music Publisher: A Documentary Sourcebook of Early 19th-Century Music.* xxviii + 398 pp. Stuyvesant, N.Y.: Pendragon Press, 1990. (Annotated reference tools in music, 3)

A source listing everything published by Ignace Pleyel et Cie., with access to additional information through a series of indexes.

Reviewed by Anik Devriès in *Revue de musicologie* 76 (1990): 247 and by Corey Field in *Notes* 47 (1991): 793–94.

9.5 Bergmans, Paul. "La typographie musicale en Belgique au XVIe siècle." In *Histoire du livre et de l'imprimerie en Belgique des origines à nos jours* 5 (1929): 47–75.

An illustrated account of 16th-century Belgian music printers and printing.

9.6 Bernstein, Jane A. "The Burning Salamander: Assigning a Printer to Some Sixteenth-Century Music Prints." In *Notes* 42 (1986): 483–501.

An article on the attribution of a number of printed works to the Venetian music publisher Girolamo Scotto.

9.7 Berz, Ernst-Ludwig. *Die Notendrucker und ihre Verleger in Frankfurt am Main von den Anfängen bis etwa 1630: Eine bibliographische und drucktechnische Studie zur Musikpublikation.* 336 pp. Kassel, Germany: International Association of Music Libraries and International Musicological Society, 1970. (Catalogus musicus, 5)

A thoroughly documented study of music printing in Frankfurt to 1630, with a bibliography of 258 printed works by 43 printers.

9.8 Bobillier, Marie (Michel Brenet, pseud.). "La librairie musicale en France de 1653 à 1790, d'après les Registres de privilèges." In *Sammelbände der Internationalen Musikgesellschaft* 8 (1906–7): 401–66.

An examination with extensive transcriptions from the archives in the Bibliothèque Nationale pertaining to licenses granted for the publication of music and books on music in Paris from 1652 to 1790. There is a thorough discussion of the inception of the royal *privilège* with transcriptions of sample 17th-century *privilèges*. This work is supplemented by Cucuel (**9.21**).

9.9 Brook, Barry. *The Breitkopf Thematic Catalogue: The Six Parts and Sixteen Supplements, 1762–1787.* Edited, with an introduction and indexes. xxvii + 888 + lxxxi pp. New York: Dover, 1966.

First published as *Catalogo delle sinfonie, partite, overture, soli, trii, quattri e concerti per il violino, flauto traverso, cembalo ed altri stromenti, che si trovano in manuscritto nella officina musica di Giovanni Gottlob Breitkopf in Lipsia* (Leipzig: Breitkopf & Härtel, 1762–65), and *Supplementi I–XVI* (1766–87).

A facsimile reproduction of the major 18th-century thematic catalog, giving almost 15,000 musical incipits and 1,300 first lines of text, representing over 1,000 composers. The thematic catalog is preceded by an informative essay and an outline of the contents. The contents are chiefly instrumental music, but there are some vocal works, from the archives of Breitkopf & Härtel. This catalog is useful in tracing or identifying the works of the period. Includes a first-line index and a general index of names and topics.

Reviewed by Bernard E. Wilson in *JAMS* 21 (1968): 400–4, by Donald W. Krummel in *Notes* 24 (1968): 697–700, and by H. C. Robbins Landon in *Haydn Yearbook* 6 (1969): 218.

9.10* Brown, A. Peter, and **Richard Griscom.** *The French Music Publisher Guéra of Lyon: A Dated List.* xxiii + 115 pp. Detroit, Mich.: Information Coordinators, 1987. (Detroit studies in music bibliography, 57)

Reviewed by H. C. Robbins Landon in *Haydn Yearbook* 11 (1980): 211–12.

9.11* *C. F. Peters Music Publishing Tradition, 1800–1975: Classical/Contemporary Highlights.* 16 pp. New York: C.F. Peters Corp., 1975.

Reviewed by Alfred Mann in *American Choral Review* 18 (1976): 29.

9.12 Calderisi, Maria. *Music Publishing in the Canadas, 1800–1867 / L'édition musicale au Canada, 1800–1867.* 128 pp. Ottawa: National Library of Canada, 1981.

A bibliographic study with a list of imprints beginning about 1800.

Reviewed by Donald W. Krummel in *Fontes* 29 (1982): 90.

9.13 Castelain, Raoul. *Histoire de l'édition musicale, ou, du droit d'éditeur au droit d'auteur, 1501–1793.* Pref. de André Siegfried. 92 pp. Paris: H. Lemoine, 1957.

A brief history of music publishing, with emphasis on legal aspects.

9.14* *Catalogue de Brandus et Cie: Musique de piano: Musique instrumentale: Musique vocale.* 64 + 68 + 46 pp. Geneva: Minkoff, 1989. (Archives de l'édition musicale française, 10)

The reprint of three publishers' catalogs originally published separately by Brandus in 1853. There is a succinct historical introduction by François Lesure.

9.15 Chrysander, Friedrich. "A Sketch of the History of Music: Printing, from the Fifteenth to the Nineteenth Century." In *MT* 18 (1877): 265–68, 324–26, 375–78, 470–75, 524–27, 584–87.

Also published in German as "Abriss einer Geschichte des Musikdruckes vom fünfzehnten bis zum neunzehnten Jahrhundert" in *Allgemeine musikalische Zeitung* 14 (1879) cols. 161–67, 177–83, 193–200, 209–14, 225–32, 241–48.

9.16 *Cinq catalogues d'éditeurs de musique à Paris (1824–34): Dufaut et Dubois, Petit, Frère, Delahante-Erard, Pleyel.* With an introduction by François Lesure. Geneva: Minkoff Reprint, 1976. (Archives de l'édition musicale française, 2)

Reprints of the catalogs of the five publishers, each classified, some with tables of contents. The introduction provides information on each firm's history. The Pleyel catalogs provide plate numbers.

Reviewed by Rita Benton in *Fontes* 25 (1978): 197–99.

9.17 *Cinque secoli di stampa musicale in Europa.* 299 pp. Naples: Electa Napoli, 1985.

An illustrated catalog for an exhibition at the Museo di Palazzo Venezia celebrating the 400th anniversary of the founding of the Accademia Nazionale di Santa Cecilia.

The exhibition was segmented into chronological periods. The catalog follows this design with introductory essays before entries for a particular period. Each entry provides a title-page transcription, collation, and indications of the library or archive holding the item. There follows a short explanation of the significance of the item for the history of music printing.

There were at least 620 scores exhibited, a large number of documents concerning music printing, many catalogs of music publishers from the 18th century forward, and at least two dozen prints and paintings with musical themes. Each of these is described. The catalog concludes with a bibliography of works concerning the iconographic items in the exhibition and a general bibliography. The emphasis is on Italian music printing, but all of the major European developments are represented.

9.18 Cohen, Paul. *Musikdruck und Drucker zu Nürnberg im 16. Jahrhundert erschienenen Noten- und Musikbücher.* 63 pp. Nuremberg: H. Zierfuss, 1927.

Also issued as a dissertation (Erlangen) under the title *Die Nürnberger Musikdrucker im sechzehnten Jahrhundert,* 1927. A historical study, with brief accounts of the individual printers, followed by a chronological list of 443 works published in Nuremberg from 1501 to 1600.

9.19 Coover, James. *Music Publishing, Copyright, and Piracy in Victorian England: A Twenty-Five Year Chronicle, 1881–1906, from the Pages of the Musical Opinion & Music Trade Review and Other English Music Journals of the Period.* 169 pp. London; New York: Mansell, 1985.

A summary of copyright reports and concerns from periodicals of the time, with helpful annotations, bibliography, and indexes.

Reviewed by David Hunter in *Notes* 45 (1988): 64–65 and by Miriam Miller in *Fontes* 33 (1986): 219–20.

9.20 Cucuel, Georges. "Notes sur quelques musiciens, luthiers, éditeurs et graveurs de musique au XVIIIe siècle." In *Sammelbände der internationalen Musikgesellschaft* 14 (1912–13): 243–52.

9.21 Cucuel, Georges. "Quelques documents sur la librairie musicale au XVIIIe siècle." In *Sammelbände der internationalen Musikgesellschaft* 13 (1911–12): 385–92.

A further study of the archives related to the licensing of music publications in France, which supplements the article by Bobillier (**9.8**).

9.22 Davidsson, Åke. *Bibliographie zur Geschichte des Musikdrucks.* 86 pp. Uppsala: Almquist & Wiksells, 1965. (Studia musicologia upsaliensis. Nova ser., 1)

A bibliography organized into a single alphabetical sequence of 598 entries, prefaced by a historical introduction devoted to an account of music publishing in different countries. This is the expansion of a bibliography first issued as part of the author's *Musikbibliographische Beiträge* (**9.24**).

9.23 Davidsson, Åke. *Danskt musiktryck intill 1700–talets mitt: Dänischer Musikdruck bis zur Mitte des 18. Jahrhunderts.* 100 pp. Uppsala: Almquist & Wiksell, 1962. (Studia musicologica Upsaliensia, 7)

A historical study of early Danish music printing, with a chronological list of Danish printed editions issued during the period under consideration. Includes a bibliography and index of names.

Reviewed by Martin Geck in *Die Musikforschung* 18 (1965): 346: 47.

9.24 Davidsson, Åke. "Die Literatur zur Geschichte des Notendrucks." In his *Musikbibliographische Beiträge,* pp. 91–115. Uppsala: A.B. Lundequistska Bokhandeln, 1954. (Uppsala Universitets Årsskrift, 1954:9)

A survey of writings on the history of music printing, with a bibliography of 268 items, superseded by the author's *Bibliographie zur Geschichte des Musikdrucks* (**9.22**).

Reviewed by Edward N. Waters in *Notes* 12 (1955): 604 and by Vincent H. Duckles in *LQ* 26 (1956): 73–74.

9.25 Davidsson, Åke. *Studier rörande svenskt musiktryck före ar 1750: Studien über schwedischen Musikdruck vor 1750.* 167 pp. Uppsala: Uppsala Akaddemisk Avhandling, 1957. (Studia musicologica Upsaliensia, 5)

A study of early Swedish music printing. The 1st section is a general survey of early Swedish music printing; the 2nd is a bibliography of 124 early Swedish imprints issued between 1585 and 1750, in chronological order. The text is in Swedish, the summary German. Includes a general bibliography and an index of persons.

Reviewed by Rudolf Gjelsness in *Notes* 15 (1958): 569–70.

9.26 Deaville, James. "The C. F. Kahnt Archive in Leipzig: A Preliminary Report." In *Notes* 42 (1986): 502–17.

An article concerning the survival and contents of the papers of one of the lesser Leipzig publishing houses.

9.27 Deutsch, Otto Erich. *Music Publishers' Numbers: A Selection of 40 Dated Lists, 1710–1900: Reprinted from the Journal of Documentation, Vol. I, no. 4 (March, 1946) and Vol. II, no. 2 (Sept., 1946), with Some Alterations and an Index.* 30 pp. London: Association of Special Libraries and Information Bureaus, 1946.

Deutsch, Otto E. *Musikverlags-Nummern: Eine Auswahl von 40 datierten Listen.* Zweite, verbesserte und erste deutsche Ausgabe. 32 pp. Berlin: Merseburger, 1961.

A revision and expansion of a list originally published in the *Journal of Documentation* 1 (1946), as "Music Publishers' Numbers: A Selection of 40 Dated Lists, 1710–1900."

A study treating 20 German, 14 Austrian, 3 Dutch, 1 English, 1 French, and 1 Swiss firm. There is an index of places and individual publishers, supplemented by the author's "Musikverlags-Nummern: Ein Nachtrag," in *Die Musikforschung* 15 (1962): 155.

Reviewed by Donald W. Krummel in *Notes* 19 (1961): 76–77 and by Richard Schaal in *Die Musikforschung* 16 (1963): 389. The 1946 ed. is reviewed by Inger Christensen in *Notes* 5 (1948): 379.

9.28 Devriès, Anik. "Un éditeur de musique 'à la tête ardenté,' Maurice Schlesinger." In *Fontes* 27 (1980): 125–36.

A brief recounting of the publishing career of the person responsible for the *Revue et gazette musicale.*

9.29 Devriès, Anik. *Édition et commerce de la musique gravée à Paris dans la première moitié du XVIIIe siècle: les Boivin, les Leclerc.* 274 pp. Geneva: Minkoff, 1976. (Archives de l'édition musicale française, 1)

A study of Parisian music engraving in the early 18th century, with particular regard for one of the principal engravers. "Catalogue général de la production des Leclerc" (pp. 127–272) is an extensive catalog, alphabetized by composer, of the works of the Leclercs.

Reviewed by Neal Zaslaw in *Notes* 33 (1977): 825–26, by Barry S. Brook in *Fontes* 24 (1977): 50–52, and by J. M. Thomson in *EM* 7 (1979): 409.

9.30 Devriès, Anik. "Les éditions musicales Sieber." In *Revue de Musicologie* 55 (1969): 20–46.

An article on the publishing history of the Parisian firm of Sieber between 1771 and 1847, including a table of the Sieber firm's addresses in Paris. Among others, Sieber published works by Stamitz, J. Haydn, W. A. Mozart, and J. Pleyel.

9.31 Devriès, Anik, and **François Lesure.** *Dictionnaire des éditeurs de musique française des origines à environ 1820.* 2 vols. in 3. Geneva: Minkoff, 1979–88. (Archives de l'édition musicale française, 4)

Contents: Vol. 1, *Des origines à environ 1820* (2 vols.); Vol. 2, *De 1820 à 1914.*

A comprehensive dictionary whose 1st vol. contains the dictionary of music publishers and dealers in France from the 16th century to 1820, including in each a biography, lists of successive addresses, lists of published catalogs, citations of privileges received, and a bibliography. Vol. 2 presents facsimiles of more than 200 catalogs by 50 publishers and forms a supplement to Cari Johansson's *French Music Publishers' Catalogues* (**9.71**). Includes an index to insignia, as well as indexes to the composers and titles in the reproduced catalogs. The source of each catalog and the rationale for attribution of date are given in a list preceding the reproductions. Vol. 2 is an alphabetical directory of French music publishers from 1820 to the start of World War I, with each entry given a chronological list of addresses, other names the firm may have used, the firm's agents (generally foreign), and their catalogs. An appendix lists provincial publishers arranged by city; includes an index to the names of Parisian streets, listing the publishers residing there, and an index of prefaces to plate numbers and names (personal, professional, and periodical).

Reviewed by Eugene K. Wolf in *JAMS* 33 (1980): 592–96 and by Lenore Coral in *Notes* 37 (1980): 61–62. The 2nd vol. is reviewed by Lenore Coral in *Fontes* 37 (1990): 199–200 and by Jean Gribenski in *Revue de musicologie* 77 (1991): 136–37.

9.32 Donà, Mariangela. *La stampa musicale a Milano fino all'anno 1700.* 167 pp. Florence: Olschki, 1961. (Biblioteca di bibliografia italiana, 39)

A list of Milanese music publishers given in alphabetical order, with chronological lists of their publications. Copies of rare works are located in major European libraries. Includes an index of composers and works and an index of persons to whom works are dedicated.

Reviewed by Richard Schaal in *Die Musikforschung* 17 (1964): 183.

9.33* Duggan, Mary Kay. *Italian Music Incunabula: Printers and Type.* 323 pp. Berkeley, Calif.: University of California Press, 1992.

A careful look at the earliest days of Italian music printing, in part through a descriptive bibliography of 152 books containing either printed music or space for the music to be added by hand.

Reviewed by Hans Lenneberg in *Fontes* 40 (1993): 347–48.

9.34 Dunning, Albert. *De muziekuitgever Gerhard Fredrik Witvogel en zijn fonds: Een bijdrage tot de geschiedenis van de Nederlandse muziekuitgeverij in de achttiende eeuw.* 64 pp. Utrecht: A. Oosthoek's Uitgevermaatschappij N.V., 1966. (Muziekhistorische monografieen, 2)

"Uitgegeven door de Vereniging voor Nederlandse Muziekgeschiedenis."

A discussion of the life and works of Witvogel, with an annotated bibliography of 95 music publications by the firm. Locations of copies are given, with a list of composers whose works were published, a bibliography, and an index of names.

9.35 Eitner, Robert. *Buch- und Musikalienhändler, Buch- und Musikaliendrucker nebst Notenstecher, nur die Musik betreffend nach den Originaldrucken verzeichnet.* 248 pp. Leipzig: Breitkopf & Härtel, 1904. (Monatshefte für Musikgeschichte, Beilage)

A source compiled as a by-product of the *Quellen-Lexikon* (**5.544**), limited to material before 1850. There is an alphabetical list of publishers, printers, and dealers with their dates of location at various addresses, changes in name, and branches (if any), with international coverage.

9.36 Elvers, Rudolf. "Musikdrucker, Musikalienhändler und Musikverleger in Berlin 1750–1850." In *Festschrift Walter Gerstenberg zum 60. Geburtstag,* pp. 37–44. Wolfenbüttel, Germany: Möseler Verlag, 1964.

A list of 155 Berlin music printers, dealers, and publishers active during the century under consideration.

9.37 Epstein, Dena J. *Music Publishing in Chicago before 1871: The Firm of Root and Cady, 1858–1871.* 243 pp. Detroit, Mich.: Information Coordinators, 1969. (Detroit studies in music bibliography, 14)

An especially careful study illuminating the work of a firm of central importance in the history of American music publishing.

Reviewed by Klaus Hortschansky in *Die Musikforschung* 24 (1971): 464–65.

9.38* Fenlon, Iain. *Music, Print, and Culture in Early Sixteenth-Century Italy.* 96 pp. London: British Library, 1995. (The Panizzi lectures, 1994)

A talk on the social aspects of music publishing in early-16th-century Italy.

9.39 Fisher, William A. *150 Years of Music Publishing in the U.S.: A Historical Sketch with Special Reference to the Pioneer Publisher Oliver Ditson Co., 1783–1933.* 156 pp. Boston, Mass.: Oliver Ditson, 1934.

A revision and extension of portions of the author's *Notes on Music in Old Boston,* Boston, 1918.

9.40 Fog, Dan. *Dänische Musikverlage und Notendruckereien: Beiträge zur Musikaliendatierung.* 27 pp. Copenhagen, 1972.

Basic factual information concerning 60 Danish music printers and publishers. Important events in the history of these firms are given chronologically.

9.41 Fog, Dan. *Notendruck und Musikhandel im 19. Jahrhundert in Dänemark: Ein Beitrag zur Musikaliendatierung und zur Geschichte der Musikvermittlung.* 336 pp. Copenhagen: Dan Fog Musikverlag, 1986.

A revised abridgment, in German, of the 2-vol. *Musikhandel og Nodetryk i Danmark efter 1750* (Copenhagen: D. Fog Musikforlag, 1984).

A guide to music publishing and music trades in Denmark after 1750 until roughly 1899, incorporating a brief section on dating music of the period by plate numbers and other characteristics. Included is a dictionary of music dealers and publishers citing plate numbers, with bibliography and indexes.

Reviewed by D. W. Krummel in *Notes* 44 (1988): 469–70.

9.42 Fog, Dan. "Random Thoughts on Music Dating and Terminology." In *Fontes* 24 (1977): 141–44.

"My main purpose in voicing these observations is to suggest that the two principal preoccupations of our present work, dating and terminology, call for a new and different way of thinking. We must break free from the conventional, book-infected concepts that are often transferred to music bibliography."

9.43* Fog, Dan. *Zur Datierung der Edition Peters: Auf Grundlage der Grieg-Ausgaben.* 36 pp. Copenhagen: D. Fog, 1990.

Reviewed by John Wagstaff in *Brio* 28 (1991): 49–50.

9.44 Fog, Dan, and **Kari Michelsen.** *Norwegian Music Publication since 1800: A Preliminary Guide to Music Publishers, Printers, and Dealers.* 30 pp. Copenhagen: Dan Fog Musikforlag, 1976.

Brief sketches, in English, with an informative introduction, of the activity of 38 Norwegian music publishers, printers, and dealers, with plate numbers given where known. The bibliography also cites rental libraries.

Reviewed by Richard Andrewes in *MT* 119 (1978): 423–24.

9.45 Forney, Kristine Koren. *Tielman Susato, Sixteenth-Century Music Printer: An Archival and Typographical Investigation.* 356 pp. Ph.D. dissertation, University of Kentucky, 1978.

An investigation of the technical aspects of Susato's output and his contributions to single-impression music printing. Susato was active in Antwerp from 1543 to 1561. The study includes a survey of music printing in the Low Countries before Susato. Includes a chapter on "The Making of a Renaissance Music Book" and another presenting an adaptation of the techniques of descriptive bibliography to identify and describe editions of chanson books issued by Susato. There are bibliographies of primary and secondary sources.

9.46 Fraenkel, Gottfried S. *Decorative Music Title Pages: 201 Examples from 1500 to 1800.* Selected, introduced, and annotated by Gottfried S. Fraenkel. 230 pp. New York: Dover, 1968.

An anthology of music title pages, whose introduction (pp. 1–15) gives a historical survey of the items in the collection. There are 201 plates with historical and descriptive annotations.

9.47 Fuld, James J., and **Frances Barulich.** "Harmonizing the Arts: Original Graphic Designs for Printed Music by World-Famous Artists." In *Notes* 43 (1987): 259–71.

A bibliography of the works of well-known artists created as illustrations to printed music, arranged in alphabetical order by artist.

9.48 Gamble, William. *Music Engraving and Printing: Historical and Technical Treatise.* 266 pp. London; New York: Pitman, 1923 [1922].

Reprinted by Arno Press, New York, 1979.

An illustrated discussion of the technical processes of music printing and engraving, with emphasis on contemporary practices.

9.49* Gates, R. Terry. "Samuel Gerrish, Publisher to the 'Regular Singing' Movement in 1720s New England," in *Notes* 45 (1988): 15–33.

A brief, well-documented account of Gerrish's activities, which are further illuminated by various tabulations of music publishing activities in the Boston area in colonial times.

9.50* *Gedruckte Musik: 225 Jahre Musikverlag Schott in Mainz.* 47 pp. Bern: Gutenberg-Museum, 1995.

A commemorative publication on the occasion of the 225th anniversary of the publication of printed music by B. Schott's Söhne.

9.51 Gericke, Hannelore. *Der Wiener Musikalienhandel von 1700 bis 1778.* 150 pp. Graz, Austria: H. Böhlaus Nachf., 1960. (Wiener musikwissenschaftliche Beiträge, 6)

Contents: Wiener Buchhändler als Verkäufer von Musikalien; Privatverkäufer, Kopisten; Kupferstecher; Verzeichnis der Wiener Musikdrucke von 1700–1778; Liste der verbotenen Musikbücher; Zusammenfassung; Literaturverzeichnis.

Reviewed by Donald W. Krummel in *Notes* 18 (1961): 229–30.

9.52 Göhler, Albert. *Verzeichnis der in den Frankfurter und Leipziger Messkatalogen der Jahre 1564 bis 1759 angezeigten Musikalien.* 4 parts in 1 vol. Leipzig: C.F. Kahns Nachf., 1902.

Reprint by F. Knuf, Hilversum, The Netherlands, 1965.

A major source of information on the activities of early music dealers, printers, and publishers. It lists music entered in the Frankfurt and Leipzig trade catalogs from 1564 to 1759.

9.53 Goovaerts, Alphonse J. M. A. *Histoire et bibliographie de la typographie musicale dans les Pays-Bas.* 608 pp. Antwerp: P. Kockx, 1880. (Extrait des Memoires de l'Academie Royale de Belgique, Collection in-8; tome 29)

Reprint issued by F. Knuf, Hilversum, The Netherlands, 1963.

Music publishing in the Netherlands. Part I (historical): a chronological discussion of music publishing in the Netherlands from 1539. Part II (bibliographical): chronological list of 1,415 music publications from 1539 to 1841. The descriptions are full, with an index of personal names, titles, and places.

9.54 Grand-Carteret, John. *Les titres illustrés et l'image au service de la musique.* 269 pp. Turin: Bocca, 1904.

Contents: Première partie (pp. 3–120), Le titre de musique sous la Révolution, le Consulat et le Premier Empire (1500–1800). Deuxième partie, Le titre de musique et la lithographie, 1: 1817–30, 2: 1830–50.

Abundantly illustrated with facsimiles of title pages, printers' devices, and pages of music.

9.55* Guidobaldi, Nicoletta. "Music Publishing in Sixteenth- and Seventeenth-Century Umbria." In *Early Music History: Studies in Medieval and Early Modern Music,* Vol. 8, pp. 1–36. Cambridge, England; New York: Cambridge University Press, 1988.

9.56* Guillo, Laurent. *Les éditions musicales de la renaissance lyonnaise.* 494 pp. Paris: Klincksieck, 1991. (Domaine musicologique, 9)

Reviewed by Henri Vanhulst in *Revue de musicologie* 79 (1993): 156–58.

9.57* Harwell, Richard B. *Confederate Music.* 184 pp. Chapel Hill, N.C.: University of North Carolina Press, 1950.

A history of music publishing in the southern United States is followed by a checklist of 648 titles, "Sheet Music Published in the Confederate States" (pp. 101–56), and a list of Confederate publishers.

Reviewed by John Tasker Howard in *Notes* 7 (1950): 468–69.

9.58 Hase, Oskar von. *Breitkopf & Härtel: Gedenkschrift und Arbeitsbericht.* 5th ed. 2 vols. in 3. Wiesbaden: Breitkopf & Härtel, 1968.

Contents: Bd. 1, *1542–1827;* Bd. 2, *1828–1918;* Bd. 3, *1918–68.*

A thorough documentation of the activities of the great Leipzig publishing house of Breitkopf & Härtel, reviewing the history of the firm, its business relationships, and its dealings with the great composers of the late 18th and 19th centuries; editorial work on the *Denkmäler* and *Gesamtausgaben.* Bd. 3, by Hellmuth von Hase, reviews the history of the firm through World War II to its establishment in Wiesbaden.

9.59 Heartz, Daniel. "La chronologie des recueils imprimés par Pierre Attaingnant." In *Revue de musicologie* 44 (1959): 178–92.

A brief survey of Attaingnant's activity as a music printer, followed by a chronological tabulation of all collections published by him from 1528 to 1537, superseded by Heartz's magisterial study (**9.60**).

9.60 Heartz, Daniel. *Pierre Attaingnant, Royal Printer of Music: A Historical Study and Bibliographical Catalogue.* 451 pp. Berkeley; Los Angeles: University of California Press, 1969.

A historical study treating the founding of the Attaingnant press, new techniques of music printing, and commercial and artistic relationships, together with selected documents, dedications, and privileges (pp. 1–204), with a bibliographical catalog of 174 works issued by the press with precise bibliographical descriptions, lists of contents, and location of surviving copies (pp. 207–377). There are 16 black-and-white plates, with a frontispiece in color. This is an outstanding work in book design and subject coverage, with chronological and alphabetical short-title lists. There are indexes of Latin and French first lines and of composers.

Reviewed by Nicolas Barker in *Book Collector* (Summer 1971): 261–70, by Samuel Pogue in *Notes* 27 (1970): 258–60, by G. Dottin in *Revue de musicologie* 57 (1971): 87–88, by Howard M. Brown in *JAMS* 24 (1971): 125–26, and by Frank Dobbins in *M&L* 51 (1970): 447–49.

9.61 Henle, Gunter. *25 Jahre G. Henle Musikverlag 1948–1973.* 75 pp. Munich: G. Henle, 1973.

A history of the firm, chiefly a reprint from part of the author's autobiography, *Weggenosse des Jahrhunderts,* published in 1968.

9.62 Hill, Richard S. "The Plate Numbers of C. F. Peters' Predecessors." In *Papers . . . of the American Musicological Society . . . 29 and 30 Dec. 1938 [c. 1940],* pp. 113–34.

A survey of the publishing activities of F. A. Hoffmeister and A. Kühnel, 1784–1814, with a detailed analysis of their production in 1801–2, plate numbers 1–102.

9.63* Hilmar, Rosemary. *Der Musikverlag Artaria & Comp.: Geschichte und Probleme der Druckproduktion.* 176 pp. Tutzing, Germany: H. Schneider, 1977. (Publikationen des Institut für Österreichische Musikdokumentation, 6)

A history and archival study of the prominent Vienna publisher that breaks new ground in dating works with the Artaria imprint. Plate numbers of the firm (with composer, brief title, and approximate printing date) were initially listed by Kathi Meyer and Eva O'Meara in *Notes,* ser. 1, no. 15 (1942): 1–42, and by Alexander Weinmann (**9.150**).

Reviewed by Thomas F. Heck in *Notes* 35 (1978): 78–79.

9.64 Hoffmann-Erbrecht, Lothar. "Der Nürnberger Musikverleger Johann Ulrich Haffner." In *Acta musicologica* 26 (1954): 114–26 and 27 (1955): 141–42.

A biography and chronologically ordered bibliography of works published by Haffner between 1742 and 1765, with an index to composers.

9.65 Hoogerwerf, Frank W. *Confederate Sheet-Music Imprints.* 158 pp. Brooklyn, N.Y.: Institute for Studies in American Music, Conservatory of Music, Brooklyn College of CUNY, 1984. (ISAM monographs, 21)

A study of music printing in the Confederate States of America during the American Civil War, citing over 800 pieces of sheet music, with full bibliographical data, library locations, and index.

9.66 Hopkinson, Cecil. *A Dictionary of Parisian Music Publishers, 1700–1950.* 131 pp. London: The author, 1954.

Reprinted by Da Capo Press, New York, in 1979.

A description of some 550 printers, tabulating their name forms and addresses where they were active during specific periods. This is a useful tool for determining dates of undated French publications, although specific sources for its datings are often not included.

Reviewed by Inger M. Christensen in *Notes* 11 (1954): 550–51 and by Vincent H. Duckles in *JAMS* 8 (1955): 62–64. Entries **9.71** and **9.72** show another approach to the dating of 18th-century French music publications. The IAML *Guide for Dating Early Published Music* (**9.85**) provides more references and techniques.

9.67 Hopkinson, Cecil. *Notes on Russian Music Publishers.* 10 pp. Printed for the author for private distribution to the Members of the IAML at the Fifth International Congress, Cambridge, England, 29 June–4 July 1959.

An ed. limited to 125 numbered copies.

9.68 Humphries, Charles, and **William C. Smith.** *Music Publishing in the British Isles from the Beginning until the Middle of the Nineteenth Century: A Dictionary of Engravers, Printers, Publishers and Music Sellers, with a Historical Introduction.* 2nd ed., with supplement. 392 pp. + 25 plates. New York: Barnes & Noble; Oxford: Blackwell and Mott, 1970.

First published in 1954 by Cassell & Co., London. The 2nd ed. differs only in the addition of a 36-page supplement.

Superseding Kidson (**9.75**), a dictionary covering more than 2,000 persons and firms associated with British music printing and publishing. An introductory essay gives an excellent survey of the field. There are indexes of firms outside London and of makers and repairers of musical instruments.

The 1st ed. is reviewed by J. M. Coopersmith in *Notes* 11 (1954): 549–50; the 2nd ed. is reviewed by William Lichtenwanger in *Notes* 27 (1971): 489–90.

9.69 Hunter, David. "Music Copyright in Britain to 1800." In *M&L* 67 (1986): 269–82.

A historical summary of the evolution of concepts of copyright and intellectual property rights in Britain, focusing principally on the 18th century, for which period documentation is more plentiful. The article also provides insights on the sociological and commercial shifts affecting composers and publishers.

9.70 Imbault, Jean-Jerôme. *Catalogue thématique des ouvrages de musique, avec un index des compositeurs cités.* [Réimpression de l'édition de Paris, c. 1792.] 284 pp. Geneva: Minkoff Reprint, 1972.

A classified thematic catalog of works published by Imbault. Each section has its own pagination.

9.71 Johansson, Cari. *French Music Publishers' Catalogues of the Second Half of the Eighteenth Century.* 2 vols. Uppsala: Almquist & Wiksell, 1955.

Contents: Vol. 1 (octavo), *Textband,* 228 pp.; Vol. 2 (folio), *Tafeln,* 145 facsimiles from catalogs by 9 French music publishing houses, as well as newspapers and announcements.

The 1st vol. analyzes and describes the contents of the catalogs, and their use for dating purposes. It is useful to compare Johansson's method with that of Hopkinson (**9.66**). There is an index of names, titles, and catalogs, chronologically arranged under the name of the firm.

Reviewed by Donald W. Krummel in *Notes* 17 (1960): 234–35, by A. Hyatt King in *M&L* 37 (1956): 376–77, and by Wolfgang Schmieder in *Die Musikforschung* 10 (1957): 180–82.

9.72 Johansson, Cari. *J. J. & B. Hummel: Music-Publishing and Thematic Catalogues.* 3 vols. Stockholm: Almquist & Wiksell, 1972. (Publications of the Library of the Royal Swedish Academy of Music, 3)

A documented history of the publishing activities of the Hummel brothers, active in 18th-century Paris. Vol. 1 contains essays on the life and work of the Parisian brothers J. J. and B. Hummel; "Aids to the Dating of Hummel Prints," transcription of the Hummel catalogs 1762–1814; a list of plate numbers; an index of names and titles; and an index of catalogs. Vol. 2 contains music publishing catalogs in facsimile. Vol. 3 is a thematic catalog, 1768–74, in facsimile.

Reviewed by Rita Benton in *JAMS* 27 (1974): 530–32 and by François Lesure in *Revue de musicologie* 59 (1973): 297–98 no. 2.

9.73 *Journal général d'annoncés des oeuvres de musique, gravures, lithographies, publié en France et à l'étranger.* Avec un index des noms cités. 1 vol. Geneva: Minkoff Reprint, 1976. (Archives de l'édition musicale française, 3)

Reprint of weekly editions of a trade paper published in 1825, most heavily weighted to French publications.

9.74 Kast, Paul. "Die Musikdrucke des Kataloges Giunta von 1604." In *Analecta musicologica* 2 (1965): 41–47.

A transcription of the music portion of a general catalog issued by the Florentine music dealer and publisher Giunta in 1604, containing masses, motets, and secular works of the late 16th century, as well as a small selection of instrumental and theoretical works.

9.75 Kidson, Frank. *British Music Publishers, Printers and Engravers . . . from Queen Elizabeth's Reign to George IV, with Select Bibliographical Lists of Musical Works Printed and Published within That Period.* 231 pp. London: W. E. Hill & Sons, 1900. Unaltered reprint by Benjamin Blom, Inc., New York, 1967.

The pioneer work on English music publishing. Not as comprehensive as Humphries and Smith (**9.68**), but many of Kidson's entries are fuller and are accompanied by lists of publications. Entries arranged alphabetically by place. There is no index.

9.76 King, A. Hyatt. "English Pictorial Music Title-Pages, 1820–1885: Their Style, Evolution and Importance." In *Library* ser. 5, Vol. 4 (1949-50): 262–72.

9.77 King, A. Hyatt. *Four Hundred Years of Music Printing.* 2nd ed. 48 pp. London: Trustees of the British Museum, 1979.

First ed., 1964, 48 pp.

A short, well-written account of the history of music printing, with a selected bibliography of 29 items on the subject. The history is illustrated with facsimile pages of early music printing. The 2nd ed., 1968, incorporates a few changes in the text and additions to the bibliography.

The 1st ed. is reviewed by Harry Carter in *Library* ser. 5, Vol. 20 (June 1965): 154–57 and by Donald W. Krummel in *Notes* 22 (1965–66): 902–3.

9.78 Kinkeldey, Otto. "Music and Music Printing in Incunabula." In *Bibliographic Society of America, Papers* 26 (1932): 89–118.

For other discussions of music incunabula, see **9.106** and **9.152**.

9.79 Kinsky, Georg. "Erstlingsdrucke der deutschen Tonmeister der Klassik und Romantik." In *Philobiblon* 7 (1934): 347–64.

Also printed separately by H. Reichner, Vienna, 1934.

A contribution by one of the leading specialists in music printing of the 18th and 19th centuries.

9.80 Kohler, Stuart A. *Music Publishing in Rochester, 1859–1930: A Checklist of the Sheet Music Printed in Rochester in the Collection of the Rochester Museum and Science Center.* 75 ll. in various foliations. Rochester, N.Y.: Rochester Museum and Science Center, 1975.

9.81* Krohn, Ernst C. *Music Publishing in St. Louis.* Completed and edited by J. Bunker Clark. xxiii + 126 pp. Warren, Mich.: Harmonie Park Press, 1988. (Bibliographies in American music, 11)

A history of music publishing in a major 19th-century American center.
Reviewed by Mary Kay Duggan in *Notes* 47 (1991): 794–95.

9.82 Krohn, Ernst C. *Music Publishing in the Middle Western States before the Civil War.* 44 pp. Detroit, Mich.: Information Coordinators, 1972. (Detroit studies in music bibliography, 23)

9.83 Krummel, Donald W. *English Music Printing, 1553–1700.* 188 pp. London: Bibliographical Society, 1975.

A history, a typographical study, and a bibliographical study. It is not a bibliography, although it is filled with useful bibliographic references. It is included here as a model of bibliographic investigation. It uses the concept of bibliographical forms and has, as an appendix, "A Chronological Synopsis of Music Type Faces." This is a successor to Steele (**9.139** and **9.140**).

Reviewed by Lenore Coral and Stanley Boorman in *Notes* 34 (1977): 65–57, by Philip Brett in *JAMS* 32 (1979): 155–58, by H. Edmund Poole in *Fontes* 23 (1976): 198–99, and by J. M. Thomson in *EM* 4 (1976): 315–17.

9.84 Krummel, Donald W. "Graphic Analysis: Its Application to Early American Engraved Music." In *Notes* 16 (1959): 213–33.

A discussion of the history of early American music publishing in terms of the printing processes used, with special reference to the work of Blake and Willig.

9.85 Krummel, Donald W. *Guide for Dating Early Published Music: A Manual of Bibliographical Practices.* 267 pp. Hackensack, N.J.: Joseph Boonin; Kassel, Germany: Bärenreiter, 1974.

The author's "Supplement to the *Guide for Dating Early Published Music*," in *Fontes* 24 (1977): 175–84, adds and corrects information in the *Guide*.

A very important compilation of information on the dating of early editions of music bearing no date of publication spearheaded by Krummel, the chair of IAML's Committee for Bibliographic Research. There is a synopsis, or systematic outline, of the methodology. Plate numbers, publishers' and dealers' addresses, publishing practices, and other kinds of evidence are discussed. There is a section organized by country discussing specifics of music publishing, including studies; directories; important publishers, printers, and engravers; plate number files; and catalogs. Also considered in each national report are copyright, announcements of music publication, design and printing practices, paper, units of currency and pricing practices, important collections, and other evidence. The first section is followed by footnotes and a bibliography, which the second section incorporates by references in each of the national reports. There is a composer index.

The contents of the IAML *Guide* are made more accessible by Linda I. Solow's "An Index to Publishers, Engravers, and Lithographers, and a Bibliography of the Literature Cited in the IAML *Guide for Dating Early Published Music*," in *Fontes* 24 (1977): 81–95, serving in effect as an appendix to the IAML *Guide*.

Reviewed by Rita Benton in *JAMS* 29 (1976): 138–40, by Simone Wallon in *Fontes* 22 (1975): 158–59, and by Clifford Bartlett in *Brio* 12 (1975): 18–19.

9.86 Krummel, Donald W. "Late 18th-Century French Music Publishers' Catalogs in the Library of Congress." In *Fontes* 7 (1960): 61–64.

9.87* Krummel, Donald W. *The Literature of Music Bibliography: An Account of the Writings on the History of Music Printing & Publishing.* 447 pp. Berkeley, Calif.: Fallen Leaf Press, 1992. (Fallen Leaf reference books in music, 21)

An overview of the history of writings on the history of music printing and publishing, in order to define the field and its boundaries. The 976 annotated entries are organized chronologically by eight topics: music bibliographical theory, historical surveys of music printing, music printing technology, printed music as graphic art, musical commerce and property, national literatures, music libraries and book dealers, and reference works. A following chapter makes suggestions for the future. There are various helpful lists: principal publishers and printers of Europe and the United States, the most represented composers in *RISM* (**5.590**), national lists of literature on printers and publishers established before 1920, and exhibition catalogs of music printing from 1834 to 1986, chronologically arranged. There are indexes of authors and subjects.

Reviewed by Christopher Grogan in *Brio* 30 (1993): 105–8, by Karl Kroeger in *Fontes* 42 (1995): 289–90, by John Wagstaff in *M&L* 75 (1994): 255–57, and by Stanley Boorman in *Notes* 51 (1994): 60–65.

9.88 Krummel, Donald W. "Musical Functions and Bibliographical Forms." In *Library* (1976): 327–50.

A most important concept, that of grouping editions into bibliographical forms, is presented.

9.89 Layer, Adolf. *Katalog des Augsburger Verlegers Lotter von 1753.* 44 pp. Kassel, Germany: Bärenreiter, 1964. (Catalogus musicus, 2)

A facsimile edition of the 1753 catalog of the music publications of the firm of Johann Jacob Lotter in Augsburg, listing some 370 titles by 170 composers of the late 17th and early 18th centuries. An Index and "Nachwort" are provided by the editor.

9.90* Lenneberg, Hans. "The Haunted Bibliographer," in *Notes* 41 (1984): 239–48.

A concise accounting of the range of 19th-century music publishing technology and the problem this variety presents the music bibliographer.

9.91 Lenz, Hans U. *Der Berliner Musikdruck von seinen Anfängen bis zur Mitte des 18. Jahrhunderts.* 116 pp. Lippstadt, Germany: Buchdruckerei Thiele, 1932.

Also issued as a dissertation, Rostock, 1932.

A discussion of the Berlin music printers, their output, and their techniques, with a chronological list of 126 printed works (pp. 27–35).

9.92 Lesure, François. *Bibliographie des éditions musicales publiées par Estienne Roger et Michel-Charles Le Cène (Amsterdam, 1696–1743).* 173 pp. Paris: Heugel/Société Française de Musicologie, 1969. (Publications de la Société Française de Musicologie, 2/12)

A documentation of the production of one of the most active music publishers of the early 18th century, some 700 volumes of vocal and instrumental music for French and Italian musicians. Includes a transcription of the catalog by Roger published in 1716 and a facsimile of a Le Cène catalog printed in Amsterdam in 1737.

9.93 Lesure, François. "Cotages d'éditeurs antérieurs à c. 1850: Liste préliminaire." In *Fontes* 14 (1967): 22–37.

A list by country of late-18th- and 19th-century music publishers who used plate numbers.

9.94 Lesure, François, and **Geneviève Thibault.** *Bibliographie des éditions d'Adrian Le Roy et Robert Ballard (1551–1598).* 304 pp. Paris: Société Française de Musicologie/Heugel et Cie, 1955. (Publications de la Société Française de Musicologie, 2/9)

An exemplary bibliography of 319 musical editions issued by the Le Roy–Ballard Press, cited chronologically with full bibliographical descriptions, lists of contents, and locations in public and private collections. Includes a brief historical introduction and an anthology of the most important prefaces, dedications, and other documents, as well as a first-line index of texts and an index of titles and personal names.

Reviewed by Kenneth Levy in *JAMS* 8 (1955): 221–23 and by Vincent H. Duckles in *Notes* 15 (1957): 102–3.

9.95 Lesure, François, and **Geneviève Thibault.** "Bibliographie des éditions musicales publiées par Nicolas Du Chemin (1549–1576)." In *Annales musicologiques* 1 (1953): 269–373.

A bibliography similar in scope and format to the preceding work, covering 100 editions published by Du Chemin, with full descriptions, lists of contents, and locations of copies. There are numerous facsimiles of title pages, a first-line index of Latin and French texts, and an index of titles and names.

9.96 Lewis, Mary S. *Antonio Gardano, Venetian Music Printer, 1538–1569: A Descriptive Bibliography and Historical Study: Vol. 1 (1538–1549).* 863 pp. + 46 pp. of plates. New York: Garland Publishing, 1988– . (Garland reference library of the humanities, 718)

The first of a proposed set of 4 vols. The first 3 vols. are to describe all 442 of Gardano's publications (madrigals, masses, chansons, motets, and a variety of instrumental music). Each volume, organized chronologically, will cover a decade in Gardano's career, with composers listed alphabetically within each year. Each entry contains a description of the edition, with title page transcriptions; a collation; a discussion of other editions; a list of watermarks, type fonts, decorative initials, and related matter; text of dedications; a list of contents, with concordant sources for each piece; a list of copies with notes on bindings, variants, and manuscript additions for each copy; and references to relevant secondary literature. The introduction includes a biography, a brief history of Gardano's printing press, and a description of his production methods (editorial practice and the paper, formats, and typography used). The bibliography proper is followed by material on bound anthologies of printed editions, lost and doubtful editions, a series of indexes, a list of primary and secondary sources consulted and their sigla, a general index, and a group of plates. Other indexes cover composers, text incipits, genre, and library. The 4th vol. is planned to give a full historical study of Gardano's press and the repertory he published.

Reviewed by David Hunter in *Notes* 46 (1989): 380–82, by Hans Lenneberg in *Fontes* 37 (1990): 201–2, and by Kristine K. Forney in *JAMS* 45 (1992): 332–38.

9.97 Littleton, Alfred H. *A Catalogue of One Hundred Works Illustrating the History of Music Printing from the 15th to the End of the 17th Century, in the Library of Alfred H. Littleton.* 38 pp. + 12 facsimile plates. London: Novello, 1911.

A catalog including both musical and theoretical works, grouped by nationality, with annotations directing attention to their interest as examples of music printing.

9.98* Love, Harold. *Scribal Publication in Seventeenth-Century England.* 379 pp. Oxford; New York: Clarendon Press; Oxford University Press, 1993.

An account of English scriptoria in the 17th century, producing manuscripts of literature and music.

9.99 Macmillan, Barclay. "Tune-Book Imprints in Canada to 1867: A Descriptive Bibliography." In *Papers of the Bibliographical Society of Canada* 16 (1977): 31–57.

A complement to the Calderisi study (**9.12**), covering imprints in Canada up to the Confederation, thus omitting any publications from the Maritime Provinces.

9.100 Marco, Guy A. *The Earliest Music Printers of Continental Europe: A Checklist of Facsimiles Illustrating their Work.* 20 pp. Charlottesville, Va.: Bibliographical Society of the University of Virginia, 1962.

An index of facsimile plates of the work of early music printers to be found in a variety of music histories, monographs, and other reference works. 101 printers from the late 15th century to 1599 are included.

9.101 Matthäus, Wolfgang. *Johann André Musikverlag zu Offenbach am Main: Verlagsgeschichte und Bibliographie, 1772–1800.* (After the death of the author, edited by Hans Schneider.) 401 pp. Tutzing, Germany: H. Schneider, 1973.

A history and description of the publishing house of Johann André, including a chronological survey of the publications listing plate numbers. There follows an extensive annotated bibliography of the publications in chronological order and an index to the composers in the bibliography.

Reviewed by Thomas Heck in *Notes* 31 (1971): 62–63 and by Rita Benton in *JAMS* 27 (1974): 530–32.

9.102 Matthäus, Wolfgang. "Quellen und Fehlerquellen zur Datierung von Musikdrucken aus der Zeit nach 1750." In *Fontes* 15 (1967): 37–42.

A discussion of the three criteria that should be used to ascertain the date of a printed work.

9.103 Meissner, Ute. *Der Antwerpener Notendrucker Tylman Susato: Eine bibliographische Studie zur niederländischen Chansonpublikation in der ersten Hälfte des 16. Jahrhunderts.* 2 vols. Berlin: Merseburger, 1967. (Berliner Studien zur Musikwissenschaft, 11)

Biographical information and an analysis of Susato's activity as a music printer (Vol. 1), and a complete chronological bibliography of Susato's publications, with an index of composers and a first-line index of compositions.

Reviewed by Howard Mayer Brown in *JAMS* 21 (1968): 215–17, by Winfried Kirsch in *Die Musikforschung* 22 (1969): 237–38, and by Donald W. Krummel in *Notes* 25 (1969): 500–1.

9.104 Meyer, Kathi, and **Inger M. Christensen.** "Artaria Plate Numbers." In *Notes* ser. 1, no. 15 (1942): 1–22.

A painstakingly assembled list of Artaria (Jean as well as Mathias) plate numbers citing composers, brief title, and approximate date of printing, with a supplementary list of Artaria plates without numbers in the copies they examined.

9.105 Meyer, Kathi, and **Eva J. O'Meara.** "The Printing of Music, 1473–1934." In *Dolphin* 2 (1935): 171–207.

A well-illustrated sketch of the history of music printing, including a bibliography of works on the subject.

9.106 Meyer-Baer, Kathi. *Liturgical Music Incunabula: A Descriptive Catalog.* 63 pp. London: Bibliographical Society, 1962.

A catalog of 257 entries, arranged alphabetically by title, treating some 800 items. References are made to the standard bibliographies of incunabula and to locations of copies in major libraries. 12 plates illustrate types of notation. Includes a chronological index and an index of printers and places.

A preliminary study by the author, "Liturgical Music Incunabula in the British Museum," appears in *Library* ser. 4, Vol. 20 (1939): 272–94. The *Catalog* is reviewed by Mariangela Donà in *Fontes* 12 (1965): 27, by Donald W. Krummel in *Notes* 21 (1964): 366–68, and anonymously in *TLS* (November 16 1962): 880.

9.107 Milliot, Sylvette. "Un couple de marchands de musique au XVIIIe siècle: Les Boivin." In *Revue de musicologie* 54 (1968): 106–13.

An article on the life and career of music publisher François Boivin and his wife, née Elizabeth Catherine Ballard, between 1721 and 1753. Ballard was the daughter and granddaughter of the famous printers of music for the king.

9.108 Mischiati, Oscar. *Indici, cataloghi e avvisi degli editori e librai musicali italiani dal 1591 al 1798.* 553 pp. Florence: Leo S. Olschki Editore, 1984. (Studi e testi per la storia della musica, 2)

Transcriptions of lists of published Italian music from contemporaneous sources with descriptions of the sources, a composer–title index to the transcriptions, an index to names cited in the text, and a list of libraries cited in the text, with page references.

Reviewed by François Lesure in *Fontes* 32 (1985): 186.

9.109 Molitor, Raphael. "Italienische Choralnotendrucke." In his *Die nachtridentische Choral-Reform zu Rom,* Vol. 1, pp. 94–119. Leipzig, 1901.

Reprinted by Olms, Hildesheim, Germany, 1982.

A general discussion of Italian printers of liturgical books of the late 15th and 16th centuries.

9.110 Müller, Hans Christian. *Bernhard Schott, Hofmusikstecher in Mainz: Die Frühgeschichte seines Musikverlages bis 1797.* Mit einem Verzeichnis der Verlagswerke 1779–1898. 219 pp. Mainz: Schott, 1977. (Beiträge zur mittelrheinischen Musikgeschichte, 16)

A historical sketch of the publishing house of Schott until 1797, followed by a bibliographic study of musical works published up to that time.

Reviewed by Rita Benton in *Fontes* 25 (1978): 194–95.

9.111 Neighbour, O. W., and **Alan Tyson.** *English Music Publishers' Plate Numbers in the First Half of the Nineteenth Century.* 48 pp. London: Faber & Faber, 1965.

Reviewed by Klaus Hortschansky in *Die Musikforschung* 21 (1968): 102.

9.112 Novello & Co. *A Century and a Half in Soho: A Short History of the Firm of Novello, Publishers and Printers of Music, 1811–1961.* 85 pp. London: Novello, 1961.

A popular history of the music publishing house that has exercised wide influence on public taste in England through the printing of inexpensive editions of the classics. Victoria Cooper-Deathridge's "The Novello Stockbook of 1858–1869: A Chronicle of Publishing Activity," in *Notes* 44 (1987): 240–51, gives a more detailed look at a segment of the Novello activities.

9.113* Oja, Carol J. "Cos Cob Press and the American Composer," in *Notes* 45 (1988): 227–52.

A history of the innovative American firm, with an appendix, arranged by publisher, indexing American composers covered in Reis's *American Composers* (**1.231**), 1932, and another of Cos Cob publications, arranged by year of issue.

9.114 Oldman, Cecil B. *Collecting Musical First Editions.* 29 pp. London: Constable, 1938. (Aspects of book collecting)

Reprinted from *New Paths in Book Collecting,* edited by John Carter, London, 1934, pp. 95–124.

An informal and inviting discussion of the pleasures of collecting early music, with bibliography (pp. 120–24).

9.115* Parkinson, John A. *Victorian Music Publishers: An Annotated List.* 315 pp. Warren, Mich.: Harmonie Park Press, 1990. (Detroit studies in music bibliography, 64)

To date, the major directory of 19th-century British music publishers, citing for each entry the names held by each firm, the various addresses, the major compositions it published, and, for major firms, historical notes.

Reviewed by Michael J. Budds in *Fontes* 39 (1992): 369–70, by David Hunter in *Notes* 48 (1992): 1,261–62, and by Peter Ward Jones in *M&L* 73 (1992): 610–11.

9.116 Pattison, Bruce. "Notes on Early Music Printing." In *Library* ser. 4, Vol. 19 (1939): 239–421.

A survey of the state of knowledge of the printing of music from 1481 to 1630, updating an earlier article by George Barclay Squire, "Notes on Early Music Printing," in *Bibliographica* 3 (1897): 99–122.

9.117 Plesske, Hans-Martin. "Bibliographie des Schrifttums zur Geschichte deutscher und österreichischer Musikverlage." In *Beiträge zur Geschichte des Buchwesens,* Band 3 (1968): 135–222.

A bibliography of 755 items listed alphabetically under the names of the firms. The first section is devoted to information in general reference works, the second to histories of music publishing.

9.118 Pogue, Samuel F. *Jacques Moderne, Lyons Music Printer of the Sixteenth Century.* 412 pp. Geneva: Librairie Droz, 1969. (Travaux d'humanisme et renaissance, 101)

An extensive bibliography of all of Moderne's output, with full bibliographical descriptions of the nonmusical books, and contents with concordances of the music books; there are 149 entries, of which 59 are for books of music.

Reviewed by Albert Dunning in *Notes* 29 (1972): 46–47, by Frank Dobbins in *JAMS* 24 (1971): 126–31, and by Charles Cudworth in *M&L* 51 (1970): 85–86.

9.119 Poole, H. Edmund. "New Music Types: Invention in the Eighteenth Century." In *Journal of the Printing Historical Society* 1 (1965): 21–38.

A review of the history of music printing, with special emphasis on the contribution of Breitkopf.

9.120* Przywecka-Samecka, Maria. *Poczatki drukarstwa muzycznego w Europie wiek XV.* 132 pp. Warsaw: Zakład Narodowy im Ossolińskich, Wydawnictwo Polskiej Akademii Nauk, 1981. (Prace Wrocławskiego Towarzystwa Naukowego/Travaux de la Société des Sciences et des Lettres de Wrocław, A 221)

A bibliography of 285 editions of 15th-century printed music, updating Meyer-Baer's bibliography (**9.106**).

Reviewed by Mary Kay Duggan in *Notes* 47 (1991): 794–95.

9.121 Redway, Virginia L. *Music Directory of Early New York City: A File of Musicians, Music Publishers and Musical Instrument Makers Listed in N.Y. Directories from 1786 through 1835, Together with the Most Important New York Music Publishers from 1836 through 1875.* 102 pp. New York: New York Public Library, 1941.

A directory divided into three main sections: musicians and teachers; publishers, printers, lithographers, and dealers, with names and addresses as they appeared in successive years; and instrument makers and dealers. The appendixes include a chronological list of firms and individuals, 1786–1811, and a list of musical societies, 1789–99.

9.122 Rheinfurth, Hans. *Der Musikverlag Lotter in Augsburg (c. 1719–1845).* 344 pp. Tutzing, Germany: H. Schneider, 1977. (Musikbibliographische Arbeiten, 3)

9.123 Robert, Henri. *Traité de gravure de musique sur planches d'étain et des divers procédés de simili gravùre de musique, precédé de l'historique du signe, de l'impression et de la gravùre de musique.* 2nd ed. 151 pp. Paris: Chez l'auteur, 1926.

First published in 1902.

A rather sketchy historical survey of music writing, printing, and engraving, followed by a description of the technical processes involved in preparing engraved plates.

9.124 Romero de Lecea, Carlos. *Introducción a los viejos libros de musica.* 138 pp. Madrid: Joyas Bibliográficas, 1976. (Collección de estudios y ensayos, 4)

A history of music printing in Spain in the 15th and 16th centuries, with numerous facsimile plates, providing a list of the earliest known examples of printed music, 1492–1511.

9.125 Ross, Ted. *The Art of Music Engraving and Processing: A Complete Manual, Reference and Text Book on Preparing Music for Reproduction and Print.* 278 pp. Miami, Fla.: Hansen Books, 1970.

A well-illustrated handbook full of historical and technical information.

9.126 Sartori, Claudio. *Bibliografia delle opere musicali stampate da Ottaviano Petrucci.* 217 pp. Florence: L.S. Olschki, 1948. (Biblioteca di bibliografia italiana, 18)

The chronological bibliography of Petrucci's work, with full descriptions, including contents, of each publication. Includes an index of titles, lists of libraries and their holdings of works printed by Petrucci, and a supporting bibliography (pp. 211–17).

Reviewed by Ernest H. Sanders in *JAMS* 2 (1949): 120–23.

9.127 Sartori, Claudio. *Casa Ricordi, 1808–1958: Profile storico.* 116 pp. + 48 plates. Milan: G. Ricordi, 1958.

A history of the prominent Italian publisher. 16 of the plates are facsimile pages of composers' autographs; the remainder are chiefly reproductions, in color, of cover designs for noteworthy Ricordi music publications.

Reviewed by Donald W. Krummel in *Notes* 17 (1960): 400–1.

9.128 Sartori, Claudio. *Dizionario degli editori musicali italiani (tipografi, incisori, librai-editori).* 215 pp. Florence: L.S. Olschki, 1958. (Biblioteca di bibliografia italiana, 32)

Italian music printers, editors, and publishers from the 16th century to the present. Some bibliographical references are given. The principal issues of the publishers are noted but no complete catalogs are given. There is an index of names, but no chronology.

Reviewed by Dragan Plamenac in *Notes* 16 (1959): 242–43 and by Gerhard Croll in *Die Musikforschung* 12 (1959): 255–56.

9.129 Schaal, Richard. *Die Kataloge des Augsburger Musikalien-Händlers Kaspar Flurschütz, 1613–1628.* Mit einer Einleitung und Registern zum ersten Mal herausgegeben von Richard Schaal. Mit einer Bibliographie zur Augsburger Musikgeschichte 1550–1650. 159 pp. Wilhelmshaven, Germany: Heinrichshofen's Verlag, 1974. (Quellenkataloge zur Musikgeschichte, 7)

A catalog with an introduction and index to the publisher/music seller Flurschütz, including a bibliography of the history of music in Augsburg from 1550–1650.

9.130* Schaal, Richard. *Musiktitel aus fünf Jahrhunderts: Eine Dokumentation zur typographischen und künstlerischen Gestaltung und Entwicklung der Musikalien.* 250 pp. Wilhelmshaven, Germany: Heinrichshofen, 1972. (Quellenkataloge zur Musikgeschichte, 5)

The bulk of the contents is illustrations, with a bibliography (pp. 23–27).

9.131* Schaefer, Hartmut. *Die Notendrucker und Musikverleger in Frankfurt am Main von 1630 bis um 1720: Eine bibliographisch-drucktechnische Untersuchung.* 2 vols. 711 pp. Kassel, Germany: Bärenreiter, 1975. (Catalogus musicus, 7)

Bibliography: pp. 663–87.

Reviewed by Liesbeth Weinhold in *Fontes* 24 (1977): 56–57.

9.132 Schmid, Anton. *Ottaviano dei Petrucci da Fossombrone, erster Erfinder des Musiknotendruckes mit beweglichen Metalltypen, und seine Nachfolger im sechzehnten Jahrhunderte.* 342 pp. Vienna: P. Rohrmann, 1845.

Reprinted by B.R. Gruner, Amsterdam, 1968. 356 pp. with 4 folded leaves.

One of the first scholarly studies of early music printing, containing important information about Petrucci's contemporaries in other European centers of music printing.

9.133 Schmidt-Phiseldeck, Josef. "Datierung der Musikalien." In *Beethoven-Zentenarfeier: Wien, 1927,* pp. 279–82. Vienna: Universal Edition, 1927.

A short article on the importance of dating music publications.

9.134* Schneider, Hans. *Der Musikverleger Heinrich Philipp Bossler, 1744–1812: Mit bibliographischen übersichten und einem Anhang, von Mariane Kirchgessner und Bossler.* 388 pp. Tutzing, Germany: H. Schneider, 1985.

Bibliography (pp. 371–82).

Reviewed by Peter Ward Jones in *M&L* 70 (1989): 259–60.

9.135* Schneider, Hans. *Der Musikverleger Johann Michael Götz (1748–1810) und seine kurfürstlich privilegierte Notenfabrique.* 2 vols. 504 + 243 pp. Tutzing, Germany: H. Schneider, 1989.

Contents: Vol. 1, *Verlagsgeschichte und Bibliographie;* Vol. 2, *Drei Sortimentskataloge aus den Jahren 1780, 1784 and 1802.*

Information on the first major Mannheim publisher, with an annotated list of publications, numerous facsimiles, and helpful, detailed indexes.

Reviewed by Mary Kay Duggan in *Notes* 47 (1991): 794–95 and by Peter Ward Jones in *M&L* 73 (1992): 109–10.

9.136 Smith, William C. *A Bibliography of the Musical Works Published by John Walsh during the Years 1695–1720.* 215 pp. + 38 plates. London: Bibliographical Society, 1948.

Reissued with corrections in 1968.

A list of 642 publications cited for the period under consideration, with numerous descriptive annotations. Includes an index of titles and works, as well as a general index.

Reviewed by J. Coopersmith in *Notes* 7 (1949): 104–6 and by A. Hyatt King in *M&L* 30 (1949): 273–76.

9.137 Smith, William C., and **Charles Humphries.** *A Bibliography of the Musical Works Published by the Firm of John Walsh during the Years 1721–1766.* 351 pp. London: Bibliographical Society, 1968.

Reviewed by J. Merrill Knapp in *Notes* 26 (1969): 274–75, by Lenore Coral in *JAMS* 23 (1970): 141–43, and by Charles Cudworth in *M&L* 50 (1969): 416–17.

9.138 Squire, William Barclay. "Publishers' Numbers." In *Sammelbände der Internationalen Musikgesellschaft* 15 (1913–14): 420–27.

An early article organizing music publishers' plate numbers.

9.139 Steele, Robert. *The Earliest English Music Printing: A Description and Bibliography of English Printed Music to the Close of the 16th Century.* 102 pp. London: Printed for the Bibliographical Society, 1903. (Illustrated monographs, 11)

A brief introduction covering methods of printing, including a chapter on early English printers of music. The bibliography of 197 items is arranged chronologically from 1495 to 1600, giving full title and collation, library locations, and notes on typography. There is a bibliography of 34 items on music printing.

Reprinted in London, 1965, with a new appendix of addenda and corrigenda.

9.140 Steele, Robert. "Early Music Printing, 1601–1640." In *Transactions of the Bibliographical Society* 11 (1909): 13–15.

The description of a project extending his *Earliest English Music Printing* (**9.139**).

9.141 Stellfeld, J. A. *Bibliographie des éditions musicales plantiniennes.* 248 pp. + 21 plates. Brussels: Palais des Academies, 1949. (Academie Royale de Belgique; Classe des beaux-arts. Memoires, V, 3)

A detailed bibliography of the 21 music imprints of Christophe Plantin (1514–89) and his immediate successors in Antwerp and Leiden, with a brief history of his press.

9.142 Valentin, Erich. *50 Jahre Gustav Bosse Verlag: Streiflichter aus der Verlagsarbeit, statt einer Festschrift.* 161 pp. Regensburg: G. Bosse, 1963.

"Verzeichnis der im Gustav Bosse Verlag erschienenen Werke" (pp. 149–61).

9.143* Vanhulst, Henri. *Catalogue des éditions de musique publiées à Louvain par Pierre Phalese et ses fils, 1545–1578.* xlvii + 383 pp. Brussels: Palais des Academies, 1990. (Memoires de la Classe des beaux-arts. Collection in 80, 2, 16, 2)

Reviewed by Samuel F. Pogue in *Notes* 49 (1993): 979–80.

9.144 Vernarecci, D. Augusto. *Ottaviano dei Petrucci da Fossombrone, inventore dei tipi mobili metalli fusi della musica nel secolo XV.* 2nd ed. 288 pp. Bologna: Romagnoli, 1882.

9.145 Voltman, B. *Russkie pechatnye noty XVIII veka.* 292 pp. Leningrad: Gosudarstvennoe muzykal´noe izdatel´stvo, 1957.

Russian printed music of the 18th century.

9.146* Weaver, Robert Lee. *A Descriptive Bibliographical Catalog of the Music Printed by Hubert Waelrant and Jan de Laet.* xxvi + 264 pp. Warren, Mich.: Harmonie Park Press, 1994. (Detroit studies in music bibliography, 73)

A work on the publications of the two 16th-century Belgians, compiled to accompany his history *Waelrant and Laet: Music Publishers in Antwerp's Golden Age* (Warren, Mich.: Harmonie Park Press, 1995).

9.147 Weinhold, Liesbeth. "Musiktitel und Datierung." In *Fontes* 13 (1966): 136–40.

9.148 Weinmann, Alexander. *Der Alt-Wiener Musikverlag im Spiegel der Wiener Zeitung.* 71 pp. Tutzing, Germany: H. Schneider, 1976. (Institut für Österreichische Musikdokumentation. Publikation, 2)

9.149 Weinmann, Alexander. *Die Anzeigen des Kopiaturbetriebes Johann Traeg in der Wiener Zeitung zwischen 1782 und 1805: Bd. 2 zu seinen Musikalienverzeichnissen von 1799 und 1804 aus der Reihe Beiträge zur Geschichte des Alt-Wiener Musikverlags.* 109 pp. Vienna: L. Krenn, 1981. (Wiener Archivstudien, 6)

9.150 Weinmann, Alexander. *Beiträge zur Geschichte des Alt-Wiener Musikverlages.*

A series of studies related to Viennese music publishing of the late 18th and early 19th centuries. They appeared under varied imprints and in two subseries: *Komponisten* (Reihe 1) and *Verleger* (Reihe 2), and are listed below in series order.

Reihe 1, Folge 1: See **6.209.**

Reihe 1, Folge 2: See **6.330.**

Reihe 1, Folge 3: See **6.331.**

Reihe 2, Folge 1a: *Verzeichnis der Verlagswerke des Musikalischen Magazins in Wien, 1784–1802, Leopold (und Anton) Kozeluch.* 2nd ed. 53 pp. Vienna: L. Krenn, 1979. First published in 1950 by Österreichischer Bundesverlag, Vienna, 31 pp.

Works without plate numbers, and with questionable plate numbers, in chronological order; works with plate numbers in numerical order, followed by an alphabetical list by composer of Kozeluch's catalog, published in 1800.

Reihe 2, Folge 2: *Vollständiges Verlagsverzeichnis Artaria & Comp.* 2nd ed. 201 pp. Vienna: L. Krenn, 1978.

First ed. published 1952.

A history of the Artaria firm, with a classified list, chronological within classifications, of its publications, giving in most cases exact dates of publication. There is an index by composers.

The 1st ed. is reviewed by Richard S. Hill in *Notes* 10 (1953): 449–50.

Reihe 2, Folge 3: "Vollständiges Verlagsverzeichnis der Musikalien des Kunst- und Industrie-Comptoirs in Wien, 1801–1819." In *Studien zur Musikwissenschaft: Beihefte der DTÖ* 22 (1955): 217–52.

A list of 802 plate numbers in numerical order, with composer, title, and date of publication of the corresponding works, as well as a composer index.

Reviewed by William Klenz in *Notes* 14 (1956): 117.

Reihe 2, Folge 4: "Verzeichnis der Musikalien des Verlages Johann Traeg in Wien, 1794–1818." In *Studien zur Musikwissenschaft: Beihefte der DTÖ* 23 (1956): 135–83.

A list of all works published by the firm, in chronological order.

Reihe 2, Folge 5: *Wiener Musikverleger und Musikalienhändler von Mozarts Zeit bis gegen 1860: Ein firmengeschichtlicher und topographischer Behelf.* 72 pp. Vienna: In Kommission bei Rudolf Rohrer, 1956. (Österreichische Akademie der Wissenschaft. Veröffentlichungen der Kommission für Musikforschung, 2)

A summary of a century of Viennese music publishers and a dated series of their addresses. Weinmann lists and discusses 38 music dealers and publishers and 19 related general book dealers and publishers, with tables showing early and existing addresses of the firms, useful in dating Viennese musical imprints of this period.

Reviewed by Richard S. Hill in *Notes* 15 (1958): 396–97.

Reihe 2, Folge 6: *Verzeichnis der Musikalien aus dem K.K. Hoftheater-Musik-Verlag.* 130 pp. Vienna: Universal Edition, 1961. (Wiener Urtext Ausgabe)

A brief history of the firm and biographical notes on the people associated with it, with a list of publications from 1796 to c. 1820, as well as plate numbers and dates of issue, if known.

Reviewed by Donald W. Krummel in *Notes* 19 (1961): 76.

Reihe 2, Folge 7: *Kataloge Anton Huberty (Wien) und Christoph Torricella.* 135 pp. Vienna: Universal Edition, 1962.

Brief histories of the firms, followed by detailed lists of their publications, giving composer, title, date of publication if known, and the location of copies in European libraries.

Reviewed by Richard Schaal in *Die Musikforschung* 18 (1965): 83.

Reihe 2, Folge 8: *Die Wiener Verlagswerke von Franz Anton Hofmeister.* 252 pp. Vienna: Universal Edition, 1964.

A book containing a biography of Hofmeister, a dated list of plate numbers, entries (largely thematic) for all of the firm's publications, and brief historical discussions of aspects of the firm's history.

Reihe 2, Folge 8a: *Addenda und Corrigenda zum Verlagsverzeichnis Franz Anton Hofmeister.* 46 pp. Vienna: L. Krenn, 1982.

Reihe 2, Folge 9: *Verlagsverzeichnis Tranquillo Mollo (mit und ohne Co.).* 111 pp. Vienna: Universal Edition, 1964.

A biography of the Mollo family and history of the firm, with transcriptions of catalogs, complete with plate numbers; there are alphabetical indexes by composers. The firm was a successor to Artaria.

Reihe 2, Folge 9a: *Ergänzungen zum Verlags-Verzeichnis Tranquillo Mollo.* 38 pp. Vienna: Universal Edition, 1972.

Reihe 2, Folge 10: *Verlagsverzeichnis Pietro Mechetti quondam Carlo (mit Portraits).* 205 pp. Vienna: Universal Edition, 1966.

Reviewed by Harald Heckmann in *Die Musikforschung* 21 (1968): 507–8.

Reihe 2, Folge 11: *Verlagsverzeichnis Giovanni Cappi bis A. O. Witzendorf.* 210 pp. Vienna: Universal Edition, 1967.

Reviewed by Imogen Fellinger in *Die Musikforschung* 25 (1972): 371.

Reihe 2, Folge 12: *Verzeichnis der Musikalien des Verlages Joseph Eder-Jeremias Bermann.* 78 pp. Vienna: Universal Edition, 1968.

Reihe 2, Folge 13: *Wiener Musikverlag "Am Rande." Ein lückenfüllender Beitrag zur Geschichte des Alt-Wiener Musikverlages.* 155 pp. Vienna: Universal Edition, 1970.

Reihe 2, Folge 14: *Verzeichnis der Musikalien des Verlages Maisch-, Sprenger-, Artaria.* With two Supplements: *Die Firma Mathias Artarias Witwe und Compagnie* and *Supplement zum Verlagsverzeichnis des Musikalischen Magazins in Wien (Kozeluch).* 95 pp. Vienna: Universal Edition, 1970. (Wiener Urtext-Ausgabe)

Reihe 2, Folge 15: *Verlagsverzeichnis Ignaz Sauer (Kunstverlag zu den Sieben Schwestern), Sauer und Leidesdorf und Anton Berka & Comp.* 100 pp. Vienna: Universal Edition, 1972.

Reihe 2, Folge 16: *Verlagsverzeichnis Johann Traeg (und Sohn).* 2nd ed. 89 pp. Vienna: Universal Edition, 1973.

Reihe 2, Folge 17: *Johann Traeg: Die Musikalienverzeichnisse von 1799 und 1804 (Handschriften und Sortiment).* 133 pp. Vienna: Universal Edition, 1973.

Facsimiles of the two lists: *Verzeichniss alter und neuer sowohl geschriebener als gestochener Musikalien* and *Erster Nachtrag zu dem Verzeichniss alter und neuer sowohl geschriebener als gestochener Musikalien.*

Reihe 2, Folge 19: *Vollständiges Verlagsverzeichnis Senefelder, Steiner, Haslinger,* Vols. 1 and 3. 2 vols. Munich; Salzburg: Musikverlag Katzbichler, 1979–83. (Musikwissenschaftliche Schriften, 14 and 16)

Contents: Bd. 1, *A. Senefelder, Chemische Druckerey, S. A. Steiner, S. A. Steiner & Comp.* (Wien, 1803–1826); Bd. 3, *Tobias Haslingers Witwe und Sohn und Carl Haslinger qdm. Tobias* (Wien, 1843–75).

Reihe 2, Folge 20: *Verzeichnis der Musikalien des Verlages Anton Pennauer.* 58 pp. Vienna: Krenn, 1981.

Reihe 2, Folge 21: *Verzeichnis der Verlagswerke J. P. Gotthard.* 55 pp. Vienna: L. Krenn, 1981.

Reihe 2, Folge 22: *Verzeichnis der Musikalien des Verlages Thadé Weigl.* 178 pp. Vienna: L. Krenn, 1982.

Reihe 2, Folge 23: *Verlagsverzeichnis Peter Cappi und Cappi & Diabelli (1816 bis 1824).* 150 pp. Vienna: Krenn, 1983.

Reihe 2, Folge 24: *Verlagsverzeichnis Anton Diabelli & Co. (1824 bis 1840).* 494 pp. Vienna: L. Krenn, 1985.

9.151* Weinmann, Alexander. *Ein erstergedruckter Verlagskatalog der Firma Anton Diabelli & Co.* 14 + 55 + 7 + 12 pp. Vienna: L. Krenn, 1979. (Wiener Archivstudien, 3)

The reprint of catalogs originally published in Vienna, 1825–28. The original title page read *Verzeichniss der Verlags-Musikalien von Anton Diabelli und Compagnie im Wien, am Graben Nro. 1133,* with title also given in French.

9.152 Wolf, Johannes. "Verzeichnis der musiktheoretischen Inkunabeln mit Fundorten." In Francesco Caza, *Tractato vulgare de canto figurato . . .,* pp. 64–92. Berlin: M. Breslauer, 1922. (Veröffentlichungen der Musikbibliothek Paul Hirsch, 1)

A list of 104 incunabula in the field of music theory, with the locations where copies are preserved, as a supplement to Wolf's ed. of Caza's treatise.

9.153* Wolfe, Richard J. *Early American Music Engraving and Printing: A History of Music Publishing in America from 1787 to 1825 with Commentary on Earlier and Later Practices.* 321 pp. Urbana, Ill.: Published in cooperation with the Bibliographical Society of America by the University of Illinois Press, 1980. (Music in American life)

9.154 Young, James Bradford. "An Account of Printed Musick, ca. 1724." In *Fontes* 29 (1982): 129–36.

A description of one of the earliest catalogs of printed music published in England. No publisher is named on the catalog, but evidence suggests that it was produced in connection with the revival of the Estienne Roger music publishing enterprise by Michel Le Cène. The article considers "the essential place of commercial factors in the development of music publishing."

9.155 Zecca-Laterza, Agostina. *Il Catalogo numerico Ricordi 1857 con date e indici.* Prefazione di Philip Gossett. Rome: Nuovo Istituto Editoriale Italiano, 1984– . Vol. 1– . (Bibliotheca musicae, 8)

Originally published in Florence by Presso Ricordi e Jouhaud, 1857.

A plate number catalog for the most important Italian publishing firm, covering the first 50 years of Ricordi's output, annotated with approximate dates of publication.

Introduction in English.

9.156 Zur Westen, Walter von. *Musiktitel aus vier Jahrhunderten: Festschrift anlässlich des 75 jährigen Bestehens der Firma C. G. Röder, Leipzig.* 115 pp. Leipzig: C.G. Röder, 1921.

A study of musical title pages from the renaissance to the end of the 19th century, with 96 facsimile illustrations.

10

DISCOGRAPHIES AND RELATED SOURCES

Within the last few decades the field of recorded sound has inspired an abundance of documentation useful to librarians, teachers, researchers, and private collectors. One effort to bring these diverse interests together resulted in the formation of the Association for Recorded Sound Collections, which in addition to producing a valuable journal for the discographer (**10.1**) has helped sponsor a number of discographical initiatives. Another organization, the International Association of Sound Archives, has issued a directory of member archives covering the holdings, services, and staffs of institutions globally (**11.34**).

Recorded music has a particular attraction for collectors, whether their areas of specialization are early vocal discs or cylinders or jazz recordings. There has been a proliferation of record reviews, listeners' guides, manufacturers' catalogs and numerical lists, and journals devoted almost exclusively to discography. Some indication of the scope and variety of the bibliographical coverage is suggested by the 3 vols. of the *Bibliography of Discographies,* edited by Michael Gray and Gerald D. Gibson (**10.2**). The last decade has produced a flood of additional titles. A representative sampling is listed in this chapter. Although this chapter omits many titles found in the 4th ed., revised, some outmoded works are included to remind the researcher of the distance traveled by discographical specialists in the course of this century.

Gordon Stevenson, in his article "Discography: Scientific, Analytical, Historical and Systematic," in *Trends in Archival and Reference Collections of Recorded Sound, Library Trends* 21 (1972): 101–35 no. 1, has provided some of the basic theoretical principles of discography. A number of articles in the *Journal of Jazz Studies* have discussed some of these same philosophical and methodological points in the course of careful examinations of discographic questions concerning jazz recordings. The *Journal* is well worth perusal even for those not engaged in jazz studies.

In this chapter, "Encyclopedias of Recorded Music" are distinguished from the various categories of "Collectors' Guides." Although the distinction is perhaps an arbitrary one, it is intended to separate the few comprehensive discographies from those directed toward the interests of collectors of classical music, jazz, ethnic music, or early discs.

BIBLIOGRAPHIES OF DISCOGRAPHIES

10.1 Association for Recorded Sound Collections. *Journal.* Vol. 1– (1968–).
The journal of the professional discographer. In addition to the regular appearance of discographies as articles in the *Journal,* there are reviews and citations of discographies. This is also known as the *ARSC Journal.*

10.2 *A Bibliography of Discographies.* 3 vols. New York: R.R. Bowker, 1977–83.
Contents: Vol. 1, *Classical Music, 1925–1975,* by Michael H. Gray and Gerald D. Gibson, 164 pp., 1977; Vol. 2, *Jazz,* by Daniel Allen, 237 pp., 1981; Vol. 3, *Popular Music,* by Michael. H. Gray, 205 pp., 1983.

The most complete and scholarly bibliographies in the field of discography. They include lists of monographs and of discographies appearing as articles or appended to articles. Each vol. is separately indexed.

The 1st vol. contains 3,307 entries arranged in subject order. Each citation includes complete bibliographic information and annotations. *Classical Music Discographies, 1976–1988,* by Michael H. Gray (Westport, Conn: Greenwood Press, 1989. 334 pp.) (Discographies, 34) was specifically compiled as a supplement to Vol. 1, adding entries for record labels citing significant numbers of classical recordings, discographies included in dissertations, and discographies appearing in program notes on sound recordings. Although the period of coverage for the most part is from 1976 to 1988, a number of citations for discographies overlooked in the earlier volumes are included.

Vol. 2 cites discographies of jazz, blues, ragtime, gospel, and rhythm and blues music published 1935–80, excluding record company catalogs, works primarily of a critical nature, and lists of records, whether to support an accompanying text or for popular consumption. Entries are arranged by subject. A list of subject headings other than personal names or names of groups is provided. Includes a list of periodicals cited and an index. Vol. 3 cites discographies of pop music, rock and country, hillbilly and bluegrass, motion picture and stage show music, and excludes record company catalogs, but includes pricing guides to out-of-print records and lists of charted popular music. Includes a list of periodical titles cited and an index. The series is updated to an extent by the "Bibliography of Discographies, Annual Cumulation" published each year in *ARSCJ* (**10.1**).

The 1st vol. is reviewed by Jean-Michel Nectoux in *Fontes* 25 (1978): 418–19 and by Garrett H. Bowles in *Notes* 35 (1979): 876–77. Vol. 2 is reviewed by J. F. Weber in *AM* 2 (1984): 99–100 no. 3, by Eileen Southern in *BPM* 12 (1984): 137–39, by Dan Morgenstern in *ARSCJ* 13 (1981): 137–38, by Nina Davis-Millis in *Notes* 39 (1982): 102–3, and by David Horn in *Popular Music* 2 (1982): 300–5. Michael H. Gray's *Classical Music Discographies, 1976–1988* is reviewed by Arne J. Arneson in *Notes* 47 (1991): 800–1 and by Jim Farrington in *Fontes* 38 (1991): 280.

10.3 Cooper, David Edwin. *International Bibliography of Discographies: Classical Music and Jazz & Blues, 1962–1972: A Reference Book for Record Collectors, Dealers, and Libraries.* 272 pp. Littleton, Colo.: Libraries Unlimited, 1975. (Keys to music bibliography, 2)

A bibliography that includes buying guides, chronologies, label discographies, and composer and performer discographies. There is a summary of national discographies, catalogs, and major review sources.

Reviewed by Stephen M. Fry in *Notes* 32 (1976): 554–55, by Morris Martin in *Fontes* 22 (1975): 156–57, and by Eric Cooper in *Brio* 12 (1975): 48–49.

10.4 Dearling, Robert, and **Celia Dearling,** with **Brian Rust.** *The Guinness Book of Recorded Sound.* 225 pp. London: Guinness, 1984.

A vast assemblage of facts about the history of recorded sound.

10.5 Foreman, Lewis. *Systematic Discography.* 144 pp. London: Clive Bingley, 1974.

A comprehensive guide to the compilation of discographies. It includes a short chapter on the importance of sound recordings in documenting 20th-century history. Includes a now-dated list of dealers in out-of-print recordings, a list of pirate record labels, a bibliography of relevant journals, another bibliography of discographies arranged by subject (wild-life, jazz, ethnic), and a general bibliography on sound recording and discography.

10.6 Rust, Brian A. L. *Brian Rust's Guide to Discography.* 133 pp. Westport, Conn.: Greenwood Press, 1980. 133 pp. (Discographies, 4)

The *Guide's* contents include purposes and functions of discography, a short history of the science of discography, the creation of a discography, securing information about discographies, labels, and a bibliography of book-length discographies.

ENCYCLOPEDIAS OF RECORDED MUSIC

10.7* Canfield, David DeBoor. *Canfield Guide to Classical Recordings.* 4th ed. c. 1200 pp. Elletsville, Ind.: Ars Antiqua, 1995.

Third ed., 1991. Second ed., 1989, 181 pp. First ed., 1988, 175 pp.

Primarily a list, with prices, of 33-1/3-rpm recordings, with separate lists for 45-rpm recordings, 78-rpm recordings, CDs, and cassette tapes.

10.8 Clough, Francis F., and **Geoffrey J. Cuming.** *The World's Encyclopedia of Recorded Music.* 890 pp. London: The London Gramophone Corp. in association with Sidgwick & Jackson, 1952.

First Supplement (April 1950 to May–June 1951) is bound with the main volume. *Second Supplement* (1951–52), London, 1952 (262 pp.); *Third Supplement* (1953–55), London, 1957 (564 pp.). Reprinted by Greenwood Press, Westport, Conn., in 1970.

A useful reference tool for the record specialist. Known by the nickname WERM, the *Encyclopedia,* concentrating on art music, is arranged alphabetically by composer, with a subclassification of works under prolific composers. Recordings of all speeds are included. Full information is given for album contents and labels. There is a special section for anthologies.

The 1952 ed. is reviewed by Philip L. Miller in *Notes* 10 (1952): 94–95. The *Third Supplement* is reviewed by Richard S. Hill in *Notes* 14 (1957): 357–59. Background information by the authors, "Problems of an International Record Catalogue," appears in *Fontes* 3 (1956): 95–108.

10.9 Eastman School of Music, Rochester, N.Y. *Sibley Music Library: Catalog of Sound Recordings.* 14 vols. Boston, Mass.: G.K. Hall, 1977.

Photoreproduction of the dictionary catalog of an extensive LP collection. Until the time of publication, the Sibley Music Library had a collection development policy to collect all current LPs of art music issued in the U.S. This catalog provides excellent coverage with numerous cross-references and added entries, but with no subject entries. The prebaroque coverage is limited, and anthologies of the earlier periods are not analyzed.

10.10* Erlewine, Michael, Chris Woodstra, and **Vladimir Bogdanov.** *All Music Guide: The Best CDs, Albums & Tapes: The Experts' Guide to the Best Releases from Thousands of Artists in All Types of Music.* 1,417 pp. San Francisco, Calif.: Miller Freeman Inc., 1994.

The 1st ed. was published in 1992, edited by Erlewine and Scott Bultman, 1,176 pp., and was also made available on CD-ROM.

A classified discography listing current recordings of rock, pop and soul, blues, gospel, country and western, contemporary instrumental, Christmas, classical, reggae, and jazz, edited by experts in the specialty. The verso of the title page describes this effort as "an ongoing database project, the largest collection of substantive album reviews ever assembled," although it is "a rather small subset (although an important one) of a much larger collection of over 100,000 albums and reviews."

10.11 Greenfield, Edward, Robert Layton, and **Ivan March.** *The Penguin Guide to Compact Discs and Cassettes.* New ed. xxii + 1,417 pp. London; New York: Penguin Books, 1994. (Penguin handbooks)

An approximately biennial international review of CDs for the amateur collector, ranking the quality of the performance by a series of easily accessible symbols. The editorial trio, with Greenfield, March, and Denis Stevens (the latter to be followed by Robert Layton), started publishing in this vein in the LP era with the *Stereo Record Guide* (Blackpool, England: Long Playing Record Library, 1960), 316 pp., an annual, with Layton replacing Stevens in 1974. Another of the trio's early titles was *A Guide to the Bargain Classics* (Blackpool, England: Long Playing Record Library, 1962), 2 vols., by Greenfield, March, and Denis Stevens, which in 1966 became *The Penguin Guide to Bargain Records* (xxiii + 584 pp.), the first Penguin guide, followed by *The Second Penguin Guide to Bargain Records* (1970) and *The Third Penguin Guide to Bargain*

Records (1972, xxii + 328 pp.). *The Penguin Stereo Record Guide* first appeared in 1975 (1,114 pp.), followed by a 2nd ed., 1977 (xxvii + 1,169 pp.). In 1979 a new format was examined in *The Penguin Cassette Guide* (xxv + 838 pp.), followed in 1980 by the *New Penguin Guide to Bargain Records (and Cassettes),* xx + 172 pp., by Greenfield, March, and Layton, followed by their *The New Penguin Stereo Record and Cassette Guide* (1982), xxii + 977 pp., and *The Complete Penguin Stereo Record and Cassette Guide* (3rd ed., 1984, 1,344 pp.).

The era of the CD was heralded by the *Penguin Guide to Compact Discs, Cassettes and LPs* (1986, xxiii + 1,217 pp.), followed in 1988 by the *New Penguin Guide to Compact Discs and Cassettes* (xix + 1,366 pp.); a supplement to the latter, labeled a "yearbook" (494 pp.), appeared the following year. 1990 saw the *Penguin Guide to Compact Discs* (1,339 pp.), as well as the subject-restricted *Penguin Guide to Opera on Compact Disc* (643 pp.), followed the next year by a supplemental "yearbook" (615 pp.) to the basic guide. *The Penguin Guide to Compact Discs and Cassettes* (1992, xviii + 1,348 pp.), issued with the *Penguin Guide to Bargain Compact Discs and Cassettes* (1992, xviii + 689 pp.), brings this list, except for the title atop this entry, up to date.

A catalog of currently available recordings. The authors are reviewers for *Gramophone.* This is a catalog of about 4,000 recordings, generally in order by composer; a final section covers anthologies, classified by medium, generally listed alphabetically under the name of the most prominent performer. Each entry supplies copious discographical and performance information and the authors' opinions of the recording. The focus is principally on recordings marketed in Great Britain and the United States. There is no index. The 1984 ed. is reviewed by Dean Tudor in *ARBA* 17 (1986): no. 1268; the 1986 ed. is reviewed by Robert Skinner in *ARBA* 19 (1988): no. 1303.

10.12* Marco, Guy A. *Encyclopedia of Recorded Sound in the United States.* xlix + 910 pp. New York: Garland Publishing, 1993. (Garland reference library of the humanities, 936)

An encyclopedic repository of information on the history of the first eighty years (to 1970) of recorded sound. The signed articles, by authorities in the field, include technical definitions, information on record labels, and short biographies of well-known recording artists, as well as a variety of related areas ("Sound Recordings Periodicals," "Sexually Explicit Lyrics," and "Christmas Records"). Includes an extensive (85-pp.) index and (37–pp.) bibliography.

Reviewed by Anthony J. Adam in *LJ* 118 (1993): 68 and by Eric Hughes in *ARSCJ* 25 (1994): 64–68.

10.13* New York Public Library. Rodgers and Hammerstein Archives of Recorded Sound. *Dictionary Catalog of the Rodgers and Hammerstein Archives of Recorded Sound.* 15 vols. Boston, Mass.: G.K. Hall, 1981.

Photoreproduction of the card catalog of the enormous sound archive at Lincoln Center. There are entries under composer, important performers, titles, and subjects.

10.14 Reid, Robert H. *The Gramophone Shop Encyclopedia of Recorded Music.* 3rd ed., revised and enlarged. 639 pp. New York: Crown Publishers, 1948.

The 1st ed. was published by the Gramophone Shop, New York, in 1936 (574 pp.). The 2nd ed. was compiled by R. D. Darrell and published in 1942 by Simon & Schuster, with George C. Leslie, supervising editor (558 pp.). The 3rd ed. was reprinted by Greenwood Press, Westport, Conn., in 1970.

A prototype for all encyclopedias of recorded music in its organization and coverage, with works arranged alphabetically under the composer and partially classified. There are brief biographical accounts of the composers. All three volumes must be consulted for full coverage because the later editions are not fully cumulative. The contents are restricted to 78-rpm discs.

The 3rd ed. is reviewed by R. D. Darrell in *Notes* 5 (1948): 563.

10.15* Sutton, Allan. *A Guide to Pseudonyms on American Records, 1892–1942.* 148 pp. Westport, Conn.: Greenwood Press, 1993.

Reviewed by Marjorie Hassen in *Notes* 51 (1994): 226 and by Guy A. Marco in *Choice* 31 (1994): 1,106.

COLLECTORS' GUIDES TO CLASSICAL MUSIC

Works on recordings of classical music cited in this section are useful to scholars because they generally include brief reviews featuring comments on the performances and often on the technical quality of the recordings. Few books intended for the amateur collector are included in the following section; the list is generally confined to more comprehensive English-language works, usually presupposing some musical knowledge on the part of the reader. Such journals as *Gramophone* and *Fanfare* provide numerous reviews of current releases.

10.16* **Alexandre, Ivan A.** *Guide de la Musique Ancienne et Baroque: Dictionnaire à l'Usage des Discophiles.* li + 1,366 pp. Paris: R. Laffont, 1993. (Bouquins)

An annotated list of preclassical period recorded music, with complete discographic citations.

10.17* **Bahr, Edward R.** *Trombone/Euphonium Discography.* xxiv + 502 pp. Stevens Point, Wisc.: Index House, 1988.

Bibliography (pp. xvii–xxiv).

Reviewed by Ann P. Basart in *CNV* 132 (1989): 22–23.

10.18 *Band Record Guide: Alphabetical Listing of Band Records by Title of Composition, Composer, Performing Group, and Record Title.* 1969 edition. 102 pp. Evanston, Ill.: Instrumentalist Co., 1969.

An index to 1,480 works by title, representing 574 composers and 170 bands. There is also a list of record manufacturers and distributors.

10.19 **Basart, Ann Phillips.** *The Sound of the Fortepiano: A Discography of Recordings on Early Pianos.* 472 pp. Berkeley, Calif.: Fallen Leaf Press, 1985. (Fallen Leaf reference books in music, 2)

A discography of pre-1985 commercially released recordings of predecessors of the modern piano or authentic reproductions of such pianos. Included are the main composer/title list, a performer list, a list of piano manufacturers, and a list by record company, with label numbers. The thorough indexes include approaches by performance medium (as piano duet, concerti), performers other than pianists, album titles, piano dates, and piano collections and individual owners.

Reviewed by Clifford Bartlett in *Brio* 23 (1986): 43–44, by Robert J. Dennis in *Notes* 47 (1991): 779–80, by Graham Sadler in *EM* 15 (1987): 163, and by David Lasocki in *EKJ* 4 (1985–86): 64–68.

10.20* **Beaumont, François de.** *L'Alto et Ses Interpretes / Die Viola und ihre Interpreten / The Viola and Its Interpreters : Discographie 1920–1980.* 4th ed. 61 ll. Auvernier, France: A. de Beaumont, 1980.

The 3rd ed. was published in 1977 (50 ll.). The complete and corrected 2nd ed. was published as *Discographie sur l'Alto (1925–1970)* (34 pp. + 11 ll.). A German ed., *Viola-Diskographie* was published in Kassel by Bärenreiter, 1973 (36 pp.).

A discography of some viola performances, with text in German, French, and English.

The German ed. is reviewed in *Orchester* (January 1976): 43–44 and by Michael H. Gray in *Notes* 31 (1974): 63–66.

10.21* **Blyth, Alan.** *Choral Music on Record.* 309 pp. Cambridge, England; New York: Cambridge University Press, 1991.

An account of the recorded history of 25 choral masterpieces, with each treated to a discographical essay by one of a team of authorities. Discographies for each work (pp. 264–98) and an index conclude the body of essays.

10.22 Blyth, Alan. *Song on Record.* 2 vols. Cambridge, England: Cambridge University Press, 1987–88.

Discursive commentary on the repertory of recorded solo vocal music beginning with the works of Haydn and Mozart. Though not a discography per se, the text is liberally laced with references to particularly favored performances and there are occasional lists of recordings. Each section is an independent essay written by one of a group of distinguished music critics, among them David Hamilton, Will Crutchfield, Robin Holloway, and Michael Kennedy. The 1st vol. has material on Lieder, and the 2nd contains more general information on songs. An index of singers' names is included.

Vol. 1 is reviewed by Ann P. Basart in *CNV* 119 (1988): 13–14 and by Stephen Johnson in *Gramophone* 65 (1987): 1,512. Vol. 2 is reviewed by Lionel Salter in *Gramophone* 66 (1988): 380 and by Arne J. Arneson in *Notes* 47 (1991): 800–80.

10.23 Blyth, Alan, and **Malcolm Walker.** *Opera on Record.* 663 pp. London: Hutchinson, 1979.

Opera on Record 2 was published in 1983, 399 pp.; the American ed. of *Opera on Record 3* was published in Dover, N.H., by Longwood Press in 1984, 375 pp.

The 2nd vol. is reviewed by Elizabeth Forbes in *MT* 125 (1984): 275; the 3rd vol. is reviewed by David Anthony Fox in *OQ* 4 (1986) 198–200 no. 2.

10.24* Chaine, Jacques. *Orphee Data-Base of Guitar Records.* 444 pp. Columbus, Ohio: Editions Orphee, 1990.

A guitar discography intended to be kept current by annual supplements.

Reviewed by Marc Crozet in *Fontes* 38 (1991): 341–42.

10.25* Cohen, Aaron I. *International Discography of Women Composers.* 254 pp. Westport, Conn.: Greenwood Press, 1984. (Discographies, 10)

Reviewed by Ann P. Basart in *AM* 4 (1986): 227–28 and by Elizabeth Hayden Pizer in *SSB* 11 (Summer 1985): 54.

10.26 Cohn, Arthur. *Recorded Classical Music: A Critical Guide to Compositions and Performances.* 2,164 pp. New York: Schirmer Books; London: Collier Macmillan, 1981.

Evaluations of the recordings of 9,000 works by more than 1,800 composers, with the entries arranged alphabetically by composer, then title. The record-label index helps the reader find which works appear together on disc. Cohn wrote *The Collector's Twentieth-Century Music in the Western Hemisphere* (1961) and *Twentieth-Century Music in Western Europe: The Compositions and the Recordings* (1956).

Reviewed by Otto Luening in *MQ* 70 (1984): 152–53 and by David Hall in *Notes* 39 (1982): 81–83.

10.27 Coover, James, and **Richard Colvig.** *Medieval and Renaissance Music on Long-Playing Records.* 122 pp. Detroit, Mich.: Information Service, 1964. (Detroit studies in music bibliography, 6)

Supplement, covering 1962–71, was published in Detroit by Information Coordinators in 1973, 258 pp. (Detroit studies in music bibliography, 26)

A well-organized, detailed guide to the recorded resources of medieval and renaissance music. Over 1,200 anthologies are analyzed, with both composer and classified performer access.

The *Supplement* is reviewed by Howard Mayer Brown in *EM* 4 (1976): 319–21. The 1964 ed. is reviewed by Klaus Speer in *Notes* 22 (1966): 1,235–36, by George F. DeVine in *JRME* 13 (1965): 260, and by Ludwig Finscher in *Die Musikforschung* 20 (1967): 84–85.

10.28 Creighton, James. *Discopaedia of the Violin, 1889–1971.* 987 pp. Toronto; Buffalo, N.Y.: University of Toronto Press, 1974.

A discography of the recordings of nearly 1,800 violinists. The main entries are arranged by artist, with recorded works listed alphabetically by composer. There are composer and popular title indexes.

10.29 Croucher, Trevor. *Early Music Discography; From Plainsong to the Sons of Bach.* 2 vols. Phoenix, Ariz.: Oryx Press, 1981.

First published by the Library Association, London.

A list of 3,164 recordings in a classified arrangement by period, with information including performing ensemble, conductor, and basic discographic data. The entries are arranged alphabetically by composer, with liturgical chant in a separate section. There are indexes to names, plainsong melodies, and titles (of anonymous works). Although this is related to the Coover–Colvig index (**10.27**), there is little overlap because the latter's coverage ends with 1971 issues.

10.30* Day, Timothy. *A Discography of Tudor Church Music.* 317 pp. London: British Library, 1989.

Reviewed by John Milsom in *EM* 19 (1991): 288–89.

10.31 De Lerma, Dominique-René. *Concert Music and Spirituals: A Selective Discography.* 44 pp. Nashville, Tenn.: Institute for Research in Black American Music, Fisk University, 1981. (Black music research, no. 1)

An earlier ed. was published as *A Discography of Concert Music by Black Composers* in Minneapolis, Minn., by The AAMOA Press, 1973, 29 pp. (AAMOA resource papers, 1).

10.32* Elste, Martin. *Modern Harpsichord Music: A Discography.* 319 pp. Westport, Conn.: Greenwood Press, 1995. (Discographies, 58)

Reviewed by Jerome F. Weber in *ARSCJ* 26 (1995): 90–91 no. 1.

10.33* Fellers, Frederick. *The Metropolitan Opera on Record: A Discography of Commercial Recordings.* 101 pp. Westport, Conn.: Greenwood Press, 1984. (Discographies, 9)

10.34* Fellers, Frederick P., and **Betty Meyers.** *Discographies of Commercial Recordings of the Cleveland Orchestra and the Cincinnati Symphony Orchestra.* 211 pp. Westport, Conn.: Greenwood Press, 1978. (Discographies, unnumbered)

A discography whose entries include information on the auxiliary ensembles associated with these two orchestras and are chronologically arranged, supplying dates, matrix number, issue number, issue date, tape number, and miscellanea. There are two indexes for each orchestra: one listing composer/title, the other the assisting artists.

Reviewed by J. F. Weber in *ARSCJ* 12 (1980): 270–72.

10.35 Frasier, Jane. *Women Composers: A Discography.* 300 pp. Detroit, Mich.: Information Coordinators, 1983. (Detroit studies in music bibliography, 50)

A list of 1,030 discs by 337 composers of art music. The main body of the book lists composers alphabetically, followed by indexes of record company with label numbers, of genres, and of titles. There is a brief bibliography.

Reviewed by Gillian Anderson in *Fontes* 32 (1985): 89–90.

10.36 Gilbert, Richard. *The Clarinetists' Solo Repertoire: A Discography.* 100 pp. New York: Grenadilla Society, 1972.

A supplement, *The Clarinetists' Discography II,* was published in 1975 (150 pp.).

More than a discography. There are reviews and critiques, portraits of leading clarinetists, bibliographies, and lists of record publishers and their addresses.

10.37* Gruber, Paul. *The Metropolitan Opera Guide to Recorded Opera.* 782 pp. New York: Metropolitan Opera Guild/W.W. Norton; London: Thames & Hudson, 1993.

A guide to the various performances available on CD of the operas that make up the repertoire of the Metropolitan Opera.

10.38 Halsey. Richard S. *Classical Recordings for Home and Library.* 340 pp. Chicago, Ill.: American Library Association, 1975.

A discography intended to provide guidance to librarians and amateur collectors in building a basic collection of classical music. The entries are arranged by genre and within genre by composer, with indexes to title and manufacturers' names and numbers. Users should ignore the idiosyncratic rating system.

10.39 Hermil, Helene. *Musique: 10,000 compositeurs du XIIe au XXe siècle, répertoire chronoethnique.* 842 pp. Paris: Production et distribution Groupe de Recherche et d'Études Musicales, 1983.

An alphabetical list of composers with dates and places of birth and death, followed by a chronological list of composers by country, showing ethnic origin. There are lists of women composers and of composers related by familial, marital, or other significant ties. Entries give record label and numbers. This is a product of the Bibliothèque Internationale de Musique Contemporaine.

10.40 Hernon, Michael. *French Horn Discography.* 291 pp. New York: Greenwood Press, 1986. (Discographies, 24)

A discography of music featuring the horn, international in scope, dating from the 15th century to the present and arranged by performance medium. There are indexes to composers, horn players, and ensembles.

Reviewed by Ann Basart in *CNV* 112 (1987): 13 and by Dominique-René de Lerma in *ARBA* 19 (1988): no. 1293.

10.41 Kondracki, Miroslaw, Marta Stonkiewicz, and **Frits C. Weiland.** *International Diskographie elektronischer Musik / International electronic music discography / Discographie internationale de la musique électronique.* 174 pp. Mainz: Schott, 1979.

A computer-generated discography arranged by composer, with entries providing title, date of issue, name of studio, university, broadcasting station or institution where composition was produced, and the title of the complete recording or album. There are lists of abbreviations of record companies and of electronic studios. There is an index of composers.

10.42 Kratzenstein, Marilou, and **Jerald Hamilton.** *Four Centuries of Organ Music: From the Robertsbridge Codex through the Baroque Era: An Annotated Discography.* 300 pp. Detroit, Mich.: Information Coordinators, 1984. (Detroit studies in music bibliography, 51)

An analysis of organ recordings, especially those issued between 1970 and 1980, with the annotation indicating the organ used, noting builder, date, and place. There are indexes of organs, performers, and composers.

Reviewed by Jean-Michel Nectoux in *Fontes* 32 (1985): 222.

10.43 Kroó, György. "New Hungarian Music." In *Notes* 39 (1983): 43–71.

An annotated discography of the works of contemporary Hungarian composers in the period 1969–82. 100 works are described in detail, with a discussion of the place of Hungarian music in the Western tradition.

10.44 Laster, James H. *A Discography of Treble Voice Recordings.* 147 pp. Metuchen, N.J.: Scarecrow Press, 1985.

10.45* Meza, Fernando A. *Percussion Discography: An International Compilation of Solo and Chamber Percussion Music.* 108 pp. New York: Greenwood Press, 1990. (Discographies, 36)

10.46 Oja, Carol J. *American Music Recordings: A Discography of 20th-Century U.S. Composers: A Project of the Institute for Studies in American Music for the Koussevitsky Music Foundation, Inc.* 368 pp. Brooklyn, N.Y.: Institute for Studies in American Music, 1982.

A list of over 13,000 disc recordings of 8,000 works by almost 1,300 American composers, excluding jazz, folk, and popular musics. There are indexes to performing groups, ensembles, vocalists and narrators, and instrumentalists, and a bibliography. The editor and R. Allen Lott

write about the origins of this book in "A Discography Is Born," in *ISAMN* 11 (1982): 1–2 no. 2.
Reviewed by Thomas F. Heck in *Fontes* 21 (1984): 132–33.

10.47* Rasmussen, Richard Michael. *Recorded Concert Band Music, 1950–1987: A Selected, Annotated Listing.* 442 pp. Jefferson, N.C.: McFarland & Company, Inc., Publishers, 1988.

A discography of 1,705 annotated entries, both original and arranged, organized by composer. A brief survey of the recorded literature also describes 17 series of recorded band music. Includes an annotated appendix, "Where to Get Records" (pp. 381–87), as well as a title, name, and musical type or theme index.

Reviewed by Robert Aken in *ARBA* 20 (1989): no. 1217, by Arne J. Arneson in *Notes* 47 (1991): 800–1, and by Ann Basart in *CNV* 132 (1989): 21–22.

10.48 Rowell, Lois. *American Organ Music on Records.* 105 pp. Braintree, Mass.: Organ Literature Foundation, 1976.

A discography with 415 entries of recorded organ music by American composers, arranged by performer, giving title, performer, location and maker of organ recorded, and discographic citation. Indexes are supplied to performers, organ makers and locations, album titles, record labels and numbers, authors of program notes, and series.

Brief review by Stephen M. Fry in *Notes* 33 (1976): 306.

10.49 Stahl, Dorothy. *A Selected Discography of Solo Song: Cumulation through 1971.* 137 pp. Detroit, Mich.: Information Coordinators, 1972. (Detroit studies in music bibliography, 24)
Supplement, 1971–1974. 99 pp. Detroit, 1976. (Detroit studies in music bibliography, 34)
Supplement, 1975–1982. 236 pp. Detroit, 1984. (Detroit studies in music bibliography, 52)
First published in 1968 and supplemented in 1970.
An index to recorded anthologies of solo song. There is no approach by performer.
Review by Jean-Michel Nectoux in *Notes* 42 (1985): 228.

10.50 Turner, Patricia. *Afro-American Singers: An Index and Preliminary Discography of Long-Playing Recordings of Opera, Choral Music, and Song.* 255 pp. Minneapolis, Minn.: Challenge, 1977.

A 44-pp. supplement was issued by the author in 1980.

10.51 Weber, Jerome F. *A Gregorian Chant Discography.* 2 vols. Utica, N.Y.: The author, 1990. (Discography series, 20)

A practical guide to Gregorian chant on records. Organized into two lists, each in 1 vol. Vol. 1 lists recordings with each entry showing recording format, country recorded, label name and number, title, performing ensemble, date of recording, type of chant, title of chant, mode, chant book source, page number of chant in printed source, and duration of chant. Vol. 2 provides entries in order of chant book sources, then by order of the chants in each book; entries show type of chant, mode, and the recordings made of each chant. Includes a table of chant recordings in chronological order, an appendix on non-Gregorian Latin chants, and records not available for analysis (a very small section). Includes a performer index, a directory of performers, a conductor index, and an index to titles of all recorded chants in alphabetical order. This work brings order and clarity to chant discography.

Reviewed by Keith Falconer in *EM* 19 (1991): 287–88.

COLLECTORS' GUIDES TO EARLY RECORDINGS

The field of discs and cylinder recordings dating from 1898 to 1925 has long been the province of private collectors. Emphasis is usually placed on the performer, particularly the vocalist, rather than on the composer. The importance of collecting in this area has been recognized on a large scale by libraries and research institutions throughout the world, as at the New York Public Library, the Library of Congress, the British Institute of Recorded Sound, the Stanford

University Archive of Recorded Sound, the Yale University Collection of Historical Sound Recordings, and Syracuse University. Lately there have been increasing numbers of musicological studies based on early recordings. To pursue this research most effectively, discographers are discovering the value of research in the catalogs issued by recording manufacturers and in their archives of contracts and logs of studio work.

10.52 Bauer, Robert. *The New Catalogue of Historical Records, 1898–1908/09.* 2nd ed. 494 pp. London: Sidgwick & Jackson, [1947].

Reprinted 1970. 1st edition, 1937.

Recordings listed under performer, grouped under label and year of pressing. Serial numbers are given, and there are brief entries for composer and title of work.

10.53 Bescoby-Chambers, John. *The Archives of Sound, Including a Selective Catalogue of Historical Violin, Piano, Spoken, Documentary, Orchestral, and Composer's Own Recordings.* 153 pp. Lingfield, Surrey, England: Oakwood Press, 1964.

Vocal recordings are fairly well documented today. Violin, piano, and orchestral recordings are rarely written about and there is a vast, almost uncharted sea of piano roll recordings that are almost forgotten today.

A valuable contribution to the discography and player piano resources for instrumental music, with brief biographies of performers and lists of their recordings. Some chapter headings include "The Violin on Record," "Historical Piano Recordings," "Orchestral Recordings," and "The Composer's Own Interpretation."

10.54 Bontinck-Küffel, Irmgard. *Opern auf Schallplatten, 1900–1962: Ein historischen Katalog vollständiger oder nahezu vollständiger Aufnahmen als Beitrag zur Geschichte der Aufführungspraxis.* Edited by Kurt Blaukopf and Manfred Wagner. 184 pp. Vienna: Universal Edition, 1974.

An early attempt to apply discography to historical research. The editors identify the first recording of each opera cited with information on cast, orchestra, and label. The discography is arranged by composer and title, with alternative titles given, as well as complete discographic information. There is a bibliography, but no index.

Reviewed by John Warrack in *M&L* 57 (1976): 168–70.

10.55* Daniels, William R. *The American 45 and 78 Rpm Record Dating Guide, 1948–1959.* 156 pp. Westport, Conn.: Greenwood Press, 1985. (Discographies, 16)

10.56 Deakins, Duane D. *Cylinder Records: A Description of the Numbering Systems, Physical Appearance, and Other Aspects of Cylinder Records Made by the Major American Companies, with Brief Remarks about the Earliest American Companies and the Foreign Record Manufacturers.* 2nd ed. 35 pp. Stockton, Calif.: Duane D. Deakins, 1958.

Reviewed by Richard S. Hill in *Notes* 16 (1959): 243–44.

10.57 Deakins, Duane D., Elizabeth Deakins, and **Thomas Grattelo.** *Comprehensive Cylinder Record Index.* Stockton, Calif.: Duane D. Deakins, 1966.

The 1st ed. was produced in 1956. 2nd ed. appeared in 1958.

Contents: Pt. 1, *Edison Amberol Records;* Pt. 2, *Edison Standard Records;* Pt. 3, *Edison Blue Amberol Records;* Pt. 4, *Indestructible Records;* Pt. 5, *U.S. Everlasting Records.*

A discography of the earliest commercially distributed recordings, drawing together information from surviving catalogs, company documents, and the cylinders themselves. The concern in these indexes is for the objects, the companies, and the manufacturing process, not for the music recorded.

10.58* Docks, Les R. *American Premium Record Guide, 1915–1965.* 3rd ed. 354 pp. Florence, Ala.: Books Americana, 1984.

First published as *1915–1965 American Premium Record Guide: Identification and Values: 78's, 45's and LP's* in 1980 (737 pp.).

A collector's price guide that includes a section illustrating over a thousand labels, with coverage including jazz, dance bands, blues, country, and rockabilly, and a performers' index.

10.59 Girard, Victor, and **Harold M. Barnes.** *Vertical-Cut Cylinders and Discs: A Catalogue of All "Hill-and-Dale" Recordings of Serious Worth Made and Issued between c. 1897–1932.* 196 pp. London: British Institute of Recorded Sound, 1971.

A facsimile reprint (corrected) of the original 1964 ed.

A major contribution to the discography of early recordings, arranged in three major categories: vocal recordings, speech recordings, and instrumental and orchestral recordings. Appendixes are devoted to complete operas and to anonymous Pathé discs. The approach is mainly by performer.

10.60 Hurst, P. G. *The Golden Age Recorded.* New and revised ed. 187 pp. Lingfield, Surrey, England: Oakwood Press, 1963.

First published by Sidgwick & Jackson, London, 1946.

A manual for private collectors. General discussions of record collecting are followed by biographical notices of the major artists, classified by voice. The appendix (pp. 147–87) gives a selected list, by performer, of important early recordings.

10.61* Jasen, David A. *Recorded Ragtime, 1897–1958.* 155 pp. Hamden, Conn.: Archon Books, 1973.

A discography of all known 78-rpm recordings of ragtime, omitting much of the relevant discographic information (date of recording and matrix number, for example).

10.62 Karlin, Fred J. *Edison Diamond Discs 50001–52651.* 160 pp. Santa Monica, Calif.: Bona Fide Publishing Co.

A numerical list of every Edison Diamond Disc issued in the 50000 series from 1912 to 1929, citing 5,200 titles as well as the performing artists, composers, and lyricists.

10.63 Koenigsberg, Allen. *Edison Cylinder Records, 1889–1912, with an Illustrated History of the Phonograph.* xlii + 159 pp. New York: Stellar Productions, 1969.

A list of Edison cylinder records, with a numerical list, a performer index, and a title index. Reviewed by Edward Colby in *Notes* 27 (1971): 499–500.

10.64* Laird, Ross. *Tantalizing Tingles: A Discography of Early Ragtime, Jazz, and Novelty Syncopated Piano Recordings, 1889–1934.* xxx + 258 pp. Westport, Conn.: Greenwood Press, 1995. (Discographies, 59)

Documentation of all known recordings of nonclassical piano music issued before 1935 on disc and cylinder recordings.

10.65 Methuen-Campbell, James. *Catalogue of Recordings by Classical Pianists.* 66 pp. Chipping Norton, Oxfordshire, England: Disco Epsom, 1984.

A 2nd vol. is projected.

This catalog aims to list all released recordings by classical pianists born up through 1872. The layout of the catalog is simple: matrix numbers, where known, are given in the left-hand column, catalog numbers in the right-hand column. The center column is reserved for the composer and the title of the work recorded. A brief biography prefaces the recording of each artist.

A discography in order by pianist, including private or never-released recordings and some reissues on LP, especially those of the International Piano Archive. There are occasional notes on individual recordings. Reported but not examined recordings are mentioned. The catalog includes Eugen d'Albert, Johannes Brahms, Claude Debussy, Enrique Granados, Alexander

Gretchaninov, Edvard Grieg, Vincent d'Indy, Ignace Paderewski, Hans Pfitzner, Camille Saint-Saëns, Florent Schmitt, and Richard Strauss. There is no index.

10.66 Moogk, Edward B. *Roll Back the Years: History of Canadian Recorded Sound and its Legacy: Genesis to 1930.* 443 pp. + 7" disc. Ottawa: National Library of Canada, 1975.

Issued also in French as *En Remontant les Années,* 1975.

A history including discographies of Canadian performers, composers, and early recordings.

10.67* Moses, Julian Morton. *American Celebrity Recordings, 1900–1925.* Revised 3rd ed. 208 pp. Dallas, Tex.: Monarch Record Enterprises, 1993.

10.68 Moses, Julian Morton. *Collectors' Guide to American Recordings, 1895–1925.* 199 pp. New York: American Record Collectors' Exchange, 1949.

Reprinted by Dover Publications in 1977. The 1st ed. was published by Concert Bureau in 1936, 44 pp.

A selective guide in which the entries for discs are arranged under the performers' names by label serial or matrix number. Also includes a numerical guide to these numbers, an index of operas and an instrumental index.

Reviewed by Philip L. Miller in *Notes* 7 (1950): 289.

10.69 *Rigler and Deutsch Record Index.* 977 microfiches. Washington, D.C.: Association for Recorded Sound Collections, 1981–83.

Originally issued on 36 reels of microfilm by Mi-Kal County-Matic, Syracuse, N.Y., in 1983.

An index to the 78-rpm recordings held by the Associated Audio Archives, five of the largest recorded-sound collections in the United States: New York Public Library, Rodgers and Hammerstein Archives of Recorded Sound; Yale University, Collection of Historical Sound Recordings; Syracuse University, Belfer Audio Laboratory and Archives; Stanford University, Archive of Recorded Sound; and the Library of Congress, Motion Picture, Broadcasting, and Recorded Sound Division. A total of 615,000 recordings held among these institutions are reflected in the *Index.*

The index is in several parts: an author/composer section, a title section, a performer section, a label name and issue number section, a label name and matrix number section, and a section in which label name and issue numbers are arranged by institution. The introduction, on the first microfiche, explains the methodology used to gather the data. No attempt was made to list the names and titles in a consistent form, with an established authority control. Nevertheless, the *Index* brought previously unknown or unlisted recordings to light. ARSC and Associated Audio Archives converted the *Index* to machine-readable form, improving the ease of use; the *Index* is available on RLIN (**12.2**).

There is an excellent, if brief, article on the *Index* by David Hamilton, "A New Way to Find Old Records," in *Opus* (December 1985): 12–13 and a review by Richard Koprowski in *Notes* 42 (1986): 535–37.

10.70 Rust, Brian A. L. *Discography of Historical Records on Cylinders and 78s.* 327 pp. Westport, Conn.: Greenwood Press, 1979.

A history of the earliest period of sound storage, with an index.

10.71* Turner, Patricia. *Dictionary of Afro-American Performers: 78 RPM and Cylinder Recordings of Opera, Choral Music, and Song, c.1900–1949.* 433 pp. New York: Garland Publishing, 1990. (Garland reference library of the humanities, 590)

A companion title by the author is *Afro-American Singers: An Index and Preliminary Discography of Long-Playing Recordings of Opera, Choral Music, and Song* (Minneapolis, Minn.: Challenge Productions, 1977), 225 pp. (**10.50**).

A discography featuring short biographical essays on early African-American classical performers, listing their recordings, with selected photographs of the performers and rare and beautiful record labels and concert and recital programs. In addition, each entry includes a selected bibliography. Archival collections and other resource materials held by institutions in the United States are noted when known. The section on spirituals identifies well-known arrangers. Another section covers recordings of the compositions of African Americans as performed by John McCormick, Fritz Kreisler, The Orpheus Quartet, and others. Included are private recordings and those of small and short-lived companies, as well as the casts and recordings of such top musicals as *Porgy and Bess, Four Saints in Three Acts,* and *Carmen Jones.*

COLLECTORS' GUIDES TO JAZZ RECORDINGS

Jazz record collectors live in a world of their own and are well equipped with reference tools designed to meet their needs. The initial impetus toward jazz documentation came from European rather than American enthusiasts; see Carl Gregor, Duke of Mecklenburg (**4.248**), Delaunay (**10.79**), and Panassie (**10.93**). Daniel Allen's *Jazz* volume in the Gibson and Gray *Bibliography of Discographies* (**10.2**) provides entries for almost 4,000 discographies. Only some of the most important ones are cited in this section.

10.72 Allen, Walter C. *Studies in Jazz Discography, I- .* New Brunswick, N.J.: Institute of Jazz Studies, Rutgers University, 1971– .

Later issues published by Greenwood Press, Westport, Conn.

A periodical consistently presenting serious and important jazz discographic work. Lists of recordings and actual discographic investigations are featured, as well as reviews of similar works published elsewhere.

Reviewed by James Patrick in *Notes* 29 (1972): 236–39.

10.73* Bruynincx, Walter. *Jazz: Swing, 1920–1985: Swing, Dance Bands & Combos.* 12 vols. c. 4,875 pp. Mechelen, Belgium: 60 Years of Recorded Jazz Team, 1986–90.

Bruynincx, Walter. *Jazz: The Vocalists, 1917–1988: Singers & Crooners.* 4 vols. c. 1,645 pp. Mechelen, Belgium: 60 Years of Recorded Jazz Team, 1988–90.

Bruynincx, Walter. *Jazz: Traditional Jazz, 1897–1985: Origins, New Orleans, Dixieland, Chicago Styles.* 6 vols. c. 3,000 pp. Mechelen, Belgium: 60 Years of Recorded Jazz Team, 1987–90.

Bruynincx, Walter. *Modern Jazz: Be-Bop, Hard Bop, West Coast.* 6 vols. c. 2,570 pp. Mechelen, Belgium: 60 Years of Recorded Jazz Team, 1984–87.

Bruynincx, Walter. *Modern Jazz: Modern Big Band.* 2 vols. c. 890 pp. Mechelen, Belgium: 60 Years of Recorded Jazz Team, 1985–89.

Bruynincx, Walter. *Progressive Jazz: Free, Third-Stream, Fusion.* 5 vols. c. 2,225 pp. Mechelen, Belgium: 60 Years of Recorded Jazz Team, 1984–89.

Spin-offs from the *60 Years of Jazz* lists. The final volume of each series includes an index of musicians.

Reviewed by Barry Kernfeld and Howard Rye in *Notes* 51 (1995): 865–77.

10.74 Bruynincx, Walter. *70 Years of Recorded Jazz: 1917–1987.* Mechelen, Belgium, 1987.

Originally issued between 1967 and 1975 as *50 Years of Recorded Jazz,* with a supplement vol. issued in 1980. *60 Years of Recorded Jazz, 1917–1977,* issued in 16 vols., 1980, with an update M–P issued in 1986.

Focused primarily on LPs, with entries arranged by name of performer or group, with brief biographical or historical information. Discographies cite all recordings with personnel and individual titles, including date and location of recording sessions. Bruynincx gives unissued and alternative takes when known. A few major artists (Louis Armstrong and Duke Ellington, for example) have comprehensive discographies that include 78-rpm discs as well as LPs. There is a separate artists index, not subjected to authority control, that treats every musician listed anywhere in the set. Although intended for the avid amateur, this work is a substantial asset to the jazz scholar.

10.75 Carey, David A., and **Albert M. McCarthy.** *The Directory of Recorded Jazz and Swing Music.* 6 vols. London: Cassell, 1950–57.

Cover title: *Jazz Directory.* Vols. 2–4 have appeared in 2nd editions, 1955–57.

An alphabetical list of performers and ensembles, with detailed information as to their recorded output and informative annotations. The work progressed through 6 vols. (as of 1957), paged continuously through p. 1,112, as far as the entry "Longshaw."

Vols. 1–4 published by the Delphic Press, Fordingbridge, Hants. The 2nd editions of Vols. 2–4 and Vols. 5 and 6 are published by Cassell, London. Continued in Jepsen (**10.84**) and McCarthy (**10.90**).

Reviewed by Barry Kernfeld and Howard Rye in *Notes* 51 (1994): 512–14.

10.76* Cook, Richard, and **Brian Morton.** *The Penguin Guide to Jazz on CD, LP, and Cassette.* New ed. 1,287 pp. London; New York: Penguin Books, 1992.

First ed., 1,287 pp., 1992.

A jazz discography with generally generous annotations, covering a variety of formats, with an international overview. The authors provide a rating system, a list of personnel, the date of the recording, and a comparative review of the recordings of each artist.

Reviewed by Tony Russell in *TLS* 4736 (January 7 1994): 15 and by John Corbett in *Down Beat* 61 (October 1994): 60.

10.77* Crawford, Richard, and **Jeffrey Magee.** *Jazz Standards on Record, 1900–1942: A Core Repertory.* xxv + 94 pp. Chicago, Ill.: Center for Black Music Research, Columbia College, Chicago, 1992. (CBMR monographs, 4)

10.78 Cullaz, Maurice. *Guide des disques de jazz: Les 1,000 meilleurs disques de spirituals, gospel songs, blues, rhytm [sic] and blues, jazz, et leur histoire.* 351 pp. Paris: Buchet/Chastel, 1971. (Collection musique)

An interesting source that provides access to a wide range of recordings based on a French discographer's opinions. Along with title pages that reproduce accolades from blues, R&B, and jazz performers such as Memphis Slim, Ray Charles, and Art Taylor, Cullaz has subdivided his list by genre and given the reader a survey of the different subjects. Each section is arranged alphabetically by the performers, with a short introduction to their work and a list of recordings annotated with reviews by the author. Four pages of black-and-white photographs complete this French look at indigenous American music.

10.79 Delauney, Charles. *New Hot Discography: The Standard Dictionary of Recorded Jazz.* Edited by Walter E. Schaap and George Avakian. 608 pp. New York: Criterion Music Corporation, 1948.

First published in France in 1936; reprinted, 1982.

Separating the "pioneers of jazz" from "post-1930 jazz," a discography, subdivided by region, with an elaborate classification system that groups recordings by major jazz personalities. There is a complete index of names.

Reviewed by Rudi Blesh in *Notes* 6 (1948): 159–60.

10.80* Fordham, John. *Jazz on CD: The Essential Guide.* Revised ed. 474 pp. London: Kyle Cathie, 1993.

A chronologically arranged discography.

10.81 Harris, Rex, and **Brian Rust.** *Recorded Jazz.* 256 pp. Harmondsworth, Middlesex, England: Penguin Books, 1958.

Although this is not a comprehensive discography, the authors present a cross-section of real jazz, together with biographical notes of performers and a critical assessment of the records listed.

Reviewed by Charles Fox in *Gramophone* 36 (June 1958): 36 and by Francis Newton and Benedict Edwards in *Jazz Journal* 11 (June 1958): 32, 36.

10.82* Harris, Steve. *Jazz on Compact Disc: A Critical Guide to the Best Recordings.* 176 pp. New York: Harmony Books, 1987.

Reviewed by Ray Spencer in *Jazz Journal International* 41 (March 1988): 18.

10.83* Harrison, Max, Charles Fox, and **Eric Thacker.** *The Essential Jazz Records.* [Vol. 1: *Ragtime to Swing*]. 566 pp. Westport, Conn.: Greenwood Press, 1984– . (Discographies, 12)

First published as *Modern Jazz: The Essential Records* (London: Aquarius Books, 1975, 140 pp.).

A chronologically arranged list of the 250 jazz recordings deemed important to these reviewers, divided by eras, with special emphasis on the 1930s. Harrison and colleagues provide critical notes, along with discographical information, to the major recordings of jazz history, closing with a section titled "Transition to Modern Jazz," taking the reader up to Charlie Parker. A substantial bibliography, as well as an index of LP titles and musicians, provide significant information for the jazz listener.

The 1st ed. is reviewed by Frank Tirro in *Notes* 33 (1976): 73–74 and by Eileen Southern in *BPM* 6 (1978): 94–96. The 1984 ed. is reviewed by W. Royal Stokes in *Down Beat* 52 (November 1985): 61 and by John White in *Popular Music* no. 5 (1982): 299–301.

10.84 Jepsen, Jørgen Grunnet. *Jazz Records: A–Z, 1942–1969: A Discography.* 11 vols. in 8. Holte, Denmark: K.E. Knudsen, 1963–70.

A pioneering reference work covering recorded jazz from 1942 to 1969. Vols. 5 and 6 were published by Nordisk Tidskrift Forlag, Copenhagen. Updated by Raben (**10.95**).

Reviewed by Brian Knight in *Jazz Journal* 16 (December 1963): 13 and by Barry Kernfeld and Howard Rye in *Notes* 51 (1994): 535–40.

10.85* Kernfeld, Barry. *The Blackwell Guide to Recorded Jazz.* 2nd ed. 474 pp. Oxford, England; Cambridge, Mass.: Blackwell, 1995. (Blackwell reference)

First ed. issued in 1991.

Six leading jazz authorities select 150 of the world's greatest jazz recordings as the basis of a comprehensive collection, organized chronologically, with longer and more considered reviews than the usual anthology of this type.

10.86* Lange, Horst H. *Die Deutsche "78er": Discographie der Hot-Dance- und Jazz-Musik: 1903–1958.* 2nd revised ed. 1,056 pp. Berlin: Colloquium Verlag, 1978.

First published by Bote & Bock in 1955, 652 pp. Second ed. published by Colloquium Verlag, Berlin, 1966, 775 pp.

One of several European compilations of jazz records, with a number of English and continental performers.

10.87* Leder, Jan. *Women in Jazz: A Discography of Instrumental Music, 1913–1969.* 305 pp. Westport, Conn.: Greenwood Press, 1985. (Discographies, 19)

An important and unique source for tracing the impact women have had as musicians on many jazz recordings. This discography was derived from the research of four sources: Delauney's *New Hot Discography* (**10.79**), Rust's *Jazz Records 1897–1942* (**10.96**), Jepsen's *Jazz Records: A–Z, 1942–1969* (**10.84**), and Bruyninckx's *60 Years of Recorded Jazz, 1917–1977* (**10.73**), supplemented by the Stash recording *Jazzwomen: A Feminist Retrospective.* The first section, an alphabetically arranged single performer's list, notes her instrument and all the recordings on which she played, as well as a chronological catalog of dates and places of recording sessions, a performer's list with instrumentation and side-players, the title of the cut, the matrix number, and the record label and number of the issue. The second section lists recordings with two or more women performing, with like entries. An index of women performers is included.

10.88* Litchfield, Jack. *The Canadian Jazz Discography, 1916–1980.* 945 pp. Toronto, Ont.; Buffalo, N.Y.: University of Toronto Press, 1982.

A discography compiled to list every jazz record recorded by a Canadian jazz artist from 1916 to 1980. It includes a biography of each artist, with entries giving the personnel of the orchestra, the city and date of recording, label name and number, and title and composer credits. Jazz artists appearing on other recordings where a substantial jazz passage is featured are also included in the discography. The bulk of the discography is arranged alphabetically by performer, with separate lists for motion pictures and piano rolls by Canadian artists. Indexes to the tune titles and the musicians accompany the work.

10.89* Lord, Tom. *The Jazz Discography,* Vols. 1–14 (to date). West Vancouver, B.C.: Lord Music Reference; Redwood, N.Y.: Cadence Books, 1992– .

An attempt to update the individual paperback versions of the Bruynincx discographies (**10.73**). Barry Kernfeld and Howard Rye thoroughly examined this set in an essay-review in *Notes* 51 (1995): 877–88. There are additional reviews by Anthony J. Adam in *LJ* 117 (1992): 128, by Kevin Whitehead in *Down Beat* 60 (January 1993): 48, and by James Farrington in *Choice* 30 (1993): 1,297.

10.90 McCarthy, Albert J. *Jazz Discography 1: An International Discography of Recorded Jazz, Including Blues, Gospel, and Rhythm-and-Blues for the Year January-December 1958.* 271 pp. London: Cassell, 1960.

The 1st vol. of a projected yearbook to cover all jazz recordings issued throughout the world. New releases are listed alphabetically by country. Full contents of each disc are listed, with personnel, place, and date of recording if known. This vol. was an attempt to carry on the work started by Carey and McCarthy in their *Directory of Recorded Jazz* (**10.75**). Only 1 vol. was published, but supplements appeared in McCarthy's periodical *Jazz Monthly.*

Reviewed by Charles Fox in *Gramophone* 38 (October 1960): 253.

10.91 McCarthy, Albert, Alun Morgan, Paul Oliver, and **Max Harrison.** *Jazz on Record: A Critical Guide to the First 50 Years: 1917–1967.* 416 pp. London: Hanover Books; New York: Oak Publications, 1968.

Supersedes a work published under the same title by Charles Fox, Peter Gammond, and Alun Morgan (London: Hutchinson, 1960).

Jazz on Record is not a gramophone catalog but a reference book to the best, the most significant, or simply the most typical recorded works of the leading jazz and blues artists to come to prominence between 1917 and 1967. A source with much biographical and critical commentary, arranged mainly by jazz artists, with additional sections devoted to styles and traditions.

Reviewed by Frank Tirro in *Notes* 26 (1970): 756–58.

10.92 Nicolausson, Harry. *Swedish Jazz Discography.* 416 pp. Stockholm: Swedish Music Information Centre, 1983.

A revision of *Svensk jazzdiskografi,* 1953; also published as *Publikationer fran jazzavdelningen, Svensk Visarchiv.*

A discography in English and Swedish, emphasizing recordings of international jazz artists issued in Sweden and providing a unique source for recordings. Entries are arranged alphabetically by performer, with recordings listed in chronological order and including personnel, date of the session, and recording information. Record company labels and numbers are included, as is an index to performers. Of special interest to non-Swedish users is the appearance of the Swedish A's and O's lists at the end of the alphabet, both in the body of the discography and in the index.

Reviewed by Chris Sheridan in *Jazz Journal International* 37 (April 1984): 18.

10.93 Panassie, Hughes. *Discographie critique des meilleurs disques de jazz.* 621 pp. Paris: Robert Laffont, 1958.

An earlier edition, Paris, Correa, 1951, 371 pp.

A discography by a prolific writer on jazz and one of the first important discographers in the field. Arrangement is by performer, with an analytical index by medium and an index of names.

10.94* Piazza, Tom. *The Guide to Classic Recorded Jazz.* 391 pp. Iowa City, Iowa: University of Iowa Press, 1995.

A discography in the narrative style, with much historical and comparative information interspersed with discographical citations. The author has divided this resource into ensembles and soloists, and further subdivided them chronologically by style (or, in the case of the soloists, by instrument) to provide a survey of recorded jazz. The epilogue recounts the author's affection for jazz recordings. An index to performers is included.

Reviewed by Paul Baker in *LJ* 120 (March 1 1995): 74, by Stanley Dance in *Jazz Times* (February 1996): 61–62, by Lee Bash in *Jazz Educators Journal* 28 (1995): 28 no. 3, and by John Corbett in *Down Beat* 62 (October 1995): 64.

10.95* Raben, Erik. *A Discography of Free Jazz: Albert Ayler, Don Cherry, Ornette Coleman, Pharaoh Sanders, Archie Shepp, Cecil Taylor.* 38 ll. Copenhagen: Knudsen, 1969.

A small discography subdivided in separate sections for each performer and arranged chronologically by the title of the albums. Entries include the performers and their instrument, the city and date of the recording session, the title of the cuts (with their issue labels and numbers), and any notes about omissions and reissues. No indexes or introductions are included.

10.96 Rust, Brian. *Jazz Records, 1897–1942.* 5th ed., revised and enlarged. 2 vols. 1,996 pp. Chigwell, England: Storyville Publications, 1982.

Contents: Vol. 1, *A–Kar;* Vol. 2, *Kar–Z.*

This work supersedes earlier editions issued variously under the titles *Jazz Records A–Z: 1897–1931* (Hatch End, London: The author, 1961), 736 pp.; *Jazz Records ii: 1932–1942, A–Z,* 1965, 680 pp.; *Jazz Records A–Z, 1897–1942.* Revised 3rd ed., 2 vols., 1,968 pp., published in London by Storyville, 1969. The 4th ed. of the current title was published by Arlington House, New Rochelle, N.Y., 1978, 1,996 pp.

A set of two books covering in the fullest possible detail all known records made between 1897 and 1942 in ragtime, jazz, and swing idioms. Only records made by American and British musicians are listed.

Performers and groups are listed alphabetically, with their records identified by matrix numbers and titles. Includes an introduction and an index of abbreviations for musical terms and record labels. An artists' index was compiled by Mary Rust. This is a rich source of information on jazz history and recording activity for the period specified.

The 4th ed. is reviewed by Donald McCormick in *Notes* 35 (1979): 638 and by R. Serge Denisoff in *Journal of Popular Culture* 12 (1979): 761.

10.97* Scott, Frank, and the staff of **Down Home Music.** *The Down Home Guide to the Blues.* 250 pp. Pennington, N.J.: A Cappella Books, 1991.

A generously illustrated, discographical guide to more than 3,000 blues and gospel LPs, CDs, and cassettes, with information on the featured artists and the quality and availability of the recordings. Genres covered include zydeco, Cajun, early jazz, boogie woogie, and R&B, among others. Part One is listed by artist and includes a biography of the artist, with a list of the record label number, title, and information on cuts. Recordings considered essential are so noted. The second part includes anthologies, divided into prewar and postwar sections, arranged by city.

Reviewed by David Lands in *Jazz International Journal* 45 (March 1992): 15.

10.98* Smith, Charles E., Frederic Ramsey, Jr., Charles Payne Rogers, and **William Russell.** *The Jazz Record Book.* 515 pp. New York: Smith and Durrell, 1942.

Reprinted in 1978 by Greenwood Press, Westport, Conn.

A survey of the history of jazz in its various regional styles (pp. 1–125) and record lists by major performers and ensembles, with critical and descriptive commentary (pp. 130–508). There is a selected bibliography of jazz, with an index of bands.

Reviewed by Barry Kernfeld and Howard Rye in *Notes* 51 (1994): 514–29.

10.99 Tudor, Dean, and **Nancy Tudor.** *Jazz.* 302 pp. Littleton, Colo.: Libraries Unlimited, 1979. (American popular music on Elpee)

A discography of American jazz on LP records for the amateur aficionado. For an update, see **10.157.**

Reviewed by Robert M. Jones in *Notes* 36 (1980): 648–49.

10.100* Tulane University. William Ransom Hogan Jazz Archive. Catalog of the William Ransom Hogan Jazz Archive: *The Collection of Seventy-Eight RPM Phonograph Recordings, Howard-Tilton Memorial Library, Tulane University.* 2 vols. Boston, Mass.: G.K. Hall, 1984.

A photoreproduction of the card catalog for older recordings of one of the most significant jazz archives in the U.S.

10.101* Wynn, Ron, and **Michael Erlewine.** *All Music Guide to Jazz: The Best CDs, Albums and Tapes.* 751 pp. San Francisco, Calif.: Miller Freeman Books; Emeryville, Calif.: Publishers Group West; Milwaukee, Wisc.: Hal Leonard Publishing, 1994.

A discography of jazz recordings, a spinoff from the *All Music Guide* (**10.129**), listing almost 1,200 musicians and ensembles, rating 9,000+ recordings. Also included are background material on jazz history, some basic jazz definitions, and guidance to jazz labels, producers, clubs, publications, and retail jazz sources.

Reviewed by James Farrington in *Choice* 32 (1995): 911 and by Amy Knutson-Strack in *Instrumentalist* 49 (December 1994): 10.

COLLECTORS' GUIDES TO MUSICAL THEATER, FILM, AND TELEVISION RECORDINGS

10.102* Gänzl, Kurt. *The Blackwell Guide to the Musical Theatre on Record.* 547 pp. Oxford; Cambridge, Mass.: Blackwell Reference, 1990. (Blackwell Reference)

A detailed discography of musical theater recordings.

Reviewed by Nigel Douglas in *M&L* 72 (1991): 305–6.

10.103* Gelfand, Steve. *Television Theme Recordings: An Illustrated Discography, 1951–1994.* 332 pp. Ann Arbor, Mich.: Popular Culture, Ink., 1994.

An earlier ed. was published in the Bronx, N.Y., by Steve Gelfand (Television Music Archives), 1985, 136 pp.

A discography of television music, arranged alphabetically by program name, including the theme number (if a different tune was used), composer, recording artists, recording format (singles or albums), record title, label and number, re-release and previous issues, whether a theme for both radio and television, public domain and classical compositions used in the recording, release date of the record, and versions. The basic discographical information is interspersed with a TV theme trivia quiz and composer biographies. Of special interest is a selected foreign discography (primarily for the U.K.), discographical notes (with various trivia), and the answers to the TV Theme Quiz.

Appendixes include the Top 10 Most Recorded TV Themes (U.S. Releases); Charted TV Themes (on *Billboard, Cash Box,* and *Record World*); Chart Statistics (year by year, 1948–93); Singles (main themes); Novelties, Parodies, and Interpolations (1953–93); Charted Themes from British series never telecast in the U.S.; a Basic LP Collection; Grammy Award Winners (1958–93); and a discography of Historical Reprints. Indexes to composers, popular recording artists, and song titles are provided for the complete TV discography.

The 1994 ed. is reviewed by James Rettig in *Wilson Library Bulletin* 69 (January 1995): 86. *Television Theme Recordings* is reviewed by B. Lee Cooper in *PMS* 11 (Summer 1987): 120, by B. Lee Cooper in *Popular Music* 7 (1988): 116–17, and by Tim Brooks in *ARSCJ* 27 (1996): 74–75 no. 1.

10.104* Harris, Steve. *Film and Television Composers: An International Discography, 1920–1989.* 302 pp. Jefferson, N.C.: McFarland & Co. Inc., 1992.

A sequel to *Film, Television and Stage Music on Phonograph Records: A Discography,* with an emphasis on composers. The list stresses commercial phonograph records, U.S. pressings, full scores, and original soundtrack performances through the end of 1989 production. The entries give no dates. There is a production title index. Harris has tightly defined what is included in this resource. Only composers of originally composed and adapted music are considered, and the productions listed must have been composed or adapted specifically for that production. It is international in scope, but lists primarily composers from the U.S., Great Britain, France, and Italy, depending on access to the information available. Limitations include the fact that composers are included only if they have at least three or four different film or TV credits to their name, and domestic U.S. recordings are favored. The most complete recording of the music is given preference over cover versions. The original soundtrack is also favored, unless the cover version has significant amounts of uncovered music. Finally, the discography lists only conventional vinyl phonograph records, excluding cassettes, CDs, and acetates. An index to the title of the production, with reference to the entry number, is provided.

Reviewed by A.J. Adam in *Choice* 29 (1992): 1,656 and by B. Lee Cooper in *PMS* 17 (Fall 1993): 106–7.

10.105* Harris, Steve. *Film, Television, and Stage Music on Phonograph Records: A Discography.* 445 pp. Jefferson, N.C.: McFarland, 1988.

A collection of 11,761 entries for U.S., Great Britain, and other important productions, arranged alphabetically by title, in separate lists for film, television, and stage, with each section having an appendix of related recordings, excluding CDs and tapes. A helpful feature is the inclusion of relevant excerpts on anthologies. Includes a bibliography and a composer index.

Reviewed by B. Lee Cooper in *ARSCJ* 20 (1988–89): 84–86 and in *PMS* 13 (Summer 1989): 120–22, by H. Stephen Wright in *Fontes* 36 (1989): 340–41, and by Steven Smolian in *Notes* 49 (1993): 1,527–28.

10.106* Hodgins, Gordon W. *The Broadway Musical: A Complete LP Discography.* 183 pp. Metuchen, N.J.: Scarecrow Press, 1980.

A list of 331 different musicals, with both original cast and featured performers but no film soundtracks, from North American record companies. The discography is an alphabetical list of Broadway musicals, including reissues of LPs and new issues of older musicals. The entries include the title, designation of whether it is the original cast, record label number, the main performers in the cast, credits (music lyrics, book), and a list of songs in order of appearance on disk. Indexes include composer (listing also the name of the show), book and lyrics writer, performer, song, composer/lyricist, and major record company sequential index (alphabetical by company), providing multiple access to the collection. An appendix listing albums for which full information is not given concludes this resource.

Reviewed by Donald McCormick in *Notes* 38 (1981): 61–63.

10.107 Hummel, David. *The Collector's Guide to the American Musical Theatre.* New revised, enlarged ed. 2 vols. Metuchen, N.J.: Scarecrow Press, 1984.

First published by the author in Grawn, Mich., 1978 and 1979.

An extensive discography arranged by show title. Each entry gives performance dates and titles of the principal members, and has extensive notes. The main body of entries is preceded by essays on British, Australian, and Canadian musicals, as well as on the pre-LP original cast recording. There is an appendix of sources of excerpts. The 2nd vol. is an index of all personal names cited.

Reviewed by Ed Glazier in *Notes* 43 (1986): 301–3 and by Doris McGinty in *BPM* 13 (1985): 227–29.

10.108* Lynch, Richard Chigley. *Broadway on Record: A Directory of New York Cast Recordings of Musical Shows, 1931–1986.* 347 pp. New York: Greenwood Press, 1987. (Discographies, 28)

A directory of original cast albums of popular Broadway and off-Broadway New York musical theater (1931–86). Performers who performed on the stage and on record are highlighted. The discography lists the shows alphabetically and gives title, date of the original show, and theater; record company and number; whether stereo or monaural; the availability on CD; composers/lyricists; musical director; primary cast members; and songs (in order on record), indicating the featured role. A chronology of productions (June 3 1931–August 10 1986) follows, which lists the date, production, and theater. An index to the production's entry in the body of the discography is provided. Includes a performer index (with dates or nationality, if not first on Broadway); a technical index lists composer, lyricist, musical director, and pianist.

Reviewed by James Rettig in *Wilson Library Bulletin* 62 (March 1988): 96 and by James Miller in *Fanfare* 12 (1988): 425–26 no. 2.

10.109* Lynch, Richard Chigley. *Movie Musicals on Record: A Directory of Recordings of Motion Picture Musicals, 1927–1987.* 445 pp. New York: Greenwood Press, 1989. (Discographies, 32)

A companion volume to **10.108,** providing an alphabetical list of recordings of movie musicals from Al Jolson's *The Jazz Singer* to *Three Amigos,* 1987. At least three musical numbers must be in the movie for it to qualify as a movie musical, and the numbers must be connected to the film's plot. The entries are primarily American and include the film title, with the name of company and year first released, the original label and number (as well as the most recent reissue), whether the recording is in stereo or monaural, and whether it is available on CD. Other facets of the entry include the major composer, lyricist, and musical conductor; cast members who sang on the recording listed (including ghost voices); and titles of songs as they appeared on recording, with the primary performer. A chronology of films (1927–87) includes the title and the album company; a performer index and a technical index (listing composers, lyricists, and musical directors) provide multiple access points.

Reviewed by Bonnie Jo Dopp in *LJ* 114 (1989): 84 and by Don McCormick in *Notes* 49 (1992): 172–73.

10.110* Lynch, Richard Chigley. *TV and Studio Cast Musicals on Record: A Discography of Television Musicals and Studio Recordings of Stage and Film Musicals.* 330 pp. New York: Greenwood Press, 1990. (Discographies, 38)

Yet another alphabetical list by Lynch, this time highlighting the recordings of TV and studio cast musicals issued on record, with the usual discographical information provided by the author. The source covers 1874–1988, with 657 entries and 6,500 song titles. Recordings listed include archival recreations (such as the Smithsonian issues), concert recordings, demo records commercially released, failed musicals, film scores, ice revues, musicals for records, original concert albums, pre-Broadway records, puppet shows, radio productions, studio cast, TV musicals, TV productions, and TV specials. Extras include a television chronology (1950–85) and a movie musical chronology (1929–78). The performer and technical index give the same information as in the other Lynch discographies.

Reviewed by Renee J. LaPerriere in *ARBA* 22 (1991): 533 and by Tim Brooks in *ARSCJ* 24 (1993): 65–66 no. 1.

10.111* Miletich, Leo N. *Broadway's Prize-Winning Musicals: An Annotated Guide for Libraries and Audio Collectors.* 255 pp. New York: Haworth Press, 1993. (Haworth library and information science)

A select list of the best and most readily available shows (original casts, revival casts, studio casts, and film casts) in order to suggest a collection of representative musicals that span the genre's history. The entries include original record and film recordings, divided into acts, which correspond to the awards given the musicals. The introduction to each "act" explains the purpose and the history of the award. Act One: The Tony Award (1949–91) appears in narrative form, and includes the title of the musical, date, composers, when the musical opened on Broadway, the original Broadway cast, a summary of the plot, and a summary of reviews. Miletich lists the personnel in all editions of the musical. The other "acts" follow the first act's format: The New York Drama Critics Circle Award (1945–91), the Pulitzer Prize (1932–85), the Grammy Award (1958–90), and A Musical World (musicals that didn't win awards although their creators or performers did). Musicals in this category were chosen for historical importance, entertainment value, the quality of their performances, or their availability. Appendixes that may be of help to the researcher include The Search (suggestions for librarians of where to find old copies), a two-page list of reference material, a list of recorded anthologies, and an updating of the resource for the 1991/92 season. A small bibliography and a general index and a song index round out this resource.

Reviewed by R. D. Johnson in *Choice* 31 (1994): 917 and by Jutta Lambrecht in *Die Musikforschung* 47 (1994): 415.

10.112* Pattillo, Craig H. *TV Theme Soundtrack Directory and Discography with Cover Versions.* 279 pp. Portland, Ore.: Braemar Books, 1990.

A discography including single recordings, album recordings, TV theme subtitles, and various subsections. There is a series index.

10.113 Pitts, Michael R., and **Louis H. Harrison.** *Hollywood on Records: The Film Stars' Discography.* 411 pp. Metuchen, N.J.: Scarecrow Press, 1978.

The beginnings of a discography listing recordings of performers with a Hollywood career.

Reviewed by Steven Smolian in *Notes* 35 (1979): 877–78.

10.114 Raymond, Jack. *Show Music on Record: The First 100 Years.* 429 pp. Washington, D.C.: Smithsonian Institution Press, 1992.

First published as *Show Music on Record: From the 1890s to the 1980s* (New York: F. Ungar, 1982), 253 pp. and 32 pp. plates.

Includes all English-language recordings that contain representative selections from a show's score. The volume is preceded by a bibliography and a list of the show numbers. The shows are arranged chronologically and given accession numbers. "Artist albums" and anthologies are separately listed. A list of LP numbers and an artist index provide access to the discography's entries.

Reviewed by B. Lee Cooper in *PMS* 16 (Winter 1992): 102 and by Paul Charosh in *SSB* 18 (1992): 138.

10.115 Smolian, Steven. *A Handbook of Film, Theater, and Television Music on Record, 1948–1969.* 128 pp. New York: Record Undertaker, 1970.

A handbook for collectors of show and soundtrack recordings, evenly divided between an alphabetical list and an index. This book is intended to assist the reader in two basic ways: to outline what has been issued and to provide information about records he or she may already have.

Reviewed by Philip L. Miller in *Notes* 28 (1972): 450.

COLLECTORS' GUIDES TO POPULAR RECORDINGS

An area of prolific publishing activity and of burgeoning interest by academic libraries, popular music discography easily justifies the separate section that follows. For the sake of this list, these resources, which include country/western, blues, R&B, and rock-n-roll, as well as the standard popular music discographies, provide a wealth of material and, in some cases, a great deal of trivial information. Resources in popular music discography have some resemblance to jazz discographies in that in both areas the collectors and the listeners want to know all the details of recording sessions, and the discographer provides this. But popular music fans also want to know more about the personal habits of their idols, which many of these sources provide for their readers and their potential audiences, the disc jockeys and the pop music radio public.

Popular music is also driven by the marketplace, and many writers have combed the music industry's publications, such as *Billboard, Cash Box, Record World,* and their British counterpart, *Melody Maker,* for lists and ratings, supplemented with what many would call gossip. The popular music industry, unlike most of the jazz music scene, also has to contend with the underground music industry of bootlegs and concert recordings, something that is also well documented in publications of rock material. Finally, individual fans have documented many of their region's popular recording activities, something that is only touched on in this list because of the concern for availability and reviews of the resources. In some cases, publications that began as personal lists have been reprinted and nationally (and, for some, internationally) distributed.

10.116* Albert, George, and **Frank Hoffmann.** *Cash Box Series* [Unlabeled]. Metuchen, N.J.: Scarecrow Press, 1988–95.

The Cash Box Album Charts, 1955–1974, with Lee Ann Hoffman. 1988, 528 pp.

The Cash Box Album Charts, 1975–1985, with Lee Ann Hoffman. 1987, 546 pp.

The Cash Box Black Contemporary Album Charts, 1975–1987, with Lee Ann Hoffman. 1989, 239 pp.

The Cash Box Black Contemporary Singles Charts, 1960–1984, with Lee Ann Hoffman. 1986, 704 pp.

The Cash Box Charts for the Post-Modern Age, 1978–1988. 1994, 589 pp.

The Cash Box Country Album Charts, 1964–1988. 1989, 290 pp.

The Cash Box Country Singles Charts, 1958–1982. 1984, 596 pp.

The Cash Box Pop Singles Charts, 1950–1993, with Pat Downey. (Englewood, Colo.: Libraries Unlimited, 1994), 526 pp.

Earlier ed. covered 1950–81, with Lee Ann Hoffmann. 1983, 860 pp.

A discographical series coordinating the record sales statistics gathered by *Cash Box,* a weekly magazine of the popular music recording industry. The standard resources these books contain include an artist index, alphabetically arranged by artist, which lists the date of entry to the chart, the title of song, the record label and number, and all the positions on the charts since the song entered the chart, with the total number of weeks.

There are indexes to song titles (alphabetical) and to the groups performing them. The appendixes include a chronological list of number-one songs (with all dates at number one on the charts); top-10 records of each year; records with the longest run on the charts; the most chart hits per artist, by artist; the most weeks at number one, by artist; and the most weeks at number one, by song.

The Cash Box Album Charts, 1955–1974, is reviewed by R. Serge Denisoff in *PMS* 12 (Summer 1988): 85. *The Cash Box Album Charts, 1975–1985* is reviewed by Laura Dankner in *Notes* 45 (1989): 520 and by Stephen L. Nugent in *Popular Music* 5 (1985): 235–44. *The Cash Box Country Album Charts, 1964–1988* is reviewed by R. S. Lehmann in *ARBA* 22 (1991): 530. *The Cash Box Country Singles Charts, 1958–1982* is reviewed by David Evans in *SSN* 12 (1986): 23–24 and by James Rettig in *Wilson Library Bulletin* 62 (1988): 106–7. *The Cash Box Black Contemporary Singles Charts, 1960–1984* is reviewed by Janice Glover in *Small Press* 13 (Winter 1995): 66. *The Cash Box Pop Singles Charts, 1950–1981* is reviewed by James Rettig in *Wilson Library Bulletin* 69 (1995): 131.

10.117* Allen, Bob. *The Blackwell Guide to Recorded Country Music.* 411 pp. Oxford, England; Cambridge, Mass.: Blackwell, 1994. (Blackwell reference) (Blackwell guides)

A discographic guide systematically covering various aspects of country music, by authorities in the field. The introduction discusses the commercial aspects of country music. The discography itself has 10 sections, each with an account of the genre, the principal performers, and the important recordings, including the essential recordings. Listings include album title, performer, record label information, and the album's contents, followed by a paragraph describing the performer and songs. Topics covered include the early years, honky-tonk, regional musics, Western music, bluegrass, the 1950s and 1960s, hillbilly, rockabilly and early country pop, the 1970s, alternative country, Irish country, 1963–93, and the 1980s and beyond. Also included are recommended readings, a glossary, and an index listing stars, titles, and other people involved in the country music industry.

Reviewed by Anthony J. Adam in *LJ* 119 (July 1994): 82.

10.118* Berry, Peter E. *". . . And the Hits Just Keep On Comin'."* 278 pp. Syracuse, N.Y.: Syracuse University Press, 1977.

Preceded by a narrative highlighting trends in music featuring the stars and hits of the rock era, as well as industry issues (such as the payola scandal in the early 1960s), a personalized look at rock-n-roll. This reference work, arranged by chapter divided by year (from 1956 to 1976), includes the five most influential artists of each year (based on the number of hits each artist has had, the number of records sold, and radio audience response). Other categories listed under each year are Top 50: Number-One Songs (based on *Cash Box* magazine), Number One Song (according to the *Billboard* charts), Most Significant Artists, Academy Award Winners, and NARAS (Grammy) Major Category Winners. Includes a "Discography of Popular Hits, 1955–1976," based on U.S. national top 40 singles only, but also listing gold or platinum albums (pp. 167–276).

10.119* Blair, John. *The Illustrated Discography of Surf Music, 1961–1965.* 3rd ed., revised. 265 pp. Ann Arbor, Mich.: Popular Culture, Ink., 1995. (Rock & roll reference series, 15)

First ed., published by J. Bee Productions, Riverside, Calif., 1983, 128 pp. Second ed., Ann Arbor, Mich.: Pierian Press, 1985, 166 pp.

Another compilation of theme music by Blair, including an alphabetical list of singles, followed by a section on albums. Each entry includes the title of the song or album, date released, label number, group members' information, reissue information, and any unusual packaging information (such as colored records or unique covers). Black-and-white photographs of record labels, posters, album covers, and groups are interspersed throughout the discography. Appendixes include compilation albums by label, Surf Music and Hollywood, Surfing Documentary Soundtrack Albums, and Surf Music on the Top 100. A bibliography of resources used in compiling the discography and an index complete this source. The index has excellent cross-references to name changes of groups and individuals.

Reviewed by B. Lee Cooper in *PMS* 11 (Spring 1987): 99–100, by C. Haka in *Choice* 28 (1990): 70, and by Richard Grefrath in *ARBA* 17 (1986): no. 1292.

10.120* Blair, John, and **Stephen J. McParland.** *The Illustrated Discography of Hot Rod Music, 1961–1965.* 167 pp. Ann Arbor, Mich.: Popular Culture, Ink., 1990. (Rock & roll reference series, 32)

The exploration of a genre not normally covered in such lists. It includes a singles discography (arranged by group, with a brief biography of the group, including personnel), followed by an alphabetical list of songs and label information. There is also information on reissues, composer (if not the original leader of the performing group), photographs of the group, and reproductions of record labels. The appendixes include Compilation Albums by Label, Glossary of Hot Rod and Racing Terms, U.S. Releases of Foreign Hot Rod Recordings, Filmography of Hot Rod Music and Hollywood, the 1960s, and Hot Rod Recordings on the Top 100 (*Billboard* listing). There are indexes for personal and group names, record label name and number, and song and album titles.

Reviewed by B. Lee Cooper in *PMS* 15 (Spring 1991): 114–15, by James Rettig in *Wilson Library Bulletin* 64 (1990): 148, and by Randall Rafferty in *ARBA* 22 (1991): 534–35.

10.121 Bronson, Fred. *The Billboard Book of Number One Hits: A Listing of Number One Hits, by Year, Beginning with 1955.* 3rd ed., revised and enlarged. xxiv + 822 pp. New York: Billboard Books, 1992.

The 1st ed., *Billboard's Book of #1 Hits,* was published in New York by American Photographic Book Publishers, 1985, xxi + 616 pp. The 2nd ed., 1988, xxiv + 712 pp.

One of many sources drawing on *Billboard*'s hit charts. This work supplements chart listings with information on the artist's life (often given by the artist) and provides background information on the song and the times. An insert includes the top five hits of each week. Photographs of each number-one performer, in black and white, appear on each chart. Appendixes include "The Biggest Jumps to Number One" (arranged from largest to smallest, with title, artist and year), "The Biggest Falls from Number One" (similarly arranged), "The Most Number Ones" (organized by artist, writer, producer, and label), and "The Most Weeks at Number One" (arranged by artist and song). The indexes include those for artists and for titles. See also **10.162**.

The 1st ed. is reviewed by Greil Marcus in *Popular Music* 6 (1987): 110–12 no. 1 and by Robert Skinner in *ARBA* 17 (1986): no. 1275. The 2nd ed. is reviewed by Charles A. Pressler in *Choice* 29 (1992): 1,199. The 3rd ed. is reviewed by James Farrington in *Choice* 32 (1994): 82, by Kip Lornell in *Notes* 51 (1995): 959–61, and by D. A. Rothschild in *ARBA* 25 (1994): 557.

10.122* Bronson, Fred. *Billboard's Hottest Hot 100 Hits.* Revised and enlarged. 497 pp. New York: Billboard Books, 1995.

First ed. published by Watson-Guptill, New York, 1991, 416 pp.

Another source by Bronson drawing on *Billboard*'s record industry charts. The listings are similar to those in **10.121**. See also **10.161**.

Reviewed by B. Lee Cooper in *PMS* 16 (Winter 1992): 94–95.

10.123 Cooper, B. Lee. *A Resource Guide to Themes in Contemporary American Song Lyrics, 1950–1985.* xxiii + 458 pp. New York: Greenwood Press, 1986.

More than 3,000 records organized to support 15 social, political, and personal themes (characters and personalities; communications media; death; education; marriage, family life, and divorce; military conflicts; occupations; materialism and workplaces; personal relationships, love, and sexuality; political protest and social criticism; poverty and unemployment; race relations; religion; transportation systems; urban life; and youth culture). There is an audio profile of the rock era, 1950–85, in discography format. The classified selective bibliography (pp. 339–65) includes books, dissertations, song lyric collections, discographies, encyclopedias, articles, reviews, and conference proceedings. There are indexes to song titles and recording artists.

Reviewed by Ann P. Basart in *CNV* 115 (1987): 13–14 and by George Louis Mayer in *ARBA* 18 (1987): no. 1260.

10.124 DeCurtis, Anthony, James Henke, and **Holly George Warren.** *The Rolling Stone Album Guide: Completely New Reviews, Every Essential Album, Every Essential Artist.* 3rd ed. 838 pp. New York: Random House, 1992.

First published as *The Rolling Stone Record Guide: Reviews and Ratings of Almost 10,000 Currently Available Rock, Pop, Soul, Country, Blues, Jazz, and Gospel Albums,* edited by Dave

Marsh with John Swensen, 1979, 631 pp. The 1983 revised, updated ed. was *The New Rolling Stone Record Guide,* edited by Dave Marsh and John Swenson, 1983, 648 pp. (**10.145**)

A list of reviews, with critical ratings for 12,000+ rock, pop, soul, country, blues, folk, and gospel albums compiled by the definitive rock-n-roll publication. This is, in effect, a survey of a large swath of recorded popular music commercially available in the United States.

The 1st ed. is reviewed by William H. Tallmadge in *AM* 1 (1983): 92–94 and by R. Serge Denisoff in *PMS* 7 (1980): 200–1. The 2nd ed. is reviewed by Lawrence Starr in *AM* 3 (1985): 352–54 and by Stephen L. Nugent in *Popular Music* 5 (1985): 235–44. The 3rd ed. is reviewed by D. A. Rothschild in *ARBA* 25 (1994): 560, by James Farrington in *Choice* 30 (1993): 1,743, and by B. Lee Cooper in *PMS* 16 (Winter 1992): 97–99.

10.125* Downey, Pat. *Top 40 Music on Compact Disc, 1955–1981.* 658 pp. Englewood, Colo.: Libraries Unlimited, 1994.

Access to past hits, reissued in CD format.

10.126* Duxbury, Janell R. *Rockin' the Classics and Classicizin' the Rock: A Selectively Annotated Discography.* 188 pp. Westport, Conn: Greenwood Press, 1985. (Discographies, 14)

First Supplement, 168 pp. (New York: Greenwood Press, 1991) (Discographies, 43).

A source that helps identify recordings of classical music influenced by rock music and rock music drawn from the classical realm. The 1st section, "Rockin' the Classics," lists recordings inspired by classical music, arranged by performer, with the date of issue, record company, and an annotation that gives the classical source information. The 2nd section, "Classicizin' the Rock," lists classical groups that have made albums of popular music, including the dates of recording, the record number, and a list of cuts, as well as notes on the performers. Other lists include rock groups or artists recording with established orchestras and choruses, rock music simulating baroque or classical period music, and rock influences on classical music. Appendixes include "Selected Big Band Versions of the Classics," "Selected Parodies of the Classics," and "Selected Country and Folk Versions of the Classics." There are indexes by performer and song title. The *First Supplement* (1985) has new entries and updates the older edition. It also includes a small bibliography of sources.

Reviewed by Richard Koprowski in *Notes* 42 (1986): 786–87. The *First Supplement* is reviewed by B. Lee Cooper in *PMS* 16 (Summer 1992): 116–17.

10.127* Eddy, Chuck. *Stairway to Hell: The 500 Best Heavy Metal Albums in the Universe.* 232 pp. New York: Harmony Books, 1991.

Reviewed by Timothy Scheurer in *Notes* 49 (1991): 625–26.

10.128* Edwards, John W. *Rock 'n' Roll through 1969: Discographies of All Performers Who Hit the Charts, Beginning in 1955.* 475 pp. Jefferson, N.C.: McFarland and Company, Inc., 1992.

Edwards, John W. *Rock 'n' Roll. 1970 through 1979: Discographies of All Performers Who Hit the Charts.* 640 pp. Jefferson, N.C.: McFarland, 1993.

An alphabetical list by performer that includes personnel (for groups), albums that made the charts, singles (with chart rating), category (R&B, etc.), and any deaths of performers and the cause of death. Some entries have black-and-white illustrations. Other features of interest include The Birthday List (by month, then year) and The Deceased Performers List (arranged in reverse chronological order by date of death, from 1991 back). An index by performer, referring to the group in which the performer played, is included.

Reviewed by Richard Grefrath in *ARBA* 25 (1994): 563–64; the 1993 publication is reviewed by Jim Farrington in *Choice* 31 (1993): 430.

10.129* Erlewine, Michael, Vladimir Bogdanov, and **Chris Woodstra.** *All Music Guide to Rock: The Best CDs, Albums & Tapes: Rock, Pop, Soul, R & B and Rap.* 973 pp. San Francisco, Calif.: Miller Freeman Books, 1995. (AMG all music guide series)

Biographies and reviews of the performers, arranged alphabetically by artist, with the biography of group or performer, category of performer, and a chronological list of albums, including title, date of release, and record label. Each section concludes with a review. Other features are "Essays of Rock Styles" and "Non-Rock Styles that Influenced Rock." Also included are reviews of rock reference books; lists of record catalogs, magazines, and newspapers; and an index.

10.130* Gambaccini, Paul, Tim Rice, and **Jonathan Rice.** *Guinness Series* [Unlabeled].
British Hit Albums. 6th ed. 448 pp. Enfield, Middlesex, England: Guinness, 1994.
5th ed., 1992, 416 pp. 4th ed., 1990, 352 pp. 3rd ed., 1988, 201 pp. Earlier editions (1st–3rd) are known as *The Guinness Book of British Hit Albums.*
British Hit Singles. 9th ed. 432 pp. Enfield, Middlesex, England: Guinness, 1993.
8th ed., 1991, 406 pp. 7th ed., 1989, 383 pp. 6th ed., 1987, 347 pp. Earlier editions had the title *Guinness British Hit Singles.*
The Guinness Book of Number One Hits. 3rd ed. 416 pp. Enfield, Middlesex, England: Guinness, 1994.
2nd ed., 1988, 272 pp. The 1st ed. (1982, 263 pp.) was issued as *Guinness Book of 500 Number One Hits.*
Top 40 Charts: Every Chart—Every Week. c. 700 pp. Enfield, Middlesex, England: Guinness, 1992.
Another compilation series, this one based on the Guinness Books Charts that provide a summary of the charts in the British source, in much the same manner that the Whitburn sources (**10.161** and **10.162**) do for the *Billboard* (American) charts. The format of the 1994 *Guinness Book of Number One Hits* is typical of the arrangement of most of the series. Section One: The Number Ones Listed Chronologically: The Full Story, 1952–1994 has listings that include title, performer, the date the record was number one and for how long, the record company and number, writers, and producers, followed by information about the tune, the performer, and some parallel cultural facts. Section Two includes over Seven Hundred Number Ones, listed alphabetically by artist. The entries include artist, date the recording made number one, the song title, and the number of weeks as Guinness' number one. Section Three: Over Seven Hundred Number Ones Listed Alphabetically by Title includes the song title, performer's name, and accession number under which the song is listed in the book.
The 5th ed. of *British Hit Albums* is reviewed by Lori L. Oling in *ARBA* 25 (1994): 558. *The Guinness Book of British Hit Singles* is reviewed by Stephen Bernard in *Popular Music* 11 (1992): 111–15.

10.131* George, Nelson. *Top of the Charts: The Most Complete Listing Ever.* 470 pp. Piscataway, N.J.: New Century Publishers, 1983.
Lists of the top 10 best-selling records in various genres, such as Pop Singles, Pop Albums, Black Singles, Jazz Albums, and Country Albums, based on *Record World Magazine.* Recordings are arranged chronologically for the 1970s and early 1980s. An afterword gives the author's recommended recordings for 1970–81.

10.132 Gillett, Charlie, and **Stephen Nugent.** *Rock Almanac: Top 20 Singles, 1955–73, and Top 20 Albums, 1964/73.* 485 pp. New York: Doubleday, 1976.
A paperback ed. was published by Anchor, 1978.
A resource that combines compilations of U.S. and British hit lists from each country's recording industry publications. The discography starts with a list of the Hot One Hundred Singles and Albums (according to the editor and noted rock-n-roll reviewers Simon Frith and Dave Marsh). This is followed by a number of logs featuring American and British top-20 singles, 1955–73; chart-topping singles, 1955–73; a roll call of hit makers (U.S.); and the log of American and British top 20 albums, 1964–73. Depending on the emphasis of the log, the entries are

arranged by artist, by year, or by chart order, with title, label (and whether U.S. or U.K.), date of chart entry, the highest position, and the number of weeks on the chart. Other entries include soundtrack albums and original cast albums.

10.133 Godrich, John, and **Robert M. W. Dixon.** *Blues and Gospel Records: 1902–1943.* 3rd revised ed. 900 pp. Essex, England: Storyville Publications, 1982.

Second ed., 1969, 912 pp. First published by Brian Rust.

An attempt to list every distinctive Black folk music record made up to the end of 1942. These records were made mostly by large national record companies and issued for an almost exclusively Black audience. In later years some of the records were reissued for a predominantly White public. Full issue and reissue details of all 78-rpm records are included in the main listing, as are the few microgroove issues involving the first appearance of previously unissued material. It also includes details of the blues and gospel recordings made for the Library of Congress by John Lomax and others. Sessions involving artists in the Library of Congress recordings whose names begin with M–Z are included in the main listing; those with names beginning with letters A–L are in the Appendix.

Each artist is listed alphabetically by surname, unless the artist is known only by a pseudonym. Information about accompanying musicians is included. The dates of recording sessions, matrix numbers, and take numbers are supplied as well. There are explanatory entries on the recording companies, an index to accompanists, and a small section of late additions. Many entries include a brief disquisition on the artists and their relationships to the recording companies. There are also explanations of the pseudonyms.

Reviewed by Dick Spottswood in *JEMFQ* 19 (1983): 252–53. The 2nd ed. is reviewed by David Illingworth in *Jazz Journal* 22 (1969): 24 no. 12 and by Frank J. Gillis in *Ethnomusicology* 14 (1970): 499–500.

10.134* Gribin, Anthony J., and **Matthew M. Schiff.** *Doo-Wop: The Forgotten Third of Rock 'n' Roll.* 616 pp. Iola, Wisc.: Krouse Publications, 1992.

A topical resource that includes a historical survey of doo-wop, discussing its nature, the culture that spawned it, information on street corner singers, and elements contributing to its demise. The arrangement is by genre, in 10 chapters. The songs (from 45s, 78s, albums, and extended play sources) are presented in an alphabetical list by artist, with song title, year of the first known release, and label name and number. The appendixes include a list of the best 500 doo-wop songs, indicating the group, the era (classic, neo, and schoolboy, for instance), tempo, sub-era, and the year of issue; a 2nd appendix lists doo-wop periodicals.

Reviewed by Kip Lornell in *Notes* 51 (1995): 959–61 and by B. Lee Cooper in *PMS* 16 (Winter 1992): 85–86.

10.135* Hadley, Frank-John. *The Grove Press Guide to the Blues on CD.* 309 pp. New York: Grove Press, 1993.

A small and personalized rated guide to 810 blues and blues-related CDs owned by four blues critics. Recordings are primarily U.S. releases with some foreign titles. *Down Beat* magazine's star system is used to rate the records. Listings are arranged by performer (including some jazz and some R&B artists), with the title of album and label name, followed by a paragraph of review. Running times, date, and whether a reissue are noted. A second list of anthologies has no listing of citations, but notes headline personnel. An addendum of lists of recordings to update the publication is provided, as well as an index by album title.

Reviewed by David Whiteis in *Down Beat* 60 (March 1993): 54 and by G. T. Johnson in *Choice* 31 (1994): 914–15.

10.136* Hall, Doug. *Country on CD: The Essential Guide.* 217 pp. North Pomfret, Vt.: Trafalgar Square; London: Kyle Cathie, 1993.

Biographies of major country artists and reviews of their best releases, including music of the current Grand Ole Opry performers. The alphabetically arranged entries (from Alabama to Yokum) provide information on the founding members (of the original as well as the new Opry) and birth and death dates, with biographical information about their recording output and careers. Each entry includes at least one CD listing, with title, record label number, and other album information on narrative fashion. Any *Billboard* or other significant music awards are mentioned. An index of artists, venues, and stage names is included.

10.137 Hounsome, Terry. *Rock Record: A Collector's Directory of Rock Album and Musicians.* 3rd ed. 752 pp. New York: Facts on File; Poole, England: Blandford, 1987.

Original limited ed. published by Rockmaster, 1978. A revised, expanded ed. was published and produced in the U.K. by Terry Hounsome, 1979. The 2nd U.S. ed., with Tim Chambre, was published in 1981, 526 pp.; the 2nd British ed., 1981, was published by Blandford Books Ltd. as *New Rock Record.* The 2nd ed. was revised as *The New Rock Record: A Collector's Directory of Rock Albums and Musicians*, 719 pp. (New York: Facts on File, 1983).

A source without narrative, offering just the facts, arranged in such categories as pop, soul, reggae, jazz rock, blues, country, folk music, and mainstream music. The 1981 ed. lists 4,500 entries, 30,000 LPs, and 25,000 musicians. With lists arranged alphabetically by artist and then by album title, *Rock Record* includes listings of each group member, the instrument played, record title, date of issue, record company, and catalog number. An index provides cross-references between maiden, stage, former, and real names. No bootleg or single records are included.

The 3rd ed. is reviewed by Eileen Southern in *BPM* 15 (1987): 122–23 and by David Lands in *Jazz Journal International* 48 (1995): 19–20. The 2nd American ed. is reviewed by Steve Simels in *Stereo Review* 47 (1982): 94 and by Michael Tearson in *Audio* 66 (August 1982): 46.

10.138* Jancik, Wayne. *The Billboard Book of One-Hit Wonders.* 420 pp. New York: Billboard Books (Watson-Guptill), 1990.

Drawing on the *Billboard* charts, a list of names appearing thereon with only one song. The entries are arranged chronologically by decade, with the name of the artist, the title of the piece, composer, record label number, and the rate and date of the chart appearance. Biographical information about the performers and facts about the song are given. Performers include those from rock, blues, country and western, and pop. Jancik often includes quotations from the performer. There are indexes by artist and song, and a list of "The Runners-Up: More One-Hit Wonders," featuring artists who made it to the chart only once, between #21 and 40 on the pop charts.

Reviewed by D. A. Rothschild in *ARBA* 22 (1991): 535.

10.139* Jasper, Tony. *The Top Twenty Book: The Official British Record Charts, 1955–1983.* 2nd ed. 367 ed. Poole, Dorset, England: Blandford Press, 1984.

Published in association with *Music Week.*

10.140 Kingsbury, Paul. *Country on Compact Disc: The Essential Guide to the Music, by the Country Music Foundation.* 286 pp. New York: Grove Press, 1993.

A team of 26 critics combined to make a comprehensive ratings list of country artists, their 2,000+ CD releases, and the dates these albums were first issued. The biographical material included is centered around the individual artists' CDs. Gold and platinum certifications by the Recording Industry Association of America are indicated and there is a concluding index of *Billboard*'s number-one country songs, 1944–92, with CD album locations.

Reviewed by D. Gordon in *Choice* 31 (1994): 1,590.

10.141* Kocandrle, Mirek. *The History of Rock and Roll: A Selective Discography.* 297 pp. Boston: G.K. Hall, 1988.

A list of significant popular music singles and albums from the 1920s through 1987, arranged chronologically within listed genres. The author billed this as a "Historical and Chronological Overview of all Important Rock 'n' Roll Styles in One Source." The source includes a "Diagram of Progression of Music Styles, from pre–World War II to Late 1960's." Genres include everything from hard rock (German, Australian, Canadian, and Japanese rock) to ragtime, boogie-woogie, and classical rock to pre– and post–World War II blues, R&B, Cajun, and zydeco. The entries give the performer under each category, in chronological order, with the date of the album and the label number. An index by performer is provided.

Reviewed by Shelley L. Rogers in *Notes* 46 (1989): 79–80.

10.142* Leadbitter, Mike, and **Neil Slaven.** *Blues Records, 1943–1970: A Selective Discography.* 2 vols. Revised ed. London: Record Information Services, 1987–94.

The 2nd vol. (L–Z), subtitled *The Bible of the Blues,* was compiled by Mike Leadbitter, Leslie Fancourt, and Paul Pelletier.

First ed. in 1 vol., 381 pp., covered 1943–66. London: Hanover Books, 1968. Distributed in the U.S. and Canada by Oak Publications, New York.

A list by artist and ensemble, with discographies as complete as the compilers could make them. Instrumentation for the groups and the recording dates are provided when possible.

The 1st ed. is reviewed by Frank Tirro in *Notes* 26 (1970): 756–58. The 2nd vol. of the revised ed. is reviewed by David Lands in *Jazz Journal International* 48 (October 1995): 19–20 and by Mary Katherine Aldin in *Living Blues* no. 121 (May 1995): 111–12.

10.143* McAleer, Dave. *All Music Book of Hit Singles: Top Twenty Charts from 1954 to the Present Day.* 432 pp. San Francisco, Calif.: Miller Freeman Books; 1994.

Pairs U.S. and U.K. monthly top 20 charts for the last 40 years.

Reviewed by Janice Glover in *Small Press* 13 (Winter 1995): 66.

10.144* Marsh, Dave. *The Heart of Rock & Soul: The 1001 Greatest Singles Ever Made.* 717 pp. New York: New American Library, 1989.

The rock-n-roll favorites of the author, a rock reviewer for *Rolling Stone,* encompassing every genre of rock with the exception of gospel. The entries are arranged in order of preference and include the title, performers, producer, writer, label number, year of issues, and the top *Billboard* placement. Each entry is followed by an extensive personal critique of the piece, with information on the song, the personnel involved, and a description of the style of music. The work concludes with an appendix that alphabetically lists songs "in the Heart of Rock & Soul," and an index of song titles, album titles, and performers.

Reviewed by Sharon Liveten in *The New York Times Book Review* (October 8 1989): 11, by Jacob Weisberg in *Washington Monthly* 21 (December 1989): 51–53, and by Joah Wilde in *Melody Maker* (November 18 1989): 14.

10.145 Marsh, Dave, and **John Swenson.** *The New Rolling Stone Record Guide.* Revised, updated ed. 648 pp. New York: Random House/Rolling Stone Press, 1983.

First published as *The Rolling Stone Record Guide* in 1979 (631 pp.).

Ratings of over 12,000 rock, pop, soul, country, blues, folk, and gospel albums, a survey of a large swath of recorded popular music.

The 1979 ed. is reviewed by William H. Tallmadge in *AM* 1 (1983): 92–94; the 1983 ed. is reviewed by Lawrence Starr in *AM* 3 (1985): 352–54.

10.146* Mawhinney, Paul C. *MusicMaster: The 45 Rpm Record Directory, 1947 to 1982.* 2 vols. New York: Facts on File, 1983.

Contents: Vol. 1, *Artist Directory;* Vol. 2., *Title Directory.*

A supplement, *MusicMaster: The 45 Rpm Singles Directory / Supplement: 44 Years of Recorded Music, 1948–1992: Alphabetically Listed by Artist,* published in Pittsburgh, Pa., by Record-Rama Sound Archives, 1992 (199 pp.).

A discography of all types of music, emphasizing popular, country and western, folk, and jazz. The entries include artist, title, label, manufacturer number, computer number, type, format (vocal, instrumental, or comedy), the year released, the flip side, and music by subject or genre. In 1992, a CD version was published as *MusicMaster: The CD-5 Singles Directory from the Beginning 1992 Alphabetically Listed by Artists/Title.*

Reviewed by Charles Hamm in *Notes* 40 (1984): 547–50.

10.147* Miles, Betty T., Daniel J. Miles, and **Martin J. Miles.** *The Miles Chart Display.* 2 vols. Boulder, Colo.: Convex Industries, 1971 (Vol. 1); New York: Arno Press, 1977 (Vol. 2).

The 2nd vol. has the title *The Miles Chart Display of Popular Music.*

Contents.: Vol. 1, *Top 100, 1955–1970;* Vol. 2, *Top 100, 1971–1975.*

A charted display of the Billboard top 100 popular records, charted to show weekly standing, by title.

10.148* Morthland, John. *The Best of Country Music.* 456 pp. Garden City, N.Y.: Doubleday, 1984.

A critic's lists of the 100 most significant albums in country music, divided by subject albums such as Nashville and Singing Cowboys, with the exception of gospel and Cajun music. Morthland covers about 50 years in his survey. Each section includes a long discussion with biographical information about performers and cuts, followed by an extensive alphabetical list of supplementary albums that include the album title, the performer, the record label, and a short summary of the album. An appendix includes domestic record company information. An index to performers, themes, and topics is provided.

Reviewed by Michael Goldberg in *Rolling Stone* (December 6 1984): 56.

10.149* Oliver, Paul. *The Blackwell Guide to Recorded Blues.* 372 pp. London; Cambridge, Mass.: Blackwell Publishing, 1991. (Blackwell guides)

Earlier version issued as *The Blackwell Guide to Blues Records* (Cambridge, Mass.: Blackwell, 1989), 347 pp.

Edited by noted blues authority Paul Oliver, an edition including 12 surveys of different blues genres by experts, including discographical details. The discography has a recommended reading list, CD supplement (noting the contributors' recommended recordings available on CD), and an index of names (with the instrument of the performer attached).

Reviewed by Dick Spottswood in *ARSCJ* 21 (1990): 266–67, by Tim LaBorie in *LJ* 114 (1989): 104, by David Lands in *Jazz Journal International* 43 (April 1990): 23, and by Michael D. Mannis in *ARBA* 22 (1991): 531.

10.150* Osborne, Jerry, and **Bruce Hamilton.** *Official Record Collector Series. Blues, Rhythm & Blues, Soul.* 160 pp. Phoenix, Ariz.: O'Sullivan Woodside, 1980.

Country Music: A Buyers-Sellers Reference Book and Price Guide. 320 pp. Tempe, Ariz.: Osborne Enterprises, 1984.

Reviewed in *Variety* (March 13 1985): 124.

55 Years of Recorded Country/Western Music. 164 pp. Phoenix, Ariz.: O'Sullivan Woodside, 1978.

Reviewed by Stephen M. Fry in *Notes* 34 (1978): 621.

A Guide to Record Collecting. 142 pp. Phoenix, Ariz.: O'Sullivan Woodside, 1979.

The Official Price Guide to Movie/TV Soundtracks and Original Cast Albums. 662 pp. New York: House of Collectibles, 1991.

First issued as *Soundtracks & Original Cast,* Phoenix, Ariz.: O'Sullivan Woodside, 1981, 177 pp.

The Official Price Guide to Compact Discs. First ed. 296 pp. New York: House of Collectibles, 1994.

The Official Price Guide to Records. 11th ed. 1,224 pp. New York: House of Collectibles, 1995. Eighth ed., 1,010 pp., 1988.

The 8th ed. is reviewed in *Variety* (May 11 1988): 128.

Rock, Rock & Roll 45's. 4th ed. 168 pp. Phoenix, Ariz.: O'Sullivan Woodside, 1978.

The 2nd ed. published in 1978 as *Popular & Rock Records, 1948–1978.* 252 pp. First ed. published in 1976 as *Record Collector's Price Guide.* Third ed. published as *Popular & Rock Price Guide for 45's: The Little Record with the Big Hole.* 3rd ed. 168 pp.

Record Albums. Fifth ed. 178 pp. Phoenix, Ariz.: O'Sullivan Woodside, 1983.

First published as *33 1/3 & 45 Extended Play Record Album Price Guide,* 1977, 166 pp. Second ed. published in 1978 as *Record Albums, 1948–1978.* Third ed., *Record Albums Price Guide,* 1980, 180 pp. Fourth ed., *Record Albums,* 1982, 155 pp.

Rockin' Records: Buyers, Sellers Reference Book and Price Guide. 16th ed. Port Townsend, Wash.: 1994–95.

First published as *Record Collector's Price Guide.* 1976, 196 pp.

Reviewed by B. Lee Cooper in *PMS* 18 (1994): 84–86 no. 3.

A series of price guides meant for the serious collector. Osborne and Hamilton have arranged the entries alphabetically by performer with record label and number and price charts based on the physical condition of the recordings. Further considerations of picture sleeves or covers, the year of release, and stickers or artist's pictures on the box or disc are included in the criteria for top dollars.

10.151* Prakel, David. *Rock 'n' Roll on Compact Disc: A Critical Guide to the Best Recordings.* London: Salamander, 1987.

First American edition published by Harmony Books, New York, 1987.

A resource written to enable its reader to build a rock-n-roll collection on CD, with an interesting illustrated section on how CDs are made. The author lists the top 100 recordings (of the 350+ reviewed). Separate sections are devoted to well-covered artists on CD and to artists who are less important or not well covered by CDs.

An alphabetical list by artist (starting with ABBA) gives the group's name, its date of formation, the nationality of its members, a narrative about the group, and a chronological list of albums transferred to CD, with ratings indicating desirability and recording quality. Prakel also gives cuts, label numbers of the CD, the date of the first issue, how the issue was recorded (analog or digital), and running time. A 1-p. index provides access to the names of the individuals or groups.

Reviewed by Art Lange in *Down Beat* 55 (April 1988): 52–53 and by B. Lee Cooper in *PMS* 16 (Winter 1992): 97–99.

10.152* Pruter, Robert. *The Blackwell Guide to Soul Recordings.* 453 pp. Oxford, England; Cambridge, Mass.: Blackwell Publishers, 1993. (Blackwell Reference)

In the format of the other Blackwell guides, a geographically arranged core discography of 400+ recordings, as contributed by seven specialists. The arrangement is primarily by U.S. cities, with a section on Great Britain and the European continent, and a separate section titled "Funk and Later Trends." The entries include album title with a discographical citation, contents, and a brief account of the artist, including artistic influences. A list of recommended readings (pp. 383–87) and a glossary (pp. 388–400) are included, with a detailed index of song titles, albums, personal names, and subjects.

Reviewed by Kip Lornell in *Notes* 51 (1995): 959–61, by B. Lee Cooper in *PMS* 18 (Fall 1994): 83–84, and by Paul Dunbar-Hall in *International Journal of Music Education* 24 (1994): 88–89.

10.153* Robbins, Ira A. *The Trouser Press Record Guide.* 4th ed. 763 pp. New York: Collier Books; Toronto: Maxwell Macmillan Canada; New York: Maxwell Macmillan International, 1991.

1983 ed. published as *The Trouser Press Guide to New Wave Records.* The 1985 ed., *New Trouser Press Record Guide,* updated and revised, was edited by Ira A. Robbins and published by Scribner (463 pp.); it covered so many divergent developments that the umbrella title had to be dropped. Third ed., 1988.

Another unique source that fills a niche in the popular music discography genre, emphasizing punk and new wave recordings. Entries are in alphabetical order by performer, with the name of album or EP disc, company, and date, followed by a review of the album by one of 14 reviewers, with information on the performers. Robbins covers every album released in the U.S. and Great Britain. To be included, the title must be an album or a "significant" 12-inch EP. Performers included are primarily English and American bands, with some European, Australian, Japanese, and Canadian groups. An appendix listing compilation albums alphabetically by record company is followed by a short list of Record Sources (distributors).

The 3rd ed. is reviewed by Daniel J. Lombardo in *LJ* 114 (1989): 66 and by Bruce Rosenstein in *ARSCJ* 21 (1990): 273–74.

10.154 Rust, Brian. *The American Dance Band Discography, 1917–1942.* 2 vols. New Rochelle, N.Y.: Arlington House, 1975.

Contents: Vol. 1, *Irving Aaronson to Arthur Lange;* Vol. 2, *Arthur Lange to Bob Zurke.*

A discography covering 2,300 dance orchestras and listing their 78-rpm recordings with matrix and label numbers, dates of recording, personnel, arrangers, vocalists, etc. There are 50,000 records cited, with an artist index of about 8,000 names. Black ensembles, Glenn Miller, and Benny Goodman are omitted, and there is no title index.

Briefly reviewed by Stephen M. Fry in *Notes* 32 (1976): 782.

10.155* Rust, Brian A. L., and **Allen G. Debus.** *The Complete Entertainment Discography, from 1897 to 1942.* 2nd ed. 794 pp. New York: Da Capo Press, 1989. (The roots of jazz)

A revised ed. of *The Complete Entertainment Discography, from the Mid-1890s to 1942,* published in 1973 by Arlington House in New Rochelle, N.Y., 677 pp.

A discography with entries organized alphabetically by entertainer's name. The individual listings are chronologically arranged by the recording, along with the recording's date and place and the record label and number.

The 2nd ed. is reviewed by Ann Basart in *CNV* 132 (1989): 23 and by Len Kunstadt in *Record Research* 239–40: 3.

10.156* Shapiro, Bill. *Rock & Roll Review: A Guide to Good Rock on CD.* 299 pp. Kansas City, Mo.: Andrews and McMeel, 1991.

First published in 1988 as *The CD Rock & Roll Library: 30 Years of Rock & Roll on Compact Disc.*

One critic's opinion of the top 30 years of rock-n-roll available on CD at the time of publication. Divided by decade, then alphabetically by artist, the entries include biographical and historical information on the performer, the album (with label information, timings, and grade), and reviews. Reviews of specific discs are grouped with the decade in which the original recording was made. The author also names his "Top 100 Rock Compact Discs (by Decade)" with performer and title, grouped by decade, a bibliography (pp. 291–99), and an index by performer, with the title of the album.

Reviewed by W. M. Gargan in *Choice* 29 (1992): 726.

10.157 Tudor, Dean. *Popular Music: An Annotated Guide to Recordings.* 647 pp. Littleton, Colo.: Libraries Unlimited, 1983.

Previous ed., *Contemporary Popular Music,* 1979, 313 pp.

A thorough updating and revision of the four separate vols. published by Libraries Unlimited in 1979 as *Jazz* (**10.99**), *Black Music* (**10.158**), *Grass Roots Music* (**10.159**), and *Contemporary Popular Music.*

Arranged by categories as indicated in the earlier vols., also with popular religious music. There is an index of artists.

Reviewed by Eileen Southern in *BPM* 12 (1984): 137–39. The previous ed. is reviewed by

Robert M. Jones in *Notes* 36 (1980): 648–49.

10.158 Tudor, Dean, and **Nancy Tudor.** *Black Music.* 262 pp. Littleton, Colo.: Libraries Unlimited, 1979. (American popular music on Elpee)
A discography of African-American music that is a representative rather than thorough treatment of the subject. A later edition is **10.157.**

10.159 Tudor, Dean, and **Nancy Tudor.** *Grass Roots Music.* 367 pp. Littleton, Colo.: Libraries Unlimited, 1979. (American popular music on Elpee)
A discography of American folk music and folk songs, including country music and bluegrass music. For a revised ed., see **10.157.**

10.160* Walters, David. *The Children of Nuggets: The Definitive Guide to "Psychedelic Sixties" Punk Rock on Compilation Albums.* 372 pp. Ann Arbor, Mich.: Popular Culture, Ink., 1990.
An index to the "forgotten music" of the mid-1960s on 333 albums, including punk, garage, and psychedelic rock-n-roll. This source is especially good for its independent labels. In six parts, there are lists of compilation album titles in alphabetical order, with album title, label name and number, contents, and performer. There follows an alphabetical list of performers, with song titles and original album information (including the compilation album on which the song may be found) for 2,600+ groups and individuals. The total performance time is given. Part Three lists 3,800 songs and gives performer, original label, catalog number, and country of origin. Part Four lists the original record numbers (with country and compilation album information, including accession number and time). The last two parts provide an identification note and index to the album photographs included throughout the discography and an alphabetical list of recent compilation album titles, providing bibliographic access to 33 extras, with label number and song titles, noting the performer.
Reviewed by M. L. Larsgaard in *Choice* 28 (1990): 84–86 and by Richard W. Grefrath in *ARBA* 22 (1991): 537.

10.161* Whitburn, Joel. [Various publications.] Menomonee Falls, Wisc.: Record Research, 1972– .
Drawing on the *Billboard* charts, compilations of those charts, enhanced by performer information, photographs, and trivia for the pop, rock, country and western, and R&B aficionado. Most publications follow a standard format of reproducing each week's or year's chart, with information detailing the top performers in boxes next to the chart. Each vol. includes an index to artists and songs. Publications included in this series are as follows:
Joel Whitburn Presents Billboard Top 1000 X 5: Five Top Rankings of America's Favorite Hits. 265 pp., 1993.
Joel Whitburn Presents Billboard's Top 10 Charts: A Week by Week History of the Hottest of the Hot 100, 1958–1988. 594 pp., 1988.
Joel Whitburn Presents Daily #1 Hits: A Day by Day Listing of the #1 Pop Records of the Past 50 Years, 1940–1989, Compiled from Billboard's Pop Singles Charts, 1940–1989. 379 pp., 1989.
First ed., 1989, covered 1940–89.
Reviewed by Louis Zelenka in *ARBA* 25 (1994): 559.
Joel Whitburn Presents the Billboard Hot 100 Charts: The Eighties: Reproductions of Billboard's Hot 100 Charts, 1980–1989. 1 vol. (unpaged), 1991.
Joel Whitburn Presents the Billboard Hot 100 Charts: The Seventies: Reproductions of Billboard's Hot 100 Charts, 1970–1979. 1 vol. (unpaged), 1990.
Joel Whitburn Presents the Billboard Hot 100 Charts: The Sixties: Reproductions of Billboard's Hot 100 Charts, 1960–1969. 1 vol. (unpaged), 1990.
Joel Whitburn Presents the Billboard Pop Album Charts, 1965–1969. 1 vol. (unpaged) 1993.
Joel Whitburn Presents the Billboard Pop Charts, 1955–1959: Reproductions of Billboard's pop singles charts. 1 vol. (unpaged), 1992.
Joel Whitburn's Bubbling under the Hot 100, 1959–1985. Compiled from *Billboard's*

"Bubbling under the Hot 100" charts, 1959–85. 377 pp., 1992.

An earlier ed. covered 1959–81, 235 pp., 1982.

The 1st ed. is reviewed by Paul Grein in *Billboard* 94 (May 22 1982): 64.

Joel Whitburn's Pop Hits, 1940–1954: Compiled from Billboard's Pop Singles Charts, 1940–1954. 398 pp., 1994.

Joel Whitburn's Pop Memories, 1890–1954: The History of American Popular Music. Compiled from America's Popular Music Charts 1980–54. 657 pp., 1986.

Reviewed by Greil Marcus in *Village Voice* 31 (October 7 1986): 65.

Joel Whitburn's Record Research. 1 vol. (unpaged), 1970.

Supplement. 2 vols. (unpaged), 1971.

Joel Whitburn's Top Country Singles: 1944–1993. Third ed. 603 pp., 1994.

The 2nd ed., covering 1944–88, was released in 1989 (535 pp.). The 1st ed. was published in 1972 as *Top Country & Western Records, 1949–1971* (152 pp.).

The 3rd ed. is reviewed by Edward Morris in *Billboard* 106 (April 23 1994): 24. The 2nd ed. is reviewed by Dean Tudor in *ARBA* 22 (1991): 531.

Joel Whitburn's Top Pop, 1955–1982: Compiled from Billboard's Pop Singles Charts, 1955–1982. 4th ed. 692 pp., 1983.

The 3rd ed. was published in 1979 as *Joel Whitburn's Top Pop Artists and Singles, 1955–1978.* 662 pp. The 2nd ed. was published in 1973 as *Top Pop Records, 1955–1972.* First ed., 1973, 88 pp.

Top Pop Albums, 1955–1985: Compiled from Billboard's Pop Album Charts, 1955–85. 508 pp., 1985.

Top Pop Singles, 1955–1986. 746 pp., 1987.

Also titled *Joel Whitburn's Pop Singles Annual.* Earlier eds. published as *Top Pop Artists & Singles, 1955–1978.* 3rd ed., 662 pp., 1979; 2nd ed. was *Top Pop Records, 1955–1972.* 88 pp., 1973.

Top Rhythm & Blues (Soul) Records, 1949–1971. 184 pp., 1973.

Updated annually, beginning in 1974. Subsequent editions titled *Top R & B Singles, 1972–1988* and *Joel Whitburn's Top Soul Singles & LP's (1978–81): Compiled from Billboard's Rhythm & Blues Charts.*

The 1988 ed. is reviewed by Nelson George in *Billboard* (January 14 1989): 21.

And finally, in this entry, perhaps special notice should be taken of the one book that covers CDs: *Joel Whitburn's Top Pop Singles CD Guide, 1955–1979* (270 pp., 1995), compiled not by Whitburn (despite the title), but by Jerry Reuss.

10.162* Whitburn, Joel [Various publications.] New York: Billboard Publications, 1985– .

Another series by Whitburn, this time under the auspices of Billboard Publications. The format used in the Record Research publications is followed here. These publications include the following:

The Billboard Book of Top 40 Hits, 1955 to the Present. 5th ed., 1992.

Fourth ed., revised and enlarged, 622 pp., 1989. The 3rd ed., 330 pp., 1991. The 3rd ed., revised and enlarged, 484 pp., 1987. Second ed., revised and enlarged, 571 pp., 1985. First ed., 1983, 509 pp.

The 5th ed. is reviewed by Charles A. Pressler in *Choice* 29 (1992): 1,198. The 2nd ed. is reviewed by Stephen Nugent in *Popular Music* 5 (1985): 235–44. The 1st ed. is reviewed by Paul Grein in *Billboard* (July 2 1983): 6+.

The Billboard Book of Top 40 Albums. 3rd ed., revised and enlarged. 400 pp., 1995.

Third ed., 347 pp., 1991. A 2nd ed. was published in 1987 (330 pp.). First ed., 1985, unpaged.

The 1987 ed. is reviewed by Tim LaBorie in *LJ* 113 (1988): 60.

Billboard's Top 2000: 1955–1985. 140 pp., 1985.

Reviewed by Charles A. Pressler in *Choice* 29 (1992): 1,198.

10.163* White, Adam. *The Billboard Book of Gold and Platinum Records.* 308 pp. New York: Billboard Books/Watson Guptill, 1990.

All the award-winning artists' songs and albums, including RIAA certifications, essential chart data, and behind-the-scenes facts, according to the author. The music industry's certified gold and platinum records are arranged alphabetically by artist and include release dates, certification ranking (whether gold or platinum), date of certification, chart peak, artist/title, songwriter, producer (singles only), and record label and number. White also includes lists of original soundtracks, original cast albums, children's records (singles and albums), and miscellaneous recordings, including television shows and concerts. An index by song title follows. Addenda include rearrangements of the various charts by gold or platinum and by artists, comparing the biggest sellers in the industry. See also Murrells (**10.227**).

Reviewed by Randall Rafferty in *ARBA* 22 (1991): 525.

10.164* White, Adam, and **Fred Bronson.** *The Billboard Book of Number One Rhythm & Blues Hits.* xxii + 505 pp. New York: Billboard Books, 1993.

A source covering 1965–90. The titles are listed by year, in chronological order of number-one hits (beginning with the Temptations' "My Girl," January 30 1965). Views of the song's placement on the *Billboard* charts for six weeks, with information on the label, writers, producer, date of entry, and number of weeks on the chart, are included. Addenda include The Most Number One R & B Hits by Artist, by Writer, by Producer, by Label, The Longest-Running Number One Hits, The Number One R & B Hits That Also Topped the Hot 100, and The Number One R & B Hits That Didn't Reach the Hot 100. Indexes are by artist and by title.

Reviewed by Kip Lornell in *Notes* 51 (1995): 959–61 and by James Farrington in *Choice* 32 (1994): 82.

10.165* Williams, Paul. *Rock and Roll: The 100 Best Singles.* 235 pp. New York: Carroll and Graf Publishers, 1993.

A chronological narrative list by the founder of *Crawdaddy,* one of the first rock-n-roll magazines. Beginning with 1937, then jumping from 1950 up to 1991, Williams has identified every song released as a 7-inch 45 rpm (except the first, by Robert Johnson, originally released on 78 rpm) in the U.S. or Great Britain that is rock-n-roll, according to the author's definition. Each entry has a 2- to 3-pp. summary of why the work was included on the list, with information on its first release (record label and number, place of release, month, and year). No index to song titles or artists is provided; the table of contents lists songs and performers.

Reviewed by David Szatmary in *LJ* 118 (1993): 94.

ETHNIC AND WORLD MUSIC ON RECORDS

Discography is to the ethnomusicologist what bibliography is to the historical musicologist: the "bibliographical" control of his or her primary source material. The documentation of the sound universe within a cultural context is vital to the ethnomusicologist's job and recordings are part of that primary source material. Originally, this was chiefly achieved through the analysis of field recordings, but of late, ethnomusicologists have been making much use of commercial music as well. Therefore, the following list is of both guides to field recordings and discographies of commercial recordings.

10.166 Barnett, Elise Braun. *A Discography of the Art Music of India.* 54 pp. Ann Arbor, Mich.: Society for Ethnomusicology, 1975. (Special series: Society for Ethnomusicology, 3)

A brief guide to 315 numbered commercial sound recordings primarily of Indian art music, arranged alphabetically by record label and indexed by sacred chants, art music (sacred and secular), Hindustani ragas, talas, performers, performing forces, dance music, folk music, and composers.

Reviewed by Michael Gray in *Notes* 32 (1975): 293–96 and by Josef Kuckertz in *IFMCY* 7 (1975): 164–65.

10.167 Biagiola, Sandro. *Ethnomusica: Catalogo della musica di tradizione orale nelle registrazioni dell'Archivio Etnico-Linguistico-Musicale della Discoteca di Stato.* 887 pp. Rome: Discoteca di Stato, Ed. Il Ventaglio, 1986.

A list of more than 11,000 recordings, the vast majority being music of oral traditions, as well as traditional liturgical music. Also included are indexes to genres, geographic locations, and performance contexts.

Reviewed by Mauricio Agamennone in *Nuova rivista musicale italiana* 21 (1987): 313–15 and by Giovanni Giuriati in *Musica/Realtà* 23 (1987): 155–56.

10.168* Bodman, Ellen-Fairbanks, and **Lorraine Sakata.** *The World of Islam, Images and Echoes: A Critical Guide to Films and Recordings.* 208 pp. New York: American Council of Learned Societies, 1980.

A list of films (by Bodman) and sound recordings (by Sakata), including the less familiar films of good quality, obtainable in North America. The arrangement of the recordings is geographic. Dealer information is provided.

Reviewed by George D. Sawa in *Ethnomusicology* 31 (1987): 131–33.

10.169* Boggs, Beverly B., and **Daniel W. Patterson.** *An Index to Selected Folk Recordings.* 75 pp. + 55 microfiches. Chapel Hill, N.C.: Curriculum in Folklore, University of North Carolina at Chapel Hill, 1984.

An index to 500 published recordings, chiefly in disc format, containing chiefly English-language Anglo- and African-American folk songs from the U.S., Canada, the Caribbean, and the British Isles. There are indexes to instrumental and speech content and to album notes. The user's guide includes a thesaurus and a collection of folklore recordings recommended for library purchase.

Reviewed by Jay Orr in *Journal of American Folklore* 100 (1987): 97–99, by William Kearns in *SSN* 12 (1986): 23, and by Susan L. Porter in *SSN* 12 (1986): 95–96.

10.170* Broughton, Simon, and **Kim Burton.** *World Music: The Rough Guide.* 697 pp. New York: Penguin Books, 1994. (The rough guides)

An introduction to selected world music idioms on record. Thirteen chapters cover such areas as "The Celtic World," "From the Baltic to the Balkans," "The Indian Subcontinent," "The Far East," "North America," and "Australia and the Pacific." Three chapters are devoted to Africa and two chapters cover Latin America and the Caribbean. Although most of the musics discussed are what might be called popular idioms, classical musics of India and Indonesia (among others) are included. In each chapter there are 6 to 10 articles written by individual scholars and critics. Styles, terminology, major artists, and historical and cultural contexts are all discussed, and discographies of currently available recordings are included.

10.171 Christensen, Dieter, and **Hans-Jürgen Jordan.** *Katalog der Tonbandaufnahmen M1–M2000 der Musikethnologischen Abteilung des Museums für Volkerkunde Berlin.* 355 pp. Berlin: Museum für Volkerkunde, 1970.

The catalog of a major field recording collection in Berlin. It provides very complete citations of some of the earlier ethnomusicological recordings in existence. Included are indexes to people, places, languages, genres, forms, occasions, cultural contents, organology, composers and authors, and collectors.

Reviewed by Ann Briegleb in *Ethnomusicology* 16 (1972): 547–50 and by Joseph Kuckertz in *Die Musikforschung* 26 (1973): 390–91.

10.172* Cohen, Norm. *Traditional Anglo-American Folk Music: An Annotated Discography of Published Sound Recordings.* 517 pp. New York: Garland Publishing, 1994. (Garland reference library of the humanities, 1469) (Garland library of musical ethnology, 2)

A selective, critical guide to 500 recordings (LP, cassette, and CD) of traditional music, with contents ranging from 19th-century popular American songs to pre–World War II country music. The four sections of the book include field recordings, field anthologies, commercial hillbilly recordings (pre-1942) of individual artists, and commercial hillbilly anthologies. Recordings by single artist or ensemble are arranged alphabetically by performer name, and anthologies by label name and number. Indexes to artists, titles, Child ballad numbers, Laws ballad numbers, and album label/numbers are included.

Reviewed by Kip Lornell in *Notes* 52 (1996): 826–27.

10.173* Cuthbert, John A. *West Virginia Folk Music: A Descriptive Guide to Field Recordings in the West Virginia and Regional Historical Collection.* 185 pp. Morgantown, W.V.: West Virginia University Press, 1982.

10.174 Danielou, Alain. *A Catalogue of Recorded Classical and Traditional Indian Music.* 236 pp. Paris: UNESCO, 1952. (Archives of recorded music, Series B: Oriental music)

A catalog of performers with lists of pieces (specific ragas, instruments played, and genres) keyed to their recordings. The work includes biographical and evaluation commentary. The text is in French and English.

10.175 Dols, Nancy, et al. *Musics of the World: A Selective Discography.* 4 vols. Los Angeles: Ethnomusicology Archive, UCLA Music Library, 1977– . (UCLA Music Library discography series, 1–4)

Vols. 2–4 are titled *Musics of the World.*

An international discography. Vol. 1 covers sub-Saharan Africa, Bulgaria, Ethiopia, Guatemala, Japan, Romania, Tibet, the USSR, the U.S., and Yugoslavia. Vol. 2, edited by Don Niles, covers Indonesia, Korea, Oceania, Taiwan, and Thailand. Vol. 3, edited by Nora Yeh, covers the U.S.: African-American, European-American, Hispanic-American, and Native American musics. Vol. 4, edited by Kenneth Culley, includes an index.

10.176 Fraser, Norman. *International Catalogue of Recorded Folk Music.* With a preface by R. Vaughan Williams and introduction by Maud Karpeles. 201 pp. London: Prepared and published for UNESCO by the International Folk Music Council in association with Oxford University Press, 1954. (Archives of recorded music, Series C: Ethnographical and folk music, 4)

An early survey of recorded folk music archives. Part I lists commercial recordings of ethnic and folk music, arranged by continent and by country. Part II surveys collections of ethnic and folk music in libraries and research institutions throughout the world.

10.177 Gillis, Frank. "The Incunabula of Instantaneous Ethnomusicological Sound Recordings, 1890–1910: A Preliminary List." In *Problems and Solutions; Occasional Essays in Musicology Presented to Alice D. Moyle,* pp. 322–55. Edited by Jamie C. Kassler and Jill Stubington. Sydney: Hale and Iremonger, 1984.

An article providing a list of the earliest ethnomusicological field recordings and their locations as of the early 1980s. Organized according to the scheme in Murdoch's *Outline of World Cultures* (the organization of the Human Relations Area File).

10.178 Gombert, Greg. *A Guide to Native American Music Recording.* 134 pp. Fort Collins, Colo.: Multi Cultural Publishing, 1994.

A source covering the entire range of music produced by Native Americans, including traditional, pan-Indian, and crossover styles. A comprehensive list of recording companies and distributers is included.

10.179* Graham, Ronnie. *The Da Capo Guide to Contemporary African Music.* 315 pp. New York: Da Capo Press, 1988.

The first serious attempt to catalog and describe the music recorded in Africa since the end of World War II. The music is classified under each country. The index of names and subjects gives helpful access.

Reviewed by Ann P. Basart in *CNV* 129 (1989): 9.

10.180 Hickmann, Hans, and **Charles Grégoire, Duc de Mecklenbourg.** *Catalogue d'enregistrements de musique folklorique égyptienne.* 78 pp. Strasbourg: Heitz, 1958. (Collection d'études musicologiques, 37)

A guide to a small collection (211 items) of Egyptian folk music assembled in 1955. Also included is a discussion of the music and organology.

10.181 Hoerburger, Felix. *Katalog der europäischen Volksmusik im Schallarchiv des Instituts für Musikforschung Regensburg.* 189 pp. Regensburg: Gustav Bosse, 1952. (Archives of recorded music, Series C: Ethnographical and folk music. 3)

The catalog of a particular collection of European folk music recordings. The material is grouped by country and province.

10.182 Indiana University. Archives of Traditional Music. *A Catalog of Phonorecordings of Music and Oral Data Held by the Archives of Traditional Music.* 541 pp. Boston, Mass.: G.K. Hall, 1975.

A facsimile of a card-catalog guide to one of the most important ethnographic sound archives in the U.S. By 1974, the collection contained 125 wire recordings, 6,000 cylinders, 25,000 discs, and 18,000 tapes of songs, tales, instrumental music, and interviews. It is particularly strong in African, African-American, Latin American, Native American, and Indian music. The catalog includes indexes by subject (including geographic areas and culture groups), names (collectors, depositors, performers, and informants), and recording company.

10.183 International Commission on Folk Arts and Folklore. *Collection Musée de l'Homme (Paris).* 74 pp. Paris: UNESCO, 1952. (Archives of Recorded Music. Series C: Ethnographical and folk music, 2)

The catalog of a collection of more than 1,000 recordings from Asia and Africa.

10.184 International Commission on Folk Arts and Folklore *.Collection Phonothèque Nationale (Paris).* 254 pp. Paris: UNESCO, 1952. (Archives of Recorded Music. Series C: Ethnographical and Folk Music, 1).

A inventory list of 4,564 discs, indexed by country.

10.185 International Institute for Comparative Music Studies and Documentation, Berlin. *Oriental Music: A Selected Discography.* 100 pp. New York: Foreign Material Center, University of the State of New York, State Education Department and National Council of Associations for International Studies, 1971. (Foreign Area Material Center: Occasional publication, 16)

A discography of commercial recordings arranged by general region and country. Each citation includes brief critical annotations and details regarding performers, genres, and instrumentation. The work also includes a list of the addresses of 55 record companies.

Reviewed by Frank J. Gillis in *Ethnomusicology* 17 (1973): 135.

10.186 *Katalog der Tonbandaufnahmen B 1–B 13,000 des Phonogrammarchives der Österreichische Akademie der Wissenschaften in Wien.* 4 vols. Vienna: Harmann Böhlaus Nachf., 1960– . (Mitteilung der Phonogrammarchivs-Kommission, Österreichische Akademie der Wissenschaften, 81–82, 84–85)

A comprehensive catalog of field recordings in the Vienna Phonogrammarchiv. In addition to the musical recordings, the archive contains linguistic and oral histories. Indexes to ethnic groups, languages, geographical locations, instruments, cultural occasions, and collectors are included.

The 1st vol. is reviewed by Fritz Bose in *Jahrbuch für musikalische Volks- und Volkerkunde* 4 (1968): 117–18. The 3rd vol. is reviewed by Ann Briegleb in *Ethnomusicology* 16 (1972): 547–50.

10.187* Keeling, Richard. *A Guide to Early Field Recordings (1900–1949) at the Lowie Museum of Anthropology.* 485 pp. Berkeley: University of California Press, 1991.

An inventory of a collection of field recordings (originally consisting of over 2,700 wax cylinders) covering Native American tribes in California. The collection itself is the third largest collection of Native American songs and spoken texts, and the largest covering a single cultural area. It encompasses source materials, published writings, and manuscripts. The guide breaks the collection down by tribe and includes indexes to tribal groups and collectors. The introduction includes a summary history of the Edison phonograph, an ethnological survey of California, a guide to other sources and documentation, an explanation of the guide, technical information, and instructions on how to use the collection.

10.188* Kinnear, Michael S. *A Discography of Hindustani and Karnatic Music.* 594 pp. Westport, Conn.: Greenwood Press, 1985. (Discographies, 17)

Comprehensive coverage of Indian classical music on commercial recordings from the mid-1930s to the mid-1980s. The discography lists around 2,700 individual items and is organized by performer. The introduction is a short history of the Indian recording industry. Indexes to ragas, talas, instruments, and styles are included, as is a glossary of terms.

Reviewed by Gregory D. Booth in *Asian Music* 18 (1986): 201–2 no. 1 and by Ravinda Nath Sharma in *ARBA* 17 (1986): no. 1240.

10.189* Laade, Wolfgang. *Neue Musik in Afrika, Asien und Ozeanien: Diskographie und historisch-stilistischer Überblick.* 110 pp. Heidelberg: Wolfgang Laade, 1971.

A general discussion of music and musical activities in the non-Western world, covering all types of music including traditional idioms. The work includes a discography of more than 650 commercial recordings.

Reviewed by Fritz Bose in *Musica* 26 (1972): 287, by Hans Oesch in *Melos* 29 (1972): 168–69, by Brigitte Schiffer in *The World of Music* 15 (1973): 55–63, and by Jürgen Wisner in *Beiträge zur Musikwissenschaft* 17 (1975): 323–27.

10.190 Lee, Dorothy Sara. *Native North American Music and Oral Data: A Catalogue of Sound Recordings, 1893–1976.* 463 pp. Bloomington, Ind.: Indiana University Press, 1979.

A guide to the holdings of recorded native North American music and oral history recordings in the Indiana University Archives of Traditional Music, including about 500 field and commercial recordings and broadcasts. Some important parts of the collection include the cylinder recordings of Franz Boas, as well as materials from Chicago's Field Museum and the University of Pennsylvania Museum. Information about collectors, performers, culture groups, and areas is provided, as well as other types of documentation. Indexes to culture groups and subject descriptions are appended.

Reviewed by G. Edward Evans in *ARBA* 11 (1980): no. 960, and, very briefly, by A. F. Leighton Thomas in *MR* 44 (1983): 67.

10.191 Lornell, Kip. *Virginia's Blues, Country, & Gospel Records, 1902–1943: An Annotated Discography.* 238 pp. Lexington, Ky.: University Press of Kentucky, 1989.

A documenting of the earliest years of the commercial recording of Virginia's traditional musics, both Anglo- and African-American. The body of the work is arranged by the artist's or group's name. Each entry includes biographical background and a list of recordings. A useful historical introduction opens the book. A bibliography, an index of artists, a guide to reissues, and 1 geographical listing provide further access.

10.192 Lumpkin, Ben Gray, and **N. L. MacNeil.** *Folksongs on Records: Issue Three, Cumulative, Including Essential Material in Issues One and Two.* 98 pp. Boulder, Colo.: Folksongs on Records; Denver, Colo.: Alan Swallow, 1950.

A list of 700 commercially recorded discs and albums of folk songs and folk music, chiefly American. This discography gives the contents of discs, with informal annotations. There are useful indexes to English and Scottish ballads, spirituals, work songs, Irish songs, and Mexican and Latin American songs, as well as a numerical list of albums.

Reviewed by Rae Korson in *Notes* 8 (1950): 180–81.

10.193 Merriam, Alan P. *African Music on L.P.: An Annotated Discography.* 200 pp. Evanston, Ill.: Northwestern University Press, 1970.

A catalog of 389 commercial recordings of African music. The compiler has attempted to be comprehensive, with one notable exception: "The Sound of Africa" series cataloged elsewhere (**10.203**). Field recordings are not included. The body of the discography is arranged according to label and number, and each entry includes contents, language, author of notes, indication of the presence of texts, artists and performing groups, and indications of photographs. The annotations are descriptive and numerous indexes are included.

Reviewed by Hugh Tracey in *Ethnomusicology* 17 (1973): 337–39.

10.194* Minegishi, Yuki. *Discography of Japanese Music.* 57 pp. Tokyo: Japan Foundation, 1980.

A guide to 673 commercial recordings issued in the late 1970s. An index to the original Japanese is included.

10.195* Moyle, Alice M. *A Handlist of Field Collections of Recorded Music in Australia and Torres Strait.* 227 pp. Canberra: Australian Institute of Aboriginal Studies, 1966. (Occasional papers in aboriginal studies, 6) (Ethnomusicology series, 1)

A list of Australian aboriginal musical recordings in all formats: cylinder, wire, tape, and phonodisc. Organized chronologically by collection, it covers field recordings dating from 1899. Citations provide very complete bibliographic information. The work contains a keyed map to musical regions, and indexes collectors' names, localities, languages and ethnic groups, and phonodiscs.

Reviewed by Frank J. Gillis and Stephen Wild in *Ethnomusicology* 11 (1967): 264–65.

10.196* Nourrit, Chantal, and **William Pruitt.** *La musique traditionelle.* 20 vols. in 2 series. Paris: Radio-France Internationale, 1979–83.

An international series, organized by country, on each country's music and available recordings. Each vol. provides introductory essays on aspects of music in the area in question, followed by annotated discographies of 78-rpm and 33-1/3-rpm discs arranged by record manufacturer. There are indexes to ethnic groups, instruments, performers and authors, and locations; historic and legendary people; subjects; and record titles. Each vol. includes a bibliography. The vols. range from 60 pp. to 260 pp.; the two series cover three regions in the Indian Ocean and 17 countries of "Afrique Noire."

10.197 Quinn, Jennifer Post. *An Index to Field Recordings in the Flanders Ballad Collection at Middlebury College, Middlebury, Vermont.* 242 pp. Middlebury, Vt.: Middlebury College, 1983.

An index to recordings of New England folk songs. Each entry includes the title as given by the performer, the uniform title, the name of the performer, and the location of the performance. Each of these elements is indexed, and a description of the collection and a bibliography are included. For more information about the collection see Dale Cockrell's "The Helen Harkness Flanders Ballad Collection, Middlebury College," in *Notes* 39 (1983): 31–42.

Reviewed by Arthur Schrader in *SSN* 12 (1986): 22–23.

10.198* Schaeffer, Deborah L. *Irish Folk Music: A Selected Discography.* 180 pp. New York: Greenwood Press, 1989 (Discographies, 31)

An annotated discography covering the Irish folk music revival since the 1970s, based on reviews of recorded performances released primarily in the U.S. and, to a lesser extent, in Ireland. Included in each entry is the artist's or group's name, personnel, title, record label and number, contents, and an evaluation. Also includes a glossary, a directory of distributors and record companies, and indexes to artists and titles.

Reviewed by David Dodd in *Notes* 47 (1990): 391–92.

10.199* Seeger, Anthony, and **Louise S. Spear.** *Early Field Recordings: A Catalogue of Cylinder Collections at the Indiana University Archives of Traditional Music.* 198 pp. Bloomington, Ind.: Indiana University Press, 1987.

A catalog providing collection-level access to almost 7,000 ethnographic cylinders recorded between 1893 and 1938. More than 150 cultural groups from all over the world are covered. Information is included on the individual collections (organized according to the name of the collector), evaluations of sound quality, and narrative annotations documenting the history and provenance of the collection. There are also indexes to names, culture groups, subjects, and geographical areas, as well as an introduction detailing the history of the collections and the problems involved in preserving them.

Reviewed by Jennifer C. Post in *Ethnomusicology* 31 (1987): 453–55.

10.200 Spottswood, Richard K. *Ethnic Music on Records: A Discography of Ethnic Recordings Produced in the United States, 1893–1942.* 7 vols. Urbana, Ill: University of Illinois Press, 1990. (Music in American life)

Contents: Vol. 1, *Western Europe;* Vol. 2, *Slavic;* Vol. 3, *Eastern Europe;* Vol. 4, *Spanish, Portuguese, Philippine, Basque;* Vol. 5, *Mid-East, Far-East, Scandinavian, English Language, American Indian, International;* Vol. 6, *Artist Index, Title Index;* Vol. 7, *Record Number, Matrix Number Index.*

A monumental discography of folk and ethnic music in the U.S., arranged hierarchically by region, country of origin, and performer's name. In 7 vols., the author has attempted to document all production of foreign-language records made in the U.S. and its possessions from 1893 to 1942, except operatic and other classical recordings, language instruction records, humorous material, Hawaiian music, reissues of non-U.S. matrices on U.S. labels, instrumental recordings, and Native American recordings of private or institutional origin.

Reviewed by Carl Rahkonen in *Notes* 48 (1992): 1,311–12.

10.201 Stone, Ruth, and **Frank J. Gillis.** *African Music and Oral Data: A Catalog of Field Recordings, 1902–1975.* 412 pp. Bloomington, Ind.: Indiana University Press, 1976.

Based on the African Field Recording Project, a catalog that is a finding aid to collections of recordings and oral data held throughout the world. The catalog itself contains information about collectors and repositories, cultural groups, size of collections, evaluations of quality, degrees of access restriction, and subject headings. Indexes are included for countries, cultural groups, and subjects.

Reviewed by David B. Coplan in *African Music* 6 (1980): 131–32 no. 1 and by Gilbert Rouget in *Fontes* 28 (1981): 254–55.

10.202* Toth, Andrew. *Recordings of the Traditional Music of Bali and Lombok.* 243 pp. Society for Ethnomusicology, 1980. (Special series, 4)

A discography that documents commercially available sound recordings released through 1977. Phonodiscs produced since 1928 (almost all of these on Western labels) and cassettes issued in Bali since 1970 are featured, and the entries include standard discographic information and cross-referencing in their original languages as they appear on the physical item. A glossary and short bibliography of Balinese music are also provided.

Reviewed by Ernst Heins in *Yearbook of the International Folk Music Council* 6 (1974): 148–50.

10.203 Tracey, Hugh. *Catalogue of the Sound of Africa Series: 210 Long Playing Records of Music and Songs from Central, Eastern, and Southern Africa.* 2 vols. Roodepoort, South Africa: International Library of African Music, 1973.

The first significant documentation of African music. Vol. 1 is an extensive introduction to the recordings in the Sound of Africa series and thus to the musical cultures; it includes data on instruments, language zones, and scales. Vol. 2 is the catalog. Recordings were made in the field, 1929–c. 1963.

10.204 U.S. Library of Congress, Music Division. *Check-list of Recorded Songs in the English Language in the Library of Congress Archive of American Folk Song to July 1940.* 3 vols. in 1. 604 pp. in all. Washington, D.C.: Library of Congress, Division of Music, 1942.

Reprinted by Arno Press, New York, 1971.

A list of songs and stories held by the Archive of Folk Song (now Archive of Folk Culture) at the Library of Congress. The list is ordered by title and includes the names and places of residence of the singer or speaker, the collector's name, and the date the item was collected; all of the entries are field recordings. A geographical index is included.

10.205 U.S. Library of Congress, Music Division. *Folk Music: A Catalog of Folk Songs, Ballads, Dances, Instrumental Pieces, and Folk Tales of the United States and Latin-America on Phonograph Records.* 107 pp. Washington, D.C.: Library of Congress, 1964.

Earlier lists of the same nature appeared in 1943, 1948, 1953, and 1959.

A catalog of field recordings remastered on vinyl disc and available for purchase. The catalog includes 107 78-rpm discs and 59 33-1/3-rpm discs. Although only 899 selections are listed, the catalog was intended to include representative examples from the 16,000+ records in the Archive at the time of publication.

10.206* Vernon, Paul. *Ethnic and Vernacular Music, 1898–1960: A Resource and Guide to Recordings.* xxii + 344 pp. Westport, Conn.: Greenwood Press, 1995. (Discographies, 62)

A historical folk music discography that includes bibliographical references.

10.207 Waterhouse, David. "Hogaku Preserved: A Select List of Long-Playing Records Issued by Japanese Record Companies of the National Music of Japan." In *Recorded Sound* 33 (January 1969): 383–402.

CURRENT OR ANNUAL DISCOGRAPHIES

Current lists and record reviews are in abundant supply, with periodicals such as *Fanfare* and *Gramophone* devoted exclusively to the interests of record collectors.

10.208* Armitage, Andrew D., and **Dean Tudor.** *Annual Index to Popular Music Record Reviews, 1972–1975.* Metuchen, N.J.: Scarecrow Press, 1973–78.

An index to popular music reviews in over 50 periodicals by two enthusiastic discographers. The 1974 ed. is noted in *Fontes* 23 (1976): 147.

10.209 *Bielefelder-Katalog; Katalog der Schallplatten klassischer Musik. Schallplatten.* Bielefeld, Germany: Bielefelder Verlagsanstalt, 1953– .

First known as *Langspielplatte.*

The German equivalent to *Opus,* with superior analytics and indexing by composer and label. It is issued semiannually.

10.210 *Bielefelder Katalog Jazz; Verzeichnis der Jazz-Schallplatten.* Bielefeld, Germany: Bielefelder Verlagsanstalt, 1953– .

Issued annually.

10.211* *CD Review Digest Annual: The Guide to English Language Reviews of All Music Recorded on Compact Disc.* Voorheesville, N.Y.: Peri Press, 1987– .

The 1st vol. is a 2-vol. retrospective (1983–87) with over 19,000 reviews of over 8,000 recordings. The 1988 vol. is a cumulation of 1988's quarterly issues of *CD Review Digest.*

A condensed accumulation of reviews, with multiple indexes whose approaches include performers, titles, record labels and numbers, and reviewers. In 1995 (Vol. 8), the title became *Schwann CD Review Digest* (Stereophile, Inc., Santa Fe, N.M.) including "all non-classical music categories."

The 1988 *Annual* is reviewed by Ann P. Basart in *CNV* 128 (1988): 9–11.

10.212 *Classical Catalogue.* Harrow, Middlesex, England: General Gramophone Publications, 1990– .

Gramophone Classical Catalogue, founded in 1953, in 1990 merged with *Gramophone Compact Disc Audio Guide and Catalogue* to form *Classical Catalogue.*

Title varies: *Gramophone Long Playing Classical Record Catalogue.*

The British version of *Schwann,* with substantially better analysis of anthologies, access by performer, and more extensive indexing. A handy feature is the indication of *Gramophone* magazine's review date for each recording's citation. The *Catalogue* is now published in cumulating issues twice each year interspersed with issues updating the semiannual cumulations. The updating issues are themselves cumulations. This is also available in CD-ROM format.

10.213 Clough, Francis F., and **Geoffrey J. Cuming.** "Phonograph Periodicals: A Survey of Some Issued outside the United States." In *Notes* 15 (1958): 537–58.

An annotated list of 28 then-current periodicals "devoted exclusively to phonographic matters" in Austria, Belgium, Canada, Denmark, France, the German Federal Republic, Great Britain, Holland, Italy, Mexico, Spain, and Sweden, with comments on coverage in general periodicals.

10.214 *Deutsche Bibliographie: Musiktonträger-Verzeichnis.* Frankfurt am Main: Buchhändler-Vereinigung, 1978–90.

Successor to the *Deutsche Bibliographie Schallplatten-Verzeichnis,* the *Musiktonträger-Verzeichnis* is a monthly publication with an annual composer/title index.

The premiere national discography, listing sound recordings not only published in the former Bundesrepublik Deutschland but also distributed there. The depth and accuracy of indexing are impressive.

10.215 *Diapason: Catalogue général.* Paris: Diapason-microsillon, 1956– .

Title varies: *Catalogue Disques et Cassettes Diapason; Catalogue Général de Musique Classique et de Diction.*

The French equivalent to the Schwann series, issued as an annual.

All issues include a classical music catalog with composer and anthology sections, occasionally with a section devoted to chant. Some issues also include spoken word recordings. Entries provide full analysis of album contents. The composers and titles recorded in anthologies are entered with cross-references in the composer section. Entries show performer, album title, manufacturer's name and number, and contents. From 1977, there is an index to performers in the catalog. A list of French record manufacturers is provided.

10.216 Gelatt, Roland. *High Fidelity Record Annual.* Vols. 1–26. Philadelphia, Pa.: J.B. Lippincott, 1955–81.

The title, imprint, and editor vary: from 1957, generally *Records in Review,* Great Barrington, Mass.: Wyeth Press. The set through Vol. 12 (1972) was reprinted by AMS Press, New York, in 1972.

Compilations of generally authoritative, signed reviews from *High Fidelity* magazine (a title that also varies), gathered annually from monthly issues of the previous year. The main list is by composer, followed by a classified section of "recitals and miscellany." Each vol. concludes with a detailed performer index.

The 18th vol., edited by Peter G. Davis, is reviewed in *Notes* 31 (1974): 63–66 by Michael H. Gray. The 19th vol. is reviewed by Michael Gray in *Notes* 32 (1975): 293–96.

10.217* *The Good CD Guide,* 1988– . Harrow, Middlesex: General Gramophone Publications Ltd./Quad Electroacoustics Ltd., 1987– .

An annual publication, based on reviews first offered in its parent publication, *Gramophone,* and noting the special awards and honors given individual discs, awards distributed by *Gramophone*. Although the work focuses on British labels, the equivalent American label information is given as well.

10.218 "Index of Record Reviews, with Symbols Indicating Opinions of Reviewers." In *Notes* 5 (March 1948)- .

Since its inception, a regular feature of *Notes*, compiled chiefly by Kurtz Myers until the end of major LP record releases, with the assistance of various specialists from time to time. A valuable guide to record selection for libraries and private collectors. The quarterly appearances of this column have been cumulated (**10.220**).

Richard Le Sueur followed Myers, succeeded by Paul Cauthen and Mark Palkovic. Beginning with Le Sueur, CDs were included and now the Index covers only CDs.

10.219 Maleady, Antoinette O. *Index to Record and Tape Reviews, 1975–82.* 7 vols. San Anselmo, Calif.: Chulainn Press, 1976–83.

An earlier series was published as *Record and Tape Reviews Index, 1971–74* in Metuchen, N.J., by Scarecrow Press, 1972–75. 4 vols.

An index to about 20 English-language periodicals reviewing classical sound recordings. The 1st section lists reviews by composer, the 2nd lists reviews by record label, and the 3rd section lists spoken recordings.

The 1972 vol. is reviewed by Michael H. Gray in *Notes* 31 (1974): 63–66.

10.220 Myers, Kurtz. *Index to Record Reviews: Based on Material Originally Published in* Notes, *the Journal of the Music Library Association, between 1949 and 1977.* 5 vols. Boston, Mass.: G.K. Hall, 1978.

Continues *Record Ratings: The Music Library Association's Index of Record Reviews*, by Myers and Richard S. Hill (New York: Crown Publishers, 1956, 440 pp.). Continued by the *Index to Record Reviews, 1978–1983* (1985, 873 pp.) and the *Index to Record Reviews, 1984–1987* (1989, 639 pp.), both compiled by Kurtz Myers and issued by G.K. Hall.

A cumulation, with two supplements, of the quarterly columns in *Notes, the Journal of the Music Library Association*. Myers's column appeared in *Notes* from June 1948; cumulations were published by the Music Library Association in 1951 and 1952, with *Record Ratings* the first commercially released index cumulation. A guidebook to a huge body of critical writings about recordings, Myers's *Index* organizes the art music recording reviews from approximately 50 periodicals and other sources, and indicates the indexer's reading of the reviewer's judgment of the quality of the performance and of the technical aspects of the recording.

The index has two sections. The first is primarily a list by composer. The second, "composite releases," is necessary for handling records containing works by more than one composer. The entries are arranged alphabetically under the name of the manufacturer, and then serially by the manufacturer's number. The names of composers appearing in the second list are indexed in Vol. 5, which also affords access to the first 4 vols. by manufacturer label and number and by performer.

The compiler has taken great pains to clarify and verify information about individual discs and their contents. These 7 vols. gather all of Myers's work on LP records; the following columns in *Notes*, first by Richard Le Sueur and then, from Vol. 49 (1992), by the team of Paul Cauthen and Mark Palkovic, index reviews of CDs. This is a major work in the field of discography.

R. D. Darrell reviews *Record Ratings* in *Notes* 13 (1956): 637–38; David Hall reviews the *Index* in *Notes* 37 (1981): 845–47.

10.221 *Phonolog Reporter.* Los Angeles, Calif.: Trade Service Publications, Phonolog Publishing Division, 1948– .

A loose-leaf service with weekly distribution of new pages to enable subscribers (generally audio stores) to stay current with new releases in an organized fashion. It was valuable for discerning currently available audio releases in the North American market. It is in two large divisions, one for classical music and another for popular music; each page is numbered and dated, but the actual pagination is difficult to discern because the page numbers are alphanumeric.

The classical division has three sections: one for entries by composer and then title, each entry providing title of album, names of principal performers, and manufacturer's name and number of disc or tape; a second for anthologies arranged by album title, providing brief titles of works featured in each anthology; and a third devoted to performing artists by name, but referring entries under conductors to the citations for the ensembles each has conducted. In the past, there were cross-references to individual titles from one section to another.

The popular division features many sections, the largest of which, "Popular titles," is arranged by song title, often with supporting bibliographic information (composer and lyricist, publishing company). The next largest section lists alphabetically albums and their contents. Other sections cover Christmas music, Hawaiian albums, Latin albums, international albums, children's music, movie soundtracks and show tunes, sacred music, specialties, and miscellaneous.

A CD-ROM version has been released as *Billboard/Phonolog Music Reference Library* by BPI Communications of New York (**12.6**). It adds vastly improved searching possibilities to the contents of *Phonolog*.

10.222 *Polart Index to Record Reviews.* 8 vols. Detroit, Mich.: Polart, 1960–67.

An annual publication indexing all record and tape reviews published in the major journals. No evaluations are given, but the length of the review is indicated. Musical works are listed under composer, with separate sections for collections and for pop and jazz recordings.

10.223 *Schwann Opus.* Santa Fe, N.M.: Stereophile, 1991– . Vol. 2, no. 4– .

Also known as *Opus.* This succeeds *The Schwann Record and Tape Guide* and its several variant titles (*New Schwann Record and Tape Guide, Schwann-1 Record and Tape Guide,* and *Schwann-2 Record and Tape Guide*), issued in Boston beginning in 1949 as monthly publications.

Currently a quarterly publication listing over 40,000 currently available classical recordings on CD and cassette tape. The recordings are listed alphabetically by composer, then by title, then by principal artist; anthologies are listed in a separate section, arranged by instrument or music type (i.e., ballet music, choral music, vocal music, guitar, organ). New releases are listed separately. Each issue includes articles, often with discographies of currently available discs. There is a list of manufacturers providing addresses and prices. There is often an "Annual" Artist Issue, listing available discs by performers; it is organized in sections (orchestras and ensembles, conductors, instrumental soloists, choral groups, and vocalists).

10.224 *Schwann Spectrum.* Santa Fe, N.M.: Stereophile, 1991– . Vol. 2, no. 4.

Also known as *Spectrum.*

A quarterly list of over 60,000 recordings on CD, LP record, and cassette tape of popular music, arranged alphabetically by performing group. Included are sections on rock and pop individual releases and collections; jazz and jazz anthologies; musicals, movies, and TV; gospel and religious music; New Age music; spoken-word and miscellaneous recordings; children's music; international pop music, arranged by country and then by performer or group; sampler discs; Christmas music; and laser discs. New releases are so labeled in the margins.

Each issue includes articles, often with discographies of current releases.

SPECIALIZED DISCOGRAPHIES

10.225* Heier, Uli, and **Rainer E. Lotz.** *Banjo on Record: A Bio-Discography.* 658 pp. Westport, Conn.: Greenwood Press, 1993. (Discographies, 48)

The recording history of the banjo on cylinders and 78-rpm discs from 1889 to the mid-1950s, arranged by performers or performing groups. Includes a history of the banjo, information on types of banjos, bibliography, title index, and reproductions of historic labels.

10.226* Jones, Phyllis J. *Every Monday Morning: A Discography of American Labor Songs in the Conservatory Library at Oberlin College.* 91 pp. Oberlin, Ohio: Oberlin College Library, 1993.

10.227* Murrells, Joseph. *Million Selling Records from the 1900s to the 1980s: An Illustrated Directory.* 530 pp. New York: Arco Pub., 1984.

Part of the 1984 ed. is based on *The Book of Golden Discs,* 1978 ed., which was first published in 1974 (London: Barrie & Jenkins, 503 pp.).

The 1984 ed. is reviewed by Dean Tudor in *ARBA* 17 (1986): no. 1242; the earlier ed. is reviewed by Dean Tudor in *ARBA* 11 (1980): no. 961.

DISCOGRAPHIES BY LABEL

10.228* Bartlette, Reginald J. *Off the Record: Motown by Master Number, 1959–1989.* Vol. 1: *Singles.* Ann Arbor, Mich.; London: Popular Culture, 1991– . (PCI collector editions) (Rock & roll reference series, 34)

Access to the popular Detroit label, with indexes.

10.229* Bennett, John R. *A Catalogue of the Vocal Recordings from the Italian Catalogues of the Gramophone Company Limited, 1899–1900; the Gramophone Company (Italy) Limited, 1899–1909; the Gramophone Company Limited, 1909; Compagnia del Grammofono, 1912–1926.* 2 vols. Lingfield, England: Oakwood Press, 1955–67. (Voices of the past, 2)

10.230 Bennett, John R. *A Catalogue of Vocal Recordings from the English Catalogues of the Gramophone Company, 1898–1899: The Gramophone Company Limited, 1899–1900; The Gramophone & Typewriter Company Limited, 1901–1907; And the Gramophone Company Limited, 1907–1925.* xlvii + 238 pp. Lingfield, England: Oakwood Press, 1956. (Voices of the past, 1)

Reprinted in Westport, Conn. by Greenwood Press, 1978.

10.231 Bennett, John R. *A Catalogue of Vocal Recordings from the 1898–1925 French Catalogues of the Gramophone Company Limited, Compagnie Française du Gramophone.* 304 pp. Lingfield, England: Oakwood Press, 1971. (Voices of the past, 9)

10.232 Bennett, John R. *A Catalogue of Vocal Recordings from the Russian Catalogues of the Gramophone Company Limited: Obshchestvo Grammofon c [i.e., s] Ogr. Otv. 1899–1915.* 220 pp. Dorset, England: Oakwood Press, 1977. (Voices of the past, 11)

10.233 Bennett, John R. *Melodiya: A Soviet Russian L.P. Discography.* xxii + 832 pp. Westport, Conn.: Greenwood Press, 1981. (Discographies, 6)

Reviewed by Eric Hughes in *ARSCJ* 3 (1981) 139–42 no. 3 and by John D. Wiser in *Fanfare* 5 (1982): 288–91 no. 3.

10.234 Bennett, John R., and **Eric Hughes.** *The International Red Label Catalogue of "DB" & "DA" His Master's Voice Recordings 1924–1956.* 2 vols. Lingfield, England: Oakwood Press, 1961–70. (Voices of the past. 4, 6)

10.235 Bennett, John R., and **Wilhelm Wimmer.** *A Catalogue of Vocal Recordings from the 1898–1925 German Catalogues of the Gramophone Company Limited, Deutsche Grammophon A.-G.* 404 pp. Lingfield, England: Oakwood Press, 1971. (Voices of the past, 7)

Reprinted in Westport, Conn., by Greenwood Press, 1978.

10.236* Bianco, David. *Heat Wave: the Motown Fact Book.* xxiii + 524 pp. Ann Arbor, Mich.: Popular Culture Press, 1988. (Rock & roll reference series, 25)

10.237* Charosh, Paul. *Berliner Gramophone Records: American Issues, 1892–1900.* xxxii + 290 pp. Westport, Conn.: Greenwood Press, 1995. (Discographies, 60)

The first discography assembled of the first disc recordings in the United States.
Reviewed by Paul Shamberger in *ARSCJ* 26 (1995): 192–94.

10.238* Cuscuna, Michael. *The Blue Note Label: A Discography.* 510 pp. New York: Greenwood Press, 1988. (Discographies, 29)

10.239 Davis, Elizabeth A. *Index to the New World Recorded Anthology of American Music: A User's Guide to the Initial One Hundred Records.* 235 pp. New York: Norton, 1981.

A guide to the contents of a series of recordings of concert music by American composers supported by the Rockefeller Foundation as part of the American Bicentennial celebration. Includes a master index providing a description of each record in numerical order and four other indexes: names and titles of all recorded works, subjects and authors in the liner notes, genres and performing forces, and dates of composition. Many of these performances were reissued in CD format.

10.240* Ginell, Cary. *The Decca Hillbilly Discography, 1927–1945.* xxiv + 402 pp. New York: Greenwood Press, 1989. (Discographies, 45)

10.241* Gramophone Company, Ltd. *Gramophone Records of the First World War: An HMV Catalogue, 1914–1918.* 480 pp. in various pagings. Newton Abbot, England; North Pomfret, Vt.: David and Charles, 1975.

Reprint of the 1914–18 issues of the *Catalogue of Gramophone Records.*

10.242* Kelly, Alan. *His Master's Voice: The French Catalogue: A Complete Numerical Catalogue of French Gramophone Recordings Made from 1898 to 1929 in France and Elsewhere by the Gramophone Company Ltd. / La Voix de son maître.* Compiled with the cooperation of the EMI Music Archive, London. xxxvi + 679 pp. Westport, Conn.: Greenwood Press, 1994. (Discographies, 37)

Reviewed by David Breckbill in *Notes* 48 (1991): 461–65.

10.243* Kelly, Alan. *His Master's Voice: The German Catalogue: A Complete Numerical Catalogue of German Gramophone Recordings Made from 1898 to 1929 in Germany, Austria, and Elsewhere by the Gramophone Company Ltd. / Die Stimme seines Herrn.* Compiled with the cooperation of the EMI Music Archive, London. lix + 1,325 pp. Westport, Conn.: Greenwood Press, 1994. (Discographies, 55)

Reviewed by Jerome F. Weber in *ARSCJ* 26 (1995): 86–87 no. 1.

10.244* Ruppli, Michel. *The Aladdin/Imperial labels: A Discography.* 727 pp. New York: Greenwood Press, 1991. (Discographies, 42)

10.245* Ruppli, Michel. *Atlantic Records: A Discography.* 4 vols. Westport, Conn.: Greenwood Press, 1979. (Discographies, 1)

Reviewed by Dan Morgenstern in *ARSCJ* 12 (1980): 128–30 and by Stephen M. Fry in *ARBA* 11 (1980): no. 963.

10.246* Ruppli, Michel. *The Chess Labels: A Discography.* 2 vols. 733 pp. Westport, Conn.: Greenwood Press, 1983. (Discography, 7)

A label specializing in blues and jazz.

10.247* Ruppli, Michel. *The King Labels: A Discography.* 2 vols. 899 pp. Westport, Conn.: Greenwood Press, 1985. (Discographies, 18)

10.248* Ruppli, Michel, and **Ed Novitsky.** *The Mercury Labels: A Discography.* 5 vols. 4,240 pp. Westport, Conn.: Greenwood Press, 1993. (Discographies, 51)

Contents: Vol. 1, *The 1945–1956 Era;* Vol. 2, *The 1956–1964 Era;* Vol. 3, *The 1964–1969 Era;* Vol. 4, *The 1969–1991 Era and Classical Recordings;* Vol. 5, *Record and Artist Indexes.*

A discography listing all recordings made or issued by the Mercury label and its subsidiaries (Blue Rock, Cumberland, Emarcy, Fontant, Limelight, Philips, Smash, and Wings), as well as leased and purchased materials and recordings by independent labels distributed by Mercury.

10.249* Ruppli, Michel, and **Bob Porter.** *The Clef/Verve Labels: A Discography.* 2 vols. 876 pp. New York: Greenwood Press, 1986.

10.250 Ruppli, Michel, and **Bob Porter.** *The Prestige Label: A Discography.* 377 pp. Westport, Conn.: Greenwood Press, 1980. (Discographies, 3)

10.251* Rust, Brian. *The American Record Label Book.* 336 pp. New Rochelle, N.Y.: Arlington House, 1978.

Reviewed by Dean Tudor in *ARBA* 11 (1980): no. 952.

10.252* Sutton, Allan. *Directory of American Disc Record Brands and Manufacturers, 1891–1943.* xxi + 282 pp. Westport, Conn.: Greenwood Press, 1994.

The history of over 330 record labels and manufacturers, which gives an in-depth examination of the growth of the American record industry from the introduction of Berliner's disc Gramophone through the Petrillo recording ban. Included are a glossary, bibliography, and index.

Reviewed by Tim Brooks in *ARSCJ* 25 (1994): 222–24.

PERFORMER DISCOGRAPHY: ART MUSIC

The following two sections list recent discographies and recording histories of individual musical soloists, composers, and ensembles. Such titles can be found in the *Bibliography of Discographies* (**10.2**) or its successor.

Beecham, Thomas

10.253* Gray, Michael H. *Beecham: A Centenary Discography.* 129 pp. New York: Holmes & Meier Publishers; London: Duckworth, 1979.

Reviewed by David Hamilton in *ARSCJ* 12 (1980): 265–69.

Bjoerling, Jussi

10.254* Henrysson, Harald. *A Jussi Björling Phonography.* 2nd ed. 382 pp. Stockholm: Svenskt musikhistoriskt arkiv, 1993. (Musik i Sverige, 6)

The 1st ed., by Jack W. Porter and Harald Henrysson, was published as *A Jussi Bjoerling Discography* by the Jussi Bjoerling Memorial Archive, Indianapolis, Ind., 1982 (192 pp.).

A complete compilation of the sound recordings from the tenor's 40-year recording career.

Callas, Maria

10.255* Ardoin, John. *The Callas Legacy: The Complete Guide to Her Recordings on Compact Disc.* 4th ed. 236 pp. Portland, Ore.: Amadeus Press, 1995.

First ed. published in 1977 by Scribner, New York, 224 pp.; British ed. published by Duckworth, London. Revised ed., 1982, 240 pp.; 3rd ed., 1991, 236 pp.

The 4th ed. is reviewed by Marc Mandel in *Fanfare* 19 (1996): 456–57 no. 3. The 1st ed. is reviewed in *Central Opera Bulletin* 20 (1978): 33 no. 2 and in *High Fidelity/Musical America* 28 (March 1978): MA39. The 3rd ed. is reviewed by Gary A. Galo in *Notes* 49: (1993): 474–76.

Gould, Glenn

10.256* Canning, Nancy. *A Glenn Gould Catalog.* xxxi + 230 pp. Westport, Conn.: Greenwood Press, 1992. (Discographies, 50)

A discography arranged by composer, with full discographical details and cross-referenced by composition opus numbers and by recording dates. Also included are radio and TV programs and unreleased recordings. Includes a bibliography of Gould's published writings and bibliographic note on writings about Gould.

Karajan, Herbert von

10.257* Hunt, John. *Philharmonic Autocrat: The Sound and Video Recordings of Herbert von Karajan, with a Concert and Opera Register, 1916–1989.* 585 pp. London: The compiler, 1994.

A documentation of the conductor's 73-year-long career.

Reviewed by Richard Osborne in *Gramophone* 72 (September 1994): 30–31.

Kleiber, Erich

10.258* Dillon, Cesar A. *Erich Kleiber: A Discography.* 143 pp. Buenos Aires: Ediciones Tres Tiempos, 1990.

A discography of the conductor's commercial and noncommercial recordings, with an appendix that gives an account of his South American conducting activity, 1926–52.

Reviewed by David Breckbill in *Notes* 50 (1994): 1,013–15.

McCormack, John

10.259* Worth, Paul W. *John McCormack: A Comprehensive Discography.* lii + 184 pp. New York: Greenwood Press, 1986. (Discographies, 21)

Souzay, Gérard

10.260* Morris, Manuel. *The Recorded Performances of Gérard Souzay: A Discography.* 238 pp. New York: Greenwood Press, 1991. (Discographies, 41)

PERFORMER DISCOGRAPHY: POPULAR MUSIC

Baez, Joan

10.261 Swanekamp, Joan. *Diamond & Rust: A Bibliography and Discography on Joan Baez.* 75 pp. Ann Arbor, Mich.: Pierian Press, 1989.

Basie, Count

10.262* Sheridan, Chris. *Count Basie: A Bio-Discography.* 1350 pp. Westport, Conn.: Greenwood Press, 1986. (Discographies, 22)

Copious information on the career and recording sessions of an important jazz and popular artist's life, including a chronological list of the recording sessions, with take numbers, group, place of recording, date, issue numbers, titles, and record labels and numbers for issues as well as reissues, delineated by medium (cassette, 78, 45, LP) and size. Appendixes include lists of Records (arranged by label, then issue numbers), Band Itinerary (chronologically arranged, with city and place), and a bibliography of 50 items. Indexes include film and videos, a general index and indexes to musicians, arrangers, and tune titles.

Beach Boys

10.263* Elliott, Brad. *Surf's Up!: The Beach Boys on Record, 1961–1981.* 494 pp. Ann Arbor, Mich.: Pierian Press, 1982. (Rock & roll reference series, 6)

A complete guide to the recorded works of the Beach Boys. A chronological discography that includes entries with the date of release, record label and number, title of album, producer, tracks (writer), and times. The source also includes the tracks of Beach Boys' songs included in other groups' repertoires. Elliott provides lots of illustrations, with footnotes on recordings, including personnel and instrumentation on individual songs. Other features are lists of international issues of Beach Boy recordings (from Great Britain, Brazil, Czechoslovakia, France, Germany, Italy, Japan, and New Zealand) arranged by LPs and singles. In Stack O'Tracks, Elliott lists the titles of the songs alphabetically, with information on lead vocals and backing musicians, indexed to main entries. The order of the discography begins with the Beach Boys' songs, then covers performances by other groups. Unreleased issues, concert tapes, and appearances on TV are listed, as well as record titles of the unreleased tracks, with status, performer, and cross-listing to main entries. Promotional records, DJ copies (albums and singles), lists of spurious recordings attributed to the Beach Boys, a section on related friends and their careers, and lists of gold albums are provided. Week-to-week positions of the Beach Boys' records on the *Billboard* charts (singles and albums) round out the statistical information. A 3-pp. bibliography lists articles and sources. An index completes the picture of this quintessential American rock group.

Reviewed by Steve Simels in *Stereo Review* 47 (1982): 94 no. 3.

Beatles

10.264* Campbell, Colin, and **Allan Murphy.** *The Things We Said Today: The Complete Lyrics and a Concordance to the Beatles' Songs, 1962–1970.* xlii + 386 pp. Ann Arbor, Mich.: Pierian Press, 1980.

Reviewed by Stephen Barnard in *Popular Music* 2 (1982): 269–74.

10.265* Castleman, Harry, and **Walter J. Padrazik.** *All Together Now: The First Complete Beatles Discography, 1961–1975.* 385 pp. Ann Arbor, Mich.: Pierian Press, 1975.

Subsequent vol. titled *The Beatles Again?* 280 pp., 1977. *The End of the Beatles?* 553 pp., 1985. (Rock & roll reference series, 10). The newer editions update the information given in the 1975 vol., and include notice of any reissues of albums and singles. *The End of the Beatles?* also includes BBC broadcast outtakes.

The original source, *All Together Now,* and the two subsequent volumes, giving a chronological history of all recording since 1961 in Britain and the U.S., with some German and Canadian releases. The entries include the date of the U.K. or U.S. release, the record label and number, and information on the recordings, including date, performers, producers, and song titles and times. Indexes to the Beatles songs (noting the parts the various players took) and a reference to chronological entries are among the resources, with lists of songs by the Beatles for others and songs by each Beatle individually for themselves and others. Includes an index by friends and a reference to the Beatles as performers. Information is included on the origins of the songs the Beatles released but didn't write as well as lists of bootlegs, spurious Beatles songs, and a chronological list of Apple albums, singles, and films. Also featured are a bibliography of books for boys and girls, a list of solid gold Beatles songs (with the date awarded), *Melody Maker* top of the charts, and placement on the American top 40 (singles and albums) based on the *Billboard* charts.

All Together Now is reviewed by Steve Smolian in *ARSCJ* 8 (1976): 108–12 no. 2–3 and by Nigel Hunter in *Gramophone* 53 (1976): 1,802. The 1977 ed. is reviewed by Duke Johns in *MEJ* 65 (September 1978): 23.

10.266* **Lewisohn, Mark.** *The Beatles: Recording Sessions.* 204 pp. New York: Harmony Books, 1988.

The British ed. published as *The Complete Beatles Recording Sessions* (London: Hamlyn, 1988). Canadian ed. published as *EMI's the Complete Beatles Recording Sessions: The Official Abbey Road Story.* Toronto: Doubleday Canada, 1988.

A study based on the compilations of recording logs compiled by John Bartlett. Lewisohn includes all EMI Records recording sessions of the Beatles, with a preface by Paul McCartney that relates anecdotes about their recording process and collaborations with John Lennon. The sessions are arranged by year, then date, with each session including information about the studio, time, recording, and producers (even to the balance engineer and second engineer) through 1970. Copious notes about the process during each session are included, as well as permutations of tunes and titles. A 2-pp. discography (U.S. and U.K. Singles, U.K. and U.S. EP's, U.S. and U.K. Albums) and a small list of reissued CDs provide information for the most zealous Beatles fan. An index and glossary are included. Includes a small preface and postlog by Ken Townshend, the general manager of Abbey Road Studios. Over 350 color and black-and-white photographs, with photographs of Recording Sheets and in-studio candid photographs, round out this unique peek at the recording process of the Fab Four.

Reviewed by David Hunter in *Notes* 46 (1990): 641–42 and Jeffrey Ressner in *Rolling Stone* no. 545 (1989): 15–17.

10.267* **McCoy, William,** and **Mitchell McGeary.** *Every Little Thing: The Definitive Guide to Beatles Recording Variations, Rare Mixes and Other Musical Oddities, 1958–1986.* 368 pp. Ann Arbor, Mich.: Popular Culture, Ink., 1990.

Reviewed by William Shaman in *Notes* 47 (1991): 1,164–66.

10.268* **McDonald, Ian** *A Revolution in the Head: The Beatles' Records & the Sixties.* 373 pp. London: Fourth Estate, 1994.

An American ed. published by Henry Holt, 1994.

A discography beginning with a sociopolitical summary of the historical significance of the Beatles, with later views of their place in popular culture. Arranged in three parts, beginning with the group's official EMI discography, the discography draws on Lewisohn (**10.266**) and adds more recording information. Each section details a different stage of the Beatles' careers as a group. Arranged in order of recording, each song's entry has copious information on the session, a description of the playing style and mixing influences, and the significance of the song to the Beatles' careers. Entries include the title, the writer, who played what instrument, the date recorded, and the U.K. and U.S. release dates (and the song's placement on the record). A chronology of the Beatles' careers, with a chart that starts in 1960 and includes parallel sections on U.K. Pop, Current Affairs, and Culture (art, music, literature, films that came out at the same time), gives a broader perspective on the influence the group had on the culture. A bibliography, glossary, and index to songs complete the in-depth look at the Beatles' careers.

Reviewed by Eric Boehlert in *Billboard* (February 4 1995): 48.

10.269* **McKeen, William.** *The Beatles: A Bio-Bibliography.* 181 pp. New York: Greenwood Press, 1989. (Popular culture bio-bibliographies)

Reviewed by William Shaman in *Notes* 47 (1991): 1,164–66.

10.270* **Stannard, Neville,** and **John Tobler.** *The Beatles' Volume 2: Working Class Heroes: The History of the Beatles' Solo Recordings.* 239 pp. New York: Avon, 1984.

A list in four sections, arranged by performer (John Lennon, Paul McCartney, George Harrison, Ringo Starr), with record releases in Great Britain, followed by those in the U.S. Information given includes the record label, the date of recording, songs on each recording (with timing), and information about the recording sessions, including personnel, and covers controversies. Also included is the historical context of each recording. Information about release and placement on charts accompanies the sections, as well as copious black-and-white photographs of albums, personnel, and advertising posters.

Appendixes include "Chronological Record Releases in Great Britain" (with record title, artists, label, catalog number, and release date); "Chronological Record Releases in the U.S." (with similar information); "With a Little Help From Their Friends" (the songs of Lennon and McCartney recorded by others), records produced by each Beatle, and sessions played on others' albums (with exact contribution included); and "The Beatles in the BMRB (British Market Research Bureau) Chart 1962–1982." These entries include the artist, song title, entry date, highest position/weeks at No. 1, and weeks on the chart. Appendix 4 lists Yoko Ono's solo releases for Britain and America and her work with the Plastic Ono Band. Includes a short bibliography and an index.

10.271* Wiener, Allen J. *The Beatles: The Ultimate Recording Guide.* 3rd ed., revised. 596 pp. Holbrook, Mass.: B. Adams, 1994.

An earlier British ed., 291 pp., published in London by Aurum, 1993. The 3rd American ed., 291 pp., published in New York by Facts on File, 1992. First published as *The Beatles: A Recording History* in Jefferson, N.C., by McFarland in 1986, 614 pp.

A guide that claims to be the most complete discography of the Beatles, with "a wealth of previously unpublished facts." Wiener draws on Lewisohn (**10.266**) for recording information, enhancing it with other features. The general chronology of the Beatles begins in 1902 with the birth of Paul McCartney's father and continues to 1992. A recording chronology follows, including all commercially released Beatles recordings, arranged by recording date. Three discographies, subdivided by the place of issue, follow, with a separate list of bootlegs and unreleased recordings (including any unreleased song titles and the name of the composer). Appendixes include information on the Beatles as supporting players, songs on singles only, songs the Beatles never sang, and videocassettes and laser discs.

A list of references and recommended periodicals, as well as a song and record title index, complete the guide.

First ed. reviewed by Ann Basart in *CNV* 128 (1988): 9 and by Andy Linehan in *Popular Music* 6 (1987): 343–46. The 1992 ed. is reviewed by James Rettig in *Wilson Library Bulletin* 67 (December 1992): 108–9, by W. M. Gargan in *Choice* 30 (1993): 947, and by Lisha E. Goldberg in *ARBA* 25 (1994): 565.

Bechet, Sidney

10.272* Maurer, Hans J. *A Discography of Sidney Bechet.* 84 + 3 pp. Copenhagen: Knudsen, 1969.

A Danish jazz contribution to discography, a chronological list of the sessions of Sidney Bechet, from 1921 through 1958. The sessions are grouped by the performing ensemble or record company and include personnel and instrumentation, take numbers, song title, and record issue labels and numbers. Indexes of musicians and song titles follow.

Cash, Johnny

10.273* Smith, John L. *The Johnny Cash Discography, 1984–1993.* 228 pp. Westport, Conn.: Greenwood Press, 1994. (Discographies, no. 57)

A 1985 Greenwood Press ed. was published as *The Johnny Cash Discography,* 210 pp. (Discographies, no. 13).

A discography first begun as a publication by the John Edwards Memorial Foundation in 1969, covering 1955–68. The bulk of this resource on a country music legend is about the sessions, with information on the date, studio, performers, titles of songs, and record labels. An index of releases in the U.S. and Europe is arranged in separate discographies, and includes label, song, and title information. A separate index of bootleg releases and one of the ABC television series conclude the discographical entries. A song title index and a songbook and book bibliography are included.

The 1985 ed. is reviewed in *SSB* 12 (1986): 15. The 1994 ed. is reviewed by R. A. McGill-Aken in *Choice* 32 (1994): 581.

Clapton, Eric

10.274* Roberty, Marc. *Eric Clapton: The Complete Recording Sessions, 1963–1992.* 192 pp. New York: St. Martin's Press, 1993.

A complete list of Eric Clapton's official recording sessions (in studio and live) and the material recorded at the sessions, whether released or not. The entries are arranged chronologically and subdivided by his career (including his stints with the Yardbirds and Cream). Information includes the type or for whom the session was recorded, the date of the recording, location and venue, title of the track, recording on which the title was released, and a list of participants (including who played which instrument, which guitar Clapton played, and the names of the producers and engineers). Information on the session and its significance to the performer's career and life is also offered. A chronologically arranged discography (grouped by band and subdivided by singles and albums), a videography, and a list of bootleg recordings complete the information. An index to song titles is also included.

Reviewed by Marilyn A. Gillen in *Billboard* (September 11 1993): 39.

Cole, Nat "King"

10.275* Teubig, Klaus. *Straighten Up and Fly Right: A Chronology and Discography of Nat "King" Cole.* 297 pp. Westport, Conn.: Greenwood Press, 1994. (Discographies, no. 56)

A discography including all known recordings, transcriptions, and films made by Cole until 1950, followed by a selection of his later jazz-related trio sides. The list is divided into sections: "The Trio" (a narrative about his group) and "The Labels" (all known labels on which Cole recorded, with technical specifics and record label numbers). The bulk of the resource is a chronology that includes discographical information as well as Cole's historical highlights. Information given includes the title of the original record and label number, reissues (of 78s and LPs to CDs), personnel, studio information, date recorded, and all revisions and writers. Indexes to songs and a recording index, arranged alphabetically by label number, with information on specific cuts, round out the source.

Reviewed in *Jazz Times* 24 (1994): 40 no. 10.

Coltrane, John

10.276* Fujioka, Yasuhiro, Lewis Porter, and **Yoh-Ichi Hamada.** *John Coltrane: A Discography and Musical Biography.* 377 pp. Metuchen, N.J.: Scarecrow Press; Newark, N.J.: Institute of Jazz Studies, Rutgers University, 1995. (Studies in jazz, 20)

"The most complete guide ever assembled to Coltrane's recordings and professional career." Preceded by a small "Reference Materials" bibliography, a guide to usage, abbreviations, and symbols, and Japanese information. Chronologically arranged by session, with name of band, personnel, information about the place of recording, cuts, lists of reissues where these pieces have appeared, and the significance of the recording. Information on jacket photo (when available) and timings is included. There is an index of numbers for issued recordings.

Reviewed by Lee Bash in *Jazz Educators Journal* 28 (January 1996): 117–18.

Darin, Bobby

10.277* Bleiel, Jeff. *That's All: Bobby Darin on Record, Stage & Screen.* 305 pp. Ann Arbor, Mich.: Popular Culture, Ink, 1993. (PCI collector editions) (Rock & roll reference series, 38)

An overview of the performer's career that includes bibliography, filmography, videography, discographies, and index.

Davis, Miles

10.278* Lohmann, Jan. *The Sound Of Miles Davis: The Discography: A Listing Of Recordings and Tapes, 1945–1991.* 396 pp. Copenhagen: JazzMedia, 1993.

Reviewed by John Corbett in *Down Beat* 61 (February 1994): 68–69 and by Mark Gilbert in *Jazz Journal International* 46 (July 1993): 18.

DeFranco, Buddy

10.279* Kuehn, John, and **Anne Astrup.** *Buddy DeFranco: A Biographical Portrait and Discography.* xii + 261 pp. Metuchen, N.J.: Scarecrow Press; New Brunswick, N.J.: Institute of Jazz Studies, Rutgers University, 1993. (Studies in jazz, 12)

Reviewed by Mark Gilbert in *Jazz Journal International* 47 (April 1994): 17.

Diddley, Bo

10.280* White, George R. *The Complete Bo Diddley Sessions.* Limited ed. 92 pp. Bradford, England: G.R. White Publications, 1993.

The most detailed and comprehensive Bo Diddley discography ever compiled. The author includes all of Bo's official U.S. and U.K. record releases from 1955 to the present day, rare foreign releases, and guest appearances on other artists' sessions. The lists are in chronological order and include recording studio information, date, personnel, take number, title of song, performers on each song, and all release information on the Sony/USA and UK labels (1955–90). The second part of the discography provides record lists, arranged by U.S. releases and singles, then U.K. releases and selected foreign releases.

Reviewed by Peter R. Aschoff in *Living Blues* 117 (September 1994): 101.

Dolphy, Eric

10.281* Reichardt, Uwe. *Like a Human Voice: The Eric Dolphy Discography.* 80 pp. Schmitten, Germany: Ruecker, 1986. (Jazz index reference series, 2)

A source containing all known recorded sessions Eric Dolphy participated in that were phonographically documented, verified, made evident, or substantiated. Private tape recordings are excluded. A list of discographical sources precedes the body of the discography, which is arranged in chronological order, with take number, date, place of recording session, personnel and instrumentation, and the issuing record label and number. A selected tape list follows, as well as four pages of discographical annotations that give information on the sessions and the personnel. There are indexes to album titles, compositions, and musicians, with a page of last-minute additions, to provide access to the discography.

Dylan, Bob

10.282* Krogsgaard, Michael. *Positively Bob Dylan: A Thirty-Year Discography, Concert & Recording Session Guide, 1960–1991.* 498 pp. Ann Arbor, Mich.: Popular Culture, 1991. (PCI collector editions) (Rock & Roll reference series, 33)

Previously issued as *Twenty Years of Recording: The Bob Dylan Reference Book,* 608 pp. (Denmark: Scandinavian Institute for Rock Research, 1981). The second Danish ed. was *Master of the Tracks: The Bob Dylan Reference Book of Recording,* 1988.

A source including all officially released recordings of songs, interviews, and press conferences; unreleased recordings that are circulated among collectors, and unreleased and generally uncirculated material to which the author has had access. The discography is limited to officially released American records, unless the record contains different or not otherwise available material, including promos and radio station discs. Recordings and releases are listed chronologically and numbered sequentially. Recording session information includes studio place, date, producer, cuts (and eventual record numbers), personnel, and the eventual use in the album. Album entries include title, record label and number, release date, and cuts (including composers and information about the tracks). An amazing array of indexes is provided, including indexes for recorded songs and interviews, songs on records and in films, chronological and alphabetical lists of Dylan's albums, a comprehensive index to commercially released recordings, a venue index to recorded concert performances, a geographic index to recorded concert performers, a label and catalog number index, and indexes to studio sessions, recorded radio and TV broadcasts, recorded interviews, recorded press conferences, Dylan-related films, and musicians. A chronological and a separate alphabetical index to Dylan's singles complete the exhaustive portrait of Bob Dylan's recorded career.

Reviewed by Craig H. Russell in *Notes* 50 (1994): 929–33, by L. A. Sullivan in *Choice* 29 (1992): 1,050, and by James Rettig in *Wilson Library Bulletin* 66 (January 1992): 128–29.

10.283* Nogowski, John. *Bob Dylan: A Descriptive, Critical Discography and Filmography, 1961–1993.* 208 pp. Jefferson, N.C.: McFarland, 1995.

Ellington, Duke

10.284* Valburn, Jerry. *Duke Ellington on Compact Disc: An Index and Text of the Recorded Work of Duke Ellington on Compact Disc: An In-Depth Study.* 253 pp. Hicksville, N.Y.: Marlor Productions, 1993.

Reviewed in *Mississippi Rag* 21 (July 1994): 29.

Goodman, Benny

10.285* Connor, D. Russell. *Benny Goodman: Listen to His Legacy.* 357 pp. Metuchen, N.J.: Scarecrow Press and the Institute of Jazz Studies, 1988. (Studies in jazz, 6)

The final installment in a procession of discographies recounting Goodman's career. The author's *Benny Goodman Off the Record* appeared in typescript editions in 1958, 1969, and 1978, and in a typeset edition, "The Record of a Legend . . . Benny Goodman," in 1984. This discographer and friend of the clarinetist lists commercial, private, and doubtful recordings with extensive commentaries and anecdotes, as well as Goodman's radio, television, and stage appearances.

Reviewed by Karl Kroeger in *Fontes* 37 (1990): 207–8, by Frank Driggs in *Audio* 72 (October 1988): 53–54, and by Chris Sheridan in *Jazz Journal International* 41 (November 1988): 14.

Henderson, Fletcher

10.286* Allen, Walter C. *Hendersonia: The Music of Fletcher Henderson and His Musicians: A Bio-Discography.* 651 pp. Highland Park, N.J.: Jazz Monographs, 1974. (Jazz monographs, 4)

Reviewed by Barry Kernfeld and Howard Rye in *Notes* 51 (1994): 506–10.

Herman, Woody

10.287* Morrill, Dexter. *Woody Herman: A Guide to the Big Band Recordings, 1936–1987.* 129 pp. Westport, Conn.: Greenwood Press, 1991. (Discographies, 40)

A discography whose entries include the date the performance was recorded, the arrangers, the vocalists, and the soloists. There are five indexes.

Reviewed by Jim Farrington in *Notes* 48 (1991): 527–28.

Holiday, Billie

10.288* Jepsen, Jørgen Grunnet, and **Knud H. Ditlevsen.** *Billie Holiday: A Complete Discography.* 30 pp. Copenhagen: Knudsen, 1960.

All the recordings by Billie Holiday as vocalist issued to the date of the discography by the avid Danish discographer. Take numbers have been included when known, with recording sessions arranged in chronological order; included are personnel and instrumentation, city and date of the session, title, and record label and issue numbers. A short biography completes the resource.

Jolson, Al

10.289* Kiner, Larry F., and **Philip R. Evans.** *The Al Jolson Discography.* xxii + 808 pp. Metuchen, N.J.: Scarecrow Press, 1992.

An earlier ed. (194 pp.) was published in Westport, Conn. by Greenwood Press, 1983.

A chronologically arranged discography of the music performed by Al Jolson. Radio broadcasts and programs, movies, and recording sessions are all included, with entries giving the place of the studio, the name of the song with its writers, the issue status of the recording, size and speed of the recording, the record label and number, and take designations. Separate indexes to conductors, costars, 78s, single records (by label), 10-inch LP record albums, 12-inch LP record albums, motion pictures (arranged chronologically), radio series, and song titles complete the picture of this important early recording artist.

The 1992 ed. is reviewed by James Fisher in *ARSCJ* 24 (1993): 204–5 and by Bruce A. Shuman in *ARBA* 25 (1994): 559–60.

Jones, Spike

10.290* Mirtle, Jack. *Thank You Music Lovers: A Bio-Discography of Spike Jones and His City Slickers, 1941 to 1965.* 426 pp. Westport, Conn.: Greenwood Press, 1986.

Previous edition was published as *Spike Jones Bio-Discography* (106 pp.) in Victoria, British Columbia, by the author, 1980.

A discography of all Jones's commercial recording sessions along with a chronological list of all of his broadcasts and their musical contents. A title and personnel list is also included.

Current ed. reviewed by Joseph M. Boonin in *Notes* 43 (1986): 309. Previous ed. reviewed by Michael Biel in *ARSCJ* 13 (1981): 116–17 no. 2.

The Kinks

10.291* Hinman, Doug, and **Jason Brabazon.** *You Really Got Me: An Illustrated World Discography of the Kinks, 1964–1993, Part One.* 559 pp. Rumford, R.I.: D. Hinman, 1994.

A source made up of chronological entries of recordings, including those produced by the Kinks (both compilation albums and those that are solely Kinks albums). Every issue (including all countries) is listed, with date of issue, record label and number, whether in stereo or monaural, and the country of release. In the case of albums, all cuts and timing (and which mix was used, if more than one) are provided. Packaging information and album history are also included. Added chapters cover rumored bootlegs and privately made copies and cover numbers performed by the Kinks, as well as works by the Kinks' leader, Ray Davies, performed by others, with all discographical information. Indexes include song titles, record titles, and U.S./U.K. transcriptions. Also included are U.S. charts (*Billboard* singles and albums), U.K. charts (*Melody Maker* singles and LPs), and a glossary.

Reviewed by Bonna J. Boettcher in *Notes* 52 (1996): 832.

Monk, Thelonious

10.292* **Jepsen, Jørgen Grunnet.** *A Discography of Thelonious Monk & Bud Powell.* 44 pp. Copenhagen: Knudsen, 1969.

As part of a larger jazz discography series compiled by Jepsen and his colleagues, these lists provide access to the recording sessions of the major jazz artists. Divided by the artist, the recording sessions are chronologically arranged and include take numbers, with recording sessions arranged in chronological order, with personnel and instrumentation, city and date of the session, title, and record label and issue numbers. No indexes are provided.

Monroe, Bill

10.293* **Rosenberg, Neil V.** *Bill Monroe and His Blue Grass Boys: An Illustrated Discography.* 122 pp. Nashville, Tenn.: Country Music Foundation Press, 1974.

A discography, arranged in chronological order. There is a chapter for each of Bill Monroe's recording labels (Victor, Columbia, and Decca, along with a small list of recordings Monroe made with other labels and compilations), 1940–73. Entries include the location of the studio or the place of the recording, date, the number list of the record with title, composer, performers, and subsequent reissue numbers. Each section is followed by a list of 78s and 45s in numerical order, with the date of release. The author also provides an index to song titles.

Reviewed by Barbara Heuman Kriss in *Guitar Player* 9 (January 1975): 55.

Parker, Charlie

10.294* **Jepsen, Jørgen Grunnet.** *A Discography of Charlie Parker.* 38 pp. Copenhagen: Knudsen, 1968.

Earlier ed. published by Debut Records, 1959, 29 ll.

A source similar to the other Jepsen/Knudsen discographies, delineating "Bird's" recording sessions. Along with the standard discographical treatment, Jepsen also includes a table of EPs and LPs, grouped by record company, with a parallel list of the American original, the British editions, and the French, German, or Danish issues of the same recording.

Powell, Bud

see Thelonious Monk.

Presley, Elvis

10.295* **Banney, Howard F.** *Return to Sender: The First Complete Discography of Elvis Tribute & Novelty Records, 1956–1986.* 318 pp. Ann Arbor, Mich.: Pierian Press, 1987. (Rock & roll reference series, 29)

A resource providing access to recordings made by others in tribute to (and sometimes, to mimic) the man called the king of rock-n-roll. The work is divided into four parts, with the final part devoted to indexes of personal names, song and album titles, and record label numbers. The first part alphabetically lists songs on 7-inch recordings, with information on the performer, the record label, the country of origin, the date, whether the recording sounds like Elvis, and whether the song and record is a cover or a promotional recording, with additional comments about whether the text of the song refers to Elvis by name. Part Two provides the same information, arranged by performer, for 12-inch recordings. Part Three has track lists for 12-inch records, arranged by record titles, with the similar information as provided in Part One.

Reviewed by B. Lee Cooper in *PMS* 12 (Fall 1988): 109–l0 and by R. Serge Denisoff in *PMS* 12 (Summer 1988): 84.

10.296* Cotten, Lee, and **Howard A Dewitt.** *Jailhouse Rock: The Bootleg Records of Elvis Presley, 1970–1983.* xxxix + 367 pp. Ann Arbor, Mich.: Pierian Press, 1983. (Rock & roll reference series, 8)

Another source devoted to an important facet of a popular recording star's career: the recordings made without the knowledge or permission of the artist. The authors begin with an introduction that has an initial list of recordings and illustrations alphabetically arranged with entry number and photo page, then an essay on bootlegs (including a history of bootlegs in general, and specifically Elvis Presley's). A section on terminology is followed by "The Bootlegged Career of Elvis Presley: A Chronological Guide" (which includes date, place of recording/performance, and songs bootlegged). The main discography, "The Bootleg Records of Elvis Presley," consists of an alphabetical list, by performance/recording, of each bootlegged performance. The record label on which the bootleg was released, the record number, date, place of release, list of song titles, information on packaging, highlights (information on the quality of the recording, places from which the bootleg was taken and circumstances), and a summary of the recording (rating, quality, etc.) are provided. Appendixes include an extensive song title index for bootlegged albums, EPs, and singles (arranged by title, date, and version or artist); a list of interviews and press conferences that have been bootlegged (with the same information given as for the music recordings), with a topical index to the interviews and press conferences; and a list of overseas pirated releases of Elvis's albums (consisting primarily of cover photographs). Another unique list is that for bootlegged novelty albums, "About Elvis," with a song title index for the albums. Indexes include a record label index; a personal name index; the list of bootlegged cassette tapes (with the date, place, time, and duration); a filmography of bootlegged Super 8 film that includes the date, program (TV shows, movies, or performances), number of feet, black and white or color, and sound; and a videography of bootlegged videotapes (with the date, TV show, movie, or performance listed).

Reviewed by B. Lee Cooper in *JEMFQ* 19 (1983): 141–43.

10.297* Tunzi, Joseph A. *Elvis Sessions: The Recorded Music of Elvis Aron Presley 1953–1977.* 347 pp. Chicago, Ill.: Jat Productions, 1993.

A discography listing the legitimate recordings of Elvis Presley, rather than information about the edges of his career. The author includes only recordings recorded, mastered, and intended for release. Presley's work is organized chronologically and grouped into various sections: First Recordings (1953–54), The Sun Years (1954–55), Elvis Moves to RCA (1956–58), The 60's Recordings, The 70's Recordings, Various Private Recordings, and the 80's Re-Recordings. Each entry under these categories includes the pertinent recording information (with the date of the recording session and session notes explaining the significance of the song). The main section is followed by the complete discography, listing every track Elvis recorded, with the year, record, and title of both sides of the singles. There are many black-and-white photographs and indexes to the songs and songwriters. Appendixes include a Current Elvis Presley Catalog, a Topping the Charts list, RIIA Gold Record Awards, Grammy Nominations and Awards, Exhibits (photocopies of recording session sheets), and a glossary of recording terms.

Rolling Stones

10.298 Aeppli, Felix. *Heart of Stone: The Definitive Rolling Stones Discography, 1962–1983.* xliv + 535 pp. Ann Arbor, Mich.: Pierian Press, 1985. (Rock & roll reference series, 17)

A chronological list of all Rolling Stones recordings from July 1962 through 1983, whether recorded by the group or by its individual musicians. Separate catalogs of group recordings and solo recordings are followed by a catalog of unverified studio recordings and bootleg recordings, as well as funkily-labeled indexes of names of musicians and of titles of individual songs and albums.

Reviewed by B. Lee Cooper in *PMS* 11 (Winter 1987): 96–97 and in *SSN* 12 (Summer 1986): 71.

Russell, Pee Wee

10.299* Hilbert, Robert, and **David Niven.** *Pee Wee Speaks: A Discography of Pee Wee Russell.* 377 pp. Metuchen, N.J.: Scarecrow Press, 1992. (Studies in jazz, 13)

A resource including all known recorded performances by Russell, including films, radio and television broadcasts, concerts, and private recordings. An introduction to Pee Wee Russell's work begins the discography, which is chronologically arranged and includes the name of group, the place and date of the recording, personnel, record number, the title of cut, and the take. Re-releases (arranged by 78, 45, 33, CD, cassette, and 8-track) are also listed. Any incidental information is included, including producer and performance information. Indexes include a personnel and title index.

Reviewed by David Rothenberg in *Notes* 51 (1994): 202, by Glenn Bowen in *Clarinet* 21 (1994): 59 no. 3, by Floyd Levin in *Jazz Journal International* 46 (September 1993): 18, and by Kevin Whitehead in *Down Beat* 60 (June 1993): 59.

Sinatra, Frank

10.300* Ackelson, Richard W. *Frank Sinatra: A Complete Recording History of Techniques, Songs, Composers, Lyricists, Arrangers, Sessions, and First-Issue Albums, 1939–1984.* 466 pp. Jefferson, N.C.: McFarland & Company, Inc., 1992.

A discography whose subtitle almost says it all, although it also includes a variety of helpful indexes. A master song index, arranged both alphabetically (pp. 41–224) and by date published (pp. 225–241), gives date of recording and identifies composer, lyricist, arranger, publisher, and other particulars, as needed; indexes to composers (pp. 271–77), lyricists (pp. 309–15), and arrangers (pp. 346–57) are also helpful.

Reviewed by Jean Bonin in *SSB* 19 (1993): 27 no. 1 and by B. Lee Cooper in *PMS* 18 (Fall 1994): 81–83.

10.301* Sayers, Scott, and **Ed O'Brien.** *Sinatra: The Man and His Music: The Recording Artistry of Francis Albert Sinatra, 1939–1992.* 2nd ed. 303 pp. Austin, Tex.: TSD Press, 1992.

First ed. titled *The Sinatra Sessions, 1939–1980.* 125 pp. Dallas, Tex.: Sinatra Society of America, 1980.

A discography of sessions by Sinatra that were recorded and mastered for release. No bootlegs were considered in the compiling of this source. Chronological lists include information on the releases of the 45, album, and CD, and include the arranger, extra performers, the master number, title of the song, record name and label, and reissue information. The sessions sections are divided by the major labels (Columbia, Capitol, and Reprise), followed by a list by title that gives the recording date and label. A separate list of unissued recordings and film recordings is included. Addenda include his recordings that made the music charts (with the date, top position, number of weeks, and title and label), a list of CDs, Grammy Awards (including all given for engineering), and a section on exhibits (with copies of record sessions sheets).

Reviewed by B. Lee Cooper in *PMS* 16 (Winter 1992): 106–7, by Bruce Crowther in *Jazz Journal International* 45 (1992): 13 no. 8, and by Louis G. Zelenka in *ARBA* 25 (1994): 560–61.

Sousa Band

10.302 Smart, James R. *The Sousa Band: A Discography.* 123 pp. Washington, D.C.: Library of Congress, 1970.

Tatum, Art

10.303 Laubich, Arnold, and **Ray Spencer.** *Art Tatum: A Guide to His Recorded Music.* xxviii + 330 pp. Metuchen, N.J.: Institute of Jazz Studies, Rutgers University; Scarecrow Press, 1982. (Studies in jazz series, 2)

A very complete resource listing jazz pianist Art Tatum's recording sessions. This resource includes a chronological discography that includes the city of the session, date, performers and instrumentation, index number (given by the authors), published title of the cut and its timing, master or matrix number, diameter of the record, record label and issue number, country of origin, and information on reissues of the take. A chronological list of unissued sessions, a compilation of issued discs (arranged by the record label), a title list (with the discography's access number, timing, and composers and lyricists), a musicians index, and lists of films, published music, and piano rolls provide a comprehensive look at Tatum's work. The appendixes include a guide to abbreviations, a matrix cross-reference list, other discographies examined, and a quick dating guide.

Reviewed by James Remet Burden in *BPM* 11 (1983): 86–88, by George Ebbs in *Jazz Journal International* 36 (February 1983): 21, and by Frank Hoffmann in *PMS* 9(1983): 88, no. 2.

Vallee, Rudy

10.304* Kiner, Larry F. *The Rudy Vallee Discography.* 190 pp. Westport, Conn.: Greenwood Press, 1985. (Discographies, 15)

A chronological list of the performer's work, from December 1921 to 1973. Information provided includes the title of the song, the date of the recording, whether it was private or a recording session, place of the recording, what type of band or solo work it was, the composer/lyricist, the size and speed of the record issued, and the label name and number. Indexes include those for conductor and accompanist; costar and vocalist; Connecticut Yankee musicians; 78-rpm single records (arranged alphabetically by label, with a separate chronological list by record imprint number); and a list of LP record albums including the record label and number, the place of issue (if not the U.S.), title of the album, and titles of songs. Indexes to motion pictures (in chronological order), song titles, and radio series provide full access to Vallee's works. The discography closes with a bibliography.

Reviewed by Bert Whyatt in *Jazz Journal International* 38 (November 1985): 19 and by Brian Rust in *Gramophone* 63 (1985): 327.

Vaughan, Sarah

10.305* Brown, Denis. *Sarah Vaughan: A Discography.* 167 pp. New York: Greenwood Press, 1991. (Discographies, 47)

A list of all known American and British issues of 78s, 45s, EP and LPs, and four CDs—in all, some 750 songs in 221 recording sessions. Recordings from other countries are listed if they are the sole versions. Also included is a list of budget and reissue recordings, as well as indexes to musicians and orchestras and a brief bibliography.

Young, Lester

10.306* Jepsen, Jørgen Grunnet. *A Discography of Lester Young.* 45 pp. Copenhagen: Knudsen, 1968.

Another entry in the jazz discography series, a discography of Lester Young featuring a table of EPs and LPs similar to that in the Charlie Parker discography by Jepsen (**10.294**); it continues the same complete access to recording sessions available in the other sources. No indexes accompany this discography.

VIDEO SOURCES

10.307* Almquist, Sharon G. *Opera Mediagraphy: Video Recordings and Motion Pictures.* 269 pp. Westport, Conn.: Greenwood Press, 1994. (Music reference collection, 40)

A list including multiple formats for 157 operas, often with several performances of these works, a list of motion picture and television productions and distributors, and indexes of singers and conductors, composers, and production locations.

Reviewed by Guy A. Marco in *Choice* 31 (1994): 1,420.

10.308* Croissant, Charles R. *Opera Performances in Video Format: A Checklist of Commercially Released Recordings.* Canton, Mass.: Music Library Association, 1991. (MLA index and bibliography series, 26)

10.309 International Music Centre, Vienna. *Music in Film and Television: An International Selective Catalogue, 1964–1974: Opera, Concert, Documentation.* 197 pp. Paris: UNESCO Press, 1975.

A list with background information of 223 films that center around music, with a variety of genres included. There are indexes by titles, composers, librettists, authors, translators, producers and directors, conductors, performing artists, orchestras and ensembles, organizations, and companies. This is the 4th in a series of UNESCO catalogs of films on the performing arts. Many of these films are now available in video cassette and laser disc formats.

Briefly reviewed by Stephen Fry in *Notes* 33 (1976): 83.

10.310* Jacobs, Richard M., and **Ed Schwartz.** *Music Videodiscs: An Annotated Guide.* 148 pp. Dubuque, Iowa: William C. Brown Publishers, 1991.

11

YEARBOOKS, DIRECTORIES, AND GUIDES

YEARBOOKS

Publications appearing under the title or label *Yearbook* can take a variety of forms. They may be annual volumes issued by learned societies, such as the Spanish *Anuario Musical,* the British *Proceedings of the Royal Musical Association,* the Swiss *Schweizerisches Jahrbuch für Musikwissenschaft,* or the *Jahrbuch für Liturgik und Hymnologie.* They may be volumes issued annually by such music publishing houses as C.F. Peters, Simrock, or Breitkopf & Härtel, or they may be publications of societies devoted to the work of a particular composer, such as *Bach Jahrbuch, Handel Jahrbuch, Mozart Jahrbuch,* or *Haydn Jahrbuch.* Finally, they may be directories or compilations of factual information covering a specific year. Works of this kind are emphasized in the following highly selective list. Yearbooks in this sense are often useful for reference purposes because they provide data on the musical activities of a specific year and give easy access to current musical activities and personalities often difficult to find otherwise. It should be remembered that the titles listed in this chapter are exemplars of their types; conscientious bibliographic sleuthing should reveal works of this genre on many subjects, societies, regions, and persons not found here.

11.1* *The Billboard Encyclopedia of Music, 1946/1947–* . Eighth annual ed. Vol. 1. 704 pp. Cincinnati, Ohio: The Billboard Publishing Company, 1946.

Earlier editions published as *The Billboard Music Year Book: the Encyclopedia and Reference Work of the Music Industry,* 5th–7th annual editions, 1943–1946.

A work whose first seven years bore the title *yearbook,* becoming an "encyclopedia" in 1946. Still a yearbook in feeling, each issue has a chronology of musical events and includes handy lists (50 or more) of varying lengths that reflect the country's musical activity.

The 1946/47 issue is reviewed by Richard S. Hill in *Notes* 4 (1947): 175–76. The 1947/48 issue is reviewed by Richard S. Hill in *Notes* 5 (1947): 98–100.

11.2 Bloom, Julius. *The Year in American Music, 1946/47–1947/48.* 2 vols. New York: Allen, Towne & Heath, Inc., 1947–48.

The 2nd vol. was edited by David Ewen.

A yearbook whose first part in each vol. is a chronological survey of the important musical events of the year, followed by a miscellany of factual information, biographical and bibliographical.

The earlier vol. is reviewed by Richard S. Hill in *Notes* 5 (1947): 98–100.

11.3 *The British Music Yearbook.* London: A.&C. Black, 1975– .

From the 10th ed., an American ed. was published by Schirmer Books, New York.

A survey and directory with statistics, addresses, and occasional topical articles. The range of coverage includes most aspects of British musical life, including broadcast performances and trade (records, instruments, music, books, and periodicals). There are directories of performers, associations, concert and rehearsal halls, offices and societies, music publishers, critics, festivals, and competitions, as well as directories of British libraries and musical museums by categories (national libraries, church and cathedral libraries, etc.) and then by place, with address and phone number.

The 1981 yearbook is reviewed by Noël Goodwin in *MT* 122 (1981): 178; the 1982 yearbook (490 pp.) is reviewed by Noël Goodwin in *MT* 123 (1982): 188; the 1983 yearbook is reviewed by Noël Goodwin in *MT* 124 (1983): 235; the 1984 yearbook (650 pp.) is reviewed by Clifford Bartlett in *Brio* 20 (1983): 82; the 1985 (648 pp.) yearbook is reviewed by Noël Goodwin in *MT* 126 (1985): 412–13.

11.4* Feather, Leonard. *The Encyclopedia Yearbooks of Jazz.* 190 and 186 pp. New York: Da Capo Press, 1993.

The works included were originally published as *The Encyclopedia Yearbook of Jazz* (New York: Horizon Press, 1956) and *The New Yearbook of Jazz* (New York: Horizon Press, 1958).

11.5 Frank, Alan. *The Year's Work in Music, 1947/48–1950/51.* 4 vols. London, New York, Toronto: Published for the British Council by Longmans, Green & Co., 1948–51.

A yearbook issued for four years, with each vol. containing a series of essays by various specialists on aspects of British musical life during the year: musical research and the making and playing of instruments. The British Broadcasting Corporation and contemporary music are covered. There is an annual (selective) bibliography by A. Hyatt King of published music and musical literature.

Reviewed by Vincent Duckles in *Notes* 9 (1952): 399–400.

11.6 *Hinrichsen's Musical Year Book,* 1944–61. 11 vols. London: Hinrichsen Edition, Ltd., 1944–61.

A series of vols. edited by Max Hinrichsen, issued at irregular intervals, remarkably varied in content. The articles range from trivia to substantial contributions by recognized authorities. Most vols. contain bibliographies of current music publications as well as numerous lists, illustrations, and chronologies. More recent vols. have been organized about some central theme: Vol. 7, "The forerunners of the Grove–Blum" (1955); Vol. 8, "The organ of Bach and matters related to this subject" (1956); Vol. 9, "John Gay and the Ballad Opera" (1956); Vol. 10, "Organ and choral aspects and prospects" (1958). Vol. 11 (1961) contains the papers read at the Joint Congress of the International Association of Music Libraries and the Galpin Society, Cambridge, England, 1959.

Vols. IV–V, 1947–48, are reviewed by Richard S. Hill in *Notes* 5 (1947): 98–100; Vol. VI, 1949–50, is reviewed by Richard S. Hill in *Notes* 6 (1949): 614–15.

11.7* *Musical Denmark Yearbook,* 1994– . Copenhagen: Danish Cultural Institute and Danish Music Information Centre, 1994– .

11.8 *Showcase International Music Book.* 27th ed. London: Showcase Publications Ltd., 1995– .

Title varies. Previously published as *Kemp's International Music & Recording Industry Year Book,* 1988–94, 21st–26th ed.

A yearbook of the British record industry, first published in 1965.

Brief review by Stephen M. Fry in *Notes* 32 (1975): 302–3.

11.9* Zaimont, Judith Lang. *The Musical Woman: An International Perspective,* Vols. I–III. 3 vols. to date. New York: Greenwood Press, 1984– .

A collection of useful essays, as well as bibliographies, discographies, and statistics, on the general subject of women and music.

The 3rd vol. is reviewed by Liane Curtis in *Fontes* 39 (1992): 192–94 and by Judy Tsou in *Notes* 47 (1990):380–81.

DIRECTORIES

Directories are lists of names of individuals or institutions covering a specific topic or sharing a common interest; they are useful in discovering current practical information about people, organizations, societies, institutions, and locations of musical interest. Many musical organizations publish a directory of members. In particular, the annual directories of members of the American Musicological Society, the Music Library Association, and the International Association of Music Libraries can be particularly useful, with addresses, telephone numbers, e-mail access, and fax numbers commonly supplied. Out-of-date directories help to place people geographically and chronologically for a variety of purposes in the writing of history. Especially important is the series of directories compiled by the individual chapters of the Music Library Association of their own region of the country. These directories, frequently updated, offer the most up-to-date information on libraries with strong music or music-related collections (**11.18, 11.22, 11.24, 11.40, 11.41,** and **11.42**), excepting only the individual institutions' home pages. The following list is a sample that shows the range of directory information available to the music researcher.

11.10* *Agenda Musical pour l'Année 1836, Contenant Tous les Renseignements Utiles aux Amateurs de Musique et aux Artistes.* 3 vols. in 1. 3 + 103 +286 +288 cols. Geneva: Minkoff Reprint, 1981. (Archives de l'Édition musicale française, 11)
> A trade directory of musical France.

11.11* Alink, Gustav A. *Piano Competitions / Klavierwettbewerbe / Concours de Piano / Concorsi Pianistici.* 3rd ed. 229 pp. G. Alink, 1993.
> A list by an enthusiast of piano performance competitions.
> The 1st ed., 1988, 248 pp.; 2nd ed., 1990, 245 pp.

11.12 *The American Musical Directory, 1861.* With a new introduction by Barbara Owen. 260 pp. New York: Da Capo Press, 1980.
> The original edition was published in New York by T. Hutchinson, 1861.
> Arranged by state and then by city, a list of persons involved in music performance, teaching, commerce, and instrument making or repair. The largest sections are devoted to New York and New England, but coverage is truly continental, including Canada as well as most of the U.S. There are two useful appendixes: one on music in the church, ordered by denomination, describing the church organs and listing the church musicians; the other on musical societies, with entries describing the societies' purposes and activities.
> Reviewed by H. Earle Johnson in *AM* 1 (1983): 93–94.

11.13 *Association for Recorded Sound Collections: A Preliminary Directory of Sound Recordings Collections in the United States and Canada.* Prepared by a committee of the Association for Recorded Sound Collections. 157 pp. New York: New York Public Library, 1967.
> Preface written for the Committee by Jean Bowen.
> A directory with the collections listed alphabetically by state. The addresses are given, with additional brief information on contents. Many private collectors are listed.
> Reviewed by Edward Colby in *Notes* 25 (1969):504–5.

11.14 Briegleb, Ann. *Directory of Ethnomusicological Sound Recording Collections in the U.S. and Canada.* 46 pp. Ann Arbor, Mich.: Society for Ethnomusicology, 1971. (Special series, 2)
> A guide to ethnomusicology sound archives and collections with significant holdings in world music, arranged alphabetically by state and city. Unfortunately, much of the information is dated, but there is nothing to supersede it.

11.15 Chamber Music America. *A Directory of Summer Chamber Music Workshops, Schools & Festivals.* 220 pp. New York: Chamber Music America, 1994.

11.16* Child, Margaret S. *Directory of Information Sources on Scientific Research Related to the Preservation of Sound Recordings, Still and Moving Images, and Magnetic Tape.* 14 pp. Washington, D.C.: Commission on Preservation and Access, 1993.

A directory of organizations currently working to prolong the usable life of non–paper-based sources.

11.17* College Music Society. *International Directory of Music Organizations, 1995– .* Missoula, Mont.: CMS Publications, 1995– .

11.18 Cornwell, Robena *Directory of Music Collections in the Southeast United States.* 3rd ed. 70 pp. Winston-Salem, N.C.: Music Library Association, Southeast Chapter, 1994.

2nd ed., edited by Shirley Marie Watts and Mark D. Squire, 1984, 27 pp.

A directory that includes information on music and music-related collections from Alabama, Arkansas, Florida, Georgia, Louisiana, Mississippi, North Carolina, South Carolina, and Tennessee. The contents include indexes of staff, institutions and collections, and subjects.

11.19* Cowden, Robert H. *Opera Companies of the World: Selected Profiles.* xxvi + 336 pp. New York: Greenwood Press, 1992.

A directory whose accompanying profiles give some pertinent information on individual opera companies and their current practice.

11.20* Craven, Robert R. *Symphony Orchestras of the United States: Selected Profiles.* xxiii + 521 pp. Westport, Conn.: Greenwood Press, 1986.

A companion volume to **11.21.**

11.21* Craven, Robert R. *Symphony Orchestras of the World: Selected Profiles.* xxiii + 468 pp. Westport, Conn.: Greenwood Press, 1987.

Reviewed by Suzanne A. Fischer in *Fontes* 36 (1989): 61–62.

11.22 Davis-Millis, Nina, and **Lakshmi Kapoor.** *Directory of Music Collections in the Greater New York Area.* 44 pp. New York: Greater New York Chapter, Music Library Association, 1982.

A directory of music collections in New York state and New Jersey.

11.23 *Directory of Music Faculties in Colleges and Universities, U.S. and Canada, 1970/1972– .* Binghamton, N.Y.: College Music Society, 1970.

Originally published as *Directory of Music Faculties in American Colleges and Universities, 1967/8,* edited by Harry B. Lincoln.

A biennial directory of over 10,000 faculty in over 1,000 institutions, in three parts. Part I is a departmental faculty list, arranged by state (in alphabetical order by Zip Code abbreviation) and institution, with each listing supplying degrees offered and address and telephone numbers. Part II lists faculty by areas of specialization. Part III lists the entire faculty in one list.

The 1967/8 ed. is reviewed by Rey M. Longyear in *JRME* 16 (1968): 220–21.

11.24* Earnest, Jeffrey, and **Kathryn P. Glennan.** *Directory of Music Collections in California.* 77 pp. Los Angeles, Calif.: Music Library Association, Northern California and Southern California Chapters, 1991.

Earlier eds. separately issued by the respective chapters.

11.25* Eichenlaub, Frank, and **Patricia Eichenlaub.** *All American Guide to Country Music.* 237 pp. Castine, Maine: Country Road Press, 1992.

An almanac of various types of country music, including bluegrass, gospel, cowboy, Cajun, and pure country, with regional lists of nightclubs, festivals, and such.

11.26 Felton, Gary S. *The Record Collector's International Directory.* 365 pp. New York: Crown Publishers, 1980.

An international directory of record dealers, emphasizing those in English-speaking countries, with lists of journals and newsletters and a sampling of directories and guides. There is an index of dealers by specialties.

11.27 Finell, Judith Greenberg. *The Contemporary Music Performance Directory: A Listing of American Performing Ensembles, Sponsoring Organizations, Performing Facilities, Concert Series, and Festivals of 20th-Century Music.* 238 pp. New York: American Music Center, 1975.

A useful but dated contact guide produced under the auspices of the American Music Center.

Briefly reviewed by Stephen M. Fry in *Notes* 32 (1976): 780–81 and by Ann P. Basart in *CNV* 1 (1976): 2.

11.28 Flemming, Bill. *Directory of Australian Music Organisations.* Revised ed. 67 pp. Sydney: Australia Music Centre, 1985.

First published in 1978.

11.29 Goertz, Harald. *Musikhandbuch für Österreich: Struktur und Organisation des österreichischen Musikwesens: Namen, Adressen, Information.* 3rd ed. 168 pp. Vienna: Doblinger, 1993.

The 1st ed. was published in 1971 by Jugend und Volk Verlag, Munich (349 pp.), the 2nd by Doblinger in Vienna and Munich, 1983 (153 pp.).

A classified directory of Austrian music organizations, whose entries provide brief descriptions of organizational function. Includes an index to designated historical sites by composers' names and an index to names of organizations.

11.30 Handel, Beatrice. *Handel's National Directory for the Performing Arts.* 5th ed. 2 vols. Dallas, Tex.: NDPA, 1992– .

Contents.: Vol. 1, *Organizations and Facilities.* Vol. 2, *Educational Institutions.*

First ed. published in Dallas by Handel, 1973, 604 pp. 3rd ed., *National Directory for the Performing Arts and Civic Centers,* published in New York by J. Wiley, 1978, 1,049 pp. 4th ed., 1988.

A source covering the U.S., organized by state and then by locality, with data on facilities, organizations devoted to instrumental music, vocal music, theater, and dance. The key management personnel are listed.

11.31* Henry, John. *Braille Music: An International Survey.* 59 pp. Stockport, England: National Library for the Blind, 1984.

A list of libraries holding musical scores in Braille notation.

11.32* Karl, Michael, and **Markus Schratzenstaller.** *Handbuch für Musiker: Adressen und Informationen aus der Musikszene.* 390 pp. Munich: Grafenstein, 1989.

A directory of music-related addresses and telephone numbers in Austria, Switzerland, and the former West Germany.

11.33* Kelly, Thomas Forrest. *Early Music in America: A Report on a Survey Conducted by Early Music America.* 31 pp. New York: Early Music America, 1989.

11.34 Koch, Grace. *International Association of Sound Archives: Directory of Member Archives.* 174 pp. London: International Association of Sound Archives, 1982. (Special publication, 3)

The 1st ed., published in 1978, was edited by Ann Briegleb and Don Niles (94 pp.).

Extensive entries modeled on the *RISM* Series C directories to music collections (**7.1**).

11.35 Kraus, Egon. *International Directory of Music Education Institutions.* 115 pp. Paris: UNESCO, 1968.

A list, with addresses, of music education institutions arranged by country and classified under 10 categories of institutions, including workshops, competitions, festivals, libraries, collections of musical instruments, organizations, and periodicals.

11.36* Laufenberg, Cindy. *Songwriter's Market, 1996: Where and How to Market Your Songs.* 504 pp. Cincinnati, Ohio: Writer's Digest Books, 1995.

First ed., 1979. Earlier eds. had other editors.

2,500 listings of music publishers, record companies and producers, audiovisual firms, managers, classical groups, and theater companies.

11.37 Levine, Michael. *The Music Address Book: How to Reach Anyone Who's Anyone in Music.* 2nd ed. 225 pp. New York: HarperPerennial, 1994.

Addresses and telephone numbers for people working in the music business, especially those connected with popular musicians likely to tour.

11.38* Madigan, Mary D. *Concert Artist Guild's Guide to Competitions.* 9th ed., expanded and revised. 135 pp. New York: Concert Artists Guild, Inc., 1995.

Editors vary.

First ed., 1987.

A list of competitions open to American solo instrumentalists, chamber ensembles, and recital/oratorio singers; composers, conductors, and opera singers are excluded. The entries are indexed by performance categories.

The 8th ed. is reviewed by Jean Morrow in *Notes* 52 (1995): 450–51.

11.39 *Music Industry Directory.* 7th ed. 678 pp. Chicago, Ill.: Marquis Publications, 1983.

Formerly the *Musician's Guide,* issued 1954–80, in 6 eds.

A classified directory of names connected with all phases of commercial music activity, with more than 50 rosters of persons, organizations, activities, and businesses concerned with the music profession. Includes an index to music publishers and a general index.

The 1957 ed. is reviewed by Richard S. Hill in *Notes* 14 (1957): 111–13. The 1968 ed. is reviewed by Thor Wood and Neil Ratliff in *Notes* 25 (1969): 736–37.

11.40* Music Library Association. *Midwest Chapter. A Directory of Music Collections in the Midwestern United States.* 114 pp. Oberlin, Ohio: The Chapter, 1990.

11.41 Music Library Association. *New England Chapter. Directory of Music Libraries and Collections in New England.* 9th ed. 97 pp. Providence, R.I.: Music Library Association, New England Chapter, 1994.

1st ed., 1970, 27 pp. 2nd ed., 1971, 44 pp.

A guide to the holdings, services, and facilities of music libraries in New England, with a detailed index. The chapter also published a *Resource Directory* in 1993 (26 pp.).

11.42 Music Library Association. *Pennsylvania Chapter. Directory of Music Collections in the Pennsylvania Chapter of the Music Library Association.* 35 pp. Indiana, Pa.: 1992.

11.43 *The Music Magazine/Musical Courier: The Annual Directory of the Concert World.* Evanston, Ill.: Summy-Birchard Co., 1957–63.

Editions for 1957–61 published as the mid-January issue of *Musical Courier,* with the title *Directory Issue of the Musical Arts and Artists.* The 1963 issue, edited by Max D. Jones, contains pertinent information on American and foreign music organizations, artist and concert managers, artist availability, current series and associations, orchestras, opera booking organizations, festivals, foundations, schools of music, publishers, periodicals, recording firms, and music dealers.

11.44* *Music Publishers' International ISMN Directory, 1995– .* New Providence: K.G. Saur; Berlin: International ISMN Agency; New Providence: R.R. Bowker, 1995– .

A comprehensive up-to-date directory of music publishers worldwide, including members of the sound recording industry.

11.45 *Musical America: International Directory of the Performing Arts,* 1993– . New York: K-III Directory Corp., 1994– .

Continues *Musical America Directory of Performing Arts,* first issued as a special issue of *Musical America,* which started in 1898 and ceased in January 1992.

A directory international in scope, but focused most heavily on North America. Intended for use by agents, impresarios, and concert hall managers, the directory lists dance and opera companies, choral groups, festivals, music schools, contests, foundations and awards, publishers, professional organizations, managers, and magazines and trade papers, amid a welter of advertisements. There is access to the performers featured in the included advertising in the Index of Advertisers, classified by type of performer.

11.46* Musiker, Reuben. *Directory of South African Music Libraries.* 61 pp. Johannesburg: South African Music Libraries Association, 1993.

11.47* Nagle, Sigrid *Directory of Historical-Instrument Makers in North America.* 39 pp. Cleveland, Ohio: Early Music America, 1992.

A classified directory with addresses, phone numbers, and special instruments produced, with a more specific classified index.

11.48 *Neue Musik in der Bundesrepublik Deutschland: Dokumentation, 1953.* Cologne: Gesellschaft für Neue Musik, Sektion Bundesrepublik Deutschlander Internationalen Gesellschaft für Neue Musik, 1953– .

A biennial sourcebook of information about the performance of new music in Germany. There is a preliminary group of essays; the accomplishments and the programs of regional radio centers are described. New music festivals and activities supporting or featuring new music are listed by city.

11.49 Pavlakis, Christopher. *The American Music Handbook, a Guide to Organized Musical Activity in the United States: An Inventory of Musical Resources: The People, Places, and Organizations.* 836 pp. New York: Free Press, 1974.

A directory focused on professional musicianship in the U.S.: organizations, vocal and instrumental ensembles, performers, composers, festivals and awards, education, radio and television, music industries, periodicals, and management. A foreign supplement treats international festivals, contests, and music publishers. The helpful index is unique in compilations of this type.

Reviewed by Susan T. Sommer in *Notes* 31 (1975): 770–71.

11.50 *Pierre Key's Music Year Book: The Standard Music Annual,* 1924–38. 6 vols. New York: Pierre Key, Inc., 1925–38.

A directory of musical organizations and musicians, chiefly performers, issued irregularly over a period of 13 years. The earlier vols. are international in scope; the later are restricted to U.S. coverage.

11.51 *The Purchasers Guide to the Music Industries.* Annual ed., 1897– . New York: Music Trades, 1897– .

Title varies: after 1958, *Directory Issue.*

Annual classified directory of American instrument manufacturers; music publishers, engravers, and printers; retail music stores; and dealers in music merchandise. Excludes performers and performing groups. Similar titles exist in other countries: Spain has the *Guia profesional del anuario de la musica.*

11.52* Richmond, Eero. *Opera Companies and American Opera: A Directory.* 2nd ed. 23 pp. New York: American Music Center, 1992.

A list of 87 opera companies that have shown an interest in performing 20th-century American operas and music theater works. Most locations include size of company, whether a chorus or orchestra is available, and the works premiered and commissioned, with information on how to submit a score.

11.53* Rose, Johanna. *Early Music Degree Programs in North America.* 10 pp. Cleveland, Ohio: Early Music America, 1992.

An earlier ed. first appeared in *Historical Performance,* Spring 1989.

A directory detailing the early music offerings of 25 institutions, discussing the degrees granted. the various programs' special features, the applied instruction available, ensembles, course requirements and electives, entrance requirements, tuition and financial aid, early music faculty, the number of full-time students, and the application deadlines.

11.54 Samuel, Harold E. "Societies, musical." In *The New Harvard Dictionary of Music* (**1.320**), pp. 773–78. Cambridge, Mass.: Harvard University Press, 1986.

A list of current professional societies, citing titles and dates of principal publications.

11.55 *Schweizer Musik-Handbuch 1991/92: Informationen über Struktur und Organisation des Schweizer Musiklebens. Guide musical suisse: informations sur la structure et l'organisation de la vie musicale suisse. Guide musicale svizzera: informazioni sulla struttura e l'organizzazione della vita svizzera.* 285 pp. Zurich: Atlantis, 1991.

Previously published in 1979 and edited by Hans Steinbeck and published by the Schweizerisches Musik-Archiv in 1983.

11.56 Smith, Julia. *Directory of American Women Composers, with Selected Music for Senior and Junior Clubs.* 51 pp. Chicago, Ill.: National Federation of Music Clubs, 1970.

An alphabetical list of more than 600 composers who have written a wide range of music, giving a then-current address, any special honors, the type of music composed, and the publishers of this music. Addenda give lists of suggested music for senior and junior club programs.

11.57 Sobotka, Mojmir. *Česky hudební adresá / Czech Music Directory: 1991.* 2nd ed. 252 pp. Prague: Vidalo Hudební informacní stredisko, Českého hudebního fondu, 1991.

A directory of music and musicians in the former Czechoslovakia.

11.58* Sommerfeld, Marion. *Handbuch der Musikbibliotheken in Deutschland: Öffentliche und wissenschaftliche Musikbibliotheken sowie Spezialsammlungen mit Musikbibliothekarischen Beständen.* 455 pp. Berlin: Deutsches Bibliotheksinstitut, 1994.

A directory of music libraries in the unified Germany.

11.59 Steinbeck, Hans. "Directory of music information centres." In *Fontes* 26 (1979): 147–59.

An article providing information on each organization including support, publications, agencies, services, and projects.

11.60* Uscher, Nancy. *The Schirmer Guide to Schools of Music and Conservatories throughout the World.* 635 pp. New York: Schirmer Books; London: Collier Macmillan, 1988.

An international descriptive directory of over 750 institutions that train students for the life of a professional musician.

Reviewed by Marion S. Gushee in *Notes* 46 (1989): 85–87 and by Ann P. Basart in *CNV* 129 (1989): 10–11.

11.61* Weerasinghe, Lali, and **Jeremy Silver.** *Directory of Recorded Sound Resources in the United Kingdom.* xxii + 173 pp. London: British Library National Sound Archive, 1989.

GEOGRAPHIC/TRAVEL GUIDES

This geographic/travel guide section is a new one, although some travel guides can be found in the last edition under "Yearbooks and Directories." Because there are many interesting travel guides on a variety of musical subjects, it seemed helpful to the user to group them together. The emphasis is on current information, published from 1980–95, although the Brody–Brook series (**11.68**), from the 1970s, is included for the scope of the information it contains. Guides to popular music are included because of the interest in American civilization and ethnomusicology; another two guides in the following group could greatly help musicians cope with touring. It is now possible to access current information on specific cities or festivals on the World Wide Web to find concert schedules and ticket pricing and purchasing.

11.62* Adams, Richard. *A Book of British Music Festivals.* 224 pp. London: Robert Rouce; Riverdale, Md.: Riverdale, 1986.

A guide covering almost 200 British music festivals. The annotations give a description, history, and several interviews about the festival scene by well-known musical figures; entries often include brief notes on local attractions and interesting photographs. The guide begins with a map and festival calendar and ends with an index and festival addresses. It can be used as a reference for which festivals to visit, or enjoyed as a good armchair read.

Reviewed in *Central Opera* 28 (1988): 72, by Richard Fairman in *Opera* (England) 38 (1988): 140–41, by Ruth Finnegan in *Ethnomusicology* 33 (1989): 530–31, and by Hilary Finch in *MT* 128 (1987): 143.

11.63* Balázs, István. *Musical Guide to Hungary.* 160 pp. Budapest: Corvina, 1992.

A concise travel guide in English, written for tourists interested in the musical scene of the regions of Hungary. It also serves as an overview of Hungarian musical culture. Beginning chapters focus on the history and culture; subsequent chapters focus on current performances in Budapest and regions in Hungary with maps, addresses, telephone numbers, and ticket information.

11.64* Barth, Jack. *Roadside Elvis: The Complete State-by-State Travel Guide for Elvis Presley Fans.* 184 pp. Chicago: Contemporary Books, 1991.

A guide whose title says it all. Arranged by state, then city, this book lists everything it can about Elvis Presley—sites he visited, places that display all manner of memorabilia—all the while relating Elvis trivia. Also listed are addresses of Elvis fan clubs.

Reviewed by John Floyd in *Journal of Country Music* 14 (2/1992): 58–59 and by George Plasketes in *PMS* 16 (1992): 113–14.

11.65* Berman, Leslie, and **Heather Wood.** *Grass Roots: International Folk Resource Directory.* 3rd ed. 384 pp. New York: Tom Doherty Associates, 1993.

First ed. published by Grass Roots Productions, New York, 1985, 198 pp.

A comprehensive directory of information on folk music organizations, festivals, instrument builders, print media, museums, radio, record companies, and venues that lists addresses, phone numbers, time period, and type of music. Also includes a section (21 pp.) of pertinent articles on folk music.

Reviewed by Susan Jurist in *Notes* 42 (June 1986): 782.

11.66* Bernstein, Ken. *Music Lovers' Europe: A Guidebook and Companion.* 202 pp. New York: Scribner's, 1983.

A compilation of fascinating musical information that can easily be enjoyed whether read before, during, or after a trip, listing places of interest (houses, cathedrals, monuments, and museums) while relating interesting stories about the great musicians and composers. The guidebook is arranged alphabetically by country and includes, as appendixes, addresses of national tourist bureaus, glossaries in English, French, Italian, and German, and an index.

11.67* Bird, Christiane. *Jazz and Blues Lover's Guide to the USA, with More than 900 Hot Clubs, Cool Joints, Landmarks, and Legends, from the Boogie-Woogie to Bop and Beyond.* Updated ed. 416 pp. Reading, Mass.: Addison Wesley, 1994.

First ed. published as *The Jazz and Blues Lover's Guide to the U.S.*, 1991, 385 pp.

A guide organized by region, then city, with each chapter divided into two sections: a brief history of jazz and blues in that city, with a list of "landmarks and legends"; and a list of "clubs, etc." with descriptions, hours, and cover charges. The appendix includes a brief history of jazz and blues along with an April–October list of major jazz festivals.

Reviewed by John Anthony Brisbin in *Living Blues* 98 (July/August 1991): 50+ and by Philip Elwood in *Notes* 49 (1992): 631–32.

11.68 Brody, Elaine, and **Claire Brook.** *The Music Guide to Austria and Germany.* 271 pp. New York: Dodd, Mead, 1975.

Brody, Elaine, and **Claire Brook.** *The Music Guide to Belgium, Luxembourg, Holland and Switzerland.* 156 pp. New York: Dodd, Mead, 1977.

Brody, Elaine, and **Claire Brook.** *The Music Guide to Great Britain: England, Scotland, Wales and Ireland.* 240 pp. New York: Dodd, Mead; London: Hale, 1975.

Brody, Elaine, and **Claire Brook.** *The Music Guide to Italy.* 233 pp. New York: Dodd, Mead, 1978.

A series of four travel guides for the musical tourist, scholar, and reference librarian, describing concert halls, opera houses, conservatories, libraries, museums, schools, musical organizations, and musical businesses of the major cities of each country. Also included is information about festivals, competitions, societies, journals, and available services. Addresses, telephone numbers, schedules, and hours of operation are provided.

The Austrian *Guide* is reviewed by Tim Crawford in *Brio* 17 (1980) 28–29, by Stephen M. Fry in *Notes* 32 (1976): 554, and by Robert Jacobson in *ON* 40 (May 1976): 47. The Belgian *Guide* is reviewed by Stephen M. Fry in *Notes* 34 (1978): 619. The *Guide to Great Britain* is reviewed by Stanley Sadie in *MT* 118 (1977): 306 and by Robert Jacobson in *ON* 40 (May 1976): 47. The Italian *Guide* is reviewed in *Music Journal* 37 (January 1979): 47.

11.69* Burton, Gary. *A Musician's Guide to the Road.* 156 pp. New York: Watson-Guptill Publications, 1981.

An excellent guide for musicians on tour. This book gives advice on travel; transporting equipment; where to stay; dealing with agents, managers, and promoters; and credit, loans, and insurance. Included in the appendixes are sample checklists, touring forms (itinerary, cash disbursement report, road manager expense record, personal record, hotel reservation confirmation letter), and sample contracts.

Reviewed in *Music Scene* 321 (September/October 1981): 14.

11.70* Couch, John Philip. *The Opera Lover's Guide to Europe.* 265 pp. New York: Limelight Editions, 1991.

A 2nd ed. anticipated.

A guide based on the premise that exciting opera performances can be found throughout Europe, away from the big tourist centers, for considerably less money than in the well-known centers. Although the big cities are included in the guide, many more smaller cities are listed, with a short history and a wealth of useful information about ticket purchase, seating, prices, opening hours, and public transportation. The organization is by country, then city. Summer festivals, useful addresses, and a currency table are found in the appendixes.

Reviewed in *Classical Music Magazine* 16 (February 1993): 26, by Richard Law in *Opera* (England) 43 (1992): 448, and by Gary Schmidgall in *ON* 55 (March 2 1991): 44.

11.71* Dingle, Jeffrey L. *Essential Radio.* 202 pp. Marblehead, Mass.: Peregrine Press, 1994.

A unique traveler's guide to AM and FM radio stations in the U.S.. The organization is by state, subdivided by city, and includes an individual map for every state. Frequency setting, station call letters, signal strength, whether AM or FM, and station program formats (of the 43 proposed) are given. A second section lists cross-references by station frequency for AM and FM stations.

11.72* Gottesman, Roberta, and **Catherine Sentman.** *The Music Lover's Guide to Europe: A Compendium of Festivals, Concerts, and Opera.* 434 pp. New York: John Wiley & Sons Inc., 1992.

According to the Foreword and Preface, a guide helped by the staff of graduate students from the Peabody Conservatory of Music, which designed detailed questionnaires sent to festivals, opera houses, and concert halls throughout Europe. Listed in the *Guide* are both special festivals and ongoing concert series, compiled from 1,500 festival and concert season brochures. Each geographic chapter begins with a map and a general musical calendar, before descriptions of the individual cities and their concert sites, which include addresses and in-country telephone (and, if available, fax) numbers. Appendixes give a list of the New York offices and European government tourist boards and a list of opera festivals and houses, arranged by country and city. There is a geographic index, by city.

Reviewed by Vroon in *ARG* 559 (1992): 283, by Arthur Lawrence in *American Organist* 27 (April 1993):75, and by Basil Ramsey in *MT* 133 (1992): 348.

11.73 Gusikoff, Lynne. *Guide to Musical America.* 347 pp. New York: Facts on File, 1984.

Not a travel guide per se, but a fascinating history of music in America, also listing historic sites and general information on festivals. The author presents historic highlights of different styles of music as they developed in particular regions of the U.S. and specifies geographic locations where one can hear different styles of music. The organization is by region (with a concise introduction), then by genre. Maps, sources for further reading, and an index are included.

Reviewed by Paula Morgan in *Notes* 41 (1985): 516–17.

11.74* Heintze, James R. *Scholars' Guide to Washington, D.C., for Audio Resources: Sound Recordings in the Arts, Humanities, and Social, Physical, and Life Sciences.* 395 pp. Washington, D.C.: Smithsonian Institution Press, 1985. (Scholar's guide to Washington, D.C., 11)

Published for the Woodrow Wilson International Center for Scholars.

A comprehensive guide to audio resources in Washington, D.C. The first section lists collections in libraries, archives and manuscript repositories, museums and galleries, embassies, religious bodies, services for the disabled, and data banks. Addresses and phone numbers, hours, entrance restrictions, and a list of holdings are all given. Section 2 has organizations categorized as broadcasting organizations, research centers, academic programs and departments, U.S. government agencies, associations and publications, and print media. Again, key information is given for each entry. Practical information is included in the appendixes, which list record stores, recording studios, radio broadcasting stations, audio collections by size, housing and transportation, and federal government holidays. There are indexes by personal name, subject, and organization and institute names.

11.75* Labinsky, Daria, and **Stan Hieronymous.** *Music Festival Directory, 1995–1996: A User's Guide to More than 1,200 Popular Music Festivals.* 69 pp. Washington, Ill.: Music Festival News, 1994.

The 1994 ed. was titled *Music Festival Directory: A User's Guide to More than 1,200 Festivals in the United States and Canada through March 1994, including Blues, Bluegrass, Cajun, Country, Folk, Jazz, Zydeco and More.*

This directory is updated almost monthly (10 issues per year) by *Music Festival News.* Organized by festival type, then date, the short listings provide festival name, site, performers, ticket price, contact person, address, and telephone number. There is an index, with festivals listed by state and town.

11.76* Lebrecht, Norman. *Music in London: A History and Handbook.* 183 pp. London: Aurum Press Limited, 1992.

The original French ed. was published in Arles (Bouches-du-Rhône) by B. Coutaz in 1991 (178 pp.).

An excellent guide to one of the world's musical capitals, with a variety of historical essays (a chronology of music in London since Caesar, pieces inspired by London, and a chapter on opera) as well as practical suggestions for concertgoing and musical sightseeing. There are many illustrations and appendixes, as well as an index.

Reviewed by John-Pierre Joyce in *MT* 133 (1992): 572.

11.77* Lee, Edward. *Musical London.* 192 pp. London: Omnibus Press, 1995.

A collection of guided tours through the City, Westminster, Kensington and Chelsea, Camden, and other areas of interest, with practical information including maps and the times buildings are open. It has a well-organized format.

11.78* Leon, Ruth. *Applause: New York's Guide to the Performing Arts.* 506 pp. New York: Applause Books, 1991.

An excellent guide to theater, concerts, dance, opera, jazz, performance art, and festivals in New York City. It includes performance times, cost, directions by subway and bus, parking information, and amenities such as air conditioning, coatrooms, snack bar, restaurant or bar, wheelchair accessibility, and hearing devices. The guide also includes a section on children's activities, seating plans for many sites, maps, and an index.

Reviewed in *JazzTimes* 23 (1/1993): 45 and in *Variety* 347 (July 20 1992): 79.

11.79* Liebman, Dave. *Guide to the Road for the Touring Musician.* 61 pp. New Albany, Ind.: Jamey Aebersold Jazz, 1994.

Reprinted with permission by *The Saxophone Journal.*

A guide containing excellent advice for musicians on tour, covering business arrangements, travel, hotel accommodations, dealing with promoters and club owners, foreign currency, personal and legal safety, and road etiquette.

11.80* Nolan, A. M. *Rock 'n' Roll Road Trip: The Ultimate Guide to the Sites, the Shrines, and the Legends Across America.* 229 pp. New York: Pharos Books, 1992.

Arranged by region, this book is a guide to the clubs, studios, record stores, and historic spots across America related to rock, blues, and soul. It includes some maps, addresses, much interesting information, and an index.

11.81 Norris, Gerald. *A Musical Gazetteer of Great Britain and Ireland.* 352 pp. Newton Abbot, England; North Pomfret, Vt.: David & Charles, 1981.

Arranged by region, county, and city (or town), a music gazetteer documenting where musicians lived (and died) in the British Isles. The information is usually brief, with an occasional interesting anecdote.

11.82* Pfeffer, Frederic, and **Joelle Heraud.** *Hauts Lieux Musicaux d'Europe.* 572 pp. Paris: Editions Autrement, 1988.

A guide to the major concert halls and festivals of Europe, arranged by country, subdivided by major city, with separate sections for "other places" and "other festivals" under each country. Useful information includes the subway and bus numbers giving access to each hall, as well as the telephone number and business hours of the ticket offices. Seating plans are given for many of the major concert halls. Includes a detailed table of contents (pp. 560–72).

11.83 Rabin, Carol Price. *Music Festivals in America: Classical, Opera, Jazz, Pops, Country, Old-Time Fiddlers, Folk, Bluegrass, Cajun.* 4th ed. 271 pp. Great Barrington, Mass.: Berkshire Traveller Press, 1990.

1st ed. published as *A Guide to Music Festivals in America,* 1979, 199 pp.

Arranged by genre (classical, opera, jazz, ragtime and Dixieland, pops and light classical, folk and traditional, bluegrass, old-time fiddlers, country and Cajun) then by state, a guide covering over 160 festivals in 40 states. Only rock festivals are excluded. Includes historic background and ticket and accommodation information. A section called "Music Festivals by Location," grouping the festivals by region and including a map of each region, is a nice feature. There are also three suggested reading lists and an index.

11.84 Rabin, Carol Price. *Music Festivals in Europe and Britain: Including Israel, Russia, Turkey and Japan.* Revised and enlarged ed. 191 pp. Stockbridge, Mass.: Berkshire Traveller Press, 1984. 1st ed. published 1980, 162 pp.

Listing 110+ festivals in 27 countries, a well-organized guide containing information on the festival site, festival history, sightseeing opportunities, ticket and accommodation information, and dress codes. It includes a list of government tourist offices in New York City, a suggested reading list, and an index.

11.85* Rossi, Nick. *Opera in Italy Today: A Guide.* 420 pp. Portland, Ore.: Amadeus Press, 1995.

An excellent guide to Italy's historic major opera houses and important regional theaters and 10 leading Italian opera festivals, with addresses, and season and ticket information. There are brief histories of each opera company, a discography, and a bibliography (pp. 377–82), with chapters on the La Scala Museum, children's operas, and opportunities for young singers.

Reviewed by Ralph V. Lucano in *Fanfare* 19 (February 1995): 546 and by Nigel Jamieson in *ON* 60 (October 1995): 60.

11.86* Stepaniak, Michael, and **Joanne Stepaniak.** *Folk & Traditional Music Festivals: 1996 Guide for the U.S. & Canada.* 143 pp. Oak Park, Ill.: Shoreline Publishers, 1995.

A current list of some 300 folk and traditional music festivals throughout the U.S. and Canada. Indexed by state and date, the information includes festival history, size, performers, special features, admission fees, festival hours, availability of camping and restaurant facilities, and contact person.

11.87* Stockdale, F. M., and **M. R. Dreyer.** *The International Opera Guide.* 342 pp. North Pomfret, Vt.: Trafalgar Square Publications, 1990.

An informative guide listing, in alphabetical order by city, major opera houses and companies throughout the world. A good historical synopsis is followed by practical information: a small map of the city, a floor plan of the opera house, and addresses, phone and fax numbers, discounts, credit cards accepted, wheelchair space, season dates, seating capacity, refreshment facilities, public transportation information, and parking facilities. Continuing sections list "Additional Opera Houses and Companies," with much less history but all the practical information given above (minus the map and seating chart); festivals; composers and operas (with a good synopsis); and an index.

Reviewed by Norma Jean Lamb in *Notes* 48 (1991): 537–38 and in *OJ* 24 (February 1991): 50.

11.88* Walker, Dave. *American Rock 'n' Roll Tour.* 260 pp. New York: Emeryville, Calif., 1992.

A guide whose author "tours" the U.S., blending a unique history of rock-n-roll with landmarks across the country, including the site of Woodstock, the Buddy Holly crash site (Clear Lake City, Iowa), an Elvis McDonald's (Tupelo, Mississippi), and Sound City Studio (Van Nuys, California), with annotations of who performed, died, or was buried there. This guide is arranged by region, then state and city. If the building is still in existence, a phone number is given.

Reviewed by B. Lee Cooper in *PMS* 16 (1992): 104–6.

11.89* Wignall, Harrison James. *In Mozart's Footsteps.* 353 pp. New York: Paragon House, 1991.

Follow in the footsteps of Mozart from January 1756 to October 1791. This fascinating book chronicles his travels through 9 countries and 69 cities. A brief introduction to each city relates its significance in Mozart's life and work. The author traveled to over 55 cities and collaborated extensively with archivists to update information. A general chronology of Mozart's travels appears at the end of the book, followed by a select bibliography.

Reviewed by Abby Tannenbaum in *MA* 112 (1992): 61–62.

11.90* Wootton, Richard. *Honky Tonkin': A Travel Guide to American Music.* 189 pp. Charlotte, N.C.: East Woods Press, 1980.

An interesting guide to finding clubs, record stores, festivals, and radio stations across America where blues, modern country music, rock, Cajun, and Tex–Mex music can be found. Organization is sometimes by city, sometimes by state, sometimes regional, but each section begins with pertinent information for the area. The guide ends with lists of radio stations, small record labels, festivals (listed by month), and the best magazines and newspapers for this music. This source brings together a lot of good information not easily found in one place.

Reviewed by TR in *Old Time Music* 30 (Autumn 1978): 30 and by B. Lee Cooper in *PMS* 16 (1992): 104–6.

11.91* Zeitz, Karyl Lynn. *Opera!: The Guide to Western Europe's Great Houses.* 287 pp. Santa Fe, N.M.: John Muir Publications; New York: W.W. Norton, 1991.

Organized by country, then city, with each listing giving a historic overview on 92 houses (background, theaters, performance history), followed by practical information (ticket information, including box office addresses and hours, a ticket table and seating plan, an English translation of a ticket, transportation and travel information, and opera schedule). This valuable and comprehensive resource is useful as a traveler's guide as well as an excellent book on the architectural and performance history of the great opera houses.

Reviewed by Walter Price in *ON* 56 (December 7 1991): 66 and by Richard Law in *Opera* (England) 46 (November 1995): 1,372.

12

ELECTRONIC INFORMATION RESOURCES

This chapter, newly organized and including a number of familiar titles, is a selection of what is currently the most rapidly evolving format of music reference works. Its contents start with the first major cataloging databases and move through other general, nonmusic databases to those concentrating on music topics. As an example of the variety of music venues available through the Internet, a list of music-connected home pages and their addresses as of August 1996 is given; the addresses may have changed numerous times since this volume's publication. The final section lists printed reference works supporting the computer applications and online services in music research.

GENERAL/NONMUSIC DATABASES AND CD-ROMS

These sources, though not strictly music reference works, are a sampling of many general works including data that gives the researcher convenient access to music information. They include the two major cataloging utilities (**12.1** and **12.2**) that contain many general works as well as music books, scores, and sound recordings.

12.1 *OCLC.* 1971– . Online Computer Library Center, Inc.

The first of the online bibliographic utilities in the United States. OCLC currently connects over 3,000 libraries, mostly American but including some European and Japanese libraries, to an immense bibliographic database in Dublin, Ohio, a suburb of Columbus. Among the important music libraries that have contributed to the OCLC database are those at the University of California at Los Angeles, Eastman School of Music, Florida State University, University of Illinois at Champaign/Urbana, Indiana University, the University of Maryland, the Newberry Library, the University of North Carolina at Chapel Hill, Oberlin Conservatory, the University of Texas at Austin, and the University of North Texas.

Although cataloging on OCLC began in 1971, numerous retrospective conversion projects have been undertaken, so the database is extraordinarily rich in music imprints of all periods. Current cataloging from the Library of Congress is loaded into the database on a regular basis. Over 34 million works are represented by bibliographic records in the database. OCLC policy is to store a single bibliographic record and to add sigla indicating which libraries hold the item in question. It is not possible to discern how the catalog of an individual library reads through the OCLC database unless the item sought is held by only one library. A few libraries have been given "enhance" status for separate and specific types of materials (books, for example), enabling them to permanently correct the main OCLC database in that format. Catalog records for scores, sound recordings, books, microforms, video discs and tapes, and other library materials are included in the database. Access to bibliographic records in the OCLC database is given through the use of truncated versions of author/composer names or titles and is made using a library staff member as an intermediary. In the past few years, there has also been access to the database through FirstSearch, which provides the public direct use of the OCLC database by author, title, or subject through the Worldcat access, so that librarians are no longer needed as intermediaries. Access to information on an individual library's holdings is also provided by the database and assists in interlibrary loan transactions, for which the service of a library employee is required. Millions of these transactions are handled each year. In the past few years the OCLC database has displayed the holdings of some RLIN libraries (see **12.2**), such as Harvard University and New York Public Library.

A number of articles on the OCLC database have been written, among them "Music in the OCLC Online Union Catalog: A Review," by Richard P. Smiraglia and Ralph R. Papakhian in *Notes* 38 (1981): 257–74 and 968. Music librarians have formed a music OCLC users group (called MOUG), and regularly publish the *Music OCLC Users Group Newsletter,* as well as holding an annual meeting.

12.2 *Research Librarians Information Network (RLIN).*

The online bibliographic service of the Research Libraries Group, a partnership of about 40 major American libraries. Among the important music libraries contributing to RLIN are those at the University of California at Berkeley, Brown University, the State University of New York at Buffalo, Cornell University, Harvard University, the University of Michigan, New York Public Library, Peabody Conservatory, Stanford University, and Yale University. Current cataloging from the Library of Congress is loaded into the database on a regular basis. The database is rich in music imprints of all periods, thanks to numerous retrospective conversion projects.

In the RLIN database each library's catalog records are stored uniquely, a contrast to OCLC's approach. Cataloging records are clustered in most of the files around a single version of the record. The database is segmented by format, with separate files for scores, sound recordings, serials, books, and so forth. There is no way of knowing how many of the cataloging records in the books file are related to books about music, but one must remember that RLIN repeats every repetition of a bibliographic record, so the number of unique records is considerably smaller than the total would indicate.

Access to the RLIN database is possible through personal and corporate names, title phrases, word in titles, and subject phrases. Names, words, and phrases may be truncated. Indexes may be combined using the Boolean operators *and, or, &,* and *and not.* Once a search on any of these indexes has been accomplished, it can be further modified by date or range of dates of imprint, by publisher, by language, by place of publication, by words in subject phrases, and by the holdings of a specific library.

The RLIN database is driven not only by the desire to share cataloging information among the partner libraries and the other libraries the network serves, but also by the programs of the various standing and special committees of the Research Libraries Group, of which the Music Program Committee was one. Interlibrary loan is a particularly effective service to users of the network.

❧

12.3* *Arts & Humanities Search.* 1 datafile. Philadelphia, Pa.: Institute for Scientific Information.

A machine-readable file of over 1.4 million records from 1980 to the present, updated weekly. Coverage includes citations to articles, letters, editorials, meeting abstracts, errata, poems, short stories, plays, music scores, excerpts from books, chronologies, bibliographies and filmographies, and citations to reviews of books, films, music, and theatrical performances that are published in the covered journals. The Institute for Scientific Information adds implicit citations whenever creative works are the subject of articles but are not formally cited; implicit citations may be added for material such as paintings, musical compositions, literary works, and films and records, as well as dance, music, and theatrical performances. This international multidisciplinary database (Dialog file 439) corresponds to the printed publication *Arts & Humanities*

Citation Index (**4.96**). The database covers 1,100 of the world's leading arts and humanities journals, plus 5,000 relevant social and natural science journals, and has additional records from the Current Contents series of publications.

12.4* *Dissertation Abstracts Online: A Firstsearch Database.* Ann Arbor, Mich.: Dissertation Publishing, 1986– .

A database giving access to information on the dissertations and theses or lists of dissertations and theses submitted by individual degree-granting institutions (or, occasionally, lists of dissertations and theses completed) to University Microfilms International (UMI). Citations for these dissertations are included in the database and in UMI printed publications such as *Dissertation Abstracts International* and *Masters Abstracts.* A list of cooperating institutions can be found in the preface to any volume of *Comprehensive Dissertation Index* or *Masters Abstracts.* *Dissertation Abstracts Online* provides subject, title, and author access to approximately 99% of all American dissertations accepted at accredited institutions since 1861, when academic degrees were first granted in the United States. Master's theses have been selectively indexed since 1962. Abstracts are included for doctoral dissertation records from July 1980 to the present. In addition, the database serves to disseminate citations for thousands of Canadian dissertations and an increasing number of papers accepted in institutions abroad. Professional and honorary degrees are not included. See also **12.21.**

12.5* *Internationaler biographischer Index / World Biographical Index.* CD-ROM. Munich: K.G. Saur, 1995.

An index to over 1 million names in six biographical archives compiled by Saur: German; American; French; Italian; Spanish, Portuguese, and Latin American; and British. Each entry is listed alphabetically by name, pseudonym, and name variant, birth and death dates, profession, biographical sources, originating biographical archive, and fiche and frame number in the original biographical archive. The six complete biographical archives have also been mined for musicians' entries, with the results now available in a 2-vol. (xl + 792 pp.) reference work, *Internationaler biographischer Index der Musik: Komponisten, Dirigenten, Instrumentalisten, und Sänger / World Biographical Index of Music: Composers, Conductors, Instrumentalists, and Singers* (**1.258**) (Munich: K.G. Saur, 1995).

MUSIC DATABASES AND CD-ROMS

12.6* *Billboard/Phonolog Music Reference Library on CD-ROM.* 1 CD-ROM. New York: BPI Communications, 1992– . Updated quarterly.

An electronic version of *Phonolog Reporter* (**10.221**), with electronic access to over 100,000 recorded song titles, able to be searched by any combination of song title, album title, label, artist/group, and guest artist for popular music, and, in addition, composer, conductor, orchestra, or instrument for classical music.

12.7* *CPM [Catalogue of Printed Music] Plus to 1990.* 1 computer optical laser disc, with machine-readable data. London: Bowker-Saur, 1993.

Provides access to all data from the British Music Library, previously published in *The Catalogue of Printed Music in the British Library to 1980* (*CPM*) (**7.258**), unpublished records from the *CPM* supplement, and the *Current Music Catalogue* to 1990.

Access to the music collection of the British Library through title, composer, keyword, arranger, place and date of publication, publisher, forces, voices, and language. The *CPM* in printed format could be searched only by composer or song title.

12.8* *International Index to Music Periodicals.* 1 CD-ROM. Alexandria, Va.: Chadwyck-Healey, 1996– .

From the former publisher of *Music Index* on CD-ROM, intended to provide easy access to

30,000 articles published in more than 400 scholarly journals on music from more than 30 countries. The indexed articles can be approached by author, title, publication, publisher, country of publication, date of publication, language, article type, broad subject headings, and thousands of subject terms including concepts, personalities, locations, and organizations. At the time of its initial release, there were 6,461 articles indexed from approximately 220 journals.

12.9* *MUSE: MUsic SEarch: RILM Abstracts of Music Literature 1969–1991 and Library of Congress Music Catalog 1960s-1993.* 1 CD-ROM. Baltimore, Md.: National Information Services Corporation, 1984– . Updated annually (cumulative).

A source providing electronic access to the *RILM Abstracts* (**4.90**) (previously available through online searching on Dialog). At present, MUSE does not include the years 1967–68 of the *Abstracts,* nor 1992 and beyond. MUSE also provides access to materials in the Library of Congress's *Music, Books on Music and Sound Recordings* (**5.22**) from the 1960s through 1993.

12.10* *The Music Catalog.* 1 CD-ROM. Washington, D.C.: Library of Congress, 1994–96.
Updated semiannually (cumulative).

A source containing all music-related records from the LC database of verified U.S. MARC records (**5.22**) (155,562), records describing the Albert Schatz Collection of Opera Librettos (11,380 records), and LC PreMARC records for opera librettos, scores, and sound recordings (30,000).

12.11* *Music Index on CD-ROM: A Guide to Music Periodical Literature.* Alexandria, Va.: Harmonie Park Press; Chadwyck-Healey, 1993.
Annual update, each disc being cumulative, of a comprehensive subject/author guide to music periodical literature.

The electronic version of the *Music Index* (**4.89**), able to be searched by authors of articles and books as well as topical headings and subheadings. Each element of the bibliographic entries is accessible by headings, fields, or full text keyword, individually or in combination. Currently the database extends from 1979 to 1993.

12.12* *MUZE: The Ultimate Mind for Music.* 1 CD ROM. New York: Muze, Inc., 1994– .
Updated quarterly.
Previously published by Ebsco Publishers, Peabody, Mass., 1992–94.

A source providing information on 100,000 CDs, cassettes, and music videos representing more than 666,000 individual songs and musical works, giving performers, durations, and release dates, including biographies of major classical composers, conductors, and soloists, as well as popular and jazz performers.

12.13* *RILM Abstracts.* 1 data file. Dublin, Ohio: OCLC FirstSearch, 1996– .
A database that corresponds to the printed *Répertoire International de Littérature Musicale* (**4.90**). RILM has about 200,000 items in its electronic database, starting with the RILM printed year of 1969. RILM records cover all aspects of music, including historical musicology, ethnomusicology, instruments and voice, dance, and music therapy. It also includes various other fields as they relate to music, including librarianship, literature, dramatic arts, visual arts, anthropology, sociology, philosophy, and physics. RILM offers citations in 202 languages, including original language title, title translations in English, full bibliographic information, abstracts in English, and in-depth subject indexes. All formats of scholarly works are included: articles, books, bibliographies, catalogs, dissertations, films and videos, conference proceedings, and more. Concert reviews, recording notes, and pedagogical manuals are also included if they are of scholarly interest.

12.14 *RISM Series A/II Music Manuscripts after 1600 / Musikhandschriften nach 1600 / Manuscrits musicaux postérieurs à 1600.* 1 CD-ROM. Munich: Saur Verlag, 1994.
A database containing complete descriptions of each manuscript indexed in *RISM* series

A/II. This series was originally conceived as a successor to Eitner's *Quellen-Lexikon* (**5.544**), and sought to inventory music manuscripts of the period 1600–1800. The closing date for relevance to the series has now been left open, however, allowing individual national groups contributing to *RISM* to inventory 19th- and 20th-century documents as well. The first release in December 1995 included more than 160,000 bibliographic records, representing 416 libraries and more than 8,000 composers. Some 20,000–50,000 new records are expected to be added with each annual update.

INTERNET MUSIC DATABASE AND ONLINE PROJECTS

12.15* *Archive of World Music.* (Harvard University) Virginia Danielson, curator. [http://www.rism.harvard.edu/MusicLibrary/AWM/AWM.html]

A database maintained by the Archive, devoted to collecting commercial and field recordings of ethnic and folk musics, with a special emphasis on the musics of Asia and the Middle East. It also has substantial holdings of Anglo-American ballads and songs.

12.16* *Archives of African American Music and Culture.* (Indiana University) Portia K. Maultsby, director. [http://www.indiana.edu/~aaamc/index.html]

A source whose collections include audio and video recordings, photographs, original scores, and oral histories, among other artifacts and ephemera related to popular, religious, and art musics and Black radio. The Archives conducts collaborative research with such units as the Afro-American Arts Institute and the Archives of Traditional Music at Indiana University, the Smithsonian Institution, and the Rhythm and Blues Foundation.

12.17* *Beethoven Bibliography Database.* (San Jose [California] State University) William R. Meredith and Patricia Elliott, administrators. [http://www.music.sjsu.edu/Beethoven/home_page.html]

A fully indexed bibliography of published material relating to Ludwig van Beethoven. The database currently includes books, articles, and first and early editions of scores from the Beethoven Center's collection. The database is a primary project of the Ira F. Brilliant Center for Beethoven Studies at San Jose State University and is funded by the University, the National Endowment for the Humanities, the American Beethoven Society, Ira F. Brilliant, the Eva B. Buck Trust, and other sources; the Center also publishes the *Beethoven Newsletter.*

If asked to LOGON, type *lib* and hit ENTER twice. Otherwise, from the menu display, select "Choose another database," then choose "Beethoven Bibliography Database."

12.18* *CAIRSS for MUSIC: Database of Music Resources.* (University of Texas, San Antonio) Charles T. Eagle, Jr., editor, Department of Music Therapy: Medicine & Health, SMU, and Donald Hodges, director, Institute for Music Research, UTSA. San Antonio, Tex.: Institute for Music Research (Donald A. Hodges, director), University of Texas at San Antonio, 1993– . [telnet://UTSAIBM.UTSA.EDU]

A joint venture between faculty and staff at UTSA and Southern Methodist University. The Computer-Assisted Information Retrieval Service System is a bibliographic database of music research literature emphasizing music education, music therapy, music psychology, and medicine. Currently there are 15 primary journals in these areas that are completely indexed, as well as selected articles from over 1,200 secondary journals that are also in the database.

At TS> !VT100,3278, press RETURN. At the UTSA screen, type *LIBRARY,* select *LOCAL,* then select *CMUS.*

12.19* *CANTUS: Database of Chants for the Divine Service.* (Catholic University) [http://www.cua.edu/www/musu/cantus/]

A database placed at the disposal of colleagues in accordance with the aims of the International Musicological Society Study Group Cantus Planus, which promotes cooperation in computer-assisted projects and the exchange of data in electronic form.

12.20* *The Centre for the History and Analysis of Recorded Music.* (University of Southampton) Mary Callaghan, Project Administrator. [http://www.soton.ac.uk/~musicbox/charm1.html]

A database based on the work of the Centre for the History and Analysis of Recorded Music (CHARM), established in fall 1995 at the University of Southampton following the acquisition of the Norman del Mar Collection of 78-rpm records. Through its archives, journal, conferences, and discography project, CHARM aims to promote the study of musical sound. Research activity at CHARM ranges from the creation of analytical tools and software to new critical approaches that highlight the importance of performance in musical culture.

12.21 *Doctoral Dissertations in Musicology.* (Indiana University) Administered by Thomas J. Mathiesen, with Nicholas Butler. [http;/www.music.indiana.edu/ddm/]

A browsable, searchable database beginning its public use September 2 1996, planned eventually to contain all the holdings listed in the printed edition (**4.136**).

12.22* *Encyclopedia of African Music: Music from Africa and the African Diaspora.* Copyright 1995, 1996 Janet Planet. [http://matisse.net/~jplanet/afmx/ahome.htm]

A compilation of Internet resources highlighting many aspects of African music.

12.23* *Folkways/Smithsonian Database.*
[http://www.si.edu/organiza/offices/folklife/database/start/start.htm]

A database maintained by the Center for Folklife Programs and Cultural Studies, Smithsonian Institution, containing over 30,000 individual songs from several thousand albums from the original Folkways/Collection, Smithsonian/Folkways, Paredon, and Cook Labels. These web pages allow the user dynamically to search the database for album or song title, year recorded, source (label), and keyword, including instrument and genre, as well as ethnic, national, and geographic attributes.

12.24* *Gaylord Music Library Necrology File.* (Washington University) Maintained by Nathan Eakin. [http://library.wustl.edu/~music/necro/]

A datafile started in 1991, recording information from the media as received in the library, including the "Obituary Index" (**1.86**) that appears annually in *Notes,* the journal of the Music Library Association.

*12.25 *Gilbert and Sullivan Collection.* (Pierpont Morgan Library, New York)
[http://www.nyu.edu/pages/curator/gs/] [212-685-0008]

A home page organized to describe the Gilbert and Sullivan Collection of the Morgan Library, the largest and most comprehensive collection devoted to Victorian composer Sir Arthur Seymour Sullivan (1842–1900) and to his collaborator, dramatist Sir William Schwenck Gilbert (1836–1911). See also **6.342.**

12.26* *The Golden Pages: University Music Departments' and Faculties' Home Pages.* (University of London, Royal Holloway) Maintained by Geoffrey Chew.
[http://www.sun.rhbnc.ac.uk/Music/Links/musdepts.html]

This page aims to include WWW addresses (http or gopher) of all music departments in higher education. Not all institutions listed here necessarily offer full academic courses in music; they are included if they maintain separate home pages for their music departments.

12.27* *International Alliance for Women in Music.* [http://music.acu.edu/www/iawm/home.html]

A resource on women composers and women-in-music topics.

12.28* *Italian Music Homepage.* Maintained by Massimo Gentili-Tedeschi.
[http://icl382.cilea.it/music/entrance.htm]

A directory of institutional lists including university, theater, and school music libraries, catalogs, associations, information centers, cities, periodicals, and personal lists of librarians and musicologists. Also included are manuals of terms for musical forms and instruments, and information on such musical events as exhibitions, conferences, and concerts.

12.29* *Latin American Music Center.* (Indiana University) Dr. Carmen Téllez, Director. [http://www.music.indiana.edu/som/lamc/]

A home page for the library of the Latin American Music Center, perhaps the most complete collection of Latin American art music in the world. The collection includes rare manuscripts and published scores, records and books, anthologies of colonial music, photographs of musicians, periodicals microfilms, and miscellaneous documents. Guillermo Espinosa's lifetime collection was recently bequeathed to Indiana University; he served as the founder and director of the Inter-American music festivals held from the late 1950s to 1982 at the Kennedy Center for the Performing Arts, Washington, D.C.

12.30* *Libretto Home Page.* Maintained by Lyle Neff. [http://copper.ucs.indiana.edu/~lneff/libretti.html]

An online source for opera and oratorio libretti in the original languages, in the public domain.

12.31* *Lieder and Songs: Texts.* Maintained by Emily Ezust. [http://www.recmusic.org/lieder/]

An online source for public-domain texts.

12.32* *Lully Web Project.* (University of North Texas) Maintained by Dorothy Keyser. [http://www.library.unt.edu:80/projects/lully/lullyhom html]

Conceived both as a multimedia thematic catalog of the UNT Music Library collection of first and second eds. of theatrical works by French baroque composer Jean-Baptiste Lully, and as a nucleus for collecting information useful to anyone studying those works.

12.33* *Music and Brain Information Database.* [telnet://mila.ps.uci.edu]

The Music and Brain Information Database (MBI) is funded by a startup grant from the National Association of Music Merchants. Its goal is to establish a comprehensive database of scientific research (reference and abstracts) on music as related to behavior, the brain, and allied fields, in order to foster interdisciplinary knowledge. Topics included are the auditory system, human and animal behavior, creativity, the human brain, the neuropsychology of music, effects of music on behavior and physiology, music education, medicine, performance, music therapy, neurobiology, perception, and psychophysics.

[LOGON: mbi PASSWORD: nammbi]

12.34* *Polish Music Reference Center.* (University of Southern California) Wanda Wilk, the PRMC director. [http://www.usc.edu/go/polish_music/]

A home page describing a unique and important resource on music of Polish origin, including more than 10,000 titles (books, scores, recordings, articles, and journals) on Polish classical, folk, and jazz music.

12.35* *Renaissance Liturgical Imprints.* (University of Michigan) David Crawford, director. [http://www-personal.umich.edu/~davidcr]

RELICS, a database of information about worship books printed before 1601, now including information on 8,890+ titles. This information is based on personal inspections of books in most of the major research libraries of the United States, as well as libraries in a few selected European cities. Some additional information derives from published bibliographies and library catalogs. The project is in progress, and corrections and additional information are solicited.

12.36* *RISM WWW Home Page.* (U.S. *RISM* Office, Harvard University) [http://rism.harvard.edu/rism/]

RISM's home page is a worldwide effort to identify and describe sources of music and writings about music from the earliest times through c. 1825. The *RISM* home page is a joint production of the *RISM* Zentralredaktion at Frankfurt am Main, Germany, and the U.S. *RISM* Office at Harvard University, Cambridge, Mass. Plans have been formed to make the *RISM* A/II database available via the Internet.

12.37* *Thesaurus Musicarum Italicarum.* (Utrecht University) Dr. Frans Wiering, project director. [http://candl.let.ruu.nl/Research/tmi/main.html]
Located at the Department of Computers and Humanities of Utrecht University, a database that recently initiated a project to publish a number of 16th- and early-17th-century music treatises in Italian on CD-ROM.

12.38* *Thesaurus Musicarum Latinarum: TML: Canon of Data Files: Including General Information on the Thesaurus Musicarum Latinarum, the TML Introduction, The Principles of Orthography, and the Table of Codes.* 6th ed. Bloomington, Ind.: Thesaurus Musicarum Latinarum, School of Music, Indiana University, 1995. Project director: Thomas J. Mathiesen. [gopher://iubvm.ucs.indiana.edu/qq/tml/]]
The *TML* is an evolving database that will eventually contain the entire corpus of Latin music theory written during the middle ages and the early renaissance (**4.387**). This home page is currently available as data files through *TML*.

12.39* *Kurt Weill Foundation.* (New York City) [http://www.kwf.org/]
As a combination library, manuscript repository, and media center, the Kurt Weill and Lotte Lenya Research Center holds original documents and recordings as well as reproductions of materials held in public or private collections worldwide. See also **6.387**.

MUSIC ASSOCIATION AND SOCIETY HOME PAGES

12.40* The following examples were selected to show the variety of music-related home pages available on the World Wide Web. Addresses (URLs) often change as sponsors and their electronic access move.
American Choral Directors Association [http://rattler.cameron.edu:80/ACDA/]
American Federation of Musicians [http://www.afm.org/]
The American Music Network (Sonneck Society) [http://aaln.org/sonneck/]
AMS (American Musicological Society)
[http://musdra.ucdavis.edu/Documents/AMS/AMS.html]
ASCAP (American Society of Composers, Authors, and Publishers)
[http://www.ascap.com/ascap.html]
Association for the Advancement of Creative Musicians, Inc.
[http://csmaclab-www.cs.uchicago.edu/AACM/GreatBlackMusic.html]
BMI (Broadcast Music, Inc.) [http://bmi.com/]
College Music Society [http://www.music.org/]
Institute of Jazz Studies (Rutgers University) [http://www.rci.rutgers.edu/~schwart/jazz.htm]
Indiana University Worldwide Internet Music Resources
[http://www.music.indiana.edu/music_resources]
MENC (Music Educators National Conference) [http://www.menc.org/]
MLA Clearinghouse (Music Library Association)
[http://www.music.indiana.edu/tech_s/mla/index.htm]
Music Educator's Home Page [athena.athenet.net/nwslow/index.html]
Music Publishers' Association [http://www.mpa.org/]
National Music Publishers Association [http://www.nmpa.org/nmpa.html]
Plainsong and Mediaeval Music Society [http://www.ncl.ac.uk/~nip2/]
Rock & Roll Hall of Fame [http://www.rockhall.com/]
Society for Electro-Acoustic Music in the United States [http://comp.music.lsu.edu/seamus/]
SMT (Society for Music Theory) [http://boethius.music.ucsb.edu/smt-list/smthome.html]
Society for 17th Century Music [http://rism.harvard.edu/sscm/]

PRINT SOURCES

12.41 Davis, Deta S. *Computer Applications in Music: A Bibliography.* 537 pp. Madison, Wisc.: A-R Editions, 1988. (The computer music and digital audio series, 4)

Supplement I. 597 pp. Madison, Wisc.: A-R Editions, 1993. (The computer music and digital audio series, 10)

A comprehensive list of works on computer applications in music. The 1st vol. lists 4,585 entries in 25 chapters (including chapters on aesthetics, composition, music printing and transcription, musical instruments, musicology and analytic applications, and sound generation for music hardware). The *Supplement* has 4,287 items in 36 chapters.

Reviewed by Eleanor Selfridge-Field in *Notes* 50 (1994): 1,019–21, by Robert Skinner in *JMR* 12 (1992): 142–45, and by Ann P. Basart in *Fontes* 36 (1989): 65–66, answered by the author in *Fontes* 36 (1989): 2.

12.42* Ehn, Hope. *On-Line Resources for Classical and Academic Musicians: A Guide through the Wilds of the Internet: Newsgroups, Mailing Lists, and Other Resources for Early Music, Classical Music, Musicology, Music Theory, and Ethnomusicology, with a Guide to Basic List-Serve Commands for Subscribing to Mailing Lists and to Getting Files by E-Mail.* 40 pp. Newton Centre, Mass.: The author, 1994.

12.43* Greenman, Ben. *Net Music: Your Complete Guide to Rock and More on the Internet and Online Services.* 393 pp. New York: Random House Electronic Publishing; Michael Wolff & Co., 1995.

A directory of computer network resources, concentrating on means of connecting on the Internet with current popular musicians.

12.44 Hewlett, Walter, and **Eleanor Selfridge-Field.** *Computing in Musicology: A Directory of Research, 1989–* . Menlo Park, Calif.: Center for Computer Assisted Research in the Humanities, 1989– .

Earlier issues (1985–88) published as *Directory of Computer Assisted Research in Musicology, 1985–88.* 4 vols.

An annual publication with a section devoted to brief notices on activities and studies pertaining to computer-assisted musicology. Current applications are categorized and described in some detail. Includes a short bibliography of recent literature and a list of names cited in the directory.

The first issue is reviewed by Richard Koprowski in *Notes* 42 (1986): 364–65. The issues of 1988–90 are reviewed by Craig Lister in *Notes* 48 (1991): 132–33. Vol. 7 (1991) is reviewed by Alan Green in *Fontes* 40 (1993): 269–71.

12.45* Hill, Brad. *Midi for Musicians: Buying, Installing and Using Today's Electronic Music Making Equipment.* 200 pp. Pennington: A Capella Books, 1994.

Written for laymen in nontechnical prose.

12.46 Lister, Craig. *The Musical Microcomputer: A Resource Guide.* 172 pp. New York: Garland, 1988.

12.47* Rothstein, Joseph. *MIDI: A Comprehensive Introduction.* 268 pp. Madison, Wisc.: A-R Editions, 1995. (The computer and digital audio series, 7)

First ed., 1992, 226 pp.

12.48* Skinner, Robert. "Microcomputers in the Music Library." In *Notes* 45 (1988): 7–14.

A study of issues and trends in dealing with the microcomputer and its software in the music library.

12.49* Troutman, Leslie. "An Internet Primer for Music Librarians: Tools, Sources, Current Awareness." In *Notes* 51 (1994): 22–41.

12.50* Waters, William J. *Music and the Personal Computer: An Annotated Bibliography.* 175 pp. New York: Greenwood Press, 1989. (Music reference collection, 22)

A comprehensive bibliography of 1,294 entries that discuss uses for the microcomputer in the world of music.

Reviewed by Richard McQuillan in *Notes* 47 (1991): 806–8.

13

BIBLIOGRAPHY, THE MUSIC BUSINESS, AND LIBRARY SCIENCE

STUDIES IN MUSIC BIBLIOGRAPHY

13.1 Coover, James B. "The Current Status of Music Bibliography." In *Notes* 13 (1956): 581–93.
A survey of the accomplishments, progress, and lacunae in music bibliography in 1956. The paper takes its point of departure from A. Hyatt King's statement in *Library* (1945) (**13.9**).

13.2 Deutsch, Otto Erich. "Music Bibliography and Catalogues." In *Library* 23 (1943): 151–70.
An article on the importance to music bibliographers and scholars for library and other catalogers to include more information rather than less in entries. The confusion arising from varying numbering schemes for important composers' works is discussed, as is the utility of publishers' plate numbers and the variety of printing techniques used to reproduce music. It concludes with a short bibliography. Overall, this is a description of the state of music bibliography and music cataloging of the time.

13.3 Duckles, Vincent H. "Music Literature, Music, and Sound Recordings." In *Bibliography, Current State and Future Trends,* pp. 158–83. Edited by Robert B. Downs and Frances B. Jenkins. Urbana, Ill.: University of Illinois Press, 1967.
First published in *Library Trends,* January 1967.

13.4* Heck, Thomas F., Timothy Cherubini, and **Sean Ferguson.** "Anything Goes?: Issues in the Bibliographic Quality Control of Music Theses and Dissertations." In *The "Music Information Explosion" and Its Implications for College Teachers and Students* (**13.50**), pp. 56–71. Missoula, Mont.: College Music Society, 1992.
An evaluation of the bibliographic research supporting 30 recent graduate theses in music, showing that in some cases even basic reference works seem not to have been consulted to make the desired contribution to advanced work.

13.5 Hoboken, Anthony van. "Probleme der musikbibliographischen Terminologie." In *Fontes* (1958): 6–15 no. 1.
A discussion centered on the difficulties of establishing music bibliography as an "exact science" in view of the variety and complexity of the materials with which it is concerned.

13.6 Hopkinson, Cecil. "The Fundamentals of Music Bibliography." In *Fontes* (1955): 122–31 no. 2.
An attempt to stimulate discussion of some basic points as to the nature, content, and procedures of music bibliography as it serves the needs of collectors, musicians, and historians.

13.7* Hunter, David. "Two Half-Centuries of Music Bibliography." In *Notes* 50 (1994): 23–38.
A pithy description of the last 50 years in music bibliography, followed by informed delineation of needs to be met in the next 50 years.

13.8* Hunter, David, et al. "Music Library Association Guidelines for the Preparation of Music Reference Works." In *Notes* 50 (1994): 1,329–38.

The work of the Subcommittee on Bibliographic Standards for Reference Works, Reference and Public Service Committee, Music Library Association, intended as guidelines for authors, editors, and publishers.

13.9 King, A. Hyatt. "Recent Work in Music Bibliography." In *Library* 26 (September–December 1945): 99–148.

A survey of the accomplishments in music bibliography during the period just before and during World War II.

13.10 Krohn, Ernst C. "The Bibliography of Music." In *MQ* 5 (1919): 231–54.

One of the first surveys of the state of music bibliography by an American scholar, useful as a statement of the accomplishments in the field at the time of writing. In a narrative style, with incomplete citations.

13.11 Krummel, Donald W. "Bibliography of Music." In *The New Grove Dictionary of Music and Musicians* (**1.48**).

An article divided into three sections: analytical and descriptive bibliography, reference bibliography, and history of music bibliography. This article provides an overview of the subject and mentions some of the principal sources. It is particularly helpful in placing music bibliography in the context of general bibliography and in a historical perspective. There is an excellent classified bibliography, with numerous references to related articles.

13.12 Luther, Wilhelm-Martin. "Bibliographie." In *MGG* (**1.9**).

A recounting of the history and a surveying of the concepts of music bibliography, with an extensive list of titles pertaining to the field.

FESTSCHRIFTS

The past decade has witnessed the publication of a number of Festschrifts celebrating the careers and achievements of prominent music librarians and scholars of music bibliography. Most of these collections have a number of essays covering topics of music bibliography and librarianship.

Hill, Richard S.

13.13 Bradley, Carol June, and **James B. Coover.** *Richard S. Hill: Tributes from Friends.* 397 pp. Detroit, Mich.: Information Coordinators, 1987. (Detroit studies in music bibliography, 58)

Reviewed by James J. Fuld in *AM* 6 (1988): 471–73 and by Thomas Heck in *Fontes* 36 (1989): 240–42.

King, Alec Hyatt

13.14 Abraham, Gerald, and **Oliver Neighbour.** *Music and Bibliography: Essays in Honor of Alec Hyatt King.* 256 pp. New York: K.G. Saur/C. Bingley, 1980.

Includes "Problems in Teaching the Bibliography of Music" by Brian Redfern.
Reviewed by Susan T. Sommer in *Notes* 37 (1981): 580–81.

Krummel, Donald W.

13.15* Hunter, David. *Music Publishing and Collecting: Essays in Honor of Donald W. Krummel.* 252 pp. Urbana, Ill.: Graduate School of Library and Information Science, University of Illinois at Urbana-Champaign, 1994.

Reviewed by Peter Ward Jones in *Notes* 52 (1996): 794–96.

Neighbour, Oliver W.

13.16* Banks, Chris, Arthur Searle, and **Malcolm Turner.** *Sundry Sorts of Music Books: Essays on the British Library Collections: Presented to O. W. Neighbour on his 70th Birthday.* 400 pp. London: British Library, 1993.

Smith, Carleton Sprague

13.17* Katz, Israel J., Marlena Kuss, and **Richard J. Wolfe.** *Libraries, History, Diplomacy and the Performing Arts: Essays in Honor of Carleton Sprague Smith.* 459 pp. Stuyvesant, N.Y.: Pendragon Press, in cooperation with New York Public Library, 1991. (Festschrift series, 9)
    Reviewed by Calvin Elliker in *Fontes* 40 (1993): 265–68.

Watanabe, Ruth

13.18* Mann, Alfred. *Modern Music Librarianship: Essays in Honor of Ruth Watanabe.* 252 pp. Stuyvesant, N.Y.: Pendragon Press; Kassel, Germany: Bärenreiter-Verlag, 1989. (Festschrift series, 8)
    Reviewed by John Druesedow in *Fontes* 38 (1991): 146–57 and by Neil Ratliff in *Notes* 47 (1991): 722–24.

CONFERENCE REPORTS

13.19* Green, Richard D. *Foundations of Music Bibliography.* xxi + 398 pp. New York: Haworth Press, Inc., 1994.
    From a 1986 conference on music bibliography at Northwestern University.

13.20* Ochs, Michael. *Music Librarianship in America.* 144 pp. Cambridge, Mass.: Eda Kuhn Music Library, Harvard University, 1991.
    Reviewed by John Druesedow in *Fontes* 39 (1992): 377–78.
    Reviewed by Linda Solow Blotner in *SSB* 18 (1992): 79–80.

MUSIC BUSINESS AND LAW

A selective look at a complex area.

13.21 Baskerville, David. *Music Business Handbook & Career Guide.* 6th ed. xxiv + 589 pp. Thousand Oaks, Calif.: Sage Publications, 1995.
    Previous eds. published in Los Angeles by Sherwood. First ed., 1975, xxi + 669 pp.; 2nd ed., 1979, xxi + 669 pp.; 3rd ed., 1981, 553 pp.; 4th ed., 1985, 537 pp.; 5th ed., 1990, 541 pp.
    More than an introduction to the music business, a book also valuable for its detailed and comprehensive discussion of the varied employment opportunities in the field. Its major sections include songwriting, publishing, and copyright; business affairs and the recording industry; music in broadcasting and film; career planning and development; and the Canadian music industry and international copyright. Although it focuses on the popular music business, areas such as environmental music, arts administration, and education are discussed. An appendix includes copyright, BMI, and ASCAP forms, a bibliography, a glossary, a list of professional organizations, and an index.

13.22 Erickson, J. Gunnar, Edward R. Hearn, and **Mark E. Halloran.** *The Musician's Guide to Copyright.* Rev. ed. 128 pp. New York: Charles Scribner's Sons, 1983.
    First ed. published 1979 (San Francisco: Bay Area Lawyers for the Arts), 86 pp.
    A concise introduction to copyright for the lay audience.
    Reviewed by Todd I. Gordon in *Notes* 40 (June 1984): 789–90.

13.23* Halloran, Mark. *The Musician's Business and Legal Guide.* Revised, 4th ed. 884 pp. Englewood Cliffs, N.J.: Prentice-Hall, 1991.

Previous editions published under the title *The Musician's Manual.* First ed., 1980 (New York: Hawthorne/Dutton), a presentation of the Beverly Hills Bar Association Barristers, Committee for the Arts. Revised ed., 1987, by the Beverly Hills Bar Association. Updated ed. anticipated for 1996.

A collection of articles on topics including copyright, live performance, music unions, performing rights organizations, jingles, film and television music, and music publishing and recording, especially useful for its inclusion, with analysis, of many sample contracts. Includes a useful list of resources and an index.

13.24 Karlin, Fred, and **Rayburn Wright.** *On the Track: A Guide to Contemporary Film Scoring.* Includes a complete CLICK BOOK by Alexander R. Brinkman. 856 pp. New York: Schirmer; London: Collier Macmillan, 1990.

Intended as a textbook for film composers, a comprehensive and practical manual detailing the prevailing techniques in contemporary film scoring. In addition, the book includes valuable information on the business of film music, as well as a filmography (pp. 643–57) of the 150 films discussed in the course of the book, a classified bibliography, and an index.

Reviewed by Robert Wykes in *Notes* 48 (December 1991): 528–29.

13.25 Krasilovsky, M. William, and **Sidney Shemel.** *More about This Business of Music.* Revised and enlarged 5th ed. 288 pp. New York: Billboard Books, 1994.

Previous eds. published in 1989, 1982, 1974, and 1967. Shemel's name appears first in these earlier editions.

A companion to the authors's *This Business of Music,* focusing on topics not covered in that work. Most notably, the businesses of "serious" music, religious music, and jazz are discussed. There are a large variety of useful forms and lists in the appendixes, and an index.

13.26 Krasilovsky, M. William, and **Sidney Shemel.** *This Business of Music.* Revised and enlarged 7th ed. xxxvii + 698 pp. New York: Billboard Books, 1995.

Previously published in 1990, 1985, 1979, 1977, 1971, and 1964. Shemel's name appears first in the earlier editions.

The standard text on the music business. A comprehensive discussion is provided, focusing primarily on the popular and commercial music trades. Included is information on recording contracts, copyright, clubs, licensing, performing rights, mechanical rights, music publishing, trademarks, and taxation, as well as extensive appendixes of forms for copyright deposit, contracts, and licenses, with extracts from relevant statutes and documents pertaining to copyright. An index and a list of reference sources are included.

13.27* Muller, Peter. *The Music Business—A Legal Perspective: Music and Live Performances.* 356 pp. Westport, Conn.: Quorum Books, 1994.

A discussion of the major legal agreements that one will encounter in the music business.

Reviewed by Robert R. Carter, Jr., in *Notes* 52 (1996): 802.

13.28* Nimmer, Melville B., and **David Nimmer.** *Nimmer on Copyright: A Treatise on the Law of Literary, Musical and Artistic Property, and the Protection of Ideas.* 6 vols. to date (Loose-leaf). New York: Matthew Bender, 1978– .

Originally published, 1963; completely revised, 1978, with new section numbering. The contents are periodically updated.

The most respected, authoritative source on copyright. Although usually found in law libraries or collections, it provides a wealth of information for anyone concerned with copyright and artistic creativity and includes chapters on music, theater, and motion pictures. Extensive appendixes provide relevant statutes, House and Senate reports, regulations, and other primary source material. Begun by Melville Nimmer, after his 1985 death it has been continued by his son. Because it is written for those with legal training, it can be dense reading for the layperson.

13.29 Orobko, William. *The Musician's Handbook: A Practical Guide to the Law and Business of Music.* 189 pp. Vancouver, B.C.: International Self-Counsel Press; Seattle, Wash.: Self-Counsel Press, 1985.

A popular introduction to practice in the music business and to Canadian and American laws relating to that business.

13.30* Passman, Donald S. *All You Need to Know about the Music Business.* Revised, updated, and expanded ed. 415 pp. New York: Simon & Schuster, 1994.

First ed., 1991, 351 pp.

An entertaining and informative overview of the music industry, with an emphasis on comprehensibility over jargon. Thirty-two chapters cover seven major areas: advisors, record deals, songwriting and music publishing, group issues, touring, merchandising, and motion picture music, with an index.

13.31 Pohlmann, Hansjörg. *Die Frühgeschichte des musikalischen Urheberrechts (ca. 1400–1800): neue Materialien zur Entwicklung des Urheberrechtsbewusstseins der Komponisten.* 315 pp. Kassel, Germany; New York: Bärenreiter, 1962. (Musikwissenschaftliche Arbeiten, 20.)

An important history of early music copyright, and one of the few works to consider sociological and psychological factors as they relate to the development of composer's rights of ownership. An appendix gives 31 original documents in transcription.

Review by Werner Braun in *Die Musikforschung* 17 (1964): 298–99.

13.32 Rachlin, Harvey. *The Encyclopedia of the Music Business.* 524 pp. New York: Harper & Row, 1981.

A somewhat dated but still useful reference tool. Entries are terms and topics pertaining to the making and marketing of music for commercial reasons, as well as entries for many organizations.

13.33 Rapaport, Diane Sward. *How to Make & Sell Your Own Recording: A Guide for the Nineties.* 243 pp. Englewood Cliffs, N.J.: Prentice Hall, 1992.

First 3 eds. published as *How to Make and Sell Your Own Record: The Complete Guide to Independent Recording.* First ed. published in 1979 (New York: Harmony Books). Revised ed. published 1984 (Tiburon, Calif.: Headlands Press) and revised 3rd ed. published 1988 (Jerome, Ariz.: Jerome Headlands Press).

Comprehensive guide to promotion, sales, printing, design, manufacturing, recording options and procedures, copyright, business, and planning, with bibliography and index.

13.34 Rothenberg, Stanley. *Copyright and the Public Performance of Music.* 188 pp. The Hague: Martinus Nijhoff, 1954.

Reprinted in 1987 by Fred B. Rothman & Co., Littleton, Colo.

A survey still valuable today for its description of American and European copyright practices and performer's rights in the mid-1950s.

13.35 Schulze, Erich. *Urheberrecht in der Musik.* 5th, newly edited ed. 543 pp. Berlin; New York: Walter de Gruyter & Co., 1981.

4th ed. published 1972; 3rd ed., 1965; 2nd ed., 1956; 1st ed., 1951. First and second eds. published as *Urheberrecht in der Musik und die deutsche Urheberrechtsgesellschaft.*

A discussion of copyright practice in Germany. Appendixes (pp. 149–538) contain legal documents, including some from East Germany, Austria, and Switzerland.

13.36 Taubman, Joseph. *In Tune with the Music Business.* 279 pp. New York: Law-Arts Publishers, 1980.

Based on the author's lectures for his course on the music business at the New School for Social Research, New York. The book emphasizes the legal and regulatory aspects of the music trades, including sections on taxation and antitrust regulation. There is a subject index.

13.37* Winson, Gail Fleming. "Music and the Law: A Comprehensive Bibliography of Law-Related Materials." In *COMM/ENT, A Journal of Communications and Entertainment* 4 (Spring 1982): 489–551.

Winson, Gail I., and **Janine S. Natter.** "Music Law and Business: A Comprehensive Bibliography, 1982–1991." In *Hastings Communications and Entertainment Law Journal (COMM/ENT)* 13 (Summer 1991): 811–929.

Extensive, classified bibliographies, geared toward those in the legal profession or with an interest in law, but useful to others dealing with copyright or any other legal issues related to music. Entries in the earlier bibliography date from the 1920s to 1981. Both lists emphasize articles from journals and law reviews, but also include books, federal government publications, loose-leaf materials, and newsletters. The more recent bibliography also includes newspaper and newsletter articles, and provides annotations for the majority of the book entries. It also has more materials on the business of music than does the first bibliography.

MUSIC LIBRARIANSHIP

13.38* Bradley, Carol June. *American Music Librarianship: A Biographical and Historical Survey.* 237 pp. New York: Greenwood Press, 1990.

A history of American music librarianship in its early, formative years, with detailed index. Reviewed by Charles Lindahl in *AM* 10 (1992): 378–80, by John Druesedow in *Fontes* 38 (1991): 146–47, and by Neil Ratliff in *Notes* 41 (1991): 723–24.

13.39 Bradley, Carol June. *Manual of Music Librarianship.* 140 pp. Ann Arbor, Mich.: Music Library Association, 1966.

A handbook on music librarianship, sponsored by MLA's Committee on Information and Organization.

13.40 Bradley, Carol June. *Music Collections in American Libraries: A Chronology.* 249 pp. Detroit, Mich.: Information Coordinators, 1981. (Detroit studies in music bibliography, 46)

A chronological documentation of the development of music librarianship in the U.S., beginning with the 1731 founding of the Library Company of Philadelphia. There is information on individual collections, their published catalogs, and citations to written descriptions of the libraries. Also included are addresses, significant dates, and an index.

Reviewed by Paula Morgan in *Notes* 39 (1982): 357–58 and by Vincent H. Duckles in *Fontes* 29 (1982): 147–48.

13.41 Bradley, Carol June. *Reader in Music Librarianship.* 340 pp. Washington, D.C.: Microcard Editions Books, 1973. (Reader series in library and information science)

A reprinting of 53 seminal articles on the practice of music librarianship, encompassing general philosophies and operational concerns, collection development and acquisitions, cataloging and classification, bibliography and exhibitions, binding, sound recordings and equipment, facilities, and education for music librarianship. Most chapters begin with a selected bibliography on the topic under discussion and help make it a useful sourcebook, now historic in nature. The index covers concepts, subjects, library names, personal names, and titles of reprinted articles as well as the bibliographic citations throughout the book.

Reviewed by Donald W. Krummel and John W. Tanno in *Notes* 31 (1974): 286–88.

13.42 Bryant, E. T., and **Guy A. Marco.** *Music Librarianship: A Practical Guide.* 2nd ed. 449 pp. Metuchen, N.J.: Scarecrow Press, 1985.

The 1st ed. was published in London by James Clarke and in New York by Hafner Publishing in 1959 (503 pp.), and was reprinted by Stechert-Hafner in 1963.

A book intended primarily for British practitioners, including chapters on music library administration, reference books and periodicals, cataloging, classification, and sound recordings. The chapter on reference works includes an annotated bibliography of works that might constitute a reference collection in small to medium-size music libraries. The chapter on cataloging presents an overview of the principal codes for cataloging material for music libraries, and similarly the chapter on classification covers the main classification schemes. The sound recordings chapter is an extended guide to the contents of recording collections and is particularly relevant to British situations. There is a bibliography and a brief index.

The 1st ed. is reviewed by Alfons Ott in *Fontes* 7 (1960): 72–73 and by Rita Benton in *Notes* 17 (1960): 397–98. The 2nd ed. is reviewed by Susan T. Sommer in *Notes* 43 (1986): 44–45 and by David Hunter in *Libraries and Culture* 24 (1989): 506–7.

13.43* Byrne, Frank P. *A Practical Guide to the Music Library: Its Function, Organization and Maintenance.* 117 pp. Cleveland, Ohio, Ludwig Music Co., 1987.

Detailed assistance in establishing and successfully running a large collection of scores and parts for a performing ensemble.

Reviewed by Marion S. Gushee in *Notes* 45 (1989): 521.

13.44* Cassaro, James P. *Space Utilization in Music Libraries.* 140 pp. Canton, Mass.: Music Library Association, 1991. (MLA technical reports, 20)

Conference proceedings recounting the special requirements to be taken into account when renovating, reorganizing, or creating a music library facility, considered in a series of papers by veterans of such projects.

13.45 Currall, Henry F. J. *Phonograph Record Libraries: Their Organisation and Practice.* With a preface by A. Hyatt King. 2nd ed. 303 pp. Hamden, Conn.: Archon Books, 1970.

The work was first published in 1963, sponsored by IAML, as *Gramophone Record Libraries,* 182 pp., and in the United States as *Phonograph Record Libraries* (Hamden, Conn.: Archon Books, 1963). The 2nd British ed., *Gramophone Record Libraries,* was published in London by Crosby Lockwood and Son, 1970.

An illustrated manual for the administration of a record library, with contributions by British librarians and sound recording experts. "A Basic Stock List" is given (pp. 131–46), and "Gramophone Librarianship: A Bibliography" is on pp. 171–76.

The 1970 ed. is reviewed by Philip L. Miller in *Notes* 28 (1972): 449.

13.46* Davidson, Mary Wallace. "American Music Libraries and Librarianship: Challenges for the Nineties." In *Notes* 38 (1981): 13–22.

As Ruth Watanabe (**13.58**) did for the 1980s, an analysis of the changing ideas that technology and changes in available resources will bring to music librarianship.

13.47 Duckles, Vincent H. *Music Libraries and Librarianship. Library Trends* 8 (1960): 495–617. Published by the University of Illinois, School of Librarianship.

A discussion of 15 specialists of various aspects of music librarianship, covering the areas of training for the profession, bibliography and selection, cataloging, services, and administration.

Reviewed by Vladimir Fédorov in *Fontes* 8 (1961): 30–31.

13.48 Fling, Robert Michael. *Shelving Capacity in the Music Library.* 36 pp. Philadelphia, Pa.: Music Library Association, 1981. (MLA technical reports, 7)

13.49* Gottlieb, Jane. *Collection Assessment in Music Libraries.* 93 pp. Canton, Mass.: Music Library Association, 1994. (MLA technical reports, 22)

13.50* Heck, Thomas F. *The "Music Information Explosion" and Its Implications for College Teachers and Students.* 72 pp. Missoula, Mont.: College Music Society, 1992. (CMS report, 9)

13.51* Jones, Malcolm. *Music Librarianship.* 130 pp. London: Clive Bingley; K.G. Saur, 1979.
   A thoughtful manual of music library expectation by a prominent British music librarian.

13.52 McColvin, Lionel Roy, and **Harold Reeves.** *Music Libraries, Including a Comprehensive Bibliography of Music Literature and a Select Bibliography of Music Scores Published since 1957.* Completely rewritten, revised, and extended by Jack Dove. 2 vols. London: A. Deutsch, 1965. (A Grafton book)
   First published 1937–38.
   A handbook of British music librarianship. Vol. 1 is a series of chapters on various aspects of music library administration and practice, including staff, binding, classification, and cataloging. There are chapters devoted to British public libraries, British university and special libraries, and overseas libraries. Vol. 2 consists of bibliographies and indexes of music literature and scores that are cited elsewhere.
   Reviewed by Harold Spivacke and K. H. Anderson in *Notes* 22 (1965): 872–77.

13.53 Ott, Alfons. "Die Musikbibliotheken." In Fritz Milkau's *Handbuch der Bibliothekswissenschaft,* 2nd ed., Vol. 2, pp. 222–42.
   Also printed separately by Harrassowitz, Wiesbaden, 1959.
   Reviewed by Cecil B. Oldman in *Fontes* 7 (1960): 71–72.

13.54* Rahkonen, Carl. *World Music in Music Libraries.* 77 pp. Canton, Mass.: Music Library Association, 1994. (MLA technical report, 24)
   Papers presented at a plenary session of the Music Library Association Conference in Baltimore, Md., in 1992.

13.55* Tatian, Carol. *Careers in Music Librarianship: Perspectives from the Field.* 81 pp. Canton, Mass.: Music Library Association, 1990. (MLA technical report, 18)
   Papers presented at a session of the 1988 Music Library Association Conference, held in Minneapolis, Minn., and sponsored by the Personnel Subcommittee of the Administration Committee.

13.56* Thomas, David H. *Archival Information Processing for Sound Recordings: The Design of a Database for the Rodgers and Hammerstein Archives of Recorded Sound.* 132 pp. Canton, Mass.: Music Library Association, 1992. (MLA technical report, 21)
   Reviewed by James P. Cassaro in *Fontes* 40 (1994): 63–64 and by Peter G. Orr in *ARSCJ* 25 (1994): 216–17.

13.57 Wassner, Hermann. "Untersuchungen zur musikbibliothekavischen Arbeit: Ein Überblick über neuer Veroffentlichungen gegenwartige Aktivitaten und vorzuchlagende Arbeitsziele. (Beitrage aus der Bundesrepublik und aus West-Berlin)." In *Fontes* 30 (1983): 82–98.
   A survey of publications from West Germany, including West Berlin, on the profession of music librarianship since 1975. There is a classified bibliography of 167 works on the subject.

13.58 Watanabe, Ruth. "American Music Libraries and Music Librarianship: An Overview in the Eighties." In *Notes* 38 (1981): 239–56.
   An overview of the American experience following World War II, with particular attention to the challenges of the 1980s in automation, sound recordings, collection development, and conservation. Mary Wallace Davidson did the same for the 1990s (**13.46**).

13.59* White, Raymond A. *Directory of Library School Offerings in Music Librarianship.* 5th ed. 42 pp. Education Committee, Music Library Association, 1994.

MUSIC CATALOGING AND CLASSIFICATION

13.60 Bradley, Carol June. *The Dickinson Classification: A Cataloguing & Classification Manual for Music: Including a Reprint of the George Sherman Dickinson Classification of Musical Compositions.* 176 pp. Carlisle, Pa.: Carlisle Books, 1968.

A classification system developed by George Sherman Dickinson, music librarian at Vassar College, 1927–53. Included is a reprint of Dickinson's 1938 *Classification of Musical Compositions* and a manual of cataloging and classification procedures based on it. A description of the classification and a demonstration of its applications are found in Bradley's "The Dickinson Classification for Music," *Fontes* 19 (1972): 13–22.

13.61 Bratcher, Perry, and **Jennifer Smith.** *Music Subject Headings, Compiled from Library of Congress Subject Headings.* 323 pp. Lake Crystal, Minn.: Soldier Creek Press, 1988. (Soldier Creek Music Series, 1)

A 2nd ed. is coming in 1996, compiled by Harriette Hemmasi.

A list of LC subject headings for music, current to September 1987, with instructions for formulating music subject headings based on LC practice.

Reviewed by Harry E. Price in *Notes* 47 (1990–91): 1,179–81.

13.62 Coates, Eric James. *The British Catalogue of Music Classification.* 56 pp. London: Council of the British National Bibliography; British Museum, 1960.

A faceted classification scheme compiled for the Council of the British National Bibliography for use in the *British Catalogue of Music* (**5.14**). The intent and use of this system was for organizing music in bibliographies, not for organizing music collections.

Reviewed by Virginia Cunningham in *Notes* 17 (1959–60): 566–67.

13.63 *Code for Cataloging Music and Phonorecords.* Prepared by a joint committee of the Music Library Association and the American Library Association, Division of Cataloging and Classification. 88 pp. Chicago, Ill.: American Library Association, 1958.

An updating of the Music Library Association's earlier *Code for Cataloging Music* (1941–42). This is the first instance in the U.S. of a single official code for cataloging both music and phonorecords.

Reviewed by E. T. Bryant in *Notes* 15 (1958): 389–90.

13.64 Deutsches Bibliotheksinstitut. Kommission für Alphabetische Katalogisierung. *Regeln für Musikalien und Musiktonträger, RAK-Musik.* 92 pp. Wiesbaden: L. Reichert, 1986. (Regeln für die alphabetische Katalogisierung, RAK, 3)

Cataloging rules developed for use in libraries in German-speaking countries.

13.65* Drone, Jeanette M., and **Mark Crook.** *Indexes to the Established Titles, Variant Titles, Obsolete Uniform Titles, and Work Numbers in the Library of Congress Name-Authority File for the Works of Bach, Beethoven, Brahms, Haydn, Mozart, Schubert, Tchaikovsky, Telemann.* 440 pp. in various pagings. Dublin, Ohio: OCLC Online Computer Library Center, Office of Research, 1988. (Research report series)

13.66* Drone, Jeanette M. *Music Subject Headings from the Machine-Readable Library of Congress Subject Authority File.* 2 vols. Dublin, Ohio: OCLC Online Library Composer Center, Office of Research, 1988.

Contents: Vol. 1, *Classified Listing;* Vol. 2, *Alphabetical Listings of Subject Headings and See From Tracings (Topical Terms).*

13.67* Elliker, Calvin. "Classification Schemes for Scores: Analysis of Structural Levels." In *Notes* 50 (1993–94): 1,269–1,320.

A description of a study of 24 classification schemes undertaken to determine the relative importance of basic elements: form, genre, medium, character, time, place, composer, and format. There are brief descriptions of each of the schemes, with each placed in historical context.

13.68* Gaeddert, Barbara Knisely. *The Classification and Cataloging of Sound Recordings, 1933–1980: An Annotated Bibliography.* 2nd ed. 36 pp. Philadelphia, Pa.: Music Library Association, 1981. (MLA Technical Reports, 4)

First published in 1977, 32 pp.

An evaluative bibliography whose emphasis is on classification, arranged chronologically, with coverage limited to the U.S., Canada, and Great Britain.

The 1st ed. is reviewed by Kären Nagy in *Notes* 34 (1977): 88, and by Richard Andrewes in *MT* 119 (1978): 424.

*13.69 Gamble, Betsy. *Music Cataloging Decisions: As Issued by the Music Section, Special Materials Cataloging Division, Library of Congress, in the **Music Cataloging Bulletin** through December 1991.* 112 pp. Canton, Mass.: Music Library Association, 1992.

Organized access, in loose-leaf format, to the music cataloging decisions issued by the Library of Congress and published in MLA's *Music Cataloging Bulletin* through Vol. 22, no. 12, December 1991. The decisions amplify *Anglo-American Cataloging Rules,* 2nd ed., 1988 rev.

13.70 Grasberger, Franz. *Der Autoren-Katalog der Musikdrucke / The Author Catalog of Published Music.* Trans. by Virginia Cunningham. 48 pp. + 12 facsimiles. Frankfurt; London; New York: C.F. Peters Corp., 1957. (Code international de catalogage de la musique, 1)

The result of the work of the Commission on Music Cataloguing of the International Association of Music Libraries.

Reviewed by Richard S. Angell in *Notes* 15 (1957): 110–11.

13.71* Harrold, Ann, and **Graham Lea.** *Musaurus: A Music Thesaurus: A New Approach to Organising Music Information.* 128 pp. London: Music Press, 1991.

A seven-part classified scheme with auxiliary supporting material.

Reviewed by Jay Weitz in *Fontes* 39 (1992): 363–64 and by Harriette Hemmasi in *Notes* 49 (1993): 1,530–32.

13.72* Hartsock, Ralph. *Notes for Music Catalogers: Examples Illustrating AACR 2 in the Online Bibliographic Record.* 355 pp. Lake Crystal, Minn.: Soldier Creek Press, 1994. (Soldier Creek Music series, 3)

Examples of 2,007 notes used in records created by the Library of Congress for scores and sound recordings. The notes are given in MARC format and in context with other fields. Pertinent rules from *Anglo-American Cataloging Rules,* 2nd ed., 1988 rev. and related LC *Rule Interpretations* and *Music Cataloging Decisions* are provided with each group of examples.

Reviewed by Holly Gardinier in *LQ* 66 (1996): 111–12.

13.73 Hemmasi, Harriette. "The Music Thesaurus: Function and Foundations." In *Notes* 50 (1994): 875–82.

An article about the characteristics of a music thesaurus and the steps that have been taken in developing one. The characteristics are "standard vocabulary, hierarchical arrangement, faceted terms, rich lead-in vocabulary, and complete syndetic structure."

13.74 International Association of Music Libraries, Archives, and Documentation Centres. *Gruppe Bundesrepublik Deutschland. Systematiken für öffentliche Musikbibliotheken.* Jeweils 3., vollständig überarbeitete Aufl. 251 pp. Berlin: Deutsches Bibliotheksinstitut, 1991.

A system of music classification devised for public libraries in Germany.

13.75 International Association of Music Libraries. International Cataloging Code Commission. *Code international de catalogage de la musique.* 5 vols. Frankfurt; New York: C.F. Peters, 1957–83.

Parallel text in German, English, and French.

Vol. 1: **Grasberger, Franz.** *Der Autoren-Katalog der Musikdrucke. The Author Catalog of Published Music.* Trans. by Virginia Cunningham. 1957, 48 pp.

A comparative history of cataloging codes for music in two principal sections: "Cataloging problems of a music library" and "The author catalog of published music," with bibliography (pp. 46–47).

Reviewed by Richard S. Angell in *Notes* 15 (1957): 110–11.

Vol. 2: **Fédoroff, Yvette.** *Code restreint. Kurzgefasste Anleitung. Limited Code.* Trans. by Simone Wallon and Virginia Cunningham. 1961, 54 pp.

The presentation of an initial limited code for cataloging printed and manuscript music, based on decisions made by the Committee for a Cataloging Code, International Association of Music Libraries, between 1952 and 1955.

Reviewed by Minnie Elmer in *Notes* 19 (1961): 247–49 and by Richard Schaal in *Die Musikforschung* 17 (1964): 295–96.

Vol. 3: **Cunningham, Virginia.** *Rules for Full Cataloging. Rules de catalogage detaillé. Regeln für die vollständige Titelaufnahme.* 1971, 116 pp.

Full cataloging rules for printed music. The scope of the rules covers identification of a work, description of an edition of the work, and the choice of heading.

Vol. 4: **Göllner, Marie Louise.** *Rules for Cataloging Music Manuscripts.* Trans. by Yvette Fédoroff and Horst Leuchtmann. 1975, 56 pp.

Rules and suggestions for the full cataloging of music manuscripts.

Reviewed by Peter Ward Jones in *M&L* 59 (1978): 359.

Vol. 5: **Wallon, Simone,** and **Kurt Dorfmüller.** *Le catalogage des enregistrements sonores. The Cataloging of Sound Recordings.* With the collaboration of Yvette Fédoroff and Virginia Cunningham. 1983, 105 pp.

Basic premises for cataloging sound recordings; recommendations that can be adapted to various library situations.

Reviewed in *Musikhandel* 35 (1984): 164.

13.76 International Federation of Library Associations and Institutions. *ISBD (NBM): International Standard Bibliographic Description for Non-Book Materials.* 2nd ed. 96 pp. London: IFLA Universal Bibliographic Control and International MARC Programme, 1987.

First published in 1977.

Standards for descriptive cataloging of nonbook materials.

13.77 International Federation of Library Associations and Institutions. *ISBD(PM): International Standard Bibliographic Description for Printed Music.* 2nd rev. ed. 73 pp. Munich; New York: K.G. Saur, 1991. (UBCIM Publications, new series, 1)

First published in 1980.

Standards for the description and identification of published printed music. The use is intended primarily for current music publications.

13.78* Kaufman, Judith. *Library of Congress Subject Headings for Recordings of Western Non-Classical Music.* 68 pp. Philadelphia, Pa: Music Library Association, 1983. (MLA technical reports, 14)

First ed., *Recordings of Non-Western Music Subject and Added Entry Access,* 36 pp. Ann Arbor, Mich.: Music Library Association, 1977. (MLA technical reports, 5)

The 1st ed. is reviewed by Joan Kunselman in *Notes* 34 (1978): 881.

13.79* Koth, Michelle. *A Handbook of Examples for Use in Authority Records Created by the NACO Music Project.* 27 pp. New Haven, Conn.: Yale University Music Library, Distributed by the Music OCLC Users Group, 1995.

The handbook used by music catalogers in the NACO Music Project to create authority records for names of composers, editors, performers, etc., and name/uniform title headings for composers and their works. It does not discuss how to establish headings themselves, but rather how to cite sources that contain information necessary for creating a specific heading.

13.80 *Library of Congress Classification: Class M, Music and Books on Music.* 3rd ed. 228 pp. Washington, D.C.: Library of Congress, Cataloging Distribution Services, 1978.

First issued in 1904, revised 1917. 2nd ed. issued in 1963. Kept up to date by the Division's quarterly publication *L.C. Classification: Additions and Changes* and by two publications irregularly issued by Gale Research, *Library of Congress Classification Schedules: A Cumulation of Additions and Changes* and *Library of Congress Classification Schedules Combined with Additions and Changes.*

Initially the work of Oscar Sonneck, a classification schedule used in most American music libraries, particularly those in universities and colleges.

The 3rd ed. reviewed by Lenore Coral in *Notes* 35 (1979): 892–93.

13.81 New York Public Library. Reference Department. *Music Subject Headings, Authorized for Use in the Catalogs of the Music Division.* 2nd ed. enlarged. 610 pp. Boston, Mass.: G.K. Hall, 1966.

A guide reproduced from cards in the subject heading file of the New York Public Library. This is an important tool for music catalogers because it reflects the practice of one of the great American music libraries.

13.82* Saheb-Ettaba, Caroline, and **Roger B. McFarland.** *ANSCR: The Alpha-Numeric System for Classification of Recordings.* 212 pp. Williamsport, Pa.: Bro-Dart Publishing, 1969.

A classification system arranged according to 36 subject categories. These categories and four terms are used for devising unique class numbers for sound recordings. There is a bibliography (pp. 197–98).

Reviewed by Ruth Hilton in *Notes* 28 (1970): 52–54.

13.83* Seibert, Donald. *The MARC Music Format: From Inception to Publication.* 42 pp. Philadelphia, Pa.: Music Library Association, 1982. (MLA technical report, 13)

The history of the development of the MARC Music Format from 1971 to 1976.

13.84* Shaw, Sarah J., and Lauralee Shiere. *Sheet Music Cataloging and Processing: A Manual.* 51 pp. Canton, Mass.: Music Library Association, 1984. (MLA technical reports, 15)

A guide to organizing a sheet music collection by current standards, explaining authority searching, cataloging, and processing, using *AACR2* rules, LC subject headings, and the MARC Scores Format, as well as solutions to problems unique to sheet music cataloging and a bibliography of secondary reference sources useful in authority work.

13.85 Smiraglia, Richard P. *Cataloging Music: A Manual for Use with AACR 2.* Edited by Edward Swanson. 2nd ed. 181 pp. Lake Crystal, Minn.: Soldier Creek Press, 1986.

An excellent guide to the descriptive cataloging of music according to *Anglo-American Cataloging Rules,* 2nd ed., *Library of Congress Rule Interpretations, Music Cataloging Decisions,* and the MARC format. This predates the 1988 revision of *AACR2.* There is a bibliography (pp. 153–60).

13.86* Smiraglia, Richard P. *Music Cataloging: The Bibliographic Control of Printed and Recorded Music in Libraries.* 222 pp. Englewood, Colo.: Libraries Unlimited, 1989.

Theoretical principles of cataloging and classification of scores and musical sound recordings. Also included is historical background as well as description of use of the MARC format. There is a bibliography (pp. 203–9).

Reviewed by Linda Barnhardt in *Notes* 47 (1990–91): 410–12, by Richard D. Burbank in *Fontes* 38 (1991): 76–77, and by R. C. Mehta in *Journal of the Indian Musicological Society* 21 (1990): 104.

13.87* Smiraglia, Richard P. *Shelflisting Music: Guidelines for Use with the Library of Congress Classification M.* 21 pp. Philadelphia, Pa: Music Library Association, 1981. (MLA Technical Reports, 9)

Guidelines that reflect LC shelf listing practices, including flowchart analyses.

13.88 Sommerfield, David. *Proceedings of the Institute on Library of Congress Music Cataloging Policies and Procedures, January 26–27, 1971, Washington, D.C.* 80 pp. Ann Arbor, Mich.: Music Library Association, 1975. (Music Library Association Technical Reports, 3)

A conference report, including discussion of *Anglo-American Cataloging Rules,* subject headings, and classification as they pertain to music materials, as well as a description of LC policies and procedures of that time. The section about shelf listing continues to be of value.

13.89* Thorin, Suzanne E., and **Carole Franklin Vidali.** *The Acquisition and Cataloging of Music and Sound Recordings: A Glossary.* 40 pp. Canton, Mass.: Music Library Association, 1984. (MLA Technical Reports, 11)

A collection of terms used in music library technical services, subdivided by print and nonprint titles. The section on scores has value for current materials; the section on sound recordings is useful for archival materials. This is particularly helpful for librarians who have minimal music background. There is a bibliography (pp. vii–viii).

Reviewed by Clifford Bartlett in *Brio* 21 (1984): 17–18.

13.90* Tucker, Ruth. *Authority Control in Music Libraries: Proceedings of the Music Library Association Preconference, March 5, 1985.* 109 pp. Canton, Mass: Music Library Association, 1989. (MLA technical report, 16)

Papers discussing aspects of authority control for music materials. Described are definitions and needs, considerations of national standards and cooperative work, and the impact and potential of automation.

Reviewed by Elizabeth Aurelle in *Notes* 47 (1990–91): 409–10.

13.91* Weitz, Jay. *Music Coding and Tagging: MARC Content Designation for Scores and Sound Recordings.* 302 pp. Lake Crystal, Minn.: Soldier Creek Press, 1990. (Soldier Creek music series, 2)

Instructions and examples for coding MARC fields and subfields for music materials.

Reviewed by Harry T. Price in *Notes* 47 (1990–91): 1,181.

13.92* Wursten, Richard. *In Celebration of Revised 780: Music in the Dewey Decimal Classification, Edition 20.* 97 pp. Canton, Mass.: Music Library Association, 1990. (MLA technical report, 19)

A conference report, with articles including a discussion of the process of revision, a description of the revised schedule, how the schedule can assist online subject retrieval, a research study of its potential impact, and discussion of use in public libraries, with bibliography (pp. 91–94).

Reviewed by Michael Colby in *Notes* 47 (1991): 1,178–79.

INDEX

Index references are to numbered items in the text except where pages are noted. Entries for names, titles, and subjects are alphabetized together, word-by-word, in one index. Initial articles are ignored in alphabetization, as are prepositions at the beginning of subheadings; however, prepositions, articles, and conjunctions within entries are not ignored. Diacritical marks are also ignored in alphabetization. Titles beginning with arabic numerals are filed at the beginning of the section, not as if spelled out. Names beginning with Mac and Mc are interfiled as if all were spelled Mac. All reviews have been grouped together at the end of each reviewer's listing.

This index includes the following kinds of entries:

(a) Name entries may be found for individual authors and reviewers; prominent editors and translators; historic publishers; and distinctive names of institutions and organizations. Generic names of institutions, organizations, and associations may be found under the country in which each is located.

(b) Direct title entries may be found for all editions of all books, except when earlier editions bear very similar titles. Articles are indexed only under the author's name. Series and translations of works are generally not indexed, although multi-lingual works are indexed under all titles.

(c) Entries may be found under specific subjects whenever possible. Broader terms have been used for materials that encompass a number of similar subjects, and to reflect multiple facets of individual works. Cross references in the index serve as guides from more general terms to the specific, as well as to related terms.

Information in the index will be more readily accessible if the following practices are noted:

Generic subheadings have been selected in order to locate similar materials together under complex entries, and to provide a system for finding similar kinds of materials throughout the index. Thus, within many entries bibliographies of printed music (i.e., scores, parts) are listed under "music (printed)" or "music (manuscripts)," whereas bibliographies of written materials (e.g., dictionaries, articles, books) are listed as "music (literature)." Similarly, the various kinds of reference resources and primary materials may be listed together under "reference works" and "primary sources," respectively.

Multiple entries have been made for important works in order to provide access via a variety of subject facets. Thus, where preference is given to a geographic arrangement of subheadings, entries also may be found directly under the specific subjects. Nevertheless, to avoid excessive duplication of entries, the index includes cross references to lead the user from national entries to major subject entries—archives, libraries, manuscripts, musical instrument collections, printing and publishing—where providing a centralized detailed listing was deemed to be of more value than scattering this information throughout the index. In addition, the user should always look under the names of individual composers and performers for the most specific information about them.

The user should remember that additional information about an item can be ascertained by comparing its citation number to the Table of Contents. The number to the left of the decimal point corresponds to the chapter number and content as presented there.

bagpipes:
museum, 8.44
music, 5.154, 5.155, 5.156, 5.157,
5.158, 5.159, 5.160
Bahr, Edward R.,
*Trombone/Euphonium
Discography*, 10.17
Baierisches Musik-Lexikon
(Lipowsky), 1.158
Baillie, Laureen, *The Catalogue of
Printed Music in the British
Library to 1980*, 7.258
Baily, Dee:
*A Checklist of Music
Bibliographies and Indexes in
Progress and Unpublished*, 4.3
reviews:
Cowden, 1.250; Reid, 1.321
Bain, Harry, *Bain's Directory of Bag-
Pipe Tunes*, 5.155
Baines, Anthony:
*The Bate Collection of Historical
Wind Instruments*, 8.93
*European and American Musical
Instruments*, 1.492
Non-Keyboard Instruments, 8.71
*The Oxford Companion to Musical
Instruments*, 1.493
reviews:
Anoyanakis/Carameour/Klint,
1.491; Haine, 8.9; Langwill,
1.592; Leeuwen Boomkamp/
Meer, 8.27; Meyer, 5.417
Bain's Directory of Bag-Pipe Tunes
(Bain), 5.155
Baird, Margery Anthea, *A
Catalogue of the Printed
Books and Manuscripts
Deposited in Guildhall
Library*, 7.272
Bajzek, Dieter, *Percussion*, 4.232
Baker, Evan:
reviews:
*Catalog of the Opera
Collections...*, 7.99; Weaver,
5.499
Baker, Paul:
reviews:
Case/Britt/Murray, 1.357;
Piazza, 10.94
Baker, Theodore:
*Baker's Biographical Dictionary of
Musicians*, 1.62, 1.249, 1.251
A Dictionary of Musical Terms,
1.270
*Schirmer Pronouncing Pocket
Manual of Musical Terms*,
1.270
Bakus, Gerald J., *A Spanish Guitar*,
4.233
Balázs, István, *Musical Guide to
Hungary*, 11.63
Bali, 10.202

Balkin, J.M.:
"Law, Music and Other
Performing Arts," 3.75
reviews, Taruskin, 3.89
ballad operas, 1.472
Ballad Scholarship (Richmond),
4.188
ballads:
American, 5.143, 5.616, 5.618,
7.315, 7.401, 10.197, 10.205
bibliographies, 4.188
British, 5.613, 5.614, 5.617, 5.620,
7.470
*Ballads and Folk Songs of the
Southwest* (Moore), 5.618
Ballard, Elizabeth Catherine, 9.100
Ballard, Robert, 9.94
Ballerini, Graziano, *I teatri*, 4.123
ballet: *See also* dance.
Denmark, 5.480
England, 1.475
France, 5.487, 5.491
Italy, 5.481, 5.482, 5.500
libretti, 7.113, 7.591
reference works, 1.416, 1.430,
1.467, 1.472, 1.476, 1.478
*Ballets, opéra, et autres ouvrages
lyriques* (La Vallière), 5.487
Balough, Teresa, *A Complete
Catalogue of the Works of
Percy Grainger*, 6.158
Balter, G., *Fachwörterbuch Musik*,
1.271
Baltzer, Rebecca A.:
Current Thought in Musicology,
3.21
reviews, Hoppin, 2.29
Bamburgh Castle, 7.156
Banchieri, Adriano, 6.34
Band Bibliography (Berger), 5.163
Band Discography (Berger), 5.163
Band Encyclopedia (Berger), 5.163
Band Music of the French Revolution
(Whitwell), 5.171
Band Music Guide, 5.162
Band Record Guide, 10.18
The Bandora (Nordstrom), 5.286
bands: *See also* names of
individual bands.
big, 1.410, 10.73, 10.154
music (literature), 1.591, 5.163,
5.172
discographies, 10.18, 10.47,
10.302
music (printed)
bibliographies, 5.162, 5.165,
5.166, 5.167, 5.168, 5.170,
5.172
French Revolution, 5.171
Italy, 5.161
Jewish, 5.85
marches, 5.169
United States, 5.122, 5.124

Bandsman (Berger), 5.163
Bane, Michael, *Who's Who in Rock*,
1.375
Banfield, Stephen:
reviews:
Gänzl, 1.439; Threlfall, 6.126
Banjo on Record (Heier/Lotz),
10.225
banjos, 1.508, 10.225
Banks, Chris, *Sundry Sorts of Music
Books*, 13.16
Banks, Margaret Downie, reviews,
Bowles, 2.42
Banks, Paul, reviews, Grasberger,
6.85
Banney, Howard F., *Return to
Sender*, 10.295
Bannister, H.M., *Monumenti vati-
cani di paleografia musicale
latina*, 7.523
Bantock, Granville, 6.35
*The Bantu Composers of Southern
Africa* (Huskisson), 1.210
Baptie, David, *Musical Scotland*,
1.161
Barber, Josephine, *German for
Musicians*, 1.272
Barber, Samuel, 6.36
Barbour, J. Murray, reviews, *The
Hymnal*, 1.623
Bargagna, Leto, *Gli strumenti musi-
cali raccolti nel Museo del R.
Istituto L. Cherubini a
Firenze*, 8.41
Barkelow, Patricia, *Song Index*,
5.371
Barker, Andrew, *Greek Musical
Writings*, 2.85
Barker, John W., *The Use of Music
and Recordings for Teaching
about the Middle Ages*, 4.198
Barker, Nicolas, reviews, Heartz,
9.60
Barlow, Harold:
A Dictionary of Musical Themes,
1.648
*A Dictionary of Opera and Song
Themes*, 1.649
A Dictionary of Vocal Themes,
1.649
Barlow, J., reviews, Godwin, 2.100
Barnes, Harold M., *Vertical-Cut
Cylinders and Discs*, 10.59
Barnes, Marilyn, reviews,
Benser/Urrows, 6.356
Barnett, Elise Braun:
*A Discography of the Art Music of
India*, 10.166
"Special Bibliography: Art Music
of India," 4.153
Barnhardt, Linda, reviews,
Smiraglia, 13.85
Barock Music (Baumgartner), 4.212

Baron, John H.:
Baroque Music, 4.206
Chamber Music, 4.219
Baroque era: *See also* early music.
  Dublin, 2.63
  England, 1.163, 4.126, 4.307,
    4.310, 4.313, 5.375, 5.493,
    7.599
    manuscripts, 7.413, 7.598, 9.98
  France, 1.148, 1.149, 3.65, 4.302,
    5.473, 5.528, 7.305
    keyboard music, 5.226, 5.227
    manuscripts, 7.48, 7.490
  Germany
    instrument makers, 1.560, 1.593
    instrumental music, 5.591,
      5.598, 7.217
    opera, 1.424, 5.471
    vocal music, 5.550, 5.650, 7.179,
      7.217
  internet resources, 12.40
  Italy
    cantatas, 7.435, 7.437
    library catalogs, 7.436, 7.438,
      7.448, 7.507, 7.508, 7.509,
      7.519
    Lucca, 4.319
    manuscripts, 5.228, 5.532
    opera, 4.374, 5.484, 5.485,
      5.495, 5.498, 5.500, 7.93,
      7.324
    vaudeville, 5.476
  Latin America, 5.602
  music (literature)
    bibliographies, 4.60, 4.206,
      4.210
    chronologies, 2.70, 5.498
    discographies, 10.16
    histories, 2.11, 2.27, 2.28, 2.30,
      2.35, 4.208
    source writings, 2.98, 2.107,
      2.118, 4.370
  music (printed), 5.518, 5.572,
    7.601
    instrumental, 5.409, 5.422,
      5.425, 5.427, 7.602
    sacred, 5.643
    stage works
      libretti, 7.351, 7.525, 7.526
      operas, 4.370, 7.534
  musical instrument makers, 1.560,
    1.593, 8.47
  performance practice, 3.65, 3.66,
    3.67, 3.80, 3.83
    meter, 3.71, 3.73
    musical rhetoric, 1.658
    temperaments, 3.81
  printing and publishing, 9.20,
    9.140
    Austria, 9.51
    Denmark, 9.23
    England, 9.83, 9.136, 9.137,
      9.154

France, 9.8, 9.29, 9.86, 9.100
Germany, 9.64, 9.89, 9.129,
  9.131
The Netherlands, 9.92
Russia, 9.145
Sweden, 9.25
Russia, 4.338, 5.489
Spain, 7.302, 7.305, 7.306
Sweden, 7.479, 7.480, 7.520
Baroque Music (Baron), 4.206
Baroque Music (Palisca), 2.31
Barrado, Archangel, *Catálogo del
  archivio musical del
  Monasterio de Guadalupe*,
  7.27
Barrand, Anthony G., reviews,
  Brunnings, 5.372
Barrett, Alexander, *A Dictionary of
  Musical Terms*, 1.331
Barrett, James E., *The Hymnary II*,
  1.618
Barry, Malcolm, reviews,
  Ho/Feofanov, 1.209
Bartel, Dietrich, *Handbuch der
  musikalischen Figurenlehre*,
  1.658
Bártfa collection, 7.95, 7.97
Barth, Herbert, *Internationale
  Wagner-Bibliographie*, 6.373
Barth, Jack, *Roadside Elvis*, 11.64
Bartha, Dénes, "Catalogue raison-
  née der Esterházy
  Opernsammlung," 7.94
Barthélémy, Maurice:
*Catalogue des imprimés musicaux
  anciens du Conservatoire
  Royal de Musique de Liège*,
  7.248
*Inventaire général des manuscrits
  anciens du Conservatoire
  Royal de Musique de Liège*,
  7.248, 7.249
Bartholomäus, Helge, *Das
  Fagottensemble*, 5.404
Bartlett, Clifford:
*The Music Collections of the
  Cambridge Libraries*, 7.101
reviews:
  Abraham, 2.3; Abravanel,
    6.119; Arnold, 1.6; Balough,
    6.158; Barker, 2.85 ; Baron,
    4.219; Basart, 10.19; Böker-
    Heil/Heckmann/Kindermann,
    5.521; *British Catalogue of
    Music*, 5.67; *The British
    Music Yearbook*, 11.3;
    Caldwell, 3.46;
    Cohen/Lacroix/Léveillé, 2.44;
    Eisen, 6.169; Jackson, 3.74;
    Koshgarian, 5.139; Krummel,
    9.85; Lowe, 6.124; Murray,
    5.438; Stevens, 3.41;
    Thorin/Franklin, 13.88;

Whitwell, 5.172
Bartlett, Hazel, *Supplement [to]
  Catalogue of Early Books on
  Music*, 7.576
Bartlett, Ian:
*Register of Dissertations and
  Theses on Music in Britain
  and Ireland*, 4.137
*Register of Theses on Music
  Accepted for Higher Degrees
  in Britain and Ireland*, 4.137
Bartlette, Reginald J., *Off the
  Record*, 10.228
Bartlitz, Eveline:
*Die Beethoven-Sammlung in der
  Musikabteilung der Deutschen
  Staatsbibliothek*, 6.41
Carl Maria von Weber, 6.384
Bartók, Béla, 6.37, 6.38, 6.39
Barulich, Frances:
"Harmonizing the Arts," 9.47
reviews, Baytelman, 6.10
Barzun, Jacques:
Pleasures of Music, 2.86
reviews, Slonimsky, 2.122
Basart, Ann P.:
"Bibliographies of Wind Music,"
  5.393
"Finding Orchestral Music,"
  5.266
"Finding String Music," 5.292
"Finding Vocal Music," 5.316
"Guide to Piano Music," 5.242
index to *The Garland Library of
  the History of Western Music*
  (Rosand), 3.38
"Index to the Manuscripts in the
  New Grove Articles on
  'Sources'," 1.48, 5.523
*Perspectives of New Music: An
  Index*, 4.98
Serial Music, 4.214
"Serials Devoted to Individual
  Composers and Musicians,"
  6.2
The Sound of the Fortepiano,
  10.19
"Whistling in the Dark No
  Longer," 4.54
Writing about Music, 4.67
reviews:
  Anderson, 5.440; Anderton,
    1.268; Arneson, 4.94;
    Arneson/Williams, 5.224;
    Baron, 4.219; Bloch, 6.273;
    Block, 6.197; Blyth, 10.22;
    Bowles, 6.206; Brockman,
    4.12; Brusse, 5.320; *BSB-
    Musik*, 7.337; Bull, 1.246;
    Cansler, 5.180; Carter, 5.123;
    CD Review Digest Annual,
    10.211; Chase/Budwig, 6.133;
    Cohen, 1.69, 10.25; Cooper,

C

Collier, Simon, reviews, Béhague, 2.31

Collins, Pamela, *Contemporary Composers*, 1.96

Collins, Willie, reviews, de Lerma, 4.21

Collins Music Encyclopedia (Westrup/Harrison), 1.60

Colombia, 1.138, 7.67

Colombo, Paola, *La musica popolare*, 4.123

Colt, C.F., *The Early Piano*, 1.523

Coltrane, John, 10.276

Colturato, Annarita, *Biblioteca nazionale Universitaria di Torino*, 7.507

Columbro, Marta, *La raccolta di libretti d'opera del Teatro San Carlo di Napoli*, 5.474

Columbus collection, 7.469

Colvig, Richard, *Medieval and Renaissance Music on Long-Playing Records*, 10.27

The Combination of Violin and Violoncello without Accompaniment (Feinland), 5.294

Combs, F. Michael, *Solo and Ensemble Literature for Percussion*, 5.276

Commander, Doris, reviews, Vannes, 1.582

Comotti, Giovanni, *La musica nella cultura greca e romana*, 2.35

Companion to Baroque Music (Sadie), 4.208

Companion to Congregational Praise (Parry), 1.626

Companion to Contemporary Musical Thought (Paynter/Howell/Orton/Seymour), 2.117

Companion to the Hymnal (Gealy/Lovelace/Young), 1.633

Companion to the United Methodist Hymnal (Young), 1.638

The Companion to Twentieth-Century Music (Lebrecht), 1.30

competitions, 1.519, 11.11, 11.35, 11.38

The Compleat Mozart (Zaslaw/Cowdry), 6.254

The Complete Beatles Recording Sessions (Lewisohn), 10.266

The Complete Bo Diddley Sessions (White), 10.280

Complete Book of the American Musical Theater (Ewen), 1.435

Complete Catalogue of Sheet Music and Musical Works (Board of

Music Trade, U.S.), 5.118

A Complete Catalogue of the Works of Percy Grainger (Balough), 6.158

A Complete Concordance to the Songs of the Early Tudor Court (Preston), 5.587

A Complete Dictionary of Music (Waring), 1.324

The Complete Dictionary of Opera and Operetta (Anderson), 1.417

Complete Encyclopædia of Music (Moore), 1.35, 1.36

The Complete Encyclopedia of Popular Music and Jazz (Kinkle), 1.395

The Complete Entertainment Discography (Rust/Debus), 10.155

complete works editions, *see* historical editions

composers: *See also* historical editions; individual composers, countries, and subjects; women.

autographs, 5.556, 5.610

biographical sources, 1.73, 1.77, 1.79, 1.80, 1.94, 1.98, 1.550, 6.2

indexes to, 1.246, 1.255, 6.4

interviews, 1.261

chronologies, 2.75

internet resources, 12.40

societies, 1.177, 1.215, 1.221, 5.70, 5.115, 5.116, 6.3

thematic catalogs, 4.13, 6.5, 6.6

twentieth century, 1.67, 1.72, 1.82, 1.96

writings, 2.104, 2.109, 2.113, 2.121, 2.122, 6.1

Composers' Autographs (Gerstenberg/Hürlimann), 5.556

Composers' Collected Editions from Europe (Harrassowitz), 5.506

Composers' Guild of Great Britain, *Catalogue of Works by Members*, 5.70

Composers in America (Reis), 1.231

Composers of the Americas (Pan American Union), 1.189

Composers of Today (Ewen), 1.72

Composers of Yesterday (Ewen), 1.72

Composers on Music (Morgenstern), 2.113

Composers on Record (Greene), 1.255

Composers since 1900 (Ewen), 1.72

Compositeurs canadiens contemporains (Beckwith/Laplante), 1.136

Les compositeurs tchecoslovaques

contemporains (Gardavský), 1.145

composition:

Baroque era, 1.658

and computers, 12.41, 12.45, 12.46, 12.47

devices, 1.658, 1.662, 1.663

for films, 13.24

melody, 1.663

notation, 1.659, 1.661

rhythm, 1.662

style, 2.37

Compositores argentinos (Senillosa), 1.117

Compositores bolivianos (Messmer), 1.128

Composium: A Quarterly Index of Contemporary Compositions, 5.16

Composium Directory of New Music (Cunning), 5.16

Compozitorisi muzicologi romă (Cosma), 1.203

A Comprehensive Bibliography of Music for Film and Television (Wescott), 4.45

Comprehensive Catalogue of Available Literature for the Double Bass (Grodner), 5.299

The Comprehensive Country Music Encyclopedia (Russell), 1.343

Comprehensive Cylinder Record Index (Deakins/Grattelo), 10.57

Comprehensive Guide to LDS Music in Print, 5.627

Compton, Sheila, *Orchestral Library*, 7.257

Computer Appplications in Music (Davis), 12.41

Computer Catalog of Nineteenth-Century American-Imprint Sheet Music (McRae), 7.115

computer music, 1.282, 1.288, 4.217, 12.40

computers, and music, 9.1, 12.41, 12.44, 12.46, 12.50

Computing in Musicology (Hewlett/Selfridge-Field), 12.44

Comuzio, Ermanno, *Film Music Lexicon*, 1.429

Conant, Robert, *Twentieth-Century Harpsichord Music*, 5.225

Conati, Marcello:

L' Italia musicale, 4.123

La musica, 4.123

Strenna teatrale europea, 4.123

Concert and Opera Conductors (Cowden), 1.249

Concert and Opera Singers (Cowden), 1.250

Aberdeen Libraries," 7.6

Cooper, Barry, reviews, Harley, 5.74

Cooper, David Edwin, *International Bibliography of Discographies*, 10.3

Cooper, Eric, reviews, (Cooper, D.), 10.3

Cooper, Martin:
The Concise Encyclopedia of Music and Musicians, 1.11
The Modern Age, 2.27
"The Scope, Method and Aim of Musicology," 3.1

Cooper-Deathridge, Victoria, "The Novello Stockbook of 1858-1869," 9.112

Coopersmith, Jacob M.:
collection, 7.125
reviews:
Humphries/Smith, 9.68; Smith, 9.136

Coover, James B.:
Antiquarian Catalogues of Musical Interest, 4.17
"A Bibliography of East European Music Periodicals," 4.69
A Bibliography of Music Dictionaries, 1.1
Catalogue of the Extensive Library of Doctor Rainbeau, 7.641
"Composite Music Manuscripts in Facsimile," 5.503
"Current National Bibliographies: Their Music Coverage," p.237
"The Current Status of Music Bibliography," 13.1
"Dictionaries and Encyclopedias of Music," 1.1
Dictionary of Musical Terms (Tinctoris), 1.335
"Lacunae in Music Dictionaries," 1.1
Medieval and Renaissance Music on Long-Playing Records, 10.27
Music at Auction: Puttick and Simpson (of London), 7.606
Music Lexicography, 1.1
"Music Manuscripts in Facsimile Edition," 5.503
Music Publishing, Copyright, and Piracy in Victorian England, 9.19
"Music Theory in Translation," 4.377
Musical Instrument Collections, 8.2
"A Non-Evaluative Checklist of Music Dictionaries and Encyclopedias, ," 1.1
Provisional Checklist of Priced

Antiquarians' Catalogues, 4.17

Richard S. Hill: Tributes from Friends, 13.13
reviews:
Allorto, 1.4; Basart, 4.214; Goléa/Vognal, 1.16; Michel, 1.34; *The Music Index*, 4.89; Smits van Waesberghe/Fischer/Haas, 4.386

Coperario, John, 6.107

Coplan, David B., reviews, Stone/Gillis, 10.201

Copland, Aaron, 6.108

copyright:
early music, 9.13, 13.31
England, 9.19
France, 9.8, 9.21
Germany, 13.35
Great Britain, 9.69
international, 13.21, 13.34
musicians' guides, 13.22, 13.23, 13.26, 13.28
United States, 5.27, 5.61, 5.450

Copyright and the Public Performance of Music (Rothenberg), 13.34

Coral, Lenore:
British Book Sale Catalogues, p.489
A Concordance of the Thematic Indexes to the Instrumental Works of Antonio Vivaldi, 6.368
Music in English Auction Sales, p.489
reviews:
Benton, 6.272; Brook, 4.13; Coover, 4.17; Devriès/Lesure, 9.31; *Dramatic Compositions Copyrighted in the United States*, 7.574; Folter, 7.607; Heyer, 5.511; Krummel, 9.83; *Library of Congress Classification*, 13.79; Ohmura, 6.370; Pruett/Slavens, 3.36; Smith/Humphries, 9.137

I corali della Biblioteca statale di Lucca (Paoli), 7.290

Corbett, John:
reviews:
Cook/Morton, 10.76; Lohmann, 10.278; Piazza, 10.94

Corbin, David R., Jr., *Euphonium Music Guide*, 5.185

Corbin, Solange, *Répertoire de manuscrits médiévaux...*, 5.533

Corbini, Sabrini, *Catalogo dei libretti del Conservatorio Benedetto Marcello*, 7.540

Cordara, Carlo, *Catalogo delle opere musicali teoriche e pratiche...*, 7.169

Cornelius, Peter, 6.109

Cornwall, J. Spencer, *Stories of Our Mormon Hymns*, 1.640

Cornwell, Robena, *Directory of Music Collections in the Southeast United States*, 11.18

Corporon, Eugene, *Wind Ensemble/Band Repertoire*, 5.170

Corrêa de Azevedo, Luiz Hector, *Bibliografia Musical Brasileira*, 4.294, reviews, 1.129

correspondence, 2.89, 2.109. *See also* manuscripts, autographs.

A Correspondence of Renaissance Musicians (Blackburn/Lowinsky/Miller), 2.89

Corrigan, Beatrice, *Catalogue of Italian Plays*, 7.499

Corry, Mary Jane, reviews, Johnson, 4.353

Cors, Paul B.:
reviews:
Daugherty/Simon, 5.202; DeVenney, 5.126, 5.128; Rogal, 1.637; Sharp, 5.211

Corte, Andrea della:
Antologia della storia della musica, 2.94
Storia della musica, 2.9

Cortot collection, 7.22, 7.247, 7.620

Cos Cob Press, 9.113

Cosma, Viorel, *Muzicieni români, compozitori si muzicologi/Romanian Musicians, Composers and Musicologists*, 1.203

Costallat [publisher], 2.77

Cotten, Lee, *Jailhouse Rock*, 10.296

Cottrell, Roger, reviews, Ruecker/Reggentin-Scheidt, 4.124

Couch, John Philip, *The Opera Lover's Guide to Europe*, 11.70

Count Basie (Sheridan), 10.262

country music: *See also* individual performers.
chronologies, 2.81
dictionaries, 1.343, 1.346, 1.347, 1.349, 1.350, 1.408
biographical, 1.344, 1.345, 1.348, 1.392
discographies, 10.2, 10.117, 10.148, 10.159, 10.191
on CD, 10.136, 10.140
Rolling Stone guides, 10.124, 10.145
instruments, 1.508

Day, David A.:
"An Inventory of Manuscript
Scores at the Royal Opera
House, Convent Gardent,"
7.277
The Message Bird, 4.123
The New York Musical World,
4.123
reviews:
Highfill/Burnim/Langhans,
1.163; Wild, 1.487
Day, James, *Music and Aesthetics in
the Eighteenth and Early
Nineteenth Centuries*, 2.107
Day, Timothy, *A Discography of
Tudor Church Music*, 10.30
Dayton C. Miller Flute Collection
(Gilliam/Lichtenwanger),
8.112
DBG-Musiklexikon (Herzfeld), 1.20
De Angelis, Alberto, *L'Italia musi-
cale d'oggi*, 1.184
De Angelis, Marcello, *Le Cifre del
melodramma*, 7.165
De Bellis, Frank V., collections,
7.457, 7.458
De Charms, Desireé, *Songs in
Collections*, 5.377
*De Fidiculis Bibliographia: Being the
Basis of a Bibliography of the
violin* (Heron-Allen), 4.236
de Hen, Ferdinand J., *Musical
Instruments in Art and
History*, 1.494
De la Fage, J. Adrien, *Histoire
générale de la musique anci-
enne et de la danse.*, 2.12
de la Motte, Diether, reviews, Bent,
2.88
de la Motte-Haber, Helga:
Systematische Musikwissenschaft,
2.11
reviews, Karbusicky, 3.27
de Lerma, Dominique-René:
A Bibliography of Black Music,
4.21
Black Concert and Recital Music,
5.125
Black Music and Musicians...,
1.220, 1.320
*The Black-American Musical
Heritage*, 4.21
Charles Edward Ives, 6.198
Concert Music and Spirituals,
10.31
*A Discography of Concert Music
by Black Composers*, 10.31
"Entries of Ethnomusicological
Interest in *MGG*," 1.9
The Fritz Busch Collection, 7.66
Igor Fedorovitch Stravinsky, 6.336
A Name List of Black Composers,
4.21

*A Selective List of Masters' Theses
in Musicology*, 4.138
reviews:
Bajzek, 4.232; Béhague, 2.31;
Block, 6.197; Block/Neuls-
Bates, 4.398; Bull, 1.246;
Carter, 5.123; Dearling/Rust,
1.664; Farish, 5.7, 5.8, 5.269;
Floyd/Reisser, 1.253, 4.347;
Fuld, 5.5; Fuszek, 5.247;
Gray, 1.254; Green, 6.4;
Greene, 1.255; Hernon,
10.40; Hobson/Richardson,
6.204; Iwaschkin, 4.267;
Jackson, 4.392; Laurence,
1.90; Meadows, 4.253;
Miller/Highsmith, 6.313;
Southern, 1.111; Spencer,
4.359; Taylor, 4.277;
Wenberg, 1.583
de Pascual, Beryl Kenyon, reviews,
Huber, 8.88
de Pury Family, 7.35
de Reede, Rein, *Catalogus van de
Nederlandse fluitliteratuur/
Catalogue of Dutch Flute
Literature*, 5.97
De Sanctis, Stefano, *Il fondo musi-
cale dell'I.R.E.*, 7.537
De Smets, Robin, *Published Music
for the Viola da Gamba and
Other Viols*, 5.301
de Val, Dorothy, reviews,
Clinkscale, 1.522
Deakins, Duane D.:
*Comprehensive Cylinder Record
Index*, 10.57
Cylinder Records, 10.56
Deakins, Elizabeth, *Comprehensive
Cylinder Record Index*, 10.57
Deale, Edgar M., *A Catalogue of
Contemporary Irish
Composers*, 1.174
Dean, J., reviews,
Blackburn/Lowinsky/Miller,
2.89
Dean, Winton:
reviews:
Burrows/Ronish, 6.167;
Clausen, 6.168; Hamilton,
1.448
Dean-Smith, Margaret, *A Guide to
English Folk Song Collections*,
5.376
Dearling, Celia:
*The Guinness Book of Music Facts
and Feats*, 1.664
*The Guinness Book of Recorded
Sound*, 10.4
Dearling, Robert:
*The Guinness Book of Music Facts
and Feats*, 1.664
*The Guinness Book of Recorded

Sound*, 10.4
Dearmer, Percy, *Songs of Praise
Discussed*, 1.619
Deathridge, John, *Wagner Werk-
Verzeichnis*, 6.376
Deatsman, Gerald, *The Pianist's
Resource Guide*, 5.260
Deaville, James A.:
Allgemeine Wiener Musik-Zeitung,
4.123
"The C.F. Kahnt Archive in
Leipzig," 9.26
DeBoer, Kee, *Daniel Pinkham*,
6.271
Debroux collection, 7.249
Debus, Allen D., *The Complete
Entertainment Discography*,
10.155
Debussy, Claude, 5.368, 6.119,
6.120, 6.121, 6.122
The Decca Hillbilly Discography
(Ginell), 10.240
Decker, Charles, reviews,
Carnovale/Doerksen, 5.181
Decorative Music Title Pages
(Fraenkel), 9.46
DeCurtis, Anthony, *The Rolling
Stone Album Guide*, 10.124
Dedel, Peter, *Johannes Brahms*,
6.76
Dedinsky, Izabella K., *Zenemüvek*,
5.77
DeFranco, Buddy, 10.279
Degláns, Kerlinda, *Catálogo de
música clásica contem-
poránea de Puerto
Rico/Puerto Rican
Contemporary Classical
Music Catalogue*, 1.235
Degrada, Francesco:
*Indici de "La rassegna musicale...e
dei "Quaderni della Rassegna
musicale"*, 4.91
[Rivista Musicale Italiana:] Indici,
4.117
del Mar collection, 12.20
Delahante-Erard [publisher], 9.16
Delattre, Pierre:
*Phonetic Readings of Songs and
Arias*, 5.348
*Word-by-Word Translations of
Songs and Arias*, 5.349
Delauney, Charles, *New Hot
Discography*, 10.79, 10.87
Delibes, Léo, 6.9
Delius, Frederick, 6.123, 6.124,
6.125, 6.126
Delius Trust, 6.124
Della Corte, Andrea, *Gli strumenti
musicali nei sipinti della
Galleria degli Uffizi*, 7.170
Della Seta, Fabrizio, *Italia e Francia
nell'Ottocento*, 2.35

de la Ville de Strasbourg,"
7.482
Koprowski, Richard:
reviews:
Barber, 1.272; Duxbury, 10.126;
Greene, 1.80;
Hewlett/Selfridge-Field,
12.44; *Rigler and Deutsch
Record Index*, 10.69
Korda, Marion, reviews, Riley,
1.576
Korea, 2.123, 4.191
Kornick, Rebecca Hodell, *Recent
American Opera*, 1.452
Kornmüller, P. Utto, *Lexikon der
kirchlichen Tonkunst*, 1.604
Korson, Rae:
reviews:
Dean-Smith, 5.376; Lawless,
1.353; Lumpkin/MacNeil,
10.192
Korte, Werner, reviews, Husmann,
3.25
Koshgarian, Richard, *American
Orchestral Music*, 5.139
Kosmos, Livraria, *Dicionário bio-
bibliográfico musical*, 1.130
Kosovsky, Robert, reviews, Palmieri,
4.227
Kossmaly, Carl, *Schlesisches-
Tonkünstler-Lexikon*, 1.157
Kostelanetz, Richard, *The Portable
Baker's Biographical
Dictionary of Musicians*, 1.62
Koster, John:
*Keyboard Musical Instruments in
the Museum of Fine Arts,
Boston*, 8.21
reviews, Clinkscale, 1.522
Koth, Michelle, *A Handbook of
Examples for Use in Authority
Records Created by the
NACO Music Project*, 13.78
Kottick, Edward L.:
The Collegium: A Handbook, 3.78
reviews, McGee, 3.82
Koury, Daniel J., *Orchestral
Performance Practices in the
Nineteenth Century*, 3.79
Kovačevič, Krešimir:
*Hrvatski kompozitori i njihova
djela*, 1.139
Muzička enciklopedija, 1.28
Kozeluch, Leopold and Anton,
9.150 (2/1a & 14)
Krader, Barbara J., reviews, *Annual
Bibliography of European
Ethnomusicology*, 4.178;
Rklitskaya/Koltypina, 7.514
Kramer, Jonathan D., "Studies in
Time and Music: A
Bibliography," 4.32
Kramer, Lawrence, reviews,

Bergeron/Bohlman, 3.4
Kranichsteiner Musikinstitut
(Internationales
Musikinstitut Darmstadt),
7.146
Krasilovsky, M. William:
*More about This Business of
Music*, 13.25
This Business of Music, 13.25
Krasker, Tommy, *Catalog of the
American Musical*, 5.452
*Kratkiĭ Biograficheskiĭ slovar´
zarubezhnykh Kompositorov*
(Mirkin), 1.94
Kratkiĭ muzykal´nyĭ slovar´
(Dolzhanskiĭ), 1.289
Kratzenstein, Marilou:
Four Centuries of Organ Music,
10.42
*Survey of Organ Literature and
Editions*, 5.233
Kraus, Egon, *International Directory
of Music Education
Institutions*, 11.35
Kraus, Gottfried, *Musik in Öster-
reich: Eine Chronik*, 2.76
Kraus, Irwin:
reviews:
Northouse, 1.459; Orrey, 1.460;
Rich, 1.465
Krause, Peter, *Katalog der vor 1800
gedruckten Opernlibretti der
Musikbibliothek der Stadt
Leipzig*, 7.244
Krautwurst, Franz:
*Das Schrifttum zur
Musikgeschichte der Stadt
Nürnberg*, 4.305
reviews, Gottwald, 7.483
Kreft, Ekkehard, *Lehrbuch der
Musikwissenschaft*, 3.31
Kreidler, J. Evan:
"Austrian Graduals, Antiphoners,
and Noted Missals...," 7.127
"A Checklist of Spanish Chant
Sources...," 7.128
Kreitner, Kenneth:
Robert Ward, 6.383
reviews:
Barker, 4.198; Hofman/Morehen,
5.561
Krenek, Ernst, 6.206
Kretschmar, Florence, *The Music
Index*, 4.89
Kretzschmar, Hermann, *Einführung
in die Musikgeschichte*, 3.32
Krienitz, Willy, *Kataloge der
Stadtischen Musikbucherei
Munchen*, 7.344
Kriss, Barbara Heuman, reviews,
Rosenberg, 10.293
Kristeller, Paul, *Latin Manuscript
Books before 1600*, p.391

Kroeger, Karl:
American Fuguing Tunes, 5.140
*Catalog of the Musical Works of
William Billings*, 6.64
reviews:
Anderson, 4.92;
Britton/Lowens, 5.120;
Butterworth, 1.224; Connor,
10.285; Cumnock, 7.587;
Duckles/Keller, 4.22; Eagon,
5.132; Heintze, 4.351;
Internationales Musikinstitut
Darmstadt, 7.145; Kaufman,
1.241; Krummel, 9.87;
Skowronski, 6.108;
Temperley/Manns, 5.212
Krogsgaard, Michael:
Master of the Tracks, 10.282
Positively Bob Dylan, 10.282
Twenty Years of Recording, 10.282
Krohn, Ernst C.:
"The Bibliography of Music," 13.10
The History of Music: An Index...,
4.110
Music Publishing in St. Louis, 9.81
*Music Publishing in the Middle
Western States before the Civil
War*, 9.82
"Musical Festschriften and
Related Publications," 4.27
reviews, Sendrey, 5.86
Krolick, Bettye, *Dictionary of Braille
Music Signs*, 1.308
Kroó, György, "New Hungarian
Music," 10.43
Kross, Erik, *Bibliographie der
Literatur zum deutschen
Volkslied*, 4.197
Kross, Siegfried, *Brahms-
Bibliographie*, 6.78
Krüger, Irmtraud, reviews, Reuter,
8.19
Kruger, Wolfgang, reviews, Benton,
7.1
Krüger-Wust, Wilhelm J., *Arabische
Musik in europäischen
Sprachen*, 4.290
Krumbiegel, Cornelia, *Katalog der
vor 1800 gedruckten
Opernlibretti der
Musikbibliothek der Stadt
Leipzig*, 7.244
Krummacher, Friedhelm:
reviews:
Bengtsson, 3.2; Munte, 6.318
Krummel, D.W.:
*Bibliographical Handbook of
American Music*, 4.354
*Bibliographical Inventory to the
Early Music in the Newberry
Library*, 7.117
"Bibliography of Music," 13.11
Bibliotheca Bolduaniana, 4.33

Record Book, 10.98

Ranade, Ashok D., *Keywords and Concepts: Hindustani Classical Music*, 1.319

Randall, Nathan A., reviews, Arnold, 5.229

Randall Thompson (Benser/Urrows), 6.356

Randel, Don M.:
in *Disciplining Music*, 3.4
Harvard Concise Dictionary of Music, 1.44
An Index to the Chants of the Mozarabic Rite, 5.639
The New Harvard Dictionary of Music, 1.320, 5.515, 5.593
reviews:
Bryden/Hughes, 5.625; Janini/Serrano, 7.301

Raney, Carolyn, reviews, Block/Neuls-Bates, 4.398

Rangel-Ribeiro, Victor, *Chamber Music*, 5.197

Rank on Rank (Liebenow), 4.226

Ranson, Phil, *By Any Other Name*, 5.658

Ranta, Suhlo, *Suomen säveltäjiä*, 1.147

rap music, 4.270, 10.129

Rap Music in the 1980s (McCoy), 4.270

Rapaport, Diane Sward, *How to Make & Sell Your Own Recording*, 13.33

Rasmussen, Mary:
"Music for Wind Instruments in Historical Editions," 5.394
A Teacher's Guide to the Literature of Brass Instruments, 5.174
A Teacher's Guide to the Literature of Woodwind Instruments, 5.401
reviews:
Brown/Lascelle, 2.43; Sadie, 1.488; Salmen, 2.41

Rasmussen, Richard Michael, *Recorded Concert Band Music*, 10.47

Rasof, Henry, *The Folk, Country and Bluegrass Musician's Catalogue*, 1.508

La rassegna musicale: Indice generale (Allorto), 4.91

La rassegna musicale, indexes, 4.91

Ratliff, Neil:
A Guide to the Jacob Coopersmith Collection..., 7.125
Music in New York during the American Revolution, 4.92
"Resources for Music Research in Greece: An Overview," 4.314
and the Whistling/Hofmeister *Handbuch der musikalischen Literatur*, 4.54

reviews:
Bradley, 13.38; Mann, 13.18; *Musician's Guide*, 11.39; Wollen, 5.466

Ratti, Leopoldo, 9.3

Rattray, David, *Masterpieces of Italian Violin Making*, 8.69

Raugel, Félix, *Larousse de la musique*, 1.16

Rauter, Harold, reviews, Ruecker/Reggentin-Scheidt, 4.124

Ravel, Maurice, 7.22

Raver, Leonard, reviews, Spelman, 5.237

Ravina, Menashe, *Who is Who in ACUM*, 1.177

Raymond, Jack, *Show Music on Record*, 10.114

Raynaud, Gaston:
Bibliographie des altfranzösischen Liedes, 5.588
Bibliographie des chansonniers français des XIIIe et XIVe siècles, 5.588

Raynor, Henry B.:
reviews:
Dahlhaus, 3.14; Neuls-Bates, 2.115; Rowen, 2.120

Read, Danny L., *The Literature of Jazz*, 4.252

Read, Gardner:
Music Notation, 1.659
Thesaurus of Orchestral Devices, 1.660

Reader in Music Librarianship (Bradley), 13.41

Readings in Black American Music (Southern), 2.124

Readings in the History of Music in Performance (MacClintock), 2.110

Real-Lexikon der Musikinstrumente (Sachs), 1.510

Reale Accademia Filarmonica (Bologna), 7.69, 7.70

Reali, Vito, "La collezione Corsini di antichi codici musicali e Girolamo Chiti," 7.439

Reallexikon der Akustik (Rieländer), 1.322

Reaney, Gilbert, *Manuscripts of Polyphonic Music*, 5.589

Recent American Opera (Kornick), 1.452

Recent Studies in Music: A Catalog of Doctoral Dissertations (UMI), 4.151

La recherche musicologique (Weber), 3.42

Recherches historiques concernant les journaux de musique (Gregoir), 4.75

Reclams Orgelmusikführer (Lukas), 5.236

Record Albums Price Guide (Osborne/Hamilton), 10.150

Record and Tape Reviews Index (Maleady), 10.219

The Record Collector's International Directory (Felton), 11.26

Record Collector's Price Guide (Osborne/Hamilton), 10.150

Record Ratings (Myers/Hill), 10.220

Record World, 10.131

Recorded Classical Music (Cohn), 10.26

Recorded Concert Band Music (Rasmussen), 10.47

Recorded Jazz (Harris/Rust), 10.81

The Recorded Performances of Gérard Souzay (Morris), 10.260

Recorded Ragtime (Jasen), 10.61

recorder:
instrument collections, 8.47, 8.112
music, 4.243, 5.418, 5.422

The Recorder (Griscom/Lasocki), 4.243

Recorders, Fifes, and Simple System Transverse Flutes of One Key (Seyfrit), 8.112

recording industry, 4.120, 7.22

Recording Industry Index, 4.120

Recordings of Non-Western Music Subject and Added Entry Access (Kaufman), 13.77

Recordings of the Traditional Music of Bali and Lombok (Toth), 10.202

Records in Review, 10.216

Records of English Court Music (Ashbee), 4.307

Recueils imprimés... (Lesure), 5.571, 5.572

Reddick, William J., *The Standard Musical Repertoire*, 5.10

Redfern, Brian:
"Problems in Teaching the Bibliography of Music," 13.14
reviews, Kennington/Read, 4.252

Redlich, Hans F.:
collection, 7.224
reviews:
Cooper, 1.11; Lockspieser, 2.109

Redmond, Bessie Carroll:
Concerto Themes, 1.650
Symphony Themes, 1.651

Redway, Virginia L., *Music Directory of Early New York City*, 9.121

Reed, Ida, reviews, Heintze, 5.134

Reed, Philip, *A Britten Source Book*, 6.84

Reed, Tony, *British Union Catalogue of Orchestral Sets*, 5.273

Tjepkema, Sandra L., *A Bibliography of Computer Music*, 4.217

TML [database], 12.38

To the World's Bassoonists, 4.119

To the World's Oboists, 4.119

Tobler, John, *A Beatles' Volume 2: Working Class Heroes*, 10.270

Toerring-Jettenbach collection, 7.38

Toffetti, Marina, reviews, Cook, 3.10

Toggenburg collection, 7.78

Tomaszewski, Wojciech, *Bibliografia Warszawskich druków muzycznych*, 5.103

Tomlinson, Gary, in *Disciplining Music*, 3.4

Tomlyn, Bo, *Electronic Music Dictionary*, 1.336

Les tonaires (Huglo), 5.564

Tonini, Guiliano, *La raccolta di manoscritti e stampe musicali "Toggenburg" di Bolzano*, 7.78

Die Tonwerke dex XVI. und XVII. Jahrhunderts (Becker), 5.518

Toomey, Kathleen M.: *Musicians in Canada/Musiciens au Canada*, 1.263
 reviews, MacMillan/Beckwith, 1.136

Top 40 Charts (Gambaccini/Rice), 10.130

Top 40 Music on Compact Disc (Downey), 10.125

Top of the Charts (Nelson), 10.131

Top Pop [Artists/Albums] (Whitburn), 10.161

The Top Twenty Book (Jasper), 10.139

Topping, Eva C., *A Guide to Byzantine Hymnography*, 4.395

Torchi, Luigi, *Catalogo della biblioteca del Liceo Musicale di Bologna*, 7.72

Törnblom, Folke H., *Bonniers Musiklexikon*, 1.57

Torrefranca collection, 7.538, 7.541

Torres Strait, 4.163, 4.174, 10.195

Torricella, Christoph, 9.150 (2/7)

Torta, Mario, *Catalogo tematico delle opere di Ferdinando Carulli*, 6.97

Tortolano, William, *Original Music for Men's Voices*, 5.213

Toskey, Burnett R., *Concertos for Violin and Viola*, 5.298

Tóth, Aladár, *Zenei lexikon*, 1.55

Toth, Andrew, *Recordings of the Traditional Music of Bali and Lombok*, 10.202

Toulouse-Philidor collection, 7.388, 7.488, 7.490

Tovey, Donald F., *Musical Articles from the Encyclopedia Britannica*, 1.19

Towers, John, *Dictionary-Catalogue of Operas and Operettas*, 1.481

Town, Stephen, reviews, Abraham, 2.27

Tracey, Hugh: *Catalogue of the Sound of Africa Series*, 10.203
 reviews, Merriam, 10.193

Traditional Anglo-American Folk Music (Cohen), 10.172

traditional music, *see* ethnomusicology

The Traditional Music of Britain and Ireland (Porter), 4.311

The Traditional Tunes of the Child Ballads (Bronson), 5.613

Traeg, Johannes, 9.149, 9.150 (2/4, 16, 17)

Traficante, Frank, "The Alfred Cortot Collection at the University of Kentucky Libraries," 7.247, 7.620

Traité de gravure de musique sur planches d'étain... (Robert), 9.123

translations: 5.654. *See also* choral music; church music; songs; vocal music.

Translations and Annotations of Choral Repertoire (Jeffers), 5.353

travel guides, *see* individual countries and topics

Treitler, Leo: "The Present as History," 2.10
 Source Readings in Music History, 2.126
 reviews, Kerman, 3.29

Trend, J.B., "Catalogue of the Music in the Biblioteca Medinaceli, Madrid," 7.300

Trenner, Franz: *Richard Strauss: thematisches Verzeichnis*, 6.333
 Richard Strauss: Werkverzeichnis, 6.335

Trezzini, Lamberto, *Due secoli di vita musicale*, 5.497

Trillo, Joám, *La música en la Catedral de Tui*, 7.511

trio sonatas, 5.409, 5.427, 5.433

Tripp, C., *Catalogue of Music*, 7.143

Trivisonno, Anna Maria, Basevi collection, 7.166

Trolda collection, 7.418

trombone: discographies, 10.17
 music, 5.175, 5.178, 5.179

Trombone Chamber Music (Arling), 5.178

Trombone/Euphonium Discography (Bahr), 10.17

Tropen- und Sequenzen-handschriften (Husmann), 5.565

Tropenmuseum, 8.5

tropes, 5.565

troubadours, 5.555, 5.586

Troutman, Leslie: "An Internet Primer for Music Librarians," 12.49
 Music: A Guide to the Reference Literature, 4.12

Trovato, Roberto, *Regesto dei manoscritti in lingua francese...*, 7.74

trumpet: instruments, 8.48
 music, 5.180, 5.181, 5.182
 performers, 5.182

Trusler, Ivan, *The Choral Director's Latin*, 5.369

Tsou, Judy: *Cecilia Reclaimed*, 3.11
 reviews:
 Boenke, 5.419; Brand, 1.153; Cohen, 1.69; Johnson, 5.309; LePage, 1.91; Sadie/Samuel, 1.103; Zaimont, 11.9

Tsuge, Gen'ichi, *Japanese Music*, 4.323

tuba: music, 5.175, 5.183, 5.186
 program notes, 5.184

Tuba Music Guide (Morris), 5.186

Tucci, Roberta, *La collezione degli strumenti musicali*, 8.95

Tucker, Mark, reviews, Hart/Eagles/Howorth, 4.264

Tucker, Ruth: *Authority Control in Music Libraries*, 13.89
 reviews, Seeger, 1.471

Tudor, Dean: *Annual Index to Popular Music Record Reviews*, 10.208
 Black Music, 10.157, 10.158
 Contemporary Popular Music, 10.157
 Grass Roots Music, 10.157, 10.159
 Jazz, 10.99, 10.157
 Popular Music, 10.157
 Popular Music Periodicals Index, 4.127
 reviews:
 Anderson/North, 1.595; Booth, 4.256; Cackett/Foege, 1.345; De Lerma, 4.21; Greenfield/Layton/March, 10.11; Hoffmann, 4.266; Holmes, 1.84; Jasper/Oliver, 1.394; Kallman/Potvin/Winters, 1.135; Kennington/Read,

W